THE PERFECT RIFLE

REGARDLESS OF WHAT FIELD...

AR-10A4
.308 CAL. / 7.62MM

- ⊕ **ACCURATE**
- ⊕ **HARD HITTING**
- ⊕ **LOW RECOIL**

IT'S MORE THAN A SERVICE RIFLE.

THE AR-10A4 FROM ArmaLite IS ONE OF THE MOST ADVANCED, ACCURATE, AND HIGHLY DEPENDABLE RIFLES ON THE MARKET TODAY. WITH A CHANGE OF LOAD OR EXCHANGE OF THE TOP END, AN AR-10A4 ASSUMES A WHOLE NEW ROLE. THIS VERSATILITY ALLOWS YOU TO SWITCH BETWEEN POLICE OR TARGET WORK TO A SUPERIOR HUNTING RIFLE. THE .308 CAL 7.62MM AR-10 HAS AMAZING ACCURACY WITH EXTREME KNOCK-DOWN POWER; ALL WHILE OFFERING RECOIL THAT IS FAR LESS THAN THE STANDARD BIG GAME RIFLE. IF YOU'RE A BIG GAME HUNTER, CHALLENGE THE PERCEPTION. IF YOU WANT A MULTIPURPOSE RIFLE, LOOK NO FURTHER THAN THE AR-10A4 FROM ArmaLite.

ArmaLite, Inc.

TO FIND THE DEALER NEAREST YOU, CALL 1.800.336.0184 OR VISIT WWW.ARMALITE.COM

SHARKS CAN TRACK A BLOOD SOURCE FROM OVER TWO MILES AWAY. AMATEURS.

FEND FOR YOURSELF®

CARNIVORE BLOOD TRACKING LIGHT™ NATURE'S MOST DEADLY PREDATOR HAS NOTHING ON THIS. A UNIQUE TRAX™ L.E.D. ARRAY MAKES BLOOD TRAILS JUMP OFF THE FOREST FLOOR. AND SHOULD YOU NEED IT, A BRILLIANT XENON LAMP LIGHTS THE TRAIL BACK TO CAMP. THE CARNIVORE ENSURES THAT YOU'LL NEVER HUNT FOR GAME TWICE. GERBERGEAR.COM

Shooter's Bible

98th Edition

Stoeger Publishing Company, Accokeek, Maryland

StoegerBooks
Great Outdoor Books Since 1924

STOEGER PUBLISHING COMPANY
is a division of Benelli U.S.A.

Benelli U.S.A.
Vice President and General Manager: Stephen Otway
Vice President of Marketing and Communications:
Stephen McKelvain

Stoeger Publishing Company
President: Jeffrey K. Reh
Managing Editor: Harris J. Andrews
Creative Director: Cynthia T. Richardson
Marketing & Communications Manager: Alex Bowers
Imaging & Pre-Press Manager: Williams Graves
National Sales Manager: Jennifer Thomas
Special Accounts Manager: Julie Brownlee
Publishing Assistants: Amy Jones, Amy Sargent
Proofreader: Amy Jones

Specifications Editor: Keith Sutton

Published by:
Stoeger Publishing Company
17603 Indian Head Highway, Suite 200
Accokeek, Maryland 20607-2501

ISBN:0-88317-326-3   BK0601
Library of Congress Control Number: 2006927287

Manufactured in the United States of America
Distributed to the book trade and the sporting goods trade by:
Stoeger Industries, Stoeger Publishing Company
17603 Indian Head Highway, Suite 200
Accokeek, Maryland 20607-2501
301 283-6300   *Fax:* 301 283-6986

Note: Every effort has been made to record specifications and
descriptions of guns, ammunition and accessories accurately, but the
Publisher can take no responsibility for errors or omissions. The prices
shown for guns, ammunition and accessories are manufacturers'
suggested retail prices (unless otherwise noted) and are furnished for
information only. These were in effect at press time and are subject
to change without notice. Purchasers of the book have complete
freedom of choice in pricing for resale.

Front Cover: This year's cover features the new Smith & Wesson
M&P Pistol and M&P15 Rifle. These two new S&W Military &
Police Series firearms have been designed for service with law
enforcement and military personnel.

OTHER PUBLICATIONS:

Gun Trader's Guide
"Complete Fully Illustrated
Guide to Modern Firearms
with Current Market Values"

Hunting & Shooting
The Bowhunter's Guide
Elk Hunter's Bible
High Performance
Muzzleloading
Big Game Rifles
High Power Rifle Accuracy:
Before You Shoot
Hunt Club
Management Guide
Hunting Tough Bucks
Hunting Whitetails
East & West
Hunting the Whitetail Rut
Shotgunning for Deer
Taxidermy Guide
Tennessee Whitetails
Trailing the Hunter's Moon
The Turkey Hunter's
Tool Kit: Shooting Savvy
The Ultimate in Rifle Accuracy
Whitetail Strategies

Firearms
Antique Guns:
A Collector's Guide
Guns & Ammo:
The Shooter's Guide to
Classic firearms
Gunsmithing Made Easy
How to Buy & Sell Used Guns
Model 1911: Automatic Pistol
Modern Beretta Firearms

Reloading
The Handloader's Manual of
Cartridge Conversions 3rd Ed.

Fishing
Big Bass Zone
Catfishing:
Beyond the Basics
Fishing Made Easy
Fishing Online:
1,000 Best Web Sites
Flyfishing for Trout A-Z
Practical Bowfishing

Cooking Game
The Complete Book of
Dutch Oven Cooking
Healthy Game & Fish Meals
Wild About Freshwater Fish
Wild About Game Birds
Wild About Seafood
Wild About Venison
Wild About Waterfowl
World's Best Catfish Cookbook

Nature
The Pocket Disaster
Survival Guide
The Pocket Outdoor
Survival Guide
U.S. Guide to Venomous
Snakes and their Mimics

Fiction
The Hunt
Wounded Moon

Nonfiction
Escape In Iraq:
The Thomas Hamill Story

Special thanks to the
National Rifle Association, for
access to their image archives.

CONTENTS

INTRODUCTION

Keith Sutton,
Specifications Editor

For the first time this year, I attended the annual Shooting, Hunting and Outdoor Trade (SHOT) Show. This year's show in Las Vegas was the biggest in the event's 28-year history. A record 40,892 people attended, including 24,366 buyers, 14,753 exhibiting personnel from 1,846 companies, 1,385 members of the press and 388 guests.

Owned and sponsored by National Shooting Sports Foundation, the SHOT Show is the world's largest showcase of firearms, hunting and outdoor products. It provides a forum like no other for the industry to show off its newest products that will adorn the shelves of gun and sporting goods shops this year. Optimism and enthusiasm were prevalent among exhibiting companies and retailers, signaling a positive outlook for the year to come.

Imagine walking through the 616,300 square-foot show floor, bigger than ten football fields, and visiting hundreds of booths where manufacturers exhibit their full product lines and the latest in shooting and hunting equipment and accessories for industry buyers. As I made my way up and down the aisles during the four-day show, I felt as giddy as a kid in a candy shop.

You can see the fruits of my visit to the SHOT Show in this, the ninety-eighth edition of Stoeger Publishing's *Shooter's Bible*. More than 125 new products are described this year, including a wide array of rifles, shotguns, handguns, black-powder guns, ammunition, optics and accessories. I never cease to be amazed at the astounding new innovations that surface at trade shows like this, and you'll be amazed, too, as you check out new introductions.

Of course, the *Shooter's Bible* isn't just about products. This is a "how-to" guide as well, with many pages of new feature articles from America's top writers that will help you get the most out of your equipment and your days afield.

I hope you enjoy this edition of the *Shooter's Bible* as much as I enjoyed the SHOT Show.

May your aim always be true.

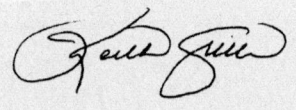

Harris J. Andrews,
Managing Editor

I'd like to welcome you to the 98th edition of Stoeger's *Shooters Bible* and second Keith's observations on this year's SHOT show. I had the privilege of attending along with several members of the Stoeger publishing team and once again I came away deeply impressed—and not a little foot-sore—after getting the opportunity to look at just a portion of the incredible variety and range of firearms and related gear on display across SHOT's "ten football fields."

In this edition of *Shooter's Bible* you'll find our pages filled with the usual wealth of detailed information and illustrations showcasing what's new and what's currently available in the world of hunting and shooting sports. Whether it's magnificent recreations of historic arms (a personal favorite) to high-tech, high-performance loads and firearms, not to mention the occasional dream gun (we can all dream, can't we?), you'll find it in these pages.

In addition to products and specifications we also present a collection of informative feature articles. Keith Sutton and Ray Sasser take you wingshooting; J.T. Uptegrove, Alan Clemmons and Dave Henderson get you ready for the field; J. Wayne Fears and Wayne vanZwoll survey famous firearms; along with much more from other great gun writers.

Finally I'd like to call your attention to our cover. This year we are featuring two innovative firearms from Smith & Wesson's Military & Police Series. These are both semi-automatic weapons intended for law enforcement and military service — Smith & Wesson's M&P Pistol series and the M&P15 Rifle.

As in every year, I'd like to thank our millions of readers for making the *Shooter's Bible* their annual of choice for firearms reference and education and for joining in the more than eight-decade tradition of the publication that our founder, Alexander F. Stoeger proudly called "America's greatest gun book."

Welcome aboard,

FEATURE ARTICLES

Choosing and Using an Ultra-light Rifle
by J.T. Uptegrove

The term "ultra-light rifle" can conjure up visions of all sorts of guns, from the most extreme versions of tactical rifles to wildly light, custom-made specialty guns. But for practical purposes, the guns that matter most in this subject are the ones big-game hunters sling over their shoulders before hiking to some backcountry destination. A gun like this may look like your everyday deer or elk rifle; the difference is how it feels after scaling a mountain or walking beyond the crowds to find a little solitude on your hunt. These rifles are designed for the spe-

cial purpose of helping you go farther while carrying less. They find their niche on the slopes of the Rocky Mountains or even more extreme environments where altitude, weather and exhaustion often catch up to hunters.

Ultra-light hunting rifles are not for everyone. The price is often a little steeper or even sticker-shocking. But there are those who long to go miles away from ordinary to find their little slice of life in the outdoors, and for those

Rapid firing can cause mountain gun barrels to heat up quickly and erode the gun's accuracy. This isn't a problem on hunts, but take note of this while shooting at the bench and work slowly to get the gun shooting perfectly.

hunters, gear means a little more than the nostalgia of having grandpa's old rifle at your side. Modern enhancements of material and design have opened up a wealth of options to big-game hunters when it's time to choose the right rifle to haul on the next adventure.

To really understand the benefits of using a lightweight rifle, you need to appreciate how much a regular scoped, loaded and slinged gun can weigh. Take your average 7½-pound rifle, put your choice of scope on it, fill the magazine with rounds, don a sling and now you've successfully given yourself a 9-pound gun if not a lot heavier. Nine pounds doesn't sound like much at first. But when it's draped over your shoulder for six hours of walking, your neck muscles might tell you a different story. Stretch that time frame to a full day, from dawn till dark, add in hills, mountains and a backpack with your gear, and now you'll start to see just how your shoulder feels about that 9-pound anchor. Take one of those long days, multiply it by seven and then you have yourself the average big-game hunt in rugged country. It's easy to see why slimming down on your rifle has benefits well beyond comfort.

Light rifles are often called "mountain guns," which is obviously earned from where most of their use takes place. But there are a number of choices on the market for them. Custom makers can build guns from scratch or even modify old standards to fit the bill. But as almost everyone knows, custom-built guns can put a real dent in your wallet. If that

puts one out of your reach, there are several more choices.

It's probable that many of the so-called youth guns will fit the bill perfectly. These guns are designed for small-framed shooters, so they often are much lighter and chambered in short-actions with shortened barrels and smaller stocks. These make a fabulous alternative.

Beyond youth and custom guns are the special-made factory guns offered by many manufacturers as their light series of rifles. Often these guns are scaled down somewhat from the old standards and come in weights that are considerably less than the average.

To have a complete rifle that ends up being light, you have to think forward and know that the weight will increase by the time you add rings, bases, scope and sling. In any case, what you are looking for is a 6¼-pound (or less) gun that is bare (without scopes, rings or accessories.) A truly light gun will come to the scale in the 5-pound range.

So what really comprises the features of a gun that qualifies for an ultra-lightweight rifle? The first and most noticeable change is the barrel. Some manufacturers just lop off several inches and call it lightweight, but for it to be a real lightweight barrel, the contour must be different. A light contour barrel thins down abruptly forward of the chamber to save weight by shaving off extra steel. This is an effective way to reduce heft, but such light barrels can heat up quickly with fast shooting of more than a handful of shots. That is something to keep in mind while sighting in from the bench, but not of serious concern on the hunt.

Extra weight resides in more places than just the barrel, and the stock is one overlooked source of it. Wood is an option, but modern synthetics go much farther to shave ounces off your shooter. Traditional black synthetics are the most common, but technology has outrun even the usefulness of those. Aramid fiber and other compounds give an even lighter, more rigid frame. Most modern factory guns boasting light weights usually have a custom-style stock developed specifically for their model. This is a huge benefit when combined with other advances in lightweight design. Aftermarket stocks are common and a viable option for some of the less expensive shelf guns.

Beyond the barrel and stock, the action is the only part left, and actions are the most difficult to lighten. This area has to be strong and reliable without sacrificing either

Choosing a Caliber

The oldest debate among shooters is exactly what caliber is best suited to each type of game animal. That only gets more complicated when dealing in light rifles with shortened barrels that dole out considerable more recoil than your average gun. In most cases, you're using these rifles in harsh conditions far from civilization in pursuit of a trophy. Those circumstances leave little to doubt that you want to use authoritative chamberings to down your trophy. But light guns are more often than not desirable in short-actions to save weight. That considered, you need to ask yourself just how effective you will be with a gun that you don't shoot reliably because of recoil issues. The new versions of short magnums go a long way to work well in light guns, but you should never overlook old standards that perform well in light hunting rifles. The 7mm-08 and .308 are perfect examples of such. The bottom line remains to choose wisely and pick cartridges effective for your game and manageable to your shoulder.

A smaller rifle that hits the scales at under 6 pounds carries easily under the extreme conditions that you might face in the wild places where you find the best trophies.

Two examples of medium-weight rifles are the Browning A-bolt micro hunter (above, bottom) in 7mm-08 and Savage Sierra 10FM (above, top) in 300 WSM. Both hit the mark for guns right at the 6-pound range without rigging.

for the sake of weight. Custom builders are the kings of scaling down actions, but some manufacturers have jumped on the band wagon and incorporated titanium to achieve the same results. The amount of weight saved in an action is negligible, and rifles built with standard actions are plenty capable of still working as mountain guns.

Below the action sits the magazine. Blind magazines are often the norm on ultra-lights because there are fewer movable parts and it means less steel to confine the shells below the bolt.

With all the choices available to hunters, which guns really fit the bill of a true ultra-light rifle? Much depends on personal preferences regarding brand, fit and feel, but there are three stellar factory options that really meet all of the specifications set forth for a genuine mountain-style gun.

Browning's A-Bolt Mountain Ti
This is a super light, tough looking shooter that hits the scales at 5½-pounds. Browning claims one pound is shaved off with a light titanium receiver and composite bolt sleeve that comes in three ounces lighter than the original. It also sports a weather-resistant, lightweight fiberglass Bell & Carlson stock finished in Mossy Oak New Break-Up camo with a Pachmayr Decelerator recoil pad. The gun comes in stainless steel and chamberings such as .270 WSM, 7mm WSM, .300 WSM, all of which are perfectly suited to the gun's intended use.

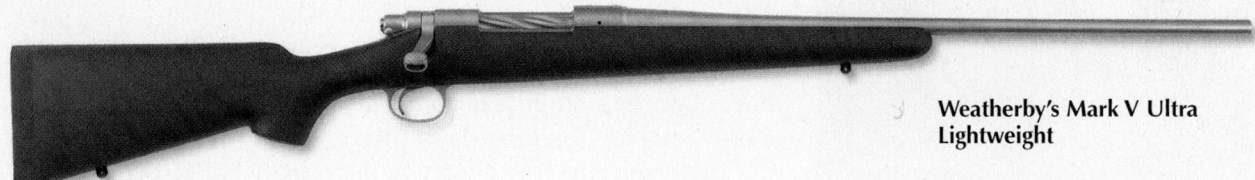

Weatherby's Mark V Ultra Lightweight

Tipping the scales at only 5¾-pounds for the non-magnum models, this gun is an ideal choice for going the extra mile. It also comes with a tan Bell & Carlson raised comb Monte Carlo composite stock with black spiderweb pattern and a Pachmayr Decelerator recoil pad. Part of its bulk is removed with a one-piece forged fluted bolt with three gas ports and a CNC-machined aluminum bedding plate. Three rings of steel surround the cartridge case head, and the recessed bolt face is surrounded by the barrel, which is surrounded by the forged and machined receiver. The gun also hosts other fancy features. Plenty of good chamberings are available for this shooter as well, including .25-06, .270, 7mm-08, .280, .308 and .30-06.

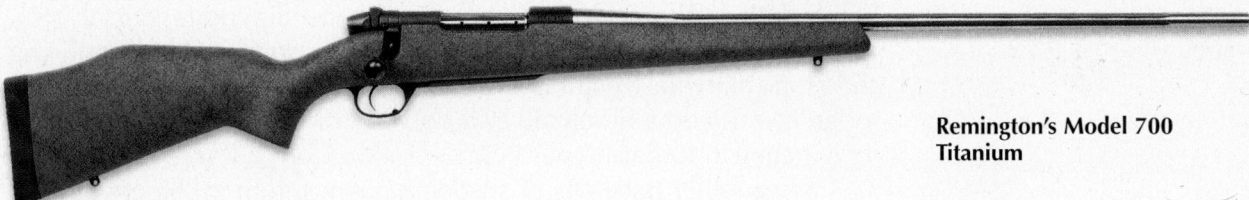

Remington's Model 700 Titanium

Remington's Model 700 Titanium

The short-action version of this gun lists as the lightest of these three, barely cresting the 5-pound mark. The receiver is machined from solid titanium, resulting in a ½-pound weight reduction over steel receivers. To further reduce weight, the bolt body is spiral fluted, and the bolt handle is skeletonized. It has a slim 22-inch mountain contour stainless-steel hammer-forged barrel. A custom designed, lightweight composite stock reinforced with carbon and aramid fibers tops off the gun's super-light form. The short action is also chambered in .260, .270, 7mm-08, .30-06 and .308.

Of course, there are many guns from many different companies that start at the 6¼-pound mark. Although these rifles are lighter than average, they're not nearly the same as a gun that starts a pound less. If you are the tinkering type, it's not hard to start with a slightly heavier gun and then re-stock it and use light accessories to get yourself into a lighter gun. But to get the rifle down to ultra-light specs, you'll probably need to employ a competent gunsmith to do the extra work in lightening up the other important parts. In the long run, you're probably not going to save enough money to warrant the effort.

Carrying an ultra-light hunting rifle has many advantages and few disadvantages. Being light means these guns are inherently quick to point and use, while being easy to carry. Shorter overall lengths enable you to maneuver the gun fast and get on target. If your arms are weary and tired, holding one to your shoulder while you wait for the right shot will be a relief. On multiple-day hunts in rugged country, you're putting

A good recoil-absorbing shooting rest like this Caldwell Lead Sled make for easy work when in comes time to tune in your ultra-light rifle. The rest steadies your shot and takes nearly all of the recoil out of the equation letting you know your gun is dead on when you need it.

that much less strain on yourself and conserving just a little energy, making the next day's hike easier.

Conversely, the low weight of the rifle makes off-hand shooting a tad shakier. The heft of normal guns does a little more to stabilize your natural tendency to waver while you sight in on an animal. A simple fix would be to get a double-duty tool like a walking stick. They aid in your travels and work amazing as a standing rest to stable your shot.

Recoil also can be a firm issue for 5-pound guns. They don't soak up the kick like weighty rifles and can give you a real complex when shooting from the bench. Because that will barely be noticeable in the field, you should take steps to ease the sighting-in process and use a good shooting vise.

When you are looking into equipping yourself with an ultra-light mountain-style gun, it all boils down to just how light you want to go in respect to the price you want to pay. There are plenty of options for the hunter with custom and factory guns, not to mention do-it-yourself project guns. Look for a gun that fits you and feels comfortable. Sacrificing shooting ability for weight is a mistake because being able to carry one for an eternity up a mountain will do you little good if you can't shoot it well enough to finish your hunt.

The few other trade-offs of shedding pounds from a rifle are far outweighed by the benefits of adding such a rifle to your armory. You'll know it for a fact the day you make it five miles into the mountains and look over your shoulder and think about just how far back you have to go.

Saving Weight with Optics

Technology has made today's rifle scopes bigger, better and somewhat cheaper. It's not uncommon these days to see very reasonably priced scopes with magnification in the teens and a 50mm bell on the end. While it may seem nice to have that kind of vision, it's often counterproductive on a lightweight rifle. Big scopes are heavy and really not necessary. You can save a lot of weight by scaling down to a low or fixed-power scope.

Consider any scope less than 16 ounces to be a good compliment to a light rifle. Plenty of manufacturers supply scopes from 2.5 to 9x magnification with objectives under 40mm, which are more than adequate for taking big game at long ranges.

Of course, scopes are not the only answer to sighting a rifle. Open sights, although not favored these days, offer an option to shave nearly a pound from your gun. Peep sights are perfectly suited for such applications. They weigh next to nothing and allow accurate shooting at long distances, plus some of the fastest target acquisition for moving game.

At left is a prime example of rigging your gun as light as possible. This 2.5x8 variable power 36mm Leupold VXIII is more than enough scope for a mountain rifle and weighs less than a pound. The sling is as basic as possible to save bulk.

TECHNOLOGY OF
PERFORMANCE
Simple
Powered by a single spring that compresses on recoil, the incredibly simple and effective Inertia Driven™ system uses only three moving parts.
Reliable
Unlike vented gas systems that require complicated action linkage, cylinders and O-rings, the Inertia Driven™ system relies on a simple basic law of physics. Without doubt Benelli's Inertia Driven™ system is the most reliable operating system ever devised.
Strong
For uncompromising strength, the over-sized lugs on the patented rotating bolt head lock-up steel-to-steel inside the barrel.
Fast
The Inertia Driven™ operating system is faster thanks to the greatly reduced mass of the parts that begin their cycle the instant that the gun fires.
Clean
The Inertia Driven™ system does not rely on gas vented into the gun's internal mechanisms to operate. Burnt powder and gas are shot out of the barrel leaving a cleaner action.
INERTIA DRIVEN™
PERFORMANCE PERFECTED
HARNESSING THE NATURAL POWER OF "INERTIA", Benelli developed an incredibly simple operating system that is driven by a single inertia spring. The new system requires no adjustments to fire everything from 2¾˝ field loads to 3½˝ magnums and stays cleaner, requiring almost no maintenance. Most significantly, Inertia Driven™ has proven to be incredibly reliable and unbelievably rugged, so much so that professional guides and hunting lodges from Argentina to Hudson Bay rely on it. Benelli called the new operating system Inertia Driven™, but the engineers simply say:
Problem Identified – Problem Solved — BENELLI TECHNOLOGY
Firing Pin
Bolt Body
Link
Locking Head Pin Channel
Inertia Spring
Locking Head Pin
Firing Pin Retaining Pin
Bolt Handle
Rotating Locking Head
Extractor
BENELLI RECOIL SYSTEM
The corrosion resistant recoil tube and spring can be accessed easily by removing the quick-detachable recoil pad.
To request a free 68 minute DVD catalog, visit FreeDVD.benelliusa.com.
PERFORMANCE WORTH THE PRICE
Benelli

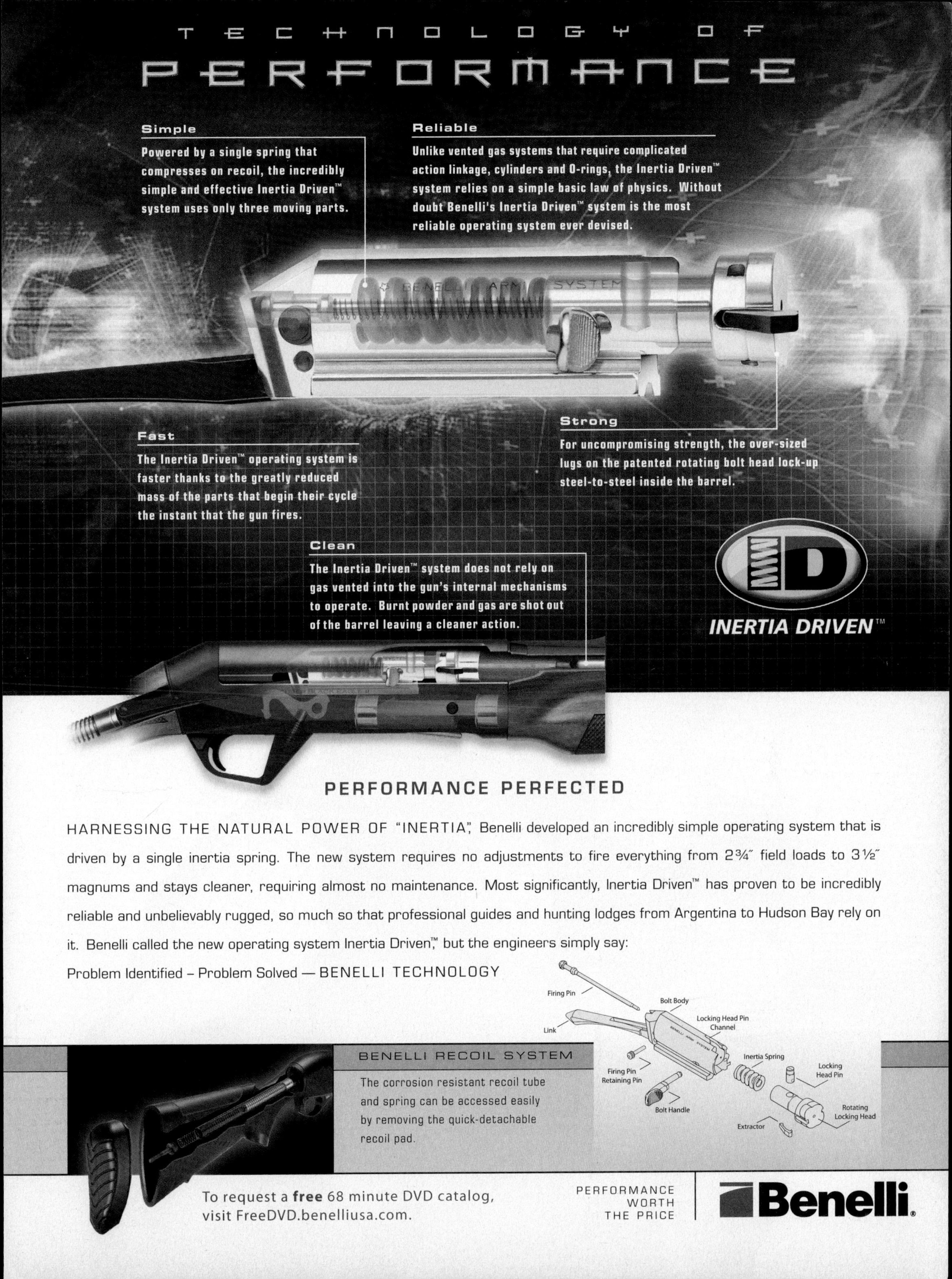

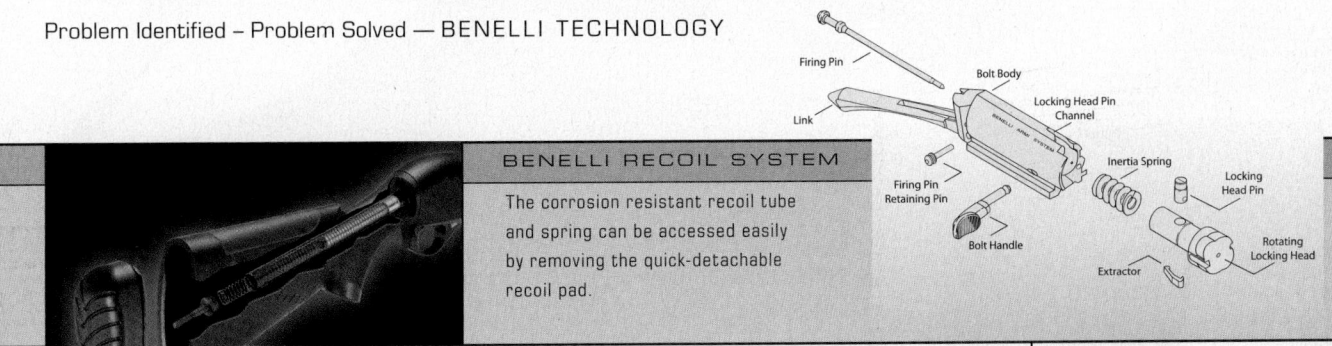

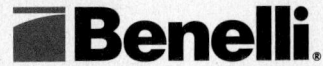

Shooting Star

by Taylor Wilson

E ven as a youngster, famed Minnesota marksman Tom Knapp found that he could pull off feats with firearms that would amaze and entertain his friends.

"It was their reactions that got me hooked," said Knapp.

Mix this strong desire to be a crowd pleaser with volumes of outdoor magazines he read as a child, influences from famed shooting greats like Winchester's Showman Shooter of the 1950s-60s, Herb Parsons, and evidently a lot—make that a whole lot—of God-given talent and the end result is an exhibition shooter like few have ever seen. Shooting for sponsors Benelli and Winchester, Tom Knapp continues his crowd-pleasing ways today at exhibitions across the country.

After years of touring and countless rounds of ammo, Knapp has a way of making the near-

Champion trapshooter and one of America's greatest exhibition shooters, Tom Knapp takes aim with a Benelli M-1.

impossible look polished and easy. In 1993, he set the world record for shooting the most hand-thrown clay targets. Using a Benelli semi-auto shotgun, he broke nine, each one with an individual shot, using no assistance and standard-sized clays.

There is some debate over the time on that. Some say 2.3 seconds, others 1.45 seconds, but time doesn't matter. He did it and consistently repeats the record at nearly all his live shows. In fact, his success rate on performing the feat is likewise phenomenal. In 106 shows, he failed to "get 'er done" only six times, and those six near misses had more to do with the weather than his shooting skills.

On July 8, 2000, Knapp used a Benelli pump gun to break eight simultaneously hand-tossed clays, smashing each one with an individual shot.

"As far as we know, no one has ever done that in the same fashion, either—shooting eight hand-thrown with individual shots for each target via a pump gun," Knapp said.

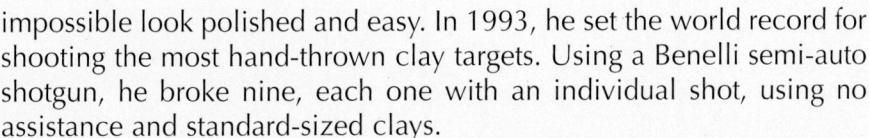

On October 20, 2004, Knapp broke his own record of nine hand-thrown targets by tossing up 10 and breaking each of them with an individual shot. Is he proud of the records? Indeed. Knapp told a crowd gathered at a recent shooting exhibition that the records that topped famed showman/shooter Parsons were in honor of the late marksman from Somerville, Tennessee. "I hope it builds on his legacy and the legacy of exhibition shooting," Knapp said.

Before he became well-known via shooting exhibitions and televisions shows such as "American Shooter," Knapp made his mark shooting trap. He led his state with a 96.8 average for six years in a row. Still, he never got to the big show: The Grand American Trapshooting Championship. "I couldn't get the sponsorship," he said.

Regardless of never getting there as a competitor, he did make it via another route. Several years ago he performed at The Grand American.

"I stood in the same two footsteps as Herb Parsons, who also performed an exhibition at The Grand American," said Knapp. "I got there, as an entertainer. I didn't need to compete."

Knapp said there is much more to being an exhibition shooter than just marksmanship, although a large percentage does spring from raw talent.

"It's a show, so you have to have flair and be a showman," he notes. "You have to be able to build drama and to have a dialogue with the crowd. You have to have the quick wit, you have to be fast on your feet, to be able to explain everything, to turn a mistake into something they (the crowd) will enjoy—a joke perhaps."

Of course, between jokes (very few are needed to cover mistakes), great exhibition shooters can always razzle-dazzle. For example, Knapp can shoot golf balls so that the balls hook the direction he desires—right, left or straight away.

While bantering with the crowd in a big, booming voice, Knapp can break targets with the gun behind his back and upside down. He can

With the camera rolling, Tom Knapp breaks his own 9-clay world record on October 20, 2004. Having tossed 10 clays aloft with one hand, Knapp proceeded to break all 10 with individual shots before any could touch the ground. Each hit is recorded in photo frames 10 to 0.

These guys would be legendary members in any rod & gun club. Famed bass angler Bill Dance, right, says it may surprise many that Shooting Star, Tom Knapp, left, is as good with a rifle as he is with a shotgun.

Tom Knapp uses a pump shotgun to pulverize a flight of clays during one of his many shooting exhibitions.

NRA official Dwight D. Van Horn presents Tom Knap with a certificate confirming his world record clay shoot at Murfresboro, Tennessee on October 20, 2004.

Tom Knapp's well-used Benelli M-1, the shotgun that he used to set the world record for hand-thrown clays. Now housed in the NRA's National Firearms Museum, Knapp fired more than 500,000 rounds through it in the course of his career as an exhibition shooter.

even toss the gun (unloaded) into the air and then catch it, load it and fire it on the mark before a falling target that he threw into the air can touch the ground.

He also can break a hand-tossed clay target and shoot the end off his empty and airborne ejected hull. And like Parsons, Knapp has a passion for igniting explosions in fruits and vegetables, turning cabbage into slaw, by way of scattergun.

Although Knapp's shooting exhibitions typically only feature shooting shotguns, Knapp's friend and fishing personality Bill Dance says the shooting star is just as good with a rifle.

"I've seen him toss aspirin in the air and powder them with a .22," Dance said.

Knapp said he learned his exhibition style from an elderly man in Michigan named George Atanasoff. Their chance meeting certainly turned out to be a blast and then some for Knapp's life and career.

"He overheard me talking in a restaurant and asked me what I really thought I knew about exhibition shooting," said Knapp. "As it turned out, I didn't know much. But he (Atanasoff) took the time to teach me, and it made all the difference."

Because there are few shots that have not been performed before, Knapp said he often relies on showmanship to put a different spin on things for the crowd. He also makes clear the distinction between exhibition shooting and trick shooting.

"Trick shooting is often an illusion," he said. "For example, it may appear a shooter is breaking eggs with a pistol, but actually the cartridges are loaded with birdshot. Sometimes the 'trick' is on the eyes.

Targets Versus Shots Taken Afield

Famed exhibition shooter Tom Knapp says there can be a world of difference between a topnotch hunter and an equally superb target shooter.

"True, a lot of it is basically practice and repetition," he said. "For example, a country boy may only own a .22 rifle, but he learns to shoot it, becomes very familiar with the rifle and the game he hunts with it. However, put him in front of some clay targets and it may take some time for him to make the pieces fit. The same could be said of the target shooter thrown in to a situation where he had to hunt with a .22.

"In both regards, there is a recipe for becoming proficient, and a lot of it is repetition, experience, or simply put, practice, practice, practice."

And, of course, no matter what kind of shooter you are, the unexpected is always going to be hard to beat. That's what you get in the field.

"Hey, it is easy for anyone to come unhinged when a pheasant flushes at your feet," said Knapp. "I consider myself an all-around shooter of sorts, fair at most shooting games, and master of few.

"There are just too many variations and surprises out in the field. You know you are supposed to put your head on the stock, but when game surprises you, you can forget. It's what makes it frustrating. It is what makes it fun."

"In exhibition shooting, however, what you see is what you get. There are no tricks played on the spectators' eyes."

Traveling the world's shooting exhibitions, Knapp is very familiar with attacks on an individual's rights to own firearms.

"In some countries, we even have to take alternate routes, because we are carrying firearms in the vehicle," Knapp said. "Many of these countries have government control on gun ownership, and they claim it is safer for their citizens. Well, all I can say is go to south Italy or some of these places and see how safe you feel."

What about in this country? Does Knapp feel Americans are in real danger of losing their rights to possess firearms?

"I feel it is paramount that we are aware of what is going on, and that's all the time, not just during an election year," he said. "Read the dockets, know what's being voted upon. Write your senators, congressmen and local officials. Tell them how you feel. It is very important; something could easily slip through and we could lose some of the rights we now enjoy."

To learn more about Knapp, readers can visit his Web site at www.tomknapp.net.

So You Want To Be An Exhibition Shooter?

Shooting Star Tom Knapp will shoot straight with you on everything, and especially about what it takes to be an exhibition shooter.

"The first thing you have got to understand is there are a lot of different shooters out there that can throw small objects up and shoot them," Knapp said. "And there are a lot of good shooters who can do amazing things, but that is not entirely what exhibition shooting is about.

"It is not based on competition, either. It is based on being able to stay consistent on demand and in order for it to reach its full potential, it absolutely has to be entertaining."

An exhibition shooter should have command of his audience—their full attention—and in a positive way. That is what sponsors and advertisers want, and it is how an exhibition shooter makes his living.

"Some guys get hung up on ego," said Knapp.

"They say 'Look at me, I can shoot an aspirin out of the air with a .22.' That's all well and good, but it is not what the business is about.

It's not all about the shooter; it's about entertaining people and making sure you bring attention to your sponsors' products."

Knapp said if someone can't convey a positive message, it doesn't matter if an exhibition shooter can break 15 targets with separate shots while riding a unicycle backward.

"If you want to get into exhibition shooting as ego, or 'look at me,' well, you would be better off going entirely into competition shooting, and that can be short-lived," said Knapp. "There's always somebody trying to knock your photo off the Wheaties box."

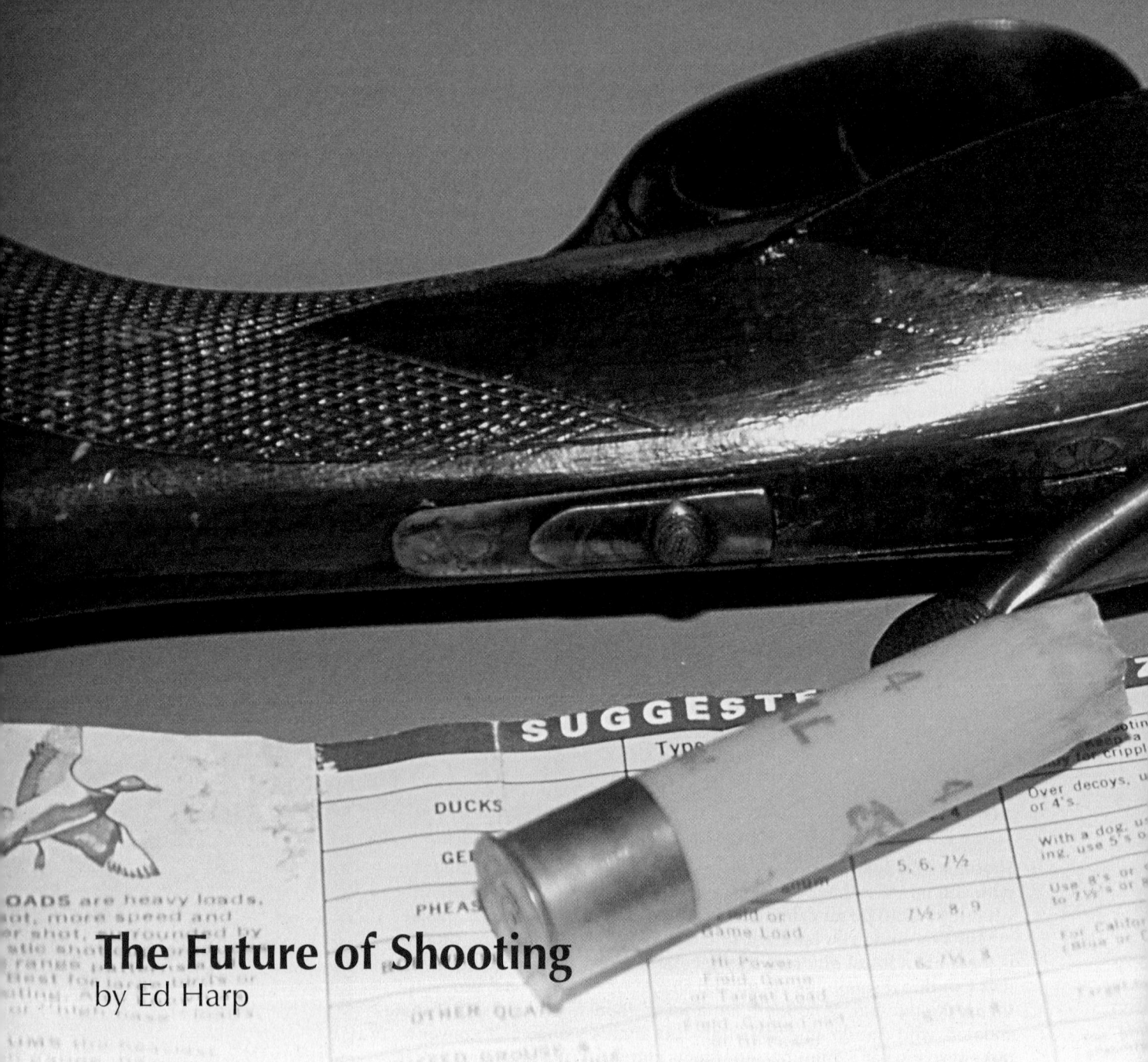

The Future of Shooting
by Ed Harp

It was, no doubt, a heck of a day. The kind of day a man never forgets, no matter what else happens in his life. That's the day, more than 1,000 years past, when a Chinese alchemist was bending over his pestle and mortar working on an elixir, searching for immortality, hoping for the best.

Somehow he stumbled upon a mixture of potassium nitrate, sulfur and charcoal. For reasons he likely never understood, the compound ignited. We don't know how, but the man was confronted with a flash of fire accompanied by smoke and gas.

His concoction didn't solve the immortality problem, but it did open up a new chapter in world history. Mankind soon found other uses for the substance that would be called gunpowder.

**SHOT PATT...
AND ...**

The amount of ...
choke in the g...
the spread or p...
charge. A "full...
shot charge c...
leaves the gun and delays...
shot to spread. As a resul...
effective at greater distanc...
range, the full choke patter...
insure being on target or...
game is ruined.

FULL CHOKE

...s are best.
Field or Ta...

. For pass s...

or 7½'s. For ...

...rly in the sea...

Valley), Gimbel...
top), Mountain a...

This old 20-gage shotgun is shown with old shells and an old Federal guide to purchasing shot and shells for hunting. At one time the side-by-side was one of the most popular shotgun designs in the country. There are better guns and shells available now but still, this outfit bagged a lot of rabbits, quail and other critters over the years. It'll do an even better job with today's improved ammunition.

Most authorities believe it was first used in fireworks and signals. Later, gunpowder morphed into use with cannon-like weapons. At some point, probably around 1304, the Arabs developed the first gun. By modern standards, it wasn't much—a bamboo tube lined with iron that propelled an arrow by means of the gasses created by burning gunpowder. And yet, that's still the basic design of our firearms today. They may not have bamboo barrels and shoot arrows, but they still use gasses from burning gunpowder to propel an object toward a distant destination. After that, it's all details.

A good place to begin to appreciate those details is with gunpowder itself. Over time, it's been transformed into smokeless powder. Sometimes it's simply referred to as a propellant. Along the way scientists

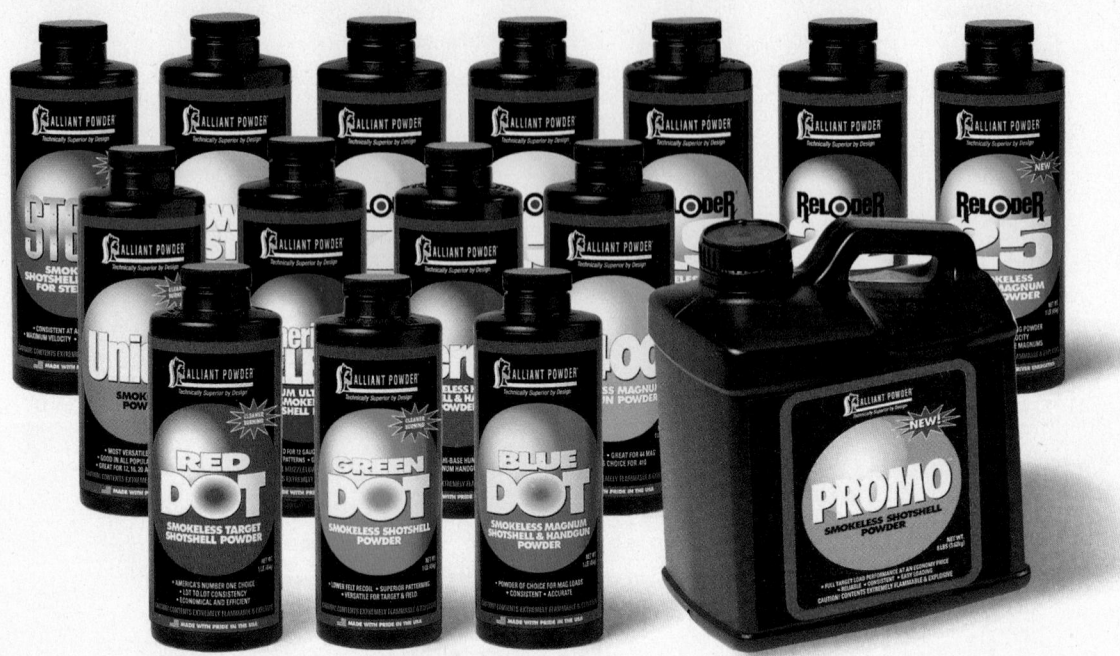

The extensive array of propellants shown above are produced by Alliant Powder, one of the many manufacturers providing smokeless powder for modern shooters. With so many varieties available, loads can be tailored for any type of shooting imaginable.

made it more powerful, more controllable and cleaner.

Their accomplishments include altering the geometric shape of the flakes or granules to include flat, hollow and honeycombed structures. Burn rates were controlled not only by the formulas used to make the powder but also by the addition of various chemicals to the exterior of the particles. Stability was improved, and shelf life increased.

These advancements offer modern shooters a wide array of choices, each designed to maximize a specific shooting experience. Alliant Powder (www.alliantpowder.com), serves as an example. They offer at least 16 grades of smokeless powder. The choices include powders designed specifically for general handgun loads, cowboy-action handgun loads, various long rifle loads and a host of shotgun applications, including trap, skeet and game.

Those choices are specific and a long way from what the Arabs used to shoot their arrows. The future is likely to be more of the same.

Most industry experts do not see anything radical on the horizon when it comes to propellants. They believe that the future will see more and better smokeless powders designed for niche or specialty markets. "If you shoot it (a bullet), somebody makes, or will make, a powder for it," said one expert.

Development of projectiles (bullets and shot), is expected to follow much the same path.

According to Jason Mash of Federal Premium (www.atk.com), much of the current improvement in bullets is in the area of projectile expansion. New construction materials and design changes are offering

shooters a more consistent rate of expansion along the flight of the bullet. This allows for greater accuracy and more consistent speed.

After that, it's a matter of making bullets and shot designed for specific purposes. Each product will be designed to enhance the shooter's experience and chances for success, be it competitive marksmanship or hunting.

But niche markets aren't the only factor driving projectile development. Environmental considerations will be important as well. Nearly every shooter is aware that in some venues lead shot has been banned. That trend is likely to continue with other substances being banned over time.

In this context, it isn't beyond the imagination of some experts that future shot, and perhaps even bullets, will be made from biodegradable materials. What and how is an open question. To some that may seem like a pipe dream, but to others it's only a matter of the evolution of shooting, moving forward one step at a time.

The Issue of Safety and Mechanical Locks

Perhaps no single issue affects gun ownership and use more than safety. Some think it's a plot by nefarious anti groups, others think it's a reasoned approach to the issue of accidental shootings. Regardless, it's a fact of life and something we must deal with.

Over the past decade or so, mechanical locks have gained popularity. Current products on the market range from mechanical trigger locks to cables that run through the breech or barrel and on toward devices that are physically inserted into the chamber. Some guns even have the lock built into the weapon itself. All have their place and all are useful deterrents on some level.

Many open with a key that's easily lost or simply laid on a table in plain view so it isn't lost. Others open with a combination—the last digits of the owner's telephone number, house address, birth date or some other easily obtained sequence of numbers.

They deter, but hardly make the

firearm secure. And, they make immediate access difficult or impossible in an emergency. How will these issues be addressed in the future?

Master Lock's Senior Product Manager Paul Schildhouse believes part of the solution lies in technology. Locks of the future may be keyed with thumbprints—they're already being used in place of time card systems in some businesses— or opened with some other form of individual identification such as voice recognition, retinal scanners or some type of DNA identification. He also points out it "may be something we haven't thought about."

So, until the perfect system comes along—and it probably never will—gun safety will continue to be a work in progress. It's unlikely, however, that technology will ever replace common sense.

Project Childsafe distributes gun locks around the country, providing locks free of charge at community events and scheduled gun safety presentations. Project Childsafe hopes to distribute some 35 million locks by the end of 2006.

Storied firearms expert, big game hunter and published author Craig Boddington offers some interesting insights into this incremental improvement process. He first points out that firearms are fundamentally the same as they were several decades ago. A bullet speed that was fast in 1915 is still fast today. Gas exit speeds haven't improved much either. What has improved—greatly improved—is the quality of factory ammunition, a combination of powder and projectile.

The reasons for this are many and varied. For starters, consider the rapid advancement of scientific knowledge. Computers have made it possible to test chemicals, metals and performance characteristics at a rate that was beyond belief only a few years ago. Those same computers allow for detailed and reliable quality control. Every load is exactly the same.

To understand how this improves shooting, consider a couple of improvements from Federal Premium: the TruBall Rifled Slug System and their Flitecontrol Wad. Both are applicable to shotguns.

The Federal TruBall Rifled Slug System uses a plastic ball that's seated between the wad and slug that locks the components together inside the barrel. This centers the slug and allows for greatly improved smoothbore accuracy. That's no small thing, especially if you hunt on a budget and can only afford one gun with one barrel.

Federal's Flitecontrol Wad uses what they call a rear-braking system that allows the wad to stay with the shot longer, in some cases up to 19 feet from the barrel. This creates a tighter shot pattern over longer

This simple bead sight perched on the muzzle of a side-by-side might not look like much, but it is quite effective in the hands of an experienced shooter. Will we see a day when fully integrated systems require nothing more than pointing a weapon? Many shooters aren't happy about the idea, at least not from a sporting point of view.

distances. That's good news for hunters, bad news for turkeys.

Neither of these developments can fairly be described as radical or revolutionary. Both rely, for the most part at least, on old technology; the same basic technology that fired an arrow from a bamboo barrel. No matter, they are meaningful incremental improvements over what has been available even a few years ago.

Now, all this doesn't do you a bit of good if you can't hit your target. To shoot with consistency you need a sight, something that helps you put the bullet or shot pattern on the target every time.

Early sights were simple enough, maybe a drop of metal or a BB on the end of the barrel. The same basic systems were employed on handguns, long guns and shotguns. They were better than nothing, but not much better. That changed soon enough. Special designs were developed for use with specific types of weapons. Perhaps the most important of these special designs was the scope.

Refinements allowed for internal adjustments to compensate for elevation, windage and other factors. Nearly distortion-free glass is now available. Most (95% at a minimum with the better manufacturers) of the available ambient light passes through the optics to the shooter's eye. All in all, things are pretty good for a 21st century shooter when it comes to sights and scopes.

Still, there are improvements on the horizon. Pat Mundy, Corporate Communications Specialist for Leupold & Stevens, Inc. (www.leupold.com) expects most of the future improvements to be small refinements. Some improvements will be in light transmission—they are already above 95% so there isn't far to go in that area—and perhaps some changes in scope construction materials. Along with that, he expects to see small improvements in optical resolution and detail.

So, it seems that shooters in the next 20 years or so can expect to see more, and better, of the same as far as individual components are concerned. There is one area, however, where major, dramatic and stunning improvements might develop. That's in the area of integration of those component parts. The Federal examples above are a part of that story. They require both powder and projectile to work together toward a better end.

Frozen at the moment of separation, a Federal Flitecontrol wad releases its load of pellets in a close group. The wad stays with the shot for about 19 yards before opening at the rear to create an air brake that pulls the shot cup/wad off the shot string.

The TruBall slug system consists of a rifled slug, (below, right bottom), a plastic wad (below, left) and the TruBal (below, center) that locks the slug and wad in place to ensure stability in the barrel. All of the components separate cleanly after leaving the muzzle.

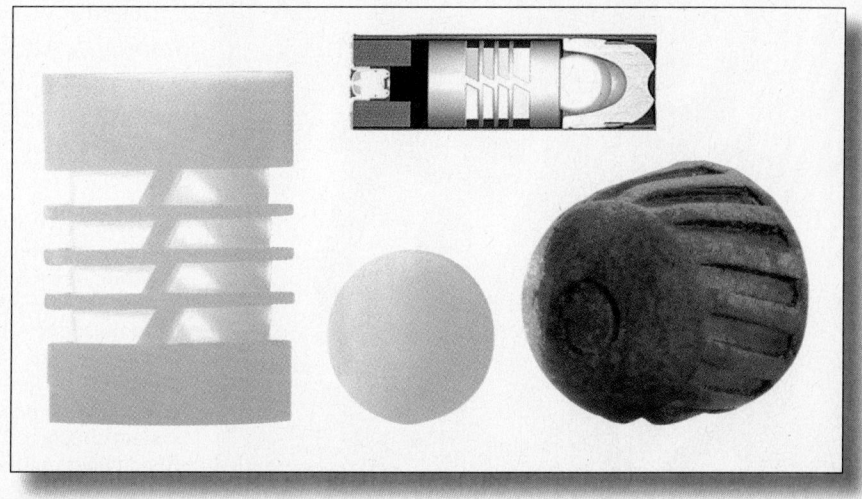

Weapons like this custom Sisk rifle are on the cutting edge of hunter technology. Fitted with a Weatherby Mark V action, Lilja barrel, Timney trigger and Kahles scope, it is one of the best available. A rifle like this will set you back about $4,700 without the scope. Depending upon shooter's skill, it will easily take-out a prairie dog at 500 yards.

Even more dramatic might be the complete integration of weapons, propellants, projectiles and sighting systems. Our military is already employing fully integrated systems in their battlefield weapons. It's no secret that operational weapons exist that will compute location and movement of the weapon, location and movement of the target, elevation, speed and ambient weather conditions. The accuracy of such systems is extraordinary.

Suppose something similar to those military systems finds its way into the civilian market? Really the question should be *when* will they find their way into civilian markets? We know they will. It's only a matter of time. When the technology becomes cost effective, it'll be available to everyone. By then the military will be using something newer and better.

That means systems will be available that will calculate the shooter's position and movement, calculate the target's position and movement, as well as read the charge and projectile all the while making any necessary corrections for elevation and windage.

The results of such a system are obvious. Hitting a running deer will be no big deal. The most challenging part of waterfowl hunting will be walking through the water to the blind. Bagging game across several hundred yards will be routine. And, competitive target shooting will be a test of computer chips, not human skill.

Is such a system on the horizon? It's probably not that close, but several experts see it coming and are worried about its effect on the sport.

Mundy admits to holding several spirited discussions in-house at Leupold on that very subject. And Craig Boddington, ever the philosopher, is "nervous" about those kinds of future developments. He's concerned that they'll take much of the skill level out of the sport and make it too easy to kill game, too easy to be a "hunter."

That sentiment is echoed in Boone and Crockett's (www.boone-crockett.org) *Fair Chase Standard*. Although some of their official positions on component integration have not yet been developed or disseminated to the public, it's clear they are concerned. And concerned

This Sisk (www.siskguns.com) custom-made rife was designed for serious competitive shooting. It's a 6.5/264 on a Remington .700 action. The Kreiger barrel, Timney trigger and Leupold scope round out the package. It's not cheap - around $6,000 - but well within the range of a serious shooter's budget. Will this weapon become obsolete when integrated systems become cost effective and available in the civilian market?

they should be; fair chase is critical to the future of hunting.

As the club's George Bettas has said, if we shooters are to survive, the nonhunting public needs to perceive us as sporting and fair. Otherwise, we're doomed. We are a small minority and will quickly be overwhelmed if the contrary is perceived or believed by the general public. Hunting must be fair to the animal.

All that said, however, there is another side to this argument. Hunting needs to be seen in its historical context. Modern shooters and hunters routinely make shots that Daniel Boone could only dream about. We do it with modern firearms, ammunition, sights and scopes. We don't need to be nearly as close to our targets as shooters and hunters did in the old days. Does that make the hunter of 2006 less sporting than the hunter of 1806?

Where's the line? Bettas believes it begins at a base point of what's legal and moves up from there. Boddington expresses a like idea somewhat differently; "It's not all about success. You can go to the grocery store for meat. It's about the challenge." That challenge is a very individual thing and changes with the times. It's a moving target.

Regardless of how you slice it, the technical side of shooting will get better and better as the component parts get better and better and as they are integrated towards working as one unit. The sporting side is likely to go the way of most things in life; it'll be what we make of it.

The custom-made Sisk rifle with its Winchester .70 action, Lilja barrel, custom trigger and high-power scope will get the job done. This example will shoot accurately across several hundred yards with ease. Daniel Boone couldn't even dream of making the amazing shots that are routine—even ordinary—with this weapon.

FRANCHI I-12

An Innovative Inertia Driven™ Shotgun From Franchi

ID
INERTIA DRIVEN™

The I-12 semiautomatic shotgun from Franchi incorporates the utterly reliable
Inertia Driven™ technology. This simple, highly efficient operating system keeps the action cleaner for low
maintenance and dependability in even the harshest environments. With no rings to change or valves to
adjust, the I-12 will cycle anything from 2¾" field loads to the heaviest 3" magnums without a hiccup.
The distinctive look of the I-12 is a sleek new design with stylish lines that stand out from the crowd.
The special gel insert recoil pad and optional 13-ounce recoil reducer can tame the most punishing magnum loads.
A shim kit is supplied regulating drop and cast to your own dimensions, making the I-12 truly yours alone. Basic black
is always in style, but the I-12 also comes in Advantage® Timber HD™, Advantage® MAX-4™ and classic walnut.
The Inertia Driven™ I-12 – simply reliable, driven to perfection.

Franchi.®

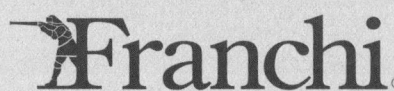

Green Timber Greenheads
by Keith Sutton

A s the shower drew near, a hush swept through the flooded timber—the calm before the storm. We watched the tempest take shape as one might watch a rain squall on the horizon, and knew, in seconds, we'd be caught in the deluge.

"My God!" one of the hunters whispered.

Then the birds began to fall.

They plummeted into the flooded trees from a single point of the compass, wings cupped, feet splayed, the emerald heads of the drakes glistening in sharp contrast to the vivid crimson and orange of the autumn-colored oaks. One landed with a splash, then another and another. In seconds, the air was full of them. The soft whistling of their wings filled our ears.

I tried guessing their numbers but it was useless. One might easier count snowflakes in a blizzard. One hundred? Five hundred? I could not determine, but in less time than it takes to tell it, they covered the shallow water before us like a warm feathered blanket. The sky, dark with their forms just seconds before, shone bluebird-blue again.

All was silent now. My hunting companions and I were afraid to move, afraid even to breath, for fear of destroying that magic moment. But despite our best intentions, the inevitable happened. Somewhere within the flock, a wary susie flushed. Something in her tiny brain told

Hunting mallards in flooded timber has a long tradition on Arkansas' Grand Prairie.

her something wasn't quite right, and she shot from the water like a stone from a catapult. The entire flock followed in an explosion of swamp water and feathers.

We watched them leave, a backward-played video on nature's TV screen. As quickly as they had come, they were gone.

I have witnessed many wonderful things during 40 years of hunting, but none more memorable than that shower of mallards. Under different circumstances, some ducks never would have left that hole. In this instance, however, not a shot was fired. My friends and I had our limits. We were simply observers.

Three hours earlier, before first light, we had boated to brush-covered blinds in the flooded timber. Sammie Faulk, a friend from Louisiana, had joined me for a hunt on the Poor Boy Duck Club just outside Stuttgart, Arkansas, the Rice and Duck Capitol of the World. Here, mallards and flooded green timber are the basic ingredients in a

Kicking the water produces splashes that look like feeding ducks.

decades-old duck-hunting recipe.

Our hunting spot, "The South Hole," was a small clearing amidst hundreds of acres of pin oaks flooded with shallow water. When we reached it, after navigating a maze of narrow woodland boat trails with a small spotlight, Sammie and I climbed into a blind. Our hosts—Vernon Baker, Bob Bendigo and George Peters—remained outside. Wearing waders and standing close beside trees in the almost-knee-deep water, the three men, almost invisible in their tree-bark garb, made the sounds of a mallards feeding, gabbing, cajoling their friends in the sky to come down. Occasionally, one man swirled his foot in the water, sending ripples through a small block of decoys. Ripples in the water convince flying ducks that their kind are feeding below.

Weather conditions were ideal for a timber hunt. The sky was robin's-egg blue with wisps of white clouds. No ice was on the water, so the birds were flying. A cold front passed the night before, and with it came a new wave of flight ducks. The sky at first light was alive with mallards.

The callers called. The ducks responded. The whole thing seemed choreographed.

A pod of greenheads and susies rocketed by at treetop height and banked sharply in response to Vern's hail call. Vern turned this way then that, trying to keep an eye on the mallards speeding through the maze of trees. A staccato burst of feeding notes was the final persuader. The birds circled once, cupped their wings and came in through the canopy. We each dropped a drake.

Timber hunting requires little in the way of equipment—just a gun, shells and waders, and if you like, a Lab to retrieve your birds.

A Legacy of Mallards

If you picture the Mississippi Flyway as a great funnel draining the plains of Canada and the United States, Stuttgart would be where the funnel first tapers down, at the beginning of the neck. This area, the Grand Prairie, has always been the prime wintering area for North America's mallards.

On December 21, 1947, St. Louis Post-Dispatch editor Ralph Coghlan wrote this about the number of ducks around Stuttgart: "... let me say that, over a hunting experience of many years, I have never seen more ducks than darkened the Arkansas skies this year. Not being a bookkeeper, an accountant, a human adding machine or a member of the federal Fish and Wildlife Service, I couldn't come within 100,000 of figuring how many I saw.

"... I watched mallards sitting in vast and solid rafts on the Arkansas reservoirs quacking raucously and happily, and at dusk, saw them start for the rice fields. They took off in successive roars like fleets of miniature B-29's, and for half an hour or more the whole sky was alive with ducks. Whether you watched them from Al Meehan's picture window overlooking the Tindall place, or at Frank Freudenberg's or Peckerwood, or Lost Island, the sight was the same. And, then at dawn, as you paddled through the timber, wave after wave of mallards got up like thundering aerial herds."

Though scenes like this were nothing but memories in recent decades, mallard numbers rebounded in the late 1990s. Hunters once again are seeing incredibly huge flocks of these magnificent birds.

Hundreds of mallards traded through the timber. George called. A flock whirled and came our way. They circled twice, then gave to the pull of gravity, falling through the trees. Two. Four. Ten. A dozen. Two dozen. When the time was right, George signaled: "Get 'em!" And some got "got."

By 10, we were celebrating our good fortune over a welcome cup of coffee back at the clubhouse. Other hunters were coming in, too, and we swapped "How'd you dos" on the front porch. All agreed it was a fine morning for hunting green-timber greenheads.

This was just one of many successful green-timber duck hunts I've enjoyed in Arkansas. Not all were as exciting as this one, but I can say with certainty Arkansas serves up the finest timber hunting in the world. Most years, the Natural State ranks number one in mallards killed, and the focal point of this harvest is the Grand Prairie region around Stuttgart.

Field shooting and reservoir hunts figure heavily in the Arkansas duck hunting equation, but these are not the essence of Stuttgart duck

A snowy duck hunt in the timber is a scene incredibly beautiful.

hunting. What symbolizes Stuttgart is shooting in flooded green timber. Hardwoods cover the bottomlands in this region. On private clubs and many public hunting grounds, water is pumped into the woods before duck season and held there by levees and stop-log structures. Mallards, wood ducks, teal, gadwalls and other puddle ducks flock to these shallow green-tree reservoirs to feed on acorns and other favored foods. When the ducks leave in spring, the water is released. Thus it does not kill the trees.

Artificial impoundments of this sort aren't the only draw for wintering ducks. Thousands of acres of naturally flooded woodlands still stretch along the region's big rivers, despite the prevalence of rice, soybean and wheat farming. These, too, draw ducks like kids to a candy store. The largest such areas are Bayou Meto Wildlife Management Area, a world-renowned green-timber waterfowling hotspot covering 34,000 acres just southwest of Stuttgart, and the 160,000-acre White River National Wildlife Refuge, part of the largest contiguous tract

of bottomland hardwoods remaining in the United States. The allure of green-timber mallard hunting attracts thousands of visitors to these areas and to scores of commercial hunting lodges around Stuttgart each year.

Timber hunting is the purest form of duck hunting and in many ways the hardest. You don't need a boat, a dog or even decoys, though these figure into most men's hunting. Timber shooting can be distilled

Big blocks of decoys aren't necessary for timber hunting. Usually a dozen or so will suffice.

down to three essentials—a man, a call and ducks.

The call is the key. Flying birds must be right over a decoy spread before they can see it. Consequently, the oversized blocks of decoys used in open water or field hunting don't work here. Sound in the form of duck talk attracts birds in green timber.

Hunters try to "read" the ducks and call when appropriate, using a combination of hail calls, feeding calls and quacks to bring birds in.

Planning a Hunt

The Stuttgart Chamber of Commerce can provide all the information you need to plan your trip. Write or call them at P.O. Box 1500, Stuttgart, AR 72160, telephone 870-673-1602. Ask for their Directory of Duck Hunting Camps (guide services), information on overnight accommodations and whatever else you might need. If you're surfing the web, you can find details on every facet of Stuttgart waterfowling by visiting their website at www.StuttgartArkansas.com.

If you plan your trip during Thanksgiving weekend, you also can take in the Wings Over the Prairie Festival in Stuttgart. The Festival includes the World Championship Duck Calling Contest, a duck gumbo cookoff, a sporting clays event and much more. This is one of the biggest shindigs in Arkansas every year, and it brings duck hunters and vendors from all over the country. The Stuttgart Chamber of Commerce

can provide more information.

To check waterfowl season dates and regulations, get a current report on water conditions and duck numbers, or buy a license and waterfowl stamp, go to the Arkansas Game & Fish Commission website at www.agfc.com, or call toll-free 800-364-GAME.

The weather during duck season can range from 10 degrees to 65 degrees in a matter of days, so bringing a wide range of camouflage clothing is smart. A face mask or face paint is required if you like watching the ducks, and always bring chest waders, especially if hunting in the timber. Hip boots seldom get you by unless you're hunting in the fields.

Most hunters shoot 12-gauge shotguns in either a 3-inch or 3.5-inch. Timber hunters usually shoot 2s,4s or 6s, while field shooters often shoot BBs, 1s and 2s.

Mallards respond differently to calling each day. The best hunters recognize this and change their approach to be successful.

The average Stuttgart duck hunter's pacifier was replaced with a duck call at a very early age, so many hunters here are experts at the craft. Those less confident in their calling skills, and those wanting an added advantage, place a dozen or so decoys in a small opening to keep the birds coming those last few critical yards. Blending into the shadow of nearby trees, some hunters call while others slosh the water with enthusiastic kicking to get the decoys moving around and create the impression of mallards feeding on acorns.

Shooting can be fast and furious. Hard-to-see ducks in tall timber can be on top of you before you realize they are near. You must decide in a split second if they're within range, if they're going to drop in or if they should be taken on the pass.

You would probably take more birds if you stuck to pass shooting exclusively, even though it's tricky to track, lead and shoot a bird in the scant seconds before it is swallowed up in the maze of branches. Too often mallards that appear to be coming in will circle and circle, then disappear when they spot something out of place. But resisting pass shots holds a special reward. Few sights in the sport of hunting are as magnificent as a flock of ducks skimming the winter-bare treetops, wings cupped in classic fashion, as they drop from the sky into a flooded forest.

Timber shooting can be distilled down to three essentials—a man, a call and ducks.

In November 1999, my son Matt and I accompanied Jim Spencer of Little Rock for a timber hunt on Bayou Meto WMA. Jim has been hunting Bayou Meto for decades, and through his generosity, Matt and I experienced a moment the two of us will always remember.

Wading into flooded timber at first light, we took a stand in a small opening and watched thousands of mallards trading back and forth overhead. Most were too high for shooting, but Jim's expert calling convinced several to drop in. At noon, when shooting hours ended, we had six mallards for our efforts.

What happened next was almost too astounding to believe. All shooting ended. We unloaded our guns and sat back to watch. Mallards that flew high all morning started dropping into the timber. It began as a trickle of ducks, but the trickle soon grew to a flood, and mallards were splashing down all around us. As the water became crowded with birds, those trying to land were forced to circle and look for open water. Thousands and thousands of them flew round about us, circling through the woods like a huge feathered whirlwind. The three of us were mesmerized.

Moments like that, after a successful hunt, embody the true green-timber experience.

The .410 Dove Challenge
by Ray Sasser

The anemic sunflower stalk wasn't nearly enough cover to conceal the spreading bulk of a middle-aged mourning dove hunter, but it was the tallest cover in the late-season field. Doves had been pouring into the field since daylight, but the October birds held advanced degrees in Hunter Avoidance.

I'd see a bird flying directly at my spot and feel confident I was about to get an easy shot. Invariably and imperceptibly, the dove would alter its course. By the time it passed my position, it would be 50 yards or farther. One careless dove seemed to venture a little closer than the others. At the last second, I stood, shouldered my sleek over-under, swung past the bird until there was plenty of pale, blue sky between the barrel and the target and touched it off.

The bird folded, dead in the air. Why is there never a witness around

Success in one of wingshooting's ultimate challenges, the author displays a brace of Texas mourning doves taken with a .410 autoloading shotgun.

when you pull off what seems like an impossible shot? I walked over to fetch my dove. Because my taller-than-normal stalk of sunflower was easy to find, I paced off the distance from where the right-angle crossing bird fell back to the spot where I'd shot. It was 49 long paces. Under normal circumstances, I would not attempt that shot with a 20-gauge, but I'd just pulled it off with a .410.

I love wingshooting, and I consider mourning doves the ultimate wingshooting challenge. Luckily, I live in Texas, a state that produces millions of resident doves each year and acts as a migration funnel for 50 million American mourning doves headed south to Mexico. In a good season, Texas dove hunters bag about 5 million birds. In an average season, more than 100 mourning doves go into my freezer.

The state's primary mourning dove flyway is a 100-mile wide band that extends from Wichita Falls to Laredo. That's pretty much where I hunt doves. If you do your homework in this neck of the woods, a slow dove hunt takes two hours and produces a limit of 12 or 15 birds (depending on the dove zone). A good dove hunt takes less than an hour and yields the same limit.

I'm not a great wing shot, and I'm not a student of the art and science of shotguns. I'm more interested in waffle cones than forcing cones. To me, back bored sounds like a good place to mount a basketball hoop. I shoot a .410 for doves because the little gun provides an added challenge and extends my time in the field. I believe that hunting doves with a .410 has made me a better wing shot, whether I'm shooting a 20-gauge for quail or pheasant or a 12-gauge for waterfowl.

Don Grogan is the first dove hunter I saw exclusively shooting a .410. At the time, Grogan owned a sporting goods store in Dallas. I was impressed that Grogan shot a Remington 1100 .410, and he usually filled a limit of doves in about the same time it took me to limit with a 20-gauge. Grogan always shot 3-inch shells, not so much for the additional shot they put in his ragged pattern but because his autoloader would not cycle the 2½-inch shells that skeet shooters use.

"The .410 has very mild recoil, anyway," says Grogan. "Shoot .410 shells

The author's .410 gets a wipe-down at the end of a successful day's shooting. The downside of hunting with a .410 autoloader is that it takes a lot of maintenance to keep the gun's smaller mechanism functional.

A .410 shotshell, even a 3-inch containing more pellets, requires greater accuracy and concentration on the part of the shooter. A standard 2½-inch .410 contains only half of an ounce of shot, about half of the load of a 20-gauge #8 shell.

through a gas-operated auto like an 1100 and there is no recoil. -It helps to own a sporting goods store and have a gunsmith who works for you."

About the same time I took up the .410, I started hunting with Wally Marshall of Garland, Texas. Marshall is best known as Mr. Crappie. He makes a handsome living teaching anglers how to catch his favorite panfish and promoting a huge assortment of tackle under the Mr. Crappie label. What most fishermen don't know about Mr. Crappie is that he loves dove hunting with a .410 almost as much as he enjoys catching slab crappie.

At the time, Marshall was shooting a reliable Browning pump. He's now switched to a Browning over-under.

"I shoot a .410 because of the challenge," says Marshall. "A shotgun is forgiving because you're putting a lot of pellets in your pattern. With the .410, you've got a lot fewer pellets. To make up for the lack of pattern density, I generally shoot a full choke. There's not much room for error. To bag a limit of doves with a .410 you've really got to be on top of your game and you've got to concentrate on every shot. There's no such thing as a 'gimme'."

To get some idea of what Marshall is talking about, let's look at the shotshell that he usually shoots. It's a 2½-inch shell loaded with ½-ounce of No. 8 shot. There are 205 pellets in that load. Most Texas dove hunters shoot a full ounce of No. 8 shot from a 20-gauge or a 12-gauge shotgun. An ounce of 8s has 410 pellets in the pattern.

Marshall scoffs at 3-inch shells for his .410. "If you're going to shoot 3-inch shells, you may as well be shooting a 28-gauge," he says.

That's a slight exaggeration. A light 28-gauge load contains ¾-ounce of shot. Three-inch .410 shells are loaded with 11/16 ounce of shot.

That's still only 282 pellets, if you're shooting No. 8s. I've shot 3-inch .410 shells loaded with No. 7½, 8 and 9 pellets and 2½-inch shells loaded with No. 7½ and No. 8 shot. I started with 3-inch 9s on the advice of my friend, Rick Pope.

Pope knows something about shotguns. He is a world-class shotgunner, former captain of the All-American Skeet Team. In 1997, Pope set what was then a world record for a skeet run with a .410. He broke 387 targets in a row. Unless you've shot skeet with a .410, you can't possibly comprehend the scope of that achievement. Pope's longest 12-gauge skeet run was 1,241 targets. On the surface, it looks like the .410 is three times as challenging as a 12-gauge.

"That's how it looks on paper," says Pope, now the president of Temple Fork Outfitters, a Dallas-based company that imports high-quality, inexpensive fly rods. "In practice, shooting skeet with a .410 is much more difficult than it seems. It's a mental grind to know how few pellets are in the .410 pattern. When you miss a target with a .410, you tend to overcompensate by becoming more careful. Skeet is a matter of confidence and swing. When you start thinking about it, you lose your confidence. In a dove field, it's best to shoot the .410 like it's a 20-gauge. If you're confident in your gun mount and your swing, the birds will fall."

Loss of confidence is one problem Marshall has never faced. His motto: if you don't believe in yourself, why should anybody else believe in you? Marshall shoots nothing but a full choke in his .410. With 2½-inch No. 7½ shot, he routinely bags birds at ranges normally reserved for 12-gauge.

Careful attention to shooting form is a genuine necessity when wingshooting with a .410. A steady, confident swing and good position will make up for the .410's smaller shot pattern.

Waterholes and ponds, particularly in dry regions, are excellent locations for developing the techniques of dove hunting with a .410. Birds moving toward watering places tend to offer closer shots.

The truth is, I can't tell the difference in the field performance of 3-inch or 2½-inch shells. That probably says more about my shooting ability than about the efficiency of the shotgun or the loads, but that's the conclusion I've reached. I've settled on 2½-inch No. 7½ shotshells as my dove load.

I'm still experimenting with choke combinations in my .410 over-under. I've tried everything from skeet choke to full choke. Skeet works great if the birds are 25 yards or closer. The skeet-choked .410 does not work for me at distances beyond 30 yards. Improved-modified and full choke will kill doves cleanly at 40 yards or more. In fact, my most effective choke is improved-modified. It's a wide enough pattern that I can hit birds that are close, but it's tight enough to make the long shots.

For a beginning .410 dove hunter, I recommend a modified choke in a single-barreled shotgun, improved-cylinder and modified in a double.

Spinning Wing Decoys

A relatively new option for the .410 dove hunter is to use a spinning wing decoy to attract birds within easy range. Spinning wing decoys are best known as duck-hunting aids. Though not widely used for doves, they work very well.

Texas dove-hunting outfitter Tom Walker sold me on spinning wing decoys early in the 2005 season. We hunted in a field that had been pounded by Walker's hunters the previous weekend. Walker set up two Mojo dove decoys, and we hid in very thin cover along a fence line. Most of the doves that passed by were well out of range. Enough birds were intrigued by the decoys that I was able to fill my limit. Without the decoys, it would have been my slowest hunt of the season.

Convinced by what I'd seen, I bought two Mojo decoys ($50 apiece). They're powered by AA batteries. On a memorable hunt later in the season, I set up the decoys in front of my wife. It was her first dove hunt of the year, and I wanted to stack the odds in her favor. Emilie stood in the deep shade between two mesquite trees growing on a fence line. I moved about 75 yards away. It was a slow morning—at least for me. When I had two doves, Emilie had 11. By the time I had five, she had filled a 15-bird limit.

As soon as Emilie had finished her limit, I moved to her spot near the decoys. In 20 minutes, I'd shot another 10 doves. I only missed one shot in my last 10, a testament to how close the decoys pulled birds. The great thing about spinning wing decoys is that you can set them within 10 yards of a good hiding place and the doves come very close. They sometimes try to land beside the decoys.

Walker believes that using decoys in tandem is much more effective than a single decoy. Be sure to place the decoys in an open area where passing birds can readily see them. I set one decoy facing my position. The second decoy is set about five yards from the first, positioned as if flying toward its partner. This setup maximizes the long-range visibility of the spinning wing action. To a passing dove, it looks like the decoys are back peddling, trying to land. Spinning wing dove decoys are very effective and ideal for drawing birds into .410 range.

Hold your shots to 30 yards or closer. To accomplish that task, you may have to become a more efficient dove hunter. That means wearing full camouflage and actively hiding from the birds until they come within effective range. It also means reading the dove field and placing yourself in the optimum position for close shots.

If you hunt in a dry region, waterhole hunting is a great way to break into .410 dove hunting. Doves typically water twice a day, after they feed. Though most waterhole hunts are late afternoon affairs, late morning is also a good time to set up at a waterhole. Texas allows all-day dove hunting. On several occasions when field hunting was slow, I'd head for a productive waterhole at about 9a.m. and finish my limit. The good thing about waterhole hunting is that birds are coming to a specific spot rather than passing through a field in random fashion. You usually can get good, close shots at a waterhole.

The author finds that the most effective choke for his .410 is an improved-modified which allows him to make longer shots while retaining a sufficiently wide pattern.

Make no mistake about it. The .410 may be the smallest shotgun, but it is not a child's shotgun. Many fathers unthinkingly start their youngsters out with a single-shot .410. Sure, the little gun has light recoil, and the single-shot models are inexpensive, small enough and light enough to be easily handled by a youngster. Single-shot shotguns are not necessarily safer, however. Most of them have a hammer that must be cocked before the gun can be fired. The hammer can slip from under a kid's thumb. If the gun is cocked in anticipation of a shot and the shot is not taken, the hammer must be eased back to a safe position.

Doves wheel low near the brush-covered margins of a Texas field. Careful choice of location can provide the edge a .410 shooter needs to take these wary, fast moving birds.

The main reason that a .410 is not a child's shotgun is because the little gun is inherently difficult to shoot effectively. Many kids will get

Common .410 Dove Loads

SHOT SIZE	LOAD WEIGHT	PELLET CT
9	½ ounce	292
9	11/16 ounce	409
8	½ ounce	205
8	11/16 ounce	282
7½	½ ounce	175
7½	11/16 ounce	24

discouraged at their inability to hit a target with a .410. They'll give up before they have a real chance at being successful. I've taught dozens of Boy Scouts to shoot clay targets with a shotgun. Many of these kids had never before handled a real gun, much less shot one. The shotgun that works best for novices is a gas-operated, 20-gauge autoloader with a skeet or cylinder choke.

Most kids who are physically strong enough to handle the gun, who follow directions fairly well and are coordinated enough to point at a straight-away target, will do fine with a 20-gauge shooting 1-ounce loads. The mildest recoil 20-gauge I've shot is the Remington 1100. Most kids can handle a 20-gauge 1100 by age nine or 10. Moreover, they can break targets or kill doves with a 20- gauge. If a kid is not ready for a 20-gauge, he's probably not strong enough to safely handle any shotgun.

Some older scouts have spent a lot of time on the range and tend to get cocky. These are kids who can break 75% of the clay targets they shoot at with a 20-gauge or a 12-gauge. When they get too cocky, I break out the .410, just to bring them down a peg or two. Their 75% average plummets, often to 25% or less.

My friend Wally Marshall hunts every kind of upland bird from quail to pheasant with a .410. I prefer more firepower for the non-migratory species. Break a wing on a passing dove and you'll find the bird very near where it fell. Doves don't spend much time on the ground, and they run slowly and awkwardly. Break a wing on a quail or pheasant and those birds will hit the ground running like a track star. They will often get away.

The .410 dove challenge is not for everyone. If you hunt where doves are abundant and you enjoy making a difficult target even more challenging, try a .410. Shooting doves with a .410 has made me a better shot. Unless I mount the gun perfectly, I have no chance of connecting on a fast-moving dove. Mourning doves are the first birds I hunt each season. That gun-mounting precision carries over into other forms of wing shooting. Because of the .410 dove challenge, I've learned to scout better, to make better use of the cover and to read fields and flyways better. In short, I'm a better hunter.

Success TAKES MANY PATHS BUT NO SHORTCUTS.

A trophy on your packmule doesn't get there easy. It's an effort worth the world's most advanced bullets, painstakingly matched to world-class brass, precision powders and the hottest primers. It's a goal worthy of the widest range of ammunition types, styles, loads and calibers available, each one crafted for a specific need. Only Federal Premium® takes this extra care, to make your hunt more successful. That's what makes it Premium®.

www.federalpremium.com

Every shot counts™

Premium through and through.
This is no place to compromise.

Mount Your Own Scope
by Monte Burch

Mounting a scope on a modern rifle is usually a straightforward chore that even a first-timer can accomplish fairly easily. Scopes can be mounted on rifles, shotguns and handguns. Mounting scopes on rifles is the most common, and what this article describes. The scope/rifle combination shown is a Remington Model 700, .30-06, with a Trijicon scope, a combination excellent for anything from whitetails to elk.

The first step is to determine what scope you desire, depending on the rifle, intended game and hunting technique or terrain and habitat. It's important to match the scope and the rifle. Scopes are mounted to guns using bases and rings. These bases and rings must match the gun make and model, and the scope size. Scopes may be one-inch or 30mm tubes. Scopes also have different size objectives, and it is important to have the correct height rings so the largest portion of the scope will clear the gun barrel.

Brownell's, the gunsmith and gun tinkerer's supply source, has scopes, rings, bases and tools to mount just about any scope on any gun you can imagine. You can order from their giant catalog or on-line. If you're not sure of the correct bases and rings, their tech staff is available to answer your questions and help select the supplies needed.

Basically you can mount most scopes using nothing more than a couple of screwdrivers. But the proper tools make the chore much easier, safer and provide a more reliable and accurate job. Two tools

Ready for sighting, a Remington 700 wears its freshly mounted Trijicon scope on the author's workbench. Mounting a scope on a modern rifle is fairly easy and an enjoyable home project.

are especially important: a good vise to hold the gun safely secured without scratching or damaging it, and the proper screwdrivers. Almost any vise, if padded, will work, but the best choice is a gunsmith's vise such as the Tipton Gun Vise from Battenfeld Technologies. This vise is highly adaptable to almost any size and shape gun and holds the gun secure. Trays in the molded bottom can hold small parts such as rings, bases and screws.

The number one rule in gunsmithing is to use the correct screwdriver to precisely fit the screws being driven, and to do this, they should be gunsmithing screwdrivers. Ordinary blade screwdrivers have tapered heads that can slip out of screw slots and mar the finish on your gun. Both Brownell's and Wheeler from Battenfeld Technologies offer a variety of excellent gunsmithing screwdriver sets.

With the gun locked securely in place, remove the tiny screw plugs in the top of the receiver. These reveal the scope base holes. Position the scope bases in place and temporarily fasten them. Hold the scope rings on the bases and make sure the scope, bases and rings will work properly, without the scope bell touching the barrel, and so forth. Note several different kinds of bases are available and the type depends on the gun model. The bases may be one- or two-piece. Two-piece bases are the most common. There are even some combination base/rings that are held in place with thumb levers. One base style, the Weaver base, is made to be used with "tip-off" style rings. Available in either aluminum

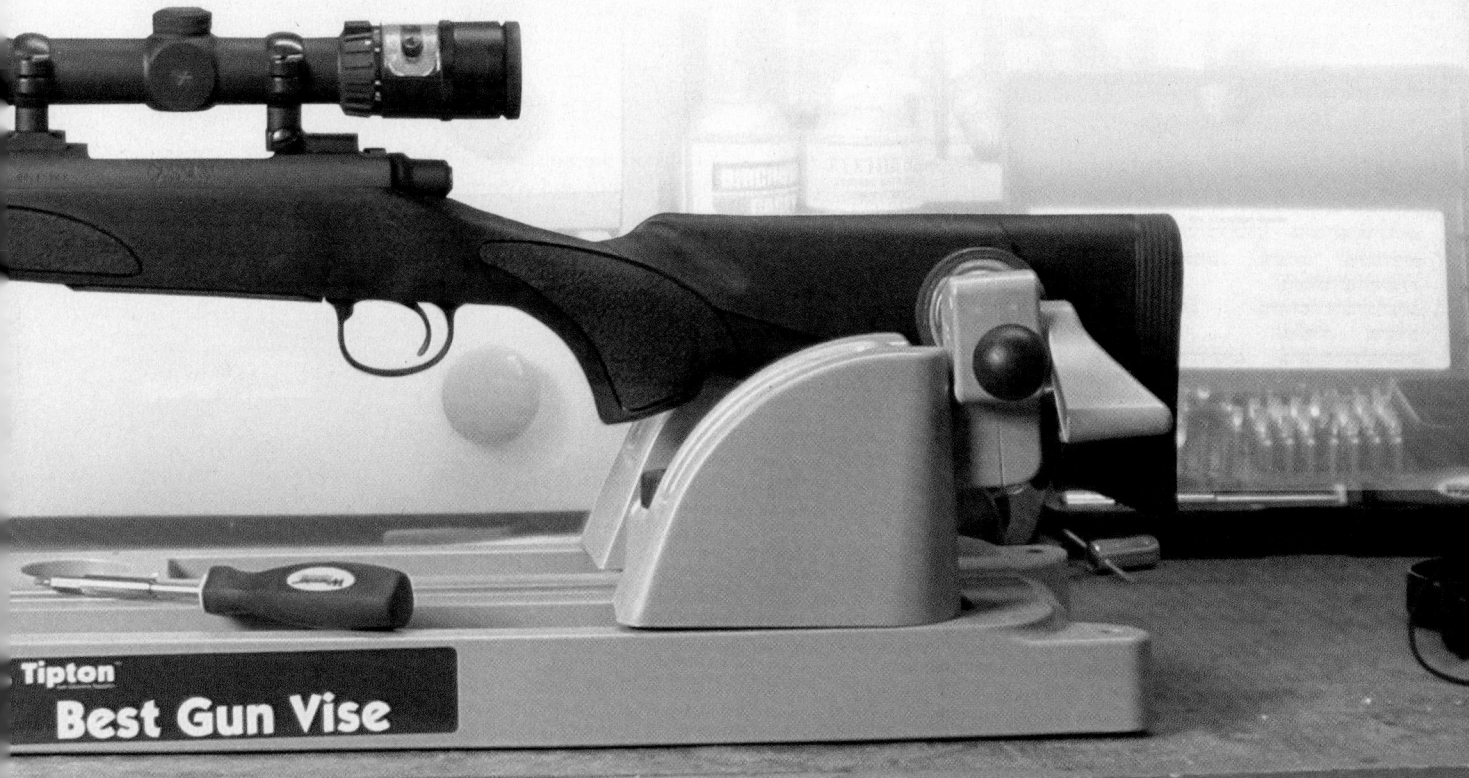

or steel, the bases have a flaring top edge and a cross slot through their center. The matching rings have screws that clamp the rings down over the flared or dovetail slot. The screw/bolt fits in the cross slot to align the rings and base. These are the most economical and commonly used base and ring combinations and are available for a wide range of both old and new guns. The rings for these bases are available in either horizontal or vertical clamping designs. The horizontal or top and bottom half rings are the most common. Some quick-detach rings that fasten at the top and bottom are also available. These are commonly used on muzzleloaders where the hunter hunts in several states, some that allow scopes and some states that don't.

Another common style of base and ring combination is the "twist-on" such as the Leupold. In this case, the rear sight has a similar

Mounting the Scope

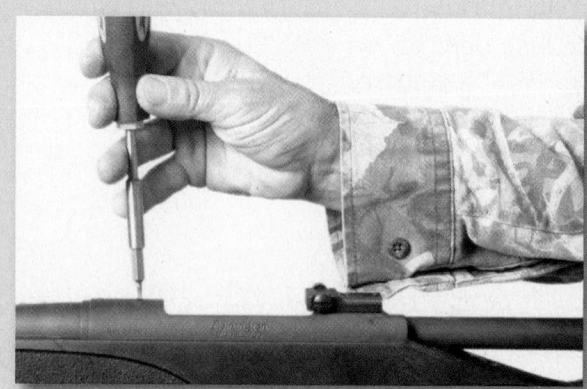

1. Remove the plug screws in the rifle receiver.

3. Install the bottom ring section. These may be held with clamps and a slotted base.

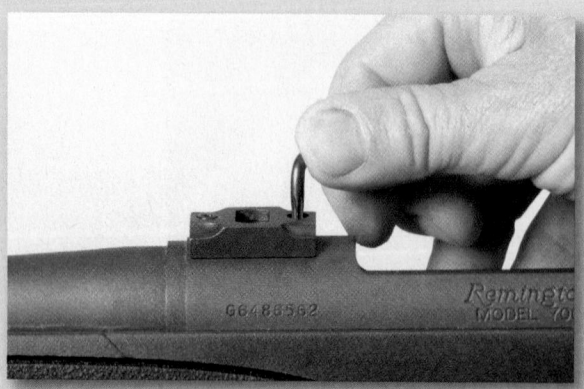

2. Mount the bases in place placing LocTite on the screw threads.

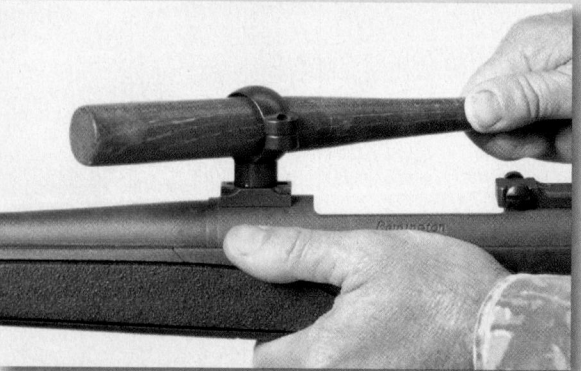

4. Some may have twist-on rings and matching bases. In the latter case the top section is temporarily locked in place, and a large wooden dowel used to twist the bottom ring in place.

screw-locking design. The front base, however, has a dovetail slot positioned crosswise. The matching ring has a matching dovetail milled into it. The bases are both fastened in place, and the dovetail of the front ring is positioned down in the dovetail slot of the base. The ring and dovetail are positioned 90° to the final location. The top of the scope ring is fastened to the bottom and a large wooden dowel used to turn the ring 90° and lock it solidly in place. The rear ring is fastened in place to the base with large screws. This type of scope mount is more expensive but more secure, and you can adjust windage easily by moving the screws on either side of the base.

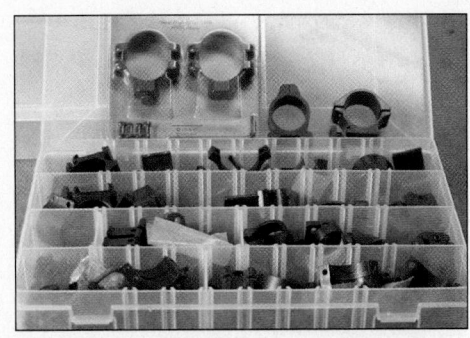

Scope bases and rings come in several different styles. It's important to choose the correct bases and rings to match the scope and rifle.

Regardless of the type of scope bases and rings chosen, the first step is to temporarily assemble and check the position of the scope, height,

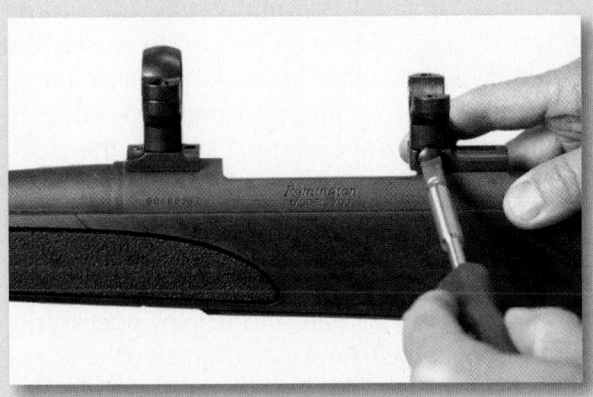

5. The rear bottom ring section is secured with large screws.

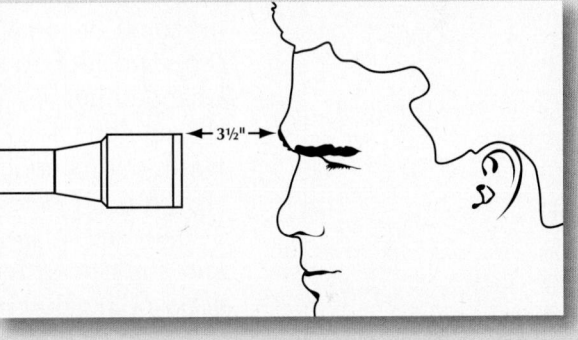

7. The scope should be adjusted for proper eye relief, traditionally 3½ inches on centerfire riflescopes and the crosshairs should be aligned with the axis of the rifle bore.

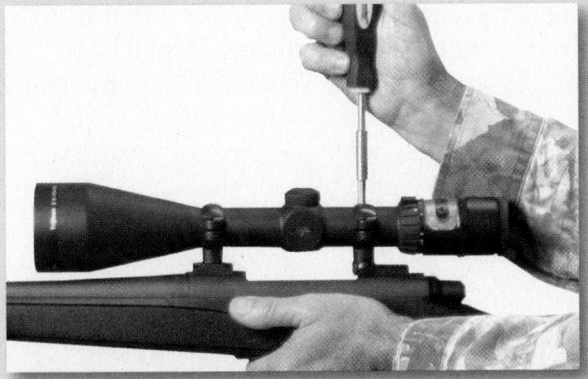

6. The scope is placed in position and the top ring sections temporarily tightened.

8. The screws are finally tightened securely in place, with LocTite placed on their threads.

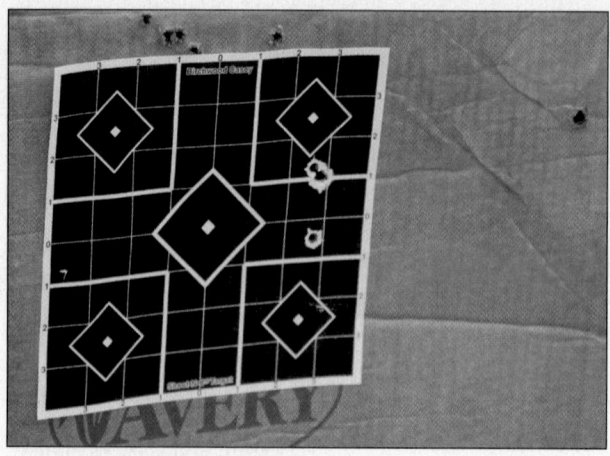

A centerfire rifle should first be sighted-in at the range at 25 yards. Shoot three shots. Adjust the scope according to the minute of angle marked on the scope adjustment knobs, which may be ¼, ½ or 1 inch at 100 yards.

eye relief and if the scope clears any type of sight that may be on the gun. Then disassemble and get ready for final assembly.

Position a base in place. Add a drop of LocTite to each screw and fasten the base securely in place. Repeat for the second base, if using two bases. Make sure all screws are tightly driven in place, but do not overtighten to the point of marring the screwhead. Fasten the bottom sections of the rings in place, using either of the two techniques mentioned for the two different types of base/rings. Make sure the rings are mounted centered, and not off to one side. Place the scope down in the bottom ring sections and temporarily fasten the top ring sections in place.

Now is the time to determine the best location for the scope. It is important to have the correct amount of eye-relief, the proper distance from the eyepiece of the scope to the shooter's eyebrow or glasses. This should be a minimum of 3½ inches. You may prefer even more on some of today's magnum rifles. It is best, however, to match the scope position to the shooter. When my wife first took up deer hunting I handed her my rifle. She couldn't get a shot at a big buck because she couldn't see through the scope. With her short stature, the stock was too long and the scope located too far away for her to pick up the sight quickly. She got a youth model Remington 7mm-08 with a Zeiss 3-9x40mm scope mounted on it to match her stature for Christmas, and she's been happily bagging whitetails since. Which brings up a good point: purchase the best scope you can afford. Not necessarily the most powerful, but choose one with a large objective lens. For instance, scopes may range from 20 to 56mm. The larger objective lenses not only offer better vision in lower light but allow for quicker target acquisition with relatively long eye relief.

When you've determined the correct eye relief, make sure the crosshairs are aligned properly, horizontally and vertically to match the axis of the rifle. Again, temporarily make sure the scope is secure by lightly tightening all screws.

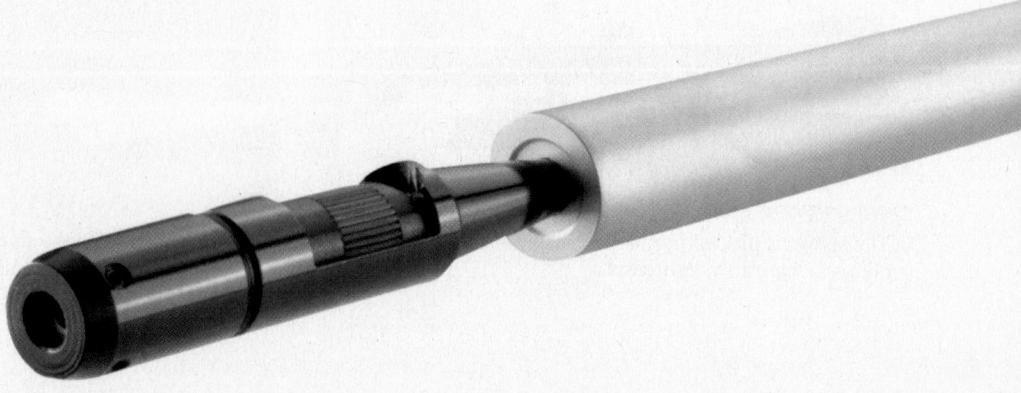

Screws for holding rings together may be either slotted, Phillips, hex or Torx. The latter have become increasingly popular on high-end scope rings. They utilize special small drivers, usually packed with the rings. Better quality gunsmithing screwdriver sets also include them. Remove a ring holding screw, place a bit of LocTite on the thread and turn it in place, but not snug. Then repeat for the remaining screws. Finally, turn all screws snugly in place, alternating turning the screws so the scope is evenly clamped in place.

With the scope mounted properly, it's time to sight it in. First step is to bore sight it. You can do this quite simply with a bolt-action rifle. Mark a large X on a piece of paper and place it on a cardboard box. Remove the rifle bolt and place the rifle on sandbags or other means of securing it. Position the box and target 25 yards away from the rifle muzzle. Peering through the breech and barrel, adjust the rifle until the X is centered in the bore. Then adjust the scope to meet the X. This will get you roughly in place. But you may still be several inches off target.

A better choice is to use a boresighter tool. These allow you to get the scope more accurately on target in your shop. Several different types are available. I've used a Simmons bore sight for many years. In use, the correct spud to fit the rifle caliber is inserted into the optical tool, then into the rifle. Peering through the scope you then adjust the windage and elevation knobs of the scope to align with a squared graph.

Now you're ready for the

The Caldwell Lead Sled is not only a secure, steady rest; it can be weighted with lead or sandbags to greatly reduce felt recoil during sight-in sessions.

The LaserLyte Super Hi-Precision Universal Laser Bore-Sighting system makes initial sight-in in the shop quick and easy and can also be used at camp to check for accuracy.

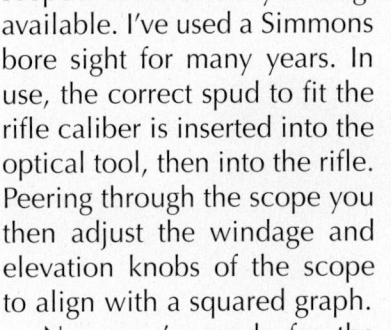
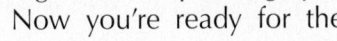
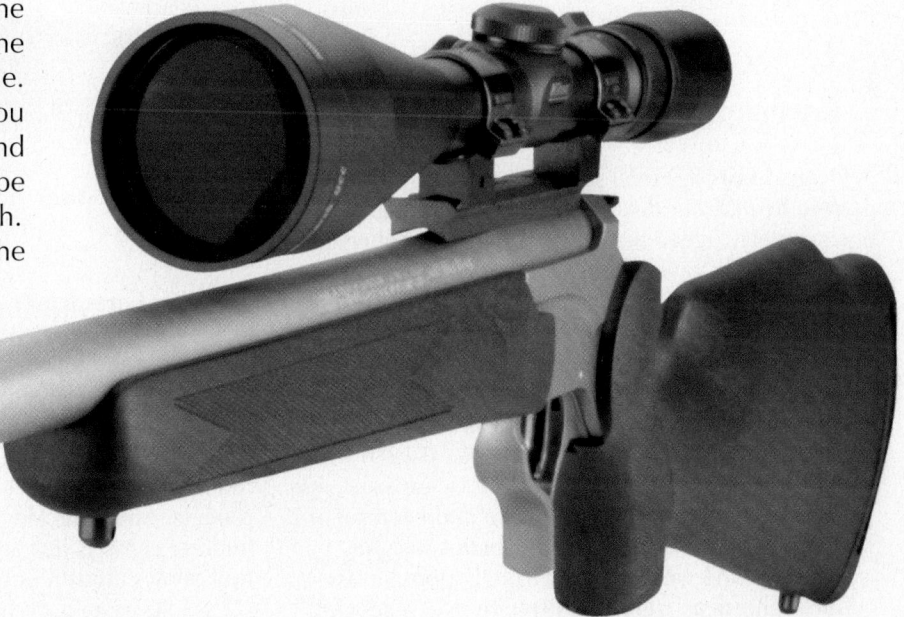

range. The rifle should be fired from a solid bench rest with the forearm, not the barrel, resting on a pad. If sighting in a centerfire rifle, first shots should be at 25 yards. For rimfires, 15 yards is best. Shots striking target zero at these ranges will put the bullet approximately one-inch high at 100 yards. Aim at the center of the target and fire three shots, making sure the gun is held secure and steady for each shot. Locate the center of the three shots. Move the windage and elevation knobs of the scope according to the scope manufacturer's directions. Scopes may have ¼, ½ or 1 minute of angle. One-fourth means moving one "click" which moves the scope crosshairs ¼ inch at 100 yards. When initialing sighting-in at 25 yards, the adjustment must be four times the amount shown on a grid. For instance moving one inch with a ¼ minute scope would require 16 "clicks." With the scope adjusted, carefully fire a second group of three. This should be at the center of the target. If not, readjust as needed.

Then move out to 100 yards and repeat the three-shot groups. For centerfire rifles, the group center should be approximately two inches high at 100 yards. This places it dead-on at 200 yards, and around eight inches low at 300 yards, for most calibers.

Mounting and sighting in your own scope is a fun chore that can also make you a better shooter.

Boresighters

Optical boresighters, such as the Simmons model, have been around for a number of years and are extremely rugged and easy to use. A number of new models have also become available. Sweany also offers their similar version, the Site-A-Line. The new Leopold Zero Point Magnetic illuminated boresighter is extremely compact, lightweight and easy to use. The boresighter uses no metal spuds or batteries, and holds securely to the muzzle with two powerful magnets. It even fits in your shirt pocket, and allows you to get your rifle on paper fast, recheck your zero and even record the zero at different ranges or bullet weights.

Lasers have become increasingly popular as boresighters as well. The Site-Lite uses a special laser target placed 25 feet away with a laser beam aimed at the target. All the boresighters mentioned above are available from Brownell's.

Another laser unit I've tested recently and found excellent is the LaserLyte Super Hi-Precision Universal Laser Bore-Sighting system. The Hi-Precision bore sighter allows perfect alignment of the laser to the central axis of the bore. By calibrating the unit while in a firearm, you can effectively achieve almost perfect bore sighting accuracy before firing the first shot. The result is not only faster, easier sight-in sessions, but reduced ammunition consumption during the process. And, checking sights after arriving in hunting camp is just as easy. The laser boresighting tool allows adjustments on guns in calibers from .22 to .50 using a set of four expandable caliber adapters that secure the unit snugly in the center of the bore. Boresighting can be done indoors or outdoors, even in broad daylight—at distances from 25 feet to 100 yards. For sighting-in during daylight hours, a special reflective Daytime Laser Target is provided with each tool set.

New for 2006

& BURRIS

4X-12X-42mm

LaserScope™
Finally, the successful integration of a high-performance laser rangefinder into a quality riflescope. Rugged construction and sophistcated micro-circuit technology at an affordable price. Includes the Ballistic Plex reticle and a patented ultra-low mounting configuration.

6X-24X XTR Xtreme Range Tactical Scope
for long to extreme range engagement. XT-1000 Xtreme Range Tactical Adjustment Knobs. Elevation knob features 50 inches of adjustment In a single revolution in 1" increments per click.

Fullfield II™ Tactical Riflescopes
Outstanding performance at a great value. Features Hi-Lume multicoatings on ALL lens surfaces, TAC-2 adjustment knobs, hard anodized, non-reflective, Type III Mil-Spec Olive Drab.

EuroDiamond™ 3P#4 ElectroDot™ Riflescopes
The ultimate in low light performance. The 1X-24X-24mm provides the largest possible field-of-view. Includes 3P#4 Electro-Dot reticle and turret-mounted illumination switch.

2X-7X-35mm Fullfield II™ Shotgun/Muzzleloader/Rifle
Ideal size, field of view, and magnification for mountain rifles, slug guns, and muzzleloaders. Ballistic Plex provides for trajectory compensation in matte or camo finishes.

2X-7X Handgun LRS
The world's most poular handgun scope is now available with a Lighted Reticle.

6X-24X-50mm

3X-9X-40mm
4.5X-14X-42mm
6.5X-20X-50mm

3X-12X-56mm

1X-4X-24mm

3P#4 E-Dot

2X-7X-35mm

2X-7X-32mm

8X-42
10X-42
10X-50
12X-50

8X-42
10X-42

Double Dovetail

Medium
.22 Signature

Medium and High
30mm Signature

XTB Xtreme
Tactical Bases

Signature Select™ Binoculars
Lens and prism coating refinements, focus calibration improvements, extremely precise collimation specifications, user-friendly eyecups and objective lens covers create the ultimate in binocular technology.

Fullfield II™ Camo Binoculars
See, but don't be seen. Here's full-size performance in a compact, lightweight, concealable binocular package.

Double Dovetail™ Rings
Now available in low, medium, and high matte black and nickel finishes.

Medium .22 Signature Rings

Medium and High 30mm Signature Zee Rings
Perfect for your Euro Diamond and Black Diamond riflescopes.

XTB Xtreme Tactical™ Bases
Solid steel bases designed for maximum mounting flexibility. Allows for the lowest possible scope mounting.

Burris Company
331 E. 8th St., Greeley, CO 80631
(970)356-1670
www.burrisoptics.com

Muzzleloader Myths
By Alan Clemons

Hunting with muzzleloaders, either with the traditional flintlock style or today's sleek inline models, gives many hunters another opportunity during special seasons to kill a doe for the freezer.

Everyone knows muzzleloaders don't work well at long distances. With all that dirty, corrosive and smelly powder, you have to use your bathtub, soapy water and some kind of suction device to clean the barrel.

You need a backpack or big fanny pack to tote around all the stuff you need to shoot one, including powder, pellets, bullets, ramrod handles, primers, a multi-tool for emergencies, tape to cover the barrel if it rains and a bullet-puller to get the bullet out if you don't fire the gun.

And the worst part is after every shot, even at the shooting range, you have to take a portion of your limited shooting time to clean the gun with all sorts of patches, solvents, rags, ramrod attachments and who knows what else?

The dirty work begins once the hunt is over, but using a muzzleloader often gives hunters more satisfaction because having only one shot puts a premium on preparation and accuracy.

Complete bunk! All those myths are propagated and spread by the unknowing, those who have heard horror stories from friends who had bad experiences or quite possibly remember the days when those myths contained more than a small grain of truth. The fact is, muzzleloaders are much easier to use and clean, and are more fun than ever.

Decades ago, muzzleloaders really didn't do well at long distances. Prior to the technological advances with inline rifles, most flintlock shooters wanted a close shot at a deer or other big game. They knew the limits of their firearm and, often, it was inside 100 yards and sometimes much less than that.

Toting gear never has required much effort. Even in the old days, a powder horn, bag of molded bullets and some pillow-ticking for patches was it. Today's hunter may carry a few more items, such as a bullet starter, spare "speed loaders" for pelletized powder and bullets, a nipple pick and possibly a few cleaning patches for a quick run-through in the field.

Cleaning is a snap today, requiring a thorough but not-too-long stay at the bench. Removable breech plugs on inline models such as the Thompson/Center Omega, CVA Kodiak or Knight Vision eliminate the need for a soak in the bathtub. By removing the plug, you can easily clean the barrel and plug, let them dry, put a few drops of lubricant on the plug threads, return it and then lube the barrel before storing it in a safe location.

"They're very much easier to use and clean today," says Ernie French of Thompson/Center in Rochester, New Hampshire. "With the expansion of the muzzleloader market, most of the industry has tried to funnel things in that direction. We know the easier and cleaner we can make it for people, the more likely they are to use them. Probably the most common thing we see is people leave their gun loaded for a year, stuck in the corner, and we'll get them back at the plant with a note saying they can't get the bullet out or the barrel's rusted.

"What happens is the powder sits in there for such long time and is corrosive, or moisture seeps inside the barrel and causes more corrosion. But with the removable breech plugs available today, that really should not be a problem. You simply remove the plug, knock out the (powder) loads and bullet, clean the gun well, season it with a little lube and you're good to go."

Keeping muzzleloaders clean, inside and out, obviously not only preserves the life of the rifle but also ensures more accurate shots at the range and in the woods.

Mark Laney is in research and development with Thompson/Center and has seen some of the nastiest, corroded barrels you can imagine. Like French, he is amazed at how some hunters simply don't take the time or believe cleaning a gun thoroughly is unnecessary.

"Powder left in a gun, whether it is loose powder or the new pellets that are so popular, actually destroys the area where the powder sits around the breech plug," he said. "It may not affect the accuracy because the barrel may not be affected along the length of it, but if you go to clean it, when you get to the bottom, the patch is just going to stick. It's not a good thing because it affects the breech plug and everything. Pyrodex and black powder are very corrosive. Pyrodex is just as corrosive, so you should be sure to clean your gun extremely well at the end of the season."

Some powder manufacturers today tout hundreds or thousands of rounds fired through a muzzleloader before a cleaning is required.

More than 414,000 women were among the 3.8 million who participated in recreational shooting or hunting with muzzleloaders in 2004.

That may work in regulated testing, but under the normal rigors of a hunting trip where fog, condensation, rain or simple neglect by the hunter come into play, it can lead to serious problems.

A good cleaning kit includes a stable work area with a bench or rest, such as a Stoney Point Cleaning Cradle. You'll also need a cleaning rod with a handle that accepts accessories such as a bronze bore brush, cleaning "mop," patches with cleaning solvent and dry ones for follow-up swabbing and a lubricant such as Natural Lube 1000-Plus Bore Butter for post-cleaning seasoning. The breech plug should be cleaned well, a nipple pick used to make sure any gunk is not in the ignition chamber and a bit of lube applied before the plug is returned.

"You can get away with wiping it out after you shoot and that's fine, but after the season you really need to take the breech plug out and give it a good cleaning with some of the products that are available, such as the pre-lubed patches or other things you prefer, before you put it away," Laney said. "If you have a very good barrel and you don't take care of it and keep it clean, it's not going to stay that way. You'll lose accuracy, so cleaning it is very important."

Data on participation compiled for the National Sporting Goods Association and National Muzzleloader Rifle Association show approximately 3.81 million people used muzzleloaders in 2004. That includes 3.4 million males and 414,000 females, with the highest-ranking male age group being 35-44 years old and second highest

Hodgdon Pyrodex and Triple Se7en muzzleloading propellants.

44-54 years old. Third highest was 25-35 years old.

That appears to be a strong sign that muzzleloaders will continue to gain popularity as older, veteran hunters assist younger hunters with advice and knowledge. In turn, the younger demographic is looking at purchasing a rifle to use for hunting and recreational shooting.

Also from that data, the "South Atlantic" region from West Virginia south led in participation with about 703,000 users. The "East North Central" area that includes Wisconsin, Illinois, Indiana, Ohio and Michigan was second with 664,000 and the "East South Central" region of Kentucky, Tennessee, Mississippi and Alabama was third with about 550,000 shooters.

While some states prohibit rifles and require muzzleloaders or shotguns for deer, others such as Alabama, Mississippi and Tennessee have specific muzzleloader-only seasons. Alabama's is five days long in November, running concurrently with the last week of archery-only season prior to the general firearms opener. The use of scopes on inline rifles also was approved for hunter's choice either-sex hunting.

Special seasons spur sales of rifles, powder, bullets and accessories. It also helps people who may be getting back into hunting, or who want to try something new instead of a regular rifle or archery equipment.

"It's sort of like people who go from shooting semi-auto rifles to bolt-actions to single-shot firearms," French said. "A lot have gone to muzzle-loaders simply because it gives them more time in the field. That was their initial excuse—more hunting time. Then they get out there and find out how much fun it is with a muzzleloader and how accurate they truly are."

Ah, yes, the accuracy question. Just how far can a muzzleloader

Muzzleloading bullets and sabots by Hornady.

Modern muzzleloading bullets, powered by Pyrodex or traditional black powder, are both accurate and effective.

shoot a bullet? More importantly, how far is an accurate trajectory for a killing shot maintained before gravity takes over and the bullet begins falling? If two Pyrodex pellets provide good accuracy, why won't three? Or four? Should I use sabot bullets or a plain, lubricated bullet?

Bullets fired from a muzzleloader can go as far as 500 yards, according to firearms companies, but most hunters are more concerned about what happens within150-200 yards. With two or three Pyrodex pellets or a 100- to 150-grain load of powder, bullets have more than enough energy to effectively penetrate hide, bone and vital organs of big-game animals to 150 yards. Better bullets with polymer tips, hollow points and bonded copper-lead bodies also are contributing to improved accuracy.

"At 100 yards, they will shoot inside two inches all day," said French, of the Thompson/Center rifles, adding the routine of the shooter and his loads should not be overlooked once accuracy is attained. "The 209 is a hotter, faster ignition, and I recommend Pyrodex pellets for a couple of reasons. One is the consistency with the manufacture of the pellets. Often we've had people loading loose powder and there's a lot

Flintlock Shooting Improves Skills

How can a rifle that belches a cloud of smoke and creates sparks and a flash near your face make you a better shooter? By causing you to do two simple things: be patient, and stay with the shot.

That's what Ernie French with Thompson/Center Arms in Rochester, N.H., believes with all his heart. He's a diehard flintlock shooter, the old-school style rifleman who needs that flint, frizzen, flash and "fa-whoom!" to get his blood going.

By keeping his head down after the flint sparks the ignition powder in the frizzen, then through the touchhole to the powder in the barrel, French knows he will keep his focus on the target.

"There's a group of us at the T/C shop who get together and shoot flintlocks quite a bit," he said. "If you don't follow through and stick with the shot, you're not going to be very accurate. It takes some getting used to because you have that fire going off beside your face, hence the name 'flinch-locks.' It is very easy to flinch, and those who have been doing it a long time even flinch."

But French said the patience and dedication required to shoot flintlocks pays off. Not only do you become a better shooter, but you become more familiar with your rifle because the corrosive powder forces you to very thoroughly clean the barrel, touchhole and frizzen every 5 to 10 shots.

"Everyone who shoots a flintlock and shoots it regularly and gets good at it has said the same thing: when you go back to shoot your centerfire rifle or even your inline muzzleloader, it makes you a better shooter," he said. "You concentrate more on the shot. It's a lot of fun. It's real common to get a hangfire in a flintlock, and after doing that a few times with the pan going off, you know you have to stay right with that shot. You'll pull the trigger, have a flash and you just stand there. You get used to it. Same thing happens with a centerfire rifle when you squeeze the trigger and follow through by keeping your head down on the gun."

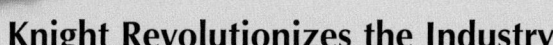

Knight Revolutionizes the Industry

After being laid off from his job with the Rock Island railroad in Illinois, Tony Knight returned to his native Missouri and began a new career repairing firearms as a gunsmith. When some of his customers had a disappointing flintlock hunt because of the weather, they asked him about helping to solve the problem of misfires. Knight took the challenge to heart, examining different guns and researching ways to create a more reliable ignition and firing system.

What resulted was a revolution for the muzzleloader industry as Knight created the first modern-day inline rifle. Introduced in 1985 and named the MK-85, for his daughter Michele, the rifle quickly became one of the most popular muzzleloaders on the market.

As his company grew, Knight moved it to Centerville, Iowa, where it is located today. In 1997, he further assisted hunters by introducing the DISC system. The ignition primer is housed in a plastic casing that fits snugly into the breech, creating a tight weatherproof housing. It's easy to use and eliminates worry about moisture seeping in to ruin the ignitor or powder in the breech.

In 2005, to celebrate Knight Rifles' 20th anniversary, the company brought the popular Bighorn rifle out of retirement. It comes with three ignition systems—No. 11 nipple, musket nipple and Extreme shotgun primer system—along with non-fiber optic sights. Additionally, the beautiful 20th anniversary Revolution debuted in a limited-edition of 1,000 rifles that features a two-piece stock, bedded barrel and detachable pivot-block action for easy cleaning.

All this because of a bad hunting trip and persistence from a guy who simply loves guns and loves to hunt.

of inconsistency. With a pre-manufactured powder you get more consistency. Obviously, second is the ease of loading (with the pellets.) Whatever you do, do it the same every time."

Inlines are the hottest thing right now in the muzzleloader industry, with their improved ignitions and ease of use. Thumbhole stocks are the rage, and consumers have an array of choices with stainless or blued metal and wooden or composite stocks. Thompson/Center shook things up three years ago with the pivoting breech, which made loading and weatherproofing a snap. It would seem the inlines can't be improved much more, but we know it will happen. Someone will design this little gizmo or that little gadget that will make things just a touch easier.

"As in almost everything else today, the speed with which this whole world moves, everyone wants to do it fast, do it efficient and do it often," French said. "With the inlines, that's essentially what you've got. We make it as easy as possible to load, as easy as possible to fire, as easy as possible to clean."

With the advances in the industry, that means it's also easy as possible to have fun with a muzzleloader.

Rabbits Without Rover
by Keith Sutton

There are basically two ways to hunt rabbits: with dogs or without. Devout dog men wouldn't think of hunting without their canine pals. But many hunters simply don't have the time, financing or inclination to manage a well-trained pack of beagles.

Where does that leave the dogless hunter? In pretty good shape, really, so long as the hunter is willing to work for his hasenpfeffer. Where rabbits are plentiful, a canine-less cottontail hunt can provide lots of action-packed excitement. But the dogless hunter can't sit on a stump and await the singing announcement of an incoming rab-

You don't need dogs to have a successful rabbit hunt, as this hunter could attest.

bit. His success, or failure, relies on his own legwork and effort and not on that of a pack of beagles.

Hunting rabbits without dogs can be productive any time, early or late in the season. In fall and early winter, hunting pressure, natural predation and weather have yet to thin the population. Rabbits are more numerous and easier to find. During late winter, rabbits are fewer, but they're more concentrated, too, avoiding cold winter weather by hiding in the thickest cover they can find. The hunter who's willing to brave the brambles can enjoy fast-paced jumpshooting, even on the coldest days.

The first order of business is identifying a good hunting area. When walking 'em up, this means an area that is: 1) fairly small or confined, so there's a better chance of flushing rabbits into the open for an easy shot; and 2) seldom hunted, so rabbits are more likely to be plentiful. Look for isolated patches and strips of cover that are not easily accessible by other hunters, and try to find several such places you can hunt during a day afield. By "spot hunting" (covering one fencerow or brush patch in an hour or so, then driving on to another potential hotspot), you'll locate more rabbits and boost your chances for finding consistent action.

Stalking rabbits in the thick cover of a woodland edge produced a nice cottontail for this "no-dogs" hunter.

If there are two or more hunters in your "no-Rover" hunting party, try hunting long narrow strips of cover such as brushy fence rows, lines of tree-shrouded thickets between cropfields, abandoned railroad rights-of-way, cover-choked ditches and such. One or two hunters walk through the middle, kicking spots of cover that may hide rabbits. The others walk the outside edges, standing ready to pick off retreating rabbits that hightail it out one side.

Planning a Safe Drive

A variation of this technique uses blockers and drivers. One or more gunners wait on stand while others attempt to flush and drive rabbits toward them by beating the cover on foot. The drivers have the hardest going, but periodically, drivers and blockers switch places so everyone gets in on the action. Blockers must be good snap shooters. They'll probably have some rip-snorting action for a moment or two as cottontails sprint past them.

Of course, safety must be foremost on everyone's mind. A strict set of rules governs every drive: 1) Only blockers carry guns; 2) To

The dogless hunter must work thoroughly and walk through even small spots of cover that may hide rabbits.

A cover of snow shouldn't deter rabbit hunters who have no dogs. Stalking is a very effective technique after a snowfall, and hunters can often pinpoint rabbits by tracking them.

increase visibility to one another, everyone wears the same hunter-orange bodywear and hats required for deer hunting; 3) No shots are taken in anyone else's direction; 4) No one shoots until their target is positively identified; 5) Blockers remain in their assigned position until the drive is over; and 6) Drivers follow their assigned route and end up where they're supposed to be. Everyone on a drive should know where his hunting buddies are at all times.

So everyone knows what's expected of them, it's a good idea to map out your hunting strategy before each drive. The person who best knows the lay of the land should be the drive boss, and everyone follows his or her instructions precisely. Using a map, a pencil and paper, or just a stick in the dirt, the drive boss illustrates exactly where the blockers will be positioned and where the drivers will work. At the completion of each drive, everyone assembles, and the hunters reorganize for the next drive.

Next to safety, the single most important aspect of a successful cottontail drive is proper deployment of the blockers. Hunters must be positioned where they can cover the rabbits' escape routes.

To best accomplish this, confine your hunting to narrow patches of cover with well-defined borders created by open fields, streams and

other features. Position blockers at one end or near small breaks or bottlenecks in the cover. The best areas are open enough so the blocker has a good shot at crossing rabbits, but not so barren or wide that rabbits will avoid crossing them.

Blockers shouldn't be positioned at the center of the bottleneck or opening, nor should they face the drivers. First, this isn't safe. Second, approaching rabbits will see the blockers immediately. Instead, blockers should stand off to the side so shots will be angled away from the drivers. This also permits fleeing rabbits to follow familiar escape routes without detecting the blockers.

Although four or five people can be used in a properly orchestrated drive, in most areas with small to moderate patches of cover, two or three hunters are plenty. The two-hunter approach worked fine on one memorable hunting trip with my buddy Jim.

We were hunting a long narrow strip of thickets, with a field of standing cotton on one side and an open plowed field on the other. Jim had hunted here before and knew flushed rabbits would invariably head straight down the strip of cover, then break to the right and cross into the cotton field. Knowing that gave us the upper hand.

Because rabbits are so well-camouflaged, stalking them is challenging. It's tough to spot the rabbit hiding in this thicket, but it's there.

The cover strip was about a quarter-mile long, so instead of driving the whole patch at once, we divided it into sections. One of us took a position up ahead in the open turnrow between the cotton field and the thicket. The other stomped through the brush to flush hiding rabbits. There were plenty of cottontails, and most headed across the turnrow and into the cotton field just as Jim had predicted. In 2½ hours, we managed to bag eight rabbits—not too bad for walking them up.

Brushpiles

When present, piles of brush and timber also merit the attention of hunters working without dogs. These woody heaps attract plenty of rabbits and concentrate them in a very small area, a key advantage for the jumpshooter. Some hunters make their own brushpiles by placing a loose covering of brush over a framework of heavy branches, then come back to hunt them after they've "seasoned out" for a few months. Others hunt brushpiles left behind by timber cutters and farmers clearing their land.

The best way to hunt a brushpile is to circle it first, trying to identify the most likely exit a cottontail will use. Look for trails through adjacent cover, large openings in the brush or anything that gives a clue as to how the rabbit will react to your intrusion. Then

position one or two hunters where there's a good view of the exit, and let another stomp through, without a gun, from the other side. Be ready. This is fast, sporty gunning, and many great wingshots and high scorers on sporting clays fields don't fare too well during their first encounters with brushpile cottontails.

Stalking

One of the most casual, yet challenging, methods of hunting rabbits is stalking them, one on one, hunter against animal. Rabbits are adept at hiding, so the hunter must use a healthy measure of cunning to score consistently when using this technique.

Much of what I know about stalking rabbits I learned from an older friend named Tommy. When I started hunting with him, I had an inclination to run full speed ahead, believing the more cover I stormed through, the more rabbits I was likely to see. Tommy, on the other hand, just poked along, rarely kicking the brush at all, but looking, always looking, canvassing every bit of cover through which he walked. His slow pace aggravated me to no end, as did his tendency to carry his gun draped over an elbow, muzzle pointing at the ground a few feet

The rabbit's round black eye is easily seen by the stalking hunter who trains himself to look for it.

Small tracts of dense cover, like this honeysuckle patch, are ideal for "no-dogs" rabbit hunting. This hunter bagged a swamp rabbit after it was flushed by his hunting partner.

Serving as blockers on a "no-dogs" cottontail drive, this father-daughter hunting team watches for more cottontails flushed by their partners.

Farm Help

Savvy rabbit hunters know that farmers are an invaluable aid for finding cottontail concentrations. Because they work their land daily and see rabbits regularly, farmers know where huntable populations are likely to be. Most are eager to keep cottontails thinned out so they don't cause crop damage.

It's a simple matter to cultivate your own contacts in farm country. Remember these things: Ask permission before hunting, every time you visit. Follow all rules the landowner asks you to abide by, like passing up shots at the coveys of quail he's nurturing. Leave everything just as you found it, and always take time to thank the farmer personally. Offer to share your game, and follow up with a thank-you note and a token of your appreciation. Make these easy-to-follow guidelines part of all your farm visits, and you'll always have prime rabbit lands on which to hunt.

ahead of his rubber knee boots, a carry from which it would obviously take half a minute to get into action. The efficient hunter, I thought, always carried his shotgun in both hands, muzzle up, ready to be thrown to the shoulder in a split instant to send a deadly shot charge on its way. Tommy didn't really match my mental image of an efficient hunter.

All of which shows how young and ignorant I was. While I was rushing around, stomping through every inch of cover, Tommy was hunting. He carefully perused everything around him, looking into thickets and briar patches, under brushpiles, between the roots of trees. And after a while, it dawned on me that he was seeing more rabbits with his casual approach that I was with my incessant hurrying.

"Hold up, boy," he'd say, pointing a finger into a thicket. "See his eye shining against the leaves?" Eventually I'd see the bright little dot of black, out of place in the crisscross of cover. Then magically, the rabbit's whole body would appear, and I'd stand there and wonder why I couldn't see one like that myself.

Thinking back, I'm sure there were many times when my helter-skelter hunting method took me right past many rabbits that sat tight, relying on their excellent camouflage to hide them. Tommy, of course, saw most of them. He looked everywhere and missed very little. And when he finished hunting a brushy draw or fencerow, there was no sense in anyone else going through it.

More Tips

In the years since I hunted with Tommy, I've learned much more about hunting rabbits without dogs. I've learned, for instance, that rabbits' soft fur does little to turn the cold, and on sunny winter days, they'll sit in a spot out of the wind where they can warm themselves in direct sunlight. Knowing this helps when I'm stalking rabbits on frigid days late in the season.

I've learned that if a rabbit isn't spooked too bad, a sharp whistle may stop it in its tracks, giving me an added few seconds to make a clean shot before my target disappears.

I've learned that rabbits in isolated patches of cover will try to sneak around behind me rather than cross open ground. Others sit tight till I pass, then squirt out behind. Glancing over my shoulder now and then while hunting helps me bag some of these renegades before they escape.

I've learned to wear heavy clothing when hunting without dogs to keep from turning myself into a lump of hamburger when thrashing through the stickers.

And best of all, I think, I've learned that hunting rabbits without dogs can be just as much fun as hunting them with a pack of beagles. Happiness, my friend, is small game hunting, no matter how you serve it up.

Dress for Success

Most good cottontail thickets have one thing in common—thorns. And if you're kicking up rabbits yourself, without the aid of dogs, you're going to have to get right down in the thickets to flush and retrieve game. It's a sure bet some type of stickers will be clawing at your ears, fingers, thighs and other tender parts. Wearing protective clothing can do wonders to make your trips afield more enjoyable and less painful.

Blue jeans are preferred by many rabbit fans, but offer little protection. A good pair of briar-busting breeches with thorn-proof material covering the front should be considered essential equipment no matter where and how you hunt. It also helps to wear a briar-resistant hunting coat, gloves and some type of hunting cap with flaps that can be pulled down over your ears.

Finally, wear hunter orange hats and bodywear on all hunts to make yourself more visible. That's a tip we all can live with.

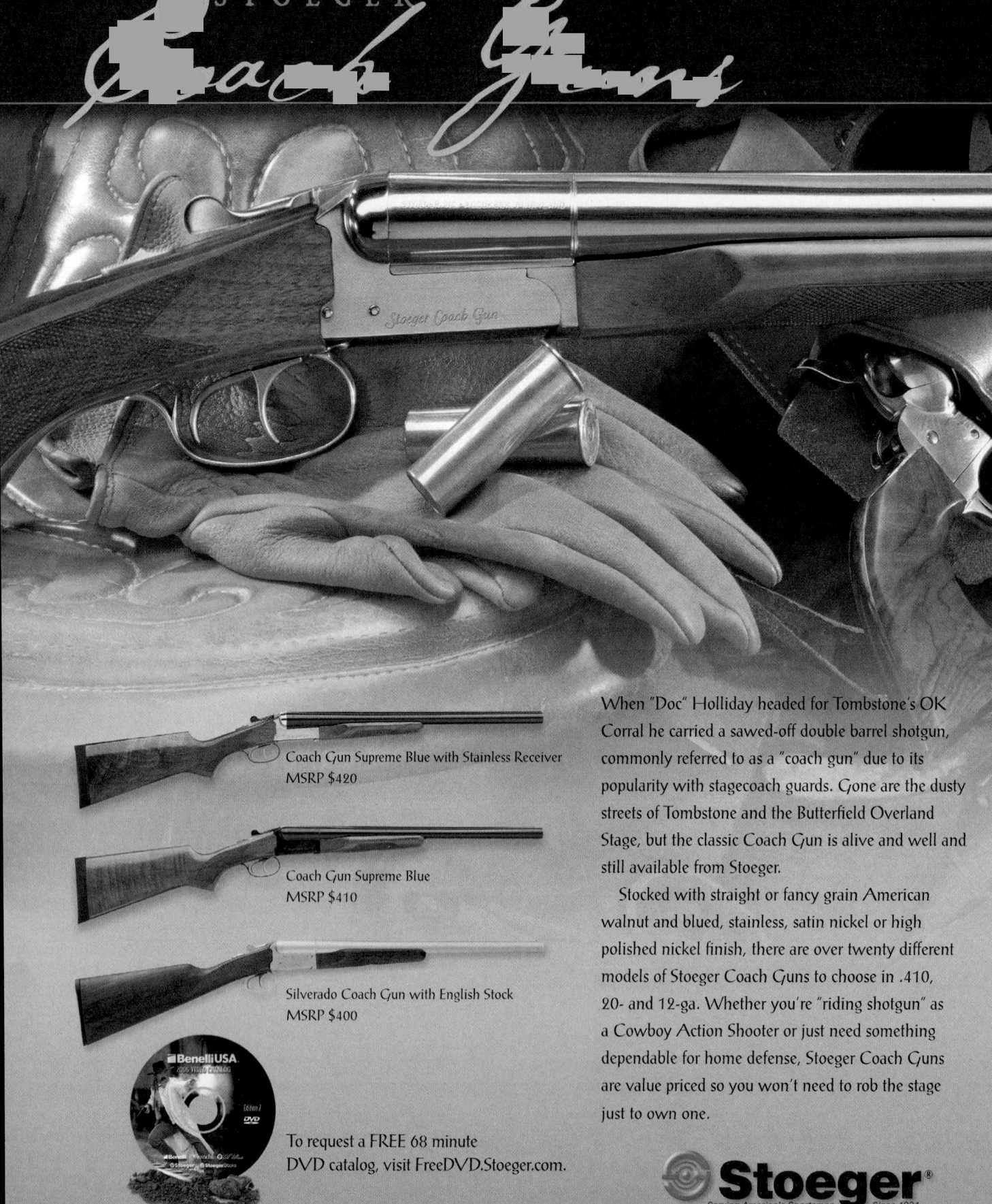

STOEGER

Coach Guns

Coach Gun Supreme Blue with Stainless Receiver
MSRP $420

Coach Gun Supreme Blue
MSRP $410

Silverado Coach Gun with English Stock
MSRP $400

To request a FREE 68 minute
DVD catalog, visit FreeDVD.Stoeger.com.

When "Doc" Holliday headed for Tombstone's OK Corral he carried a sawed-off double barrel shotgun, commonly referred to as a "coach gun" due to its popularity with stagecoach guards. Gone are the dusty streets of Tombstone and the Butterfield Overland Stage, but the classic Coach Gun is alive and well and still available from Stoeger.

Stocked with straight or fancy grain American walnut and blued, stainless, satin nickel or high polished nickel finish, there are over twenty different models of Stoeger Coach Guns to choose in .410, 20- and 12-ga. Whether you're "riding shotgun" as a Cowboy Action Shooter or just need something dependable for home defense, Stoeger Coach Guns are value priced so you won't need to rob the stage just to own one.

Stoeger®
Serving America's Sportsmen   Since 1924

Imported by Stoeger Industries   •   (301) 283-6300   •   StoegerIndustries.com

State of the Art in Slug-Shooting
by Dave Henderson

The handsome Illinois 9-pointer that I took on a friend's farm in 2004 wasn't the biggest buck I'd ever killed. Nor was the shot particularly difficult because the big guy was standing broadside 91 yards away in a fog-shrouded field of mustard grass.

And the Iowa 8-pointer I was privileged to take a month later on outfitter-writer-buddy Judd Cooney's heralded lease—in a dusky rain at more than 130 yards—similarly didn't set any personal size or shooting milestones.

If the dimensions weren't there, however, the magic sure was. In fact, the bucks could have been a forkhorn and a spike sneaking through the cut corn behind my house, and the moments would have been the same. These were my 100th and 101st whitetails with a slug gun. Given the personal milestone, achieved among friends at traditional big-buck Meccas, well, say I was immensely proud of the bucks, and leave it at that.

Those 101 deer actually brought me full circle in the slug-shooting world. The first one, some 34 years previously, had fallen to a

Author Dave Henderson poses in an Illinois field with a handsome 9-pointer, his 100th deer taken with a slug-firing shotgun.

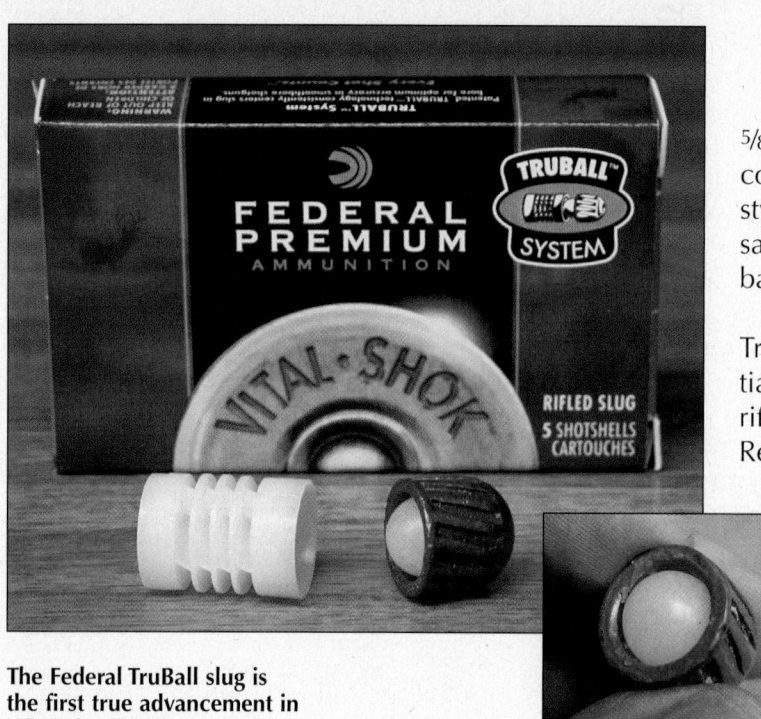

The Federal TruBall slug is the first true advancement in rifled slug design since the 1930s.

⅝-ounce 20-gauge rifled slug. The first couple dozen or so, in fact, fell to Foster-style rifled slugs or Brennekes before sabots, their many variations and rifled barrels came into vogue.

But No. 100 was felled by a Federal Tru-Ball Vital-Shok slug—which is essentially the 21st century evolution of the rifled slug—fired through a smoothbore Remington barrel. And No. 101 fell victim to a 3-inch Remington BuckHammer, which, fired through a Remington rifled barrel, packs more punch than any slug on the planet.

One hundred deer may not mean much to those who hunt where whitetails are plentiful and bag limits liberal. But for my first 25 years of hunting, one deer per season was pretty much the legal limit. It increased slightly in certain areas at home, but even last season I got only a buck tag and one antlerless tag for the shotgun season. The century mark is testimony to a peripatetic lifestyle and a meat hunter's philosophy of quantity over quality.

Both of the new loads must be considered "state of the art" for shotgunners. But "state-of-the-art," as you'll see, is a rather nebulous phrase as it pertains to slug shooting, with vastly dissimilar definitions.

The 3-inch Remington BuckHammer is a 1,500 feet per second, 1-⅛-ounce thunderclap that generates 3,232 foot pounds of energy at the muzzle. The Federal TruBall is essentially the first major step forward in slug shooting for smoothbores since the rifled slug was introduced in the 1930s and effectively increases the effective range of the industry's most popular slug design. More than 65 percent of the market is still smoothbore shotguns and rifled slugs.

Add in other new-to-the-scene loads like Hornady's revolutionary new SST slug with its polymer-tipped bullet design and Hastings' opposite-end-of-the-spectrum bulky non-discarding sabot design and you've got something new for virtually every slug shooter's preferences.

Comparing slugs and shotguns from my early days of hunting more than three decades ago with today's state-of-the-art, controlled expansion projectiles is like juxtaposing the Wright brothers' Kitty Hawk flying machine and the Space Shuttle.

In my salad days, we transformed rabbit guns into deer guns by simply changing the fodder. You bought slugs from a hardware store bin at a dime apiece with no regard brand or type. Today we're actually comparing ballistic coefficients in shotgun loads, for God's sake, and slipping the safety off when a buck appears two football fields away.

The aforementioned Remington BuckHammer, the Hastings Magnum, Brenneke's Black Magic, Gold and K.O. Sabot and Rottweil's Blitz slug are all fairly new, big, full-bore soft lead slugs that launch at 1,500-1,700 fps. They are made to penetrate and impart major shock on the animal while retaining most, if not all, of their mass.

At the same time, Hornady's unique SST slug, Winchester's Partition Gold, Remington's CoreLokt Ultra and the Winchester Platinum Tip are all high-velocity, jacketed, lead core bullets encased in cup-like sabots. The SST and 3-inch Partition Gold both eclipse 2,000 fps in muzzle velocity and pack a savage punch out to 200 yards.

The SST's polymer tip not only serves to accentuate expansion, like a hollow point, but also gives the slug a much sleeker profile and thus excellent ballistic coefficient. It's the first-ever pointed bullet loaded in a shotgun slug, its one-inch (actually about 15/16) length allowing it to be seated deep enough so that the polymer point is recessed inside the hull, far from the primer of the slug ahead of it in the magazine.

When Winchester (Partition Gold) and Remington (CoreLokt Ultra) vaulted into the 1,900-2,000 fps stratosphere, they had to reinforce the floor of the sabot by molding in metal wafers to withstand the higher pressure. Otherwise the sabots would cling to the slug and not release consistently.

But instead of reinforcing the sabot floor, Hornady places a loose cushioning wad under the slug's base to achieve the same effect. The slug starts at 2,000 feet per second yet retains 1,482 fps at 150 yards, and a whopping 1,463 foot pounds of energy.

While the SST derives its outstanding ballistics from a 300-grain

Remington BuckHammer slug.

The new Hornady SST slug represents the state of the art in high-velocity sabot slugs, built for rifled barreled shotguns.

The modern lead core, copper-jacketed high-velocity slugs like Hornady's H2K (left) and Winchester's Partition Gold, are actually large-caliber versions of pistol bullets.

OPPOSITE PAGE:
The author's 101st deer with a shotgun was this Iowa buck, taken with a state-of-the-art Remington 870 12-gauge with a Boyd's Thumbhole laminated stock and a 3-inch Remington BuckHammer slug.

Examples of high-velocity (1,700-2,000 fps muzzle velocity) sabot slugs: (l to r) Lightfield Commander, Winchester Partition Gold, Winchester Platinum Tip, Hevi-Shot sabot, Hornady SST, Federal Barnes Expanders.

bullet, sleek shape and high velocity, Remington's 3-inch BuckHammer does it with sheer mass. The slug was, as expected, a brute. With 1³/₈ of lead and an attached plastic stabilizing wad, the recoil was particularly brutal. Launched at relatively pedestrian 1,500 fps, it's still toting 1,710 foot pounds of energy at 100 yards.

The 3-inch Lightfield Commander, Hevi-Shot Sabot, the Federal Barnes EXpander, Remington Copper Solid and and Brenneke Super Sabot are also certainly state of the art without fitting neatly into either sabot niche.

The TruBall system and Winchester's Super-X Power Point rifled slug are designed for smoothbore shotguns. They'll shoot fairly accurately through rifled bores, but the soft lead will skid on the rifling and quickly (within 2-3 shots) fill the grooves, after which accuracy is severely compromised.

Similarly, don't shoot sabot slugs through a smoothbore gun. Sabots are designed to be spun by rifled barrels. Shoot them out of a smoothbore and the sabot sleeves aren't likely to release efficiently, which means very poor flight characteristics and greatly reduced range.

The Sabots

If you shoot a rifled-barreled slug gun, the evolution process for your slugs has been much shorter and more rapid. In the 1990s, when rifled bores were legalized in more and more states, the development of the sabot slug took a quantum leap forward.

Sabot slugs are smaller diameter (usually around .50 caliber for 12 gauge and .45 caliber for 20s, although designs use larger diameters and thinner sabot sleeves), more aerodynamic slugs encased in bore-filling, fall-away plastic sleeves called sabots. This allowed the ballistically cavernous shotgun bore to throw a much more efficient projectile, and the plastic sleeves grabbed the rifling and imparted a stabilizing spin on the whole unit.

The sabot's true advantage comes farther downrange where the combination of spin and weight distribution keep it stable—thereby retaining its energy well past the point where the full-bore slugs had petered out—past 100 yards.

There have been dozens of sabot designs introduced over the last 20 years, only to ultimately fade into obsolescence. The high retail price

Kinder, Gentler Slugs

One of the most noticeable effects of slug shooting, and one of its biggest deterrents, is recoil. Shotguns shooting slugs simply kick hard, which dampens enthusiasm and can adversely effect accuracy, not to mention practice sessions at the range.

That's the reason shotgun slugs have been added to the list of kinder, gentler ordnance that has swept onto the market in the last couple of years.

They are more comfortable to shoot but still serious hunting ordnance. Witness the soft-shooting "Managed Recoil" version of the BuckHammer with which I took whitetail No. 99—at 146 yards—in South Carolina. Like the other two scenarios, the shot resulted in a clean, one-shot kill. And despite the watered-down ballistics involved, it was the longest killing shot I've ever made on a whitetail.

The 1⅛-ounce slug left the barrel at 1,350 fps and was still toting sufficient energy to punch through both lungs at that distance.

Other softer slug designs for rifled bores include Hastings' Low Recoil-Youth slug, with a muzzle velocity of 1,020 fps and Lightfield Lites, which are a 1,300 fps version of the company's Hybred sabot design.

Federal has a Low Recoil version of the TruBall that launches at a comfortable 1,300 fps at the muzzle yet still carries more than 900 foot pounds of energy at 75 yards. Remington similarly recently introduced a Managed Recoil version of its vaunted Slugger rifled slugs for smoothbores.

and rapidly advancing technology, combined with technical difficulty in coordinating the separation of the slug and sabot, manufacturing problems and sometimes less-than-spectacular performance doomed many versions.

The first successful sabot was an hour glass-shaped .50-caliber lead pellet encased in a bore-filling, two-piece plastic tube (sabot) that grabbed the rifling and was discarded by the spin when the system exited the muzzle.

Winchester and Federal built new, improved versions off the BRI sabot patent in the 1990s. Their designs, which were virtually identical, were very accurate but much too hard to expand on deer-sized game and were markedly slower than fullbore slugs, putting it at a distinct disadvantage for short-range shooting in typical whitetail environments.

The tiny Lightfield Ammunition Corporation was formed to produce an expanding design sabot slug. The Lightfield Hybred, formulated by British designer Tony Kinchin, was actually much closer to the 3-inch Brenneke design, or the similar Activ attached wad design, but encased in a two-piece thin sabot.

Next in the slam-bang development of slugs came Remington's revolutionary Copper Solid—a 1-ounce, .50-caliber slug with an open, slotted nose that was machined out of solid copper bar stock.

The Copper Solid was the first actual bullet (rear-weighted rather than nose-heavy) loaded in a sabot. The second came in the late 1990s when Federal started loading the soft-copper hollow point Barnes Expander bullet. Remington actually redesigned the Copper Solid in 1998 to a softer form, much like the Barnes Expander. The soft copper 1,500 fps slugs expanded well and retained 100 percent of their mass when hitting a deer, the first sabot slug since the Lightfield Hybred to do that.

Quick on their heels, however, came the first of the high-velocity slugs. The Hornady H2K Heavy Mag, Winchester Partition Gold and later the Remington CoreLokt Ultra and Winchester Platinum Tip were all beefed up jacketed lead pistol bullets driven at velocities of 1,800-2,000 fps.

Federal joined the club by simply dropping the weight of its Barnes Expander slug to ¾-ounce, thus jacking the velocity to 1,900 fps. Lightfield introduced a totally new 3-inch design called the Commander, which boasted 1,800 fps and a 3.5-incher at 1,900 fps and Brenneke's unique articulated copper Super Sabot soon followed.

In each case, except for Lightfield, the companies followed with 20-gauge, high-velocity versions. But the high-velocity slugs' sabot designs struggle mightily with the increased force and don't shoot as accurately in many guns as the conventional velocity loads. That's probably the reason that the newest slug designs—ostensibily the Remington BuckHammer Express, Hastings Magnum, Brenneke K.O. Sabot and Black Magic, Hevi-Shot Sabot and the Rottweil Blitz—are larger diameter, all-lead (tungsten alloy in the Hevi-Shot), lower velocity slugs. They are easier to shoot accurately and kick less than their high-velocity counterparts.

The flashiest of the new sabot designs are the high-velocity (1,800-2,000 fps) versions that incorporate a big-bore, usually jacketed, lead core pistol bullet. The fastest had been Hornady's H2K Heavy Mag, which topped 2,000 fps regularly but never showed good accuracy. It was retired in 2005 in favor of the new SST slug, which is the first shotgun load to use a pointed bullet design.

The SST, which has a proven accuracy record as a muzzleloader bullet, is an inch-long, 300-grain, .50-caliber version of the company's famed polymer-tipped pistol bullet that is launched at 2,000 fps.

In 2004 Winchester introduced the 3-inch 12-gauge version of its Partition Gold sabot slug. Remington's 1-ounce CoreLokt Ultra and Federal's ¾-ounce Barnes EXpander are legitimate 1,900 fps loads, and Winchester's 400-grain, 1,700 fps Platinum Tip slug is actually a .50-caliber variant of the company's Fail Safe bullet line and is virtually identical, albeit larger caliber, to the company's pistol bullet line.

All offer flat trajectory, plenty of retained energy out past 150 yards and excellent upset performance on deer. The drawback is that they are not accurate in all guns. Some experts contend that a faster rifling twist (typically 1-turn-in-28 inches as opposed to the conventional 1-in-35) is essential in handling the high-velocity slugs.

But others will tell you that, given the pressures generated by the higher velocities and the hardness of the bullet-slug at setback, sabot-to-barrel fit (rather than twist rate) is more critical with the faster slugs than it is with the softer, slower sabots.

In fact, the difficult-to-control nature of the high-velocity slugs, and their attendant mule-like kick, are probably the reasons that the industry has put more design work into the more predictable full-bore sabot slugs in recent years.

The Hastings slug, introduced in 2004 in a 12-gauge 1¼-ounce, 1,500 fps magnum version and the 1,020 fps Low Recoil-Youth ver-

Examples of slugs built for rifled barreled shotguns:(l to r) Lightfield Commander, Hastings Magnum, Winchester Partition Gold, Remington BuckHammer, Federal Barnes Expander, Brenneke Super Sabot, Federal Premium sabot, Winchester High Impact sabot, Brenneke Gold.

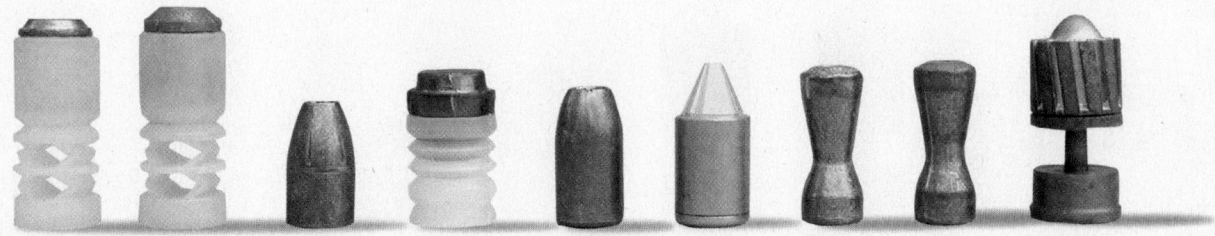

sion, is a soft lead slug encased in a non-discarding sabot and attached wad, the sabot sleeve working like a jacket on a rifle bullet. This year there is a 3-inch, 12-gauge Lazer Mag version (1,625 fps at the muzzle) and a 20-gauge version also. The Hastings' soft slug and flexible sabot allow it to swell at setback and thus fill the bore of any gun, giving it a reputation for accuracy.

Hastings uses the same Sabot Technologies sabot as the Hevi-Shot sabot, which has a much harder tungsten-alloy slug. The Lightfield 3- and 3.5-inch Commander's sabot is of a similar non-discarding design with a different lead slug and higher (1,800-1,900 fps) velocity.

Brenneke's Black Magic and Gold slugs are, like the Remington BuckHammer, full-bore slugs with attached plastic wads but no sabot sleeves. The 1⅜-ounce Brenneke versions are specially coated to reduce leading in the bore and offer 1,500-1,600 fps muzzle velocities in the 2¾- and 3-inch designs. The Brenneke K.O. Sabot is a 1-ounce slug with an encompassing sabot, different attached wad and faster velocities.

Back in 1997, when Federal first started loading a proprietary soft copper version of the Barnes XBullet as the Federal Barnes EXpander, it marked the first actual bullet (rear-weighted) loaded as a slug that expanded readily. Four years earlier, Remington's original Copper Solid was the first rear-weighted, bullet-like slug design but it fell out of favor due to problems caused by its uncompromising hardness.

Remington redesigned the Copper Solid as a virtual ballistic twin of the Federal Barnes EXpander in 1998, but when Federal sped up the Barnes EXpander as a high-velocity version in 2000, Remington took its technology toward the CoreLokt Ultra – a .50-caliber verison of its vaunted rifle bullet design.

The unique design of the Brenneke Super Sabot doesn't allow it to fit into any particular niche. A sliding copper sleeve around a soft-nosed needle core gives the 1,526 fps slug (in the 3-inch version) excellent stability, structural integrity and good expansion on impact.

The Truball

All that being said, the smoothbore slug still represents more than 65% of the slug-shooting market. The TruBall, based on an idea patented by Georgia slug innovator Jay Menefee, is a simple yet ingenious expansion of a 70-year-old design.

Examples of slugs built for smoothbore shotguns: (l to r) Rottweil Blitz, Brenneke KO, Brenneke Black Magic, Brenneke Magnum, Original Brenneke, Hevi-Shot Foster slug, Federal TruBall, conventional rifled slug as made by Winchester, Federal and Remington.

The TruBall is not a 100-yard-plus load like the sabots on the market; after all, it's still a rifled slug. But the unique design improves accuracy to the point where it will be on target at considerably longer range than its short, stubby, full-bore brethren. Understand that the typical rifled slug has not changed, in a visual sense, since ballistician Karl Foster's design was picked up by Winchester-Western and hit the market in the 1930s. It's still a cup-shaped dollop of soft lead with "rifling" grooves swaged into the outside walls.

The TruBall's unique design—essentially a polymer ball inserted into the cavity of a conventional rifled slug and driven at 1,600 feet per second by a cylindrical polymer pusher wad—doesn't make the new slug any more powerful than conventional rifled slugs. But it does make the slug much more effective.

The polymer ball keeps the slug from collapsing and forces it down the bore concentric with the tube, giving it a far better chance of flying true when it exits the muzzle. Because it's flying true, it remains stable farther down range.

In a comparative sense, the TruBall is not a re-invention of the wheel, but rather a move that essentially makes the wheel rounder; more efficient and effective.

The Tru-Ball extends the rifled slug's effective range because the design essentially guarantees concentricity to the bore and thus an undeformed emergence and subsequently truer flight.

Not to be left behind, Winchester last year introduced the Super-X Power-Point, a more stable version of the conventional 1-ounce rifled slug. Unlike other rifled slugs, the Power-Point's "rifling grooves" extend up the sides of the slug to the start of the deep hollow point nose.

Winchester's newest move into the rifled slug design came one year after Remington introduced a high-velocity (1,800 fps in 2¾-inch and 1,875 in 3-inch) version of its venerable Slugger rifled slug line. The Slugger HV is actually a reintroduction of the company's 7/8-ounce slug that was retired in the 1980s in favor of 1-ounce versions.

Remington, Winchester, Federal and Hevi-Shot all offer various versions of the conventional rifled slug design while Brenneke, Dynamit-Nobel, PMC, Fiocchi, Challenger, Wolf and others offer full-bore designs with attached wads that are designed to be shot through smoothbore barrels.

As with all slug loads, the only way to determine the best performer in your gun is to shoot several. Today's slug shooter shouldn't have any trouble finding one that fits his needs.

Savage: Alive and Very Well
by J. Wayne Fears

My guide and I watched from a canyon rim as the adventure unfolded rapidly below us. A 172-inch whitetail buck darted between mesquite trees as a hunter swung his gold-filled engraved custom rifle into action. At the first shot, the buck slowed down to see what had caused the noise. The hunter took another shot, and the buck took off again. Two more shots, and the buck disappeared down the canyon, unhurt.

That night, the hunter showed off his rifle and stated it cost many thousands of dollars. After showing the rifle, he announced that he was going to another part of the ranch and hunt wild hogs the next day. "That buck was scared out of the county," he concluded. I looked at my guide, and he winked approval.

Model 116FSAK Weather Warrior

The next morning, my guide and I waited for daylight and a fog to lift on the canyon rim. As the first rays of sunlight lit up the countryside, we could see a huge buck running three does some 200 yards to our east. "I think that is the buck we are after," the guide whispered. We both strained through our binoculars. "It is; take him when you can," he finally announced. My rifle cracked and down went the best buck of my whitetail hunting career.

At lunch, back at the ranch, the hunter who had missed the buck the day before couldn't wait to see my rifle. When I pulled out my Savage Model 116, you should have seen the look on his face. His mega thousand dollar rifle had been beaten by a $600 rifle.

That's been several years ago, but since then Savage has only gotten better. In those days, it was said that Savage built one of the best rifles made for big-game hunting, but it needed a good trigger. Ron Coburn, president and CEO of Savage Arms Company, listened and put his engineers to work. The result is the AccuTrigger with adjustable pull between 1½ and 6 pounds, capable of being adjusted by the owner, completely safe, with a crisp release that has no creep. The development of this trigger put Savage in the big league of firearms accuracy.

This is only one example of how Coburn not only listens to shooters buts goes into the field and observes first-hand his products in the hands of those who use them. As I was working on this article, I was in Casper, Wyoming, pronghorn hunting. I picked up the local paper and read where Coburn was in Wyoming guiding handicapped hunters for big game. I have hunted with him from Colorado to Alabama, testing new Savage products before they were released to the shooting public. He demands much from a new rifle, handgun or shotgun, and I have seen him stop a project cold in its tracks until a small problem was solved. He is one firearms company president who believes in getting on the grass-roots level when it comes to product testing or contributing to the shooting sports.

Model 64F Semi-Automatic .22 Magnum

Savage's Cub Mini-Youth single-shot .22 rifle is fitted with a basic rear peep sight, a good choice for beginning shooters.

During the past two decades, Savage has evolved into one of the most successful companies in the firearms business. Coburn recently told me, "Savage started a new business campaign in the early 1990s to be the best American-made firearm in the industry. We told ourselves we were the best long before the industry recognized it and ultimately agreed. Everything we do is about making the best for less. We brought in managers and staff from unrelated industries and reinvented ourselves. And we stay the course—same vision, same drive to succeed and same management group—year after year."

During that time, they have developed the SNAIL, an environmentally friendly shooting range system that has been adopted by private shooting clubs, major firearms manufacturers, military and law enforcement agencies.

Recognizing the need for quality rimfire rifles, Savage obtained a Canadian division that manufactures rimfire rifles. Today, regardless of ones need in a rimfire, Savage has a good selection, including the Model 64F semi-automatic .22 Magnum; the Model 93FVSS, a stainless steel bolt-action .22 with a AccuTrigger; the Mark II in .22 LR or .17 HM2 with AccuTrigger; and the 17 Series in .17 HMR. For youth or small-framed shooters, there is the Cub Mini-Youth single-shot rifle with scaled down dimensions and lightweight at 3.3 pounds. It shoots .22 S, L and LR cartridges. Also, there is the famous Stevens Favorite .22 lever-action, single-shot rifle and the Stevens Model Cadet-Mini Youth single-shot, an ideal starter rifle, shooting .22 S, L, LR cartridges.

The youth market appears to be growing. Savage realizes that the next generation of shooters is their lifeblood, so they cater to youth markets with suitable designs, and discounts to Boy Scouts, 4-H and numerous organizations that facilitate youth introduction to the shooting sports.

Savage also offers a good selection of youth rifles in varmint and big-game calibers. The Model 11GY, Model 11YXP3 and Model 10GY are all high-quality centerfire rifles offered in varmint or big-game calibers and are designed to fit the smaller frame shooter. Perhaps equally important is the fact that these rifles are offered at affordable prices.

Savage listened to the wishes of muzzleloading rifle hunters and developed the Model ML-II muzzleloading rifle. The ML-II is unique in that it is the first muzzleloading rifle that can use smokeless powder as a propellant as well as black powder, Pyrodex or other black powder substitutes. The bolt-action rifle features the AccuTrigger system, uses 209 primer ignition and is drilled and tapped for scope mounting.

Savage is probably best known for its varmint and big-game rifles, and the selection gets better as more of the models are now available with the AccuTrigger. The hunter who wants a "four-wheel-drive" all-weather rifle will want to check out the Model 116 Weather Warrior series with its stainless-steel hardware and synthetic stock. Those

Model 93FVSS-XP

Mark II

Cub Mini-Youth

Model 11FYXP3

Model 10GY

hunters who want a quality rifle in the hot Winchester Short Magnum calibers should see the Model 11, Model 16, Model 116 and Model 14. Varmint hunters owe it to themselves to look over the selections in Model 12 or Model 40.

Turkey and deer hunters will find the Savage Model 210 bolt-action shotguns to offer features tailored for the sport. Both are available in camo finish, drilled for scope mounting and in 3-inch 12 gauge. The Model 210FT turkey gun comes with choke tubes, and the Model 210 F

Model 10ML-II

Model 116FSAK Weather Warrior

Model 16FXP3

Model 12 Varminter Low Profile

Model 40 Varmint Hunter

Camo Slug Warrior comes with a rifled barrel.

Savage entered the imported side-by-side shotgun market with the introduction of the Stevens 12-gauge Model 411. I asked Coburn how the Model 411 sold and what the future is for Stevens. "The 411 was a success for Savage," he stated, "as we navigated the rather congested import distribution market with a good quality, reasonably priced side-by-side shotgun. It demonstrated to us that Savage can serve a broader market and we intend to develop more complimentary shotguns and rifles under the Stevens banner."

There have been rumors about Savage bringing out a line of high-end firearms under the time-honored name Fox. I asked Coburn when shooters will see the new generation of Fox products.

"Fox is a brand name that has tremendous market acceptance and his-

AccuTrigger from Savage Arms

The AccuTrigger pull is completely adjustable from a minimum of approximately 1½ lbs to a maximum of 6 lbs in the 12 Series Varmint and LE Series, and from a minimum of approximately 2½ to a maximum of 6 lbs in most centerfire hunting models, and adjusts easily by the owner to suit his or her individual preference. To adjust the trigger pull, simply remove the stock and turn the trigger return spring (A) with the special tool (B) as shown in figures 1 and 2. Insert the tool into the bottom of the trigger return spring as shown, to engage the springtail with the slot on the tool. To adjust towards the higher range of pull, turn the tool clockwise. The maximum trigger pull is at the point where the spring "clicks" when rotated (see figure 1.) To adjust for a lower pull, turn the tool counter-clockwise. The minimum pull is at the point when the large coil contacts the top of the surface of the trigger and you detect resistance (see figure 2). The spring should not be forced beyond these limits.

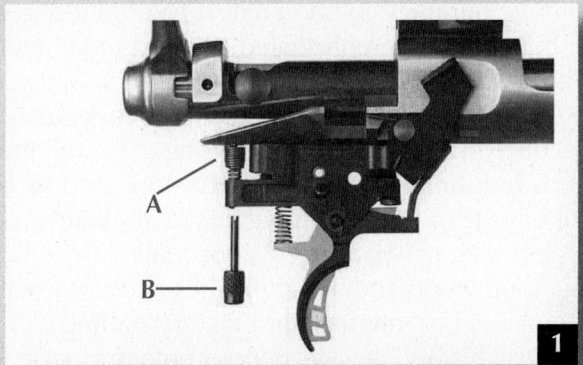

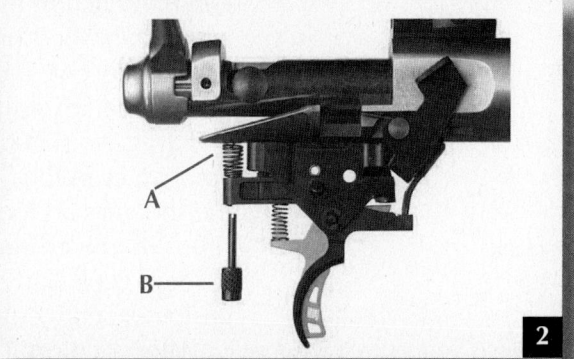

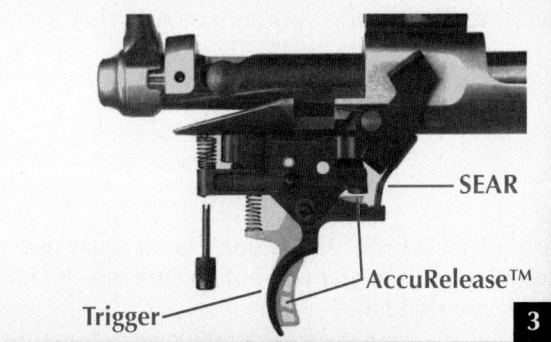

The AccuTrigger cannot accidentally discharge from being jarred or dropped even when the trigger pull is set at its lowest setting. The AccuTrigger is designed with and integrated AccuTrigger (see figure 3). The AccuTrigger must be completely depressed or the rifle cannot fire because the travel of the sear (see figure 4) is blocked (see figure 5).

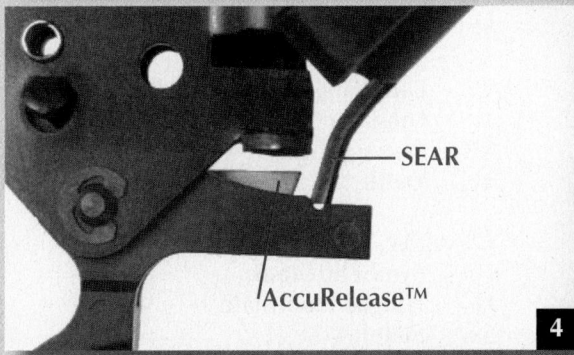

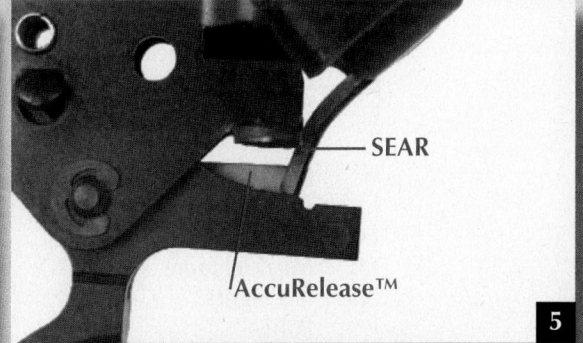

Model 210F Camo Slug Warrior

Model 411

toric significance," he told me. "We are exploring a top of the line shotgun introduction that will be our flagship on quality. Over the years, we have established niche markets, each represented by recognized brand names. Stevens is the best value in the market, Savage is the accuracy leader, and Fox will be our superior quality statement," he concluded.

Savage sold 300,000 rifles in 2005, making them one of the top three companies in the firearms industry. This will be hard to top in 2006, but the shooter can look for Savage to have AccuTriggers in all their rimfire rifles, improved removable magazines, hinged floor plates, new technology recoil pads, upgraded wood and metal finishes and even better customer service through Web site interface and factory staffing.

After a colorful 112-year history, Savage is not content to sit back and go along for the ride. Under the leadership of Ron Coburn, the company is alive and very well, and the shooters of America are reaping the benefits.

Savage Product Codes

Anyone who has not studied the Savage product codes can get confused quickly. For example, the Model 116 centerfire rifle may be shown as a Model 116FHSS. If you don't know what the letters stand for, you will not be sure which features the rifle has.

Here is how to break the code:

AK	Adjustable Muzzle Break
B	Laminate Stock
C	Clip (detachable magazine)
F	Synthetic Stock
G	Hardwood Stock
H	Hinged Floorplate
L	Left Hand
LW	Law Enforcement
ML	Muzzleloader
NS	No Sights
P	Police

SE	Safari Express
SS	Stainless Steel
U	Ultra High Lustre
V	Long Range 9Heavy Barrel)
XP	Package Gun
Y	Youth

EXAMPLE: Model 116FHSS

F	Synthetic Stock
H	Hinged Floorplate
SS	Stainless Steel

Savage®Arms
The Definition of Accuracy

STEVENS®
A Savage Arms Company

Savage History at a Glance

1894 Savage Arms Company was organized by Arthur Savage in Utica, New York.

1895 Developed the first side-ejection, hammer enclosed lever action rifle, known as Model 189. The Model 1895 became the Model 99 and is still manufactured today. Theodore Roosevelt swore by the Model 99 and used it on most of his hunting expeditions.

1902 The Stevens Favorite introduced.

1914 During WWI, Savage Arms Co. produced the Lewis aircraft machine gun, the first to be mounted on wings of airplanes and timed to shoot between the propellers.

1917 Savage developed the first washer/dryer for the consumer.

1920 Savage purchased J. Stevens Co., one of the most renowned long-distance rifle manufacturers in the world.

1930 Savage purchased A.H. Fox, well-known maker of shotguns.

1932 Savage was the largest firearm manufacturer in the free world.

1942 Savage produced 55,000 guns per month for the war effort.

1963 Black & Decker purchased the companies.

1981 Savage sold to local businessmen.

1987 Introduced "trigger locks" on all firearms, the first in the industry.

1989 Savage reorganized and has been growing since.

1992 SNAIL shooting range system developed.

1995 Purchased by its chairman/CEO in 1995 and taken private.

1998 Savage adjustable muzzle break patented. Striker hunting handgun introduced.

2000 Introduction of first smokeless powder muzzleloading rifle.

2002 Introduction of AccuTrigger.

2005 AccuTrigger available on rimfire rifles.

The Modern .22 Handgun
by Michael Burch

"*Plink!*"—the distinctive sound of a .22 round going through a Campbell's Soup can. It is a beautiful sound, and one every gun enthusiast recognizes.

I suspect many of you got the same start shooting as I did. I grew up with a .22 by my side, and many a can got riddled with cheap .22 ammunition. The lack of recoil of the gun allowed me to learn proper shooting techniques and to hone my abilities, but more importantly, it was fun and still is.

As history tells it, the common .22 short cartridge dates back to the middle 1800s and is the oldest cartridge still being loaded today. Since then, there have been many changes with the popular round, and a few different types of ammunition emerged, including the ever-popular .22 long rifle (LR) that can still be purchased by the brick for less than $15.

When it comes to hunting small game or spending all day at the range practicing or just enjoying the shoot, nothing beats a .22 handgun.

Today's Handguns

There have been a lot of great .22 guns built in the past, but you can't stop technology and progress. So what makes the modern .22 better? There are a few things that stand out, including greater accuracy, more gun selection, better safety features and improved ammunition.

The array of .22 handguns available today is amazing. Chosing those to feature in the paragraphs that follow was almost impossible. This is just a small sampling of some of the great guns on the market. With a little research, you can find the perfect .22 to fit your hand, and your budget.

As you will see from the following sample of modern .22 handguns, there is literally a handgun for any type of shooter, from the plinker to the serious competition shooter. You can spend as much or as little as you need and get an accurate .22 pistol that will be a constant range companion.

Walther P22

For you "tactical" autoloader fans, the Walther P22 is a gun that stands out. It comes with big pistol looks and features, but retains a small size and allows you to shoot all day while spending only $10 on ammunition. In other words, you get a lot of bang for your buck.

The P22 is built on a light polymer frame and can be bought with a 3.4- or 5-inch barrel. It comes in a variety of frame and slide colors, including olive drab, black and titanium. And, to fit many different hand-sizes, the P22 has interchangeable grip panels. Standard features include an internal trigger lock, loaded chamber indicator, magazine disconnect, ambidextrous safety and magazine release.

While not a target pistol, the P22 has an adjustable three dot rear sight and interchangeable front sights to allow for accurate "plinking." With its "large pistol" features and handy size, the P22 is perfect for hunting, backpacking and target shooting.

Beretta U22 Neo

Beretta fans will be pleased with their "Neo" pistol. The latest addition to the stable of Beretta handguns, this light, modern, perfectly weighted pistol

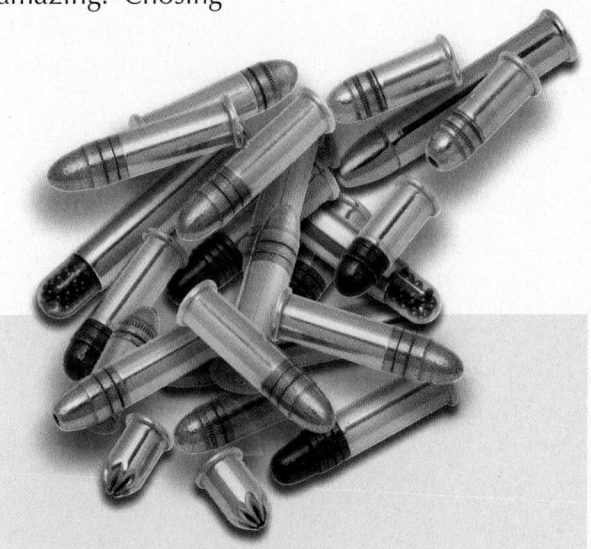

Ammo for Anything

Of the thousands and thousands of .22 shells that I've put downrange, there have been very few that haven't uncannily found their way to their target (not counting shooter faults). And I can probably count on one hand the number of misfires I've had. With that type of record, you'd think it would be hard to improve on this seemingly simple round, but as with most things, human curiosity and ingenuity found a way to engineer a variety of different .22 rounds.

These days you can purchase specialty rounds for about any type of shooting that you do. Included in the list are tracers, magnums for varmint hunting, shotshell cartridges, subsonics and many more in a variety of grain sizes. You can also buy regular ol' .22 Long Rifle ammo on the cheap for all-day plinking. Visit your local gun store or surf the web to find out what will work best in your favorite modern .22 handgun.

is ideal for beginners. But its sophisticated design and powerful accuracy make it much more than a mere "training gun."

The Neo (Greek for "new") definitely stands out from the competition with its distinctive styling. Beretta teamed up with Giugiaro Design to create the 100% American-designed and manufactured pistol with easily interchangeable barrel and grip units. The pistol is available with a 4.5 or 6-inch barrel that includes an integral rail that accepts standard Weaver-style scope mounts. Each one includes a fully adjustable target rear sight and removable front sight. Because the sight system is mounted on the barrel unit, you don't lose zero when the barrel is changed. Accessory grips with colored rubber inserts are also available.

Sigarms Sig Sauer Mosquito
Introduced in 2005, the Mosquito is another polymer-framed gun that is sized-down (90% of the size of their P226 model) to fit the needs of .22 shooters.

SIGARMS is a well-known name among handgun enthusiasts and for a good reason; they put out high-quality guns shooters can rely on round

WALTHER P22

Built around a light polymer frame, the Walther P22 is a great little gun that is perfect for backpacking, hitting the range, or just plinking away on a soup can. This well-used one has had many, many .22s though it and is still going strong.

Model:	P22
Caliber:	.22 LR
Capacity:	10
Barrel Length:	3.4"
Action:	DA/SA
Finish:	Stainless
Weight:	15.1 oz
Sights:	3-Dot Adjustable
Length:	6¾"
Width:	1.1"
Height:	4.5"

after round. The Mosquito is no exception with its wear-resistant, polymer frame outfitted with an integrated Picatinny rail. You also find the slide to be equipped with adjustable sights, and SIG's blowback system.

"Mosquito" is definitely not a misnomer with this little gun. With a barrel length of 3.98 inches, it is a handy size for carrying during your outdoor excursions. But don't let its diminutive size fool you; it has the same proven automatic drop safety and decocking lever features that are on SIG's larger guns. SIG takes it even further on the Mosquito with an ambidextrous manual safety on the slide in addition to the magazine-disconnect safety and an integrated internal lock that completely blocks the pistol's use.

Ruger Mark III
You can't discuss .22 pistols without talking about the Mark series from Ruger. Based on the original rimfire pistol built more than half a century ago, the new Mark III carries the Ruger name with pride.

The Mark II is such a solid gun that it is hard to believe it could be improved upon; but it was. The ejection ports on the Mark III pistols

BERETTA U22 NEO

Beretta teamed-up with Giugiaro Design, which was named Designer of the Century by designers from 130 countries, to create the 100% American-designed and manufactured pistol.

Model:	U22 Neos 6.0 DLX
Caliber:	22 LR
Capacity:	10
Barrel Length:	6"
Action:	SA
Grips:	Polymer with Inlays
Weight:	36.2 oz.
Sights:	Target
Length:	10.3"

have been re-contoured, and the bolt ears are tapered to improve performance and aesthetics. For comfort, the Ruger .22/45 Mark III's slim polymer grip frame features checkered grip panel areas, a serrated front strap and a checkered back strap. The grip frame is designed similarly to the popular 1911 so target shooters can get acquainted with the 1911 features without having to spend money on centerfire ammunition.

The new .22/45 Hunter is the first Ruger to have a fluted barrel and to incorporate a visible "loaded chamber" indictor. The Hunter also comes with a HiViz front sight and a Weaver-style scope adapter.

Ruger Bearcat

The Ruger Bearcat revolver is based on the old "super-six" design and is the ultimate .22 wheelgun for those who like classic styling and designs. The beautiful Bearcat has a blued finish that is accented with rosewood grips and a 4-inch barrel. The single-action revolver features the patented Ruger transfer bar safety mechanism, which provides an unparalleled measure of security against accidental discharge.

To further enhance the Civil War era looks of the gun, it has an unfluted cylinder that displays a roll mark with a bear and cougar

SIG ARMS SIG SAUER MOSQUITO

The scaled-down Mosquito is new to the gun world, but will soon become an old favorite of plinkers and hunters. Its polymer frame gives it a light weight without compromising accuracy.

Model:	Mosquito
Caliber:	.22LR
Capacity:	10 Rounds
Barrel Length:	3.9"
Action:	DA/SA
Finish:	Blued
Grips:	Composite
Weight w/ Mag:	24.6 oz
Front Sight:	Fixed
Rear Sights:	Adjustable
Length:	7.20"
Width:	1.46"
Height:	5.28"

design. All you need with this gun is a great leather holster and you'll be plinking or hunting in style.

Taurus Tracker

Taurus has been known for thinking "outside the box of shells" with their innovative wheelgun designs. They were first to offer their customers an unqualified lifetime repair policy, and their Raging Bull series of hunting handguns were highly popular. Taurus' "modern revolvers" feature yoke detent, full length ejector rods and the Taurus Security System.

The company's "Raging Bull" style and features are now available in Taurus Model 970 Tracker .22. The 6-inch barrel offers great accuracy for hunting or casual target shooting. The Model 970 holds seven rounds and wears the exclusive Taurus Rubber Grip and the Taurus Security System. It also features Taurus' transfer bar mechanism that prevents the hammer from striking the firing pin unless the trigger is pulled fully to the rear.

Taurus didn't skimp on any features for their .22 version designed in their unique revolver style. If you need a great hunting wheelgun, the Taurus Tracker .22 is the perfect match for you.

RUGER MARK III

Available in the standard or .22/45 handle configuration, the Mark III has a ton of modern features, but is still reminiscent of the first Ruger autoloader.

Model:	KMKIII678H
Caliber:	.22 LR
Capacity:	10
Barrel Length:	6⅞"
Finish:	Stainless
Grip:	Half-checkered Cocobolo
Weight:	41 oz
Front Sight:	Fiber-Optic
Rear Sight:	Adjustable
Length:	11⅛"

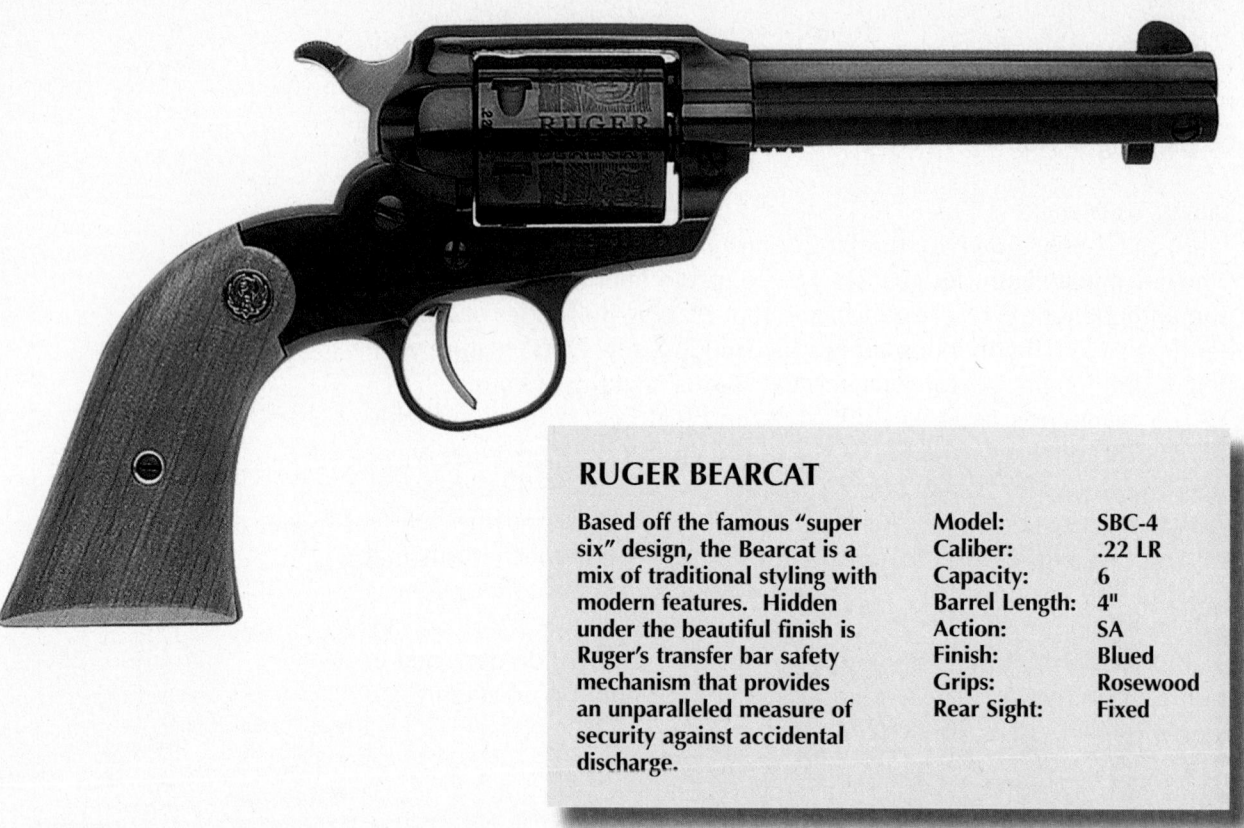

RUGER BEARCAT

Based off the famous "super six" design, the Bearcat is a mix of traditional styling with modern features. Hidden under the beautiful finish is Ruger's transfer bar safety mechanism that provides an unparalleled measure of security against accidental discharge.

Model:	SBC-4
Caliber:	.22 LR
Capacity:	6
Barrel Length:	4"
Action:	SA
Finish:	Blued
Grips:	Rosewood
Rear Sight:	Fixed

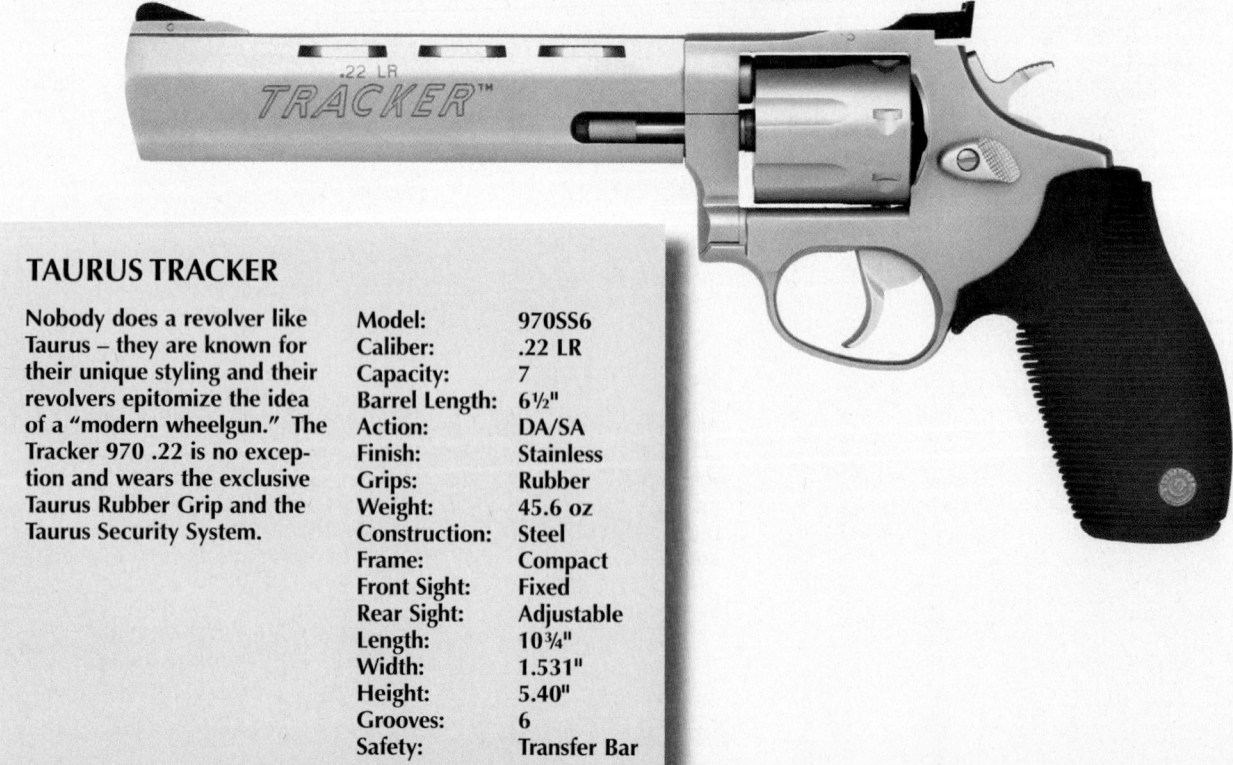

TAURUS TRACKER

Nobody does a revolver like Taurus – they are known for their unique styling and their revolvers epitomize the idea of a "modern wheelgun." The Tracker 970 .22 is no exception and wears the exclusive Taurus Rubber Grip and the Taurus Security System.

Model:	970SS6
Caliber:	.22 LR
Capacity:	7
Barrel Length:	6½"
Action:	DA/SA
Finish:	Stainless
Grips:	Rubber
Weight:	45.6 oz
Construction:	Steel
Frame:	Compact
Front Sight:	Fixed
Rear Sight:	Adjustable
Length:	10¾"
Width:	1.531"
Height:	5.40"
Grooves:	6
Safety:	Transfer Bar

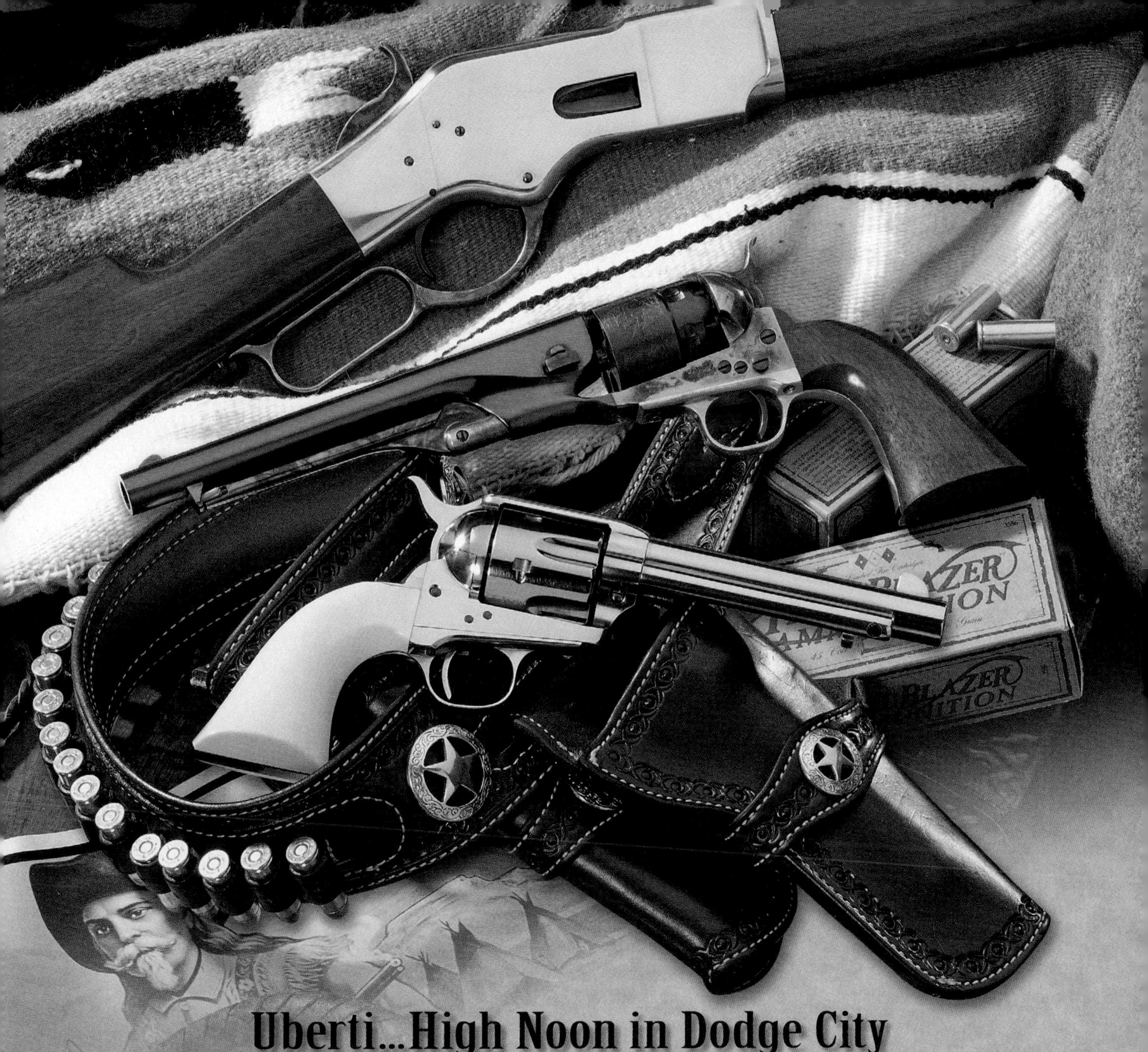

Uberti...High Noon in Dodge City

In 1878 Bat Masterson wrote a letter to the Colt Company and ordered an 1873 .45 cal. six-shooter with 4¾" barrel, nickel plating and ivory grips. Bat Masterson's old "Peacemaker" is priceless, but you can now have one just like it, made from stronger steel for today's more powerful ammunition. Or, if you're a traditionalist, there's the .44 caliber "Open Top" 1860, regarded as the most elegant cap-and-ball revolver ever built. When it came to rifles, the 1866 "Yellow Boy" was a hit with Old West lawmen and outlaws alike.

The Old West isn't gone – when you pick up an Uberti you're holding history in your hands.

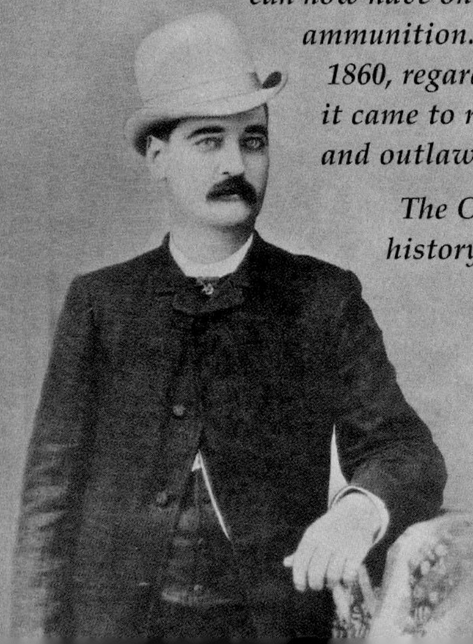

A. Uberti
HISTORY REPEATS ITSELF

To request a FREE
68 minute DVD catalog, visit
FreeDVD.uberti.com.

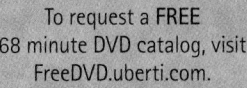
Imported by Stoeger Industries®   (301) 283-6300   Part of the Benelli USA® family

Rebirth of the American Double
by Wayne vanZwoll

Highland Hills ranch in central Oregon produced this chukar for Jeff Patterson and his Weatherby double.

The last gun Winchester Repeating Arms developed before its collapse during the Great Depression was not a rifle. The Model 21, called by many the best double shotgun ever built in the United States, survived as a custom offering long after Western Cartridge Company purchased Winchester in January, 1931. Never a gun for the masses, the 21 outlived the Parker, L.C. Smith, Lefever and A.H. Fox. It remains a symbol of better days past and, some would argue, better guns.

Double-barrel shotguns predated shotshells by centuries. Flint and percussion locks graced side-by-sides carried on the North American frontier. In those days, shotguns and rifles came from small shops that often fashioned their own parts. Eliphalet Remington started his company by building a rifle for a fellow shooter who wanted one similar to a rifle Remington had built for himself. But soon Remington was making parts for other shops. In the 1850s a customer could buy an iron Remington barrel for $2.00. Damascus barrels cost $4.00, while a matched pair of cast steel tubes for double guns was tagged at $6.50. The demand for double shotgun barrels would remain strong for another 50 years. Ironically, Remington would rank among gun firms that hamstrung the market for American double guns.

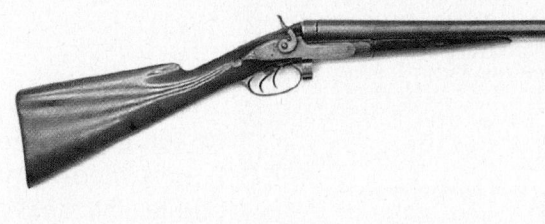
Parker 1869 Double 12 gauge

Parker: The Gold Standard

Choosing the best American shotgun of the 19th century is easy. If you don't say "Parker" you'll have to defend your alternative to an army of shotgun enthusiasts who maintain there is no alternative. Charles Parker's side-by-sides aren't the sturdiest ever built, nor the lightest. Still, they've become celebrated guns — a legendary line that comprises not just steel and walnut, but the elusive ingredients of great art. To connoisseurs, Parkers are simply what shotguns should be.

Born January 2, 1809, in Cheshire, Connecticut, Charles began his working career as an apprentice in a Southington button shop. By 1831 he had launched his own coffee mill business and by 1862 his Parker Company catalog included several hundred items — among them door knockers, waffle irons, tobacco tins, piano stools and German silver tableware. In 1868 Parker and his sons Wilbur, Charles and Dexter, established Parker Brothers Corporation to manufacture sporting guns.

Sixty years old, Charles Parker was still in vigorous good health and very much in charge of the firm. In 1874 he snagged gun designer Charles A. King from Smith & Wesson to develop a hammerless shotgun — the first of Parker's guns offered with automatic ejectors. But his best-known and most important contributions were to the locking mechanisms of Parkers. The bolting assembly was so ingenious that Parkers fired without the bolt engaged did not open! Within six years Parker listed 11 Shotgun models, priced from $45 to $250 and claimed to have the "best and hardest shooting gun in the world."

Parker's first hammerless guns appeared in 1889 and in 1910 Parker technician James P. Hayes, who had engineered and patented the top-lever bolting system, came up with a simpler design. The old mechanism had 18 parts, the new one only four!

Grading of Parker guns started as early as 1872. The first Parkers were priced according to the quality of the Damascus steel and workmanship in their barrels. While all barrel steel was initially imported from Belgium, the Damascus patterns (from the iron and steel cords wound about the mandrel) showed varying degrees of pattern complexity. The "CH," for example, with its fancy "Bernard twist" was Parker's best and most expensive gun until the company introduced fluid steel tubes after World War I.

Tight wood-to-metal fit and well-excuted engraving give this Marlin a high-quality look.

Ken Jorgensen swings a ruger Gold Label 12-gauge, a mid-priced single-trigger double.

INSET: Ruger's Gold Label is American-made, not imported. It weighs just 6$\frac{1}{3}$ lbs with 28-inch barrels.

Parker Trojan advertisement from a page in the 1939 Stoeger Arms Corporation catalog.

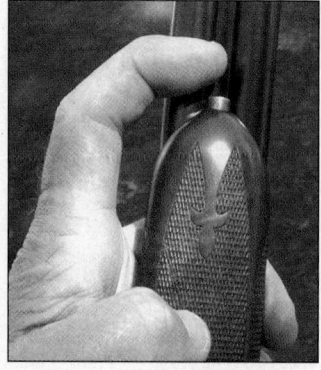

The Marlin L.C. Smith features a front forend button for disassembly.

Clean, sweeping lines and borderless fleur de lis checkering give this Marlin cosmetic appeal.

The Fatal Flaw

Parker guns were made largely by hand, the barrels filed to reduce weight or change their profile, the stocks selected by weight to ensure proper balance on individual guns, locks and ribs hand-fitted. Barrels had to be so closely "soft-fitted" to the standing breech that two pieces of tissue paper would be gripped tightly; but no metal contact was allowed! American walnut for Parker stocks was chosen by the firm's Walter King on annual visits to the Des Moines saw mills. Linseed oil, hand-rubbed, was the most common stock finish. At the height of Parker's production, fewer than 300 people worked at the Meriden plant. Compared with the 17,000 employed by Winchester during wartime! But Parkers were not guns for the masses. Only 20 to 25 guns came off the line each day.

For nearly 50 years Parker maintained the most comprehensive line of double-barrel shotguns ever produced in America, but the way Parker guns were made would prevent them from selling as cheaply as mass produced repeating shotguns. A normal year's production totaled about 4,000 shotguns of all grades. The future of the Parker — indeed, of double-barreled shotguns — must have been clear to anyone familiar with changes in factory tooling during WWI.

While Parkers changed less than some, the firm's line did evolve. The firm experimented with repeating mechanisms and over/under shotguns but never produced them. Three years after armistice, Damascus steel barrels were dropped and in 1922 Parker announced its first single trigger. A ventilated rib came along in 1926 and the first .410 Parker was introduced in 1927.

By 1929, Parker was building about 5,000 guns a year. The 200,000th Parker shotgun came along in the first months of the Depression. The Invincible was a top-of-the-line gun that was to be produced regularly in small quantities. It sold for $1,500. Unfortunately the Depression crushed the Invincible—only two were built, and the gun was not listed after 1930.

In contrast, the least expensive Parker, the Trojan, continued to sell steadily at $27.50. The Trojan's late debut (47 years after Parker started his company) made sense. Before World War I the only way to do build any double shotgun was by hand. Compared to this expense, the extra work needed to make a gun look good entailed only a little additional cost. When war

Marlin L.C. Smith

spurred more efficient manufacturing methods, Parker applied the new technology, offering the famous Parker balance and bolting system in a working-man's shotgun.

Ironically, higher production costs proved the undoing of the Trojan (and other Parkers). In 1939, its last year, a Trojan listed for $80 – three times its introductory price and a lot higher than the competition's shotguns. When Remington assumed control of Parker on June l, 1934 there were 104 guns at the plant. During the next 3½ years Remington continued to build shotguns at the Meriden facility, turning out 5,562 Parkers.

In 1937 Remington transferred the operation to its Ilion factory. Parkers were manufactured regularly until 1944, and assembled sporadically during the war. The last were shipped in 1947. From 1938 to war's end Remington finished only 1,723 Parkers, partly because the market had shifted heavily to repeating shotguns and partly because Remington's plant was better suited to high-volume manufacture of guns designed for the assembly line. The last Parker shotgun assembled, 80 years after the company's birth, bore the serial number 242,385.

Uncle Dan Lefeve, and Kin

In 1878, after a failed partnership, Dan Lefever retreated to his workbench in Syracuse, New York to fashion a gun he'd designed. Lefever's brainchild was a hammerless double shotgun. This wasn't really a new idea, as W.W. Greener had displayed a working model at the Philadelphia Exposition in 1876. Nevertheless, on June 20, 1880, Dan Lefever got a patent for the first hammerless double shotgun designed and built in the U.S.

Lefever's sleek new gun opened by means of a top-lever, just like traditional shotguns; but it also had a cocking lever on the left sideplate. Initially offered in 12 gauge, it was later built for 8- and 10-gauge shells too. Between 1880 and 1883, Lefever shipped 3,049 "side-cockers" in six grades. Internal rods replaced the side levers in 1883, cocking the gun automatically when the barrels were swung down. The hammerless gun sold so well that the next year Lefever incorporated as the Lefever Arms Company of Syracuse, New York.

While Dan Lefever's hammerless mechanism remained essentially the same for three decades, grade names and

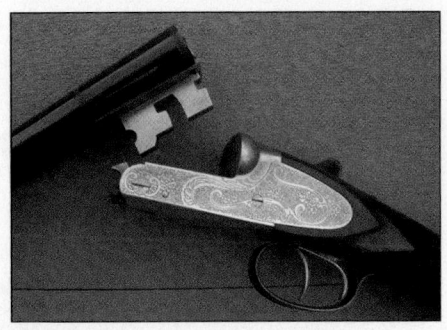

The Weatherby shotgun's massive underlugs are hidden by sleek lines and a slender profile.

Wayne van Zwoll swings an Athena d'Italia. Fine balance makes this gun feel much lighter than its 7 pounds.

INSET: Excellent engraving and skin-tight wood-metal fit mark this Weatherby side-by-side.

LEFEVER DOUBLE AND SINGLE BARREL SHOTGUNS

MODEL 1, LEFEVER NITRO SPECIAL

The Lefever Nitro Special has nonbreakable coil springs, the stock is securely fastened to the frame with draw bolt running up through the grip of the stock to the frame and the top snap may be tripped by simply pressing down with your thumb on a trip pin which comes up through the face of the frame. Made with the following standard specifications: 12 gauge, 26 and 28 inches; weight about 7 pounds. 12 gauge 30 and 32 inch about 7½ pounds. 16 gauge 26, 28 or 30 inch about 6½ pounds. 20 gauge 26 and 28 inch; weight about 6 pounds. .410 caliber 26 inch; weight about 5¾ pounds.

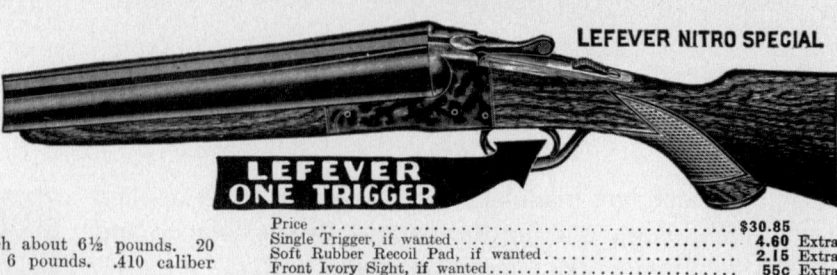

LEFEVER NITRO SPECIAL

LEFEVER ONE TRIGGER

Price	$30.85
Single Trigger, if wanted	4.60 Extra
Soft Rubber Recoil Pad, if wanted	2.15 Extra
Front Ivory Sight, if wanted	55c Extra
Rear Ivory Sight, if wanted	55c Extra

ABOVE: An Ithica boxlock "Lefever Nitro Special" appears for sale in the 1939 "Worlds Fair" Stoeger Arms Corporation catalog.

BELOW: Lefever's first shotgun, introduced in the early 1880s, featured Damascus barrels and cocking lever mounted on the side plate. The gun was opened by means of a top-mounted lever.

embellishments changed frequently. Dan Lefever was always looking for ways to improve his guns. His greatest contribution to shotgun design was the automatic ejector, first offered on Lefever guns in 1892.

Lefever guns below serial number 12,000 were sidelocks, the firing mechanisms affixed to the plates. From about 12,000 to 25,000, part of the works were attached to the plates, part to the frame. Above number 25,000 Lefever's hammerless gun still wore sideplates, but they served no function. Grade changes in the boxlock guns came as regularly as they had with Lefever's original sidelocks. By 1905 two grades had vanished, and three had been introduced. The "Uncle Dan," after Lefever's nickname, was the company's showpiece and retailed for $400.

Dan Lefever died in 1906 but his original Syracuse firm kept building shotguns, including a "One Thousand Dollar" grade. Billed as "the finest gun that can be made at any price," it cost a third more than the L.C. Smith A3 and the Parker A1 Special! Introduced in 1910 (when the average factory wage was 20 cents an hour), this was the most expensive American shotgun until 1929, when Parker, with tragic timing, trotted out its $l,500 Invincible. Two of these top-grade Lefevers are known to exist. Both are in 10-gauge.

All Lefever assets were sold to the Ithaca Gun Company in 1915. Two years later Ithaca sent out the last Lefever catalog and between 1915 to 1919 Ithaca sold some Lefever guns under its own name. In 1921 Ithaca built a boxlock "Nitro Special" shotgun and called it a Lefever—it stayed in Ithaca's line until 1947.

Between the Spanish-American War and World War II, double shotguns dominated the duck marsh and upland coverts. Repeating mechanisms didn't easily digest paper hulls dampened by salt spray and rain. But John Browning's development of the 1897 Winchester slide-action and, a few years later, of an autoloading shotgun, ensured the double's demise. A gun that required hand labor to build would lose any competitive edge during the 20th century.

Magazine Guns Give Way

In the wake of the Second World War, pump-guns and autoloaders brought waterfowl and upland birds to bag for millions of American

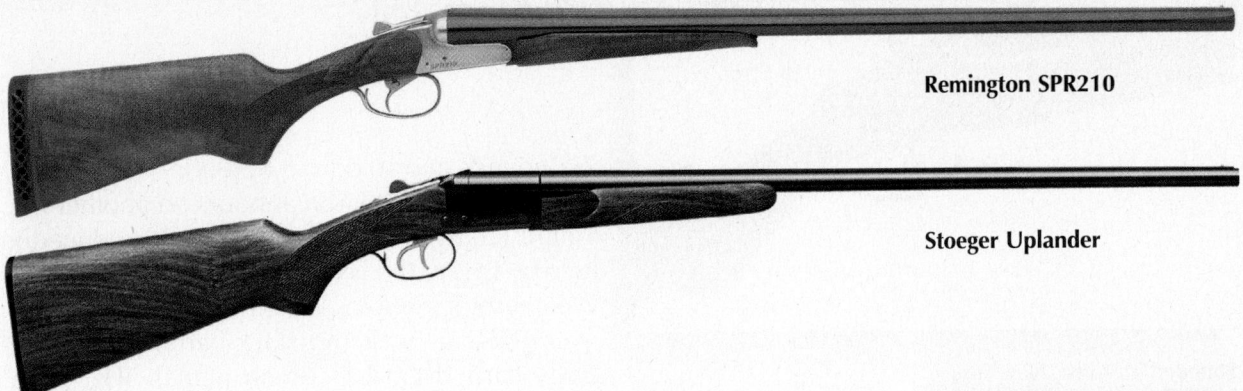

Remington SPR210

Stoeger Uplander

hunters. The advent of 3-inch shells set engineers to work, and soon repeaters could use ammunition of varying lengths. The price of doubles climbed with a shrinking pool of craftsmen and a climbing wage rate. Meanwhile, mass production of pumps and self-loaders kept their prices in check. New materials made them lighter, choke tubes made them more versatile.

But there was something a double could offer that a repeater could not. Call it feel. A double gun was shorter in the breech. It was low and sleek in profile. It never rattled. It came up clean and tight, the weight low in the forward hand. The side-by-side was still the choice of gun connoisseurs in England. Some American hunters satisfied their need for a fast gun and their wish for a single sighting plane by choosing an over/under. But purists clung to the side-by-sides. In 1956 you could have bought a Model 21 Winchester at retail for $355. List cost for this and other American doubles reflected in part a stable market for English doubles, built by hand and then still readily available.

In the early 1960s, Winchester listed its Grand American Model 21 for $3,500. This was when a Browning Superposed retailed for $315. Could a double-barrel shotgun again be profitable? Marlin tested the waters with a modified L.C. Smith in 1968; but three years and 2,000 guns later it faded. The affordable, utilitarian Model 311 Stevens double lost its long tenure in 1989.

America's double-gun scene was quiet for a decade thereafter. Then a flurry of side-by-sides blew in. Weatherby was among the first, but quality control proved troublesome, and their Spanish-built gun was discontinued. In 2005 Weatherby tried again with a new double shotgun built on the Anson and Deeley boxlock mechanism in Italy. The Athena d'Italia had double triggers, a straight grip, slender forend and engraved sideplates. Available in 12, 20 and 28 gauge, it featured automatic ejectors and chrome-lined, back-bored 26- or 28-inch barrels. The Athena d'Italias ranged in weight from 6¾ to

The Spartan SPR's forend is wide enough for a sure grip; it's also shallow, to look good in profile.

Eddie Stevenson swings on a quail with a 220 Spartan, a sturdy, functional field gun.

INSET: Remington's Spartan SPR 210 features a single selctive trigger—for around $400.

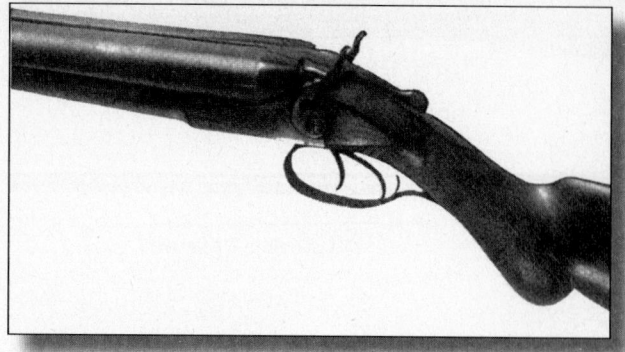

Founded in Ithica, New York in 1889, some of the first Ithaca doubles had Prince of Wales stocks and side hammers. In common with other shotguns of the era they were fitted with Damascus barrels.

7¼ pounds and sold from $2,800.

Also in 2005, Marlin announced another L.C. Smith. Really, it was a boxlock gun produced in Italy by Fausti, the venerable firm that also builds Weatherby's double. Marlin commissioned an over/under as well (no stack-barrel guns previously carried the L.C. Smith name). The "Elsie" by Marlin was stocked with a long pistol grip and semi-beavertail forend. The stock was checkered with fleur-de-lis patterns and the wood was plain-grained black walnut. The barrels and guard were polished and blued with engraving. The "Elsie" was available in 12 gauge, with 28-inch barrels chambered for 3-inch shells. The initial list price for Marlin's L.C. Smith was $1,884.

Twin Tubes, Affordable and Otherwise

Ruger came to market with its Gold Label side-by-side a couple of years before Marlin introduced the new L.C. Smith. Priced just under $2,000, the 12-bore Gold Label was a boxlock with a single trigger manufactured in straight or pistol grip.

Kimber also entered the double-gun market, with the Valier side-by-side, built in Turkey. It was a boxlock with sideplates, designed with the traditionalist in mind with a figured Turkish walnut stock with a point-pattern-checkered straight grip and slender forend. The barrels come bored in 16 and 20 gauge. Kimber's Grade I guns have color-cased plates; Grade IIs wear color case, blue or bone charcoal finish. The prices started at about $3,899.

Another knock-out is the semi-custom Dakota Superlight, designed by the late Don Allen. This boxlock comes in three grades, in 12, 16, 20, 28 and .410 borings — and in 24 and 32 gauge! The Superlight is a double-trigger gun with automatic ejectors and a raised hand-cut rib with straight, Prince of Wales or pistol grip stock.

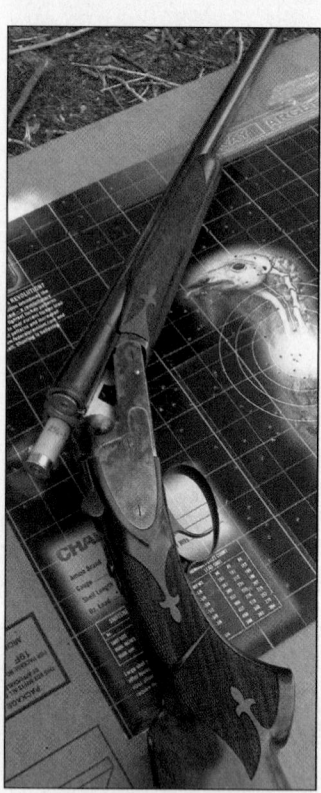

A good pattern—but if you don't like it, just change the choke tubes on this Marlin L.C. Smith.

If you're on a beer budget, you'll find the new CZ side-by-side more to your liking. It's built in a small Turkish town reported to have no restaurants or movie theaters — just sporting clays, trap and skeet ranges! The double-trigger Bobwhite is available with 12, 20 or 28 gauge barrels. Prices range from $795 to $1,045.

Even more affordable are the doubles imported by America's oldest gunmaker, Remington. Three years ago Remington announced a new division: Spartan Gunworks. The initial offering comprised hinged-breech shotguns manufactured in the Russian Baikal factory and distributed through major U.S. chain retailers. Remington has since expanded the line and upgraded the smoothbores for sale through its own distributors.

The SPR side-by-sides feature chrome-lined barrels and a checkered walnut stock. The single-trigger SPR 210 comes in 12, 16 and 20 gauge with four choke tubes. Retail price: $390. For an additional $29, you can order a 28 or .410. The 12 and 16 gauge guns have 28-inch barrels,

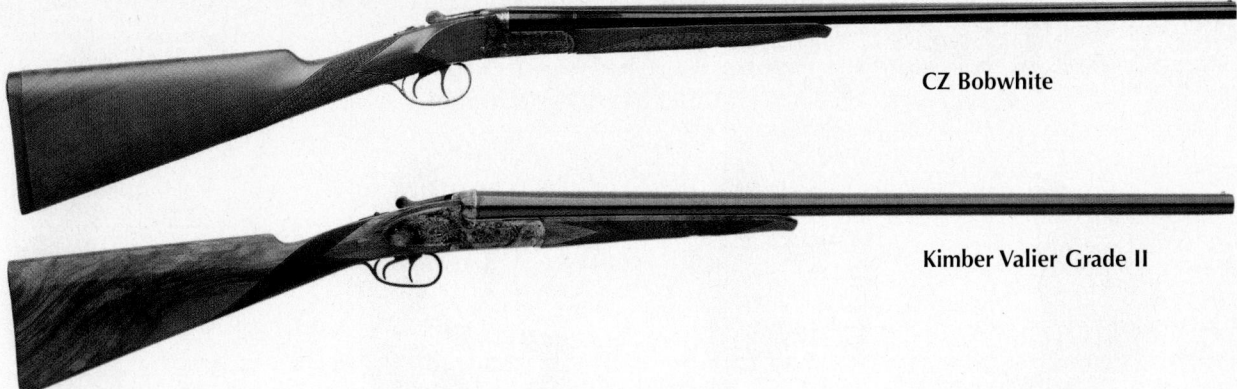

CZ Bobwhite

Kimber Valier Grade II

smaller gauges 26-inch tubes. The SPR's frame size is not gauge-specific, but small-bores are given lighter, tidier frames.

While only recently have American manufacturers offered imported double guns, companies like SKB and Charles Daly have been bringing them to American shooters for years. SKB has suspended side-by-side sales for 2006, but Charles Daly still carries both.

The name Charles Daly first popped up in hunting circles around 1875, when he teamed up with August Shoverling in a hardware and sporting goods venture in New York. The partnership sold in 1919 and the new owners chose Charles Daly's name as a brand for imported firearms. Guns from well-known Italian firms like Beretta and Japanese gunmaking giant Miroku have sold under the Daly banner. In 1996 KBI bought the name to market Spanish and Italian shotguns. The Daly line now includes "Hunter" doubles, single-trigger boxlocks in 12, 16, 20, 28 and .410 borings with straight or pistol-grip stocks.

Another double-gun source for value-conscious hunters is the venerable firm of Stoeger, now a part of the Beretta family of companies, which sells its Uplander series in four configurations, (including a two-barrel set for only $629). Uplanders are sturdy, reliable, and priced from only $350.

It's unlikely that the side-by-side will replace the pump-gun or autoloader anytime soon. But advocates of side-by-side guns point out that they handle much better than repeaters. The dust and water that can disable repeaters are easily kept from the innards of doubles. Comparisons with over/unders must start with the acknowledgement that stack-barrels remain hugely popular. But side-by-sides are slimmer in profile and, given the same barrel weights, lighter than over/unders. The deep receivers of over/unders add weight and bulk absent on trim side-by-sides. Side-by-sides need not open at such sharp angles as over/unders for ejection or loading. They aren't bothered as much from gusts of wind from the side.

In the final sift, the best shotgun for you is the gun you shoot best. Since World War II most wing-shooters have teethed on repeaters. They're most comfortable with a single rib to guide their eye; they're used to guns deep in the belly. But if you've not committed an afternoon with a side-by-side, either on the clays range or in grouse coverts, you're missing a grand experience. Wing-shooting didn't follow the Auto 5. It was first tended to by shooters with slim side-by-sides so eager to point they seemed alive. By most measures, the double gun is coming back. It's about time.

The Weatherby Athena d'Italia offers a long, slim—and comfortable—Prince of Wales grip.

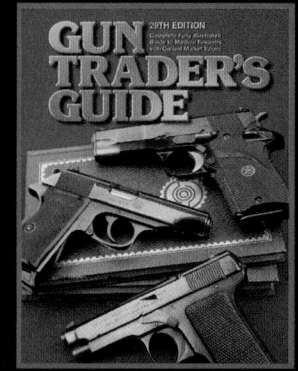
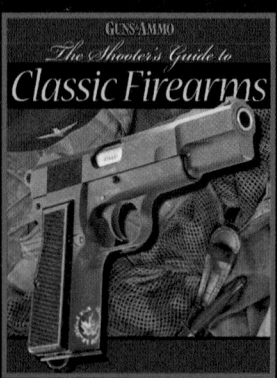

NEW Products: **Armalite Rifles**

AR-10 SUPERSASS

Action: semiautomatic
Stock: composite
Barrel: 24 in. SST T Heavy
Sights: Leupold 3.5 X 10 tactical telescopic sight
Weight: 11.97 lbs.
Caliber: .308 and 7.62mm
Magazine: 10-round box

Features: selectable gas valve; sound suppressor; full-length rail mounting system; adjustable buttstock; main accessories: flip up rear and front sights, high power throw lever rings, Harris bipod and ARMS throw lever adapter; complete rifle system: flip up front and rear sights, Leupold Vari X III 3.5-10X40 scope, high power throw lever rings, Harris bipod and ARMS throw lever adapter, Starlight case, Sniper Cleaning Kit; dummy sound suppressor available for display

MSRP: $2788
W/ main accessories: $3358
Complete system: $5221

NEW Products: **Benelli Rifles**

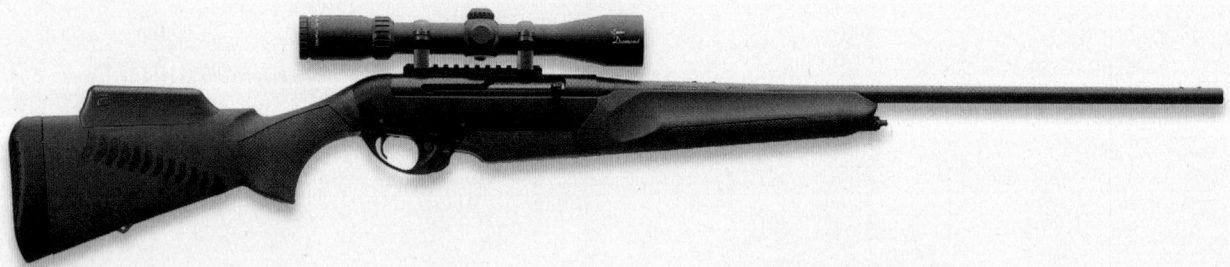

R1 RIFLE-COMFORTECH

Action: autoloader
Stock: synthetic
Barrel: 20, 24 in. (.270 & .300 Win.); 22, 22 in. (.30-06)
Sights: None
Weight: 7.3 lbs.
Caliber: .270 WSM, .30-06 Springfield, .300 WSM
Magazine: 3 rounds

Features: ComforTech recoil absorbing stock system; optional interchangeable barrels; GripTight stock and fore-end; receiver is drilled and tapped for scope mount; Picatinny rail scope base included; open sights available

MSRP: $1365

NEW Products: **Browning Rifles**

NEW PRODUCTS

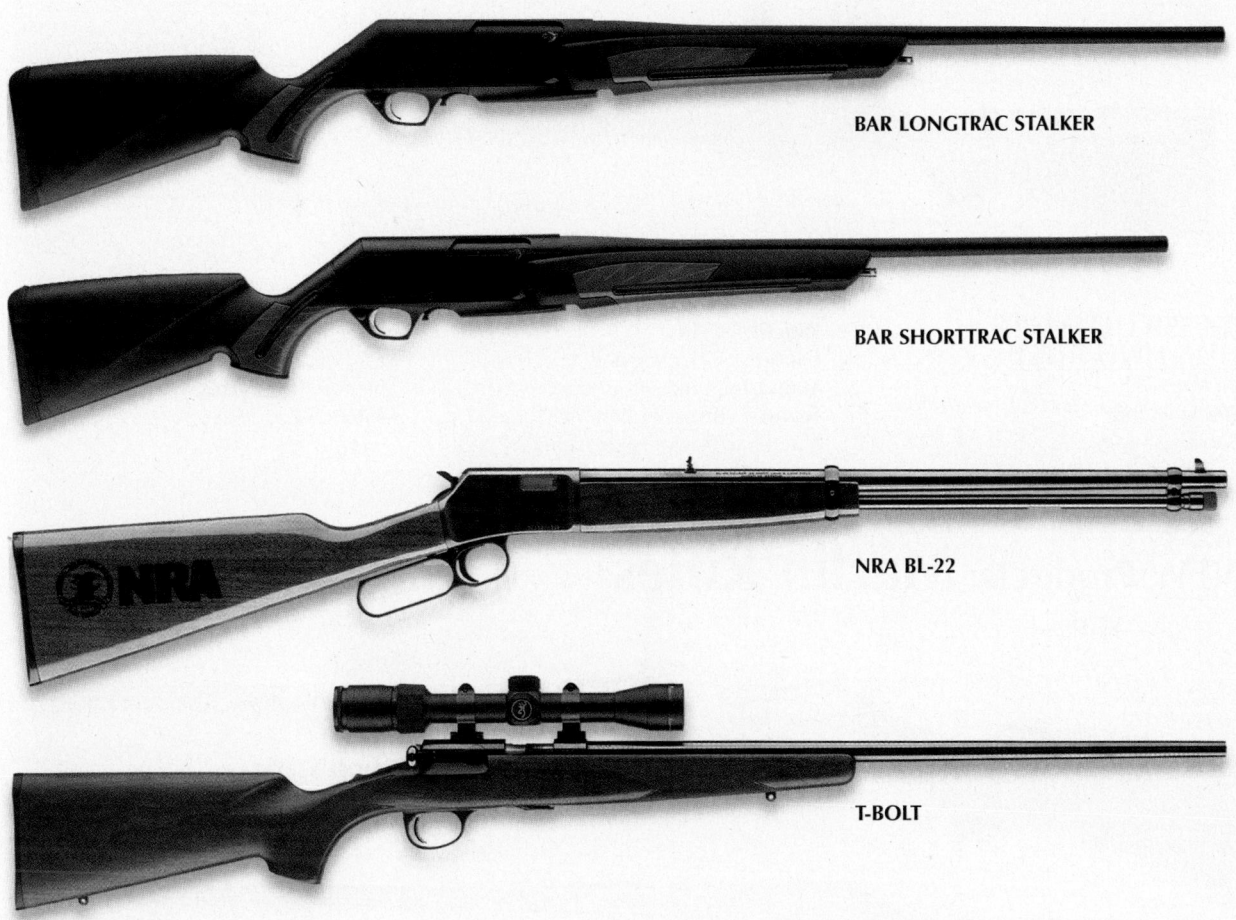

BAR LONGTRAC STALKER

BAR SHORTTRAC STALKER

NRA BL-22

T-BOLT

BAR LONGTRAC STALKER

Action: autoloader
Stock: composite
Barrel: 22 and 24 in.
Weight: 6.9 lbs. and 7.5 lbs.
Caliber: .270 Win, .30-06, 7mm Rem Mag, .300 Win Mag
Magazine: detachable box, 3-4-rounds
Features: matte black finish; recoil pad
MSRP: **$927-1010**

BAR SHORTTRAC STALKER

Action: autoloader
Stock: composite
Barrel: 22 and 23 in.
Weight: 6.9 lbs. and 7.5 lbs.
Caliber: .243 Win, .308 Win, .270

WSM, 7mm WSM, .300 WSM
Magazine: detachable box, 3-4-round
Features: matte blued finish; recoil pad
MSRP: **$927-1010**

NRA BL-22

Action: lever, short 33-degree throw
Stock: gloss finish American walnut
Barrel: 20 in.
Sights: adjustable
Weight: 5.0 lbs.
Caliber: .22 S, L and LR
Magazine: tube, 15 rounds
Features: NRA mark on buttstock; steel, blue finish receiver and barrell
MSRP: **$504**

T-BOLT

Action: bolt
Stock: checkered walnut
Barrel: 22 in.
Sights: none
Weight: 4.25 lbs. (average)
Caliber: .22 LR
Magazine: rotary box, 10-round
Features: straight-pull T-Bolt; receiver drilled and tapped for scope mounts; Double HelixT rotary box magazine; overall length 40⅛ in.
MSRP: **$611**

NEW Products: **CZ Rifles**

CZ 550 ULTIMATE HUNTING RIFLE
Action: bolt
Stock: walnut
Barrel: 23.6 in.

Sights: iron, adjustable
Weight: 7.7 lbs.
Caliber: .300 Win Mag
Magazine: box, 3 rounds
Features: broke-in hammer forged blued barrel; boresighted 5.5-22 x 50

Nightforce scope w/ R2 reticle mounted on 1 piece rings; aluminum hard case; minute of angle accuracy guarantee to 1000 yards
MSRP: **$3450**

NEW Products: **Marlin Rifles**

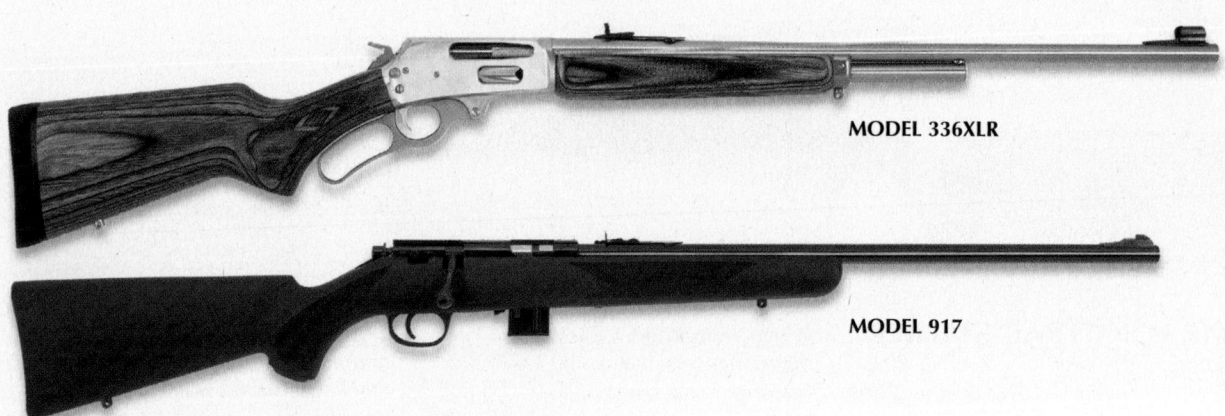

MODEL 336XLR

MODEL 917

MODEL 336XLR
Action: lever
Stock: laminated
Barrel: 24 in.
Sights: adjustable
Weight: 7.0 lbs.
Caliber: .30/30
Magazine: tube, 5 rounds
Features: 24 in. stainless barrel w/ broached Ballard rifling; stainless solid-top receiver with side-ejection—tapped for scope mount; semi-buckhorn folding rear sight, ramp front sight with Wide-Scan hood; black/gray laminated hardwood pistol grip stock, cut checkering; nickel plated swivel studs; decelerator recoil pad
MSRP: **$874**

MODEL 444XLR
Action: lever
Stock: laminated
Barrel: 24 in.
Sights: adjustable
Weight: 7.5 lbs.
Caliber: .444 Marlin
Magazine: tube, 5 rounds
Features: 24 in. stainless barrel w/ broached Ballard rifling; stainless solid-top receiver with side-ejection—tapped for scope mount; semi-buckhorn folding rear sight, ramp front sight with Wide-Scan hood; black/gray laminated hardwood pistol grip stock; cut checkering; nickel plated swivel studs; decelerator recoil pad
MSRP: **$874**

MODEL 917
Action: bolt
Stock: synthetic
Barrel: 22 in.
Sights: adjustable
Weight: 6.0 lbs.
Caliber: .17 HMR
Magazine: clip, 7 rounds
Features: Sporter barrel; adjustable T-900 trigger system; fiberglass-filled synthetic stock with full pistol grip, swivel studs and molded-in checkering; adjustable open rear, ramp front sights
MSRP: **$269**

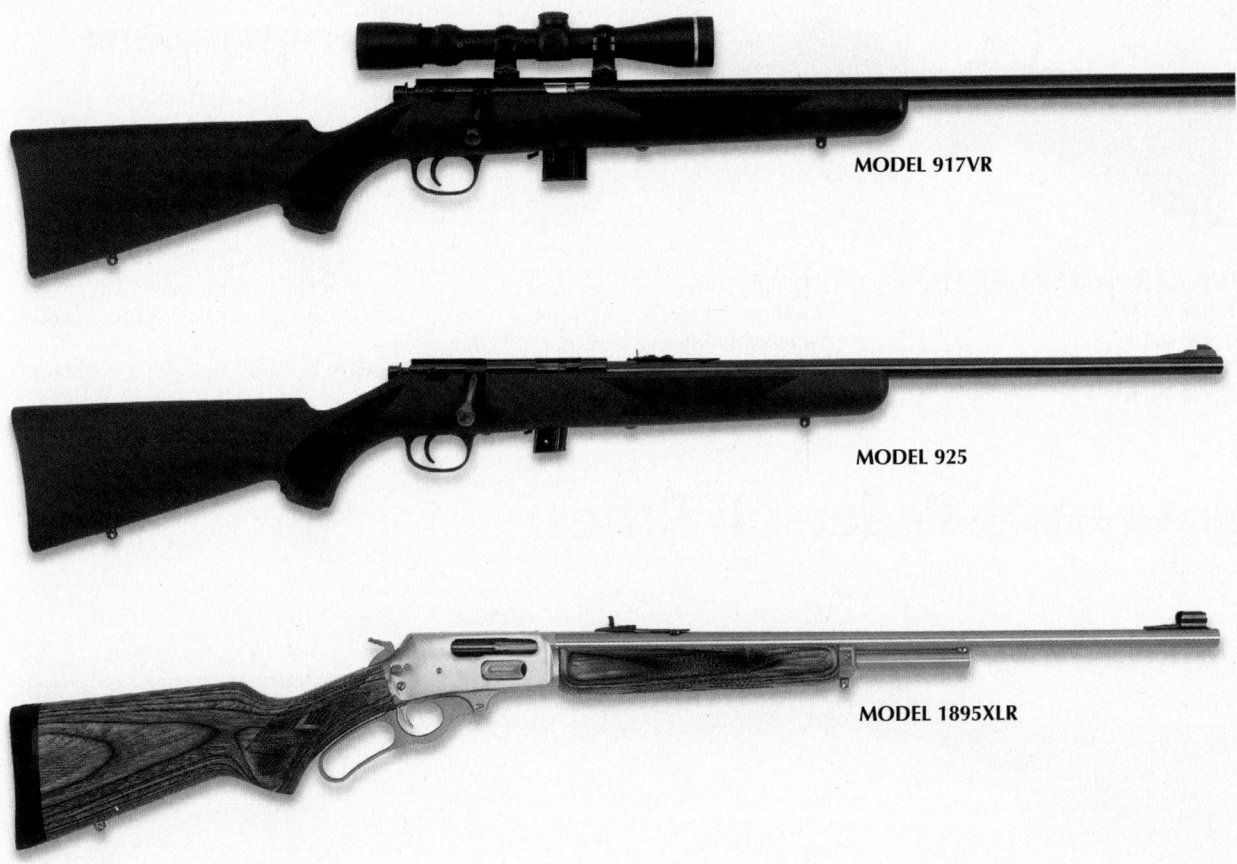

MODEL 917VR

MODEL 925

MODEL 1895XLR

MODEL 917VR

Action: bolt
Stock: synthetic
Barrel: 22 in.
Sights: none
Weight: 6.0 lbs.
Caliber: .17 HMR
Magazine: clip, 7 rounds
Features: Varmint barrel; thumb safety; red cocking indicator; receiver is grooved for scope mount; drilled and tapped for scope bases (scope bases included); fiberglass-filled synthetic stock with full pistol grip, swivel studs and molded-in checkering
MSRP: $282

MODEL 925R

Action: bolt
Stock: synthetic
Barrel: 22 in.
Sights: adjustable
Weight: 5.5 lbs.
Caliber: .22 LR
Magazine: clip, 7 rounds

Features: Micro-Groove sporter barrel; patented T-900 Fire Control System; black synthetic stock with molded-in checkering and swivel studs; adjustable open rear, ramp front sights
MSRP: $221

MODEL 1895XLR

Action: lever
Stock: laminated
Barrel: 24 in.
Sights: adjustable
Weight: 7.5 lbs.
Caliber: .45/70
Magazine: tube, 4 rounds
Features: 24 in. stainless steel barrel w/ Ballard rifling; stainless solid-top receiver with side-ejection—tapped for scope mount; semi-buckhorn folding rear sight, ramp front sight with brass bead and Wide-Scan hood; black/gray laminated hardwood pistol grip stock with fluted comb, cut checkering; nickel-plated swivel studs; decelerator recoil pad
MSRP: $874

MODEL 1895MXLR

Action: lever
Stock: laminated
Barrel: 24 in.
Sights: adjustable
Weight: 7.0 lbs.
Caliber: .450 Marlin
Magazine: tube, 4 rounds
Features: 24 in. stainless steel barrel w/ Ballard rifling; stainless solid-top receiver with side-ejection—tapped for scope mount; semi-buckhorn folding rear sight, ramp front sight with brass bead and Wide-Scan hood; black/gray laminated hardwood pistol grip stock, cut checkering; nickel-plated swivel studs; decelerator recoil pad
MSRP: $874

100 ATR SHORT-ACTION
Action: bolt
Stock: hardwood
Barrel: 22 in.
Sights: none

Weight: 7 lbs.
Caliber: .243 Win, .308 Win.
Magazine: internal box, 4 + 1 rounds
Features: free floating matte blued barrel; side-lever safety; factory installed

Weaver style scope bases; walnut finished hardwood stock; rubber recoil pad
MSRP: **$348-423**

NEW Products: **Pedersoli Rifles**

.45-70 OFFICER'S MODEL TRAPDOOR SPRINGFIELD
Action: single-shot hinged breech
Stock: walnut
Barrel: 26 in.
Sights: Creedmoor style tang

Weight: 7.72 lbs.
Caliber: .45-70
Magazine: none
Features: blued, 26 in. tapered round barrel, precision broach rifled with 6 lands and grooves with a one turn-in-

18 inches rifling twist; color case-hardened receiver, breechblock, trigger guard, barrel band, butt plate and lock plate; satin-finished American black walnut stock
MSRP: **$1200-1250**

NEW Products: **Remington Rifles**

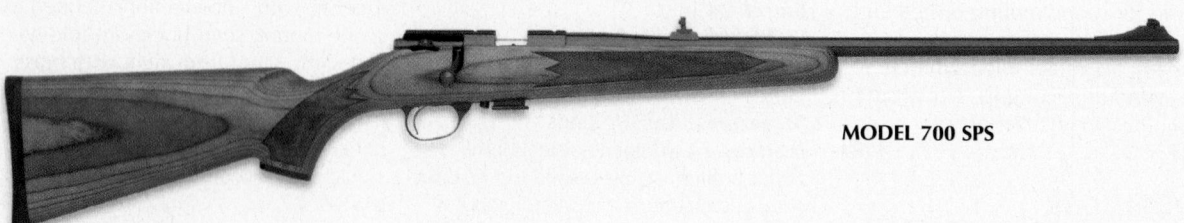

MODEL 700 SPS

MODEL FIVE
Action: bolt
Stock: laminated
Barrel: 22 in.
Sights: adjustable, open

Weight: 6.75 lbs.
Caliber: .22LR, .22WMR
Magazine: clip, 5 rounds
Features: blued barrel; receiver grooved for scope mounts; walnut fin-

ish laminated stock
.22LR: **$348**
.22WMR: **$362**

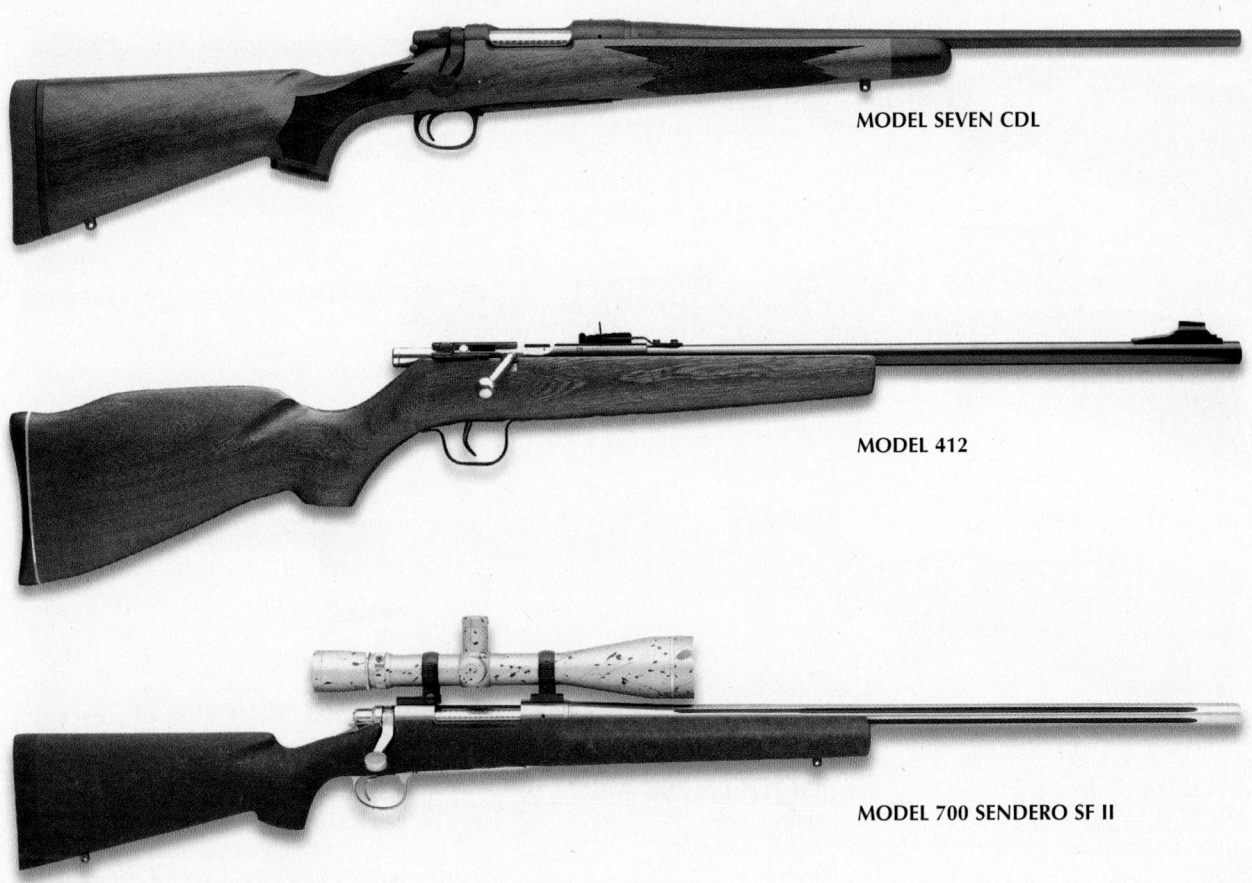

MODEL SEVEN CDL

MODEL 412

MODEL 700 SENDERO SF II

MODEL SEVEN CDL & CDL MAGNUM

Action: bolt
Stock: satin American walnut classical-styled CDL
Barrel: 20 and 22 in.
Sights: none
Weight: 6.3 lbs. (7.75 lb. for Magnums)
Caliber: .204 Ruger, .223 Rem., .22-250 Rem., .243 Win., .260 Rem., .6.8 Rem. SPC, 7mm-08 Rem., .270 WSM, 7mm Rem. SAUM, .300 Rem. SAUM, .300 WSM; .308 Win. (Model Seven CDL); .350 Rem. Mag. (Model Seven CDL Magnum)
Features: 2⅜ inches shorter overall length than Model 700 counterparts; cylindrical receiver; 350 Remington Mag. features 20 in. magnum contour barrel w/sights; R3 recoil pads; satin blued barrel
CDL: **$799**
CDL Magnum: **$589**
.350 Rem. Mag.,
   CDL Magnum: **$825**

MODEL 412

Action: bolt
Stock: hardwood
Barrel: 19¾ in.
Sights: open, adjustable
Weight: 4.25 lbs.
Caliber: .22LR
Magazine: none
Features: automatic safety; receiver is grooved for scope mounting; second-shot holder for convenient reloading
MSRP: **$136**

MODEL 700 SENDERO SF II

Action: bolt
Stock: composite
Barrel: 26 in.
Weight: 8.5 lbs.
Caliber: .264 Win. Mag., 7mm Rem. Mag., 7mm Rem. Ultra Mag., .300 Win. Mag., .300 Win. Ultra Mag.
Features: heavy-contour (0.820" Muzzle O.D.) polished stainless fluted barrel; full-length aluminum bedding blocks; black with gray webbing H.S. Precision aramid fiber reinforced composite stock with contoured beavertail forend with ambidextrous finger grooves and palm swell; twin front swivel studs for sling and a bipod
MSRP: **$1128**

NEW Products: **Remington Rifles**

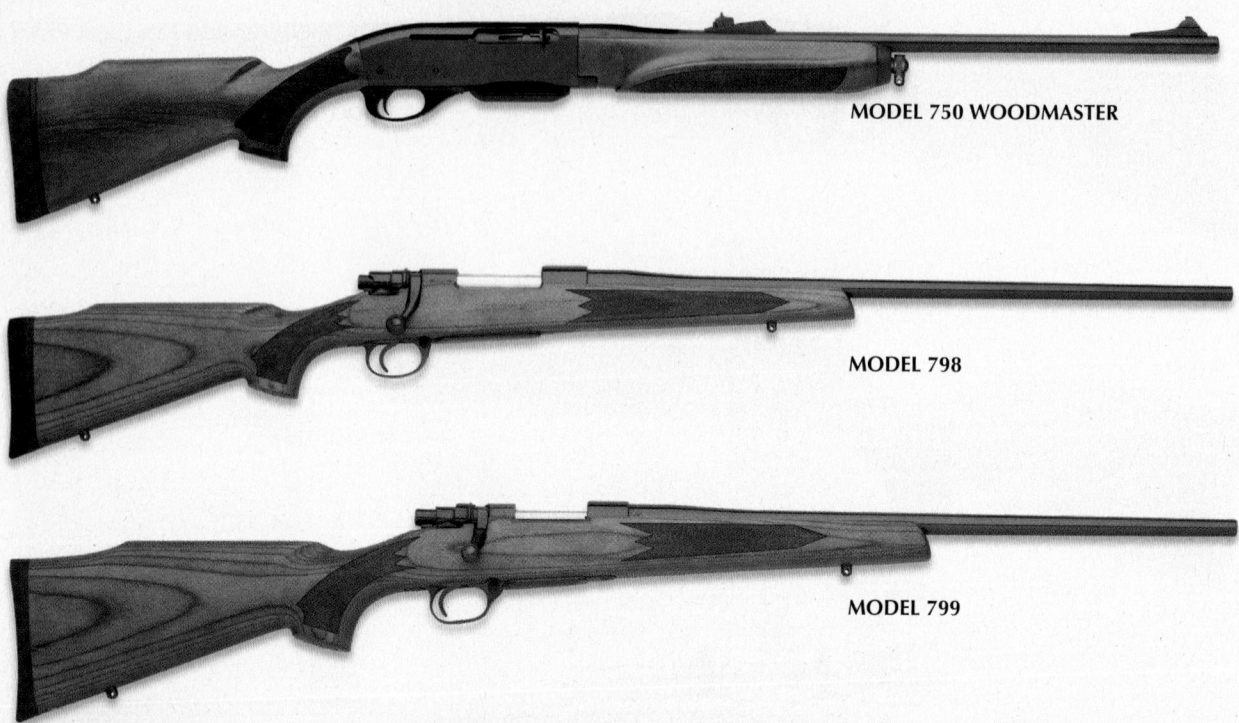

MODEL 750 WOODMASTER

MODEL 798

MODEL 799

MODEL 750 WOODMASTER

Action: autoloader
Stock: walnut
Barrel: 18.5 (carbines) and 22 in.
Sights: open, adjustable
Weight: 7.25 lbs. and 7.5 lbs.
Caliber: .243 Win., .308 Win., .270 Win., .30-06 Sprng., .35 Whelen, .308 Win. (carbine), .30-06 (carbine), .35 Whelen (carbine)
Features: improved gas system; low-profile design; R3 recoil pad; receiver drilled and tapped for Model 7400 scope mounts; satin finish American walnut forend and stock with machine-cut checkering
MSRP: **$732**

MODELS 798 AND 799

Action: bolt
Stock: laminated
Barrel: 20, 22, 24 in.
Sights: none
Weight: 7.0 lb. (798), 6.75 lbs. (799)
Caliber: .243 Win, .308 Win, .30-06, .270 Win, 7mm Rem. Mag., .300 Win. Mag., .375 H&H Mag., .458 Win. Mag. (Model 798). .22 Hornet, .222 Rem., .22-250 Rem., .223 Rem., 7.62x39mm (Model 799)
Magazine: internal (M-799 .22 Hornet) or detachable box, 5 rounds
Features: Model 98 Mauser action; M-798: 22 in. bl. (standard calibers); 24 in. bl. (long-action magnums); M-799: 20 in. bl.; hinged magazine floorplate; claw extractor; Sporter style 2-position safety; blued barrel and receiver; brown laminated stock; M-799 .22 Hornet utilizes a 5-round detachable box magazine; receivers are drilled and tapped for standard Mauser 98 long- and short-action scope mounts; one-inch rubber butt pad
Model 798: **$599-839**
Model 799: **$599**

When shotgunning, follow-through is vital. Swing the bead through the target and pull the trigger the instant the lead seems right, but never let the gun stop or you'll shoot behind the target. Keep swinging as you pull the trigger, the same way a golfer follows through on his swing after hitting the ball.

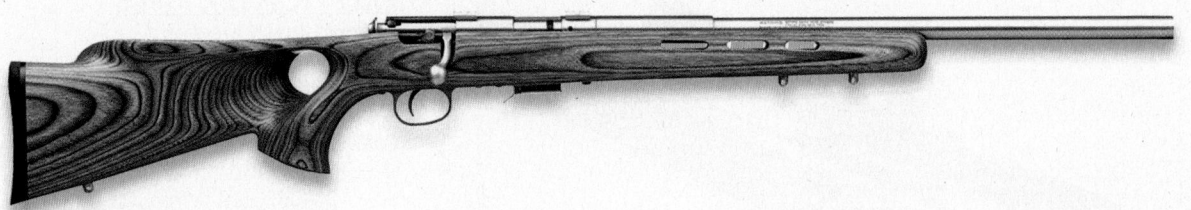

.17 SERIES MODEL 93R17BTVS

Action: bolt
Stock: laminated
Barrel: 21 in.

Sights: none
Weight: 6.0 lb.
Caliber: .17 HMR
Magazine: detachable box, 5 rounds
Features: AccuTrigger; stainless steel

bolt-action; button-rifled heavy varmint barrel; swivel studs; brown laminated vented thumbhole stock
MSRP: **$399**

NEW Products: **Smith & Wesson Rifles**

M&P15

M&P15A

M&P15T

M&P15 & M&P15A

Action: autoloader
Stock: synthetic
Barrel: 16 in.
Sights: adjustable
Weight: 6.74 lbs.
Caliber: 5.56/.223 NATO
Magazine: detachable box, 30-rounds
Features: gas-operated semi automatic; 4140 steel barrel; black anodized finish; adjustable post front sight; adjustable dual aperture rear sight; 6-position telescopic black synthetic stock—rifle measures 35 in. long when fully extended and 32 in. with the stock collapsed; M&P15A available with folding rear combat sight in place of the flat-top handle

M&P15: **$1200**
M&P15A: **$1300**

M&P15T

Action: autoloader
Stock: synthetic
Barrel: 16 in.
Sights: adjustable post front sight; adjustable dual aperture rear sight
Weight: 6.85 lbs.

Caliber: 5.56 mm NATO / .223
Magazine: detachable box, 30 rounds (5.56 mm or .223)
Features: gas-operated semi automatic; free floating chrome-lined 4140 steel barrel; black anodized finish; folding front and rear combat sights with four-sided Picatinny fore-end; 6-position telescopic hard coat black anodized synthetic stock—rifle measures 35 in. long when fully extended and 32 in. with stock collapsed; front rail system with Smith & Wesson handrails
MSRP: **$1700**

NEW Products: **Thompson/Center Rifles**

PRO HUNTER RIFLE
Action: hinged breech
Stock: synthetic
Barrel: 28 in.
Sights: none
Caliber: .204 Ruger, .22-250 Rem, .223 Rem, .243 Win, .25-06, .270 Win, .30-06, .300 Win, .308 Win, .338 Win, .7mm Mag, 7mm-08
Magazine: none
Features: stainless steel fluted barrel; machined target crown and chamber; Swing Hammer rotating hammer; all-steel one-piece extractor; FlexTech stock system
MSRP: . . . . **TBA**

NEW Products: **Uberti Rifles**

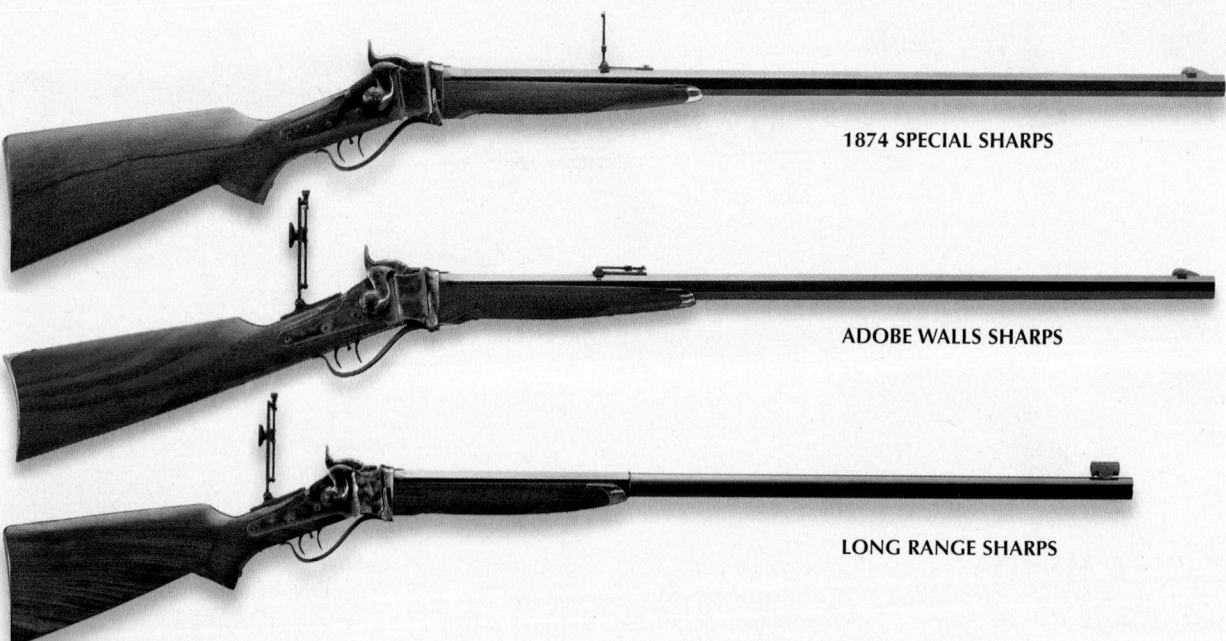

1874 SPECIAL SHARPS

ADOBE WALLS SHARPS

LONG RANGE SHARPS

1874 SHARPS RIFLE
Action: single-shot lever
Stock: walnut
Barrel: 30, 32 (Special), 34 in. (Deluxe)
Sights: adjustable ladder
Weight: 10.57 lbs.
Caliber: .45-70

Magazine: none
Features: case-hardened frame, butt-plate and lever; blued barrel; Standard model — 30 in. round barrel; Special — 32 in. octagonal barrel; Deluxe — 34 in. octagonal barrel; Down Under Sharps — 34 in. octagonal barrel; Adobe Walls Sharps — 32 in. octago-

nal barrel; Long Range Sharps — 34 in. octagonal barrel
Standard Sharps: **$1195**
Special Sharps: **$1450**
Adobe Walls Sharps: **$1750**
Down Under Sharps: **$1799**
Long Range Sharps: **$1799**
Deluxe Sharps: **$2200**

NEW Products: **Uberti Rifles**

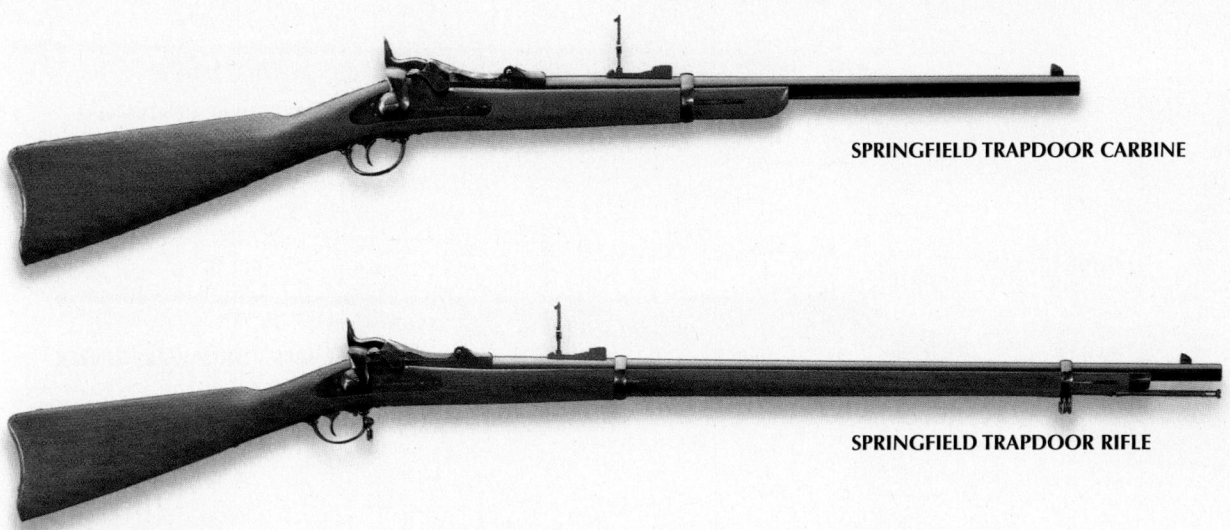

SPRINGFIELD TRAPDOOR CARBINE

SPRINGFIELD TRAPDOOR RIFLE

NEW PRODUCTS

SPRINGFIELD TRAPDOOR CARBINE

Action: hinged breech
Stock: walnut
Barrel: 22 in.
Sights: adjustable ladder
Weight: 7.27 lbs.
Caliber: .45-70
Magazine: none
Features: rear ladder sight adjustable

up to 1000 yds.; carbine ring; blued barrel and action; case-hardened buttplate
MSRP: **$1100**

SPRINGFIELD TRAPDOOR RIFLE

Action: hinged breech
Stock: walnut
Barrel: 32.5 in.

Sights: adjustable ladder
Weight: 8.81 lbs.
Caliber: .45-70
Magazine: none
Features: rear ladder sight adjustable up to 1000 yds.; blued barrel and action; case-hardened buttplate; cleaning rod
MSRP: **$1295**

NEW Products: **Weatherby Rifles**

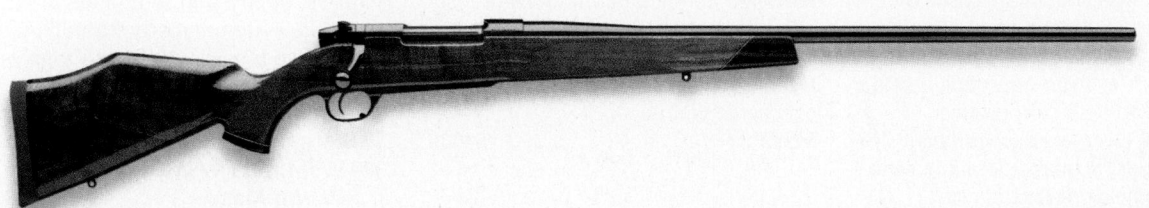

MARK V ULTRAMARK

Action: bolt
Stock: walnut
Barrel: 26 in.
Weight: 8.5 lbs.

Caliber: .257 Weatherby Magnum, .300 Weatherby Magnum
Magazine: box, 3 + 1 rounds
Features: six locking lugs for a 54-degree bolt lift; high gloss, raised

comb Monte Carlo stock from hand-selected highly figured, exhibition grade walnut
MSRP: **$2599**

Ice cubes are good targets for plinkers. They shatter explosively when hit but don't create litter. They also encourage careful marksmanship because if the target is missed, it melts down a little smaller each time.

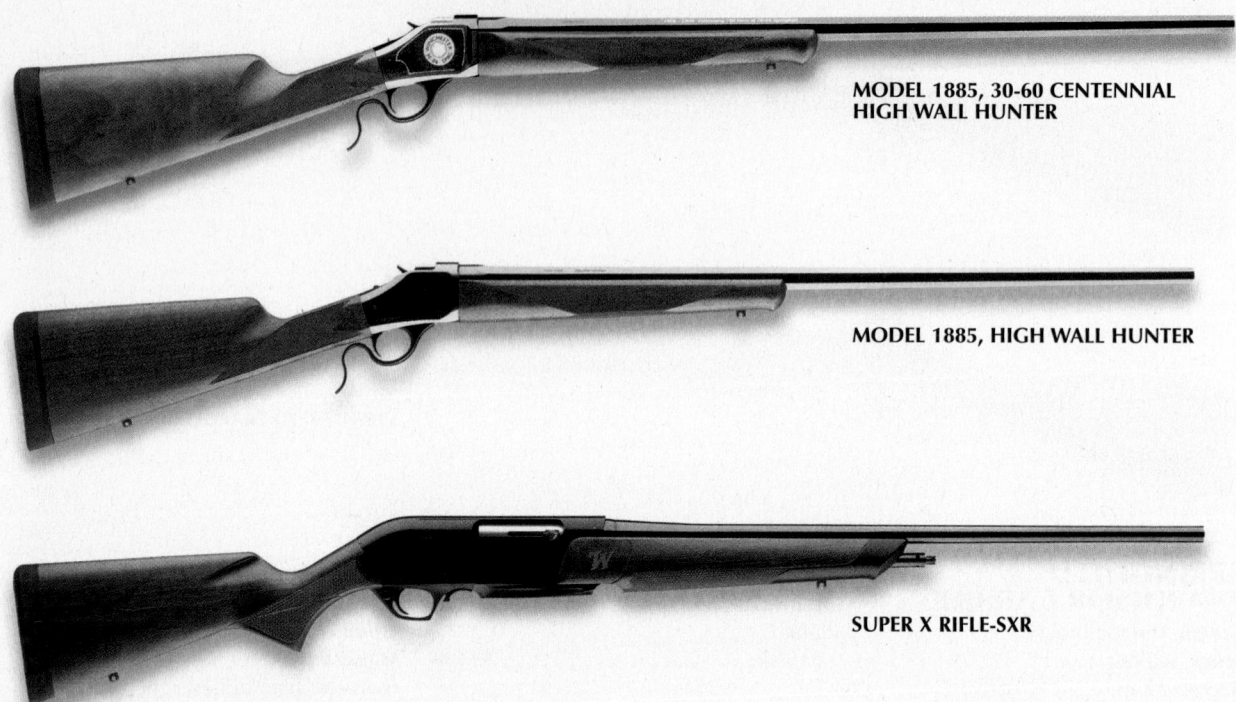

MODEL 1885, 30-60 CENTENNIAL
HIGH WALL HUNTER

MODEL 1885, HIGH WALL HUNTER

SUPER X RIFLE-SXR

MODEL 1885, 30-06 CENTENNIAL HIGH WALL HUNTER

Action: single-shot falling block
Stock: walnut
Barrel: 28 in.
Sights: none
Weight: 8.5 lbs.
Caliber: .30-06
Magazine: none
Features: free-floating full octagon barrel, drilled and tapped for scope mounts; special engraving and gold plating on receiver; adjustable trigger; ejector with deflector; premier Pachmayr Decelerator recoil pad; sling swivel studs; Schnabel forearm; satin finished checkered walnut stock
MSRP: **$1617**

MODEL 1885, HIGH WALL HUNTER

Action: single-shot falling block
Stock: walnut
Barrel: 28 in.
Sights: none
Weight: 8.5 lbs. average
Caliber: .270 WSM, 7 mm WSM, .300 WSM, .223 Rem., .22-250, .325 WSM
Magazine: none
Features: free-floated full octagon barrel; adjustable trigger; ejector with deflector; premier Pachmayr Decelerator recoil pad; satin finished checkered walnut stock
MSRP: **$1085**

SUPER X RIFLE-SXR

Action: autoloader
Stock: walnut
Barrel: 22-24 in.
Sights: none
Weight: 7.0-7.25 lbs.
Caliber: .30-06, .300 Win Mag, .300 WSM, .270 WSM
Magazine: 4 rounds (.30-06); 3 rounds (other calibers), detachable box
Features: Rotary bolt semi-auto, center-fire system; crossbolt safety; single-stage trigger w/enlarged trigger guard; Pachmayr Decelerator recoil pad; sling swivel studs
.30-06: **$811**
**.300 WSM, .270 WSM,
    .300 Win Mag:** **$839**

Some shooters like to tape the trajectory figures for a particular load to their rifle or its scope so they don't have to rely on memory in holding over or under for a target at a particular estimated range.

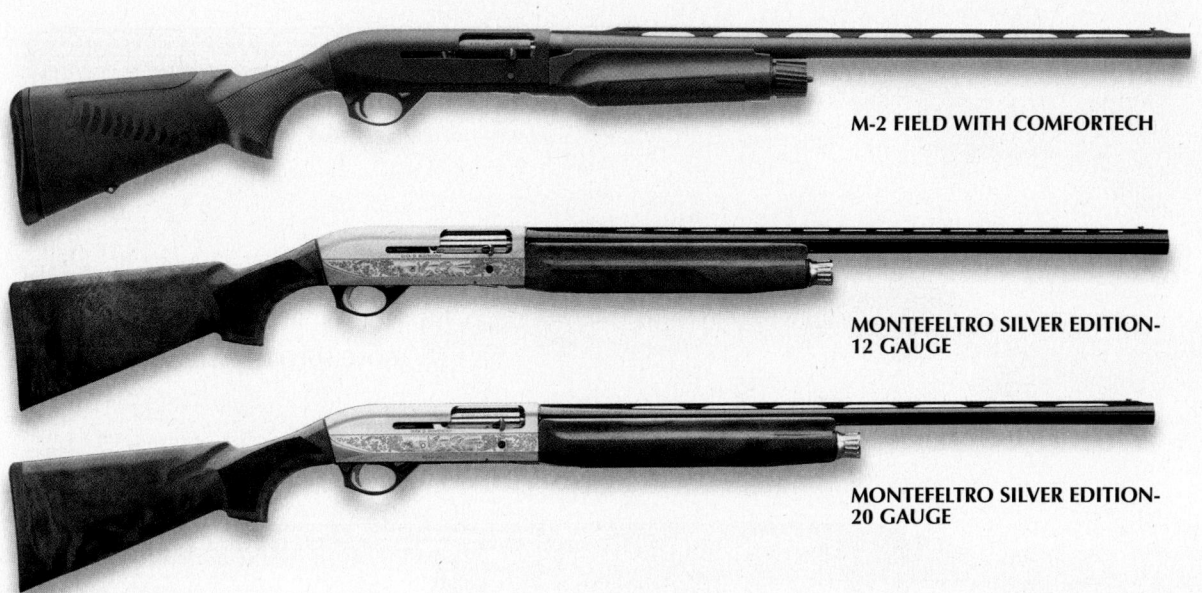

M-2 FIELD WITH COMFORTECH

MONTEFELTRO SILVER EDITION-12 GAUGE

MONTEFELTRO SILVER EDITION-20 GAUGE

M-2 FIELD WITH COMFORTECH

Action: autoloader
Stock: synthetic
Barrel: 24 and 26 in.
Chokes: screw-in tubes
Weight: 5.7-5.8 lb.
Bore/Gauge: 20
Magazine: 3 + 1 rounds
Features: Crio barrel; Comfortech recoil reduction system; inertia operated (Benelli Inertia Driven), rotating bolt with dual lugs; 3 in. chamber;

Walnut, Advantage Timber HD, Advantage–MAX-4 camo or black synthetic stock; standard chokes—C, IC, M, IM, F

Black or Advantage Timber HD
    Black synthetic: **$1175**
Advantage Timber HD: **$1305**

MONTEFELTRO SILVER EDITION

Action: autoloader
Stock: select walnut
Barrel: 26 in.

Chokes: screw-in tubes
Bore/Gauge: 20 or 12
Magazine: 4 + 1 rounds
Features: Inertia operated (Benelli Inertia Driven), rotating bolt; 3 in. chamber; lightweight, slim forend and low profile rib; figured select walnut; engraving with gold embellishments; nickel with gold finish; Red bar front sight and metal bead mid sight; choke tubes — C, IC, M, IM, F
MSRP: **$1465**

NEW Products: **Browning Shotguns**

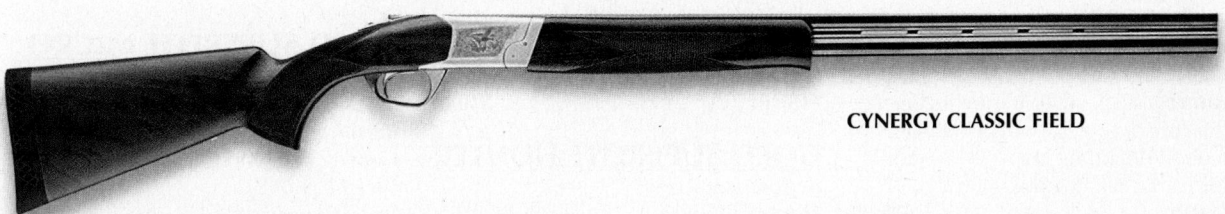

CYNERGY CLASSIC FIELD

CYNERGY CLASSIC FIELD

Action: over/under
Stock: walnut
Barrel: 26 or 28 in.
Chokes: screw-in tubes
Weight: 7.69-7.8 lbs

Bore/Gauge: 12
Magazine: none
Features: back-bored barrels; silver nitride receiver; impact ejectors; low profile Monolock hinge; mechanical triggers; Inflex recoil pad; convention-

al butt stock configuration; satin finish walnut stock; three Invector-Plus choke tubes
MSRP: **$2186**

NEW Products: **Browning Shotguns**

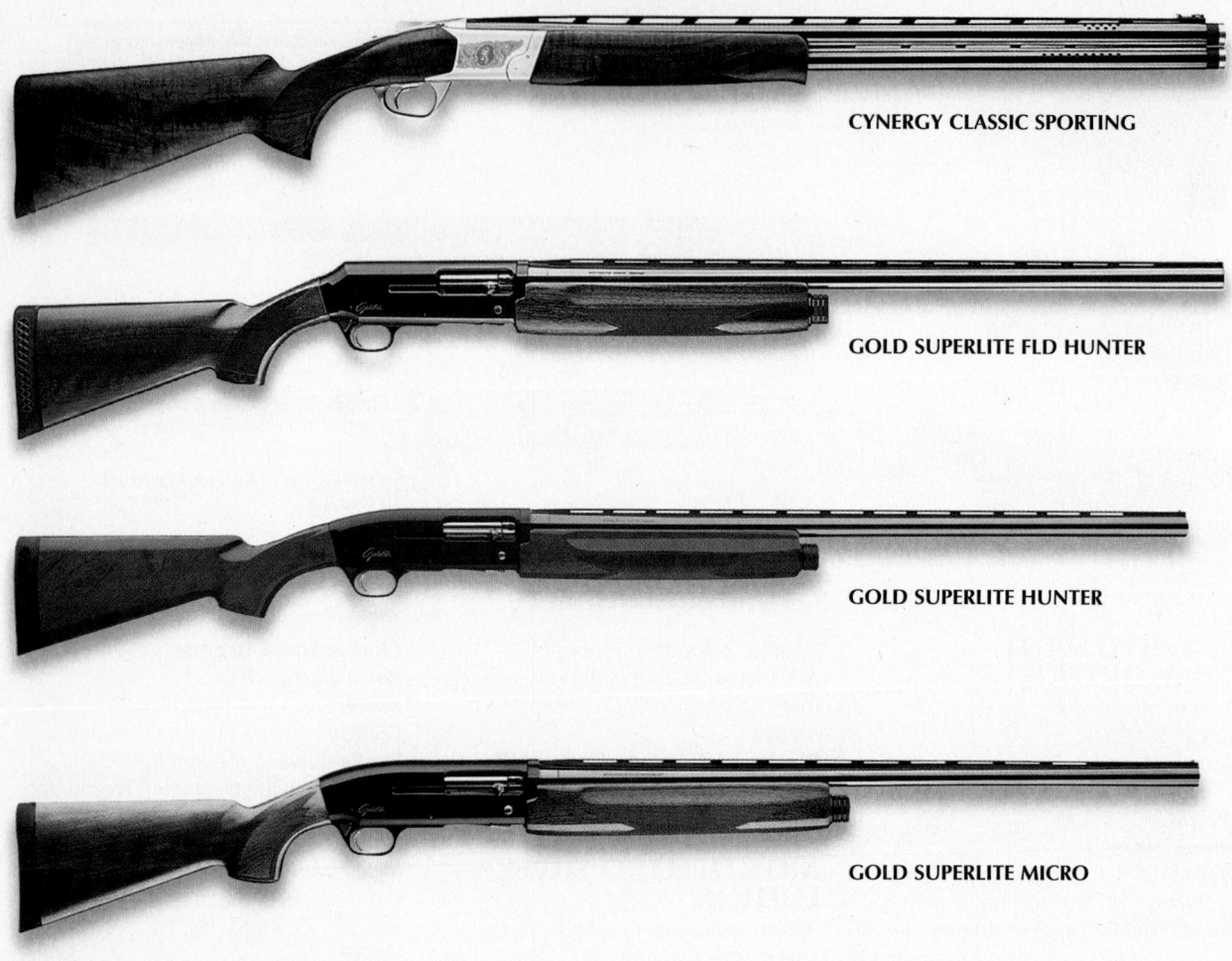

CYNERGY CLASSIC SPORTING

GOLD SUPERLITE FLD HUNTER

GOLD SUPERLITE HUNTER

GOLD SUPERLITE MICRO

CYNERGY CLASSIC SPORTING

Action: over/under
Stock: walnut
Barrel: 28, 30 or 32 in.
Chokes: screw-in tubes
Weight: 7.69-7.94 lbs.
Bore/Gauge: 12
Magazine: none
Features: steel, silver nitride receiver; ultra-low profile; MonoLock Hinge; grade III/IV walnut stock; 3 Invector-Plus Midas Grade choke tubes
MSRP: $3200

GOLD SUPERLITE FLD HUNTER

Action: autoloader
Stock: walnut
Barrel: 26 or 28 in.
Chokes: screw-in tubes

Weight: 6.4 -7 lbs.
Bore/Gauge: 20, 12
Magazine: 3 rounds
Features: aluminum alloy receiver; semi humpback design; 3 in. chamber; lightweight alloy magazine tube; shim-adjustable satin finish walnut stock with ¼ in. adjustment range; three Invector-Plus choke tubes
MSRP: $1083

GOLD SUPERLITE HUNTER

Action: autoloader
Stock: walnut
Barrel: 26 or 28 in.
Chokes: screw-in tubes
Weight: 6.32-7.13 lbs.
Bore/Gauge: 12, 20
Magazine: 3 rounds
Features: aluminum alloy receiver; lightweight alloy magazine tube; gloss

finish walnut stock; three Invector-Plus choke tubes
**Gold Superlite Hunter
(3 in.):** $1083
**Gold Superlite Hunter
(3½ in.):** $1254

GOLD SUPERLITE MICRO

Action: autoloader
Stock: walnut
Barrel: 26 in.
Chokes: screw-in tube
Weight: 9.6 lbs.
Bore/Gauge: 20, 12
Magazine: 3 rounds
Features: Aluminum alloy receiver; 3 in. chamber lightweight alloy magazine tube; magazine cut-off; compact, gloss finish walnut stock; three Invector-Plus choke tubes.
MSRP: $1083

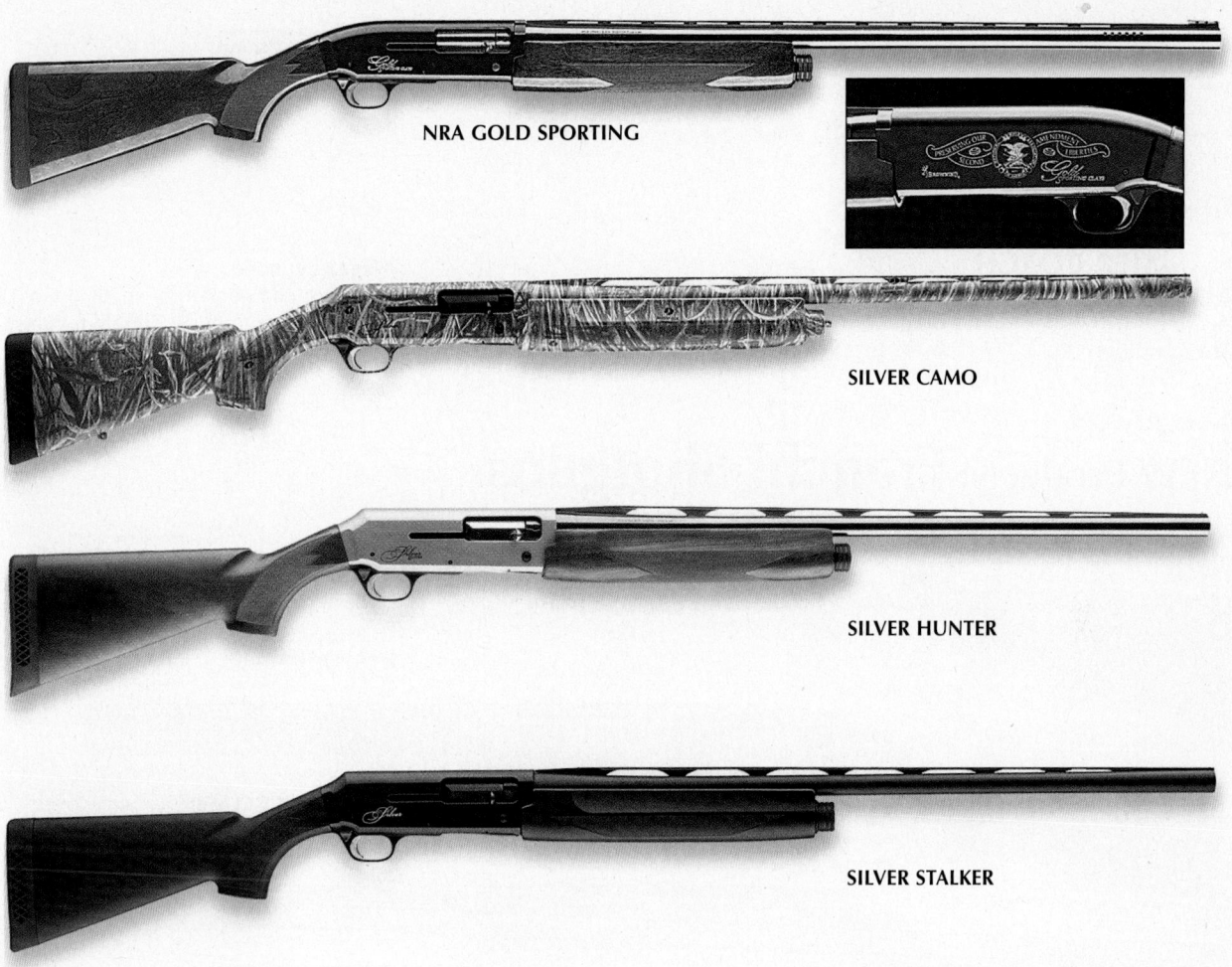

NRA GOLD SPORTING

SILVER CAMO

SILVER HUNTER

SILVER STALKER

NRA GOLD SPORTING

Action: autoloader
Stock: walnut
Barrel: 28 and 30 in.
Chokes: screw-in tubes
Weight: 7.75-7.8 lbs.
Bore/Gauge: 12
Magazine: 4 rounds
Features: limited edition with gold-filled NRA Heritage mark and motto on the receiver; 2¾ in. chamber; HiViz TriComp front sight; gloss finish walnut, shim adjustable stock with ¼ in. adjustment range; three Invector-Plus choke tubes; donation to the NRA Basic Firearms Training Program for every gun sold
MSRP: **$1137**

SILVER CAMO

Action: autoloader
Stock: composite
Barrel: 26 or 28 in.
Chokes: screw-in tube
Weight: 7.5-7.88 lbs.
Bore/Gauge: 12
Magazine: 3 rounds
Features: 3 or 3½ in. chamber; Mossy Oak New Break-Up and Mossy Oak New Shadow Grass finish, Dura-Touch armor coating; F, M and IC Invector-PlusT choke tubes
Silver Camo 3 in.: **$978**
Silver Camo 3½ in.: **$1098**

SILVER HUNTER

Action: autoloader
Stock: checkered satin finish walnut
Barrel: 26, 28 and 30 in.
Chokes: screw-in tubes
Weight: 7.25-7.56 lbs.
Bore/Gauge: 12
Magazine: 3 rounds
Features: Silver finish aluminum alloy receiver; hump back configuration; available with 3 or 3½ in. chambers; interchangeable F, M and IC Invector-PlusT tubes
Silver Hunter 3 in:. **$876**
Silver Hunter 3½ in:. **$1023**

SILVER STALKER

Action: autoloader
Stock: composite
Barrel: 26 or 28 in.
Chokes: screw-in tube
Weight: 7.5-7.56 lbs.
Bore/Gauge: 12
Magazine: 3 rounds
Features: black matte finish, 3 or 3¾ in. chamber; Dura-Touch armor coating; interchangeable F, M and IC Invector-PlusT tubes
Silver Stalker 3 in.: **$856**
Silver Stalker 3½ in.: **$975**

NEW Products: CZ Shotguns

HAMMER COACH SHOTGUN
Action: side-by-side
Stock: walnut

Barrel: 20 in.
Chokes: IC and Mod
Weight: 6.7 lbs.
Bore/Gauge: 12

Magazine: none
Features: chambered for shells up to 3 in.; external hammers; double triggers
MSRP: **$795**

NEW Products: Franchi Shotguns

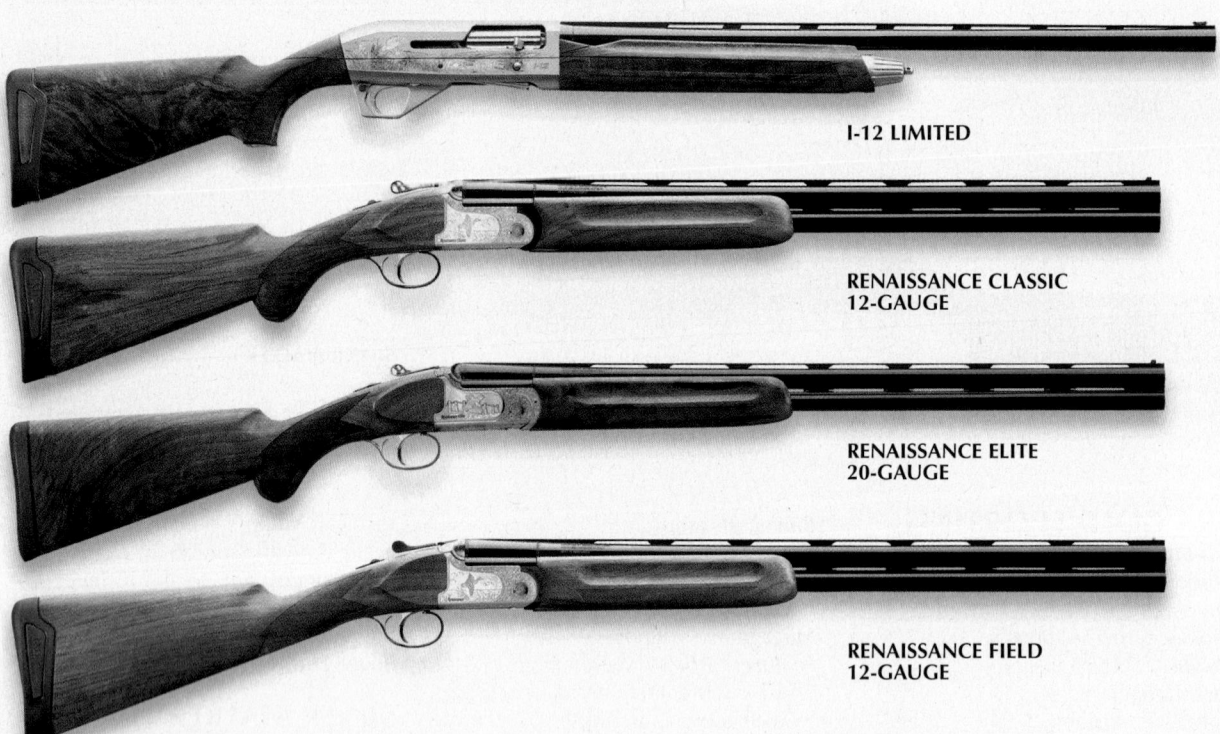

I-12 LIMITED

RENAISSANCE CLASSIC 12-GAUGE

RENAISSANCE ELITE 20-GAUGE

RENAISSANCE FIELD 12-GAUGE

I-12 LIMITED
Action: autoloader
Stock: walnut
Barrel: 28 in.
Chokes: screw-in tubes
Weight: 7.7 lbs.
Bore/Gauge: 12
Magazine: 4 + 1 rounds
Features: chambered for 3 in.; nickel receiver accented with white gold game birds; Inertia Driven operating system; Twin Shock Absorber recoil pad with special gel insert; oil finished AA-grade figured walnut stock w/ cut checkering; chokes—C, IC, M, IM, F
MSRP: $1399

RENAISSANCE SERIES FIELD, CLASSIC AND ELITE MODELS
Action: over/under
Stock: walnut
Barrel: 26 and 28 in. (20, 12 ga.); 26 in. (28 ga.)
Chokes: screw-in tubes
Weight: 6.0 lbs.
Bore/Gauge: 20, 28 and 12
Magazine: none
Features: precision-machined light-weight alloy receiver; Dual Shock-Absorber recoil pad with special gel insert; traditional oil finish select walnut stock with Prince of Wales pistol grips, cut checkering; 2 to 5 screw-in choke tubes depending on model
MSRP: $1250-2100

NEW Products: Harrington & Richardson Shotguns

EXCELL SYNTHETIC

EXCELL TURKEY

EXCELL WALNUT

EXCELL WATERFOWL

EXCELL AUTO

Action: autoloader
Stock: synthetic
Barrel: 28 in. (Synthetic, Walnut, Waterfowl); 22 in. (Turkey); 28 in. w/ventilated rib, 24 in. rifled barrel (Combo)
Chokes: screw-in tubes

Weight: 7.0 lbs.
Bore/Gauge: 12
Magazine: 5 rounds
Features: vent rib barrels (except slug barrel); 3 in. magnum capability; magazine cut-off; ventilated recoil pads; stock available in black, American walnut, Real Tree Advantage Wetlands or Real Tree Advantage Hardwoods; 4 screw-in tube chokes—IC,M,IM,F

Synthetic:	**$415**
Walnut:	**$461**
Waterfowl:	**$521**
Turkey:	**$521**
Combo:	**$583**

NEW Products: Remington Shotguns

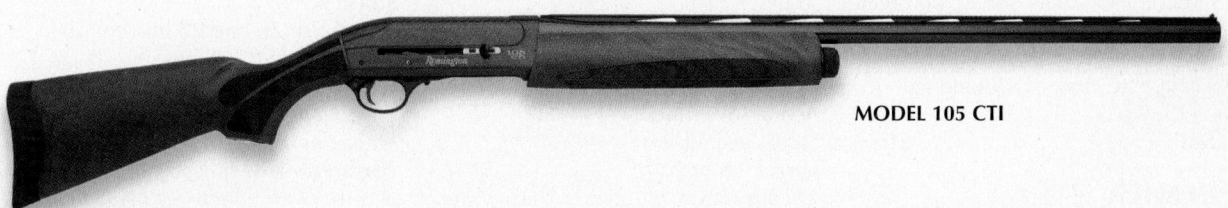

MODEL 105 CTI

MODEL 105 CTI

Action: autoloader
Stock: walnut
Barrel: 26 or 28 in.
Chokes: screw-in tubes

Weight: 7.0 lb.
Bore/Gauge: 12
Magazine: 5 rounds
Features: bottom-eject, titanium/carbon-fiber receiver; 3 in. chamber; optimized gas operation; "Double-Down" bottom feed and eject system; R3 recoil pad; FAA approved lockable hard case; 3 ProBore—IC, M, F
MSRP: **$1332**

NEW Products: Remington Shotguns

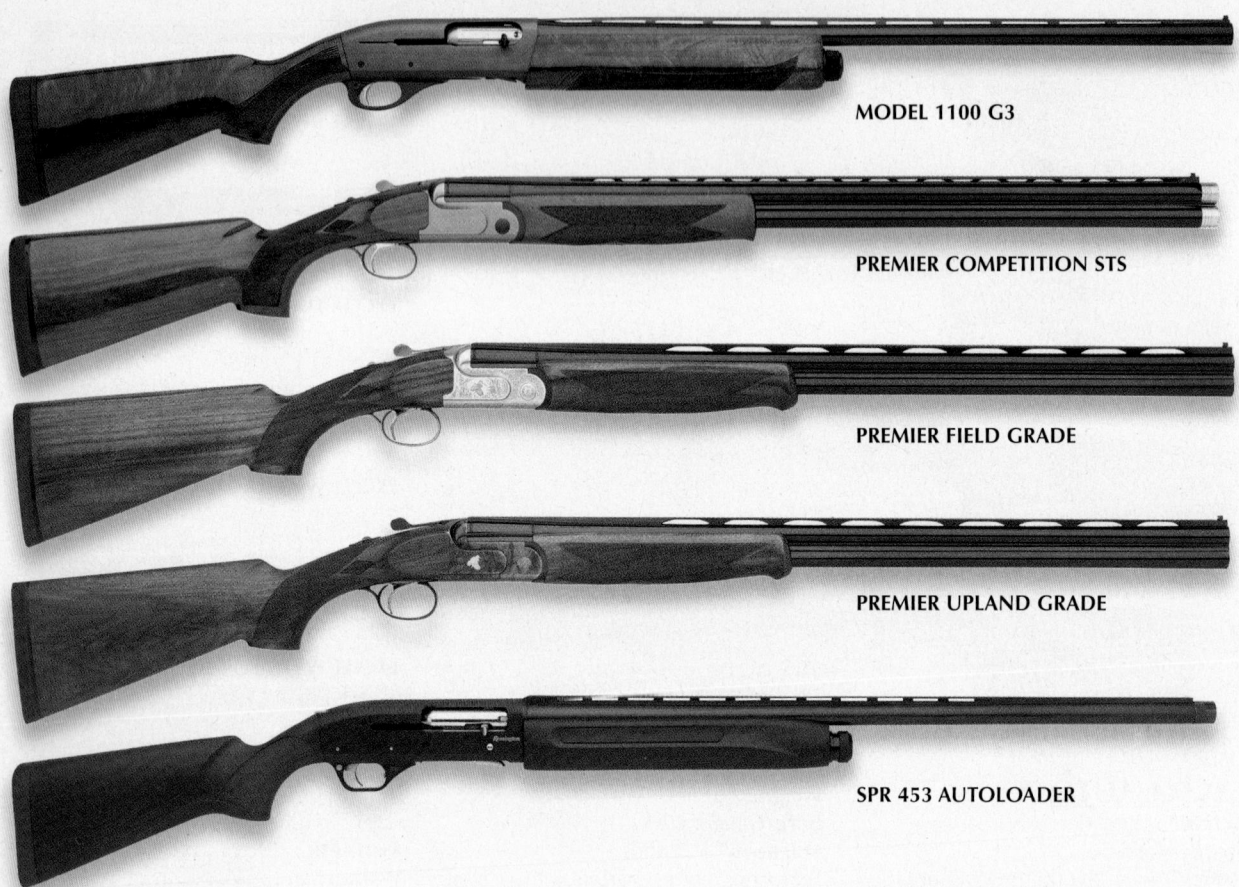

MODEL 1100 G3

PREMIER COMPETITION STS

PREMIER FIELD GRADE

PREMIER UPLAND GRADE

SPR 453 AUTOLOADER

MODEL 1100 G3

Action: autoloader
Stock: laminated   *Barrel:* 26 or 28 in.
Chokes: screw-in tubes
Weight: 6.75 lbs.
Bore/Gauge: 20, 12
Features: pressure compensated barrel; solid carbon steel receiver; honed operating parts w/ nickel-plated, Teflon coating; Titanium PVD (Physical Vapor Deposition) coating; R3 Recoil Pad; Realwood carbon reinforced walnut laminate stock; 5 choke tubes—Skeet, IC, LM, M, Full ProBore on 12 ga.; IC, LM, M, IM and Full Rem Choke on 20 ga.
MSRP: **$1065**

PREMIER COMPETITION STS

Action: over/under
Stock: walnut
Barrel: 28 or 30 in.
Chokes: screw-in tubes
Weight: 7.5-7.75 lbs.

Bore/Gauge: 12
Magazine: none
Features: Titanium PVD-finished receiver; gold trigger and engraved receiver; right-hand palm swell and target Schnabel forend; 10mm target-style rib; ivory front bead and steel midpost; gloss finish figured walnut stock; 5 extended ProBore tubes with knurled extensions: Skeet, IC, LM, M, F
MSRP: **$2240**

PREMIER FIELD GRADE AND PREMIER UPLAND GRADE

Action: over/under
Stock: walnut
Barrel: 26 or 28 in.
Chokes: screw-in tubes
Weight: 6.5-7.75 lbs.
Bore/Gauge: 20, 28, 12
Magazine: none
Features: Field w/ nickel-finished receiver; Upland w/ case-colored receiver; 7mm rib; ivory front bead

and steel midpost; traditional Schnabel forend; satin-finished premium walnut stock (Field); oil finished walnut stock (Upland); 5 flush mount ProBore tubes; 28-gauge w/ 3 flush mount ProBore tubes
Field Grade:. **$1840-1880**
Upland Grade:. **$1920-1960**

SPR 453 AUTOLOADER

Action: autoloader
Stock: synthetic
Barrel: 24, 26 and 28 in. vent rib
Chokes: screw-in tubes
Weight: 8.0-8.5 lbs.
Bore/Gauge: 12
Magazine: 4 + 1 rounds
Features: matte finished vent rib barrel and receiver; tunable gas system; dual extractors; chambers 2¾ field loads to 3½ magnums; black synthetic or Mossy Oak Break-Up stock; four extended screw-in SPR choke tubes-IC, M, F and Super-Full Turkey
MSRP: **$405-461**

NEW Products: Savage Arms Shotguns

MILANO
Action: over/under
Stock: walnut
Barrel: 28 in.
Chokes: screw-in tubes

Weight: 6.25-7.5 lbs.
Bore/Gauge: .410, 20, 28, 12
Magazine: none
Features: chrome-lined barrel w/ elongated forcing cone; automatic ejectors;

single selective trigger; fiber optic front sight with brass mid-rib bead; satin finish Turkish walnut stock; F, M, IC included; .410 chokes: M, IC
MSRP: **$1433**

NEW Products: Stoeger Shotguns

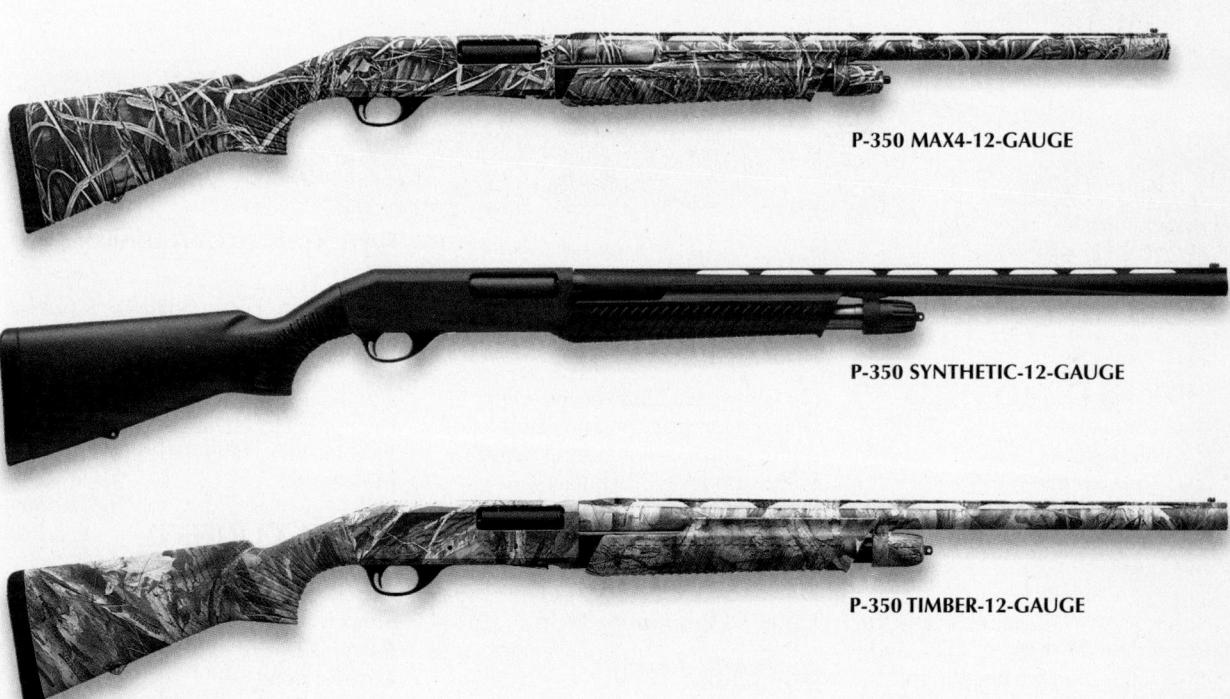

P-350 MAX4-12-GAUGE

P-350 SYNTHETIC-12-GAUGE

P-350 TIMBER-12-GAUGE

P-350, 3½ IN. MAGNUM PUMP
Action: pump
Stock: Synthetic
Barrel: 24, 26, 28 in. (ventilated rib), 18½ in. (home defense)
Chokes: screw-in tubes

Bore/Gauge: 12
Features: designed to fire all types of 12 ga. Ammunition—2¾ in., 3 in., 3½ in. Magnum, target loads, steel shot, lead shot or slugs; rotating lugs; optional 11 oz. mercury recoil reducer;black, Advantage Max-4 HD

or Advantage Timber HD camo stock; five choke tubes, including extra-full extended turkey choke
Black: **$289**
Camo: **$349**

NEW Products: Winchester Shotguns

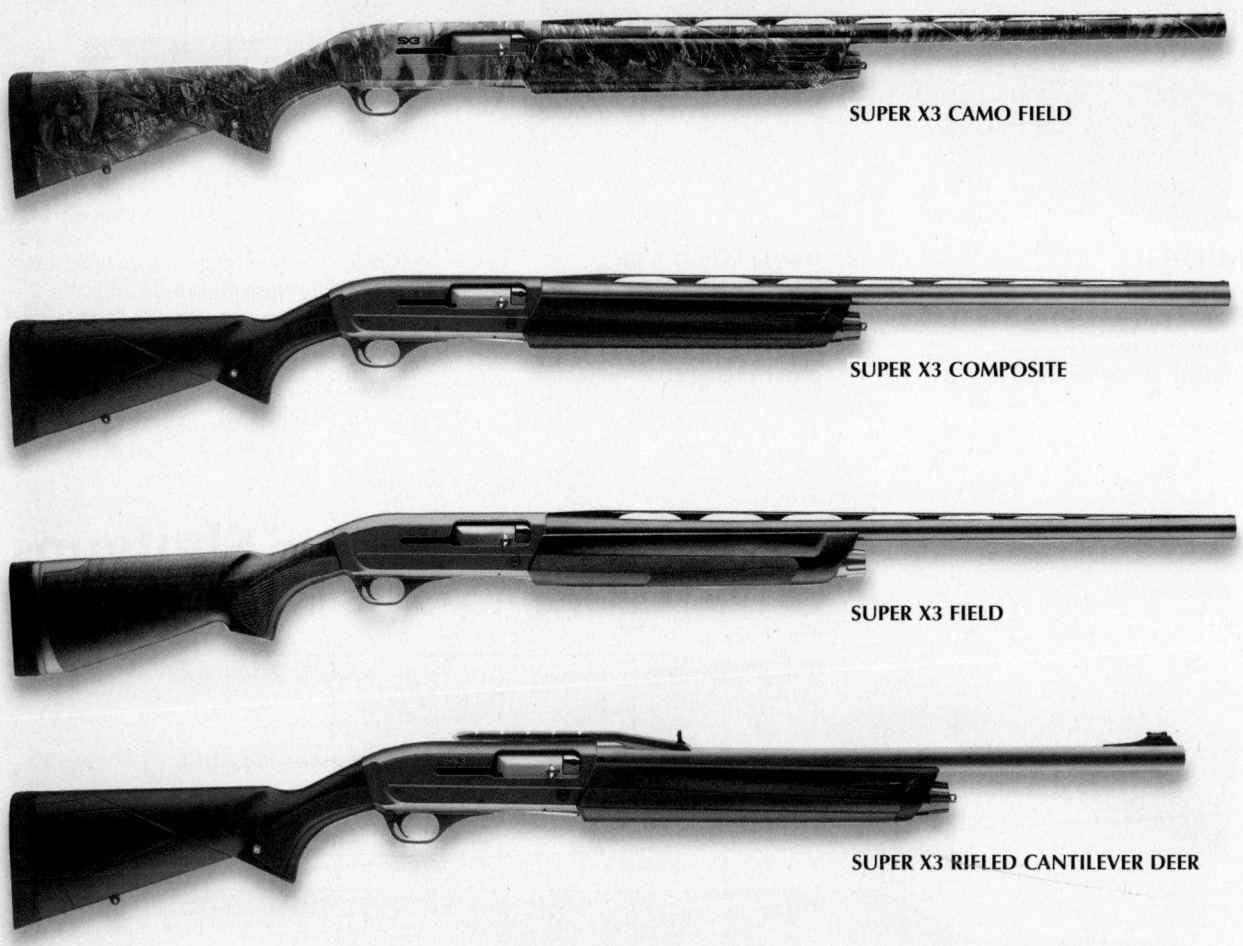

SUPER X3 CAMO FIELD

SUPER X3 COMPOSITE

SUPER X3 FIELD

SUPER X3 RIFLED CANTILEVER DEER

SUPER X3 CAMO FIELD

Action: autoloader
Stock: composite
Barrel: 26 or 28 in.
Chokes: screw-in tubes
Weight: 7.5 lbs.
Bore/Gauge: 12
Magazine: 4 rounds
Features: Mossy Oak New Break-Up finish; composite stock w/ shims and Dura-Touch Armor Coating finish; Invector-Plus choke tube system
MSRP: **$1217**

SUPER X3 COMPOSITE

Action: autoloader
Stock: composite
Barrel: 26 or 28 in.
Chokes: screw-in tubes
Weight: 7.5 lbs.
Bore/Gauge: 12
Magazine: 4 rounds
Features: slim barrel with machined rib; lightweight alloy receiver; lightweight alloy magazine tube and recoil spring system; self-adjusting Active Valve gas system; Pachmayr Decelerator recoil pad; composite stock w/ Dura-Touch Armor Coating finish; Invector-Plus choke tube system
Super X3 Composite 3 in.: **$945**
Super X3 Composite 3¾ in.: . **$1049**

SUPER X3 FIELD

Action: autoloader
Stock: walnut
Barrel: 26 or 28 in.
Chokes: screw-in tubes
Weight: 7.0 lbs.
Bore/Gauge: 12
Magazine: 4 rounds
Features: lightweight back-bored (.742 in.) barrel; machined rib; self-adjusting Active Valve gas system; chambered for 3 in.; ultralight alloy magazine tube and recoil spring; gunmetal gray Perma-Cote finish; Pachmayr Decelerator recoil pad; Invector-Plus choke tube system
MSRP: **$979**

SUPER X3 RIFLED CANTILEVER DEER

Action: autoloader
Stock: composite
Barrel: 22 in.
Chokes: none
Weight: 7.0 lb.
Bore/Gauge: 12
Magazine: 4 rounds
Features: fully rifled barrel; cantilever scope base mount and rifle style sights; lengthwise groove in the cantilever; TruGlo fiber-optic front sight; Weaver-style rail on the cantilever; composite stock w/ Dura-Touch armor coating
MSRP: **$994**

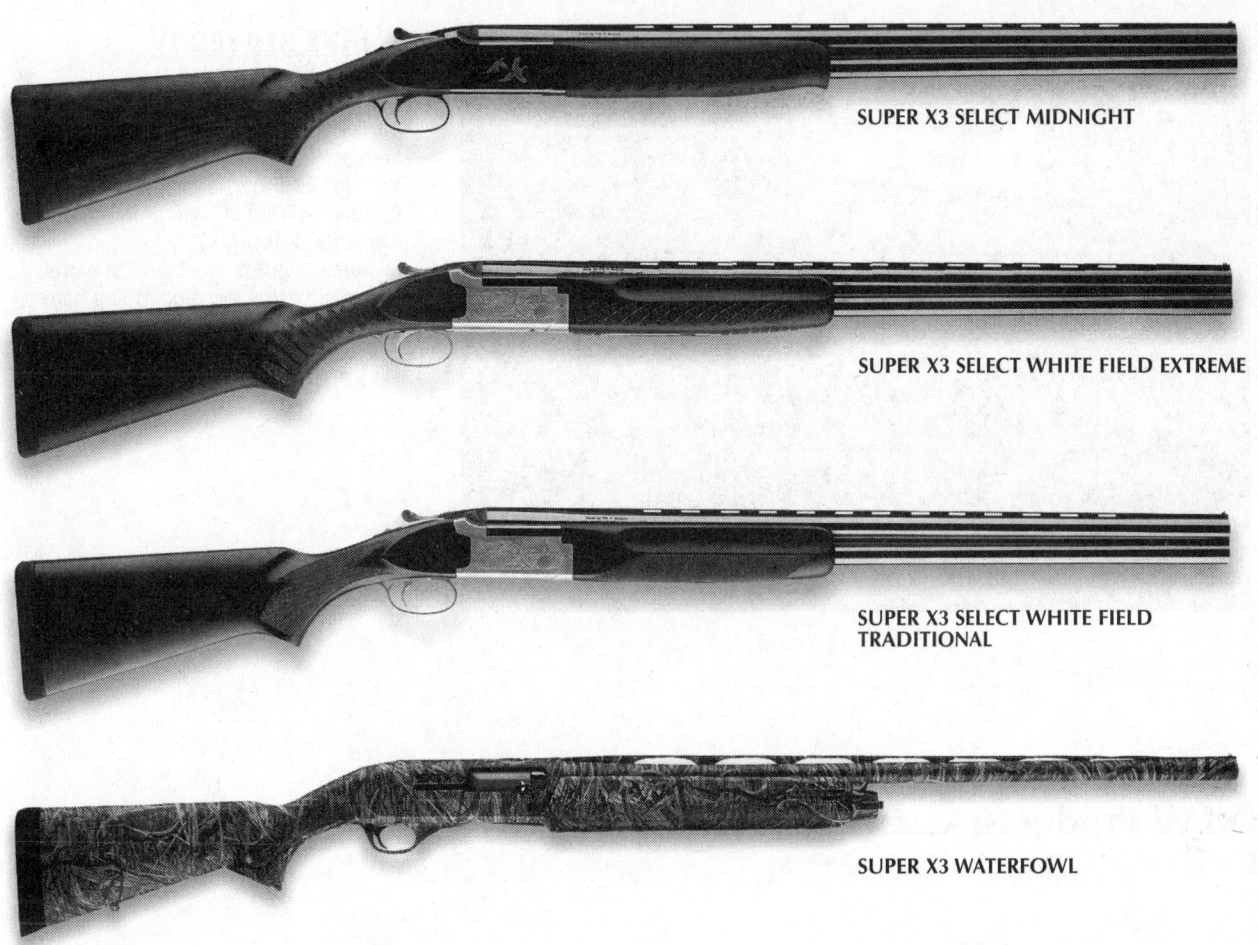

SUPER X3 SELECT MIDNIGHT

SUPER X3 SELECT WHITE FIELD EXTREME

SUPER X3 SELECT WHITE FIELD
TRADITIONAL

SUPER X3 WATERFOWL

SUPER X3 SELECT MIDNIGHT

Action: over/under
Stock: walnut
Barrel: 26 or 28 in.
Chokes: screw-in tubes
Weight: 7.0-7.25 lbs.
Bore/Gauge: 12
Magazine: none
Features: lightweight barrels; low-profile receiver with gold accented game birds and extensive engraving; high-gloss bluing on receiver and barrels; satin finished grade II/III walnut stock with oval checkering on grip; deluxe recoil pad; Invector-Plus choke system with three choke tubes—F, M, IC
MSRP: $2380

SUPER X3 SELECT WHITE FIELD EXTREME

Action: over/under
Stock: walnut
Barrel: 26 or 28 in.
Chokes: screw-in tubes
Weight: 7.0-7.25 lbs.
Bore/Gauge: 12
Magazine: none
Features: lightweight profile barrels; 3 in. chamber; low-profile engraved silver nitride receiver; walnut stock with oval-style checkering; Invector-Plus choke system with three choke tubes supplied—F, M, IC
MSRP: $1533

SUPER X3 SELECT WHITE FIELD TRADITIONAL

Stock: walnut
Barrel: 26 or 28 in.
Chokes: screw-in tubes
Weight: 7.0-7.25 lbs.
Bore/Gauge: 12
Magazine: none
Features: engraved silver nitride receiver; walnut stock with traditional cut checkering; Invector-Plus choke system with three choke tubes supplied—F, M, IC
MSRP: $1533

SUPER X3 WATERFOWL

Action: autoloader
Stock: composite
Barrel: 26 or 28 in.
Chokes: screw-in tubes
Weight: 7.5 lb.
Bore/Gauge: 12
Magazine: 4 rounds
Features: barrel with improved ventilated rib design; Active Valve system; weather-resistant composite stock and forearm with Dura-Touch Armor Coating finish; available in Mossy Oak New Shadow Grass finish; stock shims for cast and comb height adjustability; sling swivel studs are included; Invector-Plus choke tube system
MSRP: $1217

NEW Products: Bond Arms Handguns

SNAKE SLAYER IV
Action: hinged breech
Grips: rosewood
Barrel: 4.25 in.
Sights: blade front, fixed rear
Weight: 23.5 oz.
Caliber: .410/45LC with 3 in. chambers
Capacity: 2 rounds
Features: stainless steel double barrel; automatic extractor; rebounding hammer; retracting firing pins; crossbolt safety; extended custom rosewood grips
MSRP: . . . . **TBA**

NEW Products: CZ Handguns

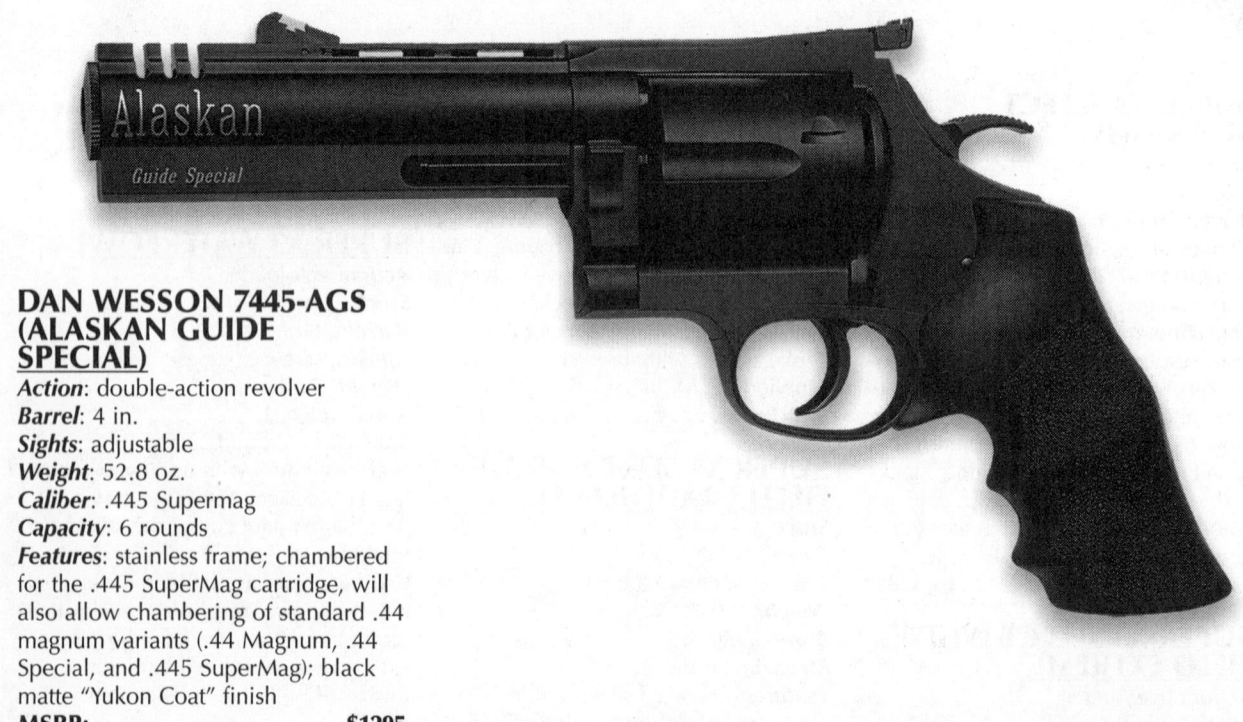

DAN WESSON 7445-AGS (ALASKAN GUIDE SPECIAL)
Action: double-action revolver
Barrel: 4 in.
Sights: adjustable
Weight: 52.8 oz.
Caliber: .445 Supermag
Capacity: 6 rounds
Features: stainless frame; chambered for the .445 SuperMag cartridge, will also allow chambering of standard .44 magnum variants (.44 Magnum, .44 Special, and .445 SuperMag); black matte "Yukon Coat" finish
MSRP: **$1295**

NEW Products: **Heckler & Koch Handguns**

COLOR FRAME PISTOLS

Heckler & Koch is offering a limited edition run of color frame versions of its most popular pistol models. These guns are functionally identical to their black-framed counterparts but are unique alternatives with molded-in colors especially suited for desert, jungle or urban environments.

Offered in select models of HK's USP, USP Compact, USP Tactical and Mark 23 pistols, Desert Tan, Green and Gray frame variations feature a tough, matte black corrosion resistant finish on all metal parts. Each color frame model comes with two magazines, a cleaning kit and nylon carry case.

Heckler & Koch color frames are available in: Gray (USP 45 & USP 40 Compact); Green (USP 45, USP 40, USP 40 Compact & USP 45 Tactical); Desert Tan (USP 45, USP 40, USP 40 Compact, USP 45 Tactical and Mark 23). Suggested retail prices for the color frame models are the same as for the black frame variation.

NEW Products: **Kahr Arms Handguns**

P SERIES KP4544

Action: autoloader
Grips: polymer
Barrel: 3.54 in.
Sights: bar-dot
Weight: 18.5 oz.
Caliber: .45 ACP
Capacity: 6 rounds
Features: black textured polymer frame; matte blackened stainless steel slide; drift-adjustable, white bar-dot combat sights (tritium night sights optional); textured polymer grips
MSRP: **$791**

NEW Products: Kel-Tec Handguns

PF-9

Action: autoloader
Grips: plastic
Barrel: 3.1 in.
Sights: open, adjustable
Weight: 12.7 oz.
Caliber: 9mm Luger
Capacity: 7+1 rounds
Features: firing mechanism, double-action only with automatic hammer-block safety; available in blued, Parkerized, and hard chrome finishes; single stack magazine; black, gray or olive drab grips
Blued: **$314**
Parkerized: **$355**
Hard chrome: **$369**

NEW Products: Kimber Handguns

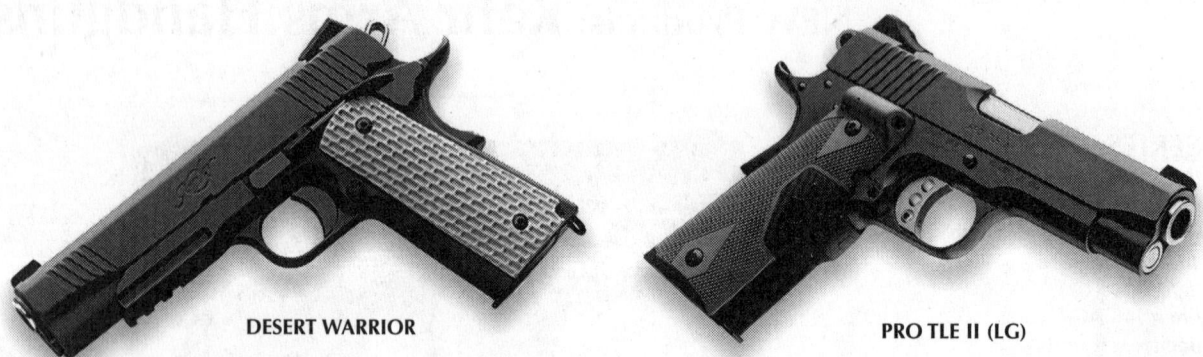

DESERT WARRIOR

PRO TLE II (LG)

DESERT WARRIOR .45ACP

Action: autoloader
Grips: synthetic
Barrel: 5 in.
Sights: Tactical wedge
Weight: 39 oz.
Caliber: .45ACP
Capacity: 7 + 1 rounds
Features: match grade solid steel barrel; ambidextrous thumb safety; bumped and grooved beavertail grip safety and bumper pad on the magazine; integral Tactical Rail; G-10 Tactical Grips; Tactical Wedge Tritium low profile night sights; KimPro II Dark Earth finish; lanyard loop
MSRP: **$1282**

PRO TLE II (LG) .45 ACP

Action: autoloader
Barrel: 4 in.
Sights: 3 dot
Weight: 36 oz.
Caliber: .45ACP
Capacity: 7 + 1 rounds
Features: bushingless match grade bull barrel; steel frame; Crimson Trace Lasergrips (normal grip pressure activates a laser mounted in a grip panel); Meprolight Tritium 3 dot night sights
MSRP: **$1231**

NEW Products: **Para Ordnance Handguns**

WARTHOG
Action: autoloader
Grips: black plastic
Barrel: 3 in.
Sights: 3 dot
Weight: 24 oz.
Caliber: .45ACP
Capacity: 10 + 1 rounds
Features: Para Power Extractor; competition hammer
MSRP: **$884**

NEW Products: **Smith & Wesson Handguns**

MODEL 29 .44 MAGNUM

MODEL 327 TRR8

MODEL 29 .44 MAGNUM 50TH ANNIVERSARY EDITION
Action: double-action revolver
Grips: African cocobolo
Barrel: 6.5 in.
Sights: target
Weight: 48.5 oz.
Caliber: .44 MAG
Capacity: 6 rounds
Features: 24kt gold-plated anniversary logo on the frame; red ramp front sight, adjustable white outline rear sight; shipped with a mahogany presentation case and a Smith & Wesson cleaning kit with screwdriver
MSRP: . . . . **TBA**

MODEL 327 TRR8
Action: double-action revolver
Grips: rubber
Barrel: 5 in., two-piece shrouded steel
Sights: interchangeable front sight, adjustable rear sight
Weight: 35.3 oz.
Caliber: .357 Magnum, .38 S&W Special
Capacity: 8 rounds
Features: precision barrel forcing cone, optimum barrel and cylinder gap; ball and detent cylinder lockup and chamfered charge holes; wide range of options for mounting optics, lights, laser aiming devices and other tactical equipment
MSRP: **$1260**

NEW PRODUCTS

M&P 9MM

SW 1911 TACRICAL RAIL

SW 1911 ROLLING THUNDER

M&P 9MM, M&P .40 AND M&P .357 SIG

Action: autoloader
Barrel: 4.25 in.
Sights: fixed open
Weight: 24 oz. (empty)
Caliber: 9mm, .40, .357 SIG
Capacity: 17 + 1 rounds (9mm), 15 + 1 rounds (.40 and.357 SIG)
Features: part of the Smith & Wesson Military & Police Pistol Series; Zytel polymer frame reinforced with a ridged steel chassis; thru-hardened black melonite stainless steel barrel and slide; dovetail-mount steel ramp front sight; steel Novak Lo-mount carry rear sight; optional Tritium sights
MSRP: . . . . **TBA**

SW1911PD AND SW1911 TACTICAL RAIL SERIES

Action: autoloader
Barrel: 5 in.
Sights: fixed open
Weight: 32 oz. (1911PD), 39 oz. (1911)
Caliber: .45 ACP
Capacity: 8 + 1 rounds
Features: Model SW1911 stainless steel slide w/ melonite finish; black anodized Scandium Alloy frame; non-reflective matte grey finish; white dot front sight and Novak Lo Mount Carry rear sight; Picatinny-style rail with standard 1911 configuration
1911PD: **$1057-1120**
1911: . . . . **TBA**

SW1911, ROLLING THUNDER COMMEMORATIVE

Smith & Wesson, in conjunction with Rolling Thunder Inc., commemorates the lives of America's men and women who have become prisoners of war or are missing in action with the SW1011 Rolling Thunder Commemorative.
Action: autoloader
Grips: ivory (imitation)
Barrel: 5 in.
Sights: fixed open
Weight: 38.5 oz.
Caliber: .45ACP
Capacity: 8 + 1 Rounds
Features: limited edition Model SW1911; machine engraving on frame with 24kt gold plated Rolling Thunder logo; white dot front sight, Novak Lo Mount Carry rear; glass top presentation case; special serial range starting with RTS0001; imitation ivory grips
MSRP: . . . . **TBA**

NEW Products: Uberti Handguns

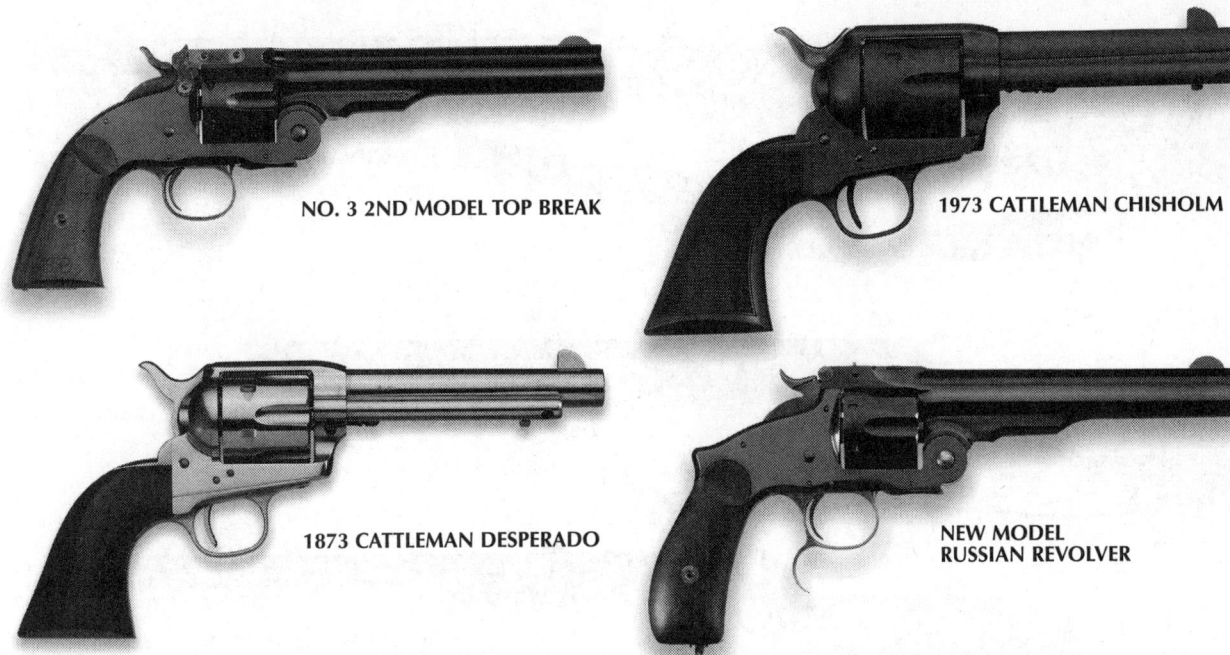

NO. 3 2ND MODEL TOP BREAK

1973 CATTLEMAN CHISHOLM

1873 CATTLEMAN DESPERADO

NEW MODEL RUSSIAN REVOLVER

NO. 3 2ND MODEL TOP BREAK
Action: single-action revolver
Grips: pearl   **Barrel**: 7 in.
Sights: open fixed
Weight: 33.0-37.0 oz.
Caliber: .38, .45 Colt; .44/40
Capacity: 6 rounds
Features: improved rounded and knurled top latch; 6-shot fluted cylinder; nickle finish; two piece mother-of-pearl grips
MSRP: **$925**

1873 CATTLEMAN CHISHOLM
Action: single-action revolver
Grips: walnut   **Barrel**: 5.75 in.
Sights: open fixed   **Weight**: 35 oz.
Caliber: .45 Colt   **Capacity**: 6 rounds
Features: 6-shot fluted cylinder; checkered walnut grip; matte blue finish
MSRP: **$385**

1873 CATTLEMAN DESPERADO
Action: single-action revolver
Grips: pearl   **Barrel**: 5.5 in.
Sights: open fixed   **Weight**: 35 oz.
Caliber: .45 Colt   **Capacity**: 6 rounds

Features: 6-shot fluted cylinder; mother-of-pearl grip; matte blue finish
MSRP: **$635**

NEW MODEL RUSSIAN REVOLVER
Action: single-action revolver
Grips: walnut   **Barrel**: 6.5 in.
Sights: open fixed   **Weight**: 40 oz.
Caliber: 44 Russian, .45 Colt
Capacity: 6 rounds
Features: improved top latch, 6-shot fluted cylinder; blued frame, barrel and backstrap; case-hardened trigger guard
MSRP: **$825**

NEW Products: Weatherby Handguns

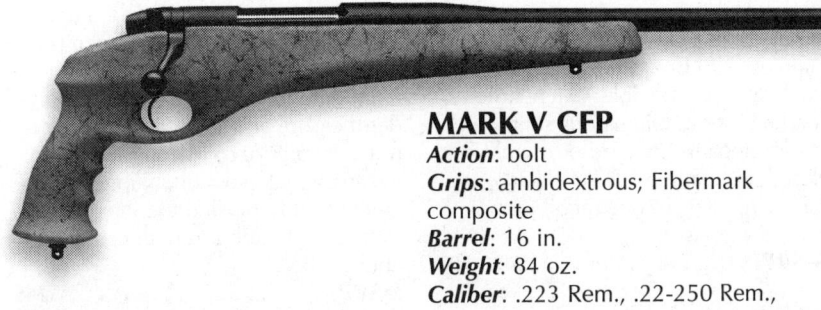

MARK V CFP
Action: bolt
Grips: ambidextrous; Fibermark composite
Barrel: 16 in.
Weight: 84 oz.
Caliber: .223 Rem., .22-250 Rem.,

.243 Win., 7mm-08 Rem.
Capacity: 5 + 1 rounds
Features: Button-rifled, #2 contour, chrome moly (4140 steel) barrel; one-piece forged and fluted bolt; cocking indicator; adjustable trigger
MSRP: **$1499**

NEW Products: **CVA Black Powder**

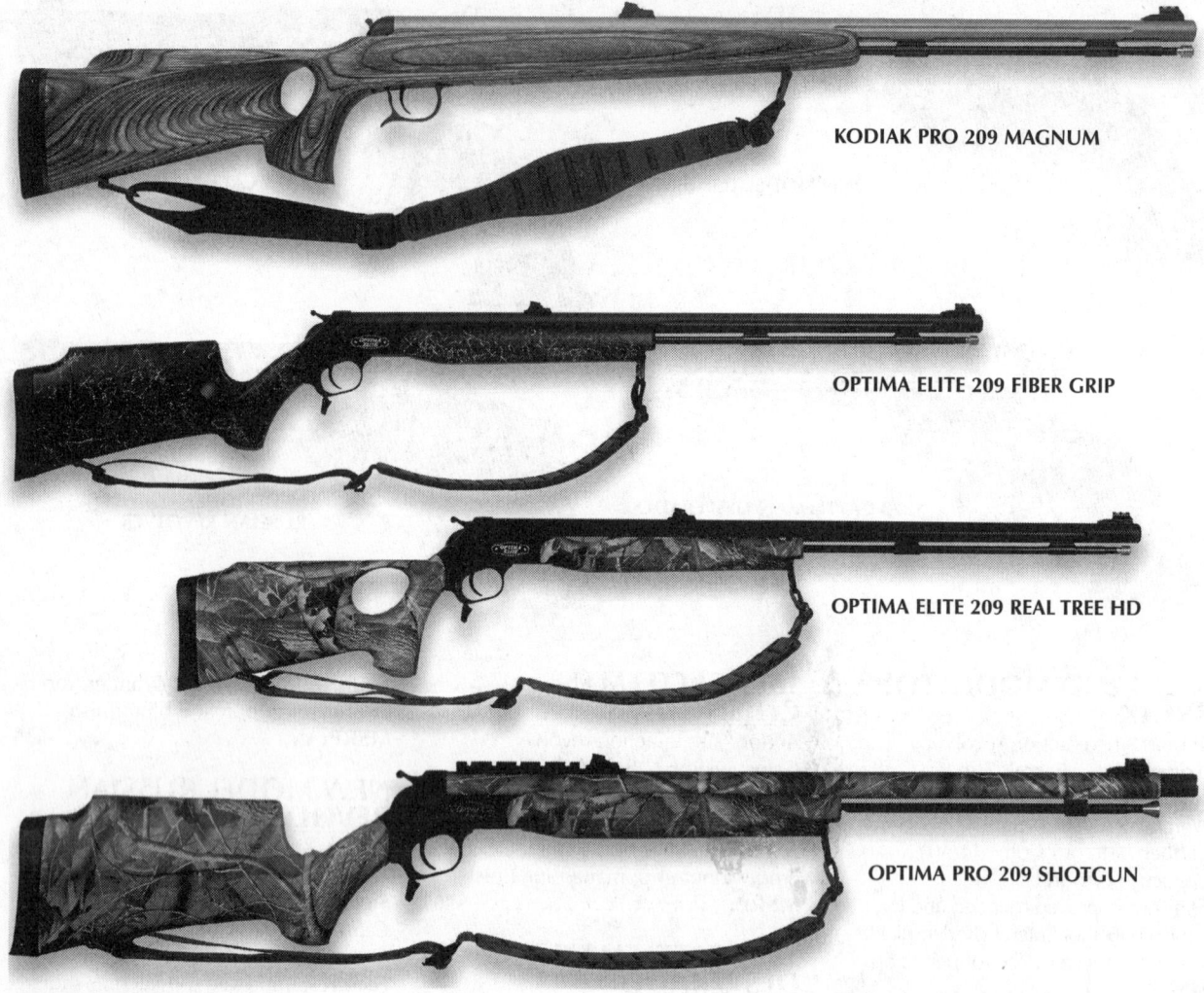

KODIAK PRO 209 MAGNUM

OPTIMA ELITE 209 FIBER GRIP

OPTIMA ELITE 209 REAL TREE HD

OPTIMA PRO 209 SHOTGUN

KODIAK PRO 209 MAGNUM

Lock: pivot block
Stock: composite or laminated
Barrel: 29 in.
Sights: DuraBright fiber optic
Weight: 7.5 lb.
Bore/Caliber: .45, .50
Features: fluted blue or stainless barrel; all metal DuraBright fiber optic sights; thumbhole or standard composite or laminated wood stock in camo or black finish; semi-solid stock comes with a Quake Claw sling and a CrushZone recoil pad
MSRP: $290-465

OPTIMA ELITE 209 MAGNUM BREAK-ACTION

Lock: in-line
Stock: composite
Barrel: 29 in. blued or stainless fluted
Sights: DuraBright adjustable fiber optic
Weight: 8.8 lb.
Bore/Caliber: .45 and .50
Features: Bergara button rifled barrel with bullet guiding muzzle (Optima Pro and Optima barrels cannot be installed on the Optima Elite frame); stainless 209 breech plug; reversible cocking spur available; extendable loading rod; ambidextrous solid composite stock in standard or thumbhole design in Realtree HD or Black FiberGrip; CrushZone recoil pad; Quake Claw sling
MSRP: $425-500

OPTIMA PRO 209 SHOTGUN

Lock: in-line
Stock: composite
Barrel: 26 in.
Sights: DuraBright fiber optic
Weight: 7.5 lbs.
Choke: screw-in tube
Bore/Caliber: 12
Features: barrel finished in Mossy Oak New Breakup camo or Matte Blue; removable, stainless steel breech plug; closed-breech receiver; extendable aluminum loading rod; includes powder measure and shot cups; ambidextrous deep-grip, solid composite stock in Mossy Oak New Breakup Camo; DuraBright sights and the integral Weaver style rail; screw in extra full choke tube
MSRP: $440

NEW Products: **Knight Black Powder**

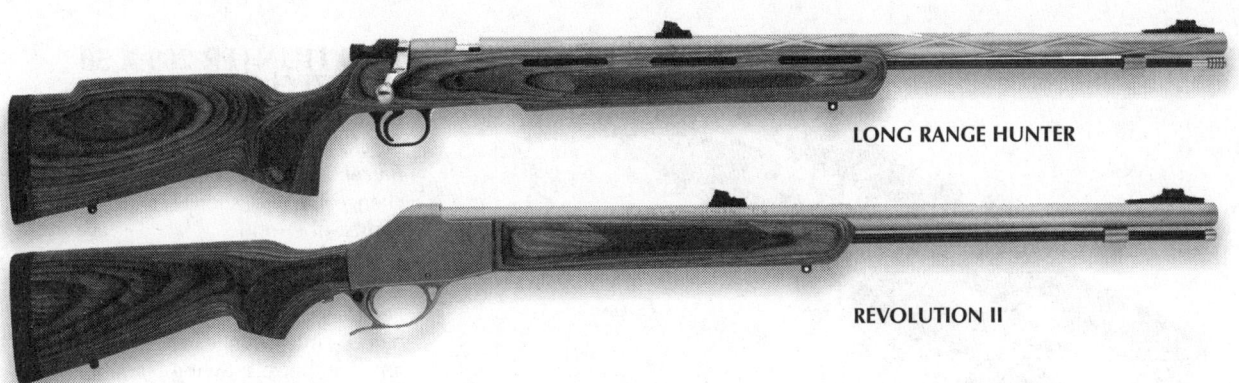

LONG RANGE HUNTER

REVOLUTION II

LONG RANGE HUNTER
Lock: in-line   *Stock*: laminated
Barrel: 27 in.
Sights: adjustable
Weight: 8.25 lbs.
Bore/Caliber: .50, .52
Features: spiral custom-fluted, stainless free floated barrel; adjustable target trigger; metallic fiber optic sights; cast-

off stock for right- and left-handed shooters w/ vent slots in forest green laminated wood or sand stone
MSRP: $725

REVOLUTION II
Lock: pivot-block drop action
Stock: composite or laminate
Barrel: 27 in.

Sights: adjustable
Weight: 7.45 lbs.
Bore/Caliber: .50, .52
Features: stainless steel barrel; quick detachable action; drilled and tapped for scope; metallic fiber optic sights; two-piece black composite, camouflage composite and wood laminate stock
MSRP: $388-482

NEW Products: **Remington Black Powder**

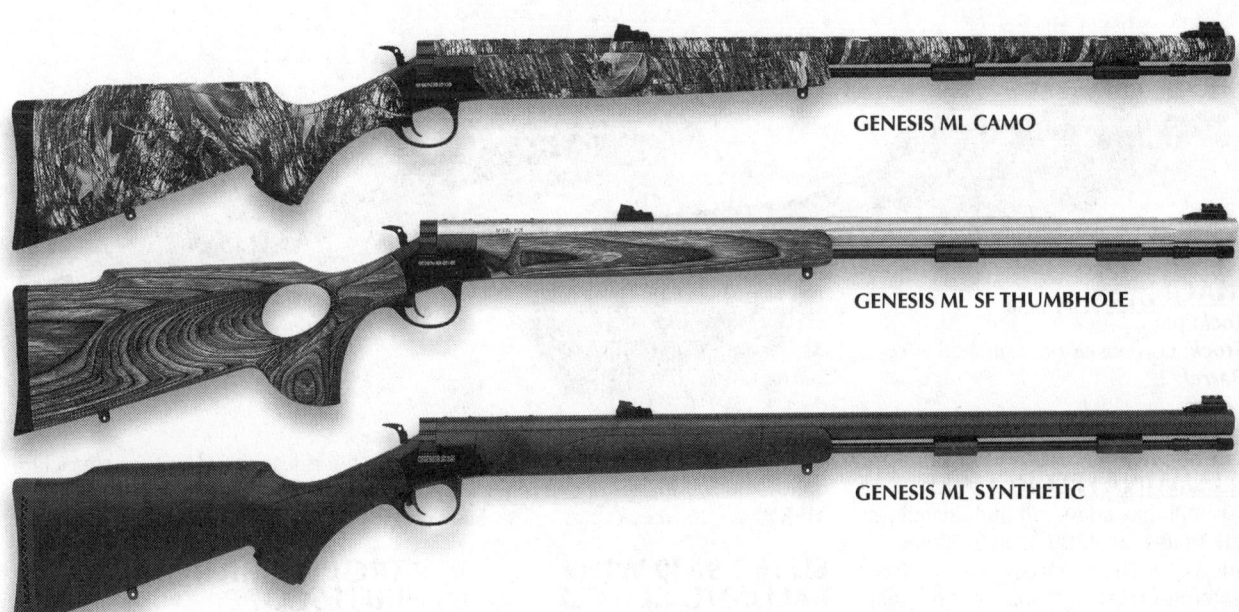

GENESIS ML CAMO

GENESIS ML SF THUMBHOLE

GENESIS ML SYNTHETIC

GENESIS
Lock: in-line
Stock: synthetic or laminate
Barrel: 28 in.
Sights: fiber-optic
Weight: 7.5-8.0 lbs.
Bore/Caliber: .50

Features: 1:28 twist barrel; ultra-compact TorchCam breech; 209 primer system; Carbon Blue Matte and Camo (ML line) barrel; stainless steel (MLS and ML SF Thumbhole lines); drilled and tapped for scope mounts; over-travel hammer w/ ambidextrous

Hammer Spur; crossbolt safety; aluminum anodized ramrod; Williams fiber-optic sights; Black Synthetic, Mossy Oak New Break-Up (ML, MLS and ML SF Thumbhole stock lines); Grey Laminate (ML SF Thumbhole line)
MSRP: $279-566

NEW Products: **Thompson/Center Black Powder**

PRO HUNTER 209 X 50 MUZZLELOADER

Lock: in-line
Stock: FlexTech composite
Barrel: 28 in., stainless, fluted; inter-changeable with shotgun and rifle barrels
Sights: fiber-optic
Weight: N/A
Bore/Caliber: .50
Features: stainless, fluted precision barrel—interchangeable with shotgun and rifle barrels; Swing Hammer design; engraved receiver; FlexTech (recoil system) composite stock in black or Realtree Hardwoods camo with or without thumbhole
Black:. **$919**
Realtree Hardwoods camo: . . . **$985**

NEW Products: **Bushnell Optics**

ELITE 2.5-10X50   **ELITE 3-9X40**

ELITE 2.5-10X50 WITH ILLUMINATED RETICLE

Bushnell has added an illuminated reticle to its Elite 4200 2.5-10x50mm riflescope. The battery-powered reticle features a small 1 M.O.A; red dot that helps shooters quickly acquire their target. The battery housing for the reticle has been moved from the top of the eyepiece to a position opposite the windage cap making it easier for the shooter to adjust the illumination while still maintaining the sight picture. The Elite 2.5-10x50mm also has a

Fast Focus eyepiece, multi-coated optics and 3.3 inches of eye relief.
MSRP: **$549**

ELITE 3-9X40 WITH BALLISTIC RETICLE

Bushnell has added a ballistic reticle to its popular 3-9x40mm 3200 Elite riflescope. Long-range target shooters can rely on the gradient lines under the crosshairs that indicate the point of impact at various distances. Shooters can also use the reticle to estimate windage. The ballistic reticle is etched

into the riflescope glass for better clarity and accuracy.
MSRP: **$279**

TROPHY MP RED DOT RIFLESCOPE

Bushnell has introduced a new Trophy 1x32mm MP Red Dot riflescope for use on tactical firearms. It has integrated Weaver style mounts, and its bright optics, low magnification and T-Dot reticle make for fast target acquisition. The Trophy MP Red Dot offers shooters a choice between a green T-Dot reticle

**TROPHY MP RED
DOT RIFLESCOPE**

**YARDAGE PRO
RIFLESCOPE**

for low-light conditions or a red T-Dot reticle under brighter conditions. It features unlimited eye relief and a compact design. It is ruggedly constructed, dry nitrogen purged and sealed with an o-ring to protect the optics against moisture and fog. Windage and elevation adjustments are ¼" M.O.A. It comes in a matte black finish.
MSRP: **$229**

YARDAGE PRO RIFLESCOPE

This new riflescope combines premium, fully multi-coated optics with a laser rangefinder that accurately ranges targets from 30 to 800 yards with Bullet Drop Compensator turrets that quickly and easily adjust elevation to the displayed range. The scope comes with five Bullet Drop Compensator (BDC) turrets calibrated to match the most popular calibers and bullet weights. In the field or at the range, the shooter uses a wireless trigger pad

to activate the laser rangefinder. Once the distance is displayed in the scope, the BDC turret is adjusted to match the range, eliminating the need for holdover. Once the shooter knows the range, the Mil Dot reticle can be used to compensate for windage and elevation. Other features include fully multi-coated optics, and waterproof/fog proof construction. Eye relief is set at 3.5 inches. It is compact in design and weighs just 25.3 ounces.
MSRP: **$899**

NEW Products: **Cabela's Optics**

PINE RIDGE .17 TACTICAL RIFLESCOPES

Cabela's new scopes are specially engineered for rifles in the .17 HMR caliber. The Pine Ridge .17 Tactical Riflescopes are incrementally calibrated to adjust for bullet drop out to 300 yards. Waterproof, fogproof and shockproof, these scopes have fully coated optics. Mounting tube is 1 inch, and eye relief is 3 inches. The scopes also have finger-adjustable windage and elevation with trajectory compensation turret and parallax adjustment. The 3-

12x40 and 6-18x40 feature side-focus parallax adjustment. These scopes have all the quality features and high-performance optics of the regular .17 Tactical Scopes above, but by repositioning the parallax setting knob location on the scope, Cabela's has

enabled the user to keep the target in sight while making adjustments from 50 to 300 yards and beyond. Side-focus models also have a larger field of view for quicker target acquisition.
MSRP: **$69.99-129.99**

NEW Products: **Kahles Optics**

CL 1-INCH RIFLESCOPE

The CL 1-inch scope line will initially be available in a 3-9x42, 3-10x50 and 4-12x52. Features include the Kahles multizero system, a revolutionary "micro-mechanic" ballistic system that will allow users to pre-set up to five different sight settings on the scope; third turret parallax; enhanced AMV Lens Coating technology on all air-to-glass surfaces which now maximizes low light performance by transmitting a higher percentage of the visible light spectrum; waterproof submersible turrets even when protective caps are removed; expanded point-of-impact total range of adjustment; and an 18% larger ocular diameter which has expanded the eye relief, expanded the field-of-view, fast focus ocular dial and enhanced the edge-to-edge resolution.

All Kahles CL riflescopes have the reticle located in the (non-magnifying) second image focal plane that maintains its size throughout the magnification range, come standard with a technologically advanced, scratch-resistant matte finish.

NEW Products: **Konus USA Optics**

PRO SHOTGUN/BLACKPOWDER

PRO VARMINT

PRO SHOTGUN/ BLACKPOWDER SCOPE

Two new KonusPro scopes in a fixed 2.5X32mm and a variable 1.5X-5X32mm configuration, both with etched reticles, are available for shotgun and blackpowder applications. Other features include long-eye relief, Aim-Pro reticle design (circle/diamond pattern), multi-coated optical glass for increased light transmission and a nitrogen purged tube assembly for 100% waterproof and fogproof integrity.

2.5X32mm:. **$80**
1.5X-5X32mm: **$115**

PRO VARMINT SCOPE

The KonusPro 6X-24X44mm Varmint Scope features an etched reticle and adjustable objective. It also includes finger-adjustable windage and elevation controls, multi-coated glass optics, nitrogen purged tube assembly and a tapered 30/30 styled reticle. The KonusPro rifle scope line all contain a glass engraved/laser etched reticle system. The reticle is etched on to precision glass rather than using a thin wire. The etched reticle system is extremely rugged and eliminates the chances of breaking or becoming misaligned.

MSRP: **$190**

"WM. MALCOLM" SCOPE AND MOUNTS

The Wm. Malcolm scope offers authentic 1870s looks and styling, but has been built with the benefits of modern scope-making technology. Unlike the originals used on Sharps, Winchester High Wall and Remington Rolling Block black powder cartridge rifles, this 6X long tube-type scope is built with light gathering full multi-coated lenses. This scope is built with a nitrogen-filled ¾ in. tube for fog-free service. The scope can be mounted on old-style rifles with barrel lengths from 28 to 34 inches using the factory cut front and rear sight dovetails. Comes with fully adjustable external mounts.
MSRP: **$419**

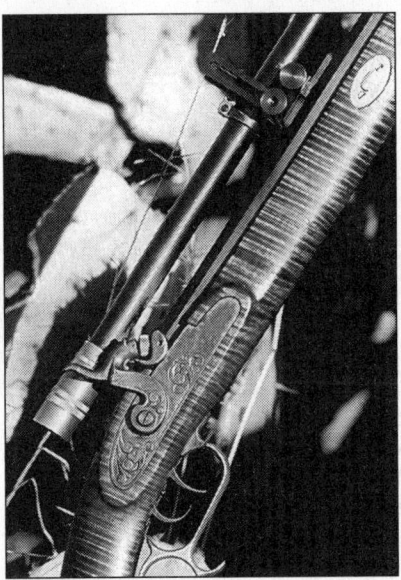

NEW Products: **Leupold Optics**

GOLDEN RING
VX-III 4.5-14X40

MARK 4 2.5-8X36

GOLDEN RING VX-III 4.5-14X40MM ADJUSTABLE OBJECTIVE RIFLESCOPE

The Leupold Golden Ring VX-III 4.5-14x40mm Adj. Obj. riflescope has a wide range of magnification. The adjustable objective makes it easy to set your parallax for specific distances. It fits easily into a scabbard and doesn't get hung up on brush, changing your parallax setting. You can adjust for parallax as close as 25 yards—ideal for target shooting or small game. Finally, you get incredible power without a lot of heft; the 1 in. maintube is incredibly strong and extremely lightweight.

MARK 4 2.5-8X36MM MR/T RIFLESCOPES

Leupold introduced its Mid Range/Tactical (MR/T) riflescopes because not all engagements occur at 1,000 yards or in close quarters. The Leupold Mark 4 2.5-8x36mm MR/T M1 and M2 riflescopes help cover that crucial middle ground. Like the original MR/T riflescopes, the 2.5-8x36mm MR/T is designed and built to military specifications with matte black finish, and either M1 or M2 finger-adjustable windage and elevation dials. Eye relief is optimized for 7.62mm NATO and other larger caliber, harder recoiling systems, aiding in the instant target acquisition you need. Available with a Mil Dot or Leupold Tactical Milling Reticle (both are available with Illumination).

NEW Products: Nikon Optics

OMEGA BLACK   OMEGA CAMO   OMEGA SILVER

OMEGA MUZZLELOADING RIFLESCOPE

The Nikon Omega 3-9x40 with BDC-250 reticle was created to help shooters take advantage of the full accuracy potential of their muzzleloaders. The Omega offers a bullet drop compensating reticle designed specifically for muzzleloading loads and ranges and was designed to utilize .50 caliber muzzleloading loads –150 grains of Pyrodex (pellets or powder), 250-grain bullets and ranges (out to 250-yards).

The BDC-250 is a trajectory-compensating reticle designed and calibrated to provide fast, simple aiming points for various shot distances. This unique system integrates a series of small "ballistic circles"—each subtending 2" @ 100 yards—allowing an unimpeded view of the target. (At 200 yards, the circles are 4"; at 250 yards, they are 5".) The reticle is designed to be sighted-in at 100 yards, with aiming-point circles at 150, 200, 225 and 250 yards. A generous 25.2 8.4-foot

field-of-view also makes getting on a trophy animal a breeze. The Omega Riflescope is equipped with precise, ¼-MOA click reticle adjustments and a full 5 inches of eye relief for even the hardest kicking, magnum charge loads. Omega measures a compact 11.3-inches in length, and weighs 13.8 ounces.

Matte:	**$250**
Silver:	**$260**
Realtree Hardwoods Green HD:	**$270**

NEW Products: Pentax Optics

GAMESEEKER
DOT SIGHT RD10

GAMESEEKER
RIFLESCOPE

GAMESEEKER DOT SIGHTS

Each of Pentax's new Gameseeker Dot Sights features a 4 MOA dot, an ideal size for most shooters, as well as 11 brightness settings for various shooting conditions and a battery that provides 72 hours of continuous use. Also featuring PentaBright Technology, each Gameseeker dot sight offers a sharp, clear image that is parallax free for accurate target acquisition.
MSRP: **$200**

GAMESEEKER RIFLESCOPES

Featuring one inch, one-piece tube construction, Pentax Gameseeker riflescopes are extremely durable and fully waterproof for the most extreme hunting situations. Each scope is nitrogen filled to prevent internal fogging of optical elements, and the fully-multi-coated optics with PentaBright technology help increase light transmission to deliver sharp, clear images. Every Gameseeker includes the new bullet

drop compensating Precision Plex reticle. Gameseeker scopes will be available in the following variable powers: 3x-9x 40mm Matte, 4x-12x 40mm Matte, 3x-9x 50mm Matte, 3.5x-10x 50mm Matte, 1.5x-6x 40mm Matte, 2.5x-10x 56mm Matte, 4x-16x 50mm Matte, 1.75x-5x 20mm Matte and in the following fixed powers: 4x 32mm Matte and 6x 42mm Matte.
MSRP: **$200**

**SOLAR POWERED
RED DOT SCOPE**

TS RED DOT SCOPE

SOLAR POWERED RED DOT SCOPE

The Solar Cell Red Dot scope solar cell technology is available in a 1x30mm. For use during low light early morning or late afternoon hours, it can be switched from solar power to a back up battery. Standard features include fully coated lenses; an illuminated 5 M.O.A. red dot reticle; Tasco Rubicon lens coating and unlimited eye relief. A rheostat lets the user dial in the brightness of the red dot to match hunting or shooting conditions.
MSRP: **$97**

TS RED DOT SCOPE

The new TS Red Dot 1x32mm scope will function as well on the range as it will in the field. With a new single mounting ring design it mounts easily on rifles, shotguns or pistols. It is also the ideal scope for use on tactical firearms. Other key features include fully coated lenses; flip-up caps on the objective and ocular lenses; an illuminated 5 M.O.A. red dot reticle and unlimited eye relief. The intensity of the red dot can be adjusted with an 11 position rheostat. It is covered by a lifetime limited warranty.
MSRP: **$170**

NEW Products: **Trijicon Optics**

**ACOG MODEL
TA31DOC**

TRIPOWER

ACOG MODEL TA31DOC

The TA31DOC combines the technology of the battle-tested Trijicon ACOG (4x32) gun sight with the Docter Optic Red Dot sight. The Trijicon ACOG model TA31DOC is an internally adjustable telescopic sight powered by Trijicon fiber optics and tritium-based technology. It's dual-illuminated reticle is designed to hold zero under the most extreme conditions and present a bright aiming point in all lighting conditions — providing excellent long-range precision targeting or even faster short range target selection using the Bindon Aiming Concept (BAC). With the field-proven Docter Optic 1x red dot sight mounted on top of the Trijicon ACOG TA31DOC, this innovative sighting system provides the user with lightening fast target acquisition in CQB situations while allowing for excellent situational awareness.
MSRP: **$1650**

TRIPOWER

The TriPower now features a durable body forged in hard-anodized aircraft aluminum alloy, a sleek scope design for maximum field of view and upgraded lens coatings. The Trijicon TriPower provides a quick and bright hunting optic for those fast-moving, close-in shots. In tactical users, it provides clearly visible aiming point for the varied lighting conditions experienced in CQB (close-quarter battle).
MSRP: **$599**

NEW Products: **Weaver Optics**

QUAD LOCK FAMILY ADDITIONS

Five new offerings add to an already popular Quad Lock series of rings. All Quad-Lock rings utilize four straps per set for added gripping strength. These rings mount to all Weaver Top Mount Bases and their all-aluminum construction offers hunters a lightweight, sturdy option. The new silver or matte Tip-Off Quad Lock rings fit a ⅜ in. dovetail receiver and three Quad Locks sets are now available in silver (medium, high and high extension).

SURE GRIP WINDAGE ADJUSTABLE RINGS

With the new Sure Grip Windage Adjustable Rings, hunters and shooters can rest assured that these rings will handle any recoil thrown at them. The four-screw system and steel cap offer shot-of-a-lifetime dependability. The new windage adjustable models ensure zeroing in your scope to the critical optical clarity zone is certain.

NEW Products: **Barnes Bullets Ammunition**

SPIT-FIRE T MZ MUZZLELOADER BULLET

The same boattail design and 100% copper construction of the Spit-Fire MZ, but with a streamlined polymer tip to enhance expansion. Higher BC for exceptional long-range performance. Stays intact at extreme velocities, expands at 1050 fps. New sabot makes loading easier without sacrificing the tight gas seal that makes the Spit-Fire MZ and Spit-Fire TMZ the most accurate muzzleloader bullets on the market. Offered in .50 caliber, 250- and 290-grain weights in 15- and 24-bullet packs.

NEW Products: **Brenneke Ammunition**

CLASSIC MAGNUM SHOTGUN SLUG

The Classic Magnum 12 gauge, 2¾ in. slug is a direct descendent of the 1898 Brenneke design. Redesigned plastic disks have been added around the Classic Magnum's felt wad, in front of a new "H-type" filler wad, resulting in 50% greater accuracy. The Classic retains the massive frontal area, weight-forward stability and power that distinguishes all Brenneke slugs. Its effectiveness has been proven on bears, moose, Cape buffalos and even elephants.

The improved Classic Magnum is capable of five-shot groups of under two inches at 50 yards, while producing 2460 ft. lbs. of energy at the muzzle. It is suitable for use in both rifled and smoothbore barrels, making it a truly "universal" round.

NEW Products: CCI Ammunition

SELECT .22LR

CCI's skilled ballistics staff has improved the lot-to-lot accuracy of this specific load; it's perfect for shooters looking for accuracy and consistency for target shooting. 1200 fps velocity. .22 Long Rifle 40-Grain Lead Round Nose.

NEW Products: Federal Premium Ammunition

V-SHOK .204 RUGER AND .22 HORNET

Federal will add the .204 Ruger to its list of V-Shok offerings. In addition, the .22 Hornet will also be available under V-Shok, further extending this line's options for varmints and predators. Federal has taken the speedy .204 Ruger round and topped it with the explosive 39-grain Sierra BlitzKing bullet. This Premium loading will give hunters legendary Sierra accuracy coupled with optimum velocity and terminal performance on varmints and predators.

The .22 Hornet offerings, available in both a 33-grain Speer TNT and a 45-grain Speer Soft Point, offer high velocities and Premium performance. Predator hunters everywhere will love the rapid-expansion and terminal performance of the TNT bullet.

MAG-SHOK TURKEY LOADS

For 2006, those in pursuit of old Tom will have several more options as they take the field. No longer is the chambering of the gun a limiting factor for turkey hunters. The same wad system that produces up to 30% tighter patterns is now available in 2¾-inch loads. In addition, HEAVYWEIGHT loads will now be available in 3 and 3½-inch #7 shot offerings.

NEW Products: Hornady Ammunition

20 GAUGE SST SHOTGUN SLUG

The SST bullet delivers true, 200 yard long range accuracy. Sub-2" groups at 100 yards. Ultra-flat trajectory. Polymer tip initiates violent expansion over a wide range of velocities.

500 S&W

6.8MM SPC

.338 LAPUA

LEVER REVOLUTION

416 RIGBY

500 S&W 300-GRAIN EVOLUTION HANDGUN AMMUNITION

Evolution bullets are the flattest shooting handgun ammunition on the market and deliver long-range accuracy and terminal performance. The Elastomer Flex Tip produces a high ballistic coefficient that delivers dramatically flatter trajectories for increased downrange energy and exceptional bullet expansion. This ammunition is new production, non-corrosive, in boxer primed, reloadable brass cases.

6.8MM SPC RIFLE AMMUNITION

Developed at the request of the U.S. Special Forces, the 6.8 SPC is a perfect sporting cartridge for game up to the size of whitetail and mule deer. This cartridge is in about the same power class as the .300 Savage, but delivers a flatter trajectory and less recoil. Hornady's 6.8 SPC ammo features either a 110 gr. BTHP bullet, specifically designed for the cartridge, or a proven 110 gr. V-MAX bullet. The 110 gr. BTHP delivers excellent expansion and maximum energy transfer at all velocities, while the 110 gr. VMAX has all the characteristics of our Varmint Express ammo—flat trajectories and rapid, violent expansion. Also new in Hornady ammunition: .338 Lapua (250 grain) and .416 Rigby (400 grain) ammunition.

LEVER/REVOLUTION RIFLE AMMUNITION

Hornady brings you an innovation in ammunition performance featuring state of the industry elastomer Flex Tip Technology that is safe in your tubular magazine. Its higher ballistic coefficient delivers dramatically flatter trajectories for fantastic downrange energy. Features include: up to 250 feet-pe-second faster muzzle velocity than conventional lever gun loads; exceptional accuracy and overwhelming downrange terminal performance; patent-pending Evolution bullet featuring elastomer Flex Tip Technology; up to 40% more energy than traditional flat point loads. Available in .30-30 Win., .35 Rem., .444 Marlin, .45-70 Gov't., .450 Marlin.

NEW Products: **PowerBelt Ammunition**

PLATINUM SERIES MUZZLELOADING BULLETS

PowerBelt Platinum Series Bullets are plated using a proprietary process that produces a harder exterior surface than standard copper plating and also results in the platinum color for which they were named. This harder plating results in reduced resistance as the bullet travels down the bore of the barrel, producing faster and more consistent velocities, thereby improving both trajectory and accuracy.

The Platinum series also benefit from an improved ballistic coefficient because of a more aggressive bullet taper. Not only does the new taper provide for a more aerodynamic flight, but it also helps control the rate of expansion, regardless of powder charge or distance.

The third innovation the PowerBelt engineers incorporated into the new Platinum design is a horizontally fluted gas check, allowing the check to be sized larger than that of a standard PowerBelt, while still being just as easy to load. The larger diameter gas check produces higher and more consistent pressures, further improving both velocity and accuracy.

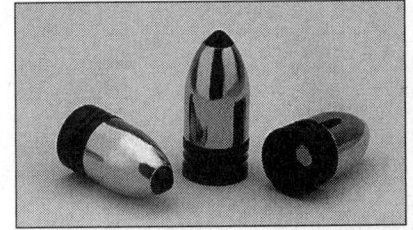

PowerBelt Platinum bullets will be available in both .45 and .50 calibers, all in the AeroTip configuration, with designated grain weights for medium sized game and larger thick-skinned game as well.

NEW Products: **Remington Ammunition**

WINGMASTER HD SHOTSHELLS

The new Wingmaster HD Shotshells effectively stretch the kill zone with a combination of pattern uniformity, higher density, high pellet count and choke responsiveness—putting a greater number of pellets on game at longer ranges, with equal pellet energy and deeper penetration than any other similar density non-toxic material.

At a density of 12.0 grams/cc, Wingmaster HD's non-toxic tungsten/bronze/iron composition is 10% denser than lead and a whopping 56% denser than steel, which dramatically enhances per-pellet energy and extended-range penetration.

Wingmaster HD's round, smooth, consistently sized pellets are key to increasing effective range and pattern density. At ranges beyond 40 yards, it proved superior to all tested waterfowl lead alternatives in combined pattern density and penetration.

Ideal density of 12.0 g/cc yields the best combination of par-pellet energy and effective performance. Approved by the USF&W and Canada.

NEW Products: **Winchester Ammunition**

SUPREME ELITE XP3 CENTERFIRE RIFLE AMMUNITION

The patent-pending 2-Stage expansion XP3 delivers precision accuracy, awesome knockdown power and deep penetration all in one package-and it's as effective on thin-skinned game such deer and antelope as it is on tough game like elk, moose, bear and African animals, at short and long ranges.

NEW Products: **Winchester Ammunition**

SUPREME ELITE XTENDED RANGE HI-DENSITY TURKEY SHOTSHELLS

Supreme Elite Xtended Range Hi-Density shotshells feature high density shot that actually performs better than lead. The "Triple Threat" of Xtended Range Hi-Density Shot: 1) weighs more than lead; 2) harder hitting and deeper penetrating than lead; and 3) longer range performance than lead. These shotshells deliver an average of 140 shot pellets into a 10 in. circle at 40 yards. Plus, the high density shot is softer than most shotgun barrels and chokes.

SUPREME ELITE XTENDED RANGE HI-DENSITY WATERFOWL SHOTSHELLS

Winchester Supreme Elite Xtended Range Hi-Density waterfowl shotshells combine patented high density shot and Drylok Wad Technology. The advantages of Xtended Range Hi-Density Shot include: non-toxic and 55% higher density than steel shot; harder hitting and deeper penetrating; consistent shot shape resulting in highly consistent patterns. Plus, the high density shot is softer than most shotgun barrels and chokes.

NEW Products: **Barnes Bullets**

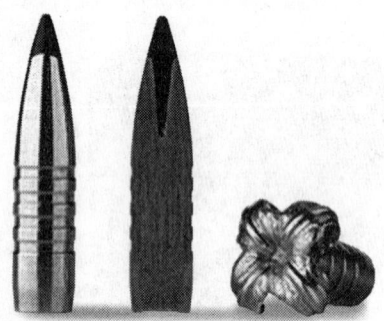

MAXIMUM-RANGE X-BULLET

The Barnes super-premium, boattail Maximum-Range X-Bullet (MRX) combines the best features and deadly killing power of Barnes' copper Triple-Shock X-Bullet with a new Delrin tip and a tungsten core. The denser-than-lead tungsten core moves the MRX bullet's center of gravity rearward, producing optimum ballistic performance, maximum penetration and exceptional accuracy. A heavy tungsten core surrounded by a controlled-expanding all-copper body means game-dropping performance no lead-core bullet can match. Unlike soft lead cores that fragment or squeeze out under pressure, the tough MRX tungsten core retains its shape on impact, maintaining bullet integrity.

The MRX bullets will be available in .270, .30, .338 and 7mm.

FRANKFORD ARSENAL MICRO RELOADING SCALE

The Micro Reloading Scale is the perfect accessory for reloaders who want a light, accurate, portable scale. The unit is suitable for use on the reloading bench, yet is at home on the shooting range or in the field. The Micro Reloading Scale weighs objects up to 750 grains. It is accurate within +/− .1 grains. The digital scale can be set to read in grains, grams, ounces, ct, dwt or ozt. It comes with a protective sleeve and is small enough to fit in your shirt pocket. A calibration weight and batteries are also included.
MSRP: $50

NEW Products: **Hornady Bullets**

.22 CAL. 80 GRAIN A-MAX BULLET

For the ultimate in long range accuracy, consistency and wind defying performance, Hornady offers the 80 grain A-MAX. Designed, refined and tested to deliver extreme accuracy and match-winning performance at the 600 yard line.
Diameter: .224
Weight: 80 gr.
Ballistic Coef.: 453
Sec. Den.: 228
Box Count: 100

NEW Products: **Hornady Reloading Accessories**

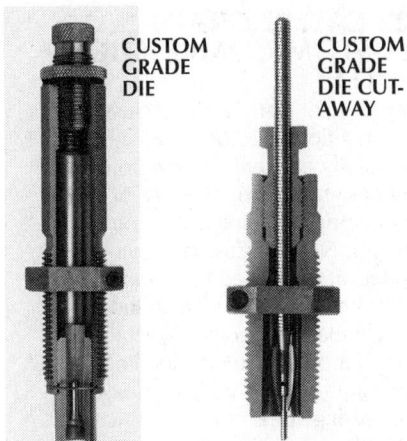

CUSTOM GRADE DIE

CUSTOM GRADE DIE CUT-AWAY

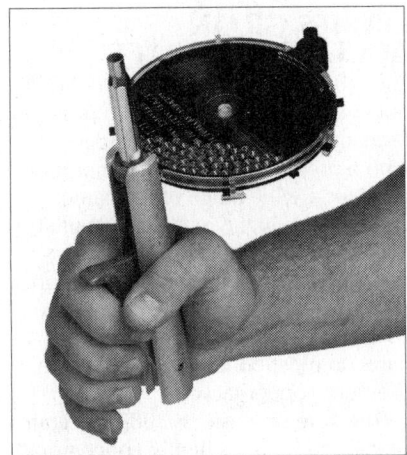

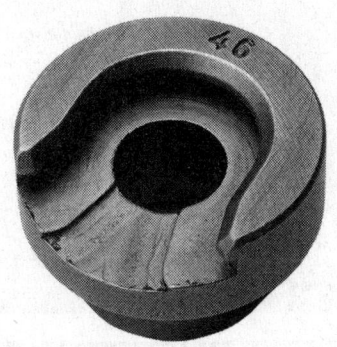

CUSTOM GRADE DIES WITH NEW & IMPROVED ZIP SPINDLE

Hornady's Custom Grade Dies are guaranteed never to break or wear out from normal use. The new Zip Spindle design features a series of light threads cut on the spindle and spindle collet. This design eliminates spindle slippage and takes the knucklebusting out of tightening the spindle lock while making spindle adjustments a snap.

HANDHELD PRIMING TOOL

Hornady's handheld priming tool features a one-piece primer tray with an improved retaining system for the lid. It also sports integral molded bushings for ultra reliable function. The new primer tray also eliminates the need for separate bushings. The system comes with an additional tray designed for use with RCBS shell holders. The body has been modified for easier change-over, and the seater punch and spring are captured inside the body; allowing shell holders and primer trays to be changed without removing them.

UNIVERSAL SHELL HOLDERS

Shell Holders for the single stage press have been improved. The mouth of the shell holder has been widened with a radius to allow easier case insertion while maintaining maximum contact area once the case is in the shell holder. Designed for use in any tool designed to use a shell holder.

NEW Products: **Nosler Bullets and Brass**

.204 RUGER 40 GRAIN BALLISTIC TIP BULLET

The Nosler .204, 40 grain Ballistic Tip (BC .239) is designed to provide varmint hunters with a very aerodynamic projectile in a popular weight for the .204 Ruger cartridge. Like other Nosler Ballistic Tip Varmint bullets, this one utilizes extremely thin-mouthed, highly concentric tapered jackets and form-fitted, pure lead cores for consistent accuracy and vio-

lent expansion across a broad spectrum of velocities and ranges. The Solid Base boattail design, long ogive and polycarbonate tip confer ballistic coefficients substantially greater than bullets of identical weight and diameter. These features greatly reduce wind deflection, enhance long range stability and allow the bullets to be fired at virtually any velocity without sacrificing accuracy or structural integrity.

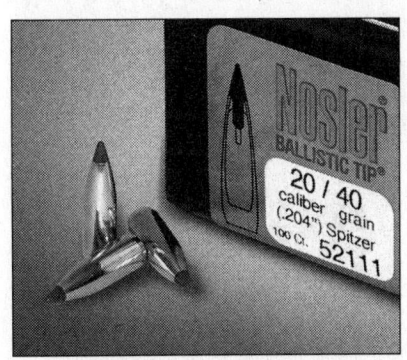

NEW Products: Nosler Bullets and Brass

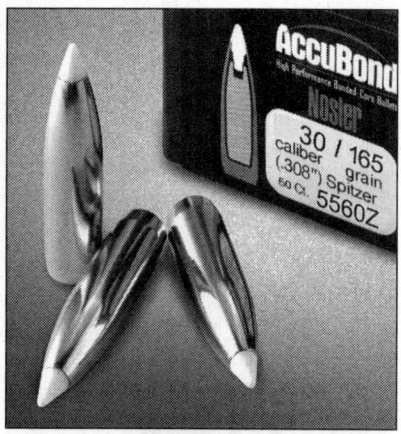

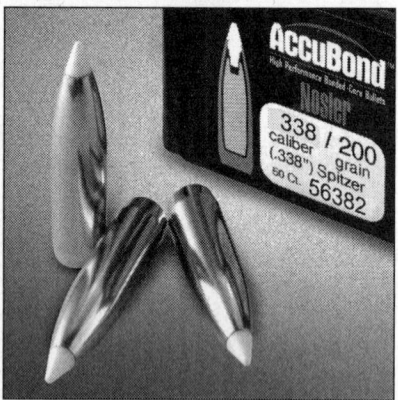

.308 165 GRAIN ACCUBOND BULLET

The .308, 165 grain Nosler AccuBond bullet (.475 BC) is designed to provide users of most 30-caliber cartridges with a premium grade bullet that is ideal for a wide range of big game. The tapered, highly concentric bullet jackets are constructed from gilding metal using Nosler's impact extrusion process. The result is a bullet that produces very little metal fouling compared to most bonded core bullets that use pure copper jackets.

The core of Nosler's .308, 165 grain AccuBond bullet is highly concentric, very uniform in weight, and made from a special lead alloy. The core is bonded to the jacket using a proprietary process that produces a virtually inseparable, void-free bond between core and jacket. This results in an absence of core/jacket separation or slippage, even during high velocity, close range impacts. All Nosler AccuBond bullets feature distinctive white polycarbonate tips that prevent deformation in the magazine, boost aerodynamic efficiency, and initiate expansion. The bullets also feature a precisely formed boattail that serves to reduce drag and provides a more efficient flight profile for higher retained energy at long range.

.338 200 GRAIN ACCUBOND BULLET

The .338 200 Grain Nosler AccuBond bullet (.414 BC) is designed to provide users of .338 caliber cartridges such as the .338 Winchester Magnum, .338-06, .338 Lapua and .340 Weatherby Magnum with a premium grade bullet in an optimum weight that is ideal for a wide range of big game. This bullet provides hunters with a judicious blend of expansion and penetration with outstanding accuracy and weight retention at all normal hunting velocities and ranges. The tapered, highly concentric bullet jackets are constructed from gilding metal using Nosler's exclusive impact extrusion process. The result is a bullet that produces very little metal fouling compared to most bonded core bullets that use pure copper jackets.

.22 CAL. 52 GRAIN CUSTOM COMPETITION BULLET

Nosler's .22 Cal. 52 Grain Custom Competition (.220 BC) is an aerodynamically efficient, hollow point boattail design, built on Nosler's extremely concentric and uniform custom bullet jackets. Nosler's Custom Competition bullets are designed for commonality with other match bullets in the same weight class. This offers several advantages for shooters: First, loading data is very similar. Second, because of similar bearing surfaces and identical weights, pressures will be very similar. Third, Nosler's Custom Competition bullets have identical flight characteristics, producing top accuracy at the same distances.

NOSLERCUSTOM CARTRIDGE BRASS

Nosler has expanded its cartridge brass line with new .204 Ruger, 6.5-284 Norma, .280 Remington, .300 Remington Ultra Magnum and .300 Weatherby Magnum introductions. Each round of NoslerCustom cartridge brass is made to exact dimensional standards and tolerances using quality materials for maximum accuracy/consistency potential and long case life. Flash holes are deburred, necks are deburred and chamfered and the brass then undergoes rigorous quality control, with every piece hand inspected, weight-sorted and packaged in custom boxes of 50. Also available in .223 Remington, .22-250 Remington, .243 Winchester, .270 Winchester, 7mm Remington, .308 Winchester, .30-06 Springfield and .300 Winchester Magnum.

Accu-Tek Rifles

ACCELERATOR

ACCELERATOR
Action: autoloading
Stock: synthetic
Barrel: 18 in.
Sights: none

Weight: 8.0 lbs.
Caliber: .17 HMR, .22 WMR
Magazine: detachable box, 9 rounds
Features: fluted stainless steel bull barrel; pistol grip stock; aluminum shroud

with integral Weaver scope and sight rail; manual safety and firing pin block; last round bolt hold-open feature
MSRP: **$465**

Anschütz Rifles

MODEL 1416

1416 D HB

MODEL 1451

MODEL 1416
Action: bolt
Stock: walnut
Barrel: 22 in.
Sights: open
Weight: 5.5 lbs.
Caliber: .22LR, .22 WMR
Magazine: detachable box, 5 rounds .22 LR, 4-round .22 WMR
Features: M64 action; 2-stage match trigger; checkered stock available in

classic or Monte Carlo
Classic: **$796**
Monte Carlo: **$819**

1416 D HB, 1502 D HB, 1517 D HB
Action: bolt
Stock: walnut
Barrel: 23 in.
Sights: none
Weight: 6.2 lbs.
Caliber: .22 LR, .17 Mach 2 and .17 HMR, respectively

Magazine: detachable box, 5 rounds
MSRP: **$813-878**

MODEL 1451
Action: bolt
Stock: Sporter Target, hardwood
Barrel: heavy 22 in.
Sights: open
Weight: 6.3 lbs.
Caliber: .22 LR
Magazine: detachable box, 10 rounds
Features: M64 action
MSRP: **$515**

MODEL 1517

1702 D HB

MODEL 1827 FORTNER

MODEL 1903

MODEL 1517

Action: bolt
Stock: walnut
Barrel: target-grade sporter, 22 in.
Sights: none
Weight: 6.0 lbs.
Caliber: .17 HMR
Magazine: 4 rounds
Features: M64 action, heavy and sporter barrels; Monte Carlo and Classic stocks available; target-grade barrel; adjustable trigger (2.5 lbs.)
Classic: **$834**
Monte Carlo: **$855**

1702 D HB

Action: bolt
Stock: walnut
Barrel: 23 in.
Sights: none
Weight: 8 lbs.
Caliber: .17 Mach 2
Magazine: detachable box, 5 rounds
MSRP: **$1512**

MODEL 1710

Action: bolt
Stock: walnut
Barrel: target-grade sporter, 22 in.
Sights: none
Weight: 6.7 lbs.   *Caliber*: .22 LR
Magazine: 5 rounds
Features: M54 action; two-stage trigger; Monte Carlo stock; silhouette stock available
Model 1710 . . . . **$1469**
   with fancy wood **$1743**
Silhouette Model 1712 . . . . . . **$1554**

MODEL 1730 AND 1740 CLASSIC SPORTER

Action: bolt
Stock: sporter, walnut   *Barrel:* 23 in.
Sights: none   *Weight:* 7.3 lbs.
Caliber: .22 Hornet and .222
Magazine: detachable box, 5 rounds
Features: M54 action; Meister grade about $250 additional
1730 .22 Hornet, Monte Carlo $1729
**1730 .22 Hornet with
   heavy barrel** **$1621**
1740 .222 with heavy barrel . . **$1621**
1740 .222, Monte Carlo **$1729**

MODEL 1827 FORTNER

Action: bolt
Stock: Biathlon, walnut
Barrel: medium 22 in.
Sights: none
Weight: 8.8 lbs.
Caliber: .22 LR
Magazine: detachable box, 5 rounds
Features: M54 action
1827: **$1850**
   with thumbhole stock: . . . **$1940**

MODEL 1903

Action: bolt
Stock: Standard Rifle, hardwood
Barrel: heavy 26 in.
Sights: none
Weight: 10.5 lbs.
Caliber: .22 LR
Magazine: none
Features: M64 action; adjustable cheekpiece; forend rail
1903: **$690**
   left-hand: **$730**

Anschütz Rifles

RIFLES

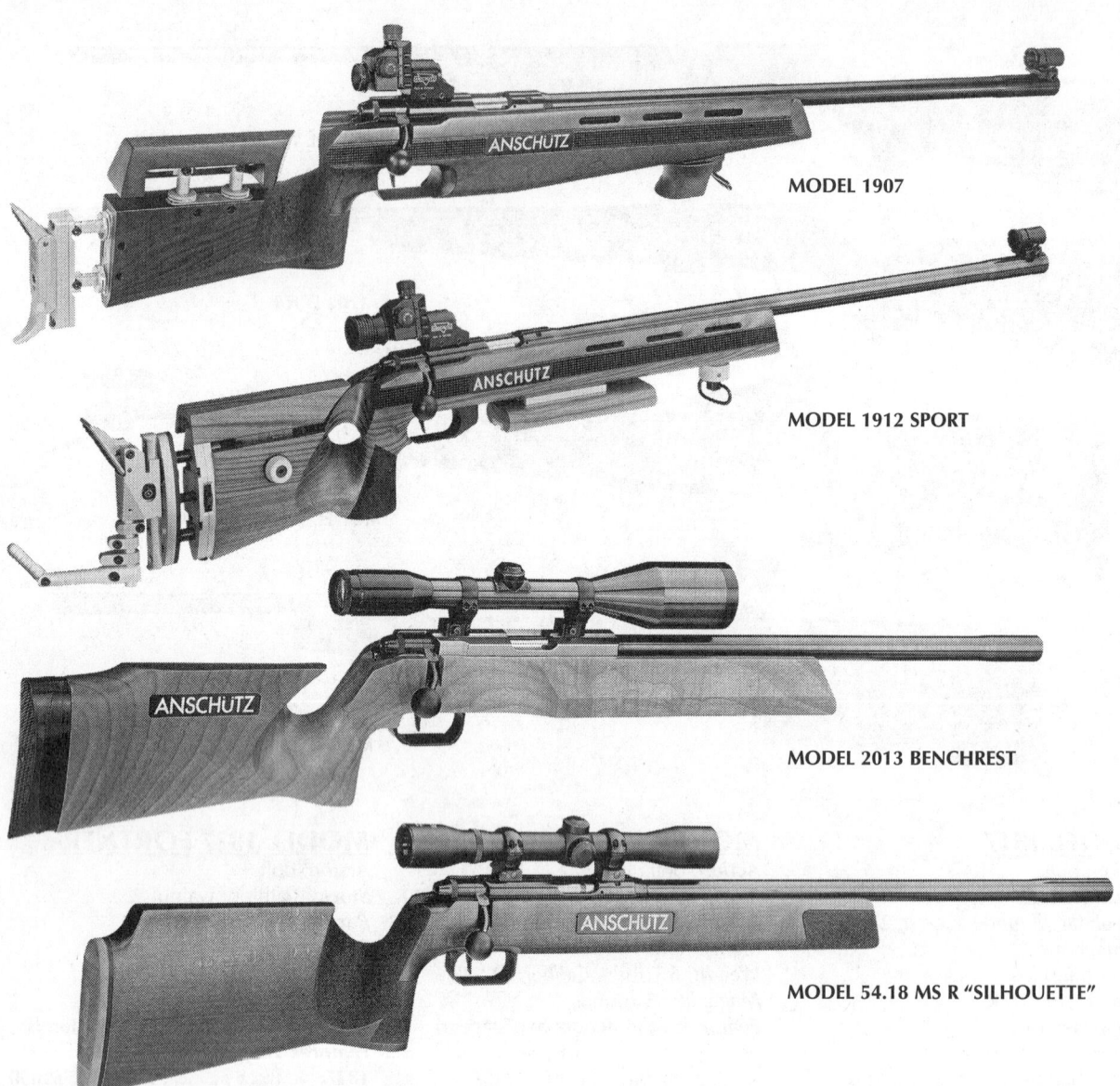

MODEL 1907

MODEL 1912 SPORT

MODEL 2013 BENCHREST

MODEL 54.18 MS R "SILHOUETTE"

MODEL 1907

Action: bolt
Stock: standard rifle, walnut
Barrel: heavy 26 in.
Sights: none
Weight: 10.5 lbs.
Caliber: .22 LR
Magazine: none
Features: M54 action; adjustable cheekpiece and butt; forend rail
1907: $1375
   left-hand: $1475

MODEL 1912 SPORT

Action: bolt
Stock: International, laminated

Barrel: heavy 26 in.
Sights: none
Weight: 11.4 lbs.
Caliber: .22 LR
Magazine: none
Features: M54 action; adjustable cheekpiece and butt; forend rail
1912: $1690
   left-hand: $1785

MODEL 2013 BENCHREST

Action: bolt
Stock: Benchrest (BR-50) walnut
Barrel: heavy 20 in.
Sights: none
Weight: 10.3 lbs.

Caliber: .22 LR
Magazine: none
Features: M54 action
MSRP: $1575

MODEL 54.18 MS

Action: bolt
Stock: Silhouette, walnut
Barrel: heavy 22 in.
Sights: none
Weight: 8.1 lbs.
Caliber: .22 LR
Magazine: none
Features: M54 action
MSRP: $1225

Armalite Rifles

AR-10A2 CARBINE

AR-10B

AR-10T

AR-10A2 CARBINE

Action: autoloading
Stock: synthetic
Barrel: 16 in.
Sights: open
Weight: 9.0 lbs.
Caliber: .308
Magazine: detachable box, 10 rounds
Features: forged A2 receiver; NM two stage trigger; chrome-lined barrel; recoil check muzzle device; green or black synthetic stock
MSRP: **$1506-1606**

AR-10A4 SPR (SPECIAL PURPOSE RIFLE)

Action: autoloading
Stock: synthetic
Barrel: 20 in.
Sights: none
Weight: 9.6 lbs.
Caliber: .308, .243 WIN
Magazine: detachable box, 10 rounds
Features: forged flattop receiver; chrome-lined heavy barrel; optional recoil-check muzzle device; green or black synthetic stock; Picatinny rail sight base
MSRP: **$1506-1606**

AR-10B

Action: autoloading
Stock: synthetic
Barrel: 20 in.
Sights: open
Weight: 9.5 lbs.
Caliber: .308
Magazine: detachable box, 20 rounds
Features: multi-slot recoil-check muzzle device; M-16 style front sight base, single stage trigger (two stage NM optional); chrome-lined barrel; forged aluminum upper receiver; M-16 style tapered handguards; AR-10 SOF with M4 type fixed stock
MSRP: **$1698**

AR-10T AND AR-10A4 CARBINE

Action: autoloading
Stock: synthetic
Barrel: 24 in.; (Carbine: 16 in.)
Sights: open; (Carbine: none)
Weight: 10.4 lbs.; (Carbine: 9 lbs.)
Caliber: .308
Magazine: detachable box, 10 rounds
Features: forged flattop receiver; stainless T heavy barrel; carbine with chrome-lined barrel and recoil check muzzle device; two stage NM trigger
AR-10T: **$2126**
AR-10A4 Carbine: **$1506-1606**

RIFLES

Armalite Rifles

AR-30

AR-50

M-15 A2 CARBINE

M-15 A4 SPRII

AR-30M RIFLE
Action: bolt
Stock: synthetic
Barrel: 26 in.
Sights: none
Weight: 12.0 lbs.
Caliber: .300 WIN MAG, .308 WIN, .338 LAPUA
Magazine: detachable box
Features: Triple lapped match grade barrel; manganese phosphated steel and hard anodized aluminum finish; forged and machined removable butt-stock; available with bipod adapter, scope rail and muzzle brake; receiver drilled and slotted for scope rail
.308 Win & .300 Win Mag: . . . $1460
.338 Lapua: $1615

AR-50
Action: bolt
Stock: synthetic
Barrel: 31 in.
Sights: none
Weight: 35.0 lbs.
Caliber: .50BMG
Magazine: none
Features: receiver drilled and slotted for scope rail; Schillen standard single stage trigger; vertically adjustable butt-plate; vertical pistol grip; manganese phosphated steel and hard anodized aluminum finish; available in right- or left-handed version
MSRP: $2885

M-15 A2, M-15 A2 CARBINE AND M-15 A2 NATIONAL MATCH RIFLE
Action: autoloading
Stock: synthetic
Barrel: 16 in., (M-15A2), 20 in.
Sights: open
Weight: 7.0 lbs. (Carbine); 8.27 lbs.
Caliber: .223 REM
Magazine: detachable box, 10 rounds; 7 rounds (Carbine)
Features: forged A2 receiver; heavy, stainless, chrome-lined floating match barrel; recoil check muzzle device; green or black synthetic stock; Carbine with M-16 style front sight base; National Match Rifle with NM two stage trigger and NM sleeved floating barrel; M-15 A4 (T) with flattop receiver and tubular handguard
M-15A2: $1100-1200
Carbine: $1100-1200
National Match Rifle: $1472

M-15 A4 SPR II (SPECIAL PURPOSE RIFLE)
Action: autoloading
Stock: synthetic
Barrel: 20 in.
Sights: none
Weight: 9.0 lbs.
Caliber: .308, .243 WIN
Magazine: detachable box, 10 rounds
Features: forged flattop receiver; NM sleeved floating stainless barrel; Picatinny rail; two stage trigger; green or black synthetic stock; Picatinny gas block front sight base
MSRP: $1472

MODEL 1927 A1

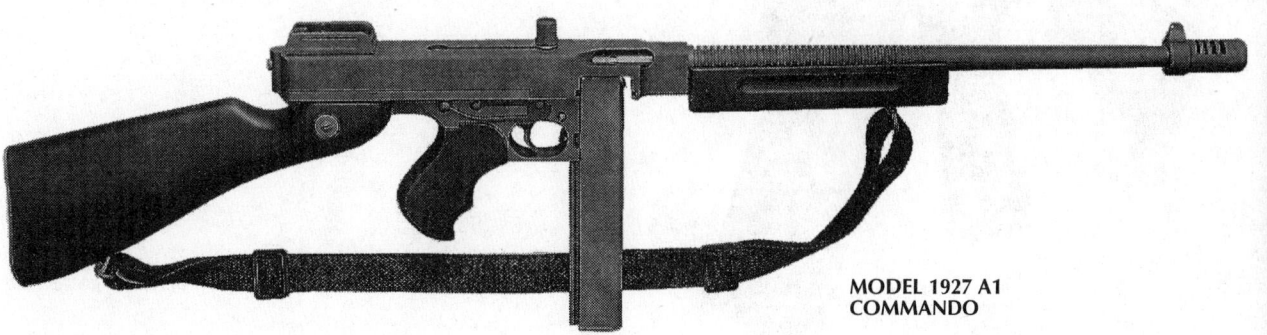

**MODEL 1927 A1
COMMANDO**

This veteran design, the Thompson Submachine Gun, became famous during the "Roaring Twenties" and World War II. These replicas are legal autoloaders, not machine guns.

MODEL 1927 A1

Action: autoloading
Stock: walnut, vertical foregrip
Barrel: 16 in.
Sights: open
Weight: 13.0 lbs.
Caliber: .45 ACP
Magazine: detachable box, 20-rounds
Features: top-cocking, autoloading blowback; lightweight version 9.5 lbs.
Standard:. **$1164**
Lightweight:. **$986**

MODEL 1927 A1 COMMANDO

Action: autoloading
Stock: walnut, horizontal fore-grip
Barrel: 16 in.
Sights: open
Weight: 13.0 lbs.
Caliber: .45 ACP
Magazine: detachable box, 20-rounds
Features: top-cocking, autoloading blowback; carbine version with side-cocking lever, 11.5 lbs.
1927: **$1143**
Carbine: **$1164**

It's a good idea to periodically check the bedding screws on your rifle. They tend to work loose over time, and loose screws can adversely affect shooting accuracy.

Barrett Rifles

MODEL 468

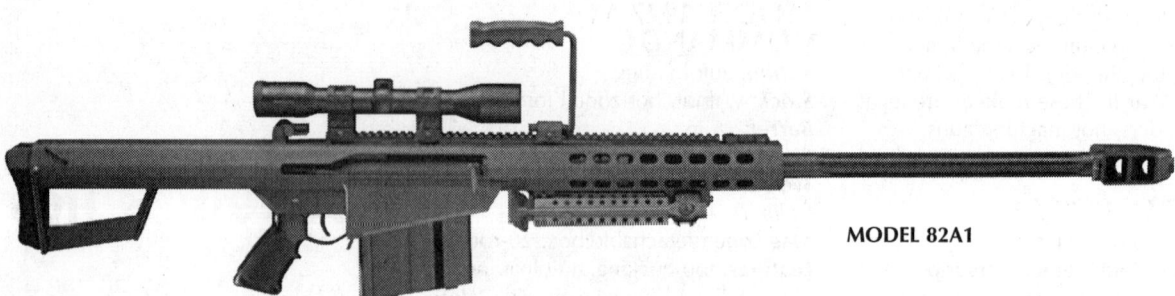

MODEL 82A1

MODEL 468
Action: semi-automatic
Stock: synthetic
Barrel: 16 in.
Sights: target
Weight: 7.3 lbs.
Caliber: 6.8 Rem SPC
Magazine: 5, 10, 30 rounds available
Features: two-stage trigger;
muzzle brake
MSRP: **$2700**

MODEL 82A1
Action: autoloading
Stock: synthetic
Barrel: 29 in.
Sights: target
Weight: 28.5 lbs.
Caliber: .50 BMG
Magazine: 10 rounds
Features: Picatinny rail and scope
mount; fluted barrel, detachable bipod
and carrying case
MSRP: **$7775**

RIFLES

Barrett Rifles

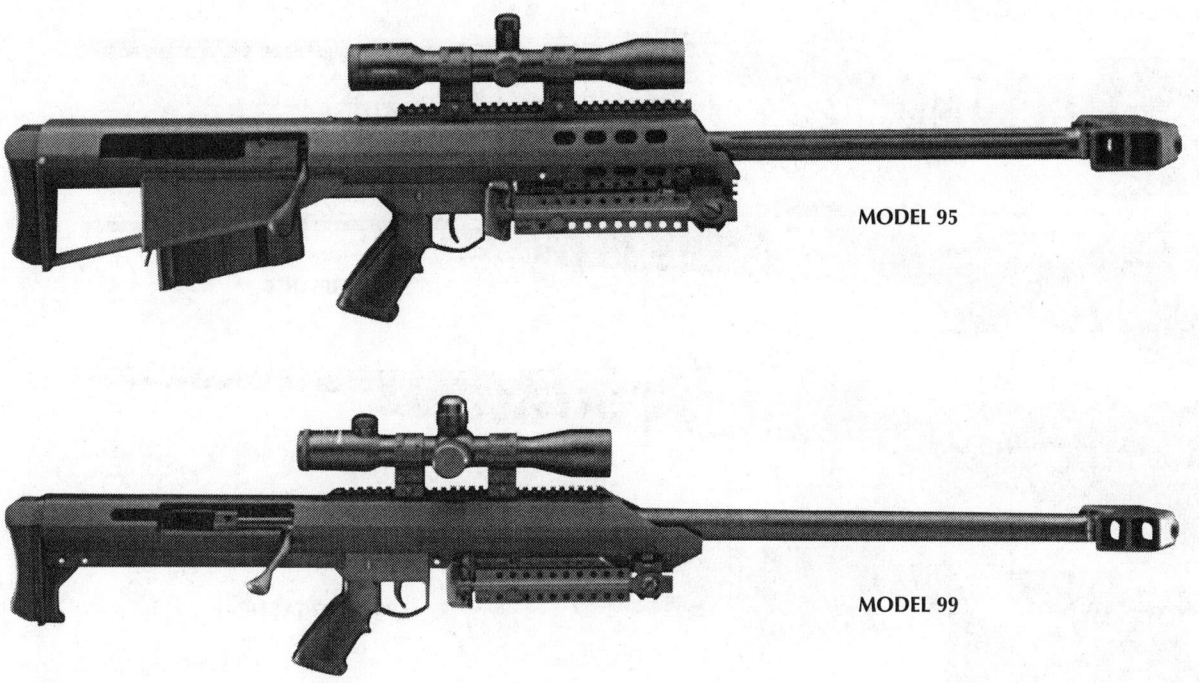

MODEL 95

MODEL 99

MODEL 95, MODEL 99
Action: bolt
Stock: synthetic
Barrel: 29 in. or 33 in. (M99)
Sights: none
Weight: 25.0 lbs.
Caliber: .50 BMG
Magazine: 5 (M95) or none (M99)

Features: Picatinny rail; detachable bipod; M95 has fluted barrel and weighs 22 lbs.
M95: **$5540**
M99: **$3675**

Benelli Rifles

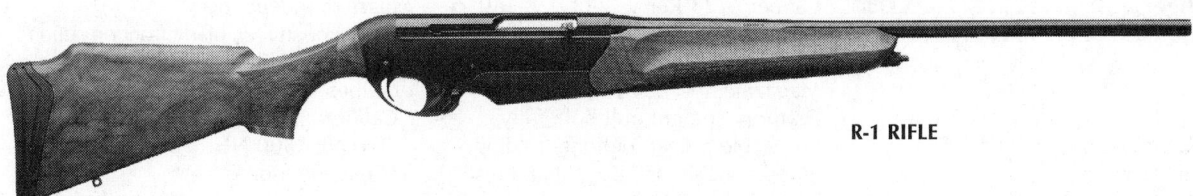

R-1 RIFLE

R-1 RIFLE
Action: autoloading
Stock: walnut
Barrel: 22 in. (Standard Rifle); 20 in. (Standard Carbine); 24 in. (Magnum Rifle), 20 in. (Magnum Carbine)
Sights: none

Weight: 7.1 lbs. (Standard Rifle); 7.0 lbs. (Standard Carbine); 7.2 lbs. (Magnum Rifle); 7.0 lbs. (Magnum Carbine)
Caliber: Standard 30-06; Magnum .300 Win. Mag., .308 Win, .270 WSM, .300WSM

Magazine: detachable box, 3-4 rounds
Features: auto-regulating gas-operated system; three lugged rotary bolt; select satin walnut stock; receiver drilled and tapped for scope mount; base included
Standard Rifle & Carbine $1200
Magnum Rifle & Carbine $1200

RIFLES

Blaser Rifles

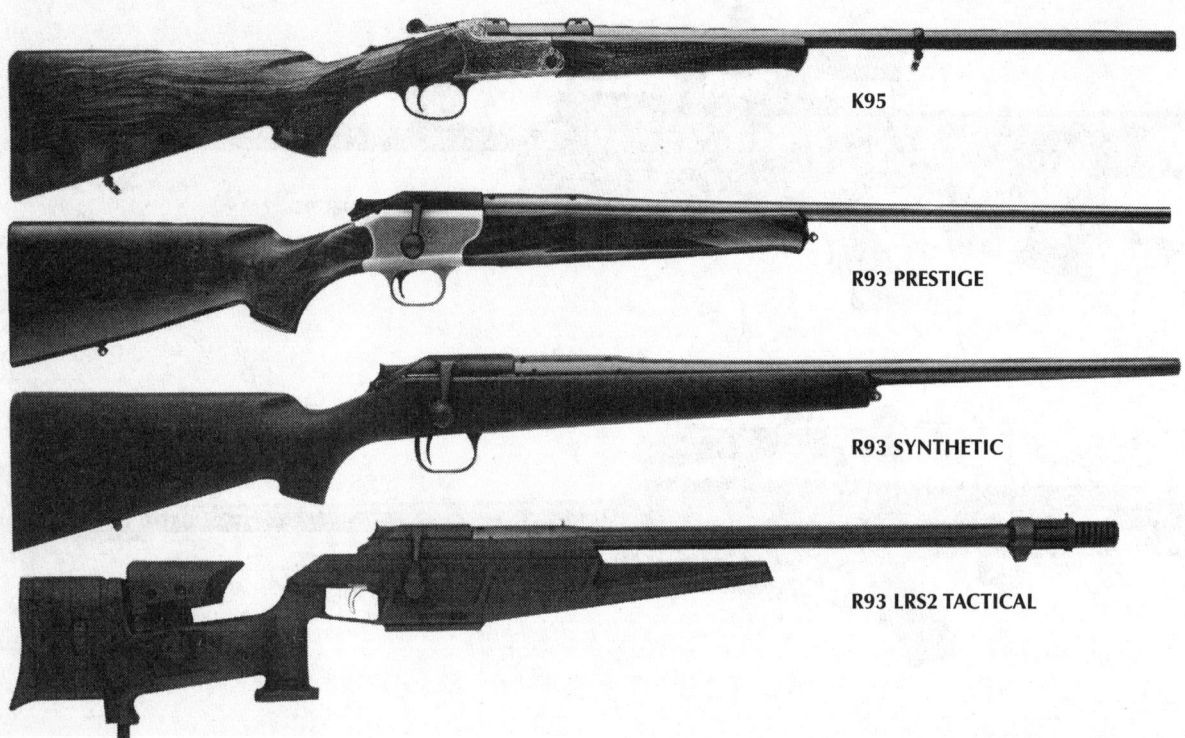

K95

R93 PRESTIGE

R93 SYNTHETIC

R93 LRS2 TACTICAL

K95
Action: hinged breech
Stock: walnut
Barrel: 24 in. and 26 in. (magnum)
Sights: none
Weight: 5.5 lbs.
Caliber: .222, .22 Hornet, .25-06, .243, .270, .308, .30-06; 7mm Rem. magnum, .300 Win., .300 Wby.
Magazine: none
Features: easy takedown with no loss of zero; magnum calibers weigh 5.8 lbs.; Luxus has hand engraving on receiver
Prestige: **$3300**
Luxus: **$3800**

R93
Action: bolt
Stock: walnut or synthetic
Barrel: 22 in.
Sights: none
Weight: 6.5 lbs., 7.0 lbs. (Magnum)
Caliber: .22-250, .243, .25-06, 6.5x55, .270, 7x57, 7mm/08, .308, .30-06; Magnums: .257 Wby. Mag., 7mm Rem. Mag., .300 Win. Mag., .300 Wby. Mag., .300 Rem UM, .338 Win. Mag., .375 H&H, .416 Rem. Mag.
Magazine: in-line box, 5 rounds
Features: straight-pull bolt with

expanding collar lockup; left-hand versions available, add $141
Synthetic: **$2000**
Prestige: **$2600**
Luxus: **$3400**
Attache: **$4800**

R93 LONG RANGE SPORTER 2
Action: bolt
Stock: tactical composite
Barrel: heavy, fluted 26 in.
Sights: none
Weight: 8.0 lbs.
Caliber: .223 Rem., .243, .22-250, 6mm Norma, 6.5x55, .308, .300 Win. Mag., .338 Lapua Mag.
Magazine: in-line box, 5 rounds
Features: straight-pull bolt; fully adjustable trigger; optional folding bipod, muzzle brake and hand rest
Long Range Sporter: **$2900**
.338 Lapua: **$3300**

R93 LRS2 TACTICAL RIFLE PACKAGE
Action: bolt
Stock: synthetic tactical with adjustments
Barrel: heavy, fluted 26 in.
Sights: none

Weight: 10.0 lbs.
Caliber: .308, .300 Win. Mag., .338 Lapua
Magazine: in-line box, 5 rounds
Features: package includes bipod, sling, Leupold Tactical scope, mirage band, muzzle brake
Long Range Tactical: **$4200**
.338 Lapua: **$5000**

S2 SAFARI
Action: tilting block, double-barrel
Stock: select Turkish walnut, checkered
Barrels: 24 in., gas-nitrated, sand-blasted, independent
Sights: open rear, blade front on solid rib
Weight: 10.1-11.2 lbs., depending on caliber
Caliber: .375 H&H, .500/.416 NE, .470 NE, .500 NE
Magazine: none
Features: selective ejectors; Pachmayr Decelerator pad; snap caps; leather sling; Americase wheeled travel case; scope mount of choice
MSRP (standard grade): **$8500**
(extra barrel set): **$5300**
Also available: S2 double rifle in standard chamberings, from .222 to 9.3x74R, 7.7 lbs.

Brown Precision Rifles

CUSTOM TEAM CHALLENGER

HIGH COUNTRY

HIGH COUNTRY YOUTH

CUSTOM TEAM CHALLENGER

Action: autoloading
Stock: composite
Barrel: heavy Shilen match grade 18 in.
Sights: open
Weight: 7.0 lbs.
Caliber: .22 LR
Magazine: rotary, 10 rounds
Features: also available with stainless barrel

Team Challenger: **$1595**
Stainless: **$1695**

HIGH COUNTRY

Action: bolt
Stock: composite classic stock
Barrel: choice of contours, lengths
Sights: none
Weight: 6.0 lbs.
Caliber: any popular standard caliber
Magazine: box, 5 rounds
Features: Remington 700 barreled action; tuned trigger; choice of stock colors and dimensions

MSRP: **$3495**

HIGH COUNTRY YOUTH

Action: bolt
Stock: composite sporter, scaled for youth
Barrel: length and contour to order
Sights: none
Weight: 5.0 lbs.
Caliber: any popular standard short action
Magazine: box, 5 rounds
Features: Remington Model 700 or Model 7 barreled action; optional muzzle brake, scopes, stock colors and dimensions; included: package of shooting, reloading and hunting accessories

MSRP: **$1895**

Brown Precision Rifles

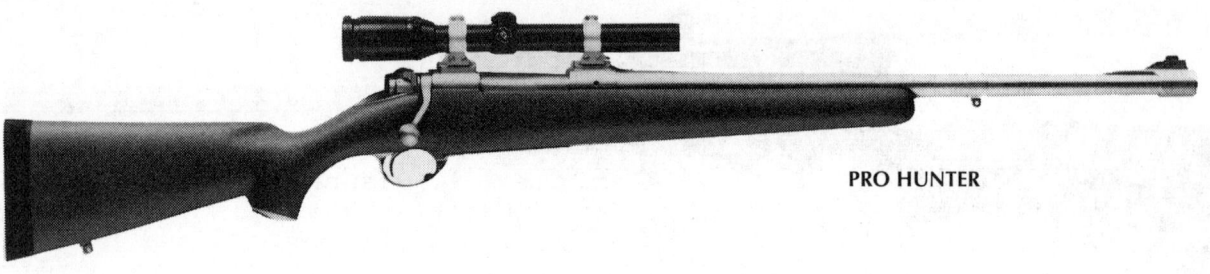

PRO HUNTER

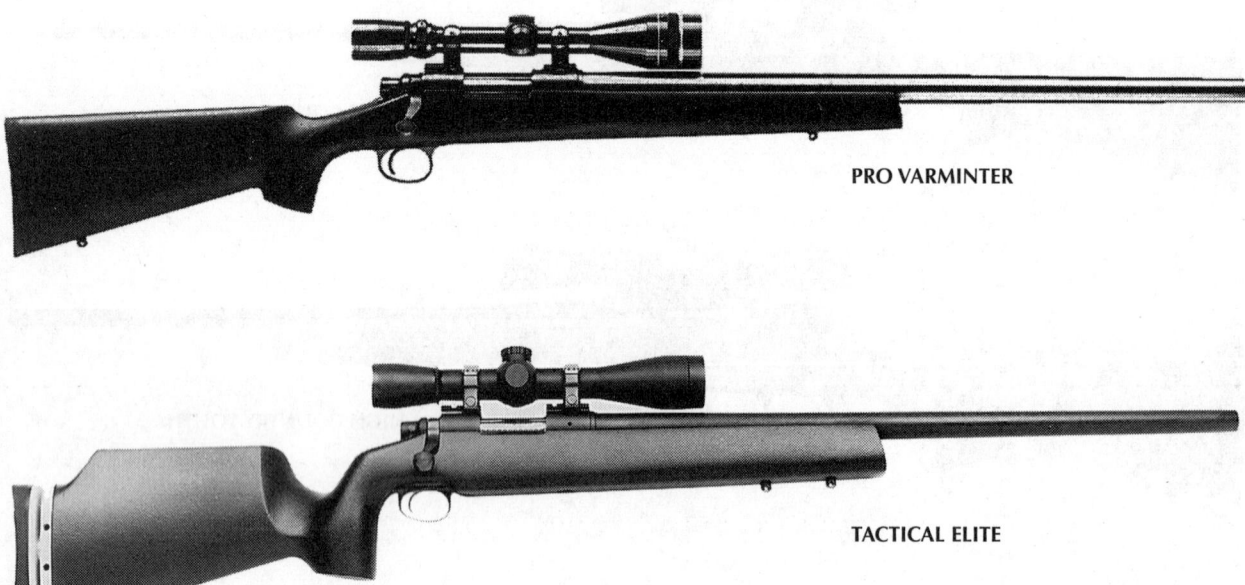

PRO VARMINTER

TACTICAL ELITE

PRO HUNTER

Action: bolt
Stock: composite sporter
Barrel: Shilen match grade stainless
Sights: none
Weight: 8.0 lbs.
Caliber: any standard and belted
Magnum caliber up to: .375 H&H
Magazine: box, 3-5 rounds
Features: Model 70 action with Mauser extractor; tuned trigger; optional Talley peep sight and banded ramp front sight or Talley mounts with 8-40 screws; optional muzzle brake, Mag-Na-Porting; Americase aluminum hard case
Pro Hunter: $4295
  left-hand:. $4395

PRO VARMINTER

Action: bolt
Stock: composite, varmint or bench rest
Barrel: heavy stainless match
Grade: 26 in.
Sights: none
Weight: 9.0 lbs.
Caliber: all popular calibers
Magazine: box (or single shot)
Features: Remington 40X or 700 action (right or left-hand); bright or bead-blasted finish; optional muzzle brake; after-market trigger; scope and mounts optional
Model 700, right-hand: $3295
Model 700, left-hand: $3595
Rem. 40X (with target trigger): $3895

TACTICAL ELITE

Action: bolt
Stock: composite tactical
Barrel: Shilen match-grade, heavy stainless
Sights: none
Weight: 9.0 lbs.
Caliber: .223, .308, .300 Win. Mag., (others on special order)
Magazine: box, 3 or 5 rounds
Features: Remington 700 action; Teflon metal finish; adjustable butt plate; tuned trigger; optional muzzle brakes, scopes
MSRP: $3995

.22 SEMI-AUTOMATIC

A-BOLT HUNTER

A-BOLT ECLIPSE HUNTER

A-BOLT HUNTER
MEDALLION BOSS

A-BOLT WSSM MEDALLION

RIFLES

.22 SEMI-AUTOMATIC

Action: autoloading
Stock: walnut
Barrel: 19 in.
Sights: open
Weight: 5.2 lbs.
Caliber: .22 LR
Magazine: tube in stock, 11 rounds
Features: Grade VI has high grade walnut, finer checkering, engraved receiver
Grade I: $546
Grade VI: $1168

A-BOLT HUNTER

Action: bolt
Stock: walnut
Barrel: 20-26 in.   **Sights:** none
Weight: 7.0 lbs.
Caliber: all popular cartridges from .22 Hornet to .30-06, including WSMs and WSSMs.

Magazine: detachable box, 4-6 rounds
Features: BOSS (Ballistic Optimizing Shooting System) available; Micro Hunters weigh 6.3 lbs. with 20 in. barrel and shorter stock; left-hand Medallion available; Eclipse thumbhole stock available with light or heavy barrel (9.8 lbs.) and BOSS
Micro Hunter: $684-714
Eclipse Hunter: $1134
Hunter: $705-755
Medallion: $805
Medallion BOSS: $936
Medallion, white gold: . $1155-1183
Medallion, white gold BOSS: . . . . .
. . . . $1235-1263

A-BOLT HUNTER MAGNUM

Action: bolt
Stock: walnut
Barrel: 23 in. and 26 in.
Sights: none
Weight: 7.5 lbs.
Caliber: popular magnums from 7mm Rem. to .375 H&H, including .270, 7mm and .300 WSM plus .25, .223 and .243 WSSMs
Magazine: detachable box, 3 rounds
Features: rifles in WSM calibers have 23 in. barrels and weigh 6.5 lbs.; WSSM have 22 in. barrels; BOSS (Ballistic Optimizing Shooting System) available; left-hand available
Magnum: $734
Medallion Magnum: $835
Medallion Magnum BOSS: . . . $915
Eclipse Magnum: $1086

Browning Rifles

A-BOLT STALKER

BAR LIGHTWEIGHT STALKER

BAR SAFARI, BOSS, WALNUT

BLR LIGHTWEIGHT 81

A-BOLT STALKER
Action: bolt
Stock: synthetic
Barrel: 22, 23 and 26 in.
Sights: none
Weight: 7.5 lbs.
Caliber: most popular calibers and magnums, including .270, 7mm and .300 WSMs; .25, .223 and .243 WSSMs
Magazine: detachable box, 3-6 rounds
Features: BOSS (Ballistic Optimizing Shooting System) available; stainless option; rifles in WSM calibers have 23 in. barrels and weigh 6.5 lbs.

Stalker: $705-734
Stainless: $897-947
Stainless, left-hand: $925-954
BOSS: $785-835
Stainless, BOSS: $977-1027
Stainless,
   left-hand, Boss: $1005-1034
Varmint Stalker: $860-913

BAR
Action: autoloading
Stock: walnut or synthetic
Barrel: 20, 23, and 24 in.
Sights: open   *Weight:* 7.5 lbs.
Caliber: .243, .25-06, .270, .308, .30-06, 7mm Rem. Mag., .300 Win. Mag., .270 WSM, 7mm WSM, .300 WSM, .338 Win. Mag.
Magazine: detachable box, 3-5 rounds
Features: gas operated; lightweight model with alloy receiver and 20 in. barrel weighs 7.2 lbs.; magnum with 24 in. barrel weighs 8.6 lbs.; BOSS (Ballistic Optimizing Shooting System) available; higher grades also available

Lightweight Stalker: $883
Safari (no sights): $889
WSMs: $964
Magnums: $972
Safari, BOSS: $988
WSM & Mag: $1071

MODEL BLR LIGHTWEIGHT 81
Action: lever
Stock: straight-grip walnut
Barrel: 20, 22 or 24 in.
Sights: open
Weight: 6.5 or 7.3 lbs.
Caliber: .22-250, .243, 7mm-08, .308, .358, .450 Marlin, .270, .30-06 (22 in.), 7mm Rem. Mag., .300 Win. Mag. (24 in.)
Magazine: 5 and 4 rounds (magnums)
Features: short action; alloy receiver, front-locking bolt; rack-and-pinion action

BLR Lightweight: $731
BLR Long Action: $775
WSMs: $802

Browning Rifles

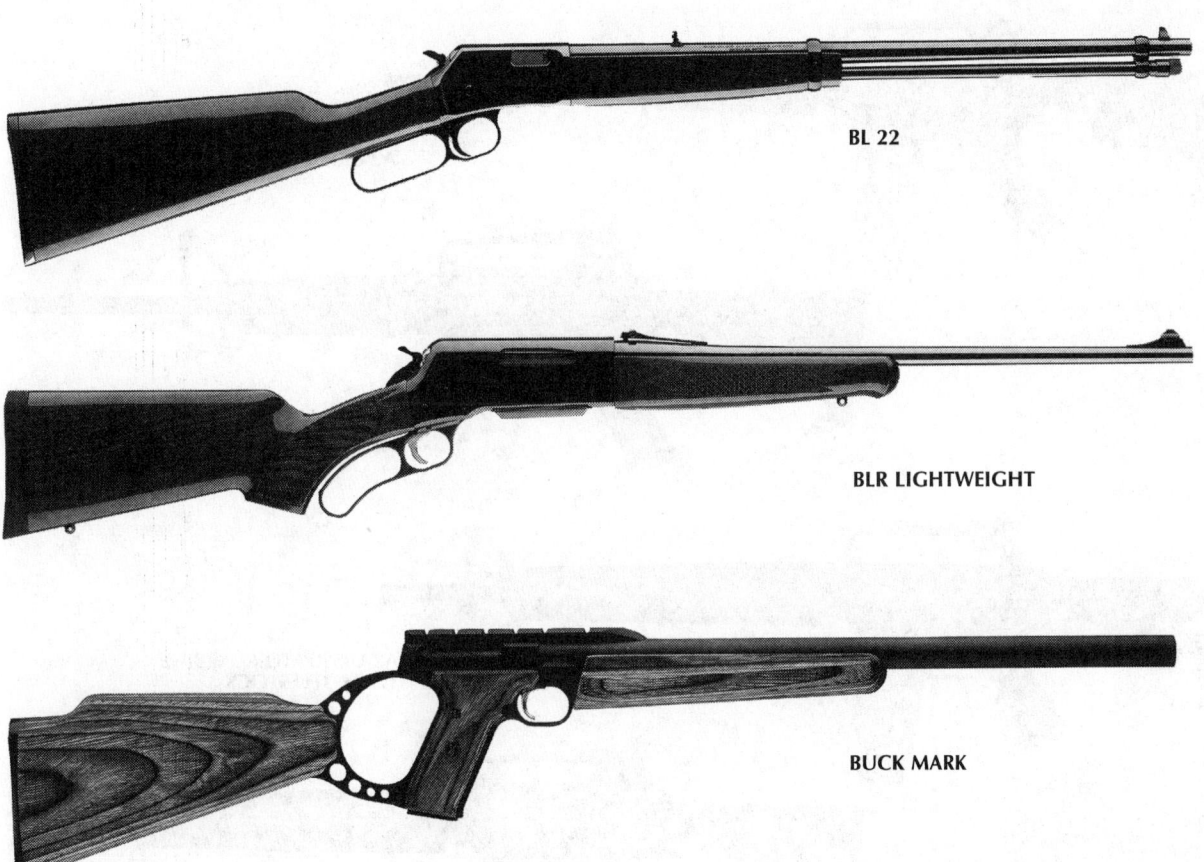

BL 22

BLR LIGHTWEIGHT

BUCK MARK

BL 22

Action: lever
Stock: walnut
Barrel: 20 or 24 in.
Sights: open
Weight: 5.0 lbs.
Caliber: .22 LR or .17 MACH2
Magazine: under-barrel tube, 15 rounds
Features: short stroke, exposed hammer, lever-action; straight grip; also available in Grade II with fine checkered walnut

Grade I: **$471**
.17 MACH2: **$484**
Grade II: **$534**
.17 MACH2: **$546**
   With 24" octagon bbl.: **$726**
.17 MACH2: **$748**
FLD Series (nickel receiver):
. . . . **$494 - $577**

BLR LIGHTWEIGHT

Action: lever
Stock: checkered walnut
Barrel: 18 or 20 in.
Sights: open
Weight: 6.5-7.75 lbs.
Caliber: .22-250, .243, 7mm-08, .308, .358, .450, .270 WSM, 7mm WSM, .300 WSM, .325 WSM, .270, .30-06, 7mm Rem. Mag., .300 Win. Mag.
Magazine: detachable box, 3-5 rounds
Features: Long- and short-actions; rotating bolt heads; sporter barrel; stock with pistol grip and Schnabel forend
MSRP: **$765-836**

BUCK MARK

Action: autoloading
Stock: laminate
Sights: open
Weight: 5.2 lbs.
Caliber: .22 LR
Magazine: detachable box, 10 rounds
Features: also in target model with heavy barrel
Sporter: **$572**
Target, heavy barrel: **$589**
Classic Carbon (3.6 lbs.): **$652**

Bushmaster Rifles

RIFLES

A2 CARBINE

AK A3 CARBINE

A2 DISSIPATOR CARBINE
WITH TELESTOCK

A3 DISSIPATOR CARBINE
WITH TELESTOCK

A2 CARBINE

Action: auto loader
Stock: polymer
Barrel: 16 in.
Sights: open, adjustable
Weight: 7.22 lbs.
Caliber: 223 Rem. (5.56mm)
Magazine: detachable box, 10 rounds
Features: lightweight forged aluminum receiver with M16 A2 design improvements; heavy profile barrel with chrome-lined bore and chamber; M16 A2 sight system; overall length 34.74 inches; manganese phosphate finish
MSRP: **$985**

A3 CARBINE, AK A3 CARBINE AND AK A2 RIFLE

Action: autoloader **Stock:** polymer
Barrel: 16 in., 14.5 in,
(AK A3 Carbine and Rifle)
Sights: open, adjustable
Weight: 6.7 lbs., 7.33 lbs.
(AK A3 Carbine and Rifle)
Caliber: .223 Rem. (5.56mm)
Magazine: detachable box, 10 rounds
Features: forged upper and lower receivers with M16 A2 design improvements; heavy-profile barrel with chrome-lined bore and chamber; M16 A2 sight system; overall length 34.75 inches; manganese phosphate finish; AK muzzle brake permanently attached
AK A2 Rifle: **$1005**
A3 Carbine: **$1085**
AK A3 Carbine: **$1105**

A2 AND A3 DISSIPATOR CARBINES

Action: autoloader
Stock: polymer
Barrel: 16 in.
Sights: adjustable
Weight: 7.68 lbs.
Caliber: .223 Rem. (5.56mm)
Magazine: detachable box, 10 rounds
Features: lightweight forged aluminum receivers; manganese phosphate finished heavy profile barrel with chrome lined bore and chamber; ribbed full length Dissipator handguards; M16 A2 sight system; removable carry handle; overall length 34.74 inches
A2 Dissipator: **$1040**
with Telestock: **$1065**
A3 Dissipator: **$1150**
with Telestock: **$1175**

Bushmaster Rifles

A3 20 INCH RIFLE

A2 .308 CARBINE

A2 .308 20-INCH RIFLE

CARBON 15 TYPE 21

A2 AND A3 20-INCH RIFLES

Action: autoloader
Stock: polymer
Barrel: 20 in.
Sights: open, adjustable
Weight: 8.27 lbs.
Caliber: 223 Rem. (5.56mm)
Magazine: detachable box, 10 rounds
Features: forged aluminum receivers; A3 upper receiver with slotted rail; optional removable carry handle; military spec. heavy barrel with chrome-lined bore and chamber; ribbed front handguard; M16 A2 rear sight system; overall length 38.25 in.; manganese phosphate finish
A2 20 inch Rifle: **$995**
A3 20 inch Rifle: **$1095**
RealTree Grey Camo Rifle: . . . **$1055**

A2 AND A3 .308 CALIBER CARBINES W/ SKELETON STOCK & IZZY BRAKE

Action: autoloader
Stock: polymer
Barrel: 16 in.

Sights: none
Weight: 8.5 lbs.
Caliber: .308 Winchester
Magazine: detachable box, 20 rounds (accepts all FN-FAL types)
Features: flat top forged aluminum upper receiver with Picatinny rail and ambidextrous controls for bolt and magazine release; heavy alloy steel barrel with Izzy muzzle brake; manganese phosphate finish
A2 Carbine: **$1800**
A3 Carbine: **$1825**

A2 .308 20-INCH RIFLE

Action: autoloader
Stock: polymer
Barrel: 20 in.
Sights: open
Weight: 9.57 lbs.
Caliber: .308 Winchester
Magazine: detachable box, 20 rounds (accepts all FN-FAL types)
Features: heavy alloy steel barrel with Bushmaster's Izzy muzzle brake; forged aluminum receiver; integral

solid carrying handle with M16 A2 rear sight; overall length 42.75 in.
A2 .308 20-inch Rifle: **$1810**
A2 .308 w/ AK Brake: **$1750**

CARBON 15 TYPE 21 RIFLE

Action: autoloader
Stock: synthetic
Barrel: 16 in.
Sights: none
Weight: 4.0 lbs.
Caliber: .223 Rem. (5.56mm)
Magazine: detachable box, 10 rounds (accepts all M16 types)
Features: carbon fiber upper and lower receivers; anodized aluminum Picatinny rail; stainless match grade barrel; quick-detach compensator; overall length 35 inches
MSRP: **$916**

Bushmaster Rifles

CARBON 15 TYPE 97

M4 A2 CARBINE

VARMINTER

VARMINTER SPECIAL

CARBON 15 TYPE 97 RIFLE

Action: autoloader
Stock: synthetic
Barrel: 16 in.
Sights: none
Weight: 3.9 lbs.
Caliber: 5.56mm., 223 Rem.
Magazine: detachable box, 10 rounds (accepts all M16 types)
Features: fluted, stainless steel match grade barrel with Quick-Detach compensator; upper receiver mounted with anodized aluminum Picatinny rail; overall length 35 in.
MSRP: **$1039**

M4 TYPE CARBINE

Action: autoloader
Stock: polymer
Barrel: 16 in.
Sights: open adjustable
Weight: 6.59 lbs.

Caliber: .223 Rem. (5.56 mm)
Magazine: detachable box, 10 rounds
Features: forged aluminum receivers with M16 A2 design improvements; M4 profile chrome-lined barrel with permanently attached Mini Y Comp muzzle brake; M16 A2 rear sight system; BATF approved, fixed position tele-style buttstock; manganese phosphate finish
MSRP: **$1110**

VARMINTER RIFLE

Action: autoloader
Stock: synthetic
Barrel: 24 in.
Sights: none
Weight: 8.75 lbs.
Caliber: .223 Remington (5.56 mm)
Magazine: detachable box, 5 rounds (accepts all M16 types)
Features: free-floating fluted heavy

DCM competition barrel; V Match tubular forend with special cooling vents and bipod stud; Bushmaster competition trigger; overall length 42.25 in.
MSRP: **$1265**

VARMINT SPECIAL RIFLE

Action: autoloader
Stock: synthetic
Barrel: 24 in.
Sights: none
Weight: 8.75 lbs.
Caliber: .223 Rem. (5.56 mm)
Magazine: detachable box, 5 rounds
Features: flat-top upper receiver with B.M.A.S. scope risers; lower receiver includes two stage competition trigger and tactical pistol grip; polished stainless steel barrel
MSRP: **$1265**

RIFLES

Bushmaster Rifles

V MATCH RIFLE

**XM15 E2S A2 20-INCH
STAINLESS STEEL**

16-INCH MODULAR CARBINE

V MATCH RIFLE AND CARBINE

Action: autoloader
Stock: synthetic
Barrel: 16 in. (Carbine),
20 in. or 24 in. (Rifle)
Sights: none
Weight: 6.9 lbs. (Carbine),
8.05 lbs. (Rifle)
Caliber: .223 Rem. (5.56mm)
Magazine: detachable box, 10 rounds
Features: forged aluminum V Match flat-top upper receiver with M16 A2 design improvements and Picatinny rail; heavy, chrome-lined free-floating barrel; front sight bases available in full sight or no sight versions; overall length 34.75 in.
Carbine: **$1045**
Rifle: **$1055**

XM15 E2S A2 20-INCH STAINLESS STEEL RIFLE

Action: autoloader
Stock: synthetic
Barrel: 20 in.
Sights: open
Weight: 8.27 lbs.
Caliber: .223 Rem. (5.56 mm)
Magazine: detachable box, 5 rounds (accepts all M16 types)
Features: heavy configuration, match grade stainless barrel; available in either A2 or A3 (with removable carry handle) configurations
MSRP: **$1055**

16-INCH MODULAR CARBINE

Action: autoloader
Stock: synthetic
Barrel: 16 in.
Sights: open adjustable
Weight: 7.3 lbs.
Caliber: .223 Rem. (5.56mm)
Magazine: detachable box, 10 rounds (accepts all M16 types)
Features: forged aluminum A3 type flat-top upper receiver; chrome-lined moly steel fluted barrel with milled gas block; A. B.M.A.S. four rail free-floater tubular forend with Picatinny rails; skeleton stock; ambidextrous pistol grip; overall length 34.5 in.
MSRP: **$1650**

Charles Daly Rifles

FIELD GRADE MAUSER

FIELD GRADE MAUSER SS

SUPERIOR GRADE MINI-MAUSER

SUPERIOR GRADE SAFARI MAUSER

FIELD GRADE MAUSER

Action: bolt, Zastava Mauser
Stock: molded black polymer, classic style with cheekpiece, reverse checkering
Barrel: hammer-forged, chrome vanadium (also stainless), 22 in. (standard) and 24 in. (magnum).
Sights: none (drilled and tapped for scope mounts)
Weight: 7.5 and 7.8 lbs.
Caliber: .22-250, .243, .25-06, .270, .308, .30-06, 7mm Rem. Mag, .300 Win. Mag.
Magazine: box, capacity 5+1 (standard), 3+1 (magnum)
Features: fully adjustable trigger; long Mauser claw extractor

MSRP (blue, standard): **$459**
(blue, magnum): **$489**
Stainless, standard: **$549**
Stainless, magnum: **$579**
Superior grade and
   Superior Mini: **$599**
Superior Magnum: **$629**
Superior Safari: **$789**

M-200

M-200C

M-310

M-400

M-200

Action: boltr
Stock: synthetic; retractable
Barrel: 30 in.
Sights: none
Weight: 27 lbs., 24lbs. (carbon fiber barrel)
Caliber: .408 CheyTac
Magazine: detachable box, 7 rounds
Features: heavy, free floated detachable fluted barrel; rear of barrel enclosed by shroud mount for bipod and handle; muzzle brake; receiver fitted with fixed MilStd Picatinny rail; fully collapsible, retractable buttstock containing integral hinged monopod.
MSRP: **$11395**

M-200C

Action: bolt
Stock: synthetic; retractable
Barrel: 25-29 in.
Sights: none
Weight: 26 lbs., 24.5 lbs. (carbon fiber barrel.)
Caliber: .408 CheyTac
Magazine: detachable box, 7 rounds

Features: heavy, free floated fluted barrel; rear part of barrel enclosed by tubular shroud as a mount for integral folding bipod and carrying handle; muzzle brake; manually operated, rotating bolt; top of receiver fitted with permanent MilStd Picatinny rail; fully collapsible retractable buttstock containing integral hinged monopod.
MSRP: **$12395**

M-310

Action: bolt
Stock: synthetic
Barrel: 29 in.
Sights: none
Weight: 16.5 lbs.
Caliber: .408 CheyTac
Magazine: single-shot or detachable box available.
Features: stainless steel match barrel — choice off fluted or non-fluted; match grade trigger; muzzle break; McMillan A-5 stock w/ adjustable cheek piece.
MSRP: **$4595**

M-400

Action: autoloader
Stock: synthetic
Barrel: 25-29 in.
Sights: none
Weight: 16.5 lbs., 14.5 lbs. (carbon fiber barrel)
Caliber: .408 CheyTac
Magazine: detachable box, 10 rounds
Features: available with steel or carbon fiber barrel; gas operated, semi-automatic system; matched upper and lower receiver; titanium firing pin; speed lock hammer; 3.5 lb. trigger pull; integral buffer system; attachable Picatinny rail.
MSRP: . . . . **upon request**

Christensen Arms Rifles

CARBON CHALLENGER THUMBHOLE

CARBON ONE CUSTOM

CARBON ONE HUNTER

CARBON RANGER

CARBON TACTICAL

RIFLES

CARBON CHALLENGE THUMBHOLE

Action: autoloading
Stock: synthetic or wood thumbhole
Barrel: graphite sleeved 20 in.
Sights: none
Weight: 4.0 lbs.
Caliber: .22 LR
Magazine: rotary, 10 rounds
Features: 10/22 Ruger action; custom trigger and bedding
Challenge: $1500
.22 Mag: $1850

CARBON ONE CUSTOM

Action: bolt
Stock: synthetic or wood sporter
Barrel: graphite sleeved 26 in.
Sights: none
Weight: 6.0 lbs.
Caliber: all popular magnums

Magazine: box, 3 rounds
Features: Remington 700 action; optional custom trigger
MSRP: $3650

CARBON ONE HUNTER

Action: bolt
Stock: synthetic
Barrel: graphite sleeved 26 in.
Sights: none
Weight: 7.0
Caliber: any popular
Magazine: box, 3 or 5 rounds
Features: Remington 700 action
MSRP: $1600

CARBON RANGER

Action: bolt
Stock: retractable tactical skeleton
Barrel: graphite sleeved, up to 36 in.
Sights: none

Weight: 18.0 lbs.
Caliber: .50 BMG
Magazine: box, 5 rounds
Features: Omni Wind Runner action; custom trigger; guaranteed 5 shots in 8 in. at 1000 yds.
MSRP: $5500

CARBON TACTICAL

Action: bolt
Stock: synthetic
Barrel: graphite sleeved, 26 in.
Sights: none
Weight: 7.0 lbs.
Caliber: most popular calibers
Magazine: box, 3 or 5 rounds
Features: guaranteed accuracy ½ in. at 100 yards; optional custom trigger, muzzle brake
MSRP: $3650

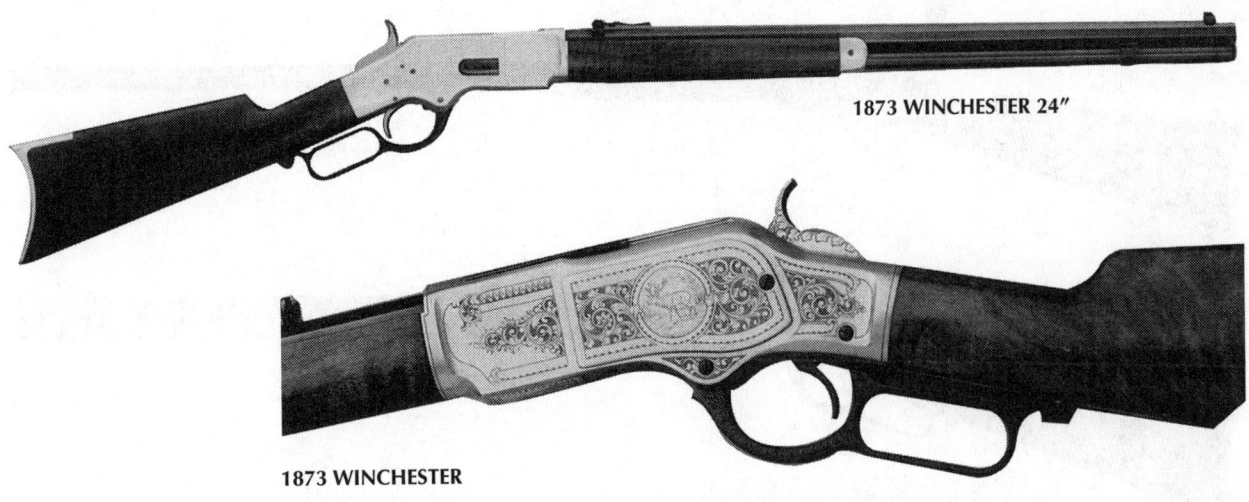

1873 WINCHESTER 24"

1873 WINCHESTER

1873 "DELUXE" SPORTING RIFLE

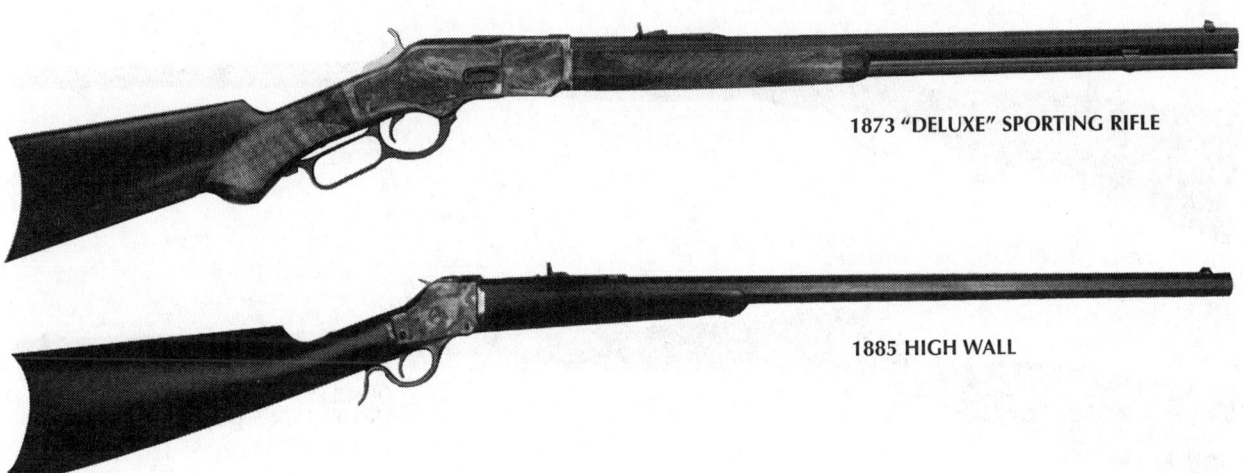

1885 HIGH WALL

RIFLES

1873 WINCHESTER

Action: lever
Stock: walnut, straight grip
Barrel: 24 in.
Sights: open
Weight: 7.5 lbs.
Caliber: .45 Colt, .44 WCF, .357, .32 WCF, .38 WCF, .44 Special
Magazine: under-barrel tube, 11 rounds
Features: Available: "Sporting" model, "Deluxe" model, "Long Range" model

(30 in. barrel), and carbine (19 in. barrel); Deluxe model has pistol grip

Sporting:	$1149
Deluxe:	$1214
Long Range:	$1079
Long Range Deluxe:	$1144
Carbine:	$1025

1885 HIGH WALL

Action: dropping block
Stock: walnut, straight grip
Barrel: octagon 30 in.

Sights: open
Weight: 9.5 lbs.
Caliber: .45-70, .45-90, .45/120, .40-65, .38-55, .348 Win., .30-40 Krag
Magazine: none
Features: reproduction of the Winchester single-shot hunting rifle popular in the 1880s

1885 Sporting:	$995
1885 Deluxe:	$1175

If you have trouble remembering which way to turn the micrometer screws to adjust your rifle sights, tape instructions to the inside of your rifle case.

Cimarron Rifles

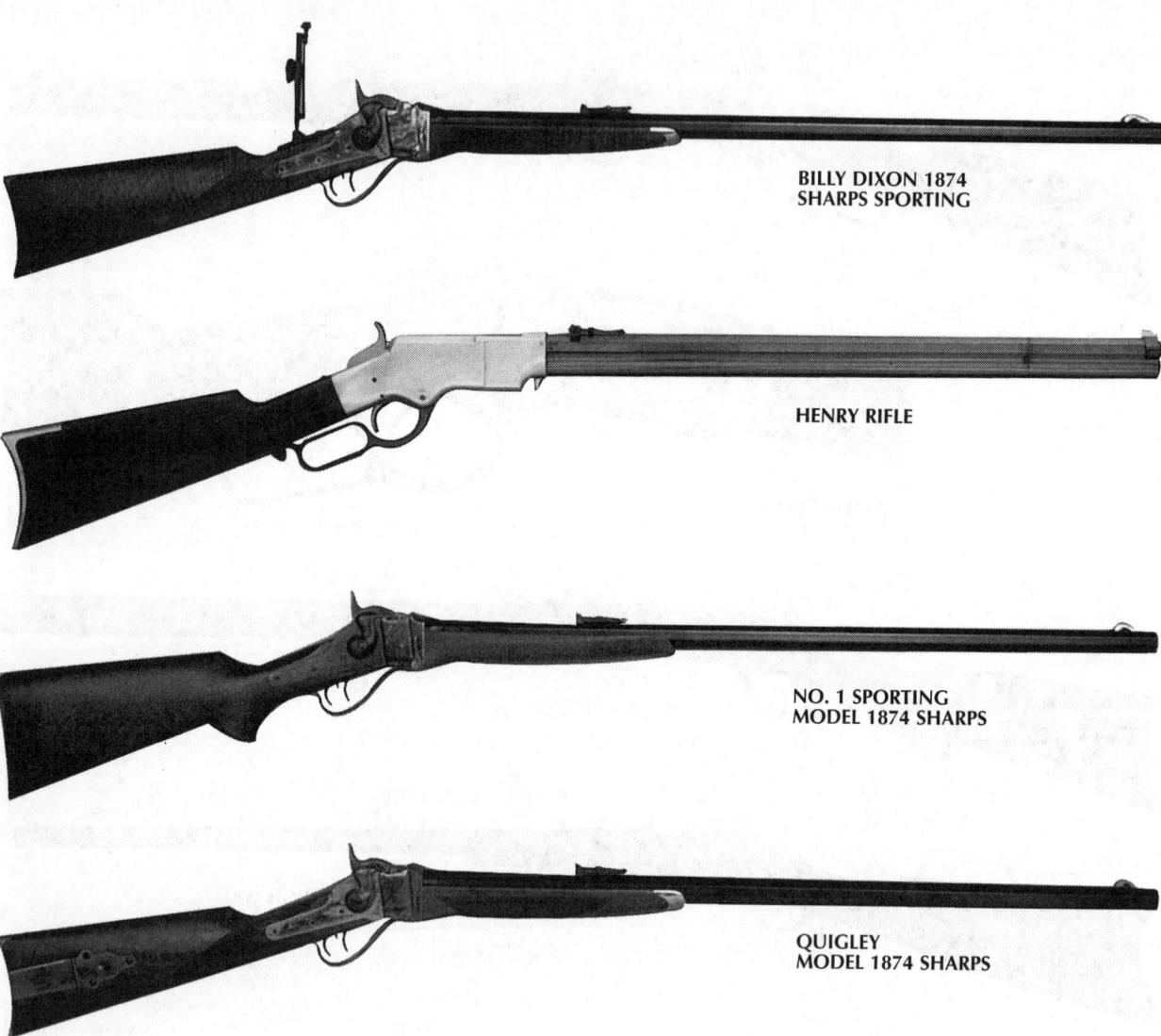

BILLY DIXON 1874
SHARPS SPORTING

HENRY RIFLE

NO. 1 SPORTING
MODEL 1874 SHARPS

QUIGLEY
MODEL 1874 SHARPS

BILLY DIXON
1874 SHARPS SPORTING
Action: dropping block
Stock: walnut, straight grip
Barrel: octagon 32 in.
Sights: open
Weight: 10.5 lbs.
Caliber: .45-70, .45-90, .45-110, .50-90
Magazine: none
Features: single-shot reproduction
MSRP: **$1349**

HENRY RIFLE
Action: lever
Stock: walnut, straight grip
Barrel: 24 in.
Sights: open   *Weight:* 7.5 lbs.
Caliber: .44 WCF, .45 LC

Magazine: under-barrel tube,
11 rounds
Features: replica of the most famous
American rifle of the Old West
MSRP: **$1149**

NO. 1 SPORTING
MODEL 1874 SHARPS
Action: dropping block
Stock: walnut, pistol grip
Barrel: 32 in. octagon
Sights: open   *Weight:* 10.5 lbs.
Caliber: .45-70, .50-70
Magazine: none
Features: single-shot reproduction;
shotgun style buttplate; barrel features
cut rifling, lapped and polished
MSRP: **$1350**

QUIGLEY
MODEL 1874 SHARPS
Action: dropping block
Stock: walnut, straight grip
Barrel: octagon 34 in.
Sights: open
Weight: 10.5 lbs.
Caliber: .45-70, .45-90, .45-120
Magazine: none
Features: single-shot reproduction
MSRP: **$1430**

RIFLES

Colt Rifles

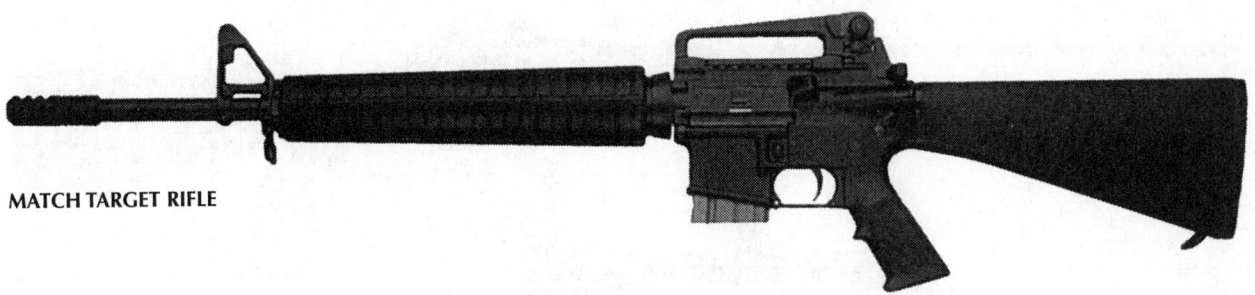

MATCH TARGET RIFLE

MATCH TARGET RIFLE
Action: autoloading
Stock: combat-style, synthetic
Barrel: 16 or 20 in.

Sights: open
Weight: 8.0 lbs.
Caliber: .223
Magazine: detachable box, 9 rounds

Features: suppressed recoil; accepts optics; 2-position safety; available with heavy barrel, compensator
MSRP: $1300

Cooper Arms Rifles

CLASSIC

WESTERN CLASSIC

CLASSIC SERIES
Action: bolt
Stock: checkered, Claro walnut
Barrel: match grade 22 in.
Sights: none
Weight: 6.5 lbs.
Caliber: .22 LR, .22 WMR, .17 HMR, .38 Hornet, .223, .308
Magazine: none

Features: single-shot; 3-lug bolt; also available in Custom Classic and Western Classic with upgraded wood
Classic: $1295-1395
Custom Classic: $1995-2195
Western Classic: $2595-2795

Cooper Arms Rifles

JACKSON SQUIRREL RIFLE

PHOENIX

VARMINTER

MODEL LVT

RIFLES

JACKSON SQUIRREL RIFLE

Action: bolt
Stock: walnut
Barrel: 22 in.
Sights: none (fitted with scope bases)
Weight: 6.5 lbs.
Caliber: .22LR, .22WMR, .17HMR, .17 Mach 2
Magazine: detachable box, 4 or 5 rounds
Features: Stainless match grade barrel; Pachmayr butt pad; matte finished
MSRP: $1499

PHOENIX

Action: bolt
Stock: synthetic (Kevlar)
Barrel: 24 in.
Sights: none (fitted with scope bases)
Weight: 7.5 lbs.
Caliber: .17 Rem, .17 Mach IV, .223 Tactical, .204 Ruger, . 221 Fireball, .222 Rem, .222 Rem Mag, .223 Rem, .223 Rem AI, .22 PPC, 6mm PPC, 6x45, 6x47, 6.8 SPC
Magazine: single shot
Features: matte stainless barrel; air-craft-grade aluminum bedding block; stock: hand-laid synthetics with Kevlar reinforcing surround; Model 21 and 22, right-hand option only.
MSRP: $1298

VARMINT SERIES

Action: bolt
Stock: checkered, Claro walnut
Barrel: stainless steel match, 24 in.
Sights: none
Weight: 7.5 lbs.
Caliber: .223, .38 Hornet, .308
Magazine: none
Features: 3-lug action in 4 sizes; also available: Montana Varminter, Varminter Extreme and Lightweight LVT
Varminter: **$1095-1295**
Montana Varminter:. . . . **$1395-1495**
Varminter Extreme: **$1795-1995**
Light Varmint Target: **$1395**

CZ (Ceska Zbrojovka Uhersky Brod) Rifles

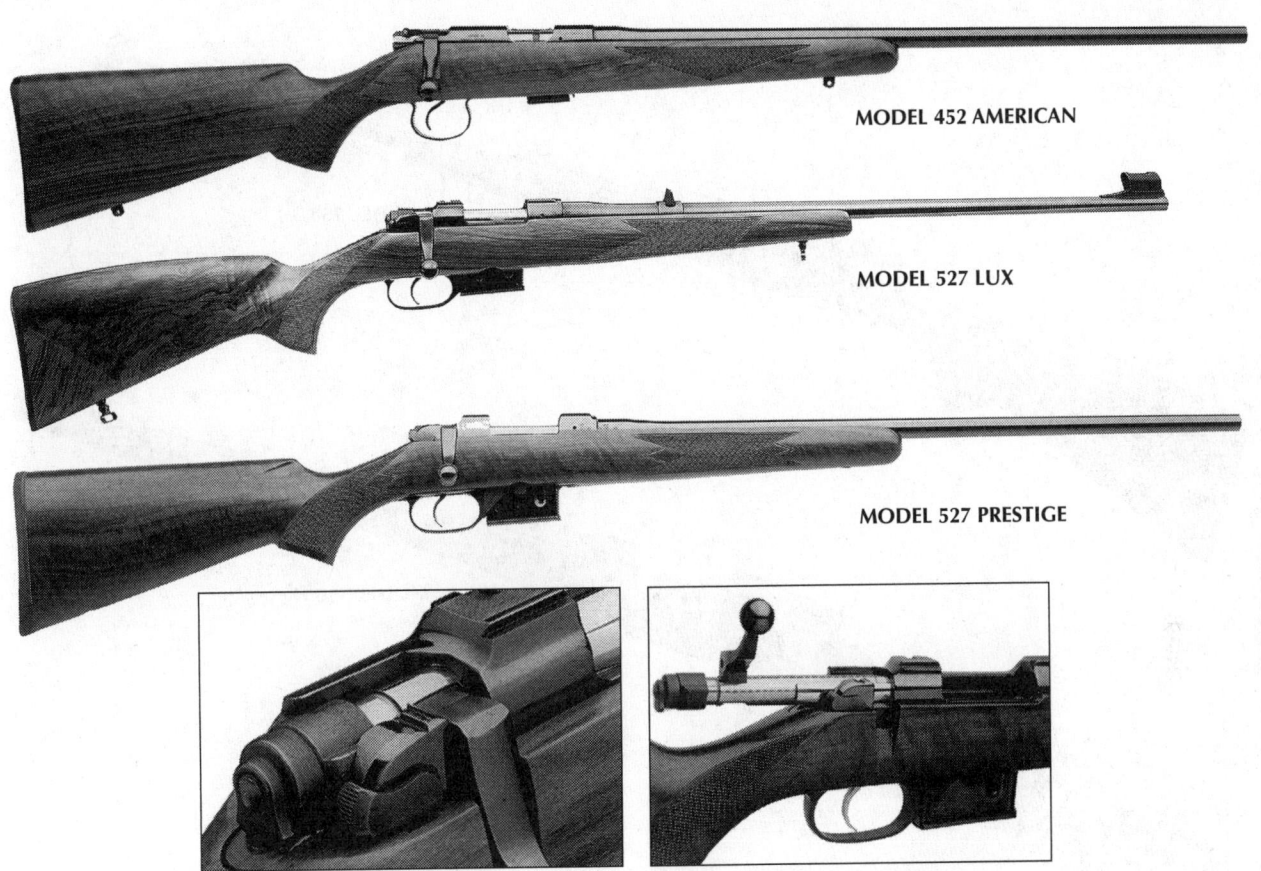

MODEL 452 AMERICAN

MODEL 527 LUX

MODEL 527 PRESTIGE

FINE MACHINING AND POLISHING ARE
CZ TRADEMARKS.

A SHORT-STROKE, LOW-LIFT BOLT AND
DETACHABLE BOX MAGAZINE ARE
DESIGNED FOR SMOOTH FEEDING.

RIFLES

MODEL 452 AMERICAN

Action: bolt
Stock: checkered walnut sporter
Barrel: 22 in.
Sights: none
Weight: 7.0 lbs.
Caliber: .22 LR, .17 HMR,
.17 MACH 2, .22 WMR
Magazine: detachable box, 5 rounds
Features: adjustable trigger; European-
style stock and open sights; Varmint
version has heavy 22 in. barrel; Youth
Scout rifle has shortened stock, 16 in.
barrel

American and Lux, .22 LR:	$389
.22 WMR:	$419
.17 HMR:	$433
.17 MACH 2:	$433

MODEL 527

Action: bolt
Stock: checkered, walnut sporter
Barrel: 24 in.
Sights: open
Weight: 6.2 lbs.
Caliber: .22 Hornet, .222, .223
Magazine: detachable box, 5 rounds
Features: CZ 527 Carbine in .223,
7.62x39, CZ 527 full stock (FS) in .22
Hornet, .222 and .223 with 20 in. bar-
rel and 527 Prestige in .22 Hornet and
.223 with 22 in. barrel

Varmint:	$597
Lux:	$599
American:	$599
Carbine:	$606
FS:	$690
Varmint Kevlar:	$799
Prestige:	$880

CZ (Ceska Zbrojovka Uhersky Brod) Rifles

MODEL 550

MODEL 550 FS

MODEL 550

Action: bolt
Stock: checkered walnut sporter
Barrel: 24 in.
Sights: open
Weight: 7.3 lbs.
Caliber: .243, 6.5x55, .270, 7x57, 7x64, .308, .30-06, 9.3x62
Magazine: box, 5 rounds
Features: adjustable single set trigger; detachable magazine optional; full-stocked model (FS) available; CZ 550 Safari Magnum has magnum length action, express sights in calibers .375 H&H, .416 Rigby, .458 Win.

American: **$623**
Medium Magnum: **$690**
FS: **$705**
Prestige: **$854**
Safari Magnum: **$875**

MODEL 550 VARMINT

Action: bolt
Stock: walnut
Barrel: heavy varmint 24 in.
Sights: open
Weight: 8.5 lbs.
Caliber: .308 Win., 22-250
Magazine: box, 5 rounds
Features: adjustable single set trigger; laminated stock optional; detachable magazine optional; also available: CZ 550 medium magnum in .7mm Rem. Mag. and .300 Win. Mag.

Varmint: **$652**
Varmint Laminate: **$749**
Medium Magnum: **$823**

Dakota Arms Rifles

MODEL 10 SINGLE-SHOT

MODEL 76

MODEL 97 HUNTER

RIFLES

MODEL 10 SINGLE-SHOT
Action: dropping block
Stock: select walnut
Barrel: 23 in.
Sights: none
Weight: 5.5 lbs.
Caliber: from .22 LR to .375 H&H;
magnum: .338 Win. to .416 Dakota
Magazine: none
Features: receiver and rear of breech
block are solid steel; removable trigger
plate
Action only: **$1675**
Barreled actions: **$2150**
Standard or Magnum: **$3995**

MODEL 76
Action: bolt
Stock: select walnut
Barrel: 23-24 in.
Sights: none
Weight: 6.5 lbs.
Caliber: Safari: from .257 Roberts to
.458 Win. Mag.; Classic: from .22-250
through .458 Win. Mag.(inc. WSM);
African: .404 Jeffery, .416 Dakota,
.416 Rigby, .450 Dakota
Magazine: box, 3-5 rounds
Features: three-position striker-block-
ing safety allows bolt operation with
safety on; stock in oil-finished English,
Bastogne or Claro walnut; African
model weighs 9.5 lbs. and the Safari is
8.5 lbs.
Classic: **$3995**
Safari: **$4995**
African: **$5795**

MODEL 97 HUNTER
Action: bolt
Stock: walnut or composite
Barrel: 24 in.
Sights: open
Weight: 7.0 lbs.
Caliber: Hunter: .25-06 through .375
Dakota; Lightweight Hunter: .22-250
through .330; Varmint hunter: .17
Rem. through .22-250
Magazine: blind box, 3-5 rounds
Features: 1 in. black recoil pad, 2 sling
swivel studs; Varmint model has #4
chrome-moly barrel, adjustable trigger,
½ in. black pad and weighs 8 lbs.
Hunter: **$1995**
**97 with semi-fancy
 wood stock:** **$2495**
Action only: **$1000**
Barreled action: **$1300**

 *Even same model rifles may shoot best with different
brands of ammunition. You'll improve your shooting
if you buy and try a variety of ammunition and select
the ammo that shoots best in your rifle.*

Dakota Arms Rifles

DOUBLE RIFLE

LONG BOW TACTICAL E.R.

PREDATOR

SHARPS RIFLE

TRAVELER

DOUBLE RIFLE
Action: hinged breech
Stock: exhibition walnut, pistol grip
Barrel: 25 in. *Sights:* open
Weight: 9.5 lbs.
Caliber: most common calibers
Magazine: none
Features: round action; elective ejectors; recoil pad; Americase
MSRP: **$27500**

LONG BOW TACTICAL E.R.
Action: bolt
Stock: McMillan fiberglass, matte finish
Barrel: stainless, 28 in. *Sights:* open
Weight: 13.7 lbs.
Caliber: .338 Lapua, .300 Dakota and .330 Dakota
Magazine: blind, 3 rounds
Features: adjustable cheekpiece; 3 sling swivel studs; bipod spike in forend; controlled round feeding; one-piece optical rail; 3-position firing pin block

safety; deployment kit; muzzle brake
Action only:. **$2400**
Tactical E.R.: **$4500**

PREDATOR
Action: bolt
Stock: checkered walnut
Barrel: match-grade stainless
Sights: none *Weight:* 9.0 lbs.
Caliber: .17 VarTarg, .17 Rem., .17 Tactical, .20 VarTarg, .20 Tactical, .20 PPC, .204 Ruger, .221 Fireball, .222 Rem., .222 Rem. Mag., .223 Rem., .22 BR, 6 PPC, 6 BR
Magazine: none
Features: many options, including fancy walnut
MSRP: **$1995**

SHARPS RIFLE
Action: dropping block
Stock: walnut, straight grip
Barrel: octagon 26 in.

Sights: open *Weight:* 8.0 lbs.
Caliber: .17 HRM to .30-40 Krag
Magazine: none
Features: small frame version of 1874 Sharps
MSRP: **$3100**

TRAVELER
Action: bolt
Stock: take-down, checkered walnut
Barrel: choice of contours, lengths
Sights: none
Weight: 8.5 lbs.
Caliber: all popular cartridges
Magazine: box, 3-5 rounds
Features: the Dakota Traveler is based on the Dakota 76 design. It features threadless disassembly. Weight and barrel length depend on caliber and version.
Classic: **$4995**
Safari: **$5995**
African: **$6795**

RIFLES

Dixie Rifles

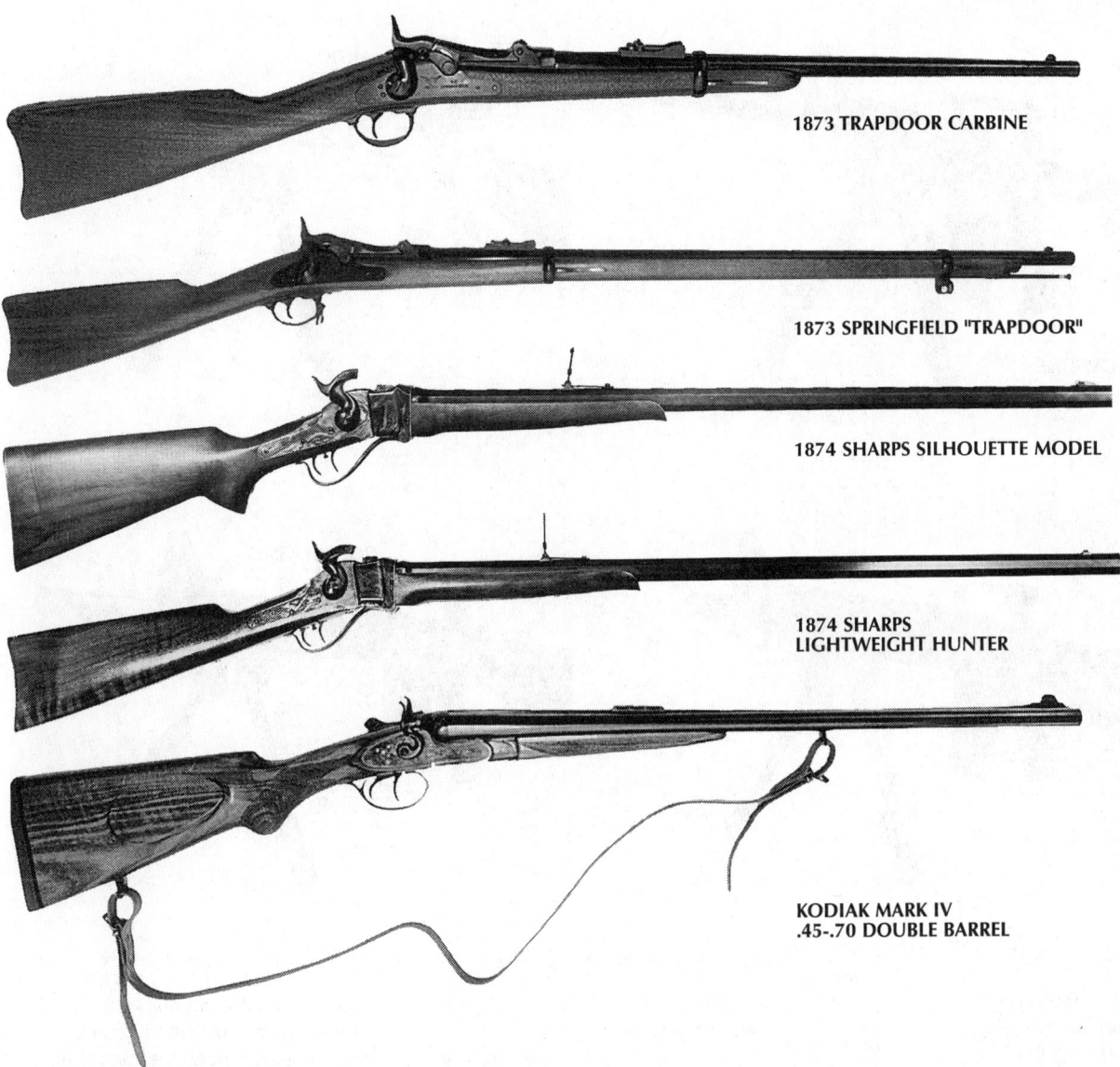

1873 TRAPDOOR CARBINE

1873 SPRINGFIELD "TRAPDOOR"

1874 SHARPS SILHOUETTE MODEL

1874 SHARPS
LIGHTWEIGHT HUNTER

KODIAK MARK IV
.45-.70 DOUBLE BARREL

RIFLES

1873 SPRINGFIELD "TRAPDOOR"

Action: hinged breech
Stock: walnut
Barrel: 26 or 32 in. (22 in carbine)
Sights: adjustable
Weight: 8.0 lbs.
Caliber: .45-70
Magazine: none
Features: single-shot rifle; first cartridge rifle of U.S. Army; Officer's Model (26 in.) has checkered stock; weight with 32 in. Barrel: 8.5 lbs. and 7.5 lbs. for carbine
1873 Springfield "Trapdoor": . . **$940**
Officer's Model: **$1125**
Carbine: **$835**

1874 SHARPS LIGHTWEIGHT HUNTER

Action: dropping block
Stock: walnut
Barrel: 30 in.
Sights: ajustable
Weight: 10.0 lbs.
Caliber: .45-70
Magazine: none
Features: case-colored receiver, drilled for tang sights; also 1874 Sharps Silhouette Hunter in .40-65 or .45-70
Hunter: **$1025**
Silhouette: **$1075**

KODIAK DOUBLE RIFLE BY PEDERSOLI

Action: hinged breech
Stock: walnut
Barrel: 24 in.
Sights: open, folding leaf
Weight: 10.0 lbs.
Caliber: .45-70
Magazine: none
Features: double-barrel rifle with exposed hammers
MSRP: **$2600**

DPMS Panther Rifles

AP4 CARBINE

ARTIC

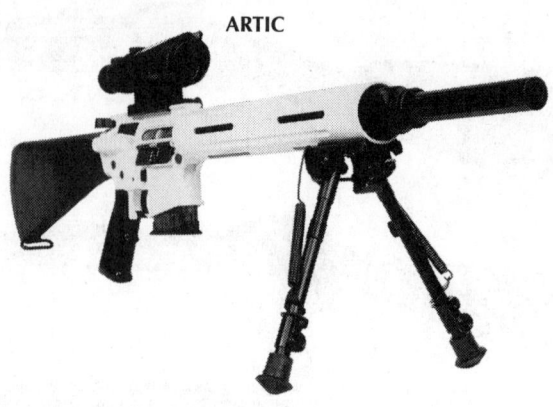

A2 TACTICAL 16-INCH

BULL CLASSIC

AP4 CARBINE
Action: autoloader
Stock: synthetic
Barrel: 16 in.
Sights: none
Weight: 6.7 lbs.
Caliber: 5.56 x 45mm
Magazine: detachable box, 30 rounds
Features: forged aluminum alloy A3 flattop upper receiver with detachable carry handle and adjustable rear sight; forged aluminum alloy lower receiver with semi-auto trigger group; chrome-moly steel barrel; telescoping stock: 36.24 in. extended, 32.5 collapsed
MSRP: $899

ARCTIC
Action: autoloader
Stock: synthetic
Barrel: 20 in.
Sights: none
Weight: 9.0 lbs.
Caliber: .223 Rem.
Magazine: detachable box, 30 rounds
Features: forged aluminum alloy A3 flattop upper receiver; forged aluminum alloy lower receiver with semi-auto trigger group; stainless steel fluted bull barrel; white coated, vented aluminum free float handguards
MSRP: $1099

A2 TACTICAL 16-INCH
Action: autoloader
Stock: synthetic
Barrel: 16 in.
Sights: open
Weight: 9.75 lbs.
Caliber: 5.56 x 45mm
Magazine: detachable box, 30 rounds
Features: forged aluminum alloy upper receiver with A2 fixed carry handle; forged aluminum alloy lower receiver with semi-auto trigger group; heavy chrome-moly steel barrel with A2 flash hider; length: 34.75 inches
MSRP: $809

BULL CLASSIC
Action: autoloader
Stock: synthetic
Barrel: 20 in.
Sights: open
Weight: 9.75 lbs.
Caliber: .223 Rem.
Magazine: detachable box, 30 rounds
Features: forged aluminum alloy upper receiver with A2 fixed carry handle; forged aluminum alloy lower receiver with semi-auto trigger group; stainless steel bull barrel; length: 38.5 inches
MSRP: $905

BULL TWENTY

SUPER BULL 24

CARBINE 16-INCH

CLASSIC

BULL SWEET SIXTEEN, TWENTY AND TWENTY-FOUR

Action: autoloader
Stock: synthetic
Barrel: 16, 20, or 24 in.
Sights: none
Weight: 7.75 lbs. (16 in.), 9.5 (20 in.), 9.8 lbs. (24 in.)
Caliber: .223 Rem.
Magazine: detachable box, 30 rounds
Features: forged aircraft aluminum alloy A3 flattop upper receiver; forged aluminum alloy lower receiver with semi-auto trigger group; stainless steel bull barrel
Bull Sweet Sixteen: $885
Bull Twenty: $915
Bull Twenty-Four: $945

BULL 24 SPECIAL & SUPER BULL 24

Action: autoloader
Stock: synthetic
Barrel: 24 in. **Sights:** none
Weight: 10.25 lbs. (Bull 24 Special), 11.75 lbs. (Super Bull)

Caliber: .223 Rem.
Magazine: detachable box, 30 rounds
Features: forged aircraft aluminum alloy A3 flattop upper receiver; flattop hi-rider upper receiver on Super Bull; forged aluminum alloy lower receiver with semi-auto trigger group; stainless steel fluted bull barrel; Super Bull with extra heavy stainless steel bull barrel (1.150-in. diameter); length: 43 inches (Bull 24 Special), 42.5 inches (Super Bull)
Bull 24 Special: $1189
Super Bull 24: $1199

CARBINE

Action: autoloader
Stock: synthetic
Barrel: 11.5 in. and 16 in.
Sights: none
Weight: 6.9 lbs. (11.5 in.), 7.06 lbs. (16 in.)
Caliber: 5.56 x 45mm
Magazine: detachable box, 30 rounds
Features: forged aluminum alloy upper receiver with A2 fixed carry handle and adjustable rear sight; forged alumi-

num alloy lower receiver with semi-auto trigger group; chrome-moly steel barrel flash hider; telescoping AP4 (6 position) stock: 35.5 in. extended, 31.75 collapsed (11.5 in.), 36.26 in. extended, 32.75 collapsed (16 in.)
11.5-inch Carbine: $799
16-Inch Carbine: $799

CLASSIC

Action: autoloader
Stock: synthetic
Barrel: 16 in., 20 in. (Classic)
Sights: open
Weight: 7.06 lbs. (Classic Sixteen), 9 lbs. (Classic)
Caliber: 5.56 x 45mm
Magazine: detachable box, 30 rounds
Features: forged aircraft aluminum alloy upper receiver with A2 fixed carry handle; forged aluminum alloy lower receiver with semi-auto trigger group; heavy chrome-moly steel barrel with A2 flash hider; chrome-plated steel bolt carrier with phosphated steel bolt
Classic Sixteen: $799
Classic: $809

DPMS Panther Rifles

DCM

LITE 16

LONG RANGE .308

LO-PRO CLASSIC

DCM

Action: autoloader
Stock: synthetic
Barrel: 20 in.
Sights: none
Weight: 9.0 lbs.
Caliber: .223 Rem.
Magazine: detachable box, 30 rounds
Features: forged aluminum alloy upper receiver with A2 fixed carry handle and adjustable NM rear sight; forged aluminum alloy lower receiver with two stage semi-auto trigger group; stainless steel heavy barrel; length: 38.5 inches
MSRP: $1099

LITE 16

Action: autoloader
Stock: synthetic
Barrel: 16 in.
Sights: open
Weight: 5.7 lbs.

Caliber: 5.56 x 45mm
Magazine: detachable box, 30 rounds
Features: forged aluminum alloy upper receiver with A1 fixed carry handle; forged aluminum alloy lower receiver with semi-auto trigger group; chrome-moly steel lite-contour barrel with A2 flash hider; chrome plated steel bolt carrier with phosphated steel bolt; A1 rear and front sights
MSRP: $720

LONG RANGE .308

Action: autoloader
Stock: synthetic
Barrel: 24 in.
Sights: none
Weight: 11.28 lbs.
Caliber: .308 Winchester
Magazine: detachable box, 9 rounds
Features: extruded aluminum upper receiver; milled aluminum lower receiver; Picatinny rail; stainless steel bull barrel; A-15 trigger group; length 43.6 in.
MSRP: $1149

LO-PRO CLASSIC

Action: autoloader
Stock: synthetic
Barrel: 16 in.
Sights: none
Weight: 7.75 lbs.
Caliber: .223 Rem.
Magazine: detachable box, 30 rounds
Features: extruded aluminum alloy flattop Lo-Pro upper receiver; forged aluminum alloy lower receiver with semi-auto trigger group; chrome-moly steel bull barrel; length: 34.75 in.
MSRP: $710

DPMS Panther Rifles

RACE GUN

TUBER

.22 LR

16-INCH AP4

RACE GUN

Action: autoloader
Stock: synthetic
Barrel: 24 in.
Sights: open
Weight: 16.0 lbs.
Caliber: .223 Rem.
Magazine: detachable box, 30 rounds
Features: extruded aluminum alloy flattop lo-pro upper receiver; forged aluminum alloy lower receiver with JP adjustable trigger group; high polish stainless steel fluted bull barrel; chrome plated steel bolt carrier with phosphated steel bolt; Hot Rod free float handguard with bipod stud installed; Badger Ordnance Tac Latch included on charge handle; JP micro adjustable rear and front sights; length: 40 in.
MSRP: $1719

SINGLE-SHOT AR RIFLE

Action: autoloader
Stock: synthetic
Barrel: 20 in.   **Sights:** open
Weight: 9 lbs.
Caliber: 5.56 x 45mm
Magazine: detachable box, 30 rounds
Features: forged aluminum alloy upper receiver with A2 fixed carry handle and adjustable rear sight; single-shot forged aluminum alloy lower receiver with standard trigger group; chrome-moly steel barrel; length: 38.25 in.
MSRP: $814

TUBER

Action: autoloader
Stock: synthetic
Barrel: 16 in.   **Sights:** none
Weight: 7.64 lbs.
Caliber: .223 Rem.
Magazine: detachable box, 30 rounds
Features: forged aluminum alloy A3 flattop upper receiver; forged aircraft aluminum alloy lower receiver with semi-auto trigger group; chrome-moly steel heavy barrel; aluminum free-float 2-inch tube handguard with M-203 handgrip; length: 34.75 in.
MSRP: $746

.22LR & DCM .22LR

Action: autoloader
Stock: synthetic
Barrel: 16 in., 20 in. (DCM)
Sights: open
Weight: 7.8 lbs., 8.7 lbs. (DCM)
Caliber: .22 LR
Magazine: detachable box, 10 rounds
Features: extruded aluminum alloy Lo-Pro flattop upper receiver; cast aluminum alloy lower receiver with semi-auto trigger group; DCM has A2 fixed carry handle; forged aluminum alloy lower receiver with semi-auto trigger group; chrome-moly steel bull barrel; heavy stainless barrel (DCM); length: 34.5 in., 38.25 in. (DCM)
.22LR: $670
DCM .22LR: $770

16-INCH AP4 POST BAN W/MICULEK COMP.

Action: autoloader
Stock: syntheic
Barrel: 16 in.
Sights: open
Weight: 7.25 lbs.
Caliber: 5.56 x 45mm
Magazine: detachable box, 30 rounds
Features: forged aluminum alloy A3 flattop upper receiver with detachable carry handle; forged aluminum alloy lower receiver with semi-auto trigger group; AP4 contour chrome-moly steel barrel with fixed Miculek compensator; length: 34 in.
MSRP: $899

Ed Brown Rifles

BUSHVELD

DAMARA

SAVANNAH

BUSHVELD

Action: bolt
Stock: McMillan composite
Barrel: 24 in., match-grade Shilen
Sights: open
Weight: 8.5 lbs.
Caliber: .375 H&H, .416 Rem. Mag., .458 Win. Mag., .458 Lott
Magazine: deep box, 4 rounds
Features: lapped barrel, 3 position safety, steel bottom metal, Talley scope mounts with 8-40 screws; optional QD scope; barrel-mounted swivel
MSRP: **$2895**

DAMARA

Action: bolt
Stock: McMillan composite
Barrel: #1.5, 22 in.
Sights: none
Weight: 6.1 lbs.
Caliber: .22-250, .243, 6mm, .260, 7mm/08, .308, .270 WSM, 7mm WSM, .300 WSM
Magazine: box, 5 rounds (WSM: 3)
Features: lapped barrel, 3 position safety, steel bottom metal; Talley scope mounts with 8-40 screws; also available in long-action: .25/06, .270, .280, 7mm Rem. Mag., 7mm Wby., .300 Win. Mag., .300 Wby. Mag.
MSRP: **$2795-2995**

SAVANNAH

Action: bolt
Stock: McMillan composite
Barrel: #3 lightweight, 24 in.
Sights: open
Weight: 7.5 lbs.
Caliber: .270 WSM, 7mm WSM, .308, .300 WSM
Magazine: box, 3 or 5 rounds
Features: short-action; lapped barrel, 3 position safety, steel bottom metal; long-action model in .270, .280, 7mm Rem. Mag., .30-06, 7mm Wby. Mag., .340 Wby., .300 Win. Mag., .300 Wby. Mag., .338 Win. Mag. with 26 in.; #4 barrel in magnums: 8.0 lbs.
MSRP: **$2795-2895**

Ed Brown Rifles

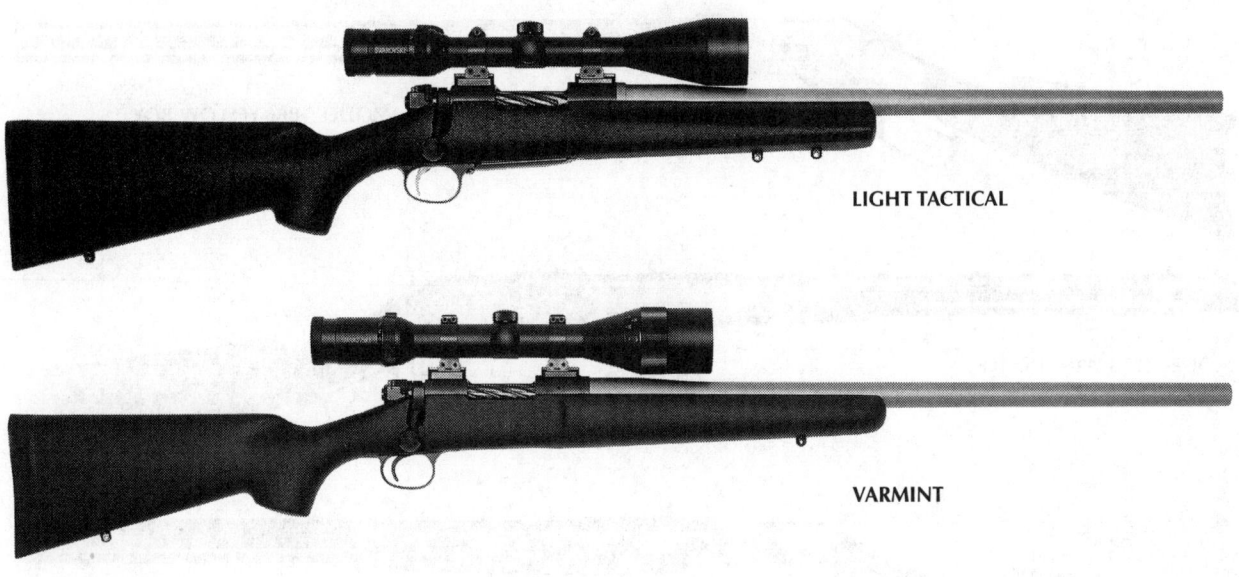

LIGHT TACTICAL

VARMINT

TACTICAL

Action: bolt
Stock: McMillan composite tactical
Barrel: heavy 26 in.
Sights: none
Weight: 11.3 lbs.
Caliber: .308, .300 Win. Mag.
Magazine: box, 3 or 5 rounds
Features: Jewell trigger; Talley scope mounts with 8-40 screws
MSRP: **$2495**

VARMINT

Action: bolt
Stock: McMillan composite varmint
Barrel: medium 24 in. or heavy 24 in.
Sights: none
Weight: 9.0 lbs.
Caliber: .22-250
Magazine: none
Features: lapped barrel, 3 position safety, steel bottom metal; optional 2 oz. trigger
MSRP: **$2495**

Get your rifle ready several weeks before hunting season opens. Fire a few rounds in a safe shooting area. Adjust your scope and/or iron sights. If repairs are needed, you'll find out before it's too late.

EMF Replica Rifles

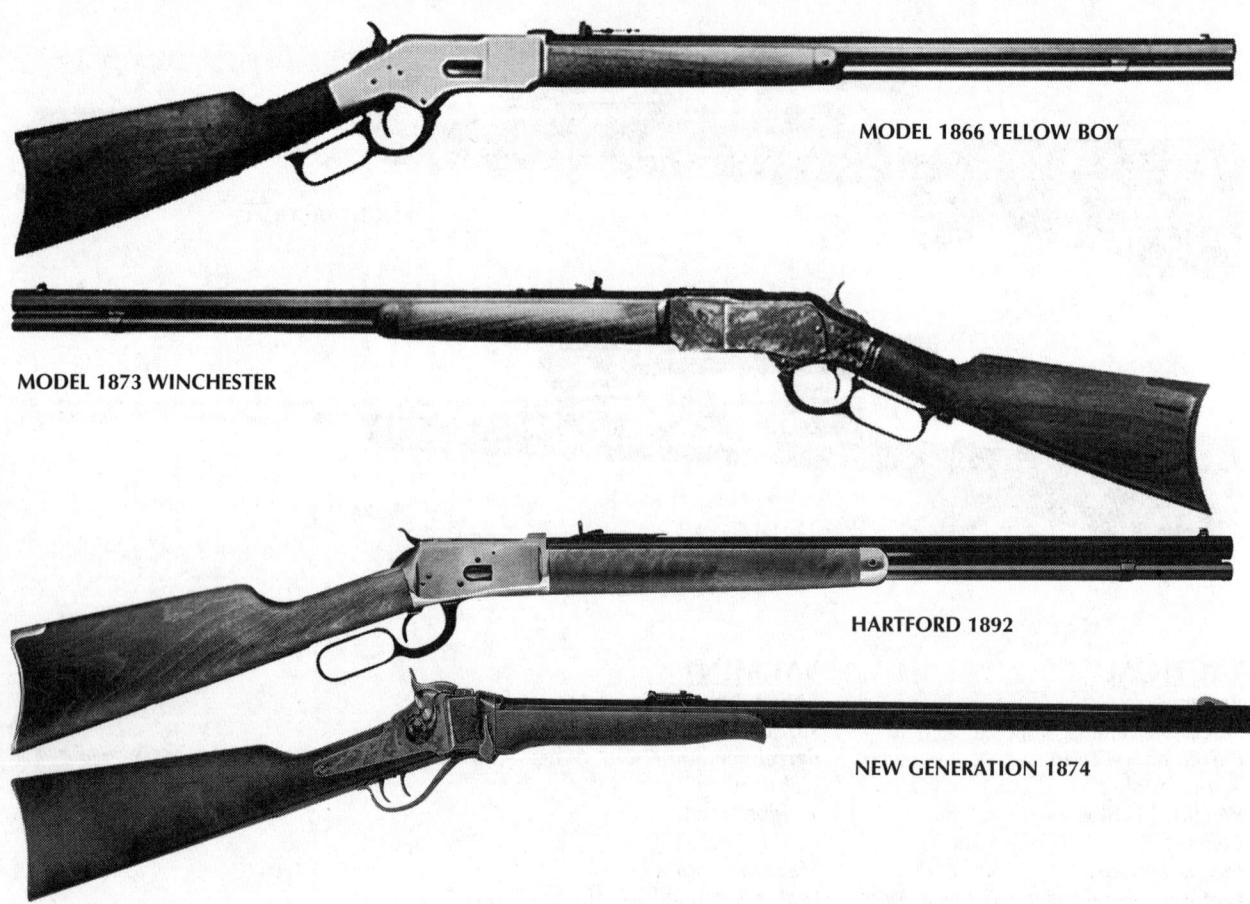

MODEL 1866 YELLOW BOY

MODEL 1873 WINCHESTER

HARTFORD 1892

NEW GENERATION 1874

RIFLES

MODEL 1860 HENRY

Action: lever
Stock: walnut
Barrel: 24 in.
Sights: open
Weight: 9.3 lbs.
Caliber: .44-40 and .45 LC
Magazine: under-barrel tube, 11 rounds
Features: blued barrel; brass frame
1860 Henry: **$1050**
White barrel: **$1160**

MODEL 1866 YELLOW BOY

Action: lever
Stock: walnut
Barrel: 24 in.
Sights: open
Weight: 8.0 lbs.
Caliber: .45 LC, .38 Special and .44-40
Magazine: under-barrel tube, 11 rounds
Features: blued barrel; brass frame
Yellow Boy: **$860**
White barrel: **$900**

MODEL 1873 WINCHESTER

Action: lever
Stock: walnut
Barrel: octagon 24 in.
Sights: open
Weight: 8.1 lbs.
Caliber: .32-20, .357, .38-40, .44-40, .45 LC; carbine: .32-30, .357, .45LC
Magazine: under-barrel tube, 11 rounds
Features: magazine tube in blued steel; frame is casehardened; carbine has 20 in. barrel
MSRP: **$990**

HARTFORD 1892

Action: lever
Stock: walnut
Barrel: octagon or round 24 in.
Sights: open
Weight: 7.5 lbs.
Caliber: .357 and .45 LC
Magazine: under-barrel tube, 11 rounds
Features: blued, casehardened or stainless steel; carbine has 20 in. barrel

Carbine, blued, round barrel: . **$380**
**Carbine, case-hardened,
 round barrel**: **$390**
**Carbine, stainless,
 round barrel**: **$425**
Case-hardened: **$450**
Blued: **$475**
Stainless: **$475**

NEW GENERATION 1874 SHARPS

Action: dropping block
Stock: walnut
Barrel: octagon 28 in.   *Sights:* open
Weight: 9.0 lbs.
Caliber: .45-70
Magazine: none
Features: created by Christian Sharps, this rifle played a major role in the Civil War. Single-shot, double-set triggers; Schnabel forearm, barrel in blue, white or brown patina
1874 Sharps: **$900**
  with brown patina: **$900**
  with white patina: **$960**

Harrington & Richardson Rifles

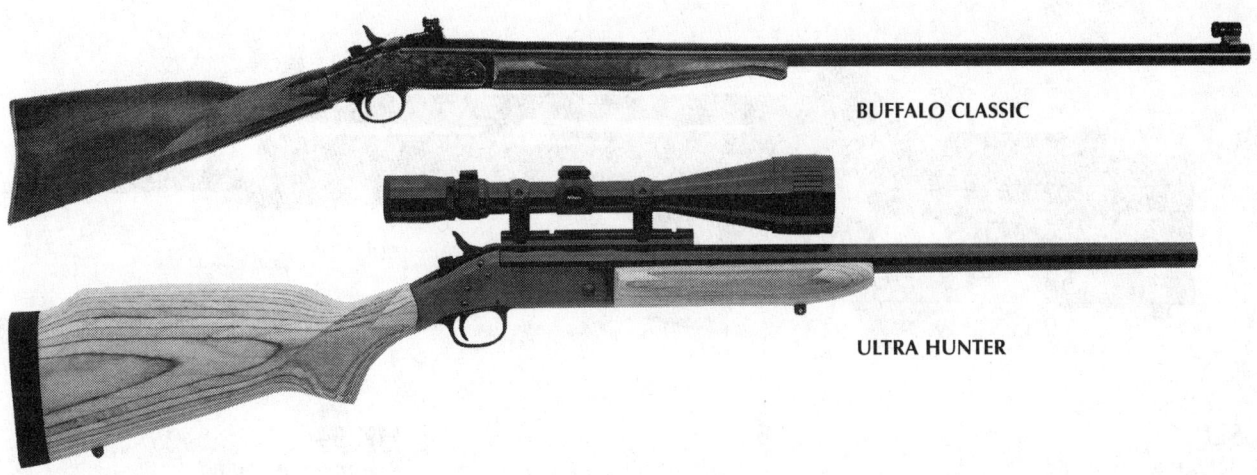

BUFFALO CLASSIC

ULTRA HUNTER

BUFFALO CLASSIC

Action: hinged breech
Stock: checkered walnut
Barrel: 32 in.
Sights: target
Weight: 8.0 lbs.
Caliber: .45-70
Magazine: none
Features: single-shot, break-open action; steel buttplate; Williams receiver sight; Lyman target front sight; antique color case-hardened frame
MSRP: $438

ULTRA HUNTER

Action: hinged breech
Stock: hand-checkered, laminate
Barrel: 22, 24, and 26 in.
Sights: none
Weight: 7.0 lbs.
Caliber: .22 WMR, .223 Rem. and .243 (Varmint), .25-06, .30-06, .270, .308 Win
Magazine: none
Features: single-shot with break-open action and side lever release; Monte Carlo stock with sling swivels on stock

and forend; scope mount included; weight varies to 8 lbs. with bull barrel
Ultra: $349
Ultra in .22 WMR: $203

Heckler & Koch Rifles

PSG1

SR9 (T) & PSG1 MARKSMAN'S RIFLE

Action: autoloading
Stock: synthetic
Barrel: 19.7 in.
Sights: open

Weight: 10.9 lbs.
Caliber: 7.62x51mm
Magazine: detachable box, 5 or 20 rounds
Features: delayed roller-locked bolt system; polygonal rifling; low-recoil

buffer system; Kevlar reinforced fiberglass thumbhole stock; adjustable buttstock (SR9 target version); overall length 42.5 in.
SR9 (T): $5000
PSG1 Marksman's Rifle: $10000

Heckler & Koch Rifles

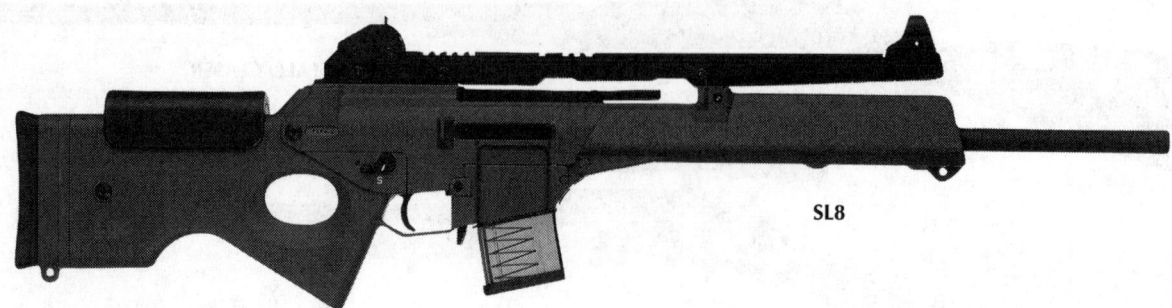

SL8

SL8
Action: autoloading
Stock: synthetic
Barrel: 20.80 in.
Sights: open
Weight: 8.60 lbs.
Caliber: 5.56x45mm
Magazine: detachable box, 10 rounds
Features: delayed roller-locked bolt system; match grade barrel with external fluting; available with Weaver type scope/sight rail or 13-inch Picitinny rail
MSRP: . . . .**not available**

SP89
Action: autoloading
Stock/grip: synthetic
Barrel: 4.5 in.
Sights: open
Weight: 4.4 lbs.
Caliber: 9mm
Magazine: detachable box, 15 or 30 rounds
Features: delayed roller-locked bolt system; overall length 13 in.; 10.25 in. sight radius
MSRP: **$4000**

HK 94
Action: autoloading
Stock: synthetic
Barrel: 16.54 in.
Sights: none
Weight: 6.43 lbs. (A2 fixed stock), 7.18 lbs. (A3 collapsible stock)
Caliber: 9x19mm Parabellum
Magazine: detachable box, 15 or 30 rounds
Features: delayed roller-locked bolt system; Stoner-style rotating bolt; A2 fixed tock or A3 collapsible stock; HK claw-lock sight mounts; sold with tool kit
MSRP: **$4400**

Henry Repeating Arms Rifles

BIG BOY

BIG BOY
Action: lever
Stock: walnut
Barrel: 20 in. octagon
Sights: open
Weight: 8.7 lbs.
Caliber: .44 Mag., .45 LC

Magazine: 10 rounds
Features: brass receiver, barrel band, buttplate
MSRP: **$775**

RIFLES

Henry Repeating Arms Rifles

GOLDEN BOY

LEVER-ACTION .22

MINI BOLT .22

PUMP-ACTION .22

GOLDEN BOY
Action: lever
Stock: walnut, straight-grip
Barrel: octagon 20 in.
Sights: open   *Weight*: 6.8 lbs.
Caliber: .22 LR, .22 WMR, .17 HMR
Magazine: under-barrel tube,
16-22 rounds
Features: brass receiver and buttplate
per Winchester 66
Golden Boy (.22 LR): $425
.22 Mag: $500
.17 HMR: $510

LEVER-ACTION .22
Action: lever
Stock: American walnut
Barrel: 18 in.

Sights: open
Weight: 5.5 lbs.
Caliber: .22 S, .22 L, .22 LR
Magazine: under-barrel tube,
15-21 rounds
Features: also available: carbine and
youth model; .22 WMR with check-
ered stock, 19 in. barrel
Rifle, carbine or youth: $290
Magnum: $410

MINI BOLT .22
Action: bolt
Stock: synthetic
Barrel: stainless 16 in.
Sights: illuminated
Weight: 3.3 lbs.
Caliber: .22 S, .22 L, .22 LR

Magazine: none
Features: single-shot; designed for
beginners
Mini Bolt: $215
Acu-Bolt (20 in. bbl. & 4x
   scope included): $350

PUMP-ACTION .22
Action: pump
Stock: walnut
Barrel: 18 in.
Sights: open
Weight: 5.5 lbs.
Caliber: .22 LR
Magazine: under-barrel tube,
15 rounds
Features: alloy receiver
MSRP: $310

Henry Repeating Arms Rifles

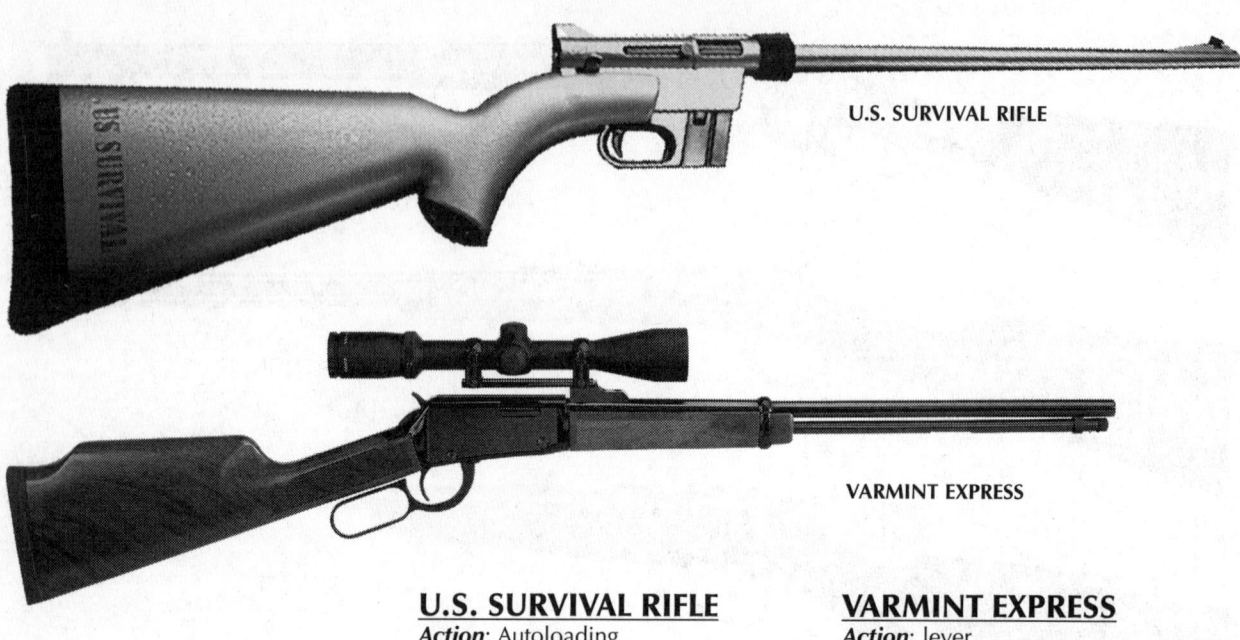

U.S. SURVIVAL RIFLE

VARMINT EXPRESS

U.S. SURVIVAL RIFLE
Action: Autoloading
Stock: synthetic butt stock
Barrel: 16 in.
Sights: open
Weight: 4.5 lbs.
Caliber: .22 LR
Magazine: detachable box, 8 rounds
Features: barrel and action stow in water-proof, floating stock
Survival Rifle (black or silver): . $215
Camo: $270

VARMINT EXPRESS
Action: lever
Stock: walnut
Barrel: 20 in.
Sights: none
Weight: 5.8 lbs.
Caliber: .17 HMR
Magazine: 11 rounds
Features: Monte Carlo stock; scope mount included
MSRP: $490

HOWA Rifles

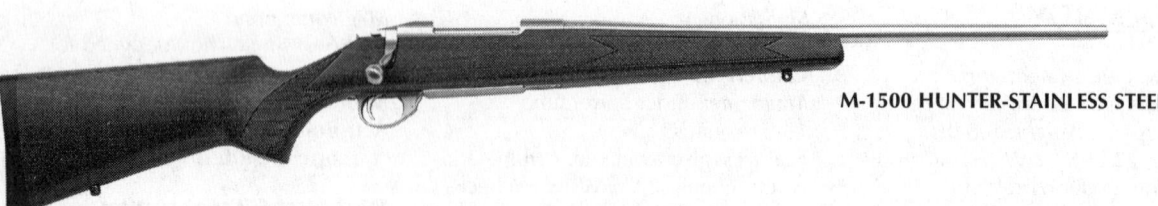

M-1500 HUNTER-STAINLESS STEEL

MODEL 1500 HUNTER
Action: bolt
Stock: American black walnut with cheekpiece
Barrel: 22 in.
Sights: none
Weight: 7.6 lbs.
Caliber: popular standard and magnum calibers from .223 Rem. to .300 WSM

Magazine: box, 5 rounds
Features: choice of blue or stainless; 22 in. (standard) or 24 in. (magnum) barrels; varmint model in .223, .22-50 and .308; checkered grips and foreend
Blue finish standard: $574
**   magnum: $595**
Stainless standard: $682
**   magnum: $704**

RIFLES

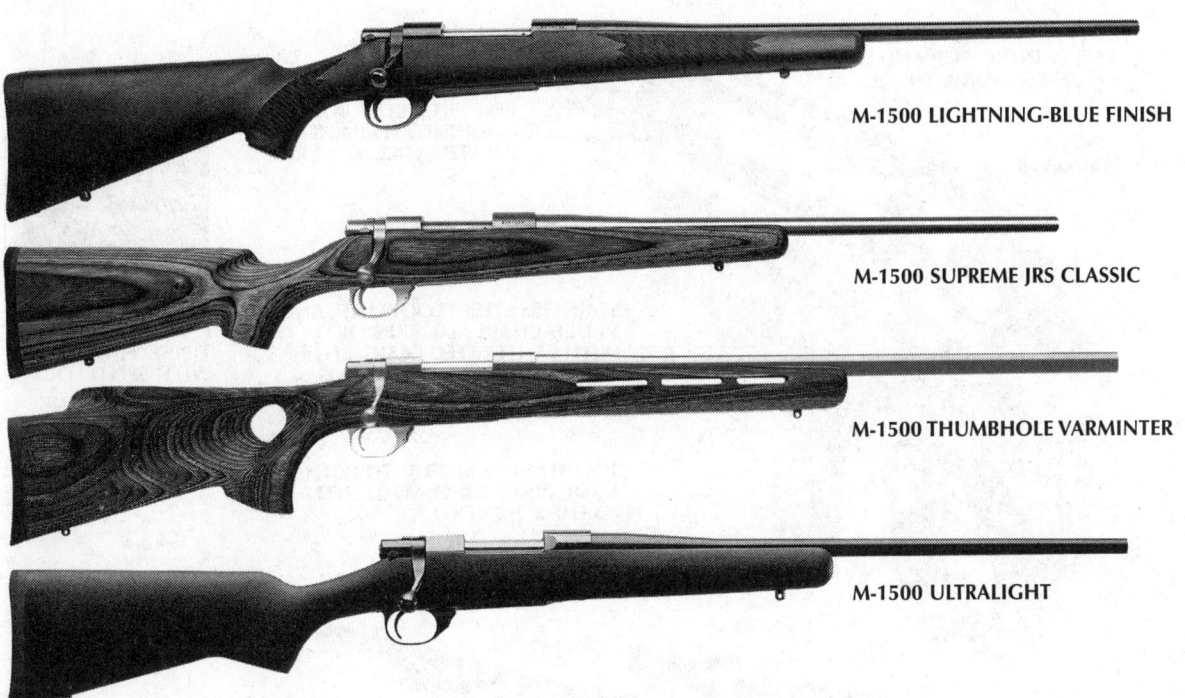

M-1500 LIGHTNING-BLUE FINISH

M-1500 SUPREME JRS CLASSIC

M-1500 THUMBHOLE VARMINTER

M-1500 ULTRALIGHT

RIFLES

MODEL 1500 LIGHTNING

Action: bolt
Stock: Black Polymer with cheekpiece or camo
Barrel: 22 in.   *Sights:* none
Weight: 7.6 lbs.
Caliber: popular standard and magnum calibers from .223 Rem. to .300 WSM
Magazine: box, 5 rounds
Features: choice of blue or stainless; 22 in. (standard) or 24 in. (magnum) barrels; new, modern checkered grips, palm swell and forend; barreled actions are available; 3-position safety

Black, blue finish standard: . . $508
   magnum:. $531
Black, stainless standard: $620
   magnum:. $649
Camo, blue finish standard: . . $545
   magnum:. $568
Camo, stainless, standard: . . . $661
   magnum:. $690

MODEL 1500 SUPREME SERIES

Action: bolt
Stock: laminated or black matte
Barrel: 22 or 24 in.   *Sights:* none
Weight: 7.6 lbs.
Caliber: .223, .25-06, .22-250, .243, 6.5x55, .270, .308, .30-06, 7mm Rem.

Mag., .300 Win. Mag., .338 Win. Mag., .270 WSM, 7mm WSM, .300 WSM
Magazine: 3 or 5 rounds
Features: stainless or blue, nutmeg or pepper stock; also: Hunter rifles with walnut stock

Blue, JRS stock: $646
Stainless, JRS stock:. $755
Magnum, blue, JRS stock: $675
Magnum, stainless, JRS stock: . $784
**Also available in
   thumbhole stock:** . . . . . .add $58

MODEL 1500 THUMBHOLE VARMINTER

Action: bolt
Stock: laminated   *Barrel*: heavy 22 in.
Sights: none
Weight: 9.9 lbs.
Caliber: .223, .22-250, .243 Win., .308
Magazine: 5 rounds
Features: nutmeg, pepper or black stock color, blued or stainless; also: Sporter thumbhole version (7.6 lbs.) in 19 calibers including WSMs

Blued sporter: $704
   magnum:. $738
Blue: $733
   stainless: $805
Stainless Sporter: $813
   magnum:. $842

MODEL 1500 VARMINT

Action: bolt
Stock: black polymer or American walnut
Barrel: 22 in.   *Sights:* none
Weight: 9.3 lbs.
Caliber: .223, .22-50 and .308
Magazine: box, 5 rounds
Features: choice of blue or stainless; 24 in. barrels; wood stocks with weather-resistant finish and laser-stippled grip and forearm panels

Blue finish black polymer: $546
Camo: $582
Walnut: $610
Stainless black polymer: $664
Camo: $704
Walnut: $719

MODEL 1500 ULTRALIGHT

Action: bolt
Stock: Black texture wood
Barrel: 20 in.   *Sights:* none
Weight: 6.4 lbs.
Caliber: .243 Win., .308, 7mm-08
Magazine: box, 5 rounds
Features: mill-cut lightweight receiver; wood stock with textured flat black finish, blue finish; Youth model available

Ultralight "Mountain Rifle": . . $539
   stainless (.308 only): $658
Ultralight "Youth Model": $539
   stainless: $658

H-S Precision Rifles

3-POSITION SAFETY WITH SAFETY INDICATOR AND COCKING INDICATOR

TANG-MOUNTED BOLT RELEASE LEVER

ONE PIECE BOLT BODY MACHINED FROM HEAT-TREATED 4142, 42-45 RC

STAINLESS STEEL FLOORPLATE AND SS DETACHABE MAGAZINE BOX WITH CENTER FEED DESIGN FOR POSITIVE CARTRIDGE FEEDING

BOLT HANDLE MACHINED WITH A 360° RING, SILVER-SOLDERED TO THE BOLT BODY

HARDENED STEEL-TIPPED FIRING PIN WITH SPEED LOCK SPRING

PHR (PROFESSIONAL HUNTER RIFLE)

VTD (VARMINT TAKE-DOWN SYSTEM)

PHR (PROFESSIONAL HUNTER RIFLE)

Action: bolt
Stock: composite
Barrel: 24-26 in.
Sights: none
Weight: 8.0 lbs.
Caliber: all popular magnum calibers up to .375 H&H and .338 Lapua
Magazine: detachable box, 3 rounds
Features: Pro series 2000 action: full-length bedding block, optional 10x Model with match-grade stainless, fluted barrel, muzzle brake, built-in recoil reducer; Lightweight SPR rifle is chambered in standard calibers
MSRP: **$2375**

TAKE-DOWN RIFLES

Action: bolt
Stock: 2-piece composite
Barrel: any contour and weight 22-26 in.
Sights: none
Weight: 8.0 lbs.
Caliber: any popular standard or magnum chambering
Magazine: detachable box, 3 or 4 rounds
Features: rifle disassembles in front of action and reassembles to deliver identical point of impact; price includes carrying case, TD versions with sporter or tactical stocks; customer's choice of barrels and chambering; left-hand model: add $200
MSRP: **$3600**

H-S Precision Rifles

VAR (VARMINT RIFLE)

VAR (VARMINT)
Action: bolt
Stock: composite
Barrel: heavy 24 in.
Sights: none

Weight: 11.0 lbs.
Caliber: all popular varmint calibers
Magazine: detachable box, 4 rounds
Features: Pro-series 2000 action; full-length bedding block; also 10x version

with fluted, stainless barrel, optional muzzle
MSRP: $2275

Jarrett Custom Rifles

ORIGNIAL BEANFIELD

PROFESSIONAL HUNTER

WIND WALKER

RIFLES

ORIGINAL BEANFIELD
Action: bolt
Stock: McMillan synthetic
Barrel: #4 match grade, 24 in.
Sights: none **Weight**: 8.5 lbs.
Caliber: any popular standard or magnum
Magazine: box, 3 or 5 rounds
Features: Shilen trigger; Remington 700 or Winchester 70 action; Talley scope mounts, case, sling, load data and 20 rounds of ammunition; Wind Walker has skeletonized 700 action (7.3 lbs.); muzzle brake
MSRP: $4850

PROFESSIONAL HUNTER
Action: bolt
Stock: synthetic
Barrel: 24 in.
Sights: open
Weight: 9.0 lbs.
Caliber: any popular standard or wildcat chambering
Magazine: 3 or 5 rounds
Features: muzzle brake; also two Leupold 1.5-5x scopes zeroed in Talley QD rings
MSRP: $9390

WIND WALKER
Action: bolt
Stock: synthetic
Barrel: 20 in.
Sights: none
Weight: 7.5 lbs.
Caliber: any popular short-action
Magazine: box, 3 or 5 rounds
Features: Remington Model 700 short-action; includes Talley scope mounts, choice of scope plus case, sling, load data and 20 rounds of ammunition
MSRP: $6650

Kimber Rifles

MODEL 84M CLASSIC

MODEL 84M MONTANA

MODEL 84M SUPER AMERICA

MODEL 8400 CLASSIC

MODEL 84M CLASSIC

Action: bolt
Stock: checkered, Claro walnut
Barrel: light sporter, 22 in.
Sights: none
Weight: 5.6 lbs.
Caliber: .243, .22-250, .260, 7mm-08, .308
Magazine: box, 5 rounds
Features: Varmint model (7.4 lbs.) in .22-250 & .204 Ruger with 26 in. stainless, fluted barrel; Long Master Classic (7.4 lbs) in .223, .243 and .308 with 24 in. stainless, fluted barrel; Long Master VT (10 lbs.) in .22-250 with stainless, bull barrel, laminated target stock; Pro Varmint with 22 in. barrel in .204 Ruger and .223 Rem., 24 in. barrel in .22-250; Short Varmint/ Target (SVT) with 18.25 in. barrel in .223 Rem.
Classic: **$1080**
Varmint: **$1038**

Long Master Classic: **$1038**
Long Master VT: **$1162**
ProVarmint: **$1115**
SVT: **$1162**

MODEL 84M MONTANA

Action: bolt
Stock: synthetic
Barrel: 22 in.
Sights: none
Weight: 5.3 lbs.
Caliber: .308, .243, .260, 7mm-08
Magazine: 5 rounds
Features: stainless steel 84M Montana, standard
MSRP: **$1124**

MODEL 84M SUPER AMERICA

Action: bolt
Stock: AAA walnut
Barrel: 22 in.
Sights: none

Weight: 5.3 lbs.
Caliber: .308, .243, .260, 7mm-08, .223 Rem.
Magazine: 5 rounds
Features: 24 LPI wrap checkering on select wood
MSRP: **$1828**

MODEL 8400 CLASSIC

Action: bolt
Stock: walnut
Barrel: 24 in.
Sights: none
Weight: 6.6 lbs.
Caliber: .270, 7mm, .325 WSM and .300 WSM
Magazine: 3 rounds
Features: 3-position safety
8400 Classic: **$1080**
8400 Montana, WSMs: **$1222**
8400 Super America: **$2023**

CLASSIC

SHORT VARMINT TARGET

CLASSIC

Action: bolt
Stock: checkered, AA walnut
Barrel: 22 in. match grade
Sights: none
Weight: 6.5 lbs.
Caliber: .22 LR
Magazine: detachable box, 5 rounds
Features: Model 70-type, 3-position safety; bead blasted finish; deluxe checkering, hand-rubbed finish; 50-yard groups less than .4 in.; also available: no-frills Hunter model; Super America with fancy AA walnut stock with wrap-around checkering; Classic Varmint with walnut stock & 20 in. fluted barrel; Pro Varmint with laminated stock; Custom Classic with AAA walnut, matte finish and ebony forend

Classic:	**$1147**
Hunter:	**$809**
Super America:	**$1865**
Classic Varmint:	**$1055**
Pro Varmint:	**$1108**
Custom Classic:	**$1507**

HS (HUNTER SILHOUETTE)

Action: bolt
Stock: high-comb walnut
Barrel: medium-heavy, half-fluted 24 in.
Sights: none
Weight: 7.0 lbs.
Caliber: .22 LR
Magazine: detachable box, 5 rounds
Features: designed for NRA rimfire silhouette competition
MSRP: **$915**

SVT (SHORT VARMINT TARGET)

Action: bolt
Stock: heavy, competition style laminate
Barrel: extra heavy, fluted, stainless 18.25 in.
Sights: none
Weight: 7.5 lbs.
Caliber: .22 LR
Magazine: detachable box, 5 rounds
Features: bead-blasted blue; gray laminated stock
MSRP: **$949**

Krieghoff Rifles

CLASSIC SIDE-BY-SIDE

CLASSIC SIDE-BY-SIDE

Action: hinged breech
Stock: select walnut
Barrel: 23.5 in.
Sights: open
Weight: 8.0 lbs.
Caliber: 7x65R, .308, .30-06, .30R Blaser, 8x57, 9.3x74, .375 H&H, .416 Rigby, .458 Win., .470 N.E., .500 N.E.
Magazine: none

Features: thumb-cocking, break-action; double triggers; optional 21.5 in. barrel; engraved side plates; weight depends on chambering and barrel contour

Standard calibers:	**$7850**
Magnum calibers:	**$9450**
Extra barrels with forearm (fitted):	**$4500**
Magnum barrels:	**$5500**

L.A.R. Rifles

GRIZZLY BIG BOAR

GRIZZLY BIG BOAR
Action: bolt
Stock: all steel sleeve with rubber butt pad
Barrel: 36 in.
Sights: none

Weight: 30.4 lbs.
Caliber: .50 BMG
Magazine: none
Features: Bull Pup single-shot; descending pistol grip; bi-pod; finish options

Grizzly:	$2350
Parkerized:	$2450
Nickel-frame:	$2600
Full nickel:	$2700
Stainless	$2600

Lazzeroni Rifles

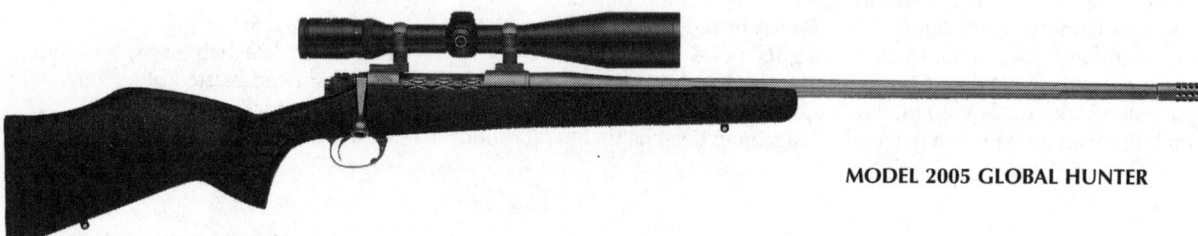

MODEL 2005 GLOBAL HUNTER

MODEL 2005 GLOBAL HUNTER
Action: bolt
Stock: synthetic
Barrel: 22 or 26 in.
Sights: none

Weight: 6.1 lbs. (short-action) or 7.4 lbs. (long-action)
Caliber: nine Lazzeroni chamberings, from 6.53 Scramjet to 10.57 Meteor
Magazine: internal box, 3 rounds
Features: fluted stainless sporter bar-rel; long- or short-action; lightweight graphite composite stock and alloy bottom metal
MSRP: $5900

The hunter does not have to be able to shooter quarter-inch, half-inch or even one-inch groups with a rifle, but it is essential to know what you and your rifle are capable of under ideal conditions. This builds confidence and lets you know what you can and cannot attempt in the field. Spend some time shooting across a solid bench rest with good ammo, and really get to know your rifle.

Legacy Sports Rifles

HOWA M-1500 JRS CLASSIC SUPREME

PUMA M-92 CARBINE

HOWA M-1500 JRS CLASSIC SUPREME

Action: bolt
Stock: laminated
Barrel: 22 in. or 24 in.
Sights: none
Weight: 7.25-7.75 lbs.
Caliber: .223, .22-250, .243, 6.5x55, .25-06, .270, .308, .30-06, 7mm Rem. Mag., .300 Win. Mag., .338 Win. Mag., .270 WSM, 7mm WSM, .300 WSM
Magazine: internal box, 3-5 rounds
Features: Improved 3-position thumb safety; Boyds stock available in black walnut or laminate; optional thumb-hole stock
Blue: $646-675
Stainless: $755-784

PUMA M-92 RIFLES AND CARBINE

Action: lever
Stock: walnut
Barrel: 16, 18, and 20 in.
Sights: open
Weight: 6.0-7.5 lbs.
Caliber: .38/.357, .44 Mag., .45 Colt, .454 Casull, .480 Ruger
Magazine: full-length tube; capacity varies with barrel length
Features: 18-inch barrel ported; available with 24-inch octagon barrel; HiViz sights; .45 carbine with large-loop lever; stainless and blued finishes available
MSRP: . . . . from $457

Les Baer Rifles

SVR

SVR

Action: autoloader
Stock: synthetic
Barrel: 18 in. and 24 in.
Sights: none
Weight: 13.0 lbs.
Caliber: .204 Ruger
Magazine: detachable box, 5-rounds
Features: Les Baer 416-R stainless barrel; chromed National Match carrier and extractor; titanium firing pin; aluminum gas block with Picatinny top; match-grade stainless; two-stage, 24-inch Jewell trigger; Picatinny rail; optional Leupold Long Range 8.5-25x50mm Vari-X III package; Versa Pod bipod; all-weather Baer Coat finish; camo finish and special rifling twist available as options
MSRP: $3075

Lone Star Rifles

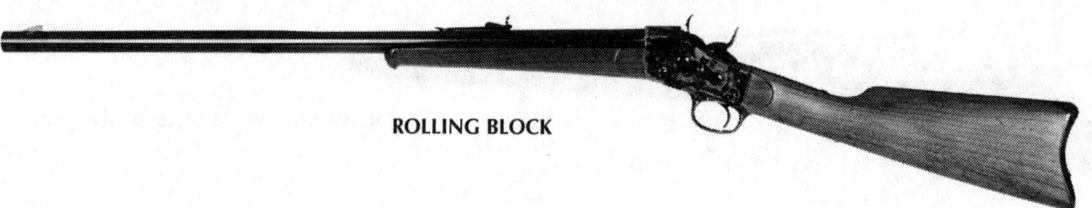

ROLLING BLOCK

ROLLING BLOCK

Action: single shot
Stock: walnut
Barrel: 28-34 in.
Sights: many options
Weight: 6.0-16.0 lbs.
Caliber: .25, .20 WCF, .25-35, .30-30, .30-40, .32-20, .32-40, .38-50, .38-55, .40-50SS, .40-50SBN, .40-70SMB, .40-70SS, .40-82, .40-90SS, .45-70, .45-90, .45-100, .45-110, .45-120, .44-60, .44-77SBN, .44-90SBN, .44-100 Rem. Sp., .50-70, .50-90, .50-140
Magazine: none
Features: true-to-form replicas of post-Civil War Remington rolling blocks; single set or double set triggers; case-colored actions on Silhouette, Creedmoor, Sporting, Deluxe Sporting, Buffalo, Custer Commemorative, #5, #7

Standard: $1595
Sporting: $1995
Buffalo Rifle: $2900
#7: $3500
Take Down: $4000

Magnum Research Rifles

BARRACUDA STOCK MAGNUMLITE

MAGNUMLITE CENTERFIRE

TACTICAL RIFLE

MAGNUMLITE CENTERFIRE

Action: bolt
Stock: composite
Barrel: graphite sleeved, 24 or 26 in.
Sights: none
Weight: 7.8 lbs.
Caliber: .280, .30-06, 7mm Rem. Mag., .300 Win. Mag., 7 WSM, .300 WSM
Magazine: box, 3 or 4 rounds
Features: adjustable trigger, free-floating match-grade barrel; platform bedding; left-hand available
Magnum Lite: $2295
Varmint model: $2295

MAGNUMLITE RIMFIRE

Action: autoloading
Stock: composite or laminated
Barrel: graphite sleeved, 16.75 in.
Sights: none
Weight: 5.2 lbs.
Caliber: .22LR, .22 WMR, .17 HMR and .17M2
Magazine: rotary, 9 rounds
Features: Ruger 10/22 action; carbon-fiber barrel with steel liner
With composite stock: $599
.17 M2: $599-759
.17 HMR: $709-999
With laminated stock: $759
Magnum with composite: $799
Magnum with laminated: $959

TACTICAL RIFLE

Action: bolt
Stock: H-S Precision, synthetic tactical
Barrel: graphite sleeved, 26 in.
Sights: none
Weight: 8.3 lbs.
Caliber: .223, .22-250, .300 WSM, .308, .300 Win. Mag.
Magazine: box, 3 or 5 rounds
Features: accurized Rem. 700 action; adjustable comb; adjustable trigger and length of pull
MSRP: $2400

RIFLES

Marlin Rifles

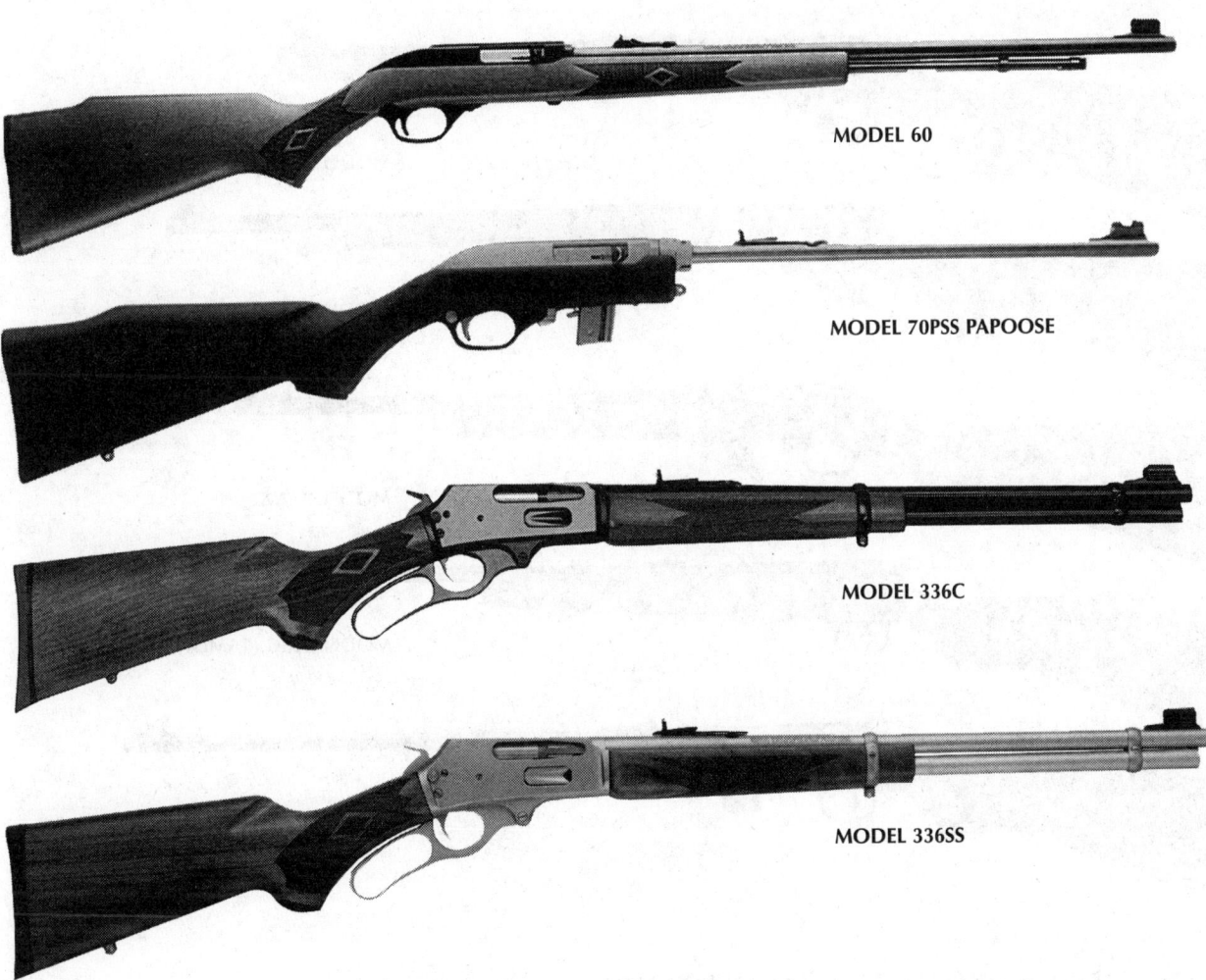

MODEL 60

MODEL 70PSS PAPOOSE

MODEL 336C

MODEL 336SS

RIFLES

MODEL 60

Action: autoloading
Stock: hardwood
Barrel: 19 in.
Sights: open
Weight: 5.5 lbs.
Caliber: .22 LR
Magazine: under-barrel tube,
14 rounds
Features: last shot hold-open device;
stainless, synthetic and laminated
stocked versions available; also
available with camo-finished stock
Standard: **$195**
Camo: **$231**
Stainless: **$247**
Stainless, synthetic: **$269**
Stainless, laminated two-tone: **$312**

MODEL 70 PSS PAPOOSE

Action: autoloading
Stock: synthetic
Barrel: 16 in.
Sights: open
Weight: 3.3 lbs.
Caliber: .22 LR
Magazine: detachable box, 7 rounds
Features: take-down rifle; nickel-plat-
ed swivel studs; floatable, padded
carrying case included
MSRP: **$318**

MODEL 336C

Action: lever
Stock: checkered walnut, pistol grip
Barrel: 20 in.
Sights: open
Weight: 7.0 lbs.
Caliber: .30-30 Win., and .35 Rem.

Magazine: tube, 6 rounds
Features: blued; hammer-block safety;
offset hammer spur for scope use
Model 336C: **$558**
Model 336A, .30-30 only,
birch stock: **$477**
Model 336W, .30-30 only,
gold-plated: **$482**

MODEL 336SS

Action: lever
Stock: checkered walnut, pistol grip
Barrel: 20 in.
Sights: open
Weight: 7.0 lbs.
Caliber: .30-30
Magazine: under-barrel tube, 6 rounds
Features: offset hammer spur for scope
use; Micro-Groove rifling
MSRP: **$692**

Marlin Rifles

MODEL 336Y SPIKEHORN

MODEL 444

MODEL 717M2

MODEL 925C (CAMO)

MODEL 925M

MODEL 336Y SPIKEHORN
Action: lever
Stock: walnut
Barrel: 16.5 in.
Sights: open
Weight: 6.5 lbs.
Caliber: .30-30
Magazine: 5 rounds
Features: pistol grip stock; 12.5-inch pull for small shooters
MSRP: **$566**

MODEL 444
Action: lever
Stock: walnut, pistol grip, fluted comb, checkering
Barrel: 22 in.
Sights: open
Weight: 7.5 lbs.
Caliber: .444 Marlin
Magazine: tube, 5 rounds
Features: blued; hammer-block safety; offset hammer spur for scope use
MSRP: **$654**

MODEL 717M2
Action: autoloading
Stock: hardwood
Barrel: 18 in.
Sights: open
Weight: 5.0 lbs.
Caliber: .17 Mach 2
Magazine: detachable box, 7 rounds
Features: Sportster barrel; last-shot bolt hold-open; manual bolt hold-open; cross-bolt safety; adjustable ramp front sight; receiver grooved for scope mount; Monte Carlo walnut-finshed laminated hardwood stock with pistol grip; 37-inch overall length
MSRP: **$264**

MODEL 925
Action: bolt
Stock: hardwood
Barrel: 22 in.
Sights: open
Weight: 5.5 lbs.
Caliber: .22 LR

Magazine: detachable box, 7 rounds
Features: T-900 Fire Control System; Micro-Groove rifling; can be ordered with scope; also available with Mossy Oak camo stock finish
925: **$223**
925 with scope: **$232**
925C (camo): **$263**

MODEL 925M
Action: bolt
Stock: hardwood
Barrel: 22 in.
Sights: open
Weight: 6.0 lbs.
Caliber: .22 WMR
Magazine: detachable box, 7 rounds
Features: T-900 Fire Control System; Micro-Groove barrel; also available with Mossy Oak camo-finish stock
925M: **$255**
925MC (camo): **$294**

Marlin Rifles

MODEL 981T

MODEL 983T

MODEL 917VSF

MODEL 1894

MODEL 981T

Action: bolt
Stock: synthetic
Barrel: 22 in. **Sights:** open
Weight: 6.0 lbs.
Caliber: .22 L, S, or LR
Magazine: under-barrel tube, 17 rounds
Features: Micro-Groove rifling; T-900 Fire Control System
918T: $225

MODEL 983T

Action: bolt
Stock: synthetic
Barrel: 22 in. **Sights:** open
Weight: 6.0 lbs.
Caliber: .22 WMR
Magazine: under-barrel tube, 12 rounds
Features: T-900 Fire Control System; Micro-Groove rifling; available as Model 983 with walnut stock or laminated stock and stainless barrel
983T: $273
Model 983: $365
Model 983S: $377

MODEL 917V

Action: bolt
Stock: hardwood
Barrel: heavy 22 in.
Sights: none
Weight: 6.0 lbs.
Caliber: .17 HMR
Magazine: detachable box, 7 rounds
Features: T-900 Fire Control System; 1-in. scope mounts provided; also available: 917VS stainless steel with laminated hardwood stock (7 lbs.)
917V: $284
917VS: $425
917 VSF (fluted barrel): $450

MODEL 1894

Action: lever
Stock: checkered American walnut
Barrel: 20 in. **Sights:** open
Weight: 6.0 lbs.
Caliber: .44 Rem. Mag./.44 Special
Magazine: tube, 10 rounds
Features: straight grip stock with Mar-Shield finish
MSRP: $591

MODEL 1894CL

Action: lever
Stock: walnut
Barrel: 22 in.
Sights: open
Weight: 6 lbs.
Caliber: .32-20 Win.
Magazine: under-barrel tube, 6 rounds
Features: Micro-Groove finish barrel; solid top receiver; hammer block safety; half-length tube magazine; Marble adjustable semi-buckhorn rear and carbine front sights; straight-grip stock with cut checkering and hard rubber butt pad; 39.5-inch overall length
MSRP: $836

Marlin Rifles

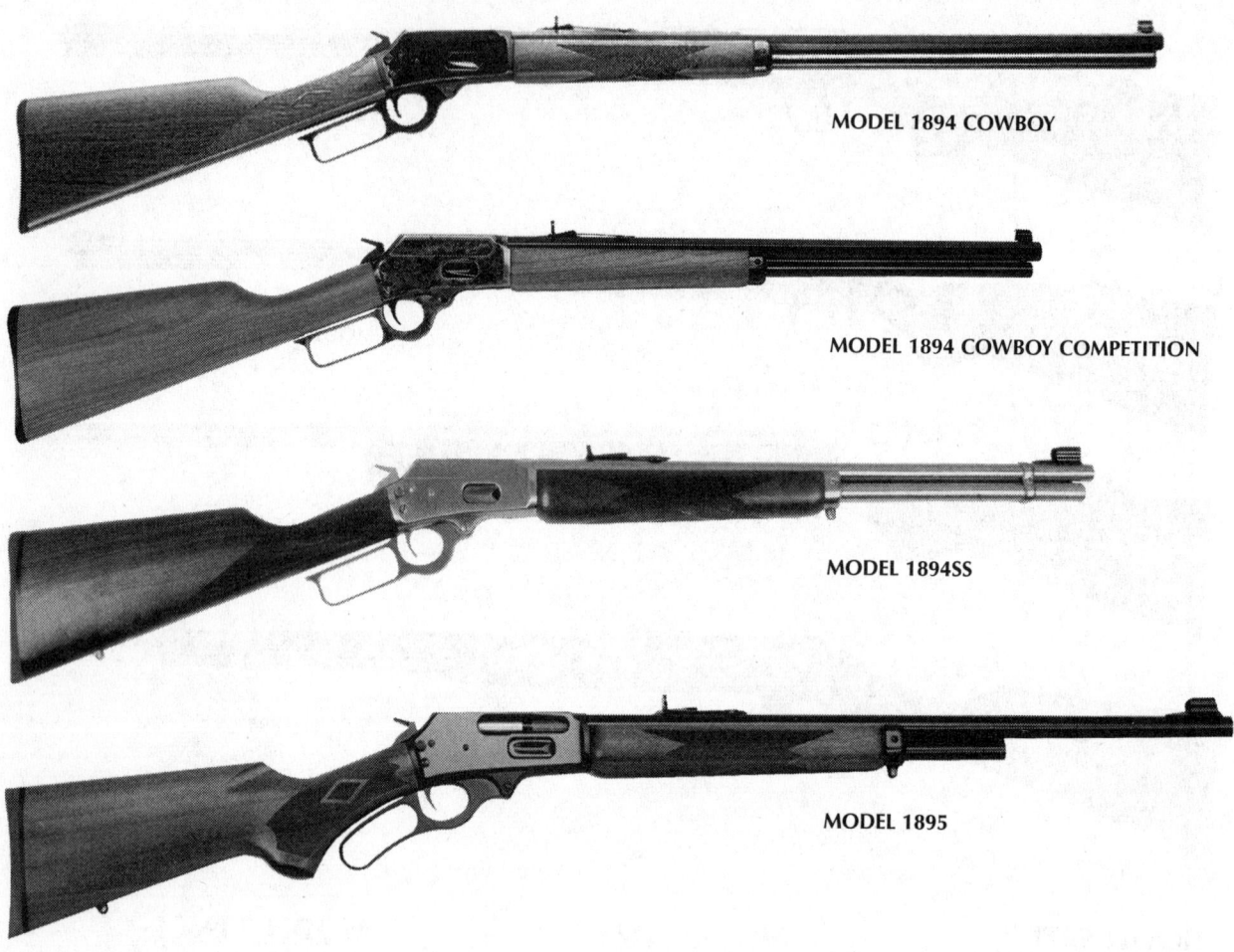

MODEL 1894 COWBOY

MODEL 1894 COWBOY COMPETITION

MODEL 1894SS

MODEL 1895

MODEL 1894 COWBOY

Action: lever
Stock: walnut, straight grip, checkered
Barrel: tapered octagon, 24 in.
Sights: open
Weight: 6.5 lbs.
Caliber: .357 Mag./.38 Special, .44 Mag./.44 Special and .45 Colt
Magazine: tube, 10 rounds
Features: blued finish; hammer-block safety; hard rubber buttplate; Competition model available in .38 Special or .45 Colt with 20 in. barrel
Cowboy in .32 H&R Mag: **$849**
1894 Cowboy: **$872**

MODEL 1894 COWBOY COMPETITION

Action: lever
Stock: walnut
Barrel: 20 in.
Sights: open
Weight: 7.0 lbs.
Caliber: .38 Spl., .45 Long Colt
Magazine: 10 rounds
Features: case-colored receiver
MSRP: **$986**

MODEL 1894SS

Action: lever
Stock: checkered walnut, straight grip
Barrel: 20 in.
Sights: open
Weight: 6.0 lbs.
Caliber: .44 Rem. Mag.
Magazine: under-barrel tube, 10 rounds
Features: Micro-groove rifling
1894C (blued): **$591**
1894 SS: **$716**
1894 CL (in .32/30 with 22 in. bbl., 6-shot): **$836**

MODEL 1895

Action: lever
Stock: checkered walnut, pistol grip
Barrel: 22 in.
Sights: open
Weight: 7.5 lbs.
Caliber: .45-70 Govt.
Magazine: tube, 4 rounds
Features: blued; hammer-block safety, offset hammer spur for scope use; Model 1895G has 18.5 in. barrel and straight grip
1895: **$654**
1895G: **$668**
1895GS in stainless steel: **$805**
1895 Cowboy (26" octagon barrel): **$849**

Marlin Rifles

MODEL 1895M

MODEL 7000

GOLDEN 39A

LITTLE BUCKAROO

MODEL 1895M

Action: lever
Stock: checkered walnut, straight grip
Barrel: Ballard rifled, 18.5 in.
Sights: open
Weight: 7.0 lbs.
Caliber: .450
Magazine: tube, 4 rounds
Features: blued finish; hammer-block safety; offset hammer spur for scope use
MSRP: **$719**

MODEL 7000

Action: autoloading
Stock: synthetic
Barrel: target weight, 28 in.
Sights: none
Weight: 5.3 lbs.
Caliber: .22 LR
Magazine: detachable box, 10 rounds
Features: also available as Model 795

and 795 SS, with sights and lighter barrel (weight: 4.5 lbs.)
7000: **$263**
795: . . . .(add) **$168**
795 SS: . . . .(add) **$247**

GOLDEN 39A

Action: lever
Stock: checkered walnut, pistol grip
Barrel: 24 in.
Sights: open
Weight: 6.5 lbs.
Caliber: .22 LR
Magazine: under-barrel tube, 19 rounds
Features: Micro-Groove rifling, single-screw take-down; swivel studs
MSRP: **$596**

LITTLE BUCKAROO

Action: bolt
Stock: hardwood
Barrel: 16 in.
Sights: open
Weight: 4.3 lbs.
Caliber: .22 S, L or LR
Magazine: none
Features: T-900 Fire Control System; stainless version available
Little Buckaroo (Model 915Y): . **$221**
Stainless (Model 915YS): **$247**

Merkel Rifles

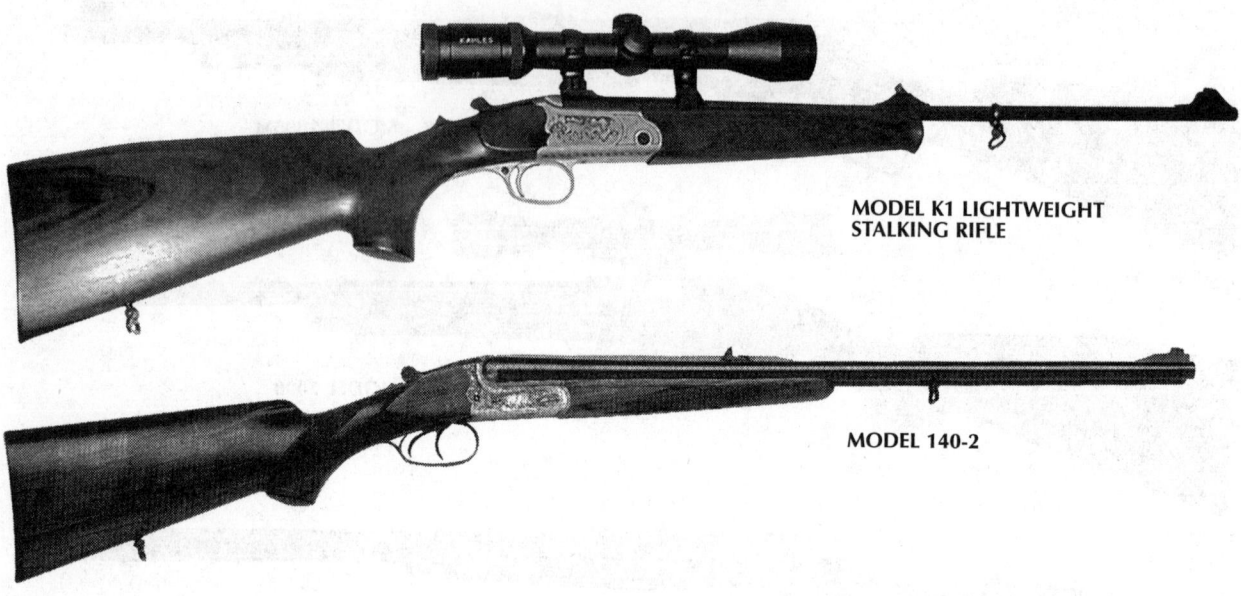

MODEL K1 LIGHTWEIGHT STALKING RIFLE

MODEL 140-2

RIFLES

MODEL K1 LIGHTWEIGHT STALKING RIFLE

Action: hinged breech
Stock: select walnut
Barrel: 24 in.
Sights: open
Weight: 5.6 lbs.
Caliber: .243, .270, 7x57R, 7mm Rem. Mag., .308, .30-06, .300 Win. Mag., 9.3x74R
Magazine: none
Features: single-shot; Franz Jager action; also available: Premium and Hunter grades
MSRP: **$3695**

SAFARI SERIES MODEL 140-2

Action: hinged breech
Stock: select walnut
Barrel: length and contour to order
Sights: open
Weight: 9.0 lbs.
Caliber: .375 H&H, .416 Rigby, .470 N.E.
Magazine: none
Features: Anson & Deely box-lock; double triggers; includes oak and leather luggage case; higher grade available; also Model 141.1, lightweight double in .308, .30-06, 9.3x74R
MSRP: **$10595**

In stormy weather, always keep your rifle barrel pointed down in order to keep water or snow from getting inside the gun.

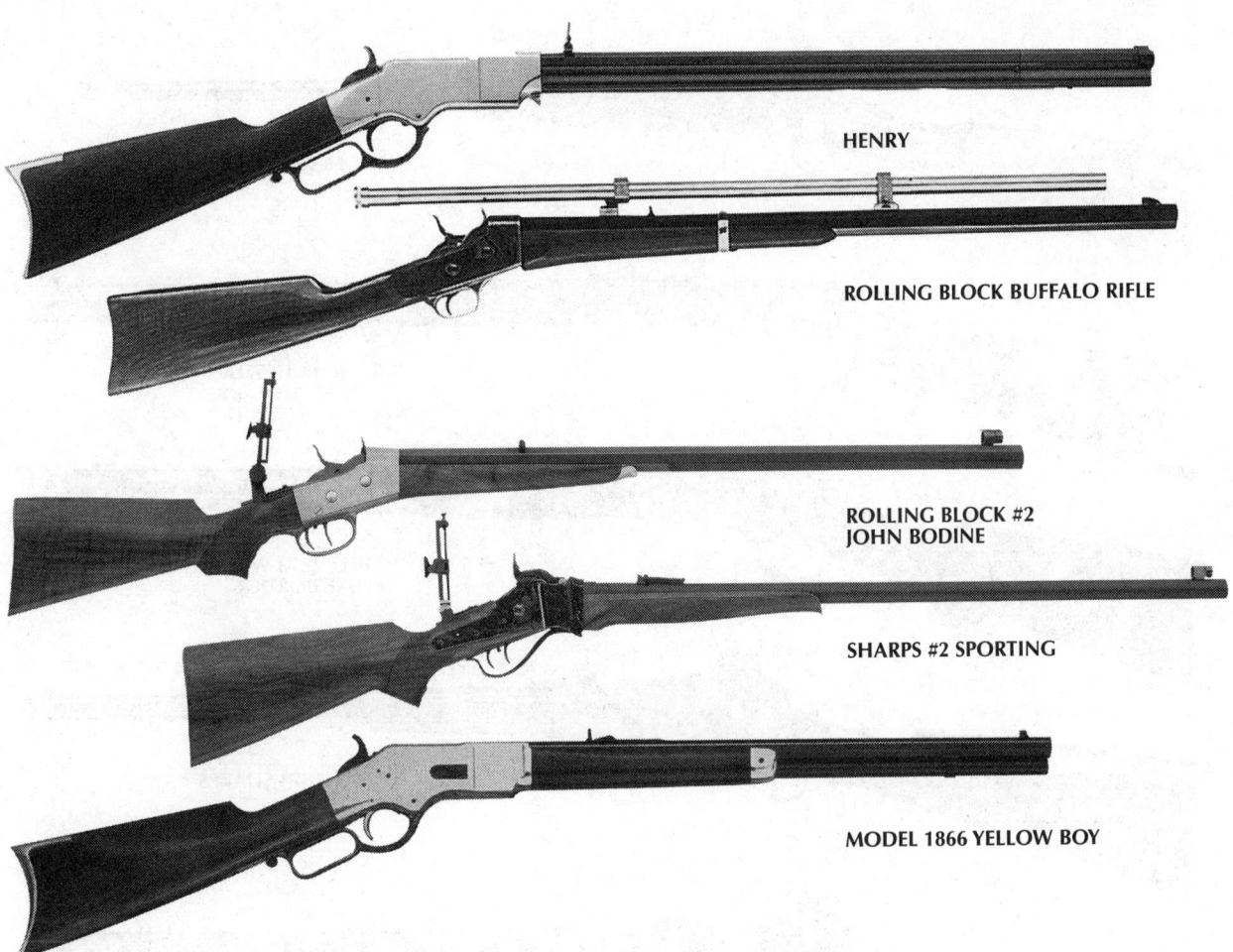

HENRY

ROLLING BLOCK BUFFALO RIFLE

ROLLING BLOCK #2
JOHN BODINE

SHARPS #2 SPORTING

MODEL 1866 YELLOW BOY

HENRY

Action: lever
Stock: walnut, straight grip
Barrel: 24 in.
Sights: open
Weight: 9.0 lbs.
Caliber: .44-40, .45 Colt
Magazine: under-barrel tube, 13 rounds
Features: blued or case-colored receiver
Military Henry: **$1164**
Henry: **$1222**

ROLLING BLOCK
BUFFALO RIFLE

Action: dropping block
Stock: walnut
Barrel: 26 in. or 30 in.
Sights: open
Weight: 9.0 lbs.
Caliber: .45-70
Magazine: none
Features: case-colored receiver;
optional brass telescopic sight; drilled

for Creedmoor sight; also checkered
#2 model with tang and globe sights
MSRP: **$910**

ROLLING BLOCK #2
JOHN BODINE

Action: dropping block
Stock: walnut
Barrel: 30 in.
Sights: adjustable tang
Weight: 12.0 lbs.
Caliber: .45-70
Magazine: none
Features: double set triggers;
nickel-finish breech
MSRP: **$1703**

MODEL SHARPS #2
SPORTING

Action: dropping block
Stock: walnut
Barrel: 30 in.
Sights: target

Weight: 10.0 lbs.
Caliber: .45-70
Magazine: none
Features: also #2 Silhouette
Creedmoor and Quigley
(with 34 in. barrel)
Sporting: **$1689**
Creedmoor: **$1689**
Silhouette: **$1689**
Quigley: **$1774**

MODEL 1866 YELLOW BOY

Action: lever
Stock: walnut, straight grip
Barrel: octagon, 20 in.
Sights: open
Weight: 7.5 lbs.
Caliber: .38 Special, .44-40, .45 Colt
Magazine: under-barrel tube, 10
rounds
Features: also available: Yellow Boy
with 24 in. barrel (8.3 lbs.)
MSRP: **$915**

RIFLES

Navy Arms Rifles

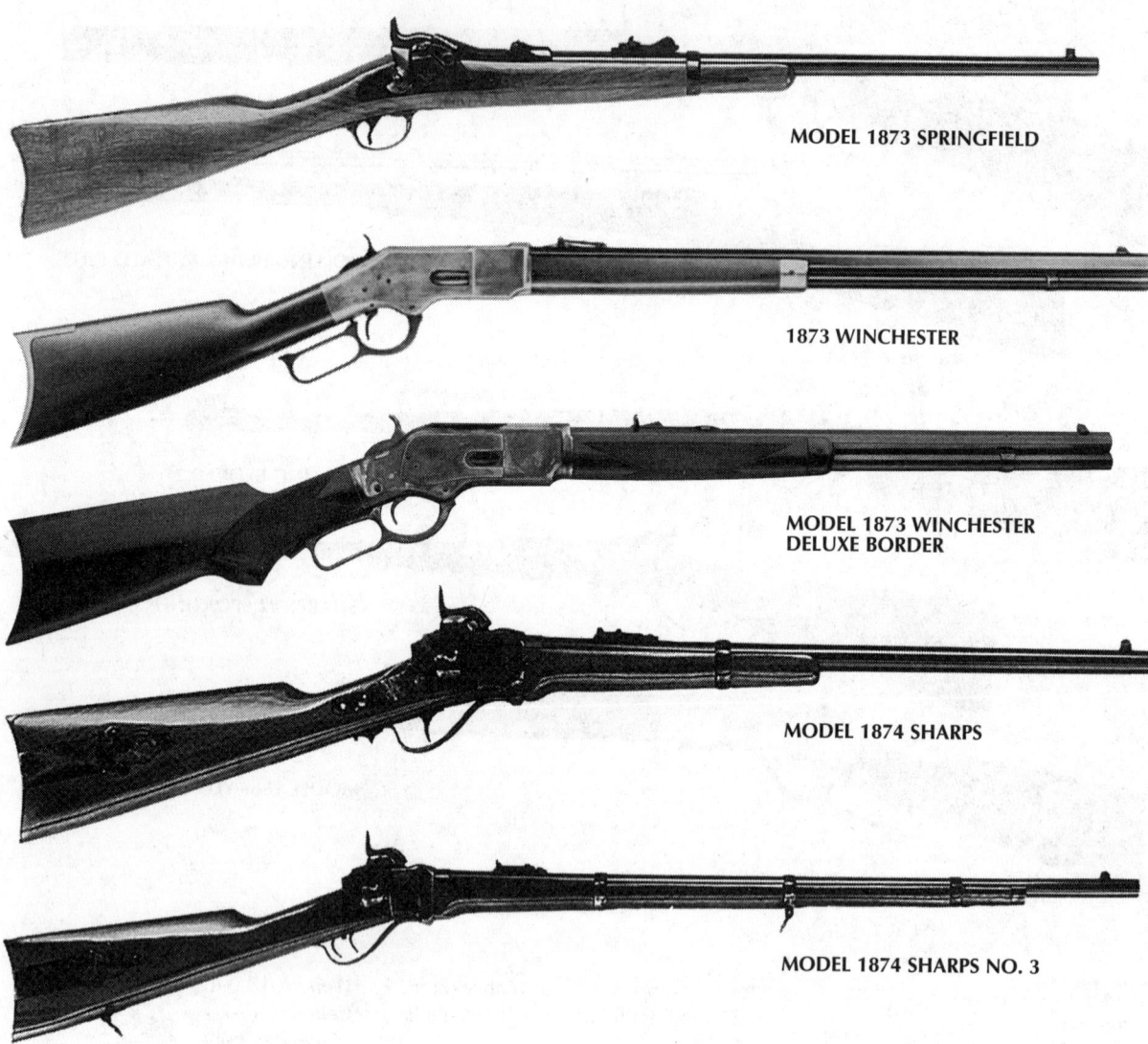

MODEL 1873 SPRINGFIELD

1873 WINCHESTER

MODEL 1873 WINCHESTER DELUXE BORDER

MODEL 1874 SHARPS

MODEL 1874 SHARPS NO. 3

MODEL 1873 SPRINGFIELD

Action: dropping block
Stock: walnut
Barrel: 22 in.
Sights: open
Weight: 7.0 lbs.
Caliber: .45-70
Magazine: none
Features: "Trapdoor" replica; saddle bar with ring
MSRP: **$1475**

MODEL 1873 WINCHESTER

Action: lever
Stock: walnut, straight grip
Barrel: 24 in.
Sights: open
Weight: 8.3 lbs.
Caliber: .357 Mag., .44-40, .45 Colt
Magazine: under-barrel tube, 13 rounds
Features: case-colored receiver; also: Carbine, Border, Deluxe (checkered) Border and Sporting models
1873 Winchester: **$1047**
Carbine: **$1025**
Border Model: **$1047**
Deluxe Border Model: **$1183**
Sporting Rifle: **$1183**

MODEL 1874 SHARPS

Action: dropping block
Stock: walnut
Barrel: 22 in.
Sights: open
Weight: 7.8 lbs.
Caliber: .45-70
Magazine: none
Features: also: No. 3 Long Range Sharps with double set triggers, 34 in. barrel (10.9 lbs.) and Buffalo Rifle with double set triggers, 28 in. octagon barrel (10.6 lbs.)
Carbine: **$1210**
No. 3: **$2205**

New England Firearms

HARDWOOD HANDI-RIFLE

SYNTHETIC HANDI-RIFLE

SPORTSTER 17 HMR

SURVIVOR

HANDI-RIFLE
Action: hinged breech
Stock: Monte Carlo synthetic or hardwood
Barrel: 22 in. or 26 in.
Sights: none
Weight: 7.0 lbs.
Caliber: .223, .22-250, .243, .270, .30-06
Magazine: none
Features: offset hammer; open-sight version of Handi-Rifle in .22 Hornet, .30-30, .357 Mag., .44 Mag., .45-70 Govt.;Youth models in .223, .243 and 7mm-08
Handi-Rifle: **$296**
With hardwood stock: **$284**
Synthetic stainless: **$354**
Youth: **$284**

SPORTSTER
17 HMR & 17 MACH2
Action: hinged breech
Stock: synthetic
Barrel: heavy varmint, 22 in.
Sights: none
Weight: 6.0 lbs.
Caliber: .17 Hornady Magnum Rimfire, .17 MACH 2
Magazine: none
Features: Monte Carlo stock; sling swivel studs; recoil pad; Sportster Youth available with 20 in. barrel (5.5 lbs.), in .22 LR or .22 WMR
Youth: **$157**
Sportster: **$183-188**

SURVIVOR
Action: hinged breech
Stock: synthetic
Barrel: 22 in. bull
Sights: open
Weight: 6.0 lbs.
Caliber: .223 & .308
Magazine: none
Features: single-shot; recoil pad; hollow synthetic stock with storage compartment; thumbscrew take down
MSRP: **$296**

New Ultra Light Arms

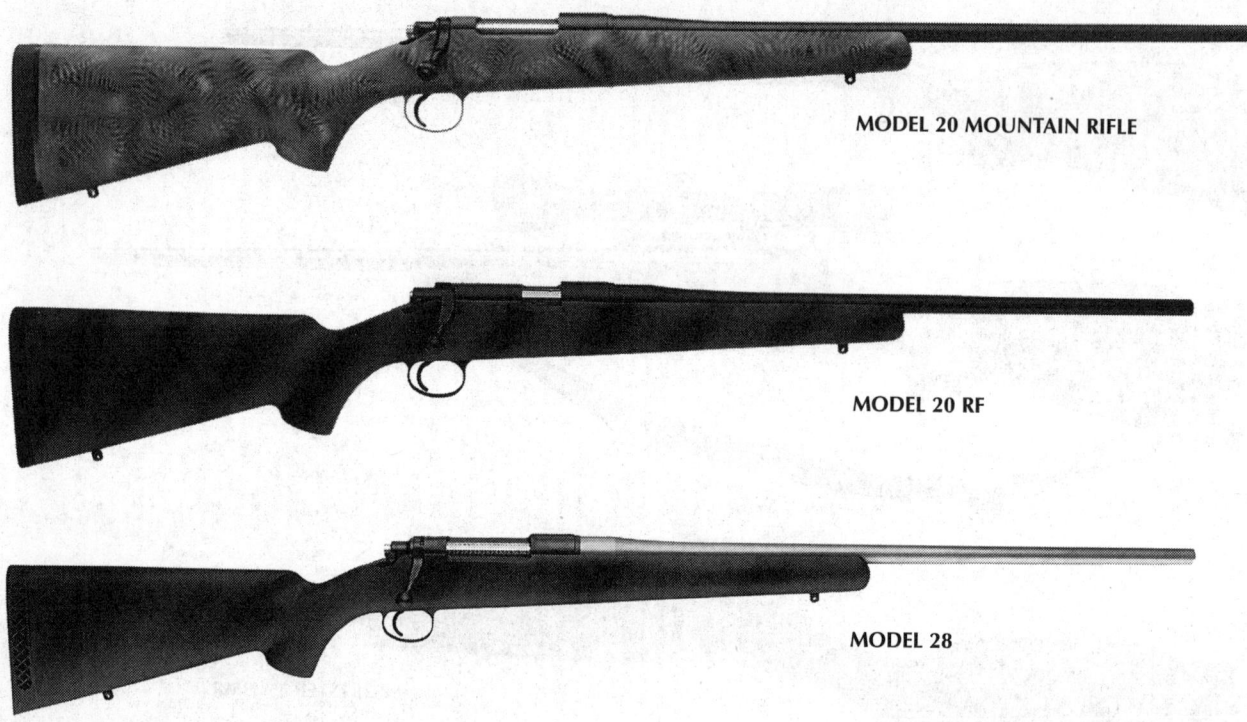

MODEL 20 MOUNTAIN RIFLE

MODEL 20 RF

MODEL 28

MODEL 20 MOUNTAIN RIFLE

Action: bolt
Stock: Kevlar/graphite composite
Barrel: 22 in.
Sights: none
Weight: 4.75 lbs.
Caliber: short action: 6mm, .17, .22 Hornet, .222, .222 Rem. Mag., .22-250, .223, .243, .250-3000 Savage, .257, .257 Ackley, 7x57, 7x57 Ackley, 7mm-08, .284, .300 Savage, .308, .358
Magazine: box, 4, 5 or 6 rounds
Features: two-position safety; choice of 7 or more stock colors; available in left-hand
Mountain Rifle: $2800
   left-hand: $2900

MODEL 20 RF

Action: bolt
Stock: composite
Barrel: Douglas Premium #1 Contour, 22 in.
Sights: none
Weight: 5.25 lbs.
Caliber: .22 LR
Magazine: none (or detachable box, 5 rounds)
Features: single-shot or repeater; drilled and tapped for scope; recoil pad, sling swivels; fully adjustable Timney trigger; 3-position safety; color options
Single-shot: $1100
Repeater: $1150

MODEL 24 AND 28

Action: bolt
Stock: Kevlar composite
Barrel: 22 in.
Sights: none
Weight: 5.25 lbs.
Caliber: long action: .270, .30-06, .25-06, .280, .280 Ackley, .338-06, .35 Whelen; Magnum (Model 28): .264, 7mm, .300, .338, .300 WSM, .270 WSM, 7mm WSM; Model 40: (magnum) .300 Wby. and .416 Rigby
Magazine: box, 4 rounds
Features: Model 28 has 24 in. bbl. and weighs 5.5 lbs.; Model 40 has 24 in. bbl. (6.5 lbs.); all available in left-hand versions
Model 24: $2900
Model 24, left-hand: $3000
Model 28 or Model 40: $3200
Model 28 or Model 40,
   left-hand: $3300

Keep ammunition out of your cleaning area. Lubes and cleaners, especially aerosols, can work their way into shells around the primer and bullet, damaging the charge.

Nosler

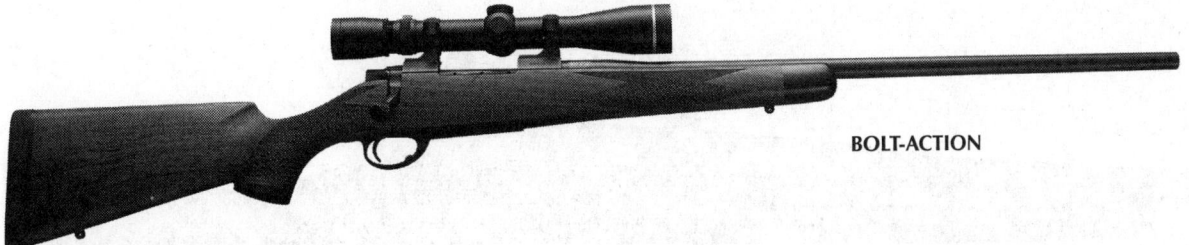

BOLT-ACTION

NOSLER BOLT-ACTION
Action: bolt
Stock: Turkish walnut
Barrel: 24 in.
Sights: optical

Weight: 7.75 lbs.
Caliber: .300 WSM
Magazine: internal box, 3-rounds
Features: hand-lapped, match-grade
Wiseman barrel; three-position safety;

Timney trigger; Leupold VX-III 2.5-
8x36 scope serial-numbered to the
rifle; production limited to 500 units
MSRP: **$3995**

Pedersoli Replica Rifles

KODIAK MARK IV DOUBLE

ROLLING BLOCK TARGET

SHARPS 1874 CAVALRY

KODIAK MARK IV DOUBLE
Action: hinged breech
Stock: walnut
Barrel: 22 in. and 24 in.
Sights: open
Weight: 8.2 lbs.
Caliber: .45-70, 9.3x74R, 8x57JSR
Magazine: none
Features: .45-70 weighs 8.2 lbs.; also
available: Kodiak Mark IV with inter-
changeable 20-gauge barrel
45-70: **$3250**
8x57, 9.3x74: **$3250**
Kodiak Mark IV: **$4925**

ROLLING BLOCK TARGET
Action: dropping block
Stock: walnut
Barrel: octagon, 30 in.
Sights: target
Weight: 9.5 lbs.
Caliber: .45-70 and .357 (10 lbs.)
Magazine: none
Features: Creedmoor sights; also avail-
able: Buffalo, Big Game, Sporting, Baby
Carbine, Custer, Long Range Creedmoor
MSRP: **$995**

SHARPS 1874 CAVALRY & INFANTRY MODEL
Action: dropping block
Stock: walnut
Barrel: 22 in.

Sights: open
Weight: 8.4 lbs.
Caliber: .45-70
Magazine: none
Features: also available: 1874 Infantry
(set trigger, 30 in. bbl.), 1874 Sporting
(.40-65 or .45-70, set trigger, 32 in.
oct. bbl.), 1874 Long Range (.45-70
and .45-90, .45-120, 34 in. half oct.
bbl., target sights)
Cavalry: **$1200**
Infantry (one trigger): **$1300**
Infantry (two triggers): **$1375**
Sporting: **$1220**
Long Range: **$1695**
Long Range Big Bore: **$1750**

RIFLES

PGW Defense Technology

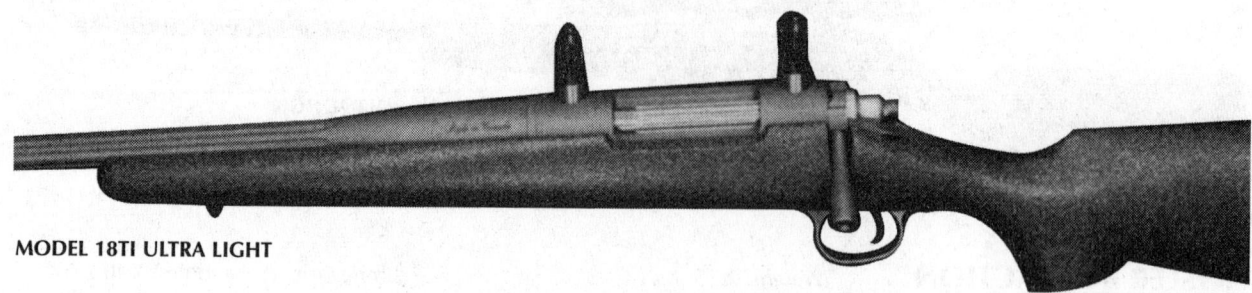

MODEL 18TI ULTRA LIGHT

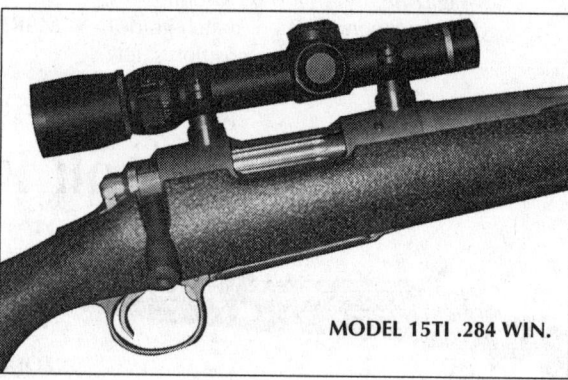

MODEL 15TI .284 WIN.

MODEL 15TI ULTRA LIGHT
Action: bolt
Stock: composite
Barrel: 22 in.
Sights: none
Weight: 5.0 lbs.
Caliber: most short-action calibers
Magazine: box, 5 rounds
Features: Rem. 700 short-action, custom alloy scope mounts; new firing pin and bolt shroud tuned; also: Model 18Ti with long 700 action
Model 15Ti: $2800
Model 18Ti: $2800

TIMBERWOLF
Action: bolt
Stock: McMillan fiberglass
Barrel: fluted, match grade
Sights: none
Caliber: .338 Lapua
Magazine: 5 rounds
Features: stainless receiver; adjustable trigger; 3-position safety, titanium rail with guide rib
Timberwolf: $5550
Also available: in .408 . . . . . . $6300
Coyote in 7.62 (5 or 10-shot
   magazine): $3700
LRT .50 caliber Take-Down: . . $4500
LRT-2 in .338 or .408: . . . $2975-3700

You cannot shoot well while inhaling or exhaling; it's imperative to hold your breath while squeezing the trigger. Take a deep breath, let part of it out and then commence your trigger squeeze. This is not so easy when you've just climbed a steep slope and a big buck bursts from cover, so it is an act that must be practiced until it becomes second nature.

Purdey

DOUBLE BARREL RIFLE
.577 NITRO

SINGLE TRIGGER

a.

b.

DOUBLE TRIGGER

c.

SPRING BLADED FRONT
TRIGGER

PURDEY'S OWN LARGE CALIBRE ACTION

PURDEY "RAIL MOUNT" SYSTEM
WITH INTEGRAL RECOIL BAR.

RIFLES

DOUBLE BARREL RIFLE .577 NITRO

Purdey's double-barrel Express rifles are built to customer specifications on actions sized to each particular cartridge. Standard chamberings include .375 H&H Magnum and .470, .577 and .600 Nitro Express. The Purdey side-by-side action patented in 1880 is still made now with only very minor changes. The action mechanism, designed by Frederick Beesley, retains a portion of the energy in the mainsprings to facilitate the opening of the gun.

The over-under is derived from the Woodward, patented in 1913. The action blocks for all guns are cut from certified forgings, for consistency of grain

throughout, and are so fitted to the barrels as to give an absolute joint. The actioner then fits the fore-part, the locks, the strikers and the safety work before finally detonating the action.

A – SINGLE TRIGGER

The Purdey single trigger works both by inertia and mechanically. It is simple, effective and fast. The firing sequence is fixed, therefore no barrel selection is possible.

B & C – DOUBLE TRIGGERS

The standard double triggers (B) can be augmented with an articulated front trigger (C). This device alleviates damage to

the back of the trigger finger on discharge.

Purdey makes its own dedicated actions for bolt rifles in the following calibers: .375 H&H, .416/450 Rigby or other, .500 and .505 Gibbs.

The action length is suited to cartridge length in each caliber. Mauser Square Bridge and Mauser '98 actions are available.

RAIL MOUNT SYSTEM

This is Purdey's own system for big bolt rifles. It is very secure and facilitates fast on/off. Rings and mounts are all made with an integral recoil bar from a single piece of steel. This system is recommended for Purdey actions and Mauser Square Bridge actions.

Remington Arms Rifles

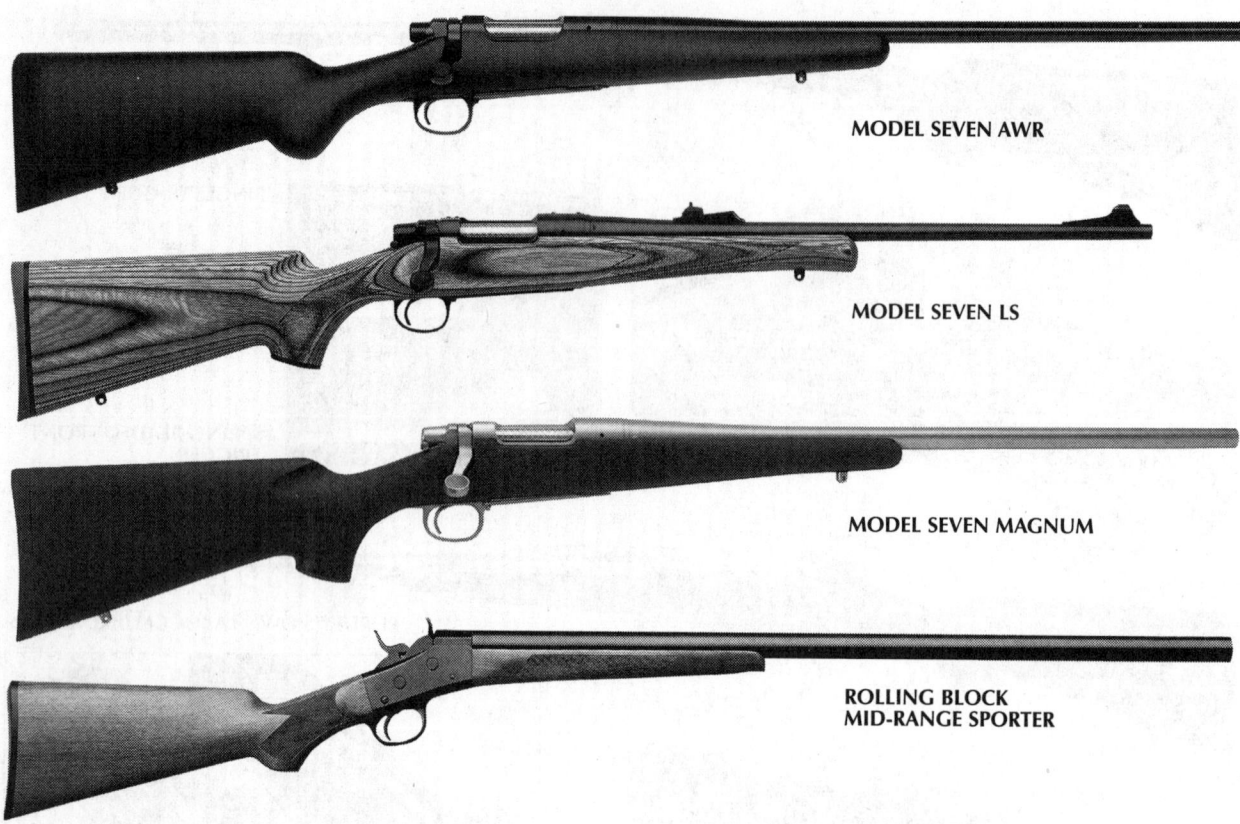

MODEL SEVEN AWR

MODEL SEVEN LS

MODEL SEVEN MAGNUM

ROLLING BLOCK
MID-RANGE SPORTER

MODEL SEVEN AWR (CUSTOM SHOP)

Action: bolt
Stock: lightweight composite
Barrel: stainless, 22 in.
Sights: none
Weight: 6.0 lbs.
Caliber: 6.8 Rem. SPC, 7mm SAUM, .300 SAUM
Magazine: box, 3 rounds
Features: Alaska Wilderness Rifle has lightweight composite stock; also MS wood, full-length stock (6.5 lbs.); Model Seven KS in standard short-action calibers has 20 in. barrel
KS (6 calibers): **$1314**
MS (12 calbiers): **$1332**
Model Seven AWR: **$1546**

MODEL SEVEN LS

Action: bolt
Stock: synthetic
Barrel: 20 in.
Sights: open
Weight: 6.5 lbs.
Caliber: .223, .243, .260, 7mm-08, .308

Magazine: box, 4 or 5 rounds
Features: synthetic stock with stainless barrel, laminate with satin finished carbon steel; youth model with short hardwood stock
LS: **$761**
LS Magnum (.300 & 7mm SAUM): **$801**
Youth (.260 Rem. only): **$580**
Stainless synthetic: **$789**
Model Seven Youth (synthetic in .223, .243, 7mm-08): **$580**

MODEL SEVEN MAGNUM

Action: bolt
Stock: synthetic or laminate
Barrel: stainless or blued, 22 in.
Sights: open
Weight: 7.25 lbs.
Caliber: 7mm SAUM, .300 SAUM
Magazine: box, 3 rounds
Features: also laminated stock versions with chrome-moly steel
LS laminated: **$801**
SS synthetic: **$829**

ROLLING BLOCK MID-RANGE SPORTER

Action: dropping block
Stock: walnut
Barrel: heavy 30 in. round barrel
Sights: Buckhorn rear, blade front
Weight: 8.75 lbs.
Caliber: .45-70
Magazine: none
Features: single set trigger
Mid-Range Sporter: **$1450**
Rolling Block Silhouette: **$1560**

XR-100 RANGEMASTER

Action: bolt
Stock: laminated thumb-hole
Barrel: 26 in.
Sights: none
Weight: 9.2 lbs.
Caliber: .204, .223, .22-250
Magazine: none
Features: Varmint-contour heavy chrome-moly barrel; 40-XB target trigger; gray laminate thumbhole stock
MSRP: **$879**

Remington Arms Rifles

MODEL 40-XBBR KS

MODEL 40-XB TACTICAL

MODEL 504

MODEL 552 SPEEDMASTER

MODEL 40-X TARGET

Action: bolt
Stock: target, benchrest or tactical
Barrel: 24 in. or 27 in.
Sights: none
Weight: 10.25-11.25 lbs.
Caliber: 18 popular standard and magnum calibers
Magazine: box, 3 or 5 rounds
Features: rimfire and single-shot versions available; walnut, laminated and composite stocks; forend rail, match trigger
40-X: $1636-2108
Left-hand: $1709-2044

MODEL 40-XBBR KS

Action: bolt
Stock: fiberglass
Barrel: 24 in.
Sights: none
Weight: 9.75 lbs.
Caliber: .22 LR
Magazine: single shot

Features: benchrest with stainless barrel; Aramid-fiber reinforced Remington green stock
MSRP: $1894

MODEL 40-XB TACTICAL

Action: bolt
Stock: black with green fiberglass
Barrel: 27.25 in.
Sights: none
Weight: 10.25 lbs.
Caliber: .308 Win.
Magazine: hinged floorplate, 5 rounds
Features: built to order
MSRP: $2108

MODEL 504

Action: bolt
Stock: checkered walnut
Barrel: 20 inches, button-rifled 1:14½
Sights: none (drilled and tapped for scope mounts)
Weight: 6.0 lbs.
Caliber: .22 LR, .17 MACH 2

Magazine: detachable box, 6 rounds
Features: fully adjustable trigger; nickel-plated bolt; removable barrel with "match" chamber
MSRP: $710
Also available:
504-T LSHB .22 LR/
.17 HMR: $799-825
504 Custom "C" Grade .22 LR: $1665

MODEL 552 BDL DELUXE SPEEDMASTER

Action: autoloading
Stock: walnut
Barrel: 21 in.
Sights: Big Game
Weight: 5.75 lbs.
Caliber: .22 S, .22 L, .22 LR
Magazine: under-barrel tube, 15-20 rounds
Features: classic autoloader made 1966 to date
MSRP: $453

Remington Arms Rifles

MODEL 572 FIELDMASTER

MODEL 597

MODEL 673

MODEL 700 AFRICAN BIG GAME

MODEL 572 BDL DELUXE FIELDMASTER

Action: pump
Stock: walnut
Barrel: 21 in.
Sights: Big Game
Weight: 5.5 lbs.
Caliber: .22 S, .22 L, .22 LR
Magazine: under-barrel tube, 15-20 rounds
Features: grooved receiver for scope mounts
MSRP: **$467**

MODEL 597

Action: autoloading
Stock: synthetic or laminated
Barrel: 20 in.
Sights: Big Game
Weight: 5.5-6.5 lbs.
Caliber: .22 LR, .22 WMR, .17 HMR

Magazine: detachable box, 10 rounds (8 in magnums)
Features: magnum version in .22 WMR and .17 HMR (both 6 lbs.); also: heavy-barrel model

Model 597:	**$156**
stainless:	**$240**
stainless laminated:	**$295**
22 WMR:	**$351**
magnum (.17 HMR):	**$377**
heavy-barrel:	**$288**
heavy-barrel magnum: . .	**$428-455**

MODEL 673

Action: bolt
Stock: laminated
Barrel: 22 in.
Sights: open
Weight: 7.5 lbs.
Caliber: .350 Rem. Mag., .308 Win., 6.5 Rem. Mag., 300 SAUM

Magazine: 3 + 1
Features: vent rib, Model Seven action
MSRP: **$859**

MODEL 700 AFRICAN BIG GAME

Action: bolt
Stock: laminated
Barrel: 26 in.
Sights: open
Weight: 9.5 lbs.
Caliber: .375 H&H, .375 RUM, .458 Win., .416 Rem.
Magazine: box, 3 rounds
Features: barrel-mounted front swivel
MSRP: **$1726**

Remington Arms Rifles

MODEL 700 AFRICAN
PLAINS RIFLE

MODEL 700 BDL

MODEL 700 CDL

MODEL 700 CLASSIC

MODEL 700 AFRICAN PLAINS RIFLE

Action: bolt
Stock: laminated
Barrel: 26 in.
Sights: none
Weight: 7.75 lbs.
Caliber: 10 offerings from 7mm Rem. Mag. to .375 RUM
Magazine: box, 3 rounds
Features: epoxy bedded action; machined steel trigger and floor plate.
MSRP: **$1716**

MODEL 700 BDL CUSTOM DELUXE

Action: bolt
Stock: walnut
Barrel: 22-26 in.
Sights: open
Weight: 7.25-7.5 lbs.

Caliber: popular standard calibers from .17 Rem. to .300 RUM
Magazine: box, 3 or 5 rounds
Features: hinged floorplate; sling swivel studs; hooded ramp front & adjustable rear sights
BDL: **$716**
BDL Magnum: **$743**
BDL Ultra-Mags: **$743**

MODEL 700 CDL

Action: bolt
Stock: walnut
Barrel: 24 in. (standard) and 26 in. (magnum, Ultra Mag)
Sights: none (drilled and tapped for scope mounts)
Weight: 7.5 lbs.
Caliber: .243, .25-06 Rem., .35 Whelen, .270, 7mm-08, 7mm Rem.

Mag., 7mm Ultra Mag, .30-06, .300 Win. Mag. .300 Ultra Mag
Magazine: box, 4 rounds (3 in magnums, Ultra Mags)
Features: fully adjustable trigger
Standard: **$743**
Ultra Mag: **$769**
Mag & Ultra Mag, lefthand (6 calibers): **$769-796**

MODEL 700 CLASSIC

Action: bolt
Stock: walnut
Barrel: 24 in.
Sights: none
Weight: 7.25 lbs.
Caliber: .308 Win.
Magazine: box, 5 rounds
Features: one-year run per caliber
MSRP: **$716**

Remington Arms Rifles

MODEL 700 CUSTOM C GRADE

MODEL 700 KS MOUNTAIN RIFLE

MODEL 700 LV SF

MODEL 700 SPS

MODEL 700 CUSTOM C GRADE

Action: bolt
Stock: fancy American walnut
Barrel: 24 in. (Ultra Mag 26 in.)
Sights: none
Weight: 7.5 lbs.
Caliber: any popular standard or magnum chambering
Magazine: 3-5 rounds
Features: some custom-shop options available
MSRP: **$1733**

MODEL 700 CUSTOM KS MOUNTAIN RIFLE

Action: bolt
Stock: lightweight composite black matte
Barrel: 24 or 26 in., blued or stainless
Sights: none
Weight: 6.5-7.0 lbs. (magnums)
Caliber: 13 choices from .270 to .375 RUM
Magazine: box, 3 or 4 rounds

Standard: **$1314**
Stainless: **$1500**
Left-hand: **$1393-1580**

MODEL 700 LIGHT VARMINT (LV SF)

Action: bolt
Stock: synthetic
Barrel: 22 in., stainless, fluted
Sights: none (drilled and tapped for scope mounts)
Weight: 6.7 lbs.
Caliber: .17 Rem., .204 Ruger, .221 Fireball, .22-250, .223
Magazine: box, 4 or 5 rounds
Features: fully adjustable trigger
MSRP: **$952**

MODEL 700 MOUNTAIN RIFLE DM

Action: bolt
Stock: walnut or laminate
Barrel: 22 in.
Sights: none
Weight: 6.5 lbs.

Caliber: .260, .270, 7mm-08, .280, .30-06
Magazine: detachable box, 4 rounds
Features: also LSS with laminated stock, stainless steel
Mountain DM: **$783**
LSS: **$833**

MODEL 700 SPS

Action: bolt
Stock: synthetic
Barrel: 24 in. or 26 in.
Sights: none
Weight: 7.25-7.5 lbs.
Caliber: .204 Ruger to .300 Ultra Mag
Magazine: detachable box, 3-5 rounds
Features: also available in youth models with 20- and 22-inch barrels; chrome-moly or stainless, sporter
MSRP: . . . . from **$520**

MODEL 700 XCR

MODEL 710

MODEL 7400

MODEL 7600

MODEL 700 TITANIUM

Action: bolt
Stock: synthetic
Barrel: stainless 22 in. (24 in. SAUM)
Sights: none
Weight: 5.25-6.25 lbs.
Caliber: .260, .270, 7mm-08, .308, .30-06, 7mm SAUM, .300 SAUM
Magazine: box, 2-4 rounds
Features: Titanium receiver; fluted bolt; skeleton handle; RC recoil pad
Titanium: **$1319**
Magnum: **$1359**

MODEL 700 VSF TARGET

Action: bolt
Stock: composite
Barrel: heavy, 26 in.
Sights: none
Weight: 9.5 lbs.
Caliber: .223, .22-250, .243, .308
Magazine: box, 5 rounds
Features: fluted barrel, stock with beavertail forend, tactical style dual front swivel studs for bi-pod; VSSF II also available in .204 Ruger and .220 Swift
VSF (desert tan): **$965**
VSSF II: **$1059**
VLS (laminate): **$785**

MODEL 700 XCR

Action: bolt
Stock: synthetic
Barrel: 24 in. or 26 in.
Sights: none
Weight: 7.5 lbs.
Caliber: 11 chamberings, from .270 to .375 Ultra Mag
Magazine: internal box, 3-5 rounds
Features: stainless barreled action; TriNyte corrosion control coating; Hogue grip panels; stock finish is Realtree Hardwoods Gray HD; R3 recoil pad
MSRP: **$993**

MODEL 710

Action: bolt
Stock: synthetic
Barrel: 22 in. or 24 in.   *Sights:* none
Weight: 7.3 lbs.
Caliber: .270, .30-06, 7mm Rem. Mag., .300 Win. Mag.
Magazine: detachable box, 3 or 4 rounds
Features: steel receiver; 60° bolt throw; includes mounted 3-9x40 Bushnell scope
MSRP: **$426**

MODEL 7400

Action: autoloading
Stock: walnut or synthetic
Barrel: 22 in.
Sights: open
Weight: 7.5 lbs.
Caliber: .243, .270, .308, .30-06
Magazine: detachable box, 4 rounds
Features: also 7400 carbine with 18 in. barrel (7.25 lbs.)
Synthetic: **$567**
Walnut: **$671**

MODEL 7600

Action: pump
Stock: walnut or synthetic
Barrel: 22 in.
Sights: open
Weight: 7.5 lbs.
Caliber: .243, .270, .308, .30-06
Magazine: detachable box, 4 rounds
Features: also 7600 carbine with 18 in. barrel (7.25 lbs.)
Synthetic: **$531**
Walnut: **$635**

Rifles, Inc.

CLASSIC

LIGHTWEIGHT STRATA STAINLESS

MASTER SERIES

SAFARI MODEL

CLASSIC
Action: bolt
Stock: laminated fiberglass
Barrel: stainless steel, match grade 24-26 in.
Sights: none
Weight: 6.5 lbs.
Caliber: all popular chamberings up to .375 H&H
Magazine: box, 3 or 5 rounds
Features: Winchester 70 or Rem. 700 action; lapped bolt; pillar glass bedded stock; adjustable trigger; hinged floorplate; also 27 in. fluted barrel, synthetic stock in .300 Rem. UM
MSRP: **$2000**

LIGHTWEIGHT STRATA STAINLESS
Action: bolt
Stock: laminated with textured epoxy
Barrel: stainless match grade 22-25 in.
Sights: none
Weight: 5.0 lbs.
Caliber: all popular chamberings up to .375 H&H
Magazine: box, 3 or 5 rounds
Features: stainless Rem. action, fluted bolt and hollowed-handle; pillar glass bedded stock; stainless metal finish; blind or hinged floorplate; custom Protektor pad; also Lightweight 70 (5.75 lbs.); Lightweight Titanium Strata
Lightweight Strata:. **$2350**
Lightweight 70: **$2250**
Titanium Strata:. **$2900**

MASTER SERIES
Action: bolt
Stock: laminated fiberglass
Barrel: match grade, 24-27 in.
Sights: none
Weight: 7.75 lbs.
Caliber: all popular chamberings up to .300 Rem. Ultra Mag.
Magazine: box, 3 rounds
Features: Remington 700 action
MSRP: **$2500**

SAFARI MODEL
Action: bolt
Stock: laminated fiberglass
Barrel: stainless match grade 23-25 in.
Sights: optional Express
Weight: 8.5 lbs.
Caliber: all popular chamberings
Magazine: box, 3 or 5 rounds, optional drop box
Features: Win. Model 70 action; drilled and tapped for 8-40 screws; stainless Quiet Slimbrake; stainless or black Teflon finish; adjustable trigger; hinged floor-plate; barrel band optional
MSRP: **$2700**

Rogue Rifle Company

CHIPMUNK

CHIPMUNK
Action: bolt
Stock: walnut, laminated black, brown or camo
Barrel: 16 in.
Sights: target
Weight: 2.5 lbs.
Caliber: Sporting rifle in .17 HMR and .17 MACH 2; Target model in .22, .22 LR, .22 WMR
Magazine: none
Features: single-shot; manual-cocking action; receiver-mounted rear sights; Target model weighs 5 lbs. and comes with competition-style receiver sight and globe front and adjustable trigger, extendable buttplate and front rail

Standard:. **$140-200**
Stainless:. **$160-220**
Bull barrel:. **$175-220**
Bull barrel/stainless: **$195-240**
Target with options:. **$350**

Rossi Rifles

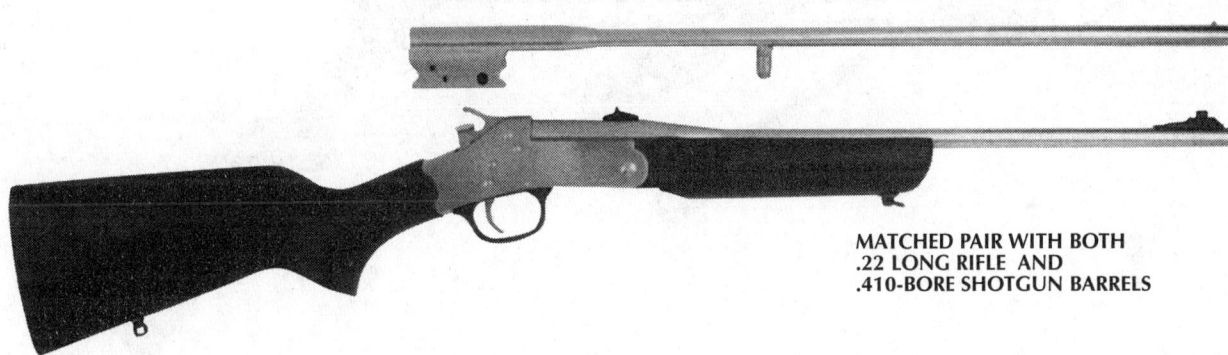

MATCHED PAIR WITH BOTH
.22 LONG RIFLE AND
.410-BORE SHOTGUN BARRELS

CENTERFIRE MATCHED PAIR
Action: hinged breech
Stock: hardwood
Barrel: 23 in. rifle or 28 in. shotgun
Sights: open
Weight: 5.0-6.0 lbs.
Caliber: 12 or 20 ga with .223 Rem., .243 Rem., .243 Win., .308, .30-06, .270 and .22-250 (Youth only)
Magazine: none
Features: carry case and sling included; adjustable sights
MSRP: **$272**

Hunters who often use their rifles in sub-zero weather should consider using a non-congealing gun lubrication product such as Remington DriLube with Teflon instead of oil. Remove old oil from all moving parts, then spray on DriLube.

Rossi Rifles

SINGLE-SHOT

RIFLES

MATCHED PAIR

SINGLE-SHOT

Action: hinged breech
Stock: hardwood
Barrel: 23 in.
Sights: open
Weight: 6.25 lbs.
Caliber: .17 HMR, .223, 243, .308, .30-06, .270, .22-250 , 7.62x39
Magazine: none
Features: single shot; recoil pad; sling swivels; extra-wide positive-action extractor; good rifle for first time shooters; all calibers except .17 HMR have Monte Carlo stock

.17 HMR blue: **$175**
.17 HMR stainless: **$222**
Single Shot with heavy barrel
  (.223, .243, .22-250): **$232**
Youth model: **$164-224**

YOUTH RIMFIRE MATCHED PAIR

Action: hinged breech
Stock: hardwood
Barrel: 18.5 in (rifle), 22 in. (shotgun)
Sights: open
Weight: 4.0-6.0 lbs.
Caliber: 20 ga/.22 LR, .410/.22 LR, .410/.17 HMR
Magazine: none
Features: single shot; blue or stainless steel; single-stage trigger, adjustable sights; full size 12 or 20 gauge with .22 LR, .22 Mag or .17 HMR

Blued: **$154**
Stainless: **$195**
.410 and .17 HMR, blue: **$196**
Stainless: **$243**
Full-size: **$160-200**

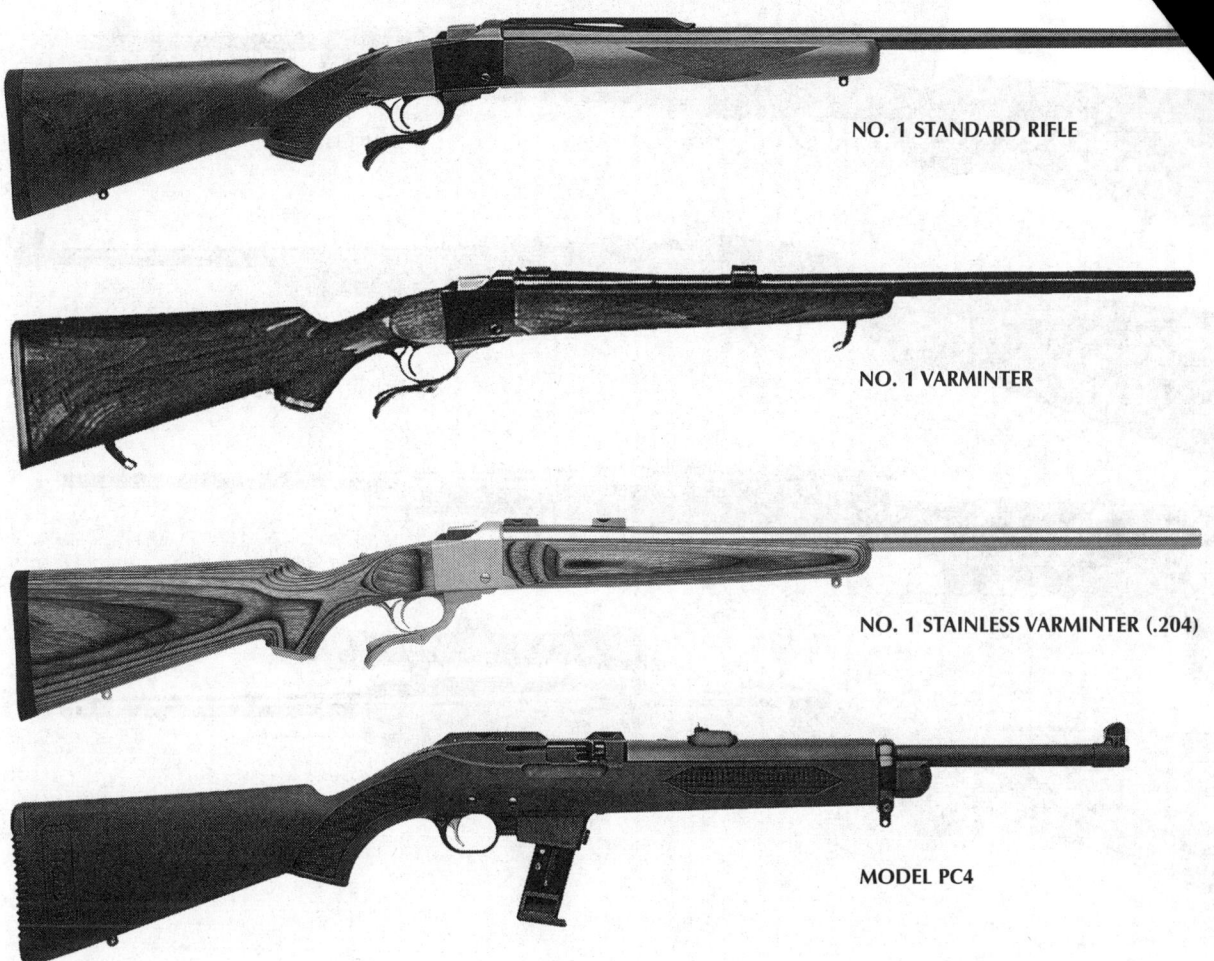

NO. 1 STANDARD RIFLE

NO. 1 VARMINTER

NO. 1 STAINLESS VARMINTER (.204)

MODEL PC4

NO. 1 SINGLE-SHOT

Action: dropping block
Stock: select checkered walnut
Barrel: 22, 24, or 26 in. (RSI: 20 in.)
Sights: open
Weight: 7.25-8.25 lbs.
Caliber: all popular chamberings in Light Sporter, Medium Sporter, Standard Rifle
Magazine: none
Features: pistol grip; all rifles come with Ruger 1" scope rings; 45-70 is available in stainless; No. 1 Stainless comes in .243, .25-06, 7mm Rem. Mag., .204, .30-06, .270, .300 Win. Mag., .308
No. 1: **$966**
Stainless steel: **$998**

NO. 1 VARMINTER

Action: dropping block
Stock: select checkered walnut
Barrel: heavy 24 or 26 in. (.220 Swift)
Sights: open
Weight: 8.75 lbs.
Caliber: .22-250, .220 Swift, .223, .25-06
Magazine: box, 5 rounds
Features: Ruger target scope block; stainless available in .22-250; also No. 1H Tropical (heavy 24 in. bbl.) in .375 H&H, .416 Rigby, .458 Lott, .458 Win. Mag., .405; No.1 RSI International (20 in. light bbl. and full-length stock) in .243, .270, .30-06, 7x57
Varmint: **$966**
Tropical: **$966**
International: **$998**
Stainless Varminter (24 - 26 in. bbl.
    in .204 Ruger or .22-250): . . . **$998**

MODEL PC4 CARBINE

Action: autoloading
Stock: synthetic
Barrel: 16.25 in.
Sights: open
Weight: 6.3 lbs.
Caliber: 9mm, .40 S&W
Magazine: detachable, 10-15 rounds
Features: delayed blowback action; optional ghost ring sight
Carbine: **$623**
    with ghost ring sights: **$647**

RANCH RIFLE

MODEL 10/22 RBM

MODEL 77R MKII

MODEL 77 MARK II FRONTIER

RIFLES

RANCH RIFLE

Action: autoloading
Stock: hardwood
Barrel: 18 in.
Sights: target
Weight: 6.5-7.0 lbs.
Caliber: .223
Magazine: detachable box, 5 rounds
Features: also stainless, stainless synthetic versions of Mini-14/5; Ranch Rifle (with scope mounts) and Mini-thirty (in 7.62x39)
Deerfield Carbine .44 Mag.: . . $702
Ranch Rifle:. $750
Ranch rifle, stainless: $809
Ranch rifle, stainless synthetic: $809
Mini-Thirty, stainless synthetic: $809

MODEL 10/22

Action: autoloading
Stock: walnut, birch, synthetic or laminated
Barrel: 18 in.

Sights: open
Weight: 5.0 lbs.
Caliber: .22 LR
Magazine: rotary, 10 rounds
Features: blowback action; also International with full-stock, heavy-barreled Target and stainless steel versions; Magnum with 9-shot magazine
Model 10/22: $275
Stainless: $304
Walnut: $324
Target: $445
Target stainless, laminated: . . . $495
Magnum:. $536
.17 HMR: $536

MODEL 77R MARK II

Action: bolt
Stock: walnut
Barrel: 22 in.
Sights: none
Weight: 7.25-8.25 lbs.
Caliber: most popular standard and

magnum calibers
Magazine: box, 3-5 rounds
Features: scope rings included; RBZ has stainless steel, laminated stock; RSBZ with sights
77R:. $716
RBZ:. $773

MODEL 77 MARK II FRONTIER

Action: bolt
Stock: laminated
Barrel: 16½-in sporter
Sights: none
Weight: 6.75 lbs.
Caliber: .243, 7mm-08, .308, .300 WSM
Magazine: internal box, 3- or 5-rounds
Features: rib for barrel-mounted scope
MSRP: $799

Ruger Rifles

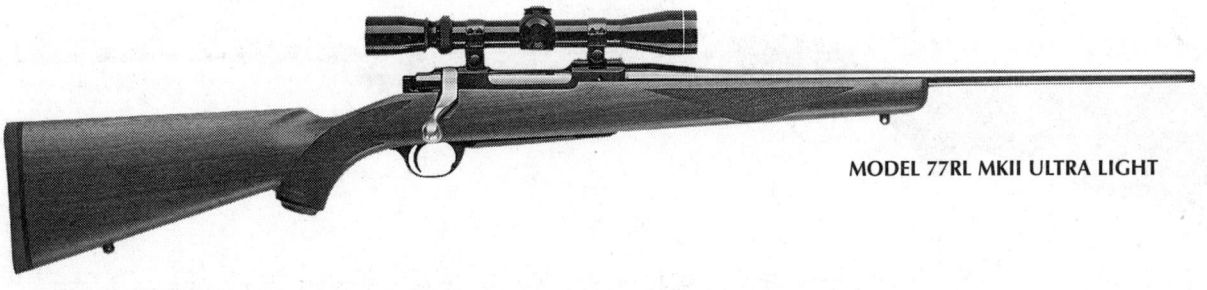

MODEL 77RL MKII ULTRA LIGHT

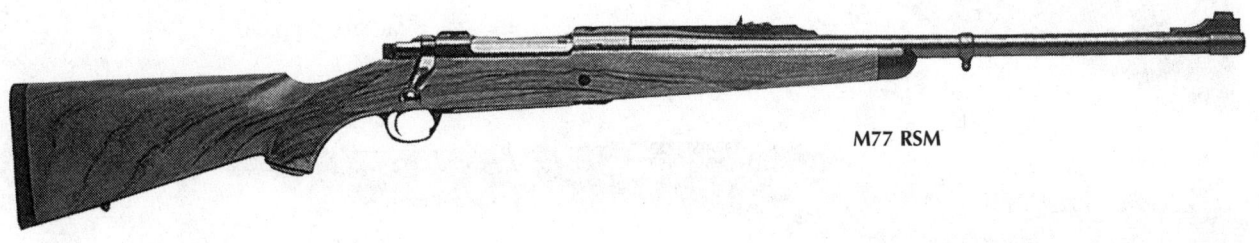

M77 RSM

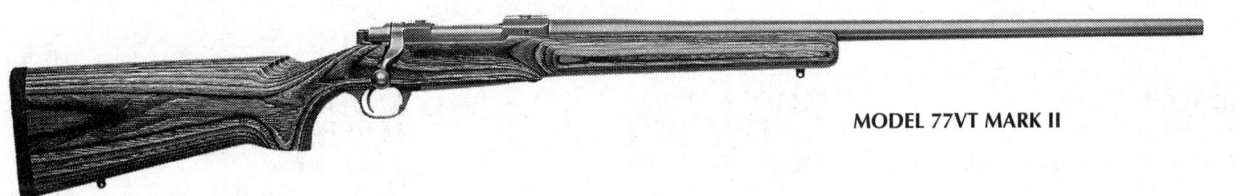

MODEL 77VT MARK II

MODEL 77 RFP MARK II

Action: bolt
Stock: synthetic
Barrel: 22 in.
Sights: none
Weight: 7.0-8.0 lbs.
Caliber: most popular standard and magnum calibers
Magazine: box, 3-5 rounds
Features: stainless steel barrel and action, (magnums with 24 in. barrel); scope rings included
MSRP: $716

MODEL 77RL MARK II ULTRA LIGHT

Action: bolt
Stock: walnut
Barrel: 20 in.
Sights: none

Weight: 6.25-6.75 lbs.
Caliber: .223, .243, .257, .270, .308
Magazine: box, 4 or 5 rounds
77RL Ultra Light: $773
**International Model
     (18 in. bbl.): $819**

MODEL 77 RSM MAGNUM

Action: bolt
Stock: Circassian walnut
Barrel: 23 in. with quarter rib
Sights: open
Weight: 9.5-10.0 lbs.
Caliber: .375 H&H, .416 Rigby (10.3 lbs.), .458 Lott
Magazine: box, 3 or 4 rounds
Features: barrel-mounted front swivel; also Express rifle in popular standard and magnum long-action calibers
MSRP: $1975

MODEL 77 VT MARK II

Action: bolt
Stock: brown laminate
Barrel: heavy stainless 26 in., target grey finish
Sights: none
Weight: 9.8 lbs.
Caliber: .223, .204, .22-250, .220 Swift, .243, .25-06, .308
Magazine: box, 4 or 5 rounds
MSRP: $870

Ruger Rifles

MODEL 77/17

MODEL 77/22VBZ

MODEL 96

MODEL 77/17
Action: bolt
Stock: walnut, synthetic or laminated
Barrel: 22 in.
Sights: none
Weight: 6.5 lbs.
Caliber: .17 HMR
Magazine: 9 rounds
Features: also stainless (P) and stain-less varmint with laminated stock (VMBBZ), 24 in. barrel (6.9 lbs.)
77/17 RM: **$613**
77/17 RMP: **$613**
K77/17 VMBBZ: **$685**
Also available:
   .17 MACH2 (20 in, blue
or stainless bbl.): **$674-746**

MODEL 77/22 RIMFIRE RIFLE
Action: bolt
Stock: walnut
Barrel: 20 in.
Sights: none
Weight: 6.0 lbs.
Caliber: .22 LR, .22 Mag., .22 Hornet
Magazine: rotary, 6-10 rounds
Features: also Magnum (M) and stain-less synthetic (P) versions; scope rings included for all; sights on S versions; VBZ has 24 in. medium stainless bar-rel (6.9 lbs.)
MSRP: **$613**
77/22RM: **$613**
K77/22RP: **$613**
K77/22 RMP: **$613**
77/22RH (.22 Hornet): **$649**
K77/22VBZ: **$685**
K77/22VMBZ: **$685**
K77/22VHZ (.22 Hornet): **$685**

MODEL 96 LEVER-ACTION RIFLE
Action: lever
Stock: hardwood
Barrel: 18½ in., blued
Sights: adjustable rear sight
Weight: 5.25 lbs.
Caliber: .17 HMR, .22 WMR, .44 Mag.
Magazine: rotary magazine, 9 rounds
Features: enclosed short-throw lever action; cross bolt safety; standard tip off scope-mount base
Model 96: **$390**
.44 Mag. (4-round): **$546**

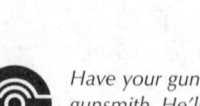

Have your guns checked periodically by a gunsmith. He'll replace worn or damaged parts before malfunctions occur.

75 GREY WOLF

MODEL 75 HUNTER

MODEL 75 VARMINT

MODEL 75 CUSTOM SINGLE-SHOT

75 GREY WOLF

Action: bolt
Stock: laminated
Barrel: 22½ in. or 24½ in.
Sights: none
Weight: 7.25-7.75 lbs.
Caliber: .223, .22-250, .243, 7mm08, .260, .308, .25-06, .270, .30-06, .270 WSM, 7mm WSM, .300 WSM
Magazine: detachable box, 4-6 rounds
Features: Satin-finished stainless cold hammer-forged barrel; four action sizes; gray laminated stock
MSRP: **$1549**

MODEL 75 HUNTER

Action: bolt
Stock: walnut or synthetic
Barrel: hammer-forged 22, 24 or 26 in.
Sights: none
Weight: 7.0 lbs.
Caliber: most popular standard and magnum calibers from .222 Rem. to .375 H&H and .300, and .270 WSM
Magazine: detachable box, 4-6 rounds
Features: barrel length depends on caliber; 4 action lengths; also stainless synthetic and short-barreled Finnlight versions; Deluxe Grade with fancy walnut stock
Hunter: $1419
.375 H&H: $1499
Stainless synthetic: $1499
Left-hand (.25-06, .270,
  .30-06): $1419
Finnlight: $1584
Deluxe: $2044
.416 Rem: $2418

MODEL 75 VARMINT

Action: bolt
Stock: varmint-style walnut
Barrel: heavy 24 in.
Sights: none
Weight: 9.0 lbs.
Caliber: .223, .260 Rem., .22-250, .243, .308, .204 Ruger
Magazine: detachable box, 5-6 rounds
Features: also single set trigger
Varmint: $1684
Varmint LS: $1959

MODEL 75 CUSTOM SINGLE-SHOT

Action: bolt
Stock: laminated
Barrel: 23 in.
Sights: none
Weight: 9.0 lbs.
Caliber: .308
Magazine: none
Features: stainless barrel; rubber butt pad
MSRP: $3448

Sako Rifles

MODEL TRG-42

QUAD

MODEL TRG-22
Action: bolt
Stock: synthetic
Barrel: 26 in.
Sights: none
Weight: 10.3 lbs.
Caliber: .308
Magazine: detachable box, 10 rounds
Features: 3-lug bolt; fully adjustable trigger; optional bipod, brake; also TRG 42 in .300 Win. Mag. and .338 Lapua (5-round magazine, 27 in. barrel, 11.3 lbs.)

TRG-22: $3589
TRG-22, folding stock: $5849
TRG-42: $3589
TRG-42, green: $3999

QUAD
Action: bolt
Stock: synthetic
Barrel: 22 in.
Sights: none
Weight: 5.75 lbs.
Caliber: .22 LR, .22 WMR, .17 Mach 2, .17 WMR

Magazine: detachable box, 5-rounds
Features: Switch-barrel combo set of four sporter-weight barrels (.22 LR, .22 WMR, .17 Mach 2, .17 HMR); color-coded barrels feature quick change system with single retaining screw; double locking lug action, bolt lift 50°; adjustable single-stage trigger; two-position sliding safety; 40 inches overall; foam-padded metal case
Single Barrel: $948
4 barrel set: $1739

Sauer Rifles

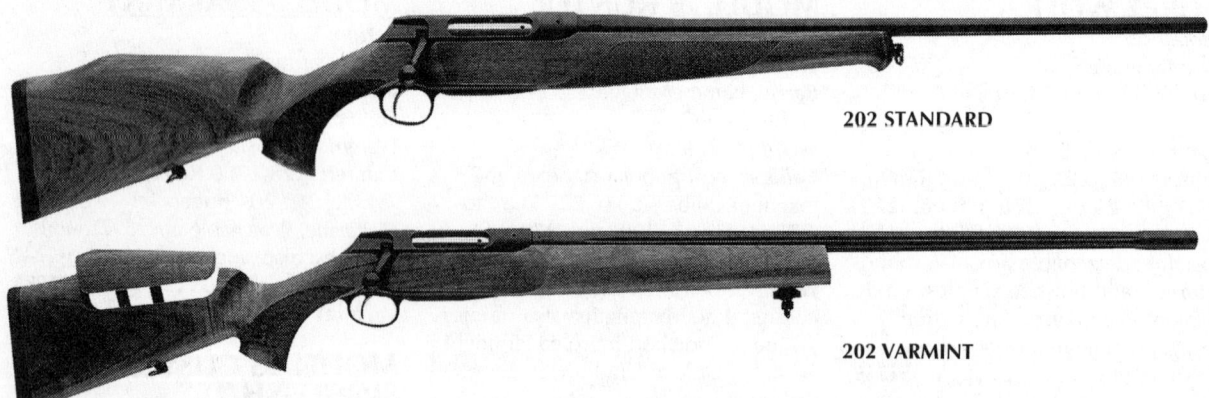

202 STANDARD

202 VARMINT

MODEL 202
Action: bolt
Stock: Claro walnut
Barrel: 24 in.   *Sights:* none
Weight: 7.7 lbs.
Caliber: .243, .25-06, 6.5x55, .270, .308, .30-06

Magazine: detachable box, 5 rounds
Features: adjustable trigger; quick-change barrel; also Supreme Magnum with 26 in. barrel in 7mm Rem., .300 Win., .300 Wby., .375 H&H; Varmint and Tactical versions too

Model 202: $2200
Magnum: $2400-2600
Synthetic: $2200-2600
Lightweight: $3400
Varmint: $3400
Left-hand (.30-06, walnut): . . . $3700
SSG 3000 Tactical: $2900-5000

RIFLES

Savage Rifles

MARK IG SINGLE-SHOT

MARK II FSS

MARK II FV HEAVY-BARREL

VARMINTER

MARK I

Action: bolt
Stock: hardwood
Barrel: 19 in. or 21 in.
Sights: open
Weight: 5.5 lbs.
Caliber: .22 S, .22 L, .22 LR
Magazine: none
Features: also MkIG Youth (19 in. barrel), MkILY Youth laminated stock, MIY Youth camo stock

Mark I FVT
 (with peep sights): **$316**
Mark I G: **$171**
G Youth: **$171**
Mark I GSB (.22 LR Short): **$171**

MARK II F

Action: bolt
Stock: synthetic
Barrel: 21 in.
Sights: open
Weight: 5.0 lbs.
Caliber: .22 LR
Magazine: detachable box, 5 rounds
Features: also MkIIG with hardwood stock, MkIIFSS stainless, MkIIGY with short stock and 19 in. barrel

F: **$169-213**
G: **$184**
FSS: **$226**
GY: **$184**
Camo: **$202**

MARK II FV HEAVY-BARREL

Action: bolt
Stock: synthetic
Barrel: heavy 21 in.
Sights: none
Weight: 6.0 lbs.
Caliber: .22 LR
Magazine: detachable box, 5 or 10 rounds
Features: Weaver scope bases included; also MkII LV with laminated stock (6.5 lbs.)

FV: **$234-240**
BV: **$285**

VARMINTER

Action: bolt
Stock: laminated
Barrel: heavy fluted stainless, button-rifled
Sights: none (drilled and tapped for scope mounts)
Weight: 9.0 lbs.
Caliber: .223 and .22-250, .204 Ruger
Magazine: 4-round box or single-shot
Features: fully adjustable AccuTrigger
MSRP: **$806**

Savage Rifles

MODEL CFM SIERRA

MODEL 11G

MODEL 12 FVSS

MODEL 12FV

MODEL CFM SIERRA

Action: bolt
Stock: synthetic
Barrel: 20-in. sporter
Sights: none
Weight: 6.0 lbs.
Caliber: .243, 7mm-08, .308, .270 WSM, .300 WSM
Magazine: detachable box, 3-5 rounds
Features: AccuTrigger
MSRP: $552

MODEL 11F

Action: bolt
Stock: synthetic
Barrel: 22 in.
Sights: none
Weight: 6.8 lbs.
Caliber: .223, .22-250, .243, 7mm-08, .308, .270 WSM, 7mm WSM, .300 WSM,
Magazine: box, 5 rounds
Features: open sights available; also 11G with walnut stock, 10 GY Youth with short stock in .223, .243, and .308
11F: $501
11G: $515

MODEL 11/111

Action: bolt
Stock: hardwood or synthetic
Barrel: 24 in.
Sights: none
Weight: 7.0 lbs.
Caliber: .270 WSM, 7mm WSM, .300 WSM, 7mm SUM, .300 SUM (all new for 2003 in various configurations)
Magazine: 3 rounds
Features: top tang safety; adjustable sights available
MSRP: . . . . from $486

MODEL 12, 112 10FP SÉRIES

Action: bolt
Stock: synthetic or laminated
Barrel: 20 in. or 26 in.
Sights: none
Weight: 8.3 lbs.
Caliber: .223, .22-250, .243, .25-06, 7mm Rem. Mag., .308, .30-06, .300 WSM, .300 Win. Mag.
Magazine: 3 or 4 rounds
Features: single-shot or box magazine;

new in these rifles for 2003 is the Savage AccuTrigger
MSRP: $934

MODEL 12FV (SHORT-ACTION)

Action: bolt
Stock: synthetic
Barrel: varmint, 26 in.
Sights: none   **Weight**: 9.0 lbs.
Caliber: .223, .22-250, .243, .308, .300 WSM, .204 Ruger
Magazine: box, 5 rounds
Features: also 12 VSS with fluted stainless barrel, Choate adjustable stock (11.3 lbs.) and V2 BVSS with stainless fluted barrel, laminated or synthetic stock (9.5 lbs.)
FV: $569
FVSS: $691
BVSS laminated: $746

MODEL 114

MODEL 16FSS

MODEL 30G

MODEL 40

MODEL 14/114

Action: bolt
Stock: checkered walnut
Barrel: 22 in. and 24 in.   *Sights:* none
Weight: 7.25 lbs.
Caliber: .223 to .300 Win. Mag.
Magazine: detachable box,
3-5 rounds
Features: AccuTrigger
MSRP: **$616**

MODEL 116FSS.
(LONG-ACTION)

Action: bolt
Stock: synthetic
Barrel: stainless 22, 24, or 26 in.
Sights: none   *Weight*: 6.5 lbs.
Caliber: .270, .30-06 (22 in.), 7mm
Rem. Mag., .300 Win. Mag., .338
Win. Mag., .300 RUM (26 in.)
Magazine: box, 3 or 4 rounds
Features: also 116BSS with checkered
laminated stock
MSRP: **$569**

MODEL 16FSS
(SHORT-ACTION)

Action: bolt
Stock: synthetic
Barrel: stainless, 22 or 24 in.
Sights: none
Weight: 6.0 lbs.
Caliber: .223, .243, .204 Ruger,
7mm WSM, .22-250 REM, 7mm-08,
.308, .270 WSM, .300 WSM
Magazine: box, 3 or 4 rounds
Features: also 16BSS with checkered
laminated stock in .300 WSM only
MSRP: **$569**

MODEL 30

Action: dropping block
Stock: walnut
Barrel: octagon, 21 in.
Sights: open
Weight: 4.3 lbs.
Caliber: .22 LR, .22 WMR, .17 HMR
Magazine: none
Features: re-creation of Steven's Favorite

30G: **$240**
30GM: **$266**
30R17: **$292**
Take-down .22: **$249**
Take-down .17: **$314**

MODEL 40 W/
ACCUTRIGGER

Action: bolt
Stock: laminated, beavertail, with third
swivel stud
Barrel: 24 in., heavy, sleeved,
free-floating
Sights: none (drilled and tapped for
scope mounts)
Weight: 8.5 lbs.
Caliber: .22 Hornet
Magazine: none
MSRP: **$452**

Savage Rifles

MODEL 64FSS

MODEL 93

MODEL 93G

MODEL 112BVSS

RIFLES

MODEL 64F

Action: autoloading
Stock: synthetic
Barrel: 21 in.
Sights: open
Weight: 5.5 lbs.
Caliber: .22 LR
Magazine: detachable box, 10 rounds
Features: also 64 FSS stainless, 64FV and FVSS heavy barrel, 64G hardwood stock
64F: **$135**
64G: **$162**

MODEL 93

Action: bolt
Stock: synthetic, hardwood or laminated
Barrel: 21 in.
Sights: none
Weight: 5.0 lbs.
Caliber: .17 HMR
Magazine: 5 rounds
Features: scope bases included; eight versions with stainless or C-M steel, different stocks; varmint models weigh 6.0 lbs.
Synthetic F: **$206**
Laminated stainless FVSS: **$298**

MODEL 93G

Action: bolt
Stock: synthetic
Barrel: 21 in.
Sights: open
Weight: 5.8 lbs.
Caliber: .22 WMR, .17 HMR
Magazine: detachable box, 5 rounds
Features: 93G with hardwood stock; 93 FSS stainless; 93FVSS with heavy barrel; 93G with hardwood stock
MSRP: **$212**

MODEL 110 LONG RANGE

Action: bolt
Stock: lightweight composite
Barrel: heavy 24 in.   *Sights:* none
Weight: 8.5 lbs.
Caliber: .25-06, 7mm Rem. Mag., .30-06, .300 Win. Mag.
Magazine: box, 4 rounds
Features: also short-action Model 10 in .223, .308
Model 110FP: **$601**
Model 110: **$601**
Model 110GY
   (youth, 22 in. bbl.): **$515**

MODEL 112 BVSS (LONG-ACTION)

Action: bolt
Stock: lightweight composite
Barrel: fluted, stainless 26 in.
Sights: none
Weight: 10.3 lbs.
Caliber: .25-06, 7mm Rem. Mag., .30-06, .300 Win. Mag.
Magazine: box, 4 rounds
Features: also 112 BVSS with laminated stock
MSRP: **$721**

MODEL 200

Action: bolt
Stock: synthetic
Barrel: 22 in. and 24 in. sporter
Sights: none
Weight: 7.5 lbs.
Caliber: 10 chamberings, from .223 to .300 Win. Mag.
Magazine: blind box
Features: pillar-bedded
MSRP: **$316**

Springfield Rifles

M1A SCOUT RIFLE

M1A STANDARD

M1 GARAND

MODEL M-6 SCOUT

RIFLES

M1A

Action: autoloading
Stock: walnut
Barrel: 22 in.
Sights: target
Weight: 9.2 lbs.
Caliber: .308
Magazine: detachable box,
5 or 10 rounds
Features: also with fiberglass stock and
M1A/Scout with 18 in. barrel and
scope mount (9.0 lbs.)
M1A: **$1531-1635**
M1A Scout Rifle: **$1658-1780**

M1 GARAND

Action: autoloading
Stock: walnut
Barrel: 24 in.
Sights: target
Weight: 9.5 lbs.
Caliber: .30-06, .308
Magazine: clip-fed, 8 rounds
Features: gas-operated; new stock,
receiver, barrel; other parts mil-spec
M1 Garand .30-06: **$1437**
M1 Garand .308: **$1467**

MODEL M-6 SCOUT

Action: hinged breech
Stock: synthetic
Barrel: 16 in.
Sights: open
Weight: 4.0 lbs.
Caliber: .22LR and .410 or
.22 Hornet and .410
Magazine: none
Features: over/under combination gun;
lockable plastic case; also stainless M-6
M-6: **$215**
M-6 stainless: **$249**

Steyr Rifles

CLASSIC

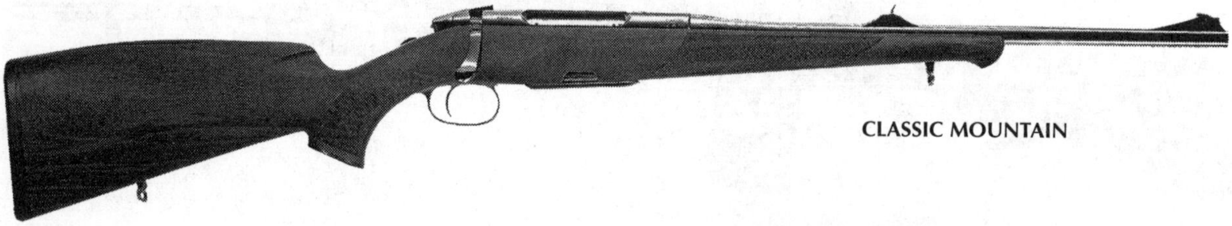

CLASSIC MOUNTAIN

SCOUT

CLASSIC MANNLICHER
Action: bolt
Stock: European walnut
Barrel: 20 in., 23.6 in. and 25.6 in.
Sights: open
Weight: 7.4 lbs., 7.7 lbs. (magnum)
Caliber: .222, .223, .243, 6.5x55 SE, 6.5x57, 25-06, .270, 7x64, 7mm-08, 308, 30-06, 8x57 JS, 9,3x62, 7 mm Rem. Mag., .300 Win. Mag., 7 mm WSM, .270 WSM, .300 WSM
Magazine: box, 4 rounds
Features: three-position roller tang safety with front locking lugs and ice/residue groove; full stock or half stock models; total length 41.7 in.; set or direct trigger; sights as optional extras on half-stock models
Half-stock: **$1566**
Mountain: **$1753**
Classic: **$1893**

SCOUT
Action: bolt
Stock: synthetic
Barrel: 19 in.
Sights: open
Weight: 7.0 lbs.
Caliber: .223, .243, 7mm-08, .308, .376 Steyr
Magazine: detachable box, 5 rounds
Features: high-strength aluminium receiver; SBS (Safe Bolt System) safety; system; three position roller tang safety full, set or direct trigger; Weaver-type rail; spare magazine in the butt stock; integral folding bipod; matte black finish; total length 38.5 in.
Scout: **$2699**

When you buy a new rifle, follow the manufacturer's break-in procedure as you squeeze off those first few shots. You'll increase the long-term accuracy of the gun, lengthen its operating life and reduce the amount of fouling.

RIFLES

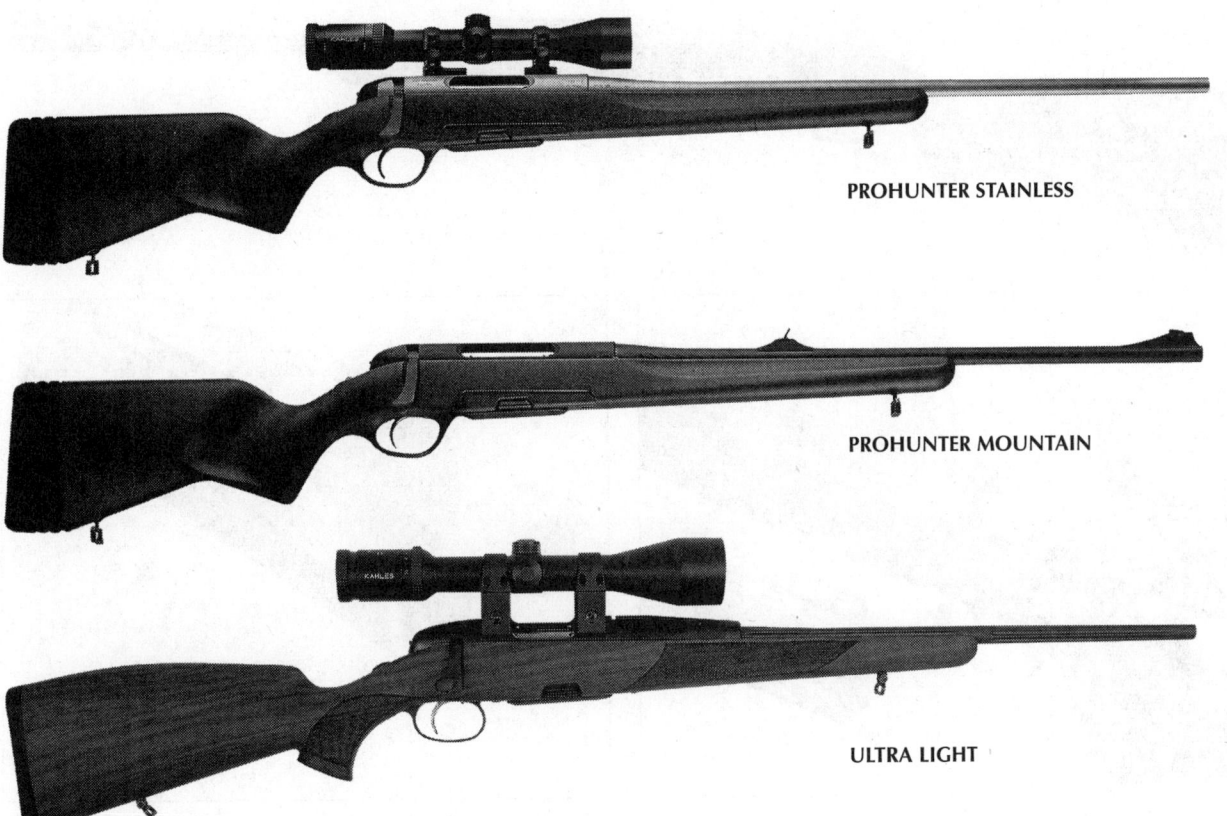

PROHUNTER STAINLESS

PROHUNTER MOUNTAIN

ULTRA LIGHT

PROHUNTER

Action: bolt
Stock: synthetic
Barrel: 20 in. (Mtn.),
23.6 in. and 25.6 in.
Sights: open
Weight: 7.8 lbs. (std.), 8.2 lbs. (mag.),
7.4 lbs. (Mtn.)
Caliber: .222, .223, .243, 6.5x55 SE,
6.5x57, .25-06, .270, 7x64, 7mm-08,
.308, .30-06, 8x57 JS, 9.3x62, 7mm
Rem. Mag., .300 Win. Mag., 7mm
WSM, .270 WSM, .300 WSM
Magazine: detachable box, 5 rounds
Features: high-strength aluminium receiver; SBS safety system; three position roller tang safety; set or direct trigger; charcoal-gray, charcoal-black or Realtree Hardwoods HD stocks; heavy barrel available in .308 or .300 Win. Mag.
ProHunter: $776
ProHunter Stainless: $861
ProHunter Mountain: $776
ProHunter
   Mountain Stainless: $861

ULTRA LIGHT

Action: bolt
Stock: European walnut
Barrel: 19 in.
Sights: none
Weight: 5.9 lbs.
Caliber: .222, .223, .243 Win.,
7mm-08 Rem., .308
Magazine: detachable box, 4 rounds
Features: high-strength aluminium receiver; bolt lugs lock into steel safety bushing; SBS (Safe Bolt System) safety system; three position roller tang safety with front locking lugs and ice/residue groove; set trigger or direct trigger; integral Weaver-type scope mounting rail; total length 38.5 in.
MSRP: $1505

Szecsei & Fuchs Rifles

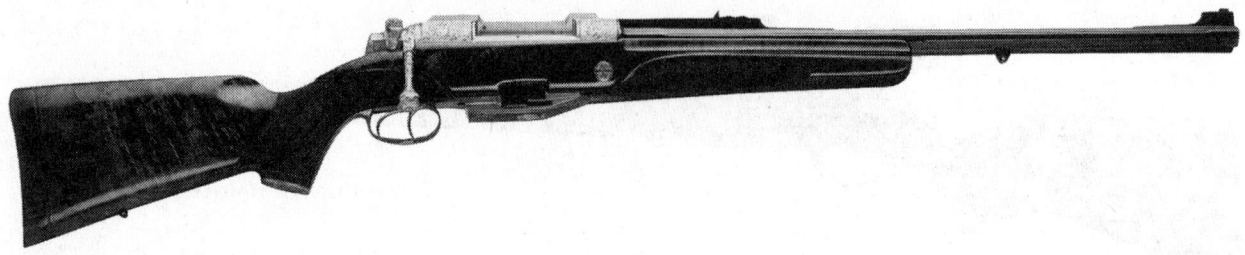

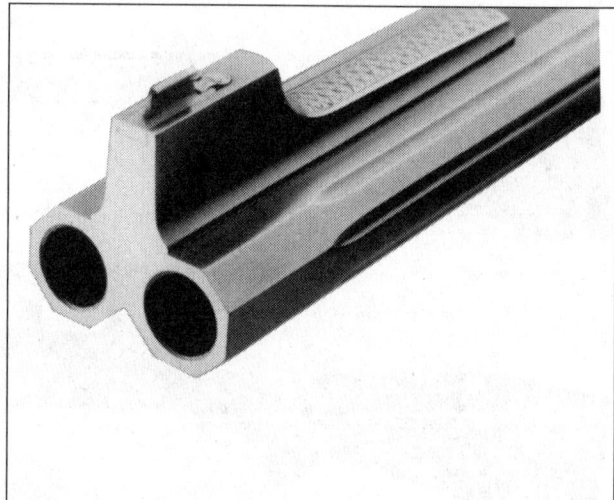

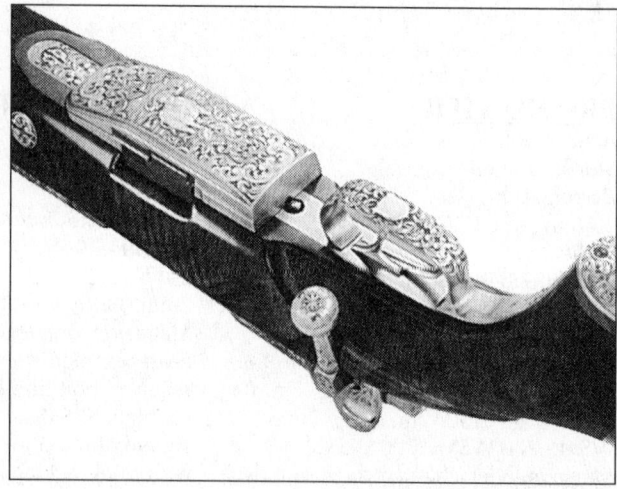

The Szecsei & Fuchs double-barrel bolt-action rifle may be the only one of its kind. Built with great care and much handwork from the finest materials, it follows a design remarkable for its cleverness. While the rifle is not light-weight, it can be aimed quickly and offers more large-caliber firepower than any competitor. The six-shot magazine feeds two rounds simultaneously, both of which can then be fired by two quick pulls of the trigger. **Chamberings**: .300 Win, 9.3 x 64, .358 Norma, .375 H&H, .404 Jeff, .416 Rem., .458 Win., .416 Rigby, .450 Rigby, .460 Short A-Square, .470 Capstick, .495 A-Square, .500 Jeffery **Weight:** 14 lbs. with round barrels, 16 with octagon barrels.
Price: . . . . **Available on request**

Tactical Rifles

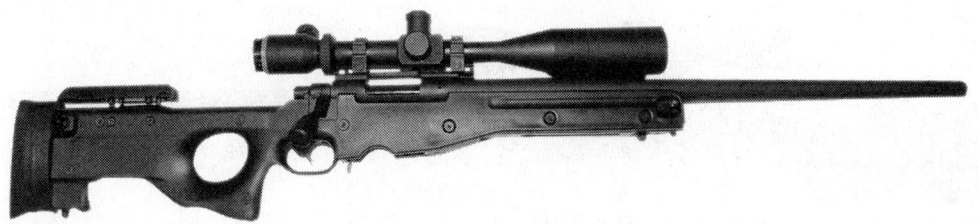

TACTICAL L.R.
Action: bolt, M700 Remington
Stock: thumbhole aluminum, with resin panels, optional adjustable cheekpiece
Barrel: heavy, match-grade, 26 in.

Sights: none (drilled and tapped for scope, supplied with Picatinny rail)
Weight: 13.4 lbs.
Caliber: 7.62 NATO (Magnum version available, in .300 WSM)
Magazine: detachable box, 5 rounds

(10-round boxes available)
Features: adjustable trigger; soft rubber recoil pad, swivel studs; options include stainless fluted barrel
MSRP: **$2450**

Taylor's Rifles

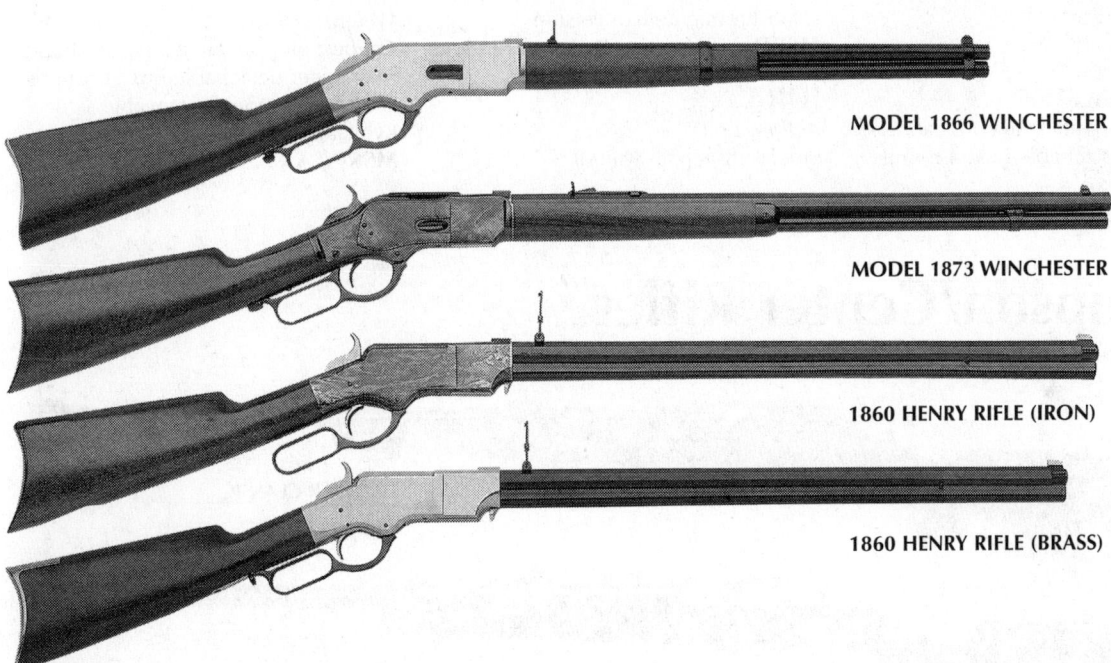

MODEL 1866 WINCHESTER

MODEL 1873 WINCHESTER

1860 HENRY RIFLE (IRON)

1860 HENRY RIFLE (BRASS)

MODEL 1866 WINCHESTER
Action: lever
Stock: walnut
Barrel: 20 in.
Sights: open
Weight: 6.5 lbs.
Caliber: .38 Spl., .45 Long Colt
Magazine: under-barrel tube, 9 rounds
Features: brass frame, octagon barrel
MSRP: **$915**

MODEL 1873 WINCHESTER RIFLE
Action: lever
Stock: walnut
Barrel: 24 in.
Sights: open
Weight: 7.5 lbs.
Caliber: .44-40, .45 Long Colt
Magazine: under-barrel tube, 13 rounds
Features: optional front globe and rear tang sights
MSRP: **$1045**

1860 HENRY RIFLE
Action: lever
Stock: walnut
Barrel: 24 in.
Sights: open
Weight: 7.5 lbs.
Caliber: .44-40, .45 Long Colt
Magazine: under-barrel tube, 13 rounds
Features: brass frame; also original-type steel-frame in .44-40 only
Brass frame: **$1160**
White finish: **$1185**
Charcoal blue: **$1220**
.44-40 Steel frame: **$1220**

Thompson & Campbell Rifles

INVER

JURA

INVER
Action: bolt
Stock: select walnut
Barrel: 22 in.
Sights: none
Weight: 8.0 lbs.
Caliber: all popular standard calibers
Magazine: detachable box, 4 rounds

Features: takedown barrels; optional removable sights and two-stage trigger; also Chromie deluxe version
MSRP: . . . .**Price on request**

JURA
Action: bolt
Stock: full-length walnut

Barrel: 17 in.
Sights: none
Weight: 7.5 lbs.
Caliber: all popular standard calibers
Magazine: detachable box, 4 rounds
Features: optional removable sights; two-stage trigger
MSRP: . . . .**Price on request**

Thompson/Center Rifles

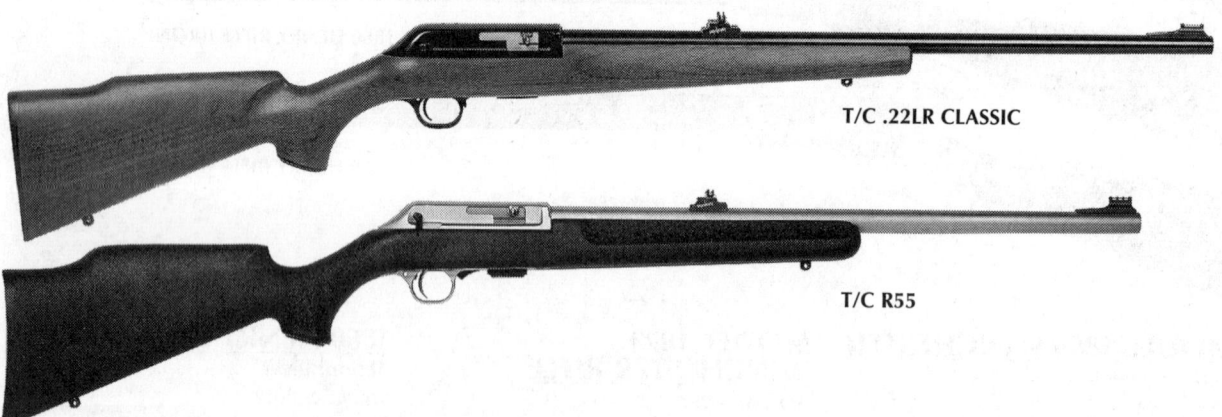

T/C .22LR CLASSIC

T/C R55

T/C.22LR CLASSIC
Action: autoloading
Stock: walnut
Barrel: 22 in.
Sights: illuminated
Weight: 5.5 lbs.
Caliber: .22 LR
Magazine: detachable box, 8 rounds
MSRP: **$397**

T/C R55
Action: blowback autoloader
Stock: synthetic/stainless or laminated/ blued
Barrel: 20 in.
Sights: adjustable, with fiber optic inserts
Weight: 5.5 lbs.
Caliber: .17 Mach 2
Magazine: detachable box, 5-rounds

Features: available in blued or stainless steel
Laminated/blued: **$479**
Synthetic/stainless: **$546**

RIFLES

Thompson/Center Rifles

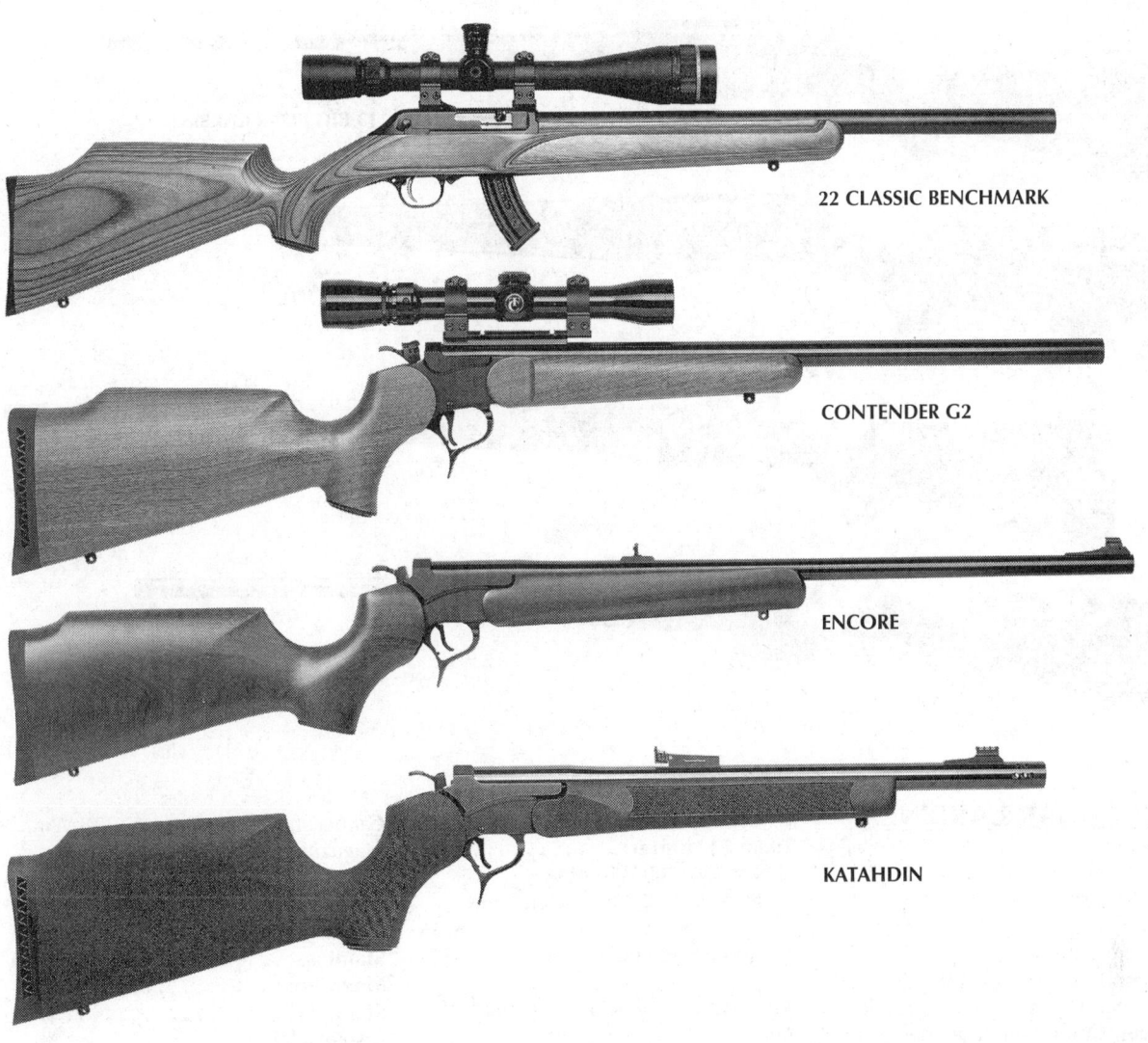

22 CLASSIC BENCHMARK

CONTENDER G2

ENCORE

KATAHDIN

RIFLES

22 CLASSIC BENCHMARK

Action: autoloading
Stock: laminated
Barrel: heavy, 18 in.
Sights: none
Weight: 6.8 lbs.
Caliber: .22 LR
Magazine: 10 rounds
Features: target rifle for bench shooting; drilled for scope
MSRP: **$506**

CONTENDER G2

Action: hinged breech
Stock: walnut
Barrel: 23 in.
Sights: none
Weight: 5.4 lbs.

Caliber: .17 HMR, .17 MACH 2, .22 LR, .223, 6.8 Rem., .30-30, .204 Ruger, .45/70, .375 JDJ
Magazine: none
Features: can recock without opening rifle
G2 Rifle: **$662**
.50 cal. Muzzleloader: **$652**

ENCORE

Action: hinged breech
Stock: walnut
Barrel: 24 and 26 in.
Sights: open
Weight: 6.8 lbs.
Caliber: most popular calibers, from .22 Hornet to .300 Win. Mag. and .45-70
Magazine: none

Features: also synthetic and stainless versions; Hunter package with .308 or .300 includes 3-9x40 T/C scope and hard case
Synthetic: **$604**
Walnut: **$649**
Stainless: **$680**

KATAHDIN CARBINE

Action: hinged breech
Stock: synthetic
Barrel: 18 in.
Sights: illuminated
Weight: 6.6 lbs.
Caliber: .450, .45-70
Magazine: none
Features: integral muzzle brake
MSRP: **$620**

Tikka Rifles

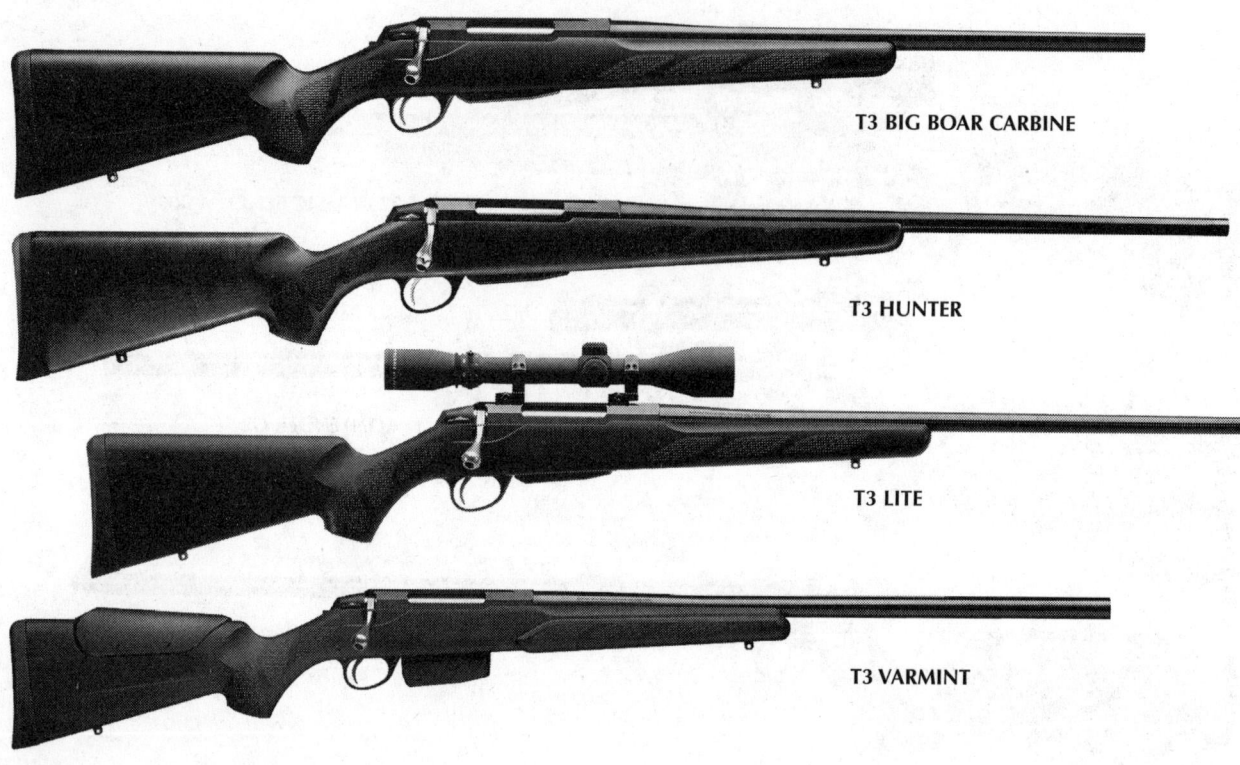

T3 BIG BOAR CARBINE

T3 HUNTER

T3 LITE

T3 VARMINT

T3 BIG BOAR CARBINE
Action: bolt
Stock: synthetic
Barrel: 19 in.
Sights: none
Weight: 6.1 lbs.
Caliber: .308, .30-06, .300 WSM
Magazine: detachable box, 3 rounds
Features: Chrome-moly sporter barrel
MSRP: $719

T3 HUNTER
Action: bolt
Stock: walnut, (T3 Lite, synthetic)
Barrel: 22⁷/₁₆, 24³/₈ in.
Sights: none
Weight: 6.63-6.8 lbs. (T3 Lite 6.2 lbs.)
Caliber: .22-250 Rem, .223 Rem, .243
Win, .25-06 Rem, .270 Win, .270
WSM, .30-06, .308 Win, 6.5 x 55
Magazine: detachable box, 3 rounds
Features: Walnut stock with distinctive
checkering pattern; blued action and
cold hammer-forged barrel; laminated
stock with stainless action and barrel,
2- to 4-pound adjustable trigger; inte-
gral scope rail, required rings are sup-
plied with each gun
T3 Lite: . . . .$ 559-$587

T3 Lite stainless: $690-725
Tikka T3 Hunter: $690
.270 WSM, 300 Win Mag,
300 WSM, 338 Win Mag 7mm
Rem Mag: $725
T3 Laminated stainless: $825

T3 LAMINATED STAINLESS
Action: two-lug bolt
Stock: laminated
Barrel: free-floating, hammer-forged,
22 in. (standard) and 24 in. (magnum)
Sights: none (drilled and tapped for
scope mounts)
Weight: 7.0 lbs.
Caliber: .243, .308, .25-06, .270, .30-
06, .270 WSM, .300 WSM, 7mm Rem.
Mag., .300 Win. Mag., .338 Win. Mag.
Magazine: detachable box, 3 rounds
Features: fully adjustable trigger
Standard: $908
Magnum: $944

T3 LITE
Action: bolt
Stock: synthetic
Barrel: 23-24 in.
Sights: none
Weight: 6.0 lbs.

Caliber: from .223 Rem to .338 Win.
Magazine: 3 or 4 rounds
Features: blue or stainless; 3-shot 1 in.
group at 100 yds. in factory testing
T3 Lite: $674
Stainless: $690
Magnums: $709
Stainless: $725
Also available:
　　T3 Hunter (walnut/blue): $759-798

T3 VARMINT
Action: bolt
Stock: synthetic
Barrel: 23³/₈ in.
Sights: none
Weight: 8.0 lbs.
Caliber: 22-250 Rem, 223 Rem, 308 Win
Magazine: detachable box, 5 rounds
Features: modular synthetic stock with
wide beavertail forend and non-reflec-
tive finish; raised-comb cheek piece;
blued or stainless steel; heavy contour
barrel
T3 Varmint: $765
Stainless: $825

Tikka Rifles

T3 TACTICAL

T3 SUPER VARMINT

T3 VARMINT AND TACTICAL
Action: two-lug bolt
Stock: synthetic
Barrel: heavy, 23 in. (Varmint), 20 in. (Tactical), free-floating, hammer-forged
Sights: none (drilled and tapped for scope mounts)
Weight: 9.0 lbs. (Varmint), 8.5 lbs. (Tactical)
Caliber: .223, .22-250,

.308 (Varmint), .223, .308 (Tactical)
Magazine: detachable box, 5 rounds
Features: fully adjustable trigger
T3 Varmint and Tactical: **$839**
Varmint, chrome-moly and
   stainless: **$908**
Tactical: **$1440**

SUPER VARMINT
Action: bolt
Stock: synthetic

Barrel: 23½-in. heavy
Sights: none   **Weight**: 9.3 lbs
Caliber: .223, .22-250, .308
Magazine: detachable box, 3 or 4 rounds
Features: stainless action and barrel, top rail and adjustable comb
MSRP: **$1668**

Uberti Rifles

LIGHTNING

1860 HENRY RIFLE

LIGHTNING
Action: pump
Stock: walnut, straight
Barrel: 20 in. and 24.75 in.
Sights: Open, fixed
Weight: 7.5 lbs
Caliber: .45 Colt, .357 mag
Magazine: 10 rounds

Features: checkered forend, blued and color case finish
MSRP: **$1099**

1860 HENRY RIFLE
Action: lever
Stock: walnut, straight grip
Barrel: octagon 18.5 in. and 24 in.

Sights: open, adjustable
Weight: 9.0 lbs (24.75 in)
Caliber: .44-40, .45 Colt
Magazine: under-barrel tube, 13 rounds
Features: brass or steel frame
Brass frame: **$1050**
Steel frame: **$1150**

Uberti Rifles

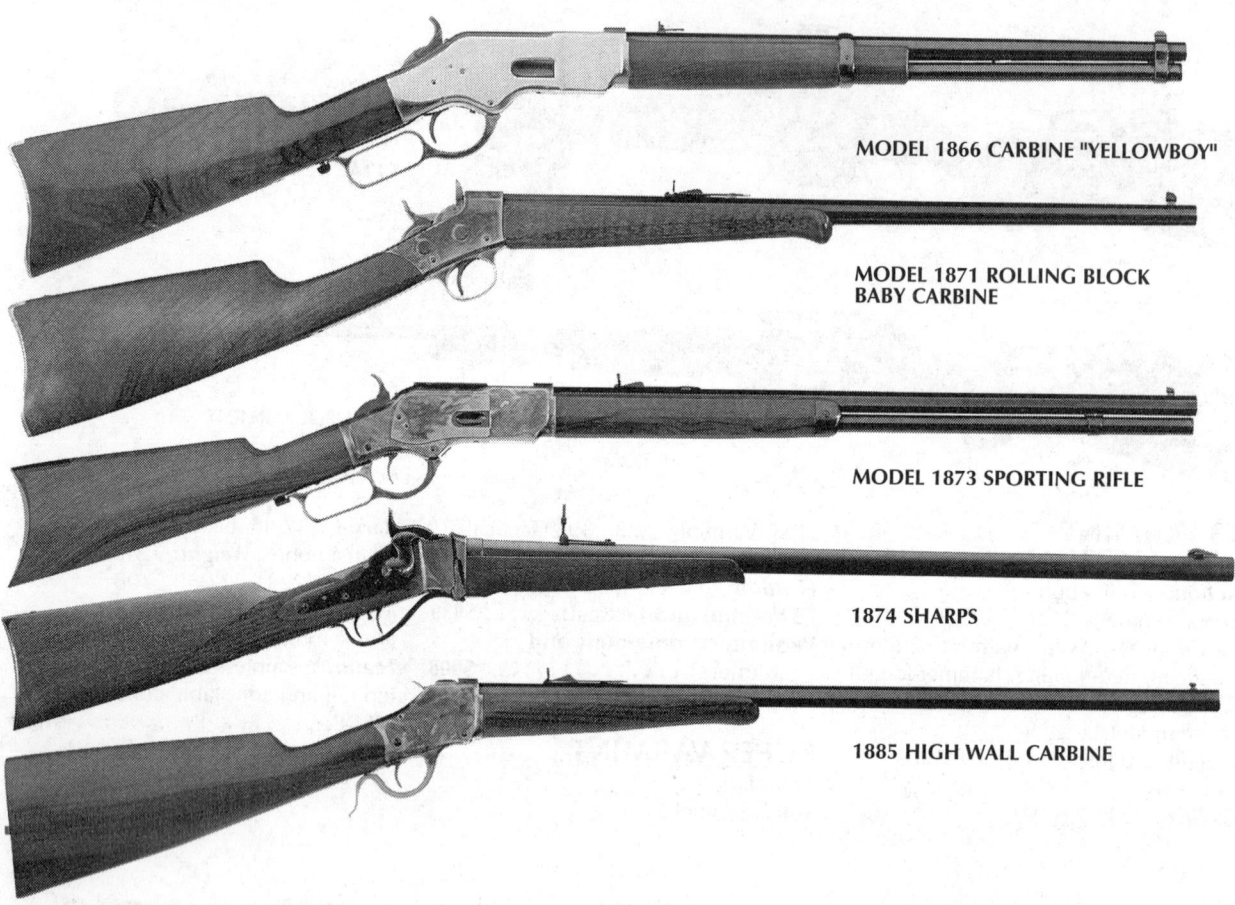

MODEL 1866 CARBINE "YELLOWBOY"

MODEL 1871 ROLLING BLOCK BABY CARBINE

MODEL 1873 SPORTING RIFLE

1874 SHARPS

1885 HIGH WALL CARBINE

MODEL 1866 WINCHESTER CARBINE "YELLOWBOY"

Action: lever
Stock: walnut, straight grip
Barrel: 19, 20, and 24.75 in.
Sights: open
Weight: 7.4 lbs.
Caliber: .38 Spl., .44-40, .45 Colt
Magazine: under-barrel tube
Features: brass frame
1866 Yellowboy Carbine: $885
1866 Rifle (24" BBL): $900

MODEL 1871 ROLLING BLOCK BABY CARBINE

Action: rolling block
Stock: walnut, straight grip
Barrel: 22 in.
Sights: open
Weight: 4.9 lbs.
Caliber: .22 LR, .22 WMR
Magazine: none
Features: case-colored receiver
Baby Carbine: $535
1871 Rifle (26" BBL): $600

MODEL 1873 WINCHESTER SPORTING RIFLE

Action: lever
Stock: walnut
Barrel: octagon 20 in., 24.75 in, (Carbine: 19 in. round)
Sights: open   *Weight:* 7.5 lbs. (20 in)
Caliber: .357 Mag., .44-40, .45 Colt
Magazine: under-barrel tube, 13 rounds
Features: straight or pistol grip stock
Straight grip (20" BBL): $945
24" BBL: $985
Pistol grip: $1100

1874 SHARPS

Action: falling block
Stock: supreme walnut
Barrel: 30, 32, and 34 in.
Sights: adjustable   *Weight:* 10.57 lbs (30")
Caliber: .45-70
Magazine: none
Features: checkered stock and forend; straight and pistol grip models available; select models come with Creedmore sights
MSRP: . . . . $1195-$2200

1885 HIGH-WALL SINGLE-SHOT RIFLE & CARBINE

Action: falling block
Stock: walnut
Barrel: 28 in. (carbine), 30 in. (rifle), 32 in. (sporting rifle)
Sights: target
Weight: 9.3 lbs. (carbine), 9.9 (rifle)
Caliber: .45-70 (carbine) .45-70, .45-90, .45-120 (rifle)
Magazine: none
Features: single shot; special sporting rifle with walnut; checkered (pistol grip stock); sporting rifles available with 30- or 32-inch octagon barrel; optional mid-range Vernier Creedmore or Lyman Creedmore sights; case-hardened frame/blued barrel
1885 High-Wall Carbine: $850
1885 High-Wall Sporting Rifle . . $850
1885 High-Wall Special
   Sporting Rifle. $1035

Walther Rifles

G22 CARBINE

Action: blowback autoloading
Stock: synthetic
Barrel: 20 in.

Sights: adjustable on handle and front strut
Weight: 6 lbs.
Caliber: .22 LR

Magazine: detachable box
Features: Weaver-style accessory rail; black or green synthetic stock
MSRP: $420

Weatherby Rifles

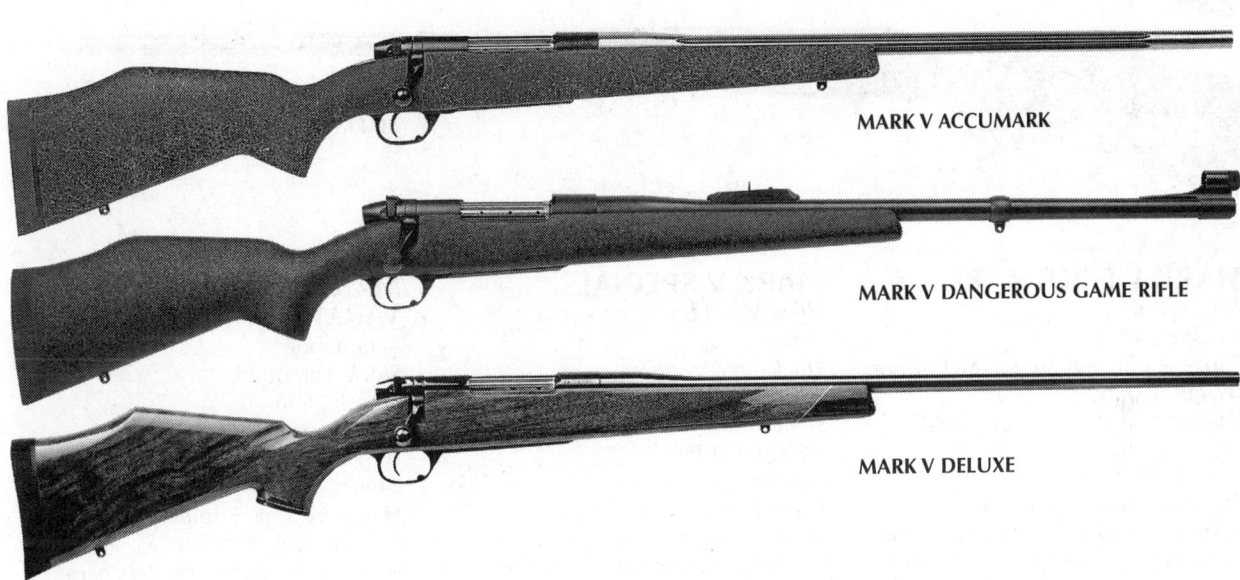

MARK V ACCUMARK

MARK V DANGEROUS GAME RIFLE

MARK V DELUXE

MARK V ACCUMARK

Action: bolt
Stock: composite
Barrel: 26 in. and 28 in.
Sights: none
Weight: 7.0 lbs.
Caliber: Wby. Magnums: .257, .270, 7mm, .300, .340, .30-378, .338-378 and .300 Win. Mag., 7mm Rem. Mag.
Magazine: box, 3 or 5 rounds
Features: weight depends on caliber; hand-laminated; raised comb, Pachmayr recoil pad
Magnums: $1761
With Accubrake: $2013

MARK V DANGEROUS GAME RIFLE

Action: bolt
Stock: composite
Barrel: 24 in. or 26 in.
Sights: open
Weight: 9.0 lbs.
Caliber: .300 Wby., .340 Wby., .375 H&H, .375 Wby., .416 Rem., .458 Win., .458 Lott; also .378, .416, .460 Wby.
Magazine: box, 3 rounds
Features: express sights, barrel band swivel
Dangerous Game Rifle: $3095
.378, .416: $3266
.460: $3360

MARK V DELUXE

Action: bolt
Stock: Claro walnut
Barrel: 26 in. and 28 in.
Sights: none
Weight: 8.5 lbs.
Caliber: .257 Wby. Mag to .460 Wby. Mag.
Magazine: box, 3 or 5 rounds
Features: 26 in. barrels for most magnum calibers; 28 in. barrel for .378, .416, .460
With Accubrake $2063
.378, .416 with Accubrake: . . . $2428
.460: $2853

Weatherby Rifles

MARK V FIBERMARK

MARK V LAZERMARK

MARK V SPECIAL VARMINT

MARK V SVM

MARK V FIBERMARK

Action: bolt
Stock: synthetic
Barrel: 24 in. and 26 in. *Sights:* none
Weight: 8.0 lbs.
Caliber: popular magnum chamberings from .257 Wby. Mag. to .375 H&H Mag.
Magazine: box, 3-5 rounds
Features: Krieger Criterion barrel; one-piece forged fluted bolt with three gas ports; hand-laminated, raised comb, pillar-bedded Monte Carlo composite stock; adjustable trigger; Pachmayr Decelerator recoil pad
Magnum:.................**$1311**
With Accubrake:..........**$1573**

MARK V LAZERMARK

Action: bolt
Stock: walnut
Barrel: 26 in. *Sights:* none
Weight: 8.5 lbs.
Caliber: Wby. Magnums from .257 to .340
Magazine: box, 3 rounds
Features: laser-carved stock; button rifled Krieger barrel
MSRP:..................**$2246**

MARK V SPECIAL VARMINT

Action: bolt
Stock: composite
Barrel: 22 in.
Sights: none
Weight: 7.3 lbs.
Caliber: .223, .22-250
Magazine: 4 and 5 rounds
Features: 6-lug action; barrel #3 contour, lapped, fluted
MSRP:..................**$1176**

MARK V SPORTER

Action: bolt
Stock: walnut
Barrel: 24 and 26 in.
Sights: none
Weight: 8.0 lbs.
Caliber: popular magnum chamberings from .257 Wby. Mag. to .340 Wby. Mag.
Magazine: box, 3 or 5 rounds
Features: checkered grip and forend
MSRP:..................**$1361**

MARK V SUPER VARMINT MASTER

Action: bolt
Stock: composite
Barrel: 26 in.
Sights: none
Weight: 8.5 lbs.
Caliber: .223, .22-250, .220 Swift, .243
Magazine: box, 5 rounds
Features: Super Varmint Master has heavy 26 in., fluted stainless barrel, flat-bottomed stock
MSRP:..................**$1772**

MARK V SYNTHETIC

Action: bolt
Stock: synthetic
Barrel: 24, 26 and 28 in.
Sights: none
Weight: 8.5 lbs.
Caliber: popular standard and magnum calibers from .22-250 to .257 Wby. Mag.
Magazine: box, 3 or 5 rounds
Features: also stainless version
Mark V Synthetic:.........**$1099**
Magnum:................**$1160**
With Accubrake:..........**$1370**

Weatherby Rifles

MARK V THREAT RESPONSE

MARK V ULTRA LIGHTWEIGHT

VANGUARD STAINLESS

VANGUARD COMPACT

VANGUARD SPORTER

MARK V THREAT RESPONSE RIFLE
Action: bolt
Stock: composite
Barrel: heavy 22 in.   **Sights:** none
Weight: 8.5 lbs.   **Caliber**: .223, .308
Magazine: box, 5 + 1 rounds
MSRP: $1737

MARK V ULTRA LIGHTWEIGHT
Action: bolt
Stock: composite
Barrel: 24 in. and 26 in.   **Sights:** none
Weight: 6.0 lbs.
Caliber: .243, .240 Wby., .25-06, .270, 7mm-08, .280, 7mm Rem. Mag., .308, .30-06, .300 Win. Mag., Wby. Magnums: .257, .270, 7mm, .300
Magazine: box, 3 or 5 rounds
Features: lightweight action; 6-lug bolt
Ultra Lightweight: $1703

Magnums: $1787

VANGUARD
Action: bolt
Stock: composite
Barrel: 24 in.   **Sights:** none
Weight: 7.8 lbs.
Caliber: .223, .22-250, .243, .270, .308, .30-06, .257 Wby. Mag., 7mm Rem. Mag., .300 Win. Mag., .300 WSM, .270 WSM, .300 Wby. Mag., .338 Win. Mag.
Magazine: internal box, 3-5 rounds
Features: 2-lug action; made in Japan; 1½-inch factory guarantee for 3-shot group
Synthetic: $509
Stainless: $637

VANGUARD COMPACT
Action: bolt
Stock: synthetic

Barrel: 20 in. sporter   **Sights:** none
Weight: 6.75 lbs.
Caliber: .22-250, .243, .308
Magazine: internal box, 5 rounds
Features: Chrome-moly or stainless steel barrel
MSRP: $587

VANGUARD SPORTER
Action: bolt
Stock: checkered walnut
Barrel: 24 in.   **Sights:** none
Weight: 7.75 lbs.
Caliber: 13 chamberings, from .223 to .338 Win. Mag.
Magazine: internal box, 3-5 rounds
Features: Chrome-moly or stainless steel barrel; pillar-bedded composite stock with Aramid, fiberglass and graphite components.
Blue: $652
Stainless: $785

Wild West Guns

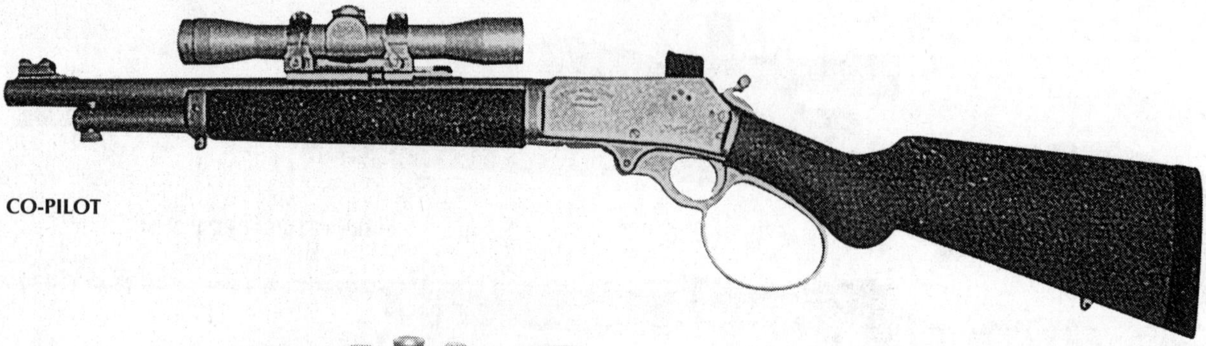

CO-PILOT

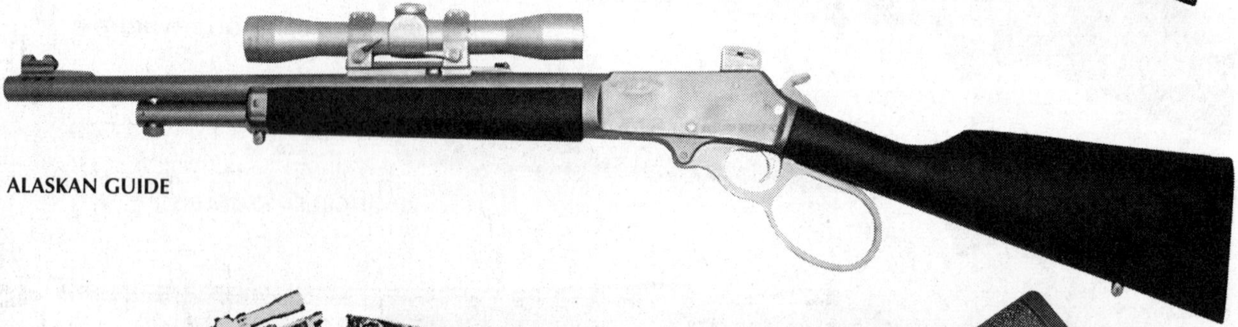

ALASKAN GUIDE

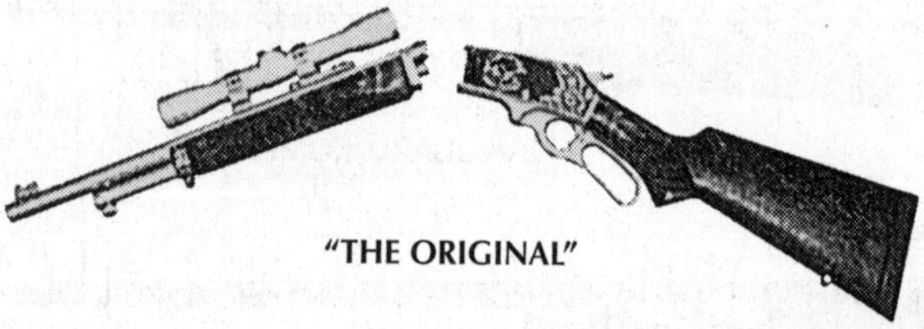

"THE ORIGINAL"

CO-PILOT

Action: lever
Stock: walnut
Barrel: 16, 18 or 20 in.
Sights: illuminated
Weight: 7.0 lbs.
Caliber: .45-70, .457 Magnum,
.50 Alaskan

Magazine: under-barrel tube
Features: 1895 Marlin action; ported
barrels; take-down feature; Alaskan
Guide similar, not take-down
.50 Alaskan conversion: $250
Alaskan on supplied 1895
 Marlin: $935
Alaskan Guide: $1320

Take-Down on supplied
 1895G: $1485
Master Guide Take-Down: . . . $1865
Co-Pilot: $1980
 on supplied 1895 Marlin: . . $1595

*One of the best ways to become a really good rifle
shot is to spend lots of time shooting a .22 rimfire.
The .22's report is mild, recoil is nonexistent, and you
can do lots of shooting for little money. A .22 is the
best tool available for curing shooting problems such
as flinching. It will also reinforce such basics as
trigger squeeze, breath control and follow-through.*

RIFLES

Winchester Rifles

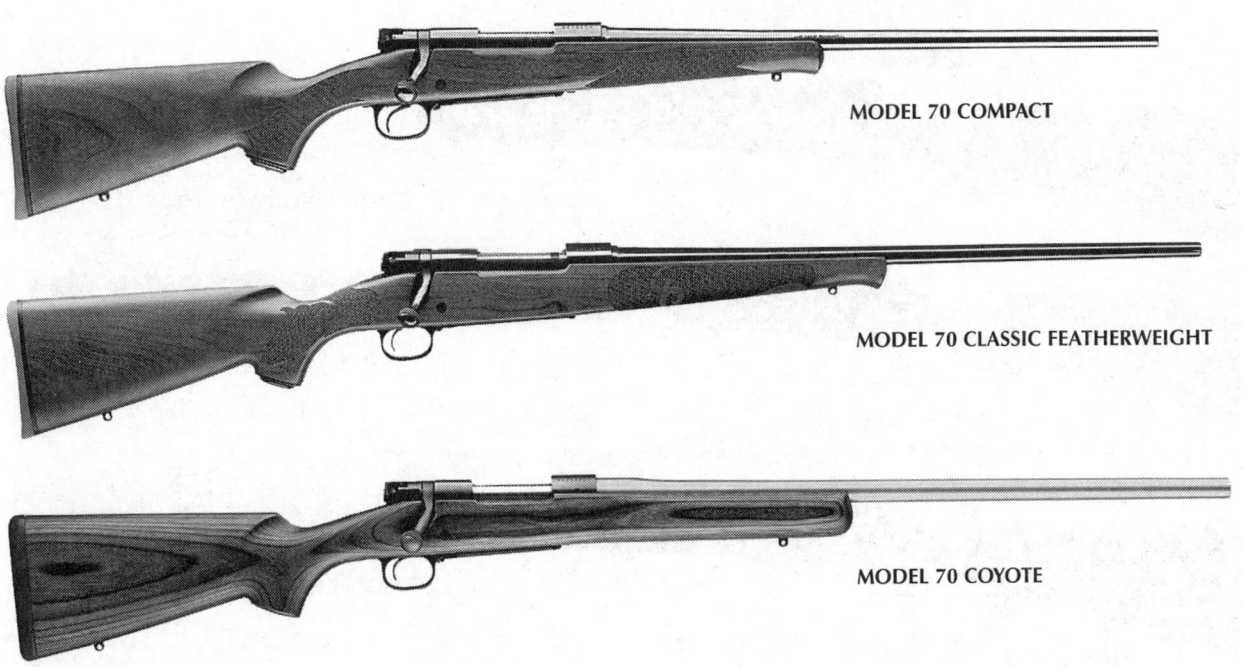

MODEL 70 COMPACT

MODEL 70 CLASSIC FEATHERWEIGHT

MODEL 70 COYOTE

RIFLES

MODEL 70 CLASSIC COMPACT

Action: bolt
Stock: walnut
Barrel: 20 in.
Sights: none
Weight: 6.0 lbs.
Caliber: .243, .308
Magazine: box, 4 rounds
Features: features 13-in. pull for small-frame people
MSRP: **$762**

MODEL 70 CLASSIC FEATHERWEIGHT

Action: bolt
Stock: walnut
Barrel: 22 in. and 24 in.
Sights: none
Weight: 7.0 lbs.
Caliber: .22-250, .243, 6.5x55, .270, .270 WSM, 7-08, 7mm WSM, .308, .30-06, .300 WSM, .223 WSSM, .243 WSSM, .25 WSSM
Magazine: box, 3 or 5 rounds
Features: stainless available in .22-250, .243, .270, .308, .30-06
Classic Featherweight: **$762**
WSM: **$792**
WSSM: **$814**

MODEL 70 CLASSIC SPORTER III

Action: bolt
Stock: walnut
Barrel: 24 in. and 26 in.   *Sights:* none
Weight: 7.8 lbs.
Caliber: .25-06, .270, 7mm Rem. Mag., .30-06, .300 Win. Mag., .338 Win. Mag., .270 WSM, 7mm WSM, .300 WSM
Magazine: box, 3 or 5 rounds
Features: also in .270, 7mm and .300 WSM with laminated stock; left-hand models available
Classic Sporter: **$742**
Magnum: **$773**
WSM: **$773-810**
Classic laminated WSM: **$810**

MODEL 70 CLASSIC STAINLESS

Action: bolt
Stock: synthetic
Barrel: 24 in. and 26 in.   *Sights:* none
Weight: 7.3 lbs.
Caliber: .270, .30-06, .300 Win. Mag., .338 Win. Mag., .375 H&H
Magazine: box, 3 or 5 rounds
Features: open sights on .375 H&H
Classic Stainless: **$817**
Magnum: **$847**
.375: **$943**

MODEL 70 CLASSIC SUPER GRADE

Action: bolt
Stock: walnut
Barrel: 24 in. and 26 in.
Sights: none
Weight: 7.8 lbs.
Caliber: .25-06, .30-06, .300 Win. Mag., .338 Win. Mag., .270 WSM, 7mm WSM, .300 WSM, .325 WSM
Magazine: box, 3 or 5 rounds
Features: also Safari Express in .375 H&H (8.5 lbs.), .416 Rem. Mag. and .458 Win. with open sights
Classic Super Grade: **$1036**
Magnum: **$1067**
Safari Express: **$1149**

MODEL 70 COYOTE

Action: bolt
Stock: laminated
Barrel: 24 in.
Sights: none
Weight: 9.0 lbs.
Caliber: .22-250, .308; also .270 WSM, 7mm WSM, .300 WSM, .223 WSSM, .243 WSSM, .25 WSSM
Magazine: box, 3-5 rounds
Features: push-feed action
Coyote, blue: **$689-742**
Stainless: **$734-787**

Winchester Rifles

MODEL 70 COYOTE LITE

M70 STEALTH II

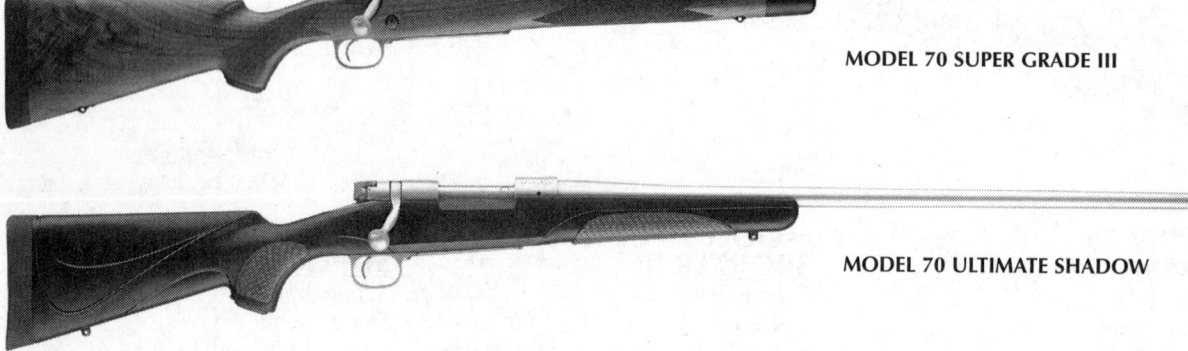

MODEL 70 SUPER GRADE III

MODEL 70 ULTIMATE SHADOW

MODEL 70 COYOTE LITE

Action: bolt
Stock: synthetic
Barrel: 24 in.
Sights: none
Weight: 7.5 lbs.
Caliber: eight chamberings, from .223 to .325 WSM (all WSSM and WSM rounds)
Magazine: internal box, 3-5 rounds
Features: chrome-moly or stainless barrel; lightweight carbon Bell & Carlson synthetic stock with double swivel studs and ventilated forend
MSRP: **$839-930**

MODEL 70 STEALTH II

Action: bolt
Stock: synthetic, beavertail forend with third stud, checkered pistol grip
Barrel: heavy, 26 in.
Sights: none (drilled and tapped for scope mounts)

Weight: 10 lbs.
Caliber: .22-250, .308, .223 WSSM, .243 WSSM, .25 WSSM
Magazine: 3-round box with hinged floorplate
Features: three-position safety; pillar bedding; matte black finish
.22-250 and .308: **$832**
WSSM:. **$886**

MODEL 70 SUPER GRADE III

Action: bolt
Stock: checkered walnut
Barrel: 24 in. and 26 in. sporter
Sights: none
Weight: 7.75-8.0 lbs.
Caliber: nine chamberings, from .25-06 to .325 WSM
Magazine: internal box, 3-5 rounds
Features: new, slimmer stock; inletted swivel studs
Standard:. **$1036**
Magnum:. **$1067**

MODEL 70 ULTIMATE SHADOW

Action: bolt
Stock: composite
Barrel: 22 in. and 24 in.
Sights: none   *Weight:* 6.5 lbs.
Caliber: .223 WSSM, .243 WSSM, .25 WSSM, .270 WSM, 7mm WSM, .300 WSM
Magazine: box, 3 rounds
Features: push-feed; Ultimate Shadow has integrated, rubberized, oval gripping surfaces on the stock pistol grip and forend
WSM: **$817**
WSSM:. **$838**
Stainless: **$914-937**
Camo: **$869-892**
Camo, stainless: **$914-937**
Super Shadow: **$554-576**

Winchester Rifles

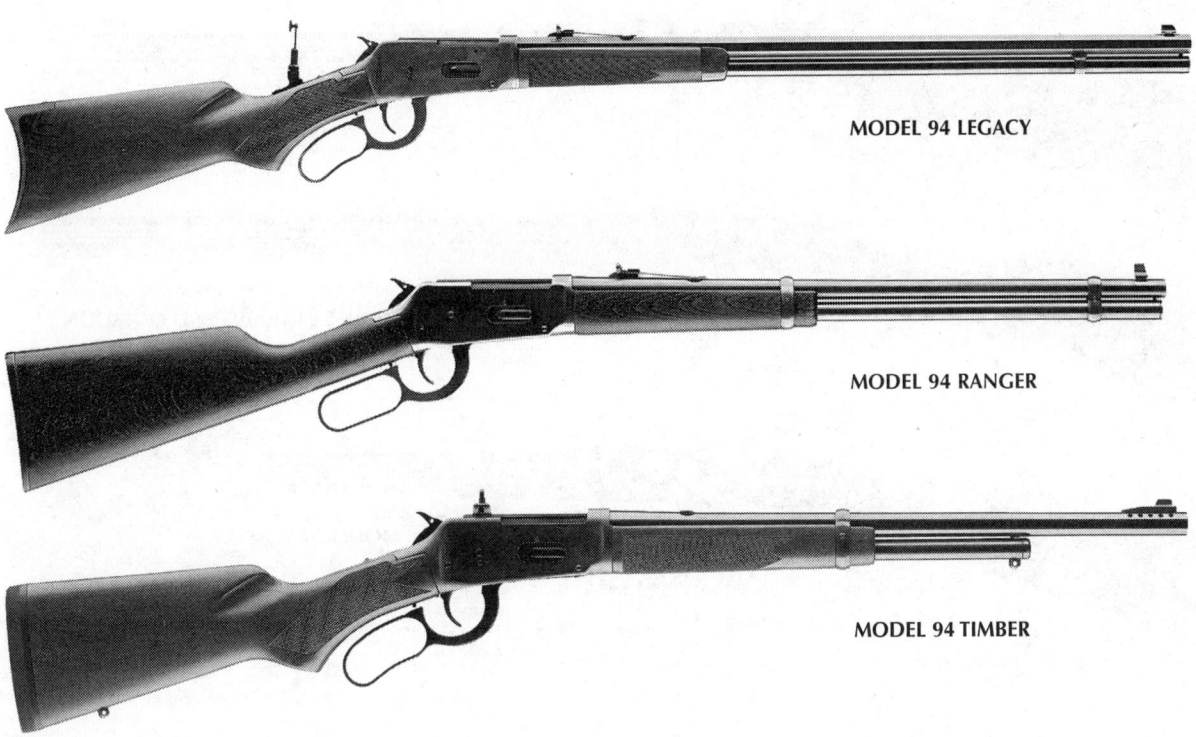

MODEL 94 LEGACY

MODEL 94 RANGER

MODEL 94 TIMBER

MODEL 70 WSSM

Action: bolt
Stock: walnut, synthetic or laminated
Barrel: 24 in.   *Sights:* none
Weight: 6.0 lbs.
Caliber: .223 WSSM, .243 WSSM, .25 WSSM
Magazine: 3 rounds
Features: shortened M70 action; new synthetic shadow stock with grip inserts; laminated Coyote weighs 9 lbs.
Super Shadow: **$576**
Coyote: **$742-930**
Featherweight:. **$814-859**
Classic: **$838-937**
Stealth: **$886**

MODEL 94 LEGACY

Action: lever
Stock: walnut
Barrel: 26 in. round or octagon
Sights: open, with rear Marble's tang peep
Weight: 7.0-7.5 lbs.
Caliber: .30-30 and .38-55
Magazine: full-length tube, 7 rounds
Features: case-colored or blued receiver; Marble adjustable tang sight; steel crescent butt and forend cap
Round blued: **$783**
Round case-colored: **$839**
Octagon blued:. **$882**
Octagon case-colored: **$939**

MODEL 94 RANGER

Action: lever
Stock: hardwood
Barrel: 20 in.
Sights: open
Weight: 4.25 lbs.
Caliber: .30-30 Win.
Magazine: under-barrel tube, 11 rounds
Features: hammer spur extension; tang-top safety; adjustable rear sight
MSRP: **$386**

MODEL 94 TIMBER

Action: exposed-hammer lever
Stock: walnut with checkered forend and pistol grip
Barrel: 18 in., ported
Sights: XS Ghost Ring rear and ramp front with bead
Weight: 6.0 lbs.
Caliber: .450 Marlin
Magazine: under-barrel 2/3-length tube, 4 rounds
Features: Pachmayr recoil pad; cross-bolt safety; receiver drilled and tapped for scope
MSRP: **$597**

Winchester Rifles

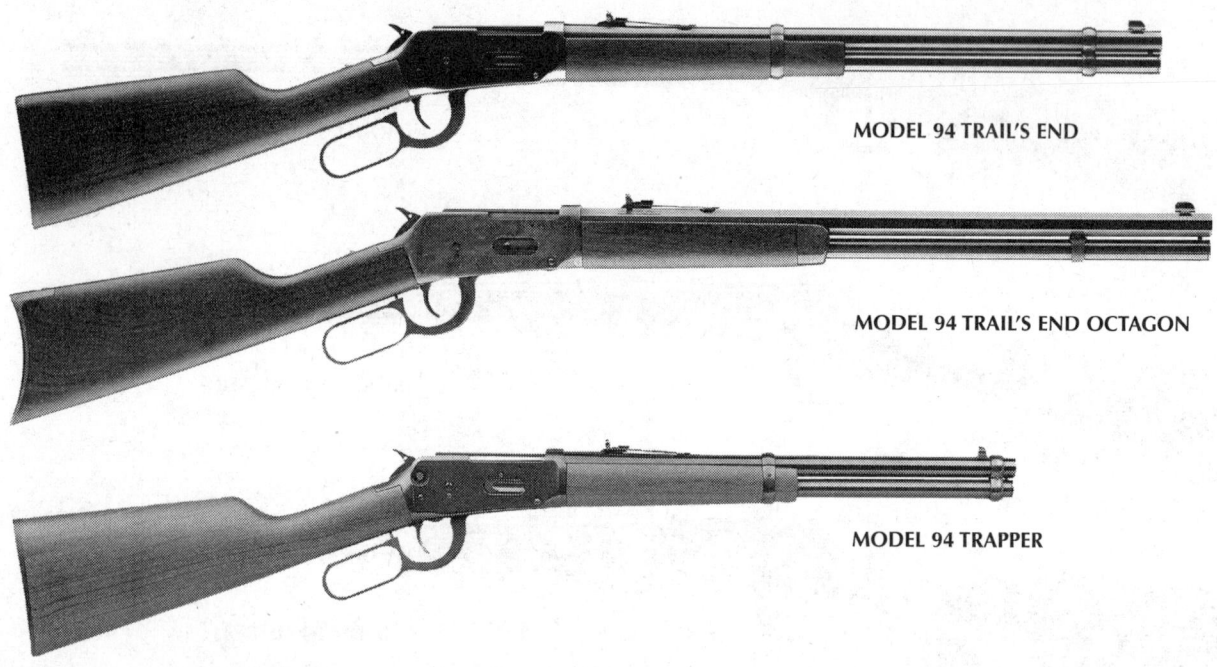

MODEL 94 TRAIL'S END

MODEL 94 TRAIL'S END OCTAGON

MODEL 94 TRAPPER

1885 LOW WALL AND HIGH WALL

Action: dropping block
Stock: checkered walnut
Barrel: 24 in. (Low Wall) 28 in. (High Wall)
Sights: open (Low Wall) and none
Weight: 8.0 lbs. (Low Wall), 8.5 lbs. (High Wall)
Caliber: .17 Mach 2 (Low Wall), and .270, 7mm and .300 WSM
Magazine: none
Features: Case-colored breech; straight-grip walnut stock with crescent butt
1885 Low Wall: $1014
1885 High Wall: $1085

MODEL 94 TRAIL'S END

Action: lever
Stock: walnut, straight grip
Barrel: 20 in.
Sights: open
Weight: 6.5 lbs.
Caliber: .357 Mag., .44 Rem. Mag., .45 Colt
Magazine: full-length tube, 11 rounds
Features: Trails End Hunter round barrel in .25-35 Win., .30-30, .38-55 Win.; large-loop option
Ranger: $377
Trails End: $468
Trails End Hunter: $468

MODEL 94 TRAILS END OCTAGON

Action: exposed-hammer lever
Stock: walnut, uncheckered, with straight grip, forend cap
Barrel: 20 in., octagonal
Sights: step-adjustable semi-buckhorn rear, bead front
Weight: 6.8 lbs.
Caliber: .357 Magnum, .44 Magnum, .45 Colt
Magazine: full-length under-barrel tube, 11 rounds
Features: case colored receiver and furniture on TECC version
Octagon: $757
Case Colored: $816

MODEL 94 TRAPPER

Action: lever
Stock: walnut
Barrel: 16 in.
Sights: open
Weight: 6.0 lbs.
Caliber: .30-30, .357 Mag., .44 Mag., .45 Long Colt
Magazine: under-barrel tube, 5 or 9 rounds
Features: saddle ring; 8 rounds only in .357, .44, .45
MSRP: $458

MODEL 94/22 TRIBUTE

Action: lever
Stock: walnut
Barrel: 20½ in. and 22½ in.
Sights: open
Weight: 6.0 lbs.
Caliber: .22 LR and .22 WMR
Magazine: tube, 15 rounds (LR) and 11 rounds (WMR)
Features: engraving; finish options, straight or pistol grip
MSRP: $516-2313

SHOTGUNS

Armsco Shotguns

MODEL 201

Features: boxlock over/under; single trigger; silver, black or case-finished breech

Canvasback, black 12 & 20: ... $695
Redhead Deluxe, silver, ejectors, 12 & 20: $795
28 & .410: $825
M103 Woodcock Deluxe, case-hardened, ejectors, 12 & 20:. $1056
28 & .410: $1129

MODEL 103
Action: over/under
Stock: walnut pistol grip
Barrel: 26, 28 or 30 in.
Chokes: improved cylinder/modified, screw-in tubes
Weight: 7.0 lbs.
Bore/Gauge: 12, 16, 20, 28, .410
Magazine: none

MODEL 201
Action: side-by-side
Stock: walnut, straight or pistol grip
Barrel: 26 in.
Chokes: improved cylinder/modified, screw-in tubes
Weight: 6.3 lbs.
Bore/Gauge: 12, 16, 20, 28, 410
Magazine: none
Features: boxlock double; single trigger; silver, black or case-finished breech; IC/M in 16 ga. and .410

12 & 20: $869
28 & .410: $1045

MODEL 712
Action: autoloader
Stock: walnut or camo
Barrel: 24, 26 or 28 in.
Chokes: screw-in tubes
Weight: 7.0 lbs.
Bore/Gauge: 12
Magazine: 4 rounds
Features: matte or polished metal
M712, 3-in., walnut: $399
Camo: $460
M720 20 ga. 3-in., walnut: $425
Camo: $499
M712 Mag., 3.5-in., walnut: ... $499
Camo: $599

AYA Shotguns

MODEL 4/53

MODEL 4/53
Action: side-by-side
Stock: walnut, straight grip
Barrel: 26, 27 or 28 in.
Chokes: improved cylinder, modified, full
Weight: 7.0 lbs.
Bore/Gauge: 12, 16, 20, 28, .410
Magazine: none
Features: boxlock; chopper lump barrels; bushed firing pins, automatic safety and ejectors
MSRP: $2795

Most sporting firearm manufacturers tailor their off-the-shelf shotguns to fit an average adult male. But if you're shorter, taller, thinner or heavier than average, your shotgun may require adjustment by a competent gunsmith. Ladies and youngsters frequently require some custom stock work to ensure a good fit.

SHOTGUNS

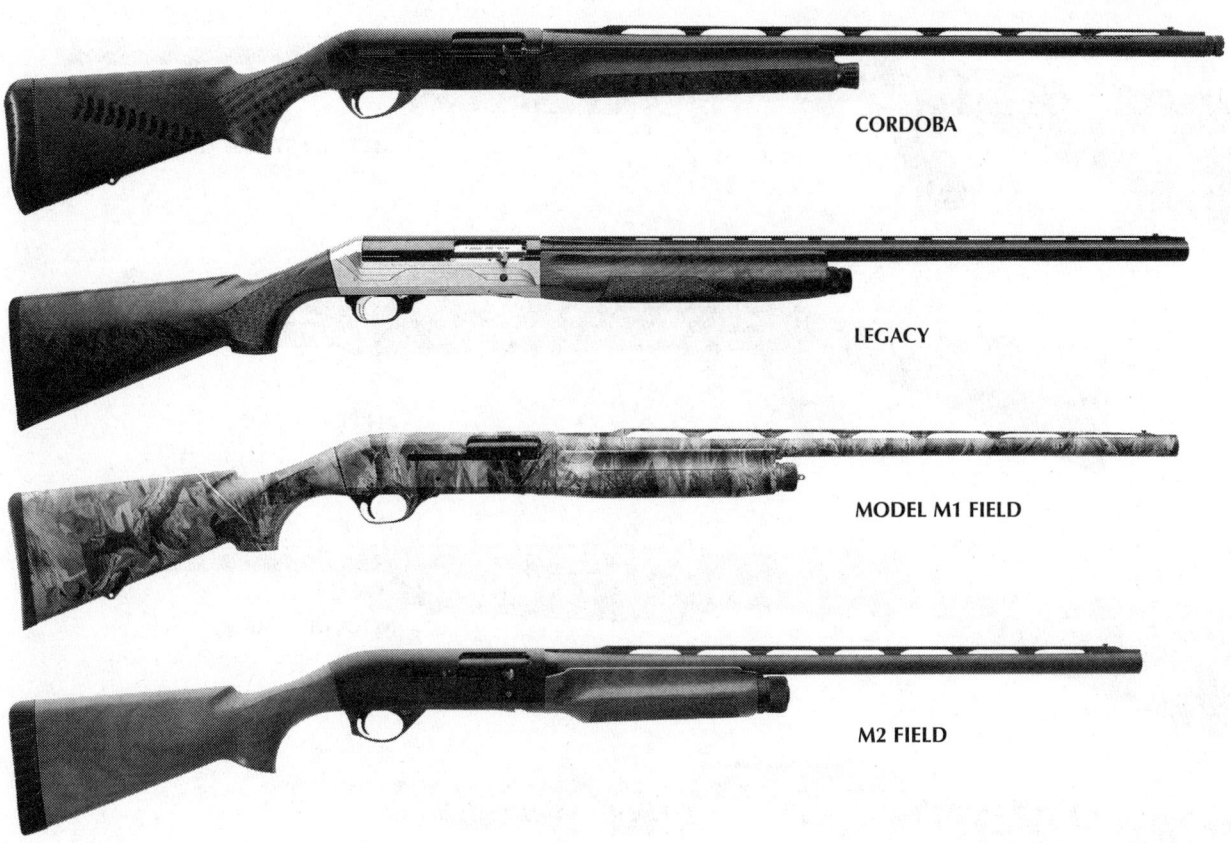

CORDOBA

LEGACY

MODEL M1 FIELD

M2 FIELD

CORDOBA

Action: autoloader
Stock: synthetic with Grip-Tight surface coating
Barrel: 28 or 30 in.
Chokes: screw-in tubes
Weight: 7.85 lbs.
Bore/Gauge: 12
Magazine: 4 rounds
Features: Comfortech recoil reduction system; ported Crio barrel; inertia operated; 3 in. chamber
MSRP: **$1665**

LEGACY

Action: autoloader
Stock: Select walnut
Barrel: 24, 26 or 28 in.
Chokes: screw-in tubes
Weight: 7.5 lbs.
Bore/Gauge: 12, 20
Magazine: 3 rounds
Features: 3 in. chambers; inertia operated; rotating bolt with dual lugs
MSRP: **$1515**

MODEL M1 FIELD

Action: autoloader
Stock: walnut, synthetic or camo
Barrel: 21, 24, 26, 28 or 30 in.
Chokes: screw-in tubes
Weight: 7.3lbs.
Bore/Gauge: 20
Magazine: 3 rounds
Features: 3 in. chambers; inertial recoil system; rotating bolt with dual lugs; rifled slug (12-gauge) about $80 more; Sport: 8 lbs., walnut, 12 ga.; Montefeltro: walnut, 5.3-7.1 lbs.

Synthetic:	**$1000**
Wood:	**$1015**
Montefeltro:	**$1035**
Tactical:	**$1040**
Camo:	**$1100**
Sport:	**$1430**

MODEL M2 FIELD

Action: autoloader
Stock: synthetic or satin walnut
Barrel: 21, 24, 26 or 28 in.
Chokes: screw-in tube
Weight: 6.9-7.1 lbs.
Bore/Gauge: 12
Magazine: 3 rounds
Features: Comfortech recoil reduction system; Crio barrel; inertia operated; 3 in. chamber; rotating bolt with dual lugs; Walnut, Advantage Timber HD, Advantage –MAX-4 camo or black synthetic stock

Walnut:	**$1110**
Synthetic:	**$1175**
Camo:	**$1295**

Benelli Shotguns

M2 FIELD STEADY GRIP

M4 PISTOL GRIP

NOVA HD TIMBER

NOVA H2O PUMP

MODEL M2 FIELD STEADY GRIP, SUPER BLACK EAGLE II STEADY GRIP

Action: autoloader
Stock: synthetic with vertical pistol grip
Barrel: 24 in.
Chokes: Crio tubes
Weight: 7.3lbs.
Bore/Gauge: 12
Magazine: 3 rounds
Features: Benelli inertia operated mechanism; Super Black Eagle II also handles 3½ in. shells
M2 SteadyGrip: **$1335**
Super Black Eagle II:
 SteadyGrip: **$1580**

MODEL M4

Action: autoloader
Stock: synthetic
Barrel: 18.5 in.
Chokes: improved cylinder, modified, full
Weight: 8.0lbs.
Bore/Gauge: 12
Magazine: 4 + 1 rounds
Features: M4 has pistol grip; ARGO gas operated; ghost-ring sight; modular buttstocks
MSRP: **$1535**

NOVA

Action: pump
Stock: synthetic
Barrel: 24, 26 or 28 in.
Chokes: screw-in tubes
Weight: 8.1lbs.
Bore/Gauge: 12, 20
Magazine: 4 rounds
Features: molded polymer (steel rein-

forced) replaces traditional stock and receiver; bolt locks into barrel
Nova synthetic: **$340**
Camo: **$405**
Rifled slug: **$505**
Rifled slug, camo: **$580**

NOVA H20 PUMP

Action: pump
Stock: synthetic
Barrel: 18.5 in.
Chokes: cylinder, fixed
Weight: 7.2 lbs.
Bore/Gauge: 12
Magazine: 4 + 1 rounds
Features: matte nickel finish; open rifle sights
MSRP: **$515**

Benelli Shotguns

SPORT II

SUPER SPORT

SUPER BLACK EAGLE II HD TIMBER

SUPER BLACK EAGLE II MAX-4

SPORT II
Action: recoil-operated autoloader
Stock: walnut, with spacers to adjust drop, cast
Barrel: hammer-forged, ported, cryogenically treated, 28 or 30 in.
Sights: red bar on tapered stepped rib
Chokes: extra-long screw-in tubes (5 provided)
Weight: 7.8 or 8.0 lbs.
Bore/Gauge: 12
Magazine: four-shot tube (2¾ in. shells); two-shot with plug
Features: fires 2¾ and 3 in. shells; light and heavy loads interchangeably without adjustment; easily disassmbled
MSRP: **$1515**

SUPER SPORT
Action: autoloader
Stock: synthetic
Barrel: 24 or 26 in.
Chokes: screw-in tubes
Weight: 7.2 lbs.
Bore/Gauge: 12
Magazine: 4 rounds
Features: Comfortech recoil reduction system; ported Crio barrel; inertia operated; 3 in. chamber; rotating bolt with dual lugs; Carbon Fiber synthetic stock
MSRP: **$1735**

SUPER BLACK EAGLE II
Action: autoloader
Stock: synthetic
Barrel: 24, 26, or 28 in.
Chokes: Crio tubes
Weight: 7.2 lbs.
Bore/Gauge: 12
Magazine: 3 rounds
Features: Comfortech recoil reduction system; Crio barrel; inertia operated; 3½ in. chamber; rotating bolt with dual lugs; Walnut, Advantage Timber HD, Advantage –MAX-4 camo or black synthetic stock.
Walnut: **$1450**
Synthetic: **$1515**
MAX-4 & HD Timber: **$1635**

Beretta Shotguns

MODEL AL391 TEKNYS GOLD

MODEL AL391 URIKA CAMO

MODEL AL391 URIKA

MODEL AL391 XTREMA2 CAMO

MODEL AL391 TEKNYS

Action: autoloader
Stock: walnut
Barrel: 26, 28, 30 or 32 in.
Chokes: screw-in tubes
Weight: 7.3 lbs. (12 ga.), 5.9 lbs. (20 ga.)
Bore/Gauge: 12, 20
Magazine: 3 rounds
Features: self-compensating gas system; Gel-Tek recoil pad; reversible cross-bolt safety; Optima-Bore overbored barrels (12-gauge); Optima Choke flush tubes; Tru-Glo front sight
AL391 Teknys: **$1425**
AL391 Teknys Gold: **$1725**
AL391 Teknys Gold Sporting: . **$1825**
AL391 Teknys Gold Trap: **$1925**

MODEL AL391 URIKA

Action: autoloader
Stock: walnut or synthetic
Barrel: 24, 26, 28 or 30 in.
Chokes: screw-in tubes
Weight: 7.3 lbs.
Bore/Gauge: 12, 20
Magazine: 3 rounds
Features: gas-operated action; alloy receiver; stock adjustment shims; high-grade "Gold" versions available
Synthetic: **$998**
Wood: **$1050**
Camo: **$1175**
Youth: **$1050**
Trap: **$1250**
Sporting: **$1250**
Parallel Target: **$1250**
Parallel Target RL: **$1250**
Parallel Target SL: **$1250**
Gold: **$1500**

MODEL A391 XTREMA2

Action: autoloader
Stock: synthetic
Barrel: 26, 28 in.
Chokes: screw-in tubes
Weight: 7.8 lbs.
Bore/Gauge: 12
Magazine: 3 rounds
Features: 3½ in. chambers; self-cleaning gas system; Kick-Off recoil reduction; spring/mass recoil reducer; Gel-Tek; Aqua Technology; stock adjustment shims; quick-detach sling swivel
Synthetic: **$1098**
 synthetic (no KO): **$1098**
 synthetic (KO): **$1498**
Camo: **$1275**
 camo (no KO): **$1198**
 camo (KO): **$1598**
Rifled: **$1450**
 rifled (no KO): **$1098**
 rifled (KO): **$1598**

Beretta Shotguns

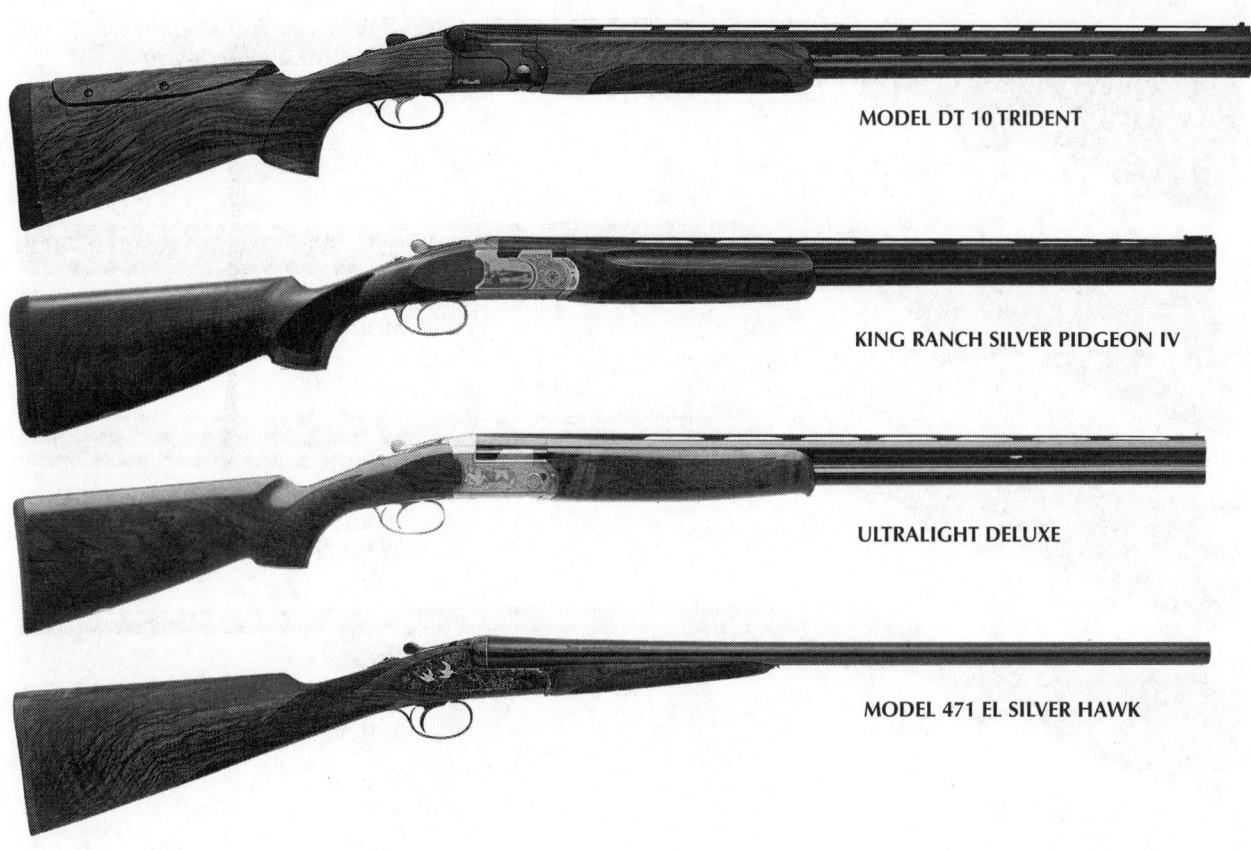

MODEL DT 10 TRIDENT

KING RANCH SILVER PIDGEON IV

ULTRALIGHT DELUXE

MODEL 471 EL SILVER HAWK

MODEL DT 10 TRIDENT

Action: over/under
Stock: walnut
Barrel: 28, 30, 32 or 34 in.
Chokes: screw-in tubes
Weight: 7.5 lbs.
Bore/Gauge: 12
Magazine: none
Features: boxlock; single selective trigger; automatic ejectors; Skeet, Trap and Sporting models are Beretta's best competition guns; combo with top single or bottom single; Trap versions available
Sporting: **$6475**
Trap: **$7125**
Trap, Bottom Single: **$7775**
Trap, Combo Top Single: . . . **$10100**

KING RANCH SERIES

Action: over/under & autoloader
Stock: walnut, oil finish
Barrel: 26, 28 in.
Chokes: Mobilchoke
Weight: various
Bore/Gauge: 12, 20, 28
Magazine: 2, 3 rounds
Features: engraving motifs derived from King Ranch executed on popular Beretta models; Limited Editions
AL391 Teknys KR: **$1825**
686 Silver Pigeon S: **$2350**
687 Silver Pigeon IV: **$3175**
687 Diamond Pigeon EELL: . . **$6995**

ULTRALIGHT SERIES

Action: O/U, improved box lock
Stock: select walnut
Barrel: 28 in.
Chokes: screw-in tubes (Mobilchoke)
Weight: 5.75 lbs.
Bore/Gauge: 12
Magazine: none
Features: aluminum, titanium-reinforced frame; single selective trigger; automatic safety; 2¾ in. chamber; Schnabel fore-end; checkered stock; gold inlay
Ultralight: **$1994**
Ultralight Deluxe: **$2408**

MODELS 471 & 471 EL SILVER HAWK

Action: side-by-side
Stock: walnut
Barrel: 26 or 28 in.
Chokes: 12 Gauge Optima Chokes, 20 Gauge Mobilechokes, or fixed chokes
Weight: 6.5 lbs. (5.9 lbs. 20 ga)
Bore/Gauge: 12, 20
Magazine: none
Features: boxlock; satin chromed or case-colored receiver; single selective trigger or double triggers; automatic ejectors; EL has case-colored receiver; gold inlay; straight or pistol grips
Model 471: **$3625**
Model 471 EL: **$8350**

Beretta Shotguns

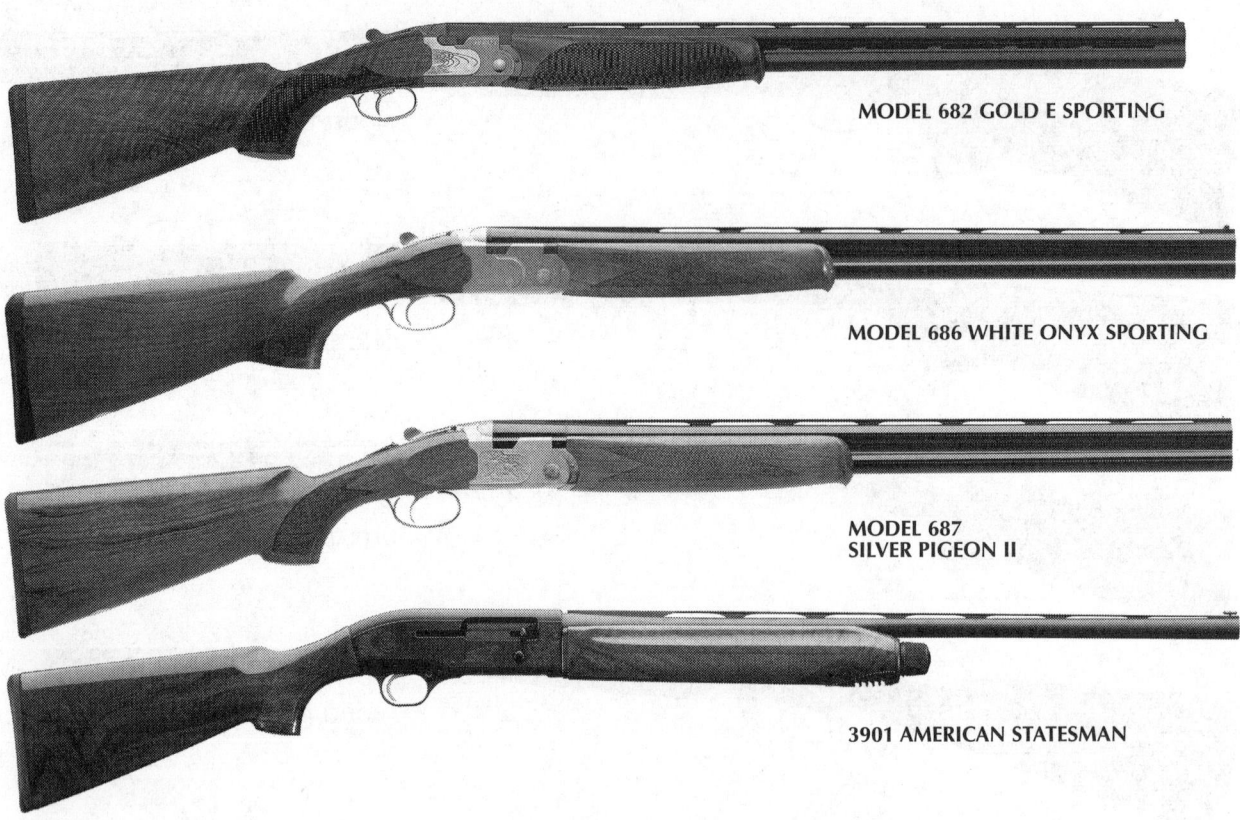

MODEL 682 GOLD E SPORTING

MODEL 686 WHITE ONYX SPORTING

MODEL 687 SILVER PIGEON II

3901 AMERICAN STATESMAN

MODEL 682 GOLD E

Action: over/under
Stock: walnut
Barrel: 28, 30 or 32 in.
Chokes: screw-in tubes
Weight: 6.5 lbs.
Bore/Gauge: 12
Magazine: none
Features: boxlock; single selective adjustable trigger; automatic ejectors; adjustable combs on Skeet and Trap models

Sporting:	**$3550**
Skeet:	**$4325**
Trap:	**$4325**
LTD Sporting:	**$5075**
Combo Trap:	**$5475**
LTD Trap Combo:	**$6775**

MODEL 686 ONYX SERIES

Action: over/under
Stock: walnut
Barrel: 26, 28, 30 in.
Chokes: screw-in tubes
Weight: 6.8-7.7lbs. (12 ga)
Bore/Gauge: 12, 20, 28, .410
Magazine: none

Features: boxlock; 3 in. chambers; single selective trigger; automatic ejectors; 3.5 has 3½ in. chambers

Onyx Pro:	**$1875**
Onyx Pro 3.5:	**$1975**
White Onyx:	**$1875**
White Onyx Sporting:	**$1975**

MODEL 687 PIGEON SERIES

Action: over/under
Stock: walnut
Barrel: 26, 28, 30 in.
Chokes: screw-in tubes
Weight: 6.8 lbs. (12 ga)
Bore/Gauge: 12, 20, 20/28 & 28/.410 Combo
Magazine: none
Features: boxlock; 3-inch chambers; single selective trigger; automatic ejectors;

Silver Pigeon S:	**$2150**
Silver Pigeon II:	**$2525**
Silver Pigeon III:	**$2650**
Silver Pigeon IV:	**$2955**
Silver Pigeon V:	**$3495**
EL Gold Pigeon II:	**$5095**
EELL Diamond Pigeon:	**$6395**

3901 AMERICAN SERIES

Action: autoloader
Stock: walnut or synthetic
Barrel: 26, 28 in.
Chokes: Mobil-choke F-M-IC
Weight: 7.4 lbs.
Bore/Gauge: 12, 20
Magazine: 3 rounds
Features: self-compensating gas operation; stock shim; Gel-Tek & Tru-Glo sights (Ambassdor); adjustable comb (Target RL only); assembled in the USA.

Citizen:	**$750**
Ambassador:	**$798**
Rifled Slug:	**$799**
Statesman:	**$898**
Target RL:	**$898**

Bernardelli Shotguns

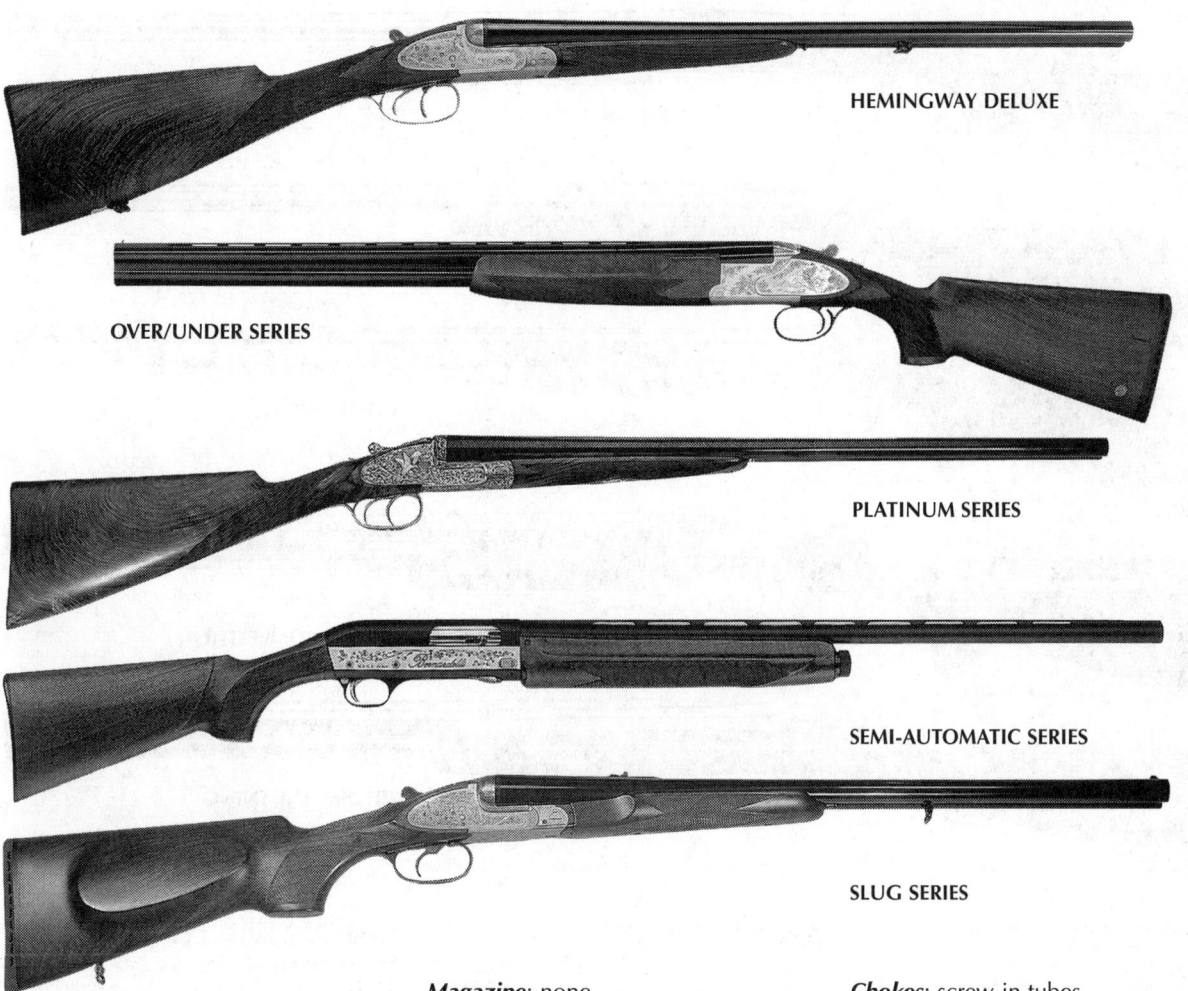

HEMINGWAY DELUXE

OVER/UNDER SERIES

PLATINUM SERIES

SEMI-AUTOMATIC SERIES

SLUG SERIES

HEMINGWAY DELUXE

Action: side-by-side
Stock: walnut, straight grip
Barrel: 26 in.
Chokes: modified, improved modified, full
Weight: 6.25 lbs.
Bore/Gauge: 16, 20, 28
Magazine: none
Features: boxlock double; single or double trigger; automatic ejectors
MSRP: . . . .**price on request**

OVER/UNDER SERIES

Action: over/under
Stock: walnut, pistol grip
Barrel: 26 or 28 in.
Chokes: modified, improved modified, full, screw-in tubes
Weight: 7.2 lbs.
Bore/Gauge: 12, 20

Magazine: none
Features: boxlock over/under; single or double triggers; vent rib, various grades
MSRP: . . . .**price on request**

PLATINUM SERIES

Action: side-by-side
Stock: walnut, straight or pistol grip
Barrel: 26 or 28 in.
Chokes: modified, improved modified, full
Weight: 6.5 lbs.
Bore/Gauge: 12
Magazine: none
Features: sidelock double; articulated single selective or double trigger; triple-lug Purdey breeching automatic ejectors; various grades
MSRP: . . . .**price on request**

SEMI-AUTOMATIC SERIES

Action: autoloader
Stock: walnut, synthetic or camo
Barrel: 24, 26 or 28 in.

Chokes: screw-in tubes
Weight: 6.7 lbs.
Bore/Gauge: 12
Magazine: 5 rounds
Features: gas-operated; concave top rib; ABS case included
MSRP: . . . .**price on request**

SLUG SERIES

Action: side-by-side
Stock: walnut, pistol grip
Barrel: 24 in.
Chokes: modified, improved modified, full
Weight: 7.0 lbs.
Bore/Gauge: 12
Magazine: none
Features: boxlock double; single or double trigger; automatic ejectors; rifle sights
MSRP: . . . .**price on request**

Browning Shotguns

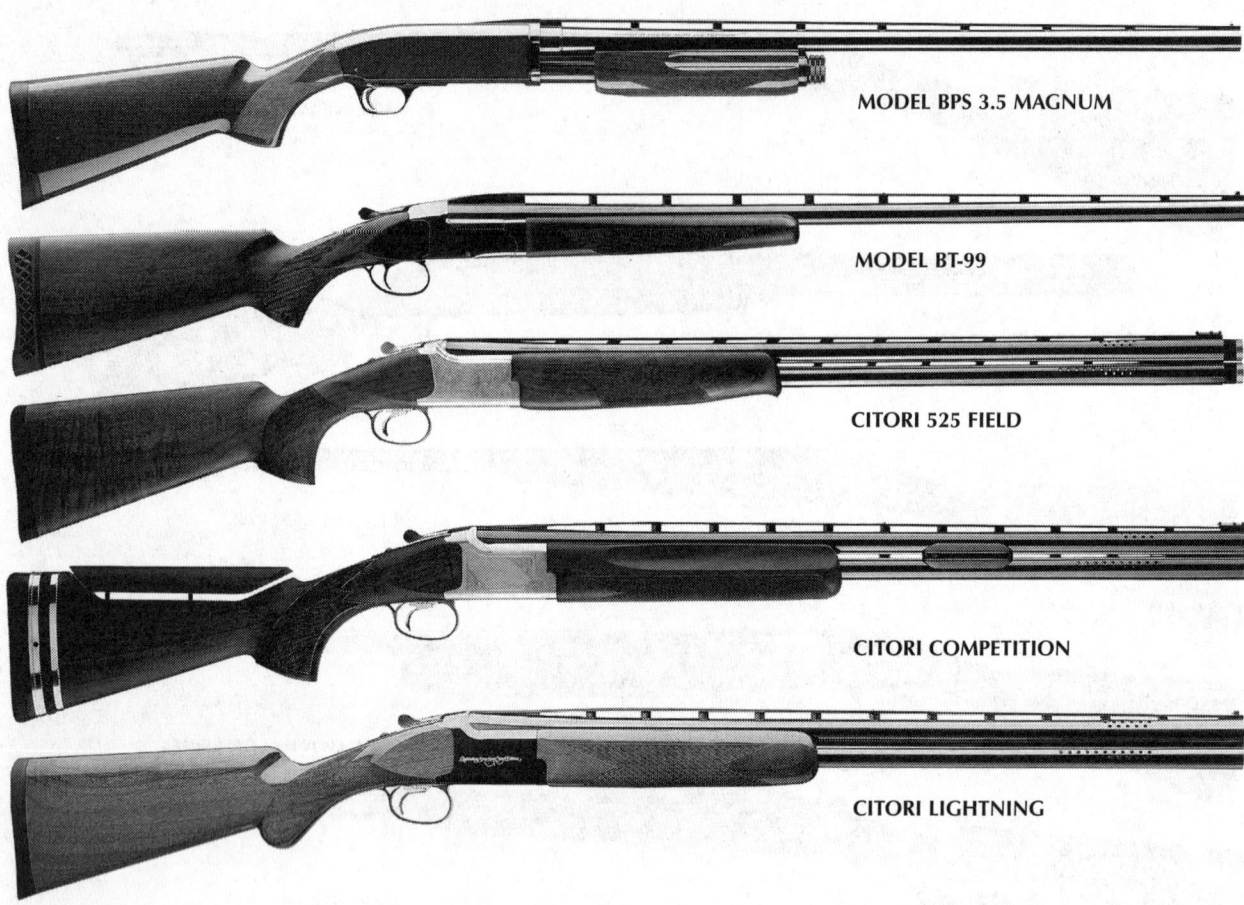

MODEL BPS 3.5 MAGNUM

MODEL BT-99

CITORI 525 FIELD

CITORI COMPETITION

CITORI LIGHTNING

MODEL BPS

Action: pump
Stock: walnut or synthetic
Barrel: 20, 22, 24, 26, 28 or 30 in.
Chokes: screw-in tubes
Weight: 8.0 lbs.
Bore/Gauge: 10, 12, 20, 28, .410
Magazine: 4 rounds
Features: Both 10 and 12 gauge available with 3½ in. chambers; Upland Special has short barrel, straight grip; Deer Special has rifled barrel; Micro BPS has short barrel, stock

Stalker (synthetic):	**$492**
Hunter (walnut):	**$509**
28 or .410:	**$544**
Upland (12, 20):	**$509**
Micro (20):	**$509**
Magnum (3.5-inch):	**$579**
Camo synthetic:	**$605**
Rifled Deer (12):	**$624**
Magnum Camo:	**$688**

MODEL BT-99

Action: hinged single-shot
Stock: walnut, trap-style
Barrel: 30, 32 or 34 in.
Chokes: screw-in tubes
Weight: 8.0 lbs.
Bore/Gauge: 12 *Magazine:* none
Features: boxlock single-shot competition gun with high-post rib

BT-99:	**$1369**
with adjustable comb:	**$1632**
Micro:	**$1369**
Golden Clays	
with adjustable comb:	**$3614**

CITORI 525

Action: over/under *Stock:* walnut
Barrel: 26, 28, 30 or 32 in.
Chokes: screw-in tubes
Weight: 7.3 lbs.
Bore/Gauge: 12, 20, 28, .410
Magazine: none
Features: boxlock; European-style stock; pronounced pistol grip; floating top and side ribs; Golden Clays has gold inlays

Field:	**$2021-2050**
Sporting Grade I:	**$2369**
Sporting:	**$2861-2871**
Golden Clays:	**$4584-4793**

CITORI COMPETITION

Action: over/under
Stock: walnut
Barrel: 26, 28 or 30 in.
Chokes: screw-in tubes
Weight: 8.0 lbs.
Bore/Gauge: 12 *Magazine:* none
Features: boxlock; XS Pro-Comp has ported barrels, adjustable stock comb, GraCoil recoil reducer; Trap and Skeet Models are stocked and barreled accordingly

XT Trap:	**$2343**
XT Trap	
with adjustable comb:	**$2625**
XT Trap Gold	
with adjustable comb:	**$4348**
XS Skeet:	**$2507**
XS Skeet	
with adjustable comb:	**$2789**

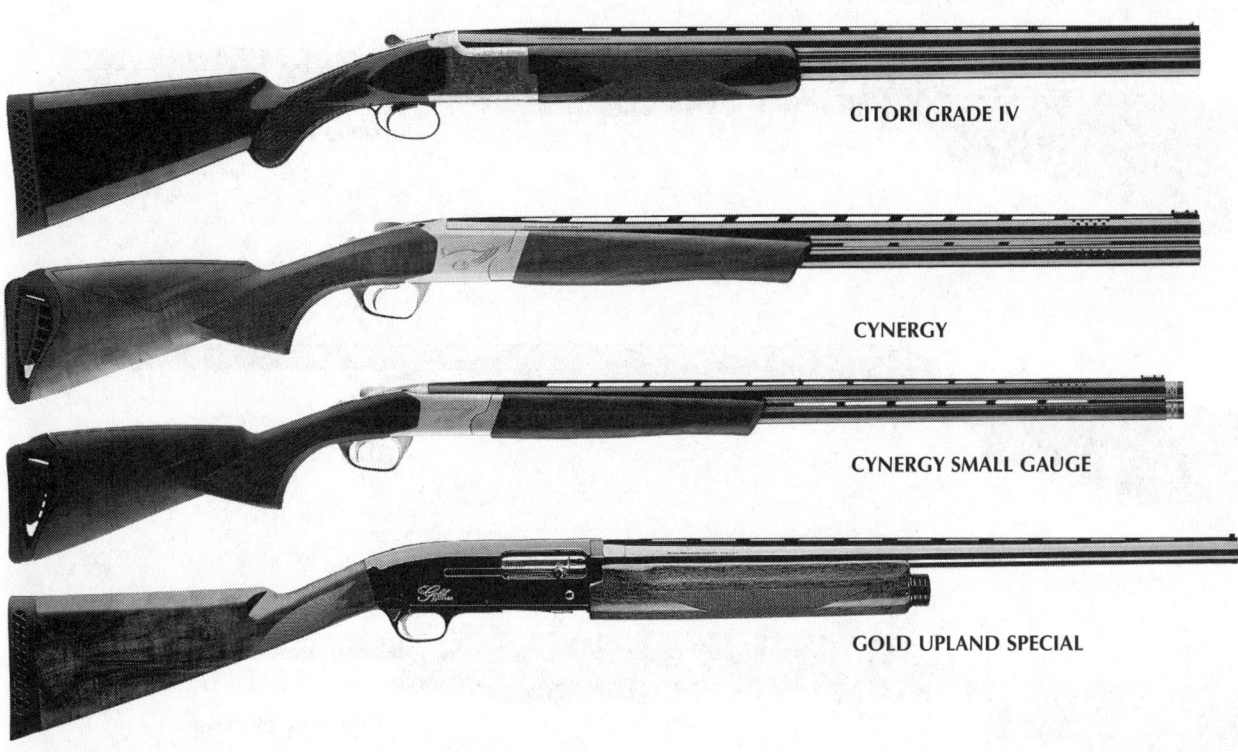

CITORI GRADE IV

CYNERGY

CYNERGY SMALL GAUGE

GOLD UPLAND SPECIAL

CITORI LIGHTNING

Action: over/under
Stock: walnut
Barrel: 26 or 28 in.
Chokes: screw-in tubes
Weight: 6.3-8.0 lbs.
Bore/Gauge: 12, 20, 28, .410
Magazine: none
Features: boxlock; single selective trigger, automatic ejectors; higher grades available; ported barrels optional
Citori Lightning: **$1678**
28 & .410: **$1743**
Citori White Lightning: **$1748**
28 & .410: **$1826**
Citori Lightning Feather: ... **$1906**
Citori Superlight Feather: ... **$1977**

CITORI GRADE IV AND VII LIGHTNING

Action: over/under
Stock: select walnut
Barrel: 26 and 28 in., backbored, 3 in. chambers in 12, 20 and .410
Chokes: screw-in tubes
Weight: 6.5-8.0 lbs.
Bore/Gauge: 12, 20, 28 and .410
Magazine: none
Features: Boxlock action with automatic ejectors; engraved receivers
12, 20 Grade IV: **$2660**

28, .410 Grade IV: **$2978**
12, 20 Grade VII: **$4229**
28, .410 Grade VII: **$4555**

CYNERGY

Action: box-lock over/under, with reverse striker firing mechanism
Stock: walnut, oil-finished and checkered, or composite, both with black recoil pad
Barrel: 26, 28, 30 or 32 in., fitted with removable choke tubes
Sights: double beads on tapered rib
Chokes: screw-in tubes (three provided)
Weight: 7.7 lbs.
Bore/Gauge: 12
Magazine: none
Features: single selective trigger; manual safety; selective ejectors
Cynergy: **$1890-3046**
Also available:
    20 & 28 ga. **$2062-3080**

CYNERGY SMALL GAUGE

Action: over/under
Stock: walnut
Barrel: 26 or 28 in. (Field), 30 or 32 in. (Sporting)
Chokes: screw-in tubes
Weight: 6.25-6.5 lbs
Bore/Gauge: 20 and 28

Magazine: none
Features: Boxlock action; 20 gauge comes with ported barrels; mechanical single trigger
Field: **$2062**
Sporting: **$3080**

GOLD

Action: autoloader
Stock: wal. (Hunter) or syn. (Stalker)
Barrel: 24, 26, 28 or 30 in.
Chokes: screw-in tubes
Weight: 8.0 lbs.
Bore/Gauge: 10, 12, 20
Magazine: 3 rounds
Features: gas-operated, 3½-inch chambers on 10 and one 12 gauge version; Youth and Ladies versions available
Stalker: **$981**
Hunter: **$1025**
Micro: **$1025**
Upland Special: **$1025**
Rifled Deer Stalker
    (22 in. bbl.): **$1086**
Sporting Clays: **$1105**
Gold Fusion: **$1129**
Rifled Deer Hunter: **$1131**
3½-inch Hunter: **$1148**
Camo: **$1127-1332**
Gold Light (10 ga.): **$1336**
Gold Fusion HighGrade: **$2095**

SHOTGUNS

Charles Daly Shotguns

EMPIRE II EDL HUNTER

FIELD HUNTER CAMO

FIELD HUNTER PUMP

EMPIRE II EDL HUNTER
Action: over/under
Stock: walnut
Barrel: 26 or 28 in.
Chokes: screw-in tubes
Weight: 7.2 lbs.
Bore/Gauge: 12, 20, 28, .410
Magazine: none
Features: boxlock; single selective trigger; automatic safety; automatic ejectors

28 ga.:	$2019
.410:	$2019
12 or 20 ga.:	$2029
Trap:	$2099

FIELD HUNTER AUTOLOADER
Action: autoloader
Stock: synthetic
Barrel: 22, 24, 26, 28 or 30 in.
Chokes: screw-in tubes
Weight: 7.5 lbs.
Bore/Gauge: 12, 20, 28
Magazine: 4 rounds
Features: ventilated rib; Superior II Grade has walnut stock, ported barrel

12 or 20 ga.:	$389
28 ga.:	$459
Camo:	$459
3.5-in. magnum synthetic:	$469
3.5-in. magnum camo:	$539
Superior Hunter:	$539
Superior Trap:	$589

FIELD HUNTER PUMP
Action: pump
Stock: synthetic
Barrel: 26 or 28 in.
Chokes: screw-in tubes
Weight: 7.0 lbs.
Bore/Gauge: 12, 20
Magazine: 4 rounds
Features: ventilated rib

Field Hunter:	$219
Camo:	$289
3.5-in. magnum synthetic:	$259
3.5-in. magnum camo:	$319

Lifting your head off the stock is one of the most frequent causes of missed targets when shotgunning. Your master eye is actually the rear sight of the gun, and to keep that rear sight on target, your head must stay on the stock. If you move your head at all, your master eye (your rear sight) moves too, and the result is almost always a miss. Keep your head down until the shot has been fired.

Charles Daly Shotguns

FIELD II

FIELD II ULTRA-LIGHT

FIELD II HUNTER SXS

SUPERIOR COMBINATION GUN

FIELD II
Action: over/under
Stock: walnut
Barrel: 26 or 28 in.
Chokes: mod/full (28 in.), imp.cyl/mod (26 in.), full/full (.410)
Weight: 7.2 lbs.
Bore/Gauge: 12, 16, 20, 28, .410
Magazine: none
Features: boxlock; single selective trigger; automatic safety

Field II: **$1029**
28-gauge: **$1129**
.410: **$1129**
Ultra-Light (12, 20): **$1199**
Superior II: **$1519**
Superior II Trap: **$1699**

FIELD II HUNTER SXS
Action: side-by-side
Stock: walnut
Barrel: 26, 28 or 30 in.
Chokes: imp.cyl/mod (26 in.), mod/full (28, 30 in.), full/full (.410)
Weight: 10.0 lbs.
Bore/Gauge: 12, 16, 20, 28, .410
Magazine: none
Features: boxlock; single selective trigger; automatic safety

12 or 20 ga.: **$1189**
16, 28 ga. or .410: **$1099**
Superior Grade: **$1629-1659**
Empire Grade: **$2119**

SUPERIOR COMBINATION GUN
Action: over/under
Stock: walnut
Barrel: 24 in.
Chokes: improved cylinder
Weight: 7.5 lbs.
Bore/Gauge: 12
Magazine: none
Features: boxlock drilling; 12 gauge over .22 Hornet, .223 or .30-06 rifle; double triggers; sling swivels

Superior: **$1479**
Empire Grade: **$2189**
Superior Express (.30-06): ... **$2259**
Empire Express (.30-06, .375 H&H, .416 Rigby): **$2949-3659**

CZ Shotguns

RINGNECK

DURANGO

WOODCOCK

712/720

AMARILLO AND DURANGO
Action: Side-by-side
Stock: walnut
Barrel: 20 in.   *Weight:* 6.0 lbs.
Bore/Gauge: 20, 12
Magazine: none
Features: Color case-hardened receiver; trigger guard and forend; single trigger (Durango); double trigger (Amarillo); hand checkered walnut stock with round knob pistol grip; overall length: 37.5 in.; 14.5 in. LOP
Amarillo: **$795**
Durango: **$795**

BOBWHITE AND RINGNECK
Action: side-by-side
Stock: Turkish walnut   *Barrel:* 26 in.
Chokes: Screw-in chokes (12 & 20); fixed chokes in .410. (IC & Mod)
Weight: 5.2 lbs.
Bore/Gauge: 20, 28, 12, .410
Magazine: none
Features: Color case-hardened finish and hand engraving; 20 and 28 gauge

built on appropriate size frame; straight English-style grip and double triggers (Bobwhite); American pistol grip with a single trigger (Ringneck); hand checkered; overall length 43 in.;14.5 in. LOP
Bobwhite: **$869**
Ringneck: **$1095**

CZ SHOTGUNS
Action: boxlock
Stock: checkered Turkish or American walnut
Barrel: 26 and 28 in.
Chokes: choke tubes in 12 and 20 gauge, fixed chokes in 28
Weight: 5.75-7.75 lbs.
Bore/Gauge: 12, 20, 28, .410
Magazine Capacity: no magazine
Features: silvered or case-colored receivers; Woodcock and Redhead Deluxe have auto ejectors; Ringneck with hand engraving.
Side-by-sides: **$795-1045**
Mallard O/U: **$487**
Single-trigger O/Us: . . . . **$695-$1129**
Woodcock O/U: **$1078**

CZ 712/720
Action: gas-operated autoloading
Stock: Turkish walnut
Barrel: 26 or 28 in., chrome-lined, with IC, Mod and Full choke tubes provided
Sights: front bead
Chokes: screw-in tubes (three provided)
Weight: 7.3 lbs.
Bore/Gauge: 12
Magazine: 4-shot without plug
Features: 3 in. chamber
CZ 712/720: **$399**
CZ 712 Magnum: **$499**

Flodman Shotguns

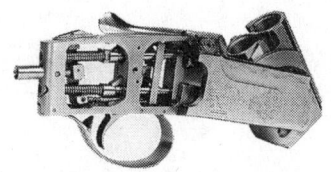

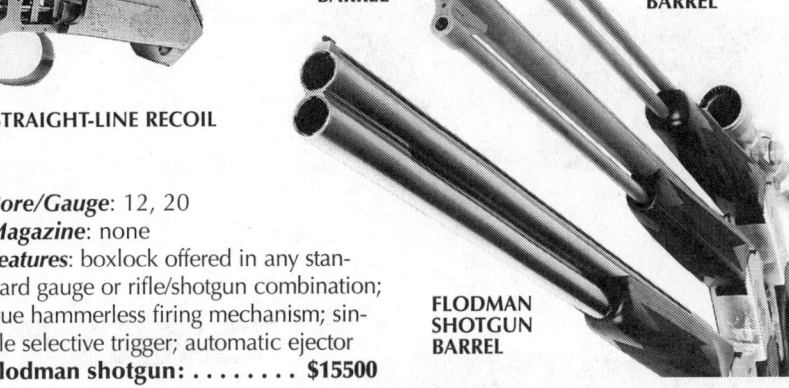

STRAIGHT-LINE RECOIL

FLODMAN COMBI BARREL

FLODMAN DOUBLE-RIFLE BARREL

FLODMAN SHOTGUN BARREL

FLODMAN SHOTGUN

Action: over/under
Stock: walnut, fitted to customer
Barrel: any standard length
Chokes: improved cylinder, modified, full
Weight: 7.0 lbs.

Bore/Gauge: 12, 20
Magazine: none
Features: boxlock offered in any standard gauge or rifle/shotgun combination; true hammerless firing mechanism; single selective trigger; automatic ejector
Flodman shotgun: **$15500**

Franchi Shotguns

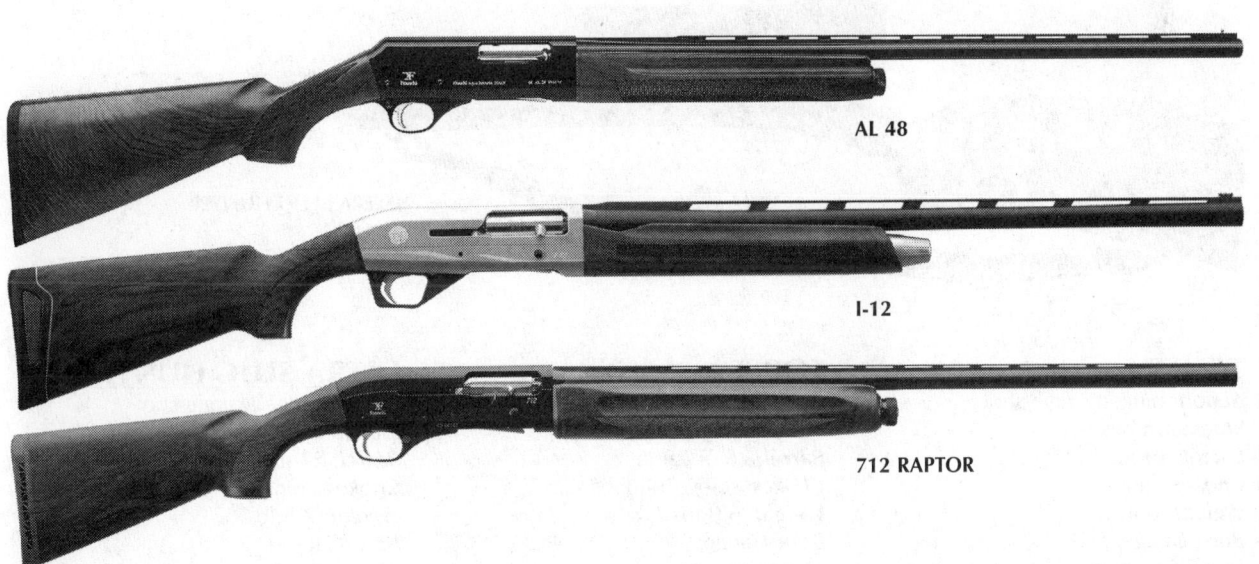

AL 48

I-12

712 RAPTOR

MODEL AL 48

Action: autoloader
Stock: walnut pistol grip or English – pistol grip only
Barrel: 24, 26 or 28 in.
Chokes: screw-in tubes
Weight: 5.6 lbs.
Bore/Gauge: 20, 28
Magazine: 4 rounds
Features: long recoil action
20 ga.: **$749**
28 ga.: **$850**
Deluxe 20: **$970**
Deluxe 28: **$1029**

MODEL I-12

Action: autoloader
Stock: walnut, black or camo synthetic
Barrel: 24, 26, or 28 in.
Chokes: screw-in tubes
Weight: 7.5 lbs.
Bore/Gauge: 12
Magazine: 4 rounds
Features: Inertia-recoil; rotary bolt; TSA recoil reduction
MSRP: . . . . **$679-$779**

712 RAPTOR, 720

Action: autoloader
Stock: walnut with WeatherCoat protection
Barrel: 30 in. (712 Raptor), 24, 26, 28 in. (720)
Chokes: screw-in tubes
Weight: 7 lbs (712), 6.25 lbs (720)
Bore/Gauge: 12 and 20
Magazine: 5 rounds (712) and 4 rounds (720)
Features: Satin nickel receiver finish; 3 in. chambers
MSRP: **$850**

SHOTGUNS

Harrington & Richardson Shotguns

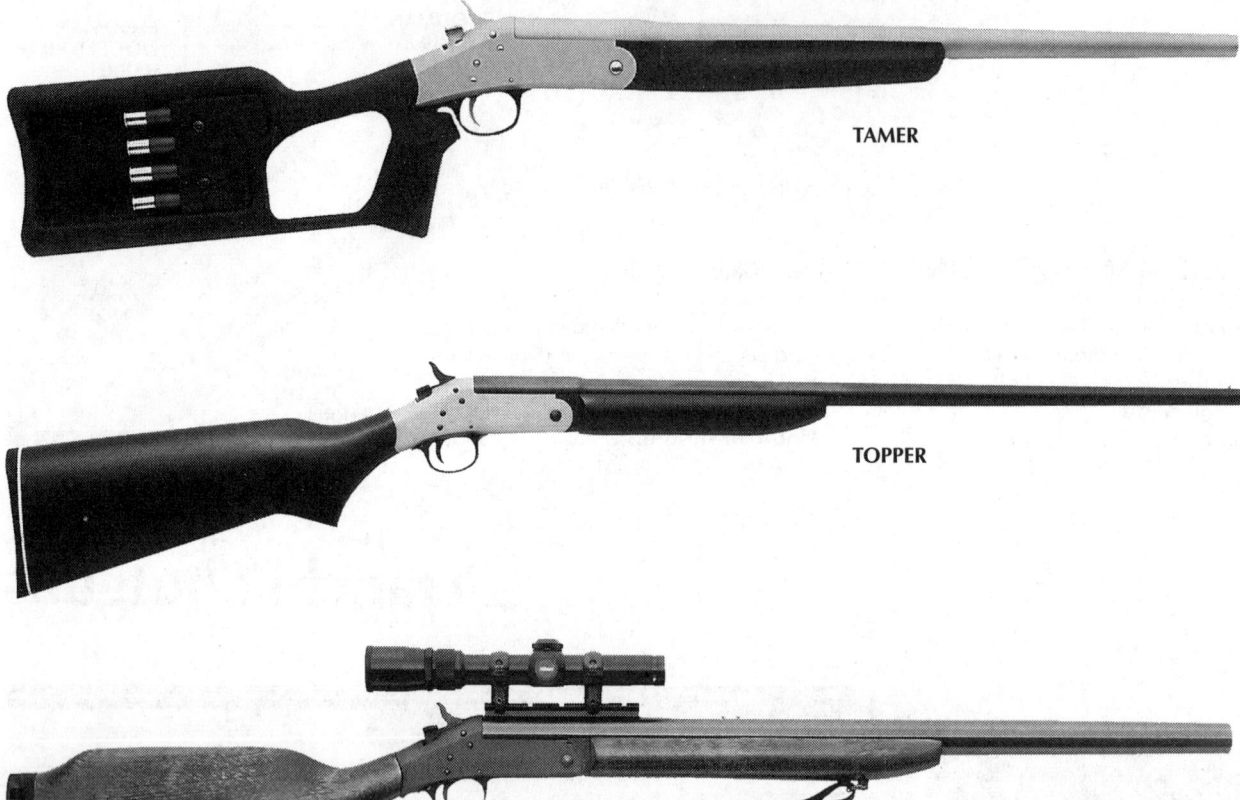

TAMER

TOPPER

ULTRA SLUG HUNTER

TAMER
Action: hinged single-shot
Stock: synthetic
Barrel: 19 in.
Chokes: full
Weight: 6 lbs.
Bore/Gauge: .410
Magazine: none
Features: thumbhole stock with recessed cavity for ammo storage
MSRP: **$169**

TOPPER
Action: hinged single-shot
Stock: hardwood
Barrel: 26 or 28 in.
Chokes: screw-in tubes
Weight: 6.0 lbs.
Bore/Gauge: 12, 20, 28, .410
Magazine: none
Features: hinged-breech with side lever release; automatic ejection
Topper: **$149**
12 gauge 3.5-inch: **$175**
Junior with walnut stock: **$193**
Deluxe Classic: **$220**

ULTRA SLUG HUNTER
Action: hinged single-shot
Stock: hardwood
Barrel: 24 in , rifled
Chokes: none
Weight: 7.5 lbs.
Bore/Gauge: 12, 20
Magazine: none
Features: factory-mounted Weaver scope base, swivels and sling
Ultra Slug Hunter: **$266**
Youth: **$266**
With camo laminated wood: . . **$328**

If your shotgun's magazine doesn't have a plug to prevent it from holding more than two cartridges, you can make one using a ½-inch-diameter wooden dowel. Measure the length of the magazine. Subtract 6 inches if your barrel is chambered for 2¾-inch shells; 6½ inches for 3-inch shells or 7½ inches for 3½-inch shells. Cut the dowel to the length of the remainder and sand it smooth. Unscrew the magazine's end cap, and place the plug inside the coil spring.

HK Fabarm Shotguns

CAMO FP6

GOLD LION MARK II

OVER/UNDER SILVER LION

MAX LION SC

REX LION

SIDE-BY-SIDE CLASSIC LION

MODEL FP6
Action: pump
Stock: walnut
Barrel: 26 or 28 in.
Chokes: screw-in tubes
Weight: 7.0 lbs.
Bore/Gauge: 12 *Magazine:* 4 rounds
Features: back-bored barrel
Camo: $469
FP6: $549

GOLDEN LION MARK II
Action: autoloader
Stock: walnut or synthetic
Barrel: 24, 26 or 28 in.
Chokes: screw-in tubes
Weight: 7.0 lbs.
Bore/Gauge: 12 *Magazine*: 4 rounds
Features: gas-operated actions; shim-adjustable buttstock
Golden Lion Mark II: $939
Sporting Clays: $1249

OVER/UNDER
Action: over/under
Stock: walnut *Barrel*: 26 or 28 in.
Chokes: screw-in tubes
Weight: 7.0 lbs.
Bore/Gauge: 12, 20 *Magazine:* none
Features: boxlock; back-bored barrels; single selective trigger
Over/Under: $1235
Silver Lion: $1315
UltraMag Camo: $1315
Sporting Clays: $1871

PARADOX LION
Action: over/under
Stock: walnut *Barrel*: 24 in.
Chokes: screw-in tubes
Weight: 7.6 lbs.
Bore/Gauge: 12, 20 *Magazine*: none
Features: boxlock; choke tube on top barrel and rifled below; case-colored receiver; 6.6 lbs for 20 gauge; also, new Max Lion Sporting Clays with adjustable stock and 32 in. tube-choked barrels (7.9 lbs.)
Paradox Lion: $1129
Max Lion SC: $1799

REX LION AND GOLD LION
Action: autoloader
Stock: walnut *Barrel*: 26 or 28 in.
Chokes: screw-in tubes
Weight: 7.7 lbs.
Bore/Gauge: 12 *Magazine:* 2 rounds
Features: gas operated; Turkish walnut stock; chrome-lined barrel
Gold Lion: $939
Rex Lion: $1049

SIDE-BY-SIDE
Action: side-by-side *Stock:* walnut
Barrel: 26 or 28 in.
Chokes: screw-in tubes
Weight: 7.0 lbs.
Bore/Gauge: 12 *Magazine:* none
Features: boxlock; back-bore barrels; single selective trigger
Grade I: $1499
Classic Lion English: $1604
Classic Lion Grade II: $2246

Ithaca Shotguns

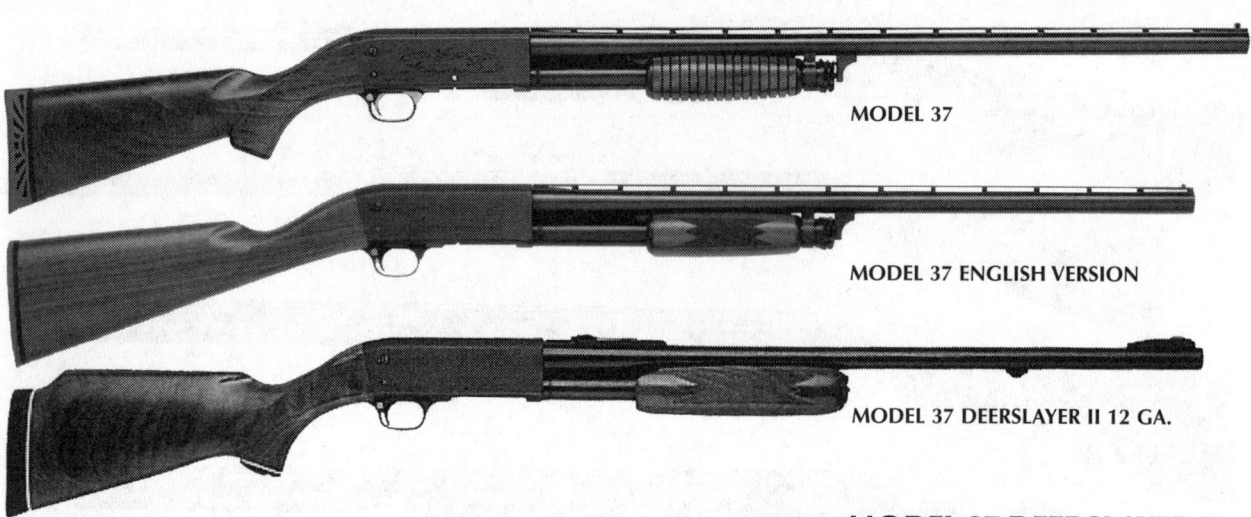

MODEL 37

MODEL 37 ENGLISH VERSION

MODEL 37 DEERSLAYER II 12 GA.

MODEL 37

Action: pump
Stock: walnut or synthetic
Barrel: 20, 22, 24, 26 or 28 in.
Chokes: screw-in tubes   *Weight*: 7.0 lbs.
Bore/Gauge: 12, 16, 20
Magazine: 4 rounds
Features: bottom ejection
M37 Guide Series slug gun,
   12 or 20: $599

Turkey Slayer Guide: $600
Deluxe vent rib: $627
Classic: $812
Ultralight 20 ga.: $834
English straight-grip: $647
Trap or Sporting Clays with
   Briley tubes, starting: $1495

MODEL 37 DEERSLAYER II

Action: pump   *Stock*: walnut
Barrel: 20 or 25 in., rifled or smoothbore
Weight: 7.0 lbs.
Bore/Gauge: 12, 16, 20   *Magazine:* 4
Features: open sights; receiver fitted
with Weaver-style scope base; also
available: Deerslayer III with 26-in.
heavy rifled barrel and Turkeyslayer (12
or 20) with 22 in. barrel, extra-full tube
Deerslayer: $591
Deerslayer II: $642

Kimber Shotguns

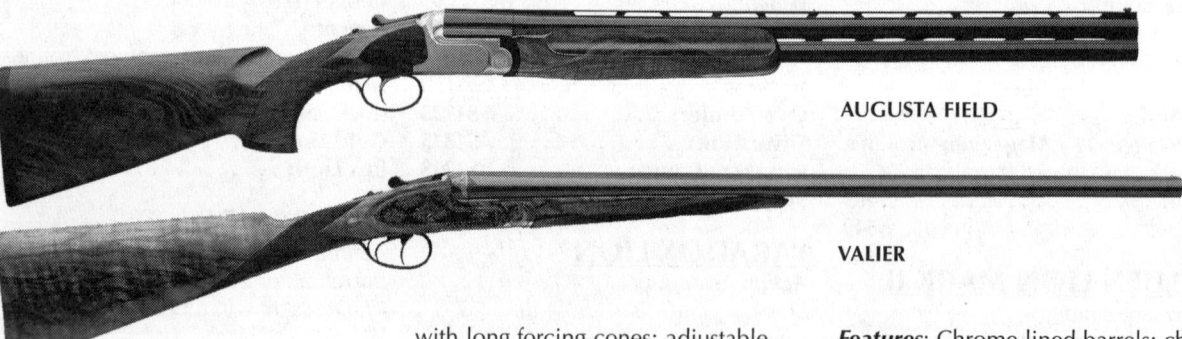

AUGUSTA FIELD

VALIER

AUGUSTA FIELD

Action: over/under
Stock: walnut
Barrel: 26, 27.5 in.
Chokes: screw-in tubes
Weight: 7.5 lbs.
Bore/Gauge: 12   *Magazine:* none
Features: boxlock; backbored barrel

with long forcing cones; adjustable
single trigger; automatic ejectors;
Hi-Viz sights (Sporting, Field, Trap
and Skeet models available)
MSRP: $5676

VALIER

Action: side-by-side, sidelock
Stock: Turkish walnut
Barrel: 26 or 28-in.
Chokes: IC & Mod.   *Bore/Gauge*: 20

Features: Chrome lined barrels; chambered for 3 in. shells; hand engraved,
case-colored receivers and furniture;
hinged forward trigger; gold line cocking indicators; straight grip, Turkish
walnut stock—14.75 in. length-of-pull;
finished in niter and rust blue; Valier
Grade I with extractors; Grade II features tuned ejectors
Grade I (20 gauge): $3879
Grade II (20 gauge): $4480

SHOTGUNS

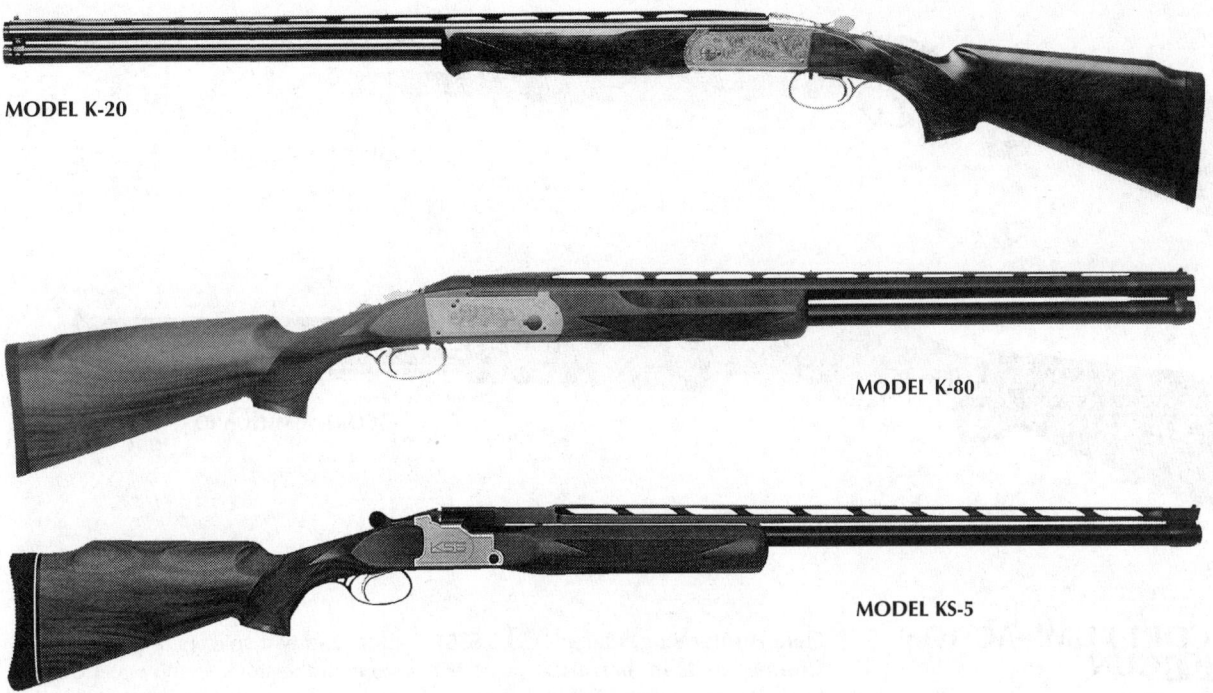

MODEL K-20

MODEL K-80

MODEL KS-5

MODEL K-20

Action: over/under
Stock: walnut
Barrel: 28 or 30 in.
Chokes: screw-in tubes
Weight: 7.2 lbs.
Bore/Gauge: 20, 28, .410
Magazine: none
Features: boxlock; single selective trigger, automatic ejectors; tapered rib; choice of receiver finish; fitted aluminum case
MSRP: . . . . .price on request

MODEL K-80

Action: over/under
Stock: walnut
Barrel: 28 or 30 in.
Chokes: screw-in tubes
Weight: 8.0 lbs.
Bore/Gauge: 12
Magazine: none
Features: boxlock; single selective trigger, automatic ejectors; tapered rib, choice of receiver finish; (Sporting Clays, Live Bird, Trap and Skeet models available)
MSRP: . . . . .price on request

MODEL KS-5

Action: hinged single-shot
Stock: walnut
Barrel: 30 in. or length to order
Chokes: screw-in tubes
Weight: 8.0 lbs.
Bore/Gauge: 12
Magazine: none
Features: boxlock; adjustable trigger (release trigger available); step rib; case-colored receiver; optional front hangers to adjust point of impact; optional adjustable comb
MSRP: . . . . .price on request

It's possible to bore-sight a scope-mounted 12-gauge shotgun barrel by removing the primers from a spent 12-gauge shell and a spent 20-gauge shell. Put the open 12-gauge shell in the chamber and insert the open 20-gauge shell in the muzzle. Secure the barrel in a vise or sandbags. Sighting through the barrel, line up the primer holes on your target. Now, simply adjust the scope to put the crosshairs on the same spot.

SHOTGUNS

Legacy Sports Shotguns

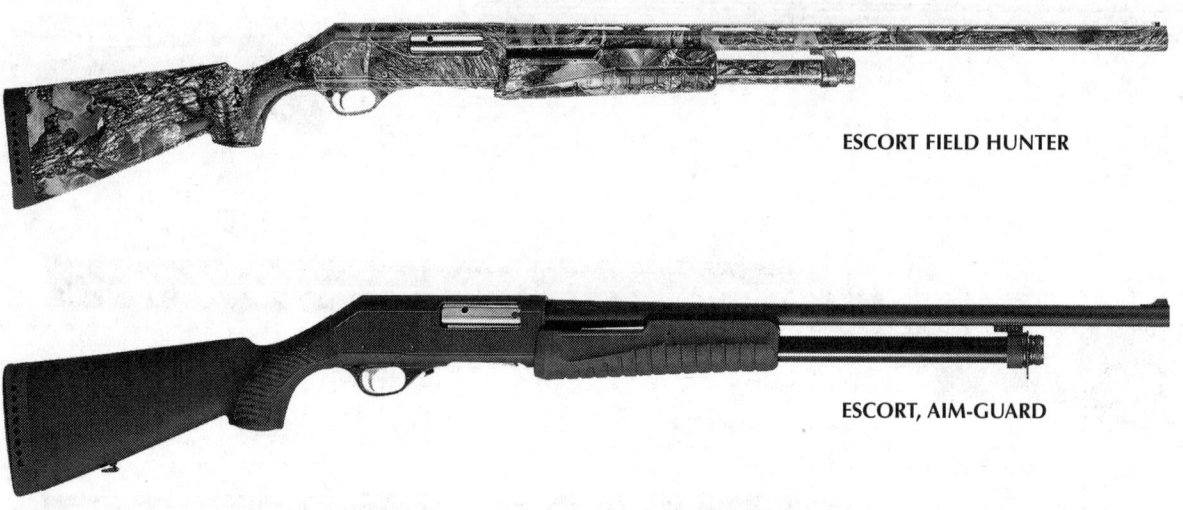

ESCORT FIELD HUNTER

ESCORT, AIM-GUARD

ESCORT PUMP-ACTION SHOTGUN

Action: pump
Stock: black or chrome polymer
Barrel: 18, 22, 26 or 28 in.
Sights: Hi Viz
Chokes: IC, M, F
Weight: 6.4-7.0 lbs.
Bore/Gauge: 12, 20
Magazine: 5-shot with cut-off button
Features: alloy receiver with 3/8 in. milled dovetail for sight mounting; black chrome or camp finish; black chrome bolt; trigger guard safety; 5-shot magazine with cut-off button; two stock adjustment shims; three choke tubes: IC, M, F (except AimGuard); 24 in. Bbl comes with extra turkey choke tube and HI Viz TriViz sight combo.

Aim Guard, 18 in. bbl.: $211
Field Hunter, black: $247
Field Hunter Camo: $312
Field Hunter slug, black: $351
Combo, 20-28 in. barrel: $270
Field Hunter, camo, TriViz
** sights: $363**
Field Hunter slug combo: $391

ESCORT SEMI-AUTOMATIC SHOTGUN

Action: autoloader
Stock: polymer or walnut
Barrel: 18, 22, 26 & 28 in.
Sights: HiViz
Weight: 6.4-7.8 lbs.
Bore/Gauge: 12, 20
Magazine: 5 rounds
Features: gas operated and chambered for 2¾ or 3in. shells; barrels are nickel-chromium-molybdenum steel with additional chrome plating internally and a ventilated anti-glare checkered rib; bolts are chrome plated; extras include three chokes, a migratory plug, and two spacers to adjust the slope of the stock; camo waterfowl and turkey combo available with Hi Viz sights, 28 in. barrel; hard case.

AS walnut: $421
AS Youth walnut: $421
PS polymer: $399
PS Aim Guard: $392
PS Slug, black: $438
PS Camo, Spark sights: $443
PS blue, 3.5 mag.: $465
PS Waterfowl & Turkey: $523
Combo, Waterfowler/Turkey
** (24-28 in. bbl., TriViz Sights,**
** Turkey choke: 574**

Mounting adjustable front and rear rifle sights on the ventilated rib of the shotgun you use for turkey hunting will allow you to center your shotgun's pattern exactly on target. Pattern your shotgun by shooting at a bull's-eye rifle target to see where your gun centers its pattern now.

SHOTGUNS

Marlin Shotguns

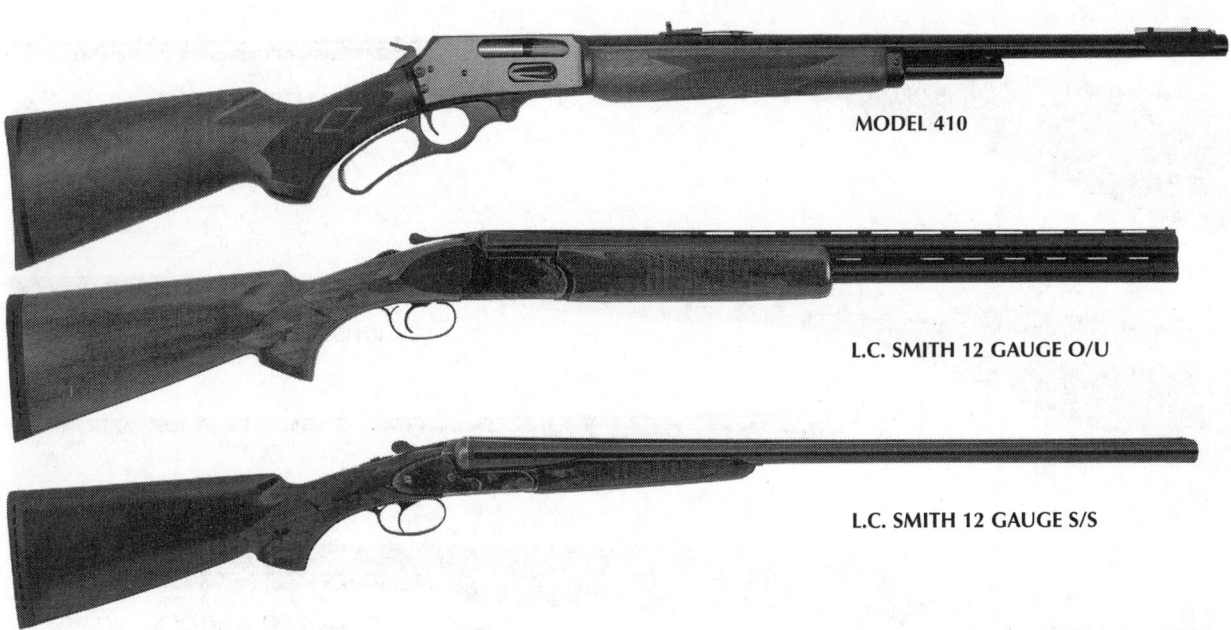

MODEL 410

L.C. SMITH 12 GAUGE O/U

L.C. SMITH 12 GAUGE S/S

MODEL 410

Action: pump
Stock: walnut, cut checkering
Barrel: 22 in.
Chokes: none
Weight: 7.3 lbs.
Bore/Gauge: .410
Magazine: 4 rounds

Features: hammer block safety; 2½ in. only
MSRP: **$614**

L.C. SMITH

Action: side-by-side and over/under
Stock: checkered walnut
Barrel: 26 and 28 in.

Chokes: screw-in tubes
Weight: 6.0 lbs. (20 gauge side-by-side), to 7.75 lbs (12 gauge O/U)
Bore/Gauge: 12, 20
Magazine: no magazine
Features: automatic ejectors; 3 in. chamber
MSRP: .. from approximately $1900

Marocchi Shotguns

MODEL 99

MODEL 99 GRADE III

MODEL 99

Action: over/under
Stock: walnut
Barrel: back-bored 28, 29, 30 or 32 in.
Chokes: screw-in tubes
Weight: 8.0 lbs.

Bore/Gauge: 12
Magazine: none
Features: boxlock; single adjustable trigger, BOSS locking system
Model 99: **$2995**
Grade III: **$4595**

Merkel Shotguns

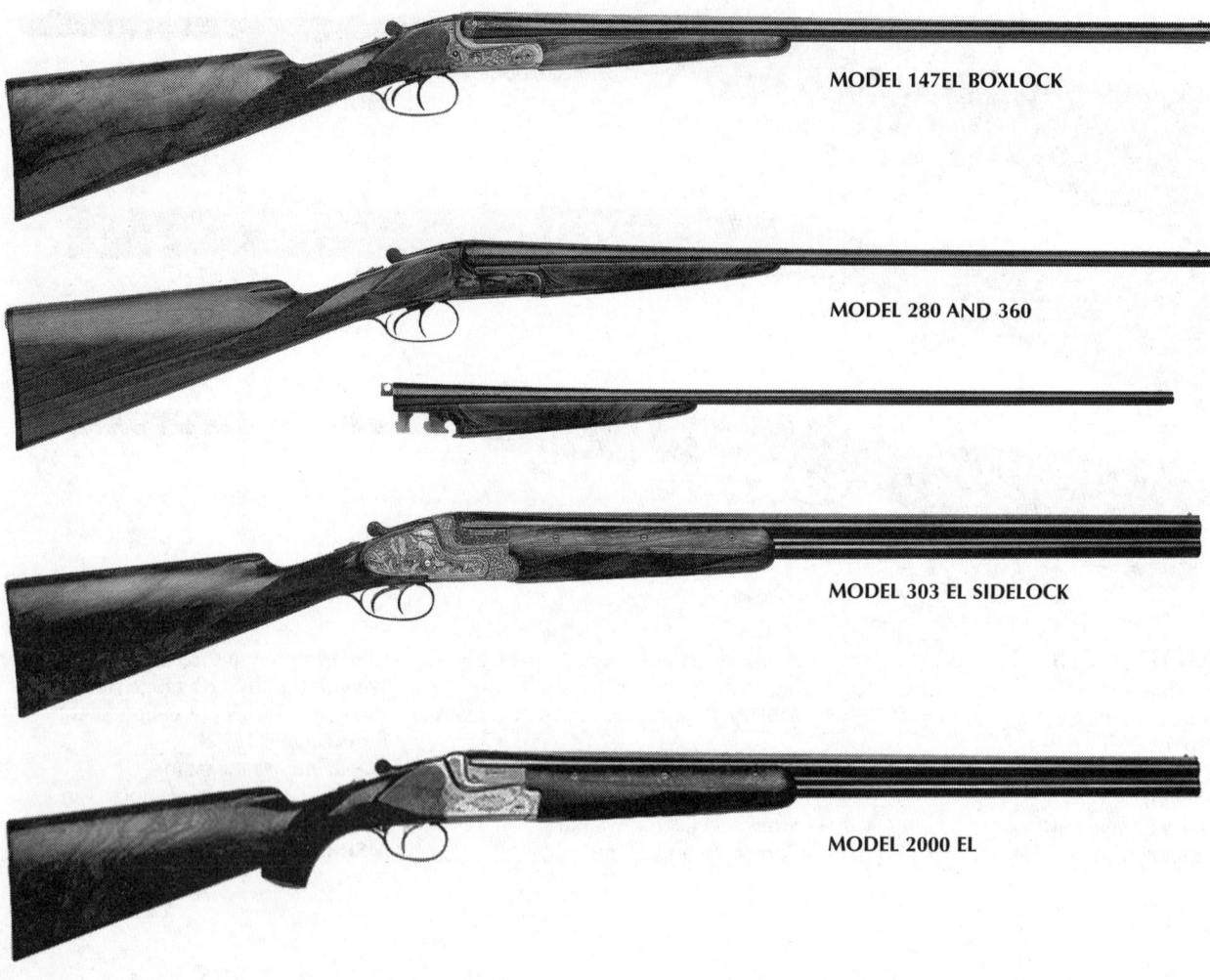

MODEL 147EL BOXLOCK

MODEL 280 AND 360

MODEL 303 EL SIDELOCK

MODEL 2000 EL

MODEL 147E

Action: side-by-side
Stock: walnut, straight or pistol grip
Barrel: 27 or 28 in.
Chokes: imp.cyl/mod or mod/full
Weight: 7.2 lbs.
Bore/Gauge: 12, 20
Magazine: none
Features: boxlock; single selective or double triggers; automatic ejectors; fitted luggage case

47E:	$3995
147E (deluxe):	$4795
147EL (super deluxe):	$5995

MODEL 280 AND 360

Action: side-by-side
Stock: walnut, straight grip
Barrel: 28 in.
Chokes: imp.cyl/mod (28 ga.), mod/full (.410)
Weight: 6.0 lbs.
Bore/Gauge: 28, .410
Magazine: none
Features: boxlock; double triggers, automatic ejectors; fitted luggage case (Model 280: 28 gauge and Model 360: .410)

Model 280 or Model 360:	$4195
Two-barrel sets:	$6495
S models with sidelocks:	$9395

MODEL 303 EL

Action: over/under
Stock: walnut, straight or pistol grip
Barrel: 27 or 28 in.
Chokes: improved cylinder, modified, full
Weight: 7.3 lbs.
Bore/Gauge: 16, 20, 28
Magazine: none
Features: sidelock; automatic ejectors; special-order features

MSRP::	$23995

MODEL 2000 EL

Action: over/under
Stock: walnut, straight or pistol grip
Barrel: 27 or 28 in.
Chokes: improved cylinder, modified, full
Weight: 7.3 lbs.
Bore/Gauge: 12, 20, 28
Magazine: none
Features: boxlock; single selective or double trigger; three-piece forend, automatic ejectors

MSRP:	$6995

Mossberg Shotguns

MODEL 500 SPORTING

MODEL 835 PUMP ULTI-MAG CAMO

MODEL 835 ULTI-MAG

MODEL 835 ULTI-MAG COMBO

MODEL 500

Action: pump
Stock: wood or synthetic
Barrel: 18, 22, 24, 26 or 28 in.
Chokes: screw-in tubes
Weight: 7.5 lbs.
Bore/Gauge: 12, 20, .410
Magazine: 5 rounds
Features: barrels mostly vent rib, some ported; top tang safety; camouflage stock finish options; 10-year warranty
Model 500: **$316**
Camo: **$364**
Bantam Ported 24 in. bbl: . . . **$355**
Two-barrel combo set: **$404**
Super Bantam Slugster: . . . **$316-364**

MODEL 500 MARINER

Action: pump
Stock: synthetic
Barrel: 18 or 20 in.
Chokes: cylinder
Weight: 7.0 lbs.
Bore/Gauge: 12
Magazine: 5 rounds
Features: top tang safety; 12-gauge has "Marinecote" metal and 10-year warranty; 20 gauge and .410 variations available in blued finish
MSRP: **$512**

MODEL 835 ULTI-MAG

Action: pump
Stock: synthetic or camo
Barrel: 24 or 28 in.
Chokes: full
Weight: 7.0 lbs.
Bore/Gauge: 12
Magazine: 4 rounds
Features: barrel ported, back-bored with vent rib; 3.5 in. chamber; top tang safety; rifled slug barrel and combination sets available; 10-year warranty
Model 835: **$394**
Model 835, camo: **$438-471**
Combo: **$502**

SHOTGUNS

New England Arms/FAIR Shotguns

MODEL 900
Action: over/under
Stock: walnut, straight or pistol grip
Barrel: all standard lengths
Chokes: screw-in tubes
Weight: 7.5 lbs.

Bore/Gauge: 12, 16, 20, 28, .410
Magazine: none
Features: boxlock; single selective trigger, automatic safety, automatic ejector; .410 has fixed choke
MSRP: $2700-3600

New England Firearms Shotguns

PARDNER YOUTH

SURVIVOR
.410/45 COLT

PARDNER PUMP

SURVIVOR AND PARDNER
Action: hinged single-shot
Stock: synthetic
Barrel: 22, 26, 28 or 32 in.
Chokes: modified, full **Weight:** 6.0 lbs.
Bore/Gauge: 12, 16, 20, 28, .410
Magazine: none
Features: Youth and camo-finish Turkey models available; Survivor has hollow pistol-grip buttstock for storage; chambers .410/.45 Colt
Pardner:. $137

Pardner Youth: $145
Pardner Turkey
   (3½ in., 10 and 12ga.): . . $187-286
Pardner Turkey Camo Youth:. . $195
Survivor blue or silver: . . . $213-232

PARDNER PUMP SHOTGUN
Action: hammerless pump
Stock: walnut , synthetic or camo
Barrel: 28 in., with vent rib, screw-in choke tube; 22 in. Turkey model; combo

comes with 22 in. rifled slug barrel
Sights: gold bead front, TruGlo front & rear on Turkey model
Chokes: screw-in Browning/ Winchester/ Mossberg tubes (one provided), turkey choke
Weight: 7.5 lbs. **Bore/Gauge:** 12
Magazine: 5-shot tube, with 2-shot plug provided
Features: twin action bars; easy take-down
MSRP: $208-305

SHOTGUNS

New England Firearms Shotguns

TRACKER II RIFLED SLUG GUN

TURKEY & SPECIAL PURPOSE

TRACKER II RIFLED SLUG GUN
Action: hinged single-shot
Stock: hardwood
Barrel: rifled 24 in.
Chokes: none
Weight: 6.0 lbs.
Bore/Gauge: 12, 20
Magazine: none
Features: adjustable rifle sights; swivel studs standard
MSRP: **$192**

TURKEY & SPECIAL PURPOSE
Action: hinged single-shot
Stock: hardwood
Barrel: 24 in. (Turkey) or 28 in. (Waterfowl)
Chokes: full, screw-in tubes
Weight: 9.5 lbs.
Bore/Gauge: 10, 12
Magazine: none
Features: Turkey and Waterfowl models available with camo finish; swivel studs standard (Turkey Gun)

Turkey Gun
   (black, tubes): $187-286
   (Camo, full choke): $195-286
Special Purpose Waterfowl
   10 ga.: $280
   With 28 in. barrel, walnut: . . $221

Perazzi Shotguns

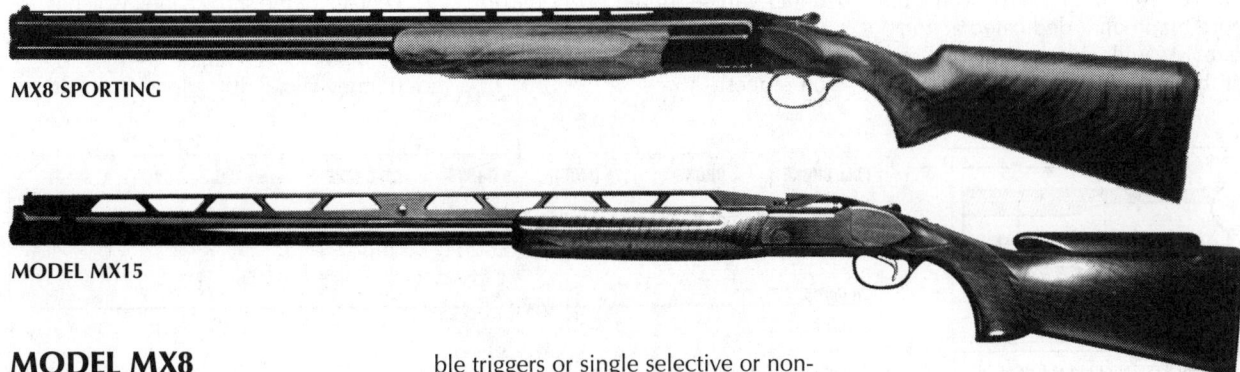

MX8 SPORTING

MODEL MX15

MODEL MX8
Action: over/under
Stock: walnut
Barrel: 28-34 in.
Chokes: screw-in tubes
Weight: 7.3 lbs.
Bore/Gauge: 12, 20
Magazine: none
Features: hinged-breech action; dou

ble triggers or single selective or non-selective trigger; Sporting, Skeet and Trap models and 28 ga. and .410 also available
MSRP: **$11166**

MODEL MX15
Action: hinged single-shot
Stock: walnut, adjustable comb

Barrel: 32 or 35 in.
Chokes: full
Weight: 8.4 lbs.
Bore/Gauge: 12
Magazine: none
Features: high trap rib
MSRP: **$9507**

SHOTGUNS

Purdey Shotguns

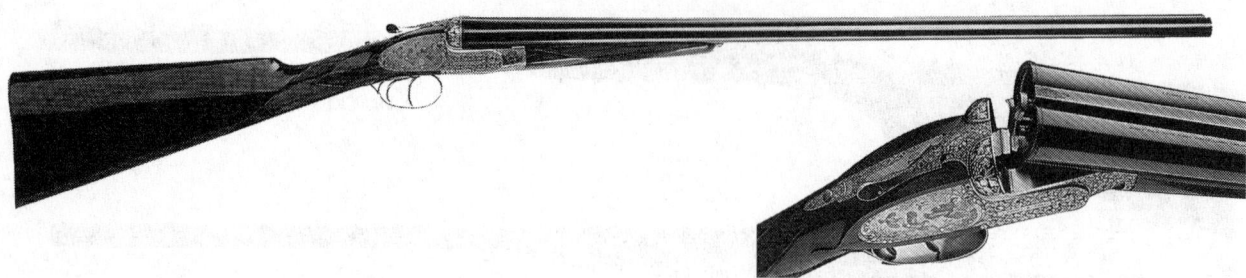

SIDE-BY-SIDE GAME GUN

Purdey easy opening action: All side-by-side guns are built on the easy opening system invented by Frederick Beesley. This system is incorporated in guns built from 1880 onwards.

Purdey offers dedicated action sizes for each of the bores 10, 12, 20, 28 & .410 cores. An extra pair of barrels can be ordered, even if you want a barrel set one gauge smaller. For example, you can have fitted 28 gauge barrels on a 20 gauge, and .410 on a 28 gauge. These guns are made with a single forend for both bores.

All Purdey barrels, both SxS and O/U, are of chopper lump construction. Each individual tube is hand filled and then "struck up" using striking files. This gives the tube the correct Purdey profile.

Once polished, the individual tubes are joined at the breech using silver solder. The loop iron is similarly fixed. Once together, the rough chokes can be cut and the internal bores finished using a traditional lead lapping technique.

Ribs are hand-filed to suit the barrel contour exactly, and then soft-soldered in place, using pine resin as the fluxing agent. Pine resin provides extra water resistance to the surfaces enclosed by the ribs.

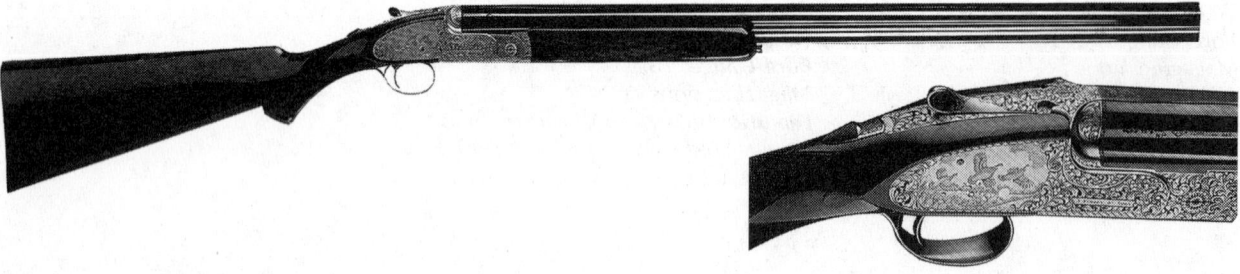

OVER/UNDER GUN

The over/under gun is available in 12, 16, 20, 28 and .410, with each bore made on a dedicated action size. As with side-by-side, the shape of the action has an effect on the weight of the gun.

Conventionally, the Purdey over-under will shoot the lower barrel first, but can be made to shoot the top barrel first if required. All prices on request.

The standard for regulating and patterning the shooting of a gun is the percentage of the shot charge, which is evenly concentrated in a circle of 30 in. diameter at a range of 40 yards. (Purdey choke restrictions 1/1000 in.)

THE CHOKE SECTION

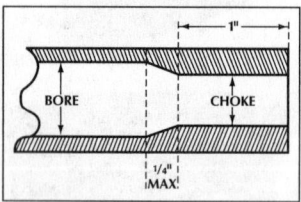

THE PERCENTAGES OF CHOKE

Cylinder	45%
Improved Cylinder	50%
1/4 Choke	55%
1/2 Choke	60%
3/4 or Modified Choke	65%
Choke	70%
Full Choke	75%
Skeet (2)	45%
Skeet (1)	40%

FULL CHOKE	CHOKE	.75 (MOD)	.5 CHOKE	.25 CHOKE	IMP CYL	CYL	SKEET
12 Bore 2.75" 1.25 oz No.6							
.038-.040	.035	.022	.016-.017	.010-.01	7-8	3	Open Bore
20 Bore 2.75"							
.038-.040	.030	.018-.019	.012-.013	7-8	6	3	Open Bore
12 Bore 2.5" 1 oz. No. 6							
.038-.040	.030	.018-.019	.012-.013	6-7	3	2	
28 Bore 2.75"							
.026	.020	.018	.015	.011	7	3	Open

Remington Shotguns

SPARTAN 210

SPARTAN 310

SPORTSMAN 11-87

SP-10 MAGNUM

SPARTAN SXS AND O/U SHOTGUNS

Action: hinged breech
Stock: walnut
Barrel: 26 or 28 in.
(also, 20 in. Coach Gun)
Chokes: screw-in tubes
(fixed chokes in 28 and .410)
Weight: 6.25-7.0 lbs. (SXS) and
7.5 lbs. (O/U)
Bore/Gauge: 12, 20, 28 and
.410 (16 in O/U)
Magazine: none
Features: chrome-lined barrels; all-steel breech; single selective trigger and selective ejectors; automatic safety; (SXS and O/U), single or double triggers
**MSRP: $320-519
(Single-shot available in 12, 20, 28 and .410 at $97; youth model in .410 and 20 gauge, 24-in barrel, $104)**

SPORTSMAN 11-87

Action: autoloading
Stock: synthetic
Barrel: 26 and 28 in.
(21 in. on Slug and Youth guns)
Chokes: RemChoke tubes
Weight: 7.75-8.5 lbs (6.5 lbs. Youth)
Bore/Gauge: 12 and 20
(12 Slug, 20 Youth)
Magazine: 4 rounds
**Field and Youth: $624
Slug: $705**

MODEL SP-10

Action: autoloader
Stock: walnut, synthetic or camo
Barrel: 26 or 30 in.
Chokes: screw-in tubes
Weight: 10.75-11.0 lbs.
Bore/Gauge: 10
Magazine: 2 rounds
Features: the only gas-operated 10 gauge made; stainless piston and sleeve; R3 recoil pad on synthetic
**SP-10:. $1387
Camo: $1524**

SHOTGUNS

Remington Shotguns

MODEL 11-87 DEER GUN

MODEL 11-87 SPS

MODEL 11-87 SPS SUPER MAGNUM

MODEL 332

MODEL 870 EXPRESS

MODEL 11-87 AUTOLOADERS

Action: autoloader
Stock: walnut or synthetic
Barrel: 21, 23, 26, 28 or 30 in.
Chokes: screw-in tubes
Weight: 6.25-8.25 lbs. **Bore/Gauge**: 12, 20
Magazine: 5 rounds
Features: gas-operated, handles 2¾ and 3 in. shells interchangeably; Deer Gun has cantilever scope mount, rifled bore; Upland Special has straight grip; Super Magnum chambers 3.5 in. shells

11-87 Premier:	**$827**
Deer Gun:	**$908**
Upland Special:	**$827**
Premier Super Mag:	**$899**
Left-Hand:	**$893**
Model 11-87 SPS Super Mag:	**$912**
SPS camo:	**$925**
SPS Super Mag camo:	**996**

SPS Waterfowl:	**$960**
SPS NWTF Turkey:	**$1016**

MODEL 332

Action: over/under
Stock: walnut, Hi-Gloss
Barrel: 26, 28 or 30 in.
Chokes: screw-in tubes
Weight: 7.5-8.0 lbs.
Bore/Gauge: 12
Magazine: none
Features: boxlock; ventilated rib; Model 332 patterned after classic Model 32

MSRP:	**$1691**

MODEL 870 EXPRESS

Action: pump
Stock: synthetic, hardwood or camo
Barrel: 18-28 in.
Chokes: screw-in tubes
Weight: 6.0-7.5 lbs.
Bore/Gauge: 12, 16, 20, 28, .410
Magazine: 5 rounds

Features: Super Magnum chambered for 3.5-inch shells; deer gun has rifled barrel, open sights

Express:	**$332**
Express Deer w/RS:	**$332**
Express Youth 16 & 20 ga.:	**$332**
Express Turkey:	**$345**
Express Deer FR:	**$372**
Express Super Magnum:	**$376**
Express LH:	**$389**
Express Super Mag. Turkey (31/2" Black synthetic):	**$389**
Youth Turkey:	**$389**
Turkey camo:	**$399**
JR NWTF:	**$419**
Express Deer w/cantilever:	**$439**
Combo with Rem choke barrel and slug barrel:	**$455-489**
Super Mag, camo:	**$500**
Express Super Mag. Turkey, camo:	**$500**
Express Super Mag. Combo with deer barrel:	**$523**

Remington Shotguns

MODEL 870 MARINE MAGNUM

MODEL 870 SPS

MODEL 870 WINGMASTER

MODEL 1100 SPORTING 13

MODEL 870 MARINE MAGNUM

Action: pump
Stock: synthetic
Barrel: 18 in.
Chokes: none, cylinder bore
Weight: 7.5 lbs.
Bore/Gauge: 12
Magazine: 7 rounds
Features: nickel-plated exterior metal; R3 recoil pad
MSRP: **$600**

MODEL 870 SPS

Action: pump
Stock: camo   *Barrel*: 20-28 in.
Chokes: screw-in tubes
Weight: 6.25-7.5 lbs.
Bore/Gauge: 12 & 20
Magazine: 4 (3: 3.5-in.) rounds
Features: turkey models available; R3 recoil pad
Turkey:. $617-621
Super Magnum camo: **$617**
   with thumbhole stock
   (12 ga., 3.5 in.): **$650**

MODEL 870 WINGMASTER

Action: pump
Stock: walnut
Barrel: 25-30 in.
Chokes: screw-in tubes
Weight: 6.5-7.5 lbs.
Bore/Gauge: 12, 16, 20, 28 & .410
Magazine: 3-4 rounds
Features: machine-cut checkering; blued receiver
3-in.: **$625**
Wingmaster Jr.: **$625**
Super Mag.: **$692**
Classic Trap: **$819**
Dale Earnhardt Special: **$820**

MODEL 1100 CLASSIC FIELD

Action: autoloader
Stock: walnut
Barrel: 26 or 28 in.
Chokes: screw-in tubes
Weight: 6.75-7.25 lbs.
Bore/Gauge: 16 and 20 (26 in. only)
Magazine: 4 rounds
Features: gas-operated autoloading; vent rib
Classic Field: **$799**
M1100 Tournament Skeet
   (12 or 20 ga.): **$901**
M1100 Sporting (12, 20,
   28 ga. & .410): **$901-935**
M1100 Classic Trap (12 ga.): . . . **$935**

Renato Gamba Shotguns

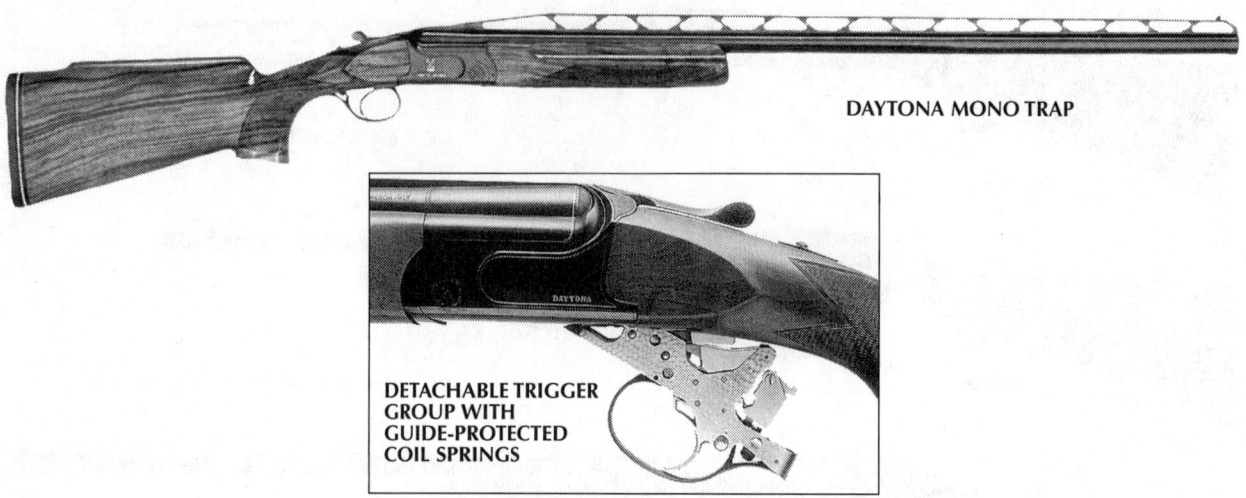

DAYTONA MONO TRAP

DETACHABLE TRIGGER GROUP WITH GUIDE-PROTECTED COIL SPRINGS

THE DAYTONA SHOTGUN

The Daytona shotgun is available in several styles oriented specifically to American Trap, International Trap, American Skeet, International Skeet, and Sporting Clays. The Daytona SL, (the side plate model), and the Daytona SLHH, (the side lock model), are the top of the Daytona line.

All employ the BOSS locking system in a breech milled from one massive block of steel.

The trigger group: The trigger group is detachable and is removable without the use of tools. The frame that contains the hammers, sears and springs is milled from a single block of special steel and jeweled for oil retention. On special order, an adjustable trigger may be produced with one inch of movement that can accomodate shooters with exceptionally large

or small hands. Internally, the hammer springs are constructed from coils that are contained in steel sleeves placed directly behind the hammers. With the fail safe capsule surrounding the springs, the shotgun will fire even if breakage occurs.

Hunter o/u: . . . . from $1390
Le Mans o/u: . . . . from $1580
Concorde o/u: . . . . from $6100
Daytona 2K o/u: . . . . from $7600

	GAUGE	BARRELS	CHAMBER	BARREL LENGTH	CHOKES	INTERCH. CHOKE
TRAP	12 - 20	heat treated special chrome-nickel-molybdenum steel	70mm (2¾") 79mm (3") on request	76-81cm 30"-32"	imp. mod/ full-mac/full	5 screw-in choke tube set available on request
DOUBLE TRAP	12 - 20	heat treated special chrome-nickel-molybdenum steel	70mm (2¾") 79mm (3") on request	76cm 30"	imp. cil./full	5 screw-in choke tube set available on request
SKEET	12 - 20	heat treated special chrome-nickel-molybdenum steel	70mm (2¾") 79mm (3") on request	68-71cm 26¾"-28"	SK/SK	5 screw-in choke tube set available on request
SPORT CLAY	12 - 20	heat treated special chrome-nickel-molybdenum steel	70mm (2¾") 79mm (3") on request	71-74cm 76-81cm 28", 29", 30", 32"	mod./full	5 screw-in choke tube set available on request
HUNTING	12 - 20	heat treated special chrome-nickel-molybdenum steel	70mm (2¾") 79mm (3") on request	68-71cm 26¾"=28"	imp. cit./imp. mod. mod./full	5 screw-in choke tube set available on request
MONO TRAP	12 - 20	heat treated special chrome-nickel-molybdenum steel	70mm (2¾") 79mm (3") on request	81-86cm 32"-34"	full	5 screw-in choke tube set available on request

Rossi Shotguns

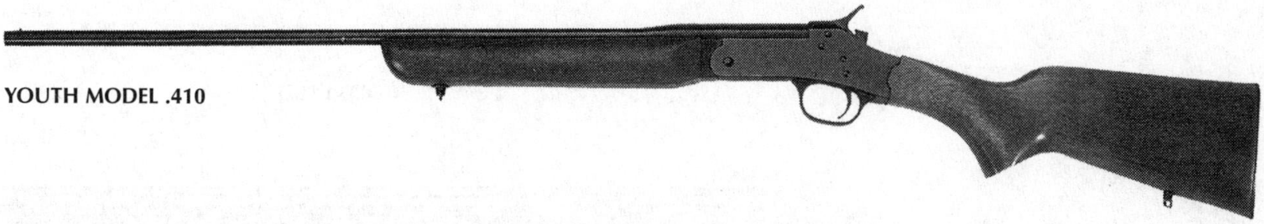

YOUTH MODEL .410

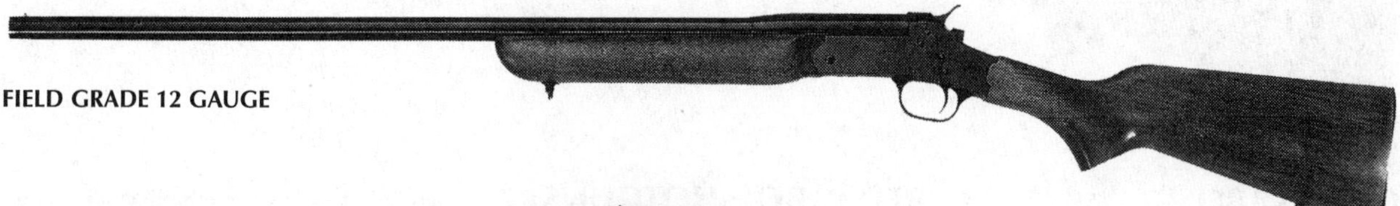

FIELD GRADE 12 GAUGE

MATCHED PAIR

SINGLE BARREL SHOTGUNS

Action: hinged single-shot
Stock: hardwood
Barrel: 28 in.
Chokes: modified, full
Weight: 5.3 lbs.
Bore/Gauge: 12, 20, .410
Magazine: none
Features: exposed-hammer, transfer-bar action; Youth model available; rifle barrels have open sights

Single-Shot: $115
Youth, 22 in. barrel: $115
Rifled barrel slug gun
(23 in. bbl., 12 or 20 ga.): . . . $190
Matched Pair (.50 cal/12 ga.
rifled slug): $275

If you have trouble hitting rising birds, the problem may be your shotgun's stock. A stock that's too long tends to make you shoot low and restricts your ability to swing with a bird. A stock that's too short makes you shoot high. Have a gunsmith check your stock and adjust it to fit your physique.

Ruger Shotguns

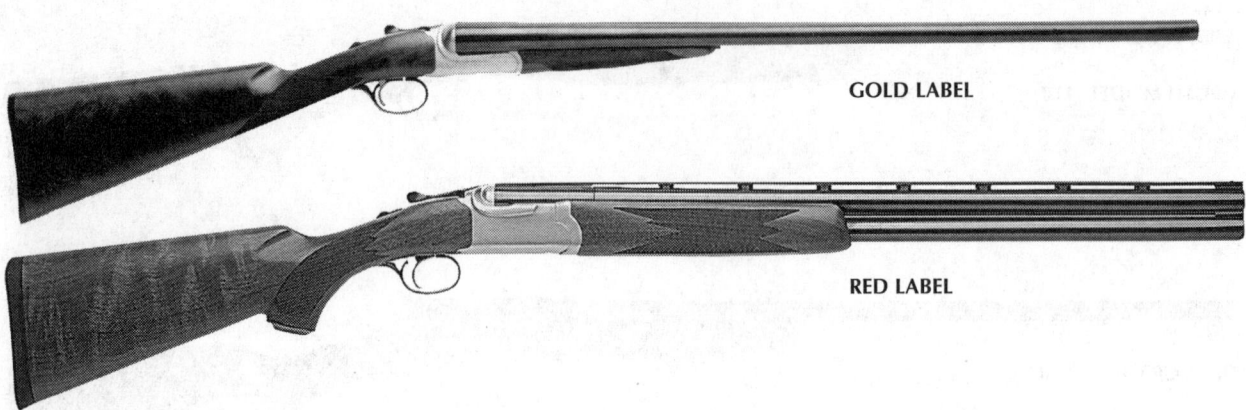

GOLD LABEL

RED LABEL

GOLD LABEL
Action: over/under
Stock: walnut, straight or pistol grip
Barrel: 28 in.
Chokes: screw-in tubes
Weight: 6.5 lbs.
Bore/Gauge: 12
Magazine: none
Features: boxlock; round stainless frame
MSRP: **$2000**

RED LABEL SHOTGUNS
Action: over/under
Stock: walnut or synthetic, straight or pistol grip
Barrel: 26, 28, 30 in.
Chokes: screw-in tubes
Weight: 6.0-8.0 lbs.
Bore/Gauge: 12, 20, 28
Magazine: none
Features: boxlock; All-Weather version

has stainless steel, synthetic stock; 28 ga. only available in 26 or 28 in. barrel
Standard or All-Weather: **$1702**
Engraved: **$1902**

Savage Shotguns

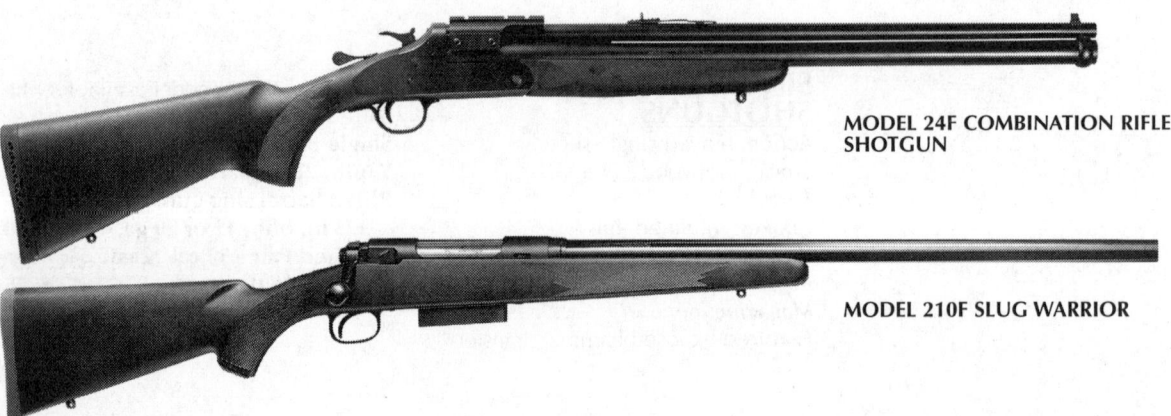

MODEL 24F COMBINATION RIFLE/ SHOTGUN

MODEL 210F SLUG WARRIOR

MODEL 24F
Action: hinged single-shot
Stock: synthetic
Barrel: rifle over shotgun, 24 in.
Chokes: none
Weight: 8.0 lbs.
Bore/Gauge: 12, 20
Magazine: none
Features: open sights; hammer-mount-

ed barrel selector; available in 20 ga./ .22LR, 20/.22 Hornet, 20/.223, 12 ga./.22 Hornet, 12/.223, 12/.30-30
20 ga.: **$628**
12 ga.: **$661**

MODEL 210F SLUG WARRIOR
Action: bolt
Stock: synthetic
Barrel: rifled, 24 in.

Chokes: none
Weight: 7.5 lbs.
Bore/Gauge: 12
Magazine: 2 rounds
Features: top tang safety; no sights; new camo version available
210F: **$475**
Camo: **$513**

SHOTGUNS

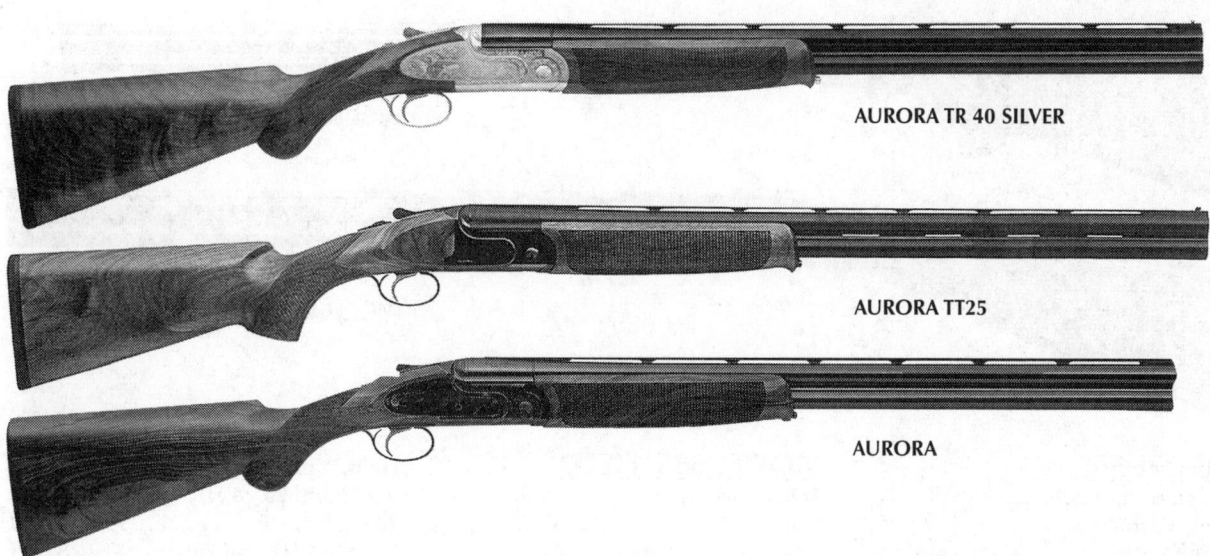

AURORA TR 40 SILVER

AURORA TT25

AURORA

AURORA

Action: over/under
Stock: walnut
Barrel: 26 or 28 in.
Chokes: screw-in tubes
Weight: 7.3 lbs.
Bore/Gauge: 12, 20, 28, .410

Magazine: none
Features: boxlock; single selective trigger; automatic ejectors; replaceable hingepin; 20 gauge weighs 6.3 lbs., 28 ga. and .410 6.0 lbs.
New Englander: **$2161**
12, 20, 28, .410: **$2250**

Series 20: **$2250**
Series 30: **$2650**
High-grade TT 25: **$2950**
Compeition: **$2950-3350**
TR 40 Gold series: **$3050**
Best-grade TT 45: **$3350**

Silma Shotguns

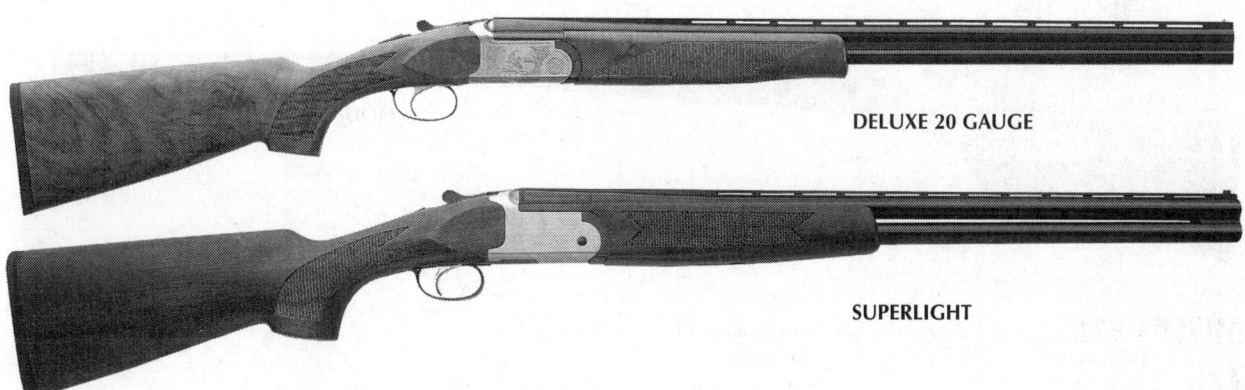

DELUXE 20 GAUGE

SUPERLIGHT

MODEL 70 EJ DELUXE

Action: box lock
Stock: walnut
Barrel: 28 in.
Bore/Gauge: 12, 20 (Standard); 12, 20, 28, .410 bore (Deluxe); 12, 20 (Superlight);12 (Superlight deluxe); 12, 20 (Clays)

Magazine: none
Features: all 12 gauge models, except Superlight, come with 3.5 in. chambers; high grade steel barrels; proofed for steel shot; all models come with single selective trigger; automatic safety; automatic ejectors; ventilated rib; recoil pad; gold plated.

Standard, 20 ga.: **$944**
Standard, 12 ga.: **$1016**
Deluxe, 12 ga.: **$1089**
Deluxe, 20 ga.: **$1016**
28 gauge & .410: **$1140**
Superlight: **$1191**
Clays: **$1387**

SHOTGUNS

SKB Shotguns

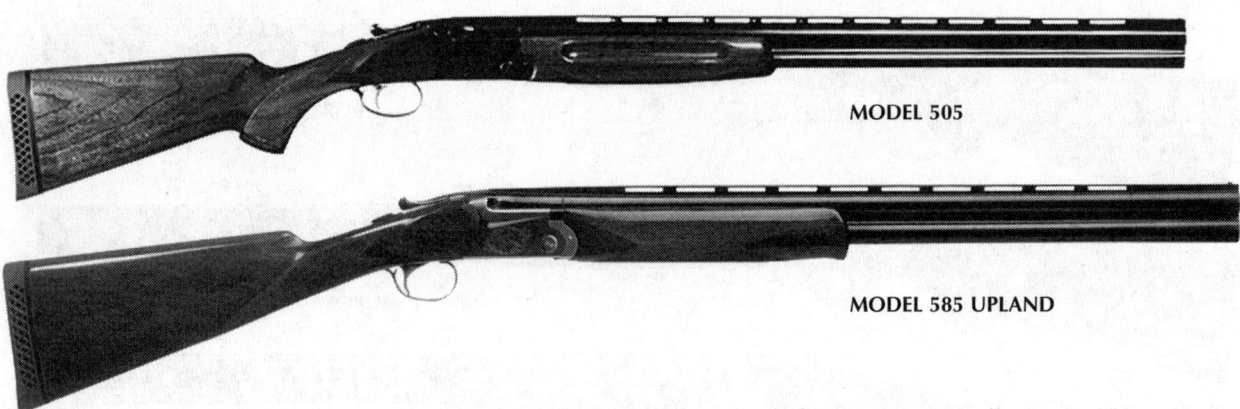

MODEL 505

MODEL 585 UPLAND

MODEL 505

Action: over/under
Stock: walnut
Barrel: 26 or 28 in.
Chokes: screw-in tubes
Weight: 8.4 lbs.
Bore/Gauge: 12, 20
Magazine: none
Features: boxlock; ventilated rib, automatic ejectors
MSRP: **$1349**

MODEL 585 FIELD

Action: over/under
Stock: walnut, straight or pistol grip
Barrel: 26 or 28 in.
Chokes: screw-in tubes
Weight: 9.0 lbs.
Bore/Gauge: 12, 20, 28, .410
Magazine: none
Features: boxlock; Field, Upland and Youth; silver and gold series available

Field, Upland, Youth
(12 and 20 ga.): **$1649**
28 ga. or .410: **$1619**
Field Set (12 and 20): **$2639**
Field Set (20 and 28): **$2719**
Field Set (28 and .410): **$2719**

Stevens Shotguns

MODEL 411

MODEL 411

Action: side-by-side
Stock: walnut
Barrel: 26 or 28 in.
Chokes: screw-in tubes
Weight: 6.8 lbs.

Bore/Gauge: 12
Magazine: none
Features: boxlock; single selective trigger, automatic safety
MSRP: **$438**

Stoeger Shotguns

MODEL 2000

MODEL 2000 ADVANTAGE TIMBER HD

MODEL 2000 MAX-4

COACH GUN SUPREME

CONDOR

MODEL 2000 WALNUT, SYNTHETIC, ADVANTÁGE TIMBER, MÁX-4
Action: autoloader
Stock: synthetic or Walnut
Barrel: 24, 26 or 28 in.
Chokes: screw-in tubes
Weight: 6.8 lbs.
Bore/Gauge: 12
Magazine: 4 rounds
Features: inertia-recoil system; ventilated rib; AdvantageTim., MAX-4 camo stock; fires 2¾ and 3 in. ammunition
MSRP: **$485**

COACH GUN
Action: side-by-side
Stock: American Walnut
Barrel: 20 or 24 in.
Chokes: screw-in or Fixed, .410 fixed
Weight: 6.4-6.5 lbs.
Bore/Gauge: 12, 20, .410
Magazine: none
Features: boxlock, double triggers; automatic safety; improved cylinder and modified screw-in chokes and fixed chokes; available with stainless receiver and blued or polished nickel finish
Standard Blued: **$340**
Supreme Blue: **$410**
Stainless Receiver: **$420**

CONDOR
Action: over/under
Stock: American Walnut
Barrel: 26, 28 in.
Chokes: IC and M
Weight: 7.0 lbs.
Bore/Gauge: 12, 20, 16 & .410
Magazine: none
Features: Standard and Supreme Grades; screw in and fixed choke models
MSRP: **$350-539**

Stoeger Shotguns

CONDOR COMBO

CONDOR COMPETITION

CONDOR SUPREME

P350

UPLANDER

CONDOR COMBO

Action: over/under
Stock: American Walnut
Barrel: 28 or 26 in.
Chokes: improved cylinder, modified
Weight: 6.8-7.4 lbs.
Bore/Gauge: 12, 20
Magazine: none
Features: boxlock; single trigger; 2 barrel sets (12 and 20 ga.)
Field: **$550**
Supreme: **$650**

CONDOR COMPETITION

Action: over/under
Stock: Supreme American Walnut
Barrel: 30 in. Ported
Chokes: screw in
Weight: 7.8 lbs (12 gauge)
Bore/Gauge: 12, 20
Magazine: none
Features: right- and left-handed models with palm swell; adjustable comb; ported barrels; barrel selector and ejectors
MSRP: **$599**

P350

Action: pump
Stock: Synthetic, Advantage Timber HD, Max 4
Barrel: 24, 26 and 28 in.
Chokes: screw-in
Weight: 6.8 lbs (26 in.)
Bore/Gauge: 12
Magazine: 4 + 1 rounds
Features: 3.5 in. chamber; Red Bead sight; recoil reducer available
MSRP: **$289-349**

UPLANDER

Action: side-by-side
Stock: American Walnut
Barrel: 24, 26 and 28 in.
Chokes: screw-in and fixed
Weight: 7.3 lbs
Bore/Gauge: 12, 20, 16, 28 and .410
Magazine: none
Features: Standard and Supreme grades; Combo sets available
MSRP: **$350-445**

Tristar Sporting Arms Shotguns

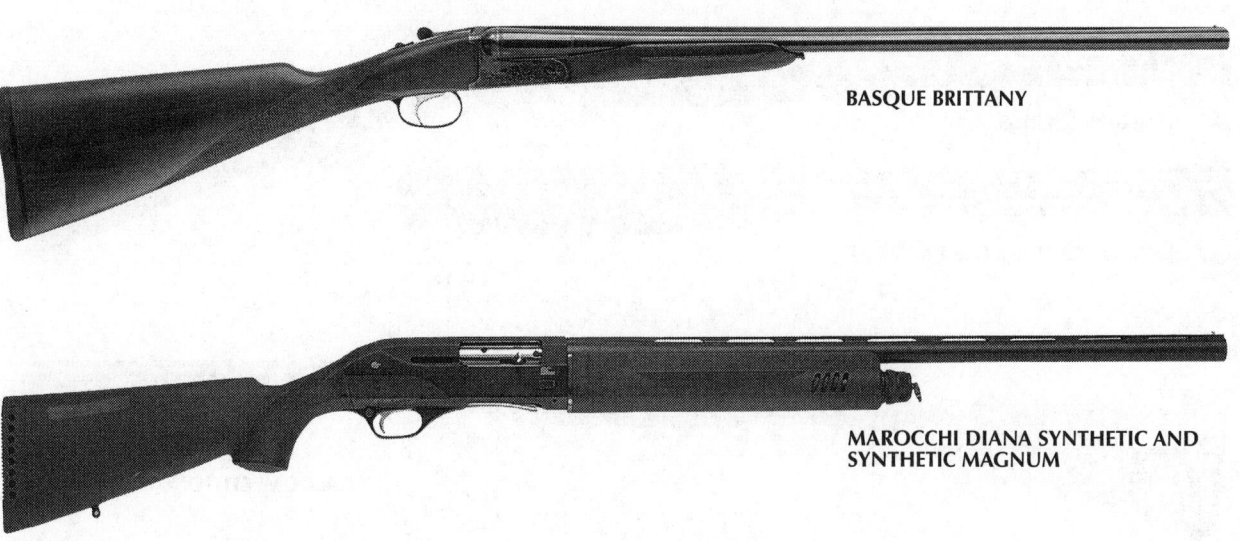

BASQUE BRITTANY

MAROCCHI DIANA SYNTHETIC AND SYNTHETIC MAGNUM

BASQUE SERIES
Action: side-by-side
Stock: walnut, straight or pistol grip
Barrel: 26 or 28 in.
Chokes: screw-in tubes
Weight: 6.8 lbs.
Bore/Gauge: 12, 16, 20, 28, .410
Magazine: none
Features: boxlock; single selective trigger; automatic ejectors; chromed bores; also: 20 in. Coach gun; chokes in 16 ga.: M/F and IC/M in 28 ga. and .410.
Gentry, 12 & 16: **$824**
20, 28 & .410: **$839**
Brittany, 12 & 20: **$943**
Brittany Sporting, 12 & 20: . . . **$1049**

MAROCCHI DIANA
Action: autoloader
Stock: walnut, synthetic or camo
Barrel: 24, 26, 28 or 30 in.
Chokes: screw-in tubes
Weight: 7.0 lbs.
Bore/Gauge: 12, 20, 28
Magazine: 4 rounds
Features: gas-operated; stock shims; slug model has sights; scope mount on rifled barrel
Synthetic, 3 in.: **$385**
Walnut, 3 in.: **$399**
Synthetic magnum, 3.5 in.: . . . **$479**

Are you flying with your shotgun to some exotic hunting destination? When packing the shotgun in an airline-approved hard case, first place it in a padded soft gun case to add extra protection.

Verona Shotguns

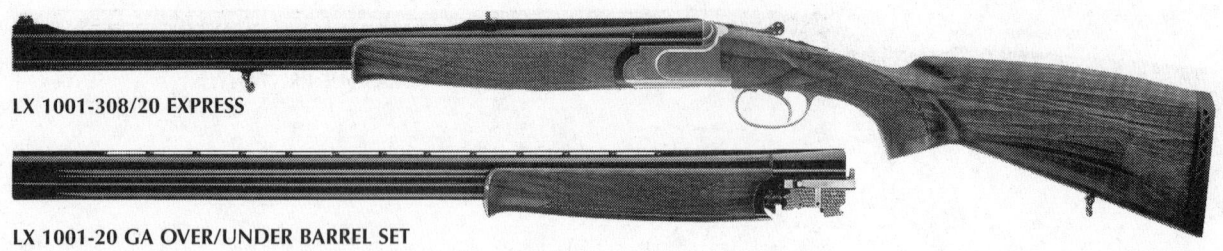

LX 1001-308/20 EXPRESS

LX 1001-20 GA OVER/UNDER BARREL SET

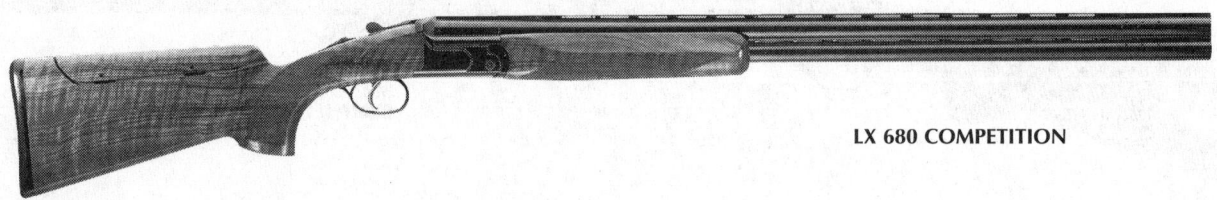

LX 680 COMPETITION

SX 801

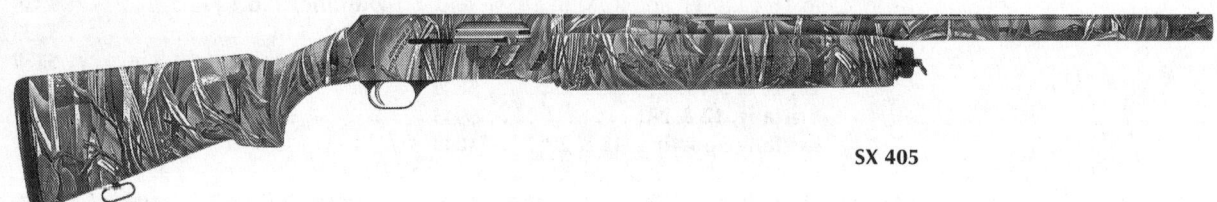

SX 405

MODEL LX EXPRESS
Action: over/under
Stock: Turkish walnut
Barrel: 28 in.
Chokes: screw-in tubes
Weight: 8.0 lbs.
Bore/Gauge: .223, .243, .270, .308 or .30-06 over 20 ga.
Magazine: none
Features: single selective tirgger; automatic ejectors
Express Combo with Express and 20 gauge over/under set: . . . $2764

MODEL LX 680 COMPETITION SERIES
Action: over/under
Stock: Turkish walnut
Barrel: 30 in. (32 in. on Trap Model)
Chokes: screw-in tubes
Weight: 7.5 lbs.
Bore/Gauge: 12
Magazine: none
Features: boxlock; removable competition trigger; ported barrels; deluxe case; also multiple-barrel sets
Verona LX 680 Sporting: $1116
LX 680 Gold Trap or Skeet:. . . $1616

MODEL SX 801
Action: autoloader
Stock: walnut
Barrel: 28 or 30 in.
Chokes: screw-in tubes
Weight: 6.8 lbs.   *Bore/Gauge:* 12
Magazine: 3 rounds
Features: gas-operated, alloy receiver; sporting and competition models available; also model SX405: synthetic or camo, 22 in. slug or 26 in. field
Verona SX 801:. $929-1139
Verona SX 405:. $353
With Docter sight:. $611

Weatherby Shotguns

ATHENA GRADE III CLASSIC FIELD

SXS ATHENA D'ITALIA

SAS FIELD

SAS MOSSY OAK CAMO

SAS SLUG GUN

SHOTGUNS

ATHENA

Action: over/under
Stock: walnut
Barrel: 26 or 28 in.
Chokes: screw-in tubes
Weight: 8.0 lbs.
Bore/Gauge: 12, 20, 28
Magazine: none
Features: boxlock; single selective mechanical trigger, automatic ejectors
Grade III Classic Field:...... **$2282**
Grade V Classic Field: **$2521**

SXS ATHENA D'ITALIA

Action: side-by-side
Stock: Turkish walnut
Barrel: 26 or 28 in.
Chokes: screw-in tubes
(fixed chokes in 28-gauge)
Weight: 6.75-7.25 lbs.
Bore/Gauge: 12, 20, 28
Magazine: none
Features: chrome-lined and back-

bored barrels; Anson and Deeley box-lock mechanism; automatic ejectors; engraved sideplates; double triggers and a straight grip, IC and M chokes in 28 ga.
MSRP: .... **from $2925**

ORION

Action: over/under
Stock: walnut, straight or pistol grip
Barrel: 26, 28, 30 or 32 in.
Chokes: screw-in tubes
Weight: 8.0 lbs.
Bore/Gauge: 12, 20 or 28
Magazine: none
Features: boxlock; single selective trigger, automatic ejectors
Upland: **$1364**
Grade II: **$1703**
Super Sporting Clays: **$2162**
Grade III:............... **$2053**

SAS

Action: autoloader
Stock: walnut, synthetic or camo
Barrel: 24, 26, 28 or 30 in., vent rib
Chokes: screw-in tubes   *Weight:* 7.8 lbs.
Bore/Gauge: 12   *Magazine:* 4 rounds
Features: gas-operated; 3 in. chamber; magazine cutoff
Synthetic: **$879**
Walnut: **$925**
Camo: **$969**
Sporting Clays: **$999**

SAS SLUG GUN

Action: autoloader
Stock: walnut   *Barrel:* 22 in. rifled
Chokes: none   *Weight:* 7.3 lbs.
Bore/Gauge: 12   *Magazine:* 4 rounds
Features: self-compensating gas system; cantilever scope base included; "smart" follower, magazine cutoff, stock has shims to alter drop, pitch, cast-off
MSRP: **$969**

Winchester Shotguns

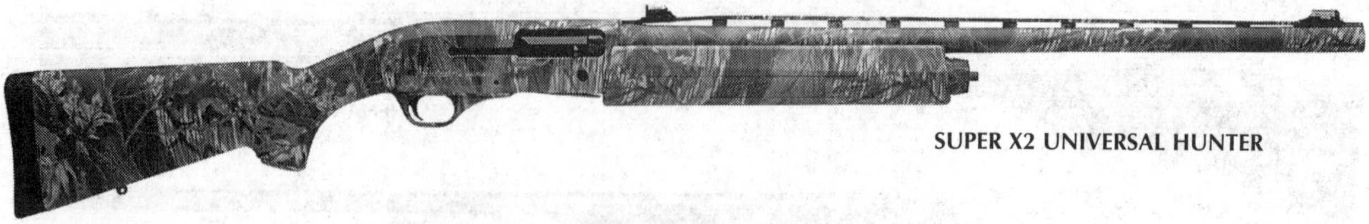

SUPER X2 UNIVERSAL HUNTER

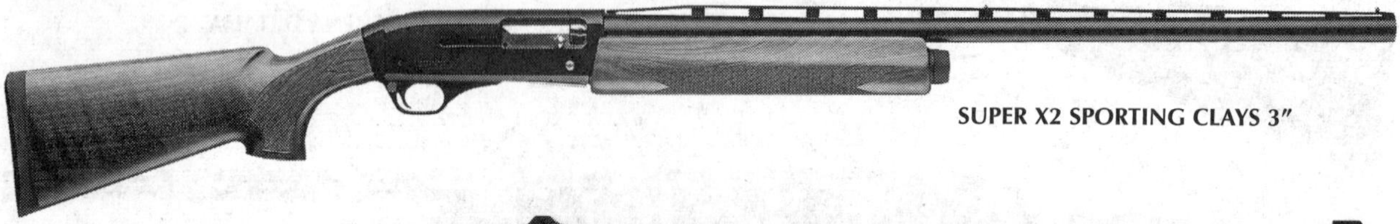

SUPER X2 SPORTING CLAYS 3"

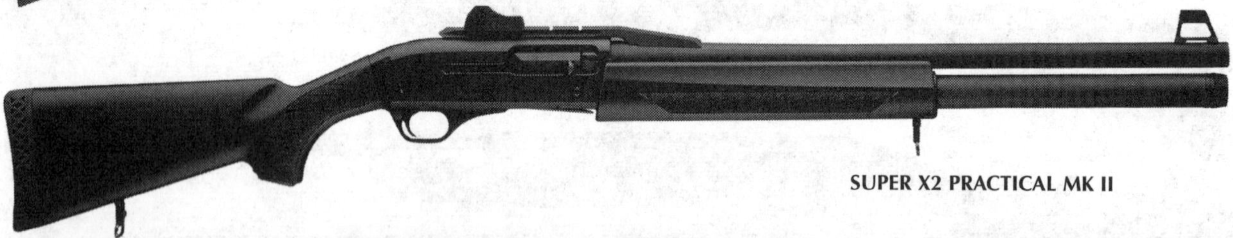

SUPER X2 PRACTICAL MK II

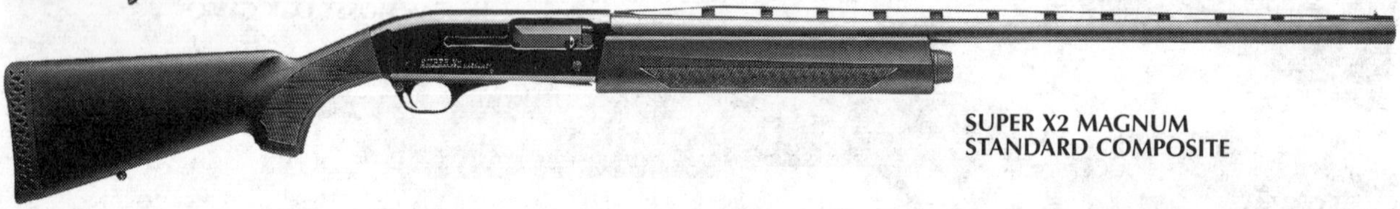

SUPER X2 MAGNUM
STANDARD COMPOSITE

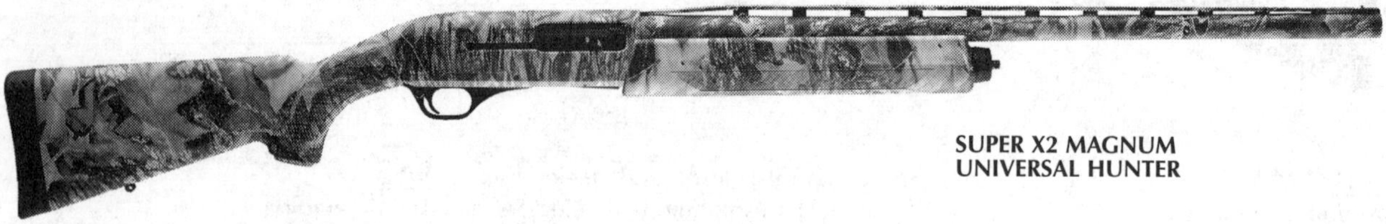

SUPER X2 MAGNUM
UNIVERSAL HUNTER

SUPER X2
Action: autoloader
Stock: walnut or synthetic
Barrel: 22, 24, 26, 28 or 30 in.
Chokes: screw-in tubes
Weight: 8.0 lbs.
Bore/Gauge: 12
Magazine: 4 rounds
Features: gas-operated mechanism, back-bored barrels; all with "Dura-Touch" finish, some with Tru-Glo sights

Super X2 Light Field:	**$945**
Sporting Clays:	**$998**
Deer, rifled barrel,	
cantilever:	**$957**
Practical MK II, extended	
magazine:	**$1287**
composite:	**$908**
Turkey:	**$1165**
Universal Hunter Turkey:	**$1179**
Practical MKI	
w/TruGlo sights:	**$1116**

Whenever you purchase a gun, photograph it and keep a record of the serial number. If a gun is stolen, or lost by an airline, a photo is handy for identification or justification of its value.

Winchester Shotguns

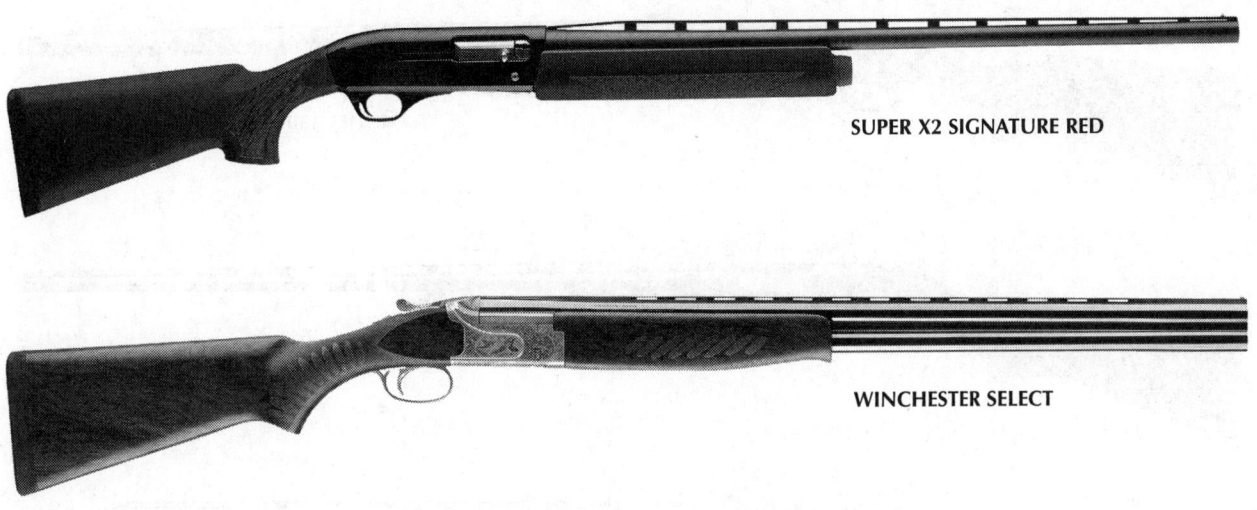

SUPER X2 SIGNATURE RED

WINCHESTER SELECT

SUPER X2 SIGNATURE RED

Action: autoloader
Stock: hardwood, "Dura-Touch" finish
Barrel: 28 or 30 in.
Chokes: screw-in tubes
Weight: 8.0 lbs.
Bore/Gauge: 12
Magazine: 4 rounds
Features: shims adjust buttstock; backbored barrel; "Dura-Touch" armor coating now available on many other Winchesters
MSRP: **$1015**

WINCHESTER SELECT

Action: boxlock over/under with low-profile breech
Stock: checkered walnut (adjustable comb available on target models, standard with palm swell)
Barrel: 26, 28 in. (field), 28, 30, 32 in. (target) threaded for Invector Plus choke tubes
Sights: bead front (TruGlo on target versions)
Weight: 7.0-7.3 lbs. (field), 7.5-7.8 lbs. (target)
Bore/Gauge: 12
Magazine: none
Features: 3 in. chambers on field guns; ventilated middle rib on target guns
Field: **$1498**
Trap and Sporting: **$1950**
Adjustable comb models: . . . **$2115**
Higher grades: **$2320**

If you hunt during warm weather and cold weather, you'll need to modify your gunstock to fit light clothing as well as heavy winter clothing. One easy solution is to have two recoil pads, one approximately an inch thinner than the other for cold-weather hunting, and change them to match your clothes.

SHOTGUNS

Winchester Shotguns

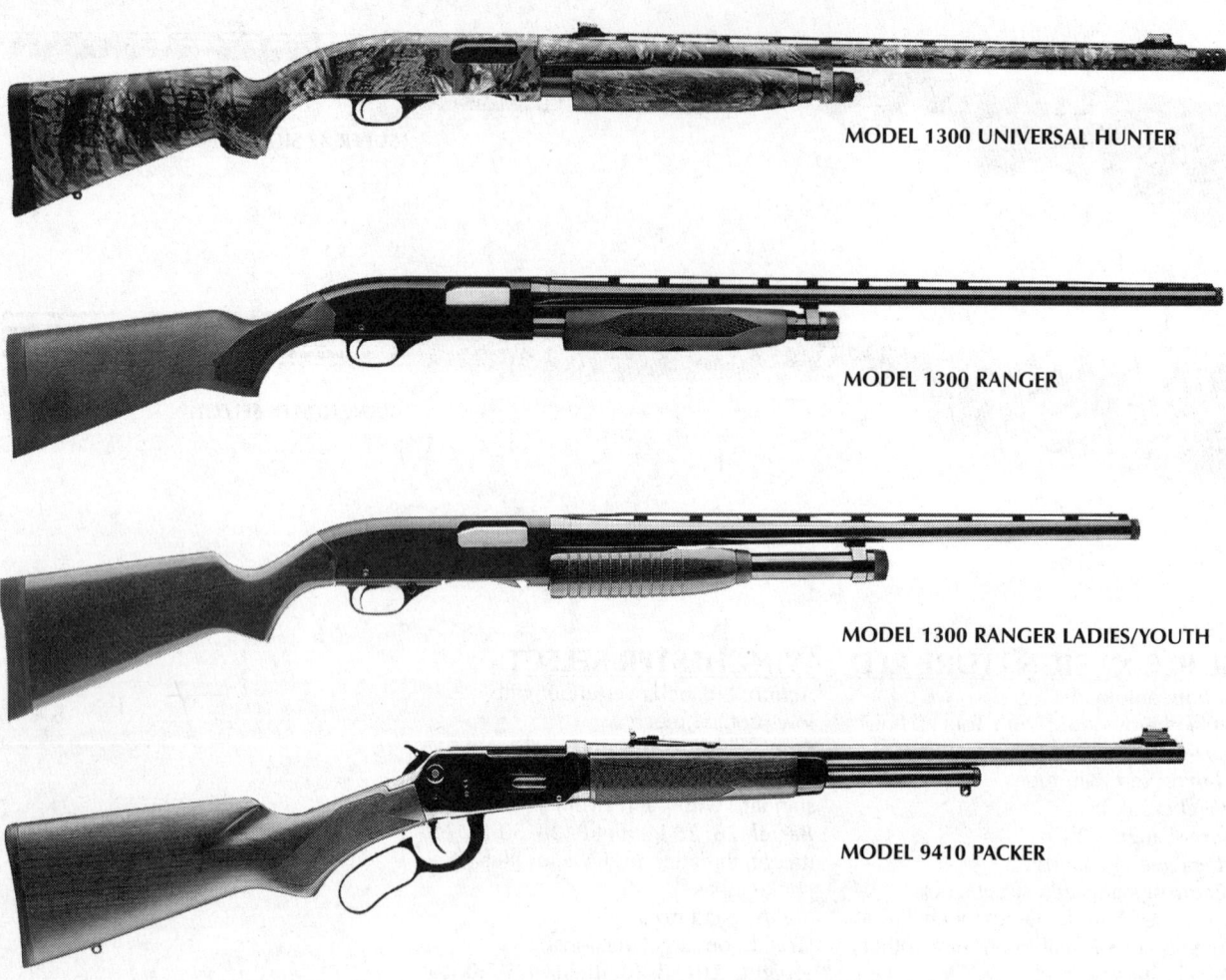

MODEL 1300 UNIVERSAL HUNTER

MODEL 1300 RANGER

MODEL 1300 RANGER LADIES/YOUTH

MODEL 9410 PACKER

SHOTGUNS

MODEL 1300
Action: pump
Stock: walnut or synthetic
Barrel: 18, 22, 24, 26 or 28 in.
Chokes: screw-in tubes
Weight: 7.5 lbs.
Bore/Gauge: 12, 20
Magazine: 4 rounds
Features: Deer versions feature either smooth or rifled 22 in. barrels, rifle sights
Synthetic: **$438**
Walnut: **$438**
Ranger, hardwood: **$366**
Turkey, camo: **$507**
Deer, synthetic: **$376**
**Deer, synthetic
   with cantilever mount:** **$420**
Deer, combo: **$453**
Universal Hunter: **$472**

MODEL 9410
Action: lever
Stock: walnut
Barrel: 20 or 24 in.
Chokes: full
Weight: 7.0 lbs.
Bore/Gauge: .410
Magazine: 9 rounds
Features: 2.5 in. chamber; Truglo front sight, shallow V rear
9410: **$626**
Packer with 20-inch barrel: . . . **$647**
**Packer w/TruGlo sights
   (no choke):** **$583**
M9410 Ranger, hardwood: **$532**

HANDGUNS

Accu-Tek Handguns

ACCELERATOR PISTOL

AT-380 II

ACCELERATOR PISTOL
Action: autoloader
Grips: composite
Barrel: 8.5 in.
Sights: target
Weight: 54.0 oz.
Caliber: .22 WMR, .17 HMR
Capacity: 9 + 1 rounds
Features: single-action; internal hammer; stainless steel bull barrel; alumi-num rib with fully adjustable target sights; integral Weaver scope base; firing pin block and last-round slide hold-open
MSRP: **$412**

AT-380 II
Action: autoloader
Grips: composite
Barrel: 2.8 in.
Sights: target
Weight: 23.5 oz
Caliber: 380.ACP
Capacity: 6 + 1 rounds
Features: exposed hammer; one-hand manual safety; European type magazine release on bottom of grip; adjustable rear sight; stainless steel magazine
MSRP: **$249**

American Derringer Handguns

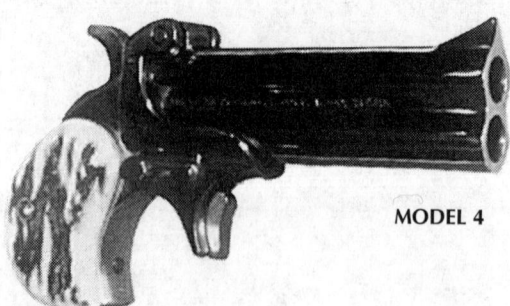

MODEL 4

.357 Mag.: $470
.357 Max.: $475
.44 Mag.: $540
Alaskan Survival
 (.45 Colt/.410): **$480**

MODEL 1
Action: hinged breech
Grips: rosewood or stag
Barrel: 3 in.   *Sights*: fixed open
Weight: 15.0 oz.
Caliber: .45 Colt, .410
Capacity: 2 rounds
Features: single-action; automatic barrel selection; manually operated hammer-block type safety
MSRP: **$423**

MODEL 4
Action: hinged breech
Grips: rosewood or stag
Barrel: 4.1 in., 6 in. (Alaskan Survival)
Sights: fixed open   *Weight*: 16.5 oz.
Caliber: .32 H&R, .357 Mag., .357 Max., .44 Mag., .45 Colt/.410, .45-70
Capacity: 2 rounds
Features: satin or high polish stainless steel finish; single-action; automatic barrel selection; manually operated hammer-block type safety

MODEL 6
Action: hinged breech
Grips: rosewood, walnut, black
Barrel: 6 in.
Sights: fixed open   *Weight*: 21.0 oz.
Caliber: .357 Mag; .45 Auto; .45 Colt/.410
Capacity: 2 rounds
Features: satin or high polish stainless steel finish; single-action; automatic barrel selection; manually operated hammer-block type safety
MSRP: **$470**

HANDGUNS

American Derringer Handguns

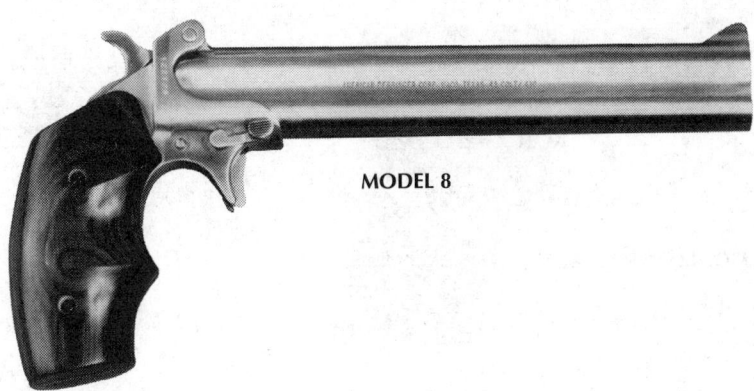

MODEL 8

MODEL 7 LIGHTWEIGHT & ULTRA LIGHTWEIGHT
Action: hinged breech
Grips: blackwood
Barrel: 3 in.
Sights: fixed open
Weight: 7.5 oz.
Caliber: .22LR; .22 Mag;.32 Mag/.32 S&W Long; .380 Auto;.38 Special; .44 Special
Capacity: 2 rounds
Features: grey matte finish; single-action; automatic barrel selection; manually operated hammer-block type safety
MSRP: **$470**

MODEL 8
Action: hinged breech
Grips: rosewood, walnut, black
Barrel: 8 in. *Sights*: red-dot scope
Weight: 24.0 oz.
Caliber: .357 Mag; .45 Auto; 45 Colt/.410
Capacity: 2 rounds

Features: satin or high polish stainless steel finish; single-action; automatic barrel selection; manually operated hammer-block type safety—automatically disengages when the hammer is cocked
.357 Mag.: **$470**
.45 Auto: **$535**
.45 Colt/.410: **$480**

Auto-Ordnance Handguns

MODEL 1911A1

1911WGSE DELUXE

MODEL 1911A1
Action: autoloader
Grips: plastic
Barrel: 5 in. *Sights*: fixed open
Weight: 39.0 oz.
Caliber: .45 ACP

Capacity: 7 + 1 rounds
Features: single-action 1911 Colt design; Deluxe version has rubber wrap-around grips, 3-dot sights; Thompson 1911C stainless; 1911 SE in blued finish

1911 SE "Standard": **$609**
Deluxe: **$615**
WWII Parkerized: **$598**

Beretta Handguns

MODEL 21 BOBCAT

MODEL 85 CHEETAH

MODEL 84 CHEETAH

MODEL 87 TARGET

MODEL 21 BOBCAT

Action: autoloader
Grips: plastic or walnut
Barrel: 2.4 in.
Sights: fixed open
Weight: 11.5 oz.
Caliber: .22 LR, .25 Auto
Capacity: 7 (.22) or 8 (.25) rounds
Features: double-action; tip-up barrel; alloy frame; walnut grips extra
Matte: **$250**
Blued: **$300**
Stainless: **$325**

MODEL 84 CHEETAH

Action: autoloader
Grips: plastic or wood
Barrel: 3.8 in.
Sights: fixed open
Weight: 23.3 oz.
Caliber: .380 Auto
Capacity: 13 + 1 rounds (10+1 restricted capacity)
Features: double-action; ambidextrous safety
Cheetah 84: **$625**
Cheetah 84 nickel: **$675**

MODEL 85 CHEETAH

Action: autoloader
Grips: plastic or wood
Barrel: 3.8 in.
Sights: fixed open
Weight: 23.3 oz.
Caliber: .380 Auto
Capacity: 8 + 1 rounds
Features: double-action; ambidextrous safety; single stacked magazine
Cheetah 85: **$575**
Cheetah 85 nickel: **$675**

MODEL 87 CHEETAH

Action: autoloader
Grips: wood
Barrel: 3.8 in.   *Sights*: fixed open
Weight: 23.3 oz.
Caliber: .22LR
Capacity: 7 + 1 rounds
Features: double-action; ambidextrous safety
MSRP: **$625**

MODEL 87 TARGET

Action: autoloader
Grips: plastic or wood
Barrel: 5.9 in. *Sights*: fixed open
Weight: 20.1 oz.
Caliber: .22 LR
Capacity: 10 + 1 rounds
Features: blowback design; Target weighs 40.9 oz. with target sights
MSRP: **$698**

Beretta Handguns

MODEL 92

MODEL 3032 TOMCAT

MODEL 92/96 VERTEC

MODEL M9

MODEL 92/96 SERIES
Action: autoloader
Grips: plastic
Barrel: 4.7 to 4.9 in. **Sights**: 3-dot
Weight: 34.4-41.0 oz.
Caliber: 9mm
Capacity: 15+ 1 rounds (10 + 1 restricted capacity)
Features: chrome-lined bore; double-action tritium sights available; reversible magazine catch; manual safety doubles as de-cocking lever; visible/touch sensitive loaded chamber indicator

Model 92FS:	**$650**
Model 92FS Inox:	**$795**
Model 92FS Vertec:	**$760**
Model Model 92 Vertec Inox:	**$825**
Model 96:	**$715**
Model 96 Inox:	**$795**
Model 96 Vertec:	**$760**

MODEL 3032 TOMCAT
Action: autoloader
Grips: plastic
Barrel: 2.5 in.
Sights: fixed open
Weight: 14.5 oz.
Caliber: .32 Auto
Capacity: 7 + 1 rounds
Features: double-action; tip-up barrel

Matte:	**$350**
Blue:	**$375**
Stainless:	**$450**
Tritium:	**$425**

MODEL M9
Action: autoloader
Grips: plastic   *Barrel*: 4.9 in.
Sights: dot and post, low profile, windage adjustable rear
Weight: 34.4 oz.
Caliber: 9mm
Capacity: 15 + 1 rounds (10 + 1 restricted capacity)
Features: chrome-lined bore; double-action; reversible magazine release button; short recoil, delayed locking block system; lightweight forged aluminum alloy frame w/ combat-style trigger guard, manual safety doubles as decocking lever; visible/touch sensitive loaded chamber indicator; open slide design; automatic firing pin block; ambidextrous manual safety; disassembly latch

MSRP:	**$650**

HANDGUNS

Beretta Handguns

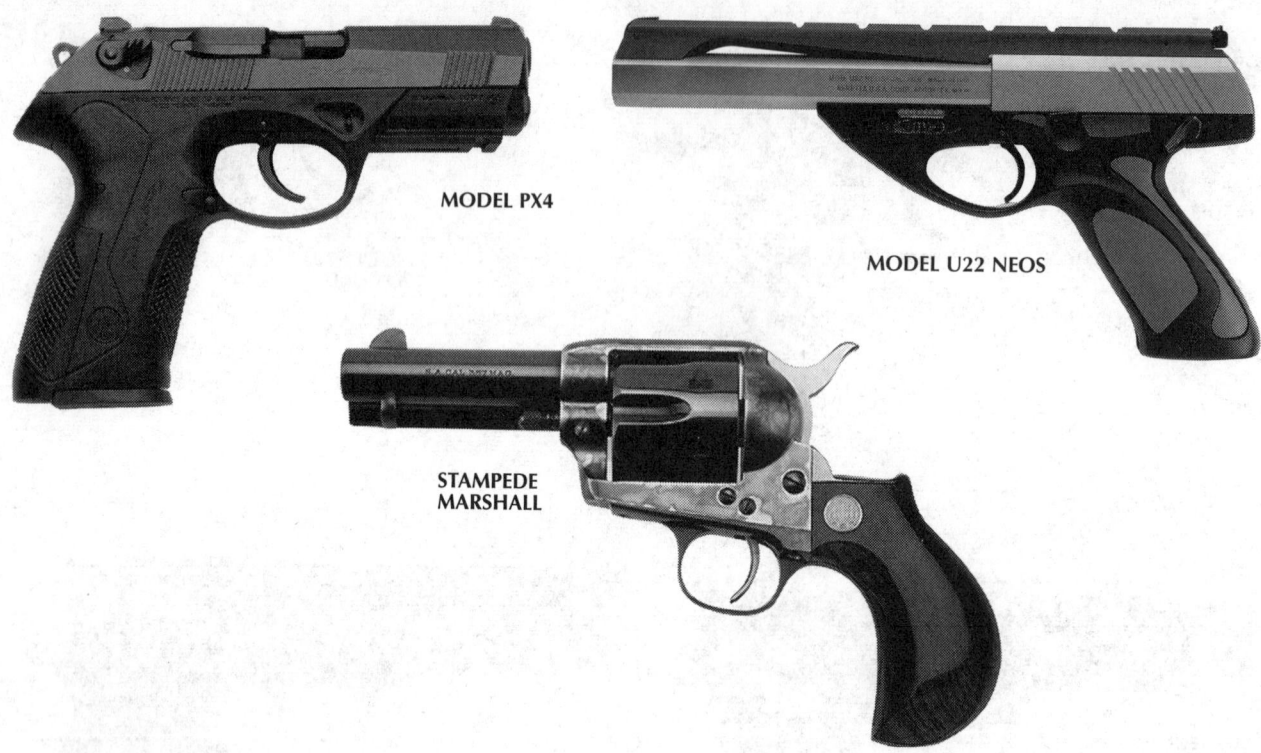

MODEL PX4

MODEL U22 NEOS

STAMPEDE MARSHALL

MODEL M9A1
Action: autoloader
Grips: plastic
Barrel: 4.9 in.
Sights: dot and post, low profile, windage adjustable rear
Weight: 34.4 oz.
Caliber: 9mm
Capacity: 15+ 1 rounds (10 + 1 restricted capacity)
Features: chrome-lined bore; double-action; reversible magazine release button; new sand resistant magazine; short recoil; delayed locking block system; lightweight forged aluminum alloy frame w/ combat-style trigger guard and integral MIL_STD-1913 "Picatinny" rail; aggressively checkered front and back strap; manual safety doubles as decocking lever; visible/touch sensitive loaded chamber indicator; open slide design, automatic firing pin block; ambidextrous manual safety; disassembly latch
MSRP: $850

MODEL PX4
Action: autoloader
Grips: 3 sizes, interchangeable polymer
Barrel: 4 in.
Sights: Super-LumiNova
Weight: .27.7 oz
Caliber: 9mm and .40 S&W
Capacity: 9mm: 17 + 1 rounds (10 + 1 restricted capacity)
Capacity: 40 S&W: 14 + 1 rounds (10 + 1 restricted capacity)
Features: double-action; cold hammer forged barrel; chrome-lined bore and chamber; MIL-STD -1913 "Picatinny" accessory rail for laser sight; flashlight; interchangeable/ambidexterous magazine release buttons; interchangeable backstraps; Night sights available as option
MSRP: $598

MODEL U22 NEOS
Action: autoloader
Grips: plastic
Barrel: 4.5 in. or 6 in.
Sights: target
Weight: 31.7 oz.
Caliber: .22 LR
Capacity: 10 + 1 rounds
Features: single-action; removable colored grip inserts; model with 6 in. barrel weighs 36.2 oz.; Deluxe model features adjustable trigger, replaceable sights; optional 7.5 in. barrel
U22 Neos: $250
Inox: $325
DLX: $350
Inox DLX: $375

STAMPEDE
Action: revolver
Grips: polymer, plastic or Walnut
Barrel: 4.75-7.5 in.
Sights: fixed, open
Weight: 36.8-38.4 oz.
Caliber: .45 Colt, ,357 Mag.
Capacity: 6 rounds
Features: single-action; color case hardened frame; blue, charcoal blue, or Inox finish
Bisley: $625
Blued: $550
Deluxe: $675
Inox: $750
Marshall: $575

HANDGUNS

Bersa Handguns

380 THUNDER

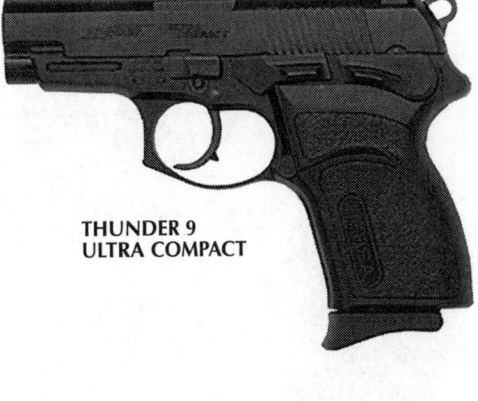

THUNDER 9
ULTRA COMPACT

THUNDER .40

THUNDER .45
ULTRA COMPACT

MODEL 380 THUNDER

Action: autoloader
Grips: black polymer
Barrel: 3 in.
Sights: fixed open
Weight: 19.75 oz.
Caliber: .380 ACP
Capacity: 7 + 1 rounds
Features: double-action; safeties: intergral locking system, manual, firing pin
Deluxe Blue: **$308**
Matte: **$275**
Matte CC: **$292**
Satin nickel: **$299**

THUNDER 9 ULTRA COMPACT

Action: autoloader
Grips: black polymer
Barrel: 3.5 in.
Sights: target
Weight: 24.5 oz.
Caliber: .9mm
Capacity: 10 + 1 rounds

Features: double-action; manual and firing pin safeties; anatomically designed grips
Matte: **$441**
Satin Nickel: **$467**
Thunder 9 High Capacity (17 rounds): **$442-467**

THUNDER .40

Action: autoloader
Grips: black polymer
Barrel: 4.2 in.
Sights: target
Weight: 28 oz.
Caliber: .40 ACP
Capacity: 16 + 1 rounds
Features: double-action; manual and firing pin safeties; anatomically designed grips
Matte: **$442**
Satin Nickel: **$467**
Thunder .40 High capacity (17 rounds): **$442-467**

THUNDER .45 ULTRA COMPACT

Action: autoloader
Grips: black polymer
Barrel: 3.6 in.
Sights: target
Weight: 27 oz.
Caliber: .45 ACP
Capacity: 7 + 1 rounds
Features: double-action; manual and firing pin safeties; anatomically designed grips
Matte: **$426**
Stainless: **$467**
Duotone: **$450**

Bond Arms Handguns

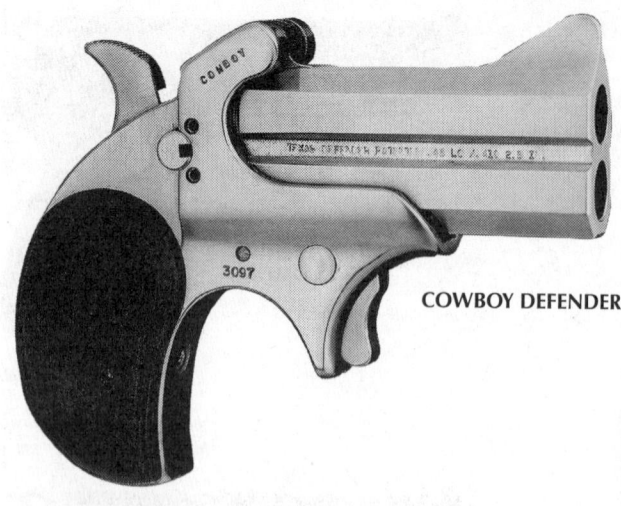

COWBOY DEFENDER

TEXAS DEFENDER

CENTURY 2000
Action: single-action
Grips: laminated
Barrel: 3.5 in.
Sights: fixed, open
Weight: 21 oz.
Caliber: .410/45LC
Capacity: 2 rounds
Features: interchangeable barrels; automatic extractor; rebounding hammer; crossbolt safety; stainless steel with satin polish finish; black ash or rosewood laminated grips
MSRP: **$404**

DEFENDER
Action: single-action
Grips: laminated
Barrel: 3 or 5 in.
Sights: fixed, open
Weight: 19 oz., 20 oz.
Caliber: .22 LR, 9 mm, 32 H & R Mag, .357 Mag/.38 Spl., .357 Max., 10 mm, .40 S&W, .45 LC; .45 ACP, .45 Glock; .44 Sp., .44-40 Win., .45 Colt/.410 Shot Shell(rifled)
Capacity: 2 rounds
Features: interchangeable barrels; automatic extractor; rebounding hammer; crossbolt safety; stainless steel with satin polish finish; black ash or rosewood laminated grips
Texas Defender: **$389**
Cowboy Defender: **$389**

SNAKE SLAYER
Action: single-action
Grips: rosewood
Barrel: 3.5 in.
Sights: fixed, open
Weight: 22 oz.
Caliber: .410/45LC
Capacity: 2 rounds
Features: interchangeable barrels; automatic extractor; rebounding hammer; crossbolt safety; stainless steel with satin polish finish; extended grips
MSRP: **$455**

Browning Handguns

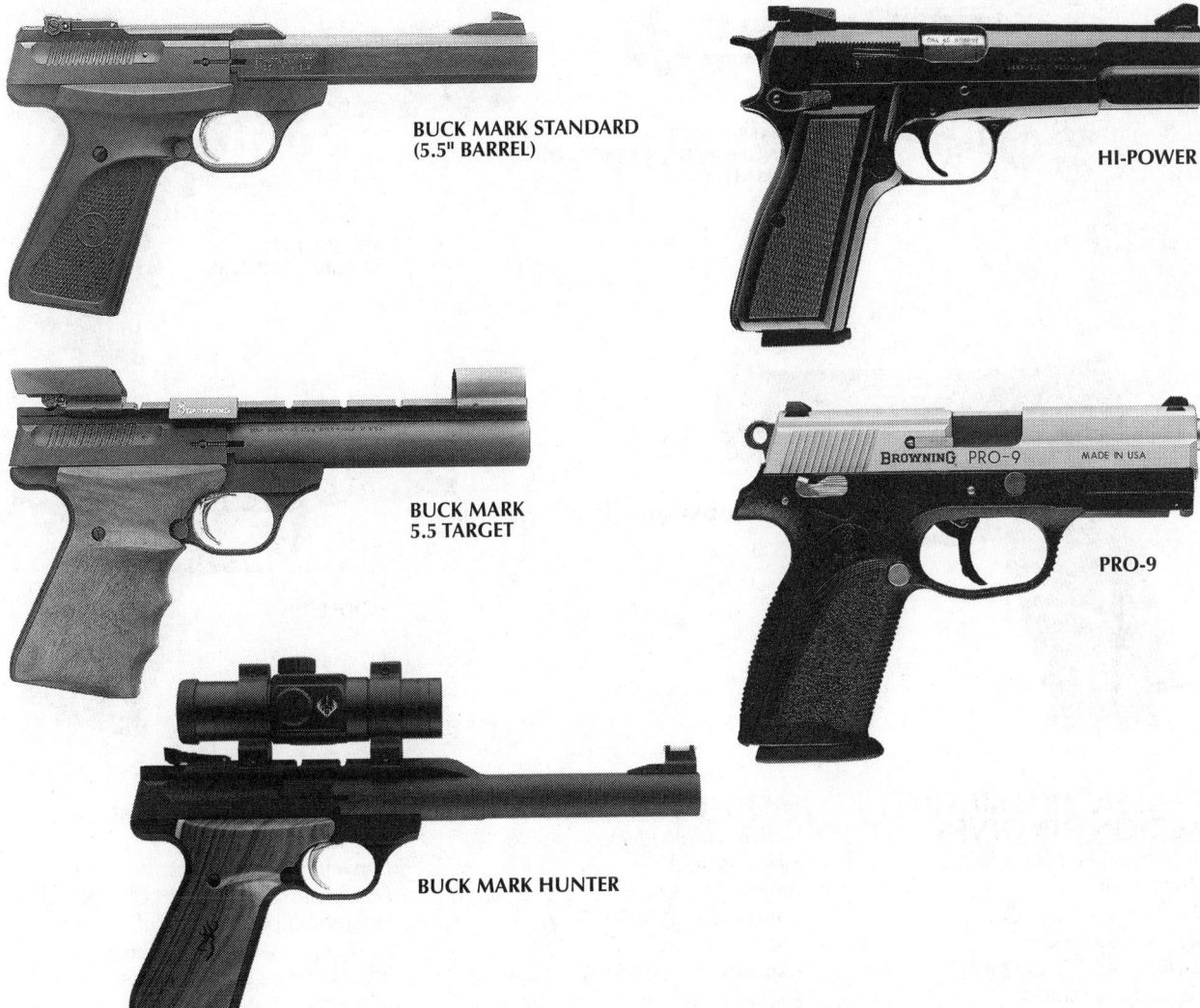

BUCK MARK STANDARD
(5.5" BARREL)

HI-POWER

BUCK MARK
5.5 TARGET

PRO-9

BUCK MARK HUNTER

BUCK MARK

Action: autoloader
Grips: composite, laminated or wood
Barrel: 4, 5.5 or 7.5 in.
Sights: target **Weight**: 34 oz.
Caliber: .22 LR **Capacity**: 10 + 1 rounds
Features: standard, camper, target, bullseye models available with various grips, barrel contours; Plus with adjustable rear and Truglo/Marble fiber-optic front sights; FLD Plus with rosewood grips and adjustable rear and Truglo/Marble fiber-optic front sights

Buck Mark:	**$324**
Stainless:	**$359**
Camper:	**$294**
Stainless:	**$323**
Field:	**$511**
Hunter (7.5 in. bbl):	**$381**

Micro (4 in. bl.):	**$324**
stainless:	**$359**
Plus:	**$390**
Nickel:	**$472**
FLD:	**$390**
Target:	**$511**

HI-POWER

Action: autoloader
Grips: walnut, rubber or composite
Barrel: 4.74 in.
Sights: fixed or adjustable
Weight: 33 oz.; 35 oz. (.40 S&W)
Caliber: 9mm, .40 S&W
Capacity: 10+1 rounds
Features: single-action; locked breech action; ambidextrous thumb safety; polished blued finish on slide
MSRP: **$549**

PRO-9 & PRO-40

Action: autoloader
Grips: polymer
Barrel: 4 in. **Sights**: fixed
Weight: 30-35 oz.
Caliber: 9mm, .40 S&W
Capacity: 10 rounds
Features: Pro-9 (9mm only) polymer receiver; has stainless steel slide and replaceable backstrap inserts; double-action; polymer receiver; stainless steel slide; under-barrel accessory rail; ambidextrous safety/decocker; interchangeable backstrap inserts

Pro-9:	**$641**
Pro-40:	**$641**

HANDGUNS

Charles Daly Handguns

CLASSIC 1873
SINGLE-ACTION REVOLVER
STAINLESS

MODEL 1911
TARGET STAINLESS

M-5 COMMANDER

MODEL 1911

CLASSIC 1873 SINGLE-ACTION REVOLVER
Action: single-action revolver
Grips: walnut
Barrel: 4.75, 5.5, 7.5 in.
Sights: fixed open
Caliber: .45 LC, .357 mag.
Capacity: 6 rounds
Features: stainless steel or color case hardened finish; available in civilian, cavalry and artillery models; brass or steel backstrap and trigger guard
1873 .45LC:. $479
1873 .357 Mag.: $479
1873 .45LC Brass Backstrap: . . . $449
1873 .357 Mag. Stainless:. $659

HI-POWER
Action: autoloader
Grips: polymer
Barrel: 4.8 in.   *Sights*:
Weight: 34.5 oz.   *Caliber*: 9mm
Capacity: 10+1 rounds
Features: single-action; carbon steel frame; thumb safety; x/s sight system; matte blue finish
MSRP:. $549

MODEL 1911 A-1
Action: autoloader
Grips: walnut
Barrel: 3.5, 4 or 5 in.   *Sights*: target
Weight: 34, 38 or 39.5 oz.
Caliber: .45 ACP
Capacity: 6+1 (ECS), 8 + 1 rounds
Features: extended hi-rise beavertail grip safety; combat trigger; combat hammer; beveled magazine well; flared and lowered ejection port; dovetailed front and low profile rear sights; ECS series with contoured left hand safety
Model 1911 A-1:. $529
Model 1911 A-1 Empire stainless:. $629
Model 1911 A-1 Empire stainless
   (ECS & EMS):. $619
Model 1911 A-1 Target: $619
Model 1911 A-1 Target stainless:. $724
Model 1911 A-1 Target Custom
   Match:. $799

MODEL M-5
Action: autoloader
Grips: walnut, rubber or composite
Barrel: 3.1, 4.4 in., 5 in.
Sights: fixed or adjustable
Weight: 28 oz., 30.5 oz., 33.5 oz.

Caliber: 9mm (Compact), .40 S&W, .45 ACP
Capacity: 10+1 rounds
Features: single-action; polymer frame; tapered bull barrel and full-length guide rod; stainless steel beaver-tail grip safeties; grip with raised contact pad with serrations
M-5:. $719
M-5 Commander: $719
M-5 Ultra X Compact: $719

ZDA PISTOL
Action: autoloader
Grips: polymer
Barrel: 3.5 in.   *Sights*: fixed
Weight: 26 oz.
Caliber: 9mm, .40 S&W
Capacity: 15, 12 rounds
Features: double-action and de-cocker; ambidextrous slide lock; low shot indicator for magazine
MSRP: $589

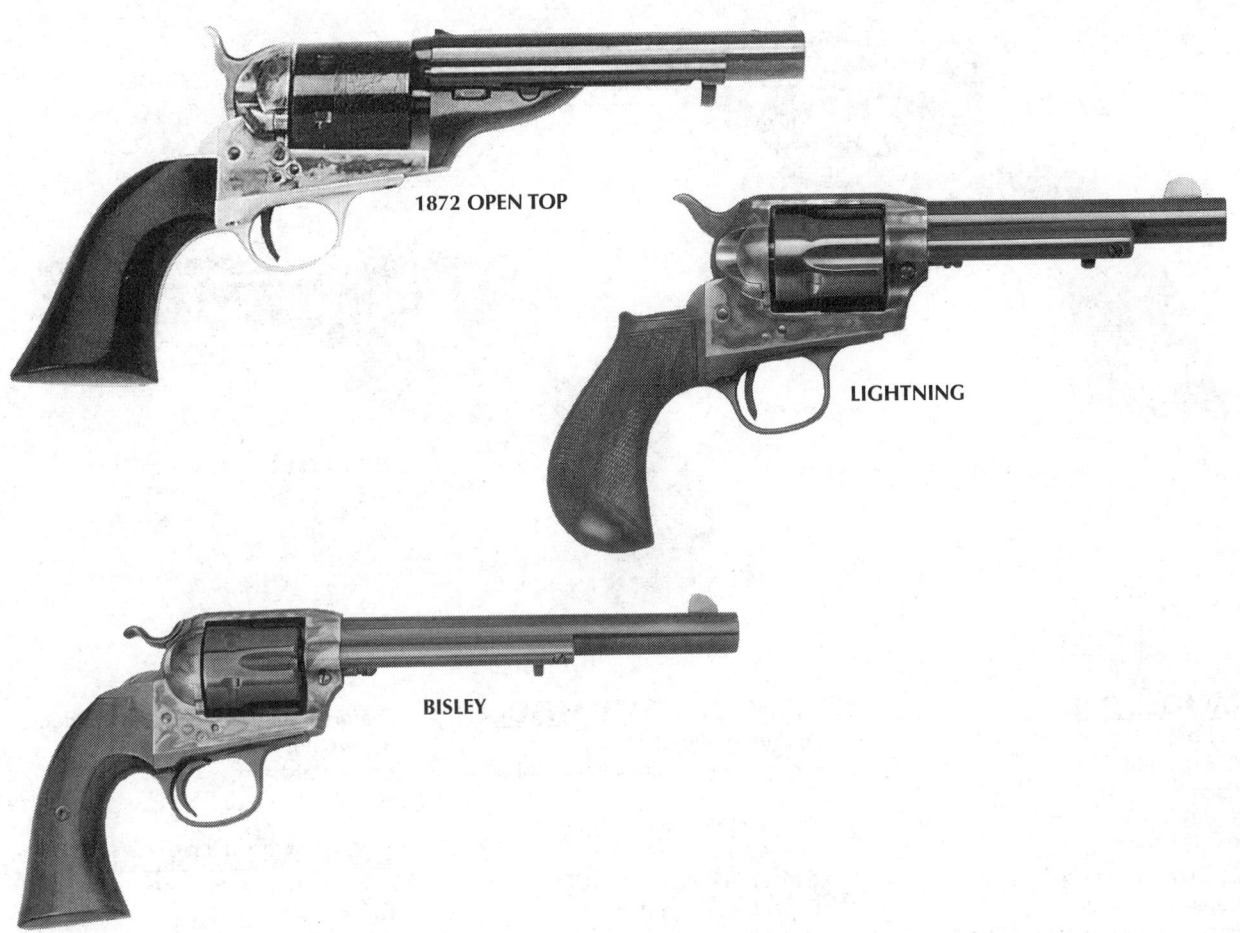

1872 OPEN TOP

LIGHTNING

BISLEY

MODEL 1872 OPEN TOP

Action: single-action revolver
Grips: walnut
Barrel: 5.5 and 7.5 in.
Sights: fixed open
Weight: 40.0 oz.
Caliber: .38 Spec, .44 Colt and .45 S&W,
Capacity: 6 rounds
Features: forged, color case-hardened frame; blue, charcoal blue or nickel finish; weight varies up to 46 oz.
1872: $529
1872 Navy grip: $529

BISLEY

Action: single-action revolver
Grips: walnut
Barrel: 4.75, 5.5 & 7.5 in.
Sights: open, fixed
Weight: 40.3, 40.6, 44.0 (.357 Mag.) oz.
Caliber: .357, .45LC, .44 Sp., and .44WCF
Capacity: 6 rounds

Features: reproduction of the original Colt Bisley; forged, color case-hardened frame; blue, charcoal blue, nickel finish
MSRP: $525

GEORGE ARMSTRONG CUSTER 7TH U.S. CAVALRY MODEL

Action: single-action revolver
Grips: walnut
Barrel: 7.5 in.
Sights: open, fixed
Weight: 40.4 oz.
Caliber: .45 LC.
Capacity: 6 rounds
Features: forged, color case-hardened frame; blue, charcoal blue or US Armory finish
MSRP: $549

LIGHTNING SA

Action: single-action revolver
Grips: walnut

Barrel: 3.5. 4.75 or 5.5 in.
Sights: open, fixed
Weight: 28.5, 29.5, 30.75 (.38 Colt) oz.
Caliber: .38 Colt and .38 Special
Capacity: 6 rounds
Features: forged, color case-hardened frame; blue, charcoal blue or nickel finish
MSRP: $489

MODEL P 1873

Action: single-action revolver
Grips: walnut, hard rubber, ivory
Barrel: 4.75, 5.5 and 7.5 in.
Sights: none
Weight: 44.0 oz.
Caliber: .32 WCP, .357, .38 WCF, 45 ACP, .45 LC, .45 Schofield, .38 WCF, .32 WCF, .44 WCF.
Capacity: 6 rounds
Features: fashioned after the 1873 Colt SAA but 20% smaller
MSRP: $499

HANDGUNS

Cimarron Handguns

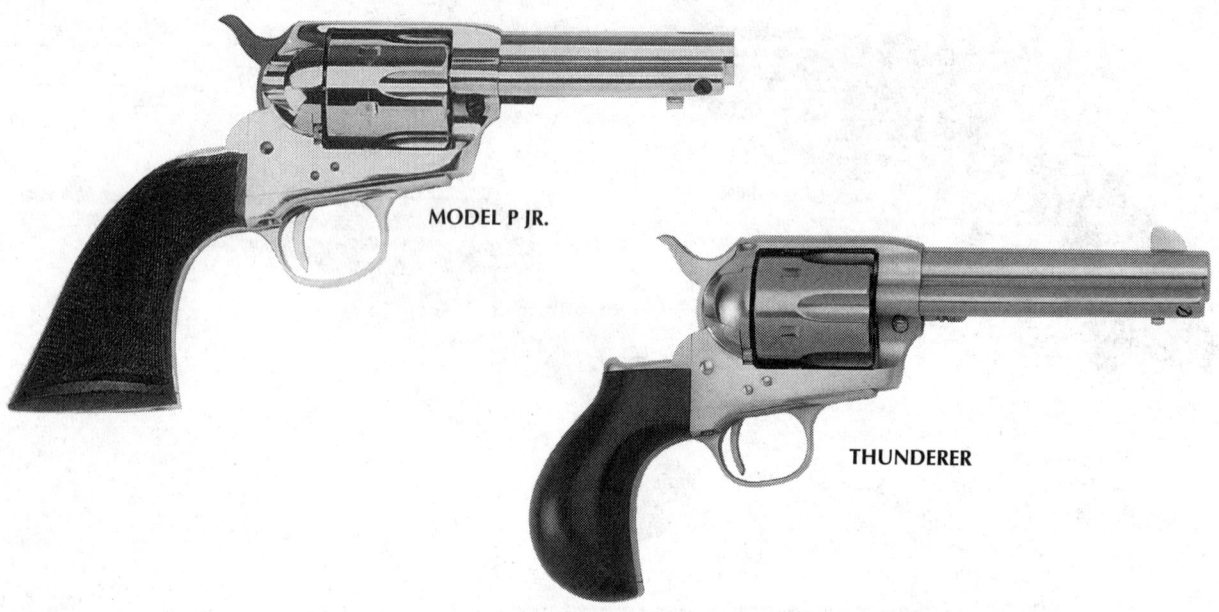

MODEL P JR.

THUNDERER

MODEL P JR.
Action: single-action revolver
Grips: walnut
Barrel: 3.5, 4.75 and 5.5 in.
Sights: open
Weight: 35.2 oz.
Caliber: .38 Special
Capacity: 6 rounds
Features: fashioned on the 1873 Colt SAA but 20% smaller; color case-hardened frame; blue, charcoal blue or nickel finish
MSRP: $499

NEW SHERIFF'S MODEL
Action: single-action revolver
Grips: walnut, black hard rubber
Barrel: 3.5 in.
Sights: open fixed
Weight: 33.5 oz.
Caliber: 45 Colt, 44 WCF,
Capacity: 6 rounds
Features: forged, color case-hardened frame; blue, charcoal blue, nickel finish
MSRP: $499

THUNDERER
Action: single-action revolver
Grips: walnut, ivory, mother of pearl or black hard rubber
Barrel: 3.5 w/ejector, 4 .75, 5.5 or 7.5 in.
Sights: open, fixed
Weight: 38, 40, 40.75, 43.60 (.357 Mag.) oz.
Caliber: .357 Mag., .44 SP, .44 WCF, .45 ACP, .45 Colt
Capacity: 6 rounds

Features: forged, color case-hardened frame; blue, charcoal blue or nickel finish
MSRP: $519

U.S.V. ARTILLERY MODEL
Action: single-action revolver
Grips: walnut
Barrel: 5.5 in.
Sights: open, fixed
Weight: 40 oz.
Caliber: .45 LC.
Capacity: 6 rounds
Features: forged, color case-hardened frame; blue, charcoal blue or US Armory finish
MSRP: $549

When using open sights, concentrate your focus on the front sight, rather than the target or rear sight. You can't focus on all three, so focus on the front sight. A good sight picture will have the rear sight and target slightly fuzzy and the front sight razor sharp.

HANDGUNS

Colt Handguns

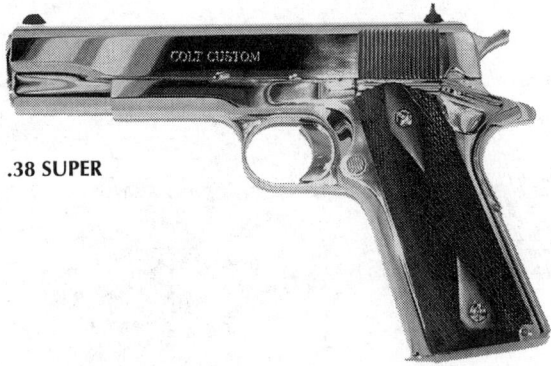

.38 SUPER

1991

DEFENDER

GOLD CUP

.38 SUPER

Action: autoloader
Grips: rosewood or composite
Barrel: 5 in.
Sights: fixed open
Weight: 39.0 oz.
Caliber: .38 Super
Capacity: 9 + 1 rounds
Features: M1911 stainless models available; aluminum trigger
Blue: $950
Stainless: $980
Bright stainless: $1200

1991 SERIES

Action: autoloader
Grips: rosewood or composite
Barrel: 5 in.

Sights: fixed open
Weight: 39.0 oz.
Caliber: .45 ACP
Capacity: 7 + 1 rounds
Features: M1911 Commander with 4.3 in. barrel available; both versions in stainless or chrome moly
1991: $870
Stainless: $920

DEFENDER

Action: autoloader
Grips: rubber finger-grooved
Barrel: 3 in.
Sights: 3-dot
Weight: 30.0 oz.
Caliber: .45 ACP
Capacity: 7 + 1 rounds

Features: stainless M1911; extended safety; upswept beavertail; beveled magazine well
MSRP: $950

GOLD CUP

Action: autoloader
Grips: black composite
Barrel: 5 in.
Sights: target
Weight: 39.0 oz.
Caliber: .45 ACP
Capacity: 8 + 1 rounds
Features: stainless or chome-moly; Bo-Mar or Eliason sights
Gold Cup, blue: $1300
Stainless: $1400

When you lubricate a revolver, remember to oil the front and back of the cylinder at the point where the main pin passes through. Also place a little good quality gun grease on the "star" at the breech end. Clean and replace the grease occasionally.

HANDGUNS

Colt Handguns

SERIES 70

XSE

SINGLE-ACTION ARMY

XSE COMMANDER

SERIES 70
Action: autoloader
Grips: walnut
Barrel: 5 in.
Sights: fixed open
Weight: 39.0 oz.
Caliber: .45 ACP
Capacity: 7 + 1 rounds
Features: single-action M1911 design
MSRP: **$990**

SINGLE-ACTION ARMY
Action: single-action revolver
Grips: composite
Barrel: 4.3, 5.5 or 7.5 in.
Sights: fixed open
Weight: 46.0 oz.
Caliber: .32/20, .357 Mag., .38 Spl.,
.44-40, .45 Colt, .38/40
Capacity: 6 rounds
Features: case-colored frame; transfer
bar; weight for .44-40, 48 oz. and 50
oz. for .45 Colt
Single-Action Army: **$1380**
Nickel: **$1530**

MODEL XSE
Action: autoloader
Grips: rosewood
Barrel: 5 in.
Sights: 3-dot
Weight: 39.0 oz.
Caliber: .45 ACP
Capacity: 8 + 1 rounds
Features: stainless; M1911 with
extended ambidextrous safety;
upswept beavertail; slotted hammer
and trigger; also available as 4.3 in.
barrel Commander
MSRP: **$1100**

MODEL 75

MODEL 75 CHAMPION

MODEL 75 COMPACT .40 S&W

MODEL 75 KADET

THE KADET ADAPTER IN ITS REAR (COCKED) POSITION

MODEL 83

MODEL 75

Action: autoloader
Grips: composite
Barrel: 4.7 in.
Sights: 3-dot
Weight: 35.0 oz.
Caliber: 9mm or .40 S&W
Capacity: 10 + 1 rounds
Features: single- or double-action
9mm: **$509**
.40 S&W: **$525**

MODEL 75 CHAMPION

Action: autoloader
Grips: composite
Barrel: 4.5 in.
Sights: target
Weight: 35.0 oz.
Caliber: 9 mm or .40 S&W

Capacity: 10 + 1 rounds
Features: also available: IPSC version with 5.4-in. barrel
Champion: **$1646**
IPSC: **$1152**

MODEL 75 COMPACT

Action: autoloader
Grips: composite
Barrel: 3.9 in.
Sights: fixed open
Weight: 32.0, 37.8 (40 S&W) oz.
Caliber: 9 mm or .40 S&W
Capacity: 10 rounds
Features: single- or double-action; ambidextrous safety
Compact: **$539**
Compact .40 S&W: **$539**

MODEL 75 KADET

Action: autoloader   **Grips**: composite
Barrel: 4.9 in.   **Sights**: target
Weight: 38.0 oz.
Caliber: .22 LR
Capacity: 10 + 1 rounds
Features: single- or double-action
Kadet: **$510**
**.22 conversion kit
   for CZ 75/85**: **$299**

MODEL 83

Action: autoloader
Grips: composite
Barrel: 3.8 in.   **Sights**: fixed open
Weight: 26.0 oz.   **Caliber**: 9mm
Capacity: 10 + 1 rounds
Features: single- or double-action
MSRP: **$420**

CZ Handguns

MODEL 85 COMBAT

MODEL 97

MODEL 100

2075 RAMI

MODEL 85 COMBAT

Action: autoloader
Grips: composite
Barrel: 4.7 in.
Sights: target
Weight: 35.0 oz.
Caliber: 9 mm
Capacity: 10 + 1 rounds
Features: single- or double-action
MSRP: $599

MODEL 97

Action: autoloader
Grips: composite
Barrel: 4.8 in.
Sights: fixed open
Weight: 41.0 oz.
Caliber: .45 ACP
Capacity: 10 + 1 rounds
Features: single- or double-action
MSRP: $663

MODEL 100

Action: autoloader
Grips: composite
Barrel: 3.9 in.
Sights: target
Weight: 24.0 oz.
Caliber: 9mm, .40 S&W
Capacity: 10 + 1 rounds
Features: single- or double-action; de-cocking lever
MSRP: $449

2075 RAMI

Action: single- and double-action autoloader
Grips: lack composite
Barrel: 3 in.
Sights: blade front, shrouded rear
Weight: 25.0 oz.
Caliber: 9mm Luger, .40 S&W
Capacity: 10 rounds (9mm), 8 rounds (.40 S&W)

Features: firing pin block; manual safety; double-stack magazine
MSRP: $576

MODEL P-01

Action: autoloader
Grips: rubber
Barrel: 3.8 in.
Sights: 3-dot
Weight: 27.3 oz.
Caliber: 9mm
Capacity: 13 + 1 rounds
Features: single- or double-action; decocking lever; safety stop on hammer; firing pin safety
MSRP: $586

HANDGUNS

Dan Wesson Handguns

**PATRIOT COMMANDER
CLASSIC BOBTAIL**

POINTMAN

RAZORBACK

PATRIOT COMMANDER CLASSIC BOBTAIL
Action: autoloader
Grips: cocobolo
Barrel: 4.74 in.   *Sights:* fixed open
Weight: 34.08 oz.
Caliber: 10mm, .45 ACP
Capacity: 8 rounds (10mm), 7 rounds (.45 ACP)
Features: series 70 stainless steel frame; forged stainless steel slide; forged one-piece stainless steel match barrel; high ride beavertail grip safety; extended thumb safety; lowered and relieved ejection port
MSRP: **$1169**

POINTMAN
Action: autoloader
Grips: exotic wood
Barrel: 5 in.
Sights: open fixed
Weight: 38.4 oz. (10mm), 38.08 oz. (.45 ACP)
Caliber: 10mm, .45 ACP
Capacity: 8 rounds (10mm), 7 rounds (.45 ACP)
Features: series 70 stainless frame; stainless slide; forged one-piece stainless match barrel; match grade trigger and sear; extended thumb safety; stainless high ride beavertail grip safety;
MSRP: **$1079**

RAZORBACK
Action: autoloader
Grips: black rubber
Barrel: 5 in.
Sights: target
Weight: 38.4 oz.
Caliber: 10 mm
Capacity: 8 rounds
Features: Series 70 stainless frame; forged stainless slide; forged one-piece stainless match barrel; solid match trigger; extended thumb safety; stainless high ride beavertail grip safety
MSRP: **$959**

Downsizer Handguns

WSP
Action: tip-up hinged breech
Grips: composite
Barrel: 2.1 in.
Sights: none
Weight: 11.0 oz.
Caliber: .357 Mag., .38 SP, .45 ACP
Capacity: 1 round
Features: double-action; stainless steel frame & barrel; internal firing pin block
MSRP: **$499**

"WORLD'S SMALLEST PISTOL"

HANDGUNS

Ed Brown Handguns

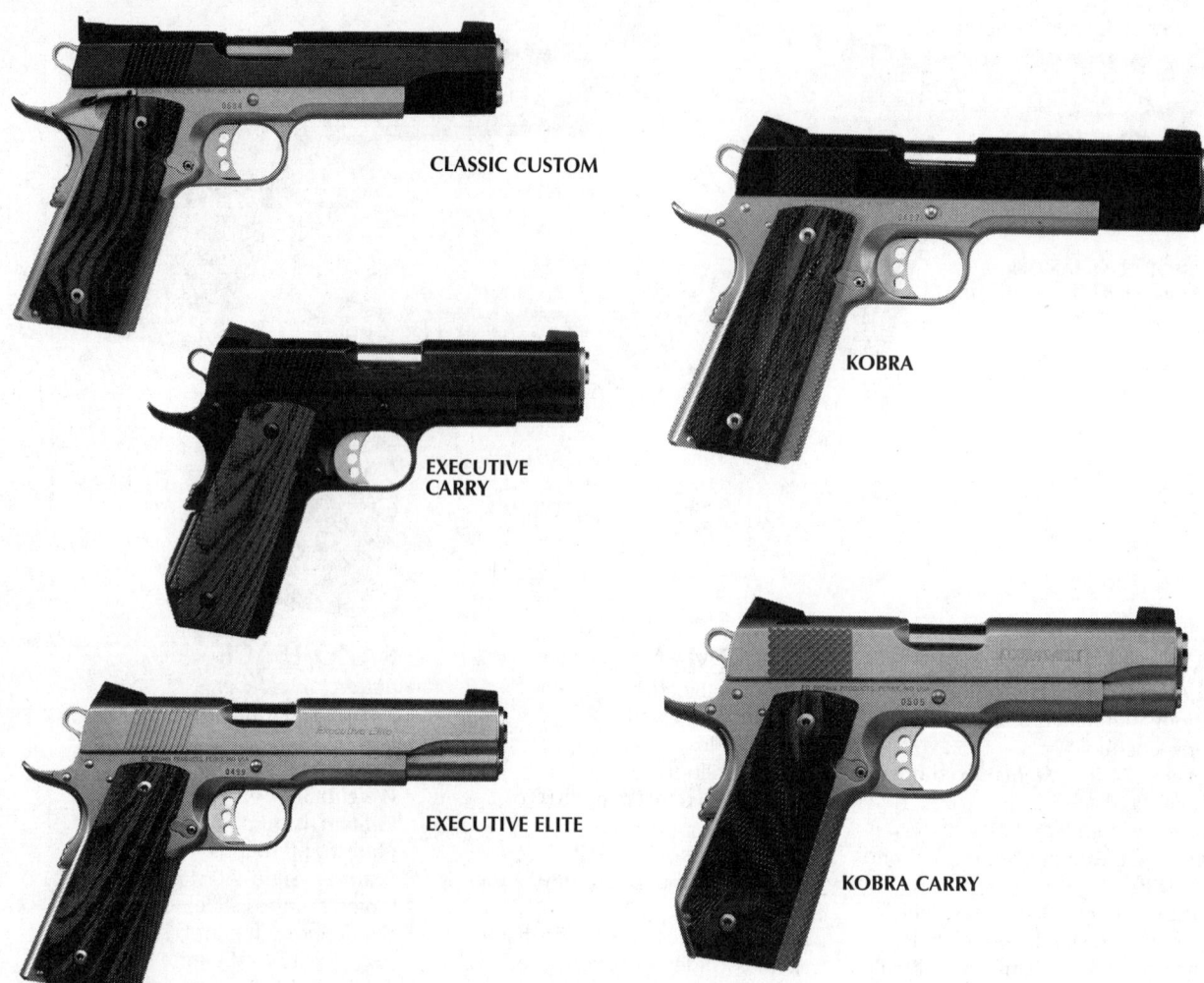

CLASSIC CUSTOM

KOBRA

EXECUTIVE CARRY

EXECUTIVE ELITE

KOBRA CARRY

CLASSIC CUSTOM

Action: autoloader
Grips: cocobolo wood
Barrel: 5 in. **Sights**: target
Weight: 37.0 oz.
Caliber: .45 ACP
Capacity: 7 + 1 rounds
Features: single-action, M1911 Colt design; Bo-Mar sights; checkered forestrap; ambidextrous safety; stainless available

Classic Custom:. $2895
Stainless/blue:. $2995
Stainless:. $3095

EXECUTIVE CARRY

Action: autoloader
Grips: checkered Cocobolo wood
Barrel: 4.25 in. **Sights**: low-profile combat
Weight: 33.0 oz.

Caliber: .45 ACP
Capacity: 7 + 1 rounds
Features: Bob-tail butt; checkered forestrap; stainless optional

Commander Bobtail:. $2495
Executive Carry:. $2295
Stainless/blue:. $2395
Stainless:. $2495

EXECUTIVE ELITE

Action: autoloader
Grips: checkered Cocobolo wood
Barrel: 5 in. **Sights**: to order
Weight: 36.0 oz.
Caliber: .45 ACP
Capacity: 7 + 1 rounds
Features: custom-grade M1911 Colt with many options to order

Elite: $2195
Stainless/blue:. $2295
Stainless:. $2395

KOBRA

Action: autoloader
Grips: cocobolo wood
Barrel: 4.3 (Kobra Carry) or .5 in.
Sights: low-profile combat
Weight: 36.0 oz.
Caliber: .45 ACP
Capacity: 7 + 1 rounds
Features: single-action M1911 Colt design; matte finish with Snakeskin treatment on forestrap; mainspring housing and rear of slide; stainless models available

Kobra: $1995
Stainless/blue:. $2095
Stainless:. $2195
Kobra Carry: $2095
Stainless/blue:. $2195
Stainless:. $2295

HANDGUNS

1873 DAKOTA

1873 PINKERTON

MODEL 1875 REMINGTON

MODEL 1890 REMINGTON POLICE

1873 HARTFORD

Action: single-action revolver
Grips: walnut
Barrel: 4, 4.75, 5.5, 7.5 in.
Sights: fixed open
Weight: 46.0 oz.
Caliber: 32/20, 38/40, 44/40, 44SP, 45LC, .357.
Capacity: 6 rounds
Features: Birdshead grip; steel back-strap and trigger guard; Great Western II features various combinations of deluxe nickel, satin nickel, casehardened or blue finish with bone, ultra stag or ultra ivory grips
1873 Hartford: $425
Dakota: $375
Great Western II: $635
Great Western II Californian (walnut grips): $450

1873 HARTFORD STALLION

Action: single-action revolver
Grips: walnut
Barrel: 3.5, 4.75, 5.5 in.
Sights: fixed open
Weight: 46.0 oz.
Caliber: 32/20, 38/40, 44/40, 44SP, 45LC, .357.

Capacity: 6 rounds
Features: Birdshead grip; steel back-strap and trigger guard
MSRP: $389

1873 PINKERTON

Action: single-action revolver
Grips: walnut, birds-head
Barrel: 4 or 4.75 in.
Sights: fixed open
Weight: 44.0 oz.
Caliber: .357, .45 Colt, .45LC
Capacity: 6 rounds
Features: case-colored frame
MSRP: $429

MODEL 1875 REMINGTON

Action: single-action revolver
Grips: walnut
Barrel: 5.5 or 7.5 in.
Sights: fixed open
Weight: 48.0 oz.
Caliber: .357 Mag., .44/40, .45 LC
Capacity: 6 rounds
Features: case-hardened colored steel frame
Model 1875: $424
Engraved: $659
Nickel: $599

MODEL 1890 REMINGTON POLICE

Action: single-action revolver
Grips: walnut
Barrel: 5.8 in.
Sights: fixed open
Weight: 48.0 oz.
Caliber: .357 Mag., .44-40, .45 Colt
Capacity: 6 rounds
Features: lanyard loop; case-colored frame
Model 1890: $450
Nickel: $675

1894 BISLEY

Action: single-action revolver
Grips: walnut
Barrel: 5.5 or 7.5 in.
Sights: fixed open
Weight: 48.0 oz.
Caliber: .45LC
Capacity: 6 rounds
Features: forged color case-hardened steel frame; Bisley grip; steel backstrap and trigger guard
MSRP: $450

HANDGUNS

Entréprise Arms Handguns

500 BOXER

ELITE

MEDALIST

**TACTICAL
P325 PLUS**

MODEL 500 BOXER
Action: autoloader
Grips: composite
Barrel: 5 in.
Sights: target
Weight: 44.0 oz.
Caliber: .40 S&W, .45 ACP
Capacity: 10 + 1 rounds
Features: match-grade components and fitting; stainless one-piece guide rod; lapped slide; flared ejection port
.45 ACP: **$1399**
.40 S&W: **$1499**

ELITE
Action: autoloader
Grips: composite
Barrel: 3.25, 4.25 or 5 in.
Sights: adjustable

Weight: 38, 40.0 oz.
Caliber: .45 ACP
Capacity: 10 + 1 rounds
Features: lowered and flared ejection port; reinforced dustcover; bolstered front strap; high grip cut; high-ride beavertail grip safety; steel flat mainspring housing; extended thumb lock; adjustable rear sights
MSRP: **$700**

MEDALIST
Action: autoloader
Grips: composite
Barrel: 5 in. *Sights*: target
Weight: 44.0 oz.
Caliber: .40 S&W, .45 ACP
Capacity: 10 + 1 rounds
Features: up-turned beavertail, stain-

less hammer and sear; flared ejection port; match trigger, lapped slide
.45: **$979**
.40 S&W: **$1099**

TACTICAL P325 PLUS
Action: autoloader
Grips: composite
Barrel: 3.3 in.
Sights: low-profile combat
Weight: 37.0 oz.
Caliber: .45 ACP
Capacity: 10 + 1 rounds
Features: extended ambidextrous safety; lapped slide; up-turned beavertail; skeleton trigger and hammer; Tactical Ghost Ring or Novak sights; (also available with 4.3 and 5.0 in. barrels)
MSRP: **$979**

A handgun scope does not always require a high magnification to be effective. A 2-power scope is often all that is needed, unless you plan to use your handgun for long range target shooting.

HANDGUNS

European American Armory Handguns

BIG BORE BOUNTY HUNTER

SMALL BORE BOUNTY HUNTER

WITNESS

WITNESS P COMPACT

BOUNTY HUNTER

Action: single-action revolver
Grips: walnut
Barrel: 4.5 or 7.5 in.
Sights: fixed open
Weight: 39.0-41.0 oz.
Caliber: .357 Mag., .44 Mag., .45 Colt
Capacity: 6 rounds
Features: case-colored or blued or nickel frame; version with 7.5 in. barrel weighs 42 oz.

Bounty Hunter: **$369-379**
Nickel: **$399**
Case color: **$369-379**
Also available:
Small Bore Bounty Hunter
  (.22 LR or .22 WMR)v **$269**
  Nickel: **$299**

THOR SINGLE-SHOT PISTOL

Action: hinged breech
Grips: rubber
Barrel: 14 in.
Sights: none
Weight: 8.0 oz.

Caliber: .30-06, .300Win, .308Win, .375Win., .44Mag, .45-70, .50SW, 7mm 08, 7mm
Capacity: 1 round
Features: single-action, steel frame, polygonal rifling, automatic ejector, grip safety, integral scope base
MSRP: **$1099**

WITNESS

Action: autoloader
Grips: rubber
Barrel: 4.5 in.
Sights: 3-dot
Weight: 33.0 oz.
Caliber: 9mm, .38 Super, .40 S&W, 10 mm, .45 ACP
Capacity: 10 + 1 rounds
Features: double-action; polymer frame available
Steel: **$459**
Polymer: **$429**
"Wonder" finish: **$459**
Gold Team: **$1699**

WITNESS COMPACT

Action: autoloader
Grips: rubber
Barrel: 3.6 in.   *Sights*: 3-dot
Weight: 29.0 oz.
Caliber: 9mm, .40 S&W, .45 ACP .45 ACP
Capacity: 10 + 1 rounds
Features: double-action; polymer frame and ported barrels available
Steel: **$459**
Polymer: **$429**
Witness P Carry: **$469**

WITNESS S/A HUNTER

Action: autoloader
Grips: rubber
Barrel: 6 in.   *Sights*: adjustable
Weight: 41.0 oz.
Caliber: 10 mm, .45 ACP
Capacity: 10+1 rounds
Features: single-action; auto firing pin block; drilled & tapped for scope mount
Hunter Pro 10: **$939**
Hunter Pro 45: **$909**

HANDGUNS

Firestorm Handguns

MODEL 45

MODEL 380

COMANCHE REVOLVER

MINI

SUPER COMANCHE SINGLE-SHOT

MODEL 45
Action: autoloader
Grips: rubber
Barrel: 4.3 or 5.2 in.   *Sights*: 3-dot
Weight: 34.0 oz.
Caliber: .45 ACP
Capacity: 7 + 1 rounds
Features: single-action; 1911 Colt design; from cocking grooves
Model 45: $333
Duotone: $341

MODEL 380
Action: autoloader
Grips: rubber   *Barrel*: 3.5 in.
Sights: 3-dot   *Weight*: 23.0 oz.
Caliber: .380
Capacity: 7 + 1 rounds
Features: double-action; also available in .22 LR; 10-shot magazine
Model 380: $274
Duotonev: $283
22 LR: $283

COMANCHE REVOLVER
Action: double-action revolver
Grips: rubber
Barrel: 3 or 6 in.   *Sights*: target
Weight: 22.0 oz.
Caliber: .38 Spl. (also in .22, .357)
Capacity: 6 rounds
Features: adjustable sights; stainless or blue finish
Comanche I (.22, 6 in.) blue: . . $236
Comanche I (.22, 6 in.) SS: . . . $258
Comanche II (.38 Spl., 3or 4 in.)
   blue: $219
Comanche II (.38 Spl., 3or 4 in.)
   SS: $236
Comanche III(.357, 3, 4 or 6 in.)
   blue: $259
Comanche III (.357, 3, 4 or 6 in.)
   SS: $284

MINI
Action: autoloader
Grips: polymer

Barrel: 3.5 in.   *Sights*: target
Weight: 24.5 oz.
Caliber: 9mm, .40 S&W, .45 ACP
Capacity: 10 + 1 rounds (7 + I in .45)
Features: double-action
Mini: $400
Duotone: $424
Duotone .45: $416
Nickel: $424
.45 nickel: $433

SUPER COMANCHE
Action: hinged breech
Grips: composite
Barrel: 10 in. *Sights*: target
Weight: 47.0 oz.
Caliber: .45 LC/.410
Capacity: 1 round
Features: adjustable sight; accepts 2.5 or 3 in. shells; rifled slugs or buckshot(.410); blue or satin nickel finish
Nickel: $192
Blue: $175

FNP 9

Action: autoloader
Grips: plastic
Barrel: 4.75in.   *Sights*: fixed, open
Weight: 25.2 oz. (24.8 Compact)
Caliber: 9mm   **Capacity**: 10 +1 rounds
Features: double/single-action operation; molded polymer frame w/tactical accessory rail; ambidextrous de-cocking levers and reversible magazine release; numerous sight configurations available; FNP 9mm Compact version available
MSRP: $553

FNP 40

Action: autoloader
Grips: plastic
Barrel: 4 in.   *Sights*: fixed, open
Weight: 26.7 oz.
Caliber: .40 S&W
Capacity: 10 + 1 rounds
Features: double/single-action operation; molded polymer frame w/ tactical accessory rail; ambidextrous de-cocking levers and reversible magazine release; numerous sight configurations available
MSRP: $553

FIVE-SEVEN USG

Action: autoloader   *Grips:* plastic
Barrel: 4.75in.   *Sights*: fixed, open
Weight: 19.2 oz.
Caliber: 5.7 x 28mm
Capacity: 10 +1 rounds
Features: single-action with internal hammer; forged barrel with hard chrome finish; polymer frame and slide cover; traditional style trigger guard, reversible magazine release
MSRP: $995

HP-SA

Action: autoloader
Grips: plastic or walnut
Barrel: 4.75 in.   *Sights*: fixed, open
Weight: 2 oz.   *Caliber*: .40 S&W
Capacity: 10 + 1 rounds
Features: original John M. Browning Hi-Power; single-action
MSRP: $797

Freedom Arms Handguns

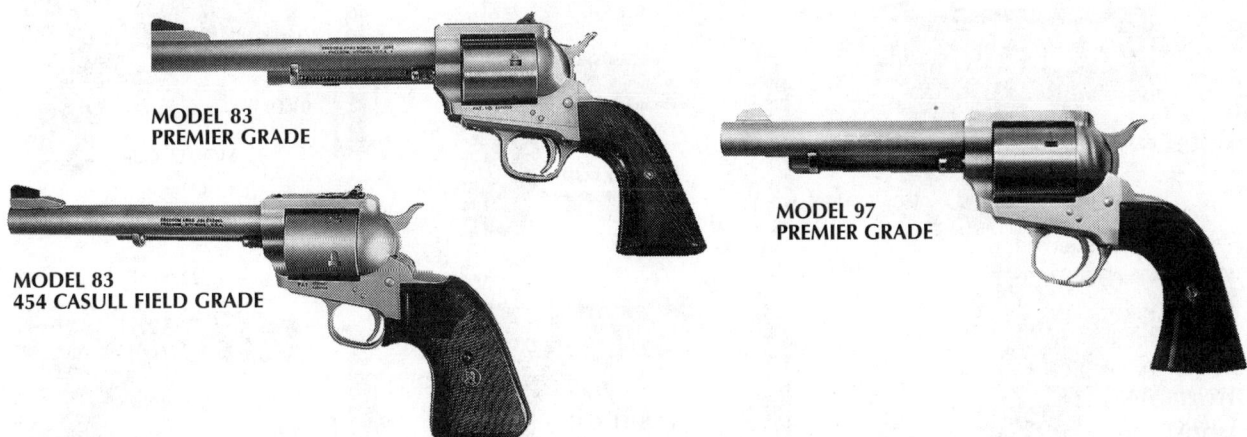

MODEL 83
PREMIER GRADE

MODEL 83
454 CASULL FIELD GRADE

MODEL 97
PREMIER GRADE

MODEL 83 PREMIER GRADE

Action: single-action revolver with manual safety bar
Grips: hardwood or optional Micarta
Barrel: 4.75, 6, 7.5, 9 or 10 in.
Sights: fixed or adjustable
Weight: 52.5 oz.
Caliber: .357 Mag., .41 Mag., .44 Mag., .454 Casull, .475 Linebaugh
Capacity: 5 rounds
Features: sights, scope mounts and extra cylinders optional
MSRP: $2035-2120

MODEL 83 RIMFIRE FIELD GRADE

Action: single-action revolver
Grips: Pachmyr or optional hardwood or Micarta
Barrel: 4.75, 6, 7.5, 9 or 10 in.
Sights: adjustable
Weight: 55.5 oz.
Caliber: .22 LR, .357 Mag., .41 mag., .44 Mag., .454 Casull, .475 Linebaugh
Capacity: 5 rounds
Features: sights, scope mounts and extra cylinders optional
MSRP: $1573-1803

MODEL 97 PREMIER GRADE

Action: single-action revolver with automatic transfer bar safety
Grips: hardwood or optional Micarta
Barrel: 4.5, 5.5, 7.5 or 10 in.
Sights: fixed or adjustable
Weight: 39.0 oz.
Caliber: .17 HMR, .22 LR, .32 H&R Mag., .357 Mag., .41 Mag., .44 Spl., .45 Colt
Capacity: 5 rounds for .41 and bigger, 6 rounds for smaller calibers
Features: sights; scope mounts and extra cylinders optional
MSRP: $1718-1784

HANDGUNS

Glock Handguns

MODEL G19

9X19

MODEL G17

MODEL G27

MODEL G23

PORTED BARREL

.40

MODEL G22

MODEL G33

MODEL G26

.357

MODEL G31

9X19

MODEL G34

MODEL G29

10MM

MODEL G20

MODEL G30

9X19

MODEL G17

.40

MODEL G35

COMPACT PISTOLS
Action: autoloader
Grips: composite
Barrel: 3.8 in.
Sights: fixed open   **Weight**: 21.2 oz.
Caliber: 9mm, .40 S&W, .357 Mag., 10mm, .45 ACP
Capacity: 9, 10, 13, 15 rounds depending on cartridge, magazine
Features: trigger safety; double-action; 10mm and .45 ACP weigh 24.0 oz.
MSRP: . . . . . . .available on request

FULL-SIZE PISTOLS
Action: autoloader
Grips: composite
Barrel: 4.5 in.
Sights: fixed open
Weight: 22.3 oz.
Caliber: 9mm, .40 S&W, .357 Mag., 10mm, .45 ACP
Capacity: 10, 13, 15, 17 rounds depending on cartridge
Features: trigger safety; double-action; 10 mm and .45 ACP weigh 26.3 oz.
MSRP: . . . . . . .available on request

SUBCOMPACT PISTOLS
Action: autoloader
Grips: composite
Barrel: 3.5 in.
Sights: fixed open
Weight: 19.8 oz.
Caliber: 9mm, .40 S&W, .357, .45
Capacity: 9, 10, 6 rounds depending on cartridge, magazine
Features: trigger safety; double-action
MSRP: . . . . . . .available on request

HANDGUNS

Glock Handguns

G-36 SLIMLINE
Action: autoloader
Grips: synthetic
Barrel: 3.8 in.
Sights: fixed open
Weight: 21.0 oz.
Caliber: .45 ACP
Capacity: 6 + 1 rounds
Features: single-stack magazine for thinner grip
MSRP: . . . .**price on request**

G-37 SLIMLINE
Action: autoloader
Grips: synthetic
Barrel: 24-30 in.
Sights:fixed open
Caliber: .45 Glock
Capacity: 10 + 1 rounds
Features: chambered for .45 Glock shortened .45 ACP cartridge
MSRP: . . . .**price on request**

G-36 SLIMLINE

G-37 SLIMLINE

Hämmerli Handguns

SP 20

X-ESSE .22 L.R.
WITH LONG BARREL

X-ESSE .22 L.R.
WITH SHORT BARREL

MODEL SP20
Action: autoloader
Grips: synthetic
Barrel: 4.6 in.
Sights: target
Weight: 40.0 oz.
Caliber: .22 LR, .32 S&W
Capacity: 5 rounds
Features: front-end magazine
.22: **$1668**
.32: **$1743**

MODEL X-ESSE SPORT
Action: autoloader
Grips: composite
Barrel: 4.5 or 5.5 in.
Sights: target
Weight: 36.0 oz.
Caliber: .22 LR
Capacity: 10 rounds
Features: single-action
MSRP: **$710**

Heckler & Koch Handguns

**MARK 23
SPECIAL OP**

P2000

MODEL P7M8

**USP 40
COMPACT LEM**

MARK 23 SPECIAL OP
Action: autoloader
Grips: polymer
Barrel: 5.9 in.
Sights: 3-dot
Weight: 42.0 oz.
Caliber: .45 ACP
Capacity: 10 + 1 rounds
Features: military version of USP
MSRP: **$2412**

MODEL P7M8
Action: autoloader
Grips: polymer
Barrel: 4.1 in.
Sights: target
Weight: 28.0 oz.
Caliber: 9mm
Capacity: 8 + 1 rounds
Features: blue or nickel finish
MSRP: **$1515**

P2000 AND P2000 SK
Action: autoloader
Grips: polymer
Barrel: 3.6 in. (2000) and 2.5 in.
(2000 SK)
Sights: 3-dot
Weight: 24 oz. (2000) and 22 oz.
(2000 SK)
Caliber: 9mm, .357 SIG, .40 S&W
Capacity: 9-13 rounds
Features: double-action; pre-cock
hammer; ambidextrous magazine
releases and interchangeable grip
straps; mounting rail for lights
and lasers
P2000: **$887**
P2000 SK: **$929**

USP 9 & 40
Action: autoloader
Grips: polymer
Barrel: 4.25 in. *Sights*: 3-dot
Weight: 27.0 oz.
Caliber: 9mm, .40 S&W
Capacity: 13 rounds
Features: short-recoil action; also in
kit form
MSRP: **$769**

USP 40 COMPACT LEM
Action: autoloader
Grips: composite
Barrel: 3.6 in. *Sights*: fixed open
Weight: 24.0 oz.
Caliber: .40 S&W
Capacity: 12 rounds
Features: double-action only with
improved trigger pull; also in 9mm
MSRP: **$799**

HANDGUNS

Heckler & Koch Handguns

USP 45
Action: autoloader
Grips: polymer
Barrel: 4.4 in.
Sights: 3-dot
Weight: 30.0 oz.
Caliber: .45 ACP
Capacity: 12 rounds
Features: short-recoil action
MSRP: **$839**

MODEL USP ELITE
Action: autoloader
Grips: composite
Barrel: 6.0 in.
Sights: target
Weight: 36.0 oz.
Caliber: 9mm, .45 ACP
Capacity: 15 rounds
Features: short recoil action, fiber-reinforced polymer frame; universal scope mounting groves, ambidextrous magazine release
USP Elite: **$1356**
**USP Expert (9mm, .45 ACP,
    .40 S&W with 5.2 in. bl.):** . . **$1356**

USP EXPERT

USP ELITE

Heritage Handguns

ROUGH RIDER

ROUGH RIDER .17 HMR

ROUGH RIDER
Action: single-action revolver
Grips: hardwood, regular or birdshead
Barrel: 3.5, 4.75, 6.5, 9 in.
Sights: fixed open
Weight: 31.0 oz.
Caliber: .22, .22 LR (.22 WMR cylinder available)
Capacity: 6 rounds
Features: action on Colt 1873 pattern; transfer bar; satin or blued finish;

weight to 38 oz. dependent on barrel length
Rough Rider: **$145**
With WMR cylinder: **$160**
Satin, with WMR cylinder: **$200**
**Satin, adjustable sights,
    WMR cylinder:** **$240**
Bird's head grip: **$159**

ROUGH RIDER IN .17 HMR
Action: single-action revolver
Grips: laminated camo
Barrel: 6.5 or 9 in.
Sights: adjustable
Weight: 38.0 oz.
Caliber: .17 HMR
Capacity: 6 rounds
Features: Williams Fire Red ramp front sight and Millet rear
MSRP: **$240**

High Standard Handguns

OLYMPIC

SUPERMATIC
CITATION MS

M1911 TARGET PISTOLS

Action: autoloader
Grips: walnut
Barrel: 5 in. (6 in. Supermatic)
Sights: fixed or target
Weight: 40 oz.
Caliber: .45 ACP
Capacity: 7 + 1 rounds
Features: Mil spec. slide; mil. spec.
barrel and bushing; flared ejection
port; beveled magazine well; match
trigger with overtravel stop; 4-pound
trigger pull; stippled front grip; avail-
able in stainless steel, blued or
Parkerized finish
Camp Perry Model
   fixed sights: **$825**
   adjustable sights: **$895**
   Supermatic Tournament: . . **$1095**

CRUSADER COMBAT

Action: autoloader
Grips: cocobolo
Barrel: 4.5 in. *Sights*: fixed open
Weight: 38 oz.
Caliber: .45 ACP
Capacity: 7+1 rounds
Features: precision fitted frame and
slide; flared ejection port; lightweight
long trigger with over-travel stop; trigger
pull tuned at 5-6 lbs.; extended slide
stop and safety; wide beavertail grip
safety; available in stainless steel, blued
or Parkerized finish
MSRP: **$463**

CRUSADER M1911 A-1

Action: autoloader
Grips: cocobolo   *Barrel*: 5 in.
Sights: fixed open
Weight: 40 oz.
Caliber: .38 Super, .45 ACP
Capacity: 7+1 (.38 Super), 9 + 1
rounds
Features: precision fitted frame and
slide; flared ejection port; lightweight
long trigger with over-travel stop; trigger
pull tuned at 5-6 lbs.; extended slide
stop and safety; wide beavertail grip
safety; available in stainless steel, blued
or Parkerized finish
MSRP: **$399**

G-MAN MODEL

Action: autoloader
Grips: cocobolo   *Barrel*: 5 in.
Sights: fixed open
Weight: 39 oz.
Caliber: .45 ACP
Capacity: 8+1 rounds
Features: custom-fit match grade stain-
less barrel and National Match bush-
ing; polished feed ramp; throated bar-
rel; lightweight trigger with over-travel
stop; flared ejection port; wide, bea-
vertail grip and ambidextrous thumb
safties; black Teflon finish
MSRP: **$1225**

OLYMPIC

Action: autoloader
Grips: walnut   *Barrel*: 5.5 in.
Sights: target   *Weight*: 44.0 oz.
Caliber: .22 Short
Capacity: 10 + 1 rounds
Features: single-action, blowback
mechanism
MSRP: **$795**

SUPERMATIC CITATION

Action: autoloader
Grips: walnut
Barrel: 10 in.
Sights: target
Weight: 54.0 oz.
Caliber: .22 LR
Capacity: 10 + 1 rounds
Features: optional scope mount; slide
conversion kit for .22 short
MSRP: **$845**

HANDGUNS

High Standard Handguns

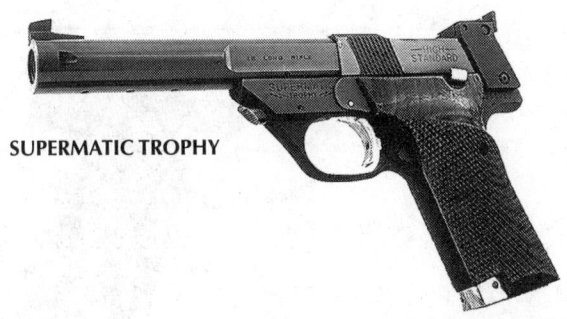

SUPERMATIC TROPHY

VICTOR

SUPERMATIC TROPHY

Action: autoloader
Grips: walnut
Barrel: 5.5 (bull) or 7.3 (fluted) in.
Sights: target
Weight: 44.0 oz.
Caliber: .22 LR
Capacity: 10 + 1 rounds
Features: left-hand grip optional

5.5 in. barrel: **$795**
7.3 in barrel (46 oz.): **$845**

VICTOR

Action: autoloader
Grips: walnut   *Barrel:* 4.5 or 5.5 in.
Sights: target   *Weight:* 45.0 oz.
Caliber: .22 LR
Capacity: 10 + 1 rounds

Features: optional slide conversion kit
for .22 Short
4.5 in. barrel: **$795**
5.5 in. barrel (46 oz.): **$795**
**4.5 in. barrel with universal scope
  base:** **$745**
**5.5 in. barrel with universal
  scope base:** **$745**

Hi-Point Handguns

CF-380 COMP

CF-380

C-9

C-9 COMP

MODEL 40S&W/POLY & .45 ACP

Action: autoloader
Grips: polymer
Barrel: 4.5 in.
Sights: 3-dot adjustable
Weight: 32 oz.
Caliber: .40 S&W, .45 ACP
Capacity: 9 + 1 rounds (10 round
magazine available for COMP)
Features: high-impact polymer frame;
last-round lock-open; quick on-and-off
thumb safety; magazine disconnect
safety; powder coat black finish
MSRP: **$179**

MODEL C-9 AND C-9 COMP

Action: autoloader
Grips: polymer
Barrel: 3.5 in.
Sights: 3-dot
Weight: 25.0, 30.0 (COMP) oz.
Caliber: 9mm
Capacity: 8 + 1 rounds (10 round
magazine available for COMP)
Features: high-impact polymer frame;
COMP models feature a compensator,
last-round lock-open
MSRP: **$169**

MODEL CF-380 AND 380 COMP

Action: autoloader
Grips: polymer
Barrel: 3.5 or 4 in. (COMP)
Sights: 3-dot adjustable
Weight: 25.0, 30.0 (COMP) oz.
Caliber: .380 ACP
Capacity: 8 + 1 rounds (10 round
magazine available for COMP)
Features: high-impact polymer frame;
last-round lock-open; COMP models
feature a compensator; powder coat
black finish with chrome rail
CF-380: **$120**
380 COMP: **$190**

HANDGUNS

Kahr Handguns

MODEL P-9

MODEL P-40

MODEL P-45

P-9 SERIES

Action: autoloader
Grips: polymer or wood
Barrel: 3.5, and 4.0 in.
Sights: fixed or adjustable
Weight: 15-26 oz.
Caliber: 9mm
Capacity: 6+1 to 8 + 1 rounds
Features: trigger cocking DAO; lock breech; "Browning-type" recoil lug; passive striker block; no magazine disconnect; black polymer frame

CW9093, polymer, matte stainless slide (3.5 in. bl, 15.8 oz.): . . $533
KT9093, Hogue grips, matte stainless (4.0 in. bl, 26.0 oz.): $741
KT9093-Novak, Hogue grips, Novak sights, matte stainless: $860
KP9093, polymer frame, matte stainless slide (3.5 in. bl, 15.8 oz.): $697
KP9094, polymer frame, blackened stainless slide w/Tungsten DLC:. $728
PM9093, polymer frame, matte stainless slide (3 in. bl, 14.0 oz.):. $728
PM9094 polymer frame, blackened stainless steel slide w/Tungsten DLC: $760
K9093, matte stainless steel (3.5 in. bl, 23.1 oz.):. $741
K9094, matte blackened stainless w/Tungsten DLC:. . . . $772
K9098 K9 Elite 2003, stainless: . . $806
M9093 matte stainless (4 in. bl, 22.1 oz.): $741
M9093-BOX, matte stainless frame, matte black slide (3 in. bl, 22.1 oz.): $475
M9098 Elite 2003, stainless steel: $806

P-40 SERIES

Action: autoloader
Grips: polymer or wood
Barrel: 3.5-4 in.
Sights: target or adjustable
Weight: 15.0-22.1 oz.
Caliber: .40 S&W
Capacity: 5+1 (Covert) to 7+1 rounds
Features: trigger cocking DAO; lock breech; "Browning-type" recoil lug; passive striker block; no magazine disconnect; black polymer frame

KT4043 4-in. barrel, Hogue grips, matte stainless (4-in. bl): . . . $741
KT4043-Novak, Hogue grips, Novak sights, matte stainless (4-in. bl): $860
KP4043 polymer frame, matte stainless slide (3.08-in. bl): . $697
KP4044 polymer frame, blackened stainless slide w/Tungsten DLC (3.5-in. bl):. $728
KPS4043 Covert, polymer frame w/shortened grip, matte stainlessslide (3.5-in.):. $697
PM4043 polymer frame, matte stainless slide (3.08-in. bl): . $728
PM4044 polymer frame, blackened stainless slide w/Tungsten DLC (3.08-in.): $760
K4043 matte stainless steel (3.5-in.): $741
K4044 matte blackened stainless w/Tungsten DLC (3.5-in. bl.): . . $772
K4048 Elite, stainless steel (3.5-in.): $806
M4043 matte stainless steel (3-in.):. $741
M4048 Elite, stainless steel (3-in.): $806

P-45 SERIES

Action: autoloader
Grips: polymer   *Barrel:* 3.54 in.
Sights: target or adjustable
Weight: 18.5 oz.   *Caliber:* .45.ACP
Capacity: 6 + 1 rounds
Features: trigger cocking DAO; lock breech; "Browning-type" recoil lug; passive striker block; no magazine disconnect; polymer frame; matte stainless slide

P45:. $760
Matte stainless slide with night sights:. $870

HANDGUNS

Kel-Tec Handguns

P-11

P-32

P-3AT

SUB RIFLE 2000

SUB RIFLE 2000 (READY TO FIRE)

MODEL P-11
Action: autoloader
Grips: polymer
Barrel: 3.1 in.
Sights: fixed open
Weight: 14.4 oz.
Caliber: 9mm
Capacity: 10 + 1 rounds
Features: locked-breech mechanism
P-11: $314
Parkerized: $355
Chrome: $368

MODEL P-32
Action: autoloader
Grips: polymer
Barrel: 2.7 in.
Sights: fixed open
Weight: 6.6 oz.
Caliber: .32 Auto

Capacity: 7 + 1 rounds
Features: locked-breech mechanism
P-32: $300
Parkerized: $340
Chrome: $355

MODEL P-3AT
Action: autoloader
Grips: polymer
Barrel: 2.8 in.
Sights: fixed open
Weight: 7.3 oz.
Caliber: .380
Capacity: 6 + 1 rounds
Features: locked-breech mechanism
P-3AT: $305
Parkerized: $345
Chrome: $360

SUB RIFLE 2000
Action: autoloader
Grips: polymer
Barrel: 16 in.
Sights: target
Weight: 64.0 oz.
Caliber: 9mm and .40 S&W
Capacity: 10 + 1 rounds
Features: take-down, uses pistol magazines
Sub Rifle:. $383
SU-16 in .223:. $640

Kimber Handguns

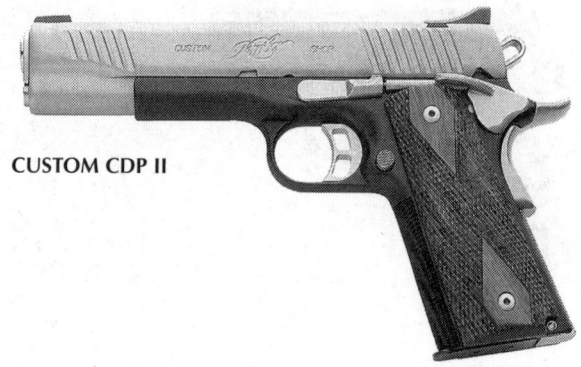

CUSTOM CDP II

CUSTOM TARGET II

COMPACT II

ECLIPSE TARGET II

CDP11 SERIES

Action: autoloader
Grips: rosewood
Barrel: 3, 4, or 5 in.
Sights: low-profile night
Weight: 25.0-31.0 oz.
Caliber: .45 ACP
Capacity: 7 + 1 rounds
Features: alloy frame, stainless slide; also in 4 in. (Pro Carry and Compact) and 3 in. (Ultra) configurations
MSRP: **$1165**

COMPACT STAINLESS II

Action: autoloader
Grips: synthetic
Barrel: 4 in.
Sights: low-profile combat
Weight: 34.0 oz.
Caliber: .45 ACP, .40 S&W
Capacity: 7 + 1 rounds
Features: shortened single-action 1911; also Pro Carry with alloy frame at 28 oz.; match-grade bushingless bull barrel

Compact II stainless: **$889**
Pro Carry II: **$789**
Pro Carry II stainless: **$862**
Pro Carry HD II: **$897**

CUSTOM II

Action: autoloader
Grips: synthetic or rosewood
Barrel: 5 in.
Sights: target or fixed
Weight: 38.0 oz.
Caliber: .38 Super, .40 S&W, .45 ACP, 10mm, 9mm
Capacity: 7 + 1 rounds
Features: single-action; 1911 Colt design; front cocking serrations; skeleton trigger and hammer

Custom II: **$760**
Stainless II: **$848**
Target II: **$854**
Stainless Target II: **$964**

ECLIPSE II

Action: autoloader
Grips: laminated
Barrel: 5 in.
Sights: 3-dot night
Weight: 38.0 oz.
Caliber: .45 ACP, 10mm
Capacity: 7 + 1 rounds
Features: matte-black oxide finish over stainless, polished bright on flats; also 3-in. Ultra and 4 in. Pro Carry versions; sights also available in low profile combat or target

Eclipse II: **$1074**
Target II: **$1177**
Ultra II: **$1074**
Pro II: **$1074**
Pro Target II: **$1177**

HANDGUNS

Kimber Handguns

GOLD COMBAT II

GOLD MATCH II
STAINLESS

ULTRA CARRY II
STAINLESS

GOLD COMBAT II

Action: autoloader
Grips: rosewood
Barrel: 5 in.
Sights: low-profile night
Weight: 38.0 oz.
Caliber: .45 ACP
Capacity: 7 + 1 rounds
Features: M1911 Colt design with
many refinements: checkered front
strap, match bushing, ambidextrous
safety, stainless match barrel
Gold Combat II: $1716
Gold Combat Stainless II: . . . $1657

GOLD MATCH II

Action: autoloader
Grips: rosewood
Barrel: 5 in.
Sights: adjustable target
Weight: 38.0 oz.
Caliber: .45 ACP
Capacity: 7 + 1 rounds

Features: single-action 1911 Colt
design; match components; ambidex-
trous safety
Gold Match II: $1192
Stainless: $1342
Stainless in .40 S&W: $1373
Team Match II: $1310

TEN II HIGH CAPACITY

Action: autoloader
Grips: polymer
Barrel: 5 in.
Sights: low-profile combat
Weight: 34.0 oz.
Caliber: .45 ACP
Capacity: 10 + 1 rounds
Features: double-stack magazine;
polymer frame; also in 4 in. (Pro
Carry) configuration, from 32 oz.
Stainless Ten II: $771
Pro Carry Ten II: $786
Gold Match Ten II: $1061

ULTRA CARRY II

Action: autoloader
Grips: synthetic
Barrel: 3 in.
Sights: low-profile combat
Weight: 25.0 oz.
Caliber: .40 S&W, .45 ACP
Capacity: 7 + 1 rounds
Features: smallest commercial 1911-
style pistol
Ultra Carry II: $783
Stainless II: $858
Stainless II in .40 S&W: $903

HANDGUNS

Llama Handguns

**MAX-I GOVERNMENT
DUOTONE FINISH**

**MICROMAX .380
MATTE FINISH**

**MINIMAX .45
SATIN CHROME FINISH**

MAX-I GOVERNMENT
Action: autoloader
Grips: rubber
Barrel: 5 in.
Sights: 3-dot
Weight: 38.0 oz.
Caliber: .45 ACP
Capacity: 7 + 1 rounds
Features: single-action M1911 Colt design; extended safety; beavertail; Duotone finish
MSRP: **$389**

MICROMAX .380
Action: autoloader
Grips: polymer
Barrel: 4 in.
Sights: 3-dot
Weight: 29.0 oz.
Caliber: .380, .32 ACP
Capacity: 7 + 1 rounds, 8 + 1 rounds
Features: extended safety
Matte: **$282**
Satin chrome: **$300**

MINIMAX .45
Action: autoloader
Grips: rubber
Barrel: 3 in.
Sights: 3-dot
Weight: 28.0 oz.
Caliber: .40 S&W, .45 ACP
Capacity: 7 + 1 rounds (.40), 6 + 1 rounds (.45)
Features: single-action M1911 Colt design; extended beavertail grip
Matte: **$309**
Duo-Tone: **$316**
Satin chrome: **$334**
Also available:
Minimax subcompact in
   .45 Auto, 10-shot matte: . . . **$316**
      Satin chrome: **$342**
      Duo-Tone: **$325**

When shooting, your "master eye" is the one you will depend on to aim your handgun. To identify your master eye, point a finger (you can use either hand) at an object with both eyes open. Alternately close one eye, then the other. Your finger will appear to remain lined up, without apparent movement, only through your master eye.

Magnum Research Handguns

BABY EAGLE
Action: autoloader
Grips: plastic composite
Barrel: 3.5, 4, 4.5 in.
Sights: 3-dot combat
Weight: 26.8-39.8 oz.
Caliber: 9mm, .40 S&W, .45 ACP
Capacity: 10 rounds (15 for 9mm)
Features: squared, serrated trigger guard
MSRP: **$499**

BFR (BIGGEST FINEST REVOLVER)
Action: single-action revolver
Grips: rubber
Barrel: 6.5, 7.5 or 10 in.
Sights: open adjustable
Weight: 50.0-67.3 oz.
Caliber: .45/70, .444, .450, .500 S&W, .30-30 Win. (long cylinder), .480 Ruger, .475 Linbaugh, .22 Hornet, .45 Colt/.410, .50 AE (short cylinder)
Capacity: 5 rounds
Features: both short and long-cylinder models entirely of stainless steel
MSRP: **$899**

IMI SP-21
Action: autoloader
Grips: polymer
Barrel: 3.9 in.
Sights: fixed, open
Weight: 26 oz. (27 oz. .45ACP)
Caliber: 9mm, .40 S&W, .45 ACP
Capacity: 10+1
Features: double-action; ambidextrous safety; integral locking mechanism; squared, serrated trigger guard
MSRP: **$499**

MARK XIX DESERT EAGLE
Action: autoloader
Grips: plastic composite
Barrel: 6 or 10 in.
Sights: fixed combat
Weight: 70.2 oz.
Caliber: .357 Mag., .44 Mag., .50 AE
Capacity: 9 + 1 rounds, 8 + 1 rounds, 7 + 1 rounds
Features: gas operated; all with polygonal rifling, integral scope bases
Desert Eagle, 6 in. barrel: . . . **$1249**
10 in. barrel (79 oz.): **$1349**
6 in. chrome or nickel: **$1489**
6 in. Titaniums/gold: **$1749**

BABY EAGLE

BFR

MARK XIX DESERT EAGLE .50 MAGNUM TITANIUM FINISH

MOA Handguns

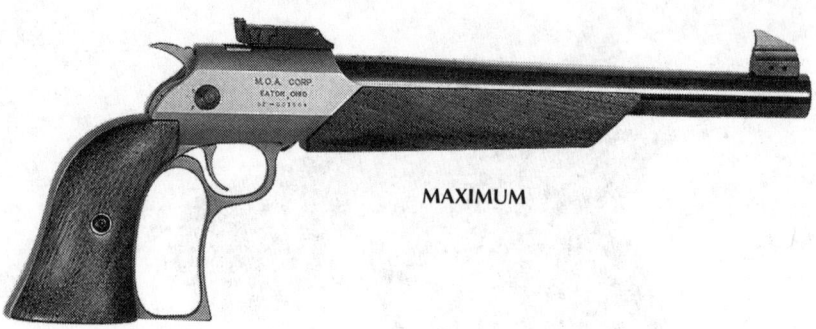

MAXIMUM

MAXIMUM

Action: hinged breech
Grips: walnut
Barrel: 8.5, 10.5 or 14 in.
Sights: target   *Weight*: 56.0 oz.
Caliber: most rifle chamberings from
.22 Hornet to .375 H&H
Features: stainless breech; Douglas
barrel; extra barrels; muzzle brake
available
Maximum: **$823**
With stainless barrel: **$919**
Extra barrels: **$269**

Navy Arms Handguns

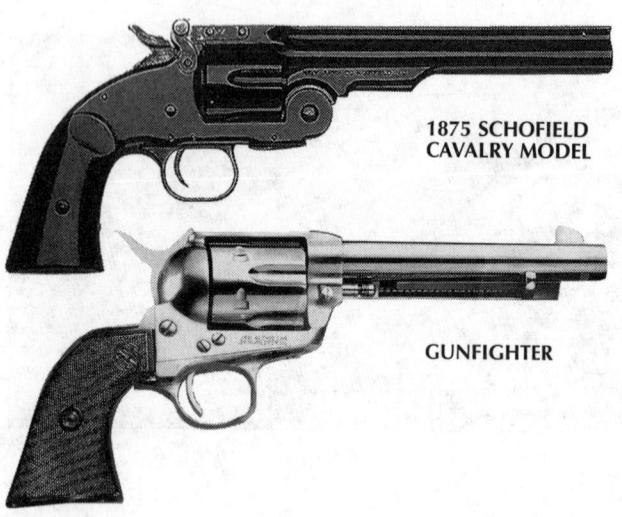

1875 SCHOFIELD
CAVALRY MODEL

GUNFIGHTER

NEW MODEL
RUSSIAN

MODEL 1875 SCHOFIELD CAVALRY MODEL

Action: double-action revolver
Grips: walnut
Barrel: 3.5, 5.0 or 7.0 in.
Sights: fixed open
Weight: 35.0 oz.
Caliber: .38 Spl.,. 44-40, .45 Colt,
Capacity: 6 rounds
Features: top-break action, automatic
ejectors; 5 in barrel (37 oz.) and 7 in.
barrel (39 oz.)
.38 Spl.: **$825**
44-40: **$825**
.45 Colt: **$825**

BISLEY

Action: single-action revolver
Grips: walnut
Barrel: 4.8, 5.5 or 7.5 in.
Sights: fixed open   *Weight*: 45.0 oz.
Caliber: .44-40, .45 Colt
Capacity: 6 rounds
Features: Bisley grip case-colored
frame; weight to 48 oz.
MSRP: **$497**

GUNFIGHTER SERIES

Action: single-action revolver
Grips: walnut
Barrel: 4.8, 5.5, 7.5 in.
Sights: fixed open
Weight: 47.0 oz.
Caliber: .357, .44-40, .45 Colt
Capacity: 6 rounds

Features: case-colored frames, after
1873 Colt design
Gunfighter: **$479**
Stainless: **$569**

NEW MODEL RUSSIAN

Action: double-action revolver
Grips: walnut
Barrel: 6.5 in.
Sights: fixed open
Weight: 40.0 oz.
Caliber: .44 Russian
Capacity: 6 rounds
Features: top-break action
MSRP: **$882**

HANDGUNS

GUARDIAN .32

Action: autoloader
Grips: polymer
Barrel: 2.5 in.　*Sights*: fixed open
Weight: 12.0 oz.
Caliber: .32 ACP or .25 NAA
Capacity: 6 + 1 rounds
Features: stainless, double-action
MSRP: **$402**

GUARDIAN .380

Action: autoloader
Grips: composite
Barrel: 2.5 in.
Sights: fixed open
Weight: 18.8 oz.
Caliber: .380 ACP or .32 NAA
Capacity: 6 rounds
Features: stainless, double-action
MSRP: **$402**

MINI MASTER SERIES REVOLVER

Action: single-action revolver
Grips: rubber
Barrel: 2 or 4 in.
Sights: fixed or adjustable
Weight: 8.8 oz (2 in.) or 10.7 oz (4 in.)
Caliber: .22LR or .22 Mag.,
.17 MACH 2, .17 HMR
Capacity: 5 rounds
Features: conversion cylinder or
adjustable sights available
**.22 Mag, LR (2 in.),
　.17 MACH2 or .17 HMR:** . . . **$258**
**.22 Mag w/conversion
　.22 LR (2 in.):** **$287**
.22 Mag or LR (4 in.): **$272**
**.22 Mag w/conversion
.22 LR (4 in.) or .17 HMR
　with .17 MACH2
　conversion:** **$301**

MINI REVOLVER

Action: single-action revolver
Grips: laminated rosewood
Barrel: 1.2 in.
Sights: fixed open
Weight: 5.0 oz.
Caliber: .22 Short, .22 LR, .22 WMR,
.17 MACH 2, .17 HMR
Capacity: 5 rounds
Features: holster grip
.22 Short, .22 LR, .17 MACH2: . **$193**
　With holster grip: **$215**
.22 Magnum, .17 HMR: **$208**
.22 Magnum with holster grip: **$229**

GUARDIAN .32

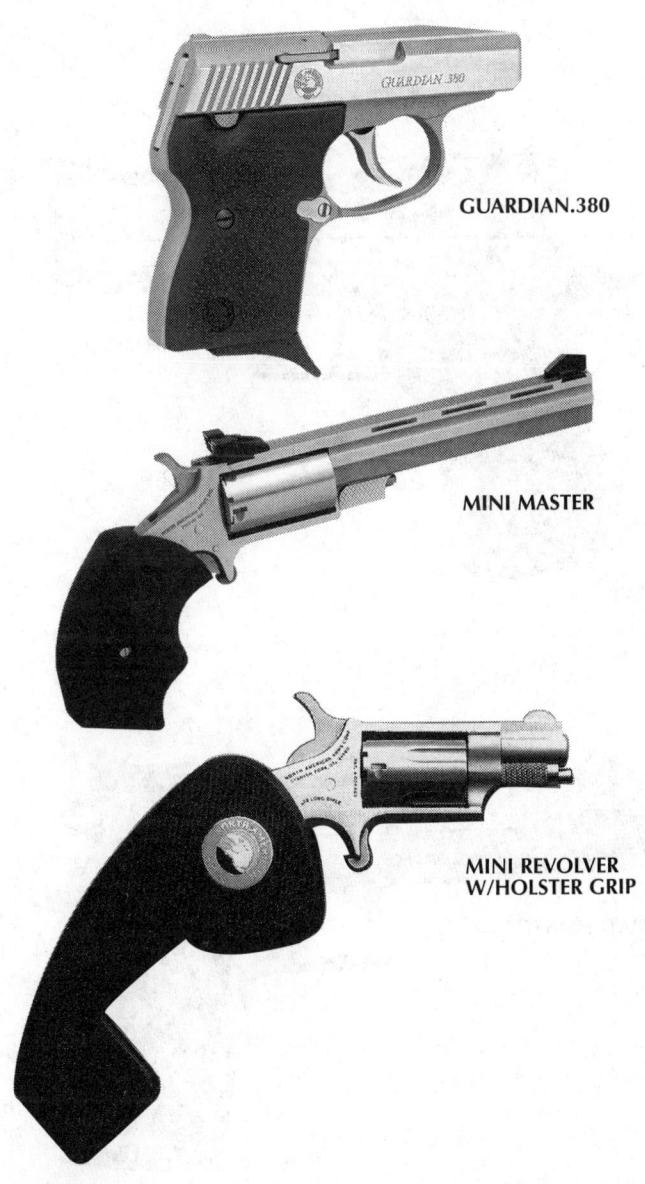

GUARDIAN.380

MINI MASTER

MINI REVOLVER
W/HOLSTER GRIP

HANDGUNS

Olympic Arms Handguns

COHORT

ENFORCER

MATCHMASTER

COHORT

Action: autoloader
Grips: walnut
Barrel: 4 in. bull   *Sights*: target
Weight: 38.0 oz.
Caliber: .45 ACP
Capacity: 7 + 1 rounds
Features: single-action on 1911 Colt design; extended beavertail; stainless or parkerized
MSRP: **$779**

ENFORCER

Action: autoloader
Grips: walnut
Barrel: 4 in. bull
Sights: low-profile combat
Weight: 36.0 oz.
Caliber: .45 ACP
Capacity: 6 + 1 rounds
Features: single-action on 1911 Colt design; extended beavertail; stainless or parkerized
MSRP: **$750**

MATCHMASTER

Action: autoloader
Grips: walnut
Barrel: 5 or 6 in. *Sights*: target
Weight: 40.0-44.0 oz.
Caliber: .45 ACP
Capacity: 7 + 1 rounds
Features: single-action on 1911 Colt design; extended beavertail; stainless or parkerized
Matchmaster 5 in.: **$714**
6 in. barrel (44 oz.): **$774**
RS (40 oz.): **$744**

WESTERNER

Action: autoloader
Grips: walnut
Barrel: 4, 5, or 6 in. *Sights*: target
Weight: 35-43 oz. *Caliber*: .45 ACP
Capacity: 7 + 1 rounds
Features: single-action; matched frames and slides; fitted and head-spaced barrels; complete ramp and throat jobs; lowered and widened ejection ports; beveled mag wells; hand-stoned-to-match hammers and sears; adjusted triggers; extended thumb safeties; wide beavertail grip safeties; adjustable rear sights; dovetail front sights
Westerner: **$834**
Trail Boss (6 in. bbl): **$959**
Constable (4 in. bbl): **$935**

HANDGUNS

Para Ordnance Handguns

PARA CCW

LDA

MODEL P12•45 ACP
(3.5" BARREL, STAINLESS)

CCW AND COMPANION CARRY
Action: double-action autoloader
Grips: cocobolo
Barrel: 2.5, 3.5 or 4.1 in.
Sights: low-profile combat
Weight: 32.0-34.0 oz.
Caliber: .45 ACP
Capacity: 7 + 1 rounds
Features: double-action; stainless; Tritium night sights available
4.25 in. CCW: **$988**
3.5 in. Companion Carry: **$988**

LDA HIGH CAPACITY
Action: autoloader
Grips: composite
Barrel: 4.25 or 5.0 in. ramped
Sights: target
Weight: 37.0-40.0 oz.
Caliber: 9mm, .40 S&W or .45 ACP
Capacity: 14 + 1 rounds, 16 + 1 rounds, 18 + 1 rounds
Features: double-action, double-stack magazine; stainless
LDA: **$899-1135**
Carry option, 3.5 in. barrel: . . **$1049**

LDA SINGLE STACK
Action: double-action autoloader
Grips: composite
Barrel: 3.5, 4.25 or 5 in.
Sights: target
Weight: 32.0-40.0 oz.
Caliber: .45 ACP
Capacity: 7 + 1 rounds
Features: ramped, stainless barrel
MSRP: **$899-1135**

P-SERIES
Action: single-action autoloader
Grips: composite
Barrel: 3.0, 3.5, 4.25, or 5.0 in.
Sights: fixed open
Weight: 24.0-40.0 oz.
Caliber: 9mm, .45 ACP
Capacity: 10 + 1 to 18 + 1 rounds
Features: customized 1911 Colt design; beveled magazine well; polymer magazine; also available with 3-dot or low-profile combat sights; stainless
MSRP: **$855-995**

Para Ordnance Handguns

PXT 1911

PXT WARTHOG

TAC-FOUR

PXT 1911 PISTOLS

Action: autoloading
Grips: cocobolo with gold medallion and beavertail extension
Barrel: 3.5, 4.25 and 5 in.
Sights: blade front, white 3 dot rear
Weight: 32.0-39.0 oz.
Caliber: .45 ACP
Magazine Capacity: 7+1 rounds
Features: single-action match trigger; extended slide lock; Para Kote Regal finish; stainless competition hammer; ramped stainless barrel
MSRP: **$840-1043**

PXT HIGH CAPACITY

Action: autoloader
Grips: polymer
Barrel: 3 in.
Sights: 3 dot
Weight: 24.0 oz.
Caliber: 9mm
Capacity: 12 rounds
Features: single-action; alloy receiver
MSRP: **$840**

PXT WARTHOG

Action: autoloader
Grips: black plastic
Barrel: 3 in.
Sights: 3 dot
Weight: 24 oz.
Caliber: .45 ACP
Capacity: 10 + 1 rounds
Features: single-action; ramped barrel; alloy receiver; spurred hammer
Warthog: **$884**
Nite Hawg: **$884**

TAC-FOUR

Action: double-action autoloader
Grips: black polymer
Barrel: 4.25 in.
Sights: low-profile combat
Weight: 36.0 oz.
Caliber: .45 ACP
Capacity: 13 + 1 rounds
Features: double-action; stainless; flush hammer; bobbed beavertail
MSRP: **$1133**

The accuracy of your shot will be determined by the position of the gun at the exact moment of firing. The things that generally destroy good position and accuracy are poor trigger technique and flinch. An effective way to control these is to dry fire as part of any practice program.

Rossi Handguns

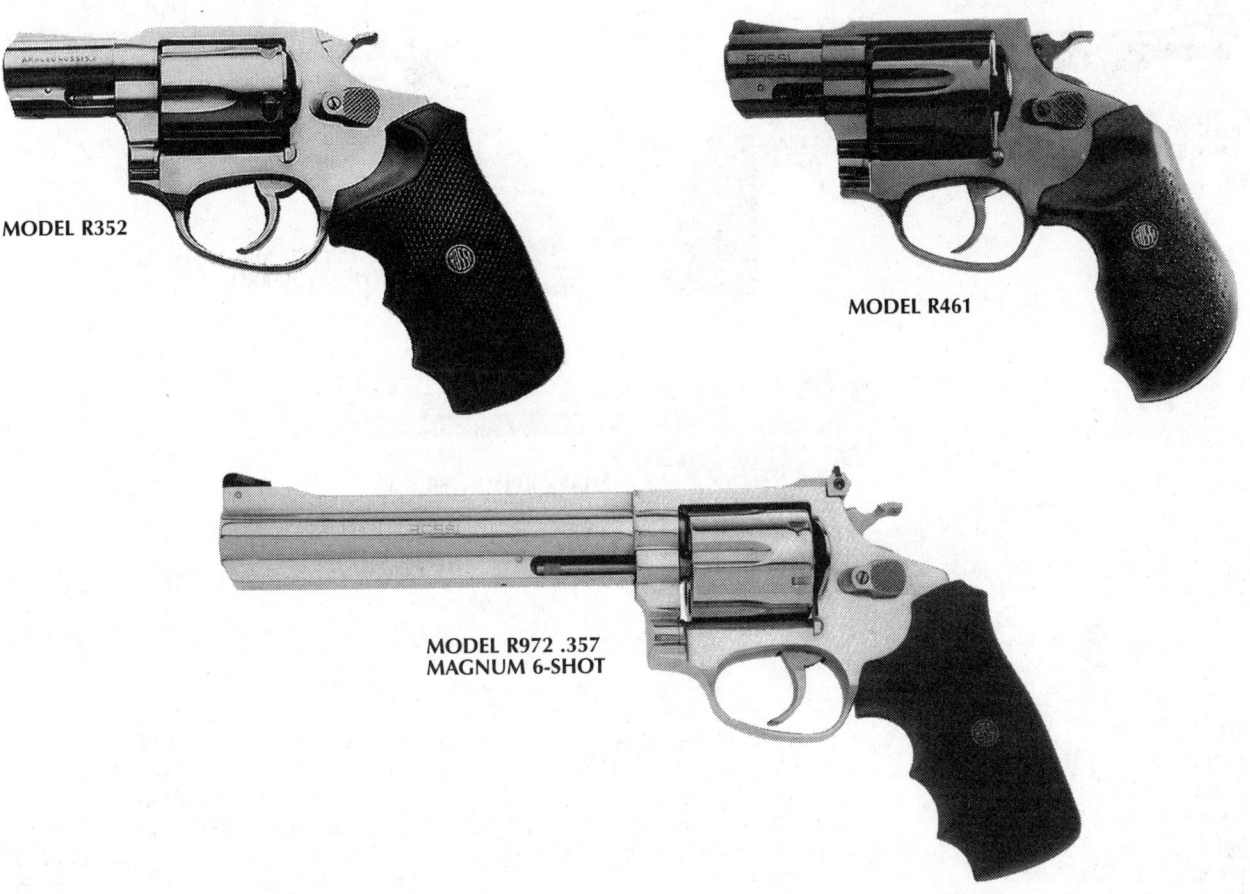

MODEL R352

MODEL R461

MODEL R972 .357
MAGNUM 6-SHOT

MODEL R351 AND R352

Action: double-action revolver
Grips: rubber
Barrel: 2 in.
Sights: fixed open
Weight: 24.0 oz.
Caliber: .38 Spl.
Capacity: 6 rounds
Features: stainless; R351 chrome-moly also available
R35202 stainless: **$362**
R35102 blue: **$313**

MODEL R462 & R461

Action: double-action revolver
Grips: rubber
Barrel: 2 in.
Sights: fixed open
Weight: 26.0 oz.
Caliber: .357 Mag.
Capacity: 6 rounds
Features: stainless; R461 chrome-moly also available
R462 stainless: **$362**
R461 blue: **$313**

MODEL R851

Action: double-action revolver
Grips: rubber
Barrel: 4 in.
Sights: adjustable
Weight: 32.0 oz.
Caliber: .38 Spl.
Capacity: 6 rounds
Features: adjustable rear sight; blue finish
R85104: **$313**

MODEL R972

Action: double-action revolver
Grips: rubber
Barrel: 6 in.
Sights: target
Weight: 34.0 oz.
Caliber: .357 Mag.
Capacity: 6 rounds
Features: stainless after S&W M19 pattern; also R971 chrome-moly with 4 in. barrel
R972 stainless: **$391**
R971 blue: **$410**

HANDGUNS

Ruger Handguns

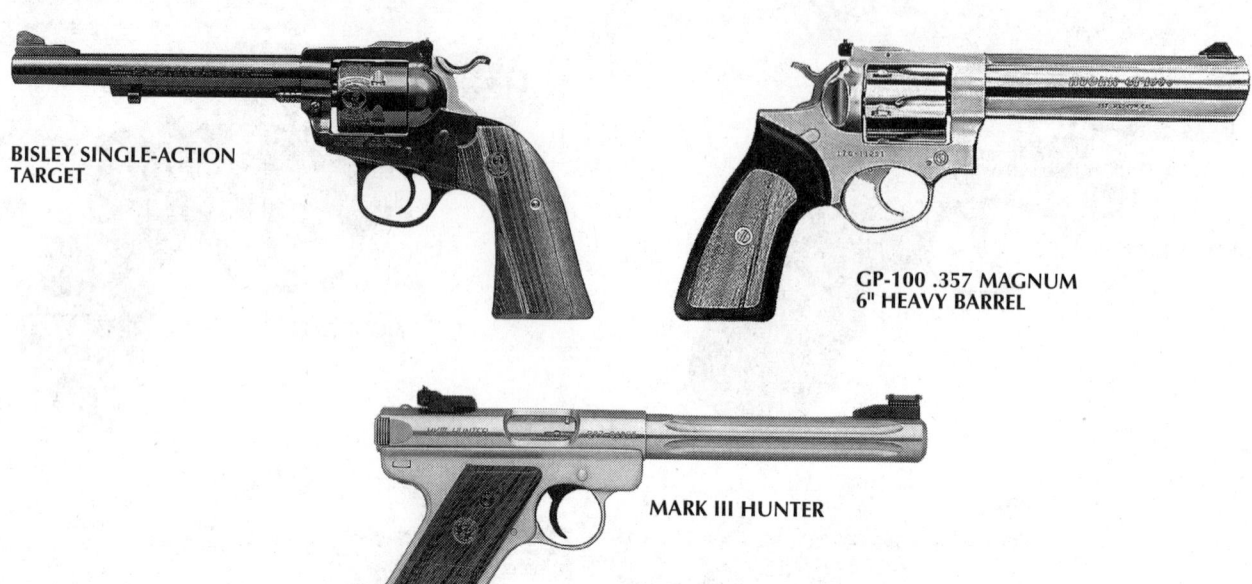

BISLEY SINGLE-ACTION TARGET

GP-100 .357 MAGNUM 6" HEAVY BARREL

MARK III HUNTER

BISLEY

Action: single-action revolver
Grips: walnut
Barrel: 6.5 (.22 LR) or 7.5 in.
Sights: target
Weight: 43.0-50.0 oz.
Caliber: .22 LR, .357 Mag., .44 Mag., .45 Colt
Capacity: 6 rounds
Features: rimfire and centerfire (48 oz.); low-profile hammer
.22LR: $475
.357, .44, .45: $597

BISLEY VAQUERO

Action: single-action revolver
Grips: rosewood
Barrel: 4.6, 5.5 in.
Sights: fixed open
Weight: 43.5-44.0 oz.
Caliber: .45 Colt or .44 Rem. Mag
Capacity: 6 rounds
Features: stainless or color case blued; transfer bar operating mechanism/ loading gate interlock
Blued: $555
Stainless: $575

MODEL GP100

Action: single-action revolver
Grips: rubber with rosewood insert
Barrel: 3.4 or 6 in.
Sights: fixed open
Weight: 38.0-46.0 oz.
Caliber: .38 Spl. or .357
Capacity: 6 rounds
Features: chrome-moly or stainless; weight to 46 oz. depending on barrel length
GP100 4-in. bl.: $557
6-in. bl.: $552
GP100 3-in. bl.: $597
4-in. bl.: $552
6-in. bl.: $615

BIRD'S HEAD VAQUERO

Action: single-action revolver
Grips: black micarta or simulated ivory
Barrel: 3.75 or 4.6 in.
Sights: fixed open
Weight: 40.0-45.0 oz.
Caliber: .45 Colt or .357
Capacity: 6 rounds
Features: gloss stainless or color case; reverse indexing pawl; bird's head grip
MSRP: $595

MARK II

Action: autoloader
Grips: synthetic or rosewood
Barrel: 4 in., 4 in. Bull, 6.7 in. Bull
Sights: open, fixed or adjustable
Caliber: .22 LR
Capacity: 10 rounds
Features: slab bull barrel; manual safety; loaded chamber indicator; magazine disconnect; adjustable rear sight; blued finish
4-in. Bull (Limited Edition rosewood grips): . . . . POR
6.7-in. Bull: $535
6.7-in slab Bull: $555

MARK III

Action: autoloader
Grips: black synthetic or wood
Barrel: 5.5 in. Bull or 6.7 in. Bull
Sights: open, adjustable
Weight: 41 oz.
Caliber: .22 LR
Capacity: 10 rounds
Features: Bull barrel; contoured ejection port and tapered bolt ears; manual safety; loaded chamber indicator; magazine disconnect; adjustable rear sight; stainless finish; drilled and tapped for a Weaver-type scope base adapter
Stainless, 5.5-in. Bull bl.: $483
Stainless, 6.7-in. bl.: $567
Stainless, 6.7-in. slab Bull bl.: $555
Blue, 4.75 in. bl.: $322
Blue, 6 in. bl.: $322
22/45 Mark III (4-in slab bull bl.): $305

Ruger Handguns

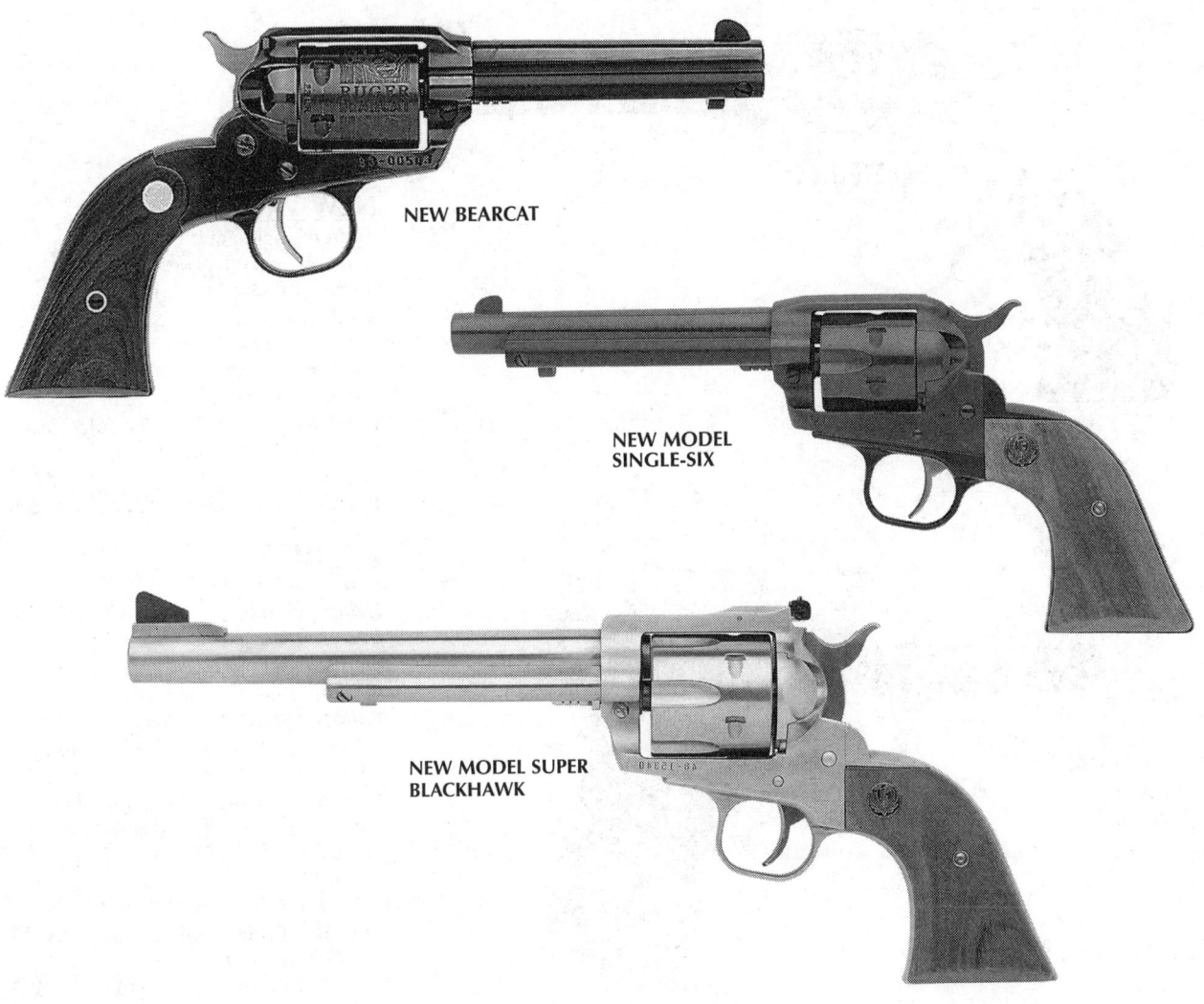

NEW BEARCAT

NEW MODEL
SINGLE-SIX

NEW MODEL SUPER
BLACKHAWK

NEW BEARCAT

Action: single-action revolver
Grips: rosewood
Barrel: 4 in.
Sights: fixed open
Weight: 24.0 oz.
Caliber: .22 LR
Capacity: 6 rounds
Features: transfer bar
New Bearcat: **$410**
Stainless: **$464**

NEW MODEL SINGLE SIX

Action: single-action revolver
Grips: rosewood or Micarta
Barrel: 4.6, 5.5, 6.5 or 9.5 in.
Sights: fixed open
Weight: 33.0-45.0 oz.
Caliber: .22 LR, .22 WMR, .17 HMR,
.17 MACH 2
Capacity: 6 rounds
Features: adjustable sights available;
weight to 38 oz. depending on
barrel length
Single Six: **$411**
Stainless: **$485-650**
.32 H&R: **$576**
17 HMR: **$617**
.17 HMR/.17 MACH2
    convertible: **$695**

NEW MODEL SUPER BLACKHAWK

Action: single-action revolver
Grips: walnut
Barrel: 4.6, 5.5, 7.5 or 10.5 in.
Sights: target
Weight: 45.0-55.0 oz.
Caliber: .41 Rem Mag, .44 Rem Mag
.45 Colt
Capacity: 6 rounds
Features: weight to 51 oz. depending
on barrel length; also available: Super
Black-hawk Hunter, stainless with 7.5
in. barrel, black laminated grips, rib,
scope rings
Blue: **$579**
Stainless: **$594-696**

HANDGUNS

Ruger Handguns

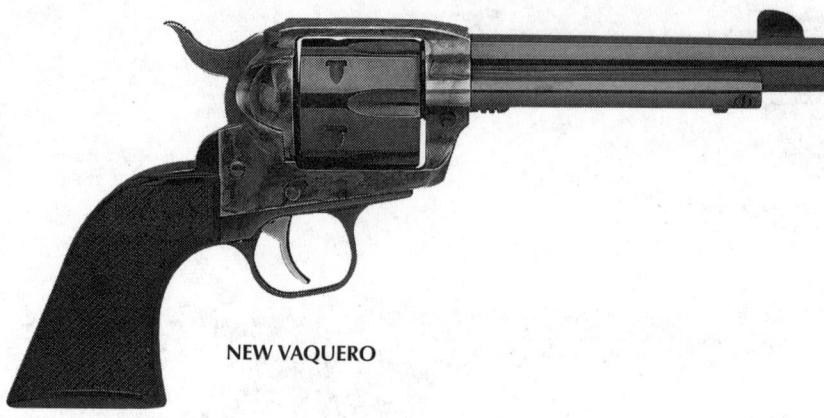

NEW VAQUERO

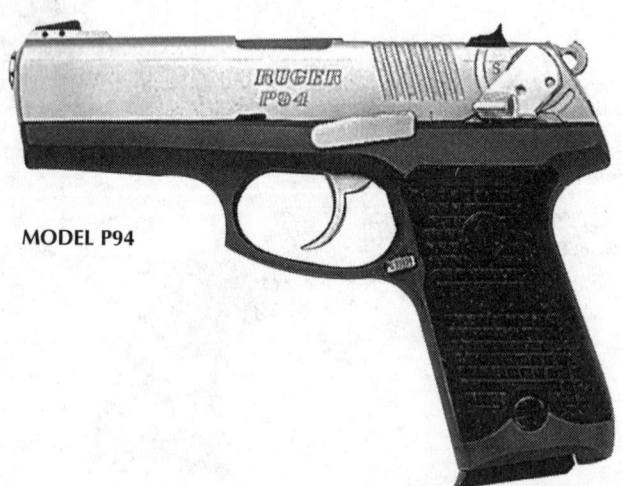

MODEL P94

P345

NEW VAQUERO
Action: single-action revolver
Grips: black, checkered
Barrel: 4.6, 5.5 or 7.5 in.
Sights: fixed open
Weight: 37.0-41.0 oz.
Caliber: .45 Colt or .357
Capacity: 6 rounds
Features: gloss stainless or color case, reverse indexing pawl
Vaquero: $590
Engraved stainless: $1000

P-SERIES
Action: autoloader
Grips: polymer
Barrel: 3.9 or 4.5 in.
Sights: fixed open
Weight: 30.0 oz.
Caliber: 9mm, .40 S&W, .45 Auto
Capacity: 10 + 1 rounds (8 + 1 in .45, 15 + 1 in 9mm)
Features: double-action; ambidextrous grip safety; decocker on some models; manual safety on others
(9 mm)
KP95PR Stainless 3.9-in. bl.: $480
P95PR Blued 3.9-in. bl.: $445
KP89 Stainless 4.5-in. bl.: . . $525
KP94 Stainless 4.1-in. bl.: . . $575
KP95 Stainless 3.9-in. bl.: . . $475
P89 Blued 4.5-in. bl.: $475
P95 Blued 3.9-in. bl.: $425
(.40 S&W)
KP94 Stainless 4.1-in. bl.: . . $575
P94 .40 S&W
Blued 4.1-in. bl.: $495
(.45 ACP)
KP345 Stainless 4.5-in. bl.:. . $540
KP345PR 4.25-in. bl.: $548
P345PR Blued 4.25-in. bl.: . . $513
KP90 Stainless 4.5-in. bl.: . . $565
P90 Blued 4.5-in. bl.: $525

HANDGUNS

**REDHAWK
STAINLESS**

REDHAWK

Action: double-action revolver
Grips: rosewood
Barrel: 5.5 or 7.5 in.
Sights: target
Weight: 49.0 oz.
Caliber: .44 Rem Mag.
Capacity: 6 rounds
Features: stainless model available;
7.5 in. version weighs 54 oz.; scope
rings available
Redhawk: **$665**
Stainless: **$730**
Stainless with rings: **$779**

MODEL SP101

Action: double-action revolver
Grips: rubber with synthetic insert
Barrel: 2.3, 3.0, or 4.0 in.
Sights: fixed open (adjustable on .32
H&R)
Weight: 25.0-30.0 oz.
Caliber: .22 LR, .32 H&R, .38 Spl., .357
Capacity: 5 or 6 rounds
Features: chrome-moly or stainless;
weight to 30 oz. depending on
barrel length
Stainless 2.25-in. bl.: **$530**
Stainless 3.1-in. bl.: **$530**
Stainless 4-in. bl: **$530**
Stainless 6-in. bl.: **$615**
.22LR: **$505**

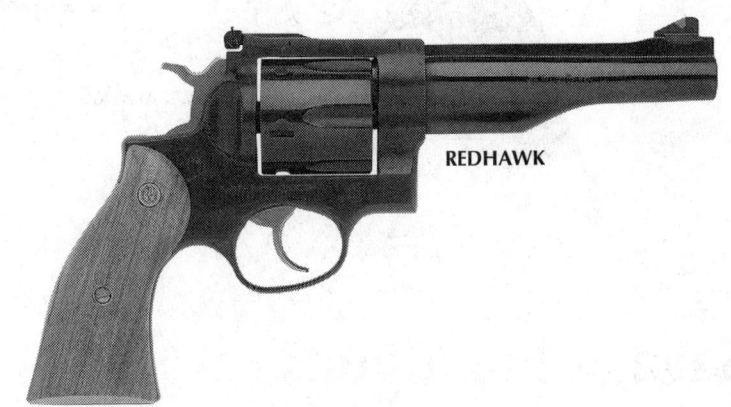

REDHAWK

MODEL SP101

*When you shoot a handgun from a rest, find a low,
stable shooting position. Then, adjust your sandbags to your position rather than squirming around
to conform your sitting posture to the sandbags.
Several small bags usually work best and allow for
more precise adjustment.*

Ruger Handguns

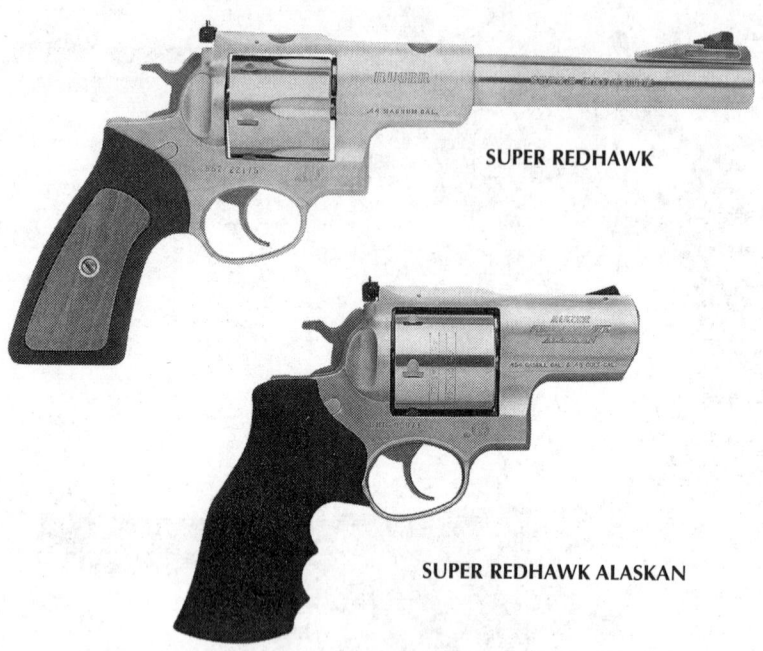

SUPER REDHAWK

SUPER REDHAWK ALASKAN

SUPER REDHAWK
Action: double-action revolver
Grips: rubber/black laminate
Barrel: 7.5 or 9.5 in.
Sights: target
Weight: 53.0 oz.
Caliber: .44 Mag., .454 Casull, .480 Ruger
Capacity: 6 rounds
Features: stainless or low glare stainless finish; 9.5 in. version weighs 58 oz.
.44 Magnum: **$779**
.454, .480 Ruger: **$860**
Alaskan: **$819**

Savage Handguns

STRIKER 516 FSAK

STRIKER 501, 502, 503
Action: bolt
Grips: synthetic
Barrel: 10 in.
Sights: none
Weight: 64.0 oz.
Caliber: .22 LR, .22 WMR, .17 HMR
Capacity: 5 + 1 rounds
Features: left-hand bolt, right-hand ejection
.22 LR: **$245**
.22 WMR: **$269**
.17 HMR: **$295**

STRIKER 516 FSAK
Action: bolt
Grips: synthetic
Barrel: 14 in.
Sights: none
Weight: 78.0 oz.
Caliber: .243, 7mm-08, .308, .270 WSM, 7mm WSM, .300 WSM
Capacity: 2 + 1 rounds
Features: stainless, with muzzle brake
MSRP: **$621**

HANDGUNS

Sigarms Handguns

MODEL P220

Action: autoloader
Grips: plastic
Barrel: 4.4 in.
Sights: adjustable
Weight: 27.8 oz.
Caliber: .45 ACP
Capacity: 8 rounds
Features: decocking lever and automatic firing pin safety block; available in blued two-tone and stainless; stainless models come with a Picatinny accessory rail

Blue: **$790**
Two-tone: **$830**

MODEL P226

Action: autoloader
Grips: polymer
Barrel: 4.4 in.
Sights: fixed
Weight: 28.3-30.6 oz
Caliber: 9mm; 357 SIG, 40 S&W with optional barrel
Capacity: 10 + 1 rounds
Features: available with alloy frame and stainless slide or all stainless; reversible magazine release; 6.3 in. sight radius; available in Nitron and two-tone finishes

Nitron: **$840**
Stainless: **$935**
W/ siglite night sight: **$1009**
P228 (Blued finish): **$840**
W/ siglite night sight: **$915**

MODEL P229

Action: autoloader
Grips: polymer
Barrel: 3.9 in.
Sights: fixed open
Weight: 24.5 oz.
Caliber: 9mm, .357 Sig, .40 S&W
Capacity: 10 + 1 rounds
Features: Nitron finish; tac rail, night sight; also available with 4.4 in. barrel

P229 Nitron: **$840**
W/ Siglite night sight: **$915**
Two-tone: **$915**

MODEL P226

MODEL P229

SIG CLASSIC
COMPACT P229 ST

Sigarms Handguns

MODEL P232

MODEL P239

MODEL PL 22
TRAILSIDE
COMPETITION

MODEL P232

Action: autoloader
Grips: polymer
Barrel: 3.6 in.
Sights: fixed open
Weight: 16.2 oz.
Caliber: .380
Capacity: 7 + 1 rounds
Features: double-action; available with Siglite night sights
P232: **$519**
W/ Siglite night sight: **$579**
Stainless: **$709**
W/ Siglite night sight: **$769**

MODEL P239

Action: autoloader
Grips: polymer
Barrel: 3.6 in.
Sights: target
Weight: 27.0 oz.
Caliber: 9mm, .357 Sig, .40 S&W
Capacity: 7 + 1 rounds
Features: double-action; lightweight alloy frame; black Nitron slide; available with Siglite night sights
P239: **$739**
With Siglite night sights: **$799**

MODEL P245

Action: autoloader
Grips: plastic
Barrel: 4.4 in.   *Sights:* adjustable
Weight: 27.8 oz.
Caliber: .45 ACP
Capacity: 7 rounds
Features: compact size; decocking lever and automatic firing pin safety block; reversible magazine release; two-toned blued finish
P245: **$840**
W/ Siglite night sight: **$915**

MODEL PL22 TRAILSIDE

Action: autoloader
Grips: rubber or walnut
Barrel: 4.5 or 6.0 in.
Sights: target
Weight: 26.0 oz.
Caliber: .22 LR
Capacity: 10 + 1 rounds
Features: all versions have a top rail for scope mounts
4.5 in. standard: **$455**
4.5 in. target: **$533**
6 in. standard: **$540**
6 in. target: **$559**
6 in. competition: **$709**

Sigarms Handguns

GSR REVOLUTION
Action: autoloader
Grips: polymer
Barrel: 5 in.
Sights: target
Weight: 40.3 oz.
Caliber: .45 ACP
Capacity: 8+1 rounds
Features: hand-fitted stainless steel frame and slide available in black Nitron finish; match grade barrel; hammer/sear set and trigger; beavertail grip safety; firing pin safety and hammer intercept notch; available with Novak night sights
Stainless: **$1396**
Nitron: **$1396**

MOSQUITO
Action: autoloader
Grips: polymer
Barrel: 4 in.
Sights: adjustable
Weight: 25 oz.
Caliber: .22 LR
Capacity: 10 rounds
Features: double-action; polymer frame; black Nitron slide; ambidextrous grip; Picatinny rail
MSRP: **$389**

PRO
Action: autoloader
Grips: polymer
Barrel: 3.9 in.
Sights: fixed open
Weight: 29.0 oz.
Caliber: .357 Sig, .40 S&W, 9mm
Capacity: 10 + 1 rounds
Features: polymer frame; Nitron finish stainless slide; double-action; Siglite night sights available
Pro: **$640**
W/ Siglite night sights: **$715**
**SP 2022 w/ Siglite night sights
& tac rail:** **$715**

MOSQUITO

PRO SP 2022

PRO TWO TONE

Smith & Wesson Handguns

MODEL SW9 VE

MODEL 22A SPORT

MODEL 10 HEAVY BARREL

MODEL 37 CHIEF'S SPECIAL AIRWEIGHT

MODEL SW9 VE

Action: autoloader
Grips: polymer
Barrel: 4 in.
Sights: 3 dot
Weight: 24.7 oz.
Caliber: 9mm
Capacity: 10 + 1 rounds
Features: double-action; stainless slide; polymer frame; finish options
SW9 VE: **$409**

MODEL 10

Action: double-action revolver
Grips: Uncle Mike's Combat
Barrel: 4.0 in. heavy
Sights: fixed open
Weight: 33.5 oz.
Caliber: .38 Spl.
Capacity: 6 rounds
Features: "military and police" model; also in stainless, K-frame
Model 10: **$572**
**Stainless with 2 in. barrel,
    round butt:** **$583**

MODEL 22A SPORT

Action: autoloader
Grips: polymer
Barrel: 4, 5.5 or 7 in.
Sights: target
Weight: 28.0 oz.
Caliber: .22 LR
Capacity: 10 + 1 rounds
Features: scope mounting rib; 5.5 in. bull barrel available
4 in.: **$293**
5.5 in. (31 oz.): **$324**
5.5 in. bull: **$407**
5.5 in. bull, Hi-Viz sights: **$429**
7 in. (33 oz.): **$367**
5.5 in. stainless: **$396**

MODEL 36-LS

Action: double-action revolver
Grips: laminated rosewood, round butt
Barrel: 1.8, 2.2, 3 in.
Sights: fixed open
Weight: 20.0 oz.
Caliber: .38 Spl.
Capacity: 5 rounds

Features: weight to 24 oz. depending on barrel length; stainless version in .357 Mag. available (60 LS)
Model 36 LS: **$596**
60 LS: **$652**

MODEL 37 CHIEF'S SPECIAL AIRWEIGHT

Action: double-action revolver
Grips: Uncle Mike's Boot
Barrel: 1.8 in.
Sights: fixed open
Weight: 11.9 oz.
Caliber: .38 Spl.
Capacity: 5 rounds
Features: alloy frame (also M37 in blue finish)
Model 637: **$450**
Model 37: **$573**

HANDGUNS

Smith & Wesson Handguns

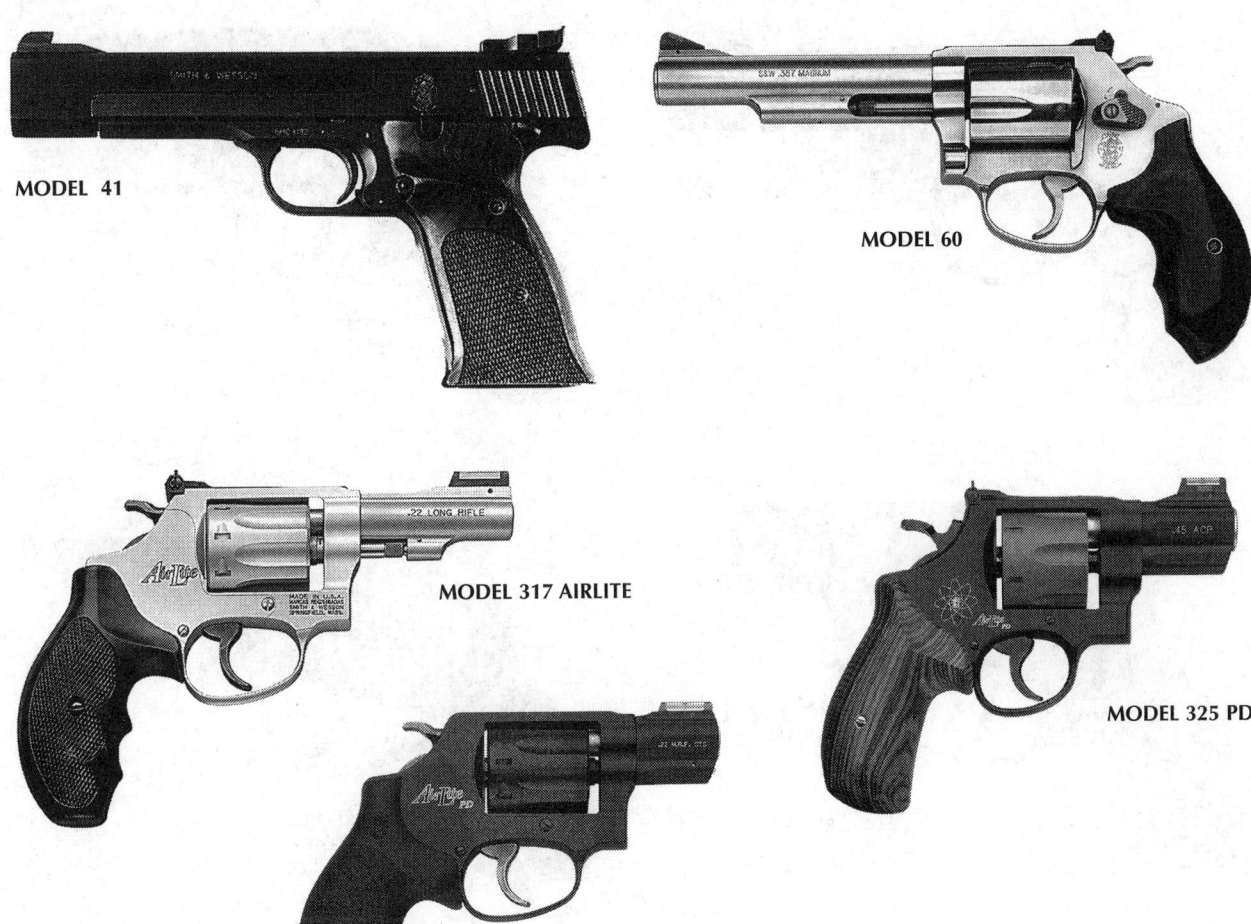

MODEL 41

MODEL 60

MODEL 317 AIRLITE

MODEL 325 PD

MODEL 351 PD

MODEL 40 SERIES
Action: autoloader
Grips: polymer
Barrel: 4 in.
Sights: 3 dot
Weight: 24.4 oz.
Caliber: .40 S&W
Capacity: 10 + 1 rounds
Features: double-action; stainless slide; polymer frame
MSRP: $409

MODEL 41
Action: autoloader
Grips: walnut
Barrel: 5.5 or 7 in.
Sights: target
Weight: 41.0 oz.
Caliber: .22 LR
Capacity: 12 + 1 rounds

Features: adjustable trigger; 7 in. barrel: 44 oz.
MSRP: $1062

MODEL 60
Action: double-action revolver
Grips: wood
Barrel: 5 in.
Sights: adjustable open
Weight: 30.5 oz.
Caliber: .357
Capacity: 5 rounds
Features: stainless frame
MSRP: $671-704

MODEL 317
Action: double-action revolver
Grips: rubber
Barrel: 1.8 or 3 in.
Sights: fixed open

Weight: 10.5 oz.
Caliber: .22 LR
Capacity: 8 rounds
Features: alloy frame
1.8 in.: $633
3 in.: $658

MODELS 325 PD AND 351 PD REVOLVER
Action: double-action revolver
Grips: wood (.45), rubber (.22)
Barrel: 2¾ in. (.45), 1⅞ in. (.22)
Sights: adjustable rear, HiViz front (.45), fixed rear, red ramp front (.22)
Weight: 21.5 oz. (.45), 10.6 oz. (.22)
Caliber: .45 ACP (Model 325), .22 WMR (Model 351)
Capacity: 6 (.45), 7 (.22) rounds
.22: $647
.45: $986-1008

HANDGUNS

Smith & Wesson Handguns

MODEL 329 PD

MODEL 360 PD
AIRLITE

MODEL 340
AIRLITE

MODEL 386
MOUNTAIN
LITE

MODEL 329 PD

Action: double-action revolver
Grips: wood
Barrel: 4 in.
Sights: adjustable fiber optic
Weight: 27.0 oz.
Caliber: .44 Mag.
Capacity: 6 rounds
Features: scandium frame,
titanium cylinder
MSRP: $1008

MODEL 340 AIRLITE

Action: double-action revolver
Grips: rubber
Barrel: 1.8 in.
Sights: fixed open
Weight: 12.0 oz.

Caliber: .357 Mag.
Capacity: 5 rounds
Features: Scandium alloy frame,
titanium cylinder
Model 340: $838-905
With Hi-Viz sight: $877

MODEL 360 AIRLITE

Action: double-action revolver
Grips: rubber
Barrel: 1.8 in.
Sights: fixed open
Weight: 12.0 oz.
Caliber: .357 Mag.
Capacity: 5 rounds
Features: Scandium alloy frame,
titanium cylinder
Model 360: $858

With Hi-Viz sight: $901
3.2 in. Kit Gun
with Hi-Viz sight: $901

MODEL 386

Action: double-action revolver
Grips: rubber
Barrel: 3.2 in.
Sights: low-profile combat
Weight: 18.5 oz.
Caliber: .357 Mag.
Capacity: 7 rounds
Features: scandium alloy frame;
titanium cylinder
Model 386: $876
2.5 in. barrel: $872

Smith & Wesson Handguns

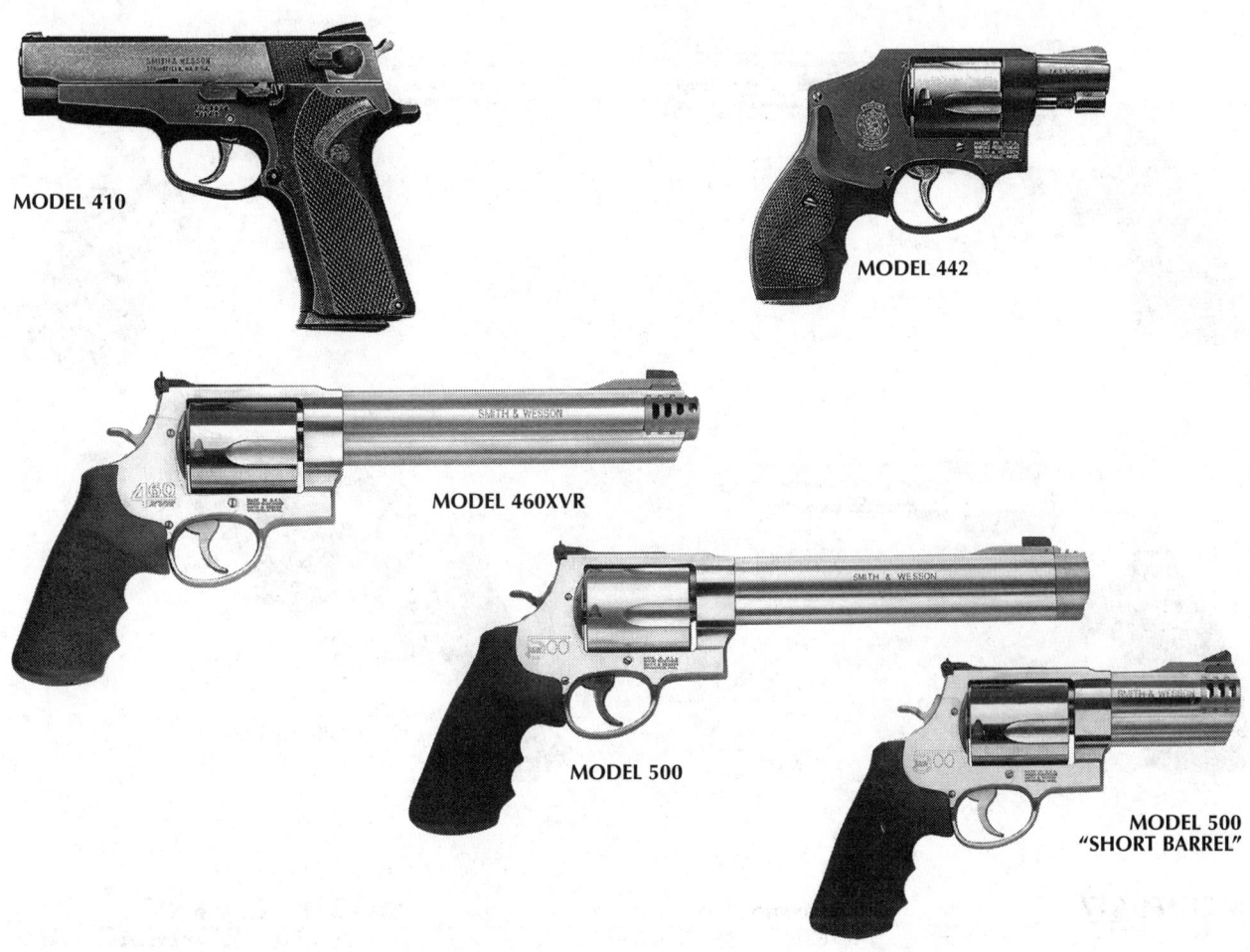

MODEL 410

MODEL 442

MODEL 460XVR

MODEL 500

MODEL 500 "SHORT BARREL"

MODEL 410, 457 & 910

Action: autoloader
Grips: rubber
Barrel: 4 in.
Sights: 3 dot
Weight: 28.5 oz.
Caliber: 9mm, .40 S&W
Capacity: 10 + 1 rounds
Features: alloy frame, chrome-moly slide, decocking lever; also M457 in .45 ACP, 7 + 1 rounds capacity; Hi-Viz sights extra
Model 910:. $587
Model 410:. $681
Model 457:. $681

MODEL 442 AIRWEIGHT

Action: double-action revolver
Grips: rubber
Barrel: 1.8 in.
Sights: fixed open
Weight: 15.0 oz.
Caliber: .38 Spl.

Capacity: 5 rounds
Features: stainless Model 642 and 442 are concealed-hammer, double-action only
Model 442:. $600

MODEL 460XVR

Action: double-action revolver
Grips: stippled rubber
Barrel: 8³⁄₈ in., stainless
Sights: adjustable open
Weight: 72 oz.
Caliber: .460 S&W
Capacity: 5 rounds
Features: ported barrel also fires .454 Casull and .45 Colt
MSRP: $1313

MODEL 500

Action: double-action revolver
Grips: Hogue Sorbathane
Barrel: ported 8.4 in.
Sights: target

Weight: 72.5 oz.
Caliber: .500 S&W
Capacity: 5 rounds
Features: X-Frame, double-action stainless revolver
Model 500:. $1186-1296
Model 460 (.460 S&W): . $1313-1401

MODEL 500 "SHORT BARREL"

Action: double-action revolver
Grips: rubber
Barrel: 4 in., sleeved, with brake
Sights: adjustable rear, red ramp front
Weight: 56 oz.
Caliber: .500 S&W
Capacity: 5
Features: double-action; Hogue grip; comes with 2 mukkle compensators
MSRP: $1256

HANDGUNS

Smith & Wesson Handguns

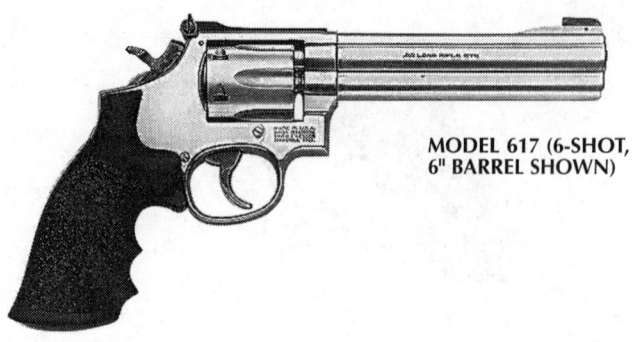

MODEL 617 (6-SHOT, 6" BARREL SHOWN)

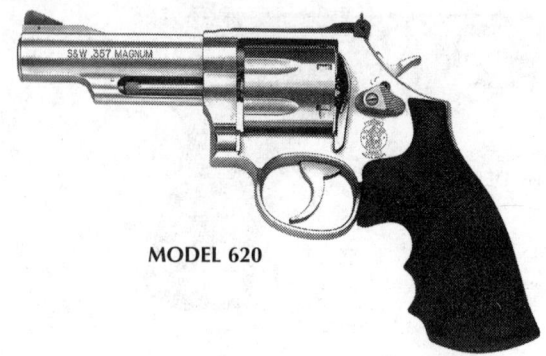

MODEL 620

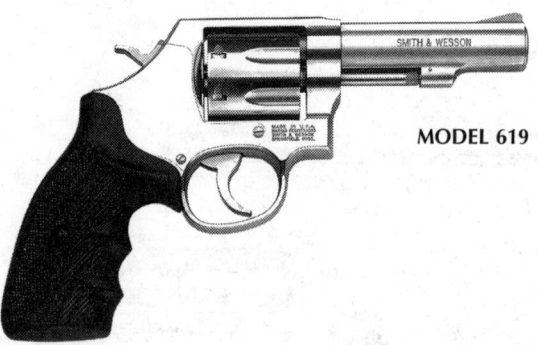

MODEL 619

MODEL 625
JERRY MICULEK

MODEL 617

Action: double-action revolver
Grips: Hogue rubber
Barrel: 4.0, 6.0, 8.4 in.
Sights: target
Weight: 42.0 oz.
Caliber: .22 LR
Capacity: 6 rounds
Features: stainless; target hammer and trigger; K-frame; weight to 54 oz. depending on barrel length
4 in.: $742
6 in.: $770
6 in., 10-shot: $751

MODELS 619 AND 620

Action: double-action revolver
Grips: checkered rubber
Barrel: 4 in.
Sights: adjustable open (M620) and fixed (M619)

Weight: 38 oz.
Caliber: .357 Magnum
Capacity: 7 rounds
Features: stainless; semi-lug barrel
M619: $664
M620: $703

MODEL 625

Action: double-action revolver
Grips: Hogue rubber, round butt
Barrel: 4 or 5 in.
Sights: target
Weight: 49.0 oz.
Caliber: .45 ACP
Capacity: 6 rounds
Features: N-frame, stainless; also in Model 610 10mm with 4 in. barrel; 5 in. barrel 51 oz.
Model 625: $858

MODEL 625 JERRY MICULEK PROFESSIONAL SERIES REVOLVER

Action: double-action revolver
Grips: wood
Barrel: 4 in.
Sights: adjustable open, removable front bead
Weight: 43 oz.
Caliber: .45 ACP
Capacity: 6 rounds
Features: wide trigger; smooth wood grip; gold bead front sight on a removable blade; comes with five full-moon clips for fast loading
MSRP: $887

Even if you are properly licensed to carry a concealed handgun, choose a method of carry that keeps your weapon hidden from the public. You never know how a stranger will react upon seeing a concealed handgun.

HANDGUNS

Smith & Wesson Handguns

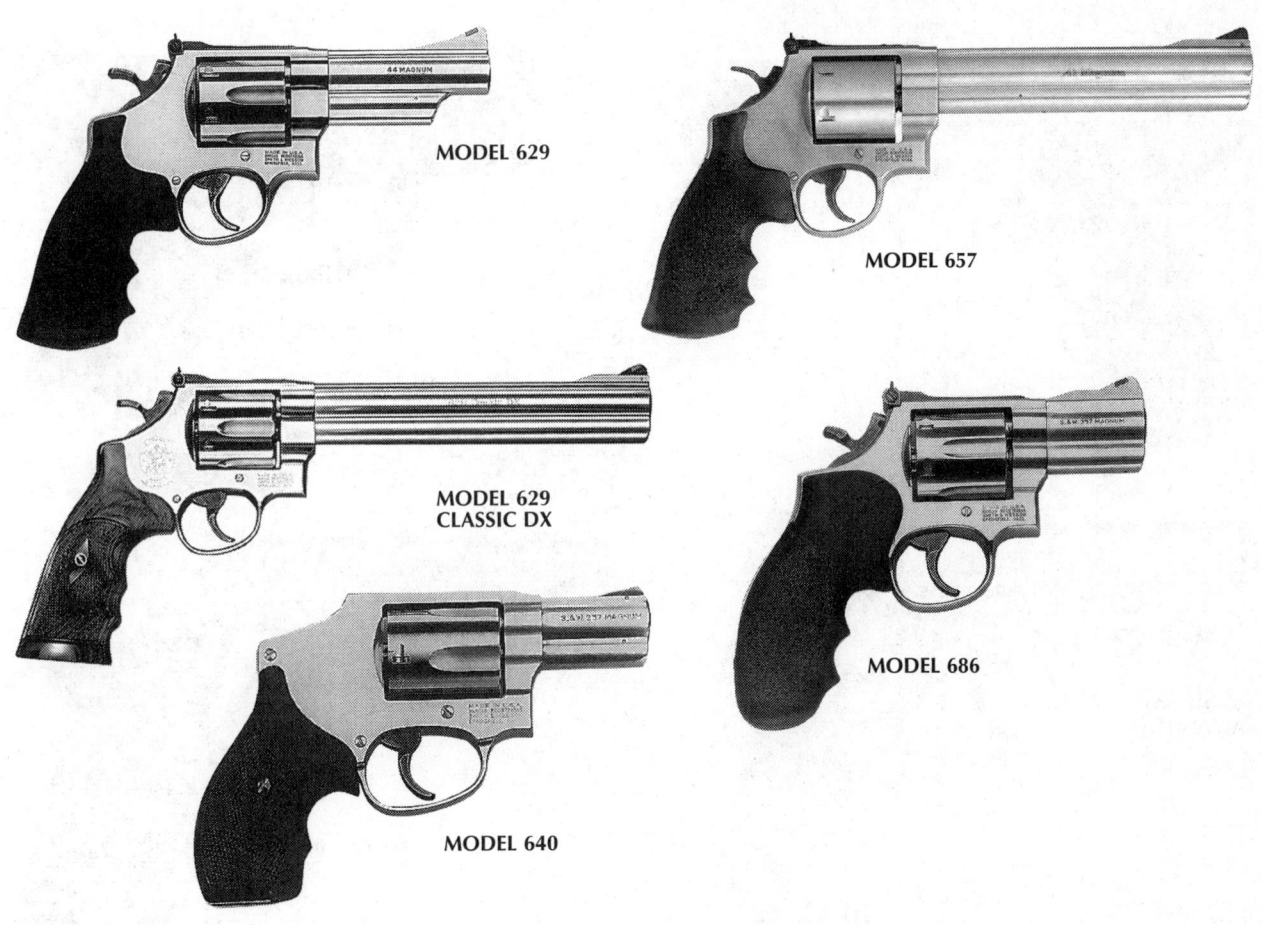

MODEL 629

MODEL 657

MODEL 629
CLASSIC DX

MODEL 686

MODEL 640

MODEL 629

Action: double-action revolver
Grips: Hogue rubber
Barrel: 4 or 6 in.
Sights: target
Weight: 44.0 oz.
Caliber: .44 Mag.
Capacity: 6 rounds
Features: N-frame, stainless; 6 in. weighs 47 oz.

4 in.:	$826
5 in.:	$885
6 in.:	$851

MODEL 629 CLASSIC

Action: double-action revolver
Grips: Hogue rubber
Barrel: 5, 6.5 or 8.4 in.
Sights: target   *Weight:* 51.0 oz.
Caliber: .44 Mag.
Capacity: 6 rounds
Features: N-frame, stainless, full lug; weight to 54 oz. depending on barrel length

5.0 or 6.5 in.:	$912
8.4 in.:	$914

MODEL 640 CENTENNIAL

Action: double-action revolver
Grips: rubber
Barrel: 2.2 in.
Sights: fixed open
Weight: 23.0 oz.
Caliber: .357
Capacity: 5 rounds
Features: stainless; concealed-hammer; double-action-only; also M649 Bodyguard single- or double-action

M640:	$658
M649:	$651

MODEL 657

Action: double-action revolver
Grips: Hogue rubber
Barrel: 7.5 in.
Sights: target
Weight: 52.0 oz.
Caliber: .41 Mag.

Capacity: 6 rounds
Features: N-frame stainless

MSRP:	$813

MODEL 686

Action: single-action revolver
Grips: combat or target
Barrel: 2.5, 4, 6, 8.4 in.
Sights: target
Weight: 34.5 oz.
Caliber: .357 Mag.
Capacity: 6 rounds
Features: stainless; K-frame 686 Plus holds 7 rounds; to 48 oz. depending on barrel length

2.5 in.:	$700
4 in.:	$728
6 in.:	$735
6 in. ported:	$784
2.5 in. Plus:	$727
4 in. Plus:	$752
6 in. Plus:	$764

Smith & Wesson Handguns

MODEL 1911

MODEL 99OL .40

MODEL 3913
LADYSMITH

MODEL 3913TSW

MODEL 990L

Action: autoloader
Grips: polymer
Barrel: 3.5, 4 or 5 in.
Sights: low-profile combat
Weight: 22.5-25.0 oz.
Caliber: .40 S&W, 9mm
Capacity: 8-16 rounds
Features: double-action pistol made in collaboration with Walther
MSRP: $773

MODEL 1911

Action: autoloader
Grips: checkered composite, checkered wood
Barrel: 5 in. (4 in. for Model 945)
Sights: adjustable open
Weight: 28-41 oz.
Caliber: .45 ACP (.38 Super in SW1911DK)
Capacity: 8+1 rounds (10 in SW1911DK)
Features: single-action; extended beavertail; match trigger
MSRP: $1008-1308

MODEL 3913 LADYSMITH

Action: autoloader
Grips: Hogue rubber
Barrel: 3.5 in.
Sights: low-profile combat
Weight: 24.8 oz.
Caliber: 9mm
Capacity: 8 + 1 rounds
Features: double-action; stainless
MSRP: $901

MODEL 3913 TSW (TACTICAL SERIES)

Action: autoloader
Grips: rubber
Barrel: 3.5 in.
Sights: 3 dot
Weight: 24.8 oz.
Caliber: 9mm
Capacity: 8 + 1 rounds
Features: alloy frame, stainless slide; also: 3953TSW double-action-only
MSRP: $1021

MODEL 4013TSW

Action: autoloader
Grips: rubber
Barrel: 3.5 in.
Sights: 3 dot
Weight: 26.8 oz.
Caliber: .40 S&W
Capacity: 9 + 1 rounds
Features: alloy frame; stainless slide; ambidextrous safety; also: 4053TSW double-action only
MSRP: **$876**

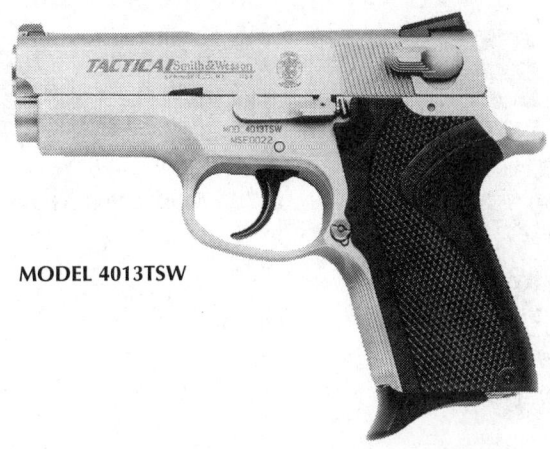

MODEL 4013TSW

MODEL 4040 PD

Action: double-action revolver
Grips: Hogue rubber
Barrel: 3.5 in.
Sights: 3 dot
Weight: 25.6 oz.
Caliber: .40 S&W
Capacity: 7 + 1 rounds
Features: first scandium-frame pistol
MSRP: **$840**

CHEIF'S SPECIAL
CS 9

CHIEF'S SPECIAL

Action: autoloader
Grips: rubber
Barrel: 3 or 3.25 in.
Sights: 3 dot
Weight: 20.8-24.0 oz.
Caliber: 9mm, .45 ACP
Capacity: 7 + 1 rounds (9mm) and 6 + 1 (.40 S&W)
Features: lightweight; compact
CS 9: **$777**
CS 45: **$826**

CHEIF'S SPECIAL
CS 45

HANDGUNS

Springfield Armory Handguns

MODEL 1911-A1

MODEL 1911-A1
CHAMPION

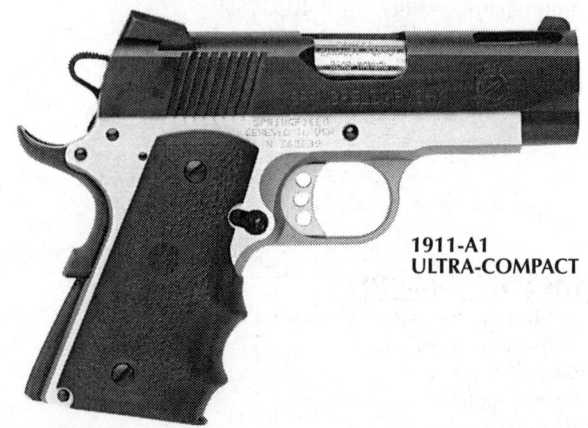

1911-A1
ULTRA-COMPACT

1911-A1
Action: autoloader
Grips: cocobolo
Barrel: 5 in.
Sights: fixed or adjustable
Weight: 38.0 oz.
Caliber: 9mm, .45 ACP
Capacity: 7 + 1 rounds
Features: steel or lightweight aluminum frames; stainless, blued and parkerized finishes; V-12 barrel porting; fixed combat or fully adjustable rear sights
Black stainless: **$904**
Stainless: **$902**
Parkerized: **$869**
Stainless: **$966**
Black Stainless w/ adjustable
   Bo Mar rear sight: **$1124**
   9 mm Service Model: $976
Lightweight (30 oz.), Bi-Tone: . **$934**
MC Operator
   (42 oz. w/ tac rail): **$1254**

MODEL 1911 A-1 CHAMPION
Action: autoloader
Grips: walnut
Barrel: 4 in.
Sights: fixed open
Weight: 28.0, 34.0 oz.
Caliber: .45 ACP
Capacity: 7 + 1 rounds
Features: fully supported ramped bull barrel; Novak sights; stainless Bi-Tone finish option
Lightweight: **$913**
Stainless: **$952**

1911-A1 COMPACT MODELS
Action: autoloader
Grips: plastic or cocobolo
Barrel: 3 (Micro-Compact) or 3.5 in.
Sights: Fixed, open
Weight: 32.0 oz.
Caliber: .45 ACP
Capacity: 6+1 rounds
Features: forged aluminum anodized alloy frame; forged steel slide; ambidextrous thumb safety
Ultra-Compact: **$952**
Micro-Compact: **$1220**

HANDGUNS

Springfield Armory Handguns

MICRO
COMPACT
1911-A1

X-TREME DUTY (XD)

MODEL 1911-A1
TROPHY MATCH

XD SUB-COMPACT W/LIGHT

1911-A1 LONG SLIDE
Action: autoloader
Grips: walnut
Barrel: 6 in.
Sights: target
Weight: 41.0 oz.
Caliber: .45 ACP
Capacity: 7 + 1 rounds
Features: slide is 1 in. longer than full-size 1911-A1
Stainless: **$1097**

1911-A1 MIL-SPEC
Action: autoloader
Grips: plastic
Barrel: 5 in.
Sights: fixed open
Weight: 35.6-39.0 oz.
Caliber: .38 Super, .45 ACP
Capacity: 7 + 1 rounds
Features: traditional M1911 A-1
Parkerized: **$660**
Stainless Steel: **$724**
.38 Super: **$1254**

MODEL 1911 A-1 TROPHY MATCH
Action: autoloader
Grips: cocobolo
Barrel: 5 in.
Sights: target
Weight: 38.0 oz.
Caliber: .45 ACP
Capacity: 7 + 1 rounds
Features: match barrel and bushing; Videcki speed trigger; serrated front strap; stainless
Trophy Match: **$1409**
Stainless: **$1452**

MODEL XD SERVICE
Action: autoloader
Grips: walnut
Barrel: 4 or 5 in.   *Sights*: fixed open
Weight: 22.8-27.0 oz.
Caliber: 9mm, .357 Sig, .40 S&W, .45 GAP
Capacity: 10 + 1 rounds
Features: single-action; short recoil; black or OD green

XD: **$536**
w/ Tritium sights: **$599**
V-10 Ported: **$566**
XD Tactical (5 in. bl.): **$566**
Bi-Tone (.45 GAP only): **$566**
Trijicon Sights: **$626**
W/ Tritium Sights: **$626**

MODEL XD SUB COMPACTS
Action: autoloader
Grips: black composite
Barrel: 3.1 in.   *Sights*: fixed, open
Weight: 20.5 oz.
Caliber: 9mm, .357 SIG, .40, .45 GAP
Capacity: 10+1 rounds
Features: cold hammer forged barrel; polymer frame with heat-treated steel slide and rails; short-recoil, locked-breech action; dual recoil springs; three safeties; cocking indicator; light rail (Mini Light optional); 3-dot sights; black or OD green finish
MSRP: **$536**

STI International Inc. Handguns

EDGE

EAGLE

LS AND BLS

EXECUTIVE

LSA LAWMAN

EAGLE
Action: autoloader
Grips: polymer
Barrel: 5 or 6 in.
Sights: target (5 in.), open fixed (6 in.)
Weight: 34.5oz. (5 in.), 40 oz. (6 in.)
Caliber: 9mm, 9X21, .38Super, .40 S&W, .45ACP
Capacity: 10+1 rounds
Features: modular steel frame; classic slide; long curved trigger; fully supported, ramped bull barrel; stainless STI grip and ambidextrous thumb safeties; blue finish
Eagle (5 in.):. **$1794**
Eagle (6 in.):. **$1894**

EDGE
Action: autoloader
Grips: polymer
Sights: target
Weight: 39 oz.
Caliber: 9mm, .40 S&W, 10mm, .45 ACP
Capacity: 6+1 rounds
Features: modular steel; long wide frame; overall length 8⅝ in.; fully supported, ramped bull barrel; long curved trigger; stainless STI grip and

ambidextrous thumb safeties; blue finish
MSRP: **$1874**

EXECUTIVE
Action: autoloader
Grips: polymer
Barrel: 5 in.
Sights: target
Weight: 39 oz.
Caliber: .40 S&W
Capacity: 10+1 rounds
Features: modular steel; long wide frame; overall length 8⅝ in.; fully supported, ramped bull barrel; long curved trigger; stainless STI grip and ambidextrous thumb safeties
MSRP: **$2389**

LS AND BLS
Action: autoloader
Grips: rosewood
Barrel: 3.4 in.
Sights: fixed open
Weight: 30 oz. (LS), 28 oz (BLS)
Caliber: 9mm, .40 S&W
Capacity: 7+1 rounds (9mm), 6+1 rounds (.40 S&W)
Features: Government size steel frame

with full size grip (BLS with officer's size grip); fully supported, ramped bull barrel; undercut trigger guard and front strap; long curved trigger; STI grip and single-sided thumb safeties; integral front sight with Heinie low-mount rear sight; flat blue finish; slide does not lock back after last round is fired
LS: **$889**
BLS: **$789**

LSA LAWMAN
Action: autoloader
Grips: rosewood
Barrel: 5 in.
Sights: fixed open
Weight: 40 oz.
Caliber: .45 ACP
Capacity: 6+1 rounds
Features: forged steel government-length frame; overall length 8.5 inches; 1911 style slide; fully supported, ramped barrel with match bushing; STI aluminum trigger; STI grip and single sided thumb STI high rise beavertail safeties; two tone polymer finish (light brown over olive drab)
MSRP: **$1344**

HANDGUNS

STI International Inc. Handguns

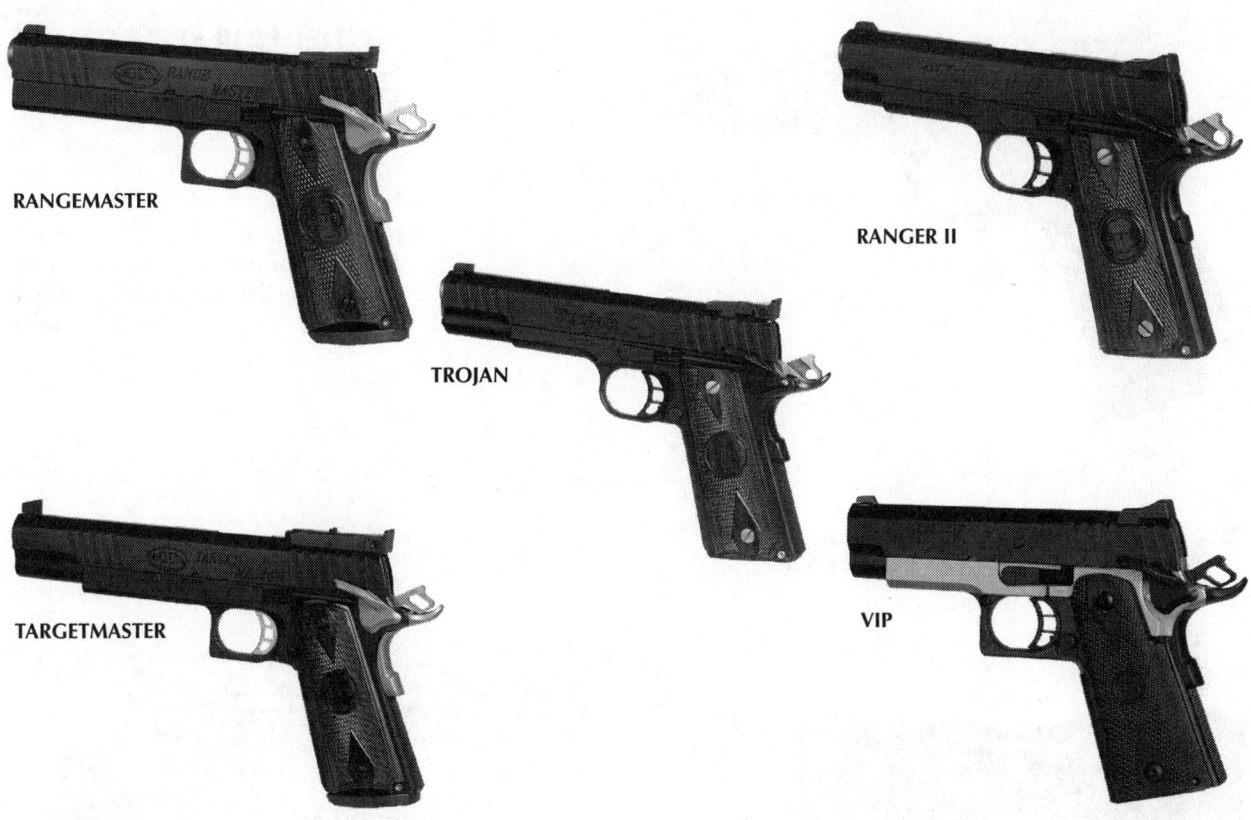

RANGEMASTER

RANGER II

TROJAN

TARGETMASTER

VIP

RANGEMASTER

Action: autoloader
Grips: rosewood
Barrel: 5 in.   *Sights*: target
Weight: 38 oz.
Caliber: 9mm, .45 ACP
Features: single stack government
length steel frame; flat top slide; full
length dust cover; fully supported,
ramped bull barrel; aluminum long
curved trigger; polished stainless grip
and ambidextrous thumb safeties; overall length 8.5 in.; polished blue finish
MSRP: **$1440**

RANGER II

Action: autoloader
Grips: rosewood
Barrel: 4.15 in.   *Sights*: fixed open
Weight: 30 oz.
Caliber: .45 ACP
Capacity: 7+1 rounds
Features: commander size with full
length 1911-style frame and fully
supported barrel; hi-rise trigger guard;
1911-style flat topped slide; long
curved trigger with stainless bow;
hi-rise grip and single sided thumb
safeties; blue finish
MSRP: **$1029**

TARGETMASTER

Action: autoloader
Grips: rosewood
Barrel: 6 in.
Sights: tarrget
Weight: 40 oz.
Caliber: 9mm, .45 ACP
Features: single stack government
length frame; classic flat top slide;
fully supported ramped match bull
barrel; overall length 9.5 in.; tri-level
adjustable sights; aluminum long
curved trigger; STI stainless grip and
ambidextrous thumb safeties; polished
blue finish
MSRP: **$1440**

TROJAN

Action: autoloader
Grips: rosewood
Barrel: 5 or 6 in.
Sights: target
Weight: 36 oz. (5 in.); 38 oz. (6 in.)
Caliber: 9mm, .38Super, .40 S&W, .45
ACP
Features: single stack government size
frame; 5 in. or 6 in. classic flat top
slide; fully supported match barrel;
high rise grip safety, STI long curved
polymer trigger and undercut trigger
guard; flat blue finish
Trojan (5 in.): **$1024**
Trojan (6 in.): **$1344**

VIP

Action: Autoloader (SA)
Grips: polymer
Barrel: 3.9 in.   *Sights*: fixed open
Weight: 25 oz.
Caliber: 9mm, .38 Super, 9X21, .40
S&W,.45 ACP
Capacity: 10 + 1 rounds
Features: modular aluminum frame;
overall length 7.5 in.; classic flat top
slide; fully supported, ramped bull bar-
rel; STI long curved trigger; STI stainless
grip and single-sided thumb safeties
MSRP: **$1653**

Swiss Arms Handguns

P210 SPORT

MODEL P210 SPORT
Action: autoloader
Grips: wood
Barrel: 4.8 in.
Sights: target
Weight: 24.0 oz.
Caliber: 9mm
Capacity: 8 + 1 rounds
Features: chrome-moly, single-action
Swiss Army Service Model: . . $3031
Target grade: $2695

Taurus Handguns

MODEL 24/7

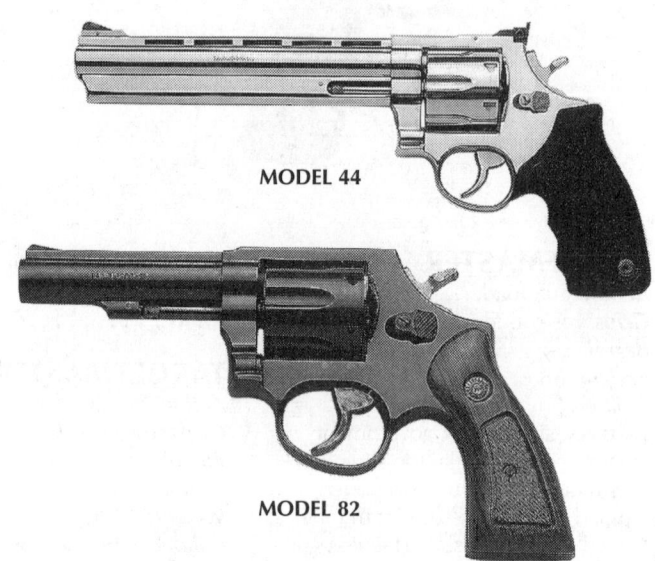

MODEL 44

MODEL 82

MODEL 24/7
Action: autoloader
Grips: polymer with rubber overlay
Barrel: 6 in.
Sights: 3 dot
Weight: 32.0 oz.
Caliber: .40 S&W
Capacity: 15 rounds
Features: double-action; reversible magazine release; Picatinny rail
MSRP: $576

MODEL 44
Action: double-action revolver
Grips: rubber
Barrel: 4, 6.5 or 8.4 in.
Sights: target
Weight: 44.0 oz.
Caliber: .44 Mag.
Capacity: 6 rounds
Features: vent rib, porting; weight to 57 oz. depending on barrel length
Stainless, 4 in.: $563
Stainless, 6.5 in.: $578
Stainless, 8.4 in.: $578

MODEL 82
Action: double-action revolver
Grips: rubber
Barrel: 4 in.
Sights: fixed open
Weight: 36.5 oz.
Caliber: .38 Spl. +P
Capacity: 6 rounds
Features: also, 21-ounce model 85 in .38 Spl, with 2 in. barrel, grip options
Model 82, blue: $352
Model 82, stainless: $398
Model 85, blue: $375
Model 85, stainless: $422

HANDGUNS

Taurus Handguns

MODEL PT-92

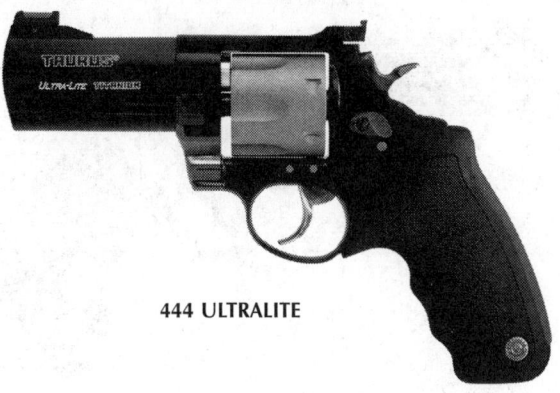

444 ULTRALITE

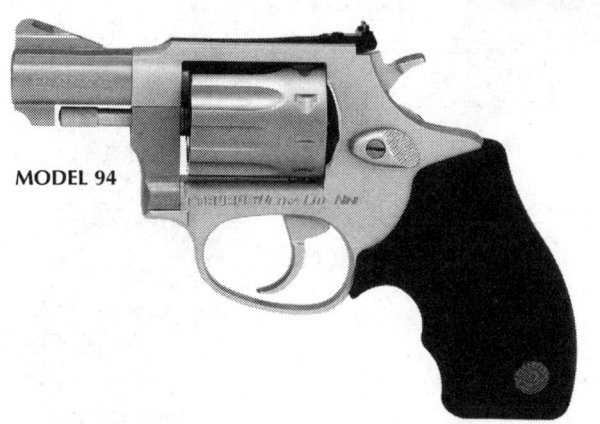

MODEL 94

MODEL 605

PROTECTOR
Action: double-action revolver
Grips: rubber
Barrel: 2 in.
Sights: fixed open
Weight: 24.5 oz.
Caliber: .357 Mag. or .38 Spl.
Capacity: 5 rounds
Features: shrouded but accessible hammer; also Titanium and UltraLight versions to 17 oz.
Blue: **$383**
Stainless: **$430**
Shadow Gray Titanium: **$547**

MODEL 92
Action: autoloader
Grips: rosewood or rubber
Barrel: 5 in.
Sights: fixed open
Weight: 34.0 oz.
Caliber: 9mm
Capacity: 10 + 1 rounds or 17 + 1
Features: double-action; also PT99 with adjustable sights

Blue: **$578**
Stainless: **$594**
Stainless gold,
  Mother of Pearl: **$656**

MODEL 94/941
Action: double-action revolver
Grips: hardwood
Barrel: 2, 4 or 5 in.
Sights: target
Weight: 18.5-27.5 oz.
Caliber: .22 LR, .22 Mag.
Capacity: 8-9 rounds
Features: small frame, solid rib
Blue: **$328**
Magnum, blue: **$344**
Stainless: **$375**
Magnum, stainless: **$391**
.22 LR, Ultralite: **$359-406**
.22 Mag., Ultralite: **$375-422**

MODEL 444 ULTRALITE
Action: double-action revolver
Grips: rubber
Barrel: 4 in.
Sights: adjustable with fiber optic insert
Weight: 28 oz.
Caliber: .44 Magnum
Capacity: 6 rounds
Features: alloy frame, titanium cylinder
Blued: **$650**
Stainless: **$699**

MODEL 605
Action: double-action revolver
Grips: rubber
Barrel: 2 in.
Sights: fixed open
Weight: 24.5 oz.
Caliber: .357 Mag.
Capacity: 5 rounds
Features: small frame, transfer bar; porting optional
Model 605: **$375**
Titanium (16 oz.): **$375**
Stainless: **$422**

HANDGUNS

Taurus Handguns

MODEL 608

MODEL M17C

MODEL 905

MODEL PT22

MODEL 608

Action: double-action revolver
Grips: rubber
Barrel: 4, 6.5 or 8.4 in., ported
Sights: target
Weight: 49.0 oz.
Caliber: .357 Mag.
Capacity: 8 rounds
Features: large frame; transfer bar; weight to 53 oz. depending on barrel length
Stainless, 4 in.: **$523**
Stainless, 6.5 or 8.4 in.: **$547**

MODEL 905

Action: double-action revolver
Grips: rubber
Barrel: 2 in.
Sights: fixed open
Weight: 21.0 oz.
Caliber: 9mm, .40 S&W, .45 ACP 9 with 2, 4 or 6.5 inch barrel)
Capacity: 5 rounds
Features: stellar clips furnished; UltraLite weighs 17 oz.

Blue: **$383**
Stainless: **$430**
.32 Mag.: **$438**

MODEL M17C

Action: double-action revolver
Grips: rubber
Barrel: 2, 4, 5, 6.5 or 12 in.
Sights: target
Weight: 18.5-26.0 oz.
Caliber: .17 HMR
Capacity: 8 rounds
Features: 8 models available in blued and stainless steel; weight varies with barrel length
Blue, 2, 4 or 5 in. barrel: **$359**
Ultralite: **$391**
Stainless: **$406**
12 in. barrel: **$430**
Ultralite stainless: **$438**

MODEL PT22

Action: autoloader
Grips: rosewood

Barrel: 2.8 in.
Sights: fixed open
Weight: 12.3 oz.
Caliber: .22 LR
Capacity: 8 + 1 rounds
Features: double-action only; blue, nickel or DuoTone finish; also in .25 ACP (PT25)
PT22: **$219**
With checkered wood: **$219**
With gold trim: **$234**
With Mother of Pearl grips: . . . **$250**

MODEL PT911 COMPACT

Action: autoloader
Grips: checkered rubber
Barrel: 4 in.
Sights: 3 dot
Weight: 28.2 oz.
Caliber: 9mm
Capacity: 10 + 1 rounds or 15 + 1
Features: double-action only; ambidextrous decocker
Blue: **$523**
Stainless: **$539**

HANDGUNS

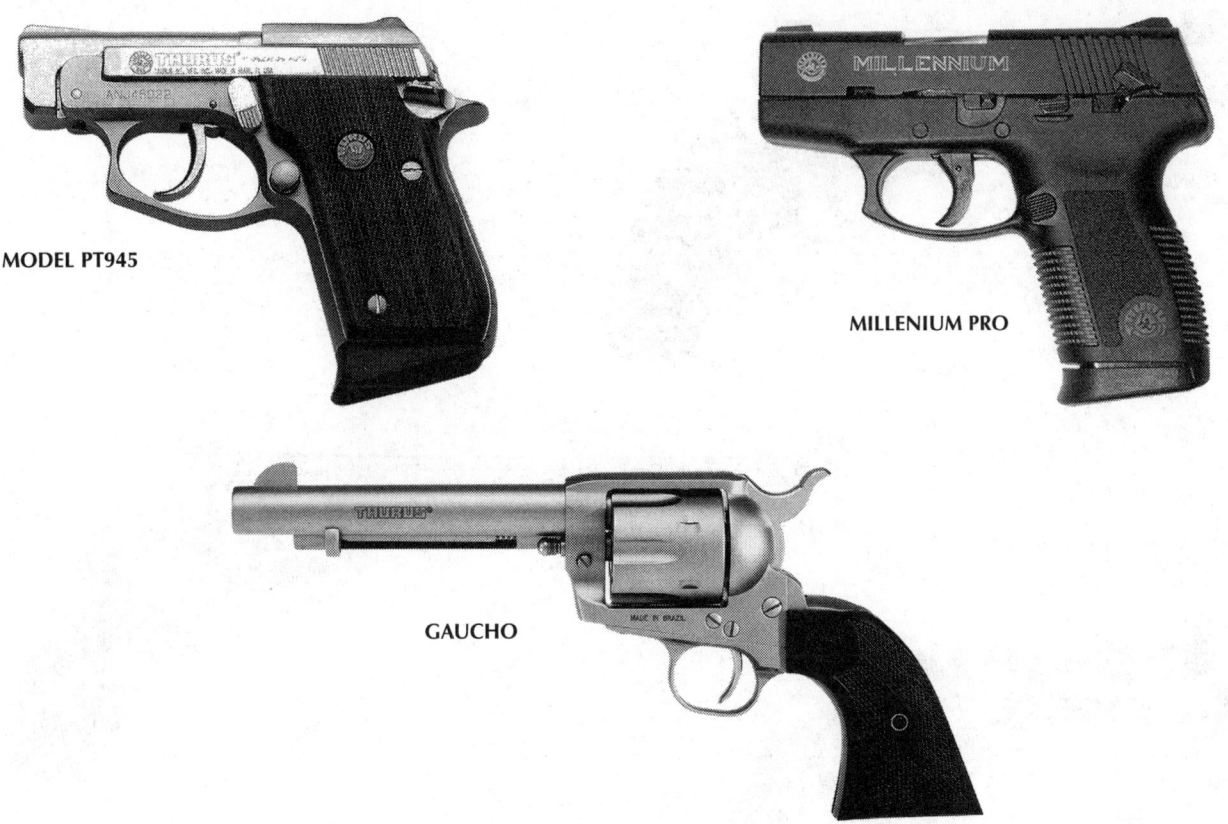

MODEL PT945

MILLENIUM PRO

GAUCHO

MODEL PT945
Action: autoloader
Grips: checkered rubber, rosewood, or Mother of Pearl
Barrel: 4.3 in.
Sights: 3 dot
Weight: 29.5 oz.
Caliber: .45 ACP, .38 Super
Capacity: 8 + 1 rounds (.38: 10 + 1)
Features: double-action; also PT38 in .38 Super
Blue: **$563**
Stainless: **$578**
**Stainless, gold,
     mother of Pearl**: **$641**
Stainless rosewood: **$625**
Model 940 blue: **$523**
Model 940 stainless: **$539**

GAUCHO
Action: single-action revolver
Grips: hard rubber
Barrel: 5.5 in.
Sights: fixed
Weight: 37 oz.
Caliber: .45 Colt
Capacity: 6 rounds
Features: single-action; transfer bar safety
Blued: **$499**
**Stainless or blued with
     case-colored frame**: **$510**

MILLENIUM PRO
Action: autoloader
Grips: polymer
Barrel: 3.25 in.   *Sights*: 3 dot
Weight: 18.7 oz.
Caliber: 9mm, .40 S&W, .45 ACP, .32 ACP, .380 ACP
Capacity: 10 + 1 rounds
Features: double-action; polymer

frame; also comes with night sights (BL or SS), add $78
.40 blue: **$461**
.40 stainless: **$476**
.45 blue/composite: **$461**
.45 stainless/composite: **$476**
9mm, .32 or .380 BL: **$422**
9mm, .32 or .380 SS: **$438**
9mm Titanium: **$508**

NINE BY SEVENTEEN
Action: autoloader
Grips: hard rubber
Barrel: 4 in.
Sights: 3 dot
Weight: 26 oz.
Caliber: 9mm
Capacity: 17 rounds
Features: double-action with de-cocker
Blued: **$523**
Stainless: **$539**

HANDGUNS

Taurus Handguns

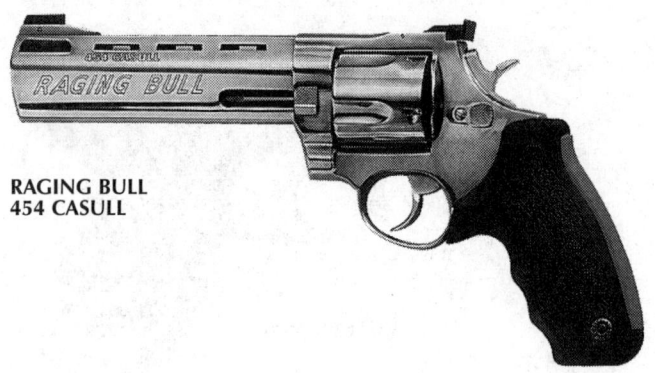

**RAGING BULL
454 CASULL**

**RAGING BULL
.500 S&W**

**TRACKER
TITANIUM**

RAGING BULL

Action: double-action revolver
Grips: rubber
Barrel: 5, 6.5 or 8.3 in.
Sights: target
Weight: 53.0-63.0 oz.
Caliber: .41 Mag., .44 Mag., .480
Ruger, .454 Casull
Capacity: 6 rounds
Features: stainless vent rib, ported;
also 72 oz. 5 round Raging Bull in
.500 Mag with 10 in. barrel

.41: **$641**
.44 Mag, blue: **$578**
stainless .44 & .480 Ruger: **$641**
454 Casull, blue: **$797**
454 Casull, stainless: **$859**
.500 Mag.: **$899**

TRACKER

Action: double-action revolver
Grips: rubber with ribs
Barrel: 4 or 6.5 in.   *Sights*: target
Weight: 24.0-45.0 oz.
Caliber: .22 LR, .41 Mag., .357 Mag.,
.44 Mag., .17 HMR, .500 S&W
Capacity: 5-7 rounds (full-moon clips)
Features: ported barrel on .44 Mag.,
.357 and .41 Mag.; available
in Titanium

.17 HMR: **$406**
.22 LR: **$391**
.357 Mag.: **$508**
.357 Mag. (Shadow Grey): **$688**
.41 Mag., stainless: **$516**
.41 Mag., Shadow Grey
    Titanium: **$688**
.44 Mag., blue: **$500**
.44 Mag., stainless: **$547**
.500 S&W: **$899**

HANDGUNS

Thompson/Center Handguns

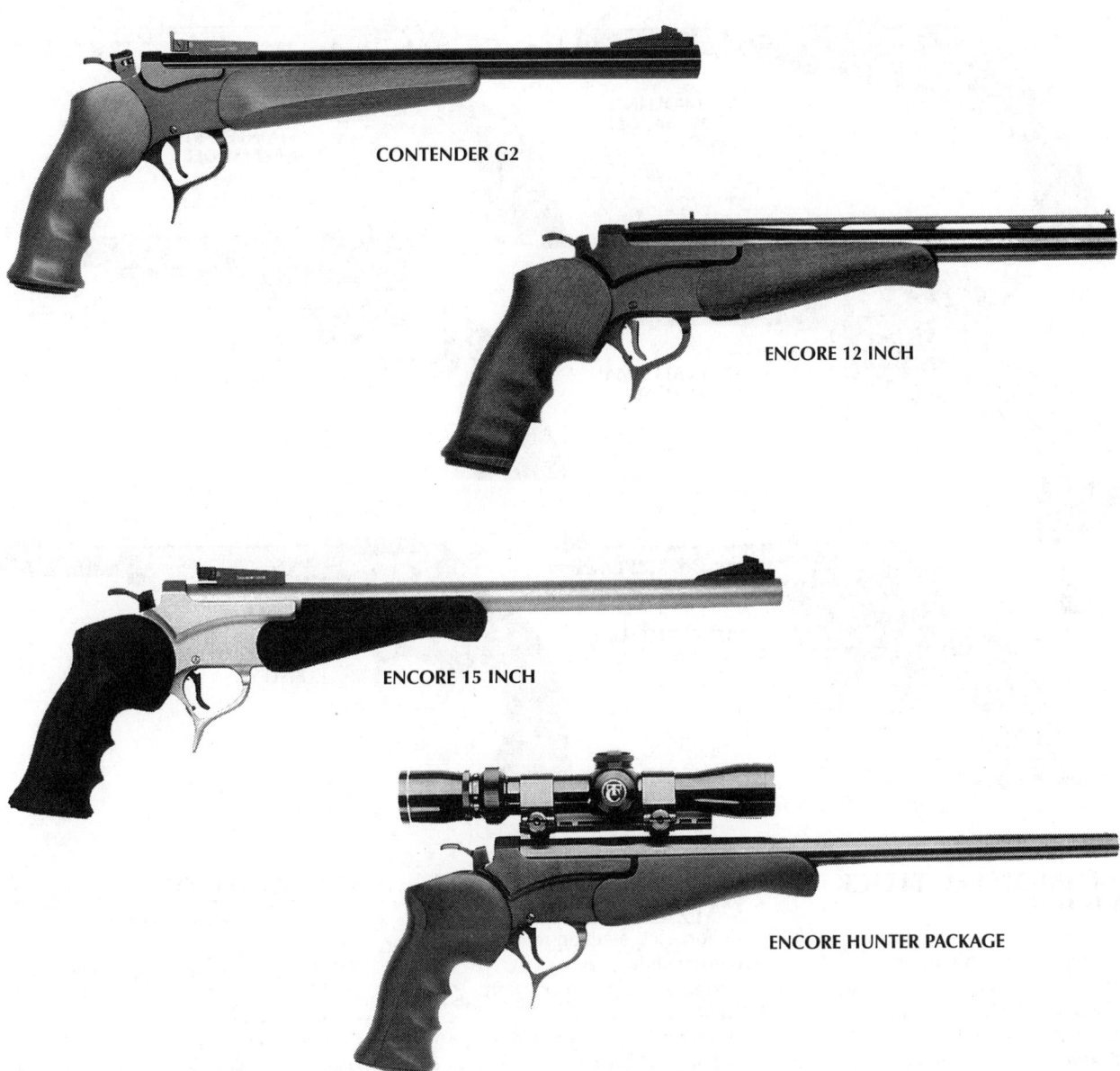

CONTENDER G2

ENCORE 12 INCH

ENCORE 15 INCH

ENCORE HUNTER PACKAGE

CONTENDER G2
Action: hinged breech
Grips: walnut
Barrel: 12 or 14 in.
Sights: target
Weight: 60.0 oz.
Caliber: .22 LR, .22 Hornet, .357
Mag., .17 MACH 2, 6.8 Rem SPC, .44
Mag., .45/.410 (12 in.), .17 HMR, .22
LR, .22 Hornet, .223, 7-30, .30-30, .44
Mag., .45/.410, .45-70 (15 in.), .204
Ruger, .375 JDJ

Capacity: 1 round
Features: improved, stronger version of
Contender
12 in.: **$562-591**
14 in. (64 oz.): **$569-605**

ENCORE
Action: hinged breech
Grips: walnut or rubber
Barrel: 12 or 15 in.
Sights: target
Weight: 68.0 oz.

Caliber: many popular rifle and big-
bore pistol rounds, from the .22
Hornet to the .30-06 and .45-70, the
.454 Casull and .480 Ruger
Capacity: 1 round
Features: also in package with 2-7x
scope, carry case; prices vary with
caliber, options
12 in.: **$583**
15 in. (72 oz.): **$591**
.45/.410 with rib: **$620**
Stainless with rubber grips: . . . **$673**

Uberti Handguns

1871 ROLLING BLOCK TARGET PISTOL

1873 CATTLEMAN STAINLESS STEEL NEW MODEL

1873 CATTLEMAN BIRD'S HEAD

1873 STALLION

1873 CATTLEMAN

1873 CATTLEMAN BISLEY

1871 ROLLING BLOCK PISTOL

Action: rolling block   **Grips**: walnut
Barrel: 9.5 in.   **Sights**: target
Weight: 45.0 oz.
Caliber: .22 LR, .22 Mag.
Capacity: 1 round
Features: case-colored breech; brass guard
MSRP: $425

1873 CATTLEMAN BIRD'S HEAD

Action: single-action revolver
Grips: walnut
Barrel: 3.5, 4, 4.5 or 5.5 in.
Sights: fixed open   **Weight**: 36.96 oz.
Caliber: .357 Mag., .44/40, .45 LC
Capacity: 6 rounds
Features: fluted cylinder; round tapered barrel; forged steel; color case-hardened frame; curved grip frame and grip; Flattop available with adjustable sights
MSRP: $450

1873 SINGLE-ACTION CATTLEMAN

Action: single-action revolver
Grips: walnut
Barrel: 4.8, 5.5, 7.5 or 18 in.
Sights: fixed open
Weight: 37.0 oz. (5.5 in.)
Caliber: .357 Mag., .44-40, .45 Colt
Capacity: 6 rounds
Features: case colored frame; Old Model/New Model available; target sights available on some models; Birds Head or Bisley grips available

1873:	$410
Nickel finish:	$490
Old West antique finish:	$490
Matte black millennium:	$270
Charcoal blue:	$465
Stainless New Model:	$495
Buntline:	$480

1873 STALLION

Action: single-action revolver
Grips: walnut
Barrel: 5.5 in.   **Sights**: open fixed
Weight: 22.24 oz.
Caliber: .22 LR, .38 SP
Capacity: 6 rounds
Features: color case-hardened steel frame; fluted cylinder
MSRP: $390

BISLEY

Action: single-action revolver
Grips: walnut
Barrel: 4.754, 5.5, 7.5 in.
Sights: adjustable
Weight: 40.16 oz. lbs.
Caliber: .357 Mag., .44/40, .45 LC
Capacity: 6 rounds
Features: Bisley style grip; color case-hardened frame; fluted cylinder

Bisley:	$450
Bisley Flattop:	$455

Uberti Handguns

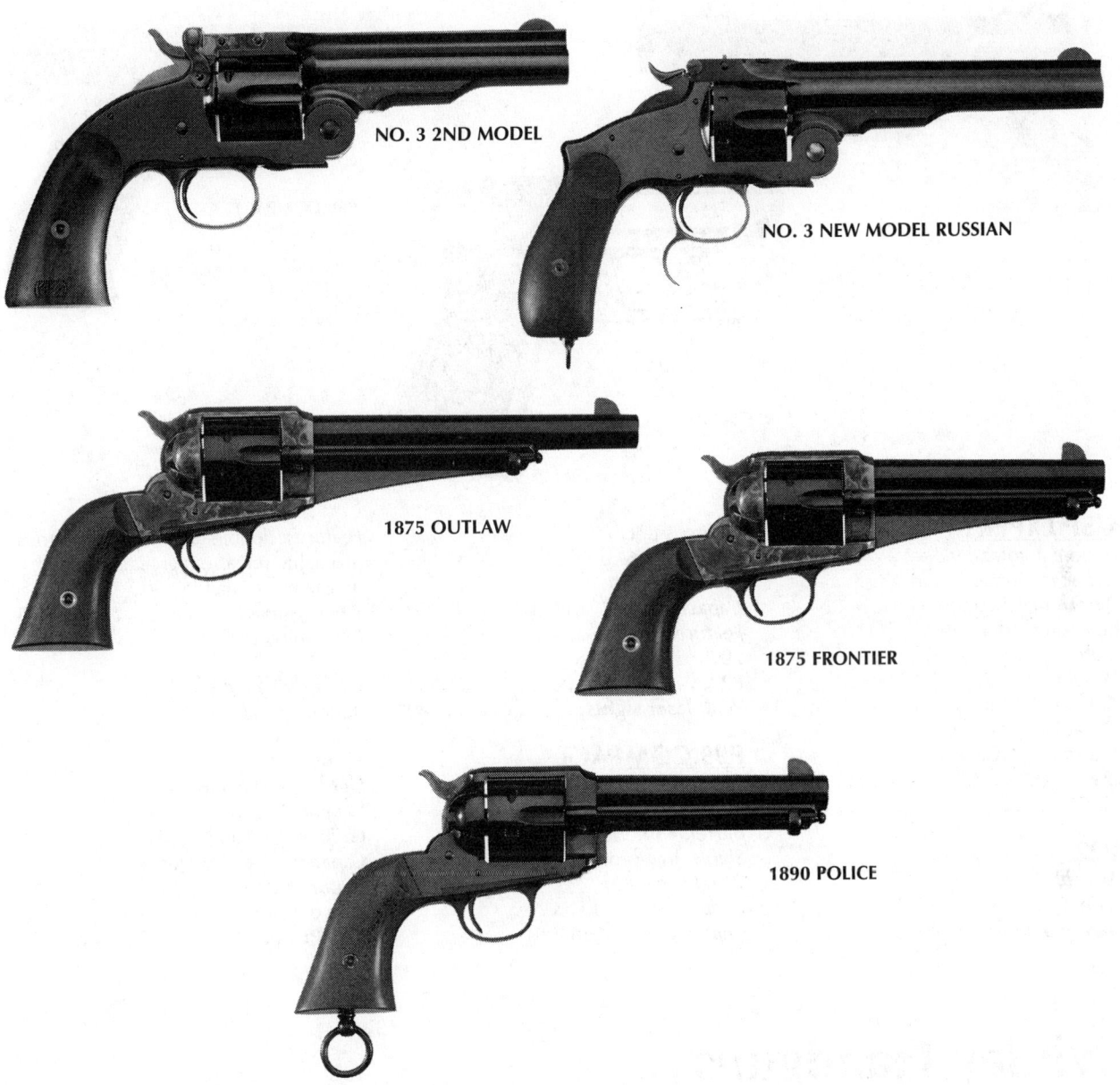

NO. 3 2ND MODEL

NO. 3 NEW MODEL RUSSIAN

1875 OUTLAW

1875 FRONTIER

1890 POLICE

TOP BREAK REVOLVERS
Action: single-action revolver
Grips: walnut
Barrel: 3.5, 5, 6.5, 7 in.
Sights: open, fixed
Weight: 36 oz. (39.5 oz. Russian)
Caliber: .44 Russian, .44/40, .45 Colt,
Capacity: 6 rounds
Features: top break action; fluted cylinder; blued finish
No. 3 2nd Model: **$775**
No 3. New Model Russian: . . . **$825**

1875 OUTLAW & FRONTIER
Action: single-action revolver
Grips: walnut
Barrel: 7.5 in. (5.5 Frontier)
Sights: open, fixed
Weight: 44.8 oz. (40 oz. Frontier)
Caliber: .45 Colt
Capacity: 6 rounds
Features: case-hardened frame with blued barrel; fluted cylinder
Outlaw: **$415**
Frontier: **$415**

1890 POLICE REVOLVER
Action: single-action revolver
Grips: walnut
Barrel: 5.5 in.
Sights: open, fixed
Weight: 41.6 oz.
Caliber: .357 Mag., .45 Colt,
Capacity: 6 rounds
Features: fluted cylinder; blued finish
MSRP: **$440**

Walther Handguns

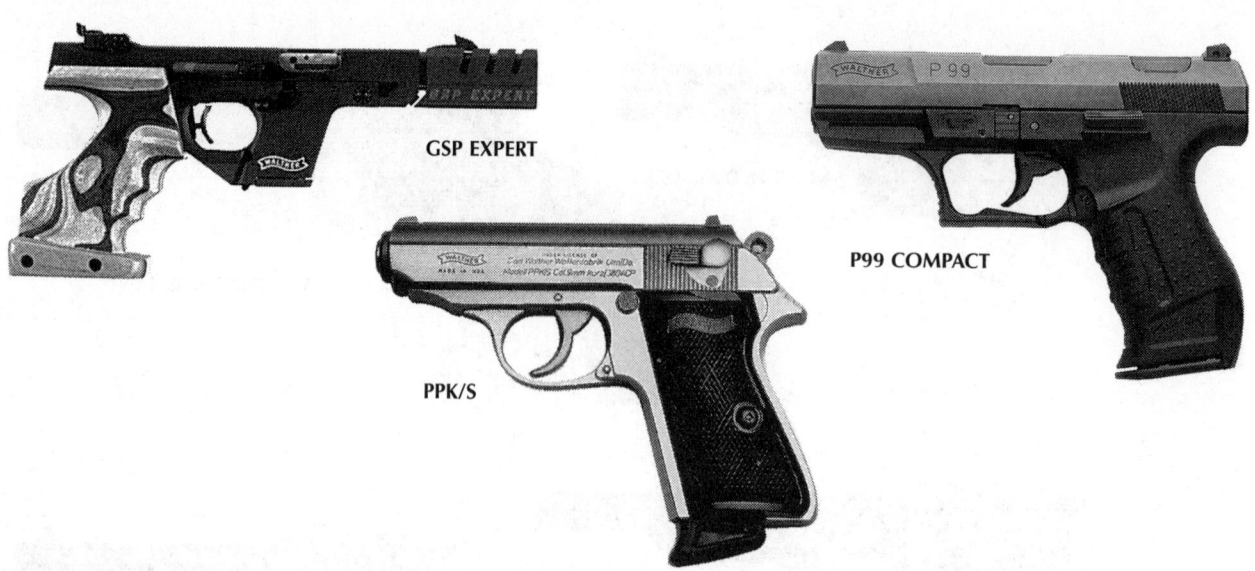

GSP EXPERT

PPK/S

P99 COMPACT

GSP EXPERT
Action: autoloader
Grips: laminated wood
Barrel: match-grade
compensated 4.2 in.
Sights: target
Weight: 29.0 oz.
Caliber: .22 LR, .32 S&W
Capacity: 5 rounds
Features: forward magazine
.22: **$1240**
.32: **$1420**

P22
Action: autoloader
Grips: polymer
Barrel: 3.4 or 5 in.

Sights: 3 dot
Weight: 19.6 oz.
Caliber: .22 LR
Capacity: 10 + 1 rounds
Features: double-action;
20.3 oz. 5 in. barrel
P22: **$295-415**
With laser sights: **$405**

P99 COMPACT
Action: autoloader
Grips: polymer
Barrel: 4 in.
Sights: low-profile combat
Weight: 25.0 oz.
Caliber: 9mm, .40 S&W
Capacity: 10 + 1 rounds

Features: double-action; ambidextrous
magazine release; high-capacity
magazines available
P99 Compact: **$665**
P99 Military: **$665**

PPK AND PPK/S
Action: autoloader
Grips: polymer
Barrel: 3.4 in.
Sights: fixed open
Weight: 22.0 oz.
Caliber: .380 and .32 ACP
Capacity: 7 + 1 rounds
Features: double-action;
blue or stainless; decocker
MSRP: **$543**

Wildey Handguns

WILDEY
AUTOMATIC PISTOL
Action: autoloader
Grips: composite
Barrel: 5, 6, 7, 8, 10, 12 or 14 in.
Sights: target
Weight: 64.0 oz.
Caliber: .45 Win. Mag.,
.44 Auto Mag, .45 and .475 Wildey
Capacity: 7 + 1 rounds
Features: gas operated; ribbed barrel
Starting at: **$1525**
Silhouette (18 in. barrel): **$2696**

Austin & Halleck Black Powder

MODEL 320 REALTREE-HARDWOODS CAMO

MODEL 420 LR CLASSIC

MODEL 420 LR MONTE CARLO

MOUNTAIN RIFLE

BOLT ACTION
MODEL 320 LR & 420 LR
Lock: in-line
Stock: curly maple, synthetic, camo
Barrel: 26 in., 1:28 twist
Sights: adjustable open
Weight: 7.8 lbs.
Bore/Caliber: .50
Features: in-line percussion w/removable weather shroud; receiver and barrel-blue or nickel-plated finishes; match trigger; drilled and tapped for

Leupold or A & H SB-N or SB-B scope bases; 47.5 in. length

Synthetic:	$419
Stainless synthetic:	$449
Camo:	$459
Stainless camo:	$489
Curly maple:	$549
Stainless maple:.	$579
Hand select maple:	$739
Monte Carlo fancy:	$549

MOUNTAIN RIFLE
Lock: traditional cap or flint
Stock: curly maple
Barrel: 32 in., 1:66 or 1:28 twist
Sights: fixed
Weight: 7.5 lbs.
Bore/Caliber: .50
Features: double set triggers

Percussion:	$539
Select percussion:.	$719
Flint:	$589
Select flint:	$769

Cabela's Black Powder

BLUE RIDGE FLINTLOCK RIFLE

TRADITIONAL HAWKEN RIFLE

KODIAK EXPRESS DOUBLE RIFLE

BLUE RIDGE FLINTLOCK RIFLE
Lock: side-hammer caplock
Stock: walnut
Barrel: 39 in., 1:48 twist
Sights: none
Weight: 7.75 lbs.
(7.25 lbs. .45, .50, .54 cal.)
Bore/Caliber: .32, .36, .45,
.50 and .54
Features: double set triggers;
case-colored locks
Flint: **$519**

DOUBLE SHOTGUN
Lock: traditional caplock
Stock: walnut
Barrel: 27, 28 or 30 in.
Sights: none
Weight: 7.0 lbs. (6.5 20 ga.)

Bore/Caliber: 20, 12 or 10 ga.
Features: screw-in choke tubes: X-Full,
Mod, IC; double triggers; weight to 10
lbs. depending on gauge
MSRP: **$659-800**

HAWKEN
Lock: traditional cap or flint
Stock: walnut
Barrel: 29 in., 1:48 twist
Sights: adjustable open
Weight: 9.0 lbs.
Bore/Caliber: .50 or .54
Features: brass furniture;
double-set trigger
**Traditional percussion
(right or left-hand):** **$300**
**Sporterized percussion
(28-in. bl.):** **$370**

KODIAK EXPRESS DOUBLE RIFLE
Lock: traditional caplock
Stock: walnut, pistol grip
Barrel: 28 in., 1:48 twist
Sights: folding leaf
Weight: 9.3 lbs.
Bore/Caliber: .50, .54, .58 and .72
Features: double triggers
MSRP from: **$900**

*Pyrodex has a relatively short shelf life and will loose
potency over time. Once the factory seal on a can has
been opened, the propellant should be used within three to
four months.*

Colt Black Powder

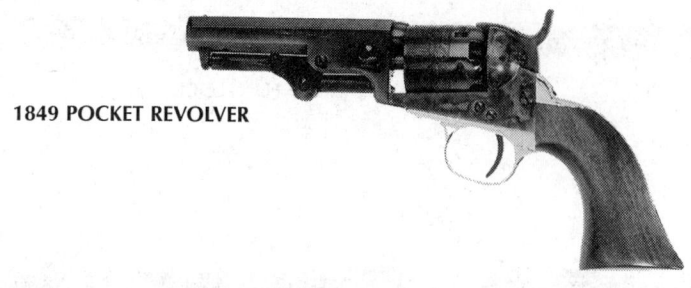

1849 POCKET REVOLVER

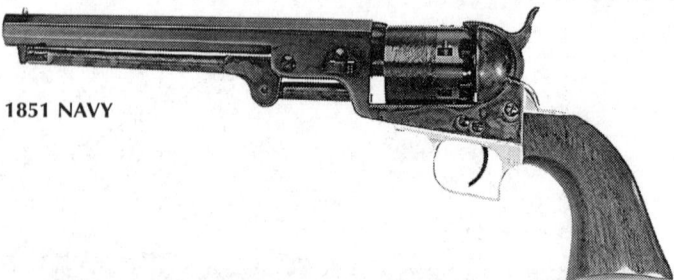

1851 NAVY

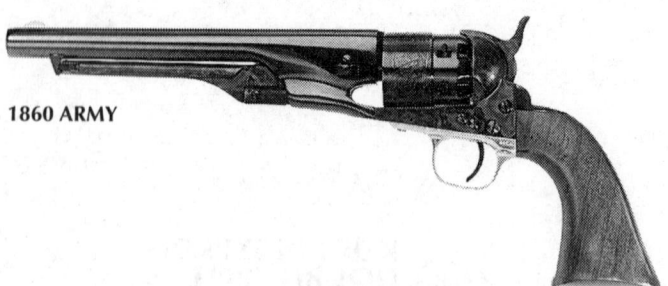

1860 ARMY

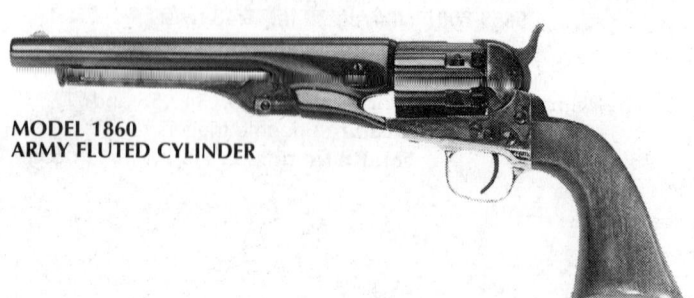

MODEL 1860
ARMY FLUTED CYLINDER

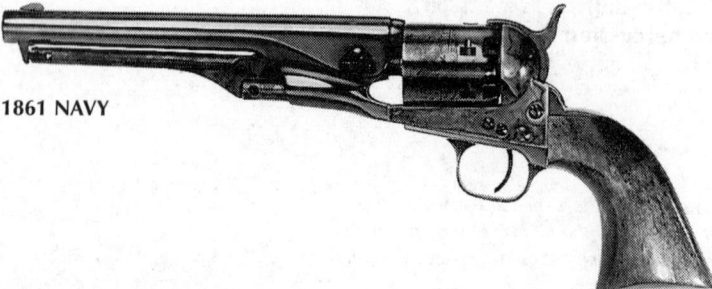

1861 NAVY

1849 POCKET REVOLVER
Lock: caplock revolver
Grips: walnut
Barrel: 4 in.
Sights: fixed
Weight: 1.5 lbs.
Bore/Caliber: .31
Features: case-colored frame
MSRP: **$675**

1851 NAVY
Lock: caplock revolver
Grips: walnut
Barrel: 7.5 in.
Sights: fixed
Weight: 2.5 lbs.
Bore/Caliber: .36
Features: case-colored frame
MSRP: **$695**

1860 ARMY
Lock: caplock revolver
Grips: walnut
Barrel: 8 in.
Sights: fixed
Weight: 2.6 lbs.
Bore/Caliber: .44
Features: case-colored frame, hammer, plunger; also with fluted cylinder and adapted for shoulder stock
MSRP: **$695**

1861 NAVY
Lock: caplock revolver
Grips: walnut
Barrel: 7.5 in.
Sights: fixed
Weight: 2.6 lbs.
Bore/Caliber: .36
Features: revolver with case-colored frame, hammer, lever, plunger
MSRP: **$695**

THIRD MODEL DRAGOON

Lock: caplock revolver
Grips: walnut
Barrel: 7.5 in.
Sights: fixed
Weight: 4.1 lbs.
Bore/Caliber: .44
Features: case-colored frame, hammer, lever, plunger
MSRP: **$750**

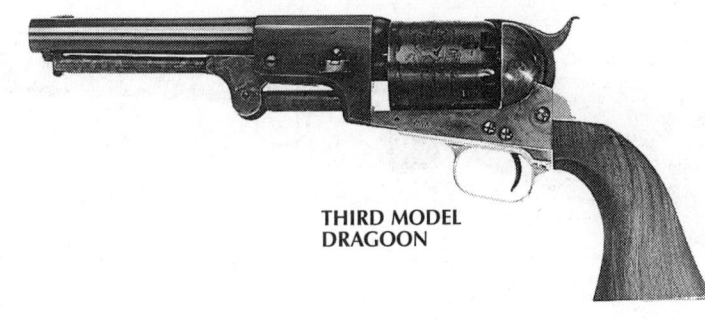

THIRD MODEL DRAGOON

TRAPPER 1862 POCKET POLICE

Lock: caplock revolver
Grips: walnut
Barrel: 3.5 in.
Sights: fixed
Weight: 1.25 lbs.
Bore/Caliber: .36
Features: revolver with case-colored frame; separate brass ramrod
MSRP: **$675**

TRAPPER 1862 POCKET POLICE

WALKER

Lock: caplock revolver
Grips: walnut
Barrel: 9 in.
Sights: fixed
Weight: 4.6 lbs.
Bore/Caliber: .44
Features: case-colored frame; authentic remake of 1847 Walker
MSRP: **$750**

COLT 1861 RIFLE

Lock: traditional caplock
Stock: walnut
Barrel: 40 in.
Sights: folding leaf
Weight: 9.2 lbs.
Bore/Caliber: .58
Features: authentic reproduction of 1861 Springfield
MSRP: **$1000**

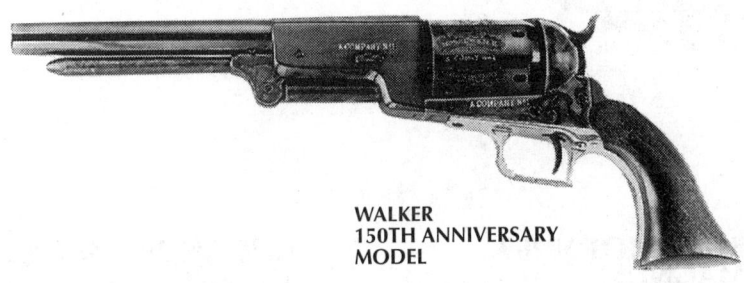

WALKER 150TH ANNIVERSARY MODEL

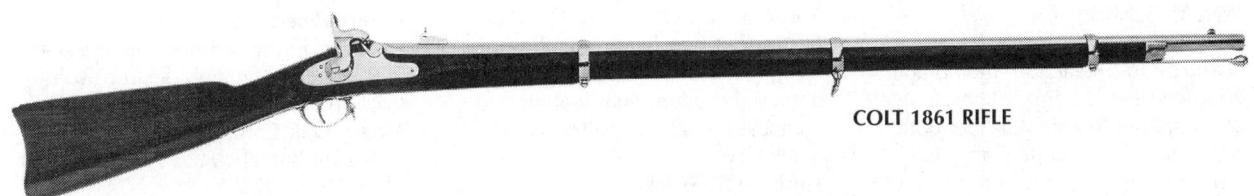

COLT 1861 RIFLE

CVA Black Powder

BUCK HORN 209 MAGNUM

ELKHORN 209 MAGNUM

KODIAK 209 MAGNUM

BUCK HORN 209 MAGNUM

Lock: in-line
Stock: synthetic
Barrel: 24 in., 1:28 twist
Sights: fiber optic
Weight: 6.3 lbs.
Bore/Caliber: .50
Features: in-line action; thumb-actuated safety; blued barrel; stainless steel 209 ignition; Illuminator fiber optic sights; solid composite stock with molded-in grip panels and sling swivel studs; drilled and tapped for scope mounts.
MSRP: **$145**

ELKHORN 209 MAGNUM

Lock: in-line, bolt-action
Stock: synthetic or camo
Barrel: 26 in. fluted,1:28 twist
Sights: adjustable fiber optic
Weight: 7.0 lbs.
Bore/Caliber: .45 or .50
Features: 3-way ignition with primer ejecting bolt face; DuraBright fiber optic sights; aluminum loading rod; composite stock in Realtree Camo or Black Fleck
Timber HD Stock/
    Blued Barrel: **$285**
Black Fleck Stock/
    Blued Barrel: **$225**

KODIAK 209 MAGNUM

Lock: in-line
Stock: synthetic
Barrel: 28 in.
Sights: fiber optic
Weight: 7.5 lbs.
Bore/Caliber: .50
Features: in-line action; stainless steel 209 breech plug; ambidextrous solid stock in black or Mossy Oak Camo
Mossy Oak Camo/
    Nickel Barrel:. **$300**
Black FiberGrip/
    Nickel Barrel:. **$255**
Black FiberGrip/
    Blue Barrel: **$225**

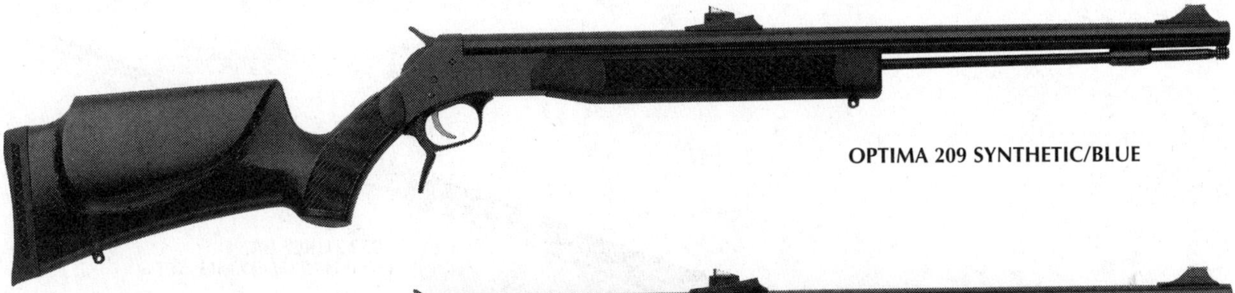

OPTIMA 209 SYNTHETIC/BLUE

OPTIMA 209 CAMO/BLUE

OPTIMA 209 CAMO/NICKEL

OPTIMA ELITE

OPTIMA 209 AND OPTIMA PRO 209

Lock: in-line
Stock: synthetic or camo
Barrel: 26 in. (29 in. on Pro), 1:28 twist
Sights: adjustable fiber optic
Weight: 8.2 lbs.
Bore/Caliber: .45 or .50
Features: stainless steel 209 breech plug, ambidextrous stock; add $75 for Pro (8.8 lbs.)

Optima, synthetic/blue: $235
camo/blue: $290
camo/nickel: $310
**Optima Pro w/camo
stock & bbl.:** $400

OPTIMA ELITE COMPACT 209 MAGNUM

Lock: in-line, break-action
Stock: synthetic or camo
Barrel: 24 in., 1:28 twist
Sights: adjustable fiber optic

Weight: 6.0 lbs.
Bore/Caliber: .45 or .50
Features: in-line break-action; available with Bergara muzzleloading barrel; ambidextrous solid composite stock; adjustable fiber optic sights; drilled and tapped for scope mounts
MSRP: $335

 Always be certain that your projectile is seated firmly against the powder charge. An air space between the projectile and powder charge can cause serious damage to the firearm and injury to the shooter.

Dixie Black Powder

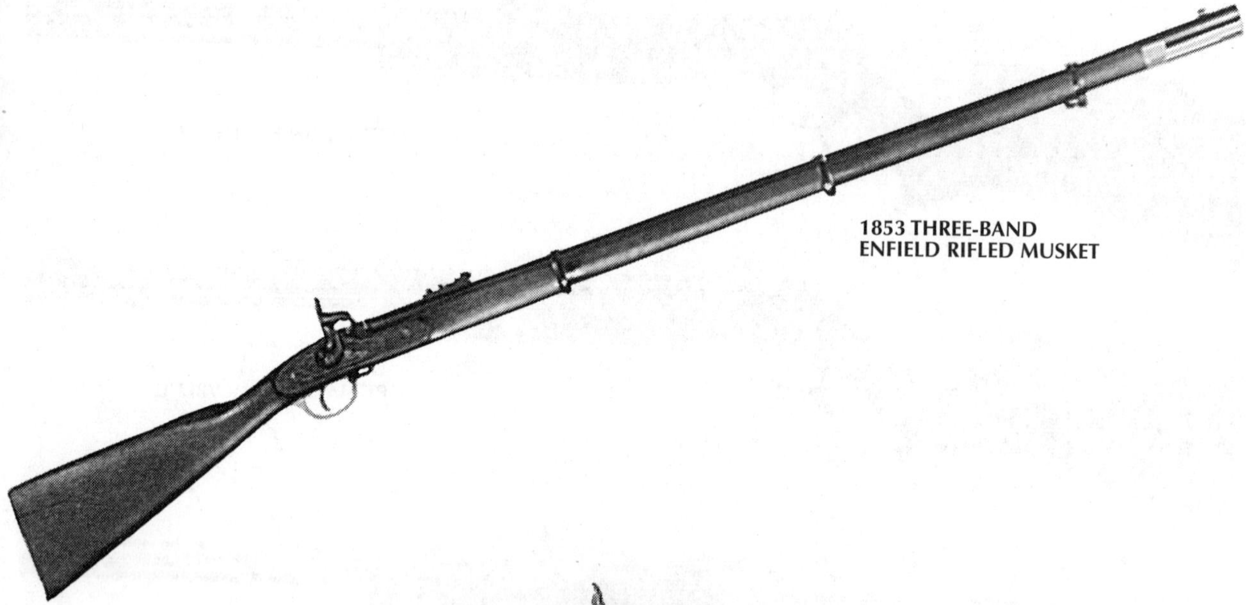

**1853 THREE-BAND
ENFIELD RIFLED MUSKET**

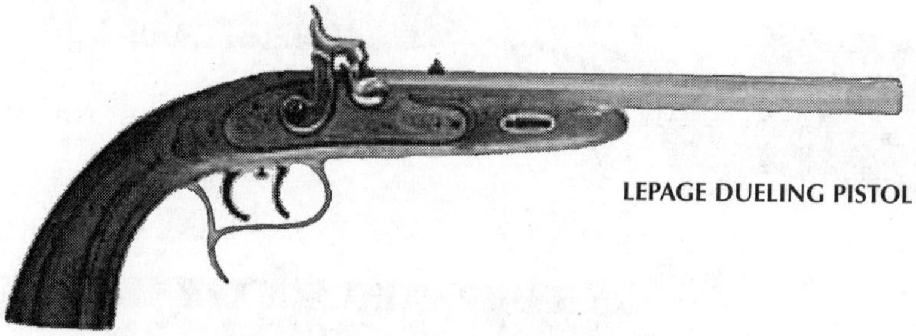

LEPAGE DUELING PISTOL

1853 THREE-BAND ENFIELD
Lock: traditional caplock
Stock: walnut
Barrel: 39 in.
Sights: fixed
Weight: 10.5 lbs.
Bore/Caliber: .58
Features: case-colored lock, brass furniture; also 1858 two-band Enfield with 33 in. barrel
Three-band: **$595**
Unfinished kit: **$595**
Two-band: **$600**

LEPAGE DUELING PISTOL
Lock: traditional caplock
Grips: hardwood
Barrel: 9 in.
Sights: fixed
Weight: 2.5 lbs.
Bore/Caliber: .45
Features: double set trigger
MSRP: **$470**

Black Powder Grades:
*Fg: coarse and slow burning—suitable for
           large smooth-bore caliber muskets*
*FFg: rifle powder—for use in
           .45-to.54-caliber inline or traditional rifles*
*FFFg: pistol and revolver powder—suitable for
           smaller bore rifles (.32-.40 caliber)*
FFFFg: priming powder for flintlocks

Dixie Black Powder

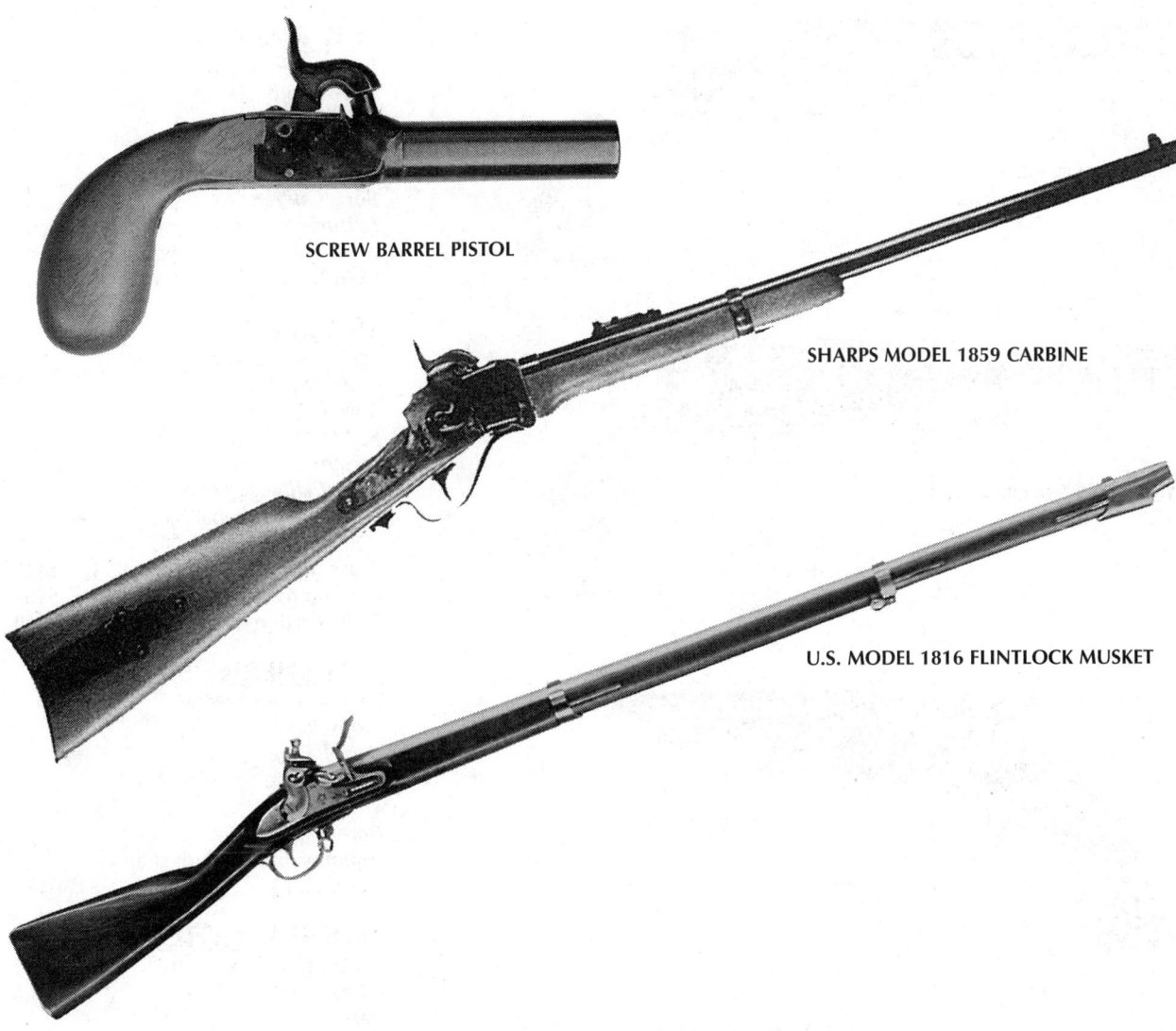

SCREW BARREL PISTOL

SHARPS MODEL 1859 CARBINE

U.S. MODEL 1816 FLINTLOCK MUSKET

SCREW BARREL PISTOL
Lock: traditional caplock
Grips: hardwood
Barrel: 3 in.
Sights: none
Weight: 0.75 lbs.
Bore/Caliber: .445
Features: barrel detaches for loading; folding trigger
MSRP: **$168**

NEW MODEL 1859 MILITARY SHARPS CARBINE
Lock: dropping block
Stock: walnut
Barrel: 22 in.
Sights: adjustable open
Weight: 7.8 lbs.
Bore/Caliber: .54
Features: case-colored furniture, including saddle ring; also 1859 military rifle with 30 in. barrel (9 lbs.); both by Pedersoli
Sharps Carbine: **$875**
with 30 in. barrel: **$995**

MODEL U.S. 1816 FLINTLOCK MUSKET
Lock: traditional flintlock
Stock: walnut
Barrel: 42 in. smoothbore
Sights: fixed
Weight: 9.8 lbs.
Bore/Caliber: .69
Features: most common military flintlock from U.S. armories, complete with bayonet lug and swivels
MSRP: **$1025**

EMF Hartford Black Powder

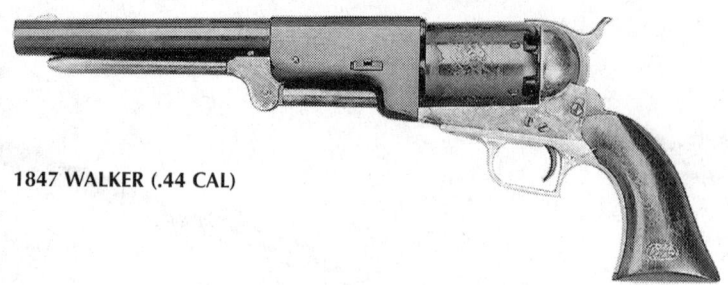

1847 WALKER (.44 CAL)

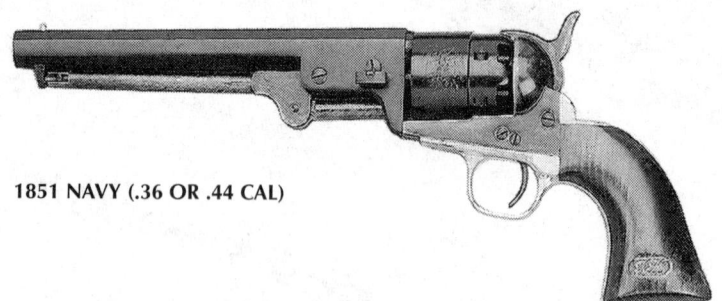

1851 NAVY (.36 OR .44 CAL)

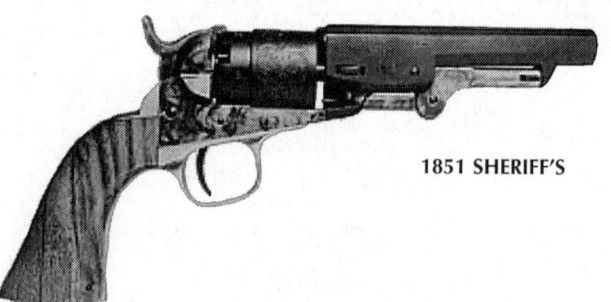

1851 SHERIFF'S

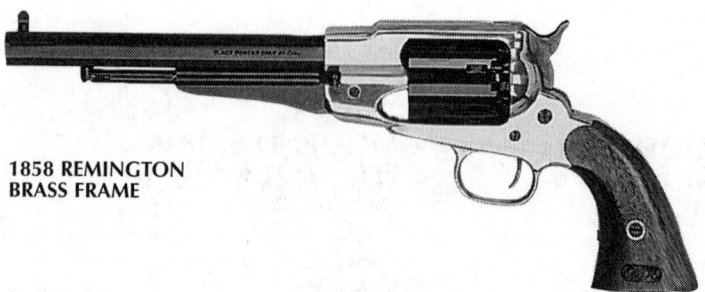

1858 REMINGTON
BRASS FRAME

1847 WALKER
Lock: caplock revolver
Grips: walnut
Barrel: 9 in.
Sights: fixed
Weight: 4.6 lbs.
Bore/Caliber: .44
Features: largest commercial Colt single-action; named after Texas Ranger
MSRP: **$320**

1851 NAVY
Lock: caplock revolver
Grips: walnut
Barrel: 7.5 in.
Sights: fixed
Weight: 2.5 lbs.
Bore/Caliber: .36 or .44
Features: octagonal barrel; brass or steel frame
Brass frame:. **$149**
London Model: **$169**
Case-hardened steel frame: . . **$180**

1851 SHERIFF'S
Lock: caplock revolver
Grips: walnut
Barrel: 5 in.
Sights: none
Weight: 2.4 lbs.
Bore/Caliber: .44
Features: brass guard; strap
MSRP: **$154-174**

1858 REMINGTON
Lock: caplock revolver
Grips: walnut
Barrel: 8 in.
Sights: fixed
Weight: 2.5 lbs.
Bore/Caliber: .44
Features: brass or stainless steel frame
Brass frame:. **$169**
Blued steel frame: **$209**
Stainless frame: **$309**

EMF Hartford Black Powder

1860 ARMY REVOLVER

Lock: caplock revolver
Stock: walnut
Barrel: 8 in.
Sights: fixed
Weight: 2.6 lbs.
Bore/Caliber: .44
Features: case-colored frame; brass guard; strap
MSRP: . . . . **$264-$209**

1863 SHARPS MILITARY CARBINE

Lock: dropping block
Stock: walnut
Barrel: 22 in.
Sights: adjustable open
Weight: 7.5 lbs.
Bore/Caliber: .54
Features: blued barrel; case-hardened frame; adjustable rear sight
MSRP: **$800**

HARTFORD MODEL 1862 POLICE REVOLVER

Lock: caplock revolver
Grips: walnut
Barrel: 5.5 in.
Sights: fixed
Weight: 2.1 lbs.
Bore/Caliber: .36
Features: 5-shot cylinder
MSRP: **$240**

SHARPS SPORTING RIFLE

Lock: dropping block
Stock: walnut
Barrel: 28 in.
Sights: adjustable open
Weight: 8.6 lbs.
Bore/Caliber: .54
Features: blued octagon barrel; adjustable rear sight
MSRP: **$870**

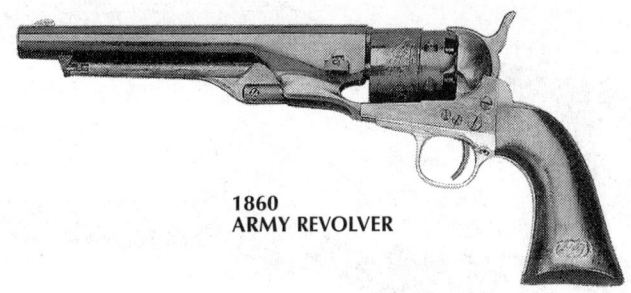

1860
ARMY REVOLVER

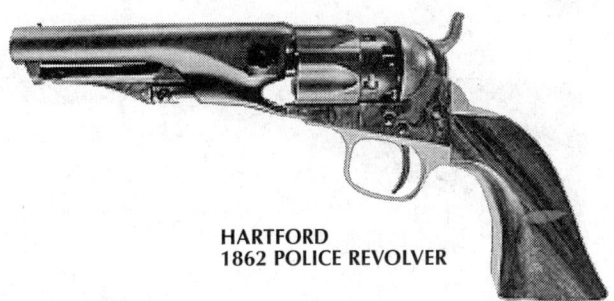

HARTFORD
1862 POLICE REVOLVER

When shooting saboted bullets in your muzzleloader, occasionally examine the expended plastic sabots for signs of tearing or rupture. A blown sabot can indicate that the plastic is not withstanding the pressure of the charge, a situation that results in diminished accuracy.

Euroarms of America Black Powder

1803 HARPER'S FERRY FLINTLOCK RIFLE

1841 MISSISSIPPI RIFLE

COOK & BROTHER
CONFEDERATE CARBINE

C.S. RICHMOND MUSKET

J.P. MURRAY CARBINE

1803 HARPER'S FERRY FLINTLOCK
Lock: traditional flintlock
Stock: walnut
Barrel: 35 in.
Sights: fixed
Weight: 10.0 lbs.
Bore/Caliber: .54
Features: half-stock, browned steel
MSRP: $735

1841 MISSISSIPPI RIFLE
Lock: traditional caplock
Stock: walnut
Barrel: 33 in.
Sights: fixed
Weight: 9.5 lbs.
Bore/Caliber: .54 or .58
Features: brass furniture
MSRP: $575

COOK & BROTHER CONFEDERATE CARBINE
Lock: traditional caplock
Stock: walnut
Barrel: 24 in.
Sights: fixed
Weight: 7.9 lbs.
Bore/Caliber: .577
Features: carbine; also rifle with 33 in. barrel
Carbine: $513
Rifle: $552

C.S. RICHMOND MUSKET
Lock: traditional caplock
Stock: walnut
Barrel: 40 in.
Sights: fixed
Weight: 9.0 lbs.
Bore/Caliber: .58
Features: 3-band furniture; swivels
MSRP: $579

J.P. MURRAY CARBINE
Lock: traditional caplock
Stock: walnut
Barrel: 23 in.
Sights: fixed
Weight: 7.5 lbs.
Bore/Caliber: .58
Features: brass furniture; replica of rare Confederate Cavalry Carbine
MSRP: $521

Euroarms of America Black Powder

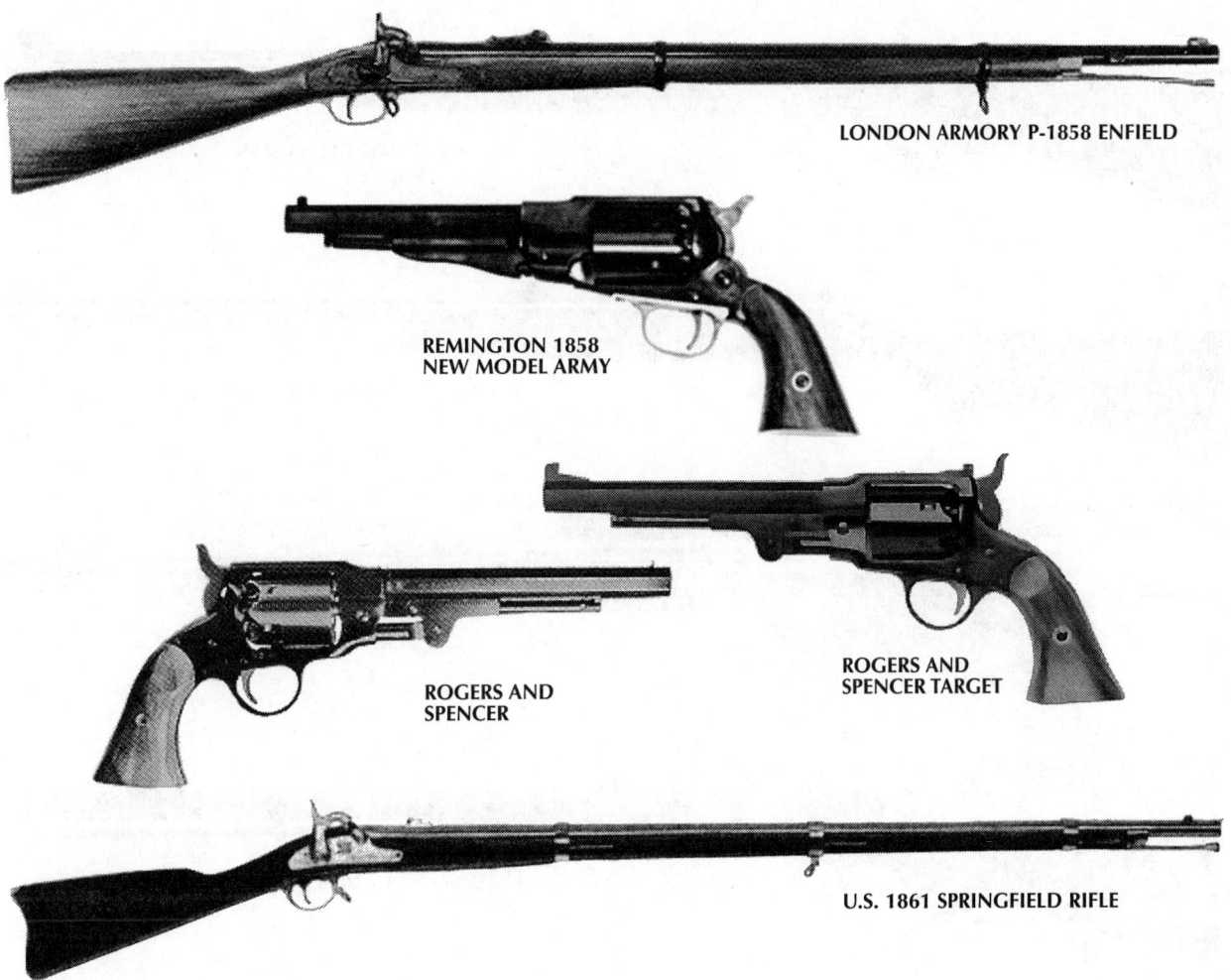

LONDON ARMORY P-1858 ENFIELD

REMINGTON 1858
NEW MODEL ARMY

ROGERS AND
SPENCER

ROGERS AND
SPENCER TARGET

U.S. 1861 SPRINGFIELD RIFLE

LONDON ARMORY P-1858 ENFIELD
Lock: traditional caplock
Stock: walnut
Barrel: 33 in.
Sights: adjustable open
Weight: 8.8 lbs.
Bore/Caliber: .58
Features: steel ramrod; 2-band
1861 London Enfield: **$475**
P-1858 Enfield: **$513**
1853 rifled musket: **$528**

REMINGTON 1858 NEW MODEL ARMY
Lock: caplock revolver
Grips: walnut
Barrel: 8 in.
Sights: fixed
Weight: 2.5 lbs.
Bore/Caliber: .44
Features: brass guard; engraved version

New Model Army: **$220**
  Engraved: **$302**

ROGERS AND SPENCER
Lock: caplock revolver
Grips: walnut
Barrel: 7.5 in.
Sights: fixed
Weight: 2.9 lbs.
Bore/Caliber: .44
Features: recommended ball diameter .451; also target model with adjustable sight
Rogers and Spencer: **$260**
  London gray finish: **$283**
Target: **$275**

U.S. 1841 MISSISSIPPI RIFLE
Lock: traditional caplock
Stock: walnut
Barrel: 33 in.

Sights: fixed
Weight: 9.5 lbs.
Bore/Caliber: .54 or .58
Features: brass furniture; also 1863 Remington Zouave rifle
Zouave: **$469**
Mississippi: **$575**

U.S. 1861 SPRINGFIELD
Lock: traditional caplock
Stock: walnut
Barrel: 40 in.
Sights: fixed
Weight: 10.0 lbs.
Bore/Caliber: .58
Features: sling swivels; also London P-1852 rifled musket; London Enfield P-1861 (7.5 lbs.)
MSRP: **$579**

Gonic Arms Black Powder

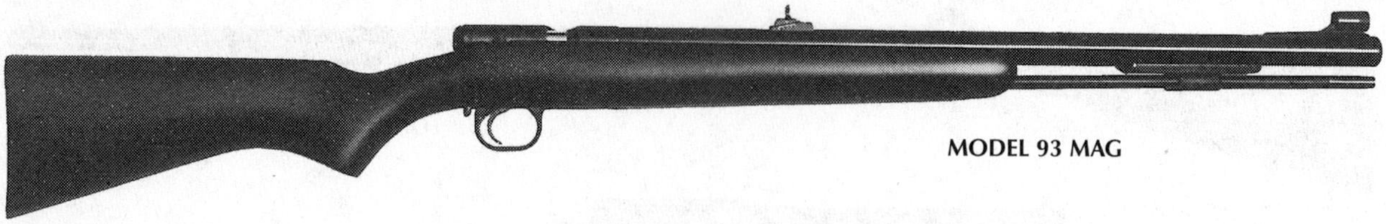

MODEL 93 MAG

MODEL 93 STANDARD

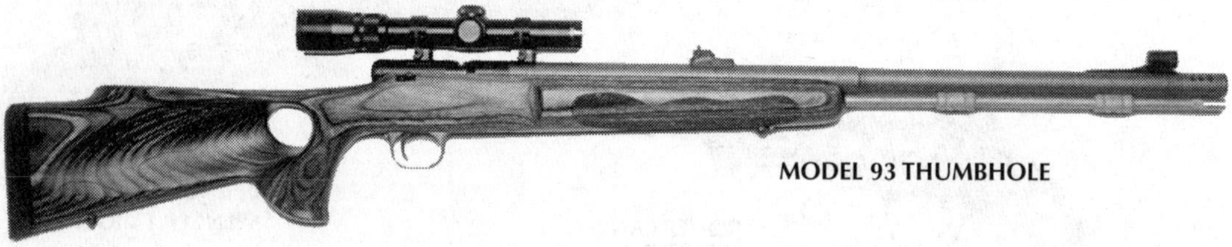

MODEL 93 THUMBHOLE

TK 2000 SHOTGUN

MODEL 93

Lock: in-line
Stock: laminated or synthetic, pillar bedded
Barrel: 26 in. stainless, 1:24 twist
Sights: adjustable open
Weight: 7.0 lbs.
Bore/Caliber: .50
Features: various stock configurations, including thumbhole; scope mounting provisions
MSRP: $999

MODEL TK 2000 SHOTGUN

Lock: in-line
Stock: synthetic or camo
Barrel: 26 in.
Sights: fiber optic
Weight: 7.6 lbs.
Bore/Caliber: 12 ga.
Features: adjustable trigger, screw-in choke tubes; uses 209 primers
Synthetic: $350
Camo: $400

All flints are not created equal. Many rifle flints available on the market are poorly knapped (the term for flint shaping) or made of inferior material. Look for careful craftsmanship and always test flints in your lock for a strong spark before you go into the field.

Knight Black Powder

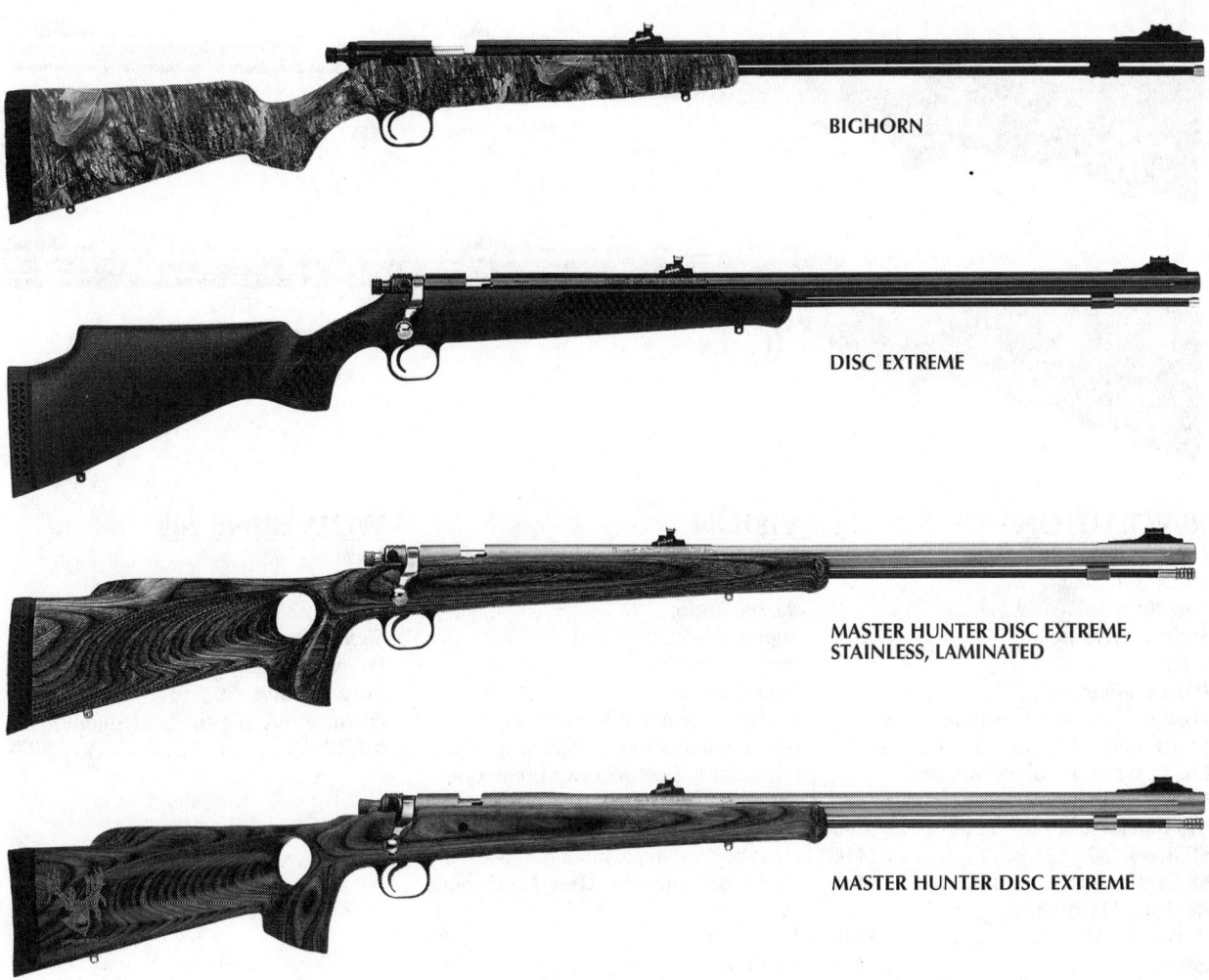

BIGHORN

DISC EXTREME

MASTER HUNTER DISC EXTREME,
STAINLESS, LAMINATED

MASTER HUNTER DISC EXTREME

BIGHORN

Lock: in-line
Stock: synthetic
Barrel: 26 in.
Sights: fiber optic or adjustable open
Weight: 7.6 lbs.
Bore/Caliber: .50
Features: 3 ignition systems: #11 nipple, musket nipple and the 209 Extreme shotgun primer system; full set of non-fiber optic sights

MS Black:	**$314**
Lefthand MS:	**$315**
SS Black:	**$356**
Lefthand SS:	**$356**
MS MO Breakup:	**$357**
SS Black Thumbhole:	**$388**
Realtree hardwoods HD:	**$400**
Phantom Thumbhole:	**$409**

DISC EXTREME

Lock: in-line
Stock: synthetic or laminated
Barrel: 26 in.
Sights: fiber optic
Weight: 7.8 lbs.
Bore/Caliber: .45, .50, .52
Features: Green Mountain action and barrel; full plastic jacket ignition system; quick-release bolt system

Blued Black:	**$503**
MS Black.45 cal.:	**$579**
Realtree Hardwood Green HD:	**$629**
.52 cal.:	**$650**
SS Black.50 cal.:	**$577**
SS Thumbhole:	**$608**
.45 cal.:	**$698**
Target:	**$699**

MASTER HUNTER DISC EXTREME

Lock: in-line
Stock: synthetic
Barrel: 26 in.
Sights: fiber optic
Weight: 7.8 lbs.
Bore/Caliber: .45, .50, .52
Features: Green Mountain action and cryogenically accurized barrel; full plastic jacket ignition system; quick-release bolt system

SS Thumbhole:	**$698**
SS Laminate Thumbhole:	**$1052**
SS Left-hand Thumbhole:	**$1052**

Knight Black Powder

REVOLUTION

WOLVERINE 209

REVOLUTION
Lock: in-line
Stock: synthetic
Barrel: 27 in.
Sights: fiber optic
Weight: 7.14 lbs.
Bore/Caliber: .50, .52
Features: 209 full plastic jacket ignition system; sling swivel studs; stainless w/laminate, blued w/black, Realtree camo available
MS Black .50: **$388**
SS Black .50: **$414**
SS Laminated: **$482**
Realtree Hardwood
Green HD: **$440**
.50 cal.: **$451**
Black Stock/Blue Barrel: **$605**

VISION
Lock: In-Line
Stock: synthetic
Barrel: 26 in.
Sights: adjustable fixed
Weight: 7.9 lbs.
Bore/Caliber: .50
Features: Green Mountain barrel; overmolded composite polymer coated stainless steel receiver break-open action; full plastic primer jackets; quick detachable trigger mechanism; cross bolt safety; available in Mossy Oak Break-Up orRealTree Hardwoods HD-Green
MS Black .50: **$399**
MO Breakup .50: **$420**
Realtree Hardwood HD: **$420**
SS Black: **$451**

WOLVERINE 209
Lock: in-line
Stock: synthetic or camo
Barrel: 22 in., 1:28 twist
Sights: fiber optic
Weight: 7.0 lbs.
Bore/Caliber: .50
Features: full plastic jacket ignition
MSRP: **$274**

Lenartz Black Powder

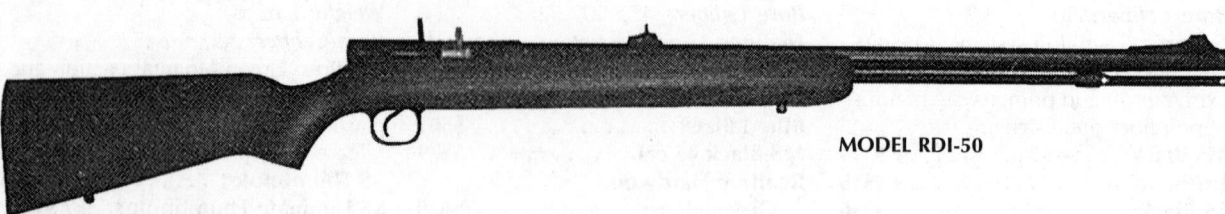

MODEL RDI-50

MODEL RDI-50
Lock: in-line
Stock: walnut
Barrel: 26 in., 1:28 twist
Sights: adjustable open

Weight: 7.5 lbs.
Bore/Caliber: .50
Features: adjustable trigger; uses 209 primers, converts to #11
MSRP: . . . .**price on request**

Lyman Black Powder

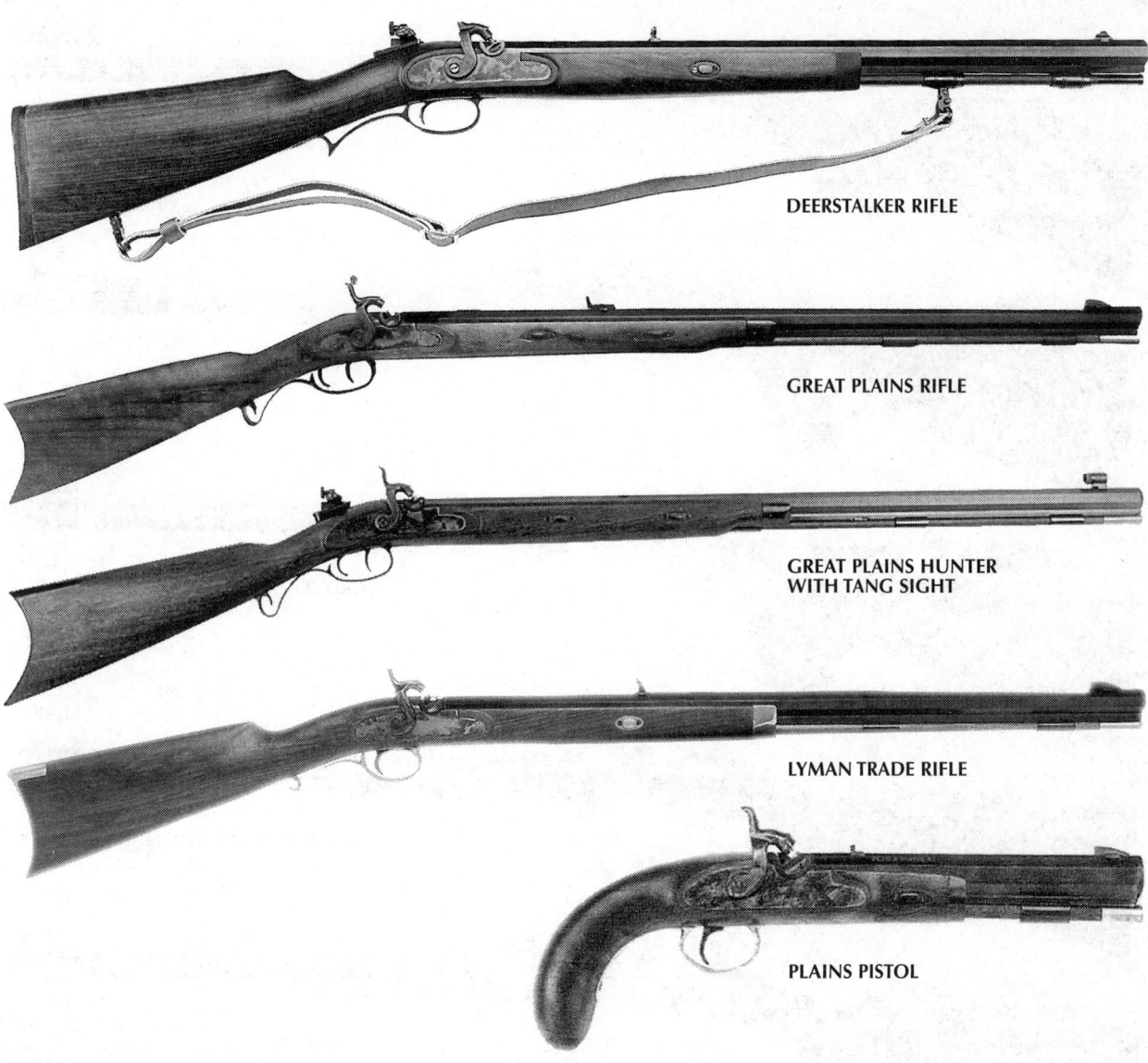

DEERSTALKER RIFLE

GREAT PLAINS RIFLE

GREAT PLAINS HUNTER WITH TANG SIGHT

LYMAN TRADE RIFLE

PLAINS PISTOL

DEERSTALKER
Lock: traditional cap or flint
Stock: walnut
Barrel: 24 in.
Sights: aperture
Weight: 7.5 lbs.
Bore/Caliber: .50 or .54
Features: left-hand models available
Caplock: **$355**
   left-hand: **$370**
Flintlock: **$410**
   left-hand: **$420**
Stainless caplock: **$465**

GREAT PLAINS RIFLE
Lock: traditional cap or flint
Stock: walnut
Barrel: 32 in., 1:66 twist

Sights: adjustable open
Weight: 8.0 lbs.
Bore/Caliber: .50 or .54
Features: double set triggers, left-hand models available; also Great Plains Hunter with 1:32 twist
Caplock: **$545**
Kit: **$418**
Flintlock: **$575**
Kit: **$450**
Hunter: **$544**

LYMAN TRADE RIFLE
Lock: traditional cap or flint
Stock: walnut
Barrel: 28 in., 1:48 twist
Sights: adjustable open
Weight: 8.0 lbs.

Bore/Caliber: .50 or .54
Features: brass furniture
Caplock: **$365**
Flint: **$400**

PLAINS PISTOL
Lock: traditional caplock
Stock: walnut
Barrel: 6 in.
Sights: fixed
Weight: 2.2 lbs.
Bore/Caliber: .50 or .54
Features: iron furniture
Plains Pistol: **$285**
Kit: **$227**

Markesbery Black Powder

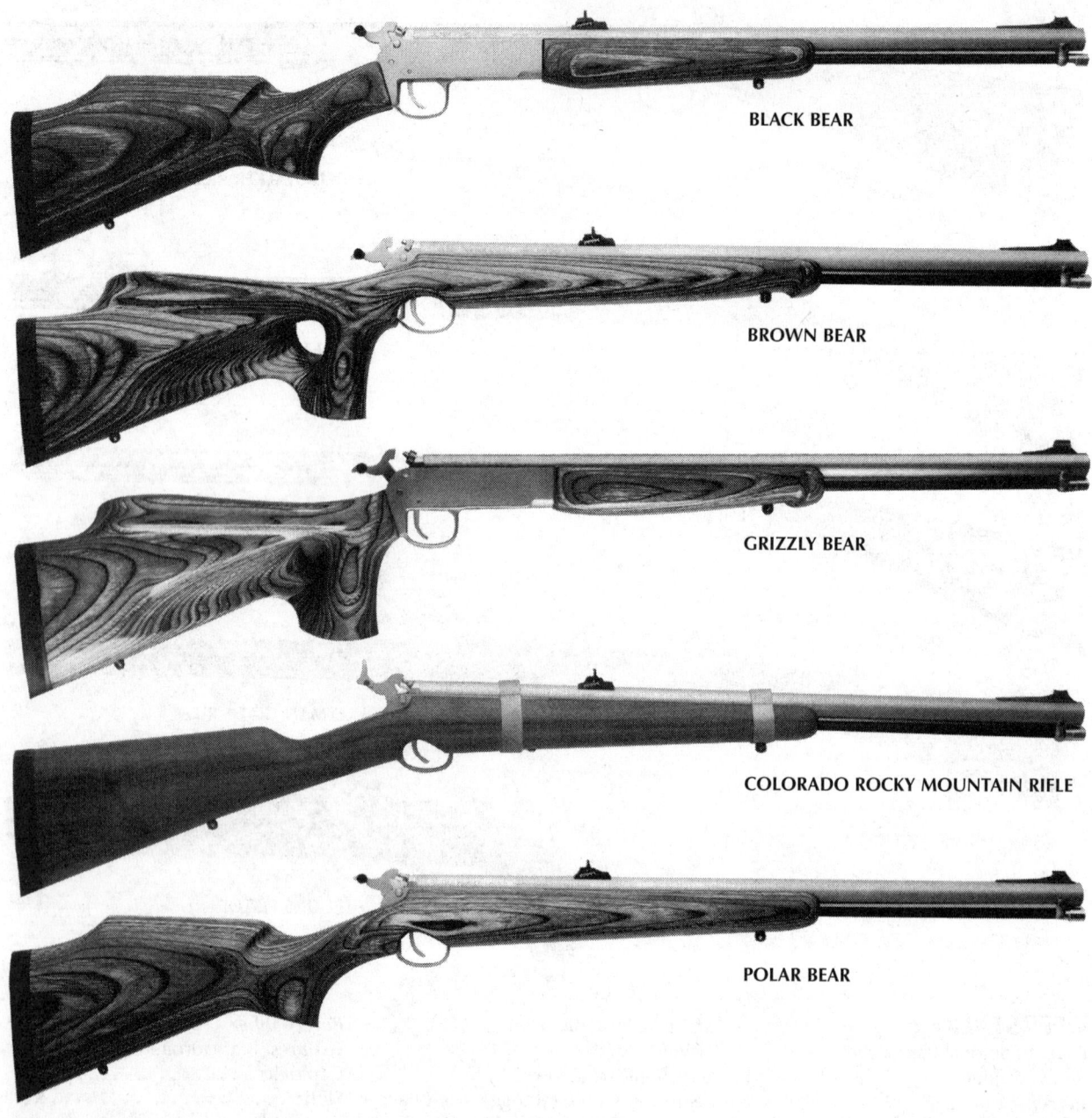

BLACK BEAR

BROWN BEAR

GRIZZLY BEAR

COLORADO ROCKY MOUNTAIN RIFLE

POLAR BEAR

BLACK BEAR
Lock: in-line
Stock: two-piece walnut, synthetic or laminated
Barrel: 24 in., 1:26 twist
Sights: adjustable open
Weight: 6.5 lbs.
Bore/Caliber: .36, .45, .50, .54
Features: also Grizzly Bear with thumbhole stock, Brown Bear with one-piece thumbhole stock, both checkered, aluminum ramrod

Black Bear:. **$536-573**
Brown Bear:. **$658-702**
Grizzly Bear: **$642-685**

COLORADO ROCKY MOUNTAIN RIFLE
Lock: in-line
Stock: walnut, laminated
Barrel: 24 in., 1:26 twist
Sights: adjustable open
Weight: 7.0 lbs.
Bore/Caliber: .36, .45, .50, .54

Features: #11 or magnum ignition
MSRP: **$546-566**

POLAR BEAR
Lock: in-line
Stock: laminated
Barrel: 24 in., 1:26 twist
Sights: adjustable open
Weight: 7.8 lbs.
Bore/Caliber: .36, .45, .50, .54
Features: one-piece stock
MSRP: **$536-570**

Navy Arms Black Powder Handguns

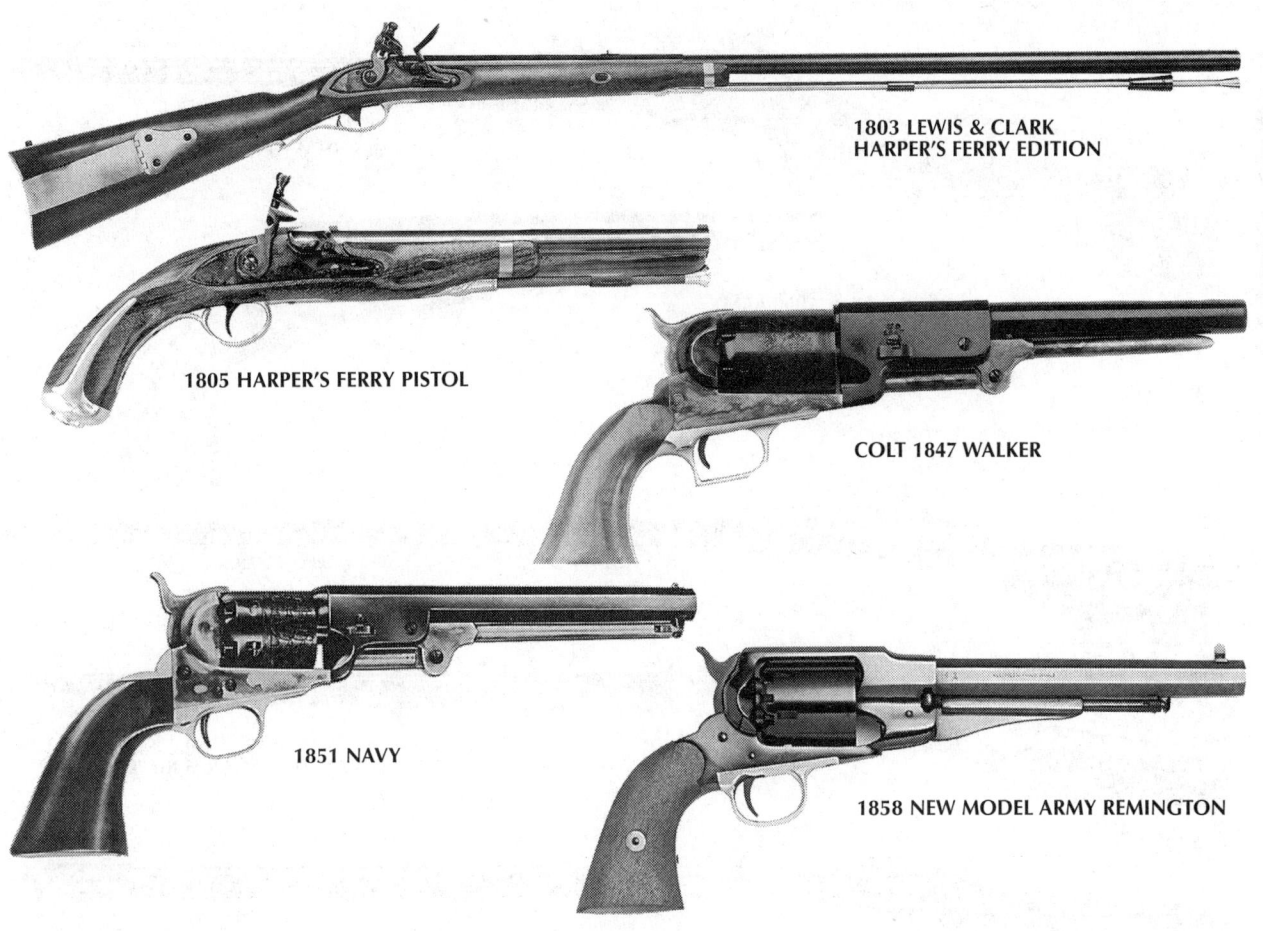

1803 LEWIS & CLARK
HARPER'S FERRY EDITION

1805 HARPER'S FERRY PISTOL

COLT 1847 WALKER

1851 NAVY

1858 NEW MODEL ARMY REMINGTON

1763 CHARLEVILLE MUSKET

Lock: traditional flintlock
Stock: walnut
Barrel: 44.75 in.
Sights: fixed
Weight: 9.8 lbs.
Bore/Caliber: .69
Features: full stock; polished steel barrel and furniture
MSRP: **$1267**

1803 LEWIS & CLARK HARPER'S FERRY EDITION

Lock: traditional flintlock
Stock: walnut
Barrel: 35 in.
Sights: fixed
Weight: 8.5 lbs.
Bore/Caliber: .54
Features: case-colored lock; brass patch box
MSRP: **$882**

1805 HARPER'S FERRY PISTOL

Lock: traditional flintlock
Stock: walnut
Barrel: 10 in.
Sights: fixed
Weight: 2.75 lbs.
Bore/Caliber: .58
Features: browned rifled barrel; case-hardened lock
MSRP: **$455**

1847 COLT WALKER

Lock: caplock revolver
Grips: walnut
Barrel: 9 in.
Sights: fixed
Weight: 4.5 lbs.
Bore/Caliber: .44
Features: case-colored frame; brass guard
MSRP: **$348**

1851 NAVY

Lock: caplock revolver
Grips: walnut
Barrel: 7.5 in.
Sights: fixed
Weight: 2.7 lbs.
Bore/Caliber: .36 and .44
Features: brass guard and strap
1851 Navy: **$242**
**1851 Navy Frontiersman
  (.36 cal., 5 in. bbl.)**: **$235**

1858 NEW MODEL ARMY REMINGTON

Lock: caplock revolver
Grips: walnut
Barrel: 8 in.
Sights: fixed
Weight: 2.5 lbs.
Bore/Caliber: .44
Features: brass guard; steel frame with top strap
1858 New Model Army Rem.: . **$269**
  with brass frame: **$183**
  stainless: **$358**
  color, case-hardened: **$320**

Navy Arms Black Powder Handguns

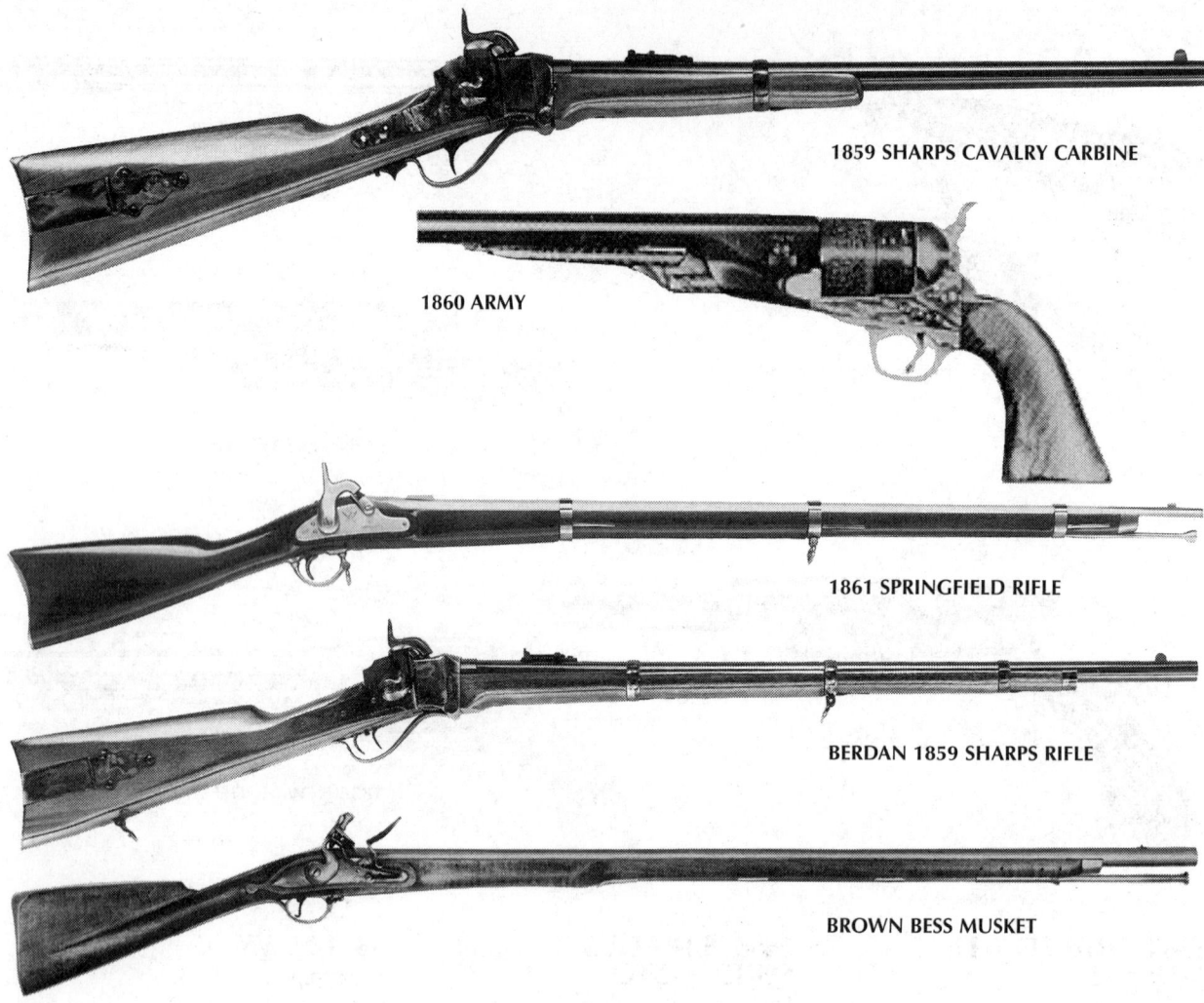

1859 SHARPS CAVALRY CARBINE

1860 ARMY

1861 SPRINGFIELD RIFLE

BERDAN 1859 SHARPS RIFLE

BROWN BESS MUSKET

1859 SHARPS CAVALRY CARBINE
Lock: percussion, dropping block
Stock: walnut
Barrel: 22 in.
Sights: adjustable open
Weight: 7.8 lbs.
Bore/Caliber: .54
Features: blued steel barrel; color case-hardened frame; saddle bar with ring
MSRP: **$1187**

1860 ARMY
Lock: caplock revolver
Grips: walnut
Barrel: 8 in.
Sights: fixed
Weight: 2.6 lbs.
Bore/Caliber: .44
Features: brass guard; steel backstrap
MSRP: **$221**

1861 SPRINGFIELD RIFLE MUSKET
Lock: traditional caplock
Stock: walnut
Barrel: 40 in.
Sights: fixed
Weight: 10.0 lbs.
Bore/Caliber: .58
Features: three-band furniture polished bright
MSRP: **$976**

BERDAN 1859 SHARPS RIFLE
Lock: traditional caplock
Stock: walnut   *Barrel*: 30 in.
Sights: adjustable open
Weight: 8.5 lbs.
Bore/Caliber: .54
Features: case-colored receiver; double set trigger

Berdan 1859 Sharps: **$1423**
Sharps Infantry Rifle: **$1386**

BROWN BESS MUSKET
Lock: traditional flintlock
Stock: walnut
Barrel: 42 in.
Sights: fixed
Weight: 9.5 lbs.
Bore/Caliber: .75
Features: full stock without bands
MSRP: **$1133**

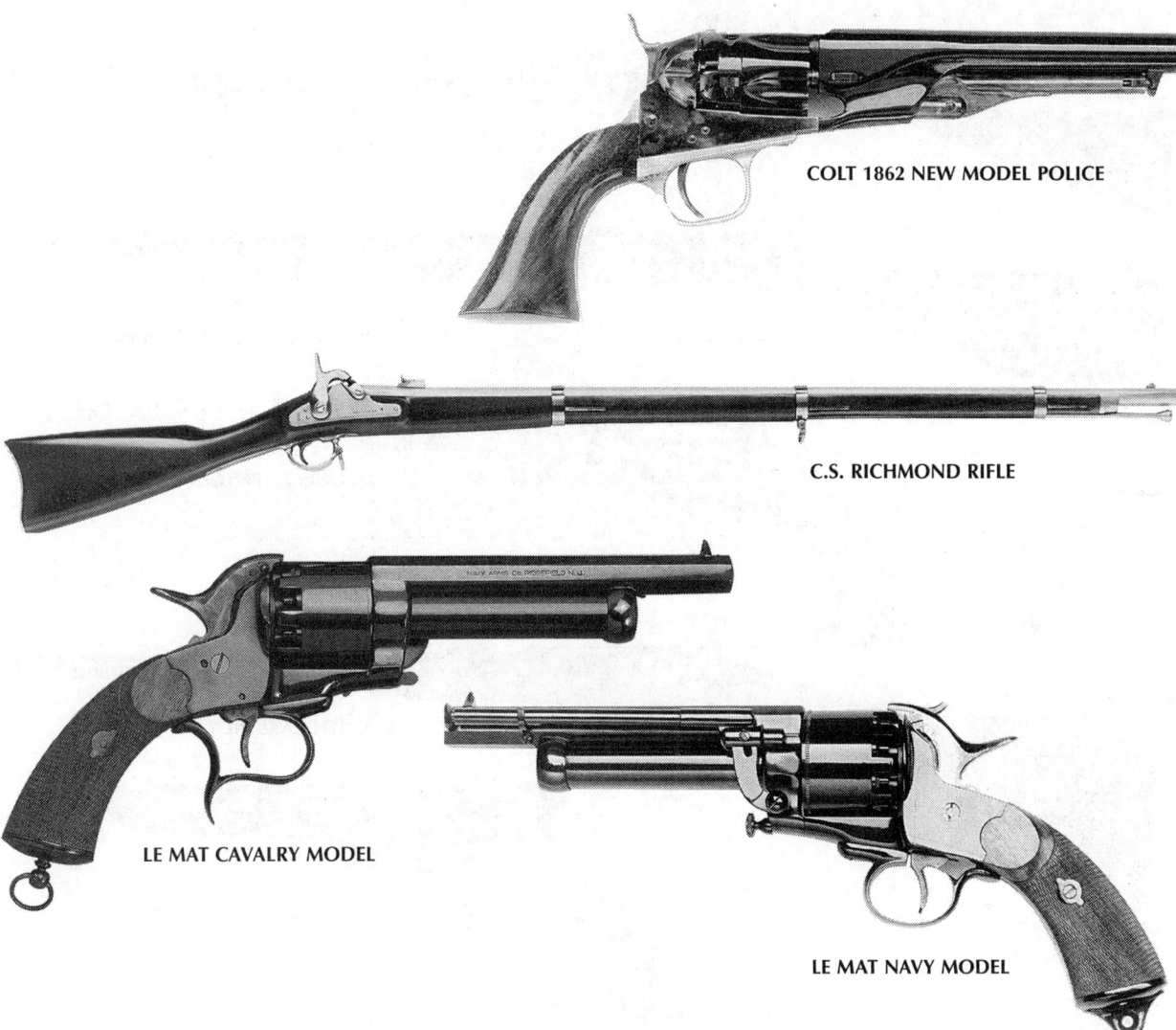

COLT 1862 NEW MODEL POLICE

C.S. RICHMOND RIFLE

LE MAT CAVALRY MODEL

LE MAT NAVY MODEL

COLT 1862 NEW MODEL POLICE
Lock: caplock revolver
Grips: walnut
Barrel: 5.5 in.
Sights: fixed
Weight: 2.7 lbs.
Bore/Caliber: .36
Features: last of the percussion Colts; has brass guard; case-colored frame
MSRP: **$266**

C.S. RICHMOND RIFLE
Lock: traditional caplock
Stock: walnut
Barrel: 40 in.
Sights: fixed
Weight: 10.0 lbs.
Bore/Caliber: .58

Features: polished furniture
MSRP: **$976**

HARPER'S FERRY FLINTLOCK PISTOL
Lock: traditional flintlock
Grips: walnut
Barrel: 10 in.
Sights: fixed
Weight: 2.6 lbs.
Bore/Caliber: .58
Features: case-colored lock; brass furniture; browned barrel
MSRP: **$412**

J. P. MURRAY CARBINE
Lock: traditional caplock
Stock: walnut
Barrel: 23.5 in.

Sights: fixed
Weight: 7.5 lbs.
Bore/Caliber: .58
Features: color case hardened lock; brass furniture
MSRP: **$748**

LE MAT REVOLVER
Lock: caplock revolver
Grips: walnut
Barrel: 7.6 in.
Sights: fixed
Weight: 3.4 lbs.
Bore/Caliber: .44
Features: 9-shot cylinder; Navy, Cavalry, Army models available
MSRP: **$748**

Navy Arms Black Powder Rifles

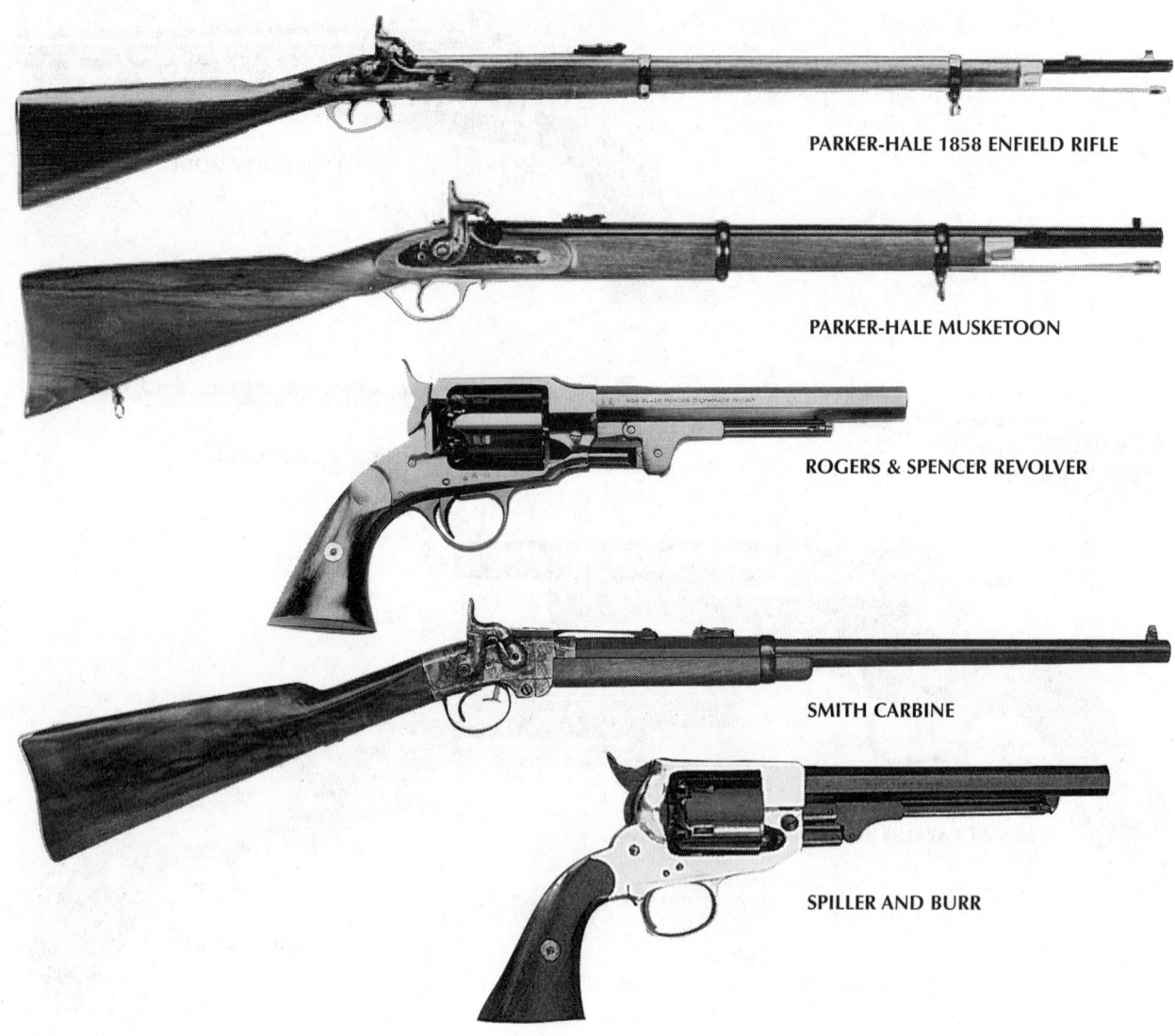

PARKER-HALE 1858 ENFIELD RIFLE

PARKER-HALE MUSKETOON

ROGERS & SPENCER REVOLVER

SMITH CARBINE

SPILLER AND BURR

PARKER-HALE 1858 ENFIELD RIFLE
Lock: traditional caplock
Stock: walnut
Barrel: 39 in. (2-band 33 in.)
Sights: adjustable open
Weight: 9.6 lbs. (2-band 8.50 lbs.)
Bore/Caliber: .58
Features: brass furniture
Parker-Hale Enfield: $848
1858 Two band Enfield: $819

PARKER-HALE MUSKETOON
Lock: traditional caplock
Stock: walnut
Barrel: 24 in.
Sights: adjustable open
Weight: 7.5 lbs.

Bore/Caliber: .58
Features: brass furniture
MSRP: $6734

ROGERS AND SPENCER
Lock: caplock revolver
Grips: walnut
Barrel: 7.5 in.
Sights: fixed
Weight: 3.0 lbs.
Bore/Caliber: .44
Features: octagonal barrel;
6-shot cylinder
MSRP: $363

SMITH CARBINE
Lock: traditional caplock
Stock: walnut
Barrel: 22 in.

Sights: adjustable open
Weight: 7.8 lbs.
Bore/Caliber: .50
Features: cavalry and artillery models
available
MSRP: $791

SPILLER AND BURR
Lock: caplock revolver
Grips: walnut
Barrel: 7 in.
Sights: fixed
Weight: 2.6 lbs.
Bore/Caliber: .36
Features: brass frame
MSRP: $197

Pedersoli Black Powder

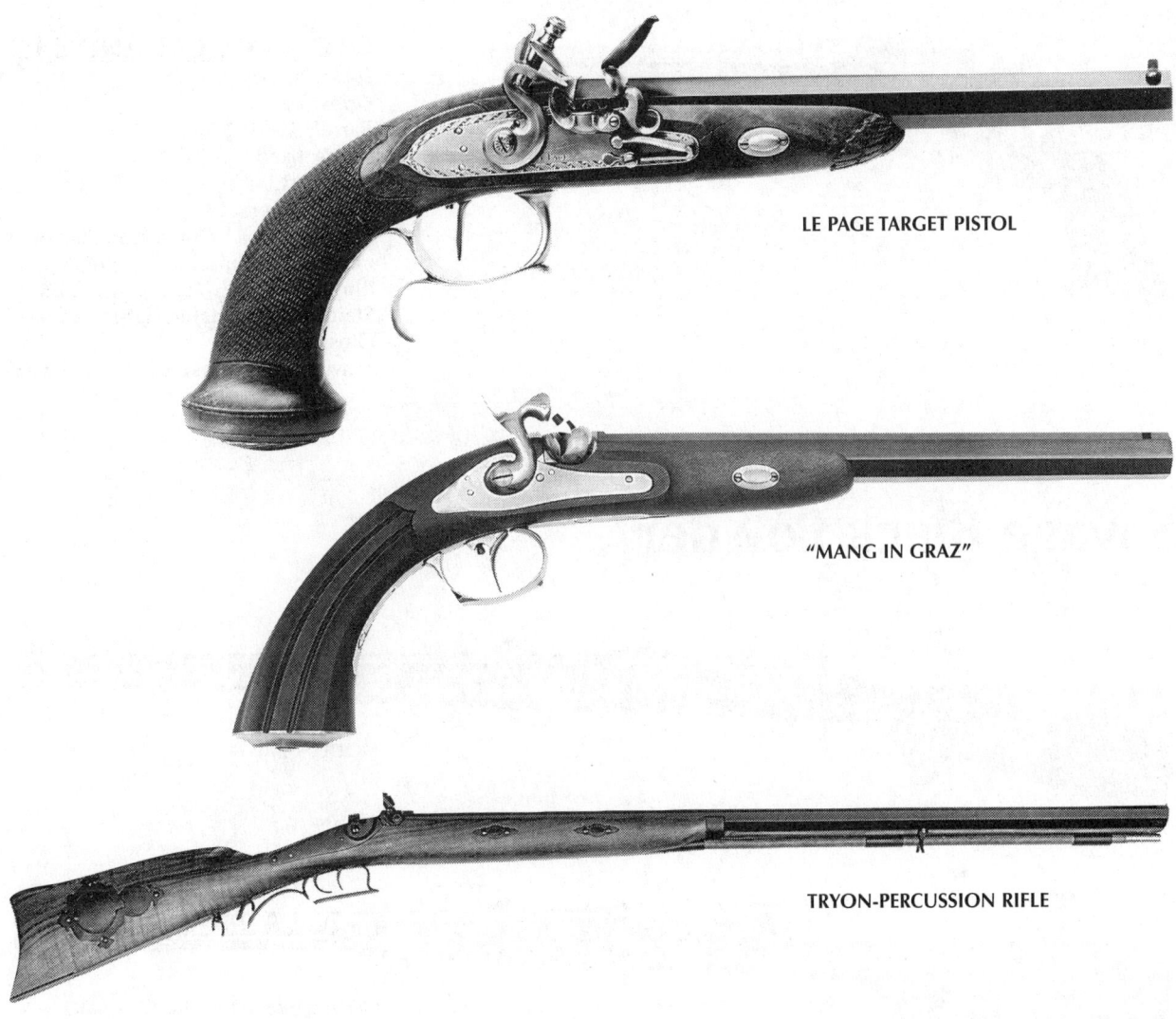

LE PAGE TARGET PISTOL

"MANG IN GRAZ"

TRYON-PERCUSSION RIFLE

LEPAGE TARGET PISTOL

Lock: traditional flintlock
Grips: walnut
Barrel: 10.5 in., 1:18 twist
Sights: fixed
Weight: 2.5 lbs.
Bore/Caliber: .44 or .45
Features: smoothbore .45 available
LePage flintlock: $900
percussion in .36, .38, .44 . . $700

"MANG IN GRAZ"

Lock: traditional caplock
Grips: walnut
Barrel: 11 in., 1:15 or 1:18 (.44) twist
Sights: fixed
Weight: 2.5 lbs.

Bore/Caliber: .38 or .44
Features: grooved butt
MSRP: $1195

MORTIMER TARGET RIFLE

Lock: flintlock
Stock: English-style European walnut
Barrel: octagon to round 36 in.
Sights: target
Weight: 8.8 lbs.
Bore/Caliber: .54
Features: case-colored lock; stock has cheekpiece and hand checkering; 7-groove barrel
MSRP: $1225

TRYON-PERCUSSION RIFLE

Lock: traditional caplock
Stock: walnut
Barrel: 32 in., 1:48 or 1:66 (.54) twist
Sights: adjustable open
Weight: 9.5 lbs.
Bore/Caliber: .45, .50, .54
Features: Creedmoor version with aperture sight available
Tyron-Percussion: $750
Creedmoor: $960

Ruger Black Powder

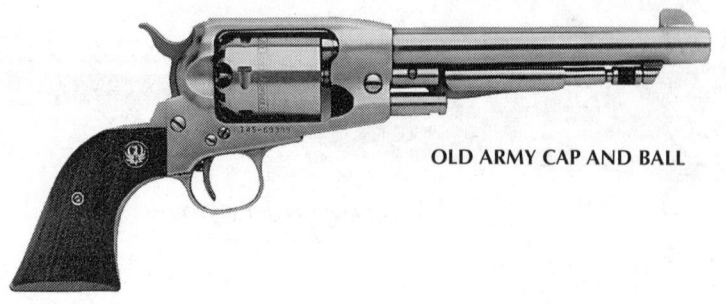

OLD ARMY CAP AND BALL

OLD ARMY CAP AND BALL

Lock: caplock revolver
Grips: walnut
Barrel: 5.5 or 7.5 in.
Sights: fixed
Weight: 3.0 lbs.
Bore/Caliber: .45
Features: Civil War-era reproduction in modern steel, music wire springs
Blue: **$541**
Stainless (adjustable sights): . . **$577**
**Gloss stainless
   with ivory grips:** **$623**

Savage Black Powder

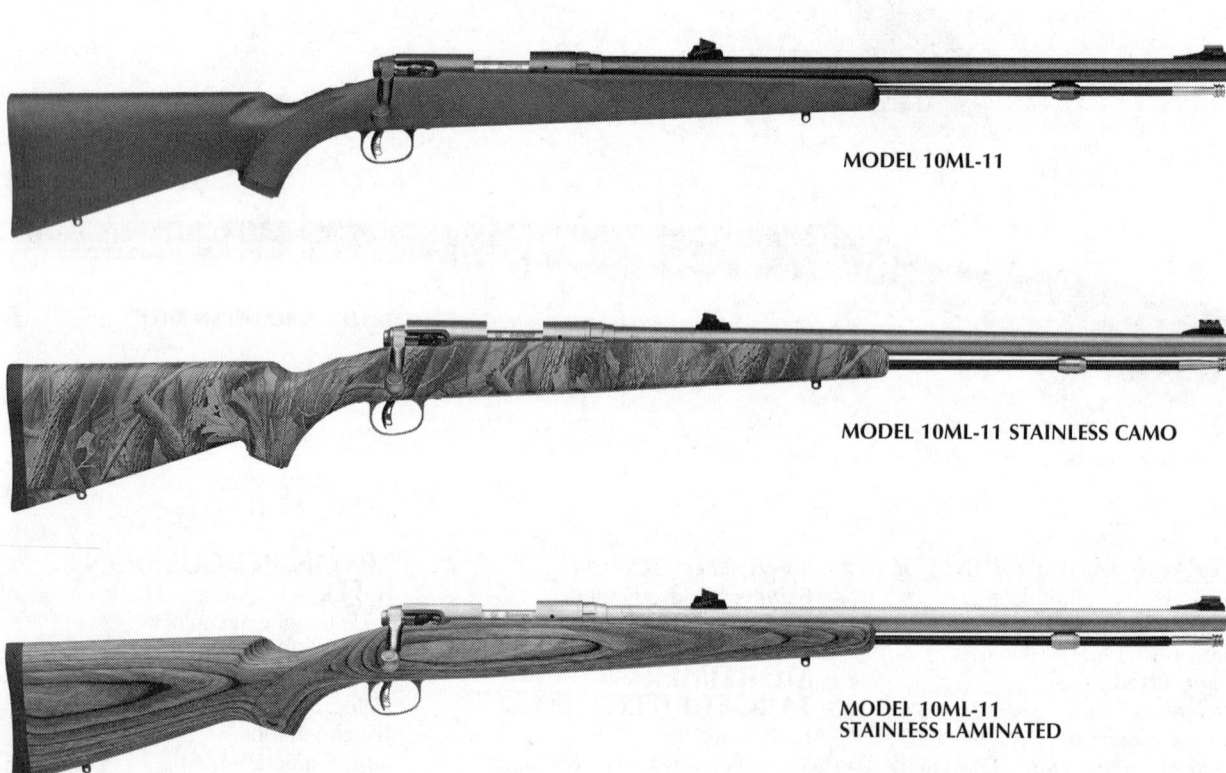

MODEL 10ML-11

MODEL 10ML-11 STAINLESS CAMO

MODEL 10ML-11
STAINLESS LAMINATED

MODEL 10ML-11 MUZZLELOADER

Lock: in-line
Stock: synthetic, camo or laminated
Barrel: 24 in.
Sights: adjustable fiber optic

Weight: 8.0 lbs.
Bore/Caliber: .50
Features: bolt-action mechanism; 209 priming
Blue synthetic: **$531**
Stainless: **$589**

Blue camo: **$569**
Stainless camo: **$628**
Stainless laminated: **$667**

Shiloh Black Powder

1863 SHARPS

**1874 CREEDMOOR TARGET RIFLE
(WITHOUT SIGHTS)**

1874 SPORTER

MODEL 1863 SHARPS

Lock: traditional caplock
Stock: walnut
Barrel: 30 in.
Sights: adjustable open
Weight: 9.5 lbs.
Bore/Caliber: .50 or .54
Features: sporting model with half-stock; double set trigger military model with 3-band full stock; also carbine with 22 in. barrel (7.5 lbs.)
Sporting rifle and carbine: . . **$1547**
Military rifle: **$1793**

MODEL 1874 CREEDMOOR TARGET

Lock: black powder cartridge
Stock: walnut
Barrel: 32 in. half octagon
Sights: none
Weight: 9.0 lbs.
Bore/Caliber: all popular black powder cartridges from .38-55 to .50-90
Features: shotgun buttstock, pistol grip; single trigger; fancy walnut, pewter tip
MSRP: **$2485**
**#2 Creedmoor Silhouette (30"
   round, tapered barrel):** . . . **$2485**

MODEL 1874 SPORTER

Lock: black powder cartridge
Stock: walnut
Barrel: 30 in. heavy or standard
Sights: adjustable open
Weight: 9.0 lbs.
Bore/Caliber: .38-55 to .50-90
Features: shotgun or military-style buttstock; double set triggers; Buckhorn rear sight, blade front
**Sporter #1 (cheek rest &
   pistol grip):** **$1638**
Sporter #3 (staight grip): **$1547**

When hunting in wet weather, cover the muzzle of your rifle with plastic wrap secured by a rubber band. If you are hunting with a traditional cap lock, seal the connection point of the nipple and breech with modeling putty.

Thompson/Center Black Powder

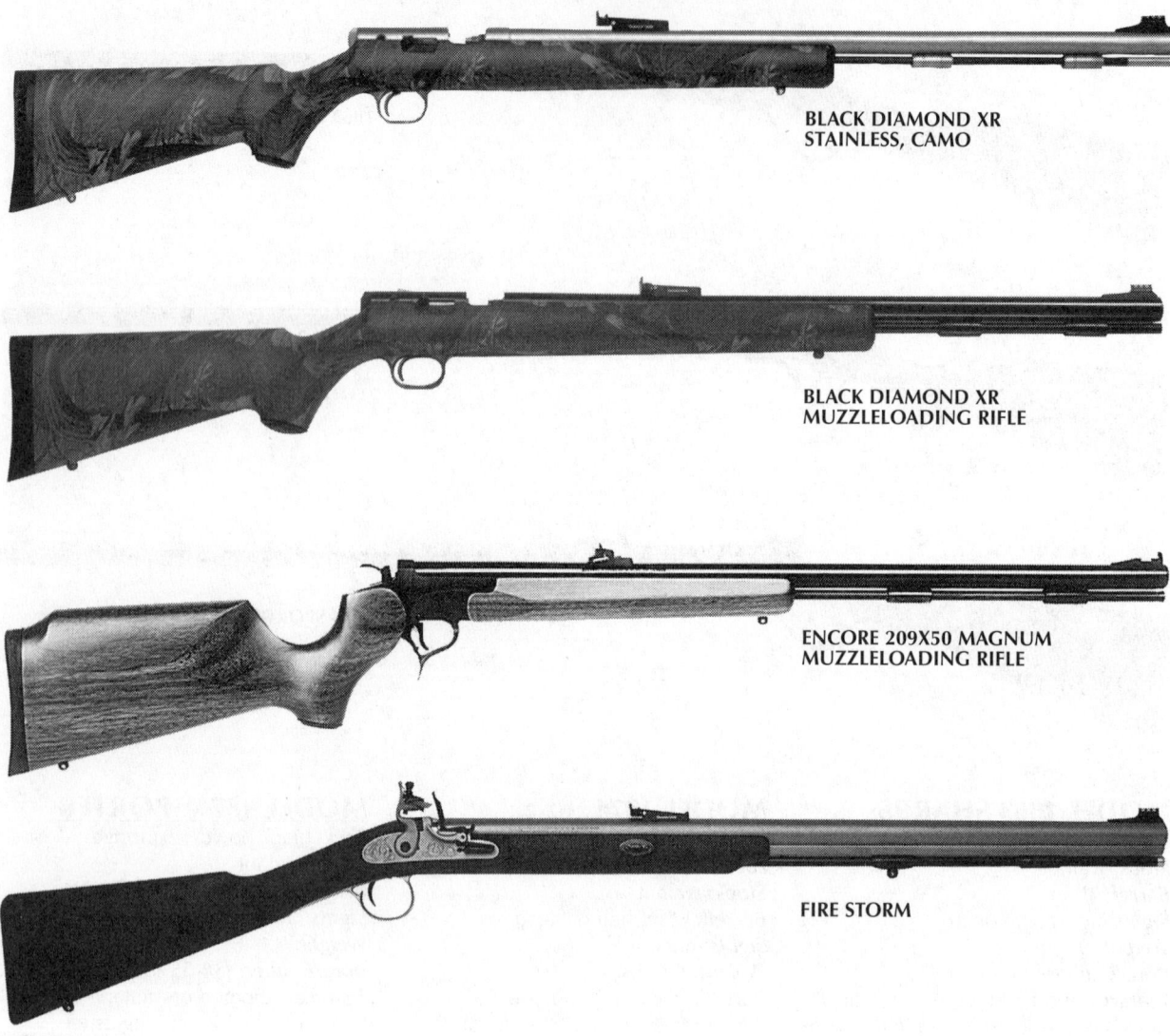

**BLACK DIAMOND XR
STAINLESS, CAMO**

**BLACK DIAMOND XR
MUZZLELOADING RIFLE**

**ENCORE 209X50 MAGNUM
MUZZLELOADING RIFLE**

FIRE STORM

BLACK DIAMOND RIFLE XR

Lock: in-line
Stock: walnut or synthetic
Barrel: 26 in., 1:28 twist
Sights: adjustable fiber optic
Weight: 6.6 lbs.
Bore/Caliber: .50
Features: musket; cap or no. 11 nipple
Blue synthetic:. **$337**
Stainless camo: **$440**

ENCORE 209X50 RIFLE

Lock: in-line
Stock: walnut or synthetic
Barrel: 26 in., 1:28 twist
Sights: adjustable fiber optic
Weight: 7.0 lbs.
Bore/Caliber: .50
Features: automatic safety; interchangeable barrel with Encore centerfire barrels; also available 209x45 9.45)
Blue synthetic:. **$637**
Blue walnut: **$678**
Blue walnut .45:. **$683**
Blue camo: **$696**
Stainless synthetic: **$713**
Stainless synthetic .45: **$727**
Stainless camo: **$772**

FIRE STORM

Lock: traditional cap or flint
Stock: synthetic
Barrel: 26 in., 1:48 twist
Sights: adjustable fiber optic
Weight: 7.0 lbs.
Bore/Caliber: .50
Features: aluminum ramrod
Blue: **$436**
Stainless: **$488**

Traditions Black Powder

1851 NAVY

1858 NEW ARMY

CROCKETT PISTOL

DEERHUNTER

1851 NAVY REVOLVER
Lock: caplock
Grips: walnut
Barrel: 7.5 in.
Sights: fixed
Weight: 2.7 lbs.
Bore/Caliber: .36
Features: blued, octagon barrel; steel or brass frame
Brass frame: $175
Steel frame: $215
1851 Navy U.S. Marshall
   (old silver, 5 in. bbl.): $325
1851 Navy Old Silver
   (7.5 in. bbl.): $279

1858 NEW ARMY REVOLVER
Lock: caplock
Grips: walnut
Barrel: 8 in.
Sights: fixed
Weight: 2.6 lbs.
Bore/Caliber: .44
Features: octagon barrel; steel frame
1858 New Army (brass): $199
1858 New Army (steel): $245
1858 New Army (stainless): . . . $399

1860 ARMY REVOLVER
Lock: caplock
Grips: walnut
Barrel: 8 in.
Sights: fixed
Weight: 2.8 lbs.
Bore/Caliber: ..44
Features: blued; round barrel; steel or brass frame
Brass frame: $189
Steel frame: $245
Nickel: $269

BUCKSKINNER FLINTLOCK CARBINE
Lock: traditional flintlock
Grips: synthetic or laminate
Barrel: 21 in., 1:48 twist
Sights: adjustable
Weight: 6.0 lbs.
Bore/Caliber: .50
Features: fully adjustable TruGlo fiber optic sights; Monte Carlo stock; hooked breech for easy barrel removal; synthetic ramrod
Buckskinner Flintlock Carbine: . . $295
Laminate/blued: $365
Laminate/nickel: $395

CROCKETT PISTOL
Lock: traditional caplock
Grips: hardwood
Barrel: 10 in.
Sights: fixed
Weight: 2.0 lbs.
Bore/Caliber: .32 caplock
Features: blued, octagon barrel
MSRP: $169

DEERHUNTER RIFLE
Lock: traditional cap or flint
Stock: hardwood, synthetic or camo
Barrel: 24 in., 1:48 twist
Sights: fixed
Weight: 6.0 lbs.
Bore/Caliber: .32, .50, .54
Features: blackened furniture; also economy-model Panther, 24 in .50 or .54
Cap, nickel, synthetic: $179
Flint, blue, synthetic: $189
Flint, nickel, cynthetic: $199
Cap, blue, hardwood: $199-205
Flint, blue, hardwood: $219
Flint, nickel, camo: $249

Traditions Black Powder

EVOLUTION PREMIER

HAWKEN

KENTUCKY PISTOL

PENNSYLVANIA RIFLE

EVOLUTION
Lock: bolt
Stock: synthetic, laminated or camo
Barrel: 26 in.
Sights: fiber optics
Weight: 7.0 lbs.
Bore/Caliber: .50
Features: fluted, tapered barrel, drilled & tapped for scope; 209 ignition; swivel studs, rubber butt pad; LD model in .45 or .50 has tru-Glo sights.
LD blue synthetic: **$249-259**
LD nickel synthetic: **$259-279**
LD blue camo: **$279**
LD nickel camo: **$289**
Premier, blue: **$349**
Premier stainless, camo: **$369**
Premier stainless: **$469**

EXPRESS DOUBLE OVER & UNDER MUZZLELOADER
Lock: 209 primer top break
Stock: synthetic
Barrel: 24 in.
Sights: adjustable
Weight: 12.5 lbs.
Bore/Caliber: .50
Features: double barrel over/under; 209-ignition system; blued barrels ; double trigger, top tang safety; fiber optic sights; drilled & tapped for a scope
MSRP: **$1399**

HAWKEN WOODSMAN RIFLE
Lock: traditional cap or flint
Stock: beech
Barrel: 28 in., 1:48 twist
Sights: adjustable open
Weight: 7.7 lbs.
Bore/Caliber: .50 or .54
Features: brass furniture
Caplock: **$295**

Lefthand caplock: **$309**
Flintlock: **$309**
Crockett (.32 caplock): **$325**

KENTUCKY PISTOL
Lock: traditional caplock
Grips: beech
Barrel: 10 in.
Sights: fixed
Weight: 2.5 lbs.
Bore/Caliber: .50
Features: brass furniture
MSRP: **$175**

PENNSYLVANIA RIFLE
Lock: traditional cap or flint
Stock: walnut
Barrel: 20 in., 1:66 twist
Sights: adjustable open
Weight: 8.5 lbs.
Bore/Caliber: .50
Features: brass furniture
MSRP: **$559**

Traditions Black Powder

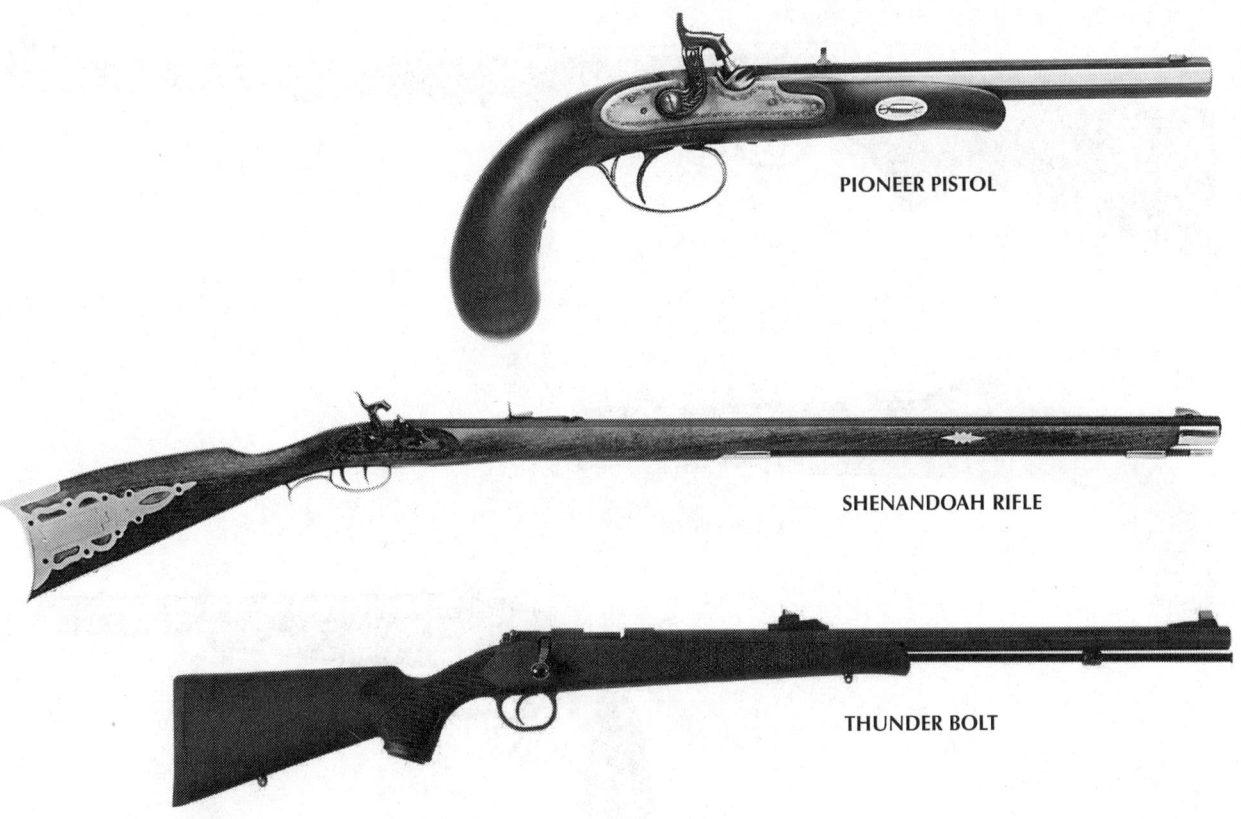

PIONEER PISTOL

SHENANDOAH RIFLE

THUNDER BOLT

PIONEER PISTOL

Lock: traditional caplock
Grips: walnut
Barrel: 9.6 in.
Sights: fixed
Weight: 1.9 lbs.
Bore/Caliber: .45
Features: German silver furniture
MSRP: $185

PURSUIT LT BREAK OPEN

Lock: break-open, 209 ignition system
Grips: synthetic
Barrel: 28 in.
Sights: adjustable
Weight: 8.25 lbs.
Bore/Caliber: .45
Features: 209-ignition; fluted barrel; cross block trigger safety; fiber optic sights

Blued/black: $299
Nickel/black: $319
Realtree Hardwoods /blue: . . . $345
Realtree Hardwoods /nickel: . . $365

SHENANDOAH RIFLE

Lock: traditional cap or flint
Stock: beech
Barrel: 33 in., 1:66 twist
Sights: fixed
Weight: 7.2 lbs.
Bore/Caliber: .50
Features: brass furniture; squirrel rifle in .36
Caplock $435
Flintlock $469
Caplock .36 . . . . $455
Flintlock .36 . . . . $485
Kentucky, flint or caplock: . . $269-325

THUNDER BOLT

Lock: bolt
Stock: synthetic
Barrel: 24 in. (21 in. youth)
Sights: adjustable
Weight: 7.0 lbs.
Bore/Caliber: .45 or .50
Features: 209-ignition; checkered stock; sling swivels; rubber butt pad; drilled & tapped for scope
Youth: $179
Blue synthetic: $179
Nickel synthetic: $189
Blue camo: $199
Nickel camo: $219

Traditions Black Powder

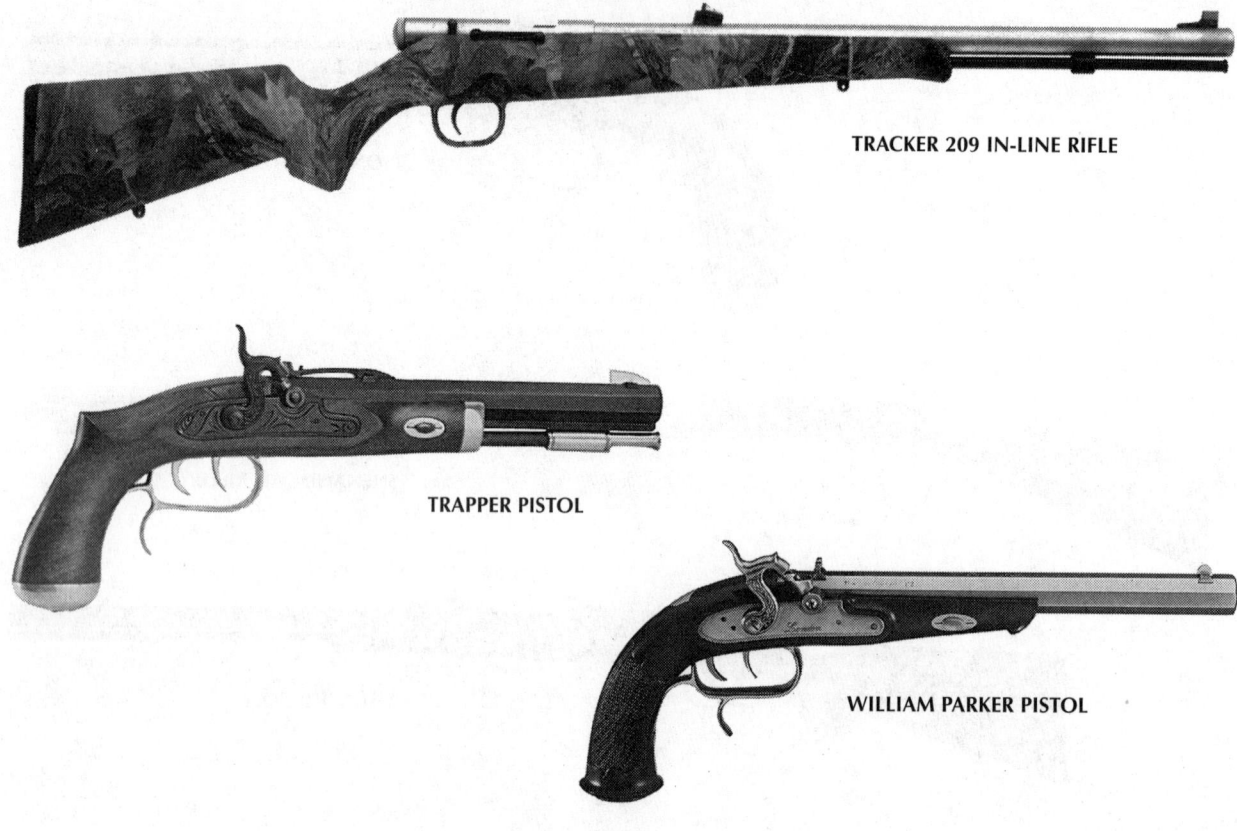

TRACKER 209 IN-LINE RIFLE

TRAPPER PISTOL

WILLIAM PARKER PISTOL

TRACKER 209
Lock: in-line
Stock: synthetic or camo
Barrel: 22 in., 1:28 twist (1:24 .45)
Sights: fiber optic
Weight: 6.5 lbs.
Bore/Caliber: .45 or .50
Features: 209 primer ignition
Blue synthetic:............. $139
Nickel synthetic: $159
Nickel camo: $199

TRAPPER PISTOL
Lock: traditional cap or flint
Grips: beech
Barrel: 9.8 in.
Sights: adjustable open
Weight: 2.9 lbs.
Bore/Caliber: .50
Features: brass furniture
Trapper:................. $235
Flintlock: $249

WILLIAM PARKER PISTOL
Lock: traditional caplock
Grips: walnut
Barrel: 10.4 in.
Sights: fixed
Weight: 2.3 lbs.
Bore/Caliber: .50
Features: checkered with brass furniture
MSRP: $309

To prevent air pressure from interfering when ramming tight-fitting wads into a muzzleloading shotgun barrel, punch two or three air holes in the wads near the edge with a small pin. This should reduce the air pressure enough to allow for smooth loading.

Uberti Black Powder

1847 WALKER

Lock: caplock revolver
Grips: walnut grips
Barrel: 9 in.
Sights: fixed
Weight: 4.45 lbs.
Bore/Caliber: .44
Features: color, case-hardened frame; brass trigger guard
MSRP: **$305**

1848 DRAGOON

Lock: caplock revolver
Grips: walnut
Barrel: 7.5 in.
Sights: fixed
Weight: 4.06 lbs.
Bore/Caliber: .44
Features: comes in 1st, 2nd and 3rd models; color, case-hardened frame; brass trigger guard
1848 Dragoon: **$285**
1848 Whiteneyville Dragoon: . . **$340**

1851 NAVY REVOLVER

Lock: caplock revolver
Grips: walnut
Barrel: 7.5 in.
Sights: fixed
Weight: 2.8lbs.
Bore/Caliber: .36
Features: case-colored frame; brass round or square trigger-guard
MSRP: **$240**

1858 REMINGTON NEW ARMY

Lock: caplock revolver
Grips: walnut
Barrel: 8 in.
Sights: fixed
Weight: 2.8lbs.
Bore/Caliber: .44
Features: octagonal barrel; brass guard
New Army: **$260**
Stainless: **$310**
18 in. barrel, carbine: **$395**

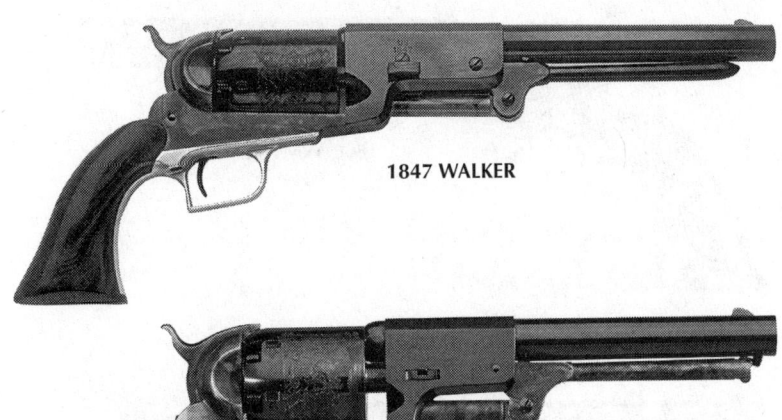

1847 WALKER

1848 3RD MODEL DRAGOON

1848 WHITENEYVILLE DRAGOON

1851 NAVY REVOLVER

1858 REMINGTON NEW ARMY

Uberti Black Powder

1860 ARMY REVOLVER

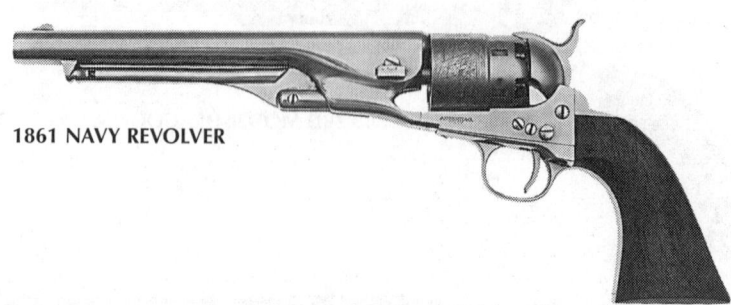

1861 NAVY REVOLVER

1862 POCKET NAVY

1862 POLICE

1860 ARMY REVOLVER
Lock: caplock revolver
Grips: walnut
Barrel: 8 in.
Sights: fixed
Weight: 2.6 lbs.
Bore/Caliber: .44
Features: case-colored frame
1860 Army:. **$260**
   fluted cylinder: **$260**

1861 NAVY REVOLVER
Lock: caplock revolver
Grips: walnut
Barrel: 7.5 in.
Sights: fixed
Weight: 2.8 lbs.
Bore/Caliber: .36
Features: case-colored frame; brass or steel trigger-guard
MSRP: **$260**

1862 POCKET NAVY
Lock: caplock revolver
Grips: walnut
Barrel: 5.5 in.
Sights: fixed
Weight: 1.68 lbs.
Bore/Caliber: .36
Features: color case-colored frame; 6-shot cylinder; forged steel barrel
MSRP: **$260**

1862 POLICE
Lock: caplock revolver
Grips: walnut
Barrel: 6.5 in
Sights: fixed
Weight: 1.59 lbs.
Bore/Caliber: .36
Features: color case-colored frame; 6-shot cylinder; forged steel barel
MSRP: **$260**

PATERSON REVOLVER

Lock: caplock revolver
Grips: walnut
Barrel: 7.5 in.
Sights: none
Weight: 2.6 lbs.
Bore/Caliber: .36
Features: 5-shot cylinder
Paterson: **$360**
   with load lever: **$390**

POCKET REVOLVERS

Lock: caplock revolver
Grips: walnut
Barrel: 4 in.
Sights: fixed
Weight: 1.46-1.56 lbs.
Bore/Caliber: .31
Features: color case-colored frame; 5-shot cylinders; forged steel barrel
1848 Baby Dragoon: **$260**
1849 Wells Fargo 4": **$260**
1849 Pocket 4": **$260**

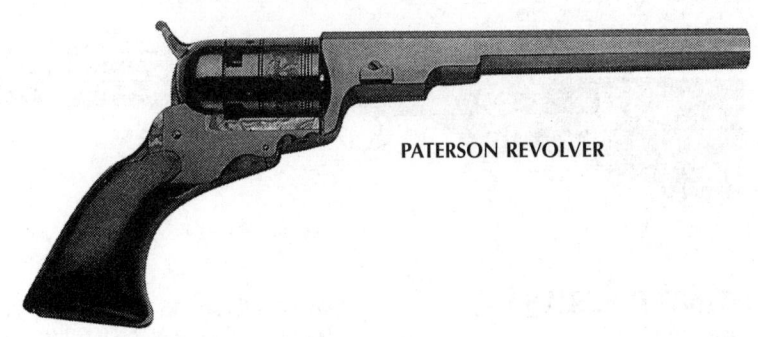

PATERSON REVOLVER

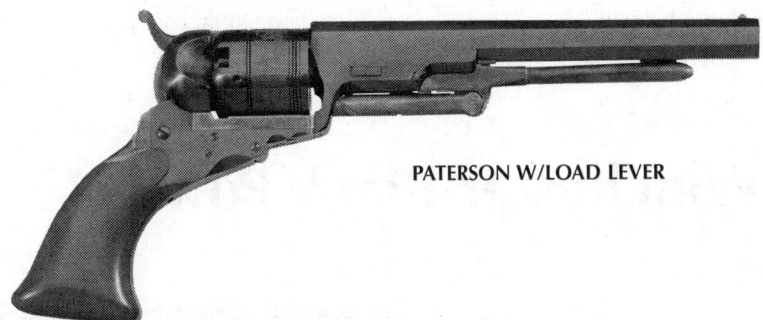

PATERSON W/LOAD LEVER

1849 POCKET

Remember, do not exceed the manufacturer's recommended powder charge in your muzzleloading rifle or pistol, particularly when using blackpowder. True blackpowder is explosive and releases most of its energy immediately upon ignition.

White Rifles Black Powder

THUNDERBOLT

HUNTER SERIES
Lock: in-line
Stock: synthetic or laminated
Barrel: stainless, 22 in. (24 in. Elite)
Sights: fiber-optic
Weight: 7.7 lbs.

Bore/Caliber: .45 or .50
Features: Elite weighs 8.6 lbs.; aluminum ramrod with bullet extractor; also: Thunderbolt bolt action with 209-ignition, 26 in. barrel

Whitetail:................ $430
Blacktail and Elite:.......... $500
Thunderbolt:.............. $600
Odyssey (ss/laminated
   thumbhole stock):....... $1300

Winchester Black Powder

APEX STAINLESS SYNTHETIC

WINCHESTER MODEL X-150

APEX MUZZLELOADER
Lock: in-line
Stock: synthetic or camo
Barrel: 28 in., 1:28 twist
Sights: fiber optic
Weight: 7.2 lbs.
Bore/Caliber: .45 or .50
Features: "swing-action" breech
Blue synthetic:............. $311
Full camo: $416
Stainless synthetic: $370
Stainless camo: $415

MODEL X-150 MUZZLELOADING RIFLE
Lock: in-line
Stock: synthetic or camo
Barrel: 26 in. fluted, 1:28 twist
Sights: fiber optic
Weight: 7.9 lbs.
Bore/Caliber: .45 or .50
Features: 209 primer ignition; stainless bolt action
Blue synthetic:............. $230
Blue camo: $280
Stainless camo: $350

Aimpoint Sights

9000

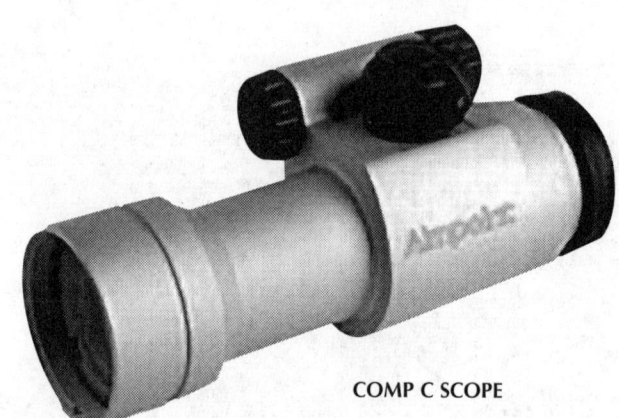

COMP C SCOPE

COMP M2 AND COMP ML2

9000

System: Passive Red Dot Collimator Reflex Sight
Optical: anti-reflex coated lens
Adjustment: 1 click = 10mm at 80 meters = 13mm at 100 meters = ½ in. at 100 yds
Length: 7.9 inches
Weight: 8.1 oz.
Objective diameter: 36mm
Diameter of dot: 2 MOA
Mounting system: 30mm ring
Magnification: 1X
Material: extruded aluminum; black finish
9000L: **$426**
9000SC: **$417**

COMP C

System: 100% Parallax free
Optics: anti-reflex coated lenses
Eye relief: Unlimited
Batteries: 3V Lithium
Adjustment: 1 click = ½ in. at 100 yards
Length: 4¾ in.
Weight: 6.5 oz.
Objective diameter: 36mm
Dot diameter: 4 MOA
Mounting system: 30mm ring
Magnification: 1X
Material: Black or stainless finish
MSRP: **$347**
CompC SM
**   (7 MOA silver metallic):** **$361**
anodized, graphite gray: **$411**

COMP ML2

System: Parallax free
Optical: Anti-reflex coated lens
Adjustment: 1 click = ½ in. at 100 yards
Length: 4.7 in.
Weight: 6.5 oz.
Objective diameter: 36mm
Diameter of dot: 2 MOA
Mounting system: 30mm ring
Magnification: 2X fixed
Material: anodized aluminum; black finish
Comp ML2: **$489**
Comp M2: **$418**

Alpen Optics

KODIAK 4-12X40

APEX 3.5-10X50

APEX AND KODIAK SCOPES

Alpen Optics offers two lines of rifle-scopes, comprising 11 models. Apex variables feature fully multi-coated lens systems, plus resettable finger-adjustable windage and elevation adjustments with ¼-minute clicks. Kodiak scopes are fully waterproof, and fogproof.

APEX SCOPES				
MAGNIFICATION (X OBJ. DIA.)	FIELD OF VIEW (FT., 100 YDS)	DIA./LENGTH (IN.)	WEIGHT (OZ.)	MSRP
3-9x42	40/14	1/12.5	17	$345
3.5-10x50	28-10	1/12.8	17	$395
4-16x50	23.6/-62	1/14.8	23	$405
6-24x50	15-4	1/16	16	$435

KODIAK SCOPES				
MAGNIFICATION (X OBJ. DIA.)	FIELD OF VIEW (FT., 100 YDS)	DIA./LENGTH (IN.)	WEIGHT (OZ.)	MSRP
4x32	34	1/12.3	12	$75
1.5-4.5x32	50-21	1/11.7	14	$86
3-9x32	37-14	1/12	12	$70
3-9x40	42-14	1/13	13	$137
2.5-10x44	42-12	1/13	20	$134
3.5-10x50	35-12	1/13.2	21	$207
4-12x40	32-11	1/13.4	16	$125
6-24x50	18-6	1/16.2	26	$238

Browning Sport Optics

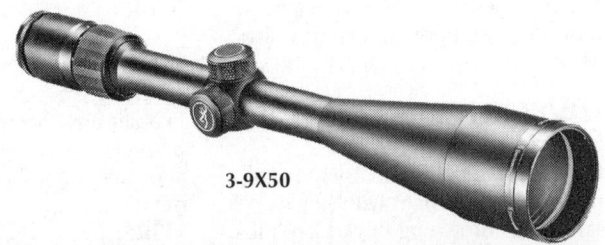

3-9X50

RIFLESCOPES

Browning's line consists of scopes featuring a fast-focus eyepiece, quarter-minute click adjustments and a one-piece water- and fogproof tube. Eye relief is 3½ inches. The lenses are all multi-coated.

RIFLESCOPES				
MAGNIFICATION (X OBJ. DIA.)	FIELD OF VIEW (FT., 100 YDS)	DIA./LENGTH (IN.)	WEIGHT (OZ.)	MSRP
2-7x32	42.5-12.1	1/11.6	16	$336
3-9x40	32-11	1/12.4	16	$352
3-9x50	30-10.5	1/15.7	16	$420
5-15x40	20.9-7	1/14.4	16	$490

Browning Sport Optics

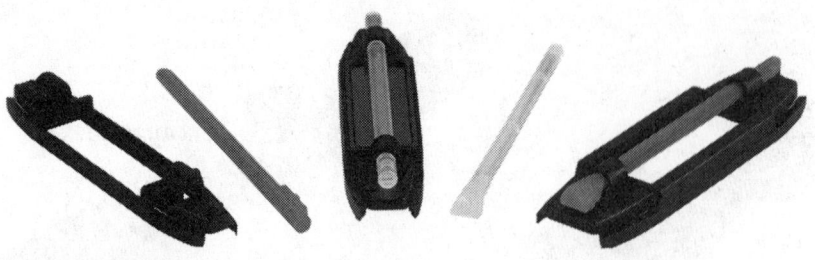

HIVIZ BIRD BUSTER MAGNETIC SHOTGUN SIGHT

HIVIZ BUCK MARK
PISTOL SIGHT

HIVIZ COMP
SIGHT

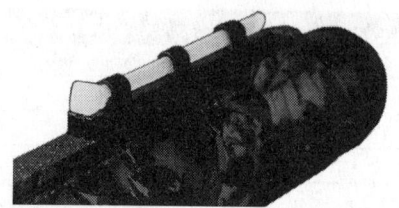

HIVIZ FLASH
POINT SIGHT

HIVIZ MAGNI-
OPTIC SIGHT

HIVIZ MID BRIGHT
SIGHT

HIVIZ SPARK
SIGHT

HIVIZ TRI-COMP
SIGHT

HIVIZ TRIVIZ
TURKEY SIGHT

HIVIZ BIRD BUSTER MAGNETIC SHOTGUN SIGHTS

Available with four interchangeable LitePipes. Fits all Browning shotguns and includes three sizes of magnetic bases. Comes in red, green or yellow.
MSRP: $19

HIVIZ BUCK MARK PISTOL SIGHT

Includes six LitePipes. Easy to install, replaces factory sight with single screw. Fits Browning Buck Mark Plus, Camper, Standard and Micro models.
MSRP $36

HIVIZ COMP SIGHT

Interchangeable LitePipes—includes eight LitePipes of different diameters and colors. Base threads directly into shotgun bead.
MSRP: $32

HIVIZ FLASH POINT SIGHT

Mounts with single screw in front bead hole of any shotgun. Includes LitePipes in various heights and colors.
MSRP: $21

HIVIZ MAGNI-OPTIC SIGHT

Enables any shotgunner to shoot with both eyes open for improved target acquisition and better hand/eye coordination.
MSRP: $35

HIVIZ MID BRIGHT SIGHT

Replaces the mid bead on many shotguns. Works well with Comp Sight, TriComp or Magnetic HiViz sights. Ensures proper barrel alignment and sight picture. Available in green or red.
MSRP: $9

HIVIZ SPARK SIGHT

Bright green fiber optic. Replaces factory bead. Thread sizes for most major shotguns.
MSRP: $8

HIVIZ TRI-COMP SIGHT

Solid steel construction with interchangeable triangular and round LitePipes.
MSRP: $31

HIVIZ TRIVIZ TURKEY SIGHT

Injection-molded optical-grade resin rear sight—fully adjustable for windage. Includes four green front sight LitePipes in different heights. Mounts on all common vent rib sizes.
MSRP: $29

BSA Scopes

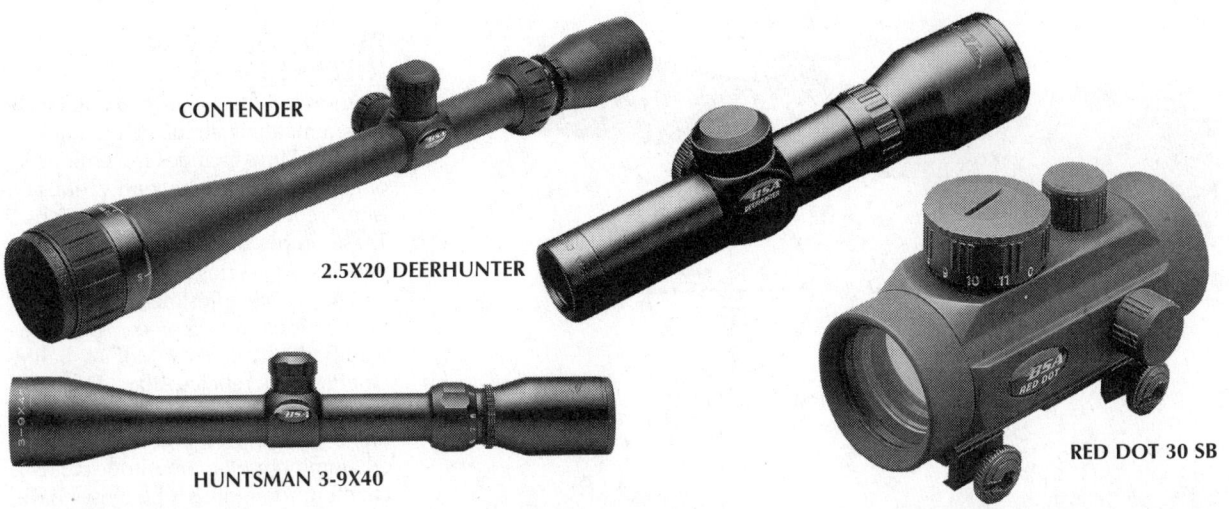

CONTENDER

2.5X20 DEERHUNTER

RED DOT 30 SB

HUNTSMAN 3-9X40

CATSEYE SCOPES

Catseye scopes have multi-coated lenses and European-style reticles; the PowerBright's reticle lights up against dark backgrounds; the Big Cat has long eye relief

1.5-4.5x32 European reticle:	$120
1.5-4.5x32 illum. reticle:	$122
3-10x44:	$152
3-10x44 illum. reticle:	$172
3.5-10x50:	$172
3.5-10x50 illum. reticle:	$192
4-16x50 AO:	$192
6-24x50:	$223

CONTENDER SCOPES

Feature multicoated lenses; eyepiece focusing from -4 to +4 diopter for duplex reticle; focusing for 10 yds. & 300 yds.; power ring & turret caps; finger adjustable windage & elevation

3-12x40 A/O TT:	$130
3-12x50	$132
4-16x40 A/O TT:	$132
6-24x40mm A/O TT:	$150
8-32x40 A/O TT:	$170

DEERHUNTER SCOPES

Deerhunter Scopes are nitrogen gas filled and feature a one piece, 1 in. tube; camera quality lenses; black textured finish; easy focus eyepiece

1.5-4.5X32mm:	$80
2.5-10X44mm:	$110
2.5X20mm (Shotgun):	$60
3-9X40mm	:$90
3-9X40mm Illuminated Reticle:	$130
3-9X40mm:	$100
3-9X50mm:	$100

HUNTSMAN SCOPES

The Huntsman series features multi-coated lenses, finger-adjustable windage and elevation and generous eye relief; warranted waterproof, fogproof and shockproof

1.5-4.5X32mm, deer/turkey reticle:	$130
3-12X50mm:	$140
3-9X40mm:	$100
3-9X44mm:	$130
4-16X40mm:	$135
4X32mm, deer/turkey reticle:	$90
18x40mmAO:	$150

MIL-DOT SCOPES

Mil-Dot scopes have multicoated objective & ocular lenses; eyepiece focusing from -4 to +4 diopter for dupleX reticle; finger adjustable windage & elevation knobs

4-16x40:	$150
6-24x40:	$170
8-32x40:	$190
6-24x40 illum:	$200
4-16x40 illum:	$180

PANTHER ALL-WEATHER SCOPES

Feature BSA Standard Reticles; fully multicoated camera quality glass lenses; ocular speed focus; European style eyeball; finger adjustable windage and elevation with "push/pull" locking system

3-10x40:	$160
2.5-10x44:	$180
3.5-10x50:	$200
6.5-20x44:	$230

PLATINUM TARGET SCOPES

Platinum target scopes are fitted with finger-adjustable windage and elevation dials; these scopes have a three-piece objective lens systems

PT 6-24x44 AO:	$222
PT 8-32x44 AO:	$242
PT 6-24x44 AO Mildot reticle:	$200
PT 8-32x44 AO Mildot reticle:	$230

RED DOT SIGHTS

Perfect sight for pistols and shotguns; a small bright red dot appears in the center; available in BSA's Shadow Black rubber; choose either a push-button control, or 11-position click rheostat

PD30BK - 30mm with rings:	$100
PD30SIL - 30mm with rings, silver:	$60
RD30 - 30mm Red Dot Sight:	$60
RD30SB - 30mm Red Dot Sight in Shadow Black Finish:	$60
RD30SIL - 30mm Red Dot Sight in Matte Silver:	$60
RD42SB - 42mm Red Dot Sight in Shadow Black Finish:	$100
RD50SB - 50mm Red Dot Sight in Shadow Black Finish:	$130
MR30BK - 30mm:	$130
RD42 - RD Red Dot Series:	$50

SWEET 17 SCOPES

Designed for the .17 HMR, these scopes feature a 1-in. mounting tube; fully-coated optics; finger-adjustable windage and elevation

2-7x32 A/O:	110
3-12x40:	$152
4-12x40:	$152
6-18x40:	$190

SIGHTS & SCOPES

Burris Scopes

SIGHTS & SCOPES

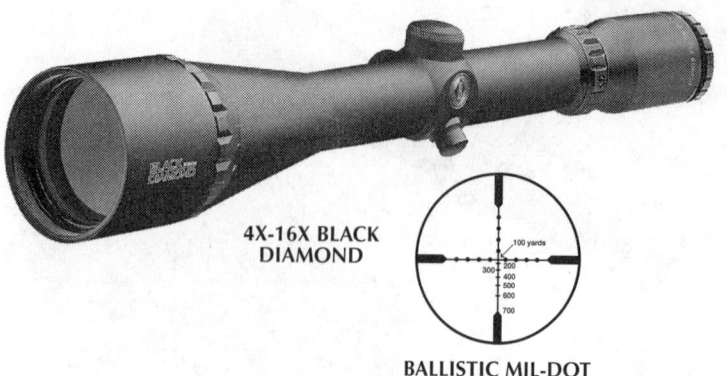

4X-16X BLACK DIAMOND

BALLISTIC MIL-DOT

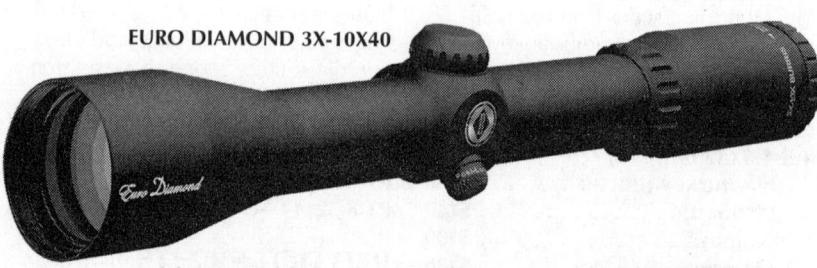

EURO DIAMOND 3X-10X40

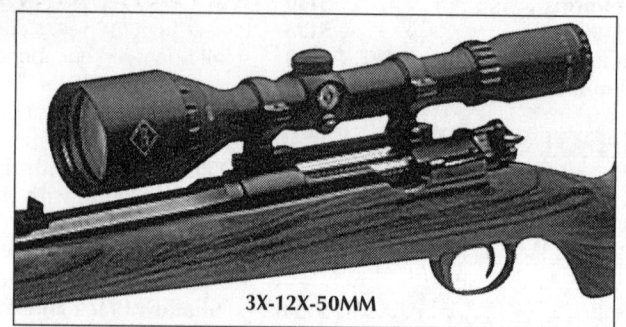

3X-12X-50MM

2.75X SCOUT

BLACK DIAMOND RIFLESCOPES

Features a 50mm objective and heavy 30mm matte finish tube. The Black Diamond line includes three models of a 30mm main tube with various finishes, reticles and adjustment knobs. These scopes have rubber-armored parallax-adjust rings, an adjustable and resettable adjustment dial and an internal focusing eyepiece. Available with BallPlex, Ballistic MilDot, BallM-Dot/PosiLock reticles. Black Diamond Titanium scopes are made of solid titanium, coated with molecularly bonded aluminum titanium nitride. Black Diamond Titanium scope lenses have a scratch-proof T-Plate coating applied to the objective and eyepiece lenses.

EURO DIAMOND SCOPES

All Euro Diamond scopes come in matte black finish, with fully multi-coated lenses and ¼-minute clicks on re-settable dials. Eye relief is 3½ to 4 inches. The eyepiece and power ring are integrated and the scopes have a helical rear ocular ring. Options include: ballistic Plex or German 3P#4 reticle and PosiLock or illuminated.

FULLFIELD II VARIABLE SCOPES

Feature one piece main tubes; multi-coated lenses; one-piece power ring/eyepiece; soft rubber eyeguard; double integral springs; available with Ballistic Plex, Ballistic MilDot, Fine Plex reticles; finished in matte, silver or black; nitrogen filled with special quad seals.

LIGHTED RETICLE SCOPES

The Burris Electro-Dot adds a bright pinpoint aiming spot to the center of the crosshair. Available with Ballistic Plex or Fast Plex reticles. Battery Life: Medium Power—50-60 hrs; High Power—40-50 hrs,

SCOUT SCOPES

For hunters who need a 7- to 14-inch eye relief for mounting in front of the ejection port; allows you to shoot with both eyes open. The 15-foot field of view and 2.75X magnification are ideal for brush guns and shotgunners.

Burris Scopes

3-9X SHORT MAG SCOPE

4.5-14X SHORT MAG SCOPE

1.5-6X SIG LRS

SPEEDDOT 135

3X10 SIG LRS

SIGHTS & SCOPES

SHORT MAG SCOPES:

Short Mag riflescopes feature top grade optical glass and index-matched HiLume lens multicoatings; generous 3½-5 in. eye relief; re-settable windage and elevation dials. Lens system formulation combines edge-to-edge clarity with 3½-5 in. of light rifle magnum eye relief. Each variable power Short Mag features a Ballistic Plex reticle.

SIGNATURE SCOPES

Features include premium quality lenses with Hi-Lume multi-coat; large internal lenses; deep relief grooves on the power ring and parallax adjust ring and centrally located adjustment turret; shooter-viewable, easy-to-grip power ring integrated with the eyepiece; non-slip ring of rubber on the internally focusable eyepiece ring. Available with Ball Plex, Ball Plex/PosiLock, Ballistic MilDot and 3P#4/PossiLock reticles.

SPEEDDOT 135

1x35mm pistol and shotgun sight. Electronic red dot reticle, 3 moa or 11 moa.

Burris Scopes

Item	Model	Reticle	Finish	Features	List
BLACK DIAMOND T-PLATES SCOPES (30MM)					
200929	4X-16X-50mm	Ballistic MDot	mat	PA	$1670
BLACK DIAMOND SCOPES (30MM)					
200954	4X-16X-50mm	Plex	mat	Side PA	$1019
200955	4X-16X-50mm	Ballistic MDot	mat	Side PA	$1153
200958	4X-16X-50mm	Ballistic MDot	mat	PLOCK/ SideP 1,202	$1226
200926	4X-16X-50mm	Ballistic Plex	mat		$1055
200933	6X-24X-50mm	Fine Plex	mat	Tar-Side /PA	$1131
200934	6X-24X-50mm	Ballistic MDot	mat	Tar-Side /PA	$1274
200942	8X-32X-50mm	Fine Plex	mat	Tar-Side /PA	$1183
200943	8X-32X-50mm	Ballistic MDot	mat	Tar-Side /PA	$1348
EURO DIAMOND SCOPES					
200960	1.5X-6X-40mm	German 3P#4	mat	Posi-Lock	$749
200961	1.5X-6X-40mm	German 3P#4	mat	Illuminated	$879
200965	3X-10X-40mm	German 3P#4	mat	Posi-Lock	$847
200967	3X-10X-40mm	German 3P#4	mat	Illuminated	$974
200966	3X-10X-40mm	Ballistic Plex	mat		$774
200919	2.5X-10X-44mm	German 3P#4	mat	Posi-Lock	$863
200918	2.5X-10X-44mm	Ballistic Plex	mat		$788
200914	3X-12X-50mm	German 3P#4	mat	Posi-Lock	$955
200915	3X-12X-50mm	German 3P#4	mat	Illuminated	$1014
200916	3X-12X-50mm	Ballistic Plex	mat		$865
FULLFIELD II SCOPES					
200052	6X-40mm	Plex	mat		$386
200057	6X-32mm HBRII	Superfine XHr	mat	Target /PA	$515
200056	6X-32mm HBRII	.375 Dot	mat	Target /PA	$538
200153	3X-9X-50mm	Plex	mat		$481
200154	3X-9X-50mm	Ballistic Plex	mat		$490
200089	1.75-5X-20mmPlex		camo		$313
200087	1.75-5X-20mmPlex		mat		$286
200160	3X-9X-40mm	Plex	blk		$336
200161	3X-9X-40mm	Plex	mat		$336
200162	3X-9X-40mm	Ballistic Plex	mat		$354

Item	Model	Reticle	Finish	Features	List
200163	3X-9X-40mm	Plex	nic		$372
200164	3X-9X-40mm	German 3P#4	mat		$372
200166	3X-9X-40mm	Ballistic Plex	blk		$354
200169	3X-9X-40mm	Ballistic Plex	nic		$390
200174	3.5X-10X-50mm	3P#4	blk		$579
200171	3.5X-10X-50mm	Plex	mat		$561
200172	3.5X-10X-50mm	Ballistic Plex	mat		$570
200180	4.5X-14X	Plex	blk	PA	$585
200181	4.5X-14X	Plex	mat	PA	$585
200183	4.5X-14X-42mm	Ballistic Plex	mat	PA	$602
200184	4.5X-14X-42	German 3P#4	mat	PA	$620
200191	6.5X-20X-50mm	Fine Plex	mat	PA	$674
200192	6.5X-20X-50mm	Fine Plex	mat	Target /PA	$715
200193	6.5X-20X-50mm	Ballistic MDot	mat	PA	808
200413	2.5X shotgun	Plex	mat		$307
LRS LIGHTED RETICLE SCOPES					
200167	3X-9X Fullfield II	Electro-Dot	mat		$531
200168	3X-9X FFII LRS	LRS Ball Plex	mat		$568
200173	3.5X-10X-50 FFII LRS	LRS Ball Plex	mat		$686
200710	1.75X-5X Sig LRS	LRS Fast Plex	mat		$792
200179	3X-9X-40 Fullfield II	Plex	mat		$568
200175	3X-10X-50 FFII	Plex	mat		$686
200185	4.5X-14X-42 FFII	Ballistic Plex	mat		$783
200186	4.5X-14X-42 FFII	Plex	mat		$783
200719	1.5X-6X-40 Sig Select	Electro-Dot	mat		$686
200565	3X-10X-40 Sig Select	Electro-Dot	mat		$817
200566	3X-10X-40 Sig Select	Ballistic Plex	mat		$863
200567	3X-10X-40 Sig Select	Ballistic Plex	mat	Posi-Lock	$908
200771	4X-16X-44 Sig Select	Electro-Dot	mat	PA	$957
200772	4X-16X-44 Sig Select	Ballistic Plex	mat	PA	$996
200773	4X-16X-44 Sig Select	Ballistic Plex	mat	Posi-Lock/ PA	$1042

SIGHTS & SCOPES

Burris Scopes

Item	Model	Reticle	Finish	Features	List
SCOUT SCOPES					
200424	1X XER	Plex	mat		$331
200269	2.75X	Heavy Plex	mat		$366
SHORT MAG SCOPES					
200424	1X XER	Plex	mat		$331
201310	4X	Plex	blk		$324
201311	4X	Plex	mat		$347
201320	2X-7X	Plex	mat		$454
201321	2X-7X	Ballistic PlexTM	mat		$472
201330	3X-9X	Plex	mat		$472
201331	3X-9X	Ballistic PlexTM	mat		$490
201340	4.5X-14X	Plex	mat	PA	$574
201341	4.5X-14X	Ballistic PlexTM	mat	PA	$593
SIGNATURE SERIES SCOPES					
200707	1.75X-5X-32 Safari	Taper Plex	mat		$618
200708	1.75X-5X-32 Safari	Taper Plex	mat	Posi-Lock	$669
200713	1.75X-5X-32 Safari	German 3P#4	mat	Posi-Lock	$706
200717	1.5X-6X-40mm	Taper Plex	mat		$618
200718	1.5X-6x-40mm	Taper Plex	mat	Posi-Lock	$669

Item	Model	Reticle	Finish	Features	List
200560	3X-10X-40mm	Ballistic Plex	mat		$685
200562	3X-10X-40mm	Plex	mat		$667
200561	3X-10X-40mm	Ballistic Plex	mat	Posi-Lock	$729
200616	3X-12X-44mm	Ballistic Plex	mat		$722
200617	3X-12X-44mm	Ballistic Plex	mat	Posi-Lock	$772
200768	4X-16X-44mm	Ballistic Plex	mat	PA	$783
200769	4X-16X-44mm	Ballistic Mdot	mat	PA	$912
200770	4X-16X-44mm	Ballistic Plex	mat	Posi-Lock/ PA	$871
200822	6X-24X-44mm	Plex	mat	PA	$810
200823	6X-24X-44mm	Fine Plex	mat	Target/PA	$847
200824	6X-24X-44mm	Ballistic MDot	mat	Target/PA	$976
200867	8X-32X	Fine Plex	mat	Target/PA	$865
200868	8X-32X	Ballistic MDot	mat	Target/PA	$994
SPEEDDOT 135 SIGHTS					
300200	1X-35mm	3 MOA Dot	mat		$297
300201	1X-35mm	11 MOA Dot	mat		$297
300203	1X-35mm	3MOA Dot	camo		$338

SIGHTS & SCOPES

Bushnell Riflescopes

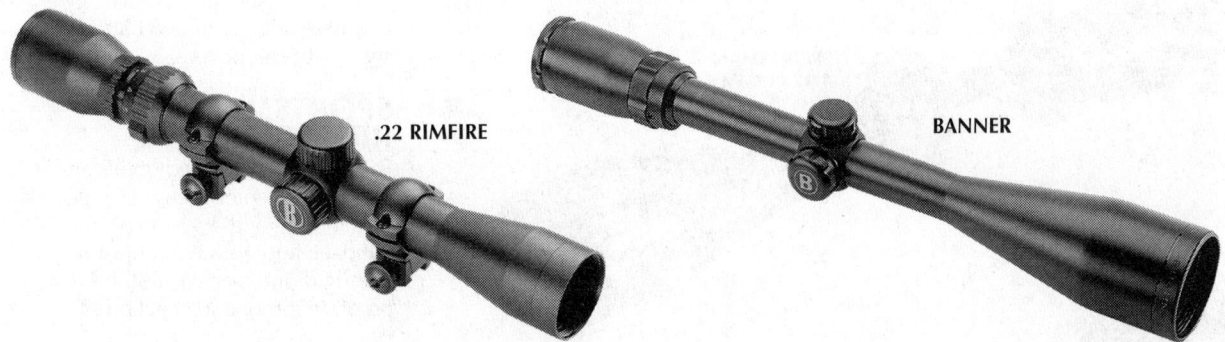

.22 RIMFIRE

BANNER

.22 RIMFIRE RIFLESCOPES

Bushnell .22 Rimfire scopes are designed with a 50-yard parallax setting and fully coated optics. The one-piece 1 in. tube is waterproof and fogproof; ¼ M.O.A. windage and elevation adjustments are fingertip-easy to turn. Scopes come with rings for grooved receivers.

BANNER RIFLESCOPES

Banner Dusk & Dawn riflescopes feature DDB multi-coated lenses to maximize dusk and dawn brightness for clarity in low and full light. A fast-focus eyepiece and wide-angle field of view complement a one-piece tube and ¼ in. M.O.A. resettable windage and elevation adjustments. An easy-trip power change ring allows fast power changes. This scope is waterproof, fogproof and shockproof.

Bushnell Riflescopes

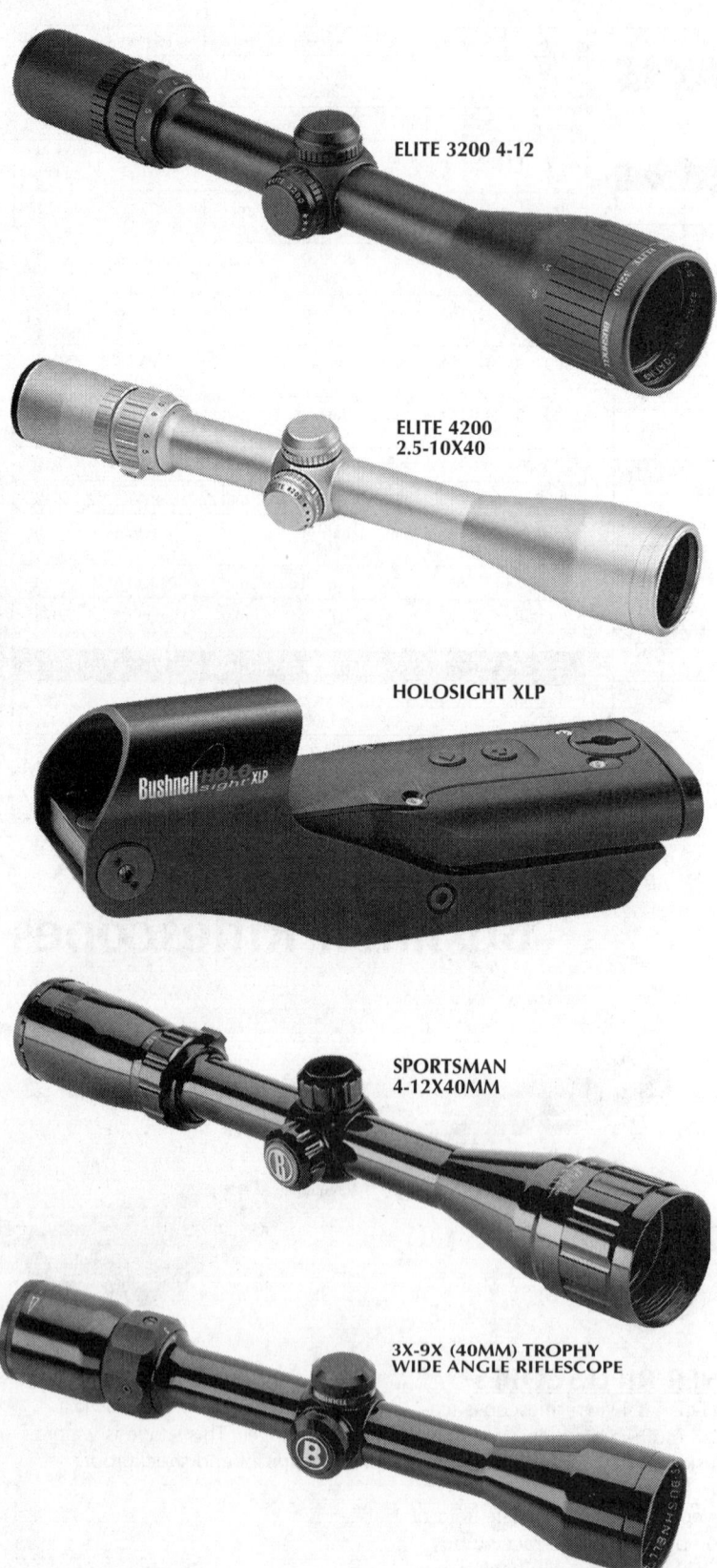

ELITE 3200 4-12

ELITE 4200
2.5-10X40

HOLOSIGHT XLP

SPORTSMAN
4-12X40MM

3X-9X (40MM) TROPHY
WIDE ANGLE RIFLESCOPE

ELITE 3200 RIFLESCOPES
Riflescopes are made with multi-coated optics and a patented Rainguard lens coating that reduces large water drops to near-microscopic specks. Bushnell's FireFly reticle is available on several 3200 models, illuminating the cross-hairs. The FireFly reticle glows green after a 10-second flashlight charge. Elite 3200 riflescopes are dry-nitrogen filled and feature a one-piece hammer-forged aluminum tube, ¼ M.O.A. fingertip, audible/resettable windage and elevation adjustment and are waterproof , fogproof, and shockproof.

ELITE 4200 RIFLESCOPES
Riflescopes feature 95% light transmission at 550nm. 4200s have multi-coated optics with hydrophobic Rainguard lens coating. These scopes feature hammer-forged one-piece aluminum/titanium alloy dry-nitrogen filled tubes, ¼ M.O.A. fingertip, audible/resettable windage and elevation adjustment; and are waterproof, fog-proof and shockproof. 4200 scopes are available with Bushnell's FireFly reticle.

HOLOSIGHT
Projects the appearance of an illuminated crosshair 50 yards in front of your gun with no projected forward light. Shockproof, waterproof and fog-proof with unlimited field of view and eye relief. Fits handguns, shotguns and rifles with a standard Weaver style mount. Available in two battery styles—N cell or AAA.

SPORTSMAN RIFLESCOPES
Featuring multi-coated optics and a fast-focus eyepiece, easy-grip power change ring and 1/4 M.O.A. fingertip windage and elevation adjustments. The rigid one-piece 1 in. tube is waterproof, fogproof and shockproof.

TROPHY RIFLESCOPES
Riflescopes feature multi-coated optics, Amber-Bright high contrast lens coating, one-piece dry-nitrogen filled tube construction, ¼ M.O.A. fingertip, audible/resettable windage and elevation adjustment, a fast-focus eyepiece and are waterproof, fogproof and shockproof.

.22 RIMFIRE

Model	Finish	Power / Obj. Lens (mm)	Reticle	Field-of-View (ft@100yds)	Weight (oz)	Length (in)	Eye Relief (in)	Exit Pupil (mm)	Click Value (in@100yds)	Adj. Range (in@100yds)	Suggested Retail
76-2239	Matte	3–9 x 32	Multi-X	40–13	11.2	11.75	3.0	10.6–3.6	.25	40	$153.95
76-2239S	Silver	3–9 x 32	Multi-X	40–13	11.2	11.75	3.0	10.6–3.6	.25	40	53.95
76-2243	Matte	4 x 32	Multi-X®	30 / 10@4x	10	11.5	3.0	8	.25	40	45.95

BANNER DUSK & DAWN

Model	Finish	Power / Obj. Lens (mm)	Reticle	Field-of-View (ft@100yds)	Weight (oz)	Length (in)	Eye Relief (in)	Exit Pupil (mm)	Click Value (in@100yds)	Adj. Range (in@100yds)	Suggested Retail
71-0432	Matte	4 x 32	Circle-X®	31.5–10.5@4x	11.1	11.3	3.3	8@4x	.25	50	$89.95
71-1432	Matte	1–4 x 32	Circle-X®	78.5–24.9	12.2	10.5	4.3	16.9@1x / 8@4x	.25	50	107.95
71-1436	Matte	1.75–4 x 32	Circle-X®	35–16	12.1	10.8	6	18.3@1.75x –6.4@4x	.25	100	101.95
71-1545	Matte	1.5–4.5 x 32	Multi-X®	67v23	10.5	10.5	4.0	17@1.5x / 7@4.5x	.25	60	101.95
71-3510	Matte	3.5–10 x 36	Multi-X®	30-10.4 15.0	12.5	3.4		10.3@ 3.5/3.6 @10	.25	85	133.95
71-3944	Matte	3–9 x 40	Circle-X®	36–13	12.5	11.5	4.0	13@3x / 4.4@9x	.25	60	109.95
71-3944MO	MosOak	3–9 x 40	Circle-X®	36/12@3x–12/4.3@9x	12.5	11.5	4.0	13@3x / 4.4@9x	.25	60	110.00
71-3946	Matte	3–9 x 40	Multi-X®	40–14	13	12	4.0	13@3x / 4.4@9x	.25	60	101.95
71-3947	Matte	3–9 x 40	Multi-X®	40–13.6	13	12	3.3	13@3x / 4.4@9x	.25	60	111.95
71-3948	Matte	3–9 x 40	Multi-X®	40–14	13	12	3.3	13.3@3x / 4.4@9x	.25	60	105.95
71-3949I	Matte	3–9 x 40	R/G illuminated	40/13.6@3x–14/4.7@9x	13	12	3.3	13.3@3x / 4.4@9x	.25	60	111.00
71-3950	Matte	3–9 x 50	Multi-X®	26–12	19	16	3.8	16@3x / 5.6@9x	.25	50	163.95
71-3951	Matte	3–9 x 50	3-2-1 Low Light™	26–12	19	16	3.8	16@3x / 5.6@9x	.25	50	163.95
71-3959I	Matte	3–9 x 50	R/G illuminated	36/12@3x–12/4@9x	20	16	3.8	16@3x / 5.6@9x	.25	50	164.00
71-4124	Matte	4–12 x 40	Multi-X®	29–11	15	12	3.3	10@4x / 3.3@12x	.25	60	138.95
71-4164I	Matte	4–16 x 40	illuminated	22/7@4x–6/2@16x	16	14	3.3	10@4x / 2.5@16x	.25	70	138.00
71-6185	Matte	6–18 x 50	Multi-X®	17–6	18	16	3.5	8.3@6x / 2.8@18x	.25	40	183.95
71-6244	Matte	6–24 x 40	Mil Dot	17–5	19.6	16.1	3.4	6.7@6x / 1.7@24x	.25	36	189.95

ELITE 3200

Model	Finish	Power / Obj. Lens (mm)	Reticle	Field-of-View (ft@100yds)	Weight (oz)	Length (in)	Eye Relief (in)	Exit Pupil (mm)	Click Value (in@100yds)	Adj. Range (in@100yds)	Suggested Retail
32-1040M	Matte	10 x 40	Mil Dot	11	15.5	11.7	3.5	4.0	.25	100	$279.95
32-1546M	Matte	1.5–4.5 x 32	FireFly™	63/21@1.5x	13	12.5	3.6	21–7.6	.25	100	307.95
32-2632M	Matte	2–6 x 32	Multi-X®	10/3@2x	10	9	20	16–5.3	.25	50	389.95
32-2632S	Silver	2–6 x 32	Multi-X®	10/3@2x	10	9	20	16–5.3	.25	50	389.95
*32-2636M	Matte	2–6 x 32	FireFly™	10/3@2x	10	9	20	16–5.3	.25	50	431.95
32-2732M	Matte	2–7 x 32	Multi-X®	44.6/15@2x	12	11.6	3.0	12.2–4.6	.25	50	265.95
32-3104M	Matte	3-10 x 40	Multi-X®	35.5/11.8 0.3x	14.5	11	3.7	13.1-4	.25	85	297.95
32-3940G	Gloss	3–9 x 40	Multi-X®	33.8/11@3x	13	12.6	3.3	13.3–4.4	.25	50	279.95
32-3940S	Silver	3–9 x 40	Multi-X®	33.8/11@3x	13	12.6	3.3	13.3–4.4	.25	50	279.95
32-3944M	Matte	3–9 x 40	Multi-X®	33.8/11@3x	13	12.6	3.3	13.3–4.4	.25	50	279.95
32-3946M	Matte	3–9 x 40	FireFly™	33.8/11@3x	13	12.6	3.3	13.3–4.4	.25	50	321.95
32-3954M	Matte	3–9 x 50	Multi-X®	31.5/10@3x	19	15.7	3.3	16–5.6	.25	50	335.95
32-3955E	Matte	3–9 x 50	European	31.5/10@3x	22	15.6	3.3	16–5.6	.36	70	561.95
32-3956M	Matte	3–9 x 50	FireFly™	31.5/1.50@3x	19	15.7	3.3	16.7–5.6	.25	50	377.95
32-3957M	Matte	3–9 x 50	FireFly™	31.5/10.5@3x	22	15.6	3.3	16.7–5.6	.25	70	603.95
32-4124A	Matte	4–12 x 40	Multi-X®	26.9/9@4x	15	13.2	3.3	10–3.33	.25	50	411.95
32-4124B	Matte	4-12x40	Ballistic	26.9/9@4x	15	13.2	3.3	10-3.33	.25	50	531.95
32-5154M	Matte	5–15 x 40	Multi-X®	21/7@5x	19	14.5	4.3	9–2.7	.25	50	439.95
32-5155M	Matte	5–15 x 50	Multi-X®	21/7@5x	24	15.9	3.4	10–3.3	.25	40	463.95
*32-5156M	Matte	5–15 x 40	FireFly™	21/7@5x	19	14.5	4.3	9–2.7	.25	50	481.95
32-7214M	Matte	7–21 x 40	MilDot	13.5/4.5@7x	15	12.8	3.3	14.6-6	.25	40	549.95

ELITE 4200

Model	Finish	Power / Obj. Lens (mm)	Reticle	Field-of-View (ft@100yds)	Weight (oz)	Length (in)	Eye Relief (in)	Exit Pupil (mm)	Click Value (in@100yds)	Adj. Range (in@100yds)	Suggested Retail
42-1636M	Matte	1.5–6 x 36	Multi-X®	61.8/20.6@1.5x	15.4	12.8	3.3	14.6–6	.25	60	$533.95
42-1637m	Matte	1.5-6 x 36	FireFly™	61.8/20.6 @65x	15.4	12.8	3.3	14.6–6	.25	60	603.95
42-2104M	Matte	2.5–10 x 40	Multi-X®	41.5/13.8@2.5x	16	13.5	3.3	15.6–4	.25	50	563.95
42-2104G	Gloss	2.5–10 x 40	Multi-X®	41.5/13.8@2.5x	16	13.5	3.3	15.6–4	.25	50	563.95
42-2104S	Silver	2.5–10 x 40	Multi-X®	41.5/13.8@2.5x	16	13.5	3.3	15.6–4	.25	50	563.95
42-2105M	Matte	2.5–10 x 50	Multi-X®	40.3/13.4@2.5x	18	14.3	3.3	15–5	.25	50	669.95
42-2106M	Matte	2.5–10 x 50	FireFly™	40.3/13.4 @25x	18	14.3	3.3	15–5	.25	50	747.95
42-2146M	Matte	2.5–10 x 40	FireFly™	41.5/13.8@2.5x	16	13.5	3.3	15.6–4	.25	50	605.95
42-2151M	Matte	2.5–10 x 50	4A w/1 M.O.A Dot	40/13.3@2.5x	22	14.5	3.3	15–5	.25	60	699.95
42-4164M	Matte	4–16 x 40	Multi-X®	26/8.7@4x	18.6	14.4	3.3	10–25	.125	40	565.95
42-4165M	Matte	4–16 x 50	Multi-X®	26/9@4x	22	15.6	3.3	12.5–3.1	.125	50	731.95
42-6242M	Matte	6–24 x 40	Mil Dot	18/6@6x	20.2	16.9	3.3	6.7–1.7	.125	26	659.95
42-6243A	Matte	6–24 x 40	¼ M.O.A. Dot	18/6@6x	20.2	16.9	3.3	6.7–1.7	.125	26	639.95
42-6244M	Matte	6–24 x 40	Multi-X®	18/4.5@6x	20.2	16.9	3.3	6.7–1.7	.125	26	639.95
42-8324M	Matte	8–32 x 40	Multi-X®	14/4.7@8x	22	18	3.3	5–1.25	.125	20	703.95

HOLO SIGHT

Model	Reticle	Mag. @ 100 yds.	Field of view ft. @ 100 yds.	Weight	Length	Eye Relief	Batteries	Brightness Adj.	Price
51-0021	Holographic	1x	Unlimited	6.4 oz.	4.12 in.	½-in.-10[1]	2 Type N	20 Levels	$389.95
53-0021	Holographic	1x	Unlimited	12 oz.	6 in.	Unlimited	AAA	20 Levels	299.95
53-0027	Holographic	1x	Unlimited	12 oz.	6 in.	Unlimited	AAA	20 Levels	299.95

Bushnell Riflescopes

SPORTSMAN® RIFLESCOPES

Model	Finish	Power / Obj. Lens (mm)	Reticle	Field-of-View (ft@100yds)	Weight (oz)	Length (in)	Eye Relief (in)	Exit Pupil (mm)	Click Value (in@100yds)	Adj. Range (in@100yds)	Suggested Retail
*72-0038	Matte	3–9 x 32	Multi-X®	37–14	13.5	12	3.5	10.6–3.6	.25	100	$69.96
**72-0039	Gloss	3–9 x 32	Multi-X®	40 13.1	163	12.2	430	3.6–11	.25	100	101.95
72-0130	Matte	1 x 23	6 M.O.A. Red Dot	60	4.9	5.5	Unlimited	2.3	.5	50	73.95
72-1393	Gloss	3–9 x 32	Multi-X®	37–14	13.5	12	3.5	10–3.6	.25	100	59.95
72-1393S	Silver	3–9 x 32	Multi-X®	37–14	13.5	12	3.5	10–3.6	.25	100	59.95
72-1398	Matte	3–9 x 32	Multi-X®	37–14	13.5	12	3.5	10–3.6	.25	100	59.95
72-1403	Matte	4 x 32	Multi-X®	29	11	11.7	3.4	8	.25	110	49.95
72-1545	Matte	1.5–4.5 x 21	Multi-X®	24–69	11.7	10.1	3.3	10–3.6	.25	210	75.95
72-1548R	Camo	1.5–4.5 x 32	Circle-X®	46.2–19.3	13.5	11.7	4.3	21–7.1	.25	100	95.95
72-3940M	Matte	3–9 x 40	Multi-X®	37–12	15	13	3.5	13–4.4	.25	100	83.95
72-3943	Matte	3–9 x 40	Lowlight	37–12	15	13	3.5	13–4.4	.25	100	83.95

*Airgun scope   **Target Airgun scope

TROPHY® RIFLESCOPES

Model	Finish	Power / Obj. Lens (mm)	Reticle	Field-of-View (ft@100yds)	Weight (oz)	Length (in)	Eye Relief (in)	Exit Pupil (mm)	Click Value (in@100yds)	Adj. Range (in@100yds)	Suggested Retail
73-0131	Matte	1 x 28	6 M.O.A. Red Dot	68–22.6	6	5.5	Unlimited	28	.5	50	$89.95
73-0134	Matte	1 x 28	4 Dial-In Electronic	68–22.6	6	5.5	Unlimited	28	.5	50	119.95
73-0135	Matte	1 x 30	4 Dial-Fn	68–22.6	6	5.5	Unlimited	28	.5	50	131.95
73-0232S	Silver	2 x 32	Multi-X®	20–7	7.7	8.7	18	16	.25	90	191.95
73-1421	Matte	1.75–4 x 32	Circle-X®	73–30	10.9	10.8	4.1	18@1.75x / 8@4x	.25	120	149.95
73-1422MO	Camo	1.75–4 x 32	Circle-X®	73–30	10.9	10.8	4.1	18@1.75x / 8@4x	.25	120	163.95
73-1500	Gloss	1.75–5 x 32	Multi-X®	68–23	12.3	10.8	4.1	18.3@1.75x / 6.4@5x	.25	120	155.95
73-2632	Matte	2–6 x 32	Multi-X®	11–4	10.9	9.1	9–26	16@2x / 5.3@6x	.25	50	251.95
73-2632S	Silver	2–6 x 32	Multi-X®	11–4	10.9	9.1	9–26	16@2x / 5.3@6x	.25	50	251.95
73-3940	Gloss	3–9 x 40	Multi-X®	42–14	13.2	11.7	3.4	13.3@3x / 4.4@9x	.25	60	139.95
73-3940S	Silver	3–9 x 40	Multi-X®	42–14	13.2	11.7	3.4	13.3@3x / 4.4@9x	.25	60	139.95
73-3946	Matte	3–9 x 40	Mil Dot	42–14	13.2	11.7	3.4	13.3@3x / 4.4@9x	.25	60	149.95
73-3948	Matte	3–9 x 40	Multi-X®	42–14	13.2	11.7	3.4	13.3@3x / 4.4@9x	.25	60	139.95
73-39481	Matte	3-9 x 40	TRX	42-14	13.2	11.7	3.4	13.3 @3x/4.4 @9x	.25	60	149.95
73-3949	Matte	3–9 x 40	Circle-X®	42–14	13.2	11.7	3.4	13.3@3x / 4.4@9x	.25	60	149.95
73-4124	Gloss	4–12 x 40	Multi-X®	32–11	16.1	12.6	3.4	10@4x / 3.3@12x	.25	60	263.95
73-4124M	Matte	4–12 x 40	Multi-X®	32–11	16.1	12.6	3.4	10@4x / 3.3@12x	.25	60	263.95
73-6184	Matte	6–18 x 40	Multi-X®	17.3–6	17.9	14.8	3.0	6.6@6x / 2.2@18x	.125	40	331.95

SIGHTS & SCOPES

Docter Sports Optics

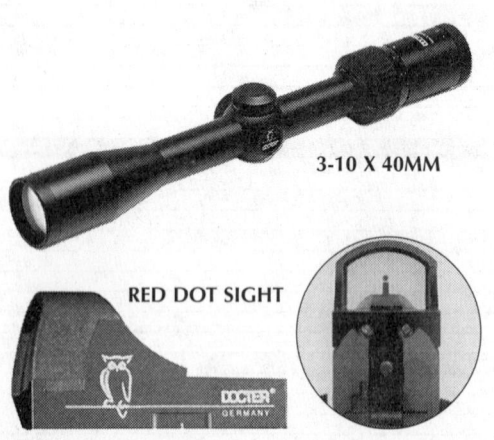

3-10 X 40MM

RED DOT SIGHT

Description	Magnification	Objective Lens Dia.	Color	Reticle	Price
ONE-INCH TUBE SCOPES					
3-9 x 40 Variable	3x to 9x	40mm	Matte Black	Plex	$454
3-9 x 40 Variable	3x to 9x	40mm	Matte Black	German #4	454
3-10 x 40 Variable	3x to 10x	40mm	Matte Black	Plex	672
3-10 x 40 Variable	3x to 10x	40mm	Matte Black	German #4	672
4.5-14 x 40 Variable	4.5x to 14x	40mm	Matte Black	Plex	730
4.5-14 x 40 Variable	4.5x to 14x	40mm	Matte Black	Dot	730
8-25 x 50 Variable	8x to 25x	50mm	Matte Black	Dot	964
8-25 x 50 Variable	8x to 25x	50mm	Matte Black	Plex	964
30mm TUBE SCOPES					
1.5-6 x 42 Variable	1.5x to 6x	42mm	Matte Black	Plex	$437
1.5-6 x 42 Variable	1.5x to 6x	42mm	Matte Black	German #4	437
1.5-6 x 42 Var., Aspherical Lens	1.5x to 6x	42mm	Matte Black	Plex	763
1.5-6 x 42 Var., Aspherical Lens	1.5x to 6x	42mm	Matte Black	German #4	437
2.5-10 x 48 Variable	2.5x to 10x	48mm	Matte Black	Plex	803
2.5-10 x 48 Variable	2.5x to 10x	48mm	Matte Black	German #4	803
2.5-10 x 48 Var., Aspherical Lens	2.5x to 10x	48mm	Matte Black	Plex	920
2.5-10 x 48 Var., Aspherical Lens	2.5x to 10x	48mm	Matte Black	German #4	858
3-12 x 56 Variable	3x to 12x	56mm	Matte Black	Plex	858
3-12 x 56 Variable	3x to 12x	56mm	Matte Black	German #4	964
3-12 x 56 Var., Aspherical Lens	3x to 12x	56mm	Matte Black	Plex	964
3-12 x 56 Var., Aspherical Lens	3x to 12x	56mm	Matte Black	German #4	964

RIFLE SCOPES

Features: High strength, one-piece tube; high grade multi-coating; joints sealed with statically and dynamically loaded ring gaskets; diopter focus; precise click-stop adjustments of ¼ in. at 100 yards for windage and elevation; more than 3 inches of eye relief; wide rubber ring on the eye-piece; wide range of adjustment (50 in.) for easier mounting error compensation.

DOCTER RED DOT SIGHT

Weighing just one ounce, it is not much bulkier than a standard rear aperture. There is no battery switch; batteries last up to five years without rest. Available in 3.5 or 7 M.D.A.

Kahles Riflescopes

2-7X36MM
AMERICAN HUNTER

CSX 1.1-4X42

HELIA CB
ILLUMINATED CB 3-12X56

HELIA COMPACT C 1,1-4X24

CL HELIA 3-9X42

CSX HELIA 1.5-6X42

AMERICAN HUNTER

Kahles rifle scopes feature 1-inch tubes and are of one piece construction, with hard anodized, scratch resistant finish. Shockproof and fogproof these scopes offer generous eye relief. The AH's reticle is mounted in the second image focal plane, so the reticle appears the same size at every power setting.

AH 2-7x36 (4A): $621
AH 2-7x36 (Plex): $621
AH 2-7x36 (Circle Plex): $621
AH 2-7x36 (TDS): $688
AH 3-9x42 (4A): $732
AH 3-9x42 (Plex): $732
AH 3-9x42 (TDS): $799
AH 3.5-10x50 (4A): $843

AH 3.5-10x50 (Plex): $843
AH 3.5-10x50 (TDS): $932

HELIA COMPACT

Kahles AMV-multi-coatings transmit up to 99.5% per air-to-glass surface. This ensures optimum use of incident light, especially in low light level conditions or at twilight. These 30mm Kahles rifle scopes are shockproof, waterproof and fogproof, nitrogen purged several times to assure the elimination of any moisture.

C 1.1-4x24 (4A or 7A): $943
C 1.5-6x42 (4A or 7A): $1043
C 2.5-10x50 (7A or Plex): $1188
C 3-12x56 (7A, Plex or 4A): . . . $1332

C 4x36 (1" tube, 4A or 7A): . . . $666
C 6x42 (1" tube, 4A or 7A): . . . $854

HELIA CB ILLUMINATED

Adjustable for illumination, and minimizes stray light. Battery life: 110 hours.

CB 1.5-6x42 (4NK or PlexN): . $1499
CB 2.5-10x50
    (4NK or PlexN): $1610
CB 3-12x56 (PlexN or 4NK): . . $1743
CSX 1.1-4x42
    (circle, Post or D-Dot): . . . $1477
CSX 1.5-6x42
    (circle, Post or D-Dot): . . . $1667
CSX 2.5-10x50
    (circle, post or D-Dot): . . . $1810

Sights & Scopes • 409

Kaps Optics Scopes

KAPS SCOPES

Headquartered in Asslar/Wetzlar, Kap scopes feature high-quality glass and state-of-the-art coatings, illuminated reticles, 30mm alloy tubes, satin finish.

KAPS				
MAGNIFICATION x OBJ. DIA.	FIELD OF VIEW (FT., 100 YDS.)	DIA./LENGTH (IN.)	WEIGHT (OZ.)	MSRP
4x36	32.8	1.18/12.8	14.1	$549
6x42	20.3	1.18/12.8	15.9	$649
8x56	18	1.18/14.2	20.8	$749
10x50	13.8	1.18/14.1	20.6	$799
1-4x22	98-33'	1.18/14.2	20.6	$819
1.5-6x42	62-23	1.18/12.4	17.3	$899
2-8x42	57-17	1.18/13.2	17.3	$949
2.5-10x50	40.7-13.8	1.18/14.1	20.6	$999
2.5-10x56	40.7-13.8	1.18/14.6	20.6	$999

Legacy Sports International

DIAMOND SPORTSMAN

GOLD CROWN

Legacy scopes made by Nikko Stirling are immersion- and shock-tested at the factory and nitrogen filled to eliminate fogging. The N-S Diamond series features first-quality, Diamond-Bright multi-coated lenses sealed in a one-piece aircraft aluminum tube with an adjustable neoprene padded eyepiece. The Diamond Sportsman riflescopes offer adjustable parallax settings from 10 yards to infinity. All other Nikko-Stirling scopes, including the Gold Crown series, are parallax set to 100 yards, effectively providing no discernible parallax between 75 yards to infinity.

DIAMOND SPORTSMAN RIFLESCOPES
10-50X60 SF: $688
10-50X60 SF: $688

GOLD CROWN RIFLESCOPES
1.5-6X42: $63
3-9X42 NO AO: $58
4.5-14X50 AO: $95
4-12X42 AO: $87
4X32: $49
4X42: $51
6X42: $51

PLATINUM NIGHTEATER RIFLESCOPES (30MM TUBE)
4-16X50 MD: $189
6-24X56 MD: $206

6-24X56 MD: $219
6-24X56 IR MD: $239
12X50 MD: $165

PLATINUM EUROHUNTER (30MM TUBE)
1.5-6X44 #4: $102
1.5-6X44 IR #4: $121
3-12X56 IR #4: $172
3-12X56 #4: $176

PLATINUM NIGHTEATER HUNTING (1-IN. TUBE)
1.5-6X36 #: $78
3.5-10X42 #4: $120
4-16X44 #4: $160
6-24X44 MD: $176
8-32X44 MD: $198
6X36 #4: $57
12X44 #4: $115

Leupold Scopes

SIGHTS & SCOPES

ULTRALIGHT VX-II 3-9X33

FX-II 2.5X28

FX-II 6X36

FX-III 6X42

VX-1 2-7X28 RIMFIRE

COMPETITION SERIES 45X45MM

FX-II 4X33

FX-II 12X40MM STANDARD

FX-II 2.2X20MM COMPACT

LPS 3.5-14X50MM SIDE FOCUS (SATIN FINISH)

ULTRALIGHT SCOPES

Ultralight riflescopes have about 17% less weight than their full-size counterparts, but retain all of the features of the larger scopes. Ultralight scopes have a Multicoat 4 lens system, are waterproof and are covered by the Leupold Full Lifetime Guarantee. They are available in matte finish with Duplex or Heavy Duplex reticles.

COMPETITION SERIES SCOPES

Leupold's new Competition series offer a bright, crisp sight picture with outstanding contrast. The side-focus parallax adjustment knob allows you to adjust your scope to be parallax-free at distances from 40 yards to infinity.

Available in matte finish with target dot or target crosshair reticle.

FX-II (FIXED POWER) SCOPES

Features: Multicoat 4 lens system; ¼ MOA click windage and elevation dials; special 9 inch eye relief; available in matte or gloss finish; duplex or wide duples reticles; Leupold full lifetime guarantee.

HANDGUN SCOPES

Features: Compact scope for handguns; multicoat 4 lens system; ¼ MOA click windage and elevation dials; special 9 inch eye relief; available in matte or gloss finish; duplex or wide duples reticles; Leupold full lifetime guarantee.

LPS PREMIERE SCOPES

Leupold's Premiere Scope (LPS) line features 30mm tubes, fast-focus eyepieces, armored power selector dials that can be read from the shooting position, 4-inch constant eye relief, Diamondcoat lenses for increased light transmission, scratch resistance, and finger-adjustable, low-profile elevation and windage adjustments.

RIMFIRE SCOPES

Adapted to the unique requirements of rimfire shooting. Features: Standard multicoat lens system; micro-friction windage and elevation dials; 60 yard parallax correction distance; Leupold full lifetime guarantee.

Leupold Scopes

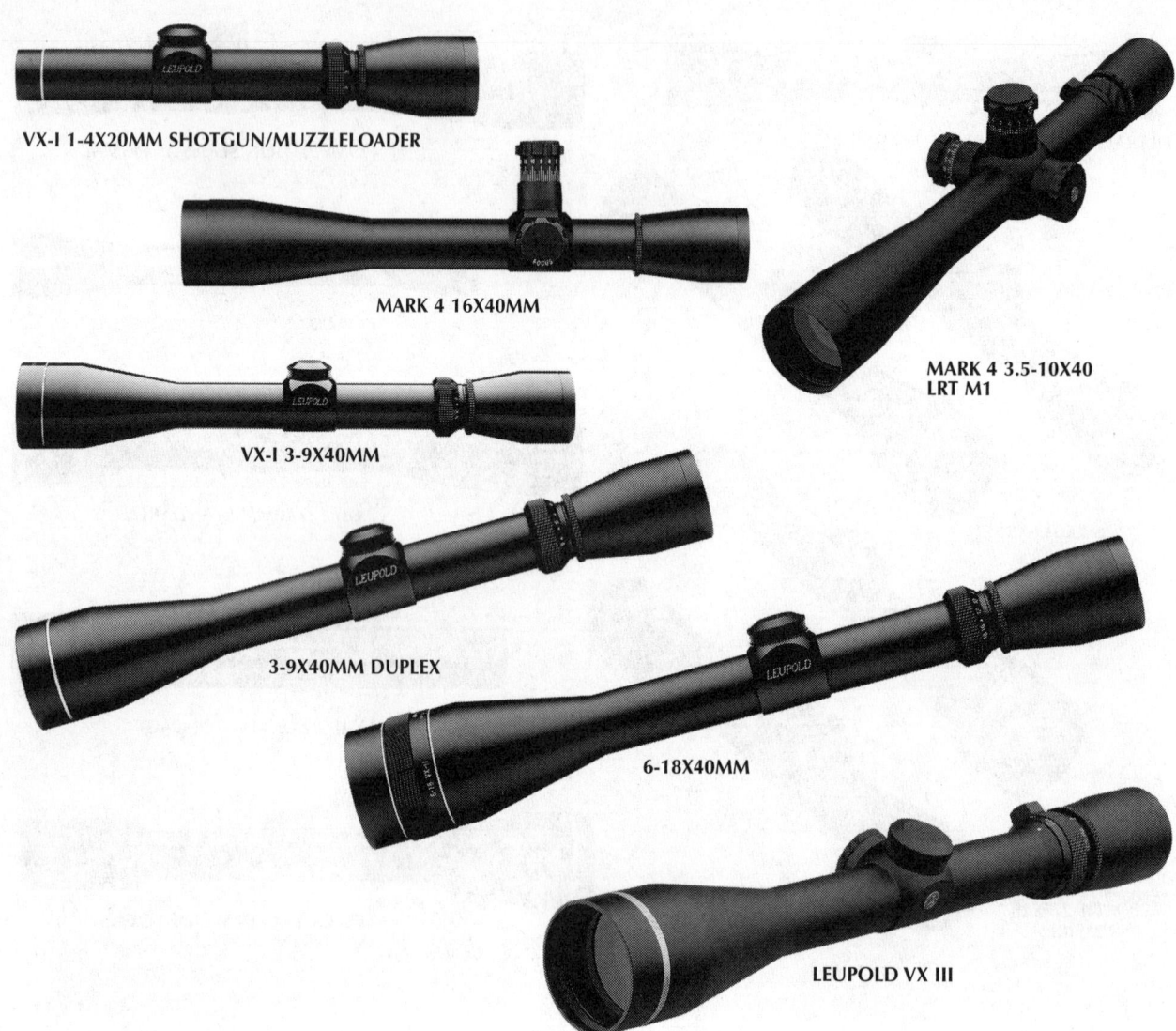

VX-I 1-4X20MM SHOTGUN/MUZZLELOADER

MARK 4 16X40MM

MARK 4 3.5-10X40 LRT M1

VX-I 3-9X40MM

3-9X40MM DUPLEX

6-18X40MM

LEUPOLD VX III

SIGHTS & SCOPES

SHOTGUN & MUZZLELOADERS SCOPES

Leupold shotgun scopes are parallax-adjusted to deliver precise focusing at 75 yards. Each scope features a special Heavy Duplex reticle that is more effective against heavy, brushy backgrounds. All scopes have matte finish and Multicoat 4 lens coating.

TACTICAL SCOPES (MARK 4)

Fixed and variable power. ¼ MOA audible click windage and elevation adjustments (Except M-3s). Duplex or MilDot reticle. Waterproof. Leupold Long Range/Tactical optics feature: 30mm (1.18 in.) maintubes–increased windage and elevation adjustment; index matched lens system; finger-adjustable dials. Fully illuminated Mil Dot, Duplex or TMR reticles available in select models. Front Focal model with the reticle in the front focal plane of the scope increases in magnification along with the image.

VX-I SERIES

A tough, gloss black finish and Duplex reticle.

VX-II SCOPES

The VX-II line offers Multi-Coated 4 lens coatings for improved light transmission; ¼ M.O.A. click adjustments; a locking eyepiece for reliable ocular adjustment; a sealed, nitrogen-filled interior for fog-free sighting.

VX-III SCOPES

The VX-III scopes, which replace the Vari-X III line, feature new lens coatings and the Index Matched Lens System (IMLS). The IMLS matches coatings to the different types of glass used in a scope's lens system. Other refinements include finger-adjustable dials with resettable pointers to indicate zero, a fast-focus, lockable eyepiece and a 30mm main tube for scopes with side-mounted focus (parallax correction) dials.

ULTRALIGHT SCOPES				
MAGNIFICATION (X OBJ. DIA.)	FIELD OF VIEW (FT., 100 YDS)	DIA./LENGTH (IN.)	WEIGHT (OZ.)	MSRP
VX-II 2-7x28mm	41.7(2x) 16.5(7x)	1/9.9	8.2	$209
VX-II 3-9x33mm	34.0(3x) 13.5(9)	1/10.96	8.8	$329
VX-II 3-9x33mm EFR	34.0(3x) 13.50(9x)	1/11.32	11.0	$455
COMPETITION SERIES SCOPES				
MAGNIFICATION (X OBJ. DIA.)	FIELD OF VIEW (FT., 100 YDS)	DIA./LENGTH (IN.)	WEIGHT (OZ.)	MSRP
35x45mm	3.3	1/15.9	20.3	$1898
40x45mm	2.7	1/15.9	20.3	$1898
45x45mm	2.5	1/15.9	20.3	$1898
FX-II (FIXED POWER)				
MAGNIFICATION (X OBJ. DIA.)	FIELD OF VIEW (FT., 100 YDS)	DIA./LENGTH (IN.)	WEIGHT (OZ.)	MSRP
2.5x28mm Scout	22.0	1/10.10	7.5	$299
4x33mm	24.0	1/10.47	9.3	$269
6x36mm	17.7	1/11.35	10.0	$280
6x42mm	17.0	1/11.90	11.3	$379
12x40mm Adj. Obj. Target	9.10	1/13.0	13.5	$529
HANDGUN SCOPES				
MAGNIFICATION (X OBJ. DIA.)	FIELD OF VIEW (FT., 100 YDS)	DIA./LENGTH (IN.)	WEIGHT (OZ.)	MSRP
FX-II 2x20mm	21.20	1/8.0	6.0	$309
FX-II 4x28mm	9.0	1/8.43	7.0	$300
LPS SCOPES				
MAGNIFICATION (X OBJ. DIA.)	FIELD OF VIEW (FT., 100 YDS)	DIA./LENGTH (IN.)	WEIGHT (OZ.)	MSRP
2.5-10x45mm	37.2(2.5x) 9.9(10x)	1/11.80	17.2	$1249
3.5-14x50mm Side Focus	27.2(3.5X) 7.1(14X)	1/13.5	19.5	$1249
RIMFIRE SCOPES				
MAGNIFICATION (X OBJ. DIA.)	FIELD OF VIEW (FT., 100 YDS)	DIA./LENGTH (IN.)	WEIGHT (OZ.)	MSRP
FX-I 4x28mm	25.5	1/9.2	7.5	$209
VX-I 2-7x28mm	41.7(2x) 16.5(7x)	1/9.9	8.2	$219
X-II 3-9x33mm EFR	34.0(3x) 13.50(9x)	1/11.32	11.0	$455
MUZZLELOADER				
MAGNIFICATION (X OBJ. DIA.)	FIELD OF VIEW (FT., 100 YDS)	DIA./LENGTH (IN.)	WEIGHT (OZ.)	MSRP
VX-I 1-4x20mm	75.0(1x) 28.5(4x)	1/9.2	9.0	$191
VX-I 2-7x33mm	42.5(2x) 17.8(7x)	1/11.0	10.5	$209
VX-I 3-9x40mm	32.9(3x) 13.1(9x)	1/12.2	12.0	$329

MARK 4 TACTICAL SCOPES				
MAGNIFICATION (X OBJ. DIA.)	FIELD OF VIEW (FT., 100 YDS)	DIA./LENGTH (IN.)	WEIGHT (OZ.)	MSRP
10x40mm LR/T M1	11.1	1.18/13.10	21.0	$1249
10x40mm LR/T M3	3.7	1.18/13.10	21.0	$1651
16x40mm LR/T M1	6.8	1.18/12.90	22.5	$1690
4 3.5-10x40mm LR/T M3	29.9(3.5x) 11.0(10x)	1.18/13.50	19.5	$1781
4.5-14x50mm LR/T M1	14.3(6.5x) 5.5(20x)	1.18/14.5	22.0	$1755
VX-I SCOPES				
MAGNIFICATION (X OBJ. DIA.)	FIELD OF VIEW (FT., 100 YDS)	DIA./LENGTH (IN.)	WEIGHT (OZ.)	MSRP
2-7x33mm	43.2(2x) 17.3(7x)	1/10.8	10.5	$246
3-9x40mm	32.9(3x) 13.1(9x)	1/12.2	12	$275
3-9x50mm	33.0(3x) 13.1(9x)	1/12.4	14.1	$290
4-12x40mm	19.9(4x) 9.4(12x)	1/12.2	13	$309
VX-II SCOPES				
MAGNIFICATION (X OBJ. DIA.)	FIELD OF VIEW (FT., 100 YDS)	DIA./LENGTH (IN.)	WEIGHT (OZ.)	MSRP
2-7x33mm	42.5(2x) 17.8(7x)	1/11.0	10.5	$499
3-9x40mm	32.3(3x) 14.0(9x)	1/12.4	12	$505
3-9x50mm	32.3(3x) 14.0(9x)	1/12.1	13.7	$600
4-12x40mm Adj. Obj.	22.8(4x) 11.0(12x)	1/12.4	14	$720
4-12x50mm	33.0(4x) 13.1(12x)	1/12.2	14.5	$767
6-18x40mm Adj. Obj.	14.5(6x) 6.6(18x)	1/13.5	15.8	$834
VX-III SCOPES				
MAGNIFICATION (X OBJ. DIA.)	FIELD OF VIEW (FT., 100 YDS)	DIA./LENGTH (IN.)	WEIGHT (OZ.)	MSRP
1.5-5x20mm	65.7(1.5x) 23.7(5x)	1/9.4	9.7 oz.	$549
1.75-6x32mm	17.0(1.75x) 6.4(6x)	1/11.23	11.2	$709
2.5-8x36mm	37.3(2.5x) 13.7(8x)	1/11.4	11.2	$709
3.5-10x40mm	29.7(3.5x) 11.0(10x)	1/12.6	13.0	$777
3.5-10x50mm	29.8(3.5x) 11.0(10x)	1/12.2	15.1	$649
4.5-14x40mm	19.9(4.5x) 7.4(14x)	1/12.6	13.2	$699
6.5-20x40mm EFR Target	14.3(6.5x) 5.6(20x)	1/14.4	19.0	$699

Lyman Sights

NO. 2 TANG SIGHT

The No. 2 Tang will fit most new and old 94 models plus Winchester Models 1885, 1887, 1890, and 1894. (The No. 2 will also fit other models when adjusted to full height).

A version is available for Marlin Models 336, 1894, 1895 and 30 series lever action-rifles. Marlin version includes adapter base. The No. 2 is all steel construction and features height index marks on the aperture post, with a maximum elevation of .800. It includes both a .093 quick sighting hunting aperture and a .040 Large Disk Target Aperture.

MSRP: **$79**

NO. 2 TANG SIGHT 1886

The Lyman No. 2 Tang Sight is now available for the Winchester 1886 lever action rifle. It fits the original Winchester Model 1886 and Browning replicas. Features include height index marks on the aperture post and an .800 maximum elevation adjustment. Also included is a .093 x 1/2 in. quick-sighting aperture and .040 x 5/8 in. target disk. Note: does not fit new rifles with Tang safety.

MSRP: **$79**

NO. 16 FOLDING LEAF SIGHT

This open rear sight with adjustable elevation blade is the perfect auxiliary sight for scope-mounted rifles. Folds close to the barrel when not in use. Designed to fit 3/8 in. dovetail slots.

MSRP: **$14**

NO. 2 TANG SIGHT

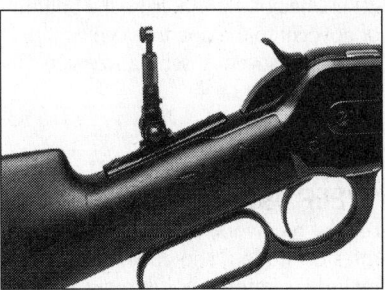

NO. 2 TANG SIGHT 1886

Lyman Sights

17 A TARGET FRONT SIGHT

20 MJT-20 LJT GLOBE

57 AND 66 RECEIVER "PEEP" SIGHT

66 WB RECEIVER SIGHT FOR 1886

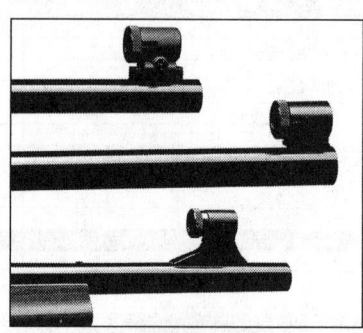

93 MATCH GLOBE FRONT SIGHT

#37 HUNTING FRONT SIGHT

SHOTGUN SIGHT

SERIES 17A TARGET FRONT SIGHTS

Machined from solid steel and designed to be mounted in 3/8 in. dovetail slots. Supplied with eight interchangeable inserts. Sight Heights (bottom of dovetail to center of aperture): 17 AHB .404; 17AMI .494; 17AUG .584
MSRP: **$31**

20 MJT-20 LJT GLOBE FRONT SIGHTS

The 20 MJT-20 LJT – 7/8 in. diameter Globe Front Sights are machined from one solid piece of steel designed to be mounted in a 3/8 in. barrel dovetail or dovetail base. 20 MJT height .700 in., 20 LJT height .825 in. from the bottom of dovetail to the aperture center supplied with seven Anschutz size steel apertures.
MSRP: **$39**

57 AND 66 RECEIVER "PEEP" SIGHTS

For flat receivers, such as lever action rifles or modern shotguns. Features include 1/4 minute audible click micrometer adjustments for elevation and windage, quick-release slide, coin-slotted "stayset" knobs and two interchangeable aperture discs (large hunting aperture and small target aperture) weight: 4 oz.
MSRP: **$77**

66 WB RECEIVER SIGHT FOR 1886

Features semi-target knobs and 1/4 minute audible clicks for windage and elevation. Supplied with hunting and target aperture disks and quick release slide.
MSRP: **$77**

90 MJT TARGET RECEIVER SIGHT

Designed to mount on Lyman and other mounting bases. Adjustable zero scales and elevation stop screw permit instantaneous return to zero. Quick release slide with release button. Large 7/8 in. non glare .040 aperture. Elevation adjustable from 1.060 to 1.560 above bore centerline.
MSRP: **$80**

93 MATCH GLOBE FRONT SIGHT

Designed to fit any rifle, the 93 match sight (7/8 in. diameter) mounts on a standard dovetail base. Supplied with seven Anschutz size inserts. The sight height is .550 from the top of the dovetail to the center of the aperture.
MSRP: **$49**

HUNTING FRONT SIGHTS

The #3 and #28 are designed to be mounted into the barrel dovetail. The #31 and #37 are designed to mount on ramps. #3 and #31 have 1/16 in. bead. #28 and #37 have 3/32 in. bead availability in ivory or gold.
MSRP: **$10**

SHOTGUN SIGHTS

Oversized ivory-like beads — easy to see under any light conditions. No. 10 Front Sights (press fit) for use on double barrel, or ribbed single barrel guns. No. 10D Front Sights (screw fit) for use on non-ribbed single barrel guns. No. 11 Middle Sight (press fit) small middle sight for use on double and ribbed single barrel guns.
MSRP: **$6**

Marble Arms Sights

CONTOUR FRONT SIGHTS

Marble's Contour Front Sights are strong, stable and give your rifle a true traditional look. Available in various widths and heights from .260 inches to .570 inches. Choose a gold, ivory or fiber optic bead.
MSRP: $12

PEEP TANG SIGHTS

The Marble's Peep Tang Sight is adjustable for windage and elevation. The adjustments are micrometer precise. Each firm detent click equals four-tenths of an inch movement at 100 yards. Each sight includes three apertures and mounting screws.
MSRP: $112

UNIVERSAL REAR SIGHTS

The #20 Universal Rear Sight system combines a strong uni-base with both peep and U-shaped semi-buckhorn uprights. All components are machined from solid steel. Marble's barrel-mounted fiber optic rear sights can be used on modern rifles, slug shotguns and muzzleloaders. Available in all standard barrel contours and a variety of heights.
#20 Universal Rear Sight. $20

Nikon Scopes

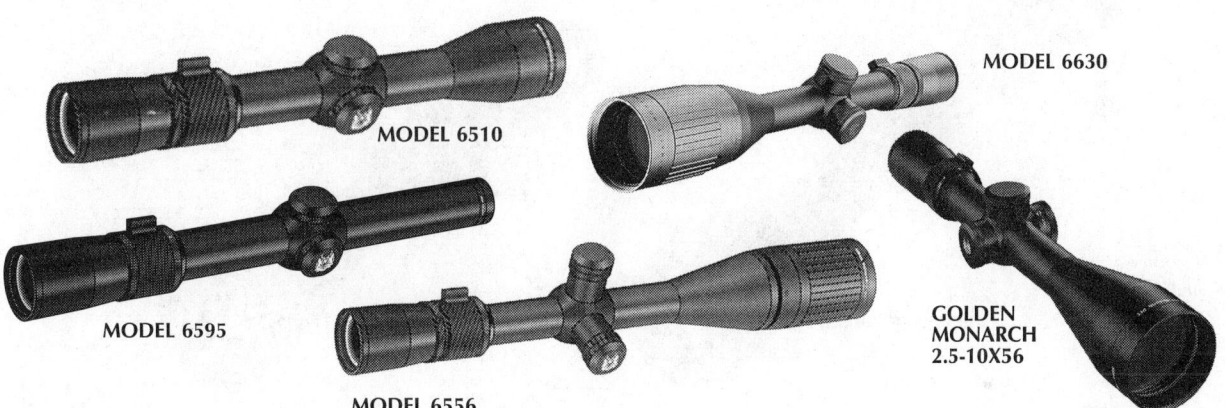

MODEL 6510
MODEL 6630
MODEL 6595
MODEL 6556
GOLDEN MONARCH 2.5-10X56

MONARCH RIFLE SCOPES

Monarch Rifle Scopes feature multi-coated Ultra ClearCoat optical system; ¼-minute positive click windage and elevation; one-piece aluminum tube construction. All Monarch scopes are shockproof, waterproof and fogproof. The Monarch series includes scopes specifically designed for use with blackpowder rifles shooting sabots or shotguns shooting sabot-style slugs. Available in matte or lustre finish.

Model 6500 4x40 Lustre:	**$230**
Model 6505 4x40 Matte:	**$230**
Model 6506 6x42 Lustre:	**$240**
Model 6508 6x42 Matte:	**$250**
Model 6510 2-7x32 Lustre:	**$406**
Model 6515 2-7x32 Matte:	**$260**
Model 6520 3-9x40 Lustre:	**$290**
Model 6525 3-9x40 Matte:	**$430**
Model 6528 3-9x40 Silver Matte:	**$430**
Model 6530 3.5-10x50 Lustre:	**$664**
Model 6535 3.5-10x50 Matte:	**$664**

Model 6537 3.3-10x44 AO Lustre:	**$380**
Model 6538 3.3-10X44 AO Matte (Mildot):	**$390**
Model 6539 3.3-10x44 AO Matte:	**$390**
Model 6540 4-12x40 AO Lustre:	**$572**
Model 6545 4-12x40 AO Matte:	**$572**
Model 6580 5.5-16.5x44 AO Black Lustre:	**$390**
Model 6585 5.5-16.5x44 AO Black Matte:	**$400**
Model 6550 6.5-20x44 AO Lustre:	**$704**
Model 6555 6.5-20x44 AO Matte:	**$704**
Model 6570 6.5-20x44 HV:	**$704**
Model 6575 6.5-20x44 HV:	**$704**
Model 6556 6.5-20x44 AO Lustre target Dot:	**$460**
Model 6558 6.5-20x44 AO Matte target Dot:	**$704**

Model 6630 3.3-10x44 AO (Titanium):	**$916**
Model 6680 5.5-16.5x44 AO (Titanium):	**$958**

HANDGUN AND SHOTGUN SCOPES

Model 6560 2x20 EER Black Lustre:	**$274**
Model 6562 2x20 EER Matte:	**$274**
Model 6565 2x20 EER Silver:	**$294**
Model 6590 1.5-4.5x20 Shotgun Black Matte:	**$240**
Model 6595 1.5-4.5x20 Sabot/Slug Black Matte:	**$304**

ILLUMINATED SCOPES

3.5-10x50 (Nikoplex or Mildot):	**$600**
6.5-20x44 (Nikoplex or Mildot):	**$680**

MONARCH GOLD

1.5-6x42:	**$840**
2.5-10x50:	**$1040**
2.5-10x56:	**$1060**

Nikon Scopes

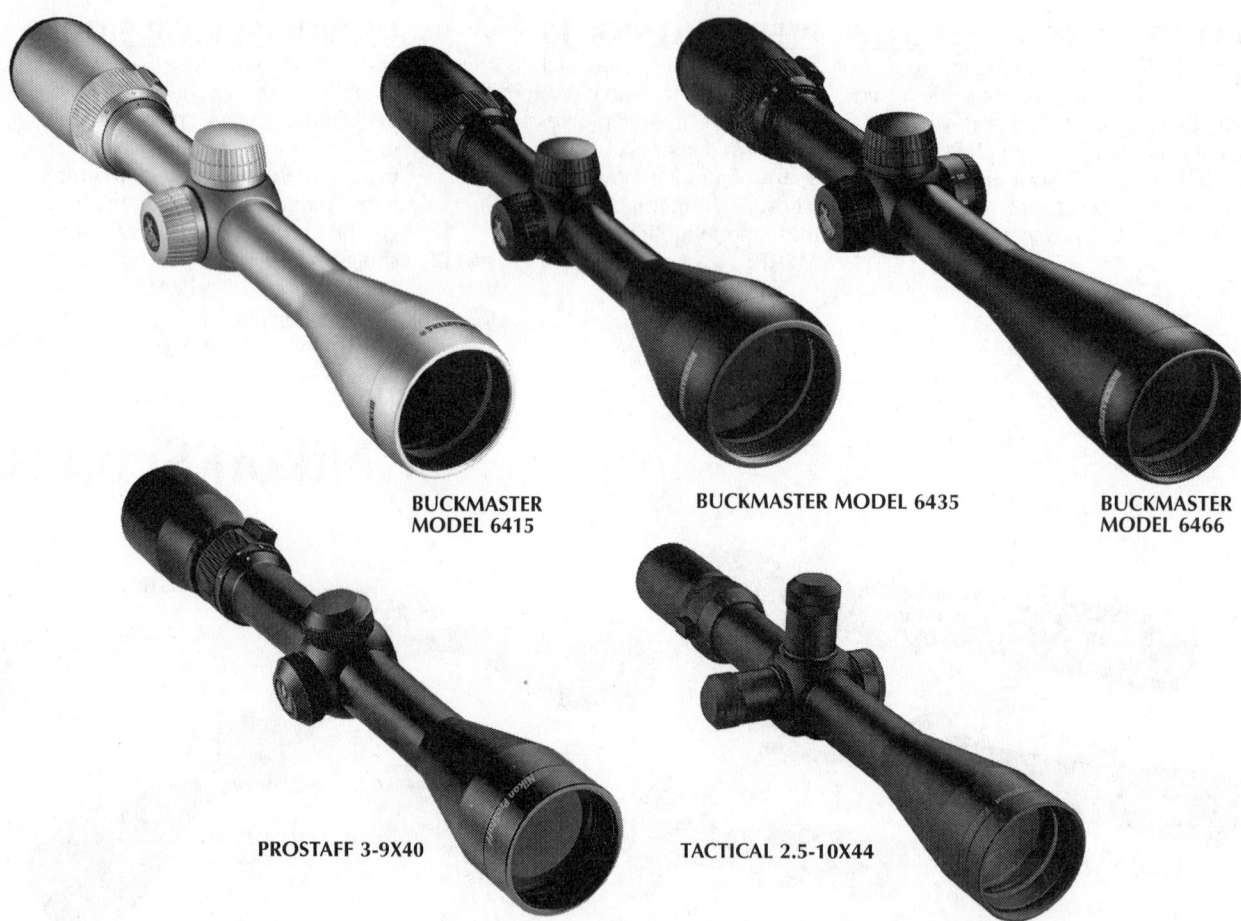

BUCKMASTER
MODEL 6415

BUCKMASTER MODEL 6435

BUCKMASTER
MODEL 6466

PROSTAFF 3-9X40

TACTICAL 2.5-10X44

BUCKMASTER SCOPES

Nikon Buckmaster scopes integrate shockproof, fogproof and waterproof construction. Nikon's Brightvue™ anti-reflective system of multicoated lenses provides over 93% anti-reflection capability for high levels of light transmission. These riflescopes are parallax-adjusted at 100 yards and have durable matte finishes that reduce glare. They also feature positive steel-to-brass, quarter-minute-click windage and elevation adjustments for instant, repeatable accuracy and a Nikoplex reticle for quick target acquisition.

Model 6465 1x20: $160
Model 6405 4x40: 160
Model 6425 3-9x40
   Black Matte: $302
Model 6415 3-9x40 Silver: $324
Model 6435 3-9x50: $300
Model 6450 4.5-14x40 AO
   Blck Matte: $440
Model 6455 4.5-14x40 AO

Silver: $460
Model 6466 4.5-14X40AO
   Matte Adj. Mildot: $440
Model 6440 4-12x50 AO Matte: $462

PROSTAFF RIFLESCOPES

Nikon's Prostaff line inclues the 4x32, 2-7x32 and 3-9x40 scopes. The 4x is parallax-corrected at 50 yards. It measures 11.2 inches long and weighs just 11.6 ounces, in silver, matte black or Realtree camo finish. The 2-7x, parallax-free at 75 yards, is a 12-ounce scope available in matte black or camo. The 13-ounce 3-9x is available in all three finishes. The Prostaff scopes have multicoated lenses and quarter-minute adjustments and are waterproof, and fogproof.

4x32 Rimfire Classic: $170
2-7x32: $190
3-9x40: $218
3-9x40 Realtree Nikoplex: $248

TACTICAL RIFLESCOPES

Nikon's Tactical Riflescopes are available in 2.5-10x44 and 4-16x50. The 2.5-10x44 features a choice of reticles: Nikoplex, Mildot, and Dual Illuminated Mildot. The 4-16 is offered with Nikoplex or Mildot. Both are equipped with turret mounted parallax adjustment knobs, have a tough, black-anodized matte finish and have easy-to-grip windage and elevation knobs for accurate field adjustments.

Tactical 2.5-10x44
   (Nikoplex or Mildot): $1360
With Illuminated Mildot: $1560
Tactical 4-16x50
   (Mildot or Nikoplex): $1460

MONARCH
DOT SIGHT

1.5-4X20
TURKEYPRO

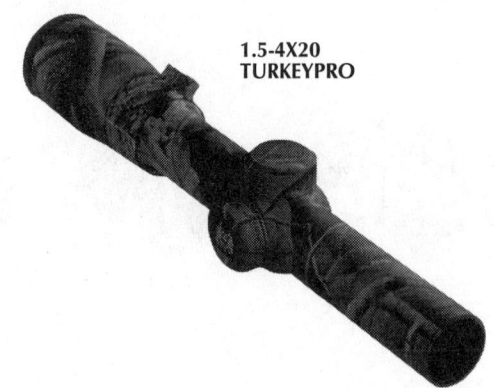

MONARCH DOT SIGHT

The Monarch Dot is waterproof, fog-proof and shockproof. Objective and ocular lenses are 30mm diameter and fully multi-coated. Nikon Dot sights have zero magnification, providing unlimited eye relief and a 47.2' field of view at 100 yards. Brightness is controlled by a lithium battery. The standard Monarch Dot Sight has a 6 MOA dot and is available in silver, black and Realtree camouflage.

Standard: **$289**
VSD: **$290**
VSD in camo: 295

1.5-4.5X20 TURKEYPRO

Available in Realtree Hardwoods camo, the 1.5-4x20 Monarch TurkeyPro is parallax-free at 50 yards.
MSRP: **$300**

2.5-8X28 EER HANDGUN SCOPE

Nikon's 2.5-8x28 EER (Extended Eye Relief) has a wide field of view at low power, but a twist of the power ring instantly supplies 8x magnification for long shots.
MSRP: **$280**

MONARCH UCC RIFLESCOPE									
Model	**4x40**	**1.5-4.5x20**	**2-7x32**	**3-9x40**	**3.5-10x50**	**4-12x40AO**	**5.5-16.5x44AO**	**6.5-20x44AO**	**2x20EER**
Lustre	6500	N/A	6510	6520	6530	6540	6580	6550/6556	6560
Matte	6505	6595	6515	6525	6535	6545	6585	6555/6558	6562
Silver	N/A	N/A	N/A	6528	N/A	N/A	N/A	N/A	6565
Actual Magnification	4x	1.5x-4.5x	2x-7x	3x-9x	3.5x-10x	4x-12x	5.5x-16.5x	6.5x-19.46x	1.75x
Objective Diameter	40mm	20mm	32mm	40mm	50mm	40mm	44mm	44mm	20mm
Exit Pupil (mm)	10	13.3-4.4	16-4.6	13.3-4.4	14.3-5	10-3.3	8-2.7	6.7-2.2	11.4
Eye Relief (in)	3.5	3.7-3.5	3.9-3.6	3.6-3.5	3.9-3.8	3.6-3.4	3.2-3.0	3.5-3.1	26.4-10.5
FOV @ 100 yds (ft)	26.9	50.3-16.7*	44.5-12.7	33.8-11.3	25.5-8.9	25.6-8.5	19.1-6.4	16.1-5.4	22
Tube Diameter	1 in.	1 in.	1 in.	1 in.	1 in.	1 in.	1 in.	1 in.	1 in.
Objective Tube(mm/in)	47.3-1.86	25.4/1	39.3-1.5	47.3-1.86	57.3-2.2	53.1-2.09	54-2.13	54-2.13	25, 4/1
Eyepiece O.D. (mm)	38	38	38	38	38	38	38	38	38
Length (in)	11.7	10	11.1	12.3	13.7	13.7	13.4	14.6	8.1
Weight (oz)	11.2	9.3	11.2	12.6	15.5	16.9	18.4	20.1	6.6
Adjustment Gradation	¼ MOA	¼ MOA	¼ MOA	¼ MOA	¼ MOA	¼ MOA	¼ MOA	1/8 MOA	¼ MOA
Max Internal Adjustment	120 MOA	120 MOA	70 MOA	55 MOA	45 MOA	45 MOA	40 MOA	38 MOA	120 MOA
Parallax Setting (yds)	100	75	100	100	100	50 to ∞	50 to ∞	50 to ∞	100

BUCKMASTER SCOPES					
Model	**1x20**	**4x40**	**3-9x40**	**3-9x50**	**4.5-14x40AO**
Matte	6465	6405	6425	6435	6450
Silver	N/A	N/A	6415	N/A	6455
Actual Magnification	1x	4x	3.3-8.5x	3.3-8.5x	4.5-13.5x
Objective Diameter	20mm	40mm	40mm	50mm	40mm
Exit Pupil (mm)	20	10	12.1-4.7	15.1-5.9	8.9-2.9
Eye Relief (in)	4.3-13.0	3.5	3.5-3.4	3.5-3.4	3.6-3.4
FOV @ 100 yds (ft)	52.5	30.6	33.9-12.9	33.9-12.9	22.5-7.5
Tube Diameter	1 in.	1 in.	1 in.	1 in.	1 in.
Objective Tube (mm/in)	27/1.06	47.3/1.86	47.3/1.86	58.7/2.3	53/2.1
Eyepiece O.D. (mm)	37	42.5	42.5	42.5	38
Length (in)	8.8	12.7	12.7	12.9	14.8
Weight (oz)	9.2	11.8	13.4	18.2	18.7
Adjustment Gradation	¼: 1 click	¼: 1 click	¼: 1 click	¼: 1 click	
Max Internal Adjustment	50	80	80	70	40
Parallax Setting (yds)	75	100	100	100	50 to ∞

Pachmayr Sights

ACCU-SET PISTOL SIGHTS

Low-profile, adjustable sights function properly with factory front sights. Constructed of carbon steel and available in blued finish. Available in plain black, white outline, or 3-dot. Micro-adjustable windage and elevation click screw for precise adjustments. Dovetail design slips easily into the factory dovetail groove and is held in place by a locking Allen screw.

MSRP: **$60**

Pentax Scopes

4X-16XAO LIGHTSEEKER 30

8.5X-32XAO LIGHTSEEKER 30

6X-24XAO LIGHTSEEKER 30

LIGHTSEEKER-XL 3-9X50

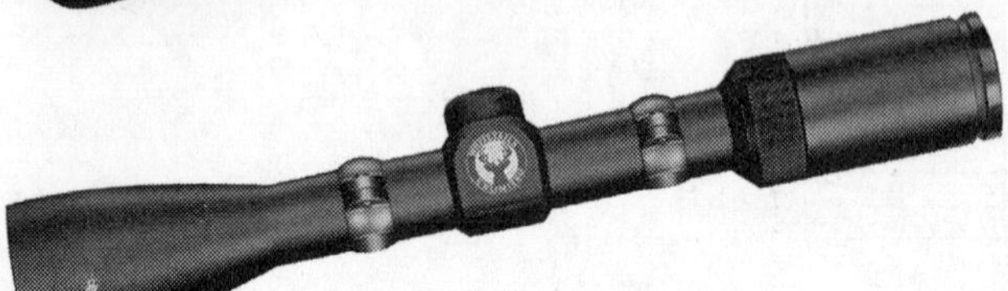

WHITETAILS UNLIMITED

LIGHTSEEKER

The Lightseeker features a scratch-resistant outer tube. High Quality cam zoom tube made of a bearing-type brass with precision machined cam slots. The zoom control screws are precision-ground to ½ of one thousandth tolerance. Power rings are sealed on a separate precision-machined seal tube. The scopes are filled with nitrogen and double-sealed with heavy-duty "O" rings, making them leakproof and fogproof. Lightseeker optics are multi-coated. The Lightseeker-30 has the same features as the Lightseeker II, but with a 30mm tube. Ballistic Plex reticles are available on the 3X-9X and 6.5X-20X Whitetails Unlimited Scopes.

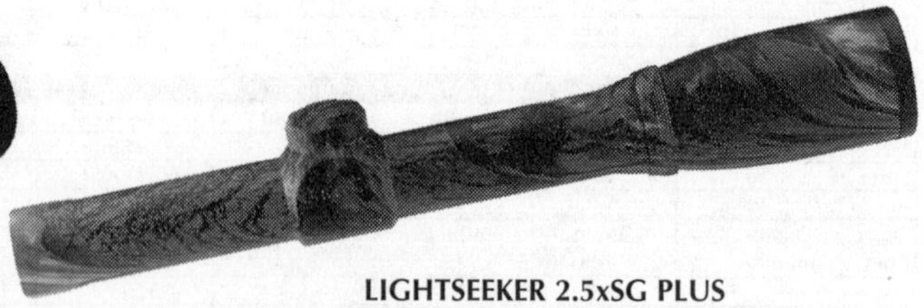

LIGHTSEEKER 2.5xSG PLUS MOSSY OAK BREAK-UP SCOPE

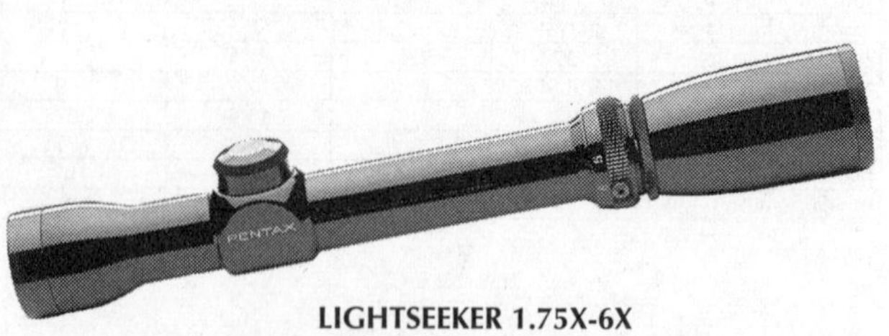

LIGHTSEEKER 1.75X-6X

Pentax Scopes

Model	Tube Diameter (in)	Objective Diameter (mm)	Eyepiece Diameter (mm)	Exit Pupil (mm)	Eye Relief (in)	Field of View (ft@ 100 yd)	Adj. Grad. (in@ 100 yd)	Max. Adjust. (in@ 100 yd)	Length (in)	Weight (oz)	Reticle	Price
RIFLE SCOPES												
Lightseeker 3X - 9X	1	40	39	12.0-5.0	3.5-4.0	36-14	¼	50	12.7	15	P, MD	$595
Lightseeker 3X - 9X	1	50	39	16.1-5.6	3.5-4.0	35-12	¼	50	13.0	19	TW, BP	$844
Lightseeker 2.5X - 10X	1	50	39	16.3-4.6	4.2-4.7	35-10	¼	100	14.1	23	TW	$844
Lightseeker 4X - 16X	1	44	36	10.4-2.8	3.5-4.0	33-9	¼	35	15.4	23.7	BP	$844
Lightseeker 2.5X SG Plus	1	25	39	7.0	3.5-4.0	55	½	60	10.0	9	DW	$364
LIGHTSEEKER-30												
3X-10X AO	30MM	40	35	13.3-4.4	3.5-4.0	34-14	¼	90	13.1	20.0	BP	$599
4X-16X AO	30mm	50	42	12-3.1	3.3-3.8	27-7.5	¼	74	15.2	23	TW, MD	$1120
6X-24X AO	30mm	50	42	7.6-2.1	3.2-3.7	18-5	1/8	52	16.9	27	MD, FP	$1076
8.5X-32X AO	30mm	50	42	6.2-1.7	3.0-3.5	14-4	1/8	39	18.0	27	MD, FP	$782-$865
WHITETAILS UNLIMITED												
2X-5X WTU	1	20	39	11.1-4.2	3.1-3.8	65-23	½	70	10.7	10	TW	$398
3X-9X WTU	1	40	39	12.9-4.7	3.1-3.8	31-13	¼	50	12.4	13	TW	$398
3.5X-10X WTU	1	50	39	13-5.1	3.1-3.8	28-11	¼	50	13.1	15	LBP	$582
3.7X-11X WTU	1	42	39	13-5.1	3.1-3.8	28-11	¼	50	13.1	15	TW	$465
4.5X-14X WTU	1	42	39	9.3-3.0	3.7-4.2	23-8	¼	52	12.9	17	BP	$497
6.5X-20X WTU	1	50	39	7.6-2.6	3.1-3.6	17-6	¼	30	14.6	19	BP	$598
3X-9X WTU	1	50	39	16.0-5.3	3.1-3.8	32-13	¼	50	13.2	17	BP	$398

Scopes are available in high gloss black, matte black, or camouflage, depending on model.
P=Penta-Plex, FP=Fine-Plex, DW=Deepwoods Plex, MD=Mil-Dot, CP=Comp-Plex, TW=Twilight Plex, BP=Ballistic Plex, LBP=Laser Ballistic Plex

Phoenix Precision Sights

PREMIUM TARGET SIGHTS

CNC machined aircraft aluminum; Zero-able, ¼ min click numbered knobs; 70 min elevation adjustment; 60 min windage adjustment; adjustable scales engraved in 3 min increments; oil impregnated bronze guide and thread bushings.

AR-15 Flat Top 1-Piece Mount Rear Sight: $350
Standard Right Hand Rear Sight: $325

AR-15 FLAT TOP REAR SIGHT

STANDARD RIGHT HAND REAR SIGHT

Redfield Optics

RIFLESCOPES

Redfield's scopes feature ED glass objective lenses; one-piece aluminum tubes; water resistant lens coating; TrueZero windage and elevation dials; 3-cam 5X zoom system; side focus adjustments (on select models); black matte finish.

5x - 25x FoV (ft.@100yds): 18.8/3.8
3x - 15x FoV (ft.@100yds): 31.5/6.3
4x - 20x FoV (ft.@100yds): 23.6/4.8
6x - 30x FoV (ft.@100yds): 15.8/3
MSRP: $500-800

3-15X52

Schmidt & Bender Scopes

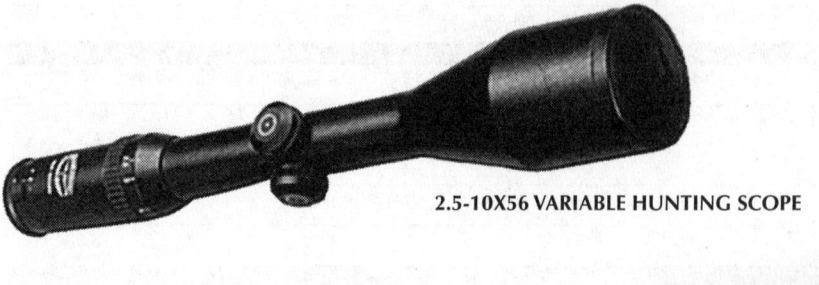

2.5-10X56 VARIABLE HUNTING SCOPE

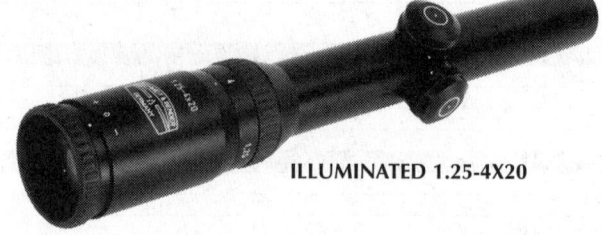

ILLUMINATED 1.25-4X20

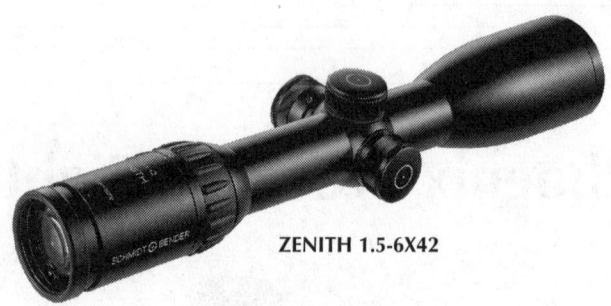

ZENITH 1.5-6X42

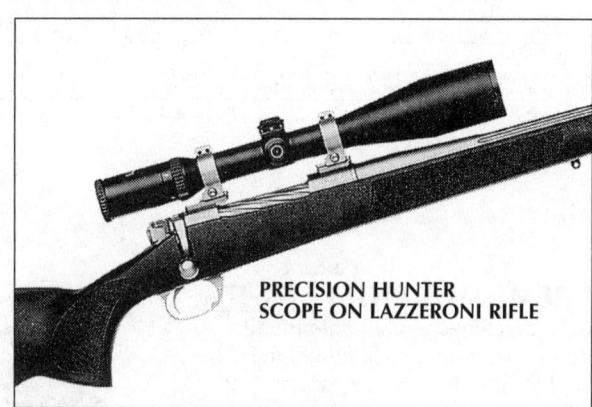

**PRECISION HUNTER
SCOPE ON LAZZERONI RIFLE**

This German firm manufactures carriage-class optics for discriminating sportsmen and tactical shooters. Variable scopes have 30mm and 34mm tubes. Note: All variable power scopes have glass reticles and aluminum tubes.

VARIABLE HUNTING SCOPES

1.5-6x42:	$1449
2.5-10x56:	$1659
3-12x42:	$1629
3-12x50:	$1629
3-12x50:	$1629
4-16x50:	$1979

FIXED POWER SCOPES

4x36:	$979
6x42:	$1069
8x56:	$1229
10x42:	$1129

ILLUMINATED SCOPES

Designed for use on magnum rifles and for quick shots at dangerous game. Long eye relief, and a wide field of view (31.5 yards at 200 yards) speed your aim. The Flash Dot reticle shows up bright against the target at the center of the crosswire. Illuminated scopes feature illuminated reticles; hard multi-coating on lenses; 30mm tubes

1.25-4x20:	$1819
1.5-6x42:	$1869
2.5-10x56:	$2089
3-12x50:	$2059
3-12x42:	$2059

PRECISION HUNTER

Precision Hunter scopes combine the optical quality of S&B hunting scopes, with a sophisticated mil-dot reticle (developed by the U.S. Marine Corps) with a bullet drop compensator to give shooters the ability and confidence to place an accurate shot at up to 500 yards.

2.5-10x56 with #9 Reticle:	$1879
3-12x42 with P3 Reticle:	$1849
3-12x50 with P3 Reticle:	$1849
4-16x50 with P3 Reticle:	$2199

PRECISION HUNTER WITH PARALLAX ADJUSTMENT

3-12x50 Parallax:	$2449
4-16x50 Parallax:	$2549

ZENITH SERIES SCOPES

1.1-4x24:	$1439
1.1-4x24:	$1869
1.5-6x42:	$1499
1.5-6x42:	$1929
2.5-10x56	$1759
2.5-10x56:	$2189
3-12x50 h:	$1759

SERIES III SCOPES

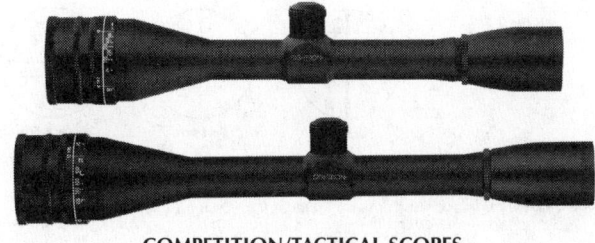

COMPETITION/TACTICAL SCOPES

SHOTGUN SCOPES

COMPACT RIFLE SCOPES

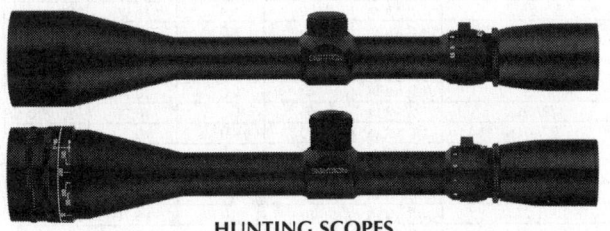

HUNTING SCOPES

SERIES I SCOPES

SIGHTS & SCOPES

SERIES 1

S1 scopes in the Sightron line include: scopes with plex reticles; multi-coated objective and ocular lenses; finger adjustable windage and elevation knobs; scopes are shockproof, waterproof and nitrogen charged. All come with Sightron's Lifetime Warranty.

1x20:	$162
2.5-10x44:	$249
2.5x32:	$115
3-9x32RF:	$156
3-9x40ST:	$205
3-9x40GL:	$205
3-9x40MD:	$248
3.5-10x50:	$276

SERIES II SCOPES

Sightron Series II riflescopes feature the patented ExacTrack windage and elevation system. All Sightron SII Series Riflescopes feature a one piece body tube with ZACT-7, seven-layer fully multi-coated optics. All SII Series scopes are waterproof, shockproof,fogproof and nitrogen filled. Available in stainless with a wide choice of reticles from plex and double diamond to mil dot..

SII SIDE FOCUS RIFLESCOPES

3.5-10x44:	$
4.5-14x44:	$
6.5-20x50:	$

SII VARIABLE POWER RIFLESCOPES

1.5-6x42:	$387
3-12x42:	$439
3-12x42 mil dot:	$445
3-12x50:	$465
3.5-10x42:	$438
3.5-10x50:	$465
3-9x36:	$402
3-9x42ST:	$371
4.5-14x42:	$501
4.5-14x50:	$493

4-16x42 mil dot:	$591
6-24x42 mil dot:	$623
24x44 mil dot:	$460

TARGET/COMPETITION SCOPES

3-6x42:	$556
4-16x42:	$501
4-16x42 dot:	$556
6-24x42:	$568
6-24x42 dot:	$586
6x42 HBRD:	$442
6-24x42:	$586

SII COMPACT SCOPES

2.5-7x32	$300
2.5-10x32:	$352
4x32:	$277
6x42:	$302

SII SHOTGUN SCOPES

SII shotgun 2.5-7x32:	$314

Sightron Scopes

RETICLE DIMENSION REFERENCES

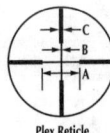

Plex Reticle · Dot Reticle · Mil Dot Reticle · Crosshair (CH) Reticle · Double Diamond Reticle · German 4A Reticle

Magnification	Objective Diameter (mm)	Field of View (ft@ 100 yd)	Eye Relief (in)	Recticle Type	Reticle Subtension Min. Power A/B/C/D/E (in.@100 yds)	Reticle Subtension Max. Power A/B/C/D/E (in.@100 yds)	Click Value	Windage Elevation Travel (in)	Tube (Dia.)	Weight (oz)	Finish
SERIES II RIFLESCOPES – Side Focus											
3.5-10X	44	25.4-8.9	4.7-3.7	Plex	102.6/10.26/3.25/2.2/.69	36/3.6/1.15/.8/.23	¼ MOA	80	1.0 in.	19.0	Satin Black
4.5-14X	44	20.5-6.8	4.7-3.7	Plex	79.0/1.33/5.32	19.8/.33/1.32	¼ MOA	70	1.0 in.	19.80	Satin Black
6.5-20X	50	14.9-4.0	4.3-3.4	Plex	79.0/1.33/5.32	19.8/.33/1.32	¼ MOA	45	1.0 in.	20.50	Satin Black
SERIES II RIFLESCOPES – Variable Power											
1.5-6X	42	50-15	4.0-3.8	Plex	79.0/1.33/5.32	19.8/.33/1.32	¼ MOA	70	1.0 in.	14.00	Satin Black
2.5-8X	42	36-12	3.6-4.2	Plex	48.0/.80/3.20	15.0/.25/1.0	¼ MOA	90	1.0 in.	12.82	Satin Black
3-9X	42	34-12	3.6-4.2	Plex	39.9/.66/2.66	13.2/.22/.88	¼ MOA	95	1.0 in.	13.22	Satin Black
3-9X	42	34-12	3.6-4.2	Plex	39.9/.66/2.66	13.2/.22/.88	¼ MOA	95	1.0 in.	13.22	Stainless
3-9X	42	34-12	3.6-4.2	Dot	4/.66	1.3/.22	¼ MOA	95	1.0 in.	13.22	Satin Black
3-12X	42	32-9	3.6-4.2	Plex	39.9/.66/2.66	9.9/.16/.66	¼ MOA	80	1.0 in.	12.99	Satin Black
3.5-10X	42	32-11	3.6	Plex	34.2/.57/2.28	12.0/.20/.80	¼ MOA	60	1.0 in.	13.80	Satin Black
4.5-14X	42	22-7.9	3.6	Plex	26.4/.44/1.76	8.5/.14/.56	¼ MOA	50	1.0 in.	16.07	Satin Black
3-9X	50	34-12	4.2-3.6	Plex	39.9/.66/2.66	13.2/.22/.88	¼ MOA	*	1.0 in.	15.40	Satin Black
3-12X	50	34-8.5	4.5-3.7	Plex	39.9/.66/2.66	9.9/.16/.66	¼ MOA	*	1.0 in.	16.30	Satin Black
3.5-10X	50	30-10	4.0-3.4	Plex	34.2/.57/2.28	12.0/.20/.80	¼ MOA	50	1.0 in.	15.10	Satin Black
4.5-14X	50	23-8	3.9-3.25	Plex	26.4/.44/1.76	8.4/.14/.56	¼ MOA	60	1.0 in.	15.20	Satin Black
SERIES II RIFLESCOPES –Variable Power Target Scopes											
4-16X	42	26-7	3.6	Plex	30/.50/2.0	7.5/.125/.50	1/8 MOA	56	1.0 in.	16.00	Satin Black
4-16X	42	26-7	3.6	Plex	30/.50/2.0	7.5/.125/.50	1/8 MOA	56	1.0 in.	16.00	Stainless
4-16X	42	26-7	3.6	Dot	1.7/.10	.425/.025	1/8 MOA	56	1.0 in.	16.00	Satin Black
4-16X	42	26-7	3.6	Dot	1.7/.10	.425/.025	1/8 MOA	56	1.0 in.	16.00	Stainless
6-24X	42	15.7-4.4	3.6	Plex	19.8/.33/1.32	4.8/.08/.32	1/8 MOA	40	1.0 in.	18.70	Satin Black
6-24X	42	15.7-4.4	3.6	Plex	19.8/.33/1.32	4.8/.08/.32	1/8 MOA	40	1.0 in.	18.70	Stainless
6-24X	42	15.7-4.4	3.6	Dot	1.12/.066	.27/.016	1/8 MOA	40	1.0 in.	18.70	Satin Black
6-24X	42	15.7-4.4	3.6	Dot	1.12/.066	.27/.016	1/8 MOA	40	1.0 in.	18.70	Stainless
3-12X	42	32-9	3.6-4.2	Mil-Dot	144/14/4.7/3.1/.7	36/3.6/1.2/.79/.1	¼ MOA	80	1.0 in.	12.99	Satin Black
4-16X	42	26-7	3.6	Mil-Dot	144/14/4.7/3.1/.6	36/3.6/1.2/.79/.1	1/8 MOA	56	1.0 in.	16.00	Satin Black
4-16X	42	26-7	3.6	Mil-Dot	144/14/4.7/3.1/.6	36/3.6/1.2/.79/.1	1/8 MOA	56	1.0 in.	16.00	Stainless
6-24X	42	15.7-4.4	3.6	Mil-Dot	144/14/4.7/3.1/.4	36/3.6/1.2/.79/.1	1/8 MOA	40	1.0 in.	18.70	Satin Black
6-24X	42	15.7-4.4	3.6	Mil-Dot	144/14/4.7/3.1/.4	36/3.6/1.2/.79/.1	1/8 MOA	40	1.0 in.	18.70	Stainless
24X	44	4.4	4.33	Dot	.27/.016	.27/.016	1/8 MOA	60	1.0 in.	15.87	Satin Black
6X	42	20	4.00	Dot	.375/.070	.375/.070	1/8 MOA	100	1.0 in.	16.00	Satin Black
SERIES II RIFLESCOPES-Compact Scopes											
4X	32	25	4.52	Plex	30/.50/2.0	30/.50/2.0	¼ MOA	120	1.0 in.	9.80	Satin Black
2.5-7X	32	41-11.8	3.8-3.2	Plex	48/.80/3.20	17.2/.29/1.2	¼ MOA	120	1.0 in.	11.60	Satin Black
2.5-10X	32	41-10.5	3.8-3.5	Plex	48/.80/3.20	12/.20/.80	¼ MOA	120	1.0 in.	10.93	Satin Black
6X	42	20	3.60	Plex	19.8/.33/1.32	19.8/.33/1.32	¼ MOA	100	1.0 in.	12.69	Satin Black
SERIES II SHOTGUN SCOPES											
2.5X	20	41	4.33	Plex	48.0/.80/3.20 ¼ MOA	48.0/.80/3.20 ¼ MOA	160	1.0 in.	9.00	Satin Black	
2.5-7X	32	41-11.8	3.8-3.2	DD	48/24/.60	17/8.5/.26	¼ MOA	120	1.0 in.	11.60	Satin Black

**Specifications not available at press time*

Simmons Scopes

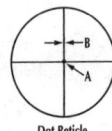

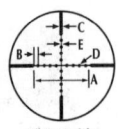

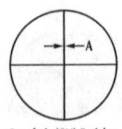

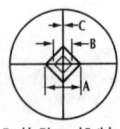

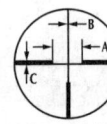

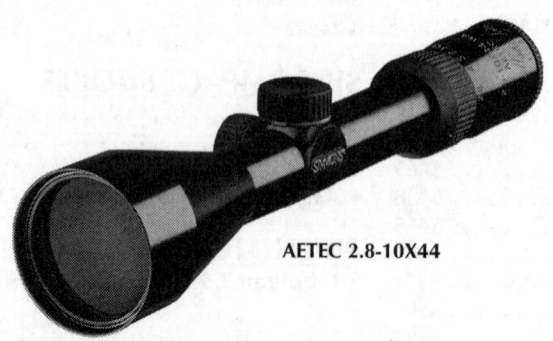

AETEC 2.8-10X44

AETEC RIFLESCOPES

Features TrueZero flex erector system; Quick Target Acquisition eyepiece, with constant minimum 3.5 inches of eye relief; one-piece tube construction; aspherical lens technology and fully multi-coated optics; HydroShield lens coating; SureGrip rubber surfaces on all eyepieces and side-focus parallax adjustments.

Simmons Scopes

BLAZER 3-9X50

PROHUNTER RIFLESCOPES

PROSPORT SCOPES

MODEL 807732 (2X)

SIGHTS & SCOPES

BLAZER RIFLESCOPES
The Blazer line of riflescopes feature the TrueZero adjustment system; QTA eyepiece; high-quality optical glass and fully coated optics; HydroShield lens coating SureGrip rubber surfaces.

PRODIAMOND SHOTGUN SCOPES
Master Series ProDiamond shotgun scopes feature TrueZero adjustment system QTA eyepiece; up to 5.5 inches of eye relief; ProDiamond reticle; one-piece tube construction; high–quality optical glass and multi-coated optics; HydroShield lens coating; SureGrip rubber surfaces on power change rings and eyepieces.

PROHUNTER HANDGUN SCOPES
ProHunter handgun scopes feature long eye relief, ½ and ¼ MOA adjustments, and are waterproof, fogproof and shockproof. Available in black and silver matte finishes.

PROHUNTER RIFLESCOPES
Master Series ProHunter rifle and shotgun scopes feature the TrueZero adjustment system; QTA eyepiece; one-piece tube construction; high-quality optical glass and multi-coated optics; HydroShield lens coating; SureGrip rubber surfaces and side-focus parallax adjustments.

PROSPORT SCOPES
Master Series ProSport scopes feature TrueZero adjustment system and QTA eyepiece with up to 5.5 inches of eye relief; one-piece tube construction; high-quality optical glass and fully coated optics; HydroShield lens coating; SureGrip rubber surfaces.

RIMFIRE RIFLESCOPES
The Rimfire collection is scaled down in size with ¾ in. tubes for smaller rifles. All are calibrated parallax free at 50 yards for shorter rimfire ranges. They come complete with a set of rings ready to be mounted on your favorite rimfire rifle.

22 MAG RIMFIRE SCOPES
Featuring TrueZero adjustment system; QTA quick target acquisition eyepiece; high-quality optical glass and fully coated optics; HydroShield lens coating; SureGrip rubber surfaces; scopes come with a set of rimfire rings. Scopes come in gloss or matte finish.

RED DOT SCOPES
Simmons Red Dot scopes work great on handguns, crossbows, shotguns and paintball guns with rapid target acquisition. Clicktype, 1 MOA windage and elevation adjustments.

Simmons Scopes

AETEC RIFLESCOPES

MAGNIFICATION (X OBJ. DIA.)	FIELD OF VIEW (FT., 100 YDS)	DIA./LENGTH (IN.)	WEIGHT (OZ.)	MSRP
2.8-10 x 44 Gloss	43.5/11.5	na	13.8	$260
2.8-10 x 44 Matte	43.5/11.5	na	13.8	$260
2.8-10 x 44 Silver	43.5/11.5	na	13.8	$260
2.8-10 x 44 Ill. Ret.	43.5/11.5	na	12.3	$300
4-14 x 44 SF Matte	29.3/8.2	na	15	$300
4-14 x 44 SF	Ill. Ret. 29.3/8.2	na	15.5	$340

BLAZER RIFLESCOPES

MAGNIFICATION (X OBJ. DIA.)	FIELD OF VIEW (FT., 100 YDS)	DIA./LENGTH (IN.)	WEIGHT (OZ.)	MSRP
3-9 x 32	31.4/10.5	na	9.6	$45
3-9 x 40	31.4/10.5	na	10.8	$45
3-9 x 50	31.4/10	na	13.2	$60
4 x 32	23.6	na	8.8	$40

PRO-DIAMOND SHOTGUN SCOPES

MAGNIFICATION (X OBJ. DIA.)	FIELD OF VIEW (FT., 100 YDS)	DIA./LENGTH (IN.)	WEIGHT (OZ.)	MSRP
1.5-5 x 32 illum.	63/20	na	9.3.	$200
1 x 20	85	na	8.4	$150
2 x 32 (ProDiamond reticle)	31.4	na	8.4	$130
1.5-5 x 20 (ProDiamond reticle)	67/20	na	9.3	$150
1.5-5 x 32 (Camo Pro Diamond)	67/20	na	9.3	$170
4X32	17	1/8.5	9.1	$135

PROHUNTER HANDGUN SCOPES

MAGNIFICATION (X OBJ. DIA.)	FIELD OF VIEW (FT., 100 YDS)	DIA./LENGTH (IN.)	WEIGHT (OZ.)	MSRP
2-6 x 32	14/4.5	na	9.7	$180
2 x 20	21.5	8.75	6.75	$140
4 x 32	15	9	8	$180

PROHUNTER RIFLESCOPES

MAGNIFICATION (X OBJ. DIA.)	FIELD OF VIEW (FT., 100 YDS)	DIA./LENGTH (IN.)	WEIGHT (OZ.)	MSRP
2 - 7 x 32	47.2	1/12.3	9.8	$120
3 - 9 x 40	31.4	1/11	10.8	$150
3–10.5 x 44	33	1/9.4	11.3	$220
4-12 x 44 SF	23.8	1/8.2	13.3	$260
6-18 x 40 SF	16	1/5.3	13	$240
6-24 x 44 SF	16	¼	13	$290
6-21 x 44 SF	16	¼.6	13.3	$269

PROSPORT SCOPES

MAGNIFICATION (X OBJ. DIA.)	FIELD OF VIEW (FT., 100 YDS)	DIA./LENGTH (IN.)	WEIGHT (OZ.)	MSRP
3-9 x 32	31.4/10.5	na	9.6	$90
3-9 x 40	31.4/10.5	na	10.8	$150
3-9 x 50	31.4/10.5	na	13.2	$100
4-32	23.6	na	8.4	$70
4-12 x 40 AO	24.8/8.1	na	13.8	$220
6-18 x 50 A/O	14.7/5.3	na	8.3	$180

RIMFIRE RIFLESCOPES

MAGNIFICATION (X OBJ. DIA.)	FIELD OF VIEW (FT., 100 YDS)	DIA./LENGTH (IN.)	WEIGHT (OZ.)	MSRP
4 x 15	18.5	¾/na	3.25	$10
4 x 20	19	¾/na	3.25	$15
3 - 7 x 20	21.75 - 9.5	¾/na	4.75	$25

22 MAG RIMFIRE SCOPES

MAGNIFICATION (X OBJ. DIA.)	FIELD OF VIEW (FT., 100 YDS)	DIA./LENGTH (IN.)	WEIGHT (OZ.)	MSRP
3 - 9 x 32	31.4/10.5	na	9.6	$60
3 - 9 x 32 A/O	31.4/10.5	na	10.8	$90
4 x 32	21	na	8.8	$50

RED DOT SCOPES

DESCRIPTION	FIELD OF VIEW	EYE RELIEF	WEIGHT	RETICLE	MSRP
30mm	Variable	Unlimited	6.5 oz.	4 MOA Dot	$50
30mm	Variable	Unlimited	5.6	Multi Reticle	$50
42mm	Variable	Unlimited	8.25	4 MOA Dot	$50

Swarovski Scopes

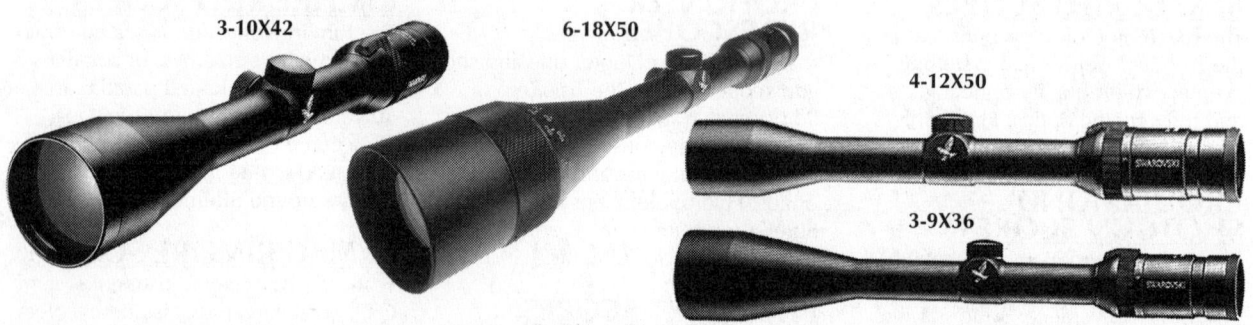

3-10X42   6-18X50   4-12X50   3-9X36

AV SERIES SCOPES

AV scopes are lightweight 1-inch scopes featuring constant-size reticles, lightweight alloy tubes and satin finish. Totally waterproof even with caps removed, these scopes have fully multi-coated lenses.

3-10X42 4A Reticle AV: $1032
3-10X42 RAIL 4A Reticle AV: . . $1088
3-10X42 PLEX Reticle AV: $1032
3-10X42 TDS Plex Reticle AV: . $1110

3-9X36 4A Reticle AV: $921
3-9X36 PLEX Reticle AV: $921
3-9X36 TDS Reticle AV: $750
4-12X50 4A Reticle AV: $1010
4-12X50 RAIL 4A Reticle AV: $1166
4-12X50 RAIL TDS Plex Reticle AV: $1243
4-12X50 TDS Plex Reticle AV: $1188
4-12x50 PLEX Reticle AV: $1032

4-12x50 RAIL PLEX Reticle AV: $1166
6-18X50 TDS Plex Reticle AV: $1243
6-18x50 4A Reticle AV: $1166
6-18x50 PLEX Reticle AV: $1166

Swarovski Scopes

PH 1.5-6X42
ILLUMINATED

PV-S
6-24X50P

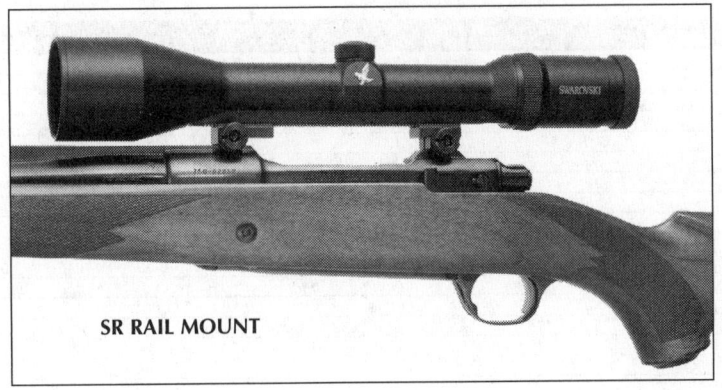

SR RAIL MOUNT

PH SERIES (PROFESSIONAL HUNTER)

"PH" riflescopes are intended for long-range target, big-game and varmint shooting. They feature waterproof parallax adjustment systems and a choice of higher powers. A non-magnifying, fine plex reticle and a fine crosshair reticle with $1/8$ in. MOA dot are available in the 6-24x50mm scope. Reticle adjustment clicks are $1/6$ 1 in. (minute) by external, waterproof target knobs. The internal optical system features a coil spring suspension system and positive reticle adjustment. The objective bell, 30mm middle tube, turret housing and ocular bell are machined from one solid bar of aluminum.

PH 1.25-4x24 w/4A Reticle:... $1277
PH 1.25-4x24 w/#24N
   High Grid Illumi:........ $1665
PH 1.25-4x24. w/3 Post
   Dot High Grid: $1666
PH 1.25-4x24 SR -#24N-High
   Grid: $1721
PH 1.5-6x42:.............. $1477
PH 1.5-6x42 w/#24 Reticle: ... $1521

PH 1.5-6x42 w/4A-IK
   High Grid: $1810
PH 1.5-6x42 Illuminated: $1810
PH 1.5-6x42 SR -#24N-High
   Grid: $1821
PH 2.5-10x42:............. $1610
PH 2.5-10x42 w/4NK Ill.
   Retic:................. $2043
PH 2.5-10x42-L-7A:......... $2440
PH 2.5-10x56:............. $1710
PH 2.5-10x56:............. $2210
PH 3-12x50: $1677
PH 3-12x50 SR-4A: $1732
PH 3-12x50 wTDS Plex Reticle: $1754
PH 3-12x50 Illuminated
   Reticle: $2143
PH 4-16x50: $1810
PH 4-16x50 w/TDS 4 Reticle: . $1888
PH 6-24x50 w/TDS 4 Reticle: . $1966
PH 6-24x50: $1999

PF / PF-N SERIES

PF fixed magnification rifle scopes feature less weight, an extra wide field of view and a telescopic dampening system for the eyecup. They also feature a scratchproof surface. The Habicht PF-N versions come with an illuminated reticle.

PF 6x42 1 Inch w/4A
   Reticle: $1154
PF 8x50 30mm w/4A
   Reticle: $1199
PF 8x56 30mm w/4A
   Reticle: $1266
PF 8x56 30mm w/PLEXN Illum.
   Reticle: $1777

SR RAIL PH SERIES

The Swarovski SR line uses an integral toothed rail on PH scopes that makes the tube stronger while eliminating the ring/tube juncture that can fail during heavy recoil.

1.25-4X24 RAIL Series #24
   Reticle: $1333
1.5-6X42 RAIL Series #4A
   Reticle: $1532
2.5-10x56 RAIL Series #4
   Reticle PH: $1832
3-12X50 RAIL Series #4A
   Reticle PH: $1732
3-12X50 RAIL Series TDS PLEX
   Reticle: $1810
3-12X50 RAIL Series Illum. #4AN
   Reticle PH: $2199
3-12X50 RAIL Series Illum. #4NK
   Reticle: $2199

SIGHTS & SCOPES

Swarovski Scopes

AV LIGHTWEIGHT	3-9x36	3-10x42	4-12x50	6-18x50
Magnification	3-9x	3.3-10x	4-12x	6-18x
Objective lens diameter: mm	36	42	50	50
Objective lens diameter: in	1.42	1.55	1.97	1.97
Exit pupil, diameter: mm	12-4	12.6-4.2	12.5-4.2	8.3-2.8
Eye relief: in	3.5	3.5	3.5	3.5
Field of view, real: m/100m	13-4.5	11-3.9	9.7-3.3	17.4-6.5
Field of view, real: ft/100yds	39-13.5	33-11.7	29.1-9.9	17.4-6.5
Diopter compensation (dpt)	± 2.6	± 2.5	± 2.5	± 2.5
Transission (%)	94	94	94	92
Twilight factor (DIN 58388)	9-18	9-21	11-25	17-30
Impact Point correction per click: in/100yds	0.25	0.25	0.25	0.25
Max. elevation/windage adjustment range: ft/100yds	4.8	4.2	3.6	3.9
Length, approx: in	11.8	12.44	13.5	14.85
Weight, approx (oz.): L	11.6	12.7	13.9	20.3
LS	–	13.6	15.2	–

L=light alloy • LS=light alloy with rail

PF & PV	PF 6x42	PF/PF-N 8X50	PF/PF-N 8X56	PV/PV-T 1.25-4X24	PV 1.5-6X42	PV/PV-N 2.5-10X42	PV/PV-N 2.5-10X56	PV/PV-N 3-1-1X50	PV 4-16X50P	PV 6-24X50P	PV-S 6-24X50P
Magnification	6x	8x	8x	1.25-4x	1.5-6x	2.5-10x	2.5-10x	3-12x	4-16x	6-24x	6-24x
Objective lens diameter: mm	42	50	56	17-24	20-42	33-42	33-56	39-50	50	50	50
Objective lens diameter: in	1.65	1.97	2.20	0.67-0.94	0.79-1.65	1.3-1.65	1.3-2.20	1.54-1.97	1.97	1.97	1.97
Exit pupil, diameter: mm	7	6.25	7	12.5-6	13.1-7	13.1-4.2	13.1-5.6	13.1-4.2	12.5-3.1	8.3-2.1	8.3-2.1
Eye relief: in	3.15	3.15	3.15	3.15	3.15	3.15	3.15	3.15	3.15	3.15	3.15
Field of view, real: m/100m	7	5.2	5	32.8-10.4	21.8-7	13.2-4.2	13.2-4.1	11-3.5	9.1-2.6	6.2-1.8	6.2-1.8
Field of view, real: ft/100yds	21	15.6	15.6	98.4-31.2	65.4-21	39.6-12.6	39.6-12.3	33-10.5	27.3-7.8	18.6-5.4	18.6-5.4
Diopter compensation (dpt)	+2. -3	+2. -3	+2. -3	+2. -3	+2. -3	+2. -3	+2. -3	+2. -3	+2. -3	+2. -3	+2. -3
Transission (%)	94	94/92	93/91	93/91	93	94/92	93/91	94/92	90	90	90
Twilight factor (DIN 58388)	16	20	21	4-10	4-16	7-21	7-24	9-25	11-28	17-35	17-35
Impact Point correction per click: in/100yds	0.36	0.36	0.36	0.54	0.36	0.36	0.36	0.36	0.18	0.18	0.17
Max. elevation/windage adjustment range: ft/100yds	3.9	3.3	3.9	9.9	6.6	3.9	3.9	3.3	E:5.4/W:3	E:3.6/W:2.1	E:3.6/W:2.1
Length, approx: in	12.83	13.94	13.27	10.63	12.99	13.23	13.62	14.33	14.21	15.43	15.43
Weight, approx (oz.): L	12.0	14.8	15.9	12.7	16.2	15.2	18.0	16.9	22.2	23.6	24.5
LS	13.4	15.9	16.9	13.8	17.5	16.4	19.0	18.3	—	—	—

L=light alloy • LS=light alloy with rail

Swift Scopes

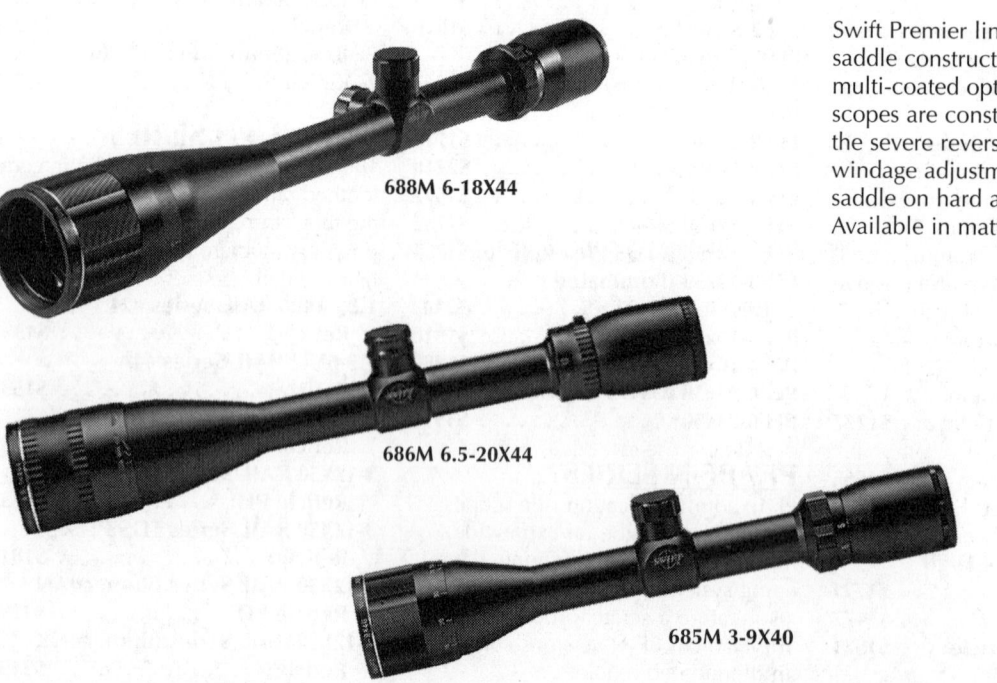

688M 6-18X44

686M 6.5-20X44

685M 3-9X40

Swift Premier line features include full saddle construction; Speed Focus; fully multi-coated optics; clear dust caps; scopes are constructed to withstand the severe reverse recoil. Elevation and windage adjustments are mounted full saddle on hard anodized 1 inch tubes. Available in matte and silver finish.

Swift Scopes

PISTOL SCOPES				
MAGNIFICATION (X OBJ. DIA.)	FIELD OF VIEW (FT., 100 YDS)	DIA./LENGTH (IN.)	WEIGHT (OZ.)	MSRP
2-6x32	14' @ 2x, 4.5' @ 6x	1/5.5	10.6	$130
4x32	6.6	1/9.4	9.9	$130
PREMIER RIFLESCOPES				
MAGNIFICATION (X OBJ. DIA.)	FIELD OF VIEW (FT., 100 YDS)	DIA./LENGTH (IN.)	WEIGHT (OZ.)	MSRP
1.5-4.5x 32	71 @ 1.5x, 25 @ 4.5x	1/10.41	12.7	$125
2-7x 40	60 @ 2x, 17 @ 7x	1/12.2	14.8	$160
3-9x 40	40 @ 3x, 14.2 @ 9x	1/12	13.1	$170
3.5-10x 44	35 @ 3.5x, 11 @ 10x	1/12.6	15.2	$230
4-12x 50	29.5' @ 4x, 9.5 @ 12x	1/13.8	15.8	$245
4-12x 40	29.5' @ 4x, 11 @ 12x	1/12.4	15.4	$190
6-18x 44	19.5' @ 6x, 7 @ 18x	1/15.4	22.6	$220
6-18x 50	19' @ 6x, 6.7 @ 18x	1/15.8	20.9	$260
STANDARD RIFLESCOPES				
MAGNIFICATION (X OBJ. DIA.)	FIELD OF VIEW (FT., 100 YDS)	DIA./LENGTH (IN.)	WEIGHT (OZ.)	MSRP
3-9x 32	38 @ 3x, 12' @ 9x	1/12	9.5	$125
3-9x40	40 @ 3x,14 @ 9x	1/12.6	12.2	$140
4x32	25	1/10	8.9	$120
4x40	35	1/12.2	11.4	$118
6x40	23 @ 100 yrds	1/12.6	10.4	$125

687M 4.5-14X44

Tasco Scopes

VARMINT 2.5-10X42

PROPOINT 1X25

RGD PRO POINT

GOLDEN ANTLER
Golden Antler riflescopes are engineered with 1-inch advanced construction for durability and feature HDC (High Definition Coating) on lens surfaces in addition to fully coated optics. Golden Antler scopes are waterproof/fogproof/shockproof. Backed by a Limited Lifetime Warranty.

TARGET & VARMINT SCOPES
Tasco Target and Varmint riflescopes share high-quality, multi-coated optics and large objective lenses along with ¼ or ⅛ minute click windage and elevation adjustments. Target and Varmint scopes are waterproof, fogproof and shockproof.

TITAN SERIES
Titan riflescopes are waterproof, fogproof and shockproof with premium, multi-coated, SuperCon optics and finger-adjustable windage and elevation controls.

PROPOINT SIGHTS
ProPoint Sights are designed for competitive pistol and revolver shooters, turkey hunters and slug gun hunters. ProPoints deliver pinpoint accuracy with a rheostat-controlled illuminated red dot, unlimited eye relief and a clear field-of-view. ProPoints are powered by lithium batteries.

Tasco Scopes

3-12X40 WORLD CLASS .22

3-9X40 WORLD CLASS 40

WORLD CLASS RIFLESCOPES

World Class riflescopes feature Tasco SuperCon multi-layered coating on the objective and ocular lenses and fully coated optics. Models feature either ProShot, 30/30 or True MilDot reticles and are waterproof, fogproof and shockproof. The scopes are built with monotube construction and carry a Limited Lifetime Warranty.

PRONGHORN RIFLESCOPES

Wide view Pronghorn scopes feature magenta multi-coating on the objective and ocular lenses for increased light transmission and are waterproof, fogproof and shockproof.

22 RIFLESCOPES

Tailor-made for .22 rimfire rifles, featuring full-sized, 1 in. Advanced Monotube Construction; 50-yard parallax setting and rings to fit standard .22 bases; magenta multi-layered lens coatings and fully coated optics; waterproof and fogproof construction.

RIMFIRE SCOPES

Tasco Rimfire scopes are designed for either .22 rifles or quality air guns, and feature lenses calibrated for short ranges and coated optics for a bright image. Rimfire scopes fit .22 and airgun receivers.

GOLDEN ANTLER			
MAGNIFICATION (X OBJ. DIA.)	FIELD OF VIEW (FT., 100 YDS)	DIA./LENGTH (IN.)	WEIGHT (OZ.)
4 x 32mm	32	1/12.75	11
3-9 x 32mm	39-13	1/13.25	12.2
2.5 x 32mm	43	1/11.4	10.1
3-9 x 40mm	41-15	1/12.75	13
TARGET & VARMINT SCOPES			
MAGNIFICATION (X OBJ. DIA.)	FIELD OF VIEW (FT., 100 YDS)	DIA./LENGTH (IN.)	WEIGHT (OZ.)
2.5-10x42	35-9	1/14	19.1
6-24x40	17-4	1/16	19.1
6-24x42	13-3.7	1/16	19.6
10-40x50	11-2.5	1/15.5	25.5
TITAN SERIES			
MAGNIFICATION (X OBJ. DIA.)	FIELD OF VIEW (FT., 100 YDS)	DIA./LENGTH (IN.)	WEIGHT (OZ.)
3.5-10x50	30-10.5	1/13	17.1
3-9x44	39-14	1/12.75	16.5
3-12x30	27-10	1/14	20.7
1.5-6x42	59 20	1/12	16.5
PROPOINT SIGHTS			
MAGNIFICATION (X OBJ. DIA.)	FIELD OF VIEW (FT., 100 YDS)	DIA./LENGTH (IN.)	WEIGHT (OZ.)
1x25mm	40	1.18/5	5.5
1x30mm	68	1.18/4.75	5.4

WORLD CLASS RIFLESCOPES			
MAGNIFICATION (X OBJ. DIA.)	FIELD OF VIEW (FT., 100 YDS)	DIA./LENGTH (IN.)	WEIGHT (OZ.)
3 - 9x40mm IR	34.50–10.50	1/12.50	16.26
1.5 - 4.5 x 32mm	77-23	1/11.25	12
2 - 8 x 32mm	50-17	1/10.5	12.5
3 - 9 x 40mm	41-15	1/12.75	13
PRONGHORN RIFLESCOPES			
MAGNIFICATION (X OBJ. DIA.)	FIELD OF VIEW (FT., 100 YDS)	DIA./LENGTH (IN.)	WEIGHT (OZ.)
2.5x32	43	1/11.4	10.1
3-9x32	39-13	1/12	11
3-9x40	39-13	1/13	12.1
4x32	32	1/12	11
22 RIFLESCOPES			
MAGNIFICATION (X OBJ. DIA.)	FIELD OF VIEW (FT., 100 YDS)	DIA./LENGTH (IN.)	WEIGHT (OZ.)
3-9x32	17.75-6	1/12.75	11.3
4x32	13.5	1/12.25	12.1
RIMFIRE SCOPES			
MAGNIFICATION (X OBJ. DIA.)	FIELD OF VIEW (FT., 100 YDS)	DIA./LENGTH (IN.)	WEIGHT (OZ.)
4x20mm	23	¾/10.5	3.8
3-7x20mm	24'–11	¾/11.5	5.7
4x15mm	20.5	¾/11	4

Trijicon Sights & Scopes

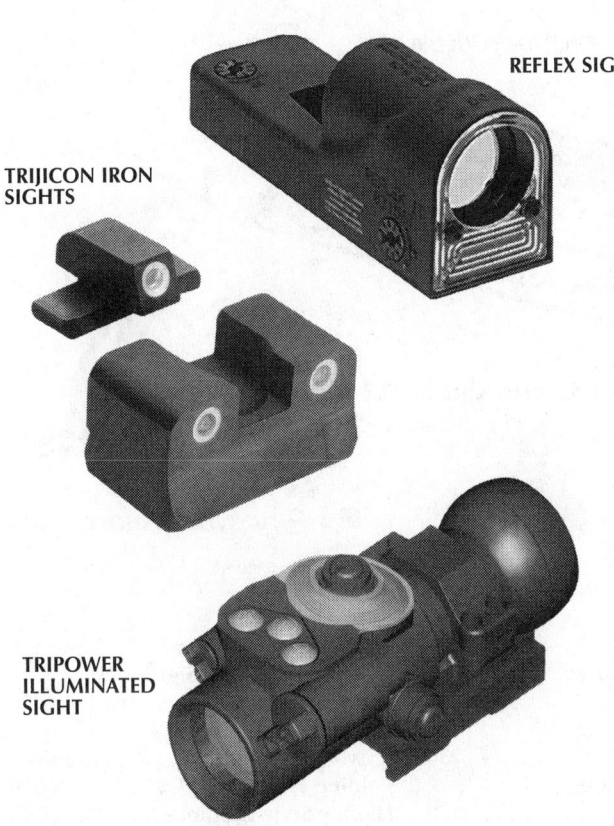

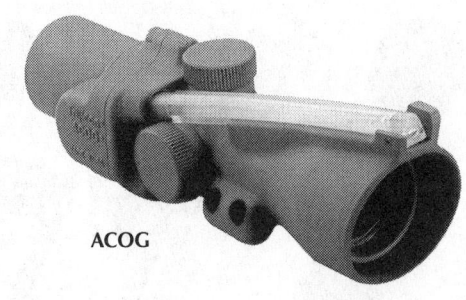

TRIJICON IRON SIGHTS

REFLEX SIGHTS

ACOG

TRIPOWER ILLUMINATED SIGHT

ACCUPOINT SCOPE

ACCUPOINT SCOPES				
MAGNIFICATION (X OBJ. DIA.)	FIELD OF VIEW (FT., 100 YDS)	DIA./LENGTH (IN.)	WEIGHT (OZ.)	MSRP
3-9x40	33.8-11.3	1.18/12.2	13.4	$720
1.25-4x24	61.6-20.5	1.18/10.2	11.4	$700
2.5-10x56	37.6-10.1	1.18/13.8	22.1	$950

ACCUPOINT SCOPES

AccuPoint's features a dual-illuminated aiming point—reticle illumination is supplied by advanced fiber optics or, in low-light conditions, by a self-contained tritium lamp. The AccuPoint scopes feature quick-focus eyepiece; water-resistant and nitrogen filled, multi-layer coated lenses; scope body crafted of hard anodized aluminum; manual brightness adjustment override; fiber-optic light collector. Choice of amber or red aiming point illuminated by a special tritium lamp.

ACOG

The ACOGs are internally-adjustable, compact telescopic sights with tritium illuminated reticle patterns for use in low light or at night. Many models are dual-illuminated, featuring fiber optics which collect ambient light for maximum brightness in day-time shooting. The ACOGs combine traditional, precise distance marksmanship with close-in aiming speed.
MSRP: $749-1600
Compact ACOG $950

NIGHT SIGHTS

Trijicon's self-luminous iron sights give shooters five times greater night fire accuracy. The light is provided by glowing tritium gas-filled lamps which are fullywarranted up to twelve years for the green or yellow rear dots and up to five years for the orange dots. Trijicon night sights also feature a white outline around the glowing dots for the highest possible daylight visibility. The tritium lamps are protected by aluminum sleeves and polished synthetic sapphire windows. In addition a silicone rubber cushion helps protect the glass lamp within the aluminum sleve. The metal body is manufactured for specific handgun makes and models. Night Sights are available for the following pistols, revolvers and rifles: Beretta, Browning, Colt, CZ, Desert Eagle, Firestar, Glock, H&K, Kimber, Remington, Ruger, SIG, Smith & Wesson, Walther, Taurus.
MSRP: $110-150

REFLEX SIGHTS

The dual-illuminated, Trijicon Reflex sight gives shooters next-generation technology for super-fast, any-light aiming without batteries. The Reflex sight features an amber aiming dot or triangle that is illuminated both by light from the target area and from a tritium lamp. Bright aiming point in low light, no light or bright light; quick target acquisition; big sight picture and realistic color.
MSRP: $375-600

TRIPOWER ILLUMINATED SIGHT

The TriPower features a red chevron-shaped reticle illuminated by three lighting sources: an integrated fiber optic system, a Tritium-Illuminated reticle and on-call battery backup. The TriPower has a 30mm tube, coated lenses, and is sealed for underwater use up to 100 feet. The TriPower is 5 inches long and weighs 6 oz.
MSRP: $620

Uberti Sights

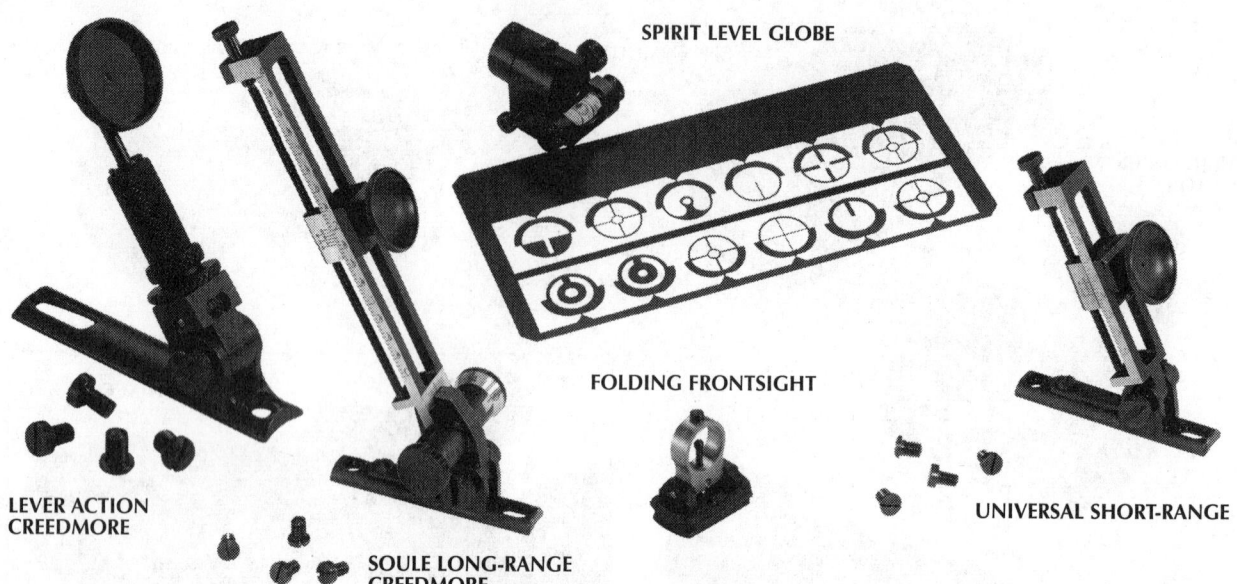

SPIRIT LEVEL GLOBE

FOLDING FRONTSIGHT

LEVER ACTION
CREEDMORE

SOULE LONG-RANGE
CREEDMORE

UNIVERSAL SHORT-RANGE

CREEDMORE TANG SIGHTS

For Sharps rifles in three heights — short-range sight good to 300 yards, mid-range to about 600 yards and long-range, about 1,200 yards. Front globe sight fitted with spirit level to level the rifle.

Soule Type Long-Range
   Creedmore $230
Soule Type Mid-Range
   Creedmore $230
Universal Long-Range
   Creedmore $170
Universal Short-Range
   Creedmore $170
Lever Action Creedmore $100

Spirit Level Globe Sight
   with 12 Inserts $125
Globe Front Sight
   with 12 Inserts $40-45
Folding Front Sight. $50
Hadley Style Eyepiece $85
Spirit Level Insert. $30
Glass Bubble Inserts (6) $30

Weaver Scopes

CLASSIC HANDGUN 1.5-4X20

K-6

CLASSIC HANDGUN SCOPES

Fixed-power scopes include 2x28 and 4x28 scopes in gloss black or silver. Variables in 1.5-4x20 and 2.5-8x28 come with a gloss black finish. Features: one-piece tubes, multi-coated lenses and generous eye relief.

2x28 gloss black or silver: $226
4x28 gloss black or silver: $245

1.5-4x20 gloss black: $300
2.5-8x28 gloss black or silver: . . $320
2.5-8x28 matte: $320
Also available:
Classic shotgun 4x32: $246
1.5-5x32: $260

CLASSIC K SERIES

Classic American scopes, the K2.5, K4 and K6 now have a sleeker look, weigh

less but deliver brighter images. K scopes–including the target model, KT-15–have one-piece tubes.

K-2.5 (2.5x20 gloss): $186
K-4 (gloss): $195
K-4 (matte): $195
K-6 (gloss): $208
K-6 (matte): $208
K-6 (matte, LER): $250
KT-15 (15x42 gloss): $394

SIGHTS & SCOPES

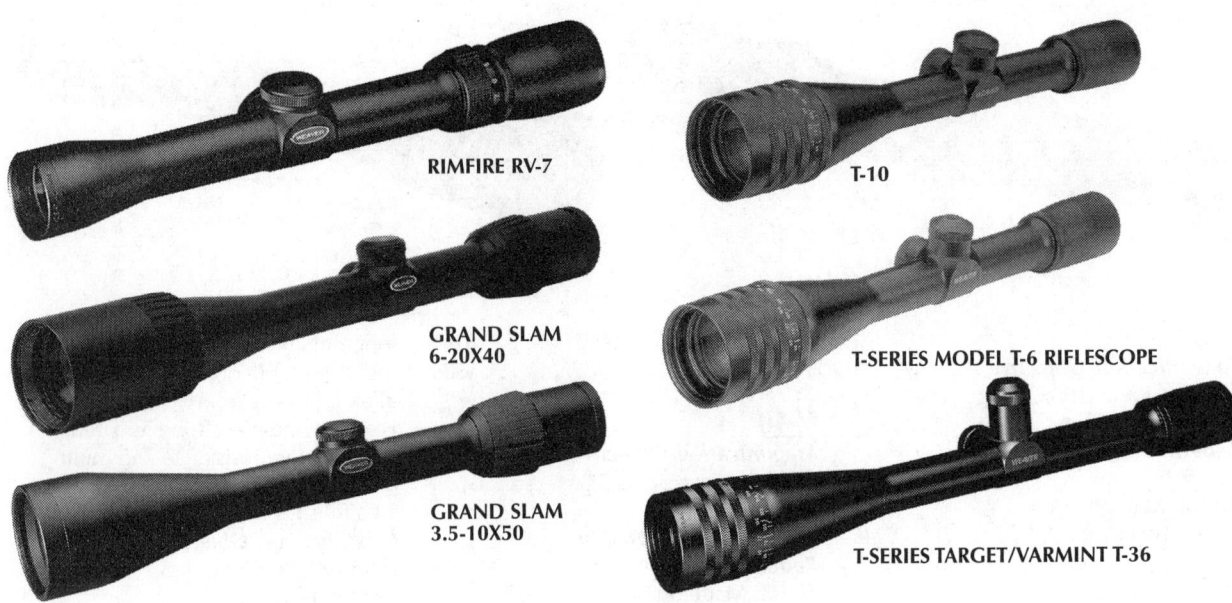

RIMFIRE RV-7

GRAND SLAM
6-20X40

GRAND SLAM
3.5-10X50

T-10

T-SERIES MODEL T-6 RIFLESCOPE

T-SERIES TARGET/VARMINT T-36

CLASSIC RIMFIRE RV4, RV-7 AND RV-9

Rimfire scopes are well suited .22s and airguns. They are designed with a sturdy one-piece aluminum housing and are waterproof and fogproof with fully multi-coated, nonglare lenses, and 28mm objective lenses. Available in fixed or variable power.

4x28 Rimfire Matte Black: **$178**
2.5-7x28 Rimfire Matte
    black or silver: **$208**
3-9x32 AO matte: **$338**

GRAND SLAM SCOPES

The Grand Slam series features an advanced one-piece tube design with a "sure-grip" power ring and AO adjustment. An offset parallax indicator lets you remain in shooting position while adjusting the scope. The eyepiece has a fast-focus adjustment ring. Grand Slam configurations include: 4.75x40mm, a fixed-power scope; 1.5-5x32mm, the ideal scope for short-range rifles; 3.5-10x40mm, the traditional choice of big-game hunters; 3.5-10x50mm, which provides the brightest view in low-light situations; 4.5-14x40mm AO, possibly the most versatile Grand Slam; and 6-20x40mm AO, target/varminter model. Windage and elevation knobs have target-type finger adjustments. Grand Slam scopes are also equipped with

Micro-Trac, Weaver's four-point adjustment system. All Grand Slam scopes are offered with a plex reticle. The scopes have a non-glare black matte or silver and black finish.

6-20x40 AO black or silver: **$580**
4.5-14x40 AO black or silver: . . **$570**
3.5-10x50 black or silver: **$520**
3-10x40 black or silver: **$430**
1.5-5x32 black: **$480**
4.75x40 black: **$400**

T-10 AND T-24 TARGET

The T-10 target model (no AO) has quarter-minute click adjustments and a 1/8-minute dot reticle. It weighs just one pound, has a 40mm objective lens and comes in black satin finish. The T-24 also has a 40mm front end. The parallax (AO) adjustment is the traditional forward ring. Weight 17 oz. Choose a 1/8-minute dot or a 1/2-minute dot.

T-10: **$598**
T-24: **$638**

T-SERIES MODEL T-6 RIFLESCOPE

Weaver's T-6 competition 6x scope is only 12.7 inches long and weighs less than 15 ounces. All optical surfaces are fully multi-coated for maximum clarity and light transmission. The T-6 features Weaver's Micro-Trac precision adjustments in 1/8-minute clicks to ensure parallel tracking. The protected target-style

turrets are a low-profile configuration combining ease of adjustment with weight reduction. A 40mm adjustable objective permits parallax correction from 50 feet to infinity without shifting the point of impact. A special AO lock ring eliminates bell vibration or shift. The T-6 comes with screw-in metal lens caps and features a competition matte black finish.

Reticles: dot, Fine Crosshair
6x40 Satin Black: **$474**

T-SERIES TARGET/VARMINT T-36

Weaver's 36x features patented Micro-Trac adjustments in a dual-spring, four-bearing housing that allows independent movement of windage and elevation. Optics are fully multi-coated and an adjustable objective allows for parallax zero from 50' to infinity. Choice of fine crosshair or dot reticles. Scopes come with sunshade, an extra pair of oversize benchrest adjustment knobs, and screw-in metal lens caps.

Magnification/Objective: 36X40mm
Field of View: 3.0'   *Eye Relief:* 3.0 in.
Length: 15.1 in.   *Weight:* 16.7 oz.
Reticle: 1/8 MOA Dot, Fine Crosshair
Finish: Matte black or silver

Matte: **$670**
Silver: **$679**
Matte Dot: **$678**
Silver Dot: **$688**

Weaver Scopes

V-3

V16

V-3
Magnification/Objective: 1-3x20
Field of View: 100x34
Eye Relief: 3.5 in.
Length: 9 in.
Weight: 9.0 oz.
Finish: Matte black
Matte black:. **$246**

V-7
2-7x32 matte: **$247**

V-9
Magnification/Objective: 3-9x38
Field of View: 34-11'
Eye Relief: 3.5 in.
Length: 12 in.   **Weight:** 11.0 oz.
Finish: Matte black, gloss

Matte black or gloss:. **$247**
3-9x50 Matte: **$335**

V-10
Magnification/Objective: 2-10X38mm
Field of View: 38.5-9.5
Eye Relief: 3.5"
Length: 12.2"   **Weight:** 11.2 oz.
Reticle: Dual-X
Finish: Matte black, silver
**Matte black, silver or
   gloss black**. **$274**
V-10 2-10x50 Matte **$386**

V-16 AND V-24
The V16 is popular for a variety of shooting applications, from close shots that require a wide field of view to long-range varmint or benchrest shooting. Adjustable objective allows a parallax-free view from 30 feet to infinity. Features one-piece tube for strength and moisture resistance and multi-coated lenses for clear, crisp images. Two finishes and three reticle options.
Magnification/Objective: 4-16X42mm
Field of View: 26.8'-6.8'
Eye Relief: 3.1 in.
Length: 13.9 in.   **Weight:** 16.5 oz.
Reticle: Choice of Dual-X, ¼ MOA Dot, or Fine Crosshair
Finish: Matte black
V-16 4-16x42: **$458**
V-24 6-24x42 black matte:. **$534**
V-24 6-24x42 with mil dot: **$554**

Williams Sights

5D SERIES

5D SERIES
5D models are available for most popular rifles and shotguns. These sights have the strength, light weight, and neat appearance of the FP, without the micrometer adjustments. 5D sights offer unobstructed vision with no knobs or side plates to blot out shooter's field of vision. Wherever possible, the manufacturers' mounting screw holes in the receivers of the guns have been utilized for easy installation. The upper staff of the Williams 5D sight is readily detachable. A set screw is provided as a stop screw so that the sight will return to absolute zero after reattaching. The Williams 5D sight is made of high grade alloy.
Most 5D models:. **$38**
Target—FP (high)
Adjustable From 1.250 in. to 1.750 in. Above Centerline of Bore.
MSRP: **$78**

**FP-GR-TK
ON REMINGTO 581**

**FP-94 SE SHOWN ON WINCHESTER
94 SIDE EJECT**

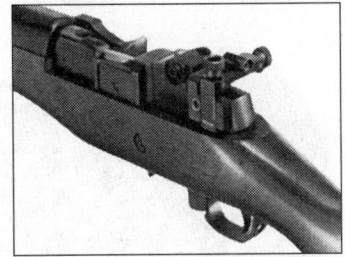

**FP MINI-14-TK
WITH SUB-BASE**

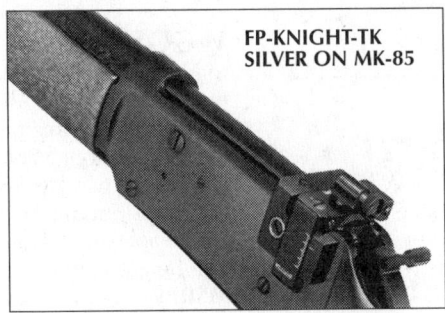

**FP-KNIGHT-TK
SILVER ON MK-85**

**FP-AG-TK
ON BEEMAN
AIR RIFLE**

FP RECEIVER SIGHT OPTIONS

STANDARD

TARGET KNOBS (TK)

**SHOTGUN/BIG
GAME APERTURE**

BLADE

**TARGET - FP
(HIGH)**

**TARGET - FP
(LOW)**

FP SERIES
The "Foolproof" series of aperture sights have internal micrometer adjustments with positive internal locks. The alloy used to manufacture this sight has a tensile strength of 85,000 pounds. Yet, the FP is light and compact, weighing only 1½ ounces. Target knobs are available on all models.

For most models:. $70
With target knobs:. $82

TARGET FP-ANSCHUTZ
Designed to fit many of the Anschutz Lightweight .22 Cal. Target and Sporter Models. No Drilling and Tapping required.
MSRP: $83

TARGET—FP (LOW)
Adjustable From .750-1.250 in. Above Centerline of Bore.
MSRP: $78

SIGHTS & SCOPES

Williams Sights

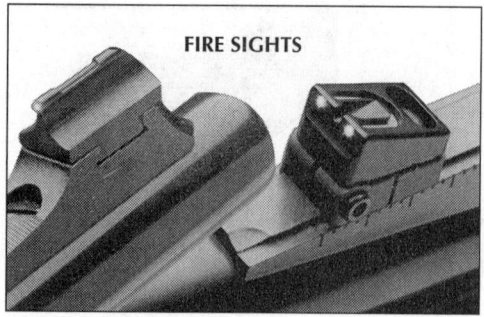

FIRE SIGHTS

WGOS

WGRS-CVA ON CVA APOLLLO

WILLIAMS

RECEIVER SIGHTS
MILITARY SIGHTS

Open and aperture for: SKS (no drilling required); AK47 (no drilling required)
MSRP: **$20-26**

FIRE SIGHTS

FireSight Steel Rifle Beads
Steel front dovetail sight beads machined to accept Fire Sight light gathering rod. A must for all shooters in low-light situations. Comes in a variety of heights. CNC machined steel beads (not plastic).
MSRP: **$18**

.22 OR MUZZLELOADER FRONT FIRESIGHT BEAD

Wide steel front bead machined to accept a FireSights fiberoptic light gathering rod. Fits all standard 3/8 in. dovetails in a variety of heights.
MSRP: **$18**

SKS RIFLE FIRESIGHT BEAD

Fiber optic, light gathering metallic front SKS sight. No gunsmithing required.
MSRP: **$19.95**

SKS RIFLE FIRESIGHT SET

Combines the FireSight Front bead with Williams fully adjustable metallic rear sight for an incredible sight picture. No gunsmithing required.
SKS Rifle FireSight Set: **$40**
Front sight: **$20**

RIFLE FIRESIGHT PEEP SETS

FireSight steel front bead and Williams WGRS rifle peep sight. Fully adjustable—no drilling and tapping required. Available for Ruger .22, Ruger 99/44, Marlin .336 and Ruger

96/22 and 96/22 Mag.
MSRP: **$48**

LEVER ACTION FIRESIGHT PEEP SET

FireSight Steel bead and Williams FP94/36 micro adjustable peep sight for Winchester or Marlin centerfire lever action rifles. (Fits: Win94 top eject, 55, 63, 64, 65, 94-22; Marlin 36, 336, 1894, 1895SS, 1895G, 444SS, 444P)
MSRP: **$81**

AR -15 STYLE FIRESIGHT

Front metallic sight that is fully adjustable for elevation. No gunsmithing required.
MSRP: **$42**

BROWNING BLR FIRESIGHT SET

Replaces rear sight and front sight bead. Fully adjustable metallic sights. No gunsmithing required.
MSRP: **$38**

RUGER 10/22 FIRESIGHT SET

Customize your 10/22 with front and rear fiber optic FireSights. The front steel sight and the fully adjustable metallic rear sight are CNC machined for a perfect fit.
MSRP: **$25**

DOVETAIL FIRESIGHT SET

Light gathering fiber optics for most lever-action rifles with ramped front sights.Fully adjustable rear metallic FireSight fits all standard 3/8 inch dovetails on most Marlin and Winchester models. Front FireSight steel bead replaces existing factory bead.
Marlin 25N & 25MN: **$30**
Dovetail Fire Sight Set: **$36**

WGOS SERIES

Made from high tensile strength aluminum. Will not rust. All parts milled—no stampings. Streamlined and lightweight with tough anodized finish. Dovetailed windage and elevation - Easy to adjust, positive locks. Interchangeable blades available in four heights and four styles.
MSRP: **$20-27**
Blades are sold separately, except "U" blades are available installed on WGOS octagon T/C and CVA.
MSRP: **$7**

WGRS SERIES

Compact Low Profile; Lightweight, Strong, Rustproof; Positive Windage and Elevation Locks In most cases these sights utilize dovetail or existing screws on top of the receiver for installation. They are made from an aluminum alloy that is stronger than many steels. Light. Rustproof. Williams quality throughout.
Most models: **$36**

WGOS SERIES

Made from high tensile strength aluminum. Will not rust. All parts milled—no stampings. Streamlined and lightweight with tough anodized finish. Dovetailed windage and elevation - Easy to adjust, positive locks. Interchangeable blades available in four heights and four styles.
MSRP: **$20-27**
Blades are sold separately, except "U" blades are available installed on WGOS octagon T/C and CVA.
MSRP: **$7**

SIGHTS & SCOPES

SMLE SCOUT SCOPE MOUNT

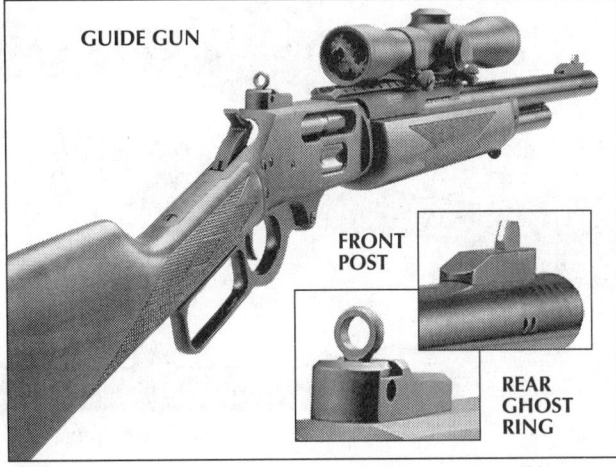

GUIDE GUN

FRONT POST

REAR GHOST RING

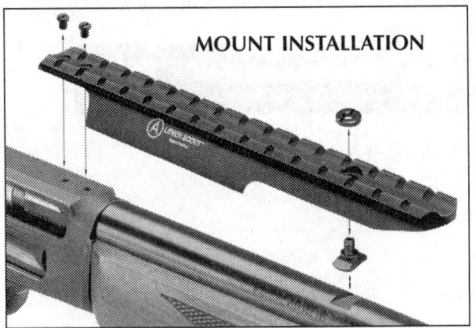

MOUNT INSTALLATION

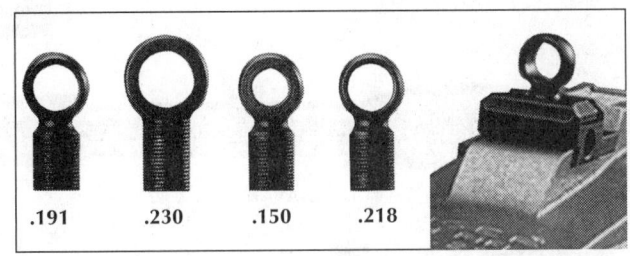

.191   .230   .150   .218

SIGHTS & SCOPES

Developed to offer hunters a faster sight and more open sight picture than are available with scopes or traditional iron sights, XS models fit most popular hunting rifles and shotguns.

XS SIGHT SYSTEMS GHOST-RING SIGHTS & LEVER SCOUT MOUNTS

Scout Scope Mount with 8 in. long Weaver-style rail and cross slots on 1/2 in. Centers. Scope mounts 1/8 in. lower than previously possible on Marlin Lever Guns. Drop-in installation, no gunsmithing required. Installs using existing rear dovetail & front two screw holes on receiver. Allows fast target acquisition with both eyes open—better peripheral vision. Affords use of Ghost-Ring Sights with Scope dismounted. Recoil tested for even the stout .45/70 and .450 Loads. Available for Marlin Lever Models: 1895 Guide Series, new .450, .444P, the .336, and 1894.

MSRP: $50
XS Lever Scout Mount
for Win 94:. $55

XS GHOST-RING HUNTING SIGHTS

Fully adjustable for windage & elevation. Available for most rifles, including blackpowder. Minimum gunsmithing for most installations; matches most existing mounting holes. Compact design, CNC machined from steel and heat treated. Perfect for low light hunting conditions and brush/timer hunting, offers minimal target obstruction.

MSRP: . . . . $90 for most

SMLE SCOUT SCOPE MOUNTS

Offers Scout Scope Mount with 7 in. long Weaver style rail. Requires no machining of barrel to fit—no drilling or tapping. Tapered counter bore for snug fit of SMLE Barrels. Circular Mount is final filled with Brownells Acraglass.
MSRP: $60

XS 24/7 TRITIUM EXPRESS SIGHTS

The original fast aacquisition sight. Now enhanced with new 24/7 tritium sight. 24/7 Express sights are the finest

sights made for fast sight acquisition under any light conditions. Light or dark just "dot the i" and put the dot on the target. Enhances low-light sight acquisition; Improves Low-Light accuracy; Low profile, snag free design; Available for most pistols.
MSRP: $90-120

XS ADJUSTABLE EXPRESS SIGHT SETS

Incorporates Adjustable Rear Express Sight with a white stripe rear, or Pro Express Rear with a Vertical Tritium Bar, fits Bomar style cut, LPA style cut, or a Kimber Target cut rear sight. Affords same Express Sight principles as fixed sight models.
Adjustable Express w/White Stripe Rear and Big Dot Front or Standard Dot Front:. $120
Adjustable Express w/White Stripe Rear and Big Dot Tritium or Standard Dot Tritium Front: $150
Adjustable Pro Express w/Tritium Rear and Big Dot Tritium or Standard Dot Tritium Front: $150

Zeiss Scopes

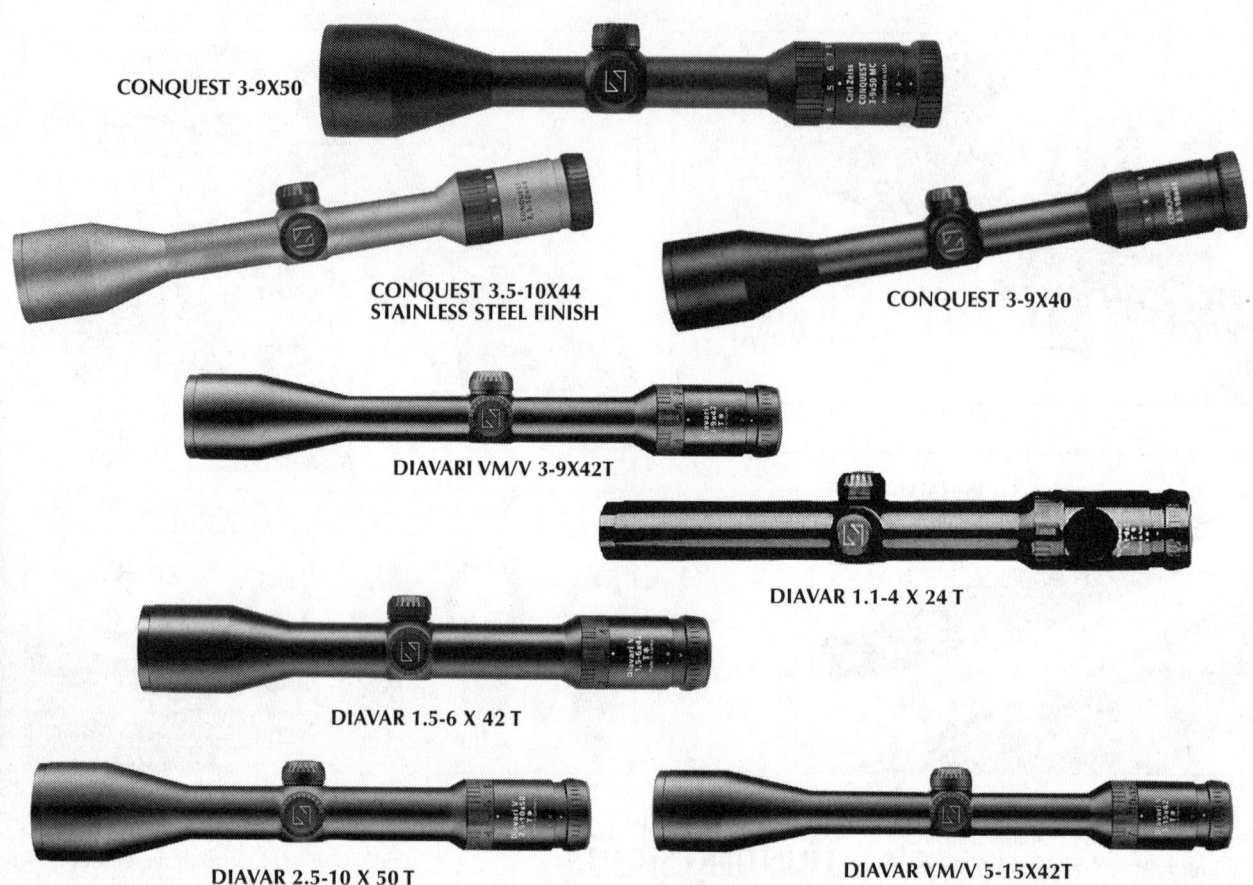

CONQUEST 3-9X50

CONQUEST 3.5-10X44 STAINLESS STEEL FINISH

CONQUEST 3-9X40

DIAVARI VM/V 3-9X42T

DIAVAR 1.1-4 X 24 T

DIAVAR 1.5-6 X 42 T

DIAVAR 2.5-10 X 50 T

DIAVAR VM/V 5-15X42T

ZEISS CONQUEST RIFLESCOPES

The Conquest series features MC anti-reflective coating, excelent low-light performance; arsenic/lead-free glass technology; Zeiss MC multicoating; Lifetime Transferable Warranty. Conquest scopes are waterproof and fogproof.

DIAVARI RIFLESCOPES

Light, compact riflescope available with illuminated varipoint reticle and wide field of view. The Diviari features easy-grip adjustment knobs and is available with bullet drop compensator.

VARIPOINT RIFLESCOPES

Compact scopes with the widest field-of-view offered by Zeiss (108 ft. at 100 yds.). The dot reticle is in the second image plane, so it's large and visible at low powers, small but distinct at high powers. The unilluminated reticle is highly visible.

CONQUEST				
MAGNIFICATION (X OBJ. DIA.)	FIELD OF VIEW (FT., 100 YDS)	DIA./LENGTH (IN.)	WEIGHT (OZ.)	MSRP
3-9x40 MC black	33.90-11.01	1/12.99	15.17	$529
3-9x40 MC stainless	33.90-11.01	1/12.99	15.17	$565
3-9x50 MC	37.5-12.9	1/12.36	16.58	$588
3-9x50 MC ss	37.5-12.9	1/12.36	16.58	$519
3.5-10x44 MC black	35.1-11.70	1/12.68	15.87	$812
3.5-10x44 MC silver	35.1-11.70	1/12.68	15.87	$729
3.5-10x50 MC	35.1-11.7	1/13.15	17.11	$706
3-12x56 MC black	27.6-9.9	1/15.3	25.8	$1142
3-12x56 MC stainless	27.6-9.9	1/15.3	25.8	$1176
4.5-14x50 MC	25.5-8.84	1/14.02	19.75	$812
4.5-14x44 AO MC black	24.9-8.4	1/13.86	17.11	$824
4.5-14x44 AO MC silver	24.9-8.4	1/13.86	17.11	$859
6.5-20x50 AO MC black	17.7-5.7	1/15.59	21.83	$1000
6.5-20x50 AO MC silver	17.7-5.7	1/15.59	21.83	$1047
DIAVARI				
MAGNIFICATION (X OBJ. DIA.)	FIELD OF VIEW (FT., 100 YDS)	DIA./LENGTH (IN.)	WEIGHT (OZ.)	MSRP
V 6-24x56T	18.6-5.10	1.18/14.84	28.40	$1980
VM/V 1.5-6x42 T	72-20.7	1.18/12.3	15	$1499
VM/V 2.5-10x50 T	43.5-12	1.18/12.5	15.9	$1670
VM/V 2.5-10x50 T w/ Illum Reticle	43.5-12	1.18/12.5	15.9	$2099
VM/V 3-12x56 T	37.5-10.5	1.18/13.54	18.38	$1699
VARIPOINT				
MAGNIFICATION (X OBJ. DIA.)	FIELD OF VIEW (FT., 100 YDS)	DIA./LENGTH (IN.)	WEIGHT (OZ.)	MSRP
1.1-4x24 T VM/V	108-30.75	1.18/11.8	15.3	$1899
1.5-6x42 T VM/V	72-20.7	1.18/12.80	15	$2050
2.5-10x50 T VM/V w/ Illum Reticle	43.5-12	1.18/12.80	20.4	$2099

Barnes Ammunition

BANDED SOLIDS

EXPANDER MZ

X – BULLET

Features: heat treated, solid copper projectile; the forward cavity causes the nose to peel back in four separate, razor-edged petals
Available in: .22, 7mm, .30/30, .30, .338, .375, .405 Winchester, .416, .458, .45/70, .50 caliber

TRIPLE-SHOCK X-BULLET

Features: ringed, all-copper construction with no fragmentation; maximum weight retention; on impact the bullet face opens to create four razor-sharp cutting edges
Available in: .22, .25, 6.5mm, 6.8mm, .270, 7mm, .30 caliber

MAXIMUM-RANGE X-BULLETS

Features: lead-free tungsten core (Silvex) with Delrin tip; available in Federal Premium Vital-Shok ammunition
Available in: .270, 7mm, .30, .338 caliber

EXPANDER MZ MUZZLELOADER BULLETS AND ALIGNERS

Features: on impact, these all-copper bullets expand into six razor-sharp petals at velocities as low as 1,100 fps.
Available in: .45, .50 and .54 calibers, 15 and 24 packs with sabots

XPB PISTOL BULLETS

Features: all-copper XPB bullets offer increased penetration and superior expansion and weight retention
Available in: 9mm, .40 S&W, .44, .45 Long Colt, .45 ACP, .454 Cassull, .480 Ruger/.475 Linebaugh, .50 S&W.

XLC BULLETS

Features: coated with Barnes' XLC solid dry film lubricant to reduce friction, fouling and heat build-up
Available in: .22, 6mm, .25, 6.5mm, .270, 7mm, .30, .577 Nitro calibers

VARMIN-A-TOR BULLETS

Features: lead-core hollowpoint design without VLC coating; Varmintor-A-Tor bullets feature a scored nose cavity and thin, tapered jacket
Available in: .22 and 6mm

ORIGINAL

Features: produced by pressure forming pure copper tubing around a pure lead core; on impact, Original bullets typically expand to more than 200 percent of their original diameter
Available in: 6mm, .348 Win, .38/55, .40/65, .458 Mag, .375 Win, .401 Win, .45/70, .50/110 Win

AMMUNITION

Black Hills Ammunition

Noted for varmint and tactical ammo, Black Hills includes softpoint offerings in its big game hunting line beginning with the .223 loaded with 60-grain Nosler Partition bullets. You'll also find a broad selection in the Black Hills Gold big game series. The .25-06 comes with 100-grain Nosler Ballistic Tips and 115-grain Barnes X-Bullets. Get 140-grain Ballistic Tips and X-Bullets in 7mm Remington Magnum cartridges.

Nosler's AccuBond joins the bullet line in several rounds, including .270 and .300 WSM, new Black Hills Gold cartridges are also available in .22-250, .243 Win, .25-06, .270, .308, .30-06, 7mm Rem. Mag. and .300 Win Mag.

The Cowboy line includes modern and traditional rounds from the .32 H&R to the .45-70. Black Hills offers an expanding line of factory-new and remanufactured ammunition for handguns and rifles. The Cowboy Action Line includes loads for the .32 H&R, .357 Magnum, .38-40, .44-40, .45 Colt, .32-20, .44 Colt, .44 Spl., .45 Schofield, .38 Spl, .38 Long Colt, .44 Russian, .45-70. Modern hand-

gun ammunition, from .40 S&W to .44 Magnum, features a variety of bullet types. Black Hills rifle cartridges include the popular .223, .308, 6.5-284, .300 Win. Mag, and the potent long-range tactical round, the .338 Lapua. There's also specialty ammo, with frangible or moly-coated bullets.

BLACK HILLS AMMUNITION
Available in: .380 Auto, 9mm Luger, .40 S&W, .45 ACP, .32 H&R Mag, .38 Special .357 Mag, .44 Mag, .223 Rem, .308 Win, .300 Win Mag, .338 Lapua

BLACK HILLS GOLD
Available in: .243 Win, .25-06 Rem, .270 Win, .308 Win, .30-06, .300 Win Mag, 7mm Rem Mag.

COWBOY ACTION AMMUNITION
Available in: .38-40, .44-40, .44 Russian, .44 Colt, .44 Special, .45 Schofield, .45 Colt, .45-70, .32 H&R, .32-20, .38 Long Colt, .38 Special, .38-55, .357 Mag.

AMMUNITION

Brenneke USA Ammunition

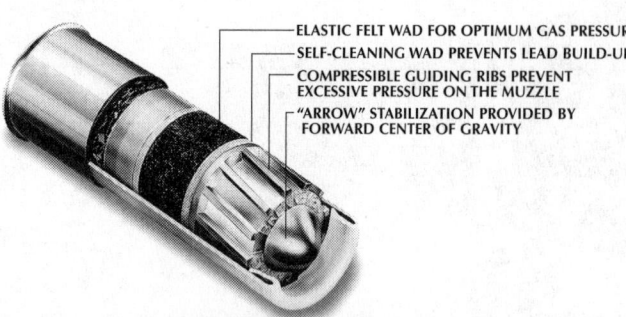

ELASTIC FELT WAD FOR OPTIMUM GAS PRESSURE RISE
SELF-CLEANING WAD PREVENTS LEAD BUILD-UP IN BORE
COMPRESSIBLE GUIDING RIBS PREVENT
EXCESSIVE PRESSURE ON THE MUZZLE
"ARROW" STABILIZATION PROVIDED BY
FORWARD CENTER OF GRAVITY

The Original Brenneke has been the standard against which other slugs have been measured for 100 years.

Brenneke USA Load	Distance (yds)	Velocity (ft./sec.)	Energy (ft./lbs.)	Trajectory (in)
Super Sabot 12 GA; 2¾"; 1⅛ oz; Rifled only	Muzzle	1407	2157	-2.0
	25	1274	1770	+0.4
	50	1165	1478	+1.6
	75	1080	1272	+1.1
	100	1017	1127	-1.3
SuperSabot 12 GA; 3"; 1⅛ oz; Rifled only	Muzzle	1526	2536	-2.0
	25	1376	2064	+0.2
	50	1248	1697	+1.2
	75	1144	1426	+0.9
	100	1065	1236	-1.1
K.O. Sabot 12 GA; 2¾"; 1 oz; Smooth or Rifled	Muzzle	1509	2184	-2.0
	25	1344	1733	+0.3
	50	1206	1395	+1.3
	75	1101	1162	+0.9
	100	1024	1007	-1.3
K.O. Sabot 12 GA; 3"; 1 oz; Smooth or Rifled	Muzzle	1673	2686	-2.0
	25	1487	2122	+0.0
	50	1325	1685	+1.0
	75	1191	1361	+0.7
	100	1090	1139	-1.1
Black Magic Short Mag 12 GA; 2¾"; 1 oz; Smooth or Rifled	Muzzle	1560	2375	-2.0
	25	1306	1664	+0.1
	50	1135	1258	+1.2
	75	1044	1063	+0.7
	100	929	842	-1.4
Black Magic Magnum 12 GA; 3"; 1⅜ oz; Smooth or Rifled	Muzzle	1502	3014	-2.0
	25	1295	2241	+0.4
	50	1136	1724	+1.6
	75	1030	1418	+1.0
	100	955	1219	-1.5
Magnum 20 GA; 3"; 1 oz; Smooth or Rifled	Muzzle	1476	2120	-2.0
	25	1322	1701	+0.4
	50	1193	1385	+1.5
	75	1094	1165	+1.2
	100	1022	1016	-1.0

Brenneke USA Ammunition

Brenneke USA Load	Distance (yds)	Velocity (ft./sec.)	Energy (ft./lbs.)	Trajectory (in)
K.O. 12 GA; 2¾"; 1 oz; Smooth or Rifled	Muzzle	1600	2491	-2.0
	25	1377	1845	+0.3
	50	1199	1399	+1.5
	75	1072	1118	+1.2
	100	987	948	-1.0
Heavy Field Short Magnum 12 GA; 2¾"; 1¼ oz; Smooth or Rifled	Muzzle	1476	2538	-2.0
	25	1310	2000	+0.4
	50	1174	1606	+1.5
	75	1075	1346	+1.0
	100	1002	1170	-1.4
Tactical Home Defense 12 GA; 2¾"; 1 oz; Smooth or Rifled	Muzzle	1378	1854	-2.0
	25	1181	1362	+0.5
	50	1066	1110	0
	75	968	915	+0.4
	100	896	785	-2.9
Magnum .410; 3"; ¼ oz; Smooth or Rifled	Muzzle	1755	781	-2.0
	25	1427	517	+0.2
	50	1179	352	+1.4
	75	1025	266	+1.0
	100	930	219	-1.4
Heavy Field Short Magnum 20 GA; 2¾"; 1 oz; Smooth or Rifled	Muzzle	1392	1890	-2.0
	25	1209	1431	-0.4
	50	1110	1201	+1.6
	75	950	884	-0.2
	100	881	761	-2.8
Gold Magnum 12 GA; 3"; 1⅜ oz; Smooth or Rifled	Muzzle	1502	3014	-2.0
	25	1295	2241	+0.4
	50	1136	1724	+1.6
	75	1030	1418	+1.0
	100	955	1219	-1.5

Federal Ammunition

The Premium label covers Federal's best big game loads, featuring bullets, including Nosler partition and Accu-Bond, Solid Base, Ballistic Tip, Trophy Bonded, and Sierra GameKing. The Barnes Triple-Shock X-Bullets are offered under the Vital Shok label. The Cape Shok list includes loads for the .375 H&H, .416 Rigby, .416 Remington Magnum, .458 Winchester and .470 Nitro Express. Choose a Partition, Bear Claw or Woodleigh Weldcore softpoint, or a Woodleigh or Trophy Bonded solid. V Shok ammunition features Ballistic Tip, Sierra Varminter and others.

The Power Shok line featuring hunting loads from the .222 to the .375 Holland and .45-70 Government, includes the .308 and .30-06 with low recoil loads. Also on the Power Shok list: the .270 and 7mm Winchester Short Magnums, with 130- and 150-grain loads at 3250 and 3200 fps.

TROPHY BONDED BEAR CLAW

This legendary Jack Carter design is ideal for medium to large dangerous game and is loaded exclusivly by Federal. The jacket and core are 100% fusion-bonded for reliable bullet expansion from 25 yards to extreme ranges. The bullet retains 95% of its weight, assuring deep penetration. The bullet jacket features a hard solid copper base tapering to a soft, copper nose section for controlled expansion.

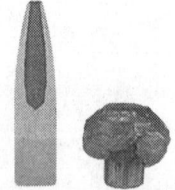

TROPHY BONDED SLEDGEHAMMER

Use it on the largest, most dangerous game in the world. This Jack Carter design maximizes stopping power and your confidence. It's a bonded bronze solid with a flat nose that minimizes deflection off bone and muscle for a deep, straight wound channel.

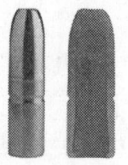

SIERRA GAMEKING BOAT-TAIL

Long ranges are its specialty. With varying calibers, it's an excellent choice for everything from varmints to big game animals. The GameKings's tapered, boat-tail design provides extremely flat trajectories. The design also gives it a higher downrange velocity, so there's more energy at the point of impact. Reduced wind drift makes it a good choice for long-range shots.

WOODLEIGH WELDCORE

Safari hunters have long respected this bonded Australian bullet for its superb accuracy and excellent stopping power. Its special heavy jacket provides 80-85% weight retention. These bullets are favored for large or dangerous game.

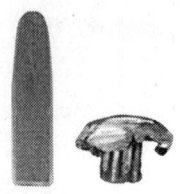

NOSLER PARTITION

This Nosler design is a proven choice for medium to large game animals. A partioned copper jacket allows the front half of the bullet to mushroom, while the rear core remains intact, driving forward for deep penetration and stopping power.

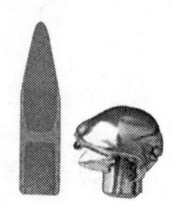

NOSLER BALLISTIC TIP

With proven fast, flat-shooting wind-defying performance, it's specially designed for long-range shots at varmints, predators and small to medium game. A color-coded polycarbonate tip provides easy identification, prevents deformation in the magazine and drives back on impact for expansion and immediate energy transfer.

AMMUNITION

Federal Ammunition

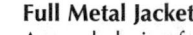

NOSLER ACCUBOND
AccuBond combines the terminal performance of a bonded bullet with the accuracy and retained energy of a Ballistic Tip. Loads in .280 Rem., 7mm-08, 7mm Rem. Mag. and 7mm Win Short Mag.

BARNES TRIPLE SHOCK X-BULLET
The TSX-Bullet delivers superior expansion and deep penetration. The all-copper design provides high weight retention for knockdown power.

NOSLER SOLID BASE BOAT-TAIL
A Federal exclusive, Solid Base is accurate and consistent. Its tapered jacket and boat-tail design provides controlled expansion and reliable performance. Available in 21 configurations.

POWER•SHOK CENTERFIRE RIFLE
Soft Point
It's a proven performer on small game and thin-skinned medium game. It has an aerodynamic tip for a flat trajectory. The exposed soft point expands rapidly for hard hits, even as velocity slows at longer ranges.

Soft Point Round Nose
For generations, hunters have made this bullet the choice for deer and bear in heavy cover. Its large exposed tip, good weight retention and specially tapered jacket provide controlled expansion for deep penetration.

Soft Point Flat Nose
This is the bullet hunters traditionally choose when headed into thick cover. It expands reliably and penetrates deep on light to medium game. The flat nose prevents accidental discharge in tubular magazines.

Full Metal Jacket Boat-Tail
These accurate, non-expanding bullets give you a flat shooting trajectory, leave a small exit hole in game, and puts clean holes in paper - great for sharpening your shooting eye. They're famous for smooth, reliable feeding into semi-automatics too.

HANDGUN BULLET STYLES
Lead Round Nose
A great economical training round for practicing at the range. It dates back to the early part of this century. This bullet is 100 lead with no jacket. It provides excellent accuracy and is very economical.

Full Metal Jacket
A good choice for range practice and reducing lead fouling in the barrel. The jacket extends from the nose to the base, preventing bullet expansion and barrel leading. It is used primarily as military ammunition and for recreational shooting.

Hi-Shok Jacketed Soft Point
It's a proven performer on small to medium-sized game.

Lead Semi-Wadcutter
The most popular all-around choice for target and personal defense, a versatile design which cuts clean holes in targets and efficiently transfers energy.

Jacketed Hollow Point
It's an ideal personal defense round in revolvers and semi-autos. Creates quick, positive expansion with proven accuracy. The specially designed jacket ensures smooth feeding into autoloading firearms.

Semi-Wadcutter Hollow Point
A good combination for both small game and personal defense. Hollow point design promotes uniform expansion.

PREMIUM HANDGUN BULLET STYLES
Hydra-Shok
Federal's unique center-post design delivers controlled expansion, and the notched jacket provides efficient energy transfer to penetrate barriers while retaining stopping power. The deep penetration of this jacketed bullet satisfies even the FBI's stringent testing requirements.

Premium Personal Defense
Has increased muzzle velocity and energy along with rapid bullet expansion that delivers instant stopping power. The recoil is significantly reduced. Our clear packaging lets you see the ammo before you open the box.

Expanding Full Metal Jacket
This revolutionary barrier-penetrating design combines a scored metal nose over an internal rubber tip that collapses on impact. Expansion is assured on every shot.

CastCore
Premium CastCore gives you a heavyweight, flat-nosed, hard cast-lead bullet that smashes through bone, without breaking apart.

Trophy Bonded Bear Claw
The Trophy Bonded Bear Claw handgun bullet has a fusion-bonded jacket and core for up to 95 percent weight retention, better penetration and more knockdown power.

AMMUNITION

Fiocchi Ammunition

Known for its shotshells and .22 rimfire ammunition, Fiocchi also markets centerfire pistol and rifle cartridges. This Italian firm has been in business since 1876.

Fiocchi Target Loads offer you many choices to suit the shell to your game: Standard 1⅛ ounce loads for everything from registered trap and skeet to sporting clays.

SHOT PELLET SIZES

Size #	9	8½	8	7½	6	5	4	3	2	1	BB	BBB	T	#4	00
Dia.In.	.08	.085	.09	.095	.11	.12	.13	.14	.15	.16	.18	.19	.20	.24	.33
Dia.MM	2.03	2.16	2.29	2.41	2.79	3.05	3.30	3.56	3.81	4.06	4.57	4.83	5.08	6.10	8.38

LOAD	Gauge	Shell Length	Dram. Equiv.	Muzzle Velocity	Shot wt./ Pellet ct.	Shot Size	Shot Type
STEEL (WATERFOWL)							
Speed Steel	12	3½"	Max	1520	1⅜	T BBB BB 1 2	Treated Steel
Heavy Steel	12	3½"	Max	1470	1⁹⁄₁₆	T BBB BB 1	Treated Steel
Speed Steel	12	3"	Max	1475	1⅛	BBB BB 1 2 3 4	Treated Steel
Steel	12	3"	Max	1320	1¼	T BBB BB 1 2 3 4	Treated Steel
Low Recoil Target	12	2¾"	Lite	1200	1	7	Treated Steel
Training Load	12	2¾"	Max	1440	⅞	7	Treated Steel
Upland Steel	12	2¾"	Max	1400	1	4 6 7	Treated Steel
Steel	12	2¾"	Max	1375	1⅛	BB 1 2 3 4 6	Treated Steel
Low Recoil Target	20	2¾"	Lite	1225	⅞	7	Treated Steel
Upland Steel	20	2¾"	Max	1470	¾	3 4 6 7	Treated Steel
Speed Steel	20	3"	Max	1500	⅞	2 3 4	Treated Steel
FIELD LOADS (UPLAND GAME)							
Heavy Field	12	2¾"	3¼	1225	1¼	6 7½ 8 9	Lead
Field Load	12	2¾"	3¼	1255	1⅛	6 7½ 8 9	Lead
Field Load	16	2¾"	2¾	1185	1⅛	6 7½ 8	Lead
Field Load	20	2¾"	2½	1165	1	6 7½ 8 9	Lead
DOVE							
Multi-Sport	12	2¾"	3	1250	1	7½ 8 9	Lead
Multi-Sport	12	2¾"	2¾	1150	1⅛	7½ 8	Lead
Game & Target	12	2¾"	3¼	1290	1	6 7½ 8 9	Lead
Game & Target	12	2¾"	3	1200	1⅛	7½ 8	Lead
Game & Target	16	2¾"	2½	1165	1	7½ 8 9	Lead
Game & Target	20	2¾"	2½	1210	⅞	7½ 8 9	Lead
Game & Target	28	2¾"	2	1200	¾	8 9	Lead
Game & Target	410	2½"	Max	1200	½	8 9	Lead
TARGET							
Target Light	12	2¾"	2¾	1150	1	7½ 8 8½ 9	Hi-Antimony Lead
Target Heavy	12	2¾"	3	1200	1	7½ 8 8½	Hi-Antimony Lead
Little Rhino	12	2¾"	HDCP	1250	1	7½ 8 8½	Hi-Antimony Lead
Crusher	12	2¾"	Max	1300	1	7½ 8 8½ 9	Hi-Antimony Lead
Super Crusher	12	2¾"	Max	1400	1	6 7½	Hi-Antimony Lead
Lite	12	2¾"	2⅞	1165	1⅛	7½ 8 9	Hi-Antimony Lead
VIP Light	12	2¾"	2¾	1150	1⅛	7½ 8 9	Hi-Antimony Lead
VIP Heavy	12	2¾"	3	1200	1⅛	7½ 8 9	Hi-Antimony Lead

AMMUNITION

Fiocchi Ammunition

LOAD	Gauge	Shell Length	Dram. Equiv.	Muzzle Velocity	Shot wt./ Pellet ct.	Shot Size	Shot Type
White Rhino	12	2¾"	HDCP	1250	1⅛	7½ 8 8½ 9	Hi-Antimony Lead
Training Load	12	2¾"	3	1200	⅞	7½ 8	Hi-Antimony Lead
International	12	2¾"	Max	1350	24 grams	7½ 8 9	Hi-Antimony Lead
Low Recoil Trap Light	12	2¾"	2¾	1140	1⅛	7½ 8	Hi-Antimony Lead
Low Recoil Trap Heavy	12	2¾"	3	1185	1⅛	7½ 8	Hi-Antimony Lead
Golden Pheasant							
Field Load	12	2¾"	3¾	1250	1⅜	4 5 6	Nickel-Plated
Field Load	12	2¾"	Max	1485	1⅜	4 5 6	Nickel-Plated
Heavy Field	12	3"	Max	1200	1¾	4 5 6	Nickel-Plated
Field Load	16	2¾"	3¼	1310	1⅛	5	Nickel-Plated
Field Load	20	2¾"	2⅞	1245	1	5 6 7½	Nickel-Plated
Heavy Field	20	3"	Max	1200	1¼	4 5 6	Nickel-Plated
Field Load	28	2¾"	Max	1300	⅞	6 7½	Nickel-Plated
HIGH VELOCITY							
High Velocity	12	2¾"	3¾	1330	1¼	4 5 6 7½ 8 9	Lead
High Velocity	12	3	Max	1330	1¾	6	Lead
High Velocity	16	2¾"	3⅛	1300	1⅛	4 6 7½ 8	Lead
High Velocity	20	2¾"	2¾	1220	1	4 5 6 7½ 8 9	Lead
High Velocity	28	2¾"	2¼	1300	¾	6 7½ 8	Lead
High Velocity	410	3"	Max	1140	1¹⁄₁₆	6 7½ 8	Lead
BUCKSHOT							
Buckshot	12	2¾"	Max	1325	27 pell.	4 Buck	Hi-Antim. Nickel-Plated
Buckshot	12	2¾"	Max	1325	9 pell.	00 Buck	Hi-Antim. Nickel-Plated
Reduced Recoil	12	2¾"	Lite	1150	9 pell.	00 Buck	Hi-Antim. Nickel-Plated
SLUGS							
Trophy Slug 70mm	12	2¾"	Max	1560	1	Rifled Slug	Lead w/attached Wad
Trophy Slug 70mm	20	2¾"	Max	1650	⅞	Rifled Slug	Lead w/attached Wad
NICKEL PLATED HUNTING							
Heavy Nickel	12	2¾"	3¼	1225	1¼	7½ 8	Nickel-Plated Lead
High Velocity Nickel	12	2¾"	3¾	1330	1¼	4 5 6 7½ 8	Nickel-Plated Lead
Golden Pheasant	12	2¾"	Max	1250	1⅜	4 5 6	Nickel-Plated Lead
Golden Pheasant 20	20	3"	Max	1200	1¼	4 5 6	Nickel-Plated Lead
INTERCEPTOR SPREADER							
Interceptor	12	2¾"	Max	1300	1	7½ 8 8½ 9	Lead
SPORTING CLAY POWER SPREADERS							
Power Spreader	12	2¾"	3	1200	1⅛	8 8½	Lead
Power Spreader	12	2¾"	Max	1250	1⅛	8 8½ 9	Lead
STEEL TARGET LOAD							
Steel Target Load	12	2¾"	Max	1440	⅞	7	Steel
Steel Target Load	12	2¾"	Max	1400	1	4 6 7	Steel
Steel Target Load	20	2¾"	Max	1470	¾	3 4 6 7	

AMMUNITION

Fiocchi Ammunition

LOAD	Gauge	Shell Length	Dram. Equiv.	Muzzle Velocity	Shot wt./ Pellet ct.	Shot Size	Shot Type
ULTRA LOW RECOIL							
Trainer	12	2¾"	Lite	1200	⅞	7½ 8	Hi-Antimony Lead
Trainer	20	2¾"	Lite	1075	¾	7½	Hi-Antimony Lead
MULTI-SPORT — GAME & TARGET							
Multi-Sport	12	2¾"	3	1250	1	7½ 8 9	Lead
Game & Target	12	2¾"	3¼	1290	1	6 7½ 8 9	Lead
Game & Target	12	2¾"	3	1200	1⅛	7½ 8	Lead
LOW RECOIL TRAP							
Low-Recoil Trap Light	12	2¾"	2¾	1140	1⅛	7½ 8	Hi-Antimony Lead
Low-Recoil Trap Heavy	12	2¾"	3	1185	1⅛	7½ 8	Hi-Antimony Lead
STEEL LOW RECOIL							
Low-Recoil Steel	12	2¾"	Lite	1200	1	7	Treated Steel
Low-Recoil Steel	20	2¾"	Lite	1225	⅞	7	Treated Steel

SHOTSHELL APPLICATION GUIDE	Game	Lead Shot	Steel Shot	Recommended Loads
	Geese	NA	T BBB BB 1	Heavy Steel, Speed Steel
	Ducks	NA	BB 1 2 3 4 6	Heavy Steel, Speed Steel, Upland Steel
	Pheasant	4 5 6	3 4 5 6	Golden Pheasant, HV, Speed Steel, Upland Steel, HVN
	Turkey	4 5 6	4 5	Turkey Tunder, HV, HVN
	Grouse/Partridge	5 6 7½ 8	4 6 7	Field Loads, Upland Steel, HV, HVN, HFN
	Quail	7½ 8 9	7	Field Loads, HV, Upland Steel, HVN, HFN
	Dove/Pigeon	6 7½ 8 9	6 7	Field Loads, GT, Dove, HV, HFN, HVN
	Rabbit/Squirrel	4 5 6 7½	6 7	Field Loads, HV, GT, Upland Steel, HFN, HVN
	Deer/Boar	00-Slug	NA	12HV00BK, 12 Gauge Slug, 20 Gauge Slug
	Trap	7½ 8 8½	6 7	TL, TH, TX, VIP, LITE, WRNO, MS, TRAPH, TRAPL
	Skeet	8 8½ 9	7	TL, TH, TX, VIP, LITE, WRNO, MS
	Sporting Clays	7½ 8 8½ 9	7	TL, TH, TX, TIP, LITE, WRNO, MS
	Steel Target			Upland Steel, Training Load

Lead Shot size	½	1/16	¾	⅞	1	1⅛	1¼	1⅜	1¾	2	Steel Shot size	¾	⅞	1	1⅛	1¼	1⅜	1⁹/₁₆
9	290	398	434	507	579	685	724				7	315	368	420				
8½				423	483						6	237		316	356			
8	204	280	305	356	407	458	509				4	143	167	191	215	239	263	
7½		238	260	303	346	389	433				3	115	134		172	191	210	
6		153	167	194	222	250	278	305	389	444	2		109		141	156	172	
5		118			171	192	214	235	299	342	1				116	129	142	161
4					135	152	169	189	236	270	BB				81	90	99	113
											BBB				69	76	84	95
											T					66	73	83

Note: When comparing steel shot to lead shot, increase shot size by two to get similar downrange results (i.e. Lead #4 to Steel #2). Check your shotgun and choke manufacturer for steel shot compatibility.

AMMUNITION

Hornady Ammunition

Hornady's .17 Mach 2 fits the mechanisms of ordinary .22s and functions in self-loaders. The tiny 17-grain V-Max bullet flies flatter than bullets from .22 Long Rifle ammunition. Hornady's .204 Ruger derives from the .222 Magnum. A 32-grain polymer-tipped, V-Max bullet, clocks 4200 fps. Hornady offers a .500 Smith & Wesson handgun cartridge with a 350-grain XTP bullet that clocks 1900 fps at the muzzle of a 7½ inch barrel.

Hornady ammunition includes a .405 Winchester cartridge loaded with a 300-grain FP bullet at 2200 fps. Other big-bore ammo: the .444 Marlin Light Magnum with a 265-grain bullet at 2335 fps and, for dangerous African game, the .458 Lott with a 500-grain bullet at 2300 fps.

Hornady's Polymer-tipped InterBond stable includes three round-nose bullets: 300-grain .375, 400-grain .416 and 500-grain .458 and a 225-grain .338 spitzer. Hornady also offers SST bullets in 154-grain 7mm Remington Magnum and 180-grain .300 Weatherby Magnum loads in its hunting ammunition line. There's also a 195-grain SP load for the 8x57 JS. The TAP personal defense series includes 9mm, .40 S&W and .45 ACP ammo, .223 and .308 rifle loads and 12-gauge 00 buckshot rounds.

Borrowing from its successful Speed Sabot system for muzzleloaders, Hornady has used the big SST bullets in a loaded shotshell. The SST slug clocks 2,000 fps and delivers 2,664 ft-lbs. of energy.

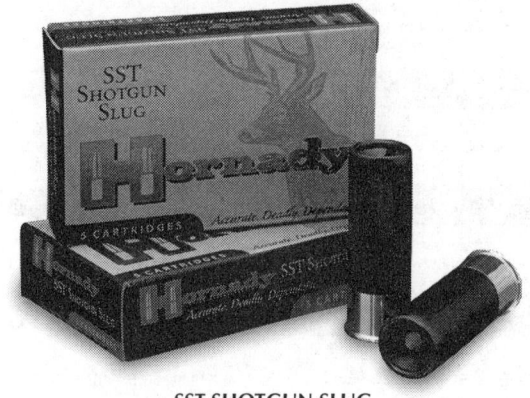

SST SHOTGUN SLUG

TAP

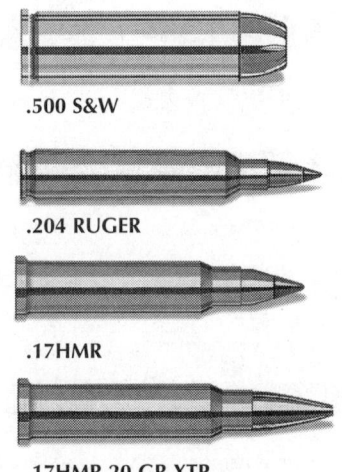

.500 S&W

.204 RUGER

.17HMR

.17HMR 20 GR XTP

.405 WINCHESTER

.17 MACH 2

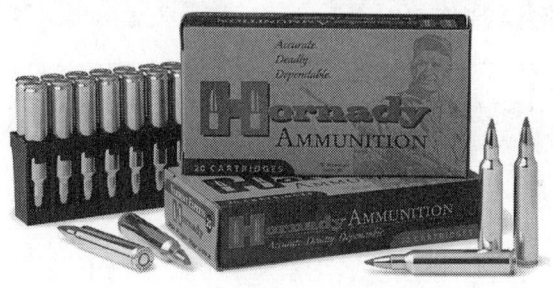

.204 RUGER

Kynoch Ammunition

480g SN/S 475 Nitro Express

410g SN/S 425 Westley Richards

14g SN/S 400/360

140g SN 6.5x54 Mannlicher

480g SN/S 472 No. 2 Eley

400g SN/S 450/400 3¾" Nitro Express

320g SN/S 360 No. 2

140g SN 275 Rigby

500g SN/S 472 No. 2 Jeffrey

400g SN/S 450/400 3" Nitro Express

270g SN 369 Purdey

220g SN/S 180g SN 300 H&H Flanged

520g SN/S 476 Nitro Express

480g SN/S 450 3¾" Nitro Express

270g SN 375 2½"

220g SN/S 180g SN 300 H&H Belted

535g SN/S 500 Jeffrey

350g SN 450 3¾" Nitro for Black

270g SN 9.5x54 Mannlicher Schoenauer

215g SN 303 British

570g SN/S 500 3" Nitro Express

480g SN/S 450 No2 Nitro Express

270g SN 400/375 Belted H&H

250g SN/S 318 Rimless Nitro Express

440g SN 500 3" Nitro for Black

480g SN/S 450 Rigby Rimless

300g SN/S 270 SN 235 SN

300g SN/S 250g SN/S 333
Jeffery Flanged

440g SN 500 3¼" Nitro for Black

480g SN/S 458 Lott

300g SN/S 270 SN 235 SN Belted Magnum

300g SN/S 333 Jeffery Rimless

525g SN/S 505 Gibbs

500g SN/S 470 Capstick

230g SN 400 Purdy

250g SN 35 Winchester

750g SN/S 577 3" Nitro Express

480g SN/S 500/450 Nitro Express

400g SN/S 404 Jeffery Nitro Express

225g SN/S 350 Rigby Magnum

900g SN/S 600 Nitro Express

480g SN/S 500/465 Nitro Express

300g SN 405 Winchester

225g SN/S 400/350 (350 No. 2 Rigby)

1000g SN/S 700 Nitro Express

500g SN/S 470 Nitro Express

410g SN/S 416 Rigby

Kenny Jarrett Ammunition

Shooters who know of Kenny Jarrett's legendary long range rifles will love Jarrett ammunition. The high-performance cartridges are in 10-round boxes. The cases are from Norma with Jarrett's headstamp. Calibers include .243, .270, 7mm Remington Magnum, .30-06, .300 Winchester Magnum, .300 Jarrett, .375 H&H and .416 Remington Magnum. Bullet options for each include Nosler Ballistic Tip and Swift A-Frame.

Magtech Ammunition

The Magtech line of pistol and revolver cartridges has 15 loadings. The most potent is the .500 Smith & Wesson, with a 400-grain semi-jacketed softpoint at 1608 fps. Almost as crushing: a 260-grain FMJ .454 Casull bullet that gets going a little faster (1800 fps). A First Defense line of ammo for autoloading pistols includes: 9mm Luger, .40 S&W, .45 ACP+P, .38 Special, .357 Magnum and .380 Auto. Features include a 100% solid copper bullet.

Solid copper hollowpoint bullets highlight Magtech's hunting ammunition. Available in .44 Magnum, .454 Casull and .500 S&W, these cartridges deliver top-rung velocities with deep penetration and high weight retention. Choose a 200-grain .44 Magnum bullet at 1,296 fps, or 225- and 240-grain .454 loads at 1,640 or 1,771 fps. The .500 kicks a 325-grain bullet downrange at 1,801 fps. Bullet types in the company stable range from semi-wadcutter lead to FMJ and jacketed hollowpoint.

SOLID COPPER HOLLOWPOINT

FIRST DEFENSE

500 S&W

GUARDIAN GOLD

CALIBER	BULLET			VELOCITY						ENERGY						MID-RANGE TRAJECTORY				TEST BARREL LENGTH	
	STYLE	WEIGHT		MUZZLE		50m	50yd	100m	100yd	MUZZLE		50m	50yd	100m	100yd	50m	50yd	100m	100yd		
		g	gr	m/s	fps	m/s	fps	m/s	fps	J	ft/lbs	J	ft/lbs	J	ft/lbs	cm	inch	cm	inch	cm	inch
.357 MAG	JHP	8.10	125	420	1378	353	1170	307	1020	714	527	505	381	382	289	1.5	0.5	7.5	2.5	1025	4-V
.380 AUTO+P	JHP	5.5	85	330	1082	303	999	282	936	300	221	252	188	219	166	3.1	1.0	13.3	4.3	9.5	3¼
.38 SPL+P	JHP	8.10	125	310	1017	295	971	282	931	389	287	352	262	322	241	3.4	1.1	14.3	4.6	10.2	4
9MM LUGER+P	JHP	7.45	115	380	1246	344	1137	318	1056	538	397	441	330	377	285	2.4	0.8	10.5	3.4	10.2	4
9MM LUGER	JHP	8.03	124	334	1096	304	1017	286	958	448	331	371	285	328	253	3.1	1.0	12.5	4.1	10.2	4
.40 S&W	JHP	10.0	155	367	1205	338	1118	317	1052	677	500	571	430	523	381	2.5	0.8	10.9	3.5	10.2	4
.40 S&W	JHP	11.66	180	302	990	282	938	268	891	532	392	463	352	419	318	3.7	1.2	13.4	4.5	10.2	4
.45 AUTO+P	JHP	12.0	185	350	1148	323	1066	303	1005	735	540	626	467	551	415	2.7	0.9	11.8	3.8	12.7	5
.45 AUTO+P	JHP	14.90	230	307	1007	290	965	279	927	702	518	626	467	580	440	4.0	1.3	12.5	4.0	12.7	5

Nosler Ammunition

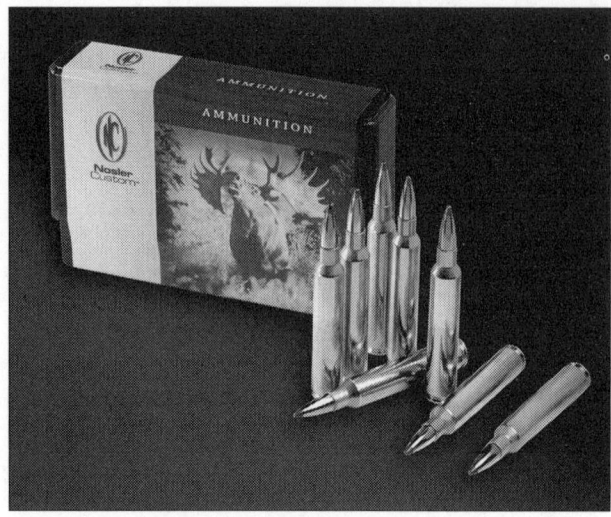

Nosler offers ammunition in the form of Nosler specification factory-loaded cartridges, using brass produced by a contractor with Nosler's headstamp. Nosler ammunition is offered in the following calibers: .22 Hornet, .221 Rem Fireball, .222 Rem, .223 Rem, .220 Swift, .240 Weatherby, .25-06 Rem, .257 Roberts (+P), .257 Weatherby Mag, .260 Rem, .264 Win, Mag, .270 Weatherby Mag, .280 Rem, 7mm Rem Mag, 7mm S.A. Ultra Mag, 7mm Weatherby Mag, 7mm STW, .308 Win, .30/06 Springfield, .300 Win Mag, .300 Win Mag, .300 S.A. Ultra Mag, .300 H&H Mag, .300 Rem Ultra Mag, .300 Weatherby Mag, .30-378 Weatherby Mag, 8x57mm JS Mauser, 8mm Rem Mag, .338 Rem Ultra Mag, .338 Win Mag, .338-06 A-Square, .338-378 Weatherby Mag, .340 Weatherby Mag, .35 Whelen, .350 Remington, 9.3x62mm Mauser, 9.3x74 R, .375 H&H Mag, .375 Rem Ultra Mag, .375 Weatherby Mag, .378 Weatherby Mag, .416 Rem Mag, .416 Rigby Mag, .416 Weatherby Magnum.

PMC Ammunition

SILVER RIFLE

PMC (Precision Made Cartridges) offers sporting and tactical centerfire rounds. Handgun ammo, from .25 Auto to .44 Magnum, includes loads specifically for Cowboy Action shooting. The centerfire rifle stable has cowboy action loads in .30-30 and .45-70, plus a wide variety of hunting and match ammunition from .222 Remington to .375 H&H Magnum. The selection of .22 rimfire rounds features hunting, plinking and match loads.

A broad choice of pistol bullets is available from PMC.

There's the quick-opening Starfire hollowpoint, a traditional jacketed hollowpoint, a jacketed softpoint and a full-metal-jacket (hardball) bullet—plus lead wadcutter, semi-wadcutter and round-nose options. Rifle bullets include the Barnes X-Bullet, .30-30 Starfire hollowpoint, Sierra boat-tail hollowpoint, Sierra boat-tail softpoint, pointed softpoint, softpoint, flat-nose softpoint and full metal jacket. PMC also manufactures shotshells, from light dove and quail and target loads to heavy steel-shot loads for geese.

PMC Ammunition

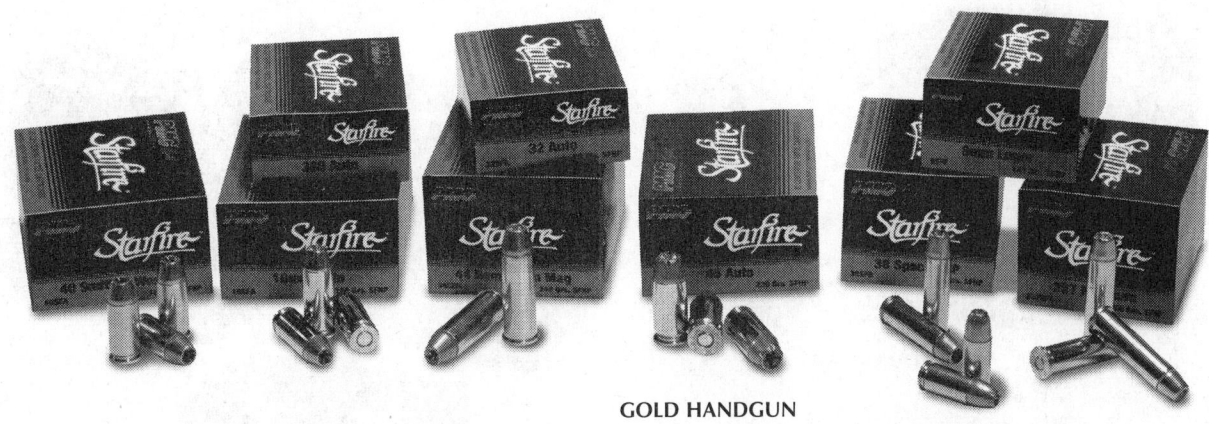

GOLD HANDGUN

GREEN PISTOL

GOLD LINE ULTIMATE HIGH VELOCITY

PMC FIELD & TARGET SHOTSHELLS

PMC's shotshell line includes the Gold Line Ultimate High Velocity shotshell. Available in 2¾-inch 12-, 20- and 28-gauge offerings and 3-inch .410, the new shells feature shot sizes ranging from 4 to 9. The 12-bore 1¼-ounce load chronographs 1400 fps. A 1-ounce 20-gauge charge leaves the muzzle at 1300, the ⅞-ounce 28 at 1250 and the 1¹/₁₆-ounce .410 at 1135. Also: extra heavy Silver Line shotshells, 12-gauge only, with 1⅜ ounces of shot at 1320 fps. Choose 4, 5, 6 or 7½ shot size. PMC has included target loads for the .410 and 28 gauge, both with a velocity of 1220 fps. To round out its shotgun ammo list, the firm has a 12-gauge deer load with a ⅞-ounce slug in a sabot sleeve.

PMC "GREEN" LINE

In centerfire ammunition, there's a PMC "Green" line with non-toxic frangible loads for the .223, .308 and 7.62x39 (bullet weights 40, 120 and 100 grains). Seven pistol rounds, from .38 Special to .357 Sig and .45 ACP are included.

PMC Gold, Silver and Bronze hunting loads range from .223 to .375 H&H, The Gold Line features Barnes XLC-HP bullets, the Silver Line Sierra BlitzKing and Match bullets, with softpoint boat-tails. The Bronze Line has softpoint and pointed softpoint bullets. New this year are .45-90 and .40-65 rifle cartridges for the Cowboy Action shooter, and Predator .22 WMR ammo with a 40-grain full-jacket bullet at 1910 fps.

Remington Ammunition

WATERFOWL LOADS

UPLAND LOADS

SLUGS

SHOTSHELL AMMUNITION

TURKEY LOADS
Nitro Buffeted Turkey Loads
Premier Hevi Shot High Velocity Magnum Turkey
Premier Hevi Shot Magnum Turkey Loads
Premier High Velocity Turkey Loads
Premier Magnum Turkey Loads
Premier Duplex Magnums
Nitro-Mag Bufered Magnums

WATERFOWL LOADS
Wingmaster HD Waterfowl Loads
Premier Hevi Shot Nitro Magnum
Nitro-Steel High Velocity Magnum
Sportsman Hi-Speed Steel

UPLAND LOADS
Nitro Pheasant Loads
Premier Hevi Shot Extra-Long Range Field Loads
Pheasant Loads
Express Extra Long Range
ShurShot High Base Pheasant Loads
ShurShot Heavy Field and Heavy Dove Loads
Lead Game Loads
Sport Loads

TARGET LOADS
Managed Recoil STS Target Loads
Premier STS Target Loads
Premier Nitro 27 Handicap Trap Loads
Premier Nitro Gold Sporting Clays Target Loads
Gun Club Target Loads

SLUGS
Premier Core-Lokt Ultra Bonded Sabot Slugs
Premier Copper Solid Sabot Slugs
BuckHammer Lead Slugs
Managed-Recoil
BuckHammer Lead Slugs
Managed-Recoil BuckHammer Lead Slugs
Slugger High Velocity Slugs
Slugger Rifled Slugs
Slugger Managed-Recoil Rifled Slug Loads

BUCKSHOT
Premier Hevi Shot Buckshot
Premier Nickel-Plated Buckshot
Express Buckshot
Managed-Recoil Express Buckshot

CENTERFIRE AMMUNITION

MANAGED-RECOIL

Managed-Recoil ammunition delivers Remington field proven hunting performance out to 200 yards with half the recoil. Bullets provide 2x expansion with over 75% weight retention on shots inside 50 yards and out to 200 yards. Available in .270 Win., 7mm Remington Mag., .30-06 Springfield, .308 Win., .300 Win Mag.

PREMIER CORE-LOKT ULTRA BONDED

The bonded bullet retains up to 95% of its original weight with maximum penetration and energy transfer. Featuring a progressively tapered jacket design, the Core-Lokt Ultra Bonded bullet initiates and controls expansion nearly 2x. Available in .243 Win., .25-06 Remington, .260 Remington, 6.8mm Remington SPC, .270 Win., 7mm Remington Mag., 7mm Rem SA Ultra Mag., 7mm Rem Ultra Mag., .30-06, .300 Win Mag., .308 Win., .300 Rem SA Ultra Mag., .300 Rem Ultra Mag., .338 Win Mag.

PREMIER SCIROCCO BONDED

The Swift Scirocco Bonded bullet combines polymer tip ballistics with weight retention. The expansion-generating polymer tip and the boat tail base defy air resistance at the front end, and reduce drag at the back. Available in .243 Win., .270 Win., 7mm Remington Mag., .30-06, .300 Win Mag., .308 Win., .300 Rem Ultra Mag., .300 WSM

PREMIER ACCUTIP

Featuring precision-engineered polymer tip bullets designed for match-grade accuracy (sub minute-of-angle), Premier AccuTip offers an unprecedented combination of super-flat trajectory and deadly down-range performance. Available in .17 Remington, .204 Ruger, .22 Hornet, .221 Rem Fireball, .222 Remington, .223 Remington, .22-250 Remington, .243 Win., .260 Remington, .270 Win., .280 Remington, 7mm-08 Remington, 7mm Remington Mag., .30-06, .300 Win Mag., .308 Win.

PREMIER A-FRAME

Loaded with dual-core A-Frame bullets for reliable expansion at long-range decreased velocities, but without over-expansion at short-range high velocities. Available in .270 Win., 7mm Remington Mag., 7mm STW, 7mm Remington Ultra Mag., .30-06, .300 Win Mag., 8mm Remington Mag., .338 Win Mag., .338 Remington Ultra Mag., .375 H&H Mag., .375 Remington Ultra Mag., .416 Remington Mag.

PREMIER MATCH

Loaded with match-grade bullets, Premier Match ammunition employs special loading practices to ensure world-class performance and accuracy with every shot. Available in .223 Remington, 6.8mm Rem. SPC, .300 Rem. SA Ultra Mag., .300 Win Mag., .308 Win.

EXPRESS CENTERFIRE

Available with Express Core-Lokt Soft Point Bullets, Express

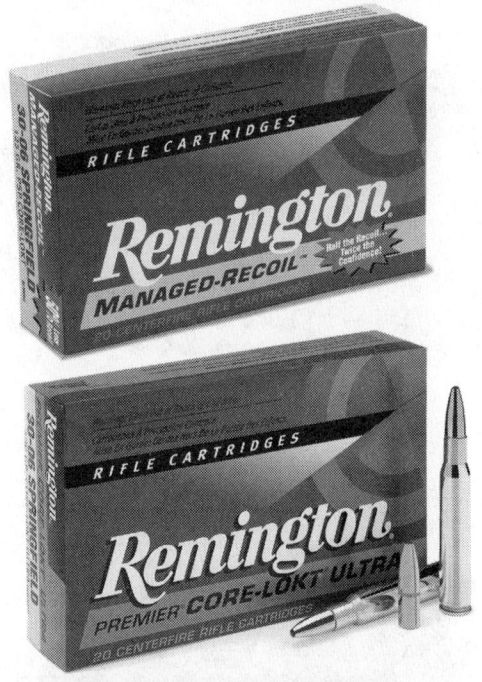

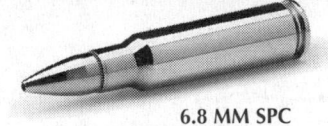

6.8 MM SPC

Core-Lokt Pointed Soft Point Bullets, Express Bronze Point Tipped Bullets, Express Power-Lokt Hollow Point Bullets in .17 Remington, .22 Hornet, .220 Swift, .222 Remington, .223 Remington, .22-250 Remington, 6mm Remington, .243 Win., .25-06 Remington, .25-20 Win, .250 Savage, .257 Roberts, 6.5X55 Swedish Mauser, 6.5mm Remington Magnum, .260 Remington, .264 Win Mag, 6.8mm Remington SPC, .270 Win, .270 WSM, .280 Remington, 7mm-08 Remington, 7mm Remington Magnum, 7mm STW, 7mm Mauser (7x57), 7mm Remington SA Ultra Mag, .30 Carbine, .30-30 Win, .30-40 Krag, .30-06 Springfield, .300 Savage, .300 WSM, .300 Win Mag, .300 Weatherby Mag, .303 British, 7.62 x 39mm, .308 Win, .300 Remington SA Ultra Mag, 8mm Mauser (8x57), .32-20 Win, .32 Win Special, .338 Win Mag, .338 Remington Ultra Mag, .35 Remington, .35 Whelen, .350 Remington Magnum, .375 H&H Mag, .375 Remington Ultra Mag, .444 Marlin, .44-40 Win, .45-70 Govt.

Remington Ammunition

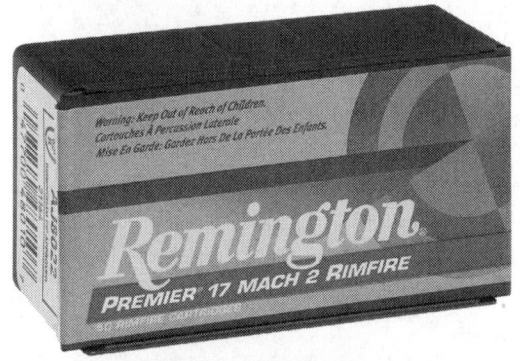

RIMFIRE AMMUNITION

RIMFIRE AMMUNITION

PREMIER GOLD BOX RIMFIRE

Premier Gold Box Rimfire ammunition uses the AccuTip-V bullet with precision-engineered polymer tip for match-type accuracy, high on-game energy and rapid expansion. Available in .17 HMR, .17 Mach 2, .22 Win Mag.

MAGNUM RIMFIRE

Premier Gold Box Rimfire ammunition features AccuTip-V bullets. Choice of Jacketed Hollow Point or Pointed Soft Point. Available in .17 HMR or .22 Win Mag.

REMINGTON-ELEY COMPETITION RIMFIRE

Remington and Eley offer three grades of premier .22 Long Rifle ammunition, Target Rifle, Club Xtra and Match EPS.

REMINGTON-ELEY COMPETITION

HANDGUN AMMUNITION

Remington handgun ammunition is available with the following bullet styles: Full Metal Case, Lead Round Nose, Jacketed Hollow Point, Lead Hollow Point, Semi-Jacketed Hollow Point, Semi-Wadcutter Lead, Soft Point and Wadcutter Match. Available in .25 (6.35mm) Auto., .32 S&W, .32 S&W Long, .32 (7.65mm) Auto., .357 Mag, 9mm Luger, 9mm Luger (+P), 9mm Luger (Subsonic), .380 Auto, .38 S&W, .38 Special, .38 Short Colt, .357 Sig, .40 S&W, .44 Remington Magnum, .44 S&W Special, .45 Colt, .45 Automatic

CORE-LOKT HIGH-PERFORMANCE

The Remington Core-Lokt Ultra bullet features bonded bullet construction, patented spiral nose cuts jacket taper and patented driving band that initiates precise bore alignment for match-grade accuracy. Available in .357 Magnum and 44 Remington Magnum.

GOLDEN SABER HPJ

The bullet diameter directly ahead of the Driving Band is reduced from groove to bore diameter, so the bullet is precisely aligned before the driving band engages the rifling. Available in .357 Mag., 9mm Luger, .380 Auto, .38 Special (+P), .40 S&W, .45 Auto.

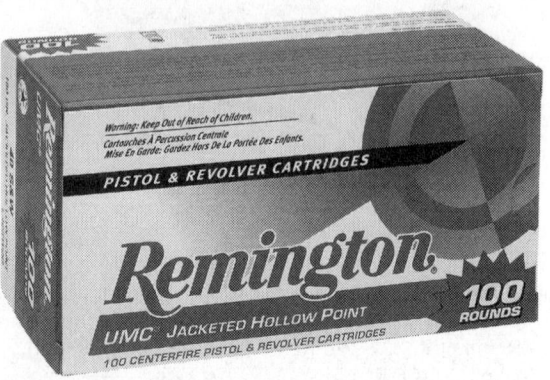

HANDGUN AMMUNITION

Ammunition that has become wet or has been submerged in water should be discarded in a safe manner. Don't try to reclaim damaged ammo by soaking it in oil or a solvent. Poor ignition, unacceptable performance or damage to your firearm and injury to yourself or may result.

AMMUNITION

RWS Ammunition

RWS .22 R50

For competitive shooters demanding the ultimate in precision. This cartridge has been used to establish several world records and is used by Olympic Gold Medalists. No finer cartridge can be bought at any price.

MSRP: **$13/box**

RWS .22 L.R. RIFLE MATCH

Perfect for the club level target competitor. Accurate and affordable.

MSRP: **$8/box**

RWS .22 L.R. SUBSONIC HOLLOW POINT

Subsonic ammunition is a favorite ammunition of shooters whose shooting range is limited to where the noise of a conventional cartridge would be a problem.

MSRP: **$5/box**

RWS .22 MAGNUM HOLLOW POINT

The soft point allows good expansion on impact, while preserving the penetration characteristics necessary for larger vermin and game.

MSRP: **$24/box**

RWS .22 SHORT R25

Designed for world class Rapid Fire Pistol events, this cartridge provides the shooter with outstanding accuracy and minimal recoil. Manufactured to exacting standards, the shooter can be assured of consistent performance.

MSRP: **$9/box**

RWS .22 L.R. TARGET RIFLE

An ideal training and field cartridge, the .22 Long Rifle Target also excels in informal competitions. The target .22 provides the casual shooter with accu-

racy at an economical price.

MSRP: **$4/box**

RWS .22 L.R. HV HOLLOW POINT

A higher velocity hollow point offers the shooter greater shocking power in game. Suitable for both small game and vermin.

MSRP: **$6/box**

RWS .22 MAGNUM FULL JACKET

Outstanding penetration characteristics of this cartridge allow the shooter to easily tackle game where penetration is necessary.

MSRP: **$24/box**

TECHNICAL DATA

Trajectory inches above (+) or below (-) line of sight

CARTRIDGES	BULLET STYLE	BULLET WT. (grains)	MAX. CHAMBER PRESSURE (psi)	MUZZLE	VELOCITY (ft./sec.) 50 yds.	100 yds.	MUZZLE	ENERGY (ft/lbs) 50 yds.	100 yds.	OPEN SIGHT @ yds.	25 yds.	50 yds.	75 yds.	100 yds.	SIGHTED @ yds.	25 yds.	50 yds.	75 yds.	100 yds.
.22 L.R. R 50	Lead	40	25.600	1.070	970	890	100	80	70	—	—	—	—	—	—	—	—	—	—
.22 Short R 25	Lead	28	18.500	560	490	—	20	15	—	—	—	—	—	—	—	—	—	—	—
.22 L.R. Rifle Match	Lead	40	25.600	1.035	945	860	95	80	65	50	+0.7	—	-3.2	-9.0	50	+0.1	—	-2.6	-7.8
.22 L.R. Target Rifle	Lead	40	25.600	1.080	990	900	100	85	70	50	+0.6	—	-3.1	-8.7	50	+0.1	—	-2.5	-7.5
.22 L.R. Subsonic	Hollow point	40	25.600	1.000	915	835	90	75	60	50	+0.8	—	-3.4	-4.7	50	+0.2	—	+2.8	-8.5
.22 L.R. HV Hollow Point	Lead coppered	40	25.600	1.310	1.120	990	150	110	85	—	—	—	—	—	—	—	—	—	—
.22 Magnum	Soft Point	40	25.600	2.020	1.710	1.430	360	260	180	100	+0.6	+1.3	+1.1	0	100	-0.3	+0.7	+0.8	0
.22 Magnum	Full Jacket	40	25.600	2.020	1.710	1.430	360	260	180	100	+0.6	+1.3	+1.1	0	100	-0.3	+0.7	+0.8	0
.45 L.R. R100	Lead	40	25.600	1.175	1.065	970	100	80	70	100	+0.6	+1.3	+1.1	0	100	-0.3	+0.7	+0.8	0
.45 AUTO+P	JHP	14.90	230	307	1007	290	965	279	927	702	518	626	467	580	440	4.0	1.3	12.5	4.0

AMMUNITION

Sierra Ammunition

For more than 50 years shooters have enjoyed the accuracy and superior ballistic performance of Sierra bullets. Sierra offers more than 160 different rifle and handgun bullets to satisfy nearly any need.

GAMEKING BULLETS are designed for hunting at long range and feature a boat-tail design to bring hunters the ballistic advantage of match bullets.

MATCHKING competition rifle bullets, manufactured to exacting tolerances, feature a hollow point boat-tail design to provide an extra margin of ballistic performance match shooters need to fire at long ranges under adverse conditions.

VARMINTER AND BLITZKING bullets are accurate and lightly constructed to provide explosive expansion while minimizing ricochets, and lightweight to obtain high velocities with flat trajectories.

PRO-HUNTER features a traditional flat base design and the custom-tapered Pro-Hunter jacket helps assure maximum expansion, optimum weight retention and deep penetration.

SPORTS MASTER handgun bullets are engineered to provide consistent, reliable expansion over a wide range of velocities. Sierra has added a "Power Jacket" to hollow cavity and hollow point bullets. On impact, the "Power Jacket" expands uniformly along the serration lines for consistent weight retention and maximum energy transfer.

TOURNAMENT MASTER handgun bullets are built to satisfy the performance demands of competitors and recreational marksmen. Their accuracy, combined with unduplicated penetrating power, make them the bullet of choice for silhouette shooters and big game hunters.

Rifles should be cleaned from the breech whenever possible and you can avoid cleaning wear by using a bore guide. You can make a bore guide by attaching a fired case to a proper sized brass tube. The neck of the case will keep the rod from rubbing on the throat and provides a good seal to keep solvents from migrating back into the action.

AMMUNITION

Winchester Ammunition

Winchester/Olin produces a wide range of quality ammunition for sporting, law enforcement and military use.

CENTERFIRE RIFLE AMMUNITION

Supreme Elite: Features XP3 bullet with 2-stage expansion design.

Supreme: Available with Ballistic Silvertip, AccuBond CT, Hollow Point Boat-tail Match, Partition Gold, Jacketed Hollow Point bullets.

Super-X: Available with Ballistic Silvertip, AccuBond, Fail Safe, Hollow Point Boat-tail Match, Partition Gold, and Jacketed Hollow Point bullets.

JHP: Available with Power Point, Hollow Soft Point, Jacketed Soft Point, Lead, Silvertip Hollow Point, Hollow Point, Positive Expanding Point, Soft Point, Silvertip, Super Clean NT Tin bullets.

USA: Available with Full Metal Jacket, JHP, Pointed Soft Point, Jacketed Hollow Point bullets.

Winchester Ammunition

HANDGUN AMMUNITION

SHOTSHELLS

HANDGUN AMMUNITION

Supreme: Available with T-Series, Platinum Tip Hollow Point and Partition Gold bullets.

Super-X: Available with Full Metal Jacket, Jacketed Flat Point, JHP, Expanding Point, Hollow Soft Point, Jacketed Soft Point, Lead Round Nose, Lead Semi-wadcutter, Lead Semi-wadcutter HP, Match, Silvertip Hollow Point.

Winchester Super Clean NT (Tin): Jacketed soft point tin core contains no lead.

Winchester WinClean: Available with Brass Enclosed Base and Jacketed Soft Point bullets.

Winchester Cowboy Loads: Available with Lead bullets.

USA: Full Metal Jacket, JHP, Full Metal Jacket-Flat Nose, Jacketed Soft Point and Lead bullets.

RIMFIRE AMMUNITION

Supreme: Available with JHP and V-Max bullets.

Super-X: Available with Full Metal Jacket, JHP, #12 Shot, Dyna Point-Plated, Lead Flat Nose, Lead Hollow Point, Lead Round Nose-Standard Velocity and Power Point-Lead Hollow Point bullets.

Xpert: Available with Lead Hollow Point bullets.

Winchester Wildcat: Available with Lead Round Nose bullets.

SHOTSHELLS

Supreme Elite: Xtended Range Hi-Density Turkey and Xtended Range Hi-Density Waterfowl loads.

Supreme: Available with slugs, buckshot, game & field loads, Partition Gold Slugs, Platinum Tip Hollow Point Slugs, turkey and waterfowl loads.

AA: Available with target loads.

Super-X: Available with slugs, buckshot, game & field loads, waterfowl, Super Pheasant, target and Super target loads.

Winchester Western: Available with target & field loads

Winchester Xpert: Available with Xpert Hi-Velocity Steel and Xpert Steel loads.

BALLISTICS

Centerfire Rifle Ballistics

Comprehensive Ballistics Tables for Currently Manufactured Sporting Rifle Cartridges

No more collecting catalogs and peering at microscopic print to find out what ammunition is offered for a cartridge, and how it performs relative to other factory loads! Shooter's Bible has assembled the data for you, in easy-to-read tables, by cartridge. Of course, this section will be updated every year to bring you the latest information.

Data is taken from manufacturers' charts; your chronograph readings may vary. Listings are current as of February the year Shooter's Bible appears (not the cover year). Listings are not intended as recommendations. For example, the data for the .44 Magnum at 400 yards shows its effective range is much shorter. The lack of data for a 285-grain .375 H&H bullet beyond 300 yards does not mean the bullet has no authority farther out. Besides ammunition, the rifle, sights, conditions and shooter ability all must be considered when contemplating a long shot. Accuracy and bullet energy both matter when big game is in the offing.

Barrel length affects velocity, and at various rates depending on the load. As a rule, figure 50 fps per inch of barrel, plus or minus, if your barrel is longer or shorter than 22 inches.

Bullets are given by make, weight (in grains) and type. Most type abbreviations are self-explanatory: BT=Boat-Tail, FMJ=Full Metal Jacket, HP=Hollow Point, SP=Soft Point—except in Hornady listings, where SP is the firm's Spire Point. TNT and TXP are trademarked designations of Speer and Norma. XLC identifies a coated Barnes X bullet. HE indicates a Federal High Energy load, similar to the Hornady LM (Light Magnum) and HM (Heavy Magnum) cartridges.

Arc (trajectory) is based on a zero range published by the manufacturer, from 100 to 300 yards. If a zero does not fall in a yardage column, it lies halfway between—at 150 yards, for example, if the bullet's strike is "+" at 100 yards and "-" at 200.

.17 REMINGTON TO .222 REMINGTON

CARTRIDGE BULLET	RANGE, YARDS:	0	100	200	300	400
.17 REMINGTON						
Rem. 20 AccuTip BT	velocity, fps:	4250	3594	3028	2529	2081
	energy, ft-lb:	802	574	407	284	192
	arc, inches:		+1.3	+1.3	-2.5	-11.8
Rem. 25 HP Power-Lokt	velocity, fps:	4040	3284	2644	2086	1606
	energy, ft-lb:	906	599	388	242	143
	arc, inches:		+1.8	0	-3.3	-16.6
.204 RUGER						
Hornady 32 V-Max	velocity, fps:	4225	3632	3114	2652	2234
	energy, ft-lb:	1268	937	689	500	355
	arc, inches:		+0.6	0	-4.2	-13.4
Hornady 40 V-Max	velocity, fps:	3900	3451	3046	2677	2335
	energy, ft-lb:	1351	1058	824	636	485
	arc, inches:		+0.7	0	-4.5	-13.9
Rem. 32 AccuTip	velocity, fps:	4225	3632	3114	2652	2234
	Energy, ft-lb:	1268	937	689	500	355
	Arc, inches:		+0.6	0	-4.1	-13.1
Rem. 40 AccuTip	velocity, fps:	3900	3451	3046	2677	2336
	energy, ft-lb:	1351	1058	824	636	485
	arc, inches:		+0.7	0	-4.3	-13.2
Win. 34 HP	velocity, fps:	4025	3339	2751	2232	1775
	energy, ft-lb:	1223	842	571	376	238
	arc, inches:		+0.8	0	-5.5	-18.1
.218 BEE						
Win. 46 Hollow Point	velocity, fps:	2760	2102	1550	1155	961
	energy, ft-lb:	778	451	245	136	94
	arc, inches:		0	-7.2	-29.4	

CARTRIDGE BULLET	RANGE, YARDS:	0	100	200	300	400
.22 HORNET						
Hornady 35 V-Max	velocity, fps:	3100	2278	1601	1135	929
	energy, ft-lb:	747	403	199	100	67
	arc, inches:		+2.8	0	-16.9	-60.4
Rem. 35 AccuTip	velocity, fps:	3100	2271	1591	1127	924
	energy, ft-lb:	747	401	197	99	66
	arc, inches:		+1.5	-3.5	-22.3	-68.4
Rem. 45 Pointed Soft Point	velocity, fps:	2690	2042	1502	1128	948
	energy, ft-lb:	723	417	225	127	90
	arc, inches:		0	-7.1	-30.0	
Rem. 45 Hollow Point	velocity, fps:	2690	2042	1502	1128	948
	energy, ft-lb:	723	417	225	127	90
	arc, inches:		0	-7.1	-30.0	
Win. 34 Jacketed HP	velocity, fps:	3050	2132	1415	1017	852
	energy, ft-lb:	700	343	151	78	55.
	arc, inches:		0	-6.6	-29.9	
Win. 45 Soft Point	velocity, fps:	2690	2042	1502	1128	948.
	energy, ft-lb:	723	417	225	127	90
	arc, inches:		0	-7.7	-31.3	
Win. 46 Hollow Point	velocity, fps:	2690	2042	1502	1128	948.
	energy, ft-lb:	739	426	230	130	92
	arc, inches:		0	-7.7	-31.3	
.221 REMINGTON FIREBALL						
Rem. 50 AccuTip BT	velocity, fps:	2995	2605	2247	1918	1622
	energy, ft-lb:	996	753	560	408	292
	arc, inches:		+1.8	0	-8.8	-27.1
.222 REMINGTON						
Federal 50 Hi-Shok	velocity, fps:	3140	2600	2120	1700	1350
	energy, ft-lb:	1095	750	500	320	200
	arc, inches:		+1.9	0	-9.7	-31.6

BALLISTICS

CARTRIDGE BULLET	RANGE, YARDS:	0	100	200	300	400
Federal 55 FMJ boat-tail	velocity, fps:	3020	2740	2480	2230	1990
	energy, ft-lb:	1115	915	750	610	484.
	arc, inches:		+1.6	0	-7.3	-21.5
Hornady 40 V-Max	velocity, fps:	3600	3117	2673	2269	1911
	energy, ft-lb:	1151	863	634	457	324
	arc, inches:		+1.1	0	-6.1	-18.9
Hornady 50 V-Max	velocity, fps:	3140	2729	2352	2008	1710.
	energy, ft-lb:	1094	827	614	448	325
	arc, inches:		+1.7	0	-7.9	-24.4
Norma 50 Soft Point	velocity, fps:	3199	2667	2193	1771	
	energy, ft-lb:	1136	790	534	348	
	arc, inches:		+1.7	0	-9.1	
Norma 50 FMJ	velocity, fps:	2789	2326	1910	1547	
	energy, ft-lb:	864	601	405	266	
	arc, inches:		+2.5	0	-12.2	
Norma 62 Soft Point	velocity, fps:	2887	2457	2067	1716	
	energy, ft-lb:	1148	831	588	405	
	arc, inches:		+2.1	0	-10.4	
PMC 50 Pointed Soft Point	velocity, fps:	3044	2727	2354	2012	1651
	energy, ft-lb:	1131	908	677	494	333
	arc, inches:		+1.6	0	-7.9	-24.5
PMC 55 Pointed Soft Point	velocity, fps:	2950	2594	2266	1966	1693
	energy, ft-lb:	1063	822	627	472	350
	arc, inches:		+1.9	0	-8.7	-26.3
Rem. 50 Pointed Soft Point	velocity, fps:	3140	2602	2123	1700	1350.
	energy, ft-lb:	1094	752	500	321	202
	arc, inches:		+1.9	0	-9.7	-31.7
Rem. 50 HP Power-Lokt	velocity, fps:	3140	2635	2182	1777	1432.
	energy, ft-lb:	1094	771	529	351	228
	arc, inches:		+1.8	0	-9.2	-29.6
Rem. 50 AccuTip BT	velocity, fps:	3140	2744	2380	2045	1740
	energy, ft-lb:	1094	836	629	464	336.
	arc, inches:		+1.6	0	-7.8	-23.9
Win. 40 Ballistic Silvertip	velocity, fps:	3370	2915	2503	2127	1786
	energy, ft-lb:	1009	755	556	402	283
	arc, inches:		+1.3	0	-6.9	-21.5
Win. 50 Pointed Soft Point	velocity, fps:	3140	2602	2123	1700	1350
	energy, ft-lb:	1094	752	500	321	202
	arc, inches:		+2.2	0	-10.0	-32.3

.223 REMINGTON

CARTRIDGE BULLET	RANGE, YARDS:	0	100	200	300	400
Black Hills 40 Nosler B. Tip	velocity, fps:	3600				
	energy, ft-lb:	1150				
	arc, inches:					
Black Hills 50 V-Max	velocity, fps:	3300				
	energy, ft-lb:	1209				
	arc, inches:					
Black Hills 52 Match HP	velocity, fps:	3300				
	energy, ft-lb:	1237				
	arc, inches:					
Black Hills 55 Softpoint	velocity, fps:	3250				
	energy, ft-lb:	1270				
	arc, inches:					
Black Hills 60 SP or V-Max	velocity, fps:	3150				
	energy, ft-lb:	1322				
	arc, inches:					
Black Hills 60 Partition	velocity, fps:	3150				
	energy, ft-lb:	1322				
	arc, inches:					
Black Hills 68 Heavy Match	velocity, fps:	2850				
	energy, ft-lb:	1227				
	arc, inches:					

CARTRIDGE BULLET	RANGE, YARDS:	0	100	200	300	400
Black Hills 69 Sierra MK	velocity, fps:	2850				
	energy, ft-lb:	1245				
	arc, inches:					
Black Hills 73 Berger BTHP	velocity, fps:	2750				
	energy, ft-lb:	1226				
	arc, inches:					
Black Hills 75 Heavy Match	velocity, fps:	2750				
	energy, ft-lb:	1259				
	arc, inches:					
Black Hills 77 Sierra MKing	velocity, fps:	2750				
	energy, ft-lb:	1293				
	arc, inches:					
Federal 50 Jacketed HP	velocity, fps:	3400	2910	2460	2060	1700
	energy, ft-lb:	1285	940	675	470	320
	arc, inches:		+1.3	0	-7.1	-22.7
Federal 50 Speer TNT HP	velocity, fps:	3300	2860	2450	2080	1750
	energy, ft-lb:	1210	905	670	480	340
	arc, inches:		+1.4	0	-7.3	-22.6
Federal 52 Sierra MatchKing BTHP	velocity, fps:	3300	2860	2460	2090	1760
	energy, ft-lb:	1255	945	700	505	360
	arc, inches:		+1.4	0	-7.2	-22.4
Federal 55 Hi-Shok	velocity, fps:	3240	2750	2300	1910	1550
	energy, ft-lb:	1280	920	650	445	295
	arc, inches:		+1.6	0	-8.2	-26.1
Federal 55 FMJ boat-tail	velocity, fps:	3240	2950	2670	2410	2170
	energy, ft-lb:	1280	1060	875	710	575
	arc, inches:		+1.3	0	-6.1	-18.3
Federal 55 Sierra GameKing BTHP	velocity, fps:	3240	2770	2340	1950	1610
	energy, ft-lb:	1280	935	670	465	315
	arc, inches:		+1.5	0	-8.0	-25.3
Federal 55 Trophy Bonded	velocity, fps:	3100	2630	2210	1830	1500.
	energy, ft-lb:	1175	845	595	410	275
	arc, inches:		+1.8	0	-8.9	-28.7
Federal 55 Nosler Bal. Tip	velocity, fps:	3240	2870	2530	2220	1920
	energy, ft-lb:	1280	1005	780	600	450
	arc, inches:		+1.4	0	-6.8	-20.8
Federal 55 Sierra BlitzKing	velocity, fps:	3240	2870	2520	2200	1910
	energy, ft-lb:	1280	1005	775	590	445
	arc, inches:		+-1.4	0	-6.9	-20.9
Federal 62 FMJ	velocity, fps:	3020	2650	2310	2000	1710
	energy, ft-lb:	1225	970	735	550	405
	arc, inches:		+1.7	0	-8.4	-25.5
Federal 64 Hi-Shok SP	velocity, fps:	3090	2690	2325	1990	1680
	energy, ft-lb:	1360	1030	770	560	400
	arc, inches:		+1.7	0	-8.2	-25.2
Federal 69 Sierra MatchKing BTHP	velocity, fps:	3000	2720	2460	2210	1980
	energy, ft-lb:	1380	1135	925	750	600
	arc, inches:		+1.6	0	-7.4	-21.9
Hornady 40 V-Max	velocity, fps:	3800	3305	2845	2424	2044
	energy, ft-lb:	1282	970	719	522	371
	arc, inches:		+0.8	0	-5.3	-16.6
Hornady 53 Hollow Point	velocity, fps:	3330	2882	2477	2106	1710
	energy, ft-lb:	1305	978	722	522	369
	arc, inches:		+1.7	0	-7.4	-22.7
Hornady 55 V-Max	velocity, fps:	3240	2859	2507	2181	1891.
	energy, ft-lb:	1282	998	767	581	437
	arc, inches:		+1.4	0	-7.1	-21.4
Hornady 55 TAP-FPD	velocity, fps:	3240	2854	2500	2172	1871
	energy, ft-lb:	1282	995	763	576	427
	arc, inches:		+1.4	0	-7.0	-21.4
Hornady 55 Urban Tactical	velocity, fps:	2970	2626	2307	2011	1739
	energy, ft-lb:	1077	842	650	494	369
	arc, inches:		+1.5	0	-8.1	-24.9

BALLISTICS

Centerfire Rifle Ballistics

.223 REMINGTON TO .22-250 REMINGTON

CARTRIDGE BULLET	RANGE, YARDS:	0	100	200	300	400
Hornady 60 Soft Point	velocity, fps:	3150	2782	2442	2127	1837.
	energy, ft-lb:	1322	1031	795	603	450
	arc, inches:		+1.6	0	-7.5	-22.5
Hornady 60 TAP-FPD	velocity, fps:	3115	2754	2420	2110	1824
	energy, ft-lb:	1293	1010	780	593	443
	arc, inches:		+1.6	0	-7.5	-22.9
Hornady 60 Urban Tactical	velocity, fps:	2950	2619	2312	2025	1762
	energy, ft-lb:	1160	914	712	546	413
	arc, inches:		+1.6	0	-8.1	-24.7
Hornady 75 BTHP Match	velocity, fps:	2790	2554	2330	2119	1926
	energy, ft-lb:	1296	1086	904	747	617
	arc, inches:		+2.4	0	-8.8	-25.1
Hornacy 75 TAP-FPD	velocity, fps:	2790	2582	2383	2193	2012
	energy, ft-lb:	1296	1110	946	801	674
	arc, inches:		+1.9	0	-8.0	-23.2
Hornady 75 BTHP Tactical	velocity, fps:	2630	2409	2199	2000	1814
	energy, ft-lb:	1152	966	805	666	548
	arc, inches:		+2.0	0	-9.2	-25.9
PMC 40 non-toxic	velocity, fps:	3500	2606	1871	1315	
	energy, ft-lb:	1088	603	311	154	
	arc, inches:		+2.6	0	-12.8	
PMC 50 Sierra BlitzKing	velocity, fps:	3300	2874	2484	2130	1809
	energy, ft-lb:	1209	917	685	504	363
	arc, inches:		+1.4	0	-7.1	-21.8
PMC 52 Sierra HPBT Match	velocity, fps:	3200	2808	2447	2117	1817
	energy, ft-lb:	1182	910	691	517	381
	arc, inches:		+1.5	0	-7.3	-22.5.
PMC 53 Barnes XLC	velocity, fps:	3200	2815	2461	2136	1840
	energy, ft-lb:	1205	933	713	537	398.
	arc, inches:		+1.5	0	-7.2	-22.2
PMC 55 HP boat-tail	velocity, fps:	3240	2717	2250	1832	1473
	energy, ft-lb:	1282	901	618	410	265
	arc, inches:		+1.6	0	-8.6	-27.7
PMC 55 FMJ boat-tail	velocity, fps:	3195	2882	2525	2169	1843
	energy, ft-lb:	1246	1014	779	574	415
	arc, inches:		+1.4	0	-6.8	-21.1
PMC 55 Pointed Soft Point	velocity, fps:	3112	2767	2421	2100	1806
	energy, ft-lb:	1182	935	715	539	398
	arc, inches:		+1.5	0	-7.5	-22.9
PMC 64 Pointed Soft Point	velocity, fps:	2775	2511	2261	2026	1806.
	energy, ft-lb:	1094	896	726	583	464
	arc, inches:		+2.0	0	-8.8	-26.1
PMC 69 Sierra BTHP Match	velocity, fps:	2900	2591	2304	2038	1791
	energy, ft-lb:	1288	1029	813	636	492
	arc, inches:		+1.9	0	-8.4	-25.3
Rem. 50 AccuTip BT	velocity, fps:	3300	2889	2514	2168	1851
	energy, ft-lb:	1209	927	701	522	380
	arc, inches:		+1.4	0	-6.9	-21.2
Rem. 55 Pointed Soft Point	velocity, fps:	3240	2747	2304	1905	1554
	energy, ft-lb:	1282	921	648	443	295
	arc, inches:		+1.6	0	-8.2	-26.2
Rem. 55 HP Power-Lokt	velocity, fps:	3240	2773	2352	1969	1627
	energy, ft-lb:	1282	939	675	473	323
	arc, inches:		+1.5	0	-7.9	-24.8
Rem. 55 AccuTip BT	velocity, fps:	3240	2854	2500	2172	1871
	energy, ft-lb:	1282	995	763	576	427
	arc, inches:		+1.5	0	-7.1	-21.7
Rem. 55 Metal Case	velocity, fps:	3240	2759	2326	1933	1587
	energy, ft-lb:	1282	929	660	456	307
	arc, inches:		+1.6	0	-8.1	-25.5
Rem. 62 HP Match	velocity, fps:	3025	2572	2162	1792	1471
	energy, ft-lb:	1260	911	643	442	298
	arc, inches:		+1.9	0	-9.4	-29.9

CARTRIDGE BULLET	RANGE, YARDS:	0	100	200	300	400
Rem. 69 BTHP Match	velocity, fps:	3000	2720	2457	2209	1975
	energy, ft-lb:	1379	1133	925	747	598
	arc, inches:		+1.6	0	-7.4	-21.9
Win. 40 Ballistic Silvertip	velocity, fps:	3700	3166	2693	2265	1879.
	energy, ft-lb:	1216	891	644	456	314
	arc, inches:		+1.0	0	-5.8	-18.4
Win. 45 JHP	velocity, fps:	3600				
	energy, ft-lb:	1295				
	arc, inches:					
Win. 50 Ballistic Silvertip	velocity, fps:	3410	2982	2593	2235	1907.
	energy, ft-lb:	1291	987	746	555	404
	arc, inches:		+1.2	0	-6.4	-19.8
Win. 53 Hollow Point	velocity, fps:	3330	2882	2477	2106	1770
	energy, ft-lb:	1305	978	722	522	369
	arc, inches:		+1.7	0	-7.4	-22.7
Win. 55 Pointed Soft Point	velocity, fps:	3240	2747	2304	1905	1554.
	energy, ft-lb:	1282	921	648	443	295
	arc, inches:		+1.9	0	-8.5	-26.7
Win. 55 Super Clean NT	velocity, fps:	3150	2520	1970	1505	1165
	energy, ft-lb:	1212	776	474	277	166
	arc, inches:		+2.8	0	-11.9	-38.9
Win. 55 FMJ	velocity, fps:	3240	2854			
	energy, ft-lb:	1282	995			
	arc, inches:					
Win. 55 Ballistic Silvertip	velocity, fps:	3240	2871	2531	2215	1923
	energy, ft-lb:	1282	1006	782	599	451
	arc, inches:		+1.4	0	-6.8	-20.8
Win. 64 Power-Point	velocity, fps:	3020	2656	2320	2009	1724
	energy, ft-lb:	1296	1003	765	574	423
	arc, inches:		+1.7	0	-8.2	-25.1
Win. 64 Power-Point Plus	velocity, fps:	3090	2684	2312	1971	1664
	energy, ft-lb:	1357	1024	760	552	393
	arc, inches:		+1.7	0	-8.2	-25.4

.5.6 x 52 R

CARTRIDGE BULLET	RANGE, YARDS:	0	100	200	300	400
Norma 71 Soft Point	velocity, fps:	2789	2446	2128	1835	
	energy, ft-lb:	1227	944	714	531	
	arc, inches:		+2.1	0	-9.9	

.22 PPC

CARTRIDGE BULLET	RANGE, YARDS:	0	100	200	300	400
A-Square 52 Berger	velocity, fps:	3300	2952	2629	2329	2049
	energy, ft-lb:	1257	1006	798	626	485
	arc, inches:		+1.3	0	-6.3	-19.1

.225 WINCHESTER

CARTRIDGE BULLET	RANGE, YARDS:	0	100	200	300	400
Win. 55 Pointed Soft Point	velocity, fps:	3570	3066	2616	2208	1838.
	energy, ft-lb:	1556	1148	836	595	412
	arc, inches:		+2.4	+2.0	-3.5	-16.3

.224 WEATHERBY MAG.

CARTRIDGE BULLET	RANGE, YARDS:	0	100	200	300	400
Wby. 55 Pointed Expanding	velocity, fps:	3650	3192	2780	2403	2056
	energy, ft-lb:	1627	1244	944	705	516
	arc, inches:		+2.8	+3.7	0	-9.8

.22-250 REMINGTON

CARTRIDGE BULLET	RANGE, YARDS:	0	100	200	300	400
Black Hills 50 Nos. Bal. Tip	velocity, fps:	3700				
	energy, ft-lb:	1520				
	arc, inches:					
Black Hills 60 Nos. Partition	velocity, fps:	3550				
	energy, ft-lb:	1679				
	arc, inches:					
Federal 40 Nos. Bal. Tip	velocity, fps:	4150	3610	3130	2700	2300
	energy, ft-lb:	1530	1155	870	645	470
	arc, inches:		+0.6	0	-4.2	-13.2

BALLISTICS

CARTRIDGE BULLET	RANGE, YARDS:	0	100	200	300	400
Federal 40 Sierra Varminter	velocity, fps:	4000	3320	2720	2200	1740
	energy, ft-lb:	1420	980	660	430	265
	arc, inches:		+0.8	0	-5.6	-18.4
Federal 55 Hi-Shok	velocity, fps:	3680	3140	2660	2220	1830
	energy, ft-lb:	1655	1200	860	605	410
	arc, inches:		+1.0	0	-6.0	-19.1
Federal 55 Sierra BlitzKing	velocity, fps:	3680	3270	2890	2540	2220
	energy, ft-lb:	1655	1300	1020	790	605
	arc, inches:		+0.9	0	-5.1	-15.6
Federal 55 Sierra GameKing BTHP	velocity, fps:	3680	3280	2920	2590	2280
	energy, ft-lb:	1655	1315	1040	815	630
	arc, inches:		+0.9	0	-5.0	-15.1
Federal 55 Trophy Bonded	velocity, fps:	3600	3080	2610	2190	1810.
	energy, ft-lb:	1585	1155	835	590	400.
	arc, inches:		+1.1	0	-6.2	-19.8
Hornady 40 V-Max	velocity, fps:	4150	3631	3147	2699	2293
	energy, ft-lb:	1529	1171	879	647	467
	arc, inches:		+0.5	0	-4.2	-13.3
Hornady 50 V-Max	velocity, fps:	3800	3349	2925	2535	2178
	energy, ft-lb:	1603	1245	950	713	527
	arc, inches:		+0.8	0	-5.0	-15.6
Hornady 53 Hollow Point	velocity, fps:	3680	3185	2743	2341	1974.
	energy, ft-lb:	1594	1194	886	645	459
	arc, inches:		+1.0	0	-5.7	-17.8
Hornady 55 V-Max	velocity, fps:	3680	3265	2876	2517	2183
	energy, ft-lb:	1654	1302	1010	772	582
	arc, inches:		+0.9	0	-5.3	-16.1
Hornady 60 Soft Point	velocity, fps:	3600	3195	2826	2485	2169
	energy, ft-lb:	1727	1360	1064	823	627
	arc, inches:		+1.0	0	-5.4	-16.3
Norma 53 Soft Point	velocity, fps:	3707	3234	2809	1716	
	energy, ft-lb:	1618	1231	928	690	
	arc, inches:		+0.9	0	-5.3	
PMC 50 Sierra BlitzKing	velocity, fps:	3725	3264	2641	2455	2103
	energy, ft-lb:	1540	1183	896	669	491
	arc, inches:		+0.9	0	-5.2	-16.2
PMC 50 Barnes XLC	velocity, fps:	3725	3280	2871	2495	2152
	energy, ft-lb:	1540	1195	915	691	514.
	arc, inches:		+0.9	0	-5.1	-15.9.
PMC 55 HP boat-tail	velocity, fps:	3680	3104	2596	2141	1737
	energy, ft-lb:	1654	1176	823	560	368
	arc, inches:		+1.1	0	-6.3	-20.2
PMC 55 Pointed Soft Point	velocity, fps:	3586	3203	2852	2505	2178
	energy, ft-lb:	1570	1253	993	766	579
	arc, inches:		+1.0	0	-5.2	-16.0
Rem. 50 AccuTip BT (also in EtronX)	velocity, fps:	3725	3272	2864	2491	2147
	energy, ft-lb:	1540	1188	910	689	512
	arc, inches:		+1.7	+1.6	-2.8	-12.8
Rem. 55 Pointed Soft Point	velocity, fps:	3680	3137	2656	2222	1832
	energy, ft-lb:	1654	1201	861	603	410
	arc, inches:		+1.9	+1.8	-3.3	-15.5
Rem. 55 HP Power-Lokt	velocity, fps:	3680	3209	2785	2400	2046.
	energy, ft-lb:	1654	1257	947	703	511
	arc, inches:		+1.8	+1.7	-3.0	-13.7
Rem. 60 Nosler Partition (also in EtronX)	velocity, fps:	3500	3045	2634	2258	1914
	energy, ft-lb:	1632	1235	924	679	488
	arc, inches:		+2.1	+1.9	-3.4	-15.5
Win. 40 Ballistic Silvertip	velocity, fps:	4150	3591	3099	2658	2257
	energy, ft-lb:	1530	1146	853	628	453
	arc, inches:		+0.6	0	-4.2	-13.4
Win. 50 Ballistic Silvertip	velocity, fps:	3810	3341	2919	2536	2182
	energy, ft-lb:	1611	1239	946	714	529.
	arc, inches:		+0.8	0	-4.9	-15.2

CARTRIDGE BULLET	RANGE, YARDS:	0	100	200	300	400
Win. 55 Pointed Soft Point	velocity, fps:	3680	3137	2656	2222	1832
	energy, ft-lb:	1654	1201	861	603	410
	arc, inches:		+2.3	+1.9	-3.4	-15.9
Win. 55 Ballistic Silvertip	velocity, fps:	3680	3272	2900	2558	2240
	energy, ft-lb:	1654	1307	1027	799	613
	arc, inches:		+0.9	0	-5.0	-15.4
Win. 64 Power-Point	velocity, fps:	3500	3086	2708	2360	2038
	energy, ft-lb:	1741	1353	1042	791	590
	arc, inches:		+1.1	0	-5.9	-18.0

.220 SWIFT

CARTRIDGE BULLET	RANGE, YARDS:	0	100	200	300	400
Federal 52 Sierra MatchKing BTHP	velocity, fps:	3830	3370	2960	2600	2230
	energy, ft-lb:	1690	1310	1010	770	575
	arc, inches:		+0.8	0	-4.8	-14.9
Federal 55 Sierra BlitzKing	velocity, fps:	3800	3370	2990	2630	2310.
	energy, ft-lb:	1765	1390	1090	850	650
	arc, inches:		+0.8	0	-4.7	-14.4
Federal 55 Trophy Bonded	velocity, fps:	3700	3170	2690	2270	1880
	energy, ft-lb:	1670	1225	885	625	430
	arc, inches:		+1.0	0	-5.8	-18.5·
Hornady 40 V-Max	velocity, fps:	4200	3678	3190	2739	2329
	energy, ft-lb:	1566	1201	904	666	482
	arc, inches:		+0.5	0	-4.0	-12.9
Hornady 50 V-Max	velocity, fps:	3850	3396	2970	2576	2215·
	energy, ft-lb:	1645	1280	979	736	545
	arc, inches:		+0.7	0	-4.8	-15.1
Hornady 50 SP	velocity, fps:	3850	3327	2862	2442	2060.
	energy, ft-lb:	1645	1228	909	662	471
	arc, inches:		+0.8	0	-5.1	-16.1
Hornady 55 V-Max	velocity, fps:	3680	3265	2876	2517	2183
	energy, ft-lb:	1654	1302	1010	772	582
	arc, inches:		+0.9	0	-5.3	-16.1
Hornady 60 Hollow Point	velocity, fps:	3600	3199	2824	2475	2156
	energy, ft-lb:	1727	1364	1063	816	619
	arc, inches:		+1.0	0	-5.4	-16.3
Norma 50 Soft Point	velocity, fps:	4019	3380	2826	2335	
	energy, ft-lb:	1794	1268	887	605	
	arc, inches:		+0.7	0	-5.1	
Rem. 50 Pointed Soft Point	velocity, fps:	3780	3158	2617	2135	1710
	energy, ft-lb:	1586	1107	760	506	325
	arc, inches:		+0.3	-1.4	-8.2	
Rem. 50 V-Max boat-tail (also in EtronX)	velocity, fps:	3780	3321	2908	2532	2185
	energy, ft-lb:	1586	1224	939	711	530
	arc, inches:		+0.8	0	-5.0	-15.4
Win. 40 Ballistic Silvertip	velocity, fps:	4050	3518	3048	2624	2238.
	energy, ft-lb:	1457	1099	825	611	445
	arc, inches:		+0.7	0	-4.4	-13.9
Win. 50 Pointed Soft Point	velocity, fps:	3870	3310	2816	2373	1972
	energy, ft-lb:	1663	1226	881	625	432
	arc, inches:		+0.8	0	-5.2	-16.7

.223 WSSM

CARTRIDGE BULLET	RANGE, YARDS:	0	100	200	300	400
Win. 55 Ballistic Silvertip	velocity, fps:	3850	3438	3064	2721	2402
	energy, ft-lb:	1810	1444	1147	904	704
	arc, inches:		+0.7	0	-4.4	-13.6
Win. 55 Pointed Softpoint	velocity, fps:	3850	3367	2934	2541	2181
	energy, ft-lb:	1810	1384	1051	789	581
	arc, inches:		+0.8	0	-4.9	-15.1
Win. 64 Power-Point	velocity, fps:	3600	3144	2732	2356	2011
	energy, ft-lb:	1841	1404	1061	789	574
	arc, inches:		+1.0	0	-5.7	-17.7

Centerfire Rifle Ballistics

6MM PPC TO 6MM REMINGTON

CARTRIDGE BULLET	RANGE, YARDS:	0	100	200	300	400
6MM PPC						
A-Square 68 Berger	velocity, fps:	3100	2751	2428	2128	1850
	energy, ft-lb:	1451	1143	890	684	516
	arc, inches:		+1.5	0	-7.5	-22.6
6x70 R						
Norma 95 Nosler Bal. Tip	velocity, fps:	2461	2231	2013	1809	
	energy, ft-lb:	1211	995	810	654	
	arc, inches:		+2.7	0	-11.3	
.243 WINCHESTER						
Black Hills 55 Nosler B. Tip	velocity, fps:	3800				
	energy, ft-lb:	1763				
	arc, inches:					
Black Hills 95 Nosler B. Tip	velocity, fps:	2950				
	energy, ft-lb:	1836				
	arc, inches:					
Federal 70 Nosler Bal. Tip	velocity, fps:	3400	3070	2760	2470	2200
	energy, ft-lb:	1795	1465	1185	950	755.
	arc, inches:		+1.1	0	-5.7	-17.1
Federal 70 Speer TNT HP	velocity, fps:	3400	3040	2700	2390	2100
	energy, ft-lb:	1795	1435	1135	890	685
	arc, inches:		+1.1	0	-5.9	-18.0
Federal 80 Sierra Pro-Hunter	velocity, fps:	3350	2960	2590	2260	1950
	energy, ft-lb:	1995	1550	1195	905	675
	arc, inches:		+1.3	0	-6.4	-19.7
Federal 85 Sierra GameKing BTHP	velocity, fps:	3320	3070	2830	2600	2380
	energy, ft-lb:	2080	1770	1510	1280	1070
	arc, inches:		+1.1	0	-5.5	-16.1
Federal 90 Trophy Bonded	velocity, fps:	3100	2850	2610	2380	2160.
	energy, ft-lb:	1920	1620	1360	1130	935
	arc, inches:		+1.4	0	-6.1	-19.2
Federal 100 Hi-Shok	velocity, fps:	2960	2700	2450	2220	1990
	energy, ft-lb:	1945	1615	1330	1090	880
	arc, inches:		+1.6	0	-7.5	-22.0
Federal 100 Sierra GameKing BTSP	velocity, fps:	2960	2760	2570	2380	2210
	energy, ft-lb:	1950	1690	1460	1260	1080
	arc, inches:		+1.5	0	-6.8	-19.8
Federal 100 Nosler Partition	velocity, fps:	2960	2730	2510	2300	2100
	energy, ft-lb:	1945	1650	1395	1170	975.
	arc, inches:		+1.6	0	-7.1	-20.9
Hornady 58 V-Max	velocity, fps:	3750	3319	2913	2539	2195
	energy, ft-lb:	1811	1418	1093	830	620
	arc, inches:		+1.2	0	-5.5	-16.4
Hornady 75 Hollow Point	velocity, fps:	3400	2970	2578	2219	1890
	energy, ft-lb:	1926	1469	1107	820	595
	arc, inches:		+1.2	0	-6.5	-20.3
Hornady 100 BTSP	velocity, fps:	2960	2728	2508	2299	2099
	energy, ft-lb:	1945	1653	1397	1174	979
	arc, inches:		+1.6	0	-7.2	-21.0
Hornady 100 BTSP LM	velocity, fps:	3100	2839	2592	2358	2138
	energy, ft-lb:	2133	1790	1491	1235	1014
	arc, inches:		+1.5	0	-6.8	-19.8
Norma 80 FMJ	velocity, fps:	3117	2750	2412	2098	
	energy, ft-lb:	1726	1344	1034	782	
	arc, inches:		+1.5	0	-7.5	
Norma 100 FMJ	velocity, fps:	3018	2747	2493	2252	
	energy, ft-lb:	2023	1677	1380	1126	
	arc, inches:		+1.5	0	-7.1	
Norma 100 Soft Point	velocity, fps:	3018	2748	2493	2252	
	energy, ft-lb:	2023	1677	1380	1126	
	arc, inches:		+1.5	0	-7.1	

CARTRIDGE BULLET	RANGE, YARDS:	0	100	200	300	400
Norma 100 Oryx	velocity, fps:	3018	2653	2316	2004	
	energy, ft-lb:	2023	1563	1191	892	
	arc, inches:		+1.7	0	-8.3	
PMC 80 Pointed Soft Point	velocity, fps:	2940	2684	2444	2215	1999
	energy, ft-lb:	1535	1280	1060	871	709
	arc, inches:		+1.7	0	-7.5	-22.1
PMC 85 Barnes XLC	velocity, fps:	3250	3022	2805	2598	2401
	energy, ft-lb:	1993	1724	1485	1274	1088
	arc, inches:		+1.6	0	-5.6	16.3
PMC 85 HP boat-tail	velocity, fps:	3275	2922	2596	2292	2009
	energy, ft-lb:	2024	1611	1272	991	761
	arc, inches:		+1.3	0	-6.5	-19.7
PMC 100 Pointed Soft Point	velocity, fps:	2743	2507	2283	2070	1869
	energy, ft-lb:	1670	1395	1157	951	776
	arc, inches:		+2.0	0	-8.7	-25.5
PMC 100 SP boat-tail	velocity, fps:	2960	2742	2534	2335	2144
	energy, ft-lb:	1945	1669	1425	1210	1021
	arc, inches:		+1.6	0	-7.0	-20.5
Rem. 75 AccuTip BT	velocity, fps:	3375	3065	2775	2504	2248
	energy, ft-lb:	1897	1564	1282	1044	842
	arc, inches:		+2.0	+1.8	-3.0	-13.3
Rem. 80 Pointed Soft Point	velocity, fps:	3350	2955	2593	2259	1951
	energy, ft-lb:	1993	1551	1194	906	676
	arc, inches:		+2.2	+2.0	-3.5	-15.8
Rem. 80 HP Power-Lokt	velocity, fps:	3350	2955	2593	2259	1951
	energy, ft-lb:	1993	1551	1194	906	676
	arc, inches:		+2.2	+2.0	-3.5	-15.8
Rem. 90 Nosler Bal. Tip (also in EtronX) or Scirocco	velocity, fps:	3120	2871	2635	2411	2199
	energy, ft-lb:	1946	1647	1388	1162	966
	arc, inches:		+1.4	0	-6.4	-18.8
Rem. 95 AccuTip	velocity, fps:	3120	2847	2590	2347	2118
	energy, ft-lb:	2053	1710	1415	1162	946
	arc, inches:		+1.5	0	-6.6	-19.5
Rem. 100 PSP Core-Lokt (also in EtronX)	velocity, fps:	2960	2697	2449	2215	1993
	energy, ft-lb:	1945	1615	1332	1089	882
	arc, inches:		+1.6	0	-7.5	-22.1
Rem. 100 PSP boat-tail	velocity, fps:	2960	2720	2492	2275	2069
	energy, ft-lb:	1945	1642	1378	1149	950
	arc, inches:		+2.8	+2.3	-3.8	-16.6
Speer 100 Grand Slam	velocity, fps:	2950	2684	2434	2197	
	energy, ft-lb:	1932	1600	1315	1072	
	arc, inches:		+1.7	0	-7.6	-22.4
Win. 55 Ballistic Silvertip	velocity, fps:	4025	3597	3209	2853	2525
	energy, ft-lb:	1978	1579	1257	994	779
	arc, inches:		+0.6	0	-4.0	-12.2
Win. 80 Pointed Soft Point	velocity, fps:	3350	2955	2593	2259	1951.
	energy, ft-lb:	1993	1551	1194	906	676
	arc, inches:		+2.6	+2.1	-3.6	-16.2
Win. 95 Ballistic Silvertip	velocity, fps:	3100	2854	2626	2410	2203
	energy, ft-lb:	2021	1719	1455	1225	1024
	arc, inches:		+1.4	0	-6.4	-18.9
Win. 100 Power-Point	velocity, fps:	2960	2697	2449	2215	1993
	energy, ft-lb:	1945	1615	1332	1089	882
	arc, inches:		+1.9	0	-7.8	-22.6.
Win. 100 Power-Point Plus	velocity, fps:	3090	2818	2562	2321	2092
	energy, ft-lb:	2121	1764	1458	1196	972
	arc, inches:		+1.4	0	-6.7	-20.0
6MM REMINGTON						
Federal 80 Sierra Pro-Hunter	velocity, fps:	3470	3060	2690	2350	2040
	energy, ft-lb:	2140	1665	1290	980	735
	arc, inches:		+1.1	0	-5.9	-18.2

464 • Shooter's Bible

CARTRIDGE BULLET	RANGE, YARDS:	0	100	200	300	400
Federal 100 Hi-Shok	velocity, fps:	3100	2830	2570	2330	2100
	energy, ft-lb:	2135	1775	1470	1205	985
	arc, inches:		+1.4	0	-6.7	-19.8
Federal 100 Nos. Partition	velocity, fps:	3100	2860	2640	2420	2220
	energy, ft-lb:	2135	1820	1545	1300	1090
	arc, inches:		+1.4	0	-6.3	-18.7
Hornady 100 SP boat-tail	velocity, fps:	3100	2861	2634	2419	2231
	energy, ft-lb:	2134	1818	1541	1300	1088
	arc, inches:		+1.3	0	-6.5	-18.9
Hornady 100 SPBT LM	velocity, fps:	3250	2997	2756	2528	2311
	energy, ft-lb:	2345	1995	1687	1418	1186
	arc, inches:		+1.6	0	-6.3	-18.2
Rem. 75 V-Max boat-tail	velocity, fps:	3400	3088	2797	2524	2267
	energy, ft-lb:	1925	1587	1303	1061	856
	arc, inches:		+1.9	+1.7	-3.0	-13.1
Rem. 100 PSP Core-Lokt	velocity, fps:	3100	2829	2573	2332	2104.
	energy, ft-lb:	2133	1777	1470	1207	983
	arc, inches:		+1.4	0	-6.7	-19.8
Rem. 100 PSP boat-tail	velocity, fps:	3100	2852	2617	2394	2183.
	energy, ft-lb:	2134	1806	1521	1273	1058
	arc, inches:		+1.4	0	-6.5	-19.1
Win. 100 Power-Point	velocity, fps:	3100	2829	2573	2332	2104
	energy, ft-lb:	2133	1777	1470	1207	983
	arc, inches:		+1.7	0	-7.0	-20.4

.243 WSSM

CARTRIDGE BULLET	RANGE, YARDS:	0	100	200	300	400
Win. 55 Ballistic Silvertip	velocity, fps:	4060	3628	3237	2880	2550
	energy, ft-lb:	2013	1607	1280	1013	794
	arc, inches:		+0.6	0	-3.9	-12.0
Win. 95 Ballistic Silvertip	velocity, fps:	3250	3000	2763	2538	2325
	energy, ft-lb:	2258	1898	1610	1359	1140
	arc, inches:		+1.2	0	5.7	16.9
Win. 100 Power Point	velocity, fps:	3110	2838	2583	2341	2112
	energy, ft-lb:	2147	1789	1481	1217	991
	arc, inches:		+1.4	0	-6.6	-19.7

.240 WEATHERBY MAG.

CARTRIDGE BULLET	RANGE, YARDS:	0	100	200	300	400
Wby. 87 Pointed Expanding	velocity, fps:	3523	3199	2898	2617	2352
	energy, ft-lb:	2397	1977	1622	1323	1069
	arc, inches:		+2.7	+3.4	0	-8.4
Wby. 90 Barnes-X	velocity, fps:	3500	3222	2962	2717	2484
	energy, ft-lb:	2448	2075	1753	1475	1233
	arc, inches:		+2.6	+3.3	0	-8.0
Wby. 95 Nosler Bal. Tip	velocity, fps:	3420	3146	2888	2645	2414
	energy, ft-lb:	2467	2087	1759	1475	1229
	arc, inches:		+2.7	+3.5	0	-8.4
Wby. 100 Pointed Expanding	velocity, fps:	3406	3134	2878	2637	2408.
	energy, ft-lb:	2576	2180	1839	1544	1287
	arc, inches:		+2.8	+3.5	0	-8.4
Wby. 100 Partition	velocity, fps:	3406	3136	2882	2642	2415
	energy, ft-lb:	2576	2183	1844	1550	1294
	arc, inches:		+2.8	+3.5	0	-8.4

.25-20 WINCHESTER

CARTRIDGE BULLET	RANGE, YARDS:	0	100	200	300	400
Rem. 86 Soft Point	velocity, fps:	1460	1194	1030	931	858
	energy, ft-lb:	407	272	203	165	141.
	arc, inches:		0	-22.9	-78.9	-173.0
Win. 86 Soft Point	velocity, fps:	1460	1194	1030	931	858.
	energy, ft-lb:	407	272	203	165	141
	arc, inches:		0	-23.5	-79.6	-175.9

.25-35 WINCHESTER

CARTRIDGE BULLET	RANGE, YARDS:	0	100	200	300	400
Win. 117 Soft Point	velocity, fps:	2230	1866	1545	1282	1097
	energy, ft-lb:	1292	904	620	427	313
	arc, inches:		+2.1	-5.1	-27.0	-70.1

.250 SAVAGE

CARTRIDGE BULLET	RANGE, YARDS:	0	100	200	300	400
Rem. 100 Pointed SP	velocity, fps:	2820	2504	2210	1936	1684.
	energy, ft-lb:	1765	1392	1084	832	630
	arc, inches:		+2.0	0	-9.2	-27.7
Win. 100 Silvertip	velocity, fps:	2820	2467	2140	1839	1569
	energy, ft-lb:	1765	1351	1017	751	547
	arc, inches:		+2.4	0	-10.1	-30.5

.257 ROBERTS

CARTRIDGE BULLET	RANGE, YARDS:	0	100	200	300	400
Federal 120 Nosler Partition	velocity, fps:	2780	2560	2360	2160	1970
	energy, ft-lb:	2060	1750	1480	1240	1030
	arc, inches:		+1.9	0	-8.2	-24.0
Hornady 117 SP boat-tail	velocity, fps:	2780	2550	2331	2122	1925
	energy, ft-lb:	2007	1689	1411	1170	963
	arc, inches:		+1.9	0	-8.3	-24.4
Hornady 117 SP boat-tail LM	velocity, fps:	2940	2694	2460	2240	2031
	energy, ft-lb:	2245	1885	1572	1303	1071
	arc, inches:		+1.7	0	-7.6	-21.8
Rem. 117 SP Core-Lokt	velocity, fps:	2650	2291	1961	1663	1404
	energy, ft-lb:	1824	1363	999	718	512
	arc, inches:		+2.6	0	-11.7	-36.1
Win. 117 Power-Point	velocity, fps:	2780	2411	2071	1761	1488
	energy, ft-lb:	2009	1511	1115	806	576.
	arc, inches:		+2.6	0	-10.8	-33.0

.25-06 REMINGTON

CARTRIDGE BULLET	RANGE, YARDS:	0	100	200	300	400
Black Hills 100 Nos. Bal. Tip	velocity, fps:	3200				
	energy, ft-lb:	2273				
	arc, inches:					
Black Hills 100 Barnes XLC	velocity, fps:	3200				
	energy, ft-lb:	2273				
	arc, inches:					
Black Hills 115 Barnes X	velocity, fps:	2975				
	energy, ft-lb:	2259				
	arc, inches:					
Federal 90 Sierra Varminter	velocity, fps:	3440	3040	2680	2340	2030
	energy, ft-lb:	2365	1850	1435	1100	825
	arc, inches:		+1.1	0	-6.0	-18.3
Federal 100 Barnes XLC	velocity, fps:	3210	2970	2750	2540	2330
	energy, ft-lb:	2290	1965	1680	1430	1205
	arc, inches:		+1.2	0	-5.8	-17.0
Federal 100 Nosler Bal. Tip	velocity, fps:	3210	2960	2720	2490	2280
	energy, ft-lb:	2290	1940	1640	1380	1150.
	arc, inches:		+1.2	0	-6.0	-17.5
Federal 115 Nosler Partition	velocity, fps:	2990	2750	2520	2300	2100
	energy, ft-lb:	2285	1930	1620	1350	1120
	arc, inches:		+1.6	0	-7.0	-20.8
Federal 115 Trophy Bonded	velocity, fps:	2990	2740	2500	2270	2050
	energy, ft-lb:	2285	1910	1590	1310	1075
	arc, inches:		+1.6	0	-7.2	-21.1
Federal 117 Sierra Pro Hunt.	velocity, fps:	2990	2730	2480	2250	2030
	energy, ft-lb:	2320	1985	1645	1350	1100
	arc, inches:		+1.6	0	-7.2	-21.4
Federal 117 Sierra GameKing BTSP	velocity, fps:	2990	2770	2570	2370	2190
	energy, ft-lb:	2320	2000	1715	1465	1240
	arc, inches:		+1.5	0	-6.8	-19.9
Hornady 117 SP boat-tail	velocity, fps:	2990	2749	2520	2302	2096
	energy, ft-lb:	2322	1962	1649	1377	1141
	arc, inches:		+1.6	0	-7.0	-20.7
Hornady 117 SP boat-tail LM	velocity, fps:	3110	2855	2613	2384	2168
	energy, ft-lb:	2512	2117	1774	1476	1220
	arc, inches:		+1.8	0	-7.1	-20.3

Centerfire Rifle Ballistics

.25-06 REMINGTON TO 6.5X55 SWEDISH

CARTRIDGE BULLET	RANGE, YARDS:	0	100	200	300	400
PMC 100 SPBT	velocity, fps:	3200	2925	2650	2395	2145
	energy, ft-lb:	2273	1895	1561	1268	1019
	arc, inches:		+1.3	0	-6.3	-18.6
PMC 117 PSP	velocity, fps:	2950	2706	2472	2253	2047
	energy, ft-lb:	2261	1900	1588	1319	1088
	arc, inches:		+1.6	0	-7.3	-21.5
Rem. 100 PSP Core-Lokt	velocity, fps:	3230	2893	2580	2287	2014
	energy, ft-lb:	2316	1858	1478	1161	901
	arc, inches:		+1.3	0	-6.6	-19.8
Rem. 115 Core-Lokt Ultra	velocity, fps:	3000	2751	2516	2293	2081
	energy, ft-lb:	2298	1933	1616	1342	1106
	arc, inches:		+1.6	0	-7.1	-20.7
Rem. 120 PSP Core-Lokt	velocity, fps:	2990	2730	2484	2252	2032
	energy, ft-lb:	2382	1985	1644	1351	1100
	arc, inches:		+1.6	0	-7.2	-21.4
Speer 120 Grand Slam	velocity, fps:	3130	2835	2558	2298	
	energy, ft-lb:	2610	2141	1743	1407	
	arc, inches:		+1.4	0	-6.8	-20.1
Win. 85 Ballistic Silvertip	velocity, fps	3470	3156	2863	2589	2331
	energy, ft-lb:	2273	1880	1548	1266	1026
	arc, inches:		+1.0	0	-5.2	-15.7
Win. 90 Pos. Exp. Point	velocity, fps:	3440	3043	2680	2344	2034
	energy, ft-lb:	2364	1850	1435	1098	827
	arc, inches:		+2.4	+2.0	-3.4	-15.0
Win. 110 AccuBond CT	velocity, fps:	3100	2870	2651	2442	2243
	energy, ft-lb:	2347	2011	1716	1456	1228
	arc, inches:		+1.4	0	-6.3	-18.5
Win. 115 Ballistic Silvertip	velocity, fps:	3060	2825	2603	2390	2188
	energy, ft-lb:	2391	2038	1729	1459	1223
	arc, inches:		+1.4	0	-6.6	-19.2
Win. 120 Pos. Pt. Exp.	velocity, fps:	2990	2717	2459	2216	1987
	energy, ft-lb:	2382	1967	1612	1309	1053
	arc, inches:		+1.6	0	-7.4	-21.8

.25 WINCHESTER SUPER SHORT MAG.

CARTRIDGE BULLET	RANGE, YARDS:	0	100	200	300	400
Win. 85 Ballistic Silvertip	velocity, fps:	3470	3156	2863	2589	2331
	energy, ft-lb:	2273	1880	1548	1266	1026
	arc, inches:		+1.0	0	-5.2	-15.7
Win. 110 AccuBond CT	velocity, fps:	3100	2870	2651	2442	2243.
	energy, ft-lb:	2347	2011	1716	1456	1228
	arc, inches:		+1.4	0	-6.3	-18.5
Win. 115 Ballistic Silvertip	velocity, fps:	3060	2844	2639	2442	2254
	energy, ft-lb:	2392	2066	1778	1523	1298
	arc, inches:		+1.4	0	-6.4	-18.6
Win. 120 Pos. Pt. Exp.	velocity, fps:	2990	2717	2459	2216	1987
	energy, ft-lb:	2383	1967	1612	1309	1053
	arc, inches:		+1.6	0	-7.4	-21.8

.257 WEATHERBY MAG.

CARTRIDGE BULLET	RANGE, YARDS:	0	100	200	300	400
Federal 115 Nosler Partition	velocity, fps:	3150	2900	2660	2440	2220.
	energy, ft-lb:	2535	2145	1810	1515	1260
	arc, inches:		+1.3	0	-6.2	-18.4
Federal 115 Trophy Bonded	velocity, fps:	3150	2890	2640	2400	2180
	energy, ft-lb:	2535	2125	1775	1470	1210
	arc, inches:		+1.4	0	-6.3	-18.8
Wby. 87 Pointed Expanding	velocity, fps:	3825	3472	3147	2845	2563
	energy, ft-lb:	2826	2328	1913	1563	1269
	arc, inches:		+2.1	+2.8	0	-7.1
Wby. 100 Pointed Expanding	velocity, fps:	3602	3298	3016	2750	2500
	energy, ft-lb:	2881	2416	2019	1680	1388
	arc, inches:		+2.4	+3.1	0	-7.7
Wby. 115 Nosler Bal. Tip	velocity, fps:	3400	3170	2952	2745	2547
	energy, ft-lb:	2952	2566	2226	1924	1656.
	arc, inches:		+3.0	+3.5	0	-7.9

CARTRIDGE BULLET	RANGE, YARDS:	0	100	200	300	400
Wby. 115 Barnes X	velocity, fps:	3400	3158	2929	2711	2504
	energy, ft-lb:	2952	2546	2190	1877	1601
	arc, inches:		+2.7	+3.4	0	-8.1
Wby. 117 RN Expanding	velocity, fps:	3402	2984	2595	2240	1921
	energy, ft-lb:	3007	2320	1742	1302	956
	arc, inches:		+3.4	+4.31	0	-11.1
Wby. 120 Nosler Partition	velocity, fps:	3305	3046	2801	2570	2350
	energy, ft-lb:	2910	2472	2091	1760	1471
	arc, inches:		+3.0	+3.7	0	-8.9

6.53 (.257) SCRAMJET

CARTRIDGE BULLET	RANGE, YARDS:	0	100	200	300	400
Lazzeroni 85 Nosler Bal. Tip	velocity, fps:	3960	3652	3365	3096	2844
	energy, ft-lb:	2961	2517	2137	1810	1526
	arc, inches:		+1.7	+2.4	0	-6.0
Lazzeroni 100 Nosler Part.	velocity, fps:	3740	3465	3208	2965	2735
	energy, ft-lb:	3106	2667	2285	1953	1661.
	arc, inches:		+2.1	+2.7	0	-6.7

6.5X50 JAPANESE

CARTRIDGE BULLET	RANGE, YARDS:	0	100	200	300	400
Norma 156 Alaska	velocity, fps:	2067	1832	1615	1423	
	energy, ft-lb:	1480	1162	904	701	
	arc, inches:		+4.4	0	-17.8	

6.5X52 CARCANO

CARTRIDGE BULLET	RANGE, YARDS:	0	100	200	300	400
Norma 156 Alaska	velocity, fps:	2428	2169	1926	1702	
	energy, ft-lb:	2043	1630	1286	1004	
	arc, inches:		+2.9	0	-12.3	

6.5X55 SWEDISH

CARTRIDGE BULLET	RANGE, YARDS:	0	100	200	300	400
Federal 140 Hi-Shok	velocity, fps:	2600	2400	2220	2040	1860
	energy, ft-lb:	2100	1795	1525	1285	1080
	arc, inches:		+2.3	0	-9.4	-27.2
Federal 140 Trophy Bonded	velocity, fps:	2550	2350	2160	1980	1810
	energy, ft-lb:	2020	1720	1450	1220	1015
	arc, inches:		+2.4	0	-9.8	-28.4
Federal 140 Sierra MatchKg. BTHP	velocity, fps:	2630	2460	2300	2140	2000
	energy, ft-lb:	2140	1880	1640	1430	1235
	arc, inches:		+16.4	+28.8	+33.9	+31.8
Hornady 129 SP LM	velocity, fps:	2770	2561	2361	2171	1994
	energy, ft-lb:	2197	1878	1597	1350	1138
	arc, inches:		+2.0	0	-8.2	-23.2
Hornady 140 SP Interlock	velocity, fps	2525	2341	2165	1996	1836
	energy, ft-lb:	1982	1704	1457	1239	1048
	arc, inches:		+2.4	0	-9.9	-28.5
Hornady140 SP LM	velocity, fps:	2740	2541	2351	2169	1999
	energy, ft-lb:	2333	2006	1717	1463	1242
	arc, inches:		+2.4	0	-8.7	-24.0
Norma 120 Nosler Bal. Tip	velocity, fps:	2822	2609	2407	2213	
	energy, ft-lb:	2123	1815	1544	1305	
	arc, inches:		+1.8	0	-7.8	
Norma 139 Vulkan	velocity, fps:	2854	2569	2302	2051	
	energy, ft-lb:	2515	2038	1636	1298	
	arc, inches:		+1.8	0	-8.4	
Norma 140 Nosler Partition	velocity, fps:	2789	2592	2403	2223	
	energy, ft-lb:	2419	2089	1796	1536	
	arc, inches:		+1.8	0	-7.8	
Norma 156 TXP Swift A-Fr.	velocity, fps:	2526	2276	2040	1818	
	energy, ft-lb:	2196	1782	1432	1138	
	arc, inches:		+2.6	0	-10.9	
Norma 156 Alaska	velocity, fps:	2559	2245	1953	1687	
	energy, ft-lb:	2269	1746	1322	986	
	arc, inches:		+2.7	0	-11.9	
Norma 156 Vulkan	velocity, fps:	2644	2395	2159	1937	
	energy, ft-lb:	2422	1987	1616	1301	
	arc, inches:		+2.2	0	-9.7	

Centerfire Rifle Ballistics

CARTRIDGE BULLET	RANGE, YARDS:	0	100	200	300	400
Norma 156 Oryx	velocity, fps:	2559	2308	2070	1848	
	energy, ft-lb:	2269	1845	1485	1183	
	arc, inches:		+2.5	0	-10.6	
PMC 139 Pointed Soft Point	velocity, fps:	2850	2560	2290	2030	1790
	energy, ft-lb:	2515	2025	1615	1270	985
	arc, inches:		+2.2	0	-8.9	-26.3
PMC 140 HP boat-tail	velocity, fps:	2560	2398	2243	2093	1949
	energy, ft-lb:	2037	1788	1563	1361	1181
	arc, inches:		+2.3	0	-9.2	-26.4
PMC 140 SP boat-tail	velocity, fps:	2560	2386	2218	2057	1903
	energy, ft-lb:	2037	1769	1529	1315	1126
	arc, inches:		+2.3	0	-9.4	-27.1
PMC 144 FMJ	velocity, fps:	2650	2370	2110	1870	1650
	energy, ft-lb:	2425	1950	1550	1215	945
	arc, inches:		+2.7	0	-10.5	-30.9
Rem. 140 PSP Core-Lokt	velocity, fps:	2550	2353	2164	1984	1814
	energy, ft-lb:	2021	1720	1456	1224	1023
	arc, inches:		+2.4	0	-9.8	-27.0
Speer 140 Grand Slam	velocity, fps:	2550	2318	2099	1892	
	energy, ft-lb:	2021	1670	1369	1112	
	arc, inches:		+2.5	0	-10.4	-30.6
Win. 140 Soft Point	velocity, fps:	2550	2359	2176	2002	1836
	energy, ft-lb:	2022	1731	1473	1246	1048.
	arc, inches:		+2.4	0	-9.7	-28.1

.260 REMINGTON

CARTRIDGE BULLET	RANGE, YARDS:	0	100	200	300	400
Federal 140 Sierra GameKing BTSP	velocity, fps:	2750	2570	2390	2220	2060
	energy, ft-lb:	2350	2045	1775	1535	1315
	arc, inches:		+1.9	0	-8.0	-23.1
Federal 140 Trophy Bonded	velocity, fps:	2750	2540	2340	2150	1970
	energy, ft-lb:	2350	2010	1705	1440	1210
	arc, inches:	+1.9	0	-8.4	-24.1	
Rem. 120 Nosler Bal. Tip	velocity, fps:	2890	2688	2494	2309	2131
	energy, ft-lb:	2226	1924	1657	1420	1210
	arc, inches:		+1.7	0	-7.3	-21.1
Rem. 120 AccuTip	velocity, fps:	2890	2697	2512	2334	2163
	energy, ft-lb:	2392	2083	1807	1560	1340
	arc, inches:		+1.6	0	-7.2	-20.7
Rem. 125 Nosler Partition	velocity, fps:	2875	2669	2473	2285	2105.
	energy, ft-lb:	2294	1977	1697	1449	1230
	arc, inches:	+1.71	0	-7.4	-21.4	
Rem. 140 PSP Core-Lokt (and C-L Ultra)	velocity, fps:	2750	2544	2347	2158	1979
	energy, ft-lb:	2351	2011	1712	1448	1217
	arc, inches:		+1.9	0	-8.3	-24.0
Speer 140 Grand Slam	velocity, fps:	2750	2518	2297	2087	
	energy, ft-lb:	2351	1970	1640	1354	
	arc, inches:		+2.3	0	-8.9	-25.8

6.5/284

CARTRIDGE BULLET	RANGE, YARDS:	0	100	200	300	400
Norma 120 Nosler Bal. Tip	velocity, fps:	3117	2890	2674	2469	
	energy, ft-lb:	2589	2226	1906	1624	
	arc, inches:		+1.3	0	-6.2	
Norma 140 Nosler Part.	velocity, fps:	2953	2750	2557	2371	
	energy, ft-lb:	2712	2352	2032	1748	
	arc, inches:		+1.5	0	-6.8	

6.5 REMINGTON MAG.

CARTRIDGE BULLET	RANGE, YARDS:	0	100	200	300	400
Rem. 120 Core-Lokt PSP	velocity, fps:	3210	2905	2621	2353	2102
	energy, ft-lb:	2745	2248	1830	1475	1177
	arc, inches:		+2.7	+2.1	-3.5	-15.5

.264 WINCHESTER MAG.

CARTRIDGE BULLET	RANGE, YARDS:	0	100	200	300	400
Rem. 140 PSP Core-Lokt	velocity, fps:	3030	2782	2548	2326	2114
	energy, ft-lb:	2854	2406	2018	1682	1389
	arc, inches:		+1.5	0	-6.9	-20.2

CARTRIDGE BULLET	RANGE, YARDS:	0	100	200	300	400
Win. 140 Power-Point	velocity, fps:	3030	2782	2548	2326	2114.
	energy, ft-lb:	2854	2406	2018	1682	1389
	arc, inches:		+1.8	0	-7.2	-20.8

6.8MM REMINGTON SPC

CARTRIDGE BULLET	RANGE, YARDS:	0	100	200	300	400
Rem. 115 Open Tip Match (and HPBT Match)	velocity, fps:	2800	2535	2285	2049	1828
	energy, ft-lb:	2002	1641	1333	1072	853
	arc, inches:		+2.0	0	-8.8	-26.2
Rem. 115 Metal Case	velocity, fps:	2800	2523	2262	2017	1789
	energy, ft-lb:	2002	1625	1307	1039	817
	arc, inches:		+2.0	0	-8.8	-26.2
Rem. 115 Sierra HPBT (2005; all vel. @ 2775)	velocity, fps:	2775	2511	2263	2028	1809
	energy, ft-lb:	1966	1610	1307	1050	835
	arc, inches:		+2.0	0	-8.8	-26.2.
Rem. 115 CL Ultra	velocity, fps:	2775	2472	2190	1926	1683
	energy, ft-lb:	1966	1561	1224	947	723
	arc, inches:		+2.1	0	-9.4	-28.2

.270 WINCHESTER

CARTRIDGE BULLET	RANGE, YARDS:	0	100	200	300	400
Black Hills 130 Nos. Bal. T.	velocity, fps:	2950				
	energy, ft-lb:	2512				
	arc, inches:					
Black Hills 130 Barnes XLC	velocity, ft-lb:	2950				
	energy, ft-lb:	2512				
	arc, inches:					
Federal 130 Hi-Shok	velocity, fps:	3060	2800	2560	2330	2110
	energy, ft-lb:	2700	2265	1890	1565	1285
	arc, inches:		+1.5	0	-6.8	-20.0
Federal 130 Sierra Pro-Hunt.	velocity, fps:	3060	2830	2600	2390	2190
	energy, ft-lb:	2705	2305	1960	1655	1390
	arc, inches:		+1.4	0	-6.4	-19.0
Federal 130 Sierra GameKing	velocity, fps:	3060	2830	2620	2410	2220.
	energy, ft-lb:	2700	2320	1980	1680	1420
	arc, inches:		+1.4	0	-6.5	-19.0
Federal 130 Nosler Bal. Tip	velocity, fps:	3060	2840	2630	2430	2230
	energy, ft-lb:	2700	2325	1990	1700	1440
	arc, inches:		+1.4	0	-6.5	-18.8
Federal 130 Nos. Partition And Solid Base	velocity, fps:	3060	2830	2610	2400	2200
	energy, ft-lb:	2705	2310	1965	1665	1400
	arc, inches:		+1.4	0	-6.5	-19.1.
Federal 130 Barnes XLC And Triple Shock	velocity, fps:	3060	2840	2620	2420	2220
	energy, ft-lb:	2705	2320	1985	1690	1425
	arc, inches:		+1.4	0	-6.4	-18.9
Federal 130 Trophy Bonded	velocity, fps:	3060	2810	2570	2340	2130
	energy, ft-lb:	2705	2275	1905	1585	1310
	arc, inches:		+1.5	0	-6.7	-19.8
Federal 140 Trophy Bonded	velocity, fps:	2940	2700	2480	2260	2060
	energy, ft-lb:	2685	2270	1905	1590	1315
	arc, inches:		+1.6	0	-7.3	-21.5
Federal 140 Tr. Bonded HE	velocity, fps:	3100	2860	2620	2400	2200.
	energy, ft-lb:	2990	2535	2140	1795	1500
	arc, inches:		+1.4	0	-6.4	-18.9
Federal 140 Nos. AccuBond	velocity, fps:	2950	2760	2580	2400	2230.
	energy, ft-lb:	2705	2365	2060	1790	1545
	arc, inches:		+1.5	0	-6.7	-19.6
Federal 150 Hi-Shok RN	velocity, fps:	2850	2500	2180	1890	1620
	energy, ft-lb:	2705	2085	1585	1185	870
	arc, inches:		+2.0	0	-9.4	-28.6
Federal 150 Sierra GameKing	velocity, fps:	2850	2660	2480	2300	2130
	energy, ft-lb:	2705	2355	2040	1760	1510
	arc, inches:		+1.7	0	-7.4	-21.4
Federal 150 Sierra GameKing HE	velocity, fps:	3000	2800	2620	2430	2260
	energy, ft-lb:	2995	2615	2275	1975	1700
	arc, inches:		+1.5	0	-6.5	-18.9

Centerfire Rifle Ballistics

.270 WINCHESTER TO .270 WINCHESTER SHORT MAG.

CARTRIDGE BULLET	RANGE, YARDS:	0	100	200	300	400
Federal 150 Nosler Partition	velocity, fps:	2850	2590	2340	2100	1880.
	energy, ft-lb:	2705	2225	1815	1470	1175
	arc, inches:		+1.9	0	-8.3	-24.4
Hornady 130 SST	velocity, fps:	3060	2845	2639	2442	2254
(or Interbond)	energy, ft-lb:	2700	2335	2009	1721	1467
	arc, inches:		+1.4	0	-6.6	-19.1
Hornady 130 SST LM	velocity, fps:	3215	2998	2790	2590	2400
(or Interbond)	energy, ft-lb:	2983	2594	2246	1936	1662
	arc, inches:		+1.2	0	-5.8	-17.0
Hornady 140 SP boat-tail	velocity, fps:	2940	2747	2562	2385	2214
	energy, ft-lb:	2688	2346	2041	1769	1524
	arc, inches:		+1.6	0	-7.0	-20.2
Hornady 140 SP boat-tail LM	velocity, fps:	3100	2894	2697	2508	2327.
	energy, ft-lb:	2987	2604	2261	1955	1684
	arc, inches:		+1.4	0	6.3	-18.3
Hornady 150 SP	velocity, fps:	2800	2684	2478	2284	2100
	energy, ft-lb:	2802	2400	2046	1737	1469
	arc, inches:		+1.7	0	-7.4	-21.6
Norma 130 SP	velocity, fps:	3140	2862	2601	2354	
	energy, ft-lb:	2847	2365	1953	1600	
	arc, inches:		+1.3	0	-6.5	
Norma 130 FMJ	velocity, fps:	2887	2634	2395	2169	
	energy, ft-lb:					
	arc, inches:		+1.8	0	-7.8	
Norma 150 SP	velocity, fps:	2799	2555	2323	2104	
	energy, ft-lb:	2610	2175	1798	1475	
	arc, inches:		+1.9	0	-8.3	
Norma 150 Oryx	velocity, fps:	2854	2608	2376	2155	
	energy, ft-lb:	2714	2267	1880	1547	
	arc, inches:		+1.8	0	-8.0	
PMC 130 Barnes X	velocity, fps:	2910	2717	2533	2356	2186
	energy, ft-lb:	2444	2131	1852	1602	1379
	arc, inches:		+1.6	0	-7.1	-20.4
PMC 130 SP boat-tail	velocity, fps:	3050	2830	2620	2421	2229
	energy, ft-lb:	2685	2312	1982	1691	1435
	arc, inches:		+1.5	0	-6.5	-19.0
PMC 130 Pointed Soft Point	velocity, fps:	2950	2691	2447	2217	2001
	energy, ft-lb:	2512	2090	1728	1419	1156
	arc, inches:		+1.6	0	-7.5	-22.1
PMC 150 Barnes X	velocity, fps:	2700	2541	2387	2238	2095
	energy, ft-lb:	2428	2150	1897	1668	1461
	arc, inches:		+2.0	0	-8.1	-23.1
PMC 150 SP boat-tail	velocity, fps:	2850	2660	2477	2302	2134
	energy, ft-lb:	2705	2355	2043	1765	1516.
	arc, inches:		+1.7	0	-7.4	-21.4
PMC 150 Pointed Soft Point	velocity, fps:	2750	2530	2321	2123	1936
	energy, ft-lb:	2519	2131	1794	1501	1248
	arc, inches:		+2.0	0	-8.4	-24.6
Rem. 100 Pointed Soft Point	velocity, fps:	3320	2924	2561	2225	1916
	energy, ft-lb:	2448	1898	1456	1099	815
	arc, inches:		+2.3	+2.0	-3.6	-16.2
Rem. 115 PSP Core-Lokt mr	velocity, fps:	2710	2412	2133	1873	1636
	energy, ft-lb:	1875	1485	1161	896	683
	arc, inches:		+1.0	-2.7	-14.2	-35.6
Rem. 130 PSP Core-Lokt	velocity, fps:	3060	2776	2510	2259	2022
	energy, ft-lb:	2702	2225	1818	1472	1180
	arc, inches:		+1.5	0	-7.0	-20.9
Rem. 130 Bronze Point	velocity, fps:	3060	2802	2559	2329	2110
	energy, ft-lb:	2702	2267	1890	1565	1285
	arc, inches:		+1.5	0	-6.8	-20.0
Rem. 130 Swift Scirocco	velocity, fps:	3060	2838	2677	2425	2232
	energy, ft-lb:	2702	2325	1991	1697	1438
	arc, inches:		+1.4	0	-6.5	-18.8

CARTRIDGE BULLET	RANGE, YARDS:	0	100	200	300	400
Rem. 130 AccuTip BT	velocity, fps:	3060	2845	2639	2442	2254
	energy, ft-lb:	2702	2336	2009	1721	1467
	arc, inches:		+1.4	0	-6.4	-18.6
Rem. 140 Swift A-Frame	velocity, fps:	2925	2652	2394	2152	1923
	energy, ft-lb:	2659	2186	1782	1439	1150
	arc, inches:		+1.7	0	-7.8	-23.2
Rem. 140 PSP boat-tail	velocity, fps:	2960	2749	2548	2355	2171
	energy, ft-lb:	2723	2349	2018	1724	1465
	arc, inches:		+1.6	0	-6.9	-20.1
Rem. 140 Nosler Bal. Tip	velocity, fps:	2960	2754	2557	2366	2187
	energy, ft-lb:	2724	2358	2032	1743	1487
	arc, inches:		+1.6	0	-6.9	-20.0
Rem. 140 PSP C-L Ultra	velocity, fps:	2925	2667	2424	2193	1975
	energy, ft-lb:	2659	2211	1826	1495	1212
	arc, inches:		+1.7	0	-7.6	-22.5
Rem. 150 SP Core-Lokt	velocity, fps:	2850	2504	2183	1886	1618
	energy, ft-lb:	2705	2087	1587	1185	872
	arc, inches:		+2.0	0	-9.4	-28.6
Rem. 150 Nosler Partition	velocity, fps:	2850	2652	2463	2282	2108
	energy, ft-lb:	2705	2343	2021	1734	1480
	arc, inches:		+1.7	0	-7.5	-21.6
Speer 130 Grand Slam	velocity, fps:	3050	2774	2514	2269	
	energy, ft-lb:	2685	2221	1824	1485	
	arc, inches:		+1.5	0	-7.0	-20.9
Speer 150 Grand Slam	velocity, fps:	2830	2594	2369	2156	
	energy, ft-lb:	2667	2240	1869	1548	
	arc, inches:		+1.8	0	-8.1	-23.6
Win. 130 Power-Point	velocity, fps:	3060	2802	2559	2329	2110
	energy, ft-lb:	2702	2267	1890	1565	1285.
	arc, inches:		+1.8	0	-7.1	-20.6
Win. 130 Power-Point Plus	velocity, fps:	3150	2881	2628	2388	2161
	energy, ft-lb:	2865	2396	1993	1646	1348
	arc, inches:		+1.3	0	-6.4	-18.9
Win. 130 Silvertip	velocity, fps:	3060	2776	2510	2259	2022.
	energy, ft-lb:	2702	2225	1818	1472	1180
	arc, inches:		+1.8	0	-7.4	-21.6
Win. 130 Ballistic Silvertip	velocity, fps:	3050	2828	2618	2416	2224
	energy, ft-lb:	2685	2309	1978	1685	1428
	arc, inches:		+1.4	0	-6.5	-18.9
Win. 140 AccuBond	velocity, fps:	2950	2751	2560	2378	2203
	energy, ft-lb:	2705	2352	2038	1757	1508
	arc, inches:		+1.6	0	-6.9	-19.9
Win. 140 Fail Safe	velocity, fps:	2920	2671	2435	2211	1999
	energy, ft-lb:	2651	2218	1843	1519	1242
	arc, inches:		+1.7	0	-7.6	-22.3
Win. 150 Power-Point	velocity, fps:	2850	2585	2336	2100	1879
	energy, ft-lb:	2705	2226	1817	1468	1175
	arc, inches:		+2.2	0	-8.6	-25.0
Win. 150 Power-Point Plus	velocity, fps:	2950	2679	2425	2184	1957
	energy, ft-lb:	2900	2391	1959	1589	1276
	arc, inches:		+1.7	0	-7.6	-22.6
Win. 150 Partition Gold	velocity, fps:	2930	2693	2468	2254	2051
	energy, ft-lb:	2860	2416	2030	1693	1402
	arc, inches:		+1.7	0	-7.4	-21.6

.270 WINCHESTER SHORT MAG.

CARTRIDGE BULLET	RANGE, YARDS:	0	100	200	300	400
Black Hills 140 AccuBond	velocity, fps:	3100				
	energy, ft-lb:	2987				
	arc, inches:					
Federal 130 Nos. Bal. Tip	velocity, fps:	3300	3070	2840	2630	2430
	energy, ft-lb:	3145	2710	2335	2000	1705
	arc, inches:		+1.1	0	-5.4	-15.8

CARTRIDGE BULLET	RANGE, YARDS:	0	100	200	300	400
Federal 130 Nos. Partition And Nos. Solid Base And Barnes TS	velocity, fps:	3280	3040	2810	2590	2380
	energy, ft-lb:	3105	2665	2275	1935	1635
	arc, inches:		+1.1	0	-5.6	-16.3
Federal 140 Nos. AccuBond	velocity, fps:	3200	3000	2810	2630	2450
	energy, ft-lb:	3185	2795	2455	2145	1865
	arc, inches:		+1.2	0	-5.6	-16.2
Federal 140 Trophy Bonded	velocity, fps:	3130	2870	2640	2410	2200
	energy, ft-lb:	3035	2570	2160	1810	1500
	arc, inches:		+1.4	0	-6.3	18.7
Federal 150 Nos. Partition	velocity, fps:	3160	2950	2750	2550	2370
	energy, ft-lb:	3325	2895	2515	2175	1870
	arc, inches:		+1.3	0	-5.9	-17.0
Norma 130 FMJ	velocity, fps:	3150	2882	2630	2391	
	energy, ft-lb:					
	arc, inches:		+1.5	0	-6.4	
Norma 130 Ballistic ST	velocity, fps:	3281	3047	2825	2614	
	energy, ft-lb:	3108	2681	2305	1973	
	arc, inches:		+1.1	0	-5.5	
Norma 140 Barnes X TS	velocity, fps:	3150	2952	2762	2580	
	energy, ft-lb:	3085	2709	2372	2070	
	arc, inches:		+1.3	0	-5.8	
Norma 150 Nosler Bal. Tip	velocity, fps:	3280	3046	2824	2613	
	energy, ft-lb:	3106	2679	2303	1972	
	arc, inches:		+1.1	0	-5.4	
Norma 150 Oryx	velocity, fps:	3117	2856	2611	2378	
	energy, ft-lb:	3237	2718	2271	1884	
	arc, inches:		+1.4	0	-6.5	
Win. 130 Bal. Silvertip	velocity, fps:	3275	3041	2820	2609	2408
	energy, ft-lb:	3096	2669	2295	1964	1673
	arc, inches:		+1.1	0	-5.5	-16.1
Win. 140 AccuBond	velocity, fps:	3200	2989	2789	2597	2413
	energy, ft-lb:	3184	2779	2418	2097	1810
	arc, inches:		+1.2	0	-5.7	-16.5
Win. 140 Fail Safe	velocity, fps:	3125	2865	2619	2386	2165
	energy, ft-lb:	3035	2550	2132	1769	1457
	arc, inches:		+1.4	0	-6.5	-19.0
Win. 150 Ballistic Silvertip	velocity, fps:	3120	2923	2734	2554	2380.
	energy, ft-lb:	3242	2845	2490	2172	1886.
	arc, inches:		+1.3	0	-5.9	-17.2
Win. 150 Power Point	velocity, fps:	3150	2867	2601	2350	2113
	energy, ft-lb:	3304	2737	2252	1839	1487
	arc, inches:		+1.4	0	-6.5	-19.4

.270 WEATHERBY MAG.

CARTRIDGE BULLET	RANGE, YARDS:	0	100	200	300	400
Federal 130 Nosler Partition	velocity, fps:	3200	2960	2740	2520	2320
	energy, ft-lb:	2955	2530	2160	1835	1550
	arc, inches:		+1.2	0	-5.9	-17.3
Federal 130 Sierra GameKing BTSP	velocity, fps:	3200	2980	2780	2580	2400
	energy, ft-lb:	2955	2570	2230	1925	1655
	arc, inches:		+1.2	0	-5.7	-16.6
Federal 140 Trophy Bonded	velocity, fps:	3100	2840	2600	2370	2150.
	energy, ft-lb:	2990	2510	2100	1745	1440
	arc, inches:		+1.4	0	-6.6	-19.3
Wby. 100 Pointed Expanding	velocity, fps:	3760	3396	3061	2751	2462
	energy, ft-lb:	3139	2560	2081	1681	1346
	arc, inches:		+2.3	+3.0	0	-7.6
Wby. 130 Pointed Expanding	velocity, fps:	3375	3123	2885	2659	2444
	energy, ft-lb:	3288	2815	2402	2041	1724
	arc, inches:		+2.8	+3.5	0	-8.4
Wby. 130 Nosler Partition	velocity, fps:	3375	3127	2892	2670	2458.
	energy, ft-lb:	3288	2822	2415	2058	1744
	arc, inches:		+2.8	+3.5	0	-8.3
Wby. 140 Nosler Bal. Tip	velocity, fps:	3300	3077	2865	2663	2470.
	energy, ft-lb:	3385	2943	2551	2204	1896
	arc, inches:		+2.9	+3.6	0	-8.4
Wby. 140 Barnes X	velocity, fps:	3250	3032	2825	2628	2438
	energy, ft-lb:	3283	2858	2481	2146	1848
	arc, inches:		+3.0	+3.7	0	-8.7
Wby. 150 Pointed Expanding	velocity, fps:	3245	3028	2821	2623	2434
	energy, ft-lb:	3507	3053	2650	2292	1973
	arc, inches:		+3.0	+3.7	0	-8.7
Wby. 150 Nosler Partition	velocity, fps:	3245	3029	2823	2627	2439.
	energy, ft-lb:	3507	3055	2655	2298	1981
	arc, inches:		+3.0	+3.7	0	-8.

7-30 WATERS

CARTRIDGE BULLET	RANGE, YARDS:	0	100	200	300	400
Federal 120 Sierra GameKing BTSP	velocity, fps:	2700	2300	1930	1600	1330.
	energy, ft-lb:	1940	1405	990	685	470
	arc, inches:		+2.6	0	-12.0	-37.6

7MM MAUSER (7X57)

CARTRIDGE BULLET	RANGE, YARDS:	0	100	200	300	400
Federal 140 Sierra Pro-Hunt.	velocity, fps:	2660	2450	2260	2070	1890.
	energy, ft-lb:	2200	1865	1585	1330	1110
	arc, inches:		+2.1	0	-9.0	-26.1
Federal 140 Nosler Partition	velocity, fps:	2660	2450	2260	2070	1890.
	energy, ft-lb:	2200	1865	1585	1330	1110
	arc, inches:		+2.1	0	-9.0	-26.1
Federal 175 Hi-Shok RN	velocity, fps:	2440	2140	1860	1600	1380
	energy, ft-lb:	2315	1775	1340	1000	740
	arc, inches:		+3.1	0	-13.3	-40.1
Hornady 139 SP boat-tail	velocity, fps:	2700	2504	2316	2137	1965
	energy, ft-lb:	2251	1936	1656	1410	1192
	arc, inches:		+2.0	0	-8.5	-24.9
Hornady 139 SP Interlock	velocity, fps:	2680	2455	2241	2038	1846
	energy, ft-lb:	2216	1860	1550	1282	1052
	arc, inches:		+2.1	0	-9.1	-26.6
Hornady 139 SP boat-tail LM	velocity, fps:	2830	2620	2450	2250	2070
	energy, ft-lb:	2475	2135	1835	1565	1330
	arc, inches:		+1.8	0	-7.6	-22.1
Hornady 139 SP LM	velocity, fps:	2950	2736	2532	2337	2152.
	energy, ft-lb:	2686	2310	1978	1686	1429
	arc, inches:		+2.0	0	-7.6	-21.5
Norma 150 Soft Point	velocity, fps:	2690	2479	2278	2087	
	energy, ft-lb:	2411	2048	1729	1450	
	arc, inches:		+2.0	0	-8.8	
PMC 140 Pointed Soft Point	velocity, fps:	2660	2450	2260	2070	1890
	energy, ft-lb:	2200	1865	1585	1330	1110.
	arc, inches:		+2.4	0	-9.6	-27.3
PMC 175 Soft Point	velocity, fps:	2440	2140	1860	1600	1380
	energy, ft-lb:	2315	1775	1340	1000	740
	arc, inches:		+1.5	-3.6	-18.6	-46.8
Rem. 140 PSP Core-Lokt	velocity, fps:	2660	2435	2221	2018	1827
	energy, ft-lb:	2199	1843	1533	1266	1037
	arc, inches:		+2.2	0	-9.2	-27.4
Win. 145 Power-Point	velocity, fps:	2660	2413	2180	1959	1754
	energy, ft-lb:	2279	1875	1530	1236	990
	arc, inches:		+1.1	-2.8	-14.1	-34.4

7X57 R

CARTRIDGE BULLET	RANGE, YARDS:	0	100	200	300	400
Norma 150 FMJ	velocity, fps:	2690	2489	2296	2112	
	energy, ft-lb:	2411	2063	1756	1486	
	arc, inches:		+2.0	0	-8.6	
Norma 154 Soft Point	velocity, fps:	2625	2417	2219	2030	
	energy, ft-lb:	2357	1999	1684	1410	
	arc, inches:		+2.2	0	-9.3	

Centerfire Rifle Ballistics

7X57 R TO .280 REMINGTON

CARTRIDGE BULLET	RANGE, YARDS:	0	100	200	300	400
Norma 156 Oryx	velocity, fps:	2608	2346	2099	1867	
	energy, ft-lb:	2357	1906	1526	1208	
	arc, inches:		+2.4	0	-10.3	

7MM-08 REMINGTON

CARTRIDGE BULLET	RANGE, YARDS:	0	100	200	300	400
Black Hills 140 AccuBond	velocity, fps:	2700				
	energy, ft-lb:					
	arc, inches:					
Federal 140 Nosler Partition	velocity, fps:	2800	2590	2390	2200	2020
	energy, ft-lb:	2435	2085	1775	1500	1265
	arc, inches:		+1.8	0	-8.0	-23.1
Federal 140 Nosler Bal. Tip And AccuBond	velocity, fps:	2800	2610	2430	2260	2100
	energy, ft-lb:	2440	2135	1840	1590	1360.
	arc, inches:		+1.8	0	-7.7	-22.3
Federal 140 Tr. Bonded HE	velocity, fps:	2950	2660	2390	2140	1900
	energy, ft-lb:	2705	2205	1780	1420	1120
	arc, inches:		+1.7	0	-7.9	-23.2
Federal 150 Sierra Pro-Hunt.	velocity, fps:	2650	2440	2230	2040	1860
	energy, ft-lb:	2340	1980	1660	1390	1150
	arc, inches:		+2.2	0	-9.2	-26.7
Hornady 139 SP boat-tail LM	velocity, fps:	3000	2790	2590	2399	2216
	energy, ft-lb:	2777	2403	2071	1776	1515
	arc, inches:		+1.5	0	-6.7	-19.4
Norma 140 Ballistic ST	velocity, fps:	2822	2633	2452	2278	
	energy, ft-lb:	2476	2156	1870	1614	
	arc, inches:		+1.8	0	-7.6	
PMC 139 PSP	velocity, fps:	2850	2610	2384	2170	1969
	energy, ft-lb:	2507	2103	1754	1454	1197
	arc, inches:		+1.8	0	-7.9	-23.3
Rem. 120 Hollow Point	velocity, fps:	3000	2725	2467	2223	1992
	energy, ft-lb:	2398	1979	1621	1316	1058
	arc, inches:		+1.6	0	-7.3	-21.7
Rem. 140 PSP Core-Lokt	velocity, fps:	2860	2625	2402	2189	1988
	energy, ft-lb:	2542	2142	1793	1490	1228
	arc, inches:		+1.8	0	-7.8	-22.9
Rem. 140 PSP boat-tail	velocity, fps:	2860	2656	2460	2273	2094
	energy, ft-lb:	2542	2192	1881	1606	1363
	arc, inches:		+1.7	0	-7.5	-21.7
Rem. 140 AccuTip BT	velocity, fps:	2860	2670	2488	2313	2145
	energy, ft-lb:	2543	2217	1925	1663	1431
	arc, inches:		+1.7	0	-7.3	-21.2
Rem. 140 Nosler Partition	velocity, fps:	2860	2648	2446	2253	2068
	energy, ft-lb:	2542	2180	1860	1577	1330
	arc, inches:		+1.7	0	-7.6	-22.0
Speer 145 Grand Slam	velocity, fps:	2845	2567	2305	2059	
	energy, ft-lb:	2606	2121	1711	1365	
	arc, inches:		+1.9	0	-8.4	-25.5
Win. 140 Power-Point	velocity, fps:	2800	2523	2268	2027	1802.
	energy, ft-lb:	2429	1980	1599	1277	1010
	arc, inches:		+2.0	0	-8.8	-26.0
Win. 140 Power-Point Plus	velocity, fps:	2875	2597	2336	2090	1859
	energy, ft-lb:	2570	1997	1697	1358	1075
	arc, inches:		+2.0	0	-8.8	26.0
Win. 140 Fail Safe	velocity, fps:	2760	2506	2271	2048	1839
	energy, ft-lb:	2360	1953	1603	1304	1051
	arc, inches:		+2.0	0	-8.8	-25.9
Win. 140 Ballistic Silvertip	velocity, fps:	2770	2572	2382	2200	2026
	energy, ft-lb:	2386	2056	1764	1504	1276
	arc, inches:		+1.9	0	-8.0	-23.8

7x64 BRENNEKE

CARTRIDGE BULLET	RANGE, YARDS:	0	100	200	300	400
Federal 160 Nosler Partition	velocity, fps:	2650	2480	2310	2150	2000
	energy, ft-lb:	2495	2180	1895	1640	1415
	arc, inches:		+2.1	0	-8.7	-24.9

CARTRIDGE BULLET	RANGE, YARDS:	0	100	200	300	400
Norma 140 AccuBond	velocity, fps:	2953	2759	2572	2394	
	energy, ft-lb:	2712	2366	2058	1782	
	arc, inches:		+1.5	0	-6.8	
Norma 154 Soft Point	velocity, fps:	2821	2605	2399	2203	
	energy, ft-lb:	2722	2321	1969	1660	
	arc, inches:		+1.8	0	-7.8	
Norma 156 Oryx	velocity, fps:	2789	2516	2259	2017	
	energy, ft-lb:	2695	2193	1768	1410	
	arc, inches:		+2.0	0	-8.8	
Norma 170 Vulkan	velocity, fps:	2756	2501	2259	2031	
	energy, ft-lb:	2868	2361	1927	1558	
	arc, inches:		+2.0	0	-8.8	
Norma 170 Oryx	velocity, fps:	2756	2481	2222	1979	
	energy, ft-lb:	2868	2324	1864	1478	
	arc, inches:		+2.1	0	-9.2	
Norma 170 Plastic Point	velocity, fps:	2756	2519	2294	2081	
	energy, ft-lb:	2868	2396	1987	1635	
	arc, inches:		+2.0	0	-8.6	
PMC 170 Pointed Soft Point	velocity, fps:	2625	2401	2189	1989	1801
	energy, ft lb:	2601	2175	1808	1493	1224
	arc, inches:		+2.3	0	-9.6	-27.9
Rem. 175 PSP Core-Lokt	velocity, fps:	2650	2445	2248	2061	1883
	energy, ft-lb:	2728	2322	1964	1650	1378
	arc, inches:		+2.2	0	-9.1	-26.4
Speer 160 Grand Slam	velocity, fps:	2600	2376	2164	1962	
	energy, ft-lb:	2401	2006	1663	1368	
	arc, inches:		+2.3	0	-9.8	-28.6
Speer 175 Grand Slam	velocity, fps:	2650	2461	2280	2106	
	energy, ft-lb:	2728	2353	2019	1723	
	arc, inches:		+2.4	0	-9.2	-26.2

7x65 R

CARTRIDGE BULLET	RANGE, YARDS:	0	100	200	300	400
Norma 150 FMJ	velocity, fps:	2756	2552	2357	2170	
	energy, ft-lb:	2530	2169	1850	1569	
	arc, inches:		+1.9	0	-8.2	
Norma 156 Oryx	velocity, fps:	2723	2454	2200	1962	
	energy, ft-lb:	2569	2086	1678	1334	
	arc, inches:		+2.1	0	-9.3	
Norma 170 Plastic Point	velocity, fps:	2625	2390	2167	1956	
	energy, ft-lb:	2602	2157	1773	1445	
	arc, inches:		+2.3	0	-9.7	
Norma 170 Vulkan	velocity, fps:	2657	2392	2143	1909	
	energy, ft-lb:	2666	2161	1734	1377	
	arc, inches:		+2.3	0	-9.9	
Norma 170 Oryx	velocity, fps:	2657	2378	2115	1871	
	energy, ft-lb:	2666	2135	1690	1321	
	arc, inches:		+2.3	0	-10.1	

.284 WINCHESTER

CARTRIDGE BULLET	RANGE, YARDS:	0	100	200	300	400
Win. 150 Power-Point	velocity, fps:	2860	2595	2344	2108	1886
	energy, ft-lb:	2724	2243	1830	1480	1185
	arc, inches:		+2.1	0	-8.5	-24.8

.280 REMINGTON

CARTRIDGE BULLET	RANGE, YARDS:	0	100	200	300	400
Federal 140 Sierra Pro-Hunt.	velocity, fps:	2990	2740	2500	2270	2060
	energy, ft-lb:	2770	2325	1940	1605	1320
	arc, inches:		+1.6	0	-7.0	-20.8
Federal 140 Trophy Bonded	velocity, fps:	2990	2630	2310	2040	1730
	energy, ft-lb:	2770	2155	1655	1250	925
	arc, inches:		+1.6	0	-8.4	-25.4
Federal 140 Tr. Bonded HE	velocity, fps:	3150	2850	2570	2300	2050
	energy, ft-lb:	3085	2520	2050	1650	1310
	arc, inches:		+1.4	0	-6.7	-20.0

BALLISTICS

CARTRIDGE BULLET	RANGE, YARDS:	0	100	200	300	400
Federal 140 Nos. AccuBond	velocity, fps:	3000	2800	2620	2440	2260
And Bal. Tip	energy, ft-lb:	2800	2445	2130	1845	1590
And Solid Base	arc, inches:		+1.5	0	-6.5	-18.9
Federal 150 Hi-Shok	velocity, fps:	2890	2670	2460	2260	2060
	energy, ft-lb:	2780	2370	2015	1695	1420
	arc, inches:		+1.7	0	-7.5	-21.8
Federal 150 Nosler Partition	velocity, fps:	2890	2690	2490	2310	2130
	energy, ft-lb:	2780	2405	2070	1770	1510.
	arc, inches:		+1.7	0	-7.2	-21.1
Federal 150 Nos. AccuBond	velocity, fps:	2800	2630	2460	2300	2150
	energy, ft-lb:	2785	2455	2155	1885	1645
	arc, inches:		+1.8	0	-7.5	-21.5
Federal 160 Trophy Bonded	velocity, fps:	2800	2570	2350	2140	1940
	energy, ft-lb:	2785	2345	1960	1625	1340
	arc, inches:		+1.9	0	-8.3	-24.0
Hornady 139 SPBT LMmoly	velocity, fps:	3110	2888	2675	2473	2280.
	energy, ft-lb:	2985	2573	2209	1887	1604
	arc, inches:		+1.4	0	-6.5	-18.6
Norma 156 Oryx	velocity, fps:	2789	2516	2259	2017	
	energy, ft-lb:	2695	2193	1768	1410	
	arc, inches:		+2.0	0	-8.8	
Norma 170 Plastic Point	velocity, fps:	2707	2468	2241	2026	
	energy, ft-lb:	2767	2299	1896	1550	
	arc, inches:		+2.1	0	-9.1	
Norma 170 Vulkan	velocity, fps:	2592	2346	2113	1894	
	energy, ft-lb:	2537	2078	1686	1354	
	arc, inches:		+2.4	0	-10.2	
Norma 170 Oryx	velocity, fps:	2690	2416	2159	1918	
	energy, ft-lb:	2732	2204	1760	1389	
	arc, inches:		+2.2	0	-9.7	
Rem. 140 PSP Core-Lokt	velocity, fps:	3000	2758	2528	2309	2102
	energy, ft-lb:	2797	2363	1986	1657	1373
	arc, inches:		+1.5	0	-7.0	-20.5
Rem. 140 PSP boat-tail	velocity, fps:	2860	2656	2460	2273	2094
	energy, ft-lb:	2542	2192	1881	1606	1363
	arc, inches:		+1.7	0	-7.5	-21.7
Rem. 140 Nosler Bal. Tip	velocity, fps:	3000	2804	2616	2436	2263
	energy, ft-lb:	2799	2445	2128	1848	1593
	arc, inches:		+1.5	0	-6.8	-19.0
Rem. 140 AccuTip	velocity, fps:	3000	2804	2617	2437	2265
	energy, ft-lb:	2797	2444	2129	1846	1594
	arc, inches:		+1.5	0	-6.8	-19.0
Rem. 150 PSP Core-Lokt	velocity, fps:	2890	2624	2373	2135	1912
	energy, ft-lb:	2781	2293	1875	1518	1217
	arc, inches:		+1.8	0	-8.0	-23.6
Rem. 165 SP Core-Lokt	velocity, fps:	2820	2510	2220	1950	1701
	energy, ft-lb:	2913	2308	1805	1393	1060.
	arc, inches:		+2.0	0	-9.1	-27.4
Speer 145 Grand Slam	velocity, fps:	2900	2619	2354	2105	
	energy, ft-lb:	2707	2207	1784	1426	
	arc, inches:		+2.1	0	-8.4	-24.7
Speer 160 Grand Slam	velocity, fps:	2890	2652	2425	2210	
	energy, ft-lb:	2967	2497	2089	1735	
	arc, inches:		+1.7	0	-7.7	-22.4
Win. 140 Fail Safe	velocity, fps:	3050	2756	2480	2221	1977
	energy, ft-lb:	2893	2362	1913	1533	1216
	arc, inches:		+1.5	0	-7.2	-21.5
Win. 140 Ballistic Silvertip	velocity, fps:	3040	2842	2653	2471	2297
	energy, ft-lb:	2872	2511	2187	1898	1640
	arc, inches:		+1.4	0	-6.3	-18.4

7MM REMINGTON MAG.

CARTRIDGE BULLET	RANGE, YARDS:	0	100	200	300	400
A-Square 175 Monolithic	velocity, fps:	2860	2557	2273	2008	1771
Solid	energy, ft-lb:	3178	2540	2008	1567	1219
	arc, inches:		+1.92	0	-8.7	-25.9
Black Hills 140 Nos. Bal. Tip	velocity, fps:	3150				
	energy, ft-lb:	3084				
	arc, inches:					
Black Hills 140 Barnes XLC	velocity, fps:	3150				
	energy, ft-lb:	3084				
	arc, inches:					
Black Hills 140 Nos. Partition	velocity, fps:	3150				
	energy, ft-lb:	3084				
	arc, inches:					
Federal 140 Nosler Bal. Tip	velocity, fps:	3110	2910	2720	2530	2360.
And AccuBond	energy, ft-lb:	3005	2630	2295	1995	1725
	arc, inches:		+1.3	0	-6.0	-17.4
Federal 140 Nosler Partition	velocity, fps:	3150	2930	2710	2510	2320
	energy, ft-lb:	3085	2660	2290	1960	1670
	arc, inches:		+1.3	0	-6.0	-17.5
Federal 140 Trophy Bonded	velocity, fps:	3150	2910	2680	2460	2250.
	energy, ft-lb:	3085	2630	2230	1880	1575
	arc, inches:		+1.3	0	-6.1	-18.1
Federal 150 Hi-Shok	velocity, fps:	3110	2830	2570	2320	2090
	energy, ft-lb:	3220	2670	2200	1790	1450
	arc, inches:		+1.4	0	-6.7	-19.9
Federal 150 Sierra GameKing BTSP	velocity, fps:	3110	2920	2750	2580	2410
	energy, ft-lb:	3220	2850	2510	2210	1930
	arc, inches:		+1.3	0	-5.9	-17.0
Federal 150 Nosler Bal. Tip	velocity, fps:	3110	2910	2720	2540	2370
	energy, ft-lb:	3220	2825	2470	2150	1865
	arc, inches:		+1.3	0	-6.0	-17.4
Federal 150 Nos. Solid Base	velocity, fps:	3100	2890	2690	2500	2310
	energy, ft-lb:	3200	2780	2405	2075	1775
	arc, inches:		+1.3	0	-6.2	-17.8
Federal 160 Barnes XLC	velocity, fps:	2940	2760	2580	2410	2240
	energy, ft-lb:	3070	2695	2360	2060	1785
	arc, inches:		+1.5	0	-6.8	-19.6
Federal 160 Sierra Pro-Hunt.	velocity, fps:	2940	2730	2520	2320	2140
	energy, ft-lb:	3070	2640	2260	1920	1620
	arc, inches:		+1.6	0	-7.1	-20.6
Federal 160 Nosler Partition	velocity, fps:	2950	2770	2590	2420	2250.
	energy, ft-lb:	3090	2715	2375	2075	1800
	arc, inches:		+1.5	0	-6.7	-19.4
Federal 160 Nos. AccuBond	velocity, fps:	2950	2770	2600	2440	2280.
	energy, ft-lb:	3090	2730	2405	2110	1845
	arc, inches:		+1.5	0	-6.6	-19.1
Federal 160 Trophy Bonded	velocity, fps:	2940	2660	2390	2140	1900
	energy, ft-lb:	3070	2505	2025	1620	1280.
	arc, inches:		+1.7	0	-7.9	-23.3
Federal 165 Sierra GameKing BTSP	velocity, fps:	2950	2800	2650	2510	2370.
	energy, ft-lb:	3190	2865	2570	2300	2050
	arc, inches:		+1.5	0	-6.4	-18.4
Federal 175 Hi-Shok	velocity, fps:	2860	2650	2440	2240	2060
	energy, ft-lb:	3180	2720	2310	1960	1640
	arc, inches:		+1.7	0	-7.6	-22.1
Federal 175 Trophy Bonded	velocity, fps:	2860	2600	2350	2120	1900
	energy, ft-lb:	3180	2625	2150	1745	1400
	arc, inches:		+1.8	0	-8.2	-24.0
Hornady 139 SPBT	velocity, fps:	3150	2933	2727	2530	2341
	energy, ft-lb:	3063	2656	2296	1976	1692
	arc, inches:		+1.2	0	-6.1	-17.7

Centerfire Rifle Ballistics

7MM REMINGTON MAG. TO 7MM REMINGTON MAG.

CARTRIDGE BULLET	RANGE, YARDS:	0	100	200	300	400
Hornady 139 SST	velocity, fps:	3150	2948	2754	2569	2391
(or Interbond)	energy, ft-lb:	3062	2681	2341	2037	1764
	arc, inches:		+1.1	0	-5.7	-16.7
Hornady 139 SST LM	velocity, fps:	3250	3044	2847	2657	2475
(or Interbond)	energy, ft-lb:	3259	2860	2501	2178	1890
	arc, inches:		+1.1	0	-5.5	-16.2
Hornady 139 SPBT HMmoly	velocity, fps:	3250	3041	2822	2613	2413
	energy, ft-lb:	3300	2854	2458	2106	1797.
	arc, inches:		+1.1	0	-5.7	-16.6
Hornady 154 Soft Point	velocity, fps:	3035	2814	2604	2404	2212
	energy, ft-lb:	3151	2708	2319	1977	1674
	arc, inches:		+1.3	0	-6.7	-19.3
Hornady 154 SST	velocity, fps:	3035	2850	2672	2501	2337
(or Interbond)	energy, ft-lb:	3149	2777	2441	2139	1867
	arc, inches:		+1.4	0	-6.5	-18.7
Hornady 162 SP boat-tail	velocity, fps:	2940	2757	2582	2413	2251
	energy, ft-lb:	3110	2735	2399	2095	1823
	arc, inches:		+1.6	0	-6.7	-19.7
Hornady 175 SP	velocity, fps:	2860	2650	2440	2240	2060.
	energy, ft-lb:	3180	2720	2310	1960	1640
	arc, inches:		+2.0	0	-7.9	-22.7
Norma 140 Nosler Bal. Tip	velocity, fps:	3150	2936	2732	2537	
	energy, ft-lb:	3085	2680	2320	2001	
	arc, inches:		+1.2	0	-5.9	
Norma 140 Barnes X TS	velocity, fps:	3117	2912	2716	2529	
	energy, ft-lb:	3021	2637	2294	1988	
	arch, inches:		+1.3	0	-6.0	
Norma 150 Scirocco	velocity, fps:	3117	2934	2758	2589	
	energy, ft-lb:	3237	2869	2535	2234	
	arc, inches:		+1.2	0	-5.8	
Norma 156 Oryx	velocity, fps:	2953	2670	2404	2153	
	energy, ft-lb:	3021	2470	2002	1607	
	arc, inches:		+1.7	0	-7.7	
Norma 170 Vulkan	velocity, fps:	3018	2747	2493	2252	
	energy, ft-lb:	3439	2850	2346	1914	
	arc, inches:		+1.5	0	-2.8	
Norma 170 Oryx	velocity, fps:	2887	2601	2333	2080	
	energy, ft-lb:	3147	2555	2055	1634	
	arc, inches:		+1.8	0	-8.2	
Norma 170 Plastic Point	velocity, fps:	3018	2762	2519	2290	
	energy, ft-lb:	3439	2880	2394	1980	
	arc, inches:		+1.5	0	-7.0	
PMC 140 Barnes X	velocity, fps:	3000	2808	2624	2448	2279
	energy, ft-lb:	2797	2451	2141	1863	1614
	arc, inches:		+1.5	0	-6.6	18.9
PMC 140 Pointed Soft Point	velocity, fps:	3099	2878	2668	2469	2279
	energy, ft-lb:	2984	2574	2212	1895	1614
	arc, inches:		+1.4	0	-6.2	-18.1
PMC 140 SP boat-tail	velocity, fps:	3125	2891	2669	2457	2255
	energy, ft-lb:	3035	2597	2213	1877	1580
	arc, inches:		+1.4	0	-6.3	-18.4
PMC 160 Barnes X	velocity, fps:	2800	2639	2484	2334	2189
	energy, ft-lb:	2785	2474	2192	1935	1703
	arc, inches:		+1.8	0	-7.4	-21.2
PMC 160 Pointed Soft Point	velocity, fps:	2914	2748	2586	2428	2276
	energy, ft-lb:	3016	2682	2375	2095	1840
	arc, inches:		+1.6	0	-6.7	-19.4
PMC 160 SP boat-tail	velocity, fps:	2900	2696	2501	2314	2135
	energy, ft-lb:	2987	2582	2222	1903	1620
	arc, inches:		+1.7	0	-7.2	-21.0
PMC 175 Pointed Soft Point	velocity, fps:	2860	2645	2442	2244	2957
	energy, ft-lb:	3178	2718	2313	1956	1644
	arc, inches:		+2.0	0	-7.9	-22.7

CARTRIDGE BULLET	RANGE, YARDS:	0	100	200	300	400
Rem. 140 PSP Core-Lokt mr	velocity, fps:	2710	2482	2265	2059	1865
	energy, ft-lb:	2283	1915	1595	1318	1081
	arc, inches:		+1.0	-2.5	-12.8	-31.3
Rem. 140 PSP Core-Lokt	velocity, fps:	3175	2923	2684	2458	2243
	energy, ft-lb:	3133	2655	2240	1878	1564
	arc, inches:		+2.2	+1.9	-3.2	-14.2
Rem. 140 PSP boat-tail	velocity, fps:	3175	2956	2747	2547	2356
	energy, ft-lb:	3133	2715	2345	2017	1726
	arc, inches:		+2.2	+1.6	-3.1	-13.4
Rem. 150 AccuTip	velocity, fps:	3110	2926	2749	2579	2415
	energy, ft-lb:	3221	2850	2516	2215	1943
	arc, inches:		+1.3	0	-5.9	-17.0
Rem. 150 PSP Core-Lokt	velocity, fps:	3110	2830	2568	2320	2085
	energy, ft-lb:	3221	2667	2196	1792	1448
	arc, inches:		+1.3	0	-6.6	-20.2
Rem. 150 Nosler Bal. Tip	velocity, fps:	3110	2912	2723	2542	2367
	energy, ft-lb:	3222	2825	2470	2152	1867
	arc, inches:		+1.2	0	-5.9	-17.3
Rem. 150 Swift Scirocco	velocity, fps:	3110	2927	2751	2582	2419
	energy, ft-lb:	3221	2852	2520	2220	1948
	arc, inches:		+1.3	0	-5.9	-17.0
Rem. 160 Swift A-Frame	velocity, fps:	2900	2659	2430	2212	2006
	energy, ft-lb:	2987	2511	2097	1739	1430
	arc, inches:		+1.7	0	-7.6	-22.4
Rem. 160 Nosler Partition	velocity, fps:	2950	2752	2563	2381	2207
	energy, ft-lb:	3091	2690	2333	2014	1730
	arc, inches:		+0.6	-1.9	-9.6	-23.6
Rem. 175 PSP Core-Lokt	velocity, fps:	2860	2645	2440	2244	2057
	energy, ft-lb:	3178	2718	2313	1956	1644
	arc, inches:		+1.7	0	-7.6	-22.1
Speer 145 Grand Slam	velocity, fps:	3140	2843	2565	2304	
	energy, ft-lb:	3174	2602	2118	1708	
	arc, inches:		+1.4	0	-6.7	
Speer 175 Grand Slam	velocity, fps:	2850	2653	2463	2282	
	energy, ft-lb:	3156	2734	2358	2023	
	arc, inches:		+1.7	0	-7.5	-21.7
Win. 140 Fail Safe	velocity, fps:	3150	2861	2589	2333	2092
	energy, ft-lb:	3085	2544	2085	1693	1361
	arc, inches:		+1.4	0	-6.6	-19.5
Win. 140 Ballistic Silvertip	velocity, fps:	3100	2889	2687	2494	2310
	energy, ft-lb:	2988	2595	2245	1934	1659.
	arc, inches:		+1.3	0	-6.2	-17.9
Win. 140 AccuBond CT	velocity, fps:	3180	2965	2760	2565	2377
	energy, ft-lb:	3143	2733	2368	2044	1756
	arc, inches:		+1.2	0	-5.8	-16.9
Win. 150 Power-Point	velocity, fps:	3090	2812	2551	2304	2071
	energy, ft-lb:	3181	2634	2167	1768	1429
	arc, inches:		+1.5	0	-6.8	-20.2
Win. 150 Power-Point Plus	velocity, fps:	3130	2849	2586	2337	2102
	energy, ft-lb:	3264	2705	2227	1819	1472
	arc, inches:		+1.4	0	-6.6	-19.6
Win. 150 Ballistic Silvertip	velocity, fps:	3100	2903	2714	2533	2359
	energy, ft-lb:	3200	2806	2453	2136	1853
	arc, inches:		+1.3	0	-6.0	-17.5
Win. 160 AccuBond	velocity, fps:	2950	2766	2590	2420	2257
	energy, ft-lb:	3091	2718	2382	2080	1809
	arc, inches:		+1.5	0	-6.7	-19.4
Win. 160 Partition Gold	velocity, fps:	2950	2743	2546	2357	2176
	energy, ft-lb:	3093	2674	2303	1974	1682
	arc, inches:		+1.6	0	-6.9	-20.1
Win. 160 Fail Safe	velocity, fps:	2920	2678	2449	2331	2025
	energy, ft-lb:	3030	2549	2131	1769	1457
	arc, inches:		+1.7	0	-7.5	-22.0

CARTRIDGE BULLET	RANGE, YARDS:	0	100	200	300	400
Win. 175 Power-Point	velocity, fps:	2860	2645	2440	2244	2057
	energy, ft-lb:	3178	2718	2313	1956	1644
	arc, inches:		+2.0	0	-7.9	-22.7

7MM REMINGTON SHORT ULTRA MAG

CARTRIDGE BULLET	RANGE, YARDS:	0	100	200	300	400
Rem. 140 PSP C-L Ultra	velocity, fps:	3175	2934	2707	2490	2283
	energy, ft-lb:	3133	2676	2277	1927	1620.
	arc, inches:		+1.3	0	-6.0	-17.7
Rem. 150 PSP Core-Lokt	velocity, fps:	3110	2828	2563	2313	2077
	energy, ft-lb:	3221	2663	2188	1782	1437
	arc, inches:		+2.5	+2.1	-3.6	-15.8
Rem. 160 Partition	velocity, fps:	2960	2762	2572	2390	2215
	energy, ft-lb:	3112	2709	2350	2029	1744
	arc, inches:		+2.6	+2.2	-3.6	-15.4
Rem. 160 PSP C-L Ultra	velocity, fps:	2960	2733	2518	2313	2117
	energy, ft-lb:	3112	2654	2252	1900	1592
	arc, inches:		+2.7	+2.2	-3.7	-16.2

7MM WINCHESTER SHORT MAG.

CARTRIDGE BULLET	RANGE, YARDS:	0	100	200	300	400
Federal 140 Nos. AccuBond	velocity, fps:	3250	3040	2840	2660	2470
	energy, ft-lb:	3285	2875	2515	2190	1900
	arc, inches:		+1.1	0	-5.5	-15.8
Federal 140 Nos. Bal. Tip	velocity, fps:	3310	3100	2900	2700	2520
	energy, ft-lb:	3405	2985	2610	2270	1975
	arc, inches:		+1.1	0	-5.2	15.2
Federal 150 Nos. Solid Base	velocity, fps:	3230	3010	2800	2600	2410
	energy, ft-lb:	3475	3015	2615	2255	1935
	arc, inches:		+1.3	0	-5.6	-16.3
Federal 160 Nos. AccuBond	velocity, fps:	3120	2940	2760	2590	2430
	energy, ft-lb:	3460	3065	2710	2390	2095
	arc, inches:		+1.3	0	-5.9	-16.8
Federal 160 Nos. Partition	velocity, fps:	3160	2950	2750	2560	2380.
	energy, ft-lb:	3545	3095	2690	2335	2015.
	arc, inches:		+1.2	0	-5.9	-16.9
Federal 160 Barnes TS	velocity, fps:	2990	2780	2590	2400	2220
	energy, ft-lb:	3175	2755	2380	2045	1750
	arc, inches:		+1.5	0	-6.6	-19.4
Federal 160 Trophy Bonded	velocity, fps:	3120	2880	2650	2440	2230
	energy, ft-lb:	3460	2945	2500	2105	1765
	arc, inches:		+1.4	0	-6.3	-18.5
Win. 140 Bal. Silvertip	velocity, fps:	3225	3008	2801	2603	2414
	energy, ft-lb:	3233	2812	2438	2106	1812
	arc, inches:		+1.2	0	-5.6	-16.4
Win. 140 AccuBond CT	velocity, fps:	3225	3008	2801	2604	2415
	energy, ft-lb:	3233	2812	2439	2107	1812
	arc, inches:		+1.2	0	-5.6	-16.4
Win. 150 Power Point	velocity, fps:	3200	2915	2648	2396	2157
	energy, ft-lb:	3410	2830	2335 1911		1550
	arc, inches:		+1.3	0	-6.3	-18.6
Win. 160 AccuBond	velocity, fps:	3050	2862	2682	2509	2342
	energy, ft-lb:	3306	2911	2556	2237	1950
	arc, inches:		1.4	0	-6.2	-17.9
Win. 160 Fail Safe	velocity, fps:	2990	2744	2512	2291	2081
	energy, ft-lb:	3176	2675	2241	1864	1538
	arc, inches:		+1.6	0	-7.1	-20.8

7MM WEATHERBY MAG.

CARTRIDGE BULLET	RANGE, YARDS:	0	100	200	300	400
Federal 160 Nosler Partition	velocity, fps:	3050	2850	2650	2470	2290
	energy, ft-lb:	3305	2880	2505	2165	1865
	arc, inches:		+1.4	0	-6.3	-18.4
Federal 160 Sierra GameKing BTSP	velocity, fps:	3050	2880	2710	2560	2400
	energy, ft-lb:	3305	2945	2615	2320	2050
	arc, inches:		+1.4	0	-6.1	-17.4

CARTRIDGE BULLET	RANGE, YARDS:	0	100	200	300	400
Federal 160 Trophy Bonded	velocity, fps:	3050	2730	2420	2140	1880.
	energy, ft-lb:	3305	2640	2085	1630	1255
	arc, inches:		+1.6	0	-7.6	-22.7
Hornady 154 Soft Point	velocity, fps:	3200	2971	2753	2546	2348.
	energy, ft-lb:	3501	3017	2592	2216	1885
	arc, inches:		+1.2	0	-5.8	-17.0
Hornady 154 SST (or Interbond)	velocity, fps:	3200	3009	2825	2648	2478
	energy, ft-lb:	3501	3096	2729	2398	2100
	arc, inches:		+1.2	0	-5.7	-16.5
Hornady 175 Soft Point	velocity, fps:	2910	2709	2516	2331	2154
	energy, ft-lb:	3290	2850	2459	2111	1803
	arc, inches:		+1.6	0	-7.1	-20.6
Wby. 139 Pointed Expanding	velocity, fps:	3340	3079	2834	2601	2380.
	energy, ft-lb:	3443	2926	2478	2088	1748
	arc, inches:		+2.9	+3.6	0	-8.7
Wby. 140 Nosler Partition	velocity, fps:	3303	3069	2847	2636	2434
	energy, ft-lb:	3391	2927	2519	2159	1841
	arc, inches:		+2.9	+3.6	0	-8.5
Wby. 150 Nosler Bal. Tip	velocity, fps:	3300	3093	2896	2708	2527
	energy, ft-lb:	3627	3187	2793	2442	2127
	arc, inches:		+2.8	+3.5	0	-8.2
Wby. 150 Barnes X	velocity, fps:	3100	2901	2710	2527	2352
	energy, ft-lb:	3200	2802	2446	2127	1842
	arc, inches:		+3.3	+4.0	0	-9.4
Wby. 154 Pointed Expanding	velocity, fps:	3260	3028	2807	2597	2397
	energy, ft-lb:	3634	3134	2694	2307	1964
	arc, inches:		+3.0	+3.7	0	-8.8
Wby. 160 Nosler Partition	velocity, fps:	3200	2991	2791	2600	2417
	energy, ft-lb:	3638	3177	2767	2401	2075.
	arc, inches:		+3.1	+3.8	0	-8.9
Wby. 175 Pointed Expanding	velocity, fps:	3070	2861	2662	2471	2288
	energy, ft-lb:	3662	3181	2753	2373	2034
	arc, inches:		+3.5	+4.2	0	-9.9

7MM DAKOTA

CARTRIDGE BULLET	RANGE, YARDS:	0	100	200	300	400
Dakota 140 Barnes X	velocity, fps:	3500	3253	3019	2798	2587
	energy, ft-lb:	3807	3288	2833	2433	2081
	arc, inches:		+2.0	+2.1	-1.5	-9.6
Dakota 160 Barnes X	velocity, fps:	3200	3001	2811	2630	2455
	energy, ft-lb:	3637	3200	2808	2456	2140
	arc, inches:		+2.1	+1.9	-2.8	-12.5

7MM STW

CARTRIDGE BULLET	RANGE, YARDS:	0	100	200	300	400
A-Square 140 Nos. Bal. Tip	velocity, fps:	3450	3254	3067	2888	2715
	energy, ft-lb:	3700	3291	2924	2592	2292
	arc, inches:		+2.2	+3.0	0	-7.3
A-Square 160 Nosler Part.	velocity, fps:	3250	3071	2900	2735	2576.
	energy, ft-lb:	3752	3351	2987	2657	2357
	arc, inches:		+2.8	+3.5	0	-8.2
A-Square 160 SP boat-tail	velocity, fps:	3250	3087	2930	2778	2631
	energy, ft-lb:	3752	3385	3049	2741	2460
	arc, inches:		+2.8	+3.4	0	-8.0
Federal 140 Trophy Bonded	velocity, fps:	3330	3080	2850	2630	2420
	energy, ft-lb:	3435	2950	2520	2145	1815
	arc, inches:		+1.1	0	-5.4	-15.8
Federal 150 Trophy Bonded	velocity, fps:	3250	3010	2770	2560	2350.
	energy, ft-lb:	3520	3010	2565	2175	1830
	arc, inches:		+1.2	0	-5.7	-16.7
Federal 160 Sierra GameKing BTSP	velocity, fps:	3200	3020	2850	2670	2530.
	energy, ft-lb:	3640	3245	2890	2570	2275
	arc, inches:		+1.1	0	-5.5	-15.7
Rem. 140 PSP Core-Lokt	velocity, fps:	3325	3064	2818	2585	2364
	energy, ft-lb:	3436	2918	2468	2077	1737
	arc, inches:		+2.0	+1.7	-2.9	-12.8

BALLISTICS

Centerfire Rifle Ballistics

7MM STW TO .30-30 WINCHESTER

CARTRIDGE BULLET	RANGE, YARDS:	0	100	200	300	400
Rem. 140 Swift A-Frame	velocity, fps:	3325	3020	2735	2467	2215
	energy, ft-lb:	3436	2834	2324	1892	1525
	arc, inches:		+2.1	+1.8	-3.1	-13.8
Speer 145 Grand Slam	velocity, fps:	3300	2992	2075	2435	
	energy, ft-lb:	3506	2882	2355	1909	
	arc, inches:		+1.2	0	-6.0	-17.8
Win. 140 Ballistic Silvertip	velocity, fps:	3320	3100	2890	2690	2499
	energy, ft-lb:	3427	2982	2597	2250	1941
	arc, inches:		+1.1	0	-5.2	-15.2
Win. 150 Power-Point	velocity, fps:	3250	2957	2683	2424	2181
	energy, ft-lb:	3519	2913	2398	1958	1584
	arc, inches:		+1.2	0	-6.1	-18.1
Win. 160 Fail Safe	velocity, fps:	3150	2894	2652	2422	2204
	energy, ft-lb:	3526	2976	2499	2085	1727
	arc, inches:		+1.3	0	-6.3	-18.5

7MM REMINGTON ULTRA MAG

CARTRIDGE BULLET	RANGE, YARDS:	0	100	200	300	400
Rem. 140 PSP Core-Lokt	velocity, fps:	3425	3158	2907	2669	2444
	energy, ft-lb:	3646	3099	2626	2214	1856
	arc, inches:		+1.8	+1.6	-2.7	-11.9
Rem. 140 Nosler Partition	velocity, fps:	3425	3184	2956	2740	2534
	energy, ft-lb:	3646	3151	2715	2333	1995
	arc, inches:		+1.7	+1.6	-2.6	-11.4
Rem. 160 Nosler Partition	velocity, fps:	3200	2991	2791	2600	2417
	energy, ft-lb:	3637	3177	2767	2401	2075
	arc, inches:		+2.1	+1.8	-3.0	-12.9

7.21 (.284) FIREHAWK

CARTRIDGE BULLET	RANGE, YARDS:	0	100	200	300	400
Lazzeroni 140 Nosler Part.	velocity, fps:	3580	3349	3130	2923	2724
	energy, ft-lb:	3985	3488	3048	2656	2308
	arc, inches:		+2.2	+2.9	0	-7.0
Lazzeroni 160 Swift A-Fr.	velocity, fps:	3385	3167	2961	2763	2574
	energy, ft-lb:	4072	3565	3115	2713	2354
	arc, inches:		+2.6	+3.3	0	-7.8

7.5x55 SWISS

CARTRIDGE BULLET	RANGE, YARDS:	0	100	200	300	400
Norma 180 Soft Point	velocity, fps:	2651	2432	2223	2025	
	energy, ft-lb:	2810	2364	1976	1639	
	arc, inches:		+2.2	0	-9.3	
Norma 180 Oryx	velocity, fps:	2493	2222	1968	1734	
	energy, ft-lb:	2485	1974	1549	1201	
	arc, inches:	+2.7	0	-11.8		

7.62x39 RUSSIAN

CARTRIDGE BULLET	RANGE, YARDS:	0	100	200	300	400
Federal 123 Hi-Shok	velocity, fps:	2300	2030	1780	1550	1350
	energy, ft-lb:	1445	1125	860	655	500.
	arc, inches:		0	-7.0	-25.1	
Federal 124 FMJ	velocity, fps:	2300	2030	1780	1560	1360
	energy, ft-lb:	1455	1135	875	670	510
	arc, inches:		+3.5	0	-14.6	-43.5
PMC 123 FMJ	velocity, fps:	2350	2072	1817	1583	1368
	energy, ft-lb:	1495	1162	894	678	507
	arc, inches:		0	-5.0	-26.4	-67.8
PMC 125 Pointed Soft Point	velocity, fps:	2320	2046	1794	1563	1350
	energy, ft-lb:	1493	1161	893	678	505.
	arc, inches:		0	-5.2	-27.5	-70.6
Rem. 125 Pointed Soft Point	velocity, fps:	2365	2062	1783	1533	1320
	energy, ft-lb:	1552	1180	882	652	483
	arc, inches:		0	-6.7	-24.5	
Win. 123 Soft Point	velocity, fps:	2365	2033	1731	1465	1248
	energy, ft-lb:	1527	1129	818	586	425
	arc, inches:		+3.8	0	-15.4	-46.3

.30 CARBINE

CARTRIDGE BULLET	RANGE, YARDS:	0	100	200	300	400
Federal 110 Hi-Shok RN	velocity, fps:	1990	1570	1240	1040	920
	energy, ft-lb:	965	600	375	260	210
	arc, inches:		0	-12.8	-46.9	
Federal 110 FMJ	velocity, fps:	1990	1570	1240	1040	920
	energy, ft-lb:	965	600	375	260	210
	arc, inches:		0	-12.8	-46.9	
Magtech 110 FMC	velocity, fps:	1990	1654			
	energy, ft-lb:	965	668			
	arc, inches:		0			
PMC 110 FMJ	(and RNSP)velocity, fps:	1927	1548	1248		
	energy, ft-lb:	906	585	380		
	arc, inches:		0	-14.2		
Rem. 110 Soft Point	velocity, fps:	1990	1567	1236	1035	923
	energy, ft-lb:	967	600	373	262	208
	arc, inches:		0	-12.9	-48.6	
Win. 110 Hollow Soft Point	velocity, fps:	1990	1567	1236	1035	923
	energy, ft-lb:	967	600	373	262	208
	arc, inches:		0	-13.5	-49.9	

.30-30 WINCHESTER

CARTRIDGE BULLET	RANGE, YARDS:	0	100	200	300	400
Federal 125 Hi-Shok HP	velocity, fps:	2570	2090	1660	1320	1080
	energy, ft-lb:	1830	1210	770	480	320
	arc, inches:		+3.3	0	-16.0	-50.9
Federal 150 Hi-Shok FN	velocity, fps:	2390	2020	1680	1400	1180
	energy, ft-lb:	1900	1355	945	650	460
	arc, inches:		+3.6	0	-15.9	-49.1
Federal 170 Hi-Shok RN	velocity, fps:	2200	1900	1620	1380	1190
	energy, ft-lb:	1830	1355	990	720	535
	arc, inches:		+4.1	0	-17.4	-52.4
Federal 170 Sierra Pro-Hunt.	velocity, fps:	2200	1820	1500	1240	1060
	energy, ft-lb:	1830	1255	845	575	425
	arc, inches:		+4.5	0	-20.0	-63.5
Federal 170 Nosler Partition	velocity, fps:	2200	1900	1620	1380	1190
	energy, ft-lb:	1830	1355	990	720	535
	arc, inches:		+4.1	0	-17.4	-52.4
Hornady 150 Round Nose	velocity, fps:	2390	1973	1605	1303	1095.
	energy, ft-lb:	1902	1296	858	565	399
	arc, inches:		0	-8.2	-30.0	
Hornady 170 Flat Point	velocity, fps:	2200	1895	1619	1381	1191
	energy, ft-lb:	1827	1355	989	720	535
	arc, inches:		0	-8.9	-31.1	
Norma 150 Soft Point	velocity, fps:	2329	2008	1716	1459	
	energy, ft-lb:	1807	1344	981	709	
	arc, inches:		+3.6	0	-15.5	
PMC 150 Starfire HP	velocity, fps:	2100	1769	1478		
	energy, ft-lb:	1469	1042	728		
	arc, inches:		0	-10.8		
PMC 150 Flat Nose	velocity, fps:	2300	1943	1627		
	energy, ft-lb:	1762	1257	881		
	arc, inches:		0	-7.8		
PMC 170 Flat Nose	velocity, fps:	2150	1840	1566		
	energy, ft-lb:	1745	1277	926		
	arc, inches:		0	-8.9		
Rem. 55 PSP (sabot) "Accelerator"	velocity, fps:	3400	2693	2085	1570	1187
	energy, ft-lb:	1412	886	521	301	172
	arc, inches:		+1.7	0	-9.9	-34.3
Rem. 150 SP Core-Lokt	velocity, fps:	2390	1973	1605	1303	1095
	energy, ft-lb:	1902	1296	858	565	399
	arc, inches:		0	-7.6	-28.8	
Rem. 170 SP Core-Lokt	velocity, fps:	2200	1895	1619	1381	1191
	energy, ft-lb:	1827	1355	989	720	535
	arc, inches:		0	-8.3	-29.9	

BALLISTICS

CARTRIDGE BULLET	RANGE, YARDS:	0	100	200	300	400
Rem. 170 HP Core-Lokt	velocity, fps:	2200	1895	1619	1381	1191.
	energy, ft-lb:	1827	1355	989	720	535
	arc, inches:		0	-8.3	-29.9	
Speer 150 Flat Nose	velocity, fps:	2370	2067	1788	1538	
	energy, ft-lb:	1870	1423	1065	788	
	arc, inches:		+3.3	0	-14.4	-43.7
Win. 150 Hollow Point	velocity, fps:	2390	2018	1684	1398	1177
	energy, ft-lb:	1902	1356	944	651	461
	arc, inches:		0	-7.7	-27.9	
Win. 150 Power-Point	velocity, fps:	2390	2018	1684	1398	1177
	energy, ft-lb:	1902	1356	944	651	461
	arc, inches:		0	-7.7	-27.9	
Win. 150 Silvertip	velocity, fps:	2390	2018	1684	1398	1177
	energy, ft-lb:	1902	1356	944	651	461
	arc, inches:		0	-7.7	-27.9	
Win. 150 Power-Point Plus	velocity, fps:	2480	2095	1747	1446	1209
	energy, ft-lb:	2049	1462	1017	697	487
	arc, inches:		0	-6.5	-24.5	
Win. 170 Power-Point	velocity, fps:	2200	1895	1619	1381	1191
	energy, ft-lb:	1827	1355	989	720	535.
	arc, inches:		0	-8.9	-31.1	
Win. 170 Silvertip	velocity, fps:	2200	1895	1619	1381	1191
	energy, ft-lb:	1827	1355	989	720	535
	arc, inches:		0	-8.9	-31.1	

.300 SAVAGE

CARTRIDGE BULLET	RANGE, YARDS:	0	100	200	300	400
Federal 150 Hi-Shok	velocity, fps:	2630	2350	2100	1850	1630
	energy, ft-lb:	2305	1845	1460	1145	885
	arc, inches:		+2.4	0	-10.4	-30.9
Federal 180 Hi-Shok	velocity, fps:	2350	2140	1940	1750	1570
	energy, ft-lb:	2205	1825	1495	1215	985
	arc, inches:		+3.1	0	-12.4	-36.1
Rem. 150 PSP Core-Lokt	velocity, fps:	2630	2354	2095	1853	1631
	energy, ft-lb:	2303	1845	1462	1143	806.
	arc, inches:		+2.4	0	-10.4	-30.9
Rem. 180 SP Core-Lokt	velocity, fps:	2350	2025	1728	1467	1252
	energy, ft-lb:	2207	1639	1193	860	626
	arc, inches:		0	-7.1	-25.9	
Win. 150 Power-Point	velocity, fps:	2630	2311	2015	1743	1500
	energy, ft-lb:	2303	1779	1352	1012	749
	arc, inches:		+2.8	0	-11.5	-34.4

.307 WINCHESTER

CARTRIDGE BULLET	RANGE, YARDS:	0	100	200	300	400
Win. 180 Power-Point	velocity, fps:	2510	2179	1874	1599	1362
	energy, ft-lb:	2519	1898	1404	1022	742
	arc, inches:		+1.5	-3.6	-18.6	-47.1

.30-40 KRAG

CARTRIDGE BULLET	RANGE, YARDS:	0	100	200	300	400
Rem. 180 PSP Core-Lokt	velocity, fps:	2430	2213	2007	1813	1632.
	energy, ft-lb:	2360	1957	1610	1314	1064
	arc, inches, s:		0	-5.6	-18.6	
Win. 180 Power-Point	velocity, fps:	2430	2099	1795	1525	1298
	energy, ft-lb:	2360	1761	1288	929	673
	arc, inches, s:		0	-7.1	-25.0	

7.62x54R RUSSIAN

CARTRIDGE BULLET	RANGE, YARDS:	0	100	200	300	400
Norma 150 Soft Point	velocity, fps:	2953	2622	2314	2028	
	energy, ft-lb:	2905	2291	1784	1370	.
	arc, inches:		+1.8	0	-8.3	
Norma 180 Alaska	velocity, fps:	2575	2362	2159	1967	
	energy, ft-lb:	2651	2231	1864	1546	
	arc, inches:		+2.9	0	-12.9	

CARTRIDGE BULLET	RANGE, YARDS:	0	100	200	300	400

.308 WINCHESTER

CARTRIDGE BULLET		0	100	200	300	400
Black Hills 150 Nosler B. Tip	velocity, fps:	2800				
	energy, ft-lb:	2611				
	arc, inches:					
Black Hills 165 Nosler B. Tip (and SP)	velocity, fps:	2650				
	energy, ft-lb:	2573				
	arc, inches:					
Black Hills 168 Barnes X (and Match)	velocity, fps:	2650				
	energy, ft-lb:	2620				
	arc, inches:					
Black Hills 175 Match	velocity, fps:	2600				
	energy, ft-lb:	2657				
	arc, inches:					
Black Hills 180 AccuBond	velocity, fps:	2600				
	energy, ft-lb:	2701				
	arc, inches:					
Federal 150 Hi-Shok	velocity, fps:	2820	2530	2260	2010	1770
	energy, ft-lb:	2650	2140	1705	1345	1050
	arc, inches:		+2.0	0	-8.8	-26.3
Federal 150 Nosler Bal. Tip.	velocity, fps:	2820	2610	2410	2220	2040
	energy, ft-lb:	2650	2270	1935	1640	1380
	arc, inches:		+1.8	0	-7.8	-22.7
Federal 150 FMJ boat-tail	velocity, fps:	2820	2620	2430	2250	2070
	energy, ft-lb:	2650	2285	1965	1680	1430
	arc, inches:		+1.8	0	-7.7	-22.4
Federal 150 Barnes XLC	velocity, fps:	2820	2610	2400	2210	2030
	energy, ft-lb:	2650	2265	1925	1630	1370
	arc, inches:		+1.8	0	-7.8	-22.9
Federal 155 Sierra MatchKg. BTHP	velocity, fps:	2950	2740	2540	2350	2170
	energy, ft-lb:	2995	2585	2225	1905	1620
	arc, inches:		+13.2	+23.3	+28.1	+26.5
Federal 165 Sierra GameKing BTSP	velocity, fps:	2700	2520	2330	2160	1990
	energy, ft-lb:	2670	2310	1990	1700	1450
	arc, inches:		+2.0	0	-8.4	-24.3
Federal 165 Trophy Bonded	velocity, fps:	2700	2440	2200	1970	1760
	energy, ft-lb:	2670	2185	1775	1425	1135
	arc, inches:		+2.2	0	-9.4	-27.7
Federal 165 Tr. Bonded HE	velocity, fps:	2870	2600	2350	2120	1890
	energy, ft-lb:	3020	2485	2030	1640	1310
	arc, inches:		+1.8	0	-8.2	-24.0
Federal 168 Sierra MatchKg. BTHP	velocity, fps:	2600	2410	2230	2060	1890
	energy, ft-lb:	2520	2170	1855	1580	1340.
	arc, inches:		+17.7	+31.0	+37.2	+35.4
Federal 180 Hi-Shok	velocity, fps:	2620	2390	2180	1970	1780
	energy, ft-lb:	2745	2290	1895	1555	1270
	arc, inches:		+2.3	0	-9.7	-28.3
Federal 180 Sierra Pro-Hunt.	velocity, fps:	2620	2410	2200	2010	1820
	energy, ft-lb:	2745	2315	1940	1610	1330
	arc, inches:		+2.3	0	-9.3	-27.1
Federal 180 Nosler Partition	velocity, fps:	2620	2430	2240	2060	1890
	energy, ft-lb:	2745	2355	2005	1700	1430.
	arc, inches:		+2.2	0	-9.2	-26.5
Federal 180 Nosler Part. HE	velocity, fps:	2740	2550	2370	2200	2030
	energy, ft-lb:	3000	2600	2245	1925	1645
	arc, inches:		+1.9	0	-8.2	-23.5
Hornady 110 TAP-FPD	velocity, fps:	3165	2830	2519	2228	1957
	energy, ft-lb:	2446	1956	1649	1212	935
	arc, inches:		+1.4	0	-6.9	-20.9
Hornady 110 Urban Tactical	velocity, fps:	3170	2825	2504	2206	1937
	energy, ft-lb:	2454	1950	1532	1189	916
	arc, inches:		+1.5	0	-7.2	-21.2

Centerfire Rifle Ballistics

.308 WINCHESTER TO .308 WINCHESTER

CARTRIDGE BULLET	RANGE, YARDS:	0	100	200	300	400
Hornady 150 SP boat-tail	velocity, fps:	2820	2560	2315	2084	1866
	energy, ft-lb:	2648	2183	1785	1447	1160
	arc, inches:		+2.0	0	-8.5	-25.2
Hornady 150 SST	velocity, fps:	2820	2593	2378	2174	1984
(or Interbond)	energy, ft-lb:	2648	2240	1884	1574	1311
	arc, inches:		+1.9	0	-8.1	-22.9
Hornady 150 SST LM	velocity, fps:	3000	2765	2541	2328	2127
(or Interbond)	energy, ft-lb:	2997	2545	2150	1805	1506.
	arc, inches:		+1.5	0	-7.1	-20.6
Hornady 150 SP LM	velocity, fps:	2980	2703	2442	2195	1964
	energy, ft-lb:	2959	2433	1986	1606	1285
	arc, inches:		+1.6	0	-7.5	-22.2
Hornady 155 A-Max	velocity, fps:	2815	2610	2415	2229	2051
	energy, ft-lb:	2727	2345	2007	1709	1448
	arc, inches:		+1.9	0	-7.9	-22.6
Hornady 155 TAP-FPD	velocity, fps:	2785	2577	2379	2189	2008
	energy, ft-lb:	2669	2285	1947	1649	1387
	arc, inches:		+1.9	0	-8.0	-23.3
Hornady 165 SP boat-tail	velocity, fps:	2700	2496	2301	2115	1937
	energy, ft-lb:	2670	2283	1940	1639	1375
	arc, inches:		+2.0	0	-8.7	-25.2
Hornady 165 SPBT LM	velocity, fps:	2870	2658	2456	2283	2078
	energy, ft-lb:	3019	2589	2211	1877	1583
	arc, inches:		+1.7	0	-7.5	-21.8
Hornady 165 SST LM	velocity, fps:	2880	2672	2474	2284	2103
(or Interbond)	energy, ft-lb:	3038	2616	2242	1911	1620
	arc, inches:		+1.6	0	-7.3	-21.2
Hornady 168 BTHP Match	velocity, fps:	2700	2524	2354	2191	2035.
	energy, ft-lb:	2720	2377	2068	1791	1545
	arc, inches:		+2.0	0	-8.4	-23.9
Hornady 168 BTHP Match LM	velocity, fps:	2640	2630	2429	2238	2056
	energy, ft-lb:	3008	2579	2201	1868	1577
	arc, inches:		+1.8	0	-7.8	-22.4
Hornady 168 A-Max Match	velocity, fps:	2620	2446	2280	2120	1972
	energy, ft-lb:	2560	2232	1939	1677	1450
	arc, inches:		+2.6	0	-9.2	-25.6
Hornady 168 A-Max	velocity, fps:	2700	2491	2292	2102	1921
	energy, ft-lb:	2719	2315	1959	1648	1377
	arc, inches:		+2.4	0	-9.0	-25.9
Hornady 168 TAP-FPD	velocity, fps:	2700	2513	2333	2161	1996
	energy, ft-lb:	2719	2355	2030	1742	1486
	arc, inches:		+2.0	0	-8.4	-24.3
Hornady 178 A-Max	velocity, fps:	2965	2778	2598	2425	2259
	energy, ft-lb:	3474	3049	2666	2323	2017
	arc, inches:		+1.6	0	-6.9	-19.8
Hornady 180 A-Max Match	velocity, fps:	2550	2397	2249	2106	1974
	energy, ft-lb:	2598	2295	2021	1773	1557
	arc, inches:		+2.7	0	-9.5	-26.2
Norma 150 Nosler Bal. Tip	velocity, fps:	2822	2588	2365	2154	
	energy, ft-lb:	2653	2231	1864	1545	
	arc, inches:		+1.6	0	-7.1	
Norma 150 Soft Point	velocity, fps:	2861	2537	2235	1954	
	energy, ft-lb:	2727	2144	1664	1272	
	arc, inches:		+2.0	0	-9.0	
Norma 165 TXP Swift A-Fr.	velocity, fps:	2700	2459	2231	2015	
	energy, ft-lb:	2672	2216	1824	1488	
	arc, inches:		+2.1	0	-9.1	
Norma 180 Plastic Point	velocity, fps:	2612	2365	2131	1911	
	energy, ft-lb:	2728	2235	1815	1460	
	arc, inches:		+2.4	0	-10.1	
Norma 180 Nosler Partition	velocity, fps:	2612	2414	2225	2044	
	energy, ft-lb:	2728	2330	1979	1670	
	arc, inches:		+2.2	0	-9.3	

CARTRIDGE BULLET	RANGE, YARDS:	0	100	200	300	400
Norma 180 Alaska	velocity, fps:	2612	2269	1953	1667	
	energy, ft-lb:	2728	2059	1526	1111	
	arc, inches:		+2.7	0	-11.9	
Norma 180 Vulkan	velocity, fps:	2612	2325	2056	1806	
	energy, ft-lb:	2728	2161	1690	1304	
	arc, inches:		+2.5	0	-10.8	
Norma 180 Oryx	velocity, fps:	2612	2305	2019	1755	
	energy, ft-lb:	2728	2124	1629	1232	
	arc, inches:		+2.5	0	-11.1	
Norma 200 Vulkan	velocity, fps:	2461	2215	1983	1767	
	energy, ft-lb:	2690	2179	1747	1387	
	arc, inches:		+2.8	0	-11.7	
PMC 147 FMJ boat-tail	velocity, fps:	2751	2473	2257	2052	1859
	energy, ft-lb:	2428	2037	1697	1403	1150
	arc, inches:		+2.3	0	-9.3	-27.3
PMC 150 Barnes X	velocity, fps:	2700	2504	2316	2135	1964
	energy, ft-lb:	2428	2087	1786	1518	1284
	arc, inches:		+2.0	0	-8.6	-24.7
PMC 150 Pointed Soft Point	velocity, fps:	2750	2478	2224	1987	1766
	energy, ft-lb:	2519	2045	1647	1315	1039
	arc, inches:		+2.1	0	-9.2	-27.1
PMC 150 SP boat-tail	velocity, fps:	2820	2581	2354	2139	1935
	energy, ft-lb:	2648	2218	1846	1523	1247.
	arc, inches:		+1.9	0	-8.2	-24.0
PMC 168 Barnes X	velocity, fps:	2600	2425	2256	2095	1940
	energy, ft-lb:	2476	2154	1865	1608	1379
	arc, inches:		+2.2	0	-9.0	-26.0
PMC 168 HP boat-tail	velocity, fps:	2650	2460	2278	2103	1936
	energy, ft-lb:	2619	2257	1935	1649	1399
	arc, inches:		+2.1	0	-8.8	-25.6
PMC 168 Pointed Soft Point	velocity, fps:	2559	2354	2160	1976	1803
	energy, ft-lb:	2443	2067	1740	1457	1212
	arc, inches:		+2.4	0	-9.9	-28.7
PMC 168 Pointed Soft Point	velocity, fps:	2600	2404	2216	2037	1866
	energy, ft-lb:	2476	2064	1709	1403	1142
	arc, inches:		+2.3	0	-9.8	-28.7
PMC 180 Pointed Soft Point	velocity, fps:	2550	2335	2132	1940	1760
	energy, ft-lb:	2599	2179	1816	1504	1238.
	arc, inches:		+2.5	0	-10.1	-29.5
PMC 180 SP boat-tail	velocity, fps:	2620	2446	2278	2117	1962
	energy, ft-lb:	2743	2391	2074	1790	1538
	arc, inches:		+2.2	0	-8.9	-25.4
Rem. 125 PSP C-L MR	velocity, fps:	2660	2348	2057	1788	1546
	energy, ft-lb:	1964	1529	1174	887	663
	arc, inches:		+1.1	-2.7	-14.3	-35.8
Rem. 150 PSP Core-Lokt	velocity, fps:	2820	2533	2263	2009	1774
	energy, ft-lb:	2648	2137	1705	1344	1048
	arc, inches:		+2.0	0	-8.8	-26.2
Rem. 150 PSP C-L Ultra	velocity, fps:	2620	2404	2198	2002	1818
	energy, ft-lb:	2743	2309	1930	1601	1320
	arc, inches:		+2.3	0	-9.5	-26.4
Rem. 150 Swift Scirocco	velocity, fps:	2820	2611	2410	2219	2037
	energy, ft-lb:	2648	2269	1935	1640	1381
	arc, inches:		+1.8	0	-7.8	-22.7
Rem. 165 AccuTip	velocity, fps:	2700	2501	2311	2129	1958.
	energy, ft-lb:	2670	2292	1957	1861	1401.
	arc, inches:		+2.0	0	-8.6	-24.8
Rem. 165 PSP boat-tail	velocity, fps:	2700	2497	2303	2117	1941.
	energy, ft-lb:	2670	2284	1942	1642	1379
	arc, inches:		+2.0	0	-8.6	-25.0
Rem. 165 Nosler Bal. Tip	velocity, fps:	2700	2613	2333	2161	1996
	energy, ft-lb:	2672	2314	1995	1711	1460
	arc, inches:		+2.0	0	-8.4	-24.3

BALLISTICS

.308 WINCHESTER TO .30-06 SPRINGFIELD

CARTRIDGE BULLET	RANGE, YARDS:	0	100	200	300	400
Rem. 165 Swift Scirocco	velocity, fps:	2700	2513	2233	2161	1996
	energy, fps:	2670	2313	1994	1711	1459
	arc, inches:		+2.0	0	-8.4	-24.3
Rem. 168 HPBT Match	velocity, fps:	2680	2493	2314	2143	1979
	energy, ft-lb:	2678	2318	1998	1713	1460
	arc, inches:		+2.1	0	-8.6	-24.7
Rem. 180 SP Core-Lokt	velocity, fps:	2620	2274	1955	1666	1414
	energy, ft-lb:	2743	2066	1527	1109	799
	arc, inches:		+2.6	0	-11.8	-36.3
Rem. 180 PSP Core-Lokt	velocity, fps:	2620	2393	2178	1974	1782
	energy, ft-lb:	2743	2288	1896	1557	1269
	arc, inches:		+2.3	0	-9.7	-28.3
Rem. 180 Nosler Partition	velocity, fps:	2620	2436	2259	2089	1927
	energy, ft-lb:	2743	2371	2039	1774	1485
	arc, inches:		+2.2	0	-9.0	-26.0
Speer 150 Grand Slam	velocity, fps:	2900	2599	2317	2053	
	energy, ft-lb:	2800	2249	1788	1404	
	arc, inches:		+2.1	0	-8.6	-24.8
Speer 165 Grand Slam	velocity, fps:	2700	2475	2261	2057	
	energy, ft-lb:	2670	2243	1872	1550	
	arc, inches:		+2.1	0	-8.9	-25.9
Speer 180 Grand Slam	velocity, fps:	2620	2420	2229	2046	
	energy, ft-lb:	2743	2340	1985	1674	
	arc, inches:		+2.2	0	-9.2	-26.6
Win. 150 Power-Point	velocity, fps:	2820	2488	2179	1893	1633
	energy, ft-lb:	2648	2061	1581	1193	888
	arc, inches:		+2.4	0	-9.8	-29.3
Win. 150 Power-Point Plus	velocity, fps:	2900	2558	2241	1946	1678
	energy, ft-lb:	2802	2180	1672	1262	938
	arc, inches:		+1.9	0	-8.9	-27.0
Win. 150 Partition Gold	velocity, fps:	2900	2645	2405	2177	1962
	energy, ft-lb:	2802	2332	1927	1579	1282
	arc, inches:		+1.7	0	-7.8	-22.9
Win. 150 Ballistic Silvertip	velocity, fps:	2810	2601	2401	2211	2028
	energy, ft-lb:	2629	2253	1920	1627	1370
	arc, inches:		+1.8	0	-7.8	-22.8
Win. 150 Fail Safe	velocity, fps:	2820	2533	2263	2010	1775
	energy, ft-lb:	2649	2137	1706	1346	1049
	arc, inches:		+2.0	0	-8.8	-26.2
Win. 168 Ballistic Silvertip	velocity, fps:	2670	2484	2306	2134	1971
	energy, ft-lb:	2659	2301	1983	1699	1449
	arc, inches:		+2.1	0	-8.6	-24.8
Win. 168 HP boat-tail Match	velocity, fps:	2680	2485	2297	2118	1948
	energy, ft-lb:	2680	2303	1970	1674	1415
	arc, inches:		+2.1	0	-8.7	-25.1
Win. 180 Power-Point	velocity, fps:	2620	2274	1955	1666	1414
	energy, ft-lb:	2743	2066	1527	1109	799
	arc, inches:		+2.9	0	-12.1	-36.9
Win. 180 Silvertip	velocity, fps:	2620	2393	2178	1974	1782
	energy, ft-lb:	2743	2288	1896	1557	1269
	arc, inches:		+2.6	0	-9.9	-28.9

.30-06 SPRINGFIELD

CARTRIDGE BULLET	RANGE, YARDS:	0	100	200	300	400
A-Square 180 M & D-T	velocity, fps:	2700	2365	2054	1769	1524
	energy, ft-lb:	2913	2235	1687	1251	928
	arc, inches:		+2.4	0	-10.6	-32.4
A-Square 220 Monolythic Solid	velocity, fps:	2380	2108	1854	1623	1424
	energy, ft-lb:	2767	2171	1679	1287	990
	arc, inches:		+3.1	0	-13.6	-39.9
Black Hills 150 Nosler B. Tip	velocity, fps:	2900				
	energy, ft-lb:	2770				
	arc, inches:					
Black Hills 165 Nosler B. Tip	velocity, fps:	2750				
	energy, ft-lb:	2770				
	arc, inches:					
Black Hills 168 Hor. Match	velocity, fps:	2700				
	energy, ft-lb:	2718				
	arc, inches:					
Black Hills 180 Barnes X	velocity, fps:	2650				
	energy, ft-lb:	2806				
	arc, inches:					
Black Hills 180 AccuBond	velocity, ft-lb:	2700				
	energy, ft-lb:					
	arc, inches:					
Federal 125 Sierra Pro-Hunt.	velocity, fps:	3140	2780	2450	2140	1850
	energy, ft-lb:	2735	2145	1660	1270	955
	arc, inches:		+1.5	0	-7.3	-22.3
Federal 150 Hi-Shok	velocity, fps:	2910	2620	2340	2080	1840
	energy, ft-lb:	2820	2280	1825	1445	1130
	arc, inches:		+1.8	0	-8.2	-24.4
Federal 150 Sierra Pro-Hunt.	velocity, fps:	2910	2640	2380	2130	1900
	energy, ft-lb:	2820	2315	1880	1515	1205
	arc, inches:		+1.7	0	-7.9	-23.3
Federal 150 Sierra GameKing BTSP	velocity, fps:	2910	2690	2480	2270	2070
	energy, ft-lb:	2820	2420	2040	1710	1430
	arc, inches:		+1.7	0	-7.4	-21.5
Federal 150 Nosler Bal. Tip	velocity, fps:	2910	2700	2490	2300	2110
	energy, ft-lb:	2820	2420	2070	1760	1485
	arc, inches:		+1.6	0	-7.3	-21.1
Federal 150 FMJ boat-tail	velocity, fps:	2910	2710	2510	2320	2150
	energy, ft-lb:	2820	2440	2100	1800	1535
	arc, inches:		+1.6	0	-7.1	-20.8
Federal 165 Sierra Pro-Hunt.	velocity, fps:	2800	2560	2340	2130	1920
	energy, ft-lb:	2875	2410	2005	1655	1360
	arc, inches:		+1.9	0	-8.3	-24.3
Federal 165 Sierra GameKing BTSP	velocity, fps:	2800	2610	2420	2240	2070
	energy, ft-lb:	2870	2490	2150	1840	1580
	arc, inches:		+1.8	0	-7.8	-22.4
Federal 165 Sierra GameKing HE	velocity, fps:	3140	2900	2670	2450	2240
	energy, ft-lb:	3610	3075	2610	2200	1845
	arc, inches:		+1.5	0	-6.9	-20.4
Federal 165 Nosler Bal. Tip	velocity, fps:	2800	2610	2430	2250	2080
	energy, ft-lb:	2870	2495	2155	1855	1585
	arc, inches:		+1.8	0	-7.7	-22.3
Federal 165 Trophy Bonded	velocity, fps:	2800	2540	2290	2050	1830
	energy, ft-lb:	2870	2360	1915	1545	1230
	arc, inches:		+2.0	0	-8.7	-25.4
Federal 165 Tr. Bonded HE	velocity, fps:	3140	2860	2590	2340	2100
	energy, ft-lb:	3610	2990	2460	2010	1625
	arc, inches:		+1.6	0	-7.4	-21.9
Federal 168 Sierra MatchKg. BTHP	velocity, fps:	2700	2510	2320	2150	1980
	energy, ft-lb:	2720	2350	2010	1720	1460
	arc, inches:		+16.2	+28.4	+34.1	+32.3
Federal 180 Hi-Shok	velocity, fps:	2700	2470	2250	2040	1850
	energy, ft-lb:	2915	2435	2025	1665	1360
	arc, inches:		+2.1	0	-9.0	-26.4
Federal 180 Sierra Pro-Hunt. RN	velocity, fps:	2700	2350	2020	1730	1470
	energy, ft-lb:	2915	2200	1630	1190	860
	arc, inches:		+2.4	0	-11.0	-33.6
Federal 180 Nosler Partition	velocity, fps:	2700	2500	2320	2140	1970
	energy, ft-lb:	2915	2510	2150	1830	1550
	arc, inches:		+2.0	0	-8.6	-24.6
Federal 180 Nosler Part. HE	velocity, fps:	2880	2690	2500	2320	2150
	energy, ft-lb:	3315	2880	2495	2150	1845
	arc, inches:		+1.7	0	-7.2	-21.0

Centerfire Rifle Ballistics

.30-06 SPRINGFIELD TO .30-06 SPRINGFIELD

CARTRIDGE BULLET	RANGE, YARDS:	0	100	200	300	400
Federal 180 Sierra GameKing BTSP	velocity, fps:	2700	2540	2380	2220	2080
	energy, ft-lb:	2915	2570	2260	1975	1720
	arc, inches:		+1.9	0	-8.1	-23.1
Federal 180 Barnes XLC	velocity, fps:	2700	2530	2360	2200	2040.
	energy, ft-lb:	2915	2550	2220	1930	1670
	arc, inches:		+2.0	0	-8.3	-23.8
Federal 180 Trophy Bonded	velocity, fps:	2700	2460	2220	2000	1800
	energy, ft-lb:	2915	2410	1975	1605	1290
	arc, inches:		+2.2	0	-9.2	-27.0
Federal 180 Tr. Bonded HE	velocity, fps:	2880	2630	2380	2160	1940
	energy, ft-lb:	3315	2755	2270	1855	1505
	arc, inches:		+1.8	0	-8.0	-23.3
Federal 220 Sierra Pro-Hunt. RN	velocity, fps:	2410	2130	1870	1630	1420
	energy, ft-lb:	2835	2215	1705	1300	985
	arc, inches:		+3.1	0	-13.1	-39.3
Hornady 150 SP	velocity, fps:	2910	2617	2342	2083	1843
	energy, ft-lb:	2820	2281	1827	1445	1131
	arc, inches:		+2.1	0	-8.5	-25.0
Hornady 150 SP LM	velocity, fps:	3100	2815	2548	2295	2058
	energy, ft-lb:	3200	2639	2161	1755	1410
	arc, inches:		+1.4	0	-6.8	-20.3
Hornady 150 SP boat-tail	velocity, fps:	2910	2683	2467	2262	2066.
	energy, ft-lb:	2820	2397	2027	1706	1421
	arc, inches:		+2.0	0	-7.7	-22.2
Hornady 150 SST (or Interbond)	velocity, fps:	2910	2802	2599	2405	2219
	energy, ft-lb:	3330	2876	2474	2118	1803
	arc, inches:		+1.5	0	-6.6	-19.3
Hornady 150 SST LM	velocity, fps:	3100	2860	2631	2414	2208
	energy, ft-lb:	3200	2724	2306	1941	1624
	arc, inches:		+1.4	0	-6.6	-19.2
Hornady 165 SP boat-tail	velocity, fps:	2800	2591	2392	2202	2020
	energy, ft-lb:	2873	2460	2097	1777	1495
	arc, inches:		+1.8	0	-8.0	-23.3
Hornady 165 SPBT LM	velocity, fps:	3015	2790	2575	2370	2176
	energy, ft-lb:	3330	2850	2428	2058	1734
	arc, inches:		+1.6	0	-7.0	-20.1
Hornady 165 SST (or Interbond)	velocity, fps:	2800	2598	2405	2221	2046
	energy, ft-lb:	2872	2473	2119	1808	1534
	arc, inches:		+1.9	0	-8.0	-22.8
Hornady 165 SST LM	velocity, fps:	3015	2802	2599	2405	2219
	energy, ft-lb:	3330	2878	2474	2118	1803.
	arc, inches:		+1.5	0	-6.5	-19.3
Hornady 168 HPBT Match	velocity, fps:	2790	2620	2447	2280	2120.
	energy, ft-lb:	2925	2561	2234	1940	1677.
	arc, inches:		+1.7	0	-7.7	-22.2
Hornady 180 SP	velocity, fps:	2700	2469	2258	2042	1846
	energy, ft-lb:	2913	2436	2023	1666	1362
	arc, inches:		+2.4	0	-9.3	-27.0
Hornady 180 SPBT LM	velocity, fps:	2880	2676	2480	2293	2114
	energy, ft-lb:	3316	2862	2459	2102	1786
	arc, inches:		+1.7	0	-7.3	-21.3
Norma 150 Nosler Bal. Tip	velocity, fps:	2936	2713	2502	2300	
	energy, ft-lb:	2872	2453	2085	1762	
	arc, inches:		+1.6	0	-7.1	
Norma 150 Soft Point	velocity, fps:	2972	2640	2331	2043	
	energy, ft-lb:	2943	2321	1810	1390	
	arc, inches:		+1.8	0	-8.2	
Norma 180 Alaska	velocity, fps:	2700	2351	2028	1734	
	energy, ft-lb:	2914	2209	1645	1202	
	arc, inches:		+2.4	0	-11.0	
Norma 180 Nosler Partition	velocity, fps:	2700	2494	2297	2108	
	energy, ft-lb:	2914	2486	2108	1777	
	arc, inches:		+2.1	0	-8.7	
Norma 180 Plastic Point	velocity, fps:	2700	2455	2222	2003	
	energy, ft-lb:	2914	2409	1974	1603	
	arc, inches:		+2.1	0	-9.2	
Norma 180 Vulkan	velocity, fps:	2700	2416	2150	1901	
	energy, ft-lb:	2914	2334	1848	1445	
	arc, inches:		+2.2	0	-9.8	
Norma 180 Oryx	velocity, fps:	2700	2387	2095	1825	
	energy, ft-lb:	2914	2278	1755	1332	
	arc, inches:		+2.3	0	-10.2	
Norma 180 TXP Swift A-Fr.	velocity, fps:	2700	2479	2268	2067	
	energy, ft-lb:	2914	2456	2056	1708	
	arc, inches:		+2.0	0	-8.8	
Norma 180 AccuBond	velocity, fps:	2674	2499	2331	2169	
	energy, ft-lb:	2859	2497	2172	1881	
	arc, inches:		+2.0	0	-8.5	
Norma 200 Vulkan	velocity, fps:	2641	2385	2143	1916	
	energy, ft-lb:	3098	2527	2040	1631	
	arc, inches:		+2.3	0	-9.9	
Norma 200 Oryx	velocity, fps:	2625	2362	2115	1883	
	energy, ft-lb:	3061	2479	1987	1575	
	arc, inches:		+2.3	0	-10.1	
PMC 150 X-Bullet	velocity, fps:	2750	2552	2361	2179	2005
	energy, ft-lb:	2518	2168	1857	1582	1339
	arc, inches:		+2.0	0	-8.2	-23.7
PMC 150 Pointed Soft Point	velocity, fps:	2773	2542	2322	2113	1916
	energy, ft-lb:	2560	2152	1796	1487	1222.
	arc, inches:		+1.9	0	-8.4	-24.6
PMC 150 SP boat-tail	velocity, fps:	2900	2657	2427	2208	2000
	energy, ft-lb:	2801	2351	1961	1623	1332
	arc, inches:		+1.7	0	-7.7	-22.5
PMC 150 FMJ	velocity, fps:	2773	2542	2322	2113	1916
	energy, ft-lb:	2560	2152	1796	1487	1222
	arc, inches:		+1.9	0	-8.4	-24.6
PMC 168 Barnes X	velocity, fps:	2750	2569	2395	2228	2067
	energy, ft-lb:	2770	2418	2101	1818	1565
	arc, inches:		+1.9	0	-8.0	-23.0
PMC 180 Barnes X	velocity, fps:	2650	2487	2331	2179	2034
	energy, ft-lb:	2806	2472	2171	1898	1652
	arc, inches:		+2.1	0	-8.5	-24.3
PMC 180 Pointed Soft Point	velocity, fps:	2650	2430	2221	2024	1839
	energy, ft-lb:	2807	2359	1972	1638	1351
	arc, inches:		+2.2	0	-9.3	-27.0
PMC 180 SP boat-tail	velocity, fps:	2700	2523	2352	2188	2030
	energy, ft-lb:	2913	2543	2210	1913	1646
	arc, inches:		+2.0	0	-8.3	-23.9
PMC 180 HPBT Match	velocity, fps:	2800	2622	2456	2302	2158
	energy, ft-lb:	3133	2747	2411	2118	1861
	arc, inches:		+1.8	0	-7.6	-21.7
Rem. 55 PSP (sabot) "Accelerator"	velocity, fps:	4080	3484	2964	2499	2080
	energy, ft-lb:	2033	1482	1073	763	528.
	arc, inches:		+1.4	+1.4	-2.6	-12.2
Rem. 125 PSP C-L MR	velocity, fps:	2660	2335	2034	1757	1509
	energy, ft-lb:	1964	1513	1148	856	632
	arc, inches:		+1.1	-3.0	-15.5	-37.4
Rem. 125 Pointed Soft Point	velocity, fps:	3140	2780	2447	2138	1853
	energy, ft-lb:	2736	2145	1662	1269	953.
	arc, inches:		+1.5	0	-7.4	-22.4
Rem. 150 AccuTip	velocity, fps:	2910	2686	2473	2270	2077
	energy, ft-lb:	2820	2403	2037	1716	1436
	arc, inches:		+1.8	0	-7.4	-21.5
Rem. 150 PSP Core-Lokt	velocity, fps:	2910	2617	2342	2083	1843
	energy, ft-lb:	2820	2281	1827	1445	1131
	arc, inches:		+1.8	0	-8.2	-24.4

BALLISTICS

.30-06 SPRINGFIELD TO .308 NORMA MAG.

CARTRIDGE BULLET	RANGE, YARDS:	0	100	200	300	400
Rem. 150 Bronze Point	velocity, fps:	2910	2656	2416	2189	1974
	energy, ft-lb:	2820	2349	1944	1596	1298
	arc, inches:		+1.7	0	-7.7	-22.7
Rem. 150 Nosler Bal. Tip	velocity, fps:	2910	2696	2492	2298	2112.
	energy, ft-lb:	2821	2422	2070	1769	1485
	arc, inches:		+1.6	0	-7.3	-21.1
Rem. 150 Swift Scirocco	velocity, fps:	2910	2696	2492	2298	2111
	energy, ft-lb:	2820	2421	2069	1758	1485
	arc, inches:		+1.6	0	-7.3	-21.1
Rem. 165 AccuTip	velocity, fps:	2800	2597	2403	2217	2039
	energy, ft-lb:	2872	2470	2115	1800	1523
	arc, inches:		+1.8	0	-7.9	-22.8
Rem. 165 PSP Core-Lokt	velocity, fps:	2800	2534	2283	2047	1825.
	energy, ft-lb:	2872	2352	1909	1534	1220
	arc, inches:		+2.0	0	-8.7	-25.9
Rem. 165 PSP boat-tail	velocity, fps:	2800	2592	2394	2204	2023
	energy, ft-lb:	2872	2462	2100	1780	1500
	arc, inches:		+1.8	0	-7.9	-23.0
Rem. 165 Nosler Bal. Tip	velocity, fps:	2800	2609	2426	2249	2080.
	energy, ft-lb:	2873	2494	2155	1854	1588
	arc, inches:		+1.8	0	-7.7	-22.3
Rem. 168 PSP C-L Ultra	velocity, fps:	2800	2546	2306	2079	1866
	energy, ft-lb:	2924	2418	1984	1613	1299
	arc, inches:		+1.9	0	-8.5	-25.1
Rem. 180 SP Core-Lokt	velocity, fps:	2700	2348	2023	1727	1466
	energy, ft-lb:	2913	2203	1635	1192	859
	arc, inches:		+2.4	0	-11.0	-33.8
Rem. 180 PSP Core-Lokt	velocity, fps:	2700	2469	2250	2042	1846
	energy, ft-lb:	2913	2436	2023	1666	1362
	arc, inches:		+2.1	0	-9.0	-26.3
Rem. 180 PSP C-L Ultra	velocity, fps:	2700	2480	2270	2070	1882
	energy, ft-lb:	2913	2457	2059	1713	1415
	arc, inches:		+2.1	0	-8.9	-25.8
Rem. 180 Bronze Point	velocity, fps:	2700	2485	2280	2084	1899.
	energy, ft-lb:	2913	2468	2077	1736	1441
	arc, inches:		+2.1	0	-8.8	-25.5
Rem. 180 Swift A-Frame	velocity, fps:	2700	2465	2243	2032	1833
	energy, ft-lb:	2913	2429	2010	1650	1343
	arc, inches:		+2.1	0	-9.1	-26.6
Rem. 180 Nosler Partition	velocity, fps:	2700	2512	2332	2160	1995
	energy, ft-lb:	2913	2522	2174	1864	1590
	arc, inches:		+2.0	0	-8.4	-24.3
Rem. 220 SP Core-Lokt	velocity, fps:	2410	2130	1870	1632	1422
	energy, ft-lb:	2837	2216	1708	1301	988
	arc, inches, s:		0	-6.2	-22.4	
Speer 150 Grand Slam	velocity, fps:	2975	2669	2383	2114	
	energy, ft-lb:	2947	2372	1891	1489	
	arc, inches:		+2.0	0	-8.1	-24.1
Speer 165 Grand Slam	velocity, fps:	2790	2560	2342	2134	
	energy, ft-lb:	2851	2401	2009	1669	
	arc, inches:		+1.9	0	-8.3	-24.1
Speer 180 Grand Slam	velocity, fps:	2690	2487	2293	2108	
	energy, ft-lb:	2892	2472	2101	1775	
	arc, inches:		+2.1	0	-8.8	-25.1
Win. 125 Pointed Soft Point	velocity, fps:	3140	2780	2447	2138	1853
	energy, ft-lb:	2736	2145	1662	1269	953
	arc, inches:		+1.8	0	-7.7	-23.0
Win. 150 Power-Point	velocity, fps:	2920	2580	2265	1972	1704
	energy, ft-lb:	2839	2217	1708	1295	967
	arc, inches:		+2.2	0	-9.0	-27.0
Win. 150 Power-Point Plus	velocity, fps:	3050	2685	2352	2043	1760
	energy, ft-lb:	3089	2402	1843	1391	1032
	arc, inches:		+1.7	0	-8.0	-24.3

CARTRIDGE BULLET	RANGE, YARDS:	0	100	200	300	400
Win. 150 Silvertip	velocity, fps:	2910	2617	2342	2083	1843
	energy, ft-lb:	2820	2281	1827	1445	1131
	arc, inches:		+2.1	0	-8.5	-25.0
Win. 150 Partition Gold	velocity, fps:	2960	2705	2464	2235	2019
	energy, ft-lb:	2919	2437	2022	1664	1358.
	arc, inches:		+1.6	0	-7.4	-21.7
Win. 150 Ballistic Silvertip	velocity, fps:	2900	2687	2483	2289	2103
	energy, ft-lb:	2801	2404	2054	1745	1473
	arc, inches:		+1.7	0	-7.3	-21.2
Win. 150 Fail Safe	velocity, fps:	2920	2625	2349	2089	1848
	energy, ft-lb:	2841	2296	1838	1455	1137
	arc, inches:		+1.8	0	-8.1	-24.3
Win. 165 Pointed Soft Point	velocity, fps:	2800	2573	2357	2151	1956
	energy, ft-lb:	2873	2426	2036	1696	1402
	arc, inches:		+2.2	0	-8.4	-24.4
Win. 165 Fail Safe	velocity, fps:	2800	2540	2295	2063	1846
	energy, ft-lb:	2873	2365	1930	1560	1249
	arc, inches:		+2.0	0	-8.6	-25.3
Win. 168 Ballistic Silvertip	velocity, fps:	2790	2599	2416	2240	2072
	energy, ft-lb:	2903	2520	2177	1872	1601
	arc, inches:		+1.8	0	-7.8	-22.5
Win. 180 Ballistic Silvertip	velocity, fps:	2750	2572	2402	2237	2080
	energy, ft-lb:	3022	2644	2305	2001	1728
	arc, inches:		+1.9	0	-7.9	-22.8
Win. 180 Power-Point	velocity, fps:	2700	2348	2023	1727	1466
	energy, ft-lb:	2913	2203	1635	1192	859
	arc, inches:		+2.7	0	-11.3	-34.4
Win. 180 Power-Point Plus	velocity, fps:	2770	2563	2366	2177	1997
	energy, ft-lb:	3068	2627	2237	1894	1594
	arc, inches:		+1.9	0	-8.1	-23.6
Win. 180 Silvertip	velocity, fps:	2700	2469	2250	2042	1846
	energy, ft-lb:	2913	2436	2023	1666	1362
	arc, inches:		+2.4	0	-9.3	-27.0
Win. 180 AccuBond	velocity, fps:	2750	2573	2403	2239	2082
	energy, ft-lb:	3022	2646	2308	2004	1732
	arc, inches:		+1.9	0	-7.9	-22.8
Win. 180 Partition Gold	velocity, fps:	2790	2581	2382	2192	2010
	energy, ft-lb:	3112	2664	2269	1920	1615
	arc, inches:		+1.9	0	-8.0	-23.2
Win. 180 Fail Safe	velocity, fps:	2700	2486	2283	2089	1904
	energy, ft-lb:	2914	2472	2083	1744	1450
	arc, inches:		+2.1	0	-8.7	-25.5

.300 H&H MAG.

CARTRIDGE BULLET	RANGE, YARDS:	0	100	200	300	400
Federal 180 Nosler Partition	velocity, fps:	2880	2620	2380	2150	1930
	energy, ft-lb:	3315	2750	2260	1840	1480
	arc, inches:		+1.8	0	-8.0	-23.4
Win. 180 Fail Safe	velocity, fps:	2880	2628	2390	2165	1952
	energy, ft-lb:	3316	2762	2284	1873	1523
	arc, inches:		+1.8	0	-7.9	-23.2

.308 NORMA MAG.

CARTRIDGE BULLET	RANGE, YARDS:	0	100	200	300	400
Norma 180 TXP Swift A-Fr.	velocity, fps:	2953	2704	2469	2245	
	energy, ft-lb:	3486	2924	2437	2016	
	arc, inches:		+1.6	0	-7.3	
Norma 180 Oryx	velocity, fps:	2953	2630	2330	2049	
	energy, ft-lb:	3486	2766	2170	1679	
	arc, inches:		+1.8	0	-8.2	
Norma 200 Vulkan	velocity, fps:	2903	2624	2361	2114	
	energy, ft-lb:	3744	3058	2476	1985	
	arc, inches:	0	+1.8	0	-8.0	

Centerfire Rifle Ballistics

.300 WINCHESTER MAGNUM TO .300 WINCHESTER MAGNUM

.300 WINCHESTER MAG.

CARTRIDGE BULLET	RANGE, YARDS:	0	100	200	300	400
A-Square 180 Dead Tough	velocity, fps:	3120	2756	2420	2108	1820
	energy, ft-lb:	3890	3035	2340	1776	1324
	arc, inches:		+1.6	0	-7.6	-22.9
Black Hills 180 Nos. Bal. Tip	velocity, fps:	3100				
	energy, ft-lb:	3498				
	arc, inches:					
Black Hills 180 Barnes X	velocity, fps:	2950				
	energy, ft-lb:	3498				
	arc, inches:					
Black Hills 180 AccuBond	velocity, fps:	3000				
	energy, ft-lb:	3597				
	arc, inches:					
Black Hills 190 Match	velocity, fps:	2950				
	energy, ft-lb:	3672				
	arc, inches:					
Federal 150 Sierra Pro Hunt.	velocity, fps:	3280	3030	2800	2570	2360.
	energy, ft-lb:	3570	3055	2600	2205	1860
	arc, inches:		+1.1	0	-5.6	-16.4
Federal 150 Trophy Bonded	velocity, fps:	3280	2980	2700	2430	2190
	energy, ft-lb:	3570	2450	2420	1970	1590
	arc, inches:		+1.2	0	-6.0	-17.9
Federal 180 Sierra Pro Hunt.	velocity, fps:	2960	2750	2540	2340	2160
	energy, ft-lb:	3500	3010	2580	2195	1860
	arc, inches:		+1.6	0	-7.0	-20.3
Federal 180 Barnes XLC	velocity, fps:	2960	2780	2600	2430	2260
	energy, ft-lb:	3500	3080	2700	2355	2050
	arc, inches:		+1.5	0	-6.6	-19.2
Federal 180 Trophy Bonded	velocity, fps:	2960	2700	2460	2220	2000
	energy, ft-lb:	3500	2915	2410	1975	1605
	arc, inches:		+1.6	0	-7.4	-21.9
Federal 180 Tr. Bonded HE	velocity, fps:	3100	2830	2580	2340	2110
	energy, ft-lb:	3840	3205	2660	2190	1790
	arc, inches:		+1.4	0	-6.6	-19.7
Federal 180 Nosler Partition	velocity, fps:	2960	2700	2450	2210	1990
	energy, ft-lb:	3500	2905	2395	1955	1585
	arc, inches:		+1.6	0	-7.5	-22.1
Federal 190 Sierra MatchKg. BTHP	velocity, fps:	2900	2730	2560	2400	2240
	energy, ft-lb:	3550	3135	2760	2420	2115
	arc, inches:		+12.9	+22.5	+26.9	+25.1
Federal 200 Sierra GameKing BTSP	velocity, fps:	2830	2680	2530	2380	2240
	energy, ft-lb:	3560	3180	2830	2520	2230
	arc, inches:		+1.7	0	-7.1	-20.4
Federal 200 Nosler Part. HE	velocity, fps:	2930	2740	2550	2370	2200
	energy, ft-lb:	3810	3325	2885	2495	2145
	arc, inches:		+1.6	0	-6.9	-20.1
Federal 200 Trophy Bonded	velocity, fps:	2800	2570	2350	2150	1950
	energy, ft-lb:	3480	2935	2460	2050	1690
	arc, inches:		+1.9	0	-8.2	-23.9
Hornady 150 SP boat-tail	velocity, fps:	3275	2988	2718	2464	2224
	energy, ft-lb:	3573	2974	2461	2023	1648
	arc, inches:		+1.2	0	-6.0	-17.8
Hornady 150 SST (and Interbond)	velocity, fps:	3275	3027	2791	2565	2352
	energy, ft-lb:	3572	3052	2593	2192	1842
	arc, inches:		+1.2	0	-5.8	-17.0
Hornady 165 SP boat-tail	velocity, fps:	3100	2877	2665	2462	2269.
	energy, ft-lb:	3522	3033	2603	2221	1887
	arc, inches:		+1.3	0	-6.5	-18.5
Hornady 165 SST	velocity, fps:	3100	2885	2680	2483	2296
	energy, ft-lb:	3520	3049	2630	2259	1930
	arc, inches:		+1.4	0	-6.4	-18.6
Hornady 180 SP boat-tail	velocity, fps:	2960	2745	2540	2344	2157
	energy, ft-lb:	3501	3011	2578	2196	1859
	arc, inches:		+1.9	0	-7.3	-20.9
Hornady 180 SST	velocity, fps:	2960	2764	2575	2395	2222
	energy, ft-lb:	3501	3052	2650	2292	1974
	arc, inches:		+1.6	0	-7.0	-20.1.
Hornady 180 SPBT HM	velocity, fps:	3100	2879	2668	2467	2275
	energy, ft-lb:	3840	3313	2845	2431	2068
	arc, inches:		+1.4	0	-6.4	-18.7
Hornady 190 SP boat-tail	velocity, fps:	2900	2711	2529	2355	2187
	energy, ft-lb:	3549	3101	2699	2340	2018
	arc, inches:		+1.6	0	-7.1	-20.4
Norma 150 Nosler Bal. Tip	velocity, fps:	3250	3014	2791	2578	
	energy, ft-lb:	3519	3027	2595	2215	
	arc, inches:		+1.1	0	-5.6	
Norma 150 Barnes TS	velocity, fps:	3215	2982	2761	2550	
	energy, ft-lb:	3444	2962	2539	2167	
	arc, inches:		+1.2	0	-5.8	
Norma 165 Scirocco	velocity, fps:	3117	2921	2734	2554	
	energy, ft-lb:	3561	3127	2738	2390	
	arc, inches:		+1.2	0	-5.9	
Norma 180 Soft Point	velocity, fps:	3018	2780	2555	2341	
	energy, ft-lb:	3641	3091	2610	2190	
	arc, inches:		+1.5	0	-7.0	
Norma 180 Plastic Point	velocity, fps:	3018	2755	2506	2271	
	energy, ft-lb:	3641	3034	2512	2062	
	arc, inches:		+1.6	0	-7.1	
Norma 180 TXP Swift A-Fr.	velocity, fps:	2920	2688	2467	2256	
	energy, ft-lb:	3409	2888	2432	2035	
	arc, inches:		+1.7	0	-7.4	
Norma 180 AccuBond	velocity, fps:	2953	2767	2588	2417	
	energy, ft-lb:	3486	3061	2678	2335	
	arc, inches:		+1.5	0	-6.7	
Norma 180 Oryx	velocity, fps:	2920	2600	2301	2023	
	energy, ft-lb:	3409	2702	2117	1636	
	arc, inches:		+1.8	0	-8.4	
Norma 200 Vulkan	velocity, fps:	2887	2609	2347	2100	
	energy, ft-lb:	3702	3023	2447	1960	
	arc, inches:		+1.8	0	-8.2	
Norma 200 Oryx	velocity, fps:	2789	2510	2248	2002	
	energy, ft-lb:	3455	2799	2245	1780	
	arc, inches:		+2.0	0	-8.9	
PMC 150 Barnes X	velocity, fps:	3135	2918	2712	2515	2327
	energy, ft-lb:	3273	2836	2449	2107	1803
	arc, inches:		+1.3	0	-6.1	-17.7
PMC 150 Pointed Soft Point	velocity, fps:	3150	2902	2665	2438	2222
	energy, ft-lb:	3304	2804	2364	1979	1644.
	arc, inches:		+1.3	0	-6.2	-18.3
PMC 150 SP boat-tail	velocity, fps:	3250	2987	2739	2504	2281
	energy, ft-lb:	3517	2970	2498	2088	1733
	arc, inches:		+1.2	0	-6.0	-17.4
PMC 180 Barnes X	velocity, fps:	2910	2738	2572	2412	2258
	energy, ft-lb:	3384	2995	2644	2325	2037
	arc, inches:		+1.6	0	-6.9	-19.8
PMC 180 Pointed Soft Point	velocity, fps:	2853	2643	2446	2258	2077
	energy, ft-lb:	3252	2792	2391	2037	1724
	arc, inches:		+1.7	0	-7.5	-21.9
PMC 180 SP boat-tail	velocity, fps:	2900	2714	2536	2365	2200
	energy, ft-lb:	3361	2944	2571	2235	1935
	arc, inches:		+1.6	0	-7.1	-20.3
PMC 180 HPBT Match	velocity, fps:	2950	2755	2568	2390	2219
	energy, ft-lb:	3478	3033	2636	2283	1968
	arc, inches:		+1.5	0	-6.8	-19.7

BALLISTICS

.300 WINCHESTER MAGNUM TO .300 WINCHESTER SHORT MAG.

CARTRIDGE BULLET	RANGE, YARDS:	0	100	200	300	400
Rem. 150 PSP Core-Lokt	velocity, fps:	3290	2951	2636	2342	2068
	energy, ft-lb:	3605	2900	2314	1827	1859
	arc, inches:		+1.6	0	-7.0	-20.2
Rem. 150 PSP C-L MR	velocity, fps:	2650	2373	2113	1870	1646
	energy, ft-lb:	2339	1875	1486	1164	902
	arc, inches:		+1.0	-2.7	-14.3	-35.8
Rem. 150 PSP C-L Ultra	velocity, fps:	3290	2967	2666	2384	2120
	energy, ft-lb:	3065	2931	2366	1893	1496
	arc, inches:		+1.2	0	-6.1	-18.4
Rem. 180 AccuTip	velocity, fps:	2960	2764	2577	2397	2224
	energy, ft-lb:	3501	3053	2653	2295	1976
	arc, inches:		+1.5	0	-6.8	-19.6
Rem. 180 PSP Core-Lokt	velocity, fps:	2960	2745	2540	2344	2157
	energy, ft-lb:	3501	3011	2578	2196	1424
	arc, inches:		+2.2	+1.9	-3.4	-15.0
Rem. 180 PSP C-L Ultra	velocity, fps:	2960	2727	2505	2294	2093
	energy, ft-lb:	3501	2971	2508	2103	1751
	arc, inches:		+2.7	+2.2	-3.8	-16.4
Rem. 180 Nosler Partition	velocity, fps:	2960	2725	2503	2291	2089
	energy, ft-lb:	3501	2968	2503	2087	1744
	arc, inches:		+1.6	0	-7.2	-20.9
Rem. 180 Nosler Bal. Tip	velocity, fps:	2960	2774	2595	2424	2259.
	energy, ft-lb:	3501	3075	2692	2348	2039
	arc, inches:		+1.5	0	-6.7	-19.3
Rem. 180 Swift Scirocco	velocity, fps:	2960	2774	2595	2424	2259
	energy, ft-lb:	3501	3075	2692	2348	2039
	arc, inches:		+1.5	0	-6.7	-19.3
Rem. 190 PSP boat-tail	velocity, fps:	2885	2691	2506	2327	2156
	energy, ft-lb:	3511	3055	2648	2285	1961
	arc, inches:		+1.6	0	-7.2	-20.8
Rem. 190 HPBT Match	velocity, fps:	2900	2725	2557	2395	2239
	energy, ft-lb:	3547	3133	2758	2420	2115
	arc, inches:		+1.6	0	-6.9	-19.9
Rem. 200 Swift A-Frame	velocity, fps:	2825	2595	2376	2167	1970
	energy, ft-lb:	3544	2989	2506	2086	1722
	arc, inches:		+1.8	0	-8.0	-23.5
Speer 180 Grand Slam	velocity, fps:	2950	2735	2530	2334	
	energy, ft-lb:	3478	2989	2558	2176	
	arc, inches:		+1.6	0	-7.0	-20.5
Speer 200 Grand Slam	velocity, fps:	2800	2597	2404	2218	
	energy, ft-lb:	3481	2996	2565	2185	
	arc, inches:		+1.8	0	-7.9	-22.9
Win. 150 Power-Point	velocity, fps:	3290	2951	2636	2342	2068.
	energy, ft-lb:	3605	2900	2314	1827	1424
	arc, inches:		+2.6	+2.1	-3.5	-15.4
Win. 150 Fail Safe	velocity, fps:	3260	2943	2647	2370	2110
	energy, ft-lb:	3539	2884	2334	1871	1483
	arc, inches:		+1.3	0	-6.2	-18.7
Win. 165 Fail Safe	velocity, fps:	3120	2807	2515	2242	1985
	energy, ft-lb:	3567	2888	2319	1842	1445
	arc, inches:		+1.5	0	-7.0	-20.0
Win. 180 Power-Point	velocity, fps:	2960	2745	2540	2344	2157
	energy, ft-lb:	3501	3011	2578	2196	1859
	arc, inches:		+1.9	0	-7.3	-20.9
Win. 180 Power-Point Plus	velocity, fps:	3070	2846	2633	2430	2236
	energy, ft-lb:	3768	3239	2772	2361	1999
	arc, inches:		+1.4	0	-6.4	-18.7
Win. 180 Ballistic Silvertip	velocity, fps:	2950	2764	2586	2415	2250
	energy, ft-lb:	3478	3054	2673	2331	2023
	arc, inches:		+1.5	0	-6.7	-19.4
Win. 180 AccuBond	velocity, fps:	2950	2765	2588	2417	2253
	energy, ft-lb:	3478	3055	2676	2334	2028
	arc, inches:		+1.5	0	-6.7	-19.4

CARTRIDGE BULLET	RANGE, YARDS:	0	100	200	300	400
Win. 180 Fail Safe	velocity, fps:	2960	2732	2514	2307	2110
	energy, ft-lb:	3503	2983	2528	2129	1780
	arc, inches:		+1.6	0	-7.1	-20.7
Win. 180 Partition Gold	velocity, fps:	3070	2859	2657	2464	2280
	energy, ft-lb:	3768	3267	2823	2428	2078
	arc, inches:		+1.4	0	-6.3	-18.3

.300 REMINGTON SHORT ULTRA MAG

CARTRIDGE BULLET	RANGE, YARDS:	0	100	200	300	400
Rem. 150 PSP C-L Ultra	velocity, fps:	3200	2901	2672	2359	2112
	energy, ft-lb:	3410	2803	2290	1854	1485
	arc, inches:		+1.3	0	-6.4	-19.l
Rem. 165 PSP Core-Lokt	velocity, fps:	3075	2792	2527	2276	2040
	energy, ft-lb:	3464	2856	2339	1828	1525
	arc, inches:		+1.5	0	-7.0	-20.7
Rem. 180 Partition	velocity, fps:	2960	2761	2571	2389	2214
	energy, ft-lb:	3501	3047	2642	2280	1959
	arc, inches:		+1.5	0	-6.8	-19.7
Rem. 180 PSP C-L Ultra	velocity, fps:	2960	2727	2506	2295	2094
	energy, ft-lb:	3501	2972	2509	2105	1753
	arc, inches:		+1.6	0	-7.1	-20.9
Rem. 190 HPBT Match	velocity, fps:	2900	2725	2557	2395	2239
	energy, ft-lb:	3547	3133	2758	2420	2115
	arc, inches:		+1.6	0	-6.9	-19.9

.300 WINCHESTER SHORT MAG.

CARTRIDGE BULLET	RANGE, YARDS:	0	100	200	300	400
Black Hills 175 Sierra MKing	velocity, fps:	2950				
	energy, ft-lb:	3381				
	arc, inches:					
Black Hills 180 AccuBond	velocity, fps:	2950				
	energy, ft-lb:	3478				
	arc, inches:					
Federal 150 Nosler Bal. Tip	velocity, fps:	3200	2970	2755	2545	2345
	energy, ft-lb:	3410	2940	2520	2155	1830.
	arc, inches:		+1.2	0	-5.8	-17.0
Federal 165 Nos. Partition	velocity, fps:	3130	2890	2670	2450	2250
	energy, ft-lb:	3590	3065	2605	2205	1855.
	arc, inches:		+1.3	0	-6.2	-18.2
Federal 165 Nos. Solid Base	velocity, fps:	3130	2900	2690	2490	2290
	energy, ft-lb:	3590	3090	2650	2265	1920
	arc, inches:		+1.3	0	-6.1	-17.8
Federal 180 Barnes TS And Nos. Solid Base	velocity, fps:	2980	2780	2580	2400	2220
	energy, ft-lbs:	3550	3085	2670	2300	1970
	arc, inches:		+1.5	0	-6.7	-19.5
Federal 180 Grand Slam	velocity, fps:	2970	2740	2530	2320	2130
	energy, ft-lb:	3525	3010	2555	2155	1810
	arc, inches:		+1.5	0	-7.0	-20.5
Federal 180 Trophy Bonded	velocity, fps:	2970	2730	2500	2280	2080
	energy, ft-lb:	3525	2975	2500	2085	1725
	arc, inches:		+1.5	0	-7.2	-21.0
Federal 180 Nosler Partition	velocity, fps:	2975	2750	2535	2290	2126
	energy, ft-lb:	3540	3025	2570	2175	1825
	arc, inches:		+1.5	0	-7.0	-20.3
Federal 180 Nos. AccuBond	velocity, fps:	2960	2780	2610	2440	2280
	energy, ft-lb:	3500	3090	2715	2380	2075
	arc, inches:		+1.5	0	-6.6	-19.0
Federal 180 Hi-Shok SP	velocity, fps:	2970	2520	2115	1750	1430
	energy, ft-lb:	3525	2540	1785	1220	820
	arc, inches:		+2.2	0	-9.9	-31.4
Norma 150 FMJ	velocity, fps:	2953	2731	2519	2318	
	energy, ft-lb:					
	arc, inches:		+1.6	0	-7.1	
Norma 150 Barnes X TS	velocity, fps:	3215	2982	2761	2550	
	energy, ft-lb:	3444	2962	2539	2167	
	arc, inches:		+1.2	0	-5.7	

Centerfire Rifle Ballistics

.300 WINCHESTER SHORT MAG. TO .300 PEGASUS

CARTRIDGE BULLET	RANGE, YARDS:	0	100	200	300	400
Norma 180 Nosler Bal. Tip	velocity, fps:	3215	2985	2767	2560	
	energy, ft-lb:	3437	2963	2547	2179	
	arc, inches:		+1.2	0	-5.7	
Norma 180 Oryx	velocity, fps:	2936	2542	2180	1849	
	energy, ft-lb:	3446	2583	1900	1368	
	arc, inches:		+1.9	0	-8.9	
Win. 150 Power-Point	velocity, fps:	3270	2903	2565	2250	1958
	energy, ft-lb:	3561	2807	2190	1686	1277
	arc, inches:		+1.3	0	-6.6	-20.2
Win. 150 Ballistic Silvertip	velocity, fps:	3300	3061	2834	2619	2414
	energy, ft-lb:	3628	3121	2676	2285	1941
	arc, inches:		+1.1	0	-5.4	-15.9
Win. 165 Fail Safe	velocity, fps:	3125	2846	2584	2336	2102
	energy, ft-lb:	3577	2967	2446	1999	1619
	arc, inches:		+1.4	0	-6.6	-19.6
Win. 180 Ballistic Silvertip	velocity, fps:	3010	2822	2641	2468	2301.
	energy, ft-lb:	3621	3182	2788	2434	2116
	arc, inches:		+1.4	0	-6.4	-18.6
Win. 180 AccuBond	velocity, fps:	3010	2822	2643	2470	2304
	energy, ft-lb:	3622	3185	2792	2439	2121
	arc, inches:		+1.4	0	-6.4	-18.5
Win. 180 Fail Safe	velocity, fps:	2970	2741	2524	2317	2120
	energy, ft-lb:	3526	3005	2547	2147	1797
	arc, inches:		+1.6	0	-7.0	-20.5
Win. 180 Power Point	velocity, fps:	2970	2755	2549	2353	2166
	energy, ft-lb:	3526	3034	2598	2214	1875
	arc, inches:		+1.5	0	-6.9	-20.1

.300 WEATHERBY MAG.

CARTRIDGE BULLET	RANGE, YARDS:	0	100	200	300	400
A-Square 180 Dead Tough	velocity, fps:	3180	2811	2471	2155	1863.
	energy, ft-lb:	4041	3158	2440	1856	1387
	arc, inches:		+1.5	0	-7.2	-21.8
A-Square 220 Monolythic Solid	velocity, fps:	2700	2407	2133	1877	1653
	energy, ft-lb:	3561	2830	2223	1721	1334
	arc, inches:		+2.3	0	-9.8	-29.7
Federal 180 Sierra GameKing BTSP	velocity, fps:	3190	3010	2830	2660	2490
	energy, ft-lb:	4065	3610	3195	2820	2480
	arc, inches:		+1.2	0	-5.6	-16.0
Federal 180 Trophy Bonded	velocity, fps:	3190	2950	2720	2500	2290
	energy, ft-lb:	4065	3475	2955	2500	2105
	arc, inches:		+1.3	0	-5.9	-17.5
Federal 180 Tr. Bonded HE	velocity, fps:	3330	3080	2850	2750	2410
	energy, ft-lb:	4430	3795	3235	2750	2320
	arc, inches:		+1.1	0	-5.4	-15.8
Federal 180 Nosler Partition	velocity, fps:	3190	2980	2780	2590	2400
	energy, ft-lb:	4055	3540	3080	2670	2305
	arc, inches:		+1.2	0	-5.7	-16.7
Federal 180 Nosler Part. HE	velocity, fps:	3330	3110	2810	2710	2520
	energy, ft-lb:	4430	3875	3375	2935	2540
	arc, inches:		+1.0	0	-5.2	-15.1
Federal 200 Trophy Bonded	velocity, fps:	2900	2670	2440	2230	2030
	energy, ft-lb:	3735	3150	2645	2200	1820
	arc, inches:		+1.7	0	-7.6	-22.2
Hornady 150 SST (or Interbond)	velocity, fps:	3375	3123	2882	2652	2434
	energy, ft-lb:	3793	3248	2766	2343	1973
	arc, inches:		+1.0	0	-5.4	-15.8
Hornady 180 SP	velocity, fps:	3120	2891	2673	2466	2268.
	energy, ft-lb:	3890	3340	2856	2430	2055
	arc, inches:		+1.3	0	-6.2	-18.1
Hornady 180 SST	velocity, fps:	3120	2911	2711	2519	2335
	energy, ft-lb:	3890	3386	2936	2535	2180
	arc, inches:		+1.3	0	-6.2	-18.1

CARTRIDGE BULLET	RANGE, YARDS:	0	100	200	300	400
Rem. 180 PSP Core-Lokt	velocity, fps:	3120	2866	2627	2400	2184
	energy, ft-lb:	3890	3284	2758	2301	1905
	arc, inches:		+2.4	+2.0	-3.4	-14.9
Rem. 190 PSP boat-tail	velocity, fps:	3030	2830	2638	2455	2279
	energy, ft-lb:	3873	3378	2936	2542	2190.
	arc, inches:		+1.4	0	-6.4	-18.6
Rem. 200 Swift A-Frame	velocity, fps:	2925	2690	2467	2254	2052
	energy, ft-lb:	3799	3213	2701	2256	1870
	arc, inches:		+2.8	+2.3	-3.9	-17.0
Speer 180 Grand Slam	velocity, fps:	3185	2948	2722	2508	
	energy, ft-lb:	4054	3472	2962	2514	
	arc, inches:		+1.3	0	-5.9	-17.4
Wby. 150 Pointed Expanding	velocity, fps:	3540	3225	2932	2657	2399
	energy, ft-lb:	4173	3462	2862	2351	1916
	arc, inches:		+2.6	+3.3	0	-8.2
Wby. 150 Nosler Partition	velocity, fps:	3540	3263	3004	2759	2528
	energy, ft-lb:	4173	3547	3005	2536	2128
	arc, inches:		+2.5	+3.2	0	-7.7
Wby. 165 Pointed Expanding	velocity, fps:	3390	3123	2872	2634	2409
	energy, ft-lb:	4210	3573	3021	2542	2126
	arc, inches:		+2.8	+3.5	0	-8.5
Wby. 165 Nosler Bal. Tip	velocity, fps:	3350	3133	2927	2730	2542
	energy, ft-lb:	4111	3596	3138	2730	2367
	arc, inches:		+2.7	+3.4	0	-8.1
Wby. 180 Pointed Expanding	velocity, fps:	3240	3004	2781	2569	2366
	energy, ft-lb:	4195	3607	3091	2637	2237
	arc, inches:		+3.1	+3.8	0	-9.0
Wby. 180 Barnes X	velocity, fps:	3190	2995	2809	2631	2459
	energy, ft-lb:	4067	3586	3154	2766	2417
	arc, inches:		+3.1	+3.8	0	-8.7
Wby. 180 Bal. Tip	velocity, fps:	3250	3051	2806	2676	2503
	energy, ft-lb:	4223	3721	3271	2867	2504
	arc, inches:		+2.8	+3.6	0	-8.4
Wby. 180 Nosler Partition	velocity, fps:	3240	3028	2826	2634	2449
	energy, ft-lb:	4195	3665	3193	2772	2396
	arc, inches:		+3.0	+3.7	0	-8.6
Wby. 200 Nosler Partition	velocity, fps:	3060	2860	2668	2485	2308
	energy, ft-lb:	4158	3631	3161	2741	2366
	arc, inches:		+3.5	+4.2	0	-9.8
Wby. 220 RN Expanding	velocity, fps:	2845	2543	2260	1996	1751.
	energy, ft-lb:	3954	3158	2495	1946	1497
	arc, inches:		+4.9	+5.9	0	-14.6

.300 DAKOTA

CARTRIDGE BULLET	RANGE, YARDS:	0	100	200	300	400
Dakota 165 Barnes X	velocity, fps:	3200	2979	2769	2569	2377
	energy, ft-lb:	3751	3251	2809	2417	2070
	arc, inches:		+2.1	+1.8	-3.0	-13.2
Dakota 200 Barnes X	velocity, fps:	3000	2824	2656	2493	2336
	energy, ft-lb:	3996	3542	3131	2760	2423
	arc, inches:		+2.2	+1.5	-4.0	-15.2

.300 PEGASUS

CARTRIDGE BULLET	RANGE, YARDS:	0	100	200	300	400
A-Square 180 SP boat-tail	velocity, fps:	3500	3319	3145	2978	2817
	energy, ft-lb:	4896	4401	3953	3544	3172
	arc, inches:		+2.3	+2.9	0	-6.8
A-Square 180 Nosler Part.	velocity, fps:	3500	3295	3100	2913	2734
	energy, ft-lb:	4896	4339	3840	3392	2988
	arc, inches:		+2.3	+3.0	0	-7.1
A-Square 180 Dead Tough	velocity, fps:	3500	3103	2740	2405	2095
	energy, ft-lb:	4896	3848	3001	2312	1753
	arc, inches:		+1.1	0	-5.7	-17.5

.300 REMINGTON ULTRA MAG TO 8MM MAUSER (8X57)

.300 Remington Ultra Mag

Cartridge Bullet	RANGE, YARDS:	0	100	200	300	400
Federal 180 Trophy Bonded	velocity, fps:	3250	3000	2770	2550	2340
	energy, ft-lb:	4220	3605	3065	2590	2180
	arc, inches:		+1.2	0	-5.7	-16.8
Rem. 150 Swift Scirocco	velocity, fps:	3450	3208	2980	2762	2556
	energy, ft-lb:	3964	3427	2956	2541	2175
	arc, inches:		+1.7	+1.5	-2.6	-11.2
Rem. 180 Nosler Partition	velocity, fps:	3250	3037	2834	2640	2454
	energy, ft-lb:	4221	3686	3201	2786	2407
	arc, inches:		+2.4	+1.8	-3.0	-12.7
Rem. 180 Swift Scirocco	velocity, fps:	3250	3048	2856	2672	2495
	energy, ft-lb:	4221	3714	3260	2853	2487
	arc, inches:		+2.0	+1.7	-2.8	-12.3
Rem. 180 PSP Core-Lokt	velocity, fps:	3250	2988	2742	2508	2287
	energy, ft-lb:	3517	2974	2503	2095	1741
	arc, inches:		+2.1	+1.8	-3.1	-13.6
Rem. 200 Nosler Partition	velocity, fps:	3025	2826	2636	2454	2279
	energy, ft-lb:	4063	3547	3086	2673	2308
	arc, inches:		+2.4	+2.0	-3.4	-14.6

.30-378 Weatherby Mag.

Cartridge Bullet	RANGE, YARDS:	0	100	200	300	400
Wby. 165 Nosler Bal. Tip	velocity, fps:	3500	3275	3062	2859	2665
	energy, ft-lb:	4488	3930	3435	2995	2603
	arc, inches:		+2.4	+3.0	0	-7.4
Wby. 180 Nosler Bal. Tip	velocity, fps:	3420	3213	3015	2826	2645
	energy, ft-lb:	4676	4126	3634	3193	2797
	arc, inches:		+2.5	+3.1	0	-7.5
Wby. 180 Barnes X	velocity, fps:	3450	3243	3046	2858	2678.
	energy, ft-lb:	4757	4204	3709	3264	2865
	arc, inches:		+2.4	+3.1	0	-7.4
Wby. 200 Nosler Partition	velocity, fps:	3160	2955	2759	2572	2392.
	energy, ft-lb:	4434	3877	3381	2938	2541
	arc, inches:		+3.2	+3.9	0	-9.1

7.82 (.308) Warbird

Cartridge Bullet	RANGE, YARDS:	0	100	200	300	400
Lazzeroni 150 Nosler Part.	velocity, fps:	3680	3432	3197	2975	2764
	energy, ft-lb:	4512	3923	3406	2949	2546.
	arc, inches:		+2.1	+2.7	0	-6.6
Lazzeroni 180 Nosler Part.	velocity, fps:	3425	3220	3026	2839	2661
	energy, ft-lb:	4689	4147	3661	3224	2831
	arc, inches:		+2.5	+3.2	0	-7.5
Lazzeroni 200 Swift A-Fr.	velocity, fps:	3290	3105	2928	2758	2594.
	energy, ft-lb:	4808	4283	3808	3378	2988
	arc, inches:		+2.7	+3.4	0	-7.9

7.65x53 Argentine

Cartridge Bullet	RANGE, YARDS:	0	100	200	300	400
Norma 174 Soft Point	velocity, fps:	2493	2173	1878	1611	
	energy, ft-lb:	2402	1825	1363	1003	
	arc, inches:		+2.0	0	-9.5	
Norma 180 Soft Point	velocity, fps:	2592	2386	2189	2002	
	energy, ft-lb:	2686	2276	1916	1602	
	arc, inches:		+2.3	0	-9.6	

.303 British

Cartridge Bullet	RANGE, YARDS:	0	100	200	300	400
Federal 150 Hi-Shok	velocity, fps:	2690	2440	2210	1980	1780
	energy, ft-lb:	2400	1980	1620	1310	1055
	arc, inches:		+2.2	0	-9.4	-27.6
Federal 180 Sierra Pro-Hunt.	velocity, fps:	2460	2230	2020	1820	1630
	energy, ft-lb:	2420	1995	1625	1315	1060
	arc, inches:		+2.8	0	-11.3	-33.2
Federal 180 Tr. Bonded HE	velocity, fps:	2590	2350	2120	1900	1700
	energy, ft-lb:	2680	2205	1795	1445	1160
	arc, inches:		+2.4	0	-10.0	-30.0
Hornady 150 Soft Point	velocity, fps:	2685	2441	2210	1992	1787
	energy, ft-lb:	2401	1984	1627	1321	1064
	arc, inches:		+2.2	0	-9.3	-27.4
Hornady 150 SP LM	velocity, fps:	2830	2570	2325	2094	1884.
	energy, ft-lb:	2667	2199	1800	1461	1185
	arc, inches:		+2.0	0	-8.4	-24.6
Norma 150 Soft Point	velocity, fps:	2723	2438	2170	1920	
	energy, ft-lb:	2470	1980	1569	1228	
	arc, inches:		+2.2	0	-9.6	
PMC 174 FMJ (and HPBT)	velocity, fps:	2400	2216	2042	1876	1720
	energy, ft-lb:	2225	1898	1611	1360	1143
	arc, inches:		+2.8	0	-11.2	-32.2
PMC 180 SP boat-tail	velocity, fps:	2450	2276	2110	1951	1799
	energy, ft-lb:	2399	2071	1779	1521	1294
	arc, inches:		+2.6	0	-10.4	-30.1
Rem. 180 SP Core-Lokt	velocity, fps:	2460	2124	1817	1542	1311
	energy, ft-lb:	2418	1803	1319	950	687
	arc, inches, s:			0	-5.8	-23.3
Win. 180 Power-Point	velocity, fps:	2460	2233	2018	1816	1629
	energy, ft-lb:	2418	1993	1627	1318	1060
	arc, inches, s:			0	-6.1	-20.8

7.7x58 Japanese Arisaka

Cartridge Bullet	RANGE, YARDS:	0	100	200	300	400
Norma 174 Soft Point	velocity, fps:	2493	2173	1878	1611	
	energy, ft-lb:	2402	1825	1363	1003	
	arc, inches:		+2.0	0	-9.5	
Norma 180 Soft Point	velocity, fps:	2493	2291	2099	1916	
	energy, ft-lb:	2485	2099	1761	1468	
	arc, inches:		+2.6	0	-10.5	

.32-20 Winchester

Cartridge Bullet	RANGE, YARDS:	0	100	200	300	400
Rem. 100 Lead	velocity, fps:	1210	1021	913	834	769
	energy, ft-lb:	325	231	185	154	131
	arc, inches:		0	-31.6	-104.7	
Win. 100 Lead	velocity, fps:	1210	1021	913	834	769
	energy, ft-lb:	325	231	185	154	131
	arc, inches:		0	-32.3	-106.3	

.32 Winchester Special

Cartridge Bullet	RANGE, YARDS:	0	100	200	300	400
Federal 170 Hi-Shok	velocity, fps:	2250	1920	1630	1370	1180
	energy, ft-lb:	1910	1395	1000	710	520
	arc, inches:		0	-8.0	-29.2	
Rem. 170 SP Core-Lokt	velocity, fps:	2250	1921	1626	1372	1175
	energy, ft-lb:	1911	1393	998	710	521
	arc, inches:		0	-8.0	-29.3	
Win. 170 Power-Point	velocity, fps:	2250	1870	1537	1267	1082
	energy, ft-lb:	1911	1320	892	606	442
	arc, inches:		0	-9.2	-33.2	

8mm Mauser (8x57)

Cartridge Bullet	RANGE, YARDS:	0	100	200	300	400
Federal 170 Hi-Shok	velocity, fps:	2360	1970	1620	1330	1120
	energy, ft-lb:	2100	1465	995	670	475
	arc, inches:		0	-7.6	-28.5	
Hornady 195 SP	velocity, fps:	2550	2343	2146	1959	1782
	energy, ft-lb:	2815	2377	1994	1861	1375
	arc, inches:		+2.3	0	-9.9	-28.8.
Hornady 195 SP (2005)	velocity, fps:	2475	2269	2074	1888	1714
	energy, ft-lb:	2652	2230	1861	1543	1271
	arc, inches:		+2.6	0	-10.7	-31.3
Norma 123 FMJ	velocity, fps:	2559	2121	1729	1398	
	energy, ft-lb:	1789	1228	817	534	
	arc, inches:		+3.2	0	-15.0	
Norma 196 Oryx	velocity, fps:	2395	2146	1912	1695	
	energy, ft-lb:	2497	2004	1591	1251	
	arc, inches:		+3	0	-12.6	

BALLISTICS

Centerfire Rifle Ballistics

8MM MAUSER (8X57) TO .338 WINCHESTER MAG.

CARTRIDGE BULLET	RANGE, YARDS:	0	100	200	300	400
Norma 196 Vulkan	velocity, fps:	2395	2156	1930	1720	
	energy, ft-lb:	2497	2023	1622	1289	
	arc, inches:		3.0	0	-12.3	
Norma 196 Alaska	velocity, fps:	2395	2112	1850	1611	
	energy, ft-lb:	2714	2190	1754	1399	
	arc, inches:		0	-6.3	-22.9	
Norma 196 Soft Point (JS)	velocity, fps:	2526	2244	1981	1737	
	energy, ft-lb:	2778	2192	1708	1314	
	arc, inches:		+2.7	0	-11.6	
Norma 196 Alaska (JS)	velocity, fps:	2526	2248	1988	1747	
	energy, ft-lb:	2778	2200	1720	1328	
	arc, inches:		+2.7	0	-11.5	
Norma 196 Vulkan (JS)	velocity, fps:	2526	2276	2041	1821	
	energy, ft-lb:	2778	2256	1813	1443	
	arc, inches:		+2.6	0	-11.0	
Norma 196 Oryx (JS)	velocity, fps:	2526	2269	2027	1802	
	energy, ft-lb:	2778	2241	1789	1413	
	arc, inches:		+2.6	0	-11.1	
PMC 170 Pointed Soft Point	velocity, fps:	2360	1969	1622	1333	1123
	energy, ft-lb:	2102	1463	993	671	476
	arc, inches:		+1.8	-4.5	-24.3	-63.8
Rem. 170 SP Core-Lokt	velocity, fps:	2360	1969	1622	1333	1123
	energy, ft-lb:	2102	1463	993	671	476
	arc, inches:		+1.8	-4.5	-24.3	-63.8.
Win. 170 Power-Point	velocity, fps:	2360	1969	1622	1333	1123
	energy, ft-lb:	2102	1463	993	671	476
	arc, inches:		+1.8	-4.5	-24.3	-63.8

.325 WSM

CARTRIDGE BULLET	RANGE, YARDS:	0	100	200	300	400
Win. 180 Ballistic ST	velocity, fps:	3060	2841	2632	2432	2242
	energy, ft-lb:	3743	3226	2769	2365	2009
	arc, inches:		+1.4	0	-6.4	-18.7
Win. 200 AccuBond CT	velocity, fps:	2950	2753	2565	2384	2210
	energy, ft-lb:	3866	3367	2922	2524	2170
	arc, inches:		+1.5	0	-6.8	-19.8
Win. 220 Power-Point	velocity, fps:	2840	2605	2382	2169	1968
	energy, ft-lb:	3941	3316	2772	2300	1893
	arc, inches:		+1.8	0	-8.0	-23.3

8MM REMINGTON MAG.

CARTRIDGE BULLET	RANGE, YARDS:	0	100	200	300	400
A-Square 220 Monolythic Solid	velocity, fps:	2800	2501	2221	1959	1718
	energy, ft-lb:	3829	3055	2409	1875	1442
	arc, inches:		+2.1	0	-9.1	-27.6
Rem. 200 Swift A-Frame	velocity, fps:	2900	2623	2361	2115	1885
	energy, ft-lb:	3734	3054	2476	1987	1577
	arc, inches:		+1.8	0	-8.0	-23.9

.338-06

CARTRIDGE BULLET	RANGE, YARDS:	0	100	200	300	400
A-Square 200 Nos. Bal. Tip	velocity, fps:	2750	2553	2364	2184	2011
	energy, ft-lb:	3358	2894	2482	2118	1796
	arc, inches:		+1.9	0	-8.2	-23.6
A-Square 250 SP boat-tail	velocity, fps:	2500	2374	2252	2134	2019
	energy, ft-lb:	3496	3129	2816	2528	2263
	arc, inches:		+2.4	0	-9.3	-26.0
A-Square 250 Dead Tough	velocity, fps:	2500	2222	1963	1724	1507
	energy, ft-lb:	3496	2742	2139	1649	1261
	arc, inches:		+2.8	0	-11.9	-35.5
Wby. 210 Nosler Part.	velocity, fps:	2750	2526	2312	2109	1916
	energy, ft-lb:	3527	2975	2403	2074	1712
	arc, inches:		+4.8	+5.7	0	-13.5

.338 WINCHESTER MAG.

CARTRIDGE BULLET	RANGE, YARDS:	0	100	200	300	400
A-Square 250 SP boat-tail	velocity, fps:	2700	2568	2439	2314	2193
	energy, ft-lb:	4046	3659	3302	2972	2669
	arc, inches:		+4.4	+5.2	0	-11.7
A-Square 250 Triad	velocity, fps:	2700	2407	2133	1877	1653
	energy, ft-lb:	4046	3216	2526	1956	1516
	arc, inches:		+2.3	0	-9.8	-29.8
Federal 210 Nosler Partition	velocity, fps:	2830	2600	2390	2180	1980
	energy, ft-lb:	3735	3160	2655	2215	1835
	arc, inches:		+1.8	0	-8.0	-23.3
Federal 225 Sierra Pro-Hunt.	velocity, fps:	2780	2570	2360	2170	1980
	energy, ft-lb:	3860	3290	2780	2340	1960
	arc, inches:		+1.9	0	-8.2	-23.7
Federal 225 Trophy Bonded	velocity, fps:	2800	2560	2330	2110	1900
	energy, ft-lb:	3915	3265	2700	2220	1800
	arc, inches:		+1.9	0	-8.4	-24.5
Federal 225 Tr. Bonded HE	velocity, fps:	2940	2690	2450	2230	2010
	energy, ft-lb:	4320	3610	3000	2475	2025
	arc, inches:		+1.7	0	-7.5	-22.0
Federal 225 Barnes XLC	velocity, fps:	2800	2610	2430	2260	2090
	energy, ft-lb:	3915	3405	2950	2545	2190
	arc, inches:		+1.8	0	-7.7	-22.2
Federal 250 Nosler Partition	velocity, fps:	2660	2470	2300	2120	1960
	energy, ft-lb:	3925	3395	2925	2505	2130.
	arc, inches:		+2.1	0	-8.8	-25.1
Federal 250 Nosler Part HE	velocity, fps:	2800	2610	2420	2250	2080
	energy, ft-lb:	4350	3775	3260	2805	2395
	arc, inches:		+1.8	0	-7.8	-22.5
Hornady 225 Soft Point HM	velocity, fps:	2920	2678	2449	2232	2027
	energy, ft-lb:	4259	3583	2996	2489	2053
	arc, inches:		+1.8	0	-7.6	-22.0
Norma 225 TXP Swift A-Fr.	velocity, fps:	2740	2507	2286	2075	
	energy, ft-lb:	3752	3141	2611	2153	
	arc, inches:		+2.0	0	-8.7	
Norma 230 Oryx	velocity, fps:	2756	2514	2284	2066	
	energy, ft-lb:	3880	3228	2665	2181	
	arc, inches:		+2.0	0	-8.7	
Norma 250 Nosler Partition	velocity, fps:	2657	2470	2290	2118	
	energy, ft-lb:	3920	3387	2912	2490	
	arc, inches:		+2.1	0	-8.7	
PMC 225 Barnes X	velocity, fps:	2780	2619	2464	2313	2168
	energy, ft-lb:	3860	3426	3032	2673	2348.
	arc, inches:		+1.8	0	-7.6	-21.6
Rem. 200 Nosler Bal. Tip	velocity, fps:	2950	2724	2509	2303	2108
	energy, ft-lb:	3866	3295	2795	2357	1973
	arc, inches:		+1.6	0	-7.1	-20.8
Rem. 210 Nosler Partition	velocity, fps:	2830	2602	2385	2179	1983
	energy, ft-lb:	3734	3157	2653	2214	1834
	arc, inches:		+1.8	0	-7.9	-23.2
Rem. 225 PSP Core-Lokt	velocity, fps:	2780	2572	2374	2184	2003
	energy, ft-lb:	3860	3305	2815	2383	2004
	arc, inches:		+1.9	0	-8.1	-23.4
Rem. 225 PSP C-L Ultra	velocity, fps:	2780	2582	2392	2210	2036
	energy, ft-lb:	3860	3329	2858	2440	2071
	arc, inches:		+1.9	0	-7.9	-23.0
Rem. 225 Swift A-Frame	velocity, fps:	2785	2517	2266	2029	1808
	energy, ft-lb:	3871	3165	2565	2057	1633
	arc, inches:		+2.0	0	-8.8	-25.2
Rem. 250 PSP Core-Lokt	velocity, fps:	2660	2456	2261	2075	1898
	energy, ft-lb:	3927	3348	2837	2389	1999
	arc, inches:		+2.1	0	-8.9	-26.0
Speer 250 Grand Slam	velocity, fps:	2645	2442	2247	2062	
	energy, ft-lb:	3883	3309	2803	2360	
	arc, inches:		+2.2	0	-9.1	-26.2
Win. 200 Power-Point	velocity, fps:	2960	2658	2375	2110	1862
	energy, ft-lb:	3890	3137	2505	1977	1539
	arc, inches:		+2.0	0	-8.2	-24.3

BALLISTICS

Centerfire Rifle Ballistics

CARTRIDGE BULLET	RANGE, YARDS:	0	100	200	300	400
Win. 200 Ballistic Silvertip	velocity, fps:	2950	2724	2509	2303	2108
	energy, ft-lb:	3864	3294	2794	2355	1972
	arc, inches:		+1.6	0	-7.1	-20.8
Win. 225 AccuBond	velocity, fps:	2800	2634	2474	2319	2170
	energy, ft-lb:	3918	3467	3058	2688	2353
	arc, inches:		+1.8	0	-7.4	-21.3
Win. 230 Fail Safe	velocity, fps:	2780	2573	2375	2186	2005
	energy, ft-lb:	3948	3382	2881	2441	2054
	arc, inches:		+1.9	0	-8.1	-23.4
Win. 250 Partition Gold	velocity, fps:	2650	2467	2291	2122	1960
	energy, ft-lb:	3899	3378	2914	2520	2134
	arc, inches:		+2.1	0	-8.7	-25.2

.340 Weatherby Mag.

CARTRIDGE BULLET	RANGE, YARDS:	0	100	200	300	400
A-Square 250 SP boat-tail	velocity, fps:	2820	2684	2552	2424	2299
	energy, ft-lb:	4414	3999	3615	3261	2935
	arc, inches:		+4.0	+4.6	0	-10.6
A-Square 250 Triad	velocity, fps:	2820	2520	2238	1976	1741
	energy, ft-lb:	4414	3524	2781	2166	1683
	arc, inches:		+2.0	0	-9.0	-26.8
Federal 225 Trophy Bonded	velocity, fps:	3100	2840	2600	2370	2150
	energy, ft-lb:	4800	4035	3375	2800	2310
	arc, inches:		+1.4	0	-6.5	-19.4
Wby. 200 Pointed Expanding	velocity, fps:	3221	2946	2688	2444	2213
	energy, ft-lb:	4607	3854	3208	2652	2174
	arc, inches:		+3.3	+4.0	0	-9.9
Wby. 200 Nosler Bal. Tip	velocity, fps:	3221	2980	2753	2536	2329
	energy, ft-lb:	4607	3944	3364	2856	2409
	arc, inches:		+3.1	+3.9	0	-9.2
Wby. 210 Nosler Partition	velocity, fps:	3211	2963	2728	2505	2293
	energy, ft-lb:	4807	4093	3470	2927	2452
	arc, inches:		+3.2	+3.9	0	-9.5
Wby. 225 Pointed Expanding	velocity, fps:	3066	2824	2595	2377	2170
	energy, ft-lb:	4696	3984	3364	2822	2352
	arc, inches:		+3.6	+4.4	0	-10.7
Wby. 225 Barnes X	velocity, fps:	3001	2804	2615	2434	2260
	energy, ft-lb:	4499	3927	3416	2959	2551
	arc, inches:		+3.6	+4.3	0	-10.3
Wby. 250 Pointed Expanding	velocity, fps:	2963	2745	2537	2338	2149
	energy, ft-lb:	4873	4182	3572	3035	2563
	arc, inches:		+3.9	+4.6	0	-11.1
Wby. 250 Nosler Partition	velocity, fps:	2941	2743	2553	2371	2197
	energy, ft-lb:	4801	4176	3618	3120	2678
	arc, inches:		+3.9	+4.6	0	-10.9

.330 Dakota

CARTRIDGE BULLET	RANGE, YARDS:	0	100	200	300	400
Dakota 200 Barnes X	velocity, fps:	3200	2971	2754	2548	2350
	energy, ft-lb:	4547	3920	3369	2882	2452
	arc, inches:		+2.1	+1.8	-3.1	-13.4
Dakota 250 Barnes X	velocity, fps:	2900	2719	2545	2378	2217
	energy, ft-lb:	4668	4103	3595	3138	2727
	arc, inches:		+2.3	+1.3	-5.0	-17.5

.338 Remington Ultra Mag

CARTRIDGE BULLET	RANGE, YARDS:	0	100	200	300	400
Federal 210 Nosler Partition	velocity, fps:	3025	2800	2585	2385	2190
	energy, ft-lb:	4270	3655	3120	2645	2230
	arc, inches:		+1.5	0	-6.7	-19.5
Federal 250 Trophy Bonded	velocity, fps:	2860	2630	2420	2210	2020
	energy, ft-lb:	4540	3850	3245	2715	2260
	arc, inches:		+0.8	0	-7.7	-22.6
Rem. 250 Swift A-Frame	velocity, fps:	2860	2645	2440	2244	2057
	energy, ft-lb:	4540	3882	3303	2794	2347
	arc, inches:		+1.7	0	-7.6	-22.1

CARTRIDGE BULLET	RANGE, YARDS:	0	100	200	300	400
Rem. 250 PSP Core-Lokt	velocity, fps:	2860	2647	2443	2249	2064
	energy, ft-lb:	4540	3888	3314	2807	2363
	arc, inches:		+1.7	0	-7.6	-22.0

.338 Lapua

CARTRIDGE BULLET	RANGE, YARDS:	0	100	200	300	400
Black Hills 250 Sierra MKing	velocity, fps:	2950				
	energy, ft-lb:	4831				
	arc, inches:					
Black Hills 300 Sierra MKing	velocity, fps:	2800				
	energy, ft-lb:	5223				
	arc, inches:					

.338-378 Weatherby Mag.

CARTRIDGE BULLET	RANGE, YARDS:	0	100	200	300	400
Wby. 200 Nosler Bal. Tip	velocity, fps:	3350	3102	2868	2646	2434
	energy, ft-lb:	4983	4273	3652	3109	2631
	arc, inches:	0	+2.8	+3.5	0	-8.4
Wby. 225 Barnes X	velocity, fps:	3180	2974	2778	2591	2410.
	energy, ft-lb:	5052	4420	3856	3353	2902
	arc, inches:	0	+3.1	+3.8	0	-8.9
Wby. 250 Nosler Partition	velocity, fps:	3060	2856	2662	2475	2297
	energy, ft-lb:	5197	4528	3933	3401	2927
	arc, inches:	0	+3.5	+4.2	0	-9.8

8.59 (.338) Titan

CARTRIDGE BULLET	RANGE, YARDS:	0	100	200	300	400
Lazzeroni 200 Nos. Bal. Tip	velocity, fps:	3430	3211	3002	2803	2613
	energy, ft-lb:	5226	4579	4004	3491	3033
	arc, inches:		+2.5	+3.2	0	-7.6
Lazzeroni 225 Nos. Partition	velocity, fps:	3235	3031	2836	2650	2471
	energy, ft-lb:	5229	4591	4021	3510	3052
	arc, inches:		+3.0	+3.6	0	-8.6
Lazzeroni 250 Swift A-Fr.	velocity, fps:	3100	2908	2725	2549	2379
	energy, ft-lb:	5336	4697	4123	3607	3143
	arc, inches:		+3.3	+4.0	0	-9.3

.338 A-Square

CARTRIDGE BULLET	RANGE, YARDS:	0	100	200	300	400
A-Square 200 Nos. Bal. Tip	velocity, fps:	3500	3266	3045	2835	2634
	energy, ft-lb:	5440	4737	4117	3568	3081
	arc, inches:		+2.4	+3.1	0	-7.5
A-Square 250 SP boat-tail	velocity, fps:	3120	2974	2834	2697	2565.
	energy, ft-lb:	5403	4911	4457	4038	3652
	arc, inches:		+3.1	+3.7	0	-8.5
A-Square 250 Triad	velocity, fps:	3120	2799	2500	2220	1958
	energy, ft-lb:	5403	4348	3469	2736	2128
	arc, inches:		+1.5	0	-7.1	-20.4.

.338 Excaliber

CARTRIDGE BULLET	RANGE, YARDS:	0	100	200	300	400
A-Square 200 Nos. Bal. Tip	velocity, fps:	3600	3361	3134	2920	2715
	energy, ft-lb:	5755	5015	4363	3785	3274
	arc, inches:		+2.2	+2.9	0	-6.7
A-Square 250 SP boat-tail	velocity, fps:	3250	3101	2958	2684	2553
	energy, ft-lb:	5863	5339	4855	4410	3998
	arc, inches:		+2.7	+3.4	0	-7.8
A-Square 250 Triad	velocity, fps:	3250	2922	2618	2333	2066
	energy, ft-lb:	5863	4740	3804	3021	2370
	arc, inches:		+1.3	0	-6.4	-19.2

.348 Winchester

CARTRIDGE BULLET	RANGE, YARDS:	0	100	200	300	400
Win. 200 Silvertip	velocity, fps:	2520	2215	1931	1672	1443.
	energy, ft-lb:	2820	2178	1656	1241	925
	arc, inches:		0	-6.2	-21.9	

.357 Mag.

CARTRIDGE BULLET	RANGE, YARDS:	0	100	200	300	400
Federal 180 Hi-Shok HP Hollow Point	velocity, fps:	1550	1160	980	860	770
	energy, ft-lb:	960	535	385	295	235
	arc, inches:		0	-22.8	-77.9	-173.8

Centerfire Rifle Ballistics

.357 MAGNUM TO .375 H&H MAGNUM

CARTRIDGE BULLET	RANGE, YARDS:	0	100	200	300	400
Win. 158 Jacketed SP	velocity, fps:	1830	1427	1138	980	883
	energy, ft-lb:	1175	715	454	337	274
	arc, inches:		0	-16.2	-57.0	-128.3

.35 REMINGTON

CARTRIDGE BULLET	RANGE, YARDS:	0	100	200	300	400
Federal 200 Hi-Shok	velocity, fps:	2080	1700	1380	1140	1000
	energy, ft-lb:	1920	1280	840	575	445
	arc, inches:		0	-10.7	-39.3	
Rem. 150 PSP Core-Lokt	velocity, fps:	2300	1874	1506	1218	1039
	energy, ft-lb:	1762	1169	755	494	359
	arc, inches:		0	-8.6	-32.6	
Rem. 200 SP Core-Lokt	velocity, fps:	2080	1698	1376	1140	1001
	energy, ft-lb:	1921	1280	841	577	445
	arc, inches:		0	-10.7	-40.1	
Win. 200 Power-Point	velocity, fps:	2020	1646	1335	1114	985
	energy, ft-lb:	1812	1203	791	551	431
	arc, inches:		0	-12.1	-43.9	

.356 WINCHESTER

CARTRIDGE BULLET	RANGE, YARDS:	0	100	200	300	400
Win. 200 Power-Point	velocity, fps:	2460	2114	1797	1517	1284
	energy, ft-lb:	2688	1985	1434	1022	732
	arc, inches:		+1.6	-3.8	-20.1	-51.2

.358 WINCHESTER

CARTRIDGE BULLET	RANGE, YARDS:	0	100	200	300	400
Win. 200 Silvertip	velocity, fps:	2490	2171	1876	1610	1379
	energy, ft-lb:	2753	2093	1563	1151	844
	arc, inches:		+1.5	-3.6	-18.6	-47.2

.35 WHELEN

CARTRIDGE BULLET	RANGE, YARDS:	0	100	200	300	400
Federal 225 Trophy Bonded	velocity, fps:	2600	2400	2200	2020	1840
	energy, ft-lb:	3375	2865	2520	2030	1690.
	arc, inches:		+2.3	0	-9.4	-27.3
Rem. 200 Pointed Soft Point	velocity, fps:	2675	2378	2100	1842	1606
	energy, ft-lb:	3177	2510	1958	1506	1145
	arc, inches:		+2.3	0	-10.3	-30.8
Rem. 250 Pointed Soft Point	velocity, fps:	2400	2197	2005	1823	1652
	energy, ft-lb:	3197	2680	2230	1844	1515
	arc, inches:		+1.3	-3.2	-16.6	-40.0

.358 NORMA MAG.

CARTRIDGE BULLET	RANGE, YARDS:	0	100	200	300	400
A-Square 275 Triad	velocity, fps:	2700	2394	2108	1842	1653
	energy, ft-lb:	4451	3498	2713	2072	1668
	arc, inches:		+2.3	0	-10.1	-29.8
Norma 250 TXP Swift A-Fr.	velocity, fps:	2723	2467	2225	1996	
	energy, ft-lb:	4117	3379	2748	2213	
	arc, inches:		+2.1	0	-9.1	
Norma 250 Woodleigh	velocity, fps:	2799	2442	2112	1810	
	energy, ft-lb:	4350	3312	2478	1819	
	arc, inches:		+2.2	0	-10.0	
Norma 250 Oryx	velocity, fps:	2756	2493	2245	2011	
	energy, ft-lb:	4217	3451	2798	2245	
	arc, inches:		+2.1	0	-9.0	

.358 STA

CARTRIDGE BULLET	RANGE, YARDS:	0	100	200	300	400
A-Square 275 Triad	velocity, fps:	2850	2562	2292	2039	1764
	energy, ft-lb:	4959	4009	3208	2539	1899.
	arc, inches:		+1.9	0	-8.6	-26.1

9.3x57

CARTRIDGE BULLET	RANGE, YARDS:	0	100	200	300	400
Norma 232 Vulkan	velocity, fps:	2329	2031	1757	1512	
	energy, ft-lb:	2795	2126	1591	1178	
	arc, inches:		+3.5	0	-14.9	
Norma 232 Oryx	velocity, fps:	2362	2058	1778	1528	
	energy, ft-lb:	2875	2182	1630	1203	
	arc, inches:		+3.4	0	-14.5	

CARTRIDGE BULLET	RANGE, YARDS:	0	100	200	300	400
Norma 285 Oryx	velocity, fps:	2067	1859	1666	1490	
	energy, ft-lb:	2704	2188	1756	1404	
	arc, inches:		+4.3	0	-16.8	
Norma 286 Alaska	velocity, fps:	2067	1857	1662	1484	
	energy, ft-lb:	2714	2190	1754	1399	
	arc, inches:		+4.3	0	-17.0	

9.3x62

CARTRIDGE BULLET	RANGE, YARDS:	0	100	200	300	400
A-Square 286 Triad	velocity, fps:	2360	2089	1844	1623	1369
	energy, ft-lb:	3538	2771	2157	1670	1189
	arc, inches:		+3.0	0	-13.1	-42.2
Norma 232 Vulkan	velocity, fps:	2625	2327	2049	1792	
	energy, ft-lb:	3551	2791	2164	1655	
	arc, inches:		+2.5	0	-10.8	
Norma 232 Oryx	velocity, fps:	2625	2294	1988	1708	
	energy, ft-lb:	3535	2700	2028	1497	
	arc, inches:		+2.5	0	-11.4	
Norma 250 A-Frame	velocity, fps:	2625	2322	2039	1778	
	energy, ft-lb:	3826	2993	2309	1755	
	arc, inches:		+2.5	0	-10.9	
Norma 286 Plastic Point	velocity, fps:	2362	2141	1931	1736	
	energy, ft-lb:	3544	2911	2370	1914	
	arc, inches:		+3.1	0	-12.4	
Norma 286 Alaska	velocity, fps:	2362	2135	1920	1720	
	energy, ft-lb:	3544	2894	2342	1879	
	arc, inches:		+3.1	0	-12.5	

9.3x64

CARTRIDGE BULLET	RANGE, YARDS:	0	100	200	300	400
A-Square 286 Triad	velocity, fps:	2700	2391	2103	1835	1602
	energy, ft-lb:	4629	3630	2808	2139	1631
	arc, inches:		+2.3	0	-10.1	-30.8

9.3x74 R

CARTRIDGE BULLET	RANGE, YARDS:	0	100	200	300	400
A-Square 286 Triad	velocity, fps:	2360	2089	1844	1623	
	energy, ft-lb:	3538	2771	2157	1670	
	arc, inches:		+3.6	0	-14.0	
Norma 232 Vulkan	velocity, fps:	2625	2327	2049	1792	
	energy, ft-lb:	3551	2791	2164	1655	
	arc, inches:		+2.5	0	-10.8	
Norma 232 Oryx	velocity, fps:	2526	2191	1883	1605	
	energy, ft-lb:	3274	2463	1819	1322	
	arc, inches:		+2.9	0	-12.8	
Norma 285 Oryx	velocity, fps:	2362	2114	1881	1667	
	energy, ft-lb:	3532	2829	2241	1758	
	arc, inches:		+3.1	0	-13.0	
Norma 286 Alaska	velocity, fps:	2362	2135	1920	1720	
	energy, ft-lb:	3544	2894	2342	1879	
	arc, inches:		+3.1	0	-12.5	
Norma 286 Plastic Point	velocity, fps:	2362	2135	1920	1720	
	energy, ft-lb:	3544	2894	2342	1879	
	arc, inches:		+3.1	0	-12.5	

.375 WINCHESTER

CARTRIDGE BULLET	RANGE, YARDS:	0	100	200	300	400
Win. 200 Power-Point	velocity, fps:	2200	1841	1526	1268	1089
	energy, ft-lb:	2150	1506	1034	714	
	arc, inches:		0	-9.5	-33.8	

.375 H&H MAG.

CARTRIDGE BULLET	RANGE, YARDS:	0	100	200	300	400
A-Square 300 SP boat-tail	velocity, fps:	2550	2415	2284	2157	2034
	energy, ft-lb:	4331	3884	3474	3098	2755
	arc, inches:		+5.2	+6.0	0	-13.3
A-Square 300 Triad	velocity, fps:	2550	2251	1973	1717	1496
	energy, ft-lb:	4331	3375	2592	1964	1491
	arc, inches:		+2.7	0	-11.7	-35.1

BALLISTICS

.375 H&H MAGNUM TO .378 WEATHERBY MAGNUM

CARTRIDGE BULLET	RANGE, YARDS:	0	100	200	300	400
Federal 250 Trophy Bonded	velocity, fps:	2670	2360	2080	1820	1580
	energy, ft-lb:	3955	3100	2400	1830	1380
	arc, inches:		+2.4	0	-10.4	-31.7
Federal 270 Hi-Shok	velocity, fps:	2690	2420	2170	1920	1700
	energy, ft-lb:	4340	3510	2810	2220	1740
	arc, inches:		+2.4	0	-10.9	-33.3
Federal 300 Hi-Shok	velocity, fps:	2530	2270	2020	1790	1580
	energy, ft-lb:	4265	3425	2720	2135	1665
	arc, inches:		+2.6	0	-11.2	-33.3
Federal 300 Nosler Partition	velocity, fps:	2530	2320	2120	1930	1750
	energy, ft-lb:	4265	3585	2995	2475	2040
	arc, inches:		+2.5	0	-10.3	-29.9
Federal 300 Trophy Bonded	velocity, fps:	2530	2280	2040	1810	1610
	energy, ft-lb:	4265	3450	2765	2190	1725
	arc, inches:		+2.6	0	-10.9	-32.8
Federal 300 Tr. Bonded HE	velocity, fps:	2700	2440	2190	1960	1740
	energy, ft-lb:	4855	3960	3195	2550	2020
	arc, inches:		+2.2	0	-9.4	-28.0
Federal 300 Trophy Bonded Sledgehammer Solid	velocity, fps:	2530	2160	1820	1520	1280.
	energy, ft-lb:	4265	3105	2210	1550	1090
	arc, inches, s:		0	-6.0	-22.7	-54.6
Hornady 270 SP HM	velocity, fps:	2870	2620	2385	2162	1957
	energy, ft-lb:	4937	4116	3408	2802	2296
	arc, inches:		+2.2	0	-8.4	-23.9
Hornady 300 FMJ RN HM	velocity, fps:	2705	2376	2072	1804	1560
	energy, ft-lb:	4873	3760	2861	2167	1621
	arc, inches:		+2.7	0	-10.8	-32.1
Norma 300 Soft Point	velocity, fps:	2549	2211	1900	1619	
	energy, ft-lb:	4329	3258	2406	1747	
	arc, inches:		+2.8	0	-12.6	
Norma 300 TXP Swift A-Fr.	velocity, fps:	2559	2296	2049	1818	
	energy, ft-lb:	4363	3513	2798	2203	
	arc, inches:		+2.6	0	-10.9	
Norma 300 Oryx	velocity, fps:	2559	2292	2041	1807	
	energy, ft-lb:	4363	3500	2775	2176	
	arc, inches:		+2.6	0	-11.0	
Norma 300 Barnes Solid	velocity, fps:	2493	2061	1677	1356	
	energy, ft-lb:	4141	2829	1873	1234	
	arc, inches:		+3.4	0	-16.0	
PMC 270 PSP	velocity, fps:					
	energy, ft-lb:					
	arc, inches:					
PMC 270 Barnes X	velocity, fps:	2690	2528	2372	2221	2076
	energy, ft-lb:	4337	3831	3371	2957	2582
	arc, inches:		+2.0	0	-8.2	-23.4
PMC 300 Barnes X	velocity, fps:	2530	2389	2252	2120	1993
	energy, ft-lb:	4263	3801	3378	2994	2644
	arc, inches:		+2.3	0	-9.2	-26.1
Rem. 270 Soft Point	velocity, fps:	2690	2420	2166	1928	1707
	energy, ft-lb:	4337	3510	2812	2228	1747
	arc, inches:		+2.2	0	-9.7	-28.7
Rem. 300 Swift A-Frame	velocity, fps:	2530	2245	1979	1733	1512
	energy, ft-lb:	4262	3357	2608	2001	1523
	arc, inches:		+2.7	0	-11.7	-35.0
Speer 285 Grand Slam	velocity, fps:	2610	2365	2134	1916	
	energy, ft-lb:	4310	3540	2883	2323	
	arc, inches:		+2.4	0	-9.9	
Speer 300 African GS Tungsten Solid	velocity, fps:	2609	2277	1970	1690	
	energy, ft-lb:	4534	3453	2585	1903	
	arc, inches:		+2.6	0	-11.7	-35.6
Win. 270 Fail Safe	velocity, fps:	2670	2447	2234	2033	1842
	energy, ft-lb:	4275	3590	2994	2478	2035
	arc, inches:		+2.2	0	-9.1	-28.7

CARTRIDGE BULLET	RANGE, YARDS:	0	100	200	300	400
Win. 300 Fail Safe	velocity, fps:	2530	2336	2151	1974	1806
	energy, ft-lb:	4265	3636	3082	2596	2173
	arc, inches:		+2.4	0	-10.0	-26.9

.375 DAKOTA

CARTRIDGE BULLET	RANGE, YARDS:	0	100	200	300	400
Dakota 270 Barnes X	velocity, fps:	2800	2617	2441	2272	2109
	energy, ft-lb:	4699	4104	3571	3093	2666
	arc, inches:		+2.3	+1.0	-6.1	-19.9
Dakota 300 Barnes X	velocity, fps:	2600	2316	2051	1804	1579
	energy, ft-lb:	4502	3573	2800	2167	1661
	arc, inches:		+2.4	-0.1	-11.0	-32.7

.375 WEATHERBY MAG.

CARTRIDGE BULLET	RANGE, YARDS:	0	100	200	300	400
A-Square 300 SP boat-tail	velocity, fps:	2700	2560	2425	2293	2166
	energy, ft-lb:	4856	4366	3916	3503	3125
	arc, inches:		+4.5	+5.2	0	-11.9
A-Square 300 Triad	velocity, fps:	2700	2391	2103	1835	1602
	energy, ft-lb:	4856	3808	2946	2243	1710
	arc, inches:		+2.3	0	-10.1	-30.8
Wby. 300 Nosler Part.	velocity, fps:	2800	2572	2366	2140	1963
	energy, ft-lb:	5224	4408	3696	3076	2541
	arc, inches:		+1.9	0	-8.2	-23.9

.375 JRS

CARTRIDGE BULLET	RANGE, YARDS:	0	100	200	300	400
A-Square 300 SP boat-tail	velocity, fps:	2700	2560	2425	2293	2166.
	energy, ft-lb:	4856	4366	3916	3503	3125
	arc, inches:		+4.5	+5.2	0	-11.9
A-Square 300 Triad	velocity, fps:	2700	2391	2103	1835	1602
	energy, ft-lb:	4856	3808	2946	2243	1710
	arc, inches:		+2.3	0	-10.1	-30.8

.375 REMINGTON ULTRA MAG

CARTRIDGE BULLET	RANGE, YARDS:	0	100	200	300	400
Rem. 270 Soft Point	velocity, fps:	2900	2558	2241	1947	1678
	energy, fps:	5041	3922	3010	2272	1689
	arc, inches:		+1.9	0	-9.2	-27.8
Rem. 300 Swift A-Frame	velocity, fps:	2760	2505	2263	2035	1822
	energy, fps:	5073	4178	3412	2759	2210
	arc, inches:		+2.0	0	-8.8	-26.1

.375 A-SQUARE

CARTRIDGE BULLET	RANGE, YARDS:	0	100	200	300	400
A-Square 300 SP boat-tail	velocity, fps:	2920	2773	2631	2494	2360
	energy, ft-lb:	5679	5123	4611	4142	3710
	arc, inches:		+3.7	+4.4	0	-9.8
A-Square 300 Triad	velocity, fps:	2920	2596	2294	2012	1762
	energy, ft-lb:	5679	4488	3505	2698	2068
	arc, inches:		+1.8	0	-8.5	-25.5

.376 STEYR

CARTRIDGE BULLET	RANGE, YARDS:	0	100	200	300	400
Hornady 225 SP	velocity, fps:	2600	2331	2078	1842	1625
	energy, ft-lb:	3377	2714	2157	1694	1319
	arc, inches:		+2.5	0	-10.6	-31.4
Hornady 270 SP	velocity, fps:	2600	2372	2156	1951	1759
	energy, ft-lb:	4052	3373	2787	2283	1855
	arc, inches:		+2.3	0	-9.9	-28.9

.378 WEATHERBY MAG.

CARTRIDGE BULLET	RANGE, YARDS:	0	100	200	300	400
A-Square 300 SP boat-tail	velocity, fps:	2900	2754	2612	2475	2342
	energy, ft-lb:	5602	5051	4546	4081	3655
	arc, inches:		+3.8	+4.4	0	-10.0
A-Square 300 Triad	velocity, fps:	2900	2577	2276	1997	1747
	energy, ft-lb:	5602	4424	3452	2656	2034
	arc, inches:		+1.9	0	-8.7	-25.9
Wby. 270 Pointed Expanding	velocity, fps:	3180	2921	2677	2445	2225
	energy, ft-lb:	6062	5115	4295	3583	2968
	arc, inches:		+1.3	0	-6.1	-18.1

Centerfire Rifle Ballistics

.378 WEATHERBY MAGNUM TO 10.57 (.416) METEOR

CARTRIDGE BULLET	RANGE, YARDS:	0	100	200	300	400
Wby. 270 Barnes X	velocity, fps:	3150	2954	2767	2587	2415
	energy, ft-lb:	5948	5232	4589	4013	3495
	arc, inches:		+1.2	0	-5.8	-16.7
Wby. 300 RN Expanding	velocity, fps:	2925	2558	2220	1908	1627.
	energy, ft-lb:	5699	4360	3283	2424	1764
	arc, inches:		+1.9	0	-9.0	-27.8
Wby. 300 FMJ	velocity, fps:	2925	2591	2280	1991	1725
	energy, ft-lb:	5699	4470	3461	2640	1983
	arc, inches:		+1.8	0	-8.6	-26.1

.38-40 WINCHESTER

CARTRIDGE BULLET	RANGE, YARDS:	0	100	200	300	400
Win. 180 Soft Point	velocity, fps:	1160	999	901	827	
	energy, ft-lb:	538	399	324	273	
	arc, inches:		0	-23.4	-75.2	

.38-55 WINCHESTER

CARTRIDGE BULLET	RANGE, YARDS:	0	100	200	300	400
Black Hills 255 FN Lead	velocity, fps:	1250				
	energy, ft-lb:	925				
	arc, inches:					
Win. 255 Soft Point	velocity, fps:	1320	1190	1091	1018	
	energy, ft-lb:	987	802	674	587	
	arc, inches:		0	-33.9	-110.6	

.41 MAG.

CARTRIDGE BULLET	RANGE, YARDS:	0	100	200	300	400
Win. 240 Platinum Tip	velocity, fps:	1830	1488	1220	1048	
	energy, ft-lb:	1784	1180	792	585	
	arc inches:		0	-15.0	-53.4	

.450/.400 (3")

CARTRIDGE BULLET	RANGE, YARDS:	0	100	200	300	400
A-Square 400 Triad	velocity, fps:	2150	1910	1690	1490	
	energy, ft-lb:	4105	3241	2537	1972	
	arc, inches:		+4.4	0	-16.5	

.450/.400 (3 1/4")

CARTRIDGE BULLET	RANGE, YARDS:	0	100	200	300	400
A-Square 400 Triad	velocity, fps:	2150	1910	1690	1490	
	energy, ft-lb:	4105	3241	2537	1972	
	arc, inches:		+4.4	0	-16.5	

.404 JEFFERY

CARTRIDGE BULLET	RANGE, YARDS:	0	100	200	300	400
A-Square 400 Triad	velocity, fps:	2150	1901	1674	1468	1299
	energy, ft-lb:	4105	3211	2489	1915	1499
	arc, inches:		+4.1	0	-16.4	-49.1

.405 WINCHESTER

CARTRIDGE BULLET	RANGE, YARDS:	0	100	200	300	400
Hornady 300 Flatpoint	velocity, fps:	2200	1851	1545	1296	
	energy, ft-lb:	3224	2282	1589	1119	
	arc, inches:		0	-8.7	-31.9	
Hornady 300 SP Interlock	velocity, fps:	2200	1890	1610	1370	
	energy, ft-lb:	3224	2379	1727	1250	
	arc, inches:		0	-8.3	-30.2	

.416 TAYLOR

CARTRIDGE BULLET	RANGE, YARDS:	0	100	200	300	400
A-Square 400 Triad	velocity, fps:	2350	2093	1853	1634	1443
	energy, ft-lb:	4905	3892	3049	2371	1849
	arc, inches:		+3.2	0	-13.6	-39.8

.416 HOFFMAN

CARTRIDGE BULLET	RANGE, YARDS:	0	100	200	300	400
A-Square 400 Triad	velocity, fps:	2380	2122	1879	1658	1464
	energy, ft-lb:	5031	3998	3136	2440	1903
	arc, inches:		+3.1	0	-13.1	-38.7

.416 REMINGTON MAG.

CARTRIDGE BULLET	RANGE, YARDS:	0	100	200	300	400
A-Square 400 Triad	velocity, fps:	2380	2122	1879	1658	1464
	energy, ft-lb:	5031	3998	3136	2440	1903
	arc, inches:		+3.1	0	-13.2	-38.7

CARTRIDGE BULLET	RANGE, YARDS:	0	100	200	300	400
Federal 400 Trophy Bonded Sledgehammer Solid	velocity, fps:	2400	2150	1920	1700	1500
	energy, ft-lb:	5115	4110	3260	2565	2005
	arc, inches:		0	-6.0	-21.6	-49.2
Federal 400 Trophy Bonded	velocity, fps:	2400	2180	1970	1770	1590
	energy, ft-lb:	5115	4215	3440	2785	2245
	arc, inches:		0	-5.8	-20.6	-46.9
Rem. 400 Swift A-Frame	velocity, fps:	2400	2175	1962	1763	1579
	energy, ft-lb:	5115	4201	3419	2760	2214
	arc, inches:		0	-5.9	-20.8	

.416 RIGBY

CARTRIDGE BULLET	RANGE, YARDS:	0	100	200	300	400
A-Square 400 Triad	velocity, fps:	2400	2140	1897	1673	1478
	energy, ft-lb:	5115	4069	3194	2487	1940
	arc, inches:		+3.0	0	-12.9	-38.0
Federal 400 Trophy Bonded	velocity, fps:	2370	2150	1940	1750	1570
	energy, ft-lb:	4990	4110	3350	2715	2190
	arc, inches:		0	-6.0	-21.3	-48.1
Federal 400 Trophy Bonded Sledgehammer Solid	velocity, fps:	2370	2120	1890	1660	1460
	energy, ft-lb:	4990	3975	3130	2440	1895
	arc, inches:		0	-6.3	-22.5	-51.5
Federal 410 Woodleigh Weldcore	velocity, fps:	2370	2110	1870	1640	1440
	energy, ft-lb:	5115	4050	3165	2455	1895
	arc, inches:		0	-7.4	-24.8	-55.0
Federal 410 Solid	velocity, fps:	2370	2110	2870	1640	1440
	energy, ft-lb:	5115	4050	3165	2455	1895
	arc, inches:		0	-7.4	-24.8	-55.0
Norma 400 TXP Swift A-Fr.	velocity, fps:	2350	2127	1917	1721	
	energy, ft-lb:	4906	4021	3266	2632	
	arc, inches:		+3.1	0	-12.5	
Norma 400 Barnes Solid	velocity, fps:	2297	1930	1604	1330	
	energy, ft-lb:	4687	3310	2284	1571	
	arc, inches:		+3.9	0	-17.7	

.416 RIMMED

CARTRIDGE BULLET	RANGE, YARDS:	0	100	200	300	400
A-Square 400 Triad	velocity, fps:	2400	2140	1897	1673	
	energy, ft-lb:	5115	4069	3194	2487	
	arc, inches:		+3.3	0	-13.2	

.416 DAKOTA

CARTRIDGE BULLET	RANGE, YARDS:	0	100	200	300	400
Dakota 400 Barnes X	velocity, fps:	2450	2294	2143	1998	1859
	energy, ft-lb:	5330	4671	4077	3544	3068
	arc, inches:		+2.5	-0.2	-10.5	-29.4

.416 WEATHERBY

CARTRIDGE BULLET	RANGE, YARDS:	0	100	200	300	400
A-Square 400 Triad	velocity, fps:	2600	2328	2073	1834	1624
	energy, ft-lb:	6004	4813	3816	2986	2343
	arc, inches:		+2.5	0	-10.5	-31.6
Wby. 350 Barnes X	velocity, fps:	2850	2673	2503	2340	2182
	energy, ft-lb:	6312	5553	4870	4253	3700
	arc, inches:		+1.7	0	-7.2	-20.9
Wby. 400 Swift A-Fr.	velocity, fps:	2650	2426	2213	2011	1820
	energy, ft-lb:	6237	5227	4350	3592	2941
	arc, inches:		+2.2	0	-9.3	-27.1
Wby. 400 RN Expanding	velocity, fps:	2700	2417	2152	1903	1676
	energy, ft-lb:	6474	5189	4113	3216	2493
	arc, inches:		+2.3	0	-9.7	-29.3
Wby. 400 Monolithic Solid	velocity, fps:	2700	2411	2140	1887	1656
	energy, ft-lb:	6474	5162	4068	3161	2435
	arc, inches:		+2.3	0	-9.8	-29.7

10.57 (.416) METEOR

CARTRIDGE BULLET	RANGE, YARDS:	0	100	200	300	400
Lazzeroni 400 Swift A-Fr.	velocity, fps:	2730	2532	2342	2161	1987
	energy, ft-lb:	6621	5695	4874	4147	3508
	arc, inches:		+1.9	0	-8.3	-24.0

Centerfire Rifle Ballistics

10.57 (.416) METEOR TO .458 WINCHESTER MAGNUM

CARTRIDGE BULLET	RANGE, YARDS:	0	100	200	300	400
.425 EXPRESS						
A-Square 400 Triad	velocity, fps:	2400	2136	1888	1662	1465
	energy, ft-lb:	5115	4052	3167	2454	1906
	arc, inches:		+3.0	0	-13.1	-38.3
.44-40 WINCHESTER						
Rem. 200 Soft Point	velocity, fps:	1190	1006	900	822	756
	energy, ft-lb:	629	449	360	300	254
	arc, inches:		0	-33.1	-108.7	-235.2
Win. 200 Soft Point	velocity, fps:	1190	1006	900	822	756
	energy, ft-lb:	629	449	360	300	254
	arc, inches:		0	-33.3	-109.5	-237.4
.44 REMINGTON MAG.						
Federal 240 Hi-Shok HP	velocity, fps:	1760	1380	1090	950	860
	energy, ft-lb:	1650	1015	640	485	395
	arc, inches:		0	-17.4	-60.7	-136.0
Rem. 210 Semi-Jacketed HP	velocity, fps:	1920	1477	1155	982	880
	energy, ft-lb:	1719	1017	622	450	361
	arc, inches:		0	-14.7	-55.5	-131.3
Rem. 240 Soft Point	velocity, fps:	1760	1380	1114	970	878
	energy, ft-lb:	1650	1015	661	501	411
	arc, inches:		0	-17.0	-61.4	-143.0
Rem. 240 Semi-Jacketed Hollow Point	velocity, fps:	1760	1380	1114	970	878
	energy, ft-lb:	1650	1015	661	501	411
	arc, inches:		0	-17.0	-61.4	-143.0
Rem. 275 JHP Core-Lokt	velocity, fps:	1580	1293	1093	976	896
	energy, ft-lb:	1524	1020	730	582	490
	arc, inches:		0	-19.4	-67.5	-210.8
Win. 210 Silvertip HP	velocity, fps:	1580	1198	993	879	795
	energy, ft-lb:	1164	670	460	361	295
	arc, inches:		0	-22.4	-76.1	-168.0
Win. 240 Hollow Soft Point	velocity, fps:	1760	1362	1094	953	861
	energy, ft-lb:	1650	988	638	484	395
	arc, inches:		0	-18.1	-65.1	-150.3
Win. 250 Platinum Tip	velocity, fps:	1830	1475	1201	1032	931
	energy, ft-lb:	1859	1208	801	591	481
	arc, inches:		0	-15.3	-54.7	-126.6
.444 MARLIN						
Rem. 240 Soft Point	velocity, fps:	2350	1815	1377	1087	941
	energy, ft-lb:	2942	1755	1010	630	472
	arc, inches:		+2.2	-5.4	-31.4	-86.7
Hornady 265 FP LM	velocity, fps:	2335	1913	1551	1266	
	energy, ft-lb:	3208	2153	1415	943	
	arc, inches:		+2.0	-4.9	-26.5	
.45-70 GOVERNMENT						
Black Hills 405 FPL	velocity, fps:	1250				
	energy, ft-lb:					
	arc, inches:					
Federal 300 Sierra Pro-Hunt. HP FN	velocity, fps:	1880	1650	1430	1240	1110
	energy, ft-lb:	2355	1815	1355	1015	810
	arc, inches:		0	-11.5	-39.7	-89.1
PMC 350 FNSP	velocity, fps:					
	energy, ft-lb:					
	arc, inches:					
Rem. 300 Jacketed HP	velocity, fps:	1810	1497	1244	1073	969
	energy, ft-lb:	2182	1492	1031	767	625
	arc, inches:		0	-13.8	-50.1	-115.7
Rem. 405 Soft Point	velocity, fps:	1330	1168	1055	977	918
	energy, ft-lb:	1590	1227	1001	858	758
	arc, inches:		0	-24.0	-78.6	-169.4

CARTRIDGE BULLET	RANGE, YARDS:	0	100	200	300	400
Win. 300 Jacketed HP	velocity, fps:	1880	1650	1425	1235	1105
	energy, ft-lb:	2355	1815	1355	1015	810
	arc, inches:		0	-12.8	-44.3	-95.5
Win. 300 Partition Gold	velocity, fps:	1880	1558	1292	1103	988
	energy, ft-lb:	2355	1616	1112	811	651
	arc, inches:		0	-12.9	-46.0	-104.9.
.450 MARLIN						
Hornady 350 FP	velocity, fps:	2100	1720	1397	1156	
	energy, ft-lb:	3427	2298	1516	1039	
	arc, inches:		0	-10.4	-38.9	
.450 NITRO EXPRESS (3 ¼")						
A-Square 465 Triad	velocity, fps:	2190	1970	1765	1577	
	energy, ft-lb:	4952	4009	3216	2567	
	arc, inches:		+4.3	0	-15.4	
.450 #2						
A-Square 465 Triad	velocity, fps:	2190	1970	1765	1577	
	energy, ft-lb:	4952	4009	3216	2567	
	arc, inches:		+4.3	0	-15.4	
.458 WINCHESTER MAG.						
A-Square 465 Triad	velocity, fps:	2220	1999	1791	1601	1433
	energy, ft-lb:	5088	4127	3312	2646	2121
	arc, inches:		+3.6	0	-14.7	-42.5
Federal 350 Soft Point	velocity, fps:	2470	1990	1570	1250	1060
	energy, ft-lb:	4740	3065	1915	1205	870
	arc, inches:		0	-7.5	-29.1	-71.1
Federal 400 Trophy Bonded	velocity, fps:	2380	2170	1960	1770	1590
	energy, ft-lb:	5030	4165	3415	2785	2255
	arc, inches:		0	-5.9	-20.9	-47.1
Federal 500 Solid	velocity, fps:	2090	1870	1670	1480	1320
	energy, ft-lb:	4850	3880	3085	2440	1945
	arc, inches:		0	-8.5	-29.5	-66.2
Federal 500 Trophy Bonded	velocity, fps:	2090	1870	1660	1480	1310
	energy, ft-lb:	4850	3870	3065	2420	1915
	arc, inches:		0	-8.5	-29.7	-66.8
Federal 500 Trophy Bonded Sledgehammer Solid	velocity, fps:	2090	1860	1650	1460	1300
	energy, ft-lb:	4850	3845	3025	2365	1865
	arc, inches:		0	-8.6	-30.0	-67.8
Federal 510 Soft Point	velocity, fps:	2090	1820	1570	1360	1190
	energy, ft-lb:	4945	3730	2790	2080	1605
	arc, inches:		0	-9.1	-32.3	-73.9
Hornady 500 FMJ-RN HM	velocity, fps:	2260	1984	1735	1512	
	energy, ft-lb:	5670	4368	3341	2538	
	arc, inches:		0	-7.4	-26.4	
Norma 500 TXP Swift A-Fr.	velocity, fps:	2116	1903	1705	1524	
	energy, ft-lb:	4972	4023	3228	2578	
	arc, inches:		+4.1	0	-16.1	
Norma 500 Barnes Solid	velocity, fps:	2067	1750	1472	1245	
	energy, ft-lb:	4745	3401	2405	1721	
	arc, inches:		+4.9	0	-21.2	
Rem. 450 Swift A-Frame PSP	velocity, fps:	2150	1901	1671	1465	1289
	energy, ft-lb:	4618	3609	2789	2144	1659
	arc, inches:		0	-8.2	-28.9	
Speer 500 African GS Tungsten Solid	velocity, fps:	2120	1845	1596	1379	
	energy, ft-lb:	4989	3780	2828	2111	
	arc, inches:		0	-8.8	-31.3	
Speer African Grand Slam	velocity, fps:	2120	1853	1609	1396	
	energy, ft-lb:	4989	3810	2875	2163	
	arc, inches:		0	-8.7	-30.8	
Win. 510 Soft Point	velocity, fps:	2040	1770	1527	1319	1157
	energy, ft-lb:	4712	3547	2640	1970	1516
	arc, inches:		0	-10.3	-35.6	

BALLISTICS

Ballistics • **489**

Centerfire Rifle Ballistics

.458 LOTT TO .700 NITRO EXPRESS

CARTRIDGE BULLET	RANGE, YARDS:	0	100	200	300	400
.458 LOTT						
A-Square 465 Triad	velocity, fps:	2380	2150	1932	1730	1551
	energy, ft-lb:	5848	4773	3855	3091	2485
	arc, inches:		+3.0	0	-12.5	-36.4
Hornady 500 RNSP or solid	velocity, fps:	2300	2022	1776	1551	
	energy, ft-lb:	5872	4537	3502	2671	
	arc, inches:		+3.4	0	-14.3	
Hornady 500 InterBond	velocity, fps:	2300	2028	1777	1549	
	energy, ft-lb:	5872	4535	3453	2604	
	arc, inches:		0	-7.0	-25.1	
.450 ACKLEY						
A-Square 465 Triad	velocity, fps:	2400	2169	1950	1747	1567
	energy, ft-lb:	5947	4857	3927	3150	2534
	arc, inches:		+2.9	0	-12.2	-35.8
.460 SHORT A-SQUARE						
A-Square 500 Triad	velocity, fps:	2420	2198	1987	1789	1613
	energy, ft-lb:	6501	5362	4385	3553	2890
	arc, inches:		+2.9	0	-11.6	-34.2
.450 DAKOTA						
Dakota 500 Barnes Solid	velocity, fps:	2450	2235	2030	1838	1658
	energy, ft-lb:	6663	5544	4576	3748	3051
	arc, inches:		+2.5	-0.6	-12.0	-33.8
.460 WEATHERBY MAG.						
A-Square 500 Triad	velocity, fps:	2580	2349	2131	1923	1737
	energy, ft-lb:	7389	6126	5040	4107	3351
	arc, inches:		+2.4	0	-10.0	-29.4
Wby. 450 Barnes X	velocity, fps:	2700	2518	2343	2175	2013
	energy, ft-lb:	7284	6333	5482	4725	4050
	arc, inches:		+2.0	0	-8.4	-24.1
Wby. 500 RN Expanding	velocity, fps:	2600	2301	2022	1764	1533.
	energy, ft-lb:	7504	5877	4539	3456	2608
	arc, inches:		+2.6	0	-11.1	-33.5
Wby. 500 FMJ	velocity, fps:	2600	2309	2037	1784	1557
	energy, ft-lb:	7504	5917	4605	3534	2690
	arc, inches:		+2.5	0	-10.9	-33.0
.500/.465						
A-Square 480 Triad	velocity, fps:	2150	1928	1722	1533	
	energy, ft-lb:	4926	3960	3160	2505	
	arc, inches:		+4.3	0	-16.0	
.470 NITRO EXPRESS						
A-Square 500 Triad	velocity, fps:	2150	1912	1693	1494	
	energy, ft-lb:	5132	4058	3182	2478	
	arc, inches:		+4.4	0	-16.5	
Federal 500 Woodleigh Weldcore	velocity, fps:	2150	1890	1650	1440	1270
	energy, ft-lb:	5130	3965	3040	2310	1790
	arc, inches:		0	-9.3	-31.3	-69.7
Federal 500 Woodleigh Weldcore Solid	velocity, fps:	2150	1890	1650	1440	1270.
	energy, ft-lb:	5130	3965	3040	2310	1790
	arc, inches:		0	-9.3	-31.3	-69.7
Federal 500 Trophy Bonded	velocity, fps:	2150	1940	1740	1560	1400
	energy, ft-lb:	5130	4170	3360	2695	2160
	arc, inches:		0	-7.8	-27.1	-60.8
Federal 500 Trophy Bonded Sledgehammer Solid	velocity, fps:	2150	1940	1740	1560	1400
	energy, ft-lb:	5130	4170	3360	2695	2160
	arc, inches:		0	-7.8	-27.1	-60.8
Norma 500 Woodleigh SP	velocity, fps:	2165	1975	1795	1627	
	energy, ft-lb:	5205	4330	3577	2940	
	arc, inches:		0	-7.4	-25.7	
Norma 500 Woodleigh FJ	velocity, fps:	2165	1974	1794	1626	
	energy, ft-lb:	5205	4328	3574	2936	
	arc, inches:		0	-7.5	-25.7	
.470 CAPSTICK						
A-Square 500 Triad	velocity, fps:	2400	2172	1958	1761	1553
	energy, ft-lb:	6394	5236	4255	3445	2678
	arc, inches:		+2.9	0	-11.9	-36.1
.475 #2						
A-Square 480 Triad	velocity, fps:	2200	1964	1744	1544	
	energy, ft-lb:	5158	4109	3240	2539	
	arc, inches:		+4.1	0	-15.6	
.475 #2 JEFFERY						
A-Square 500 Triad	velocity, fps:	2200	1966	1748	1550	
	energy, ft-lb:	5373	4291	3392	2666	
	arc, inches:		+4.1	0	-15.6	
.495 A-SQUARE						
A-Square 570 Triad	velocity, fps:	2350	2117	1896	1693	1513
	energy, ft-lb:	6989	5671	4552	3629	2899
	arc, inches:		+3.1	0	-13.0	-37.8
.500 NITRO EXPRESS (3")						
A-Square 570 Triad	velocity, fps:	2150	1928	1722	1533	
	energy, ft-lb:	5850	4703	3752	2975	
	arc, inches:		+4.3	0	-16.1	
.500 A-SQUARE						
A-Square 600 Triad	velocity, fps:	2470	2235	2013	1804	1620
	energy, ft-lb:	8127	6654	5397	4336	3495
	arc, inches:		+2.7	0	-11.3	-33.5
.505 GIBBS						
A-Square 525 Triad	velocity, fps:	2300	2063	1840	1637	
	energy, ft-lb:	6166	4962	3948	3122	
	arc, inches:		+3.6	0	-14.2	
.577 NITRO EXPRESS						
A-Square 750 Triad	velocity, fps:	2050	1811	1595	1401	
	energy, ft-lb:	6998	5463	4234	3267	
	arc, inches:		+4.9	0	-18.5	
.577 TYRANNOSAUR						
A-Square 750 Triad	velocity, fps:	2460	2197	1950	1723	1516
	energy, ft-lb:	10077	8039	6335	4941	3825
	arc, inches:		+2.8	0	-12.1	-36.0
.600 NITRO EXPRESS						
A-Square 900 Triad	velocity, fps:	1950	1680	1452	1336	
	energy, ft-lb:	7596	5634	4212	3564	
	arc, inches:		+5.6	0	-20.7	
.700 NITRO EXPRESS						
A-Square 1000 Monolithic Solid	velocity, fps:	1900	1669	1461	1288	
	energy, ft-lb:	8015	6188	4740	3685	
	arc, inches:		+5.8	0	-22.2	

Centerfire Handgun Ballistics

Centerfire Handgun Ballistics

Data shown here is taken from manufacturers' charts; your chronograph readings may vary. Barrel lengths for pistol data vary, and depend in part on which pistols are typically chambered in a given cartridge. Velocity variations due to barrel length depend on the baseline bullet speed and the load. Velocity for the .30 Carbine, normally a rifle cartridge, was determined in a pistol barrel.

Listings are current as of February the year Shooter's Bible appears (not the cover year). Listings are not intended as recommendations. For example, the data for the .25 Auto gives velocity and energy readings to 100 yards. Few hand-gunners would call the little .25 a 100-yard cartridge.

Abbreviations: Bullets are designated by loading company, weight (in grains) and type, with these abbreviations for shape and construction: BJHP=brass-jacketed hollow-point; FN=Flat Nose; FMC=Full Metal Case; FMJ=Full Metal Jacket; HP=Hollowpoint; L=Lead; LF=Lead-Free; +P=a more powerful load than traditionally manufactured for that round; RN=Round Nose; SFHP=Starfire (PMC) Hollowpoint; SP=Softpoint; SWC=Semi Wadcutter; TMJ=Total Metal Jacket; WC=Wadcutter; CEPP, SXT and XTP are trademarked designations of Lapua, Winchester and Hornady, respectively.

.25 AUTO TO .32 S&W LONG

CARTRIDGE BULLET	RANGE, YARDS:	0	25	50	75	100
.25 AUTO						
Federal 50 FMJ	velocity, fps:	760	750	730	720	700
	energy, ft-lb:	65	60	60	55	55
Hornady 35 JHP/XTP	velocity, fps:	900		813		742
	energy, ft-lb:	63		51		43
Magtech 50 FMC	velocity, fps:	760		707		659
	energy, ft-lb:	64		56		48
PMC 50 FMJ	velocity, fps:	754	730	707	685	663
	energy, ft-lb:	62				
Rem. 50 Metal Case	velocity, fps:	760		707		659
	energy, ft-lb:	64		56		48
Speer 35 Gold Dot	velocity, fps:	900		816		747
	energy, ft-lb:	63		52		43
Speer 50 TMJ (and Blazer)	velocity, fps:	760		717		677
	energy, ft-lb:	64		57		51
Win. 45 Expanding Point	velocity, fps:	815		729		655
	energy, ft-lb	66		53		42
Win. 50 FMJ	velocity, fps:	760		707		
	energy, ft-lb	64		56		
.30 LUGER						
Win. 93 FMJ	velocity, fps:	1220		1110		1040
	energy, ft-lb	305		255		225
7.62x25 TOKAREV						
PMC 93 FMJ	velocity and energy figures not available					
.30 CARBINE						
Win. 110 Hollow SP	velocity, fps:	1790		1601		1430
	energy, ft-lb	783		626		500
.32 AUTO						
Federal 65 Hydra-Shok JHP	velocity, fps:	950	920	890	860	830
	energy, ft-lb:	130	120	115	105	100
Federal 71 FMJ	velocity, fps:	910	880	860	830	810
	energy, ft-lb:	130	120	115	110	105
Hornady 60 JHP/XTP	velocity, fps:	1000		917		849
	energy, ft-lb:	133		112		96
Hornady 71 FMJ-RN	velocity, fps:	900		845		797
	energy, ft-lb:	128		112		100

CARTRIDGE BULLET	RANGE, YARDS:	0	25	50	75	100
Magtech 71 FMC	velocity, fps:	905		855		810
	energy, ft-lb:	129		115		103
Magtech 71 JHP	velocity, fps:	905		855		810
	energy, ft-lb:	129		115		103
PMC 60 JHP	velocity, fps:	980	849	820	791	763
	energy, ft-lb:	117				
PMC 70 SFHP	velocity, fps:	velocity and energy figures not available				
PMC 71 FMJ	velocity, fps:	870	841	814	791	763
	energy, ft-lb:	119				
Rem. 71 Metal Case	velocity, fps:	905		855		810
	energy, ft-lb:	129		115		97
Speer 60 Gold Dot	velocity, fps:	960		868		796
	energy, ft-lb:	123		100		84
Speer 71 TMJ (and Blazer)	velocity, fps:	900		855		810
	energy, ft-lb:	129		115		97
Win. 60 Silvertip HP	velocity, fps:	970		895		835
	energy, ft-lb	125		107		93
Win. 71 FMJ	velocity, fps:	905		855		
	energy, ft-lb	129		115		
.32 S&W						
Rem. 88 LRN	velocity, fps:	680		645		610
	energy, ft-lb:	90		81		73
Win. 85 LRN	velocity, fps:	680		645		610
	energy, ft-lb	90		81		73
.32 S&W LONG						
Federal 98 LWC	velocity, fps:	780	700	630	560	500
	energy, ft-lb:	130	105	85	70	55
Federal 98 LRN	velocity, fps:	710	690	670	650	640
	energy, ft-lb:	115	105	100	95	90
Lapua 83 LWC	velocity, fps:	240		189*		149*
	energy, ft-lb:	154		95*		59*
Lapua 98 LWC	velocity, fps:	240		202*		171*
	energy, ft-lb:	183		130*		93*
Magtech 98 LRN	velocity, fps:	705		670		635
	energy, ft-lb:	108		98		88
Magtech 98 LWC	velocity, fps:	682		579		491
	energy, ft-lb:	102		73		52
Norma 98 LWC	velocity, fps:	787	759	732		683
	energy, ft-lb:	136	126	118		102

Centerfire Handgun Ballistics

.32 S&W LONG TO 9MM LUGER

CARTRIDGE BULLET	RANGE, YARDS:	0	25	50	75	100
PMC 98 LRN	velocity, fps:	789	770	751	733	716
	energy, ft-lb:	135				
PMC 100 LWC	velocity, fps:	683	652	623	595	569
	energy, ft-lb:	102				
Rem. 98 LRN	velocity, fps:	705		670		635
	energy, ft-lb:	115		98		88
Win. 98 LRN	velocity, fps:	705		670		635
	energy, ft-lb:	115		98		88

.32 SHORT COLT

CARTRIDGE BULLET	RANGE, YARDS:	0	25	50	75	100
Win. 80 LRN	velocity, fps:	745		665		590
	energy, ft-lb	100		79		62

.32-20

CARTRIDGE BULLET	RANGE, YARDS:	0	25	50	75	100
Black Hills 115 FPL	velocity, fps:	800				
	energy, ft-lb:					

.32 H&R MAG

CARTRIDGE BULLET	RANGE, YARDS:	0	25	50	75	100
Black Hills 85 JHP	velocity, fps	1100				
	energy, ft-lb	228				
Black Hills 90 FPL	velocity, fps	750				
	energy, ft-lb					
Black Hills 115 FPL	velocity, fps	800				
	energy, ft-lb					
Federal 85 Hi-Shok JHP	velocity, fps:	1100	1050	1020	970	930
	energy, ft-lb:	230	210	195	175	165
Federal 95 LSWC	velocity, fps:	1030	1000	940	930	900
	energy, ft-lb:	225	210	195	185	170

9MM MAKAROV

CARTRIDGE BULLET	RANGE, YARDS:	0	25	50	75	100
Federal 90 Hi-Shok JHP	velocity, fps:	990	950	910	880	850
	energy, ft-lb:	195	180	165	155	145
Federal 90 FMJ	velocity, fps:	990	960	920	900	870
	energy, ft-lb:	205	190	180	170	160
Hornady 95 JHP/XTP	velocity, fps:	1000		930		874
	energy, ft-lb:	211		182		161
PMC 100 FMJ-TC	velocity, fps:	velocity and energy figures not available				
Speer 95 TMJ Blazer	velocity, fps:	1000		928		872
	energy, ft-lb:	211		182		161

9x21 IMI

CARTRIDGE BULLET	RANGE, YARDS:	0	25	50	75	100
PMC 123 FMJ	velocity, fps:	1150	1093	1046	1007	973
	energy, ft-lb:	364				

9MM LUGER

CARTRIDGE BULLET	RANGE, YARDS:	0	25	50	75	100
Black Hills 115 JHP	velocity, fps:	1150				
	energy, ft-lb:	336				
Black Hills 115 FMJ	velocity, fps:	1150				
	energy, ft-lb:	336				
Black Hills 115 JHP +P	velocity, fps:	1300				
	energy, ft-lb:	431				
Black Hills 115 EXP JHP	velocity, fps:	1250				
	energy, ft-lb:	400				
Black Hills 124 JHP +P	velocity, fps:	1250				
	energy, ft-lb:	430				
Black Hills 124 JHP	velocity, fps:	1150				
	energy, ft-lb:	363				
Black Hills 124 FMJ	velocity, fps:	1150				
	energy, ft-lb:	363				
Black Hills 147 JHP subsonic	velocity, fps:	975				
	energy, ft-lb:	309				
Black Hills 147 FMJ subsonic	velocity, fps:	975				
	energy, ft-lb:	309				
Federal 105 EFMJ	velocity, fps:	1225	1160	1105	1060	1025
	energy, ft-lb:	350	315	285	265	245
Federal 115 Hi-Shok JHP	velocity, fps:	1160	1100	1060	1020	990
	energy, ft-lb:	345	310	285	270	250
Federal 115 FMJ	velocity, fps:	1160	1100	1060	1020	990
	energy, ft-lb:	345	310	285	270	250
Federal 124 FMJ	velocity, fps:	1120	1070	1030	990	960
	energy, ft-lb:	345	315	290	270	255
Federal 124 Hydra-Shok JHP	velocity, fps:	1120	1070	1030	990	960
	energy, ft-lb:	345	315	290	270	255
Federal 124 TMJ TMF Primer	velocity, fps:	1120	1070	1030	990	960
	energy, ft-lb:	345	315	290	270	255
Federal 124 Truncated FMJ Match	velocity, fps:	1120	1070	1030	990	960
	energy, ft-lb:	345	315	290	270	255
Federal 124 Nyclad HP	velocity, fps:	1120	1070	1030	990	960
	energy, ft-lb:	345	315	290	270	255
Federal 124 FMJ +P	velocity, fps:	1120	1070	1030	990	960
	energy, ft-lb:	345	315	290	270	255
Federal 135 Hydra-Shok JHP	velocity, fps:	1050	1030	1010	980	970
	energy, ft-lb:	330	315	300	290	280
Federal 147 Hydra-Shok JHP	velocity, fps:	1000	960	920	890	860
	energy, ft-lb:	325	300	275	260	240
Federal 147 Hi-Shok JHP	velocity, fps:	980	950	930	900	880
	energy, ft-lb:	310	295	285	265	255
Federal 147 FMJ FN	velocity, fps:	960	930	910	890	870
	energy, ft-lb:	295	280	270	260	250
Federal 147 TMJ TMF Primer	velocity, fps:	960	940	910	890	870
	energy, ft-lb:	300	285	270	260	245
Hornady 115 JHP/XTP	velocity, fps:	1155		1047		971
	energy, ft-lb:	341		280		241
Hornady 124 JHP/XTP	velocity, fps:	1110		1030		971
	energy, ft-lb:	339		292		259
Hornady 124 TAP-FPD	velocity, fps:	1100		1028		967
	energy, ft-lb:	339		291		257
Hornady 147 JHP/XTP	velocity, fps:	975		935		899
	energy, ft-lb:	310		285		264
Hornady 147 TAP-FPD	velocity, fps:	975		935		899
	energy, ft-lb:	310		285		264
Lapua 116 FMJ	velocity, fps:	365		319*		290*
	energy, ft-lb:	500		381*		315*
Lapua 120 FMJ CEPP Super	velocity, fps:	360		316*		288*
	energy, ft-lb:	505		390*		324*
Lapua 120 FMJ CEPP Extra	velocity, fps:	360		316*		288*
	energy, ft-lb:	505		390*		324*
Lapua 123 HP Megashock	velocity, fps:	355		311*		284*
	energy, ft-lb:	504		388*		322*
Lapua 123 FMJ	velocity, fps:	320		292*		272*
	energy, ft-lb:	410		342*		295*
Lapua 123 FMJ Combat	velocity, fps:	355		315*		289*
	energy, ft-lb:	504		397*		333*
Magtech 115 JHP +P	velocity, fps:	1246		1137		1056
	energy, ft-lb:	397		330		285
Magtech 115 FMC	velocity, fps:	1135		1027		961
	energy, ft-lb:	330		270		235
Magtech 115 JHP	velocity, fps:	1155		1047		971
	energy, ft-lb:	340		280		240
Magtech 124 FMC	velocity, fps:	1109		1030		971
	energy, ft-lb:	339		292		259
Norma 84 Lead Free Frangible (Geco brand)	velocity, fps:	1411				
	energy, ft-lb:	371				
Norma 124 FMJ (Geco brand)	velocity, fps:	1120				
	energy, fps:	341				
Norma 123 FMJ	velocity, fps:	1099	1032	980		899
	energy, ft-lb:	331	292	263		221

CARTRIDGE BULLET	RANGE, YARDS:	0	25	50	75	100
Norma 123 FMJ	velocity, fps:	1280	1170	1086		972
	energy, ft-lb:	449	375	323		259
PMC 75 Non-Toxic Frangible	velocity, fps:	1350	1240	1154	1088	1035
	energy, ft-lb:	303				
PMC 95 SFHP	velocity, fps:	1250	1239	1228	1217	1207
	energy, ft-lb:	330				
PMC 115 FMJ	velocity, fps:	1157	1100	1053	1013	979
	energy, ft-lb:	344				
PMC 115 JHP	velocity, fps:	1167	1098	1044	999	961
	energy, ft-lb:	350				
PMC 124 SFHP	velocity, fps:	1090	1043	1003	969	939
	energy, ft-lb:	327				
PMC 124 FMJ	velocity, fps:	1110	1059	1017	980	949
	energy, ft-lb:	339				
PMC 124 LRN	velocity, fps:	1050	1006	969	937	908
	energy, ft-lb:	304				
PMC 147 FMJ	velocity, fps:	980	965	941	919	900
	enerby, ft-lb:	310				
PMC 147 SFHP	velocity, fps:	velocity and energy figures not available				
Rem. 101 Lead Free Frangible	velocity, fps:	1220		1092		1004
	energy, ft-lb:	334		267		226
Rem. 115 FN Enclosed Base	velocity, fps:	1135		1041		973
	energy, ft-lb:	329		277		242
Rem. 115 Metal Case	velocity, fps:	1135		1041		973
	energy, ft-lb:	329		277		242
Rem. 115 JHP	velocity, fps:	1155		1047		971
	energy, ft-lb:	341		280		241
Rem. 115 JHP +P	velocity, fps:	1250		1113		1019
	energy, ft-lb:	399		316		265
Rem. 124 JHP	velocity, fps:	1120		1028		960
	energy, ft-lb:	346		291		254
Rem. 124 FNEB	velocity, fps:	1100		1030		971
	energy, ft-lb:	339		292		252
Rem. 124 BJHP	velocity, fps:	1125		1031		963
	energy, ft-lb:	349		293		255
Rem. 124 BJHP +P	velocity, fps:	1180		1089		1021
	energy, ft-lb:	384		327		287
Rem. 124 Metal Case	velocity, fps:	1110		1030		971
	energy, ft-lb:	339		292		259
Rem. 147 JHP subsonic	velocity, fps:	990		941		900
	energy, ft-lb:	320		289		264
Rem. 147 BJHP	velocity, fps:	990		941		900
	energy, ft-lb:	320		289		264
Speer 90 Frangible	velocity, fps:	1350		1132		1001
	energy, ft-lb:	364		256		200
Speer 115 JHP Blazer	velocity, fps:	1145		1024		943
	energy, ft-lb:	335		268		227
Speer 115 FMJ Blazer	velocity, fps:	1145		1047		971
	energy, ft-lb:	341		280		241
Speer 115 FMJ	velocity, fps:	1200		1060		970
	energy, ft-lb:	368		287		240
Speer 115 Gold Dot HP	velocity, fps:	1200		1047		971
	energy, ft-lb:	341		280		241
Speer 124 FMJ Blazer	velocity, fps:	1090		989		917
	energy, ft-lb:	327		269		231
Speer 124 FMJ	velocity, fps:	1090		987		913
	energy, ft-lb:	327		268		230
Speer 124 TMJ-CF (and Blazer)	velocity, fps:	1090		989		917
	energy, ft-lb:	327		269		231
Speer 124 Gold Dot HP	velocity, fps:	1150		1030		948
	energy, ft-lb:	367		292		247
Speer 124 Gold Dot HP+P	velocity, ft-lb:	1220		1085		996

CARTRIDGE BULLET	RANGE, YARDS:	0	25	50	75	100
	energy, ft-lb:	410		324		273
Speer 147 TMJ Blazer	velocity, fps:	950		912		879
	energy, ft-lb:	295		272		252
Speer 147 TMJ	velocity, fps:	985		943		906
	energy, ft-lb:	317		290		268
Speer 147 TMJ-CF (and Blazer)	velocity, fps:	985		960		924
	energy, ft-lb:	326		300		279
Speer 147 Gold Dot	velocity, fps:	985		960		924
	energy, ft-lb:	326		300		279
Win. 105 Jacketed FP	velocity, fps:	1200		1074		989
	energy, ft-lb:	336		269		228
Win. 115 Silvertip HP	velocity, fps:	1225		1095		1007
	energy, ft-lb:	383		306		259
Win. 115 Jacketed HP	velocity, fps:	1225		1095		
	energy, ft-lb:	383		306		
Win. 115 FMJ	velocity, fps:	1190		1071		
	energy, ft-lb:	362		293		
Win. 115 EB WinClean	velocity, fps:	1190		1088		
	energy, ft-lb:	362		302		
Win. 124 FMJ	velocity, fps:	1140		1050		
	energy, ft-lb:	358		303		
Win. 124 EB WinClean	velocity, fps:	1130		1049		
	energy, ft-lb:	352		303		
Win. 147 FMJ FN	velocity, fps:	990		945		
	energy, ft-lb:	320		292		
Win. 147 SXT	velocity, fps:	990		947		909
	energy, ft-lb:	320		293		270
Win. 147 Silvertip HP	velocity, fps:	1010		962		921
	energy, ft-lb:	333		302		277
Win. 147 JHP	velocity, fps:	990		945		
	energy, ft-lb:	320		291		
Win. 147 EB WinClean	velocity, fps:	990		945		
	energy, ft-lb:	320		291		

9 x 23 WINCHESTER

CARTRIDGE BULLET	RANGE, YARDS:	0	25	50	75	100
Win. 124 Jacketed FP	velocity, fps:	1460		1308		
	energy, ft-lb:	587		471		
Win. 125 Silvertip HP	velocity, fps:	1450		1249		1103
	energy, ft-lb:	583		433		338

.38 S&W

CARTRIDGE BULLET	RANGE, YARDS:	0	25	50	75	100
Rem. 146 LRN	velocity, fps:	685		650		620
	energy, ft-lb:	150		135		125
Win. 145 LRN	velocity, fps:	685		650		620
	energy, ft-lb:	150		135		125

.38 SHORT COLT

CARTRIDGE BULLET	RANGE, YARDS:	0	25	50	75	100
Rem. 125 LRN	velocity, fps:	730		685		645
	energy, ft-lb:	150		130		115

.38 LONG COLT

CARTRIDGE BULLET	RANGE, YARDS:	0	25	50	75	100
Black Hills 158 RNL	velocity, fps:	650				
	energy, ft-lb:					

.380 AUTO

CARTRIDGE BULLET	RANGE, YARDS:	0	25	50	75	100
Black Hills 90 JHP	velocity, fps:	1000				
	energy, ft-lb:	200				
Black Hills 95 FMJ	velocity, fps:	950				
	energy, ft-lb:	190				
Federal 90 Hi-Shok JHP	velocity, fps:	1000	940	890	840	800
	energy, ft-lb:	200	175	160	140	130
Federal 90 Hydra-Shok JHP	velocity, fps:	1000	940	890	840	800
	energy, ft-lb:	200	175	160	140	130
Federal 95 FMJ	velocity, fps:	960	910	870	830	790
	energy, ft-lb:	190	175	160	145	130

Centerfire Handgun Ballistics

.380 AUTO TO .38 SPECIAL

CARTRIDGE BULLET	RANGE, YARDS:	0	25	50	75	100
Hornady 90 JHP/XTP	velocity, fps:	1000		902		823
	energy, ft-lb:	200		163		135
Magtech 85 JHP + P	velocity, fps:	1082		999		936
	energy, ft-lb:	221		188		166
Magtech 95 FMC	velocity, fps:	951		861		781
	energy, ft-lb:	190		156		128
Magtech 95 JHP	velocity, fps:	951		861		781
	energy, ft-lb:	190		156		128
PMC 77 NT/FR	velocity, fps:	1200	1095	1012	932	874
	energy, ft-lb:	223				
PMC 90 FMJ	velocity, fps:	910	872	838	807	778
	energy, ft-lb:	165				
PMC 90 JHP	velocity, fps:	917	878	844	812	782
	energy, ft-lb:	168				
PMC 95 SFHP	velocity, fps:	925	884	847	813	783
	energy, ft-lb:	180				
Rem. 88 JHP	velocity, fps:	990		920		868
	energy, ft-lb:	191		165		146
Rem. 95 FNEB	velocity, fps:	955		865		785
	energy, ft-lb:	190		160		130
Rem. 95 Metal Case	velocity, fps:	955		865		785
	energy, ft-lb:	190		160		130
Rem. 102 BJHP	velocity, fps:	940		901		866
	energy, ft-lb:	200		184		170
Speer 88 JHP Blazer	velocity, fps:	950		920		870
	energy, ft-lb:	195		164		148
Speer 90 Gold Dot	velocity, fps:	990		907		842
	energy, ft-lb:	196		164		142
Speer 95 TMJ Blazer	velocity, fps:	945		865		785
	energy, ft-lb:	190		160		130
Speer 95 TMJ	velocity, fps:	950		877		817
	energy, ft-lb:	180		154		133
Win. 85 Silvertip HP	velocity, fps:	1000		921		860
	energy, ft-lb:	189		160		140
Win. 95 SXT	velocity, fps:	955		889		835
	energy, ft-lb:	192		167		147
Win. 95 FMJ	velocity, fps:	955		865		
	energy, ft-lb:	190		160		
Win. 95 EB WinClean	velocity, fps:	955		881		
	energy, ft-lb:	192		164		

.38 SPECIAL

CARTRIDGE BULLET	RANGE, YARDS:	0	25	50	75	100
Black Hills 125 JHP +P	velocity, fps:	1050				
	energy, ft-lb:	306				
Black Hills 148 HBWC	velocity, fps:	700				
	energy, ft-lb:					
Black Hills 158 SWC	velocity, fps:	850				
	energy, ft-lb:					
Black Hills 158 CNL	velocity, fps:	800				
	energy, ft-lb:					
Federal 110 Hydra-Shok JHP	velocity, fps:	1000	970	930	910	880
	energy, ft-lb:	245	225	215	200	190
Federal 110 Hi-Shok JHP +P	velocity, fps:	1000	960	930	900	870
	energy, ft-lb:	240	225	210	195	185
Federal 125 Nyclad HP	velocity, fps:	830	780	730	690	650
	energy, ft-lb:	190	170	150	130	115
Federal 125 Hi-Shok JSP +P	velocity, fps:	950	920	900	880	860
	energy, ft-lb:	250	235	225	215	205
Federal 125 Hi-Shok JHP +P	velocity, fps:	950	920	900	880	860
	energy, ft-lb:	250	235	225	215	205
Federal 125 Nyclad HP +P	velocity, fps:	950	920	900	880	860
	energy, ft-lb:	250	235	225	215	205

CARTRIDGE BULLET	RANGE, YARDS:	0	25	50	75	100
Federal 129 Hydra-Shok JHP+P	velocity, fps:	950	930	910	890	870
	energy, ft-lb:	255	245	235	225	215
Federal 130 FMJ	velocity, fps:	950	920	890	870	840
	energy, ft-lb:	260	245	230	215	205
Federal 148 LWC Match	velocity, fps:	710	670	630	600	560
	energy, ft-lb:	165	150	130	115	105
Federal 158 LRN	velocity, fps:	760	740	720	710	690
	energy, ft-lb:	200	190	185	175	170
Federal 158 LSWC	velocity, fps:	760	740	720	710	690
	energy, ft-lb:	200	190	185	175	170
Federal 158 Nyclad RN	velocity, fps:	760	740	720	710	690
	energy, ft-lb:	200	190	185	175	170
Federal 158 SWC HP +P	velocity, fps:	890	870	860	840	820
	energy, ft-lb:	280	265	260	245	235
Federal 158 LSWC +P	velocity, fps:	890	870	860	840	820
	energy, ft-lb:	270	265	260	245	235
Federal 158 Nyclad SWC-HP+P	velocity, fps:	890	870	860	840	820
	energy, ft-lb:	270	265	260	245	235
Hornady 125 JHP/XTP	velocity, fps:	900		856		817
	energy, ft-lb:	225		203		185
Hornady 140 JHP/XTP	velocity, fps:	825		790		757
	energy, ft-lb:	212		194		178
Hornady 140 Cowboy	velocity, fps:	800		767		735
	energy, ft-lb:	199		183		168
Hornady 148 HBWC	velocity, fps:	800		697		610
	energy, ft-lb:	210		160		122
Hornady 158 JHP/XPT	velocity, fps:	800		765		731
	energy, ft-lb:	225		205		188
Lapua 123 HP Megashock	velocity, fps:	355		311*		284*
	energy, ft-lb:	504		388*		322*
Lapua 148 LWC	velocity, fps:	230		203*		181*
	energy, ft-lb:	254		199*		157*
Lapua 150 SJFN	velocity, fps:	325		301*		283*
	energy, ft-lb:	512		439*		388*
Lapua 158 FMJLF	velocity, fps:	255		243*		232*
	energy, ft-lb:	332		301*		275*
Lapua 158 LRN	velocity, fps:	255		243*		232*
	energy, ft-lb:	332		301*		275*
Magtech 125 JHP +P	velocity, fps:	1017		971		931
	energy, ft-lb:	287		262		241
Magtech 148 LWC	velocity, fps:	710		634		566
	energy, ft-lb:	166		132		105
Magtech 158 LRN	velocity, fps:	755		728		693
	energy, ft-lb:	200		183		168
Magtech 158 LFN	velocity, fps:	800		776		753
	energy, ft-lb:	225		211		199
Magtech 158 SJHP	velocity, fps:	807		779		753
	energy, ft-lb:	230		213		199
Magtech 158 LSWC	velocity, fps:	755		721		689
	energy, ft-lb:	200		182		167
Magtech 158 FMC-Flat	velocity, fps:	807		779		753
	energy, ft-lb:	230		213		199
PMC 85 Non-Toxic Frangible	velocity, fps:	1275	1181	1109	1052	1006
	energy, ft-lb:	307				
PMC 110 SFHP +P	velocity, fps:	velocity and energy figures not available				
PMC 125 SFHP +P	velocity, fps:	950	918	889	863	838
	energy, ft-lb:	251				
PMC 125 JHP +P	velocity, fps:	974	938	906	878	851
	energy, ft-lb:	266				
PMC 132 FMJ	velocity, fps:	841	820	799	780	761
	energy, ft-lb:	206				
PMC 148 LWC	velocity, fps:	728	694	662	631	602
	energy, ft-lb:	175				

BALLISTICS

.38 Special

CARTRIDGE BULLET	RANGE, YARDS:	0	25	50	75	100
PMC 158 LRN	velocity, fps:	820	801	783	765	749
	energy, ft-lb:	235				
PMC 158 JSP	velocity, fps:	835	816	797	779	762
	energy, ft-lb:	245				
PMC 158 LFP	velocity, fps:	800		761		725
	energy, ft-lb:	225		203		185
Rem. 101 Lead Free Frangible	velocity, fps:	950		896		850
	energy, ft-lb:	202		180		162
Rem. 110 SJHP	velocity, fps:	950		890		840
	energy, ft-lb:	220		194		172
Rem. 110 SJHP +P	velocity, fps:	995		926		871
	energy, ft-lb:	242		210		185
Rem. 125 SJHP +P	velocity, ft-lb:	945		898		858
	energy, ft-lb:	248		224		204
Rem. 125 BJHP	velocity, fps:	975		929		885
	energy, ft-lb:	264		238		218
Rem. 125 FNEB	velocity, fps:	850		822		796
	energy, ft-lb:	201		188		176
Rem. 125 FNEB +P	velocity, fps:	975		935		899
	energy, ft-lb:	264		242		224
Rem. 130 Metal Case	velocity, fps:	950		913		879
	energy, ft-lb:	261		240		223
Rem. 148 LWC Match	velocity, fps:	710		634		566
	energy, ft-lb:	166		132		105
Rem. 158 LRN	velocity, fps:	755		723		692
	energy, ft-lb:	200		183		168
Rem. 158 SWC +P	velocity, fps:	890		855		823
	energy, ft-lb:	278		257		238
Rem. 158 SWC	velocity, fps:	755		723		692
	energy, ft-lb:	200		183		168
Rem. 158 LHP +P	velocity, fps:	890		855		823
	energy, ft-lb:	278		257		238
Speer 125 JHP +P Blazer	velocity, fps:	945		898		858
	energy, ft-lb:	248		224		204
Speer 125 Gold Dot +P	velocity, fps:	945		898		858
	energy, ft-lb:	248		224		204
Speer 158 TMJ +P (and Blazer)	velocity, fps:	900		852		818
	energy, ft-lb:	278		255		235
Speer 158 LRN Blazer	velocity, fps:	755		723		692
	energy, ft-lb:	200		183		168
Speer 158 Trail Blazer LFN	velocity, fps:	800		761		725
	energy, ft-lb:	225		203		184
Speer 158 TMJ-CF +P (and Blazer)	velocity, fps:	900		852		818
	energy, ft-lb:	278		255		235
Win. 110 Silvertip HP	velocity, fps:	945		894		850
	energy, ft-lb:	218		195		176
Win. 110 Jacketed FP	velocity, fps:	975		906		849
	energy, ft-lb:	232		201		176
Win. 125 Jacketed HP	velocity, fps:	945		898		
	energy, ft-lb:	248		224		
Win. 125 Jacketed HP +P	velocity, fps:	945		898		858
	energy, ft-lb:	248		224		204
Win. 125 Jacketed FP	velocity, fps:	850		804		
	energy, ft-lb:	201		179		
Win. 125 Silvertip HP + P	velocity, fps:	945		898		858
	energy, ft-lb:	248		224		204
Win. 125 JFP WinClean	velocity, fps:	775		742		
	energy, ft-lb:	167		153		
Win. 130 FMJ	velocity, fps:	800		765		
	energy, ft-lb:	185		169		
Win. 130 SXT +P	velocity, fps:	925		887		852
	energy, ft-lb:	247		227		210
Win. 148 LWC Super Match	velocity, fps:	710		634		566
	energy, ft-lb:	166		132		105
Win. 150 Lead	velocity, fps:	845		812		
	energy, ft-lb:	238		219		
Win. 158 Lead	velocity, fps:	800		761		725
	energy, ft-lb:	225		203		185
Win. 158 LRN	velocity, fps:	755		723		693
	energy, ft-lb:	200		183		168
Win. 158 LSWC	velocity, fps:	755		721		689
	energy, ft-lb:	200		182		167
Win. 158 LSWC HP +P	velocity, fps:	890		855		823
	energy, ft-lb:	278		257		238

.38-40

CARTRIDGE BULLET		0	25	50	75	100
Black Hills 180 FPL	velocity, fps:	800				
	energy, ft-lb:					

.38 SUPER

CARTRIDGE BULLET		0	25	50	75	100
Federal 130 FMJ +P	velocity, fps:	1200	1140	1100	1050	1020
	energy, ft-lb:	415	380	350	320	300
PMC 115 JHP	velocity, fps:	1116	1052	1001	959	923
	energy, ft-lb:	318				
PMC 130 FMJ	velocity, fps:	1092	1038	994	957	924
	energy, ft-lb:	348				
Rem. 130 Metal Case	velocity, fps:	1215		1099		1017
	energy, ft-lb:	426		348		298
Win. 125 Silvertip HP +P	velocity, fps:	1240		1130		1050
	energy, ft-lb:	427		354		306
Win. 130 FMJ +P	velocity, fps:	1215		1099		
	energy, ft-lb:	426		348		

.357 SIG

CARTRIDGE BULLET		0	25	50	75	100
Federal 125 FMJ	velocity, fps:	1350	1270	1190	1130	1080
	energy, ft-lb:	510	445	395	355	325
Federal 125 JHP	velocity, fps:	1350	1270	1190	1130	1080
	energy, ft-lb:	510	445	395	355	325
Federal 150 JHP	velocity, fps:	1130	1080	1030	1000	970
	energy, ft-lb:	420	385	355	330	310
Hornady 124 JHP/XTP	velocity, fps:	1350		1208		1108
	energy, ft-lb:	502		405		338
Hornady 147 JHP/XTP	velocity, fps:	1225		1138		1072
	energy, ft-lb:	490		422		375
PMC 85 Non-Toxic Frangible	velocity, fps:	1480	1356	1245	1158	1092
	energy, ft-lb:	413				
PMC 124 SFHP	velocity, fps:	1350	1263	1190	1132	1083
	energy, ft-lb:	502				
PMC 124 FMJ/FP	velocity, fps:	1350	1242	1158	1093	1040
	energy, ft-lb:	512				
Rem. 104 Lead Free Frangible	velocity, fps:	1400		1223		1094
	energy, ft-lb:	453		345		276
Rem. 125 Metal Case	velocity, fps:	1350		1146		1018
	energy, ft-lb:	506		422		359
Rem. 125 JHP	velocity, fps:	1350		1157		1032
	energy, ft-lb:	506		372		296
Speer 125 TMJ (and Blazer)	velocity, fps:	1350		1177		1057
	energy, ft-lb:	502		381		307
Speer 125 TMJ-CF	velocity, fps:	1350		1177		1057
	energy, ft-lb:	502		381		307
Speer 125 Gold Dot	velocity, fps:	1375		1203		1079
	energy, ft-lb:	525		402		323
Win. 105 JFP	velocity, fps:	1370		1179		1050
	energy, ft-lb	438		324		257
Win. 125 FMJ FN	velocity, fps:	1350		1185		
	energy, ft-lb	506		390		

BALLISTICS

Centerfire Handgun Ballistics

.357 SIG TO .40 S&W

CARTRIDGE BULLET	RANGE, YARDS:	0	25	50	75	100
.357 MAGNUM						
Black Hills 125 JHP	velocity, fps:	1500				
	energy, ft-lb:	625				
Black Hills 158 CNL	velocity, fps:	800				
	energy, ft-lb:					
Black Hills 158 SWC	velocity, fps:	1050				
	energy, ft-lb:					
Black Hills 158 JHP	velocity, fps:	1250				
	energy, ft-lb:					
Federal 110 Hi-Shok JHP	velocity, fps:	1300	1180	1090	1040	990
	energy, ft-lb:	410	340	290	260	235
Federal 125 Hi-Shok JHP	velocity, fps:	1450	1350	1240	1160	1100
	energy, ft-lb:	580	495	430	370	335
Federal 130 Hydra-Shok JHP	velocity, fps:	1300	1210	1130	1070	1020
	energy, ft-lb:	490	420	370	330	300
Federal 158 Hi-Shok JSP	velocity, fps:	1240	1160	1100	1060	1020
	energy, ft-lb:	535	475	430	395	365
Federal 158 JSP	velocity, fps:	1240	1160	1100	1060	1020
	energy, ft-lb:	535	475	430	395	365
Federal 158 LSWC	velocity, fps:	1240	1160	1100	1060	1020
	energy, ft-lb:	535	475	430	395	365
Federal 158 Hi-Shok JHP	velocity, fps:	1240	1160	1100	1060	1020
	energy, ft-lb:	535	475	430	395	365
Federal 158 Hydra-Shok JHP	velocity, fps:	1240	1160	1100	1060	1020
	energy, ft-lb:	535	475	430	395	365
Federal 180 Hi-Shok JHP	velocity, fps:	1090	1030	980	930	890
	energy, ft-lb:	475	425	385	350	320
Federal 180 Castcore	velocity, fps:	1250	1200	1160	1120	1080
	energy, ft-lb:	625	575	535	495	465
Hornady 125 JHP/XTP	velocity, fps:	1500		1314		1166
	energy, ft-lb:	624		479		377
Hornady 125 JFP/XTP	velocity, fps:	1500		1311		1161
	energy, ft-lb:	624		477		374
Hornady 140 Cowboy	velocity, fps:	800		767		735
	energy, ft-lb:	199		183		168
Hornady 140 JHP/XTP	velocity, fps:	1400		1249		1130
	energy, ft-lb:	609		485		397
Hornady 158 JHP/XTP	velocity, fps:	1250		1150		1073
	energy, ft-lb:	548		464		404
Hornady 158 JFP/XTP	velocity, fps:	1250		1147		1068
	energy, ft-lb:	548		461		400
Lapua 150 FMJ CEPP Super	velocity, fps:	370		527*		303*
	energy, ft-lb:	664		527*		445*
Lapua 150 SJFN	velocity, fps:	385		342*		313*
	energy, ft-lb:	719		569*		476*
Lapua 158 SJHP	velocity, fps:	470		408*		359*
	energy, ft-lb:	1127		850*		657*
Magtech 158 SJSP	velocity, fps:	1235		1104		1015
	energy, ft-lb:	535		428		361
Magtech 158 SJHP	velocity, fps:	1235		1104		1015
	energy, ft-lb:	535		428		361
PMC 85 Non-Toxic Frangible	velocity, fps:	1325	1219	1139	1076	1025
	energy, ft-lb:	331				
PMC 125 JHP	velocity, fps:	1194	1117	1057	1008	967
	energy, ft-lb:	399				
PMC 150 JHP	velocity, fps:	1234	1156	1093	1042	1000
	energy, ft-lb:	512				
PMC 150 SFHP	velocity, fps:	1205	1129	1069	1020	980
	energy, ft-lb:	484				
PMC 158 JSP	velocity, fps:	1194	1122	1063	1016	977
	energy, ft-lb:	504				

CARTRIDGE BULLET	RANGE, YARDS:	0	25	50	75	100
PMC 158 LFP	velocity, fps:	800		761		725
	energy, ft-lb:	225		203		185
Rem. 110 SJHP	velocity, fps:	1295		1094		975
	energy, ft-lb:	410		292		232
Rem. 125 SJHP	velocity, fps:	1450		1240		1090
	energy, ft-lb:	583		427		330
Rem. 125 BJHP	velocity, fps:	1220		1095		1009
	energy, ft-lb:	413		333		283
Rem. 125 FNEB	velocity, fps:	1450		1240		1090
	energy, ft-lb:	583		427		330
Rem. 158 SJHP	velocity, fps:	1235		1104		1015
	energy, ft-lb:	535		428		361
Rem. 158 SP	velocity, fps:	1235		1104		1015
	energy, ft-lb:	535		428		361
Rem. 158 SWC	velocity, fps:	1235		1104		1015
	energy, ft-lb:	535		428		361
Rem. 165 JHP Core-Lokt	velocity, fps:	1290		1189		1108
	energy, ft-lb:	610		518		450
Rem. 180 SJHP	velocity, fps:	1145		1053		985
	energy, ft-lb:	542		443		388
Speer 125 Gold Dot	velocity, fps:	1450		1240		1090
	energy, ft-lb:	583		427		330
Speer 158 JHP Blazer	velocity, fps:	1150		1104		1015
	energy, ft-lb:	535		428		361
Speer 158 Gold Dot	velocity, fps:	1235		1104		1015
	energy, ft-lb:	535		428		361
Speer 170 Gold Dot SP	velocity, fps:	1180		1089		1019
	energy, ft-lb:	525		447		392
Win. 110 JFP	velocity, fps:	1275		1105		998
	energy, ft-lb:	397		298		243
Win. 110 JHP	velocity, fps:	1295		1095		
	energy, ft-lb:	410		292		
Win. 125 JFP WinClean	velocity, fps:	1370		1183		
	energy, ft-lb:	521		389		
Win. 145 Silvertip HP	velocity, fps:	1290		1155		1060
	energy, ft-lb:	535		428		361
Win. 158 JHP	velocity, fps:	1235		1104		1015
	energy, ft-lb:	535		428		361
Win. 158 JSP	velocity, fps:	1235		1104		1015
	energy, ft-lb:	535		428		361
Win. 180 Partition Gold	velocity, fps:	1180		1088		1020
	energy, ft-lb:	557		473		416
.40 S&W						
Black Hills 155 JHP	velocity, fps:	1150				
	energy, ft-lb:	450				
Black Hills 165 EXP JHP	velocity, fps:	1150 (2005: 1100)				
	energy, ft-lb:	483				
Black Hills 180 JHP	velocity, fps:	1000				
	energy, ft-lb:	400				
Black Hills 180 JHP	velocity, fps:	1000				
	energy, ft-lb:	400				
Federal 135 Hydra-Shok JHP	velocity, fps:	1190	1050	970	900	850
	energy, ft-lb:	420	330	280	245	215
Federal 155 FMJ Ball	velocity, fps:	1140	1080	1030	990	960
	energy, ft-lb:	445	400	365	335	315
Federal 155 Hi-Shok JHP	velocity, fps:	1140	1080	1030	990	950
	energy, ft-lb:	445	400	365	335	315
Federal 155 Hydra-Shok JHP	velocity, fps:	1140	1080	1030	990	950
	energy, ft-lb:	445	400	365	335	315
Federal 165 EFMJ	velocity, fps:	1190	1060	970	905	850
	energy, ft-lb:	520	410	345	300	265

.40 S&W

CARTRIDGE BULLET	RANGE, YARDS:	0	25	50	75	100
Federal 165 FMJ	velocity, fps:	1050	1020	990	960	935
	energy, ft-lb:	405	380	355	335	320
Federal 165 FMJ Ball	velocity, fps:	980	950	920	900	880
	energy, ft-lb:	350	330	310	295	280
Federal 165 Hydra-Shok JHP	velocity, fps:	980	950	930	910	890
	energy, ft-lb:	350	330	315	300	290
Federal 180 High Antim. Lead	velocity, fps:	990	960	930	910	890
	energy, ft-lb:	390	365	345	330	315
Federal 180 TMJ TMF Primer	velocity, fps:	990	960	940	910	890
	energy, ft-lb:	390	370	350	330	315
Federal 180 FMJ Ball	velocity, fps:	990	960	940	910	890
	energy, ft-lb:	390	370	350	330	315
Federal 180 Hi-Shok JHP	velocity, fps:	990	960	930	910	890
	energy, ft-lb:	390	365	345	330	315
Federal 180 Hydra-Shok JHP	velocity, fps:	990	960	930	910	890
	energy, ft-lb:	390	365	345	330	315
Hornady 155 JHP/XTP	velocity, fps:	1180		1061		980
	energy, ft-lb:	479		387		331
Hornady 155 TAP-FPD	velocity, fps:	1180		1061		980
	energy, ft-lb:	470		387		331
Hornady 180 JHP/XTP	velocity, fps:	950		903		862
	energy, ft-lb:	361		326		297
Hornady 180 TAP-FPD	velocity, fps:	950		903		862
	energy, ft-lb:	361		326		297
Magtech 155 JHP	velocity, fps:	1025		1118		1052
	energy, ft-lb:	500		430		381
Magtech 180 JHP	velocity, fps:	990		933		886
	energy, ft-lb:	390		348		314
Magtech 180 FMC	velocity, fps:	990		933		886
	energy, ft-lb:	390		348		314
PMC 115 Non-Toxic Frangible	velocity, fps:	1350	1240	1154	1088	1035
	energy, ft-lb:	465				
PMC 155 SFHP	velocity, fps:	1160	1092	1039	994	957
	energy, ft-lb:	463				
PMC 165 JHP	velocity, fps:	1040	1002	970	941	915
	energy, ft-lb:	396				
PMC 165 FMJ	velocity, fps:	1010	977	948	922	899
	energy, ft-lb:	374				
PMC 180 FMJ/FP	velocity, fps:	985	957	931	908	885
	energy, ft-lb:	388				
PMC 180 SFHP	velocity, fps:	985	958	933	910	889
	energy, ft-lb:	388				
Rem. 141 Lead Free Frangible	velocity, fps:	1135		1056		996
	energy, ft-lb:	403		349		311
Rem. 155 JHP	velocity, fps:	1205		1095		1017
	energy, ft-lb:	499		413		356
Rem. 165 BJHP	velocity, fps:	1150		1040		964
	energy, ft-lb:	485		396		340
Rem. 180 JHP	velocity, fps:	1015		960		914
	energy, ft-lb:	412		368		334
Rem. 180 FN Enclosed Base	velocity, fps:	985		936		893
	energy, ft-lb:	388		350		319
Rem. 180 Metal Case	velocity, fps:	985		936		893
	energy, ft-lb:	388		350		319
Rem. 180 BJHP	velocity, fps:	1015		960		914
	energy, ft-lb:	412		368		334
Speer 105 Frangible	velocity, fps:	1380		1128		985
	energy, ft-lb:	444		297		226
Speer 155 TMJ Blazer	velocity, fps:	1175		1047		963
	energy, ft-lb:	475		377		319
Speer 155 TMJ	velocity, fps:	1200		1065		976
	energy, ft-lb:	496		390		328
Speer 155 Gold Dot	velocity, fps:	1200		1063		974
	energy, ft-lb:	496		389		326
Speer 165 TMJ Blazer	velocity, fps:	1100		1006		938
	energy, ft-lb:	443		371		321
Speer 165 TMJ	velocity, fps:	1150		1040		964
	energy, ft-lb:	484		396		340
Speer 165 Gold Dot	velocity, fps:	1150		1043		966
	energy, ft-lb:	485		399		342
Speer 180 HP Blazer	velocity, fps:	985		951		909
	energy, ft-lb:	400		361		330
Speer 180 FMJ Blazer	velocity, fps:	1000		937		886
	energy, ft-lb:	400		351		313
Speer 180 FMJ	velocity, fps:	1000		951		909
	energy, ft-lb:	400		361		330
Speer 180 TMJ-CF (and Blazer)	velocity, fps:	1000		951		909
	energy, ft-lb:	400		361		330
Speer 180 Gold Dot	velocity, fps:	1025		957		902
	energy, ft-lb:	420		366		325
Win. 140 JFP	velocity, fps:	1155		1039		960
	energy, ft-lb:	415		336		286
Win. 155 Silvertip HP	velocity, fps:	1205		1096		1018
	energy, ft-lb:	500		414		357
Win. 165 SXT	velocity, fps:	1130		1041		977
	energy, ft-lb:	468		397		349
Win. 165 FMJ FN	velocity, fps:	1060		1001		
	energy, ft-lb:	412		367		
Win. 165 EB WinClean	velocity, fps:	1130		1054		
	energy, ft-lb:	468		407		
Win. 180 JHP	velocity, fps:	1010		954		
	energy, ft-lb:	408		364		
Win. 180 FMJ	velocity, fps:	990		936		
	energy, ft-lb:	390		350		
Win. 180 SXT	velocity, fps:	1010		954		909
	energy, ft-lb:	408		364		330
Win. 180 EB WinClean	velocity, fps:	990		943		
	energy, ft-lb:	392		356		

10 MM AUTO

CARTRIDGE BULLET	RANGE, YARDS:	0	25	50	75	100
Federal 155 Hi-Shok JHP	velocity, fps:	1330	1230	1140	1080	1030
	energy, ft-lb:	605	515	450	400	360
Federal 180 Hi-Shok JHP	velocity, fps:	1030	1000	970	950	920
	energy, ft-lb:	425	400	375	355	340
Federal 180 Hydra-Shok JHP	velocity, fps:	1030	1000	970	950	920
	energy, ft-lb:	425	400	375	355	340
Federal 180 High Antim. Lead	velocity, fps:	1030	1000	970	950	920
	energy, ft-lb:	425	400	375	355	340
Federal 180 FMJ	velocity, fps:	1060	1025	990	965	940
	energy, ft-lb:	400	370	350	330	310
Hornady 155 JHP/XTP	velocity, fps:	1265		1119		1020
	energy, ft-lb:	551		431		358
Hornady 180 JHP/XTP	velocity, fps:	1180		1077		1004
	energy, ft-lb:	556		464		403
Hornady 200 JHP/XTP	velocity, fps:	1050		994		948
	energy, ft-lb:	490		439		399
PMC 115 Non-Toxic Frangible	velocity, fps:	1350	1240	1154	1088	1035
	energy, ft-lb:	465				
PMC 170 JHP	velocity, fps:	1200	1117	1052	1000	958
	energy, ft-lb:	543				
PMC 180 SFHP	velocity, fps:	950	926	903	882	862
	energy, ft-lb:	361				
PMC 200 TC-FMJ	velocity, fps:	1050	1008	972	941	912
	energy, ft-lb:	490				

BALLISTICS

Centerfire Handgun Ballistics

10 MM AUTO TO .44-40

CARTRIDGE BULLET	RANGE, YARDS:	0	25	50	75	100
Rem. 180 Metal Case	velocity, fps:	1150		1063		998
	energy, ft-lb:	529		452		398
Speer 200 TMJ Blazer	velocity, fps:	1050		966		952
	energy, ft-lb:	490		440		402
Win. 175 Silvertip HP	velocity, fps:	1290		1141		1037
	energy, ft-lb:	649		506		418

.41 REMINGTON. MAGNUM

CARTRIDGE BULLET	RANGE, YARDS:	0	25	50	75	100
Federal 210 Hi-Shok JHP	velocity, fps:	1300	1210	1130	1070	1030
	energy, ft-lb:	790	680	595	540	495
PMC 210 TCSP	velocity, fps:	1290	1201	1128	1069	1021
	energy, ft-lb:	774				
PMC 210 JHP	velocity, fps:	1289	1200	1127	1068	1020
	energy, ft-lb:	774				
Rem. 210 SP	velocity, fps:	1300		1162		1062
	energy, ft-lb:	788		630		526
Win. 175 Silvertip HP	velocity, fps:	1250		1120		1029
	energy, ft-lb:	607		488		412
Win. 240 Platinum Tip	velocity, ft-lb:	1250		1151		1075
	energy, ft-lb:	833		706		616

.44 COLT

CARTRIDGE BULLET	RANGE, YARDS:	0	25	50	75	100
Black Hills 230 FPL	velocity, fps:	730				
	energy, ft-lb:					

.44 RUSSIAN

CARTRIDGE BULLET	RANGE, YARDS:	0	25	50	75	100
Black Hills 210 FPL	velocity, fps:	650				
	energy, ft-lb:					

.44 SPECIAL

CARTRIDGE BULLET	RANGE, YARDS:	0	25	50	75	100
Black Hills 210 FPL	velocity, fps:	700				
	energy, ft-lb:					
Federal 200 SWC HP	velocity, fps:	900	860	830	800	770
	energy, ft-lb:	360	330	305	285	260
Federal 250 CastCore	velocity, fps:	1250	1200	1150	1110	1080
	energy, ft-lb:	865	795	735	685	645
Hornady 180 JHP/XTP	velocity, fps:	1000		935		882
	energy, ft-lb:	400		350		311
Magtech 240 LFN	velocity, fps:	750		722		696
	energy, ft-lb:	300		278		258
PMC 180 JHP	velocity, fps:	980	938	902	869	839
	energy, ft-lb:	383				
PMC 240 SWC-CP	velocity, fps:	764	744	724	706	687
	energy, ft-lb:	311				
PMC 240 LFP	velocity, fps:	750		719		690
	energy, ft-lb:	300		275		253
Rem. 246 LRN	velocity, fps:	755		725		695
	energy, ft-lb:	310		285		265
Speer 200 HP Blazer	velocity, fps:	875		825		780
	energy, ft-lb:	340		302		270
Speer 200 Trail Blazer LFN	velocity, fps:	750		714		680
	energy, ft-lb:	250		226		205
Speer 200 Gold Dot	velocity, fps:	875		825		780
	energy, ft-lb:	340		302		270
Win. 200 Silvertip HP	velocity, fps:	900		860		822
	energy, ft-lb:	360		328		300
Win. 240 Lead	velocity, fps:	750		719		690
	energy, ft-lb	300		275		253
Win. 246 LRN	velocity, fps:	755		725		695
	energy, ft-lb:	310		285		265

.44 REMINGTON MAGNUM

CARTRIDGE BULLET	RANGE, YARDS:	0	25	50	75	100
Black Hills 240 JHP	velocity, fps:	1260				
	energy, ft-lb:	848				

CARTRIDGE BULLET	RANGE, YARDS:	0	25	50	75	100
Black Hills 300 JHP	velocity, fps:	1150				
	energy, ft-lb:	879				
Federal 180 Hi-Shok JHP	velocity, fps:	1610	1480	1370	1270	1180
	energy, ft-lb:	1035	875	750	640	555
Federal 240 Hi-Shok JHP	velocity, fps:	1180	1130	1080	1050	1010
	energy, ft-lb:	740	675	625	580	550
Federal 240 Hydra-Shok JHP	velocity, fps:	1180	1130	1080	1050	1010
	energy, ft-lb:	740	675	625	580	550
Federal 240 JHP	velocity, fps:	1180	1130	1080	1050	1010
	energy, ft-lb:	740	675	625	580	550
Federal 300 CastCore	velocity, fps:	1250	1200	1160	1120	1080
	energy, ft-lb:	1040	960	885	825	775
Hornady 180 JHP/XTP	velocity, fps:	1550		1340		1173
	energy, ft-lb:	960		717		550
Hornady 200 JHP/XTP	velocity, fps:	1500		1284		1128
	energy, ft-lb:	999		732		565
Hornady 240 JHP/XTP	velocity, fps:	1350		1188		1078
	energy, ft-lb:	971		753		619
Hornady 300 JHP/XTP	velocity, fps:	1150		1084		1031
	energy, ft-lb:	881		782		708
Magtech 240 SJSP	velocity, fps:	1180		1081		1010
	energy, ft-lb:	741		632		623
PMC 180 JHP	velocity, fps:	1392	1263	1157	1076	1015
	energy, ft-lb:	772				
PMC 240 JHP	velocity, fps:	1301	1218	1147	1088	1041
	energy, ft-lb:	900				
PMC 240 TC-SP	velocity, fps:	1300	1216	1144	1086	1038
	energy, ft-lb:	900				
PMC 240 SFHP	velocity, fps:	1300	1212	1138	1079	1030
	energy, ft-lb:	900				
PMC 240 LSWC-GCK	velocity, fps:	1225	1143	1077	1025	982
	energy, ft-lb:	806				
Rem. 180 JSP	velocity, fps:	1610		1365		1175
	energy, ft-lb:	1036		745		551
Rem. 210 Gold Dot HP	velocity, fps:	1450		1276		1140
	energy, ft-lb:	980		759		606
Rem. 240 SP	velocity, fps:	1180		1081		1010
	energy, ft-lb:	721		623		543
Rem. 240 SJHP	velocity, fps:	1180		1081		1010
	energy, ft-lb:	721		623		543
Rem. 275 JHP Core-Lokt	velocity, fps:	1235		1142		1070
	energy, ft-lb:	931		797		699
Speer 240 JHP Blazer	velocity, fps:	1200		1092		1015
	energy, ft-lb:	767		636		549
Speer 240 Gold Dot HP	velocity, fps:	1400		1255		1139
	energy, ft-lb:	1044		839		691
Speer 270 Gold Dot SP	velocity, fps:	1250		1142		1060
	energy, ft-lb:	937		781		674
Win. 210 Silvertip HP	velocity, fps:	1250		1106		1010
	energy, ft-lb:	729		570		475
Win. 240 Hollow SP	velocity, fps:	1180		1081		1010
	energy, ft-lb:	741		623		543
Win. 240 JSP	velocity, fps:	1180		1081		
	energy, ft-lb:	741		623		
Win. 250 Partition Gold	velocity, fps:	1230		1132		1057
	energy, ft-lb:	840		711		620
Win. 250 Platinum Tip	velocity, fps:	1250		1148		1070
	energy, ft-lb:	867		732		635

.44-40

CARTRIDGE BULLET	RANGE, YARDS:	0	25	50	75	100
Black Hills 200 RNFP	velocity, fps:	800				
	energy, ft-lb:					

CARTRIDGE BULLET	RANGE, YARDS:	0	25	50	75	100
Hornady 205 Cowboy	velocity, fps:	725		697		670
	energy, ft-lb:	239		221		204
Magtech 225 LFN	velocity, fps:	725		703		681
	energy, ft-lb:	281		247		232
PMC 225 LFP	velocity, fps:	725		723		695
	energy, ft-lb:	281		261		242
Win. 225 Lead	velocity, fps:	750		723		695
	energy, ft-lb:	281		261		242

.45 AUTOMATIC (ACP)

CARTRIDGE BULLET	RANGE, YARDS:	0	25	50	75	100
Black Hills 185 JHP	velocity, fps:	1000				
	energy, ft-lb:	411				
Black Hills 200 Match SWC	velocity, fps:	875				
	energy, ft-lb:	340				
Black Hills 230 FMJ	velocity, fps:	850				
	energy, ft-lb:	368				
Black Hills 230 JHP	velocity, fps:	850				
	energy, ft-lb:	368				
Black Hills 230 JHP +P	velocity, fps:	950				
	energy, ft-lb:	460				
Federal 165 Hydra-Shok JHP	velocity, fps:	1060	1020	980	950	920
	energy, ft-lb:	410	375	350	330	310
Federal 165 EFMJ	velocity, fps:	1090	1045	1005	975	942
	energy, ft-lb:	435	400	370	345	325
Federal 185 Hi-Shok JHP	velocity, fps:	950	920	900	880	860
	energy, ft-lb:	370	350	335	315	300
Federal 185 FMJ-SWC Match	velocity, fps:	780	730	700	660	620
	energy, ft-lb:	245	220	200	175	160
Federal 200 Exp. FMJ	velocity, fps:	1030	1000	970	940	920
	energy, ft-lb:	470	440	415	395	375
Federal 230 FMJ	velocity, fps:	850	830	810	790	770
	energy, ft-lb:	370	350	335	320	305
Federal 230 FMJ Match	velocity, fps:	855	835	815	795	775
	energy, ft-lb:	375	355	340	325	305
Federal 230 Hi-Shok JHP	velocity, fps:	850	830	810	790	770
	energy, ft-lb:	370	350	335	320	300
Federal 230 Hydra-Shok JHP	velocity, fps:	850	830	810	790	770
	energy, ft-lb:	370	350	335	320	305
Federal 230 FMJ	velocity, fps:	850	830	810	790	770
	energy, ft-lb:	370	350	335	320	305
Federal 230 TMJ TMF Primer	velocity, fps:	850	830	810	790	770
	energy, ft-lb:	370	350	335	315	305
Hornady 185 JHP/XTP	velocity, fps:	950		880		819
	energy, ft-lb:	371		318		276
Hornady 200 JHP/XTP	velocity, fps:	900		855		815
	energy, ft-lb:	358		325		295
Hornady 200 HP/XTP +P	velocity, fps:	1055		982		925
	energy, ft-lb:	494		428		380
Hornady 200 TAP-FPD	velocity, fps:	1055		982		926
	energy, ft-lbs:	494		428		380
Hornady 230 FMJ/RN	velocity, fps:	850		809		771
	energy, ft-lb:	369		334		304
Hornady 230 FMJ/FP	velocity, fps:	850		809		771
	energy, ft-lb:	369		334		304
Hornady 230 HP/XTP +P	velocity, fps:	950		904		865
	energy, ft-lb:	462		418		382
Hornady 230 TAP-FPD	velocity, fps:	950		908		872
	energy, ft-lb:	461		421		388
Magtech 185 JHP +P	velocity, fps:	1148		1066		1055
	energy, ft-lb:	540		467		415
Magtech 200 LSWC	velocity, fps:	950		910		874
	energy, ft-lb:	401		368		339

CARTRIDGE BULLET	RANGE, YARDS:	0	25	50	75	100
Magtech 230 FMC	velocity, fps:	837		800		767
	energy, ft-lb:	356		326		300
Magtech 230 FMC-SWC	velocity, fps:	780		720		660
	energy, ft-lb:	310		265		222
PMC 145 Non-Toxic Frangible	velocity, fps:	1100	1045	999	961	928
	energy, ft-lb:	390				
PMC 185 JHP	velocity, fps:	903	870	839	811	785
	energy, ft-lb:	339				
PMC 200 FMJ-SWC	velocity, fps:	850	818	788	761	734
	energy, ft-lb:	321				
PMC 230 SFHP	velocity, fps:	850	830	811	792	775
	energy, ft-lb:	369				
PMC 230 FMJ	velocity, fps:	830	809	789	769	749
	energy, ft-lb:	352				
Rem. 175 Lead Free Frangible	velocity, fps:	1020		923		851
	energy, ft-lb:	404		331		281
Rem. 185 JHP	velocity, fps:	1000		939		889
	energy, ft-lb:	411		362		324
Rem. 185 BJHP	velocity, fps:	1015		951		899
	energy, ft-lb:	423		372		332
Rem. 185 BJHP +P	velocity, fps:	1140		1042		971
	energy, ft-lb:	534		446		388
Rem. 185 MC	velocity, fps:	1015		955		907
	energy, ft-lb:	423		375		338
Rem. 230 FN Enclosed Base	velocity, fps:	835		800		767
	energy, ft-lb:	356		326		300
Rem. 230 Metal Case	velocity, fps:	835		800		767
	energy, ft-lb:	356		326		300
Rem. 230 JHP	velocity, fps:	835		800		767
	energy, ft-lb:	356		326		300
Rem. 230 BJHP	velocity, fps:	875		833		795
	energy, ft-lb:	391		355		323
Speer 140 Frangible	velocity, fps:	1200		1029		928
	energy, ft-lb:	448		329		268
Speer 185 Gold Dot	velocity, fps:	1050		956		886
	energy, ft-lb:	453		375		322
Speer 185 TMJ/FN	velocity, fps:	1000		909		839
	energy, ft-lb:	411		339		289
Speer 200 JHP Blazer	velocity, fps:	975		917		860
	energy, ft-lb:	421		372		328
Speer 200 Gold Dot +P	velocity, fps:	1080		994		930
	energy, ft-lb:	518		439		384
Speer 200 TMJ/FN	velocity, fps:	975		897		834
	energy, ft-lb:	422		357		309
Speer 230 FMJ (and Blazer)	velocity, fps:	845		804		775
	energy, ft-lb:	363		329		304
Speer 230 TMJ-CF (and Blazer)	velocity, fps:	845		804		775
	energy, ft-lb:	363		329		304
Speer 230 Gold Dot	velocity, fps:	890		845		805
	energy, ft-lb:	405		365		331
Win. 170 JFP	velocity, fps:	1050		982		928
	energy, ft-lb:	416		364		325
Win. 185 Silvertip HP	velocity, fps:	1000		938		888
	energy, ft-lb:	411		362		324
Win. 185 FMJ FN	velocity, fps:	910		861		
	energy, ft-lb:	340		304		
Win. 185 EB WinClean	velocity, fps:	910		835		
	energy, ft-lb:	340		286		
Win. 230 JHP	velocity, fps:	880		842		
	energy, ft-lb:	396		363		
Win. 230 FMJ	velocity, fps:	835		800		
	energy, ft-lb:	356		326		

BALLISTICS

Centerfire Handgun Ballistics

.45 AUTOMATIC (ACP) TO .500 SMITH & WESSON

CARTRIDGE BULLET	RANGE, YARDS:	0	25	50	75	100
Win. 230 SXT	velocity, fps:	880		846		816
	energy, ft-lb:	396		366		340
Win. 230 JHP subsonic	velocity, fps:	880		842		808
	energy, ft-lb:	396		363		334
Win. 230 EB WinClean	velocity, fps:	835		802		
	energy, ft-lb:	356		329		

.45 GAP

CARTRIDGE BULLET	RANGE, YARDS:	0	25	50	75	100
Federal 185 Hydra-Shok JHP And Federal TMJ	velocity, fps:	1090	1020	970	920	890
	energy, ft-lb:	490	430	385	350	320
Federal 230 Hydra-Shok And Federal FMJ	velocity, fps:	880	870	850	840	820
	energy, ft-lb:	395	380	3760	355	345
Win. 185 STHP	velocity, fps:	1000		938		887
	energy, ft-lb:	411		361		323
Win. 230 JHP	velocity, fps:	880		842		
	energy, ft-lb:	396		363		
Win. 230 EB WinClean	velocity, fps:	875		840		
	energy, ft-lb:	391		360		
Win. 230 FMJ	velocity, fps:	850		814		
	energy, ft-lb:	369		338		

.45 WINCHESTER MAGNUM

CARTRIDGE BULLET	RANGE, YARDS:	0	25	50	75	100
Win. 260 Partition Gold	velocity, fps:	1200		1105		1033
	energy, ft-lb:	832		705		616
Win. 260 JHP	velocity, fps:	1200		1099		1026
	energy, ft-lb:	831		698		607

.45 SCHOFIELD

CARTRIDGE BULLET	RANGE, YARDS:	0	25	50	75	100
Black Hills 180 FNL	velocity, fps:	730				
	energy, ft-lb:					
Black Hills 230 RNFP	velocity, fps:	730				
	energy, ft-lb:					

.45 COLT

CARTRIDGE BULLET	RANGE, YARDS:	0	25	50	75	100
Black Hills 250 RNFP	velocity, fps:	725				
	energy, ft-lb:					
Federal 225 SWC HP	velocity, fps:	900	880	860	840	820
	energy, ft-lb:	405	385	370	355	340
Hornady 255 Cowboy	velocity, fps:	725		692		660
	energy, ft-lb:	298		271		247
Magtech 250 LFN	velocity, fps:	750		726		702
	energy, ft-lb:	312		293		274
PMC 250 LFP	velocity, fps:	800		767		736
	energy, ft-lb:	355		331		309
PMC 300 +P+	velocity, fps:	1250	1192	1144	1102	1066
	energy, ft-lb:	1041				
Rem. 225 SWC	velocity, fps:	960		890		832
	energy, ft-lb:	460		395		346
Rem. 250 RLN	velocity, fps:	860		820		780
	energy, ft-lb:	410		375		340
Speer 200 FMJ Blazer	velocity, fps:	1000		938		889
	energy, ft-lb:	444		391		351
Speer 230 Trail Blazer LFN	velocity, fps:	750		716		684
	energy, ft-lb:	287		262		239
Speer 250 Gold Dot	velocity, fps:	900		860		823
	energy, ft-lb:	450		410		376
Win. 225 Silvertip HP	velocity, fps:	920		877		839
	energy, ft-lb:	423		384		352
Win. 255 LRN	velocity, fps:	860		820		780
	energy, ft-lb:	420		380		345
Win. 250 Lead	velocity, fps:	750		720		692
	energy, ft-lb:	312		288		266

.454 CASULL

CARTRIDGE BULLET	RANGE, YARDS:	0	25	50	75	100
Federal 300 Trophy Bonded	velocity, fps:	1630	1540	1450	1380	1300
	energy, ft-lb:	1760	1570	1405	1260	1130
Federal 360 CastCore	velocity, fps:	1500	1435	1370	1310	1255
	energy, ft-lb:	1800	1640	1500	1310	1260
Hornady 240 XTP-MAG	velocity, fps:	1900		1679		1483
	energy, ft-lb:	1923		1502		1172
Hornady 300 XTP-MAG	velocity, fps:	1650		1478		1328
	energy, ft-lb:	1813		1455		1175
Magtech 260 SJSP	velocity, fps:	1800		1577		1383
	energy, ft-lb:	1871		1437		1104
Rem. 300 Core-Lokt Ultra	velocity, fps:	1625		1472		1335
	energy, ft-lb:	1759		1442		1187
Speer 300 Gold Dot HP	velocity, fps:	1625		1477		1343
	energy, ft-lb:	1758		1452		1201
Win. 250 JHP	velocity, fps:	1300		1151		1047
	energy, ft-lb:	938		735		608
Win. 260 Partition Gold	velocity, fps:	1800		1605		1427
	energy, ft-lb:	1871		1485		1176
Win. 260 Platinum Tip	velocity, fps:	1800		1596		1414
	enuryg, ft-lb:	1870		1470		1154
Win. 300 JFP	velocity, fps:	1625		1451		1308
	energy, ft-lb:	1759		1413		1141

.460 SMITH & WESSON

CARTRIDGE BULLET	RANGE, YARDS:	0	25	50	75	100
Hornady 200 SST	velocity, fps:	2250		2003		1772
	energy, ft-lb:	2248		1395		1081

.475 LINEBAUGH

CARTRIDGE BULLET	RANGE, YARDS:	0	25	50	75	100
Hornady 400 XTP-MAG	velocity, fps:	1300		1179		1093
	energy, ft-lb:	1501		1235		1060

.480 RUGER

CARTRIDGE BULLET	RANGE, YARDS:	0	25	50	75	100
Hornady 325 XTP-MAG	velocity, fps:	1350		1191		1076
	energy, ft-lb:	1315		1023		835
Hornady 400 XTP-MAG	velocity, fps:	1100		1027		971
	energy, ft-lb:	1075		937		838
Speer 275 Gold Dot HP	velocity, fps:	1450		1284		1152
	energy, ft-lb:	1284		1007		810
Speer 325 SP	velocity, fps:	1350		1224		1124
	energy, ft-lb:	1315		1082		912

.50 ACTION EXPRESS

CARTRIDGE BULLET	RANGE, YARDS:	0	25	50	75	100
Speer 300 Gold Dot HP	velocity, fps:	1550		1361		1207
	energy, ft-lb:	1600		1234		970
Speer 325 UCHP	velocity, fps:	1400		1232		1106
	energy, ft-lb:	1414		1095		883

.500 SMITH & WESSON

CARTRIDGE BULLET	RANGE, YARDS:	0	25	50	75	100
Hornady 350 XTP Mag	velocity, fps:	1900		1656		1439
	energy, ft-lb:	2805		2131		1610
Hornady 500 FP-XTP	velocity, fps:	1425		1281		1164
	energy, ft-lb:	2254		1823		1505
Win. 400 Platinum Tip	velocity, fps:	1800		1647		1505
	energy, ft-lb:	2877		2409		2012

BALLISTICS

Barnes Bullets

ALL COPPER X-BULLET

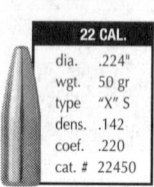

22 CAL.
dia. .224"
wgt. 50 gr
type "X" S
dens. .142
coef. .220
cat. # 22450

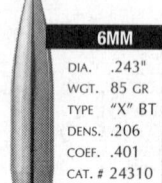

6MM
DIA. .243"
WGT. 85 GR
TYPE "X" BT
DENS. .206
COEF. .401
CAT. # 24310

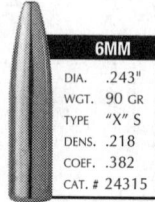

6MM
DIA. .243"
WGT. 90 GR
TYPE "X" S
DENS. .218
COEF. .382
CAT. # 24315

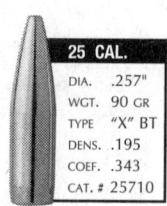

25 CAL.
DIA. .257"
WGT. 90 GR
TYPE "X" BT
DENS. .195
COEF. .343
CAT. # 25710

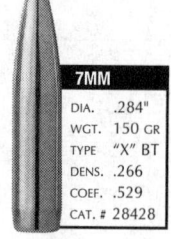

7MM
DIA. .284"
WGT. 150 GR
TYPE "X" BT
DENS. .266
COEF. .529
CAT. # 28428

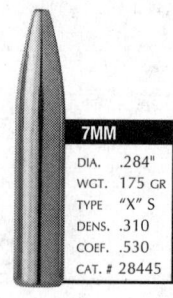

7MM
DIA. .284"
WGT. 175 GR
TYPE "X" S
DENS. .310
COEF. .530
CAT. # 28445

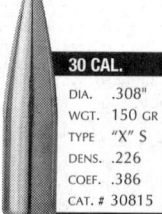

30 CAL.
DIA. .308"
WGT. 150 GR
TYPE "X" S
DENS. .226
COEF. .386
CAT. # 30815

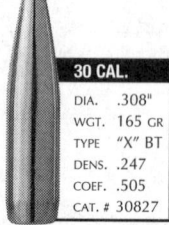

30 CAL.
DIA. .308"
WGT. 165 GR
TYPE "X" BT
DENS. .247
COEF. .505
CAT. # 30827

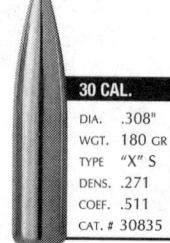

30 CAL.
DIA. .308"
WGT. 180 GR
TYPE "X" S
DENS. .271
COEF. .511
CAT. # 30835

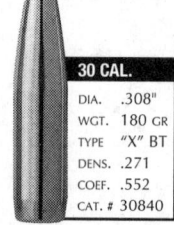

30 CAL.
DIA. .308"
WGT. 180 GR
TYPE "X" BT
DENS. .271
COEF. .552
CAT. # 30840

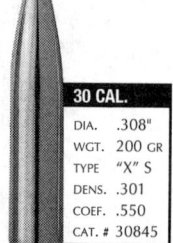

30 CAL.
DIA. .308"
WGT. 200 GR
TYPE "X" S
DENS. .301
COEF. .550
CAT. # 30845

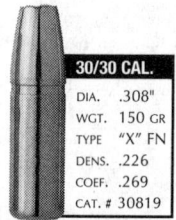

30/30 CAL.
DIA. .308"
WGT. 150 GR
TYPE "X" FN
DENS. .226
COEF. .269
CAT. # 30819

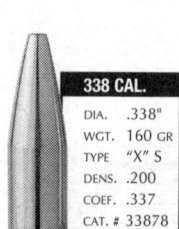

338 CAL.
DIA. .338"
WGT. 160 GR
TYPE "X" S
DENS. .200
COEF. .337
CAT. # 33878

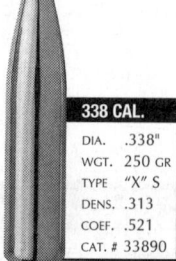

338 CAL.
DIA. .338"
WGT. 250 GR
TYPE "X" S
DENS. .313
COEF. .521
CAT. # 33890

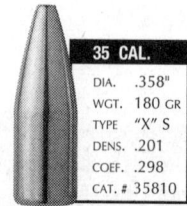

35 CAL.
DIA. .358"
WGT. 180 GR
TYPE "X" S
DENS. .201
COEF. .298
CAT. # 35810

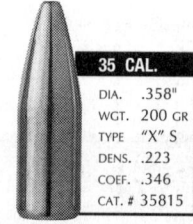

35 CAL.
DIA. .358"
WGT. 200 GR
TYPE "X" S
DENS. .223
COEF. .346
CAT. # 35815

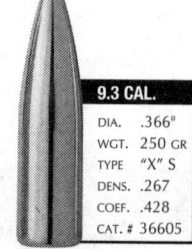

9.3 CAL.
DIA. .366"
WGT. 250 GR
TYPE "X" S
DENS. .267
COEF. .428
CAT. # 36605

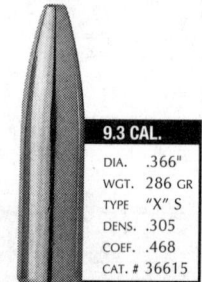

9.3 CAL.
DIA. .366"
WGT. 286 GR
TYPE "X" S
DENS. .305
COEF. .468
CAT. # 36615

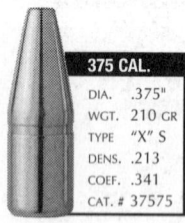

375 CAL.
DIA. .375"
WGT. 210 GR
TYPE "X" S
DENS. .213
COEF. .341
CAT. # 37575

405 WIN.
DIA. .411"
WGT. 300 GR
TYPE "X" S
DENS. .254
COEF. .313
CAT. # 41178

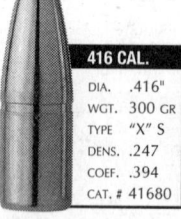

416 CAL.
DIA. .416"
WGT. 300 GR
TYPE "X" S
DENS. .247
COEF. .394
CAT. # 41680

458 MAG
DIA. .458"
WGT. 300 GR
TYPE "X" S
DENS. .204
COEF. .340
CAT. # 45802

458 MAG
DIA. .458"
WGT. 350 GR
TYPE "X" S
DENS. .283
COEF. .402
CAT. # 45805

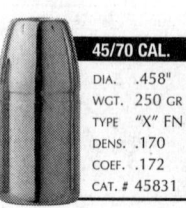

45/70 CAL.
DIA. .458"
WGT. 250 GR
TYPE "X" FN
DENS. .170
COEF. .172
CAT. # 45831

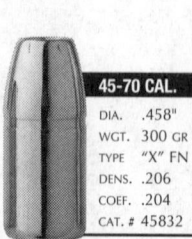

45-70 CAL.
DIA. .458"
WGT. 300 GR
TYPE "X" FN
DENS. .206
COEF. .204
CAT. # 45832

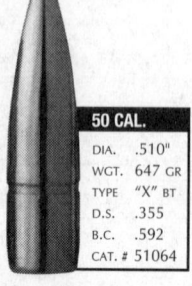

50 CAL.
DIA. .510"
WGT. 647 GR
TYPE "X" BT
D.S. .355
B.C. .592
CAT. # 51064

Barnes Bullets

TRIPLE-SHOCK X-BULLET

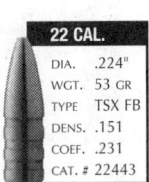

22 CAL.
DIA.	.224"
WGT.	53 GR
TYPE	TSX FB
DENS.	.151
COEF.	.231
CAT. #	22443

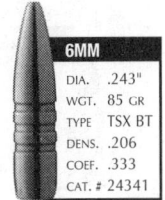

6MM
DIA.	.243"
WGT.	85 GR
TYPE	TSX BT
DENS.	.206
COEF.	.333
CAT. #	24341

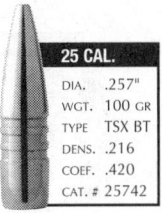

25 CAL.
DIA.	.257"
WGT.	100 GR
TYPE	TSX BT
DENS.	.216
COEF.	.420
CAT. #	25742

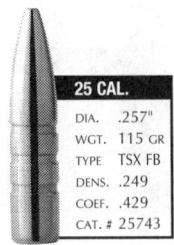

25 CAL.
DIA.	.257"
WGT.	115 GR
TYPE	TSX FB
DENS.	.249
COEF.	.429
CAT. #	25743

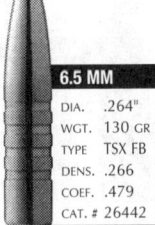

6.5 MM
DIA.	.264"
WGT.	130 GR
TYPE	TSX FB
DENS.	.266
COEF.	.479
CAT. #	26442

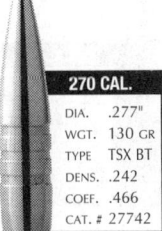

270 CAL.
DIA.	.277"
WGT.	130 GR
TYPE	TSX BT
DENS.	.242
COEF.	.466
CAT. #	27742

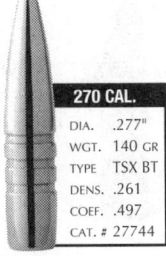

270 CAL.
DIA.	.277"
WGT.	140 GR
TYPE	TSX BT
DENS.	.261
COEF.	.497
CAT. #	27744

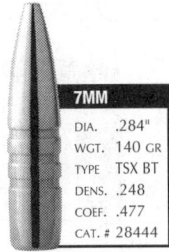

7MM
DIA.	.284"
WGT.	140 GR
TYPE	TSX BT
DENS.	.248
COEF.	.477
CAT. #	28444

7MM
DIA.	.284"
WGT.	160 GR
TYPE	TSX FB
DENS.	.283
COEF.	.508
CAT. #	28446

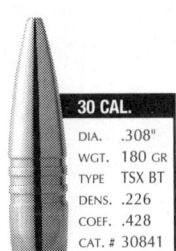

30 CAL.
DIA.	.308"
WGT.	180 GR
TYPE	TSX BT
DENS.	.226
COEF.	.428
CAT. #	30841

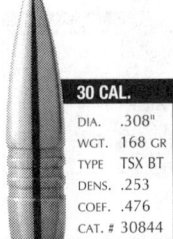

30 CAL.
DIA.	.308"
WGT.	168 GR
TYPE	TSX BT
DENS.	.253
COEF.	.476
CAT. #	30844

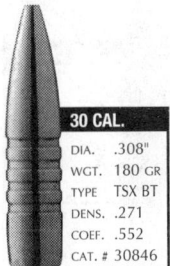

30 CAL.
DIA.	.308"
WGT.	180 GR
TYPE	TSX BT
DENS.	.271
COEF.	.552
CAT. #	30846

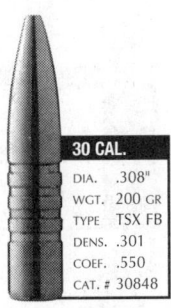

30 CAL.
DIA.	.308"
WGT.	200 GR
TYPE	TSX FB
DENS.	.301
COEF.	.550
CAT. #	30848

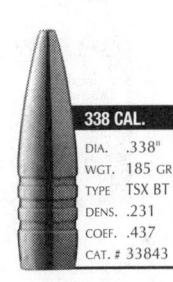

338 CAL.
DIA.	.338"
WGT.	185 GR
TYPE	TSX BT
DENS.	.231
COEF.	.437
CAT. #	33843

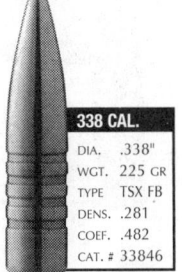

338 CAL.
DIA.	.338"
WGT.	225 GR
TYPE	TSX FB
DENS.	.281
COEF.	.482
CAT. #	33846

EXPANDER MZ MUZZLELOADER BULLET

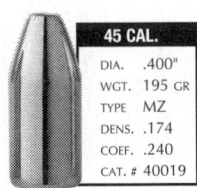

45 CAL.
DIA.	.400"
WGT.	195 GR
TYPE	MZ
DENS.	.174
COEF.	.240
CAT. #	40019

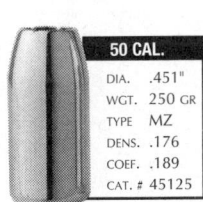

50 CAL.
DIA.	.451"
WGT.	250 GR
TYPE	MZ
DENS.	.176
COEF.	.189
CAT. #	45125

50 CAL.
DIA.	.451"
WGT.	300 GR
TYPE	MZ
DENS.	.211
COEF.	.207
CAT. #	45130

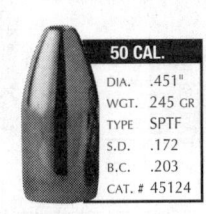

50 CAL.
DIA.	.451"
WGT.	245 GR
TYPE	SPTF
S.D.	.172
B.C.	.203
CAT. #	45124

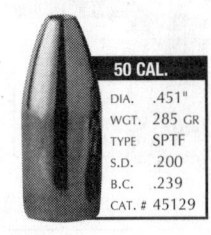

50 CAL.
DIA.	.451"
WGT.	285 GR
TYPE	SPTF
S.D.	.200
B.C.	.239
CAT. #	45129

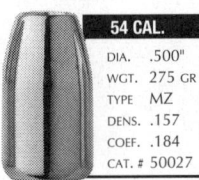

54 CAL.
DIA.	.500"
WGT.	275 GR
TYPE	MZ
DENS.	.157
COEF.	.184
CAT. #	50027

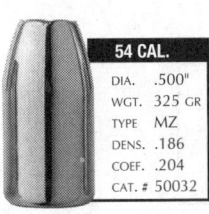

54 CAL.
DIA.	.500"
WGT.	325 GR
TYPE	MZ
DENS.	.186
COEF.	.204
CAT. #	50032

45 CAL. ALIGNER
CAT. #	04500

50 CAL. ALIGNER
CAT. #	05000

54 CAL. ALIGNER
CAT. #	05400

Barnes Bullets

XLC COATED X-BULLET

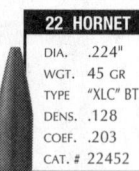

22 HORNET
DIA. .224"
WGT. 45 GR
TYPE "XLC" BT
DENS. .128
COEF. .203
CAT. # 22452

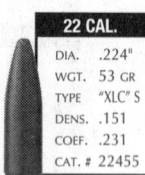

22 CAL.
DIA. .224"
WGT. 53 GR
TYPE "XLC" S
DENS. .151
COEF. .231
CAT. # 22455

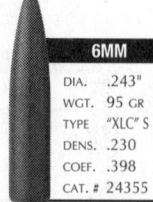

6MM
DIA. .243"
WGT. 95 GR
TYPE "XLC" S
DENS. .230
COEF. .398
CAT. # 24355

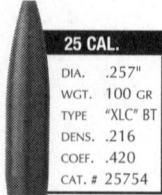

25 CAL.
DIA. .257"
WGT. 100 GR
TYPE "XLC" BT
DENS. .216
COEF. .420
CAT. # 25754

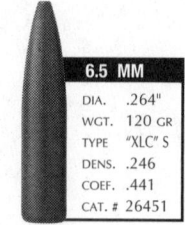

6.5 MM
DIA. .264"
WGT. 120 GR
TYPE "XLC" S
DENS. .246
COEF. .441
CAT. # 26451

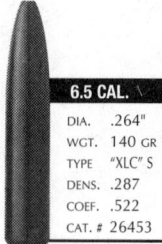

6.5 CAL.
DIA. .264"
WGT. 140 GR
TYPE "XLC" S
DENS. .287
COEF. .522
CAT. # 26453

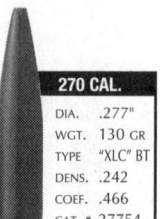

270 CAL.
DIA. .277"
WGT. 130 GR
TYPE "XLC" BT
DENS. .242
COEF. .466
CAT. # 27754

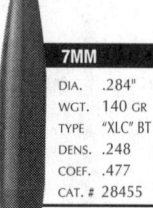

7MM
DIA. .284"
WGT. 140 GR
TYPE "XLC" BT
DENS. .248
COEF. .477
CAT. # 28455

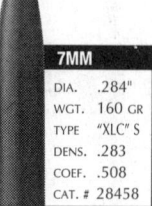

7MM
DIA. .284"
WGT. 160 GR
TYPE "XLC" S
DENS. .283
COEF. .508
CAT. # 28458

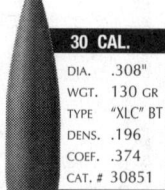

30 CAL.
DIA. .308"
WGT. 130 GR
TYPE "XLC" BT
DENS. .196
COEF. .374
CAT. # 30851

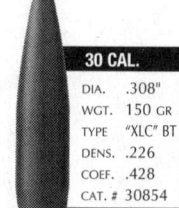

30 CAL.
DIA. .308"
WGT. 150 GR
TYPE "XLC" BT
DENS. .226
COEF. .428
CAT. # 30854

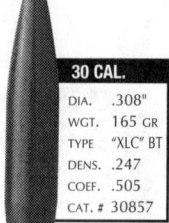

30 CAL.
DIA. .308"
WGT. 165 GR
TYPE "XLC" BT
DENS. .247
COEF. .505
CAT. # 30857

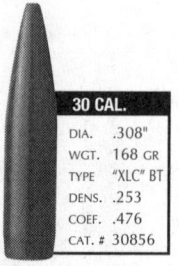

30 CAL.
DIA. .308"
WGT. 168 GR
TYPE "XLC" BT
DENS. .253
COEF. .476
CAT. # 30856

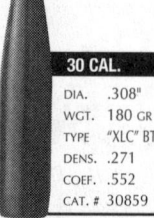

30 CAL.
DIA. .308"
WGT. 180 GR
TYPE "XLC" BT
DENS. .271
COEF. .552
CAT. # 30859

8MM
DIA. .323"
WGT. 200 GR
TYPE "XLC" S
DENS. .274
COEF. .429
CAT. # 32312

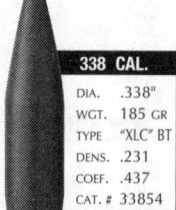

338 CAL.
DIA. .338"
WGT. 185 GR
TYPE "XLC" BT
DENS. .231
COEF. .437
CAT. # 33854

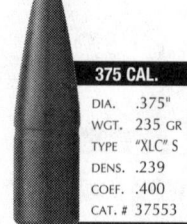

375 CAL.
DIA. .375"
WGT. 235 GR
TYPE "XLC" S
DENS. .239
COEF. .400
CAT. # 37553

470 NITRO
DIA. .474"
WGT. 500 GR
TYPE "XLC" S
DENS. .326
COEF. .318
CAT. # 47550

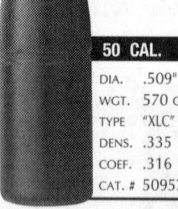

50 CAL.
DIA. .509"
WGT. 570 GR
TYPE "XLC" S
DENS. .335
COEF. .316
CAT. # 50957

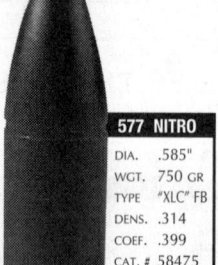

577 NITRO
DIA. .585"
WGT. 750 GR
TYPE "XLC" FB
DENS. .314
COEF. .399
CAT. # 58475

BURNER VARMIN-A-TOR BULLET

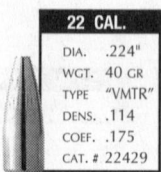

22 CAL.
DIA. .224"
WGT. 40 GR
TYPE "VMTR"
DENS. .114
COEF. .175
CAT. # 22429

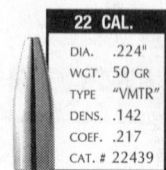

22 CAL.
DIA. .224"
WGT. 50 GR
TYPE "VMTR"
DENS. .142
COEF. .217
CAT. # 22439

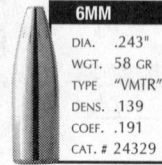

6MM
DIA. .243"
WGT. 58 GR
TYPE "VMTR"
DENS. .139
COEF. .191
CAT. # 24329

6MM
DIA. .243"
WGT. 72 GR
TYPE "VMTR"
DENS. .174
COEF. .244
CAT. # 24339

Barnes Bullets

COPPER-JACKET/LEAD CORE ORIGINAL

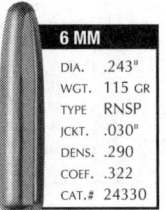

6 MM
DIA.	.243"
WGT.	115 GR
TYPE	RNSP
JCKT.	.030"
DENS.	.290
COEF.	.322
CAT.#	24330

348 WIN.
DIA.	.348"
WGT.	220 GR
TYPE	FNSP
JCKT.	.032"
DENS.	.260
COEF.	.301
CAT.#	34805

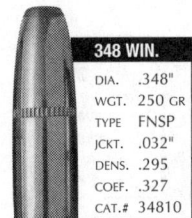

348 WIN.
DIA.	.348"
WGT.	250 GR
TYPE	FNSP
JCKT.	.032"
DENS.	.295
COEF.	.327
CAT.#	34810

375 WIN.
DIA.	.375"
WGT.	255 GR
TYPE	FNSP
JCKT.	.032"
DENS.	.259
COEF.	.290
CAT.#	375W20

38/55 CAL.
DIA.	.375"
WGT.	255 GR
TYPE	FNSP
JCKT.	.032"
DENS.	.259
COEF.	.290
CAT.#	38/5510

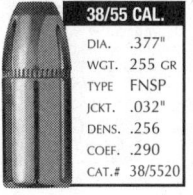

38/55 CAL.
DIA.	.377"
WGT.	255 GR
TYPE	FNSP
JCKT.	.032"
DENS.	.256
COEF.	.290
CAT.#	38/5520

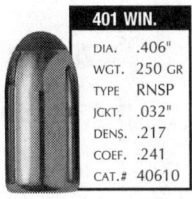

401 WIN.
DIA.	.406"
WGT.	250 GR
TYPE	RNSP
JCKT.	.032"
DENS.	.217
COEF.	.241
CAT.#	40610

40/65 WIN.
DIA.	.406"
WGT.	250 GR
TYPE	FNSP
JCKT.	.032"
DENS.	.217
COEF.	.231
CAT.#	40611

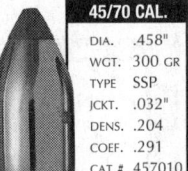

45/70 CAL.
DIA.	.458"
WGT.	300 GR
TYPE	SSP
JCKT.	.032"
DENS.	.204
COEF.	.291
CAT.#	457010

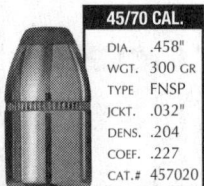

45/70 CAL.
DIA.	.458"
WGT.	300 GR
TYPE	FNSP
JCKT.	.032"
DENS.	.204
COEF.	.227
CAT.#	457020

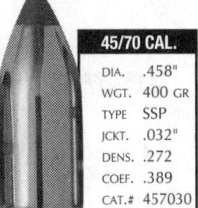

45/70 CAL.
DIA.	.458"
WGT.	400 GR
TYPE	SSP
JCKT.	.032"
DENS.	.272
COEF.	.389
CAT.#	457030

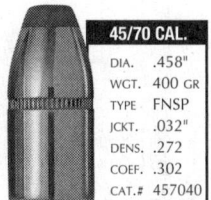

45/70 CAL.
DIA.	.458"
WGT.	400 GR
TYPE	FNSP
JCKT.	.032"
DENS.	.272
COEF.	.302
CAT.#	457040

458 MAG.
DIA.	.458"
WGT.	600 GR
TYPE	RNSP
JCKT.	.049"
DENS.	.409
COEF.	.454
CAT.#	45860

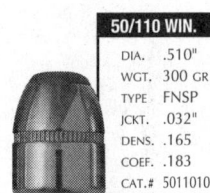

50/110 WIN.
DIA.	.510"
WGT.	300 GR
TYPE	FNSP
JCKT.	.032"
DENS.	.165
COEF.	.183
CAT.#	5011010

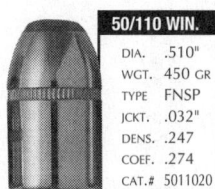

50/110 WIN.
DIA.	.510"
WGT.	450 GR
TYPE	FNSP
JCKT.	.032"
DENS.	.247
COEF.	.274
CAT.#	5011020

XPB PISTOL BULLET

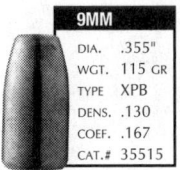

9MM
DIA.	.355"
WGT.	115 GR
TYPE	XPB
DENS.	.130
COEF.	.167
CAT.#	35515

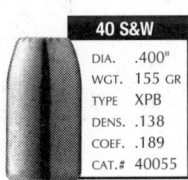

40 S&W
DIA.	.400"
WGT.	155 GR
TYPE	XPB
DENS.	.138
COEF.	.189
CAT.#	40055

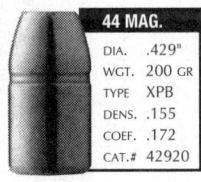

44 MAG.
DIA.	.429"
WGT.	200 GR
TYPE	XPB
DENS.	.155
COEF.	.172
CAT.#	42920

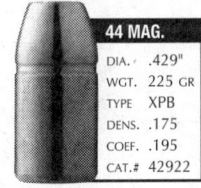

44 MAG.
DIA.	.429"
WGT.	225 GR
TYPE	XPB
DENS.	.175
COEF.	.195
CAT.#	42922

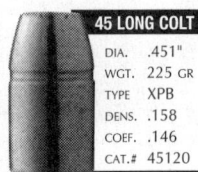

45 LONG COLT
DIA.	.451"
WGT.	225 GR
TYPE	XPB
DENS.	.158
COEF.	.146
CAT.#	45120

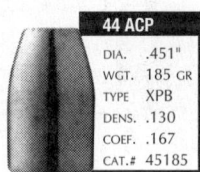

44 ACP
DIA.	.451"
WGT.	185 GR
TYPE	XPB
DENS.	.130
COEF.	.167
CAT.#	45185

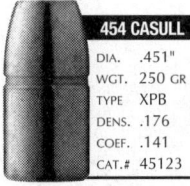

454 CASULL
DIA.	.451"
WGT.	250 GR
TYPE	XPB
DENS.	.176
COEF.	.141
CAT.#	45123

480 RUGER 475 LINEBAUGH
DIA.	.475"
WGT.	275 GR
TYPE	XPB
DENS.	.174
COEF.	.155
CAT.#	48010

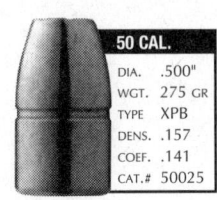

50 CAL.
DIA.	.500"
WGT.	275 GR
TYPE	XPB
DENS.	.157
COEF.	.141
CAT.#	50025

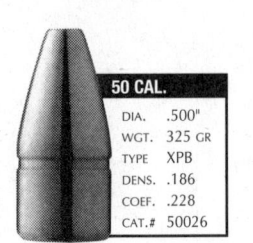

50 CAL.
DIA.	.500"
WGT.	325 GR
TYPE	XPB
DENS.	.186
COEF.	.228
CAT.#	50026

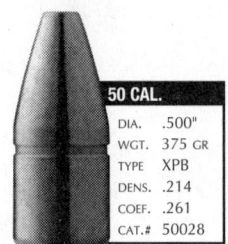

50 CAL.
DIA.	.500"
WGT.	375 GR
TYPE	XPB
DENS.	.214
COEF.	.261
CAT.#	50028

Barnes Bullets

SOLIDS

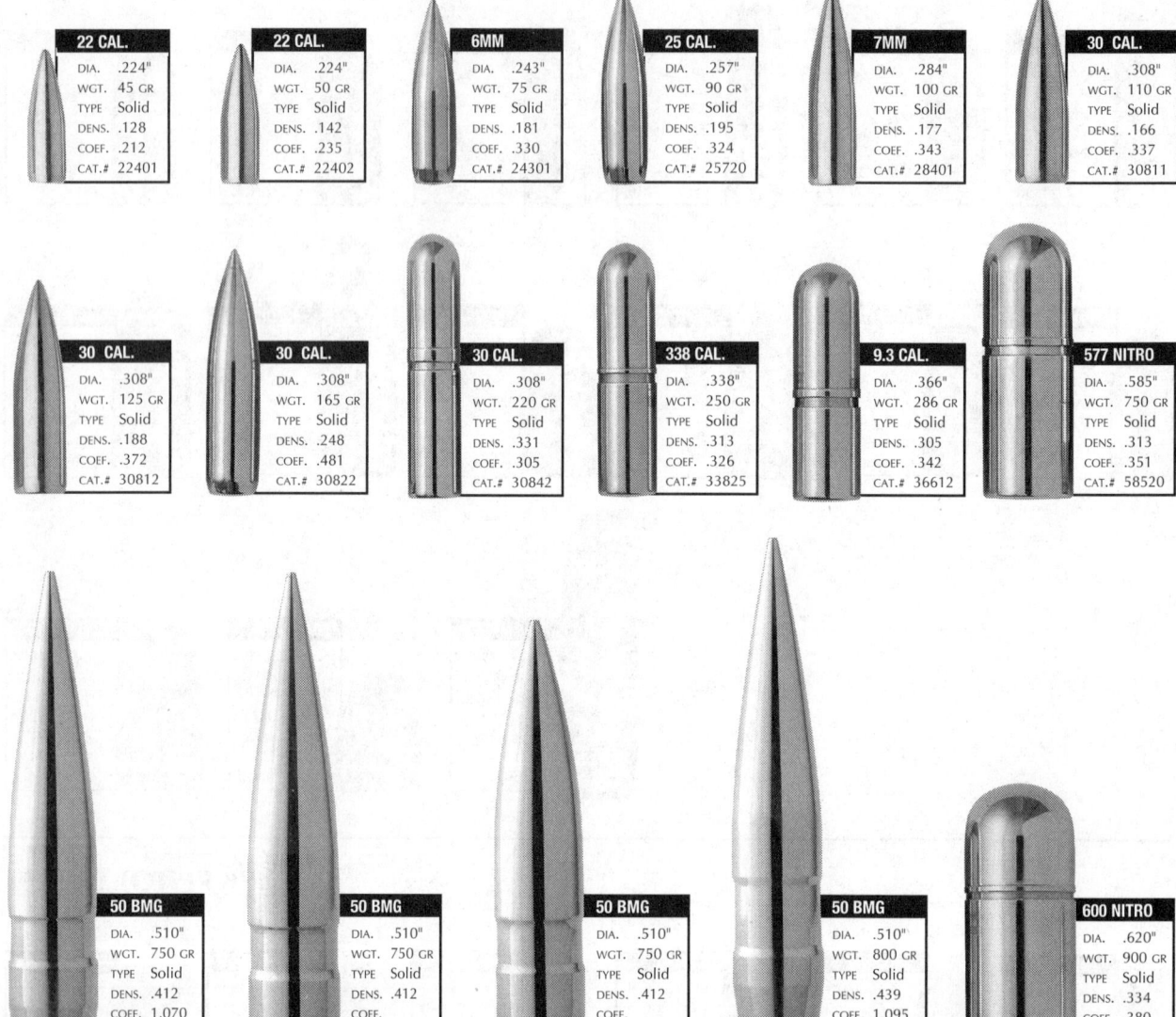

22 CAL.
DIA.	.224"
WGT.	45 GR
TYPE	Solid
DENS.	.128
COEF.	.212
CAT.#	22401

22 CAL.
DIA.	.224"
WGT.	50 GR
TYPE	Solid
DENS.	.142
COEF.	.235
CAT.#	22402

6MM
DIA.	.243"
WGT.	75 GR
TYPE	Solid
DENS.	.181
COEF.	.330
CAT.#	24301

25 CAL.
DIA.	.257"
WGT.	90 GR
TYPE	Solid
DENS.	.195
COEF.	.324
CAT.#	25720

7MM
DIA.	.284"
WGT.	100 GR
TYPE	Solid
DENS.	.177
COEF.	.343
CAT.#	28401

30 CAL.
DIA.	.308"
WGT.	110 GR
TYPE	Solid
DENS.	.166
COEF.	.337
CAT.#	30811

30 CAL.
DIA.	.308"
WGT.	125 GR
TYPE	Solid
DENS.	.188
COEF.	.372
CAT.#	30812

30 CAL.
DIA.	.308"
WGT.	165 GR
TYPE	Solid
DENS.	.248
COEF.	.481
CAT.#	30822

30 CAL.
DIA.	.308"
WGT.	220 GR
TYPE	Solid
DENS.	.331
COEF.	.305
CAT.#	30842

338 CAL.
DIA.	.338"
WGT.	250 GR
TYPE	Solid
DENS.	.313
COEF.	.326
CAT.#	33825

9.3 CAL.
DIA.	.366"
WGT.	286 GR
TYPE	Solid
DENS.	.305
COEF.	.342
CAT.#	36612

577 NITRO
DIA.	.585"
WGT.	750 GR
TYPE	Solid
DENS.	.313
COEF.	.351
CAT.#	58520

50 BMG
DIA.	.510"
WGT.	750 GR
TYPE	Solid
DENS.	.412
COEF.	1.070
CAT.#	510750A

50 BMG
DIA.	.510"
WGT.	750 GR
TYPE	Solid
DENS.	.412
COEF.	
CAT.#	510750

50 BMG
DIA.	.510"
WGT.	750 GR
TYPE	Solid
DENS.	.412
COEF.	
CAT.#	510750T

50 BMG
DIA.	.510"
WGT.	800 GR
TYPE	Solid
DENS.	.439
COEF.	1.095
CAT.#	510800A

600 NITRO
DIA.	.620"
WGT.	900 GR
TYPE	Solid
DENS.	.334
COEF.	.380
CAT.#	62020

Berger Bullets

Famous for their superior performance in benchrest matches, Berger bullets now include hunting designs. From .17 to .30, all Bergers feature 14 jackets with wall concentricity tolerance of .0003. Lead cores are 99.9% pure and swaged in dies to within .0001 of round. Berger's line includes several profiles: Low Drag, Very Low Drag, Length Tolerant, Maximum-Expansion, besides standard flat-base and standard boat-tail.

ITEM	WEIGHT	TWIST
17 Cal.	15 Gr. Varmint	12
17 Cal.	18 Gr. Varmint	12
17 Cal.	20 Gr.*	12
17 Cal.	22 Gr.*	11
17 Cal.	25 Gr.*	10
17 Cal.	37 Gr. VLD	6
20 Cal.	30 Gr. Varmint	14
20 Cal.	35 Gr. Varmint	14
20 Cal.	40 Gr. BT Varmint	12
20 Cal.	50 Gr. BT Varmint	9
22 Cal.	30 Varmint	15
22 Cal.	35 Varmint	15
22 Cal.	40 Varmint	15
22 Cal.	45 Gr.*	15
22 Cal.	50 Gr.*	14
22 Cal.	52 Gr.*	14
22 Cal.	55 Gr.*	14
22 Cal.	60 Gr.*	12
22 Cal.	62 Gr.*	12
22 Cal.	64 Gr.*	12
22 Cal.	70 Gr. VLD	9
22 Cal.	70 Gr.BT	10
22 Cal.	73 Gr. BT	9
22 Cal.	75 Gr. VLD	9
22 Cal.	80 Gr. VLD	8
(6mm) Cal.	60 Gr.*	14
(6mm) Cal.	62 Gr.*	14
(6mm) Cal.	65 Gr.*	13
(6mm) Cal.	65 Gr. Short	14
(6mm) Cal.	65 Gr. BT	13
(6mm) Cal.	66 Gr. High BC FB	13
(6mm) Cal.	68 Gr.*	13
(6mm) Cal.	69 Gr. High BC FB	12
(6mm) Cal.	70 Gr.*	13
(6mm) Cal.	71 Gr. BT*	12
(6mm) Cal.	74 Gr.*	13
(6mm) Cal.	80 Gr.*	12
(6mm) Cal.	88 Gr. High BC FB	10
(6mm) Cal.	90 Gr. BT*	10
(6mm) Cal.	95 Gr. VLD	9
(6mm) Cal.	105 Gr. LTB	9
(6mm) Cal.	105 Gr. VLD	8
(6mm) Cal.	115 Gr. VLD	7
25 Cal.	72 Gr.*	15
25 Cal.	78 Gr.*	13
25 Cal.	82 Gr.*	14
25 Cal.	87 Gr.*	13
25 Cal.	95 Gr.*	12
25 Cal.	110 Gr.*	12
25 Cal.	115 Gr. VLD	10
(6.5mm) Cal.	140 Gr. VLD	9
(7mm) Cal.	168 Gr. VLD	10
(7mm) Cal.	180 Gr. VLD	9
30 Cal.	110 Gr.*	19
30 Cal.	125 Gr.*	19
30 Cal.	135 Gr.*	16
30 Cal.	150 Gr.*	15
30 Cal.	155 Gr. LTB	14
30 Cal.	155 Gr. VLD	14
30 Cal.	168 Gr. LTB	13
30 Cal.	168 Gr. VLD	13
30 Cal.	175 Gr. VLD	13
30 Cal.	185 Gr. VLD	12
30 Cal.	190 Gr. VLD	12
30 Cal.	210 Gr. VLD	11

Hornady Rifle Bullets

The 200-grain .40 and 250- and 300-grain .45 bullets are meant for use in sabot sleeves. They feature a jacketed lead core with the signature red polymer tip. The SST has lead also to Hornady's newest big game bullet, the Interbond. Essentially, it's an SST with a thicker jacket that has an inner "expansion control ring" near the front of the shank. Jacket and core are also bonded to ensure deep penetration and high weight retention. Though it typically opens to double its initial diameter, the Interbond bullet can be expected to hold 90 percent of its weight in the animal.

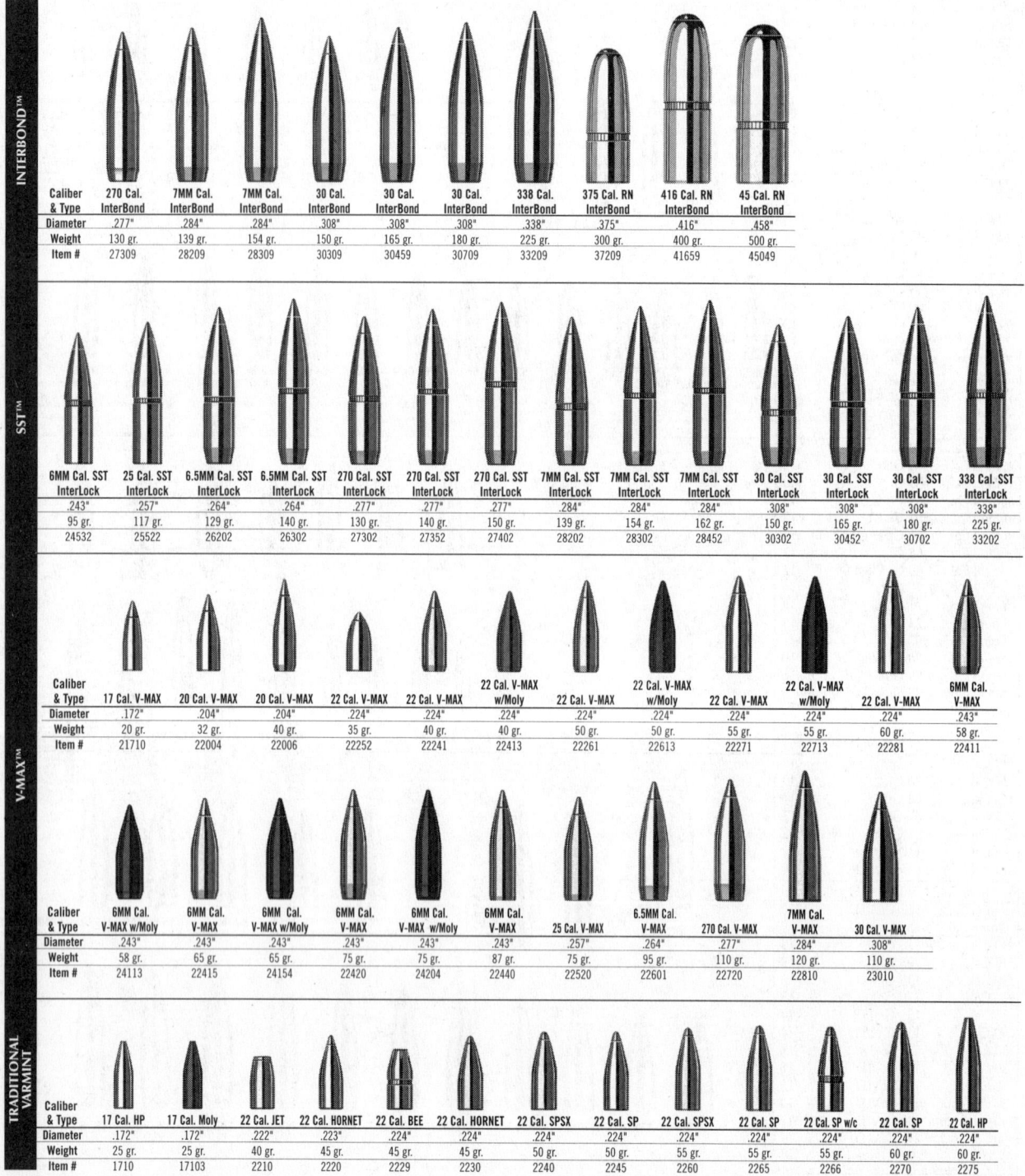

INTERBOND™

Caliber & Type	270 Cal. InterBond	7MM Cal. InterBond	7MM Cal. InterBond	30 Cal. InterBond	30 Cal. InterBond	30 Cal. InterBond	338 Cal. InterBond	375 Cal. RN InterBond	416 Cal. RN InterBond	45 Cal. RN InterBond
Diameter	.277"	.284"	.284"	.308"	.308"	.308"	.338"	.375"	.416"	.458"
Weight	130 gr.	139 gr.	154 gr.	150 gr.	165 gr.	180 gr.	225 gr.	300 gr.	400 gr.	500 gr.
Item #	27309	28209	28309	30309	30459	30709	33209	37209	41659	45049

SST™

	6MM Cal. SST InterLock	25 Cal. SST InterLock	6.5MM Cal. SST InterLock	6.5MM Cal. SST InterLock	270 Cal. SST InterLock	270 Cal. SST InterLock	270 Cal. SST InterLock	7MM Cal. SST InterLock	7MM Cal. SST InterLock	7MM Cal. SST InterLock	30 Cal. SST InterLock	30 Cal. SST InterLock	30 Cal. SST InterLock	338 Cal. SST InterLock
	.243"	.257"	.264"	.264"	.277"	.277"	.277"	.284"	.284"	.284"	.308"	.308"	.308"	.338"
	95 gr.	117 gr.	129 gr.	140 gr.	130 gr.	140 gr.	150 gr.	139 gr.	154 gr.	162 gr.	150 gr.	165 gr.	180 gr.	225 gr.
	24532	25522	26202	26302	27302	27352	27402	28202	28302	28452	30302	30452	30702	33202

V-MAX™

Caliber & Type	17 Cal. V-MAX	20 Cal. V-MAX	20 Cal. V-MAX	22 Cal. V-MAX	22 Cal. V-MAX	22 Cal. V-MAX w/Moly	22 Cal. V-MAX	22 Cal. V-MAX w/Moly	22 Cal. V-MAX	22 Cal. V-MAX w/Moly	22 Cal. V-MAX	6MM Cal. V-MAX
Diameter	.172"	.204"	.204"	.224"	.224"	.224"	.224"	.224"	.224"	.224"	.224"	.243"
Weight	20 gr.	32 gr.	40 gr.	35 gr.	40 gr.	40 gr.	50 gr.	50 gr.	55 gr.	55 gr.	60 gr.	58 gr.
Item #	21710	22004	22006	22252	22241	22413	22261	22613	22271	22713	22281	22411

Caliber & Type	6MM Cal. V-MAX w/Moly	6MM Cal. V-MAX	6MM Cal. V-MAX w/Moly	6MM Cal. V-MAX	6MM Cal. V-MAX w/Moly	6MM Cal. V-MAX	25 Cal. V-MAX	6.5MM Cal. V-MAX	270 Cal. V-MAX	7MM Cal. V-MAX	30 Cal. V-MAX
Diameter	.243"	.243"	.243"	.243"	.243"	.243"	.257"	.264"	.277"	.284"	.308"
Weight	58 gr.	65 gr.	65 gr.	75 gr.	75 gr.	87 gr.	75 gr.	95 gr.	110 gr.	120 gr.	110 gr.
Item #	24113	22415	24154	22420	24204	22440	22520	22601	22720	22810	23010

TRADITIONAL VARMINT

Caliber & Type	17 Cal. HP	17 Cal. Moly	22 Cal. JET	22 Cal. HORNET	22 Cal. BEE	22 Cal. HORNET	22 Cal. SPSX	22 Cal. SP	22 Cal. SPSX	22 Cal. SP	22 Cal. SP w/c	22 Cal. SP	22 Cal. HP
Diameter	.172"	.172"	.222"	.223"	.224"	.224"	.224"	.224"	.224"	.224"	.224"	.224"	.224"
Weight	25 gr.	25 gr.	40 gr.	45 gr.	45 gr.	45 gr.	50 gr.	50 gr.	55 gr.	55 gr.	55 gr.	60 gr.	60 gr.
Item #	1710	17103	2210	2220	2229	2230	2240	2245	2260	2265	2266	2270	2275

Hornady Rifle Bullets

TRADITIONAL VARMINT

Caliber & Type	6MM SP	6MM HP	6MM BTHP	25 Cal. HP	25 Cal. SP	270 Cal. SP	270 Cal. HP	7MM HP	7MM SP	7MM HP	30 Cal. SJ	30 Cal. SP
Diameter	.243"	.243"	.243"	.257"	.257"	.277"	.277"	.284"	.284"	.284"	.308"	.308"
Weight	70 gr.	75 gr.	87 gr.	75 gr.	87 gr.	100 gr.	110 gr.	100 gr.	120 gr.	120 gr.	100 gr.	110 gr.
Item #	2410	2420	2442	2520	2530	2710	2720	2800	2810	2815	3005	3010

Caliber & Type	22 Cal. SP	6MM SP	6MM SP InterLock	6MM BTSP InterLock	6MM RN InterLock	25 Cal. FP	25 Cal. SP InterLock	25 Cal. BTSP InterLock	25 Cal. RN InterLock	25 Cal. HP InterLock	6.5MM Cal. SP
Diameter	.227"	.243"	.243"	.243"	.243"	.257"	.257"	.257"	.257"	.257"	.264"
Weight	70 gr.	87 gr.	100 gr.	100 gr.	100 gr.	60 gr.	100 gr.	117 gr.	117 gr.	120 gr.	100 gr.
Item #	2280	2440	2450	2453	2455	2510	2540	2552	2550	2560	2610

TRADITIONAL HUNTING

Caliber & Type	6.5MM Cal. SP InterLock	6.5MM Cal. SP InterLock	6.5MM Cal. RN InterLock	Carcano 6.5MM Cal. RN	270 Cal. SP InterLock	270 Cal. BTSP InterLock	270 Cal. SP InterLock	270 Cal. RN InterLock	7MM Cal. SP InterLock	7MM Cal. BTSP InterLock
Diameter	.264"	.264"	.264"	.267"	.277"	.277"	.277"	.277"	.284"	.284"
Weight	129 gr.	140 gr.	160 gr.	160 gr.	130 gr.	140 gr.	150 gr.	150 gr.	139 gr.	139 gr.
Item #	2620	2630	2640	2645	2730	2735	2740	2745	2820	2825

Caliber & Type	7MM Cal. SP InterLock	7MM Cal. RN InterLock	7MM Cal. BTSP InterLock	7MM Cal. SP InterLock	7MM Cal. RN InterLock	30 Cal. RN InterLock	30 Cal. SP InterLock	30 Cal. SP InterLock	30 Cal. BTSP InterLock	30 Cal. RN (30-30) InterLock	30 Cal. SP InterLock
Diameter	.284"	.284"	.284"	.284"	.284"	.308"	.308"	.308"	.308"	.308"	.308"
Weight	154 gr.	154 gr.	162 gr.	175 gr.	175 gr.	110 gr.	130 gr.	150 gr.	150 gr.	150 gr.	165 gr.
Item #	2830	2835	2845	2850	2855	3015	3020	3031	3033	3035	3040

Caliber & Type	30 Cal. BTSP InterLock	30 Cal. FP (30-30) InterLock	30 Cal. SP InterLock	30 Cal. BTSP InterLock	30 Cal. RN InterLock	30 Cal. BTSP InterLock	30 Cal. RN InterLock	7.62 X 39MM Cal. SP	303 Cal. SP InterLock	303 Cal. RN InterLock
Diameter	.308"	.308"	.308"	.308"	.308"	.308"	.308"	.310"	.312"	.312"
Weight	165 gr.	170 gr.	180 gr.	180 gr.	180 gr.	190 gr.	220 gr.	123 gr.	150 gr.	174 gr.
Item #	3045	3060	3070	3072	3075	3085	3090	3140	3120	3130

Hornady Rifle Bullets

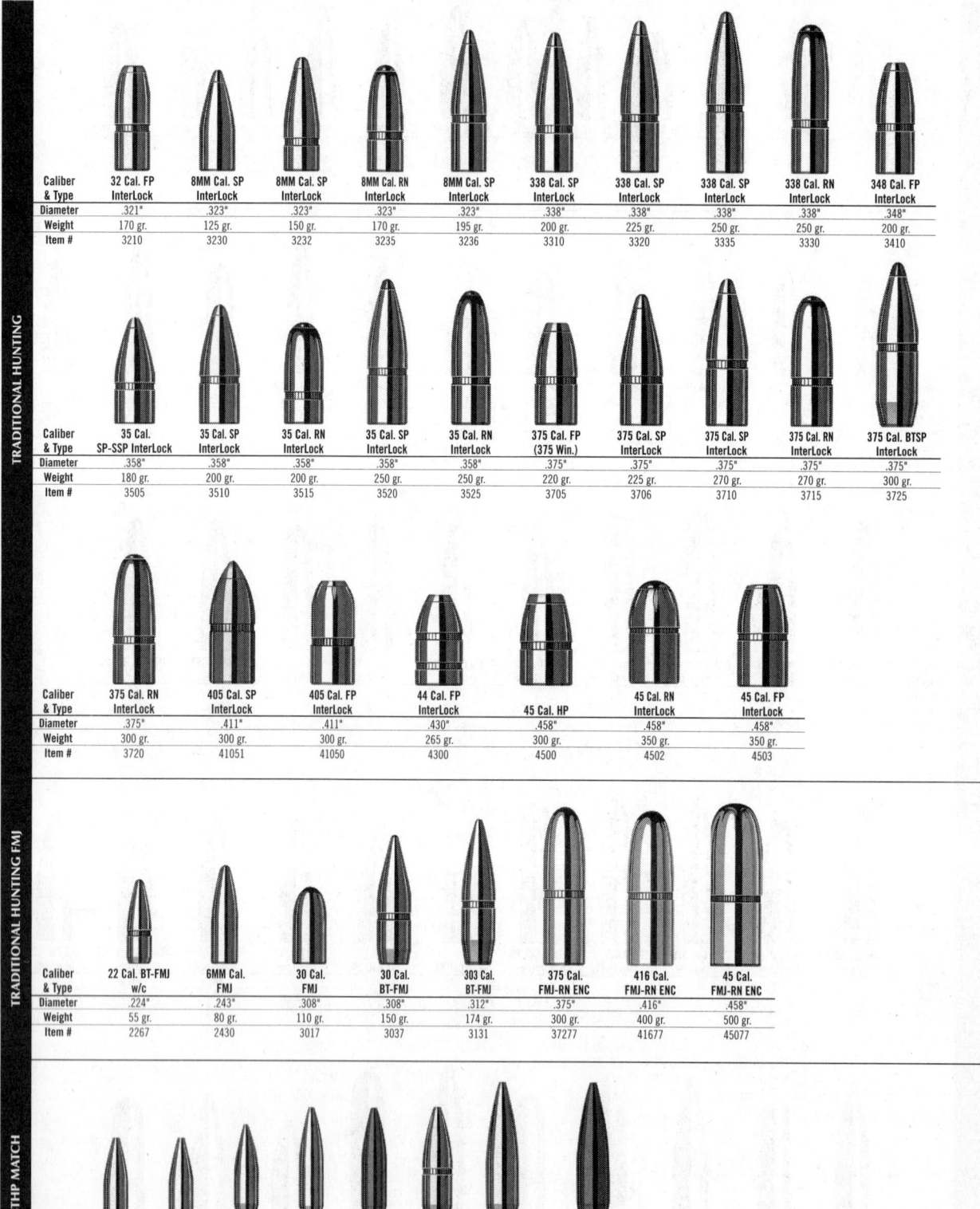

Caliber & Type	32 Cal. FP InterLock	8MM Cal. SP InterLock	8MM Cal. SP InterLock	8MM Cal. RN InterLock	8MM Cal. SP InterLock	338 Cal. SP InterLock	338 Cal. SP InterLock	338 Cal. SP InterLock	338 Cal. RN InterLock	348 Cal. FP InterLock
Diameter	.321"	.323"	.323"	.323"	.323"	.338"	.338"	.338"	.338"	.348"
Weight	170 gr.	125 gr.	150 gr.	170 gr.	195 gr.	200 gr.	225 gr.	250 gr.	250 gr.	200 gr.
Item #	3210	3230	3232	3235	3236	3310	3320	3335	3330	3410

Caliber & Type	35 Cal. SP-SSP InterLock	35 Cal. SP InterLock	35 Cal. RN InterLock	35 Cal. SP InterLock	35 Cal. RN InterLock	375 Cal. FP (375 Win.)	375 Cal. SP InterLock	375 Cal. SP InterLock	375 Cal. RN InterLock	375 Cal. BTSP InterLock
Diameter	.358"	.358"	.358"	.358"	.358"	.375"	.375"	.375"	.375"	.375"
Weight	180 gr.	200 gr.	200 gr.	250 gr.	250 gr.	220 gr.	225 gr.	270 gr.	270 gr.	300 gr.
Item #	3505	3510	3515	3520	3525	3705	3706	3710	3715	3725

Caliber & Type	375 Cal. RN InterLock	405 Cal. SP InterLock	405 Cal. FP InterLock	44 Cal. FP InterLock	45 Cal. HP	45 Cal. RN InterLock	45 Cal. FP InterLock
Diameter	.375"	.411"	.411"	.430"	.458"	.458"	.458"
Weight	300 gr.	300 gr.	300 gr.	265 gr.	300 gr.	350 gr.	350 gr.
Item #	3720	41051	41050	4300	4500	4502	4503

Caliber & Type	22 Cal. BT-FMJ w/c	6MM Cal. FMJ	30 Cal. FMJ	30 Cal. BT-FMJ	303 Cal. BT-FMJ	375 Cal. FMJ-RN ENC	416 Cal. FMJ-RN ENC	45 Cal. FMJ-RN ENC
Diameter	.224"	.243"	.308"	.308"	.312"	.375"	.416"	.458"
Weight	55 gr.	80 gr.	110 gr.	150 gr.	174 gr.	300 gr.	400 gr.	500 gr.
Item #	2267	2430	3017	3037	3131	37277	41677	45077

Caliber & Type	22 Cal. BTHP	22 Cal. HP	22 Cal. BTHP	22 Cal. BTHP	22 Cal. BTHP w/Moly	6.8MM BTHP w/c	30 Cal. BTHP	30 Cal. BTHP w/Moly
Diameter	.224"	.224"	.224"	.224"	.224"	.277"	.308"	.308"
Weight	52 gr.	53 gr.	68 gr.	75 gr.	75 gr.	115 gr.	168 gr.	168 gr.
Item #	2249	2250	2278	2279	22793	2715	30501	30503

Hornady Rifle Bullets

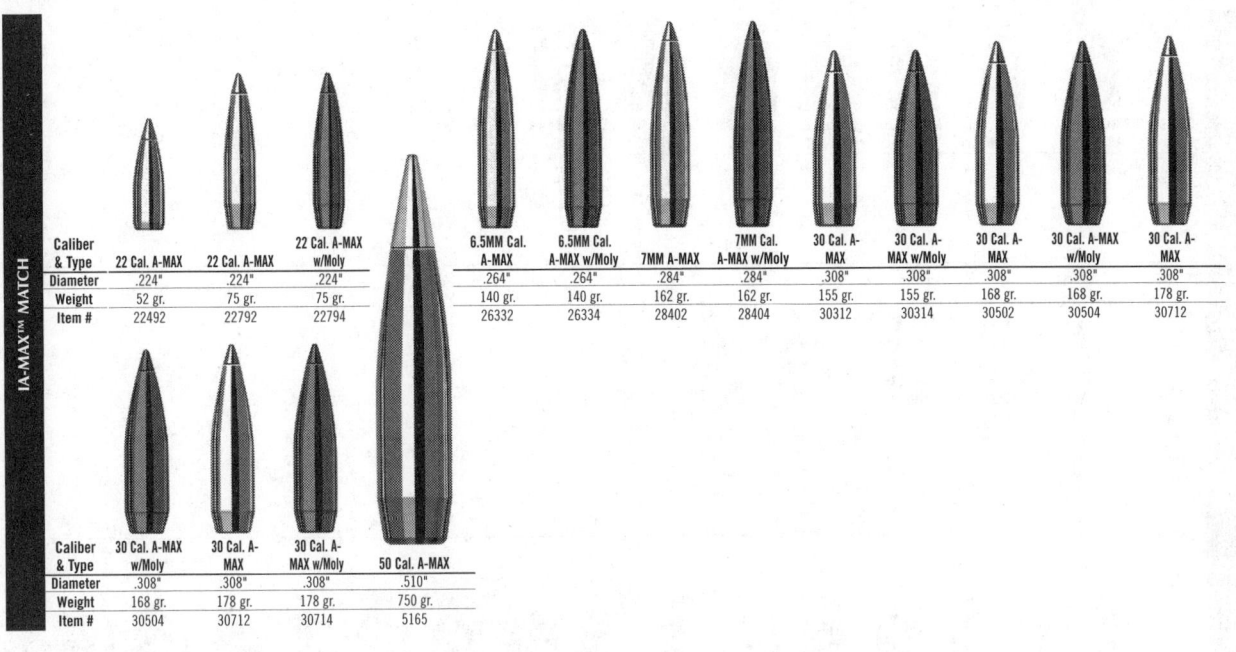

IA-MAX™ MATCH

Caliber & Type	22 Cal. A-MAX	22 Cal. A-MAX	22 Cal. A-MAX w/Moly	6.5MM Cal. A-MAX	6.5MM Cal. A-MAX w/Moly	7MM A-MAX	7MM Cal. A-MAX w/Moly	30 Cal. A-MAX	30 Cal. A-MAX w/Moly	30 Cal. A-MAX	30 Cal. A-MAX w/Moly	30 Cal. A-MAX
Diameter	.224"	.224"	.224"	.264"	.264"	.284"	.284"	.308"	.308"	.308"	.308"	.308"
Weight	52 gr.	75 gr.	75 gr.	140 gr.	140 gr.	162 gr.	162 gr.	155 gr.	155 gr.	168 gr.	168 gr.	178 gr.
Item #	22492	22792	22794	26332	26334	28402	28404	30312	30314	30502	30504	30712

Caliber & Type	30 Cal. A-MAX w/Moly	30 Cal. A-MAX	30 Cal. A-MAX w/Moly	50 Cal. A-MAX
Diameter	.308"	.308"	.308"	.510"
Weight	168 gr.	178 gr.	178 gr.	750 gr.
Item #	30504	30712	30714	5165

Hornady Handgun Bullets

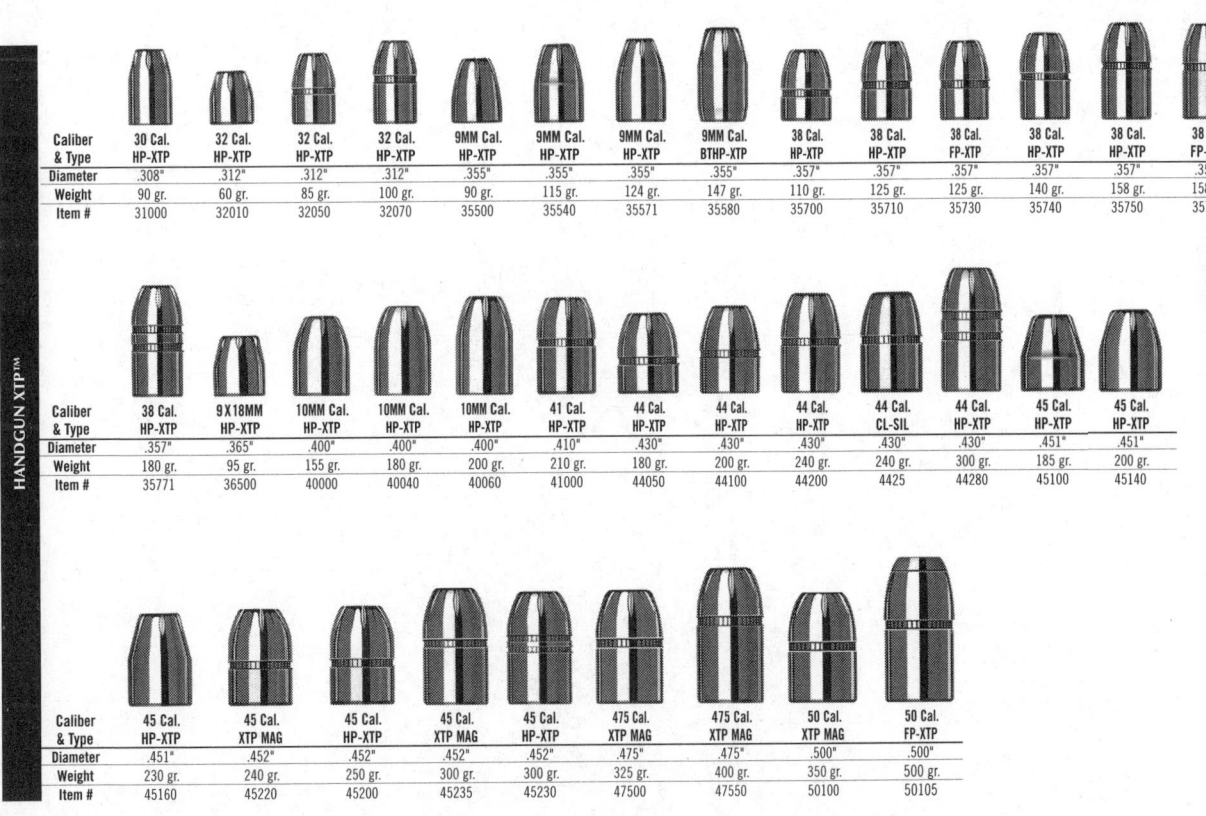

HANDGUN XTP™

Caliber & Type	30 Cal. HP-XTP	32 Cal. HP-XTP	32 Cal. HP-XTP	32 Cal. HP-XTP	9MM Cal. HP-XTP	9MM Cal. HP-XTP	9MM Cal. HP-XTP	9MM Cal. BTHP-XTP	38 Cal. HP-XTP	38 Cal. HP-XTP	38 Cal. FP-XTP	38 Cal. HP-XTP	38 Cal. HP-XTP	38 Cal. FP-XTP
Diameter	.308"	.312"	.312"	.312"	.355"	.355"	.355"	.355"	.357"	.357"	.357"	.357"	.357"	.357"
Weight	90 gr.	60 gr.	85 gr.	100 gr.	90 gr.	115 gr.	124 gr.	147 gr.	110 gr.	125 gr.	125 gr.	140 gr.	158 gr.	158 gr.
Item #	31000	32010	32050	32070	35500	35540	35571	35580	35700	35710	35730	35740	35750	35780

Caliber & Type	38 Cal. HP-XTP	9 X 18MM HP-XTP	10MM Cal. HP-XTP	10MM Cal. HP-XTP	10MM Cal. HP-XTP	41 Cal. HP-XTP	44 Cal. HP-XTP	44 Cal. HP-XTP	44 Cal. HP-XTP	44 Cal. CL-SIL	44 Cal. HP-XTP	45 Cal. HP-XTP	45 Cal. HP-XTP
Diameter	.357"	.365"	.400"	.400"	.400"	.410"	.430"	.430"	.430"	.430"	.430"	.451"	.451"
Weight	180 gr.	95 gr.	155 gr.	180 gr.	200 gr.	210 gr.	180 gr.	200 gr.	240 gr.	240 gr.	300 gr.	185 gr.	200 gr.
Item #	35771	36500	40000	40040	40060	41000	44050	44100	44200	4425	44280	45100	45140

Caliber & Type	45 Cal. HP-XTP	45 Cal. XTP MAG	45 Cal. HP-XTP	45 Cal. XTP MAG	45 Cal. HP-XTP	475 Cal. XTP MAG	475 Cal. XTP MAG	50 Cal. XTP MAG	50 Cal. FP-XTP
Diameter	.451"	.452"	.452"	.452"	.452"	.475"	.475"	.500"	.500"
Weight	230 gr.	240 gr.	250 gr.	300 gr.	300 gr.	325 gr.	400 gr.	350 gr.	500 gr.
Item #	45160	45220	45200	45235	45230	47500	47550	50100	50105

Hornady Handgun Bullets

HANDGUN FMJ

Caliber & Type	9MM Cal. FMJ RN-ENC	9MM Cal. FMJ FP-ENC	9MM Cal. FMJ RN-ENC	45 Cal. FMJ SWC-ENC	45 Cal. FMJ CT-ENC	45 Cal. FMJ RN-ENC	45 Cal. FMJ FP-ENC
Diameter	.355"	.355"	.355"	.451"	.451"	.451"	.451"
Weight	115 gr.	124 gr.	124 gr.	185 gr.	200 gr.	230 gr.	230 gr.
Item #	35557	35567	35577	45137	45157	45177	45187

HANGUN HAP™

Caliber & Type	9MM Cal. HAP	9MM Cal. HAP	10MM Cal. HAP	10MM Cal. HAP	45 Cal. HAP
Diameter	.356"	.356"	.400"	.400"	.451"
Weight	121 gr.	125 gr.	180 gr.	200 gr.	230 gr.
Item #	35530B	35572B	40042B	40061B	45161B

FRONTIER™/LEAD

Caliber & Type	32 Cal. SWC	32 Cal. HBWC	38 Cal. FP Cowboy	38 Cal. HBWC	38 Cal. SWC	38 Cal. HP-SWC	38 Cal. LRN	44 Cal. FP Cowboy	44 Cal. FP Cowboy	44 Cal. SWC	44 Cal. HP-SWC	45 Cal. SWC	45 Cal. L-C/T	45 Cal. LRN	45 Cal. FP Cowboy
Diameter	.314"	.314"	.358"	.358"	.358"	.358"	.358"	.427"	.430"	.430"	.430"	.452"	.452"	.452"	.454"
Weight	90 gr.	90 gr.	140 gr.	148 gr.	158 gr.	158 gr.	158 gr.	205 gr.	180 gr.	240 gr.	240 gr.	200 gr.	200 gr.	230 gr.	255 gr.
Item #	10008	10028	10078	10208	10408	10428	10508	11208	11058	11108	11118	12108	12208	12308	12458

Lapua precision bullets are made from the best raw materials and meet the toughest of precision specifications. Each bullet is subject to visual inspection and tested with advanced measurement devices.

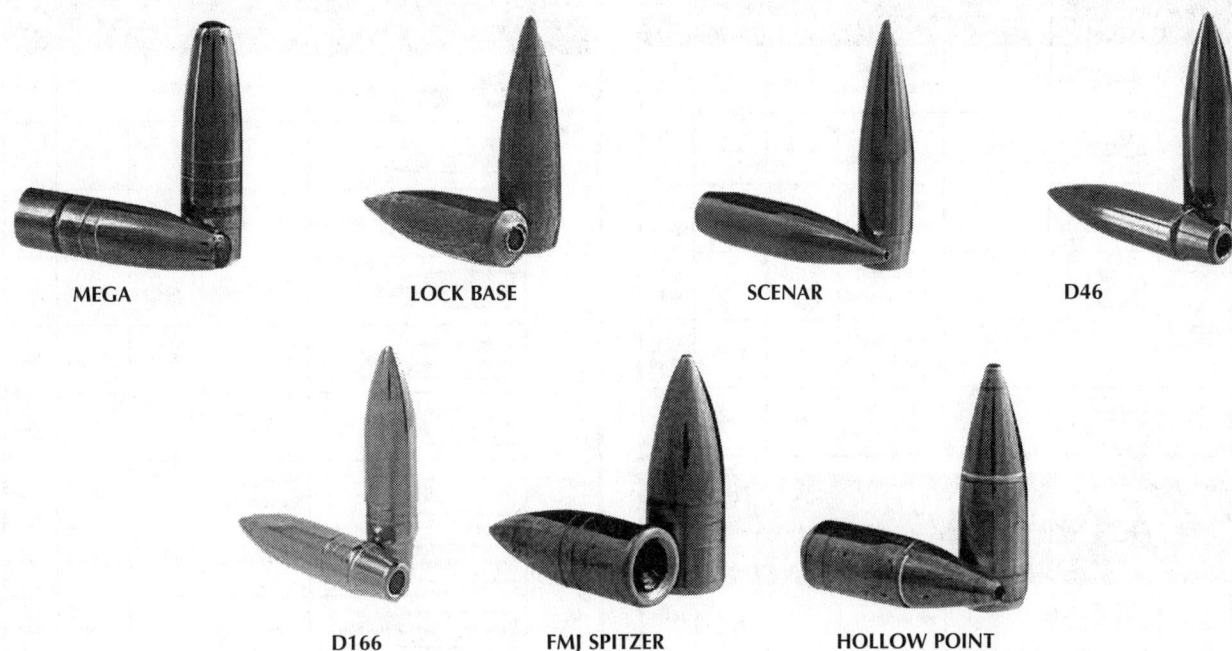

MEGA   LOCK BASE   SCENAR   D46

D166   FMJ SPITZER   HOLLOW POINT

MEGA

Mega is a soft point bullet with a protective copper jacket with quadruple expansion on impact, which causes rapid energy transfer. Mega's lead alloy core achieves up to 97% weight retention.

LOCK BASE

The construction of Lock Base bullet makes it possible to use maximum pressures and to achieve higher velocities without damaging the base of the bullet. FMJBT configuration reduces drag and provides a flatter trajectory.

SCENAR

The Scenar hollow point boat tail bullet provides low drag and a superb ballistic coefficient. These bullets deliver superb performance at long ranges and benchrest shooting. All Scenar bullets are also available in a coated Silver Jacket version.

D46

The D46 bullet is manufactured to the strictest tolerances for concentricity and uniformity of shape and weight.

D166

The Lapua's unique D166 construction has remained the same since the late 1930's: superb accurate FMJBT bullet, the only right choice for your 7.62x53R and 7.62x54R cartridges.

FMJ SPITZER

The FMJ Spitzer is exceptionally accurate. Ten rounds (S374 in .308 Win) from a hundred meters easily achieve groupings less than 30 mm.

HOLLOW POINT

This HPCE bullet cuts a clean and easily distinguishable hole in your target. With ten rounds (G477 in .308 Win) fired at 100 m, this bullet typically achieves groupings of under 25 mm— sometimes even less than 15 mm!

Nosler Bullets

CUSTOM COMPETITION™

Caliber/ Diameter	Bullet Weight & Style	Sectional Density	Ballistic Coefficient	Part #
22/ .224"	69 Gr. HPBT 250 Ct. Bulk Pack	0.196	0.305	17101 53065
22/ .224"	77 Gr. HPBT 250 Ct. Bulk Pack	0.219	0.340	22421 53064
22/ .224"	80 Gr. HPBT 250 Ct. Bulk Pack	0.228	0.415	25116 53080
30/ .308"	155 Gr. HPBT 250 Ct. Bulk Pack	0.233	0.450	53155 53169
30/ .308"	168 Gr. HPBT 250 Ct. Bulk Pack	0.253	0.462	53164 53168
45/ .451"	185 Gr. JHP 250 Ct. Bulk Pack	0.130	0.142	44847

PARTITION®

Caliber/ Diameter	Bullet Weight & Style	Sectional Density	Ballistic Coefficient	Part #
22/ .224"	60 Gr. Spitzer	0.171	0.228	16316
6mm/ .243"	85 Gr. Spitzer	0.206	0.315	16314
6mm/ .243"	95 Gr. Spitzer	0.230	0.365	16315
6mm/ .243"	100 Gr. Spitzer	0.242	0.384	35642
25/ .257"	100 Gr. Spitzer	0.216	0.377	16317
25/ .257"	115 Gr. Spitzer	0.249	0.389	16318
25/ .257"	120 Gr. Spitzer	0.260	0.391	35643
6.5mm/ .264"	100 Gr. Spitzer	0.205	0.326	16319
6.5mm/ .264"	125 Gr. Spitzer	0.256	0.449	16320
6.5mm/ .264"	140 Gr. Spitzer	0.287	0.490	16321
270/ .277"	130 Gr. Spitzer	0.242	0.416	16322
270/ .277"	140 Gr. Spitzer	0.261	0.432	35200
270/ .277"	150 Gr. Spitzer	0.279	0.465	16323
270/ .277"	160 Gr. Semi Spitzer	0.298	0.434	16324

PARTITION®

Caliber/ Diameter	Bullet Weight & Style	Sectional Density	Ballistic Coefficient	Part #
7mm/ .284"	150 Gr. Spitzer	0.266	0.456	16326
7mm/ .284"	160 Gr. Spitzer	0.283	0.475	16327
7mm/ .284"	175 Gr. Spitzer	0.310	0.519	35645
30/ .308"	150 Gr. Spitzer	0.226	0.387	16329
30/ .308"	165 Gr. Spitzer	0.248	0.410	16330
30/ .308"	170 Gr. Round Nose	0.256	0.252	16333
30/ .308"	180 Gr. Protected Point	0.271	0.361	25396
30/ .308"	180 Gr. Spitzer	0.271	0.474	16331
30/ .308"	200 Gr. Spitzer	0.301	0.481	35626
30/ .308"	220 Gr. Semi Spitzer	0.331	0.351	16332
8mm/ .323"	200 Gr. Spitzer	0.274	0.350	35277
8mm/ .323"	210 Gr. Spitzer	0.263	0.400	16337
338/ .338"	225 Gr. Spitzer	0.281	0.454	16336
338/ .338"	250 Gr. Spitzer	0.313	0.473	35644
35/ .358"	225 Gr. Spitzer	0.251	0.430	44800
35/ .358"	250 Gr. Spitzer	0.279	0.446	44801
9.3mm/ .366"	286 Gr. Spitzer (18.5 gram)	0.307	0.482	44750
375/ .375"	260 Gr. Spitzer	0.264	0.314	44850
375/ .375"	300 Gr. Spitzer	0.305	0.398	44845
416/ .416"	400 Gr. Spitzer	0.330	0.390	45200
45-70/ .458"	300 Gr. Protected Point	0.204	0.199	45325

Nosler Bullets

BALLISTIC TIP® HUNTING

Caliber/Diameter	Bullet Weight & Style	Sectional Density	Ballistic Coefficient	Part #
6mm/.243"	90 Gr. Spitzer (Purple Tip)	0.218	0.365	24090
	95 Gr. Spitzer (Purple Tip)	0.230	0.379	24095
25/.257"	100 Gr. Spitzer (Blue Tip)	0.216	0.393	25100
	115 Gr. Spitzer (Blue Tip)	0.249	0.453	25115
6.5mm/.264"	100 Gr. Spitzer (Brown Tip)	0.205	0.350	26100
	120 Gr. Spitzer (Brown Tip)	0.246	0.458	26120
270/.277"	130 Gr. Spitzer (Yellow Tip)	0.242	0.433	27130
	140 Gr. Spitzer (Yellow Tip)	0.261	0.456	27140
	150 Gr. Spitzer (Yellow Tip)	0.279	0.496	27150
7mm/.284"	120 Gr. Spitzer (Red Tip)	0.213	0.417	28120
	140 Gr. Spitzer (Red Tip)	0.248	0.485	28140
	150 Gr. Spitzer (Red Tip)	0.266	0.493	28150
30/.308"	125 Gr. Spitzer (Green Tip)	0.188	0.366	30125
	150 Gr. Spitzer (Green Tip)	0.226	0.435	30150
	165 Gr. Spitzer (Green Tip)	0.248	0.475	30165
	180 Gr. Spitzer (Green Tip)	0.271	0.507	30180
8mm/.323"	180 Gr. Spitzer (Gunmetal Tip)	0.247	0.357	32180
338/.338"	180 Gr. Spitzer (Maroon Tip)	0.225	0.372	33180
	200 Gr. Spitzer (Maroon Tip)	0.250	0.414	33200
35/.358"	225 Gr. Whelen (Buckskin Tip)	0.251	0.421	35225
9.3mm/.366"	250 Gr. Spitzer (Olive Tip)	0.267	0.494	36250

BALLISTIC TIP® VARMINT

Caliber/Diameter	Bullet Weight & Style	Sectional Density	Ballistic Coefficient	Part #
22/.224"	40 Gr. Spitzer (Orange Tip) 250 Ct. Varmint Pak™	0.114	0.221	39510 / 39555
	45 Gr. Hornet (Soft Lead Tip)	0.128	0.144	35487
	50 Gr. Spitzer (Orange Tip) 250 Ct. Varmint Pak™	0.142	0.238	39522 / 39557
	55 Gr. Spitzer (Orange Tip) 250 Ct. Varmint Pak™	0.157	0.267	39526 / 39560
6mm/.243"	55 Gr. Spitzer (Purple Tip) 250 Ct. Varmint Pak™	0.133	0.276	24055 / 39565
	70 Gr. Spitzer (Purple Tip) 250 Ct. Varmint Pak™	0.169	0.310	39532 / 39570
	80 Gr. Spitzer (Purple Tip)	0.194	0.329	24080
25/.257"	85 Gr. Spitzer (Blue Tip)	0.183	0.329	43004

CT® BALLISTIC SILVERTIP® HUNTING

Caliber/Diameter	Bullet Weight & Style	Sectional Density	Ballistic Coefficient	Part #
6mm/.243"	95 Gr. Spitzer	0.230	0.379	51040
25/.257"	85 Gr. Spitzer	0.183	0.329	51045
	115 Gr. Spitzer	0.249	0.453	51050
270/.277"	130 Gr. Spitzer	0.242	0.433	51075
	150 Gr. Spitzer	0.279	0.496	51100
7mm/.284"	140 Gr. Spitzer	0.248	0.485	51105
	150 Gr. Spitzer	0.266	0.493	51110
30/.308"	150 Gr. Spitzer	0.226	0.435	51150
	168 Gr. Spitzer	0.253	0.490	51160
	180 Gr. Spitzer	0.271	0.507	51170
338/.338"	200 Gr. Spitzer	0.250	0.414	51200

Nosler Bullets

CT® FAIL SAFE®

Caliber/Diameter	Bullet Weight & Style	Sectional Density	Ballistic Coefficient	Part #
270/.277"	140 Gr. HP Spitzer	0.261	0.322	53140
7mm/.284"	140 Gr. HP Spitzer	0.248	0.323	53150
	160 Gr. HP Spitzer	0.283	0.382	53160
30/.308"	150 Gr. HP Spitzer	0.226	0.310	53170
	165 Gr. HP Spitzer	0.248	0.314	53175
	180 Gr. HP Spitzer	0.271	0.391	53180
338/.338"	230 Gr. HP Spitzer	0.288	0.436	53230
375/.375"	270 Gr. HP Spitzer	0.274	0.393	53350
	300 Gr. HP Spitzer	0.305	0.441	53360

ACCUBOND®

Caliber/Diameter	Bullet Weight & Style	Sectional Density	Ballistic Coefficient	Part #
25/.257"	110 Gr. Spitzer	0.238	0.418	53742
270/.277"	140 Gr. Spitzer	0.261	0.496	54765
7mm/.284"	140 Gr. Spitzer	0.248	0.485	59992
	160 Gr. Spitzer	0.283	0.531	54932
30/.308"	150 Gr. Spitzer	0.226	0.435	56719
	180 Gr. Spitzer	0.271	0.507	54825
	200 Gr. Spitzer	0.301	0.588	54618
8mm/.323"	200 Gr. Spitzer	0.274	0.379	54374
338/.338"	180 Gr. Spitzer	0.225	0.372	57625
	225 Gr. Spitzer	0.281	0.550	54357
375/.375"	260 Gr. Spitzer	0.264	0.473	54413

CT® BALLISTIC SILVERTIP® VARMINT

Caliber/Diameter	Bullet Weight & Style	Sectional Density	Ballistic Coefficient	Part #
22/.224"	40 Gr. Spitzer	0.114	0.221	51005
	50 Gr. Spitzer	0.142	0.238	51010
	55 Gr. Spitzer	0.157	0.267	51031
6mm/.243"	55 Gr. Spitzer	0.133	0.276	51030

PARTITION-HG™

Caliber/Diameter	Bullet Weight & Style	Sectional Density	Ballistic Coefficient	Part #
38/.357"	180 Gr. HP	0.202	0.201	35180
44/.429"	250 Gr. HP	0.194	0.200	44250
45/.451"	260 Gr. HP	0.182	0.174	45260
	300 Gr. Protected Point	0.211	0.199	45350

SPORTING HANDGUN™

Caliber/Diameter	Bullet Weight & Style	Sectional Density	Ballistic Coefficient	Part #
9mm/.355"	115 Gr. JHP 250 Ct. Bulk Pack	0.130	0.109	44848
38/.357"	158 Gr. JHP 250 Ct. Bulk Pack	0.177	0.182	44841
10mm/.400"	135 Gr. JHP 250 Ct. Bulk Pack	0.121	0.093	44852
	150 Gr. JHP 250 Ct. Bulk Pack	0.134	0.106	44860
41/.410"	210 Gr. JHP	0.178	0.170	43012
	200 Gr. JHP 250 Ct. Bulk Pack	0.155	0.151	44846
44/.429"	240 Gr. JHP 250 Ct. Bulk Pack	0.186	0.173	44842
	240 Gr. JSP 250 Ct. Bulk Pack	0.186	0.177	44868
	300 Gr. JHP	0.233	0.206	42069
45 Colt/.451"	250 Gr. JHP	0.176	0.177	43013

Sierra Bullets
Rifle Bullets

.20 Caliber Hornet (.204 diameter)

32 gr. Blitz #1032

39 gr. Blitz #1039

.22 Caliber Hornet (.223/5.66mm diameter)

40 gr. Hornet
Varminter #1100

45 gr. Hornet
Varminter #1110

.22 Caliber Hornet (.223/5.66mm diameter)

40 gr. Hornet
Varminter #1200

45 gr. Hornet
Varminter #1210

.22 Caliber Hornet (.223/5.66mm diameter)

40 gr. HP
Varminter #1385

40 gr.
BlitzKing #1440

45 gr. SPT
Varminter #1310

50 gr. SMP
Varminter #1320

50 gr. SPT
Varminter #1330

50 gr.
BlitzKing #1450

52 gr. HPBT
MatchKing #1410

53 gr. HP
MatchKing #1400

55 gr. Blitz
Varminter #1345

55 gr. SMP
Varminter #1350

55 gr. FMJBT
GameKing #1355

65 gr. SBT
GameKing #1395

55 gr. SBT
GameKing #1365

55 gr. HPBT
GameKing #1390

55 gr.
BlitzKing #1455

60 gr. HP
Varminter #1375

63 gr. SMP
Varminter #1370

65 gr. SBT
GameKing #1395
7-10" TWST BBLS

.22 Caliber (.224/5.69mm diameter)

69 gr. HPBT
MatchKing #1380
7"-10" TWST BBLS

6MM .243 Caliber (.243/6.17mm diameter)

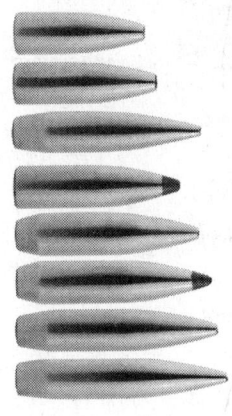

55 gr.
BlitzKing #1502

60 gr. HP
Varminter #1500

70 gr. HPBT
MatchKing #1505

70 gr.
BlitzKing #1507

75 gr. HP
Varminter #1510

80 gr. Blitz
Varminter #1515

80 gr. SPT SSP
Pro-Hunter #7150

85 gr. SPT
Varminter #1520

85 gr. HPBT
GameKing #1530

90 gr. FMJBT
GameKing #1535

100 gr. SPT
Pro-Hunter #1540

100 gr. SBT
GameKing #1560

107 gr. HPBT
MatchKing #1570
7"-8" TWST BBLS

.25 Caliber (.257/6.53mm diameter)

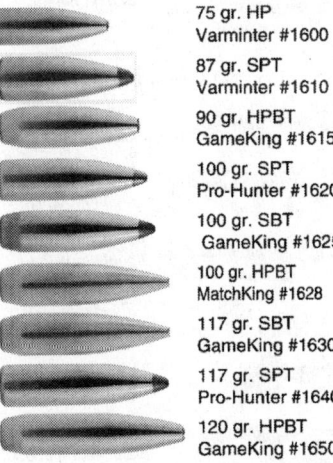

75 gr. HP
Varminter #1600

87 gr. SPT
Varminter #1610

90 gr. HPBT
GameKing #1615

100 gr. SPT
Pro-Hunter #1620

100 gr. SBT
GameKing #1625

100 gr. HPBT
MatchKing #1628

117 gr. SBT
GameKing #1630

117 gr. SPT
Pro-Hunter #1640

120 gr. HPBT
GameKing #1650

6.5MM .264 Caliber (.264/6.7mm diameter)

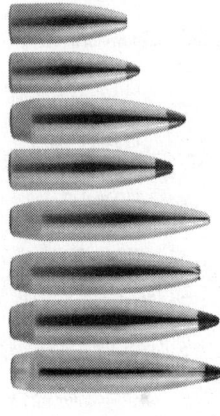

85 gr. HP
Varminter #1700

100 gr. HP
Varminter #1710

107 gr. HPBT
MatchKing #1715

120 gr. SPT
Pro-Hunter #1720

120 gr. HPBT
MatchKing #1725

140 gr. SBT
GameKing #1730

140 gr. HPBT
MatchKing #1740

142 gr. HPBT
MatchKing #1742

.270 Caliber (.277/7.04mm diameter)

90 gr. HP
Varminter #1800

110 gr. SPT
Pro-Hunter #1810

130 gr. SBT
GameKing #1820

130 gr. SPT
Pro-Hunter #1830

135 gr. HPBT
MatchKing #1833

140 gr. HPBT
GameKing #1835

140 gr. SBT
GameKing #1845

150 gr. SBT
GameKing #1840

7MM .284 Caliber (.284/7.21mm diameter)

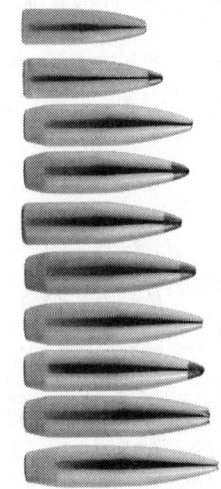

100 gr. HP
Varminter #1895

120 gr. SPT
Pro-Hunter #1900

130 gr. HPBT
MatchKing #1903

130 gr. SPT SSP
Pro-Hunter #7250

140 gr. SPT
Pro-Hunter #1910

150 gr. SBT
GameKing #1913

150 gr. HPBT
MatchKing #1915

160 gr. SBT
GameKing #1920

160 gr. HPBT
GameKing #1925

168 gr. HPBT
MatchKing #1930

Sierra Bullets

7MM .284 Caliber (cont.)
(.284/7.21mm diameter)

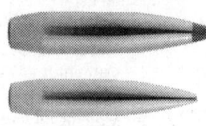

175 gr. SBT
GameKing #1940

175 gr. HPBT
MatchKing #1975
8.5" TWST BBLS

.30 (.03-30)Caliber (.308/7.82mm diameter)

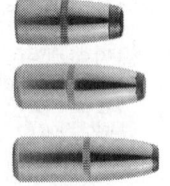

125 gr. HP/FN
Pro-Hunter #2020

150 gr. FN
Pro-Hunter #2000
POWER JACKET

170 gr. FN
Pro-Hunter #2010
POWER JACKET

.30 Caliber 7.62mm (.308/7.82mm diameter)

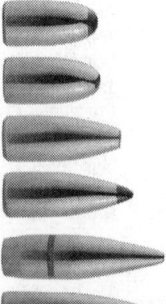

110 gr. RN
Pro-Hunter #2100

110 gr. FMJ
Pro-Hunter #2105

110 gr. HP
Varminter #2110

125 gr. SPT
Pro-Hunter #2120

150 gr. FMJBT
GameKing #2115

150 gr. SPT
Pro-Hunter #2130

150 gr. SBT
GameKing #2125

150 gr. HPBT
MatchKing #2190

150 gr. RN
Pro-Hunter #2135

155 gr. HPBT
PALMA
MatchKing #2155

165 gr. SBT
GameKing #2145

165 gr. HPBT
GameKing #2140

168 gr. HPBT
MatchKing #2200

175 gr. HPBT
MatchKing #2275

180 gr. SPT
Pro-Hunter #2150

180 gr. SBT
GameKing #2160

180 gr. HPBT
MatchKing #2220

.30 Caliber 7.62mm(cont.)
(.308/7.82mm diameter)

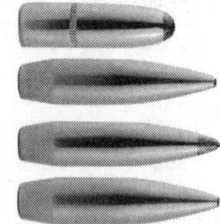

180 gr. RN
Pro-Hunter #2170

190 gr. HPBT
MatchKing #2210

200 gr. SBT
GameKing #2165

200 gr. HPBT
MatchKing #2230

220 gr. HPBT
MatchKing #2240

220 gr. RN
Pro-Hunter #2180

.303 Caliber 7.7mm (.311/7.90mm diameter)

125 gr. SPT
Pro-Hunter #2305

150 gr. SPT
Pro-Hunter #2300

174 gr. HPBT
MatchKing #2315

180 gr. SPT
Pro-Hunter #2310

8MM .323 Caliber (.323/8.20mm diameter)

150 gr. SPT
Pro-Hunter #2400

175 gr. SPT
Pro-Hunter #2410

200 gr. HPBT
MatchKing
#2415

220 gr. SBT
GameKing #2420

.338 Caliber (.338/8.59mm diameter)

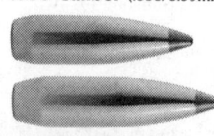

215 gr. SBT
GameKing #2610

250 gr. SBT
GameKing #2600

200 gr. HPBT
MatchKing
#2415

.35 Caliber (.358/9.09mm diameter)

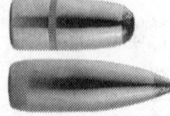

200 gr. RN
Pro-Hunter #2800

225 gr. SBT
GameKing #2850

.375 Caliber (.375/9.53mm diameter)

200 gr. FN
Pro-Hunter #2900

7MM .284 Caliber (cont.)
(.284/7.21mm diameter)

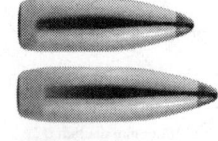

250 gr. SBT
GameKing #2950

300 gr. SBT
GameKing #3000

1.63MM Diameter)

300 gr. HP/FN
Pro-Hunter #8900

LONG RANGE SPECIALTY BULLETS

.22 Caliber, .224/5.69 Diameter
77 gr. HPBT MatchKing #9377
7"-8" TWST BBLS

22 Caliber, .224/5.69 Diameter
80 gr. HPBT MatchKing #9390
7"- 8" TWST BBLS

.30 Caliber, 7.62MM
240 gr. HPBT MatchKing #9245
9" TWST BBLS

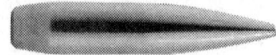

.338 Caliber, 8.59MM
300 gr. HPBT MatchKing #9300
10" TWST BBLS

ABBREVIATIONS

SBT	=	Spitzer Boat Tail
SPT	=	Spitzer
JHP	=	Jacketed Hollow Point
HP	=	Hollow Point
JHC	=	Jacketed Hollow Cavity
FN	=	Flat Nose
RN	=	Round Nose
JSP	=	Jacketed Soft Point
HPBT	=	Hollow Point Boat Tail
FMJ	=	Full Metal Jacket
FPJ	=	Full Profile Jacket
SMP	=	Semi-Pointed
FMJBT	=	Full Metal Jacket Boat Tail
SSP	=	Single Shot Pistol

Sierra Bullets
Handgun Bullets

.25 Caliber (.251/6.38mm diameter)

50 gr. FMJ
Tournament Master #8000

.30 Caliber (.308/7.82mm diameter)

85 gr. RN
Sports Master #8005

.32 Caliber 7.65MM (.312/7.92mm diameter)

71 gr. FMJ
Tournament Master #8010

.32 Caliber (.312/7.92mm diameter)

90 gr. JHC
Sports Master #8030
POWER JACKET

9MM .355 Caliber (.355/9.02mm diameter)

90 gr. JHP
Sports Master #8100
POWER JACKET

95 gr. FMJ
Tournament Master #8105

115 gr. JHP
Sports Master #8110
POWER JACKET

115 gr. FMJ
Tournament Master #8115

125 gr. JHP Sports Master
#8125 POWER JACKET

125 gr. FMJ
Tournament Master #8120

.38 Caliber (.357/9.07mm diameter)

110 gr. JHC Blitz
Sports Master #8300
POWER JACKET

125 gr. JSP
Sports Master #8310

125 gr. JHC
Sports Master #8320
POWER JACKET

140 gr. JHC
Sports Master #8325
POWER JACKET

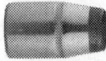
158 gr. JSP
Sports Master #8340

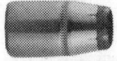
158 gr. JHC
Sports Master #8360
POWER JACKET

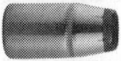
170 gr. JHC
Sports Master #8365
POWER JACKET

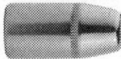
180 gr. FPJ Match
Tournament Master #8370

9MM Makarov (.363/9.22mm diameter)

100 gr. FPJ
Tournament Master #8210

10MM .400 Caliber (.400/10.16mm diameter)

135 gr. JHP
Sports Master #8425
POWER JACKET

150 gr. JHP
Sports Master #8430
POWER JACKET

165 gr. JHP
Sports Master #8445
POWER JACKET

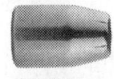
180 gr. JHP
Sports Master #8460
POWER JACKET

190 gr. FPJ
Tournament Master #8480

.41 Caliber (.410/10.41mm diameter)

170 gr. JHC
Sports Master #8500
POWER JACKET

210 gr. JHC
Sports Master #8520
POWER JACKET

.44 Caliber (.4295/10.91mm diameter)

180 gr. JHC
Sports Master #8600
POWER JACKET

210 gr. JHC
Sports Master #8620
POWER JACKET

220 gr. FPJ Match
Tournament Master #8605

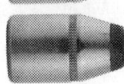
240 gr. JHC
Sports Master #8610
POWER JACKET

250 gr. FPJ Match
Tournament Master #8615

300 gr. JSP
Sports Master #8630

.45 Caliber (.4515/11.47mm diameter)

185 gr. JHP
Sports Master #8800
POWER JACKET

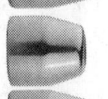
185 gr. FPJ Match
Tournament Master #8810

200 gr. FPJ Match
Tournament Master #8825

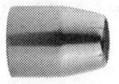
230 gr. JHP
Sports Master #8805
POWER JACKET

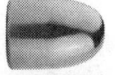
230 gr. FMJ Match
Tournament Master #8815

240 gr. JHC
Sports Master #8820
POWER JACKET

300 gr. JSP
Sports Master #8830

.50 Caliber (.5000/12.7mm diameter)

350 gr. JHP
Sports Master #5350
POWER JACKET

400 gr. JHP
Sports Master #5400
POWER JACKET

ABBREVIATIONS

SBT	=	Spitzer Boat Tail
SPT	=	Spitzer
JHP	=	Jacketed Hollow Point
HP	=	Hollow Point
JHC	=	Jacketed Hollow Cavity
FN	=	Flat Nose
RN	=	Round Nose
JSP	=	Jacketed Soft Point
HPBT	=	Hollow Point Boat Tail
FMJ	=	Full Metal Jacket
FPJ	=	Full Profile Jacket
SMP	=	Semi-Pointed
FMJBT	=	Full Metal Jacket Boat Tail
SSP	=	Single Shot Pistol

Speer Bullets

Gold Dot Handgun Bullets

Caliber & Description	25 Auto Gold Dot HP	32 Auto Gold Dot HP	380 Auto Gold Dot HP	9mm Luger Gold Dot HP	9mm Luger Gold Dot HP	9mm Luger Gold Dot HP SB	9mm Luger Gold Dot HP	357 SIG/38 Super Gold Dot HP	38 Special Gold Dot HP	38 Spl 357 Mag Gold Dot HP SB	38 Spl 357 Mag Gold Dot HP SB	357 Magnum Gold Dot HP	357 Magnum Gold Dot HP	357 Magnum Gold Dot SP	9x18mm Makarov Gold Dot HP	40/10mm Gold Dot HP	40/10mm Gold Dot HP
Diameter, Inches	.251	.312	.355	.355	.355	.355	.355	.355	.357	.357	.357	.357	.357	.357	.364	.400	.400
Weight, grains	35	60	90	115	124	124	147	125	110	135	147	125	158	170	90	155	165
BC	.091	.118	.101	.125	.134	.134	.164	.141	.117	.141	.153	.140	.168	.185	.107	.123	.138
Part Number	3985	3986	3992	3994	3998	4000	4002	4360	4009	4014	4016	4012	4215	4230	3999	4400	4397
Bullets/box	100	100	100	100	100	100	100	100	100	100	100	100	100	100	100	100	100
Bullet Construction	UC	UC	UC	UC	UC	UC	UC	UC	UC	UC	UC	UC	UC	UC	UC	UC	UC

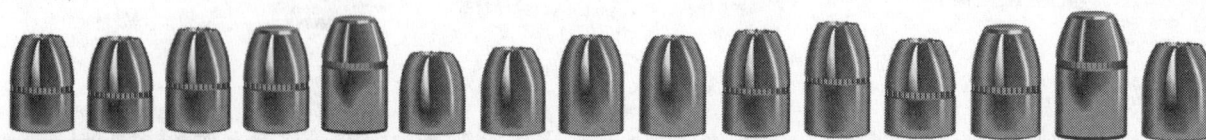

Caliber & Description	44 Special Gold Dot HP	44 Magnum Gold Dot HP	44 Magnum Gold Dot HP	44 Magnum Gold Dot SP	44 Magnum Gold Dot SP	45 Auto Gold Dot HP	45 Auto Gold Dot HP	45 Auto Gold Dot HP	45 Auto Gold Dot HP SB	45 Colt Gold Dot HP	454 Casull Gold Dot HP	480 Ruger Gold Dot HP	480 Ruger Gold Dot SP	475 Linebaugh Gold Dot SP†	50 Action Express Gold Dot HP
Diameter, Inches	.429	.429	.429	.429	.429	.451	.451	.451	.451	.452	.452	.475	.475	.475	.500
Weight, grains	200	210	240	240	270	185	200	230	230	250	300	275	325	400	300
BC	.145	.154	.175	.175	.193	.109	.138	.143		.165	.233	.162	.191	.242	.155
Part Number	4427	4428	4455	4456	4461	4470	4473	4483		4484	3974	3973	3978	3976	4493
Bullets/box	100	100	100	100	50	100	100	100	100	50	50	50	50	50	50
Bullet Construction	UC	UC	UC	UC	UC	UC	UC	UC	UC	UC	UC	UC	UC	UC	UC

†=475 Linebaugh is a registered trademark of Timothy B. Sundles

Uni-Cor Handgun Bullets

Caliber & Description	25 Auto TMJ	380 Auto TMJ	9mm Luger TMJ	9mm Luger UCSP	9mm Luger TMJ Match	9mm Luger TMJ	357 SIG 38 Super TMJ	38 Spl 357 Magnum UCHP	38 Spl 357 Magnum UCSP	38 Spl 357 Magnum UCHP	38 Spl 357 Magnum TMJ	38 Spl 357 Magnum UCHP	357 Magnum UCHP	357 Magnum UCSP	357 Magnum TMJ	357 Magnum Sil. Match TMJ	357 Magnum Sil. Match TMJ
Diameter, Inches	.251	.355	.355	.355	.355	.355	.355	.357	.357	.357	.357	.357	.357	.357	.357	.357	.357
Weight, grains	50	95	115	124	130	147	125	110	125	125	125	140	158	158	158	180	200
BC	.110	.131	.151	.115	.165	.188	.147	.113	.129	.129	.146	.145	.163	.164	.173	.230	.236
Part Number	3982	4001	3995	3992	4010	4906	4362	4007	4011	4013	4015	4203	4211	4217	4207	4229	4231
Bullets/box	100	100	100	100	100	100	100	100	100	100	100	100	100	100	100	100	100
Bullet Construction	UC	UC	UC	UC	UC	UC	UC	UC	UC	UC	UC	UC	UC	UC	UC	UC	UC

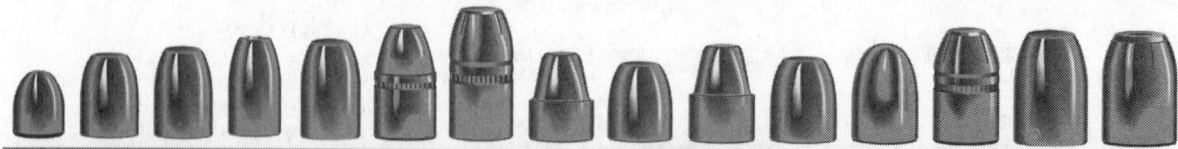

Caliber & Description	9x18 Mak.prov TMJ	40/10mm TMJ	40/10mm TMJ	40/10mm TMJ	40/10mm TMJ	44 Magnum Sil. Match TMJ	44 Magnum UCSP	45 Auto SWC Match TMJ	45 Auto FN TMJ	45 Auto SWC Match TMJ	45 Auto FN TMJ	45 Auto RN TMJ	45 Colt UCSP	50 Action Express FN TMJ	50 Action Express UCHP
Diameter, Inches	.364	.400	.400	.400	.400	.429	.429	.451	.451	.451	.451	.451	.451	.500	.500
Weight, grains	95	155	165	180	200	240	300	185	185	200	200	230	300	300	325
BC	.127	.125	.135	.143	.168	.206	.213	.090	.094	.128	.102	.153	.199	.157	.169
Part Number	4375	4399	4410	4402	4403	4459	4462	4473	4476	4475	4471	4490	4425	4490	4495
Bullets/box	100	100	100	100	100	100	50	100	100	100	100	100	50	50	50
Bullet Construction	UC	UC	UC	UC	UC	UC	UC	UC	UC	UC	UC	UC	UC	UC	UC

Jacketed Handgun Bullets

Caliber & Description	32 Revolver JHP	32 Revolver JHP	38 Spl 357 Magnum SWC-JHP	41 Magnum SWC-JHP	41 Magnum SWC-JSP	44 Magnum JHP	44 Magnum SWC-JHP	44 Magnum SWC-JSP	44 Magnum JHP	44 Magnum JSP	45 Colt JHP	45 Colt JHP
Diameter, Inches	.312	.312	.357	.410	.410	.429	.429	.429	.429	.429	.451	.451
Weight, grains	85	100	146	200	220	200	225	240	240	240	225	260
BC	.121	.167	.159	.113	.137	.122	.146	.157	.165	.164	.169	.183
Part Number	3987	3981	4205	4405	4417	4425	4435	4447	4453	4457	4479	4481
Bullets/box	100	100	100	100	100	100	100	100	100	100	100	100
Bullet Construction	C	C	C	C	C	C	C	C	C	C	C	C

Lead Handgun Bullets

Caliber & Description	32 S&W HBWC	9mm Luger RN	38 Bevel-Base WC	38 Double-Ended WC	38 Hollow-Base WC	38 SWC	38 SWC HP	38 RN	44 SWC	45 Auto SWC	45 Auto RN	45 Colt SWC
Diameter, Inches	.314	.356	.358	.358	.358	.358	.358	.358	.430	.452	.452	.452
Weight, grains	98	125	148	148	148	158	158	158	240	200	230	250
Part No	–	4601	4605	–	4617	4623	4627	4647	4660	4677	4690	4683
Box Count	–	100	100	–	100	100	100	100	100	100	100	100
Bulk Part No.	4600	4602	4606	4611	4618	4624	4628	4648	4661	4678	4691	4684
Bulk Count	1000	500	500	500	500	500	500	500	500	500	500	500

Idaho Territory Bullets

Caliber & Description	38 FN Lead	44 FN Lead	45 FN Lead	45-70 FN Lead
Diameter, Inches	.358	.430	.454	.459
Weight, grains	158	200	230	405
BC	.136	.130	.139	.224
Part No	4629	4662	4680	2480
Box Count	100	100	100	25
Bulk Part No.	4630	4663	4681	2481
Bulk Count	500	500	500	350

Abbreviation Key

BT—boat tail
C—conventional construction
FB—fusion bonded
FMJ—full metal jacket
FN—flat nose
GD—Gold Dot®
HC—Hot-Cor®
HP—hollow point
L—lead

MHP™—molybdenum disulfide impregnated
SB™—for short-barrel firearms
SP—soft point
TMJ®—encased-core full jacket
RN—round nose
SWC—semi-wadcutter
UC—Uni-Cor®
WC—wadcutter

TNT Rifle Bullets

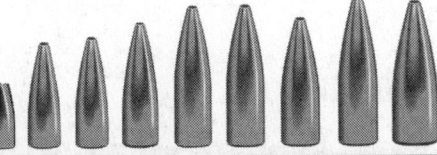

Caliber & Description	22 Hornet TNT	22 TNT HP	22 TNT HP Hi-Vel.	6mm TNT HP	25 TNT HP	6.5mm TNT HP	270 TNT HP	7mm TNT HP	30 TNT HP
Diameter, Inches	.224	.224	.224	.243	.257	.264	.277	.284	.308
Weight, grains	33	50	55	70	87	90	90	110	125
BC	.080	.228	.233	.279	.337	.281	.303	.384	.341
Part Number	1014	1030	1032	1206	1246	1445	1446	1616	1986
Bullets/box	100	100	100	100	100	100	100	100	100
Bullet Construction	UC	C	C	C	C	C	C	C	C

MHP Rifle Bullets

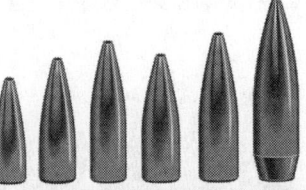

Caliber & Description	22 MHP HP	6mm MHP HP	25 MHP HP	270 MHP HP	7mm MHP HP	30 MHP Match BTHP
Diameter, Inches	.224	.243	.257	.277	.284	.308
Weight, grains	50	70	90	90	110	168
BC	.234	.296	.344	.310	.398	.541
Part Number	1031	1207	1347	1457	1615	2039
Bullets/box	100	100	100	100	100	100
Bullet Construction	MHP	MHP	MHP	MHP	MHP	MHP

Speer Bullets

JACKETED RIFLE BULLETS

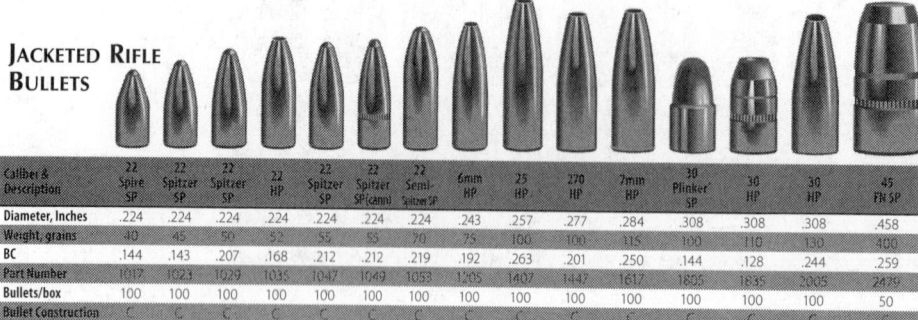

Caliber & Description	22 Spire SP	22 Spitzer SP	22 Spitzer SP	22 HP	22 Spitzer SP	22 Spitzer SP (cann)	22 Semi-Spitzer SP	6mm HP	25 HP	270 HP	7mm HP	30 Plinker SP	30 HP	30 HP	45 FN SP
Diameter, Inches	.224	.224	.224	.224	.224	.224	.224	.243	.257	.277	.284	.308	.308	.308	.458
Weight, grains	40	45	50	52	55	55	70	75	100	100	115	100	110	130	400
BC	.144	.143	.207	.168	.212	.212	.219	.192	.263	.201	.250	.144	.128	.244	.259
Part Number	1017	1023	1029	1035	1047	1049	1053	1205	1407	1447	1617	1855	1835	2005	2479
Bullets/box	100	100	100	100	100	100	100	100	100	100	100	100	100	100	50
Bullet Construction	C	C	C	C	C	C	C	C	C	C	C	C	C	C	C

HOT-COR BULLETS

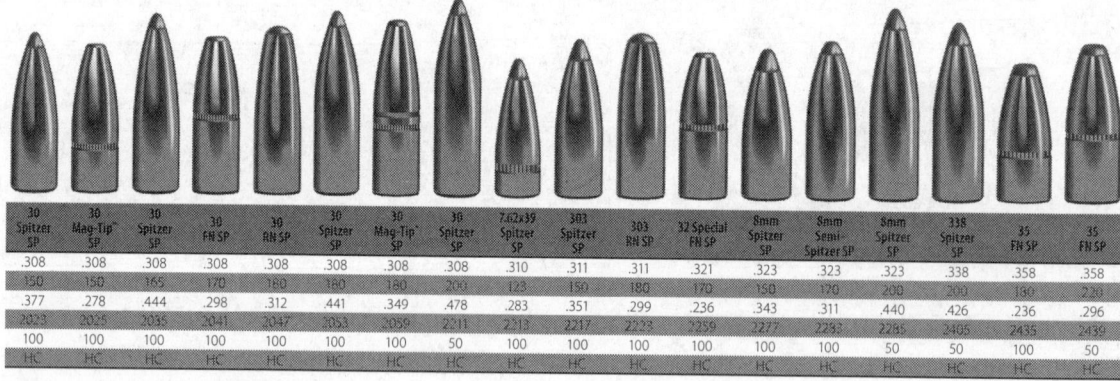

Caliber & Description	6mm Spitzer SP	6mm Spitzer SP	6mm Spitzer SP	25 Spitzer SP	25 Spitzer SP	25 Spitzer SP	6.5mm Spitzer SP	6.5mm Spitzer SP	270 Spitzer SP	270 Spitzer SP	7mm Spitzer SP	7mm Spitzer SP	7mm Mag-Tip‡ SP	7mm Mag-Tip‡ SP	30 Carbine SP	30 Spire SP	30 FN SP	30 FN SP	30 RN SP
Diameter, Inches	.243	.243	.243	.257	.257	.257	.264	.264	.277	.277	.284	.284	.284	.284	.308	.308	.308	.308	.308
Weight, grains	80	90	105	100	120	120	120	140	130	150	130	145	160	169	175	110	110	130	150	150
BC	.325	.365	.424	.300	.334	.405	.392	.498	.383	.455	.368	.416	.504	.340	.382	.136	.245	.213	.255	.235
Part Number	1211	1217	1229	1241	1405	1411	1435	1441	1459	1605	1623	1629	1635	1637	1641	1845	1855	2007	2011	2017
Bullets/box	100	100	100	100	100	100	100	100	100	100	100	100	100	100	100	100	100	100	100	100
Bullet Construction	HC	HC	HC	HC	HC	HC	HC	HC	HC	HC	HC	HC	HC	HC	HC	HC	HC	HC	HC	HC

‡ Not recommended for lever-action rifles.

Caliber & Description	30 Spitzer SP	30 Mag-Tip‡ SP	30 Spitzer SP	30 FN SP	30 RN SP	30 Spitzer SP	30 Mag-Tip‡ SP	30 Spitzer SP	7.62x39 Spitzer SP	303 Spitzer SP	303 RN SP	32 Special FN SP	8mm Spitzer SP	8mm Semi-Spitzer SP	8mm Spitzer SP	338 Spitzer SP	35 FN SP	35 FN SP
Diameter, Inches	.308	.308	.308	.308	.308	.308	.308	.308	.310	.311	.311	.321	.323	.323	.323	.338	.358	.358
Weight, grains	150	150	165	170	180	180	180	200	123	150	180	170	150	170	200	209	180	220
BC	.377	.278	.444	.298	.312	.441	.349	.478	.283	.351	.299	.236	.343	.311	.440	.426	.236	.296
Part Number	2023	2025	2035	2041	2047	3053	2059	2211	2213	2217	2223	2259	2277	2283	2285	2405	2435	2439
Bullets/box	100	100	100	100	100	100	100	50	100	100	100	100	100	100	50	50	100	50
Bullet Construction	HC	HC	HC	HC	HC	HC	HC	HC	HC	HC	HC	HC	HC	HC	HC	HC	HC	HC

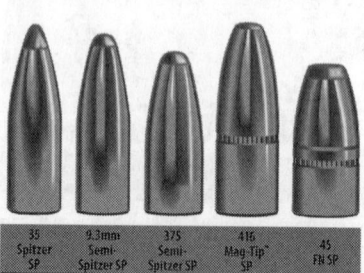

Caliber & Description	35 Spitzer SP	9.3mm Semi-Spitzer SP	375 Semi-Spitzer SP	416 Mag-Tip‡ SP	45 FN SP
Diameter, Inches	.358	.366	.375	.416	.458
Weight, grains	250	270	235	350	350
BC	.422	.361	.301	.332	.218
Part Number	2453	2459	2471	2477	2479
Bullets/box	50	50	50	50	50
Bullet Construction	HC	HC	HC	HC	HC

SPECIAL PURPOSE RIFLE BULLETS

Caliber & Description	218 Bee FN SP	22 FMJ BT	22 FMJ BT	25-20 Win FN SP	7-30 Waters FN SP	30 Carbine TMJ	30 FMJ BT	32-20 Win FN HP	45 UCHP
Diameter, Inches	.224	.224	.224	.257	.284	.308	.308	.312	.458
Weight, grains	46	55	62	75	130	110	150	100	300
BC	.087	.269	.307	.135	.257	.179	.425	.167	.206
Part Number	1024	1044	1050	1237	1625	1846	2018	3991	2482
Bullets/box	100	100	100	100	100	100	100	100	50
Bullet Construction	C	C	C	HC	HC	UC	UC	C	UC

‡ Recommended for twist rates of 1 in 10″ or faster.

Speer Bullets

Boat Tail Rifle Bullets

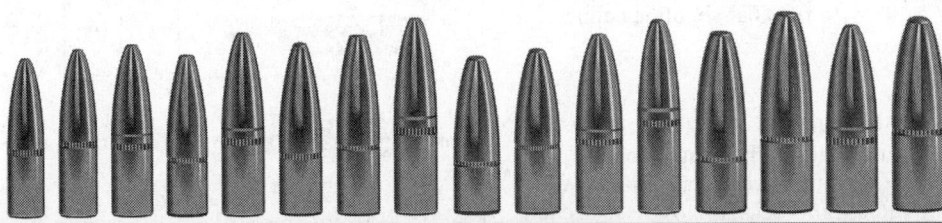

Caliber & Description	22 Match* BTHP	6mm Spitzer BTSP	6mm Spitzer BTSP	25 Spitzer BTHP	25 Spitzer BTSP	270 Spitzer BTSP	270 Spitzer BTSP	7mm Spitzer BTSP	7mm Spitzer BTSP	7mm Match* BTHP	7mm Spitzer RTSP	30 Spitzer BTSP	30 Spitzer BTSP	30 Match* BTHP	30 Spitzer BTSP	338 Spitzer BTSP	375 Spitzer BTSP
Diameter, Inches	.224	.243	.243	.257	.257	.277	.277	.284	.284	.284	.284	.308	.308	.308	.308	.338	.375
Weight, grains	52	85	100	100	120	130	150	130	145	145	160	150	165	168	180	225	270
BC	.230	.380	.446	.393	.480	.412	.489	.424	.472	.468	.519	.417	.520	.534	.545	.497	.478
Part Number	1036	1213	1220	1408	1410	1458	1604	1624	1628	1631	1634	2022	2034	2040	2052	2406	2472
Bullets/box	100	100	100	100	100	100	100	100	100	100	100	100	100	100	100	50	50
Bullet Construction	C	C	C	C	C	C	C	C	C	C	C	C	C	C	C	C	C

*Match bullets are not recommended for use on game animals.

Grand Slam

Caliber & Description	6mm Grand Slam SP	25 Grand Slam SP	6.5mm Grand Slam SP	270 Grand Slam SP	270 Grand Slam SP	7mm Grand Slam SP	7mm Grand Slam SP	7mm Grand Slam SP	30 Grand Slam SP	30 Grand Slam SP	30 Grand Slam SP	30 Grand Slam SP	338 Grand Slam SP	338 Grand Slam SP	35 Grand Slam SP	375 Grand Slam SP
Diameter, Inches	.243	.257	.264	.277	.277	.284	.284	.284	.308	.308	.308	.308	.338	.338	.358	.375
Weight, grains	100	120	140	130	150	145	160	175	150	165	180	200	225	250	250	285
BC	.327	.356	.385	.332	.378	.353	.389	.436	.295	.354	.374	.453	.382	.436	.353	.354
Part Number	1222	1415	1444	1465	1608	1632	1638	1643	2026	2038	2063	2213	2407	2408	2455	2473
Bullets/box	50	50	50	50	50	50	50	50	50	50	50	50	50	50	50	50
Bullet Construction	HC	HC	HC	HC	HC	HC	HC	HC	HC	HC	HC	HC	HC	HC	HC	HC

Trophy Bonded Bear Claw

Caliber & Description	22 TBBC	25 TBBC	6.5mm TBBC	270 TBBC	7mm TBBC	7mm TBBC	7mm TBBC	30 TBBC	30 TBBC	30 TBBC	30 TBBC	338 TBBC	35 Whelen TBBC	375 TBBC	375 TBBC	416 TBBC	458 TBBC	470 Nitro Express TBBC
Diameter, Inches	.224	.257	.264	.277	.284	.284	.284	.308	.308	.308	.308	.338	.358	.375	.375	.416	.458	.474
Weight, grains	55	115	140	140	140	160	175	150	165	180	200	225	225	250	300	400	500	500
BC	.201	.372	.405	.392	.360	.380	.400	0.335	.342	.357	.392	.376	.350	.286	.336	.374	.340	.330
Part Number	1725	1730	1735	1740	1745	1750	1755	1760	1765	1770	1775	1777	1778	1780	1785	1790	1795	
Bullets/box	50	25	25	25	25	25	25	25	25	25	25	25	25	25	25	25	25	25
Bullet Construction	FB	FB	FB	FB	FB	FB	FB	FB	FB	FB	FB	FB	FB	FB	FB	FB	FB	FB

Abbreviation Key

BT—boat tail
C—conventional construction
FB—fusion bonded
FMJ—full metal jacket
FN—flat nose
GD—Gold Dot®
HC—Hot-Cor®
HP—hollow point
L—lead

MHP™—molybdenum disulfide impregnated
SB™—for short-barrel firearms
SP—soft point
TMJ®—encased-core full jacket
RN—round nose
SWC—semi-wadcutter
UC—Uni-Cor®
WC—wadcutter

Swift
A-Frame and Scirocco Bullets

SWIFT SCIROCCO BONDED 30 CAL. (.308") 180-GR. POLYMER TIP/BOAT TAIL SPITZER Tapered jacket and proprietary bonding process produce controlled mushrooming with high weight retention. Ideally suited to fast, flat-shooting calibers.

THE SWIFT BULLET COMPANY

The Scirocco rifle bullet starts with a tough, pointed polymer tip that reduces air resistance, prevents tip deformation, and blends into the radius of its secant ogive nose section. A moderate 15-degree boat-tail base reduces drag and eases seating. The thick base prevents bullet deformation during launch. Scirocco's shape creates two other significant advantages. One is an extremely high ballistic coefficient. The other, derived from the secant ogive nose, is a comparatively long bearing surface for a sharply pointed bullet, a feature that improves rotational stability.

Inside, the Scirocco has a bonded-core construction with a pure lead core encased in a tapered, progressively thickening jacket of pure copper. Pure copper was selected because it is more malleable and less brittle than less expensive gilding metal. Both jacket and core are bonded by Swift's proprietary process so that the bullet expands without break-up as if the two parts were the same metal. In tests, the new bullet mushroomed effectively at velocities as low as 1440 fps, yet stayed together at velocities in excess of 3,000 fps, with over 70 percent weight retention.

Swift A-Frame bullet, with its mid-section wall of copper, is still earning praise for its deep-driving dependability in tough game. Less aerodynamic than the Scirocco, it produces a broad mushroom while carrying almost all its weight through muscle and bone. Available in a wide range of weights and diameters, it is also a bonded-core bullet.

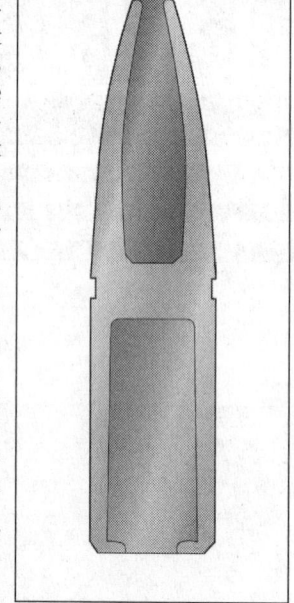

A-Frame Bullet

Cal.	Scirocco Rifle Bullet	Dia.	Wt. (gr.)	Profile	Sect. Den.	Ball. Coef.
224	1.085"	.224"	75	BTS	.214	.419
6mm	1.132"	.243"	90	BTS	.218	.419
6.5mm	1.353"	.264	130	BTS	.265	.571
270	1.315"	.277"	130	BTS	.242	.450
7mm	1.385"	.284"	150	BTS	.266	.515
30	1.270"	.308"	150	BTS	.226	.430
30	1.350"	.308"	165	BTS	.248	.470
30	1.435"	.308"	180	BTS	.271	.520
338	1.393"	.338"	210	BTS	.263	.507

1. 1440 FPS   2. 1730 FPS   3. 2245 FPS   4. 2700+ FPS

Swift SciroccoTM Expands dependably over a wide range of velocities, and maintains high jacket/core integrity.

Cal.	A-Frame Rifle Bullet	Dia.	Wt. (gr.)	Profile	Sect. Den.	Ball. Coef.
25	1.015"	.257"	100	AF/SS	.216	.318
25	1.150"	.257"	120	AF/SS	.260	.382
6.5	1.115"	.264"	120	AF/SS	.246	.344
6.5	1.245"	.264"	140	AF/SS	.287	.401
270	1.090"	.277"	130	AF/SS	.242	.323
270	1.190"	.277"	140	AF/SS	.261	.414
270	1.230"	.277"	150	AF/SS	.279	.444
7mm	1.115"	.284"	140	AF/SS	.248	.335
7mm	1.270"	.284"	160	AF/SS	.283	.450
7mm	1.365"	.284"	175	AF/SS	.310	.493
30	1.140"	.308"	165	AF/SS	.248	.367
30	1.215"	.308"	180	AF/SS	.271	.400
30	1.315"	.308"	200	AF/SS	.301	.444

Cal.	A-Frame Rifle Bullet	Dia.	Wt. (gr.)	Profile	Sect. Den.	Ball. Coef.
8mm	1.235"	.323"	200	AF/SS	.274	.357
8mm	1.325"	.323"	220	AF/SS	.301	.393
338	1.245"	.338"	225	AF/SS	.281	.384
338	1.335"	.338"	250	AF/SS	.313	.427
338	1.435"	.338"	275	AF/SS	.344	.469
35	1.140"	.358"	225	AF/SS	.251	.312
35	1.237"	.358"	250	AF/SS	.279	.347
35	1.345"	.358"	280	AF/SS	.312	.388
9.3mm	1.120"	.366"	250	AF/SS	.267	.285
9.3mm	1.310"	.366"	300	AF/SS	.320	.342
375	1.085"	.375"	250	AF/SS	.254	.271
375	1.200"	.375"	270	AF/SS	.274	.349
375	1.270"	.375"	300	AF/SS	.305	.325

BTS = Boat Tail Spitzer   AF/SS = A-Frame Semi-Spitzer   AF/FN = A-Frame Flat Nose   AF/RN = A-Frame Round Nose   AF/HP = A-Frame Hollow Point

Swift
A-Frame Rifle, Revolver and Muzzleloader Bullets

Cal.	A-Frame Rifle Bullet	Dia.	Wt. (gr.)	Profile	Sect. Den.	Ball. Coef.
416	1.260"	.416"	350	AF/SS	.289	.321
416	1.405"	.416"	400	AF/SS	.330	.367
404	1.380"	.423"	400	AF/SS	.319	.375
458	.960"	.458"	350	AF/FN	.238	.170
458	1.130"	.458"	400	AF/FN	.272	.258
458	1.310"	.458"	450	AF/SS	.307	.325
458	1.430"	.458"	500	AF/SS	.341	.361
470	1.280"	.475"	500	AF/RN	.329	.364

Cal.	A-Frame Revolver Bullet	Dia.	Wt. (gr.)	Profile	Sect. Den.	Ball. Coef.
357				Available in 2006		
41				Available in 2006		
44	.755"	.430"	240	AF/HP	.185	.119
44	.845"	.430"	280	AF/HP	.216	.139

Cal.	A-Frame Revolver Bullet	Dia.	Wt. (gr.)	Profile	Sect. Den.	Ball. Coef.
44	.910"	.430"	300	AF/HP	.232	.147
45	.750"	.452"	265	AF/HP	.185	.129
45	.840"	.452"	300	AF/HP	.210	.153
45	.895"	.452"	325	AF/HP	.227	.171
50				Available in 2006		

Cal.	A-Frame Muzzle Loader	Dia.	Wt. (gr.)	Profile	Sect. Den.	Ball. Coef.
50		.430"	240	AF/HP	.185	.119
50		.430"	300	AF/HP	.232	.147
54		.452"	265	AF/HP	.185	.129
54		.452"	325	AF/HP	.227	.153

The Swift A-Frame, noted for deep penetration in tough game, is loaded in Remington Premier ammunition.

Woodleigh Premium Bullets

WELDCORE SOFT NOSE

A product of Australia, Woodleigh weldcore Soft Nose bullets are made from 90/100 gilding metal (90% copper; 10% zinc) 1.6 mm thick. Maximum retained weight is obtained by fusing the pure lead to the gilding metal jacket.

FULL METAL JACKET

Fashioned from gilding metal-clad steel 2mm thick, jackets on FMJ bullets are heavy at the nose for extra impact resistance. The jacket then tapers towards the base to assist rifling engraving.

Calibre Diameter	Type	Weight Grain	SD	BC
700 Nitro .700"	SN	1000	.292	.340
	FMJ	1000	.292	.340
600 Nitro .620"	SN	900	.334	.371
	FMJ	900	.334	.334
577 Nitro .585"	SN	750	.313	.346
	FMJ	750	.313	.351
	SN	650	.271	.292
	FMJ	650	.271	.292
577 B.P. .585"	SN	650	.271	.320
500 Nitro .510"	SN	570	.313	.474
	FMJ	570	.313	.434
500 B.P. .510"	SN	440	.242	.336
500 Jeffery .510"	PP	535	.304	.460
	SN	535	.304	.460
	FMJ	535	.304	.422
	PP	600	.330	.423
	FMJ	600	.330	.330
505 Gibbs .505"	PP	600	.336	.450
	SN	525	.294	.445
	FMJ	525	.294	.408
	FMJ	600	.366	.450
475 No2 Jeffery .488"	SN	500	.300	.420
	FMJ	500	.300	.416
475 No2 .483"	SN	480	.303	.400
	FMJ	480	.303	.410
476 W.R. .476"	SN	520	.328	.420
	FMJ	520	.328	.455
475 Nitro .476"	SN	480	.227	.307
	FMJ	480	.227	.257
470 Nitro .474"	SN	500	.318	.411
	FMJ	500	.318	.410
465 Nitro .468"	SN	480	.318	.410
	FMJ	480	.318	.407
450 Nitro .458"	SN	480	.327	.419
	FMJ	480	.327	.410
458 Mag. .458"	SN	500	.341	.430
	SN	550	.375	.480
	FMJ	500	.341	.405
	FMJ	550	.375	.426
	PP	400	.272	.420
	RN	350	.238	.305
45/70 .458"	FN	405	.276	.250
11.3x62 Schuler .440"	SN	401	.296	.411
425 W.R. .435"	SN	410	.310	.344
	FMJ	410	.310	.336
404 Jeffery .423"	SN	400	.319	.354
	FMJ	400	.319	.358
	SN	350	.279	.357
10.75x68mm .423"	SN	347	.277	.355
	FMJ	347	.277	.307
416 Rigby .416"	SN	410	.338	.375
	FMJ	410	.338	.341
	PP	340	.281	.425
	SN	450	.372	.402
450/400 Nitro .411" or .408"	SN	400	.338	.384
	FMJ	400	.338	.433

Calibre Diameter	Type	Weight Grain	SD	BC
.408	SN	400	.338	.384
.408	FMJ	400	.338	.433
375 Mag. .375"	PP	235	.239	.331
	RN	270	.275	.305
	SP	270	.275	.380
	PP	270	.275	.352
	RN	300	.305	.340
	SP	300	.305	.425
	PP	300	.305	.420
	FMJ	300	.305	.307
	RN	350	.354	.354
	PP	350	.354	.440
	FMJ	350	.354	.372
405 Win., .411"	SN	300	.254	.194
9.3mm .366"	SN	286	.305	.331
	PP	286	.305	.381
	FMJ	286	.305	.324
	SN	250	.267	.296
360 No2 .366"	SN	320	.341	.378
	FMJ	320	.341	.362
	PP	320	.343	.428
358 Cal .358"	SN	225	.250	.277
	FMJ	225	.250	.298
	SN	250	.285	.365
	SN	310	.346	.400
	FMJ	310	.346	.378
338 Mag .338"	PP	225	.281	.425
	SN	250	.313	.332
	PP	250	.313	.470
	FMJ	250	.313	.326
	SN	300	.375	.416
	FMJ	300	.375	.398
333 Jeffery .333"	SN	250	.328	.400
	SN	300	.386	.428
	FMJ	300	.386	.419
318 W.R. .330"	SN	250	.328	.420
	FMJ	250	.328	.364
8mm .323"	SN	196	.268	.370
	SN	220	.302	.363
	SN	250	.343	.389
8X57	SN	200	.282	.370
303 British .312	SN	174	.257	.342
	PP	215	.316	.359
308 Cal .308"	FMJ	220	.331	.359
	RN	220	.331	.367
	PP	180	.273	.376
	PP	165	.250	.320
	PP	150	.226	.301
Win Mag.	PP	180	.273	.435
	PP	200	.301	.450
275 H&H .287"	PP	160	.275	.474
	PP	175	.301	.518
7mm .284"	PP	140	.247	.436
	PP	160	.282	.486
	PP	175	.312	.530
270 Win .277"	PP	130	.241	.409
	PP	150	.278	.463

SP = Semi-point • PP = Protected Point • FN = Flat Nose • RN = Round Nose • FMJ = Full Metal Jacket
All PP, FN, RN, SP, SN bullets are Weldcore Softnose

98% & 95% RETAINED WEIGHT 300 WIN MAG 180GR PP

458 X 500GN SN RECOVERED FROM BUFFALO

270 WIN 150GN PP 86% RETAINED WEIGHT

94% RETAINED WEIGHT 300 WIN MAG 180GR PP

500/465 RECOVERED FROM BUFFALO

Accurate Powder

	NG*	Avgerage Length/Thickness in./mm.	Avgerage Diameter inches	Avgerage Diameter millimeters	Bulk Density gram/cc	VMD cc/grain	Comparative Powders*** Ball	Comparative Powders*** Extruded
BALL PROPELLANTS - Handguns/Shotshell								
No.2 Imp.	14.0		0.018	0.457	0.650	0.100	WIN 231	Bullseye
No. 5	18.0		0.027	0.686	0.950	0.068	WIN 540	
No. 7	12.0		0.012	0.305	0.985	0.066	WIN 630	
No. 9	10.0		1.015	0.381	0.935	0.069	WIN 296	
1680	10.0		0.014	0.356	0.950	0.068	WIN 680	
Solo 4100	10.0		0.011	0.279	0.960	0.068	WIN 296	
BALL PROPELLANTS -Rifle								
2230	10.0		0.022	0.559	0.980	0.066	BL C2, WIN 748	
2460	10.0		0.022	0.559	0.990	0.065	BL C2, WIN 748	
2520	10.0		0.022	0.559	0.970	0.067		
2700	10.0		0.022	0.559	0.960	0.068	WIN 760	
MAGPRO	9.0		0.030	0.762	0.970	0.067		
8700	10.0		0.030	0.762	0.960	0.068	H870	
EXTRUDED PROPELLANTS - Shotshell/Handguns								
Nirto 100	21.0	0.010/ 0.254	0.058	1.473	0.505	0.128		700X, Red Dot
Solo 1000		0.010/ 0.254	0.052	1.321	0.510	0.127		Green Dot
Solo 1250		0.013/ 0.033	0.051	1.295	0.550	0.118		PB
EXTRUDED PROPELLANTS - Rifle/handgun								
5744	20.00	0.048/ 1.219	0.033	0.838	0.880	0.074		
EXTRUDED PROPELLANTS - Rifle								
2015		0.039/ 0.991	0.031	0.787	0.880	0.074		H322,N201 IMR 4198
2495		0.068/ 1.727	0.029	0.737	0.880	0.074		IMR 4895
4064		0.050/ 1.270	0.035	0.889	0.890	0.072		IMR 4064
4350		0.083/ 0.038	0.038	0.965	0.890	0.072		IMR 4350
3100		0.083/ 0.038	0.038	0.965	0.920	0.070		IMR 4831

*NG-NItroglycerin ***For comparison only, not a loading recommendation

Alliant Smokeless Powders

BULLSEYE
America's best known pistol powder. Unsurpassed for .45 ACP target loads. *Available in 8-lb., 4-lb., and 1-lb. canisters.*

POWER PISTOL
Designed for high performance in semi-automatic pistols and is the powder of choice for 9mm, .40 S&W and .357 SIG. *Available in 4-lb. and 1-lb. canisters.*

2400
Legendary for its performance in .44 magnum and other magnum pistol loads. Originally developed for the .22 Hornet, it's also the shooter's choice for .410 bore. *Available in 8-lb., 4-lb., and 1-lb. canisters.*

UNIQUE
The most versatile shotgun/handgun powder made. Great for 12, 16, 20 and 28 gauge. loads. Use with most hulls, primers and wads. *Available in 8- lb., 4-lb., and 1- lb. canisters.*

RELODER 7
Designed for small caliber varmint loads, it meters consistently, and meets the needs of the most demanding bench rest shooter. Great in .45-70 and .450 Marlin. *Available in 5-lb. and 1-lb. canisters.*

RELODER 10X
Best choice for light bullet applications in .222 Rem, .223 Rem, .22-250 Rem and key bench rest calibers. Also great in light bullet .308 Win loads. *Available in 5 lb. and 1 lb. containers.*

RELODER 15
The best all-around medium speed rifle powder. It provides excellent .223 and .308 cal. performance. Selected as the powder for U.S. Military's M118 Special Ball Long Range Sniper Round. *Available in 5-lb. and 1-lb. canisters.*

RELODER 19
Provides superb accuracy in most medium and heavy rifle loads and is the powder of choice for 30-06 and .338 calibers. *Available in 5-lb. and 1-lb. canisters.*

RELODER 22
This top performing powder for big game loads provides excellent metering, and is the powder of choice for .270, 7mm magnum and .300 Win. magnum. *Available in 5-lb. and 1-lb. canisters.*

RELODER 25
This new, advanced powder for big game hunting features improved slower burning, and delivers the high ener-gy that heavy magnum loads need. *Available in 5-lb. and 1-lb. canisters.*

Alliant Shotshell Powders

RED DOT
America's #1 choice for clay target loads, now 50% cleaner. Since 1932, more 100 straights than any other powder. *Available in 8-lb., 4-lb., and 1-lb. canisters.*

E³
The first of a new generation of high performance powders.

GREEN DOT
It delivers precise burn rates for uniformly tight patterns, and you'll appreciate the lower felt recoil. Versatile for target and field. *Available in 8-lb., 4-lb., and 1-lb. canisters.*

AMERICAN SELECT
Our "ultra clean" burning premium powder makes a versatile target load and superior 1-oz. load for improved clay target scores. Great for Cowboy Action handgun loading too! *Available in 8-lb., 4-lb., and 1-lb. canisters.*

410
Cleanest .410 bore powder on the market.

STEEL
Designed for waterfowl shotshell. Gives steel shot high velocity within safe pressure limits for 10 and 12 gauge loads. *Available in 4-lb. and 1-lb. canisters.*

BLUE DOT
The powder of choice for magnum lead shotshell loads. 10, 12, 16, and 20 gauge. Consistent and accurate. Doubles as magnum handgun powder. *Available in 5-lb., and 1-lb. canisters.*

HERCO
Since 1920, a proven powder for heavy shotshell loads, including 10, 12, 16, 20 and 28 gauge target loads. The ultimate in 12 gauge, 1¼ oz. upland game loads. *Available in 8-lb., 4-lb., and 1-lb. canisters.*

Hodgdon Smokeless Powder

Hodgdon Powder Company offers its popular sulfur-free Triple Seven powder in 50-grain pellets. Formulated for use with 209 shotshell primers, Triple Seven leaves no rotten egg smell, and the residue is easy to clean from the bore with water only. The pellets are sized for 50-caliber muzzleloaders and can be used singly (for target shooting or small game) as well as two at a time.

PYRODEX PELLETS
Both rifle and pistol pellets eliminate powder measures, speeds shooting for black powder enthusiasts.

EXTREME H4198
H4198 was developed especially for small and medium capacity cartridges.

EXTREME H322
This powder fills the gap between H4198 and BL-C9(2). Performs best in small to medium capacity cases.

EXTREME BENCHMARK
A fine choice for small rifle cases like the .223 Rem and PPC competition rounds. Appropriate also for the 300-30 and 7x57.

SPHERICAL BL-C2
Best performance is in the 222, .308 other cases smaller than 30/06.

SPHERICAL H335
Similar to BL-C(2), H335 is popular for its performance in medium capacity cases, especially in 222 and 308 Winchester.

EXTREME VARGET
Features small extruded grain powder for uniform metering, plus higher velocities/normal pressures in such calibers as .223, 22-250, 306, 30-06, 375 H&H

EXTREME H4895
4895 gives desirable performance in almost all cases from 222 Rem. to 458 Win. Reduced loads, to as low as 3/5 maximum, still give target accuracy.

SPHERICAL H380
Fills a gap between 4320 and 4350. It

is excellent in 22/250, 220 Swift, the 6mm's, 257 and 30/06.

SPHERICAL H414
In many popular medium to medium-large calibers, pressure velocity relationship is better.

EXTREME H4350
Gives superb accuracy at optimum velocity for many large capacity metallic rifle cartridges.

EXTREME H4831
Outstanding performance with medium and heavy bullets in the 6mm's, 25/06, 270 and Magnum calibers. Also available with shortened grains (H4831SC) for easy metering.

EXTREME H1000 EXTRUDED POWDER
Fills the gap between H4831 and H870. Works especially well in overbore capacity cartridges (1,000-yard shooters take note).

EXTREME H50 BMG
Designed for the 50 Browning Machine Gun cartridge. Highly insensitive to extreme temperature changes.

CLAYS
Tailored for use in 12 ga., 7/8, 1-oz. and 1 1/8-oz. loads. Performs well in many handgun applications, including .38 Special, .40 S&W and 45 ACP. Perfect for 1 1/8 and 1 oz. loads.

UNIVERSAL CLAYS
Loads nearly all of the straight-wall pistol cartridges as well as 12 ga. 1.25 oz. thru 28 ga. 3/4 oz. target loads.

INTERNATIONAL CLAYS
Ideal for 12 and 20 ga. autoloaders who want reduced recoil.

TITEWAD
This 12 ga. flattened spherical shotgun powder is ideal for 7/8, 1 and 1 1/8 oz. loads, with minimum recoil and mild muzzle report. The fastest fuel in Hodgdon's line.

HS-6 AND HS-7
HS-6 and HS-7 for Magnum field loads are unsurpassed. Deliver uniform charg-

es and are dense to allow sufficient wad column for best patterns.

LONGSHOT
Spherical powder for heavy shotgun loads.

HP38
A fast pistol powder for most pistol loading. Especially recommended for mid-range 38 specials.

TITEGROUP
Excellent for most straight-walled pistol cartridges, incl. 38 Spec., 44 Spec., 45 ACP. Low charge weights, clean burning; position insensitive and flawless ignition.

H110
A spherical powder made especially for the 30 M1 carbine. H110 also does very well in 357, 44 spec., 44 Mag. or 410 ga. shotshell. Recommended for consistent ignition.

H4227
An extruded powder similar to H110, recommended for the 22 Hornet and some specialized loading in the 45-70 caliber. Excellent in magnum pistol and .410 shotgun.

LIL' GUN
Developed specifically for the .410 shotgun but works very well in rifle cartridges like the .22 Hornet and in the .44 magnum.

RETUMBO
Designed for such cartridges as the 300 Rem. Ultra Mag., 30-378 Weatherby, the 7mm STW and other cases with large capacities and small bores. Expect up to 40-100 feet per second more velocity than other magnum powders.

TRIPLE SEVEN
A muzzleloading propellant that does not use sulfur, keeping shooter's hand clean. No offensive odor and cleaning is as easy as running a water soaked patch down the barrel followed by 3 or 4 dry patches!

IMR Powders

RIFLE POWDERS

IMR 3031 — A propellant with many uses, IMR 3031 is a favorite of 308 match shooters using 168 grain match bullets. It is equally effective in small capacity varmint cartridges from 223 Remington to 22-250 Remington and a great 30-30 Winchester powder.

IMR 4060 — The most versatile propellant in the IMR spectrum. 223 Remington, 22-250 Remington, 220 Swift, 6mm Remington, 243 Winchester Super Short Magnum, 308 Winchester, 338 Winchester Magnum etc.

IMR 4198 — This fast burning rifle powder gives outstanding performance in cartridges like the 222 Remington, 221 Fireball, 45-70 and 450 Marlin.

IMR 4227 — The choice for true magnum velocities and performance. In rifle, this powder delivers excellent velocity and accuracy in such cartridges as the 22 Hornet and 221 Fireball.

IMR 4320 — Short granulation, easy metering and perfect for the 223 Remington, 22-250 Remington, 250 Savage and other medium burn rate cartridges. It has long been a top choice for the vintage 300 Savage cartridge as well.

IMR 4350 — The number one choice for the new short magnums, both Remington and Winchester versions. For magnums with light to medium bullet weights, IMR 4350 is the best choice.

IMR — 4832 Slightly slower in burn speed than IMR 4350, IMR 4831 gives top velocities and performance with heavier bullets in medium sized magnums.

IMR — 4895 Originally a military powder featured in the 30-06, IMR 4895 is extremely versatile. From 17 Remington to the 243 Winchester to the 375 H&H Magnum, accuracy and performance are excellent. In addition, it is a long time favorite of Match shooters.

IMR — 7828 The Big magnum powder. This slow burner gives real magnum performance to the large over-bored magnums, such as the 300 Remington Ultra Mag, the 30-378 Weatherby Magnum and 7mm Remington Ultra Magnum.

HANDGUN & SHOTGUN POWDERS

"Hi Skor" 700-X — This extruded flake type powder is ideally suited for shotshell in 12 and 16 gauge where clay target and light field loads are the norm. It doubles as an excellent pistol target powder for such cartridges as the 38 Special and 45 ACP and many more.

"Hi Skor" 800-X — This large grained flake powder is at its best when used in heavy field loads from 10 gauge to 28 gauge. In handgun cartridges, 800-X performs superbly in cartridges like the 10mm Auto, 357 Magnum and 44 Remington Magnum.

PB — Named for the porous base structure of its grains by which the burning rate is controlled, PB is an extremely clean-burning single-base powder. It gives very low pressure in 12 and 20 ga. shotshell target loads and performs well in a wide variety of handgun loads.

SR 4756 — This fine grained, easy metering propellant has long been a favorite of upland and waterfowl handloaders. SR4756 performs extremely well in the big handgun cartridges.

SR 4759 — This bulky handgun powder works great in the magnums, but really shines as a reduced load propellant for rifle cartridges. It's large grain size gives good loading density for reduced loads, enhancing velocity uniformity.

SR 7625 — SR7625 covers the wide range of shotshells from 10 gauge to 28 gauge in both target and field loadings. This versatile powder is equally useful in a large array of handgun cartridges for target, self-defense and hunting loads.

Ramshot Powders

Ramshot (Western Powders, Inc.) powders are all double-base propellants, meaning they contain nitrocellulose and nitroglycerine. While some spherical or ball powders are known for leaving plenty of residue in barrels, Ramshots people say these new fuels burn very clean. They meter easily, as do all ball powders. Plastic canisters are designed for spill-proof use and include basic loading data on the labels.

RAMSHOT COMPETITION is for the clay target shooter. A fast-burning powder comparable to 700-X or Red Dot it performs well in a variety of 12-gauge target loads, offering low recoil, consistent pressures and clean combustion.

RAMSHOT TRUE BLUE was designed for small to medium-size handgun cartridges. Similar to Winchester 231 and Hodgdon HP-38, it has enough bulk to nearly fill most cases, thereby better positioning the powder for ignition.

RAMSHOT ZIP, a fast-burning target powder for cartridges like the .38 Special and .45 ACP, gives competitors uniform velocities.

RAMSHOT SILHOUETTE is ideal for the 9mm handgun cartridge, from light to heavy loads. It also works well in the .40 Smith & Wesson and combat loads for the .45 Auto.

RAMSHOT ENFORCER is a match for high-performance handgun hulls like the .40 Smith & Wesson. It is designed for full-power loading and high velocities. Ramshot X-Terminator, a fast-burning rifle powder, excels in small-caliber, medium-capacity cartridges. It has the versatility to serve in both target and high-performance varmint loads.

RAMSHOT TAC was formulated for tactical rifle cartridges, specifically the .223 and .308. It has produced exceptional accuracy with a variety of bullets and charge weights.

RAMSHOT BIG GAME is a versatile propellant for cartridges as diverse as the .30-06 and the .338 Winchester, and for light-bullet loads in small-bore magnums.

RAMSHOT MAGNUM is the slowest powder of the Western line, and does its best work in cartridges with lots of case volume and small to medium bullet diameter. It is the powder of choice in 7mm and .30 Magnums.

RAMSHOT X-TERMINATOR is a clean burning powder designed for the .222 Rem., 223 Rem., and .22 Benchrest calibers.

VihtaVuori

N110 — A very fast burning propellant that can be used in applications which previously used Hercules 2400, Hodgdon H110, or Winchester 296. Typical applications include: .22 Hornet, .25-20 Winchester, .357 S&W Magnum, .357 Maximum, .44 Magnum and .45 Winchester Magnum.

N120 — A limited application propellant. This speed develops higher pressure than N110 in order to optimize burning. Burning rate falls near the various 4227s. It works well with light bullets in .22 caliber cartridges.

N130 — Burning rate is between IMR 4227 and the discontinued Winchester 680. This is the powder used in factory loaded .22 and 6mm PPC.

N133 — This powder's speed is very close to IMR 4198 in quickness. Thus, it is ideal for the .222 Remington, .223 Remington, and .45-70 Government and other applications where a relatively fast burning rifle propellant is needed.

N135 — This is a moderate burning propellant. It will fit applications similar to Hercules Reloader 12, IMR-4895 or IMR 4064. Applications range from the .17 Remington to the .458 Winchester.

N140 — This powder can usually be used in place of Hercules Reloader 15, IMR 4320, and Hodgdon H380. Applications include: .222 Remington Magnum, .22-250 Remington (factory powder), .30-.30 Winchester, .308 Winchester, .30-06 Springfield, .375 H&H Magnum, and so on.

N150 — This is a moderately slow powder that can help refine rifle cartridge ballistics when N140 is too fast and N160 is too slow. Works well in many applications previously filled by 760, H414, and IMR 4350.

N160 — A relatively slow powder ideally suited to many magnum and standard rounds requiring a slow propellant. It has characteristics that make it work well for applications previously using various 4350s, Hercules Reloader 19, and the various 4831s. For example, some ideal applications are: .243 Winchester, .25-06 Remington, .264 Winchester Magnum, .270 Winchester (factory load), 7mm Remington Magnum, .30-06 Springfield, .300 Winchester Magnum, .338 Winchester Magnum, .375 H&H Magnum, etc.

N165 — A very slow burning magnum propellant for use with heavy bullets. Applications begin with heavy bullets in the .30-06, and include the .338 Winchester Magnum.

N170 — VihtaVuori's slowest speed propellant and the slowest canister reloading powder generally available from any manufacturer.

N500 Series
VihtaVuori calls powders that have nitroglycerol added (maximum 25%) producing the high energy NC-powders that form the N500 series. Geometrically the powders in the N500 series are equal to the N100 series. Although these new powders have a higher energy content, they do not cause greater wear to the gun. This is because the surface of the powder has been treated with an agent designed to reduce barrel wear. N500 series powders work well at different temperatures.

N530 — Burning rate close to N135. Especially for .223 Remington. Excellent also for .45-70 Government.

N540 — Burning rate like N140. Especially for the .308 Winchester.

N550 — Burning rate like N150. Especially for the .308 Winchester and .30-06 Springfield.

N560 — Burning rate like N160. Especially for .270 Winchester and 6.5 x 55 Swedish Mauser.

Dillon Precision Reloaders

MODEL SL900

MODEL RL550B

SL900R

Based on Dillon's proven XL 650 O-frame design, the SL 900 progressive press features an automatic case insert system, an electric case collator, adjustable case-activated shot and powder bars. Should the operator forget to insert a wad during the reloading process, the SL 900 will not dispense shot into the powder-charged hull. Both powder and shot systems are based on Dillon's adjustable powder bar design, which is accurate to within a few tenths of a grain. Simply adjust the measures to dispense the exact charges required.

An interchangeable tool-head makes it quick and easy to change from one gauge to another using a collet-type sizing die that re-forms the base of the shotshell to factory specifi-

cations. The SL 900 also has an extra large, remote shot hopper that holds an entire 25-pound bag of shot, making it easy to fill with a funnel. The shot reservoir/dispenser helps ensure that a consistent volume of shot is delivered to each shell. The heat-treated steel crimp-die forms and folds the hull before the final taper crimp die radiuses and blends the end of the hull and locks the crimp into place.
MSRP: **$699-899**

RL 550

The RL 550 will load over 120 different rifle and pistol calibers. Its quick-change tool-head allows the user to change calibers without having to readjust dies. Used with Dillon three-die pistol sets, the RL 550 allows crimping to be done separately in the

last station. Features: Automatic indexing; auto powder/priming systems; automatic case-feeder; swages military primer pockets; eight stations; accommodates over 120 calibers; interchangeable tool-head assembly; auto powder/priming systems; uses standard 7/8" x 14 dies.
MSRP: **$1480-1565**

MODEL RL550B PROGRESSIVE LOADER

- Accommodates over 120 calibers
- Interchangeable toolhead assembly
- Auto/Powder priming systems
- Uses standard 7/8" by 14 dies
- Loading rate: 500-600 rounds per hour

MSRP: **$370-380**

HANDLOADING

Dillon Precision Reloaders

MODEL SQUARE DEAL B

MODEL XL 650

THE SQUARE DEAL B

Designed to produce up to 400 or 500 handgun rounds per hour. The Square Deal B comes with a factory adjusted carbide die set. Square Deal B is available in all popular handgun calibers and you can change from one caliber to another in minutes with a Square Deal B caliber conversion kit. Features: Automatic indexing; auto powder/priming systems; available in 14 handgun calibers; loading dies standard.

MSRP: **$310**

MODEL XL 650

The XL 650 loads virtually every popular pistol and rifle cartridge utilizing standard dies. The optional powder charge check die on the third station sounds an alarm if the powder charge in a round is out of limits either high or low. An exclusive primer system uses a rotary indexing plate that positively controls each primer and keeps a steel shield between the primers and the operator. Features: Automatic indexing; five-station interchangeable tool-head; auto powder / priming systems; uses standard 7/8" x 14 dies rotary indexing plate for primers;

MSRP: **$495**

Forster Reloading

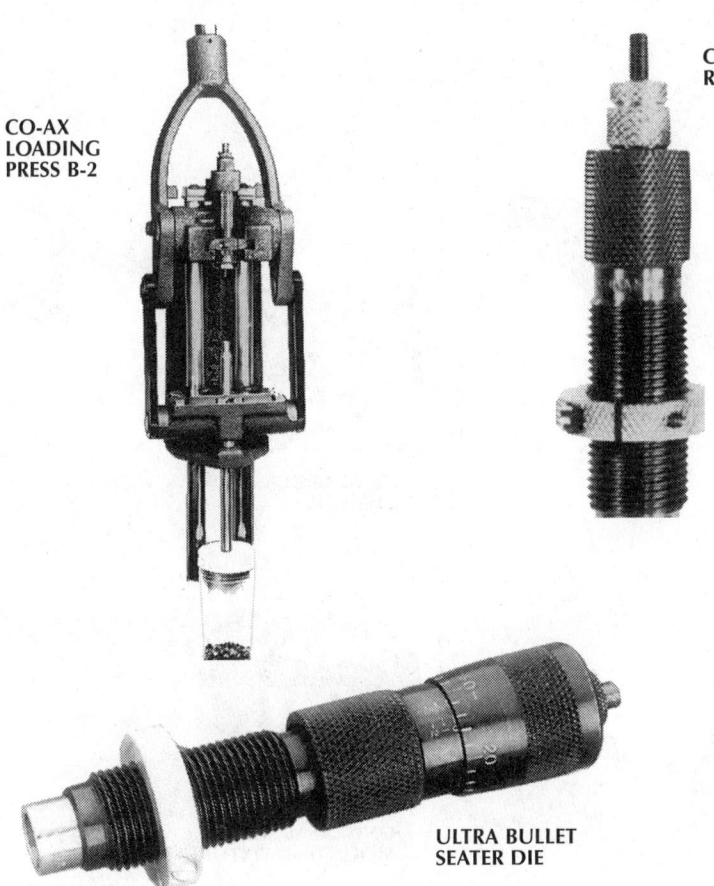

CO-AX
LOADING
PRESS B-2

CO-AX BENCH REST
RIFLE DIES

ULTRA BULLET
SEATER DIE

BENCH REST
POWDER MEASURE

CO-AX LOADING PRESS MODEL B-2

Designed to make reloading easier and more accurate, this press offers the following features: Snap-in and snap-out die change; positive spent primer catcher; automatic self-acting shell holder; floating guide rods; top priming device seats primers to factory specifications; uses any standard 7/8" x 14 dies.

MSRP: $343

CO-AX BENCH REST RIFLE DIES

Bench Rest Rifle Dies are glass-hard and polished mirror-smooth with special attention given to headspace, tapers and diameters. Sizing die has an elevated expander button to ensure better alignment of case and neck.

Bench Rest Die Set. $83
Bench Rest Seating Die $48
Ultra Bench Rest Die Set $115
Full Length Sizer $40

ULTRA BULLET SEATER DIE

The micrometer-style Ultra Die is available in 61 calibers. Adjustment is identical to that of a precision micrometer—the head is graduated to .001" increments with .025" bullet movement per revolution. The cartridge case, bullet and seating stem are completely supported and perfectly aligned in a close-fitting chamber before and during the bullet seating operation.

MSRP: $76

POWDER MEASURES

Bench Rest Powder Measure
When operated uniformly, this measure will throw uniform charges from 2 1/2 grains Bullseye to 95 grains #4320. No extra drums are needed. Powder is metered from the charge arm, allowing a flow of powder without extremes in variation while minimizing powder shearing. Powder flows through its own built-in baffle, entering the charge arm uniformly.

MSRP: $127

CASE PREPARATION

"Classic 50" Case Trimmer
Handles more than 100 different big bore calibers–500 Nitro Express, 416 Rigby, 50 Sharps, 475 H&H, etc. Also available: .50 BMG Case Trimmer, designed specifically for reloading needs of .50 Cal. BMG shooters.

"Classic 50" Case Trimmer $102
.50 BMG Case Trimmer $106

Forster Reloading

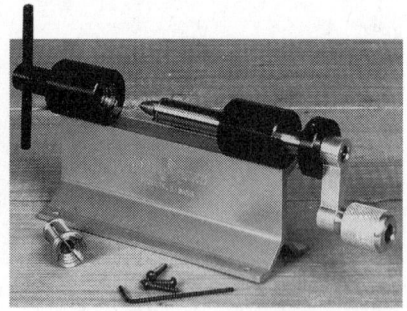

HAND CASE TRIMMER

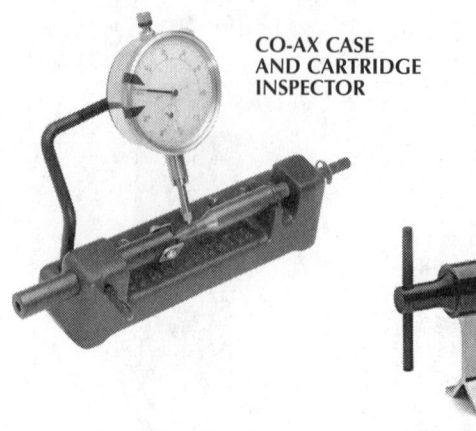

CO-AX CASE AND CARTRIDGE INSPECTOR

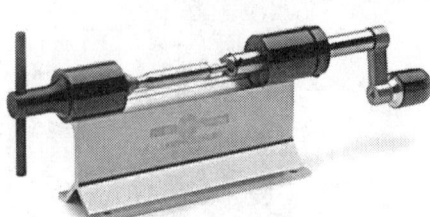

PRIMER POCKET CLEANER

PRIMER SEATER

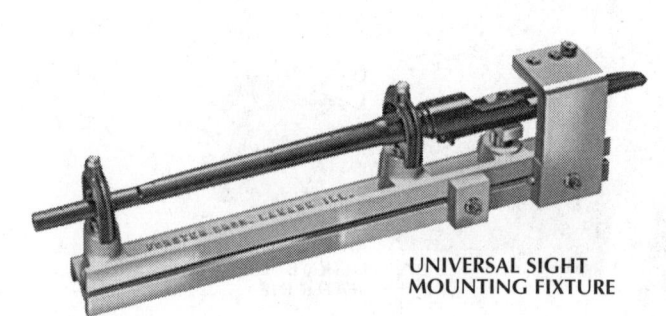

UNIVERSAL SIGHT MOUNTING FIXTURE

HAND CASE TRIMMER

Shell holder is a Brown & Sharpe-type collet. Case and cartridge conditioning accessories include inside neck reamer, outside neck turner, deburring tool, hollow pointer and primer pocket cleaners. The case trimmer trims all cases, ranging from 17 to 458 Winchester caliber.
MSRP: **$70**

CO-AX CASE AND CARTRIDGE INSPECTOR

Forster's Co-Ax Case & Cartridge Inspector provides the ability to ensure uniformity by measuring three critical dimensions: neck wall thickness; case neck concentricity; bullet run-out. Measurements are in increments of one-thousandth of an inch. The Inspector checks both the bullet and case alignment in relation to the centerline (axis) of the entire cartridge or case.
MSRP: **$94**

PRIMER POCKET CLEANER

The Primer Pocket Cleaner helps ensure consistent ignition and reduce the incidence of misfires by removing powder and primer residue from the primer pockets of your cases. This tool is easy to use by holding the case mouth over the Primer Pocket Center with one hand while you quickly and easily clean the primer pockets by turning the Case Trimmer Handle.
MSRP: **$8**

PRIMER SEATER

Bonanza Primer Seater—Designed so that primers are seated co-axially (primer in line with primer pocket). Mechanical leverage allows primers to be seated fully without crushing. With the addition of one extra set of disc shell holders and one extra Primer Unit, all modern cases, rim or rimless, from 222 up to 458 Magnum, can be primed. Shell holders are easily adjust-ed to any case by rotating to contact rim or cannelure of the case.
Primer Seater **$82**

UNIVERSAL SIGHT MOUNTING FIXTURE

The fixture handles any single-barrel gun—bolt-action, lever-action or pump-action—as long as the barrel can be laid into the "V" blocks of the fixture. Rifles with tube magazines are drilled in the same manner by removing the magazine tube. The fixture's main body is made of aluminum casting. The two "V" blocks are adjustable for height and are made of hardened steel ground accurately on the "V" as well as the shaft.
MSRP: **$414**

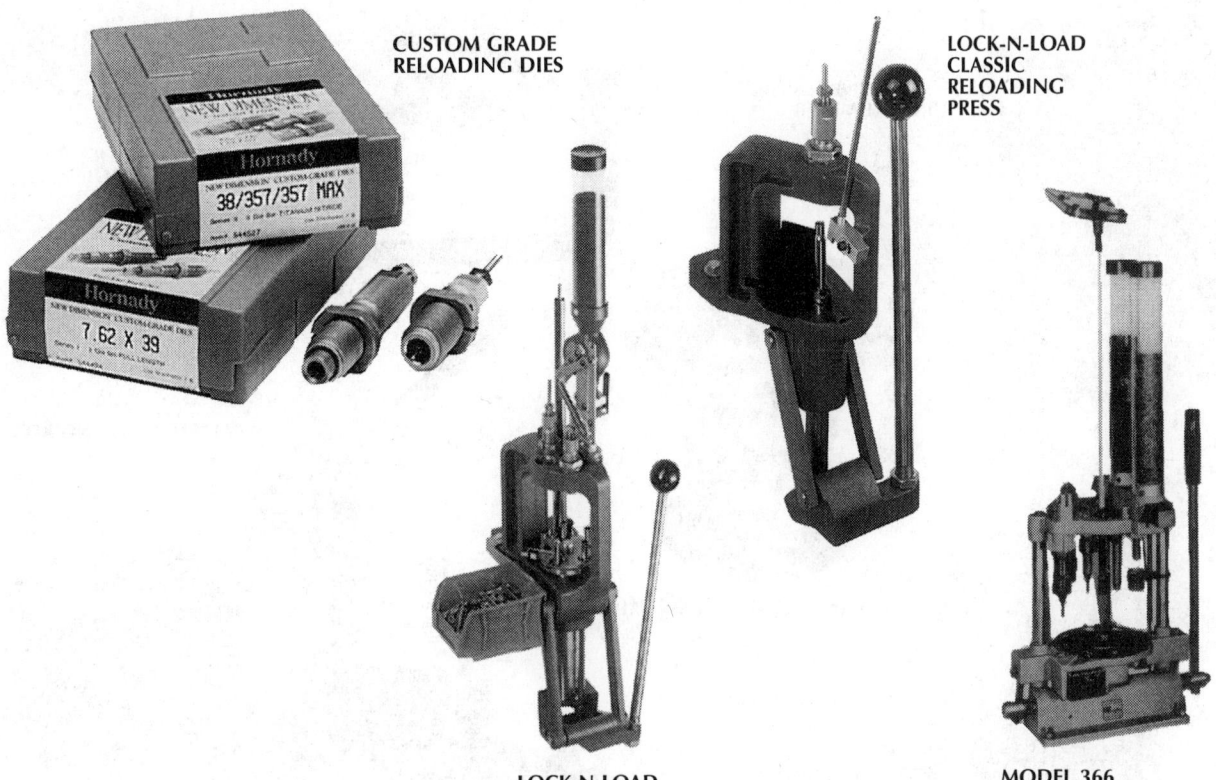

CUSTOM GRADE
RELOADING DIES

LOCK-N-LOAD
CLASSIC
RELOADING
PRESS

LOCK-N-LOAD

MODEL 366

CUSTOM GRADE RELOADING DIES

An Elliptical Expander in Hornady dies minimizes friction and reduces case neck stretch. Other design features include a hardened steel decap pin and a bullet seater alignment sleeve. Dimension Reloading Dies include: collar and collar lock to center expander precisely; one-piece expander spindle with tapered bottom for easy cartridge insertion; wrench flats on die body, Sure-Loc lock rings and collar lock for easy tightening; and built-in crimper.

Series I	$33
Series II Three-die Rifle Set	$36
Series III	$40
Match Grade	$39

LOCK-N-LOAD CLASSIC PRESS

Lock-N-Load is available on Hornady's single stage and progressive reloader models. This bushing system locks the die into the press like a rifle bolt. Instead of threading dies in and out of the press, you simply lock and unlock them with a slight twist. Dies are held firmly in a die bushing that stays with the die and retains the die setting. Features: Easy-grip handle; O-style high-strength alloy frame; positive priming system.

MSRP: Lock-N-Load Press	$129
Lock-N-Load Classic Press Kit	$347
Also Available:	
Lock-N-Load 50 Cal. BMG Press	$295
Lock-N-Load 50 Cal. BMG Press Kit	$542

LOCK-N-LOAD AUTO PROGRESSIVE PRESS

The Lock-N-Load Automatic Progressive reloading press features the Lock-N-Load bushing system. Dies and powder measure are inserted into Lock-N-Load die bushings. The bushings remain with the die and powder measure and can be removed in seconds. Other features include: deluxe powder measure, automatic indexing, off-set handle, power-pac linkage, case ejector.

Lock-N-Load Auto Progressive Press (w/ five die bushings, shellplate, primer catcher, Positive Priming System, powder drop, Deluxe Powder Measure, automatic primer feed)	$416

MODEL 366 AUTO SHOTSHELL RELOADER

The 366 Auto features full-length resizing with each stroke, automatic primer feed, swing-out wad guide, three-state crimping featuring Taper-Loc for factory tapered crimp, automatic advance to the next station and automatic ejection. The turntable holds 8 shells for 8 operations with each stroke. Automatic charge bar loads shot and powder, dies and crimp starters for 6 point, 8 point and paper crimps.

Model 366 Auto Shotshell Reloader:	
12, 20, 28 gauge	$575
.410	$708

Lyman Reloading Tools

HANDLOADING

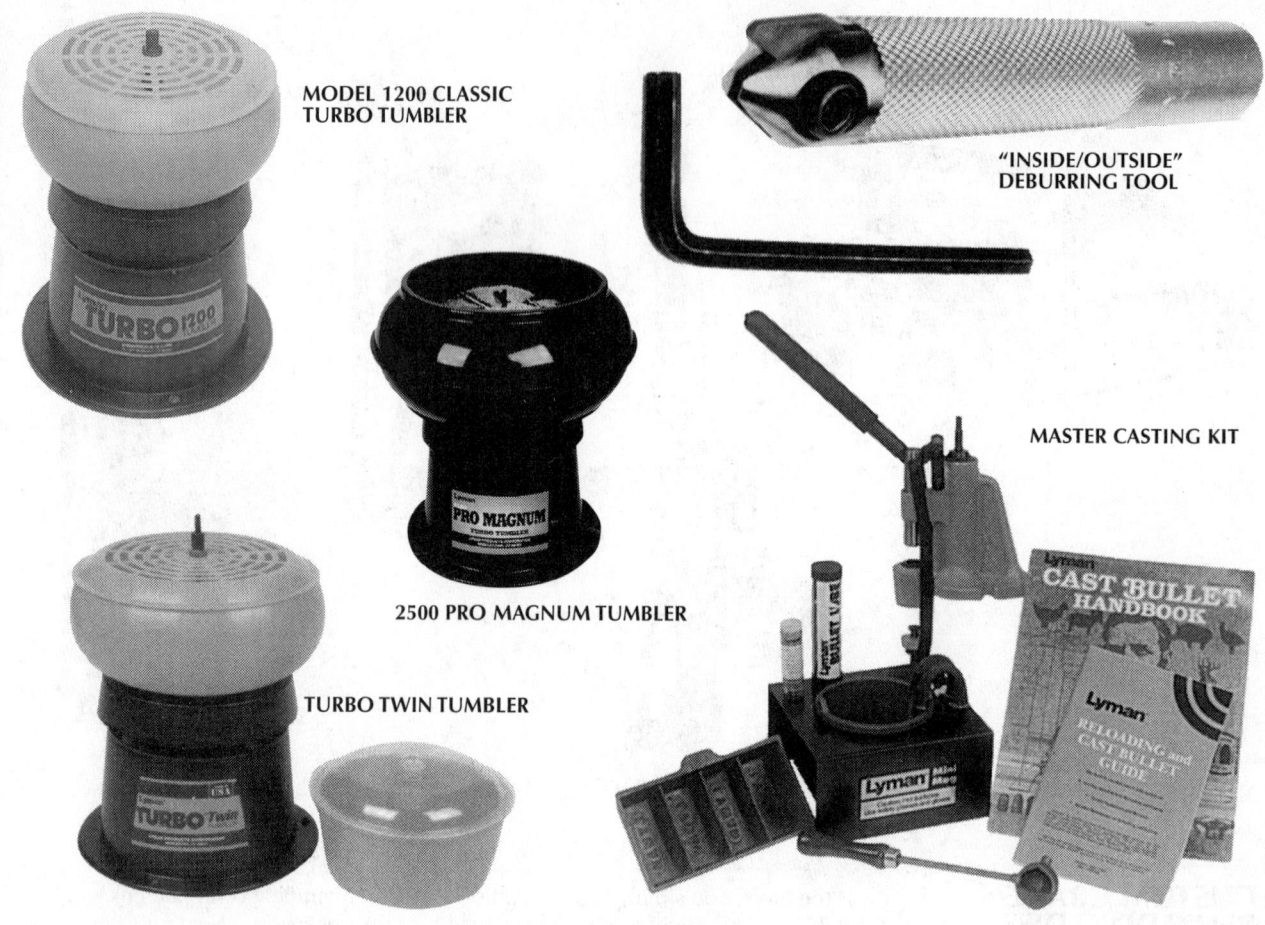

MODEL 1200 CLASSIC
TURBO TUMBLER

"INSIDE/OUTSIDE"
DEBURRING TOOL

MASTER CASTING KIT

2500 PRO MAGNUM TUMBLER

TURBO TWIN TUMBLER

RELOADING TOOLS

Model 1200 Classic Turbo Tumbler
This case tumbler features an improved base and drive system, plus a stronger suspension system and built-in exciters for better tumbling action and faster cleaning.

Model 1200 Classic. $100
Model 1200 Auto-Flo $100
Also available:
Model 600 . . . . $70
Model 2200 Auto-Flo $138
Model 3200 Auto-Flo $185

2500 PRO MAGNUM TUMBLER

The Lyman 2500 Pro Magnum tumbler handles up to 900 .38 Special cartridges at once.

2500 Pro Magnum Tumbler $95
w/ Auto Flow feature $130

"INSIDE/OUTSIDE" DEBURRING TOOL

This tool features an adjustable cutting blade that adapts easily to the mouth of any rifle or pistol case from 22 to 45 caliber with a simple hex wrench adjustment. Inside de-burring is completed by a conical internal section with slotted cutting edges, thus providing uniform inside and outside de-burring in one simple operation. The de-burring tool is mounted on an anodized aluminum handle that is machine-knurled for a sure grip.
MSRP: $14

TURBO TWIN TUMBLER

The Twin features Lyman 1200 Pro Tumbler with an extra, 600 bowl system. Reloaders may use each bowl interchangeably for small or large capacity loads. 1200 Pro Bowl System has a built-in sifter lid for easy sifting

of cases and media at the end of the polishing cycle. The Twin Tumbler features the Lyman Hi-Profile base design with built-in exciters and anti-rotation pads for faster, more consistent tumbling action.
MSRP: $80

MASTER CASTING KIT

Designed especially to meet the needs of blackpowder shooters, this kit features Lyman's combination round ball and maxi ball mould blocks. It also contains a combination double cavity mould, mould handle, mini-mag furnace, lead dipper, bullet lube, a user's manual and a cast bullet guide. Kits are available in 45, 50 and 54 caliber.
MSRP: $195

Lyman Reloading Tools

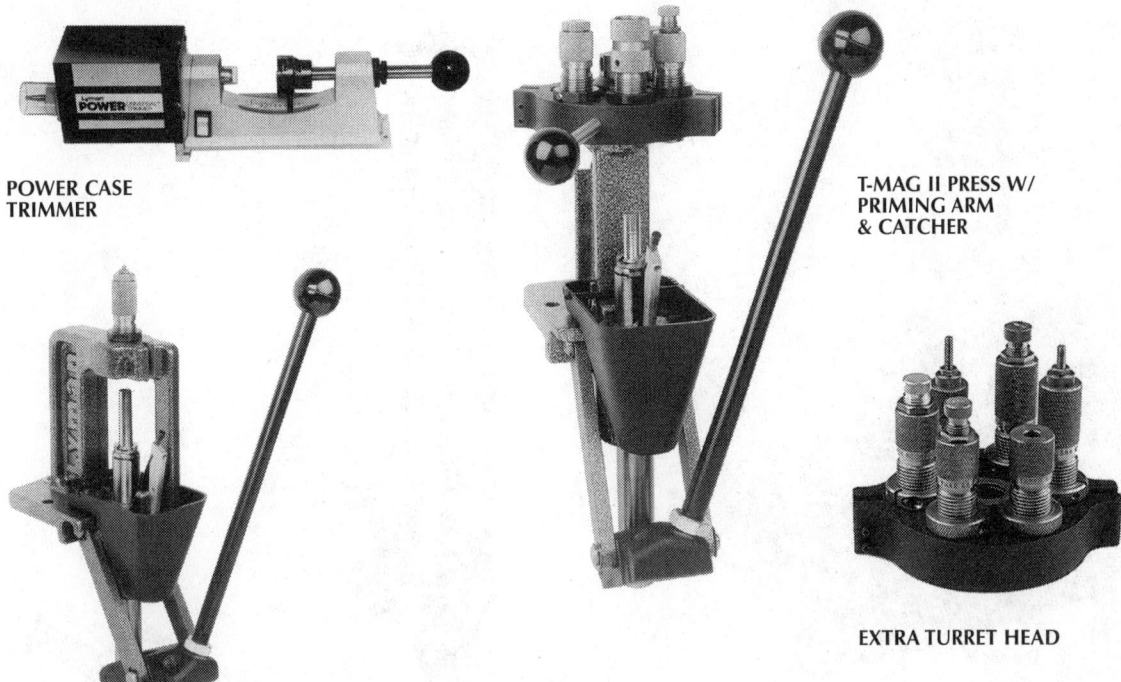

POWER CASE TRIMMER

CRUSHER II

T-MAG II PRESS W/ PRIMING ARM & CATCHER

EXTRA TURRET HEAD

POWER CASE TRIMMER

The Lyman Power Trimmer is powered by a fan-cooled electric motor designed to withstand the severe demands of case trimming. The unit, which features the Universal Chuckhead, allows cases to be positioned for trimming or removed easily. The Power Trimmer package includes Nine-Pilot Multi-Pack, two cutter heads and a pair of wire end brushes for cleaning primer pockets. Other features include safety guards, on-off rocker switch, heavy cast base with receptacles for nine pilots and bolt holes for mounting on a work bench. Power Trimmer is Available for 110- or 220-volt systems.

110 V Model **$237**
220 V Model **$245**

ACCULINE OUTSIDE NECK TURNER

(not shown)

To obtain perfectly concentric case necks, Lyman's Outside Neck Turner assures reloaders of uniform neck wall thickness and outside neck diameter. The unit fits Lyman's Universal Trimmer and AccuTrimmer. Rate of feed is adjustable and a mechanical stop controls length of cut. Mandrels are available for calibers from .17 to .375; cutter blade can be adjusted for any diameter from .195" to .405".

Outside Neck Turner w/extra blade, 6 mandrels **$32**
Individual Mandrels **$4**

CRUSHER II RELOADING PRESS

The only press for rifle or pistol cartridges that offers the advantage of powerful compound leverage combined with a true Magnum press opening. A unique handle design transfers power easily to the center of the ram. A 41/2-inch press opening accommodates even the largest cartridges.

With Priming Arm and Catcher $135

CRUSHER II PRO KIT

Includes press, loading block, case lube kit, primer tray, Model 500 Pro scale, powder funnel and Lyman Reloading Handbook.

MSRP: **$195**

T-MAG II TURRET RELOADING PRESS

With the T-Mag II, up to six different reloading dies can be mounted on one turret — dies can be precisely mounted, locked in and ready to reload at all times. The T-Mag works with all 7/8 x 14 dies. The T-Mag II turret with quick-disconnect release system is held in alignment by a 3/4-inch steel stud. The T-Mag II features Lyman's Crusher II compound leverage system.

T-Mag II Press w/Priming Arm & Catcher **$190**
Extra Turret Head **42**
Also available:
Expert Kit: (T-MAG II Press, Universal Case Trimmer and pilot Multi-Pak, Model 500 powder scale and Model 50 powder measure, plus accessories. Available in calibers 30-06, .270 and .308

MSRP: **$400**

Lyman Reloading Tools

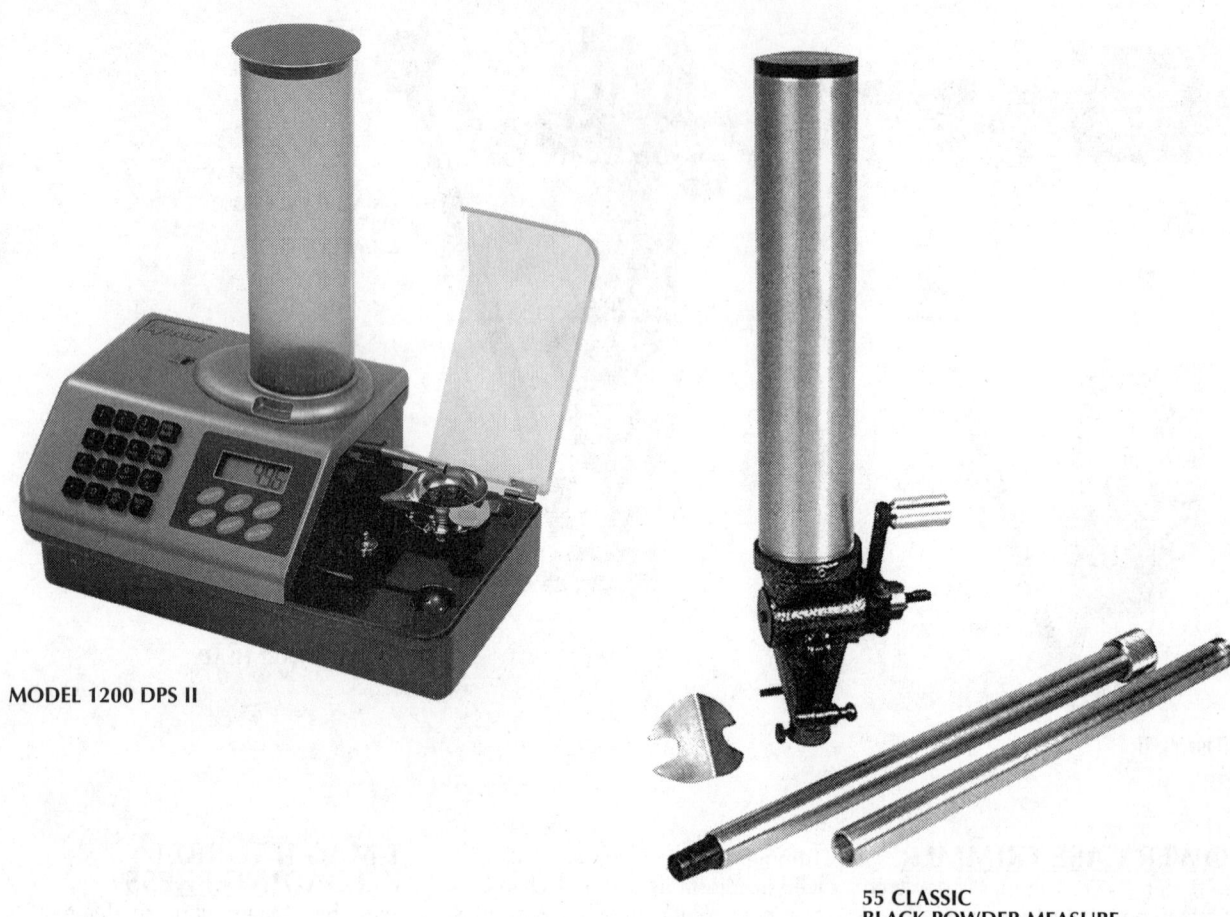

MODEL 1200 DPS II

**55 CLASSIC
BLACK POWDER MEASURE**

MODEL 1200 DPS II (DIGITAL POWDER SYSTEM)

The 1200 DPS dispenses powder quickly, with .1-grain precision. The 4500 Lube sizer, with a one-piece base casting and a built-in heating element (choose 110- or 220-volt). The long ball-knob handle offers the leverage for sizing and lubricating big bullets. It comes with a gas check seater.

1200 DPS **$350**
4500 Lube sizer **$170**

55 CLASSIC BLACK POWDER MEASURE

Lyman's 55 Classic Powder Measure is ideal for the Cowboy Action Competition or black powder cartridge shooters. The one-pound-capacity aluminum reservoir and brass powder meter eliminate static. The internal powder baffle assures highly accurate and consistent charges. The 24" powder compacting drop tube allows the maximum charge in each cartridge. Drop tube works on calibers 38 through 50 and mounts easily to the bottom of the measure.

55 Classic Powder Measure (std model-no tubes): **$125**
55 Classic Powder Measure (with drop tubes): **$140**
Powder Drop Tubes only: **$40**

Lyman Reloading Tools

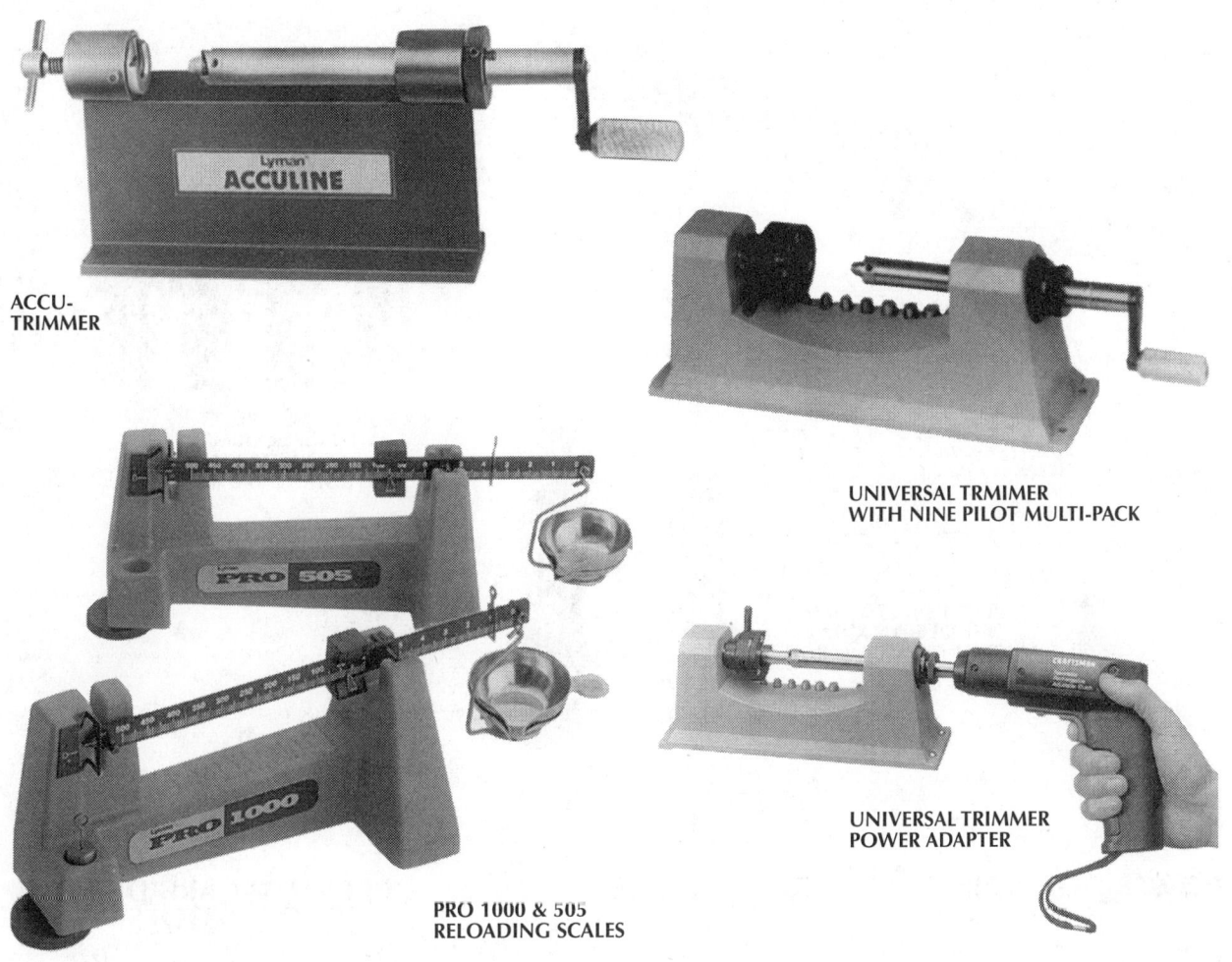

ACCU-
TRIMMER

UNIVERSAL TRMIMER
WITH NINE PILOT MULTI-PACK

UNIVERSAL TRIMMER
POWER ADAPTER

PRO 1000 & 505
RELOADING SCALES

ACCU-TRIMMER

Lyman's Accu Trimmer can be used for all rifle and pistol cases from .22 to .458 Winchester Magnum. Standard shellholders are used to position the case, and the trimmer incorporates standard Lyman cutter heads and pilots. Mounting options include bolting to a bench, C-clamp or vise.

Accu Trimmer w/9-pilot
   Multi-Pak: $53

UNIVERSAL TRIMMER

This trimmer with patented chuckhead accepts all metallic rifle or pistol cases, regardless of rim thickness. To change calibers, simply change the case head pilot. Other features include coarse and fine cutter adjustments, an oil-impregnated bronze bearing, and a rugged cast base to assure precision alignment. Optional carbide cutter available.

Trimmer Multi-Pack (9 pilots: 22, 24, 27, 28/7mm, 30, 9mm, 35, 44 and 4A): $75
Universal Trimmer
   Power Adapter: $20
Power Trimmer—110 V.: 237

PRO 1000 & 505 RELOADING SCALES

Features include improved platform system; hi-tech base design of high-impact styrene; extra-large, smooth leveling wheel; dual agate bearings; larger damper for fast zeroing; built-in counter weight compartment; easy-to-read beam.

Pro 1000 scale: $70
Pro 500 scale: $54
Metric scale: $55

Lyman Reloading Tools

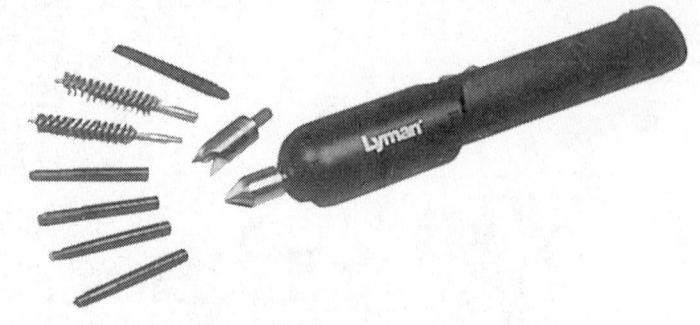

POWER DEBURRING KIT

PREMIUM 4-DIE SET WITH TAPER CRIMP AND POWDER CHARGE EXPANDING DIE

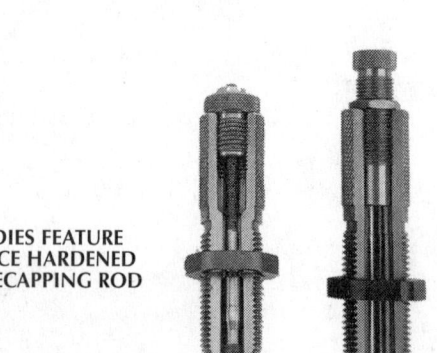

PISTOL DIES FEATURE ONE PIECE HARDENED STEEL DECAPPING ROD

POWER DEBURRING KIT
Features a high torque, rechargeable power driver plus a complete set of accessories, including inside and outside deburr tools, large and small reamers and cleaners and case neck brushes. No threading or chucking required. Set also includes battery recharger and standard flat and Phillips driver bits.
MSRP: **$55**

RIFLE DIE SETS
Lyman precision rifle dies feature fine adjustment threads on the bullet seating stem to allow for precision adjustments of bullet seating depth. Lyman dies fit all popular presses using industry standard 7/8 x 14 threads, including RCBS, Lee, Hornady, Dillon, Redding and others. Each sizing die for bottle-necked rifle cartridges is carefully vented. This vent hole is precisely placed to prevent air traps that can damage cartridge cases. Each sizing die is polished and heat-treated for toughness.

RIFLE 2-DIE SETS
Set consists of a full-length resizing die with de-capping stem and neck expanding button and a bullet-seating die for loading jacketed bullets in bottlenecked rifle cases. For those who load cast bullets, use a neck-expanding die, available separately.
MSRP: **$33**

RIFLE 3-DIE SETS
Straight wall rifle cases require these three die sets consisting of a full length resizing die with decapping stem, a two step neck expanding (M) die and a bullet seating die. These sets are ideal for loading cast bullets due to the inclusion of the neck-expanding die.
MSRP: **$43**
Classic Calibers: **$54**
Classic Neck Size Dies: **$36**

PREMIUM CARBIDE 4-DIE SETS FOR PISTOLS
Lyman 4-Die Sets feature a separate taper crimp die and powder charge/expanding die. The powder charge/expand die has a special hollow 2-step neck expanding plug which allows powder to flow through the die from a powder measure directly into the case. The powder charge/expanding die has a standard 7/8 x 14 thread and will accept Lyman's 55 Powder Measure, or most other powder measures.
MSRP: **$58**

3-DIE CARBIDE PISTOL DIE SETS
Lyman originated the Tungsten Carbide (T-C) sizing die and the addition of extra seating screws for pistol die sets and the two step neck expanding die. Multi-Deluxe Die sets offer these features; a one-piece hardened steel decapping rod and extra seating screws for all popular bullet nose shapes; all-steel construction.
MSRP: **$45**

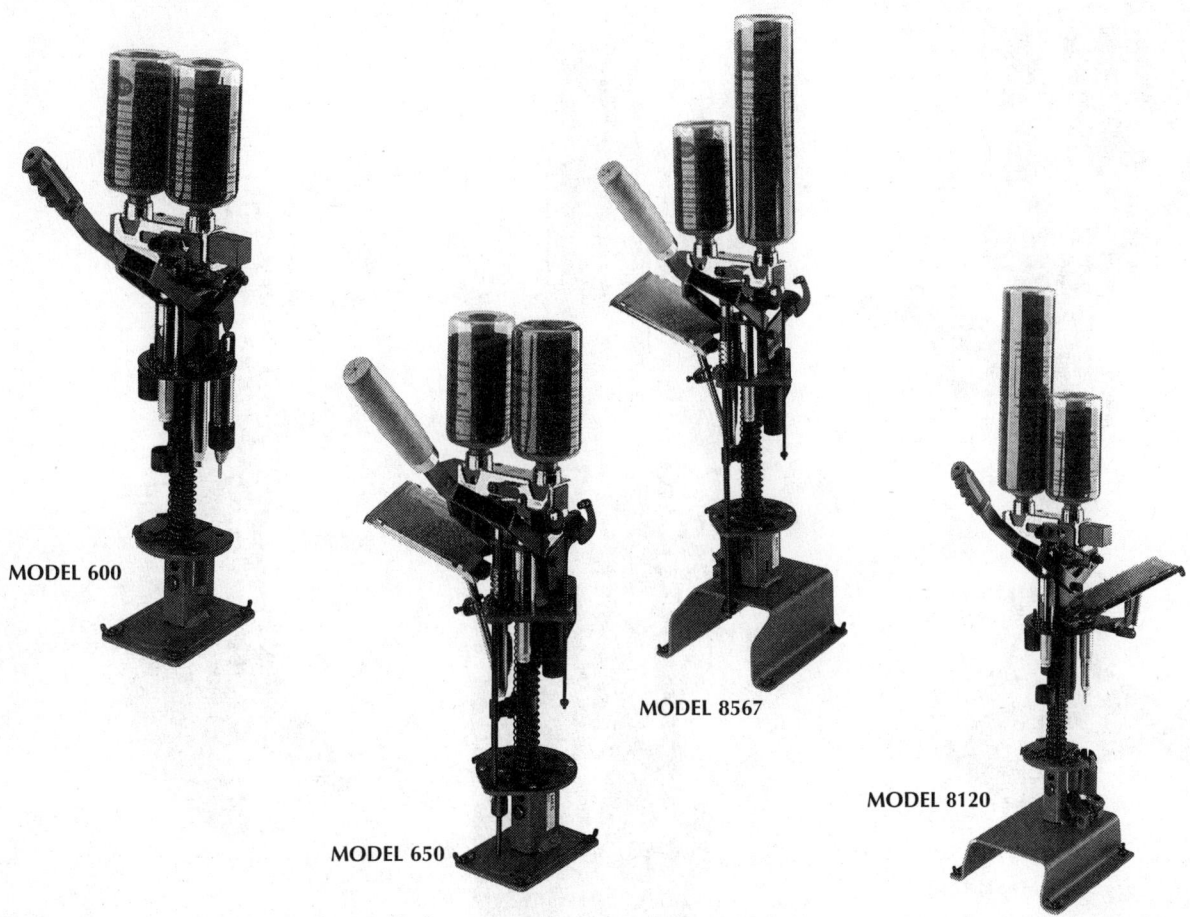

MODEL 600

MODEL 650

MODEL 8567

MODEL 8120

MODEL 600 JR. MARK V

This single-stage reloader features a cam-action crimp die to ensure that each shell returns to its original condition. MEC's 600 Jr. Mark 5 can load 6 to 8 boxes per hour and can be updated with the 285 CA primer feed. Press is adjustable for 3 in. shells.
MSRP: $120

MODEL 650

This reloader works on 6 shells at once. A reloaded shell is completed with every stroke. The MEC 650 does not resize except as a separate operation. Automatic primer feed is standard. Simply fill it with a full box of primers and it will do the rest. Reloader has 3 crimping stations: the first one starts the crimp, the second closes the crimp, and the third places a taper on the shell. Available in 12, 16, 20 and 28 gauge and .410 bore. No die sets available.
MSRP: $240

MODEL 8567 GRABBER

This reloader features 12 different operations at all 6 stations, producing finished shells with each stroke of the handle. It includes a fully automatic primer feed and Auto-Cycle charging, plus MEC's exclusive 3-stage crimp. The "Power Ring" resizer ensures consistent, accurately sized shells without interrupting the reloading sequence. Simply put in the wads and shell casings, then remove the loaded shells with each pull of the handle. Optional kits to load 3 in. shells and steel shot make this reloader tops in its field. Resizes high and low base shells. Available in 12, 16, 20, 28 gauge and .410 bore.
MSRP: $338

MODEL 8120 SIZEMASTER

Sizemaster's "Power Ring" collet resizer returns each base to factory specifications. This resizing station handles brass or steel heads, both high and low base. An 8-fingered collet squeezes the base back to original dimensions, then opens up to release the shell easily. The E-Z Prime auto primer feed is standard equipment (not offered in .410 bore). Press is adjustable for 3 in. shells and is available in 10, 12, 16, 20, 28 gauge and .410 bore. Die sets are available at: $88.67 ($104.06 in 10 ga.)
MSRP: $182

MEC Reloading

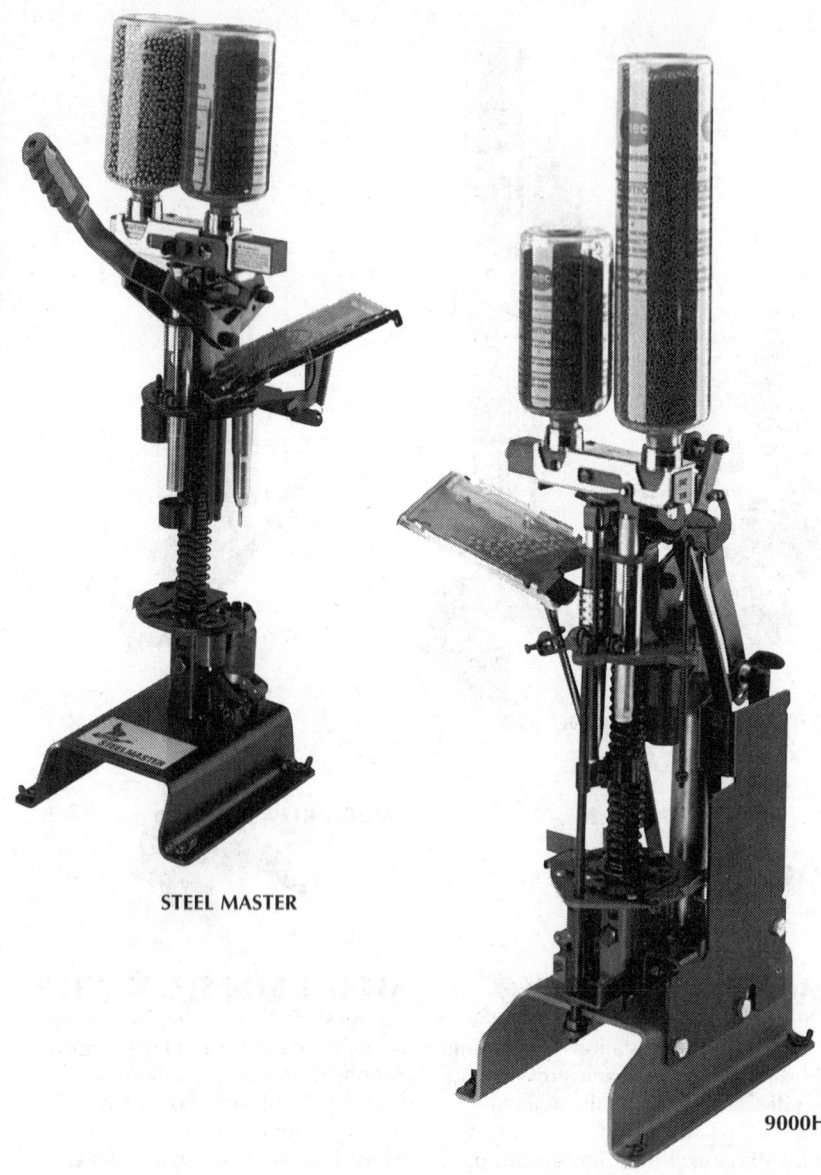

STEEL MASTER

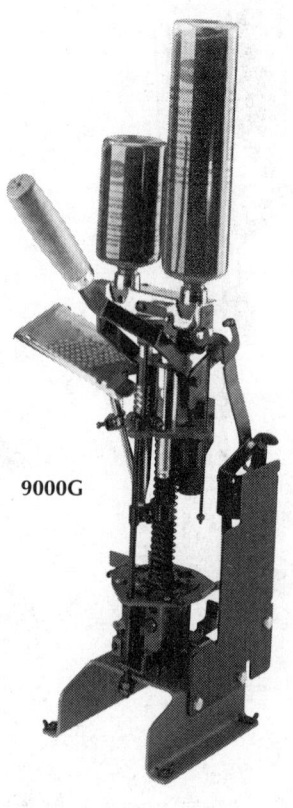

9000G

9000H

STEELMASTER SINGLE STATE

Equipped to load steel shotshells as well as lead ones. Every base is resized to factory specs by a precision "power ring" collet. Handles brass or steel heads in high or low base. The E-Z prime auto primer feed dispenses primers automatically and is standard equipment. Separate presses are available for 12 gauge 23/4", 3", 31/2" and 10 gauge.

8639 Steelmaster 10 & 12 ga. . . $197
8755 Steelmaster
    12 ga. 31/2" only $220

9000 SERIES SHOTSHELL RELOADER

MEC's 9000 Series features automatic indexing and finished shell ejection for quicker and easier reloading. The factory set speed provides uniform movement through every reloading stage. Dropping the primer into the reprime station no longer requires operator "feel." The reloader requires only a minimal adjustment from low to high brass domestic shells, any one of which can be removed for inspection from any station. Can be set up for automatic or manual indexing.

Available in 12, 16, 20 and 28 gauge and .410 bore. No die sets are available.

MEC 9000HN $958
MEC 9001HN without pump. . . . 525
MEC 9000GN Series $407
MEC Super Sizer $67

RCBS Reloading Tools

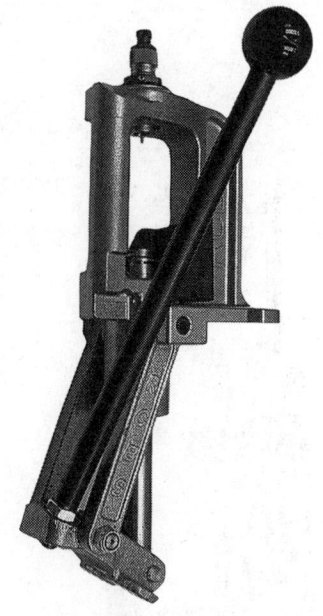

ROCK CHUCKER SUPREME

**AMMOMASTER-2
SINGLE STAGE**

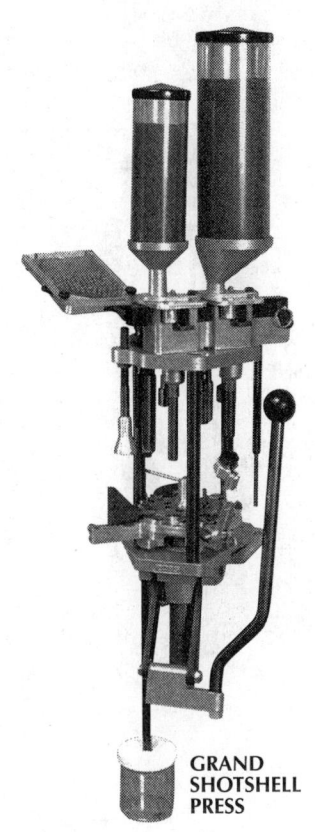

**GRAND
SHOTSHELL
PRESS**

PRESSES

ROCK CHUCKER SUPREME PRESS

With its easy operation, outstanding strength and versatility, a Rock Chucker Supreme press serves beginner and pro alike. It can also be upgraded to a progressive press with an optional Piggyback conversion unit.
• Heavy-duty cast iron for easy case-resizing
• Larger window opening to accommodate longer cartridges
• 1" ram held in place by 12.5 sq. in. of rambearing surface
• Ambidextrous handle
• Compound leverage system
• 7/8"-14 thread for all standard reloading dies and accessories
MSRP: **$156**

AMMOMASTER-2 RELOADING SYSTEM

The AmmoMaster offers handloaders the freedom to configure a press to particular needs and preferences. It covers the complete spectrum of reloading, from single stage through fully automatic progressive reloading, from .25 Auto to .50 caliber. The AmmoMaster Auto has all the features of a five-station press.
MSRP: **$259**

.50 BMG PACK

The Pack includes the press, dies, and accessory items needed, all in one box. The press is the Ammo Master® Single Stage rigged for 1.5-inch dies. It has a 1.5-inch solid steel ram and plenty of height for the big .50. The kit also has a set of RCBS .50 BMG, 1.5-inch reloading dies, including both full-length sizer and seater. Other items are a shell holder, ram priming unit, and a trim die.
MSRP: **$617**

GRAND SHOTSHELL PRESS

Features: The combination of the Powder system and shot system and Case Holders allows the user to reload shells without fear of spillage. The powder system is case-actuated: no hull, no powder. Cases are easily removed with universal 12 and 20 gauge case holders allowing cases to be sized down to the rim. Priming system: Only one primer feeds at a time. Steel size ring: Provides complete resizing of high and low base hulls. Holds 25 lbs. of shot and 11/2 lbs. of powder. Lifetime warranty.
MSRP: **$775**
Grand Conversion kit. **$370**

RCBS Reloading Tools

MINI-GRAND SHOTSHELL PRESS

PRO-2000 PROGRESSIVE PRESS

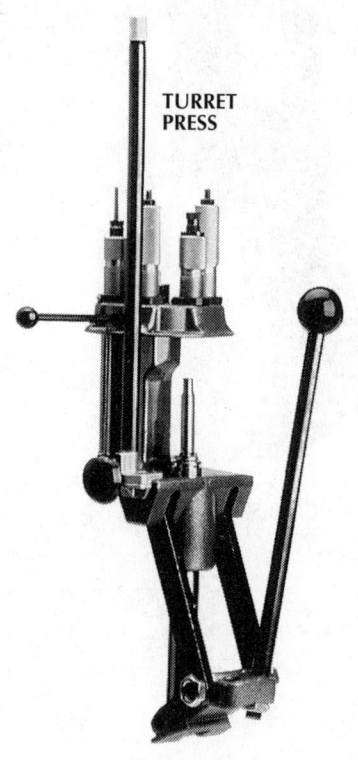

TURRET PRESS

MINI-GRAND SHOTSHELL PRESS

The Mini-Grand shotgun press, a seven-station single-stage press, loads 12- and 20-gauge hulls, from 2¾ to 3½ inches in length. It utilizes RCBS, Hornady and Ponsness Warren powder and shot bushings, with a half-pound capacity powder hopper and 12½-pound capacity shot hopper. The machine will load both lead and steel shot.
MSRP: $139

ROCK CHUCKER SUPREME MASTER RELOADING KIT

The Rock Chucker Master Reloading Kit includes all the tools and accessories needed to start handloading: Rock Chucker Press; RCBS 505 Reloading Scale; Speer Manual #13; Uniflow Powder Measure; deburring tool; case loading block; Primer Tray-2; Hand priming tool; powder funnel; case lube pad; case neck brushes; fold-up hex key set; Trim Pro Manual Case Trimmer Kit.
MSRP: $359

PARTNER PRESS

Easy-to-use, durable press in a compact package. Features compound linkage, durable steel links, priming arm. Reloads most standard calibers.
MSRP: $139
Partner Press Reloading Kit: . . $139

PRO-2000 PROGRESSIVE PRESS

Constructed of cast iron, the Pro-2000 features five reloading stations. The case-actuated powder measure assures repeatability of dispensing powder. A Micrometer Adjustment Screw allows precise return to previously recorded charges. All dies are standard ⅞-14, including the Expander Die. The press incorporates the APS Priming System.

Allows full-length sizing in calibers from .32 Auto to.460 Weatherby Mag.
Pro 2000 Progressive Press: . . . **$560**
**Pro 2000 Deluxe
  Reloading Kit:** **$959**

TURRET PRESS

With pre-set dies in the six-station turret head, the Turret Press can increase production from 50- to 200-rounds per hour. The frame, links, and toggle block are constructed of cast iron and the handle offers compound leverage for full-length sizing of any caliber from .25 ACP to .460 Weatherby Magnum. Six stations allow for custom set-up. The quick-change turret head makes caliber changes fast and easy. This press accepts all standard ⅞-14 dies and shell holders.
MSRP: **$225**
Turret Deluxe Reloading Kit: . . **$435**

RCBS Reloading Tools

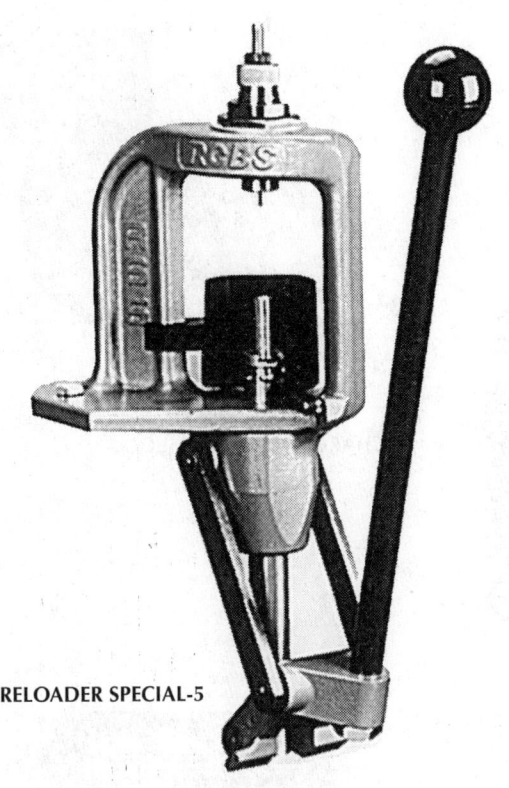

RELOADER SPECIAL-5

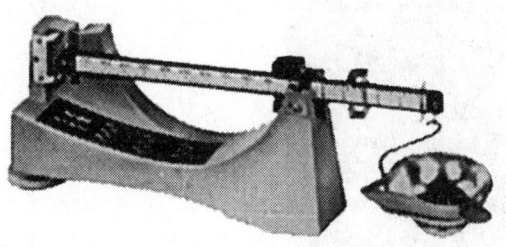

RELOADING SCALE MODEL 5-0-5

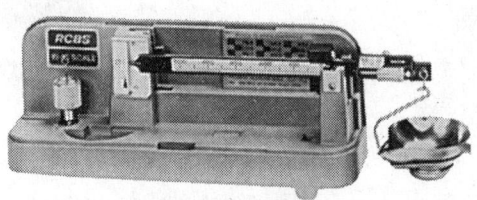

RELOADING SCALE MODEL 10-10
UP TO 1010 GRAIN CAPACITY

RELOADER SPECIAL-5 PRESS

The Reloader Special press features a ball handle and primer arm so that cases can be primed and resized at the same time. Other features include a compound leverage system; Solid aluminum "O" frame offset; corrosion-resistant baked-powder finish; 7/8-14 thread for all standard reloading dies and accessories; optional Piggyback II conversion unit.

MSRP: **$127**
Reloading Starter Kit **$290**

PIGGYBACK III CONVERSION KIT (NOT SHOWN)

The Piggyback III conversion unit moves from single-stage reloading to 5-station, manual-indexing, progressive reloading in one step. The Piggyback III will work with the RCBS Rock Chucker, Reloader Special-3, and Reloader Special-5.

MSRP: **$344**

RELOADING SCALES

MODEL 5-0-5 RELOADING SCALE

This 511-grain capacity scale has a three-poise system with widely spaced, deep beam notches. Two smaller poises on right side adjust from 0.1 to 10 grains, larger one on left side adjusts in full 10-grain steps. The scale uses magnetic dampening to eliminate beam oscillation. The 5-0-5 also has a sturdy die-cast base with large leveling legs and self-aligning agate bearings support the hardened steel beam pivots for a guaranteed sensitivity to 0.1 grains.

MSRP: **$92**

MODEL 1010 RELOADING SCALE

Normal capacity is 510 grains, which can be increased without loss of sensitivity by attaching the included extra weight up to 1010 grains. Features include micrometer poise for quick, precise weighing, special approach-to-weight indicator, easy-to-read graduation, magnetic dampener, agate bearings, anti-tip pan, and dustproof lid snaps on to cover scale for storage. Sensitivity is guaranteed to 0.1 grains.

MSRP: **$154**

RCBS Reloading Tools

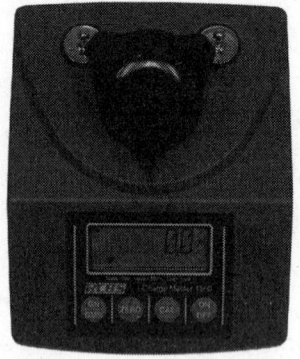

CHARGEMASTER 1500

CHARGEMASTER COMBO

RANGEMASTER 750

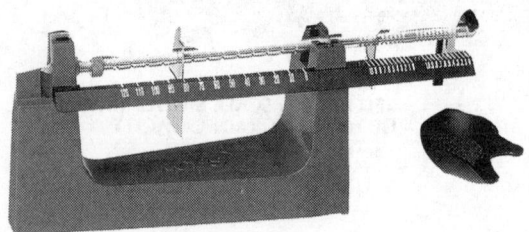

RC-130 MECHANICAL SCALE

APS PRIMER STRIP LOADER

CHARGEMASTER 1500 SCALE

High performance reloading scale with 1500 grain capacity. Scale reads in grains or grams; calibration weights included. Available in 110- or 220-volt — AC adaptor included. Can be upgraded to an automatic dispensing system with the RCBS ChargeMaster

MSRP: **$203**

CHARGEMASTER COMBO

Performs as a scale or as a complete powder dispensing system. Scale can be removed and used separately. Dispenses from 2.0 to 300 grains. Reads and dispenses in grains or grams Stores up to 30 charges in memory for quick recall of favorite

loads. 110 volt or 220 volt adaptor included

MSRP: **$387**

RANGEMASTER 750 SCALE

Compact, lightweight and portable with 750-grain capacity. Scale reads in grams or grains; calibration weights included. Accurate to + or – 1/10 of a grain • fast calibration; • Powered by AC or 9-volt battery — AC adaptor included. 110- or 220-volt model available.

MSRP: **$129**

RC-130 MECHANICAL SCALE

The RC130 features a 130-grain capacity and maintenance-free move-

ment, plus a magnetic dampening system for fast readings. A 3-poise design incorporates easy adjustments with a beam that is graduated in increments of 10 grains and 1 grain. A micrometer poise measures in 0.1-grain increments with accuracy to ±0.1 grain.

MSRP: **$46**

HANDLOADING ACCESSORIES

APS PRIMER STRIP LOADER

For those who keep a supply of CCI primers in conventional packaging, the APS primer strip loader allows quick filling of empty strips. Each push of the handle seats 25 primers.

MSRP: **$30**

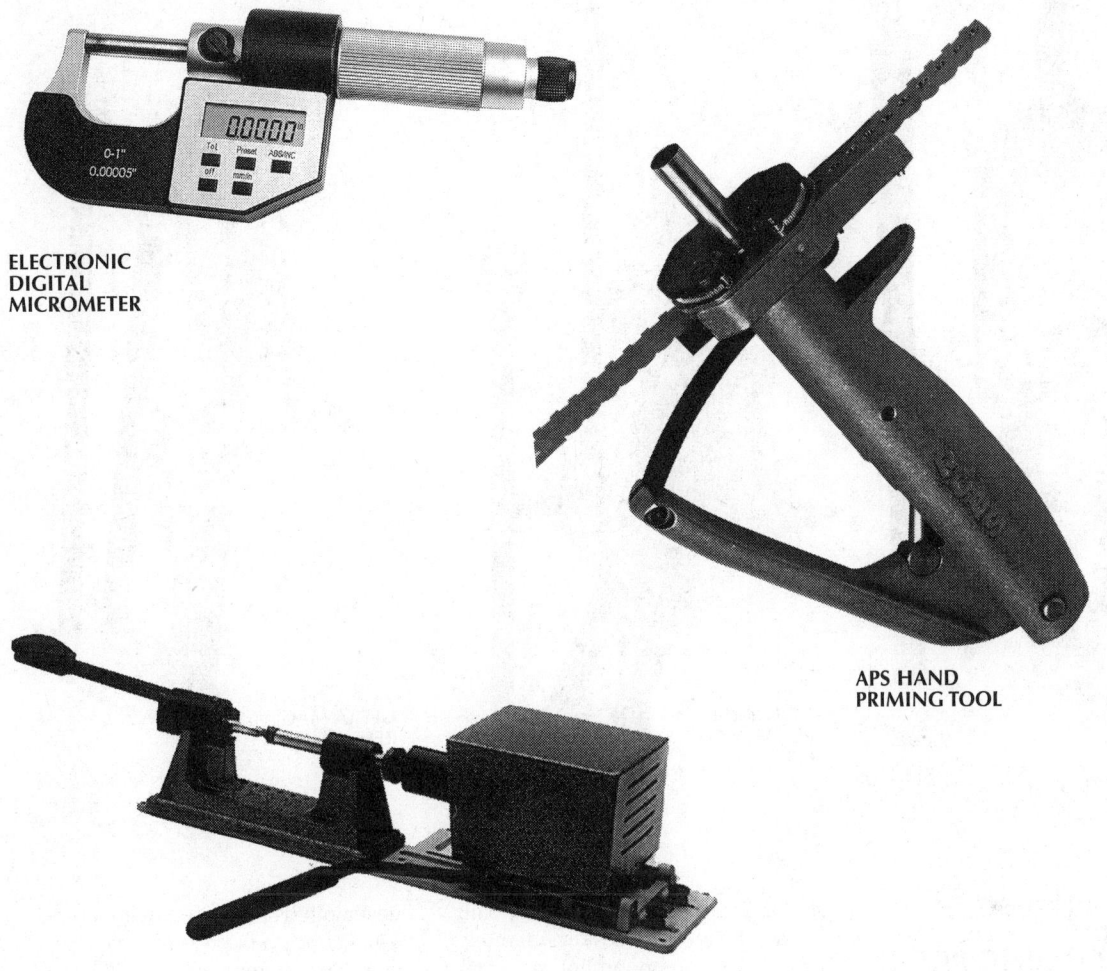

ELECTRONIC DIGITAL MICROMETER

APS HAND PRIMING TOOL

TRIM PRO CASE TRIMMER

ELECTRONIC DIGITAL MICROMETER
• Instant reading • Large, easy to read numbers for error reduction with instant inch/millimeter conversion • Zero adjust at any position • thimble lock for measuring like objects • replaceable silver oxide cell—1.55 Volt • auto off after 5 minutes for longer battery life • adjustment wrench included • fitted wooden storage cases
MSRP: **$114**

HAND PRIMING TOOL
A patented safety mechanism separates the seating operation from the primer supply, virtually eliminating the possibility of tray detonation. Fits in your hand for portable primer seating.

Primer tray installation requires no contact with the primers. Uses the same RCBS shell holders as RCBS presses. Made of cast metal.
MSRP: **$35**

POW'R PULL BULLET PULLER
The RCBS Pow'r Pull bullet puller features a three-jaw chuck that grips the case rim—just rap it on any solid surface like a hammer, and powder and bullet drop into the main chamber for re-use. A soft cushion protects bullets from damage. Works with most centerfire cartridges from .22 to .45 (not for use with rimfire cartridges).
MSRP: **$16**

TRIM PRO CASE TRIMMER
Cases are trimmed quickly and easily. The lever-type handle is more accurate to use than draw collet systems. A flat plate shell holder keeps cases locked in place and aligned. A micrometer fine adjustment bushing offers trimming accuracy to within .001-in. Made of die-cast metal with hardened cutting blades.
Power 120 Vac Kit: **$276**
Manual Kit: **$101**
Trim Pro Case
• **Trimmer Stand:** **$21**

Redding Reloading Tools

HANDLOADING

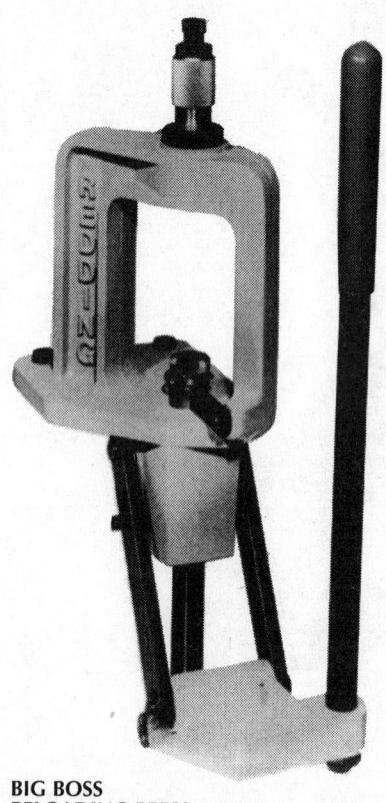

**BIG BOSS
RELOADING PRESS**

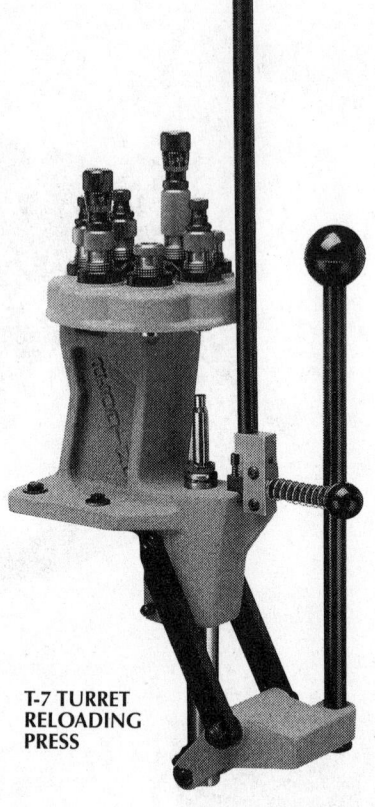

**T-7 TURRET
RELOADING
PRESS**

**ULTRA MAG
RELOADING
PRESS**

HANDLOADING PRESSES

BOSS RELOADING PRESS

This "O" type reloading press features a rigid cast iron frame whose 36° off-set provides the best visibility and access of comparable presses. Its "Smart" primer arm moves in and out of position automatically with ram travel. The priming arm is positioned at the bottom of ram travel for lowest leverage and best feel. Model 721 accepts all standard 7/8-14 threaded dies and universal shell holders.

MSRP: **$156**
w/ Shellholder and 10A Dies:. . $207
Boss Pro-Pak Reloading Kit: . . $419
w/o dies and shellholder: $360

BIG BOSS
RELOADING PRESS

A larger version of the Boss reloading press built on a heavier frame with a longer ram stroke for reloading magnum cartridges. It features a 1-inch diameter ram with over 3.8 inches of

stroke; Smart primer arm; offset ball handle; heavy duty cast iron frame; heavy duty compound linkage; steel adapter bushing accepts all standard 7/8 in.-14 threaded dies

MSRP **$200**

T-7 TURRET RELOADING
PRESS

Features 7 station turret head, heavy duty cast iron frame, 1in. diameter ram, optional "Slide Bar Automatic Primer Feeder System". This feeder eliminates handling of primers during sizing and speeds up reloading operations.

T-7 Turret Press: **$336**
**Kit (press, shellholder and
    10A dies):** **$383**
**Slide Bar Automatic
    Primer Feeder System:** **$50**

ULTRAMAG
RELOADING PRESS

The Ultramag's compound leverage system is connected at the top of the press frame. This allows the reloader to

develop tons of pressure without the usual concern of press frame deflection. Huge frame opening will handle 50 x 3¼-inch Sharps with ease.

MSRP: **$351**
**Kit, includes shell holder
    and one set of 10A dies:** . . . **$396**

DIES & BUSHINGS

BODY DIES

Designed to full-length resize the case body and bump the shoulder position for proper chambering without disturbing the case neck. They are intended for use only to resize cases that have become increasingly difficult to chamber after repeated firing and neck sizing. Small Base Body Dies are available in .223 Rem, 6mm P.P.C, 6mm B. R. Rem, 6mm/284 Win, .260 Rem, 6.5mm/284 Win, .284 Win, .308 Win, .30-06.

Category I: **$33**
Category II: **$39.90**
Category III: **$49.50**
Small Base Body Dies: **$39.90**

Redding Reloading Dies

COMPETITION BULLET
SEATING DIE

COMPETITION
BUSHING STYLE - NECK
SIZING DIE

NECK SIZING
BUSHINGS

FORM & TRIM
DIES

NECK SIZING
DIES

PISTOL TRIM
DIES

COMPETITION BULLET SEATING DIE FOR HANDGUN & STRAIGHT-WALL RIFLE CARTRIDGES

The precision seating stem moves well down into the die chamber to accomplish early bullet contact. The seating stem's spring loading provides positive alignment bias between the tapered nose and the bullet ogive. Thus spring loading and bullet alignment are maintained as the bullet and cartridge case move upward until the actual seating of the bullet begins. The Competition Bullet Seating Die features dial-in micrometer adjustment calibrated in .001-in. increments, is infinitely adjustable and has a "zero" set feature that allows setting desired load to zero. The die is compatible with all progressive reloading presses and has industry standard 7/8 x 14 threaded extended die bodies. An oversize bell-mouth chamfer with smooth radius has been added to the bottom of the die.

MSRP: $93

COMPETITION BUSHING-STYLE NECK SIZING DIE

This die allows you to fit the neck of your case perfectly in the chamber. As in the Competition Seating Die, the cartridge case is completely supported and aligned with the sizing bushing and remains supported in the sliding sleeve as it moves upward while the resizing bushing self-centers on the case neck. The micrometer adjustment of the bushing position delivers precise control to the desired neck length. All dies are supplied without bushings.

Category I $122
Category II $147
Category III $179

NECK SIZING BUSHINGS

Redding Neck Sizing Bushings are available in two styles. Both share the same external dimensions (1/2" O.D. x 3/8" long) and freely interchange in all Redding Bushing style Neck Sizing Dies. They are available in .001" size increments throughout the range of .185" thru .365", covering all calibers from .17 to .338.

MSRP: $15
Heat treated steel bushings: . . . $27

FORM & TRIM DIES

Redding trim dies file trim cases without unnecessary resizing because they are made to chamber dimensions. For case forming and necking brass down from another caliber, Redding trim dies can be the perfect intermediate step before full length resizing.

Series A $32
Series B $44
Series C $54
Series D $60

NECK SIZING DIES

These dies size only the necks of bottleneck cases to prolong brass life and improve accuracy. These dies size only the neck and not the shoulder or body, fired cases should not be interchanged between rifles of the same caliber. Available individually or in Deluxe Die Sets.

Series A $36
Series B $48
Series C $62
Series D $69

PISTOL TRIM DIES

Redding trim dies for pistol calibers allow trimming cases without excessive resizing. Pistol trim dies require extended shellholders.

Series A $32
Series B $44
Series C $54
Series D $60

Redding Reloading Tools

PROFILE CRIMP DIES

TAPER & CRIMP DIES

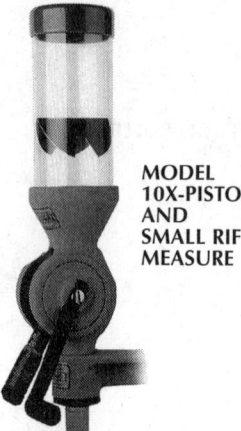

MODEL 10X-PISTOL AND SMALL RIFLE MEASURE

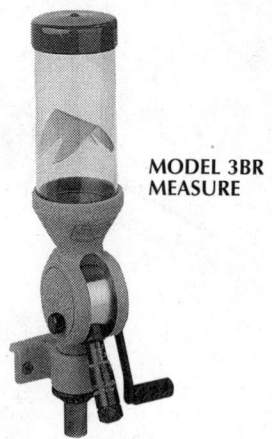

MODEL 3BR MEASURE

PROFILE CRIMP DIES

For handgun cartridges which do not head-space on the case mouth. These dies were designed for those who want the best possible crimp. Profile crimp dies provide a tighter, more uniform roll type crimp, and require the bullet to be seated to the correct depth in a previous operation.

Series A $29
Series B $36
Series C $43
Series D $48

TAPER & CRIMP DIES

Designed for handgun cartridges which headspace on the case mouth where conventional roll crimping is undesirable. Also available for some revolver cartridges, for those who prefer the uniformity of a taper crimp. Available in the following rifle calibers: 223 Rem., 7.62MM x 39, 30-30, 308 Win, 30-06, 300, Win Mag

Series A $29
Series B $36
Series C $43
Series D $48

TYPE S–BUSHING STYLE DIES

The new Type S - Bushing Style Neck Sizing Die provides reloaders with a simple means to precisely control case neck size and tension. The Type-S features: interchangeable sizing bushings available in .001" increments; adjustable decapping rod with standard size button; self-centering resizing bushing; decapping pin retainer. All dies are supplied without bushings.

Category I $66
Category II $81
Category III $99

HANDLOADING ACCESSORIES

COMPETITION MODEL 10X-PISTOL AND SMALL RIFLE POWDER MEASURE

Combines all of the features of Competition Model BR-30, with a drum and metering unit designed to provide uniform metering of small charge weights. To achieve the best metering possible at the targeted charge weight of approximately 10 grains, the diameter of the metering cavity is reduced and the metering plunger is given a hemispherical shape. Charge range: 1 to 25 grains. Drum assembly easily changed from right to left-handed operation.

MSRP: $228

COMPETITION MODEL BR-30 POWDER MEASURE

This powder measure features a drum and micrometer that limit the overall charging range from a low of 10 grains to a maximum of 50 grains. The diameter of Model 3BR's metering cavity has been reduced, and the metering plunger has a unique hemispherical shape, creating a powder cavity that resembles the bottom of a test tube. The result: irregular powder settling is alleviated and charge-to-charge uniformity is enhanced.

MSRP: $228

MATCH-GRADE POWDER MEASURE MODEL 3BR

Interchange Universal- or pistol-metering chambers. Measures charges up to 100 grains. Unit is fitted with lock ring for fast dump with large clear plastic reservoir. See-thru drop tube accepts all calibers from .22 to .600. Precision-fitted rotating drum is critically honed to prevent powder escape. Knife-edged powder chamber shears coarse-grained powders with ease, ensuring accurate charges.

Match Grade 3BR measure: . . $189
3BR Kit, with both
   chambers: $234
Pistol Metering chamber
   (0-10 grains): $57

Redding Reloading Tools

HANDLOADING

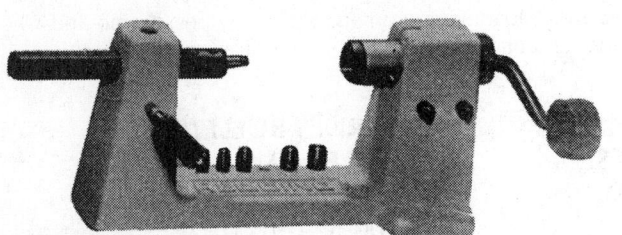

MODEL TR-1400 TRIMMER

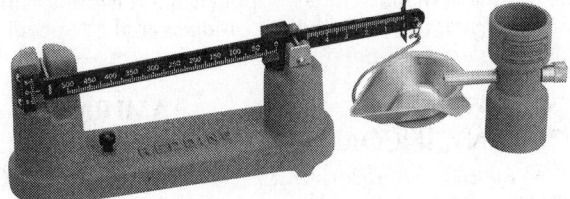

MODEL NO. 2SCALE

EZ FEED SHELL HOLDERS

EXTENDED SHELL HOLDERS

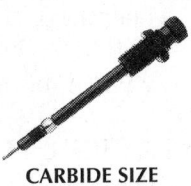

CARBIDE SIZE BUTTON KIT

HEAD SPACE & BULLET COMPARATOR

MODEL 3 POWDER MEASURE

The Model 3 has a micrometer metering chamber in front for easy setting and reading. The frame is precision machined cast iron with hand honed fit between the frame and hard surfaced drum to easily cut and meter powders. The Model 3 features a large capacity clear powder reservoir; see thru drop tube; body w/ standard 7⁄8 in.–14 thread to fit mounting bracket and optional bench stand; cast mounting bracket included.

Powder Measure 3 with universal metering chamber: **$155**
Powder Measure 3K, w/ two metering chambers: **$186**
Handgun Metering Chamber: . . **$42**

CASE TRIMMERS

MASTER CASE TRIMMER MODEL TR-1400

This unit features a universal collet that accepts all rifle and pistol cases. The frame is cast iron with storage holes in the base for extra pilots. Coarse and fine adjustments are provided for case length. The Master Case Trimmer also features: six pilots (22, 6mm, 25, 270, 7mm and 30 cal.); universal collet; two neck cleaning brushes (22 thru 30 cal.); two primer pocket cleaners (large and small); tin coated replaceable cutter; accessory power screwdriver adaptor

Master Case Trimmer: **$108**
Pilots: **$5**

POWDER SCALES

MODEL NO. 2 MASTER POWDER AND BULLET SCALE

Model No. 2 features 505-grain capacity and .1-grain accuracy, a dampened beam and hardened knife edges and milled stainless bearing seats for smooth, consistent operation and a high level of durability
MSRP: **$87**

SHELLHOLDERS

EZ FEED SHELLHOLDERS

Redding shellholders are of a Universal "snap-in" design recommended for use with all Redding dies and presses, as well as all other popular brands. They are precision machined to very close tolerances and heat treated to fit cases and eliminate potential resizing problems. The outside knurling makes them easier to handle and change.
MSRP: **$10**

EXTENDED SHELL HOLDERS

Extended shellholders are required when trimming short cases under 1½ in. O.A.L. They are machined to the same tolerances as standard shellholders except they're longer.
MSRP: **$16**

HANDLOADING TOOLS

CARBIDE SIZE BUTTON KITS

Make inside neck sizing smoother and easier without lubrication. Now die sets can be upgraded with a carbide size button kit. Available for bottleneck cartridges .22 thru .338 cal. The carbide size button is free-floating on the decap rod, allowing it to self-center in the case neck. Kits contain: carbide size button, retainer and spare decapping pin. These kits also fit all Type-S dies.
MSRP: **$28**

INSTANT INDICATOR HEADSPACE & BULLET COMPARATOR

The Instant Indicator checks the headspace from the case shoulder to the base. Bullet seating depths can be compared and bullets can be sorted by checking the base of bullet to give dimension. Case length can be measured. Available for 33 cartridges from .222 Rem to .338 Win. Mag., including new WSSM cartridges.
w/Dial Indicator: **$135**
w/o Dial Indicator: **$104**

Directory of Manufacturers & Suppliers

The following manufacturers, suppliers and distributors of firearms, reloading equipment, sights, scopes, ammo and accessories all appear with their products in the "Specifications" and/or "Manufacturers' Showcase" sections of this edition of *Shooter's Bible*.

ACCURATE ARMS COMPANY, INCORPORATED
c/o Western Powders, Inc.
P.O. Box 158
Miles City, MT 59301
406-234-0422
www.accuratepowder.com

ACCU-TEK FIREARMS
Excel Industries, Inc.
4510 Carter Ct.
Chino, CA 91710
909-627-2404
www.accu-tekfirearms.com

ADIRONDACK OPTICS
P.O. Box 303
Keesville, NY 12944
518-834-7093
www.adkoptics.com

AIMPOINT INCORPORATED
14103 Mariah Ct.
Chantilly, VA 20151
703-263-9795
www.aimpoint.com

ALLIANT POWDER
P.O. Box 6
Radford, VA 24143
800-276-9337
www.alliantpowder.com

ALPEN OUTDOOR CORPORATION
10329 Dorset St.
Rancho Cucamonga, CA 91730
909-987-8370
www.alpenoutdoor.com

AMERICAN DERRINGER CORPORATION
127 North Lacy Dr.
Waco, TX 76705
817-799-9111
www.amderringer.com

AMERICAN HUNTING RIFLES, INCORPORATED
(AHR rifles)
P.O. Box 300
Hamilton, MT 59840
406-961-1410
www.hunting-rifles.com

ANSCHUTZ, J.G.,
GmbH & Co.
www.anschutz-sporters.com
See Tristar Sporting Arms

ARMALITE INCORPORATED
P.O. Box 299
Geneseo, IL 61254
800-336-0184
www.armalite.com

ARMSCO
1247 Rand Rd.
Des Plaines, IL 60016
847-768-1000
www.armsco.net

ATK AMMUNITION
5050 Lincoln Dr.
Edina, MN 55436
952-351-3000
www.atk.com

AUSTIN & HALLECK
2150 South 950 E
Provo, UT 84606
801-371-0412
www.austinhalleck.com

AUTO-ORDNANCE CORPORATION
See Kahr Arms

AYA
See New England Custom Gun Service

BARNES BULLETS
P.O. Box 215
American Fork UT 84003
800-574-9200
www.barnesbullets.com

BARRETT FIREARMS MFG.
P.O. Box 1077
Murfreesboro, TN 37133
615-896-2938
www.barrettrifles.com

BATTENFELD TECHNOLOGIES, INC.
P.O. Box 1035
Columbia, MO 65203
573-445-9200
www.battenfeldtechnologies.com

B.C. OUTDOORS
Eldorado Cartridge Co.
(PMC ammo, Docter scopes and Verona shotguns)
P.O. Box 61497
Boulder City, NV 89006
702-294-3056
www.pmcammo.com

BENELLI U.S.A. CORP.
17603 Indian Head Hwy,
Suite 200
Accokeek, MD 20607
301-283-6981
www.benelliusa.com

BERETTA U.S.A. CORP.
17601 Beretta Dr.
Accokeek, MD 20607
301-283-2191
www.berettausa.com

BERGER BULLETS, INC.
4275 N. Palm St.
Fullerton, CA 92835
714-447-5478
www.bergerbullets.com

Directory of Manufacturers & Suppliers

BERNARDELLI
See Armsport

BERSA
See Eagle Imports Inc.

BLACK HILLS AMMUNITION
P.O. Box 3090
Rapid City, SD 57709
605-348-9827
www.black-hills.com

BLACK POWDER PRODUCTS, INCORPORATED
(CVA & Winchester Blackpowder)
5988 Peachtree Corners E
Norcross, GA 30071
800-320-8767
www.bpiguns.com

BLASER USA, INCORPORATED
See Sig Arms

BONANZA
See Forster Products

BOND ARMS INCORPORATED
P.O. Box 1296
Granbury, TX 76048
817-573-4445
www.bondarms.com

BRENNEKE OF AMERICA LTD.
P.O. Box 1481
Clinton, IA 52733
800-753-9733
www.brennekeusa.com

BROWN, ED, PRODUCTS, INC.
P.O. Box 492
Perry, MO 63462
573-565-3261
www.edbrown.com

BROWNING
1 Browning Place
Morgan, UT 84050
801-876-2711
www.browning.com

BROWNING SPORT OPTICS
See Bushnell

BROWN PRECISION, INC.
P.O. Box 270 W
Los Molinos, CA 96055
530-384-2506
www.brownprecision.com

BRUNTON
620 East Monroe Ave.
Riverton, WY 82501
307-857-4700
www.brunton.com

BSA OPTICS, INC.
3911 SW 47th Ave., Suite 914
Ft. Lauderdale, FL 33314
954-581-2144
www.bsaoptics.com

BURRIS COMPANY, INC.
P.O. Box 1899
Greeley, CO 806321
970-356-1670
www.burrisoptics.com

BUSHMASTER FIREARMS INC.
P.O. Box 1479
Windham, ME 04062
800-998-7928
www.bushmaster.com

BUSHNELL OUTDOOR PRODUCTS
9200 Cody
Overland Park, KS 66214
913-752-3400
www.bushnell.com

CABELA'S INCORPORATED
1 Cabela Dr.
Sidney, NE 69160
308-254-5505
www.cabelas.com

CCI/SPEER-BLOUNT, INC.
2299 Snake River Ave.
Lewiston, ID 83501

208-746-2351
www.cci-ammunition.com
www.speer-bullets.com

CHEY TAC ASSOCIATES LTD.
363 Sunset Dr.
Arco, ID 83213
208-527-8614
www.cheytac.com

CHRISTENSEN ARMS
192 E. 100 N
Fayette, UT 84630
888-517-8855
www.christensenarms.com

CIMARRON FIREARMS CO.
P.O. Box 906
Fredericksburg, TX 78624
830-997-9090
www.cimarron-firearms.com

COLT BLACKPOWDER ARMS COMPANY
110 8th St.
Brooklyn, NY 11215
718-499-4678

COLT'S MFG. COMPANY, LLC
P.O. Box 1868
Hartford, CT 06144
800-962-COLT
www.colt.com

COMANCHE
See Eagle Imports

CONNECTICUT SHOTGUN MANUFACTURING CO.
(A.H. Fox shotguns)
P.O. Box 1692
New Britain, CT 06051
860-225-6581
www.connecticutshotgun.com

COOPER ARMS OF MONTANA, INCORPORATED
P.O. Box 114
Stevensville, MT 59870

MANUFACTURERS

Directory of Manufacturers & Suppliers

406-777-0373
www.cooperfirearms.com

COR-BON/GLASER
P.O. Box 369
Sturgis, SD 57785
605-347-4544
www.corbon.com

CVA
(Connecticut Valley Arms)
5988 Peachtree Corners E
Norcross, GA 30071
800-320-8767
www.cva.com

CZ-USA
P.O. Box 171073
Kansas City, KS 66117
800-955-4486
www.cz-usa.com

DAKOTA ARMS
1310 Industry Rd.
Sturgis, SD 57785
605-347-4686
www.dakotarms.com

CHARLES DALY
See K.B.I., Inc.

DAYTONA
See Renato Gamba U.S.A.

DESERT EAGLE
See Magnum Research Inc.

**DILLON PRECISION
PRODUCTS, INC.**
8009 East Dillons Way
Scottsdale, AZ 85260
800-223-4570
www.dillonprecision.com

DIXIE GUN WORKS
P.O. Box 130
Union City, TN 38281
800-238-6785
www.dixiegun.com

DKG TRADING INC.
(Eley ammunition, Famous
Maker scopes)
8791 Stringtown Rd.
Evansville, IL 62242
877-354-2666
www.dkgtrading.com

DOCTER SCOPES
See B.C. Outdoors

DOWNSIZER CORPORATION
P.O. Box 710316
Santee, CA 92072
619-448-5510

DYNAMIT NOBEL/RWS
(Rottweil shotguns and ammunition, Steyr Mannlicher)
81 Ruckman Rd.
Closter, NJ 07624
201-767-1995
www.dnrws.com

**EAGLE IMPORTS,
INCORPORATED**
(Bersa, Comanche, Llama and
Firestorm handguns)
1750 Brielle Ave., Suite B1
Wanamassa, NJ 07712
732-493-0333
www.bersafirearmsusa.com

E.D.M. ARMS
421 Business Center Ct.
Redlands, CA 92373
909-798-2770
www.edmarms.com

**E.M.F. COMPANY,
INCORPORATED**
(Dakota handguns; Uberti
handguns, blackpower
arms, rifles)
1900 East Warner Ave.,
Suite 1-D
Santa Ana, CA 92705
949-261-6611
www.emf-company.com

ELEY LIMITED
Selco Way, 1st Ave.
Minworth Industrial Estate
Sutton Coldfield
West Midlands,
England B76 1BA
011 (44) 121 313 4567
www.eleyhawkltd.com

ENTRÉPRISE ARMS
15861 Business Center Dr.
Irwindale, CA 91706
626-962-8712
www.entreprise.com

ESCORT
See Legacy Sports Intl.

EUROARMS OF AMERICA INC.
P.O. Box 3277
Winchester, VA 22604
540-662-1863
www.euroarms.net

**EUROPEAN AMERICAN
ARMORY CORPORATION**
(E.A.A. handguns, rifles)
P.O. Box 1299
Sharpes, FL 32959
321-639-4842
www.eaacorp.com

FABARMS
See Heckler & Koch

FAMOUS MAKER SCOPES
See DKG Trading Inc.

FEDERAL CARTRIDGE CO.
900 Ehlen Dr.
Anoka, MN 55303
800-322-2342
www.federalcartridge.com

FLODMAN GUNS SWEDEN
640 60 Akers styckebruk
Jarsta, Sweden
46 159308 61
www.flodman.com

Directory of Manufacturers & Suppliers

FIRESTORM PISTOLS
See Eagle Imports

FIOCCHI OF AMERICA
6930 Fremont Rd.
Ozark, MO 65721
800-721-AMMO
www.fiocchiusa.com

FLINTLOCKS, ETC.
(Davide Pedersoli replica rifles)
P.O. Box 181
Richmond, MA 01254
413-698-3822
www.flintlocksetc.com

FNH USA, INCORPORATED
P.O. Box 697
McLean, VA 22101
703-288-1292
www.fnhusa.com

FORSTER PRODUCTS
310 East Lanark Ave.
Lanark, IL 61046
815-493-6360
www.forsterproducts.com

A.H. FOX
See Connecticut Shotgun Manufacturing Corporation

FRANCHI
See Beretta

FRANKFORD ARSENALS
See Battenfield Technologies

FREEDOM ARMS
P.O. Box 150
Freedom, WY 83120
307-883-2468
www.freedomarms.com

GLOCK, INCORPORATED
6000 Highlands Parkway
Smyrna, GA 30082
770-432-1202
www.glock.com

GONIC ARMS
134 Flagg Rd.
Gonic, NH 03839

GSI (GUN SOUTH INC.)
(Mauser rifles; Merkel shotguns)
P.O. Box 129
Trussville, AL 35173
205-655-8299
www.gsifirearms.com

HARRINGTON & RICHARDSON, H&R 1871 INCOPORATED
(Harrington & Richardson shotguns, New England Firearms shotguns)
60 Industrial Rowe
Gardner, MA 01440
978-630-8220
www.hr1871.com

H-S PRECISION
1301 Turbine Dr.
Rapid City, SD 57703
605-341-3006
www.hsprecision.com

HAMMERLI U.S.A.
19296 Oak Grove Cir.
Groveland, CA 95321
209-962-5311
www.hammerliusa.com

HECKLER & KOCH
(handguns, rifles; and Fabarm shotguns)
7661 Commerce Lane
Trussville, AL 35173
205-655-8299
www.hecklerkoch-usa.com

HENRY REPEATING ARMS COMPANY
110 8th St.
Brooklyn, NY 11215
718-499-5600
www.henryrepeating.com

HERITAGE MANUFACTURING
4600 NW 135th St.
Opa Locka, FL 33054
305-685-5966
www.heritagemfg.com

HEYM RIFLE
See PSI

HI-POINT FIREARMS
MKS Supply, Inc.
8611-A North Dixie Dr.
Dayton, OH 45414
877-425-4867
www.hi-pointfirearms.com

HIGH STANDARD MANUFACTURING CO.
5200 Mitchelldale, Suite E-17
Houston, TX 77092
800-272-7816
www.highstandard.com

HODGDON POWDER CO., INCOPORATED
P.O. Box 2932
Shawnee Mission, KS 66201
913-362-9455
www.hodgdon.com

HORNADY MFG. CO.
P.O. Box 1848
Grand Island, NE 68803
308-382-1390
www.hornady.com

HOWA
See Legacy Sports Intl.

HUNTER COMPANY, INC.
(Hunter Wicked Optics)
3300 W. 71st Ave.
Westminster, CO 80030
303-427-4626
www.huntercompany.com

IMR POWDER CO. INC.
See Hodgdon Powder
www.imrpowder.com

Directory of Manufacturers & Suppliers

ITHACA GUN COMPANY
420 N. Warpole St.
Sandusky, OH 43351
419-294-4113
www.ithacagun.com

**JARRETT RIFLES
INCORPORATED**
383 Brown Rd.
Jackson, SC 29831
803-471-3616
www.jarrettrifles.com

JOHANNSEN EXPRESS RIFLE
See New England Custom Guns

KAHLES
2 Slater Rd.
Cranston, RI 02920
866-606-8779
www.kahlesoptik.com

KAHR ARMS
P.O. Box 1518
Pearl River, NY 10965
845-652-8535
www.kahr.com

KAPS OPTICS
Karl Kaps Gmbh
Europastrasse
35614 Asslar/Wetzlar
Germany
49-6441-80704

K.B.I., INCORPORATED
(rifles, handguns, shotguns;
Charles Daly rifles, shotguns;
FEG handguns)
P.O. Box 6625
Harrisburg, PA 17112
866-325-9486
www.charlesdaly.com

KEL-TEC CNC
P.O. Box 236009
Cocoa, FL 32926
321-631-0068
www.kel-tec.com

**KIMBER MANUFACTURING,
INCOPORATED**
1 Lawton St.
Yonkers, NY 10705
800-880-2418
www.kimberamerica.com

KNIGHT RIFLES
21852 Hwy. J46
Centerville, IA 52544
641-856-2626
www.knightrifles.com

KONUS USA
7275 NW 87th Ave.
Miami, FL 33178
305-592-5500
www.konususa.com

**KRIEGHOFF INTERNATIONAL
INCOPORATED**
P.O. Box 549
Ottsville, PA 18942
610-847-5173
www.krieghoff.com

KYNOCH AMMUNITION
Kynamco Limited
The Old Railway Station
Mildenhall, IP28 7DT England
+44 (0) 1638 711999

LAPUA
See Vihtavuori
www.lapua.com

**L.A.R. MANUFACTURING,
INCOPORATED**
(Grizzly rifles)
4133 W. Farm Rd.
West Jordan, UT 84088
801-280-3505
www.largrizzly.com

LAZZERONI ARMS CO.
1415 S. Cherry Ave.
Tucson, AZ 85713
888-4-WAR-BIRD
www.lazzeroni.com

**LEATHERWOOD/
HI-LUX OPTICS**
2535 West 237th St., Suite 106
Torrance, CA 90505
310-257-8142
www.leatherwoodoptics.com

LEGACY SPORTS INTL.
(Howa, Mauser & Puma rifles,
Escort shotguns)
4750 Longley Ln., Suite 208
Reno, NV 89502
703-548-4837
www.legacysports.com

LENARTZ MUZZLELOADING
8001 Whitneyville Rd.
Alto, MI 49302
616-891-0372
www.lenartz.com

LEUPOLD & STEVENS, INC.
14400 NW Greenbrier Pkwy.
Beaverton, OR 97006
503-646-9171
www.leupold.com

LLAMA
See Eagle Imports

**LONE STAR RIFLE
COMPANY, INCORPORATED**
11231 Rose Rd.
Conroe, TX 77303
936-856-3363
www.lonestarrifle.com

LPA SIGHTS
Via Alfieri
26-25063 Gardone
Val Trumpia (B5) Italy
++39(30)89-11-481
www.lpasights.com

LYMAN PRODUCTS CORP.
475 Smith St.
Middletown, CT 06457
800-225-9626
www.lymanproducts.com

Directory of Manufacturers & Suppliers

MAGNUM RESEARCH INC.
7110 University Ave. NE
Minneapolis, MN 55432
800-772-6168
www.magnumresearch.com

MAGTECH AMMUNITION CO. INCOPORATED
6845 20th Ave. S, Suite 120
Centerville, MN 55038
800-466-7191
www.magtechammunition.com

MARBLE ARMS
420 Industrial Park
Gladstone, MI 49837
906-428-3710
www.marblearms.com

MARKESBERY MUZZLELOADERS, INC.
7785 Foundation Dr., Suite 6
Florence, KY 41042
606-342-5553
www.markesbery.com

MARLIN FIREARMS COMPANY
100 Kenna Dr.
North Haven, CT 06473
203-239-5621
www.marlinfirearms.com

MAROCCHI
(Conquista shotguns)
See Precision Sales Int'l.

MEADE INSTRUMENTS
(Scopes: Simmons, Redfield, Weaver)
6001 Oak Canyon
Irvine, CA 92618
800-626-3233
www.meade.com

MEC INCORPORATED
c/o Mayville Engineering Co.
715 South St.
Mayville, WI 53050

800-797-4632
www.mecreloaders.com

MERKEL
See GSI (Gun South Inc.)
www.gsifirearms.com

M.O.A. CORPORATION
285 Government Valley Rd.
Sundance, WY 82729
307-283-3030
www.moaguns.com

O.F. MOSSBERG & SONS, INCORPORATED
7 Grasso Ave.
North Haven, CT 06473
203-230-5300
www.mossberg.com

MTM MOLDED PRODUCTS
3370 Obco Ct.
Dayton, OH 45414
937-890-7461
www.mtmcase-gard.com

NAVY ARMS COMPANY, INCORPORATED
219 Lawn St.
Martinsburg, WV 25401
304-262-1651
www.navyarms.com

NEW ENGLAND ARMS CORP./ FAIR TECHNI MEC
P.O. Box 278
Kittery Point, ME 03905
207-439-0593
www.newenglandarms.com

NEW ENGLAND CUSTOM GUN LTD.
(AYA shotguns and Schmidt-Bender scopes)
438 Willow Brook Rd.
Plainfield, NH 03781
603-469-3450
www.newenglandcustomgun.com

NEW ENGLAND FIREARMS CO. INCOPORATED
60 Industrial Rowe
Gardner, MA 01440
978-632-9393
www.hr1871.com

NEW ULTRA LIGHT ARMS
P.O. Box 340
Granville, WV 26534
304-292-0600
www.newultralight.com

NIKON INCORPORATED
1300 Walt Whitman Rd.
Melville, NY 11747
631-547-4200
www.nikonsportoptics.com

NORTH AMERICAN ARMS
2150 S. 950 East
Provo, UT 84606
800-821-5783
www.northamericanarms.com

NOSLER INCORPORATED
P.O. Box 671
Bend, OR 97709
541-382-3921
www.nosler.com

OLIN
See Winchester

OLYMPIC ARMS, INCORPORATED
624 Old Pacific Hwy. SE
Olympia, WA 98513
360-456-3471
www.olyarms.com

PACHMAYR
A Division of Lyman Products,
475 Smith Street
Middletown, CT 06457
800-423-9704
www.lymanproducts.com

Directory of Manufacturers & Suppliers

PARA-ORDNANCE MANUFACTURING, INC.
980 Tapscott Rd.
Scarborough, ON Canada
M1X 1C3
416-297-7855
www.paraord.com

PEDERSOLI, DAVIDE
See Flintlocks Etc.
www.davide-pedersoli.com

PENTAX IMAGING COMPANY
600 12th St., Suite 300
Golden, CO 80401
800-877-0155
www.pentaximaging.com

PERAZZI U.S.A.
1010 W. 10th St.
Azusa, CA 91702
626-334-1234
www.perazzi.com

PGW DEFENSE TECHNOLOGIES
(Prairie Gun Works rifles)
1-761 Marion St.
Winnipeg, Manitoba,
Canada R2J0K6
204-231-2976
www.pgwdti.com

PHOENIX PRECISION
19745 159th St
Elk River, MN 55330
763-263-3327
www.phoenixprec.com

PMC CARTRIDGES
See B.C. Outdoors
www.pmcammo.com

POWERBELT BULLETS
2316 E. Railroad St.
Nampa, ID 83687
800-376-4010
www.powerbeltbullets.com

JAMES PURDEY & SONS LTD.
Audley House
57 - 58 South Audley St.
London W1K 2ED
+44 (0)20 7499 1801
www.purdey.com

RAMSHOT PROPELLANT
See Western Powders

RCBS
605 Oro Dam Blvd.
Oroville, CA 95965
800-533-5000
www.rcbs.com

REDDING RELOADING EQUIPMENT
1089 Starr Rd.
Cortland, NY 13045
607-753-3331
www.redding-reloading.com

REDFIELD USA
201 Plantation Oak Dr.
Thomasville, GA 31792
800-323-3191
www.redfieldoptics.com

REMINGTON ARMS CO., INCORPORATED
P.O. Box 700
Madison, NC 27025
800-243-9700
www.remington.com

RENATO GAMBA U.S.A. INCORPORATED
(Daytona shotguns)
25063 Gardone Val Trompia
Brescia, Italy
+39 308911640

RIFLES, INCORPORATED
3580 Leal Rd.
Pleasanton, TX 78064
830-569-2055
www.riflesinc.com

RIZZINI
1140 McDermott Dr., Suite 103
West Chester, PA 19380
610-344-7730
www.rizziniusa.com

ROGUE RIFLE COMPANY
1140 36th St. N, Suite B
Lewiston, ID 83501
208-743-4355
www.roguerifle.com

ROSSI FIREARMS
BrazTech Intl.
16175 NW 49th Ave.
Miami, FL 33014
305-474-0401
www.rossiusa.com

ROTTWEIL BRENNEKE
See Brenneke

RUGER
See Sturm, Ruger & Co., Inc.

RWS
See Dynamit Nobel

SAKO
See Beretta U.S.A. Corp.

SAUER
c/o Paul Company, Inc.
27385 Pressonville Rd.
Wellsville, KS 66092
913-883-4444

SAVAGE ARMS, INCORPORATED
118 Mountain Rd.
Suffield, CT 06078
866-233-4776
www.savagearms.com

SCHMIDT AND BENDER
Am Grossacker 42
Biebertal, Germany 35444
011-49-8115-0
www.schmidt-bender.de

Directory of Manufacturers & Suppliers

SHILOH RIFLE MANUFACTURING
P.O. Box 279
Big Timber, MT 59011
406-932-4454
www.shilohrifle.com

SIERRA BULLETS
1400 W. Henry St.
Sedalia, MO 65301
888-223-3006
www.sierrabullets.com

SIGARMS INCORPORATED
(Sig-Sauer shotguns, handguns, Blaser rifles)
18 Industrial Dr.
Exeter, NH 03833
603-772-2302
www.sigarms.com

SIGHTRON, INCORPORATED
100 Jeffrey Way, Suite A
Youngsville, NC 27596
919-562-3000
www.sightron.com

SILMA SHOTGUNS
See Legacy Sports

SIMMONS OUTDOOR CORPORATION
(scopes, Weaver, Redfield)
201 Plantation Oak Dr.
Thomasville, GA 31792
229-227-9053
www.simmonsoptics.com

SKB SHOTGUNS
4325 S. 120th St.
Omaha, NE 68137
800-752-2767
www.skbshotguns.com

SMITH & WESSON
2100 Roosevelt Ave.
Springfield, MA 01104
800-331-0852
www.smith-wesson.com

SPEER
See CCI/Speer-Blount, Inc.

SPRINGFIELD ARMORY
420 W. Main St.
Geneseo, IL 61254
309-944-8994
www.springfield-armory.com

STEVENS
See Savage Arms Co.

STEYR-MANNLICHER
See Dynamit/Nobel
www.dnrws.com

STOEGER INDUSTRIES
17603 Indian Head Hwy., Suite 200
Accokeek, MD 20607
301-283-6300
www.stoegerindustries.com

STURM, RUGER & COMPANY, INCOPORATED
1 Lacey Pl.
Southport, CT 06890
203-259-7843
www.ruger.com

SWAROVSKI OPTIK NORTH AMERICA
2 Slater Rd.
Cranston, RI 02920
800-426-3089
www.swarovskioptik.com

SWIFT BULLET COMPANY
P.O. Box 27
Quinter, KS 67752
785-754-3959
www.swiftbullets.com

SWIFT OPTICS
2055 Gateway Pl., Suite 500
San Jose, CA 95110
800-523-4544
www.swift-optics.com

SWISS ARMS AG
Industrieplatz
8212 Neuhausen am Rheinfall
Switzerland
+41 52 674 6565

SZECSEI & FUCHS
450 Charles St.
Windsor, Ontario N8X 371
Canada
001 519 966 1234

TACTICAL RIFLES – DOW ARMS
19250 Hwy. 301
Dade City, FL 33523
352-999-0599
www.tacticalrifles.net

TASCO WORLDWIDE, INCORPORATED
See Bushnell
www.tasco.com

TAURUS INTL. MFR., INCORPORATED
16175 NW 49th Ave.
Miami, FL 33014
800-327-3776
www.taurususa.com

TAYLOR'S & COMPANY INCORPORATED
304 Lenoir Dr.
Winchester, VA 22603
540-722-2017
ww.taylorsfirearms.com

THOMPSON & CAMPBELL
Cromarty – The Black Isle
Ross-Shire IV11 8YB Scotland
+44 (0) 1381 600 536
www.rifle.co.uk

THOMPSON/CENTER ARMS
P.O. Box 5002
Rochester, NH 03866
603-332-2394
www.tcarms.com

Directory of Manufacturers & Suppliers

TIKKA
See Beretta U.S.A.

**TRADITIONS
PERFORMANCE FIREARMS**
(blackpowder arms, Rizzini
Shotguns)
P.O. Box 776
Old Saybrook, CT 06475
860-388-4656
www.traditionsfirearms.com

TRIJICON
P.O. Box 930059
Wixom, MI 48393
800-338-0563
www.trijikon.com

TRISTAR SPORTING ARMS, LTD.
1816 Linn St.
North Kansas City, MO 64116
816-421-1400
www.tristarsportingarms.com

A. UBERTI
c/o Stoeger Industries
17603 Indian Head Highway,
Suite 200
Accokeek MD 20607
301-283-6300
www.uberti.com

U.S. REPEATING ARMS CO.
(Winchester rifles, shotguns)
275 Winchester Ave.
Morgan, UT 84050
801-876-3440
www.winchesterguns.com

VERONA SHOTGUNS
See B.C. Outdoors
www.veronashotguns.com

VIHTAVUORI/LAPUA
(powder and Lapua ammunition)
1241 Ellis St.
Bensenville, IL 60106
630-350-1116
www.vihtavuori-lapua.com

WALTHER
2100 Roosevelt Ave.
Springfield, MA 01104
800-372-6454
www.waltheramerica.com

**WEATHERBY,
INCORPORATED**
3100 El Camino Real
Atascadero, CA 93422
800-227-2016
www.weatherby.com

WEAVER
See Simmons
www.weaveroptics.com

WESTERN POWDERS
(Ramshot powder)
P.O. Box 158
Miles City, MT 59301
406-232-0422
www.westernpowders.com

WHITE RIFLES
234 South 1250 West
Lindon, UT 84042
877-684-4867
www.whiterifles.com

WILDEY F.A. INCORPORATED
45 Angevine Rd.
Warren, CT 06754
860-355-9000
www.wildeyguns.com

**WILD WEST GUNS,
INCORPORATED**
(Summit rifles)
7100 Homer Dr.
Anchorage, AK 99518
800-992-4570
www.wildwestguns.com

WILLIAMS GUN SIGHT CO.
7389 Lapeer Rd.
Davison, MI 48423
800-530-9028
www.williamsgunsight.com

WINCHESTER
Division of Olin Corp.
427 N. Shamrock St.
East Alton, IL 62024
618-258-2365
www.winchester.com

WINCHESTER FIREARMS
See U.S. Repeating Arms Co.
www.winchester-guns.com

**WINCHESTER
MUZZLELOADING**
See Blackpowder Products

WOODLEIGH BULLETS
P.O. Box 15
Murrabit, Victoria,
Australia 3579
011-61-3-54572226
www.woodleighbullets.com.au

XS SIGHT SYSTEMS
2401 Ludelle St.
Fort Worth, TX 76105
888-744-4880
www.xssights.com

ZEISS SPORTS OPTICS
13005 N. Kingston Ave.
Chester, VA 23836
804-530-5841
www.zeiss.com/sports

Z-HAT CUSTOM DIES
4010A S. Poplar, Suite 72
Casper, WY 82601
307-577-7443
www.z-hat.com

**ZANDER'S
SPORTING GOODS**
(Eley ammunition)
See DKG Trading Inc.

MANUFACTURERS

Manufacturer's Showcase

MODEL G9977 WOOD MILL™ WITH POWER FEED

FOR METALWORKING & WOODWORKING!

Specifications:
- Motor: 1½ HP, 110V/220V single-phase
- Precision ground cast iron table: 10" x 33¾"
- Table travel (longitudinal): 17¾"
- Table travel (cross): 12"
- Spindle taper: R-8
- Spindle travel: 3½"
- Max. spindle to column: 16½"
- Max. spindle to table: 20⁷⁄₁₆"
- 9 Speeds: 420-5000 RPM
- Approx. shipping wt: 1610 lbs.

Includes:
- Way chip protectors
- Drawbar

The **G9977** is **$2,695.00** and is shipped in the lower 48 states for $225.00.

Please check current pricing before ordering!

3 LOCATIONS
Bellingham, WA / Muncy, PA / Springfield, MO

grizzly.com Visit our Web site!

8170

TEL: 1-800-523-4777 • FAX: 1-800-438-5901

MODEL G9249 12" x 37" BELT DRIVE GAP BED LATHE

Specifications:
- Motor: 2 HP, 220V, single-phase
- Swing over bed: 12"
- Swing over gap: 18⅞"
- Distance between centers: 37"
- Spindle nose taper: MT#5
- Spindle bore: 1⁷⁄₁₆"
- Speeds: 12, 50-1200 RPM
- Tailstock barrel taper: MT#3
- Tailstock barrel travel: 3"
- Approx. shipping weight: 1136 lbs.

Includes:
- 6" 3-jaw chuck • 8" 4-jaw chuck
- 10" face plate • Steady rest
- Follow rest • Chip tray
- Heavy-duty stand • 4 way tool post
- Dual inch/metric dials

The **G9249** is **$2,195.00** and is shipped in the lower 48 states for $225.00.

Please check current pricing before ordering!

3 LOCATIONS
Bellingham, WA / Muncy, PA / Springfield, MO

grizzly.com Visit our Web site!

8170

TEL: 1-800-523-4777 • FAX: 1-800-438-5901

MODEL G4016 13½" x 40" GEAR-HEAD LATHE WITH STAND

Specifications:
- Motor: 2 HP, 220V, single-phase
- Swing over bed: 13½"
- Swing over gap: 19"
- Distance between centers: 40"
- Spindle: D1-4 Camlock
- Spindle bore: 1⁷⁄₁₆"
- 8 Speeds: 78-2100 RPM
- Tailstock barrel taper: MT#3
- Tailstock barrel travel: 3½"
- Approx. shipping weight: 1330 lbs.

Includes:
- 6" 3-jaw chuck • 8" 4-jaw chuck
- 12" face plate
- 4-way turret tool post
- Two MT#3 dead centers
- Live center
- Steady rest • Follow rest
- Jog button & emergency stop
- Tool box
- Stand, chip pan & splash guard

The **G4016** is **$2,995.00** and is shipped in the lower 48 states for $225.00.

Please check current pricing before ordering!

3 LOCATIONS
Bellingham, WA / Muncy, PA / Springfield, MO

grizzly.com Visit our Web site!

8170

TEL: 1-800-523-4777 • FAX: 1-800-438-5901

MODEL G9901 9" x 42" VERTICAL MILL WITH POWER FEED

Specifications:
- Motor: 2 HP, 110V/220V single-phase
- Precision ground cast iron table: 9" x 42"
- Table travel (longitudinal): 25⅞"
- Table travel (cross): 12½"
- Max. dist. spindle to table: 18"
- Max. dist. spindle to column: 17½"
- 8 Speeds: 78-2000 R.P.M.
- Approx. shipping weight: 2379 lbs.

Features:
- One-shot pump lubrication
- Power down feed • R-8 spindle
- Quill feeds/Spindle rev.: .0019", .0035", .0058"
- Auto stop w/ micro adjustable stop
- Longitudinal power feed
- Adjustable micrometer quill depth stop
- Hardened & ground table surface
- Chrome plated, precision ground quill

The **G9901** is **$3,595.00** and is shipped in the lower 48 states for $375.00.

Please check current pricing before ordering!

3 LOCATIONS
Bellingham, WA / Muncy, PA / Springfield, MO

grizzly.com Visit our Web site!

8170

TEL: 1-800-523-4777 • FAX: 1-800-438-5901

Manufacturer's Showcase

Gunfinder Index

To help you find the model of your choice, the following index includes every firearm found in this edition of Shooter's Bible, listed by type of gun.

Gunfinder Index

Gunfinder Index

GUNFINDER INDEX

Gunfinder Index

GUNFINDER IND

Gunfinder Index

Gunfinder Index

GUNFINDER INDEX